THE OXFORD HANDBOOK OF

SHAKESPEARE'S POETRY

Situated within the Oxford Handbooks of Literature series, the Oxford Handbooks to Shakespeare are designed to record past and present investigations and renewed and revised judgements by both familiar and younger Shakespearean specialists. Each of these volumes is edited by one or more internationally distinguished Shakespeareans; together, they comprehensively survey the entire field.

The Oxford Handbook of Shakespeare's Poetry contains thirty-eight original essays written by leading Shakespeareans around the world. Collectively, these essays seek to return readers to a revivified understanding of Shakespeare's verbal artistry in both the poems and the drama. The volume understands poetry to be not just a formal category designating a particular literary genre but to be inclusive of the dramatic verse as well, and of Shakespeare's influence as a poet on later generations of writers in English and beyond. Focusing on a broad set of interpretive concerns, the volume tackles general matters of Shakespeare's style, earlier and later; questions of influence from classical, continental, and native sources; the importance of words, line, and rhyme to meaning; the significance of songs and ballads in the drama; the place of gender in the verse, including the relationship of Shakespeare's poetry to the visual arts; the different values attached to speaking 'Shakespeare' in the theatre; and the adaptation of Shakespearean verse (as distinct from performance) into other periods and languages. The volume also devotes ten essays to detailed readings of the major poems, including *Venus and Adonis*, *The Rape of Lucrece*, the Sonnets, 'A Lover's Complaint', and 'The Phoenix and the Turle'.

Jonathan F. S. Post is Distinguished Professor of English at UCLA and the founding director of the UCLA Summer Shakespeare Program in Stratford-upon-Avon and London.

THE OXFORD HANDBOOK OF

SHAKESPEARE'S POETRY

Edited by
JONATHAN F. S. POST

OXFORD
UNIVERSITY PRESS

OXFORD
UNIVERSITY PRESS

Great Clarendon Street, Oxford, OX2 6DP,
United Kingdom

Oxford University Press is a department of the University of Oxford.
It furthers the University's objective of excellence in research, scholarship,
and education by publishing worldwide. Oxford is a registered trade mark of
Oxford University Press in the UK and in certain other countries

© Oxford University Press 2013

The moral rights of the authors have been asserted

First published 2013
First published in paperback 2016

Published in the United States of America by Oxford University Press
198 Madison Avenue, New York, NY 10016, United States of America

British Library Cataloguing in Publication Data
Data available

Library of Congress Cataloging in Publication Data
Data available

ISBN 978–0–19–960774–7 (Hbk.)
ISBN 978–0–19–877801–1 (Pbk.)

PREFACE

JONATHAN F. S. POST

The general motive for *The Oxford Handbook of Shakespeare's Poetry* is simple. After more than 400 years, Shakespeare's poetry remains one of the chief glories of the English language. Although the quaint image of every schoolboy carrying a copy of the bard's writings in his satchel no longer holds, Shakespeare's verse remains a vital part of Western thinking, both a cornerstone of the academic curriculum, one of the few remaining in the humanities, and a rich source of inspiration and pleasure to a great variety of people, whether his words are spoken on the stage, used to solemnize a marriage, or pored over—or 'burned through' if you're John Keats—in the privacy of one's own room, by reader, writer, critic, or poet. How right, in retrospect, that the authorial subject of this *Handbook* should have penned the lines: 'Not marble nor the gilded monuments | Of princes shall outlive this powerful rhyme' (Sonnet 55). So far-sighted, and so true.

The scholarly cue is more specific. For the last three decades, the study of Shakespeare has been largely dominated by a number of theoretical perspectives ranging from new historicism and cultural materialism to performance studies, including gender studies, perspectives that have nearly displaced a knowledgeable understanding of, and interest in, what an earlier generation of critics would have assumed to be the central working conditions of Shakespeare's muse: that his writings, first and foremost, belonged to the broader field of verbal art or poesis.

There are clear signs of a re-emphasis and correction already taking place, both editorially and critically. The former is most evident in Colin Burrow's exemplary Oxford edition of *The Complete Sonnets and Poems* (2002), exemplary, in part, because 'complete.' The first edition since the late nineteenth century to include all the poems, it serves as a judiciously annotated counterweight to the many editions of Shakespeare's plays, beginning with the 1623 Folio (FIGURE P.1), in which the poems have appeared, if at all, in an obscure or marginal relationship to the drama, a positioning often manifested in critical assumptions as well: that the narrative poems were written while—or because—the theatres were closed and for a limited elite audience (FIGURES P.2 and P.3); that the Sonnets appeared largely as a belated afterthought to the 1590s rage or as imperfect renderings of passions more suited to the theatre (FIGURE P.4); or that 'The Phoenix and the Turtle,' as it came to be called, was Shakespeare's attempt around 1601 to sound like John Donne. If Shakespeare were ever to be accused of writing with the left hand, it would not be for his prose, almost all of which appears in the drama, but for his poems.

Burrow has hardly been alone in this venture, either as editor or critic, and at the moment there exist in print an exceptional number of fine editions of Shakespeare's poems available to students and scholars alike. (A comparison of different editions of the Sonnets forms the subject of Chapter 24.)[1] There have also been, especially of late (although with valuable recent antecedents), important critical monographs and essay collections that seek to make the poetry an essential part of our understanding of Shakespeare's oeuvre, including the idea that Shakespeare came to regard (or present) himself as a poet and not merely a writer of scripts to be performed by an acting company in which he was a shareholder. Central to this ongoing debate, sounded as recently as Katherine Duncan-Jones' *Shakespeare: Upstart Crow to Sweet Swan, 1592–1623* (Arden, 2011), has been David Schalkwyk's *Speech and performance in Shakespeare's sonnets and plays* (Cambridge, 2002), Lukas Erne's *Shakespeare as Literary Artist* (Cambridge, 2003), Patrick Cheney's *Shakespeare, National Poet-Playwright* (Cambridge, 2004), followed by his edition of critical essays for *The Cambridge Companion to Shakespeare's Poetry* (2007), and the longer but more selectively focused *Blackwell Companion to Shakespeare's Sonnets*, ed. Michael Schoenfeldt (2007).

The Oxford Handbook of Shakespeare's Poetry contributes to this critical reassessment of the place of the poems in Shakespeare's career, but it casts a deliberately wider net than can be found in these earlier collections. It understands poetry to be not just a formal category designating a particular literary genre (narrative poem, sonnet, complaint, lyric, song, or epitaph) but to be inclusive of the dramatic verse as well, and of Shakespeare's influence as a poet on later generations of writers in English and beyond. To that end, the volume focuses on a broad set of interpretive concerns: general matters of style, earlier and later; questions of influence from classical, continental, and native sources; the importance of words, line, and rhyme to meaning; the significance of song and ballads in the drama; the place of gender in the verse, including the relationship of Shakespeare's poetry to the visual arts; the different values attached to speaking 'Shakespeare' in the theater; and the adaptation of Shakespearean verse (as distinct from performance) into other periods and languages. If the collection's circumference is deliberately wide, the volume nonetheless includes a traditional center in the section—indeed the largest section in the volume—devoted to the poems themselves, including 'A Lover's Complaint.' Whatever controversy surrounds the authorship of this poem, it has become (like Donne's 'Sappho to Philaenis') an important site of criticism in the early modern period.

In spite of its breadth, it is important to insist that coverage was never simply the goal of the volume—coverage, in any event, being an exceptionally illusory goal in the case of Shakespeare. The essays pursue individual arguments, make distinct claims; they follow out, as essays should, the lines of their own reasoning. Sometimes in dialogue with one another, but more often with readers and writers across the centuries, their major point

[1] To those editions in print, cited in Chapter 24, should be added Kenneth J. Larsen's online *Essays on Shakespeare's Sonnets*, with introduction, text, and commentary, at <http://www.williamshakespeare-sonnets.com/> (accessed on 1 July 2012.)

in common is to keep Shakespeare's poetry (sometimes minutely perceived, other times broadly construed) in the foreground of their thinking. Although the division of the volume into seven categories reflects the general disposition of topics, these boundaries are also quite elastic, as a glance at the Table of Contents will reveal. It should also be said that if the volume as a whole urges renewed involvement in the complex matter of Shakespeare's poetry, it does so, as the individual essays testify, by way of responding to critical trends and discoveries made during the last three decades.

All the essays were written specifically for this volume. For the willing efforts and great talent of the contributors, I am especially grateful. A few deserve special mention for early help in thinking through the lines of inquiry such a volume might take: Albert Braunmuller, Colin Burrow, Paul Edmondson, Linda Gregerson, John Kerrigan, Russ McDonald, Melissa Sanchez, Bruce Smith, and Gordon Teskey. Thanks to the generosity of the UCLA Center for Medieval and Renaissance Studies and the good work of Karen Burgess and Brett Landenberger, a number of the essays enjoyed an early airing at a conference held at UCLA in May, 2011, 'Where has all the Verse Gone? Shakespeare's Poetry on the Page & Stage'.

The *Oxford Handbook of Shakespeare's Poetry* is part of a series of Oxford Handbooks on Shakespeare under the general direction of Arthur Kinney. I want to thank him for inviting me to take on this project. At Oxford University Press, Andrew McNeillie offered early words of encouragement. I am especially grateful to Jacqueline Baker for commissioning the volume and seeing it through to publication, and to Rachel Platt for her timely response to many queries. The gratification in putting together a large collection like this one, enabled in part by an excellent research assistant, Claire Byun, with further help from Heather Sontong, is not simply seeing a book finally emerge but also the friendships made or renewed along the way. Among the most important to acknowledge here is the always calmly resourceful Jeanette Gilkison, in the Department of English at UCLA, and Susan Green of the Huntington Library. I also want to acknowledge, with thanks, the Academic Senate and the Council on Research at UCLA for continuing to support my scholarship over the years, including generous help with the publication of this book, and the UCLA Center for Seventeenth- and Eighteenth-Century Studies and Amy Gordainer for her excellent work preparing the index. For the past twenty summers, it has been my pleasure to teach, with my colleague Albert Braunmuller, many students who have learned to walk the pentameter line (and much else) while participating in the UCLA Shakespeare Program in London and Stratford. I like to think they will be eager and wise readers of the essays in this volume. Neither the program nor this book would exist, however, without the help of my companion in this and all else, Susan Gallick.

Unless otherwise noted, all quotations from Shakespeare are from *The Oxford Shakespeare: The Complete Works*, Stanley Wells and Gary Taylor (eds), (2nd edn Oxford: Oxford University Press, 2005).

A CATALOGVE

of the feuerall Comedies, Hiftories, and Tragedies contained in this Volume.

COMEDIES.

He Tempeft.	Folio 1.
The two Gentlemen of Verona.	20
The Merry Wiues of Windfor.	38
Meafure for Meafure.	61
The Comedy of Errours.	85
Much adoo about Nothing.	101
Loues Labour loft.	122
Midfommer Nights Dreame.	145
The Merchant of Venice.	163
As you Like it.	185
The Taming of the Shrew.	208
All is well, that Ends well.	230
Twelfe-Night, or what you will.	255
The Winters Tale.	304

HISTORIES.

The Life and Death of King John.	Fol. 1.
The Life & death of Richard the fecond.	23
The Firft part of King Henry the fourt'b.	46
The Second part of K.Henry the fourth.	74
The Life of King Henry the Fift.	69
The Firft part of King Henry the Sixt.	96
The Second part of King Hen. the Sixt.	120
The Third part of King Henry the Sixt.	147
The Life & Death of Richard the Third.	173
The Life of King Henry the Eight.	205

TRAGEDIES.

The Tragedy of Coriolanus.	Fol.1.
Titus Andronicus.	31
Romeo and Juliet.	53
Timon of Athens.	80
The Life and death of Julius Cæfar.	109
The Tragedy of Macbeth.	131
The Tragedy of Hamlet.	152
King Lear.	283
Othello, the Moore of Venice.	310
Anthony and Cleopater.	346
Cymbeline King of Britaine.	369

FIGURE P.1. The catalogue of the thirty-five plays included in the 1623 Folio, excluding the poems. By permission of the Folger Shakespeare Library.

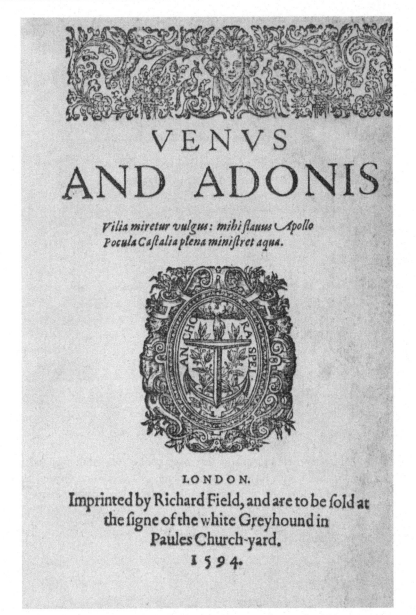

FIGURE P.2. Highly crafted quarto title page of the 1594 edition of *Venus and Adonis*. First published in 1593, the poem went through sixteen editions by 1640. The Latin epigraph from Ovid's *Amores* reads: 'Let the common herd be amazed by worthless things; but for me let gold Apollo provide cups full of the water of the Muses.' By permission of The Huntington Library.

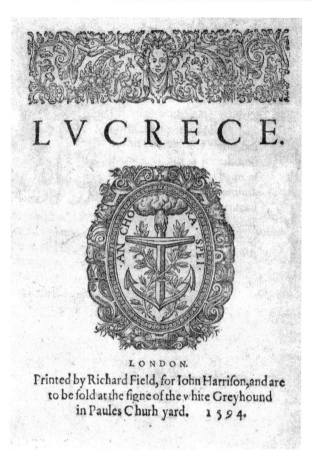

FIGURE P.3. A slightly more severe quarto title page of the 1594 edition of *Lucrece* by the same printer, Richard Field, with identical ornamentation. Shakespeare's 'graver labour' went through eight editions by 1640. By permission of the Folger Shakespeare Library.

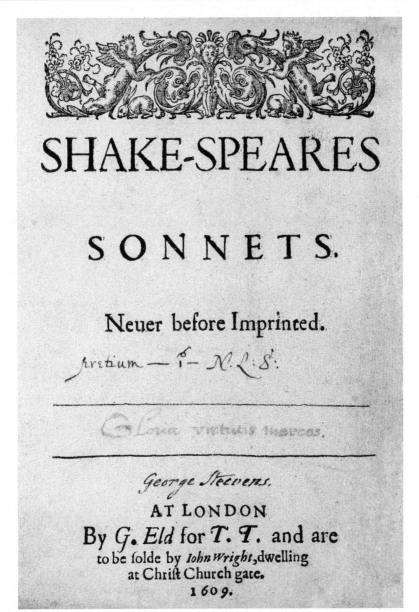

FIGURE P.4. Marked-up copy of the 1609 quarto title page of the Sonnets, bearing Shakespeare's name. Although John Benson published an eccentrically miscellaneous version of the Sonnets in 1640, it was not until a hundred years later, in 1709, that Bernard Lintot reprinted the quarto in the order of 1609, thus beginning the slow process of rescuing the poems. The process was significantly furthered by the owner of this copy, 'George Steevens.' Although scandalized by the Sonnets' subject matter, Steevens, in conjunction with Samuel Johnson and Edmund Malone in the latter eighteenth century, established the modern canon of Shakespeare's plays and poems. By permission of The Huntington Library.

CONTENTS

PART III   SONGS, LYRICS, AND BALLADS

PART IV   SPEAKING ON STAGE

PART V   READING SHAKESPEARE'S POEMS

PART VI   LATER REFLECTIONS

PART VII TRANSLATING SHAKESPEARE

LIST OF FIGURES

LIST OF CONTRIBUTORS

Gavin Alexander   University Senior Lecturer in the Faculty of English, University of Cambridge, and a Fellow of Christ's College. His publications include *Writing After Sidney* (Oxford, 2006), *Sidney's 'The Defence of Poesy' and Selected Renaissance Literary Criticism* (Penguin Classics, 2004), and numerous articles and book chapters on literary and musicological topics. An edition of *The Model of Poesy* by William Scott, a late-Elizabethan manuscript poetics treatise, is forthcoming from Cambridge University Press.

Belén Bistué   Tenured Researcher in Comparative Literature and Assistant Professor of English at the Universidad Nacional de Cuyo, in Mendoza, Argentina. She specializes in translation history. Her essay 'The Task(s) of the Translator(s): Multiplicity as Problem in Renaissance European Thought' received the A. Owen Aldridge Award from the American Comparative Literature Association, and she is currently writing a book on the use of collaborative and multilingual translation in early modern Europe.

A. R. Braunmuller   Teaches English and European drama, 1500 to the present, at UCLA. He has written about Brecht and Pinter, Chapman and Peele, Ibsen and Shakespeare, about early modern private letters and manuscript collections, and about the practice and theory of editing among other topics. He serves as Associate General Editor of the New Cambridge Shakespeare and is co-General Editor of the Pelican Shakespeare with Stephen Orgel. He anticipates completing the Arden 3 edition of *Measure for Measure* soon.

Colin Burrow   Senior Research Fellow at All Souls College, Oxford. He is the author of *Epic Romance: Homer to Milton* (Oxford, 1993), and the editor of *The Complete Sonnets and Poems* for the Oxford Shakespeare (2002), as well as of the poems for the *Cambridge Edition of the Works of Ben Jonson* (2012). Forthcoming projects include *The Elizabethans* for the Oxford English Literary History, a book on imitation, and a study of Shakespeare and classical antiquity.

Katharine A. Craik   Senior Lecturer in Early Modern Literature at Oxford Brookes University. She is the author of *Reading Sensations in Early Modern England* (Palgrave, 2007), a contributor to *The Cambridge Works of Ben Jonson* (Cambridge, 2012), and the co-editor of *Shakespearean Sensations: Experiencing Literature in Early Modern England* (Cambridge, 2013). She is particularly interested in the history of the body and emotions in early modern literature and culture.

Paul Edmondson Head of Research and Knowledge for The Shakespeare Birthplace Trust and Director of the Stratford-upon-Avon Poetry Festival. His publications include *Shakespeare's Sonnets* (co-authored with Stanley Wells, Oxford, 2004) and *Twelfth Night: A Guide to the Text and Its Theatrical Life* (Palgrave, 2005). He is a series editor for Manchester University Press's Revels Plays Companions, Palgrave's Renaissance Handbooks, and co-supervisory editor of the Penguin Shakespeare. He is a priest in the Church of England. See <http://www.bloggingshakespeare.com @ paul_edmondson>.

Margaret Ferguson Distinguished Professor of English at the University of California at Davis; she has also taught at Yale, Columbia, and the University of Colorado. She will serve as President of the Modern Language Association in 2014–15. Her publications include articles on Shakespeare, Augustine, Behn, and Freud, among others; a book on *Renaissance Defenses of Poetry*; another on *Gender, Literacy and Empire in Early Modern England and France*; and thirteen co-edited volumes, among them the *Norton Anthology of Poetry*.

Alison Findlay Professor of Renaissance Drama and Director of the Shakespeare Programme at Lancaster University (UK). She is the author of *Illegitimate Power* (1994), *A Feminist Perspective on Renaissance Drama* (1998), *Women in Shakespeare* (2010) and, most recently, *Much Ado About Nothing: a guide to the text in performance* (2011). She has also produced and published widely on early modern women's drama. She and Dr Liz Oakley-Brown are currently editing *Twelfth Night: New Critical Essays* for Arden.

Linda Gregerson Caroline Walker Bynum Distinguished University Professor of English at the University of Michigan. Her publications include *The Reformation of the Subject: Spenser, Milton, and the English Protestant Epic* and *Negative Capability: Contemporary American Poetry*, as well as five volumes of poetry. She is also the editor, with Susan Juster, of *Empires of God: Religious Encounters in the Early Modern Atlantic*.

Judith Hall Visiting writer at California Institute of Technology. She is the author of four poetry collections, including *To Put The Mouth To* (Morrow, 1992), a National Poetry Series selection, and *Three Trios*, translations from the imaginary poet J II (Northwestern, 2007). She has received awards from the Guggenheim Foundation, the Ingram Merrill Foundation, and the NEA. She also serves as poetry editor of *Antioch Review*.

Christa Jansohn Professor of British Culture and Director of the Centre for British Studies at the University of Bamberg, Germany. Her books include *Shakespeare-Apocrypha and their Reception in Germany* (2000), and the forthcoming *History of the German Shakespeare Society: 1945–1964*. She is co-editor of *German Shakespeare Studies at the Turn of the Twenty-first Century* (2006), *Shakespeare's World: World Shakespeare. The Selected Proceedings of the International Shakespeare Association World Congress,*

Brisbane 2006 (2008), and *Shakespeare without Boundaries. Essays in Honor of Dieter Mehl* (2010). Together with Dieter Mehl she is currently updating Rollins' *New Variorum Edition of Shakespeare's Poems.*

John Kerrigan   Professor of English 2000 at the University of Cambridge. Among his publications are an edition of Shakespeare's *Sonnets and A Lover's Complaint* (1986), a study in comparative literature, *Revenge Tragedy: Aeschylus to Armageddon* (1996), a collection of essays *On Shakespeare and Early Modern Literature* (2001), and *Archipelagic English: Literature, History, and Politics 1603–1707* (2008). He is currently writing books on British and Irish poetry since the 1960s and on *Shakespeare's Binding Language.*

Alysia Kolentsis   Assistant Professor of English at St. Jerome's, University of Waterloo. She completed a PhD at the University of Toronto and a postdoctoral fellowship at Stanford University, is assistant editor of the forthcoming *Shakespeare Encyclopedia* (Greenwood), and has recently published articles on Shakespeare, early modern English, and early modern representations of time.

Efraín Kristal   Professor and Chair of UCLA's Department of Comparative Literature. He is author of *Invisible Work. Borges and Translation* (2002); the essay on aesthetics and literature for the *Blackwell Companion to Comparative Literature,* (2012); and the essay on philosophical and theoretical approaches to translation for the forthcoming *Blackwell Companion to Translation Studies.*

James Longenbach   Author of four books of poems, most recently *The Iron Key* (W.W. Norton, 2010), and six books of literary criticism, most recently *The Virtues of Poetry* (Graywolf, 2013). He has also written about Shakespeare in *The Art of the Poetic Line* (Graywolf, 2008). He is the Joseph Gilmore Professor of English at the University of Rochester.

Jeremy Lopez   Associate Professor of English at the University of Toronto and the theatre-review editor for *Shakespeare Bulletin.* He is the author of numerous books and articles on the drama of Shakespeare and his contemporaries.

Russ McDonald   Professor of English Literature at Goldsmiths College, University of London, has written mainly on Shakespearean poetics, notably in *Shakespeare and the Arts of Language* (Oxford, 2001) and *Shakespeare's Late Style* (Cambridge, 2006). Author of the widely adopted *Bedford Companion to Shakespeare,* he has recently edited, with Nicholas Nace and Travis D. Williams, *Shakespeare Up Close: Reading Early Modern Texts.* His chapter is part of a new book to be called *Elizabethan Poetics and the Culture of Symmetry.*

Anthony Mortimer   Emeritus Professor at the University of Fribourg, Switzerland, and also taught for many years at the University of Geneva. His major interests are in Renaissance poetry and verse translation. Among his recent publications are *Variable Passions: A Reading of Shakespeare's 'Venus and Adonis'* (2000) and *Petrarch's Canzoniere* *in The English Renaissance* (2005). His verse translations include *Petrarch: Canzoniere, Selections* (2002), *Michelangelo: Poems and Letters* (2007), *Cavalcanti, Complete Poems* (2010), *Dante: Vita Nuova* (2011), *Angelus Silesius: Sacred Epigrams* (2012), and *Villon: Poems* (2013).

Subha Mukherji   Senior Lecturer in English at Cambridge University. Her publications include *Law and Representation in Early Modern Drama* (2006) and numerous articles, mainly on Shakespeare and Renaissance literature. She has also co-edited *Early Modern Tragicomedy* (2007), edited and contributed to *Thinking on Thresholds: the Poetics of Transitive Spaces* (2011), and co-edited and contributed to *Fictions of Knowledge: Fact, Evidence, Doubt* (2012). Her book-in-progress focuses on doubt and epistemology in early modern literature.

Steve Newman   Teaches English at Temple University. Among his publications are *Ballad Collection, Lyric, and the Canon: The Call of the Popular from The Restoration to the New Criticism* (2007) and essays on *The Beggar's Opera*, Allan Ramsay and the South Sea Bubble, and personal statements for medical school. He is currently working on a book entitled, *Time for the Humanities: Competing Narratives of Value from the Scottish Enlightenment to the 21st Century Academy*.

Catherine Nicholson   Assistant Professor of English at Yale University, where she teaches and writes about Renaissance literature and literary theories. She is completing a book-length study of stylistic eccentricity and has published articles on Marlowe, Spenser, and Shakespeare.

Michael O'Neill   Professor of English at Durham University. Recent books include (co-edited with Anthony Howe and with the assistance of Madeleine Callaghan) *The Oxford Handbook of Percy Bysshe Shelley* (2012) and (with Michael D. Hurley) *The Cambridge Introduction to Poetic Form* (2012). He is writing a book on Shakespeare and English poetry for Oxford University Press.

Jonathan F. S. Post   Distinguished Professor of English at UCLA and the founding director of the UCLA Summer Shakespeare Program in Stratford and London. His publications include studies with a special focus on poetry of the early modern and modern periods: *English Lyric Poetry: The Early Seventeenth Century* (Routledge, 1999, rpt. 2002); *Green Thoughts, Green Shades: Contemporary Poets on the Early Modern Lyric* (California, 2002); and *The Selected Letters of Anthony Hecht* (Johns Hopkins University Press, 2013). He is currently writing a critical study of Anthony Hecht's poetry for Oxford University Press.

Anne Lake Prescott   Helen Goodhart Altschul Professor (emerita) at Barnard College, is the author of *French Poets and the English Renaissance* and *Imagining Rabelais in the English Renaissance*, as well as essays on topics from Louise Labé to Donne's satires. Co-editor of *Spenser Studies*, and past president of the Spenser Society, the Sixteenth

Century Society, and the Donne Society, she is currently exploring the image of David and Saul in the Renaissance.

Sophie Read   University Lecturer in English and fellow of Christ's College, Cambridge, where she teaches Renaissance and eighteenth-century literature and pursues research interests in rhetoric and poetics. Her first monograph is *Eucharist and the Poetic Imagination in Early Modern England* (Cambridge University Press, 2013); previous publications include articles on Lancelot Andrewes, Milton, and Swift, as well as on contemporary poetry.

Peter Robinson   Professor of English and American Literature and Head of Department at the University of Reading. Has been awarded the Cheltenham Prize, the John Florio Prize, and two Poetry Book Society Recommendations for his poems and translations. He has published four volumes of literary criticism, three with Oxford University Press, and is editor of *The Oxford Handbook of Contemporary British and Irish Poetry* (2013).

Abigail Rokison   Began her career as a professional actor. She is now Lecturer in Shakespeare and Theatre at the Shakespeare Institute, University of Birmingham. Her first book, *Shakespearean Verse Speaking* (Cambridge, 2009), won the Shakespeare's Globe First Book Award. She has just completed a second book—*Shakespeare for Young People: Production, Versions and Adaptations*, and has written a number of journal articles and chapters on Shakespeare.

Melissa E. Sanchez   Associate Professor of English at the University of Pennsylvania. She is the author of *Erotic Subjects: The Sexuality of Politics in Early Modern English Literature*, along with numerous articles on gender, sexuality, and politics in sixteenth- and seventeenth-century England. She is currently writing a book on the relation between feminism and queer theory in early modern studies.

David Schalkwyk   Director of Research at the Folger Shakespeare Library in Washington DC and editor of the *Shakespeare Quarterly*. He is also Professor of English at the University of Cape Town. His monographs include *Speech and Performance in Shakespeare's Sonnets and Plays* (Cambridge, 2002), *Literature and the Touch of the Real* (Delaware University Press, 2004), *Shakespeare, Love and Service* (Cambridge, 2008) and *Hamlet's Dreams: The Robben Island Shakespeare* (Arden, 2013). He is currently working on love in Shakespeare.

Joshua Scodel   Helen A. Regenstein Professor in English, Comparative Literature, and the College at the University of Chicago, is the author of *The English Poetic Epitaph from Jonson to Wordsworth* (1991), *Excess and the Mean in Early Modern English Literature* (2002), and numerous articles on Renaissance literature. He coedited *Elizabeth I: Translations, 1544–1589* (2009) and *Elizabeth I: Translations, 1592–1598* (2009), which won the MLA's Distinguished Scholarly Edition prize.

Charlotte Scott   Senior Lecturer at Goldsmiths College, University of London. She has written widely on Shakespeare, including *Shakespeare and the Idea of the Book* (Oxford, 2007). Her most recent book, *Shakespeare's Husbandry,* is forthcoming with OUP and builds on her interest in the relationships between the social and linguistic worlds of Shakespeare's plays and poems.

L. E. Semler   Teaches in the Department of English and is Director of The Medieval and Early Modern Centre at the University of Sydney. His recent books include the co-edited volumes: *Word and Self Estranged in English Texts, 1550–1660* (with P. Kelly) (Ashgate, 2010); *What is the Human? Australian Voices from the Humanities* (with B. Hodge and P. Kelly) (Australian Scholarly Publishing, 2012); and *Teaching Shakespeare Beyond the Centre: Australasian Perspectives* (with P. Gay and K. Flaherty) (Palgrave, 2012).

Bruce R. Smith   Dean's Professor of English at the University of Southern California, is the author of six books, most recently *Phenomenal Shakespeare* (Wiley-Blackwell, 2010) and *The Key of Green: Passion and Perception in Renaissance Culture* (University of Chicago Press, 2009). He is a former president of the Shakespeare Association of America. He currently serves as general editor of the Cambridge World Shakespeare project.

David Sofield   Samuel Williston Professor of English at Amherst College, where he has taught Shakespeare, as well as early modern and twentieth-century poetry, since 1965. He co-edited, with Herbert J. Tucker, and contributed to *Under Criticism* (1998); his poems are collected in *Light Disguise* (2003).

Goran Stanivukovic   Professor of English at Saint Mary's University, Canada, and editor most recently of *Remapping the Mediterranean World in Early Modern English Writings* (2007). He has completed a book manuscript, *Knights in Arms: Travels in the Eastern Mediterranean and Romances in Early Modern England (1570–1640).* Currently he is a Marie Curie Research Fellow in the School of English at University College Cork. He is working on a book on Shakespeare's early style.

Gordon Teskey   Professor of English at Harvard University, is author of *Allegory and Violence* (1996) and of *Delirious Milton* (2006); he is editor of the Norton Edition of *Paradise Lost* (2005). A graduate of Trent University and the University of Toronto, he taught at Cornell University from 1982 to 2002.

Herbert F. Tucker   John C. Coleman Chair in English at the University of Virginia, where he serves on the editorial boards of *New Literary History* and of the University Press's Victorian series. He has written books on Browning (1980), Tennyson (1988), and epic in nineteenth-century Britain (2008), and has edited several anthologies addressing Victorian literature and culture.

Marion Wells   A member of the English and American Literatures Department at Middlebury College. She has a BA in Classics and Modern Languages from Oxford

University and a PhD in Comparative Literature from Yale University. In 2007 Stanford University Press published her book on the relationship between melancholy and romance, entitled *The Secret Wound: Love-Melancholy and Early Modern Romance*. She is currently at work on a book on the intersection of theories of emotion and gender in the early modern period, entitled *The Nightingale's Song: Passionate Voices in Early Modern Europe*.

PART I

STYLE AND LANGUAGE

CHAPTER 1

....

SHAKESPEARE'S STYLES

....

GORDON TESKEY

An author's writing style may be defined as the sum of all the close-grained, idiosyncratic, subtly altering habits of syntax, rhythm, word-choice, and ornament that confer distinctiveness on the artistic arrangement of words. Such an account of literary style has traditional roots in the ancient Greek rhetorical treatises, especially in the authors known as Longinus and Demetrius, the former concerned with one style in particular, the sublime, the latter with elocution in general. In both these theorists, however, there is an emerging idea of style as a synthesis of diverse elements, greater than the sum of its parts, now commonly referred to as 'voice.' As Heinrich von Kleist says, the arch stands because every stone wants to fall at the same time.[1]

Over the course of his approximately twenty-year career, Shakespeare's style quite naturally changed, so much so we may speak of him writing in a succession of styles, all of them distinctly his own. Shakespeare's style matured, because he got better at his craft. Writing verse, or tight, vigorous prose, is an athletic skill, involving muscle memory and unconscious processing. As time went on there was more wrist in Shakespeare's language game, giving it increased subtlety and power. But Shakespeare's style also matured simply because he got older, because he saw life differently as he saw more of it, and because he felt differently about language, the medium through which his life was lived.

As to how Shakespeare's verbal art changed across his career, the familiar accounts go something like this. The early plays are almost entirely in verse, and the verse has a higher concentration of end-stops and rhyme; it tends to fall into set speeches, 'like a ... poem ... spoken from the stage', as George T. Wright puts it.[2] As Shakespeare matured, he turned increasingly to a vigorous but comparatively unchanging prose. A higher proportion of prose to verse appears in the middle to late plays, but especially in the middle

---

[1] Longinus' *On the Sublime*, 8.1. Demetrius, *On Style* 106, in *Aristotle, 'The Poetics'; Longinus 'On the Sublime'; Demetrius 'On Style'*, Loeb Classical Library (Cambridge: Harvard University Press, 1973). Heinrich von Kleist, letter # 28, to Wilhelmine von Zenge, 18 November 1800, *Sämtliche Werke und Briefe* 2, 9th edn, Helmut Semdner (ed.), (Munich: Hanser, 1993) 593.

[2] George T. Wright, *Shakespeare's Metrical Art* (Berkeley: University of California Press, 1988), a rich account of the evolution of Shakespeare's verse. See 'The Play of Phrase and Line', 207–28.

plays, as in *Much Ado about Nothing*.[3] At the same time, Shakespeare's verse becomes increasingly like prose, good prose, which is to say, imitating speech, but more concentrated than speech ever is.

There is much crowding on of sail in the verse after the mid-1590s, for greater speed and force, as if the thought were too fast for the words. In contrast with this, rhyming couplets tend to slow the verse down, to make it more pointed and witty in the self-contained units created by rhyme, as in Helena's soliloquy in *A Midsummer Night's Dream*:

> How happy some o'er other some can be!
> Through Athens I am thought as fair as she.
> But what of that? Demetrius thinks not so
> He will not know what all but he do know ...
> Love looks not with the eyes but with the mind,
> And therefore is winged Cupid painted blind.
>
> *A Midsummer Night's Dream* (I. i. 226–35)

Later in the same play, Oberon says to Robin Goodfellow:

> What hast thou done? Thou hast mistaken quite,
> And laid the love-juice on some true love's sight.
> Of thy misprision must perforce ensue
> Some true love turned and not a false turned true
>
> *A Midsummer Night's Dream* (III. ii. 88–91)

In these passages, each rhyming thought turns in on itself before being added to the next. The effect is like that of a mosaic, which glitters brilliantly. But there is no intention of showing the speaker's thought groping for expression as it moves swiftly and impulsively onward. The thought is as perfectly in balance with itself as is the couplet through which it is expressed. The speaker already knows what she thinks, or what he thinks, all the time. Nor is this effect exclusively the consequence of rhyme. It is embedded in the style. In the following, unrhymed passage from *Love's Labour's Lost*, as Biron condemns the god Cupid, his thoughts fall neatly into parcels, as if he *were* rhyming, although he is not:

> This wimpled, whining, purblind, wayward boy,
> This Signor Junior, giant dwarf, Dan Cupid,
> Regent of love-rhymes, lord of folded arms,
> Th'anointed sovereign of sighs and groans,
> Liege of all loiterers and malcontents,
> Dread prince of plackets, king of codpieces,
> Sole imperator and great general
> Of trotting paritors—O my little heart!
> And I to be a corporal of his field,
> And wear his colours like a tumbler's hoop!
>
> *Love's Labour's Lost* (III. i. 174–83)

---

[3] Brian Vickers, *The Artistry of Shakespeare's Prose* (London: Methuen, 1968) 433.

You cannot rush lines like these, either when you speak them or when you read them. They have to be well spaced, so that each parcel of sense is delivered just in time.

After such plays as *The Comedy of Errors*, *Love's Labour's Lost*, *Richard II*, *Romeo and Juliet*, and *A Midsummer Night's Dream*, there is less rhyme, except to mark the end of a scene: 'I'll so offend to make offence a skill, | Redeeming time when men think least I will'; 'Uncle, adieu. O, let the hours be short | Till fields and blows and groans applaud our sport!' (*1 Henry IV*, I. ii. 213–14, and I. iii. 295–6). Unrhymed verse affords greater naturalism and promotes a feeling of intimacy with the characters. Rhyme, therefore, is no longer part of the texture of a play. Instead, it is so placed as to give formality and structure where needed. This is usually at the end of speeches and scenes. But the blank verse that replaces rhyme achieves more than naturalism and intimacy. It imitates hurried, importunate thought.

In the years running up to *Hamlet* (1600–1), Shakespeare increasingly uses blank verse with frequent enjambments to achieve greater concentration of thought—but also, as was noted, to make us feel the thought rushing forward too rapidly to be clearly expressed. Rhyme is now employed at the end of speeches, for summary, and for a *ritardando*, a slowing down of the action and thought for emphasis and formal effect. In the great scene between King Henry and Prince Harry in *2 Henry IV*, the gravely ill king's thoughts rush out of him on a sudden. At the end of his life, while there is still time, he is desperate to transmit the secrets of power, these being an inheritance as precious as the crown, or rather, the means by which the precious crown is to be kept. We have the feeling of a mind working at full pitch while the dying voice strives to keep up:

> God knows, my son,
> By what bypaths and indirect crook'd ways
> I met this crown; and I myself know well
> How troublesome it sat upon my head …
> Thou art not firm enough, since griefs are green,
> And all thy friends—which thou must make thy friends—
> Have but their stings and teeth newly ta'en out,
> By whose fell working I was first advanced,
> And by whose power I well might lodge a fear
> To be again displaced; which to avoid
> I cut them off, and had a purpose now
> To lead out many to the Holy Land,
> Lest rest and lying still might make them look
> Too near unto my state. Therefore, my Harry,
> Be it thy course to busy giddy minds
> With foreign quarrels, that action hence borne out
> May waste the memory of the former days.
> More would I, but my lungs are wasted so
> That strength of speech is utterly denied me.

2 Henry IV (IV. iii. 312–46)

In contrast with this rushing style, the king concludes (despite his being incapable, as he says, of further speech) with a summary couplet: 'How I came by the crown, O God forgive, | And grant it may with thee in true peace live!' (IV. iii. 347–8). The effect of this couplet is unnatural, in contrast with what has gone before, but it is also our reward for our earlier efforts to keep up with the sense. The *ritardando* then becomes a *largo*—stately, slow, and grand—as Prince Harry responds with two couplets of his own. He is no longer what Hotspur said he is, nimble footed (*1 Henry IV*, IV. i. 95). Instead, he strides:

> You won it, wore it, kept it, gave it me;
> Then plain and right must my possession be,
> Which I with more than with a common pain
> 'Gainst all the world will rightfully maintain.
>
> *2 Henry IV* (IV. iii. 350–3)

As we approach 1600, in *As You Like It* and *Hamlet*, terminal couplets are followed by unrhymed half lines, giving a sense of life bursting the chains of rhyme: 'Thus must I from the smoke into the smother, | From tyrant Duke unto a tyrant brother.— | But heavenly Rosalind!' (*As You Like It*, I. ii. 277–9); 'O cursèd spite | That ever I was born to set it right! | Nay come, let's go together' (*Hamlet*, I. v. 189–91).

Enjambment greatly increases, as do feminine endings, by a factor of three, and there are more hypermetrical lines, often with the extra, unstressed syllable tucked in the middle, at the caesura, strengthening the medial pause. The syntactical regime of the grammatical phrase increasingly challenges the rhythmical one of the iambic pentameter. It becomes harder to tell where one line ends and another begins, or even to tell prose from verse as thought presses onward, impelled by the rapid association of ideas. The verse often seems to say more than it actually does, as in the opening of *Measure for Measure*.[4] The important thing is to imitate thought, but not always to think:

> Of government the properties to unfold
> Would seem in me t'affect speech and discourse,
> Since I am put to know that your own science
> Exceeds in that the lists of all advice
> My strength can give you. Then no more remains
> But this: to your sufficiency, as your worth is able,
> And let them work.
>
> *Measure for Measure* (I. i. 3–9)

Starting in *Hamlet* and continuing thereafter, in *All's Well that Ends Well*, for example, and in *Troilus and Cressida*, Shakespeare will smear his verse (as in a Francis Bacon

---

    [4] Wright (1988) 160, 165–6, and 173. Simon Palfrey and Tiffany Stern, *Shakespeare in Parts* (Oxford: Oxford University Press, 2007) 328–52, and 380–90. Frank Kermode, *Shakespeare's Language* (New York: Farrar, Strauss, Giroux, 2000) 275–8.

painting), or make it like prose, for example, in Ulysses' speech on degree, which for all its orderliness betrays a state of high intellectual excitement:

> Take but degree away, untune that string,
> And hark what discord follows. Each thing meets
> In mere oppugnancy ...
> Force should be right—or rather, right and wrong,
> Between whose endless jar justice resides,
> Should lose their names, and so should justice too.
> Then everything includes itself in power,
> Power into will, will into appetite;
> And appetite, an universal wolf,
> So doubly seconded with will and power,
> Must make perforce an universal prey,
> And last eat up himself.

Troilus and Cressida (I. iii. 109–24)

What we hear in Shakespeare's mature style sounds less like prose or verse and more like passionate thinking in passionate speech, as in Macbeth's dark groping with the problems of opportunity, consequence, and time (I. vii. 1–12) or Othello's great speech before his suicide. Yet for all his passion Othello is one of Shakespeare's most organized, calculatedly rhetorical speakers. A successful general, Othello is used to setting out in speech to order the world before him and finding the world ready to comply. Unlike Hamlet, he does not think ahead of what he is saying at the moment, or distractedly to the side. He is always on message. Unlike Lear, he is not given to explosions of unpremeditated eloquence. Unlike Macbeth, he is not an ad hoc, undisciplined (though vigorous) thinker. His extravagances of expression and image are tactical. Even brief phrases, such as 'for the sea's worth' (I. ii. 28) and 'deserts idle' (I. iii. 140), slow the pace down, briefly paralyzing the hearer with wonder.

These elements of the style Shakespeare has conferred on the Noble Moor of Venice—rhetorical order, deliberate pace, and the immobilizing image—remain present in his final speech. But as he strives to extenuate what he has done, or at least to recover his dignity, he is no longer the master of what he is saying, or even of what he is thinking. No longer does his rhetoric move the levers of the world. As a result, there is a certain futility in these relics of a style and in that futility, pathos:

OTHELLO.   Soft you, a word or two before you go.
    I have done the state some service, and they know't.
    No more of that. I pray you, in your letters,
    When you shall these unlucky deeds relate,
    Speak of me as I am. Nothing extenuate,
    Nor set down aught in malice. Then must you speak
    Of one that loved not wisely but too well,
    Of one not easily jealous but, being wrought,
    Perplexed in the extreme; of one whose hand,

> Like the base Indian, threw a pearl away
> Richer than all his tribe; of one whose subdued eyes,
> Albeit unusèd to the melting mood,
> Drop tears as fast as the Arabian trees
> Their medicinable gum. Set you down this,
> And say besides that in Aleppo once,
> Where a malignant and a turbaned Turk
> Beat a Venetian and traduced the state,
> I took by th' throat the circumcisèd dog,
> And smote him thus.
>   *He stabs himself*
> LODOVICO.   O bloody period!
> GRATIANO.   All that is spoke is marred.
> OTHELLO.   (*to Desdemona*)
> I kissed thee ere I killed thee. No way but this:
> Killing myself, to die upon a kiss.
>
>   *Othello* (V. ii. 347–65)

It sounds orderly and indeed it is, at the outset, by habit. Othello bids his captors pause, 'soft you', before *they* go. He alludes to his service to the state before dismissing that service as irrelevant to the matter in hand, although it is, and he will return to it. He asks that in their letters they give a balanced view of the murder and of what incited him to it, neither extenuating his guilt nor reporting that guilt with malice. If they follow this imaginary middle course they *must* speak of him in respect of four things, each preceded by the phrase, 'of one who.' He is one who loved not wisely, which is true, but 'too well', which is false. He is one who is not easily jealous, which is false, but when wrought upon by Iago 'perplexed in the extreme', which is true—and perplexed *to* extremes. As I said, his rhetoric is no longer moving the levers of the world, and he senses it, too. But he doesn't give it up, even after the two failed antitheses. Keeping to the phrase, 'of one who', he adds two poetic images: a base Indian and Arabian trees. The first image is arresting and the second startling, having the immobilizing force noted before. I said Othello's extravagances of expression and image are tactical, and these images create a useful distraction in the moments before Othello draws his sword. The precious jewel the base Indian threw away has become many precious drops of medicinal gum oozing from the bark of Arabian trees. They are Othello's own tears, falling fast, as he stands there before his hearers, weeping. There is a moment of dissonance, of contrary motion in the simile's flow of comparison contributing to its mesmerizing effect: it is Othello's tears that fall rapidly; gum oozes slowly. 'Set you down this'—another distraction, in the habitual mode of command. One imagines Lodovico and Gratiano thinking, 'do we write down the *trees*, too?' Whereupon Othello returns to his service to the state and his short way with a turbaned and circumcised Turk: 'And say besides, that in Aleppo once …'. The remaining lines of the passage are verse camouflaged as ordinary speech, including the last line, which Othello shares with Lodovico. Othello stabs himself, in the caesura: 'And smote him thus. ! O bloody period'. The naturalism is supported further by the half line spoken by Gratiano: 'All that is spoke is marred'. Othello's final couplet, with the extra, unstressed syllable at the caesura of the first line ('killed thee'), gives his death a formal, poetic cadenza. But the intensity and grace of that cadenza are enhanced by contrast with the roughness of the camouflaged verses that precede it.

Perhaps an even more striking example of this concealment of verse is the death of King Lear (in the Folio version), which occurs in the caesura of a regular, iambic pentameter line, although in the theatre we are unlikely to notice that Lear's last words, and the bystanders' cries of alarm, make a single line of verse: 'Look there, look there. [*He dies*] He faints. My lord, my lord!' (V. iii. 287). In what Sir Philip Sidney calls the 'breathing place in the midst of the verse', Lear stops breathing.[5]

In the last plays, the so-called romances, which shun psychological realism for puppet-like characters who seem not to know they are puppets, poetry returns in its own likeness, almost independent of the characters that speak it, as at the beginning of Shakespeare's career.[6] The plays become lyrical, and the poetic speeches no longer reveal the interior of characters. Instead, pretty speeches embellish the melodic line of the tale. In the late plays Shakespeare can slide in and out of verse almost before we notice the change has taken place, as when we walk in mountain valleys and are startled to find ourselves suddenly above the clouds.

Can we speak of larger structures as belonging to Shakespeare's style? The management of imagery, for example, the construction of character, or even the composition of scenes, in short, *mimesis*? We are used to thinking of these as belonging to technical mastery, not to style, which works closer to the actual words of the text, on the level of diction. But isn't style something more pervasive? Let us, for the moment, allow the words *style*, *poetics*, and *imitation* or *mimesis* to speak for themselves.

The word *style* is from L. *stilus*, a sharp writing instrument. Its origin should remind us that a style, however much it changes, is as distinctive to its author as handwriting. Style is said to be the man himself: *le style est l'homme même*. But the Latin phrase from which this *bon mot* derives puts it more carefully: the pen discloses something of the man: *stilus virum arguit*. The verb *arguo*, 'to show', is from Greek *argos* 'bright', which has the same root as the ancient literary term, *enargeia* 'clearness', the supreme quality of Homer's style. A style is a brightening, a revealing. It is a kind of truth. Not the truth of resemblance, of *mimesis*, of which more in a moment, but of bringing to light, the truth of coming into appearance from which we take the words *phenomenal* and *phenomenology* (Gr. *phainein* 'to appear, to shine forth'). *Stilus mundum arguit*, 'style lights the world' but also, 'style makes the world appear and shine forth.'

Since Aristotle, the term *poesis* goes with a still more familiar one from the vocabulary of dramatic theory, a word I have mentioned above in connection with style: *mimesis* 'imitation' or, to define it more fully, the production of something different from the

    [5] *Defence of Poesie*, in *The Prose Works of Sir Philip Sidney*, ed. Albert Feuillerat, vol. 3 (Cambridge: Cambridge University Press, 1968) 44.
    [6] Anne Barton, 'Leontes and the Spider: Language and the Speaker in Shakespeare's Last Plays', in Philip Edwards, Inga-Stina Ewbank, and G. K. Hunter (eds), *Shakespeare's Styles: Essays in Honour of Kenneth Muir* (Cambridge: Cambridge University Press, 1980) 131–50.

world which is yet an imitation of the world, or a part of it. Mimesis is repetition with difference. All *that* world—the staged, imaginary realm produced by mimetic technique—is imitative resemblance. But mimesis is lit up by style, or rather style causes it to shine from within. For while it might be supposed Shakespeare's style shines *upon* what is already modelled on the stage, it actually shines *out of* it, or through it, causing it to appear. Style is prior to and deeper than mimesis. This does not mean that mimesis is superficial and not connected intimately with style. It means instead that the technical art of mimesis is brought to life in Shakespeare by his style, such that we may think of a succession of mimetic styles. These, I shall argue, afford a more grounded way of distinguishing the plays than does the traditional distribution of them into genres, which goes back to the First Folio, but not to Shakespeare.

Shakespeare may well have thought of himself as writing comedies, histories, and tragedies, but such categories were not as definitive as one would suppose when looking at almost all collected editions since the First Folio. *Lear* is a tragedy in the Folio, but a history in the Quarto; some histories in the Folio are called tragedies when published in Quarto; the category of the romances, introduced in the later 19th century by Edward Dowden, didn't exist, and the word *romance* meant something different to Shakespeare.[7] *Cymbeline* is listed in the Folio as last of the tragedies; *Troilus and Cressida* is slipped in late between the histories and the tragedies, having affinities with each of these genres but belonging to neither.

A famous definition of comedy as mimesis, attributed to Cicero, became a commonplace in the Renaissance: '*imitatio vitae, speculum consuetudinis, imago veritatis*', 'an imitation of life, a mirror of manners, an image of truth'.[8] Its mirror image was supposed (wrongly, as it appears) to have been inscribed over the door of Shakespeare's Globe Theatre; *totus mundus agit histrionem*, 'everyone in the world plays the actor', or, in Shakespeare's version, all the world's a stage (*As You Like It*, II. vii. 139–66).[9] No account of Shakespeare's style can be complete unless it is joined to this mimetic figure underlying his plays: the stage is a repetition of the world, but a repetition with a difference made by an underlying style. Through all Shakespeare's characters in their human entanglements, a Shakespearean style shines: the framing of verses; the management of the imagery; the pillaging of sources; the architectonics of scenes; and the larger rhythm, the 'mood' or *Stimmung* of each of the plays.

---

[7] Lawrence Danson, *Shakespeare's Dramatic Genres* (Oxford: Oxford University Press, 2000) 11–14. For *romance*, see George Puttenham, *The Art of English Poesy: A Critical Edition*, Frank Whigham and Wayne A. Rebhorn (eds), (Ithaca: Cornell University Press, 2007) 175. For tragicomedy, see John Fletcher, preface to *Faithful Shepherdess*, Cyrus Hoy (ed.), in vol. 3 of Fredson Bowers (gen. ed.), *The Dramatic Works in the Beaumont and Fletcher Canon* (Cambridge: Cambridge University Press, 1976) 497.

[8] Germaine Greer, *Shakespeare: A Very Short Introduction* (Oxford: Oxford University Press, 1986) 28. The definition was attributed to Cicero by the ancient commentator, Donatus, and appeared in Renaissance editions of Terence and in Ben Jonson's *Everyman Out of his Humour* (1599) III. vi. 204–7, in C. H. Herford and Percy Simpson (eds), *Ben Jonson* (Oxford: Clarendon Press, 1966) vol. 3, 515.

[9] See Tiffany Stern, 'Was *Totus Mundus Agit Histrionem* ever the Motto of the Globe Theatre?', *Theatre Notebook* 51 (1997) 122–7.

To begin with the smallest of these, who of Shakespeare's contemporaries could make such a strong line of a subordinate clause—'That from the hunter's aim had ta'en a hurt'—without compromising the rhythm of the larger phrase in which it is enclosed? 'To the which place a poor sequestered stag | That from the hunter's aim had ta'en a hurt | Did come to languish' (*As You Like It*, II. i. 33–5). Technically, we have two and a half lines. But they read like a single rhythmic unit as well, with a dying fall. Who else would show us, in the words immediately preceding these, an oak's root undermining the bank of a stream, as if the root could hear the running water and were stretching towards it: 'Under an oak, whose antic root peeps out | Upon the brook that brawls along this wood' (II. i. 31–2)? Or who else would show us, later in the same play, an oak dying from its crown: 'Under an old oak, whose boughs were mossed with age | And high top bald with dry antiquity' (IV. iii. 105–6)? The efficient rhythm of the verse, binding the restless diction—'brawls along', 'dry antiquity', and 'mossed' (this last a characteristic turning of a noun into a verb)—provides a drone-note that sounds beneath the almost painfully intense imagery drawn from the observation of nature.

There is style in Shakespeare's scene construction, too. Who else could construct the astonishing but not untypical second scene of *As You Like It*, which lights up seven distinct characters in a single, impulsive, continually changing flow of action? The scene begins with the bantering, intimate conversation of Rosalind and Celia; it registers growing tension as other characters appear—the clown Touchstone, and then Le Beau, with his report of the father weeping for his sons, who have been injured, perhaps mortally, only a moment ago, by the Duke's prize wrestler, Charles; it turns still darker with the appearance of the brutal, usurping Duke and his court; and it reaches climax with the wrestling of Orlando and Charles, the great public centre of the scene. But the real climax comes after this and after the Duke's menacing departure. It is the quiet but intense exchange between Rosalind and Orlando, when she surprisingly gives him the chain around her neck, an intimate, physical gesture. It surprises even her. The scene draws towards its somber close with the unexpected appearance of the auxiliary and, as we had formerly thought, shallow character, Le Beau, who longs to see a better world: 'Sir, fare you well. / Hereafter, in a better world than this, / I shall desire more love and knowledge of you' (I. ii. 273–5). The scene closes with Orlando alone, delivering that terminal couplet quoted before, followed by the exclamation, 'heavenly Rosalind!' (I. ii. 279).

If the concept of genre is not fundamental to Shakespeare, but adventitious, so too is the distinction between dramaturgy on the one hand and literariness—the patterning of imaginative language—on the other. Splendid imaginative flights, such as Titania's speech on the disordering of nature—'And on old Hiems' thin and icy crown | An odorous chaplet of sweet summer buds | Is, as in mock'ry, set' (*A Midsummer Night's Dream*, II. i. 109–11); gorgeous set pieces, such as Gertrude's description of Ophelia's flowery and then muddy death (a lyrical display that stands out the more for being so far out of character for the speaker); Ovidian myths; copious classical allusions, especially early in Shakespeare's career; and also early in his career, notably in *Love's Labour's Lost*, flashy rhetorical patterning, and wit: these are among the most obvious manifestations of that literary making and shaping with words we refer to as *style*. But style is not something laid on top. It illuminates the world of the play from within.

So too does every action performed on the stage, every moment we like to call dramatic, invoking the ancient connection of this word with Greek *draô* 'to do', the root of *drama*, which means, literally, 'a deed, act'.[10] Whether it is Queen Margaret wiping the Duke of York's face with a handkerchief soaked in his young son's blood; or Antipholus of Ephesus preparing to lay siege to the door of his own house, with one of the twin Dromios on either side of the door; or Titus Andronicus killing the sons of Tamora, Queen of the Goths, and baking them in a pie, deliciously called a 'coffin' (V. ii. 187); or Romeo shaking off 'the yoke of inauspicious stars' (V. iii. 111); or Pyramus stabbing himself as he speaks the words, 'Now die, die, die, die, die' (V. i. 301); or Casca being the first to stab Caesar, 'speak hands for me' (III. i. 76); or Portia outsmarting Shylock; or Rosalind arranging all the marriages; or Hamlet foregoing to kill Claudius at prayer and then killing Polonius behind the arras (he can kill when he doesn't have to see what he's doing); or Othello smothering Desdemona; or Cornwall thumbing out Gloucester's eyes, frenziedly incited thereto by his wife; or Macbeth, offstage, killing Duncan, and Macbeth's hired murderers, onstage, killing Macduff's son, 'What, you egg!' (IV. ii. 83); or Antony with the shirt of Nessus on him, deciding to fight by sea; or Coriolanus gruffly standing as candidate, or turning his back on Rome, 'I banish you' (III. iii. 127), or being broken at last by his mother, 'O mother, mother! | What have you done?' (V. iii. 183–4); or Pericles burying Thaisa at sea, 'scarcely coffined, in the ooze'—'a terrible childbed hast thou had, my dear, | No light, no fire. Th' unfriendly elements | Forgot thee utterly' (Scene xi lines 55–7); or Polixenes fleeing Sicilia; or Prospero commanding the spirits to raise a tempest and make the strong-based promontory shake, catching his enemies in the net of his magic—none of this is possible without the words that make the stage shine forth as a world. In the theatre, your body has to speak the words: '*speak*, hands!'

And so to *Hamlet*, who can't seem to let his hands do the speaking. Let us pause over this play, at the dead centre of Shakespeare's career, ending with the roar of cannons. The most brilliant wielder of language among Shakespeare's characters speaks prose more often than is generally thought, and much of the verse he does speak sounds like prose—or rather, like ordinary speech. Hamlet's excitable mind may be the collateral damage of his creator's desire to push the language faster than it is used to going. Even the prince's droll habit of spinning doggerel contributes to the effect, by setting formality in verse at a still greater distance. The famous set-piece beginning, 'I have of late—but wherefore I know not—lost all my mirth', and containing the phrase, 'what a piece of work is a man!', is in prose (II. ii. 297–8; 305). But it is a prose intended to sound like verse, only to be deflated: 'This majestical roof fretted with golden fire— why, it appears no other thing to me than a foul and pestilent congregation of vapours' (lines 302–4).

---

[10] Aristotle, *Poetics* 1448a4–1448b1.

The most famous soliloquy in Shakespeare, beginning 'To be, or not to be', sounds in its first eleven lines like mixed prose and verse, up to that suddenly regular line, 'When we have shuffled off this mortal coil':

> To be, or not to be; that is the question:
> Whether 'tis nobler in the mind to suffer
> The slings and arrows of outrageous fortune,
> Or to take arms against a sea of troubles,
> And, by opposing, end them. To die, to sleep—
> No more, and by a sleep to say we end
> The heartache and the thousand natural shocks
> That flesh is heir to—'tis a consummation
> Devoutly to be wished. To die, to sleep.
> To sleep, perchance to dream. Ay, there's the rub,
> For in that sleep of death what dreams may come
> When we have shuffled off this mortal coil
> Must give us pause.
>
> *Hamlet* (III. i. 58–70)

At the outset, there is a softening of the iambic rhythm to make it sound like thought seeking a way and straying from the way. The first four lines have feminine terminations—*question, suffer, fortune, troubles*—with an enjambment in the second line. The fifth line is hypermetrical—there is that extra, unstressed syllable ('end') before the caesura ('them'), and this and the next three lines are enjambed. The result is a slackening of tension between the iambic rhythm and the rhythm of the grammatical phrase, pushing the iambic rhythm into the background. The effect is confirmed by the repetition of the phrase 'to sleep', and by the meditative dialogue tag, 'Ay, there's the rub'.

Hamlet has a pedantic tic, nicely balancing his love of doggerel, of abruptly shifting to semi-formal lectures addressed to anyone present, or to himself, often with the authoritative—but not the royal—*we*. The change of tone is signalled by a more pronounced verse rhythm: 'For in that sleep of death what dreams may come | When we have shuffled off this mortal coil'.

The difficulty of 'to die, to sleep— | No more' imitates the difficulty of the thought. Dying is the end of all sleep; to die is to sleep no more; therefore, dying isn't sleep. A moment later, however, the thought collapses back into cliché (dying is sleeping), and the verse tells us so by its momentary regularity, imitating the mind falling into one of its habitual courses: 'and by a sleep to say we end | The heartache and the thousand natural shocks | That flesh is heir to'. Remarkably, the effect of first disjoining sleep and death and then joining them again is now repeated: 'To die, to sleep. | To sleep, perchance to dream. Ay, there's the rub'.

The rub, the irritation, as from a shoe that is too tight, is not that death is altogether different from sleep, when formerly it was comforting to think death was just a sleep. The rub is that death might be too much like sleep, not extinguishing consciousness but prolonging it in nightmare. That gives one pause. Hamlet expatiates inside that pause in a regular style, enumerating miseries inflicted by the 'unworthy'—whips and scorns, insolence, pride, disdain, oppression, spurning, and delay—which are endured by Mr. Patient Merit, 'When he himself might his quietus make | With a bare bodkin' (lines 77–8). We might expect noble Hamlet to say whips and scorns are to be endured because one must do one's duty in life, facing it with courage. Instead, he says we ignobly endure these things because the fear of Hell 'puzzles the will, | And makes us rather bear those ills we have | Than fly to others that we know not of' (lines 82–4).

After the lugubrious humour of grunting and sweating under fardels, the soliloquy ends with some heavily sententious verses that rather grunt and sweat themselves. The subject matter is surprisingly bland, a pseudo-Senecan meditation on the disadvantage to virtue of Christian belief in an afterlife:

> Thus conscience does make cowards of us all,
> And thus the native hue of resolution
> Is sicklied o'er with the pale cast of thought,
> And enterprises of great pith and moment
> With this regard their currents turn awry,
> And loose the name of action. Soft you, now ...

> (lines 85–90)

The third line of this passage, set amongst the march-step rhythms surrounding it, falls out of line to throw up, nauseous from thinking too precisely on the event, 'sicklied o'er with the pale cast of thought'. But the martial and censorious tone of the whole, lecturing us on how 'enterprises ... lose the name of action' when weaklings are in charge, sounds like something Fortinbras would say, which is the point. Fortinbras is what a part of Hamlet wants to be.

Hamlet dies in the thick of much interruption and confusion, where the causes of action are not linear, as in classical tragedy, but reticulated, as in a network, so that plot events occurring in one place are entangled at a distance with others. In the final scene, the strings of the net are pulled tight in an entanglement of styles imitating the dreadful entanglement of causes. Nowhere does *Hamlet* proclaim its modernity more clearly than in this scene, in which distraction rules.

The dying Laertes asks for forgiveness, or, rather churlishly, since he has already forgiven Hamlet, for an *exchange* of forgiveness: 'Exchange forgiveness with me, noble Hamlet' (V. ii. 281). To this, Hamlet replies generously, although an instant too late for Laertes to hear, as he recognizes: 'Heaven make thee free of it. I follow thee' (line 284). Then, with perhaps a note of surprise, Hamlet observes, 'I am dead, Horatio' (line 285), for he soon will be, and he intends to commission Horatio to report on events. The sight of his mother's corpse distracts Hamlet, however, provoking the grim farewell: 'Wretched Queen, adieu!' (line 285). Recalling the Danish courtiers who are watching, the presumptive king of Denmark, lying on the ground, composes himself to address them, reverting to his public speaking mode for four lines, before giving it up:

> You that look pale and tremble at this chance,
> That are but mutes or audience to this act,

> Had I but time—as this fell sergeant Death
> Is strict in his arrest—O, I could tell you—
> But let it be.

(lines 286–90)

The speed of death's onset makes him resume his previous, dropped purpose: 'Horatio [as I was saying], I am dead' (line 290):

> Thou liv'st. Report me and my cause aright
> To the unsatisfied.
> HORATIO   Never believe it.
> I am more an antique Roman than a Dane.
> Here's yet some liquor left.
> HAMLET As thu'rt a man,
> Give me the cup. Let go. By heaven, I'll ha't.

(lines 291–5)

Only now, after an undignified struggle over the poisoned cup, does Hamlet resume his commission: 'O God, Horatio, what a wounded name, | Things standing thus unknown, shall live behind me!':

> If thou didst ever hold me in thy heart,
> Absent thee from felicity a while,
> And in this harsh world draw thy breath in pain
> To tell my story.

(lines 296–301)

What *is* his story? It is a tangled skein of causes, which might now be untangled for us in an orderly and linear, narrative form. So we hope. But there's a new interruption, and it comes after the caesura: 'What warlike noise is this?' (line 301). A messenger enters—it's the lapwing, Osric—reporting that Fortinbras (what's he doing back?) delivers this 'warlike volley' (line 303) not to the Danish court but (we wait for it) to the English ambassadors, who have just arrived looking to be rewarded for Rosencrantz and Guildenstern's death. You would have thought we could by now forget about Rosencrantz and Guildenstern—they've gone 'to't' (V. ii. 57), as Horatio says—but Shakespeare is scrupulous in tying up loose ends, and his further intention is to strangle eloquence with interruption.

When Hamlet declares for the third time the enormous fact, 'O, I die, Horatio' (line 304), you sense he wishes people would stop shooting off ordinance, beating drums, and rushing in to announce ambassadors so that he might at last complete a sentence. The most pathetic words he speaks are 'I could tell you' (line 289), but he can't.

Hamlet's last words to Horatio likewise convey this sense of haste and interruption. He says he won't last long enough to hear the news from England, but he guesses—the connective force of this 'but' is obscure, as is typical of hurried statements—the Lords of Denmark, an elective monarchy, will choose Fortinbras to rule them. To this, Hamlet gives his 'dying voice':

> I cannot live to hear the news from England,
> But I do prophesy th' election lights
> On Fortinbras. He has my dying voice.
> So tell him.
>
> (lines 306–9)

At last, a part of Hamlet—his dying voice—gets to be Fortinbras.

In the little masterpiece of compression that follows—it's a strangled oration—Hamlet resumes for the last time his commission to Horatio, who is to tell Fortinbras all the circumstances, large and small, that have led to this outcome: 'So tell him, with th' occurrents, more and less, | Which have solicited' (lines 309–10). Solicited what? And who solicits? The verb *to solicit* is common enough in Shakespeare, but this is the only time it is used without a personal subject, without someone to do the soliciting. The events have been soliciting the event. Etymologically, *to solicit* means to put the whole in motion (L. *sollus + ciere*, OED, *solicit*, definition 4), and the Riverside edition's 'incited' is as good a gloss as any because it has the same verbal root, although for that reason it is no less obscure.[11] Who incites? And what is incited? Is the answer to *what* is incited just the tragic loading of the stage, or is it that plus Fortinbras' succession to the Danish throne? In the stress and urgency of the moment, the thought is completed in Hamlet's mind but remains incomplete in ours. The words, 'the rest is silence', are our only answer. After them, Hamlet cries in agony, and dies:

> HAMLET   O, I die, Horatio!
> The potent poison quite o'ercrows my spirit.
> I cannot live to hear the news from England,
> But I do prophesy th' election lights
> On Fortinbras. He has my dying voice.
> So tell him, with th' occurrents, more and less,
> Which have solicited. The rest is silence.
> O, O, O, O!   *He dies*
>
> (lines 304–11)

Only now is Hamlet seen off with some dignity—'Now cracks a noble heart'—but not without further interruption, and a trace of irritation: 'Good night, sweet prince, | And flights of angels sing thee to thy rest.— | Why does the drum come hither?' (lines 312–14). The dismissal of Hamlet to 'flights of angels' may have been necessary, given the Christian setting, but it is uncharacteristic of Horatio's Roman spirit, which is why the interrupting drum should drown those angels out.

---

[11] *The Riverside Shakespeare*, 2nd edn, G. Blakemore Evans and J. J. Tobin (Boston: Houghton Mifflin, 1997).

The entire action of the play, its *mythos* in Aristotle's sense, the plot, or 'standing all together of events' (*tôn pragmatôn systasis*), is compressed in that phrase, 'th'occurrents more and less | Which have solicited'.[12] Horatio's promise to unpack it by telling 'how these things came about' is to be fulfilled offstage, after the end of the play, and we rather wish we could hear it. For the present, with his usual skill, Shakespeare has Horatio review why these intruders are crowding in on the stage: 'since so jump upon this bloody question | You from the Polack wars, and you from England, | Are here arrived' (lines 329–31). Horatio then asks that order be given for the four bodies to be displayed in the Roman manner on a 'stage', that is, on a raised bier, thus preventing further violence in the state by an open declaration of all that has occurred:

> So shall you hear
> Of carnal, bloody, and unnatural acts,
> Of accidental judgements, casual slaughters,
> Of deaths put on by cunning and forced cause;
> And, in this upshot, purposes mistook
> Fall'n on th'inventors' heads. All this can I
> Truly deliver.
> FORTINBRAS Let us haste to hear it,
> And call the noblest to the audience.

(lines 334–41)

In 'carnal, bloody, and unnatural acts', we could be hearing of a tragedy by Seneca. But 'accidental' and 'casual' and 'purposes mistook' put us in the modern world—as Tom Stoppard recognized—of cross-purposes and too much information. This is not a murky style. It is a style that lights up the murkiness of murk.

Shakespeare's style changed because he got better, as I have said, more fluidly naturalistic, and broader, which are technical reasons. But his style also changed because he got older, which is an existential reason. Separating the two is one of the harder questions any examination of Shakespeare's poetics must answer.

An obvious comparison in this regard would be between *Romeo and Juliet* (1594–5) and *Antony and Cleopatra* (1606–7), which are separated by more than a decade. Part of the difference is technical improvement on the micro and macro levels, in prosody and architectonic construction. In *Antony and Cleopatra* we see a surer command of the action within the play's total structure, shortening scenes, intercutting them, and increasing their number, so that many actions flow smoothly together without waste or delay. There is no pausing for speeches that are not immediate to what is occurring. The verse of *Antony and Cleopatra* is more supple, more muscular, continuous and strong; it doesn't prance, and it doesn't need rhyme. The rare displays of virtuosity have a reason to be there, as with Enobarbus' description of Cleopatra's barge, showing us both how vital and how calculating of effect Cleopatra is, though we are happy to be taken in by it, too: 'O, rare for Antony!' (II. ii. 212). There is nothing like that in *Romeo and Juliet*, not

---

[12] Aristotle, *Poetics* 1450a12. Cf. 1450a8: *synthesis tôn pragmatôn*

that we miss it when reading that play. But when we set it beside *Antony and Cleopatra* we feel the progression from a young genius whose talent is explosively on display to a mature, understated, effortlessly powerful master.

Antony and Cleopatra is about middle-aged love. It is their last fling and they know it. It is only right they put on a show for each other, and it's a performance in every sense of the word. Romeo and Juliet never *imitate* love for each other, even when making a sonnet together (I. v. 92–105): that would be insincere, which when we are young we imagine is a terrible thing to be. There is no room in which irony might open a space between what Romeo and Juliet say and what they think: they say what they think, spontaneously and brilliantly, and it falls into art. But insincerity—not lying, which is unwise, but insincerity, the play of tiny differences and even ironies—is inevitable in love because attraction is a kind of art as well, one superbly practised by Cleopatra. Antony and Cleopatra perform all the time (that is, they *play*)—their first kiss in the opening scene is in public, and is applauded—and there is lots of space between what they say and what they think. The performative character of love is a truth you can't figure out, even if you're Shakespeare in his early thirties, writing *Romeo and Juliet*. You have to put in more years.

Instead of three or four dramatic genres, I propose we consider five kinds of mimesis which emerge more or less sequentially in Shakespeare's career: *elevated, articulated, reticulated, saturated,* and *evacuated.* These constitute Shakespeare's mimetic styles, where *style* refers to an order of practices, including the minutiae of verbal patterning, the architectonics of scene construction, the organization of plot, the interaction of characters, the mixture of generic codes, and the deep orientation of the work within the larger, meta-literary order of myth. As we saw at the outset, a style is idiosyncratic because it is an interweaving of technical practices and also an involuntary, unconscious, and inspired distortion of these practices as they flow together in the work of a single artist. When they do so productively, in any of the styles named above, the effect is what we call 'Shakespearean': *stilus virum arguit.* But because these stylistic practices are at the foundations of the mimetic, as the style itself reveals a world, one we say Shakespeare creates: *stilus mundum arguit.*

In *elevated mimesis*—in *Titus Andronicus,* for example, or *Richard III*; in *The Comedy of Errors, Two Gentlemen of Verona,* and *The Taming of the Shrew*; and in the plays on the Wars of the Roses—the characters are individually vivid but strangely isolated from one another, as if they have trouble imagining other minds. This gives way to the articulated mimesis of the early mature plays, such as *Romeo and Juliet, A Midsummer Night's Dream,* and, looking forward, *Much Ado about Nothing,* where characters irritate one another into being what they are. It is at this stage that the hieratic difference between upper-class lovers and their lower-class servants is, so to speak, turned on its side. The models from which this difference of class is taken are Henry Medwall's *Fulgens and Lucrece* and the early Shakespeare plays, *Two Gentlemen of Verona* and *The Comedy of Errors,* where the lower-class characters are comic grotesques, Launce with his dog, whom he tenderly loves, more than his toothless milkmaid, who yet can sew and brew good ale; and Dromio of Ephesus' greasy, orbicular love, whom he imagines lighting like a candle and fleeing from her by her own light. A clear hierarchy is established in which the coarsely comic, lower-class characters set off the refined sentiments of their social betters. But between the characters, there is little of that sort of dramatic interaction by which each forces the other into taking firmer outlines, into becoming what she or he is.

The change to articulated mimesis is confirmed in *Much Ado about Nothing* (a play that admittedly comes after *1 Henry IV*, which I shall shortly discuss), where the social difference between low and high becomes the aesthetic difference between foreground and background, with the lower, not the higher characters brought to the fore. In general, the higher class characters—and the older men, Don Pedro and Leonato—speak in verse, and the more familiar ones speak in prose. Benedick and Beatrice, speaking in prose, are of course socially improved and no longer grotesque, but they remain inferior in rank and they also remain the source of the humor, in keeping with their lower-class prototypes. Hero and Claudio, like Fulgens and Lucrece, are in the background, speaking in verse. More importantly, Benedick and Beatrice are the whetstones of each other's wit, and of each other's love. Among the most beautiful lines of the play are the self-consciously poetical ones spoken by the character with highest authority, one who has little part in the action:

> Good morrow, masters, put your torches out.
> The wolves have preyed, and look, the gentle day
> Before the wheels of Phoebus round about
> Dapples the drowsy east with spots of grey.
>
> (V. iii. 24–7)

This is Don Pedro, and he is the occasion, earlier, for Beatrice's most intriguing and beautiful words:

> DON PEDRO   Will you have me, lady?
> BEATRICE   No, my lord, unless I might have another for working days.
>   Your grace is too costly to wear every day. But I beseech your grace,
>   pardon me. I was born to speak all mirth and no matter.
> DON PEDRO   Your silence most offends me, and to be merry best
>   becomes you; for out o' question, you were born in a merry hour.
> BEATRICE   No, sure, my lord, my mother cried. But then there was a
>   star danced, and under that was I born.
>
> (II. ii. 305–14)

Beatrice is provoked by this slightly awkward exchange into being more deeply who she is, in a moment of dramatic articulation with Don Pedro. She has perhaps overstepped slightly the bounds of harmless flirtation, telling Don Pedro she would take a husband if he were one of Don Pedro's father's making—and does the Don perhaps have a brother? Don Pedro can hardly say other than what he does say, although he knows it will put her on the spot: will you have me? Beatrice recovers beautifully with the remark about working days and holidays, acknowledging Don Pedro's rank (instead of his age!)

and so turning the proposal aside, apologizing for the carelessness of her humor—'all mirth and no matter'. Don Pedro accepts the apology by showing it to be unnecessary: he would always want her to speak freely as she does, being, as she is, 'born in a merry hour'. Then comes the surprise: 'No, my lord, my mother cried'. Then another: 'But then there was a star danced, and under that was I born'. Beatrice is orphaned, and we now wonder, did her mother die at her birth? Or, as is more likely, on reflection, is Beatrice recalling to Don Pedro's mind, and to her own, that a birth entails more than the position of the stars, however merry: there must be pain, and crying. This is a comedy; Beatrice is after all going to be married; and at some level she knows it. A depth of sensitivity and remembrance is revealed which we have not seen before in Beatrice, and which we will not forget. It comes from the same place that will make her say, 'Kill Claudio' (IV. i. 290). The command given at this later moment shocks us, but we know where it comes from: we've been subtly prepared.

Articulated mimesis doesn't work only one way. It is reflexive. We have seen how much more of Beatrice is revealed in the exchange with Don Pedro, perhaps even to herself. But the character of Don Pedro gains depth, too. It is this extra depth of sensitivity and graciousness which allows him (without incredulity on our part) those marvelous lines on the dawn.

We begin to meet reticulated mimesis in the plays of the later 1590s, *As You Like It*, *Julius Caesar*, and especially the two parts of *Henry IV*, where the different characters appear to be disposed at the interstices of a network extending out of sight beyond the borders of the play. In *As You Like It*, the contrast between the cruelty of the court, where 'breaking of ribs [is] sport for ladies' (I. ii. 128–9), and the savage forest with its bumpkin purlieus is morally reticulated with a complexity not to be found in the contrast between city and forest in *A Midsummer Night's Dream*. The same is true, in *1 Henry IV*, of the Boar's Head Tavern, Gads Hill, the court, and Shrewsbury field. Sir Walter Blunt arrives in scene one, 'new lighted from his horse, | Stained with the variation of each soil | Betwixt that Holmedon and this seat of ours' (I. i. 63–5). We are surprised there is any passage at all from one dramatic region to another, and indeed very few make the journey. The principle of the Gestalt may come to our aid, for example, if we compare the feeling these intruded worlds create to the circles of the space stations in *2001: A Space Odyssey*, where what is shown on the screen is part of a much larger structure we are forced to imagine. In *1 Henry IV*, what we feel when we see the mud on Sir Walter Blunt and his horse is not the power of English history, or the power of the past, but rather the power of contemporary English life, the hugeness of the country, the multiplicity in it of projects and lives, among which even the struggle for the throne is only one project entangled with innumerable others.

At the outset of Act II, not long before dawn, when the big dipper is descending— 'Charles' Wain is over the new chimney' (II. i. 2)—we see an inn where rising carters call for lamps and grumble about fleas in the beds and the bad feed for their horses. Shakespeare seems interested in letting other worlds shine out for their own sakes, picking up technical phrases and odd tricks of speech: 'beat cut's saddle, put a few flocks in the point. Poor jade is wrung in the withers, out of all cess' (II. i. 5–7). Here are people with projects of their own, tangential to the play: 'I have a gammon of bacon and two races of ginger to be delivered as far as Charing Cross' (II. i. 24–5). The main characters seem to be spinning in worlds of their own, no longer standing before us, like Richard III, in splendid and stable isolation.

Consider Prince Hal's interview and reconciliation with his father, the crucial human scene of the play (III. ii.). We have already considered their reconciliation scene in *Henry IV* and much the same thing occurs here. There is keen awareness of actions not visible to us on the stage. The king and the prince are pulled together towards the showdown with their enemies at Shrewsbury field. But each is alone. It is as if the net is being pulled from one side, towards the battlefield, and everyone tends in the direction of the pull.

We pass next to the *saturated mimesis* of the series of great tragedies beginning with *Othello* and *King Lear* and ending with *Coriolanus*, but anticipated back in 1601, with the over-determined character of Hamlet. In *Romeo and Juliet*, we love the principals and dread the event. In the great tragedies, we dread the heroes themselves, about whom we have so much strangely superfluous knowledge: Othello's martial and romantic youth in North Africa; Lear's marriage and his feelings about women; Macbeth's enslavement to his wife; Coriolanus' enslavement to his mother; all of this is useless but enthralling. The characters of these later tragedies are oozing information about themselves and we admire their wasteful intensity.

What about Antony and Cleopatra? Oddly, the extra information we have about them now seems important for understanding what they are: Antony's drinking horse piss in the Alps, Cleopatra's salad days with Caesar. They do not leak information: their information fields are magnetized by powerful myths—Isis-Aphrodite and Hercules— which draw all things in the world and in the past towards them. In the future as well, when they enter into art, a translation to which Cleopatra will refer, with inadvertent irony, through the boy actor that plays her as she speaks:

> The quick comedians
> Extemporally will stage us, and present
> Our Alexandrian revels. Antony
> Shall be brought drunken forth, and I shall see
> Some squeaking Cleopatra boy my greatness
> I'th'posture of a whore.

(V. ii. 212–17)

One is squeaking now. Antony and Cleopatra have already fallen into art as she speaks, and they have done so as unconsciously as Romeo and Juliet fall into a sonnet. Cleopatra believes this falling awaits her in the future; but the future has arrived. We begin to understand that this future performance, with its 'absurd intents' (V. ii. 222), is not a sad derivative of Antony and Cleopatra's stronger existence, which is how Cleopatra sees the matter. She recoils with horror from what she foresees, her slow and undignified leaking away into art, instead of the magnificent departure she merits, with its nimbus of immortal longings. She will have that, too. What she does not see is how all those future performances of *Antony and Cleopatra*, including the one we are watching, are like clouds that travel from the sea to the origin of the Nile, re-enriching it with rains in the Ethiopian highlands.

The silt that the Nile deposits on the land, making it fertile, recalls the slime of the fatal asp's trail, at once disgusting and excitingly fertile, a primordial muck. Enobarbus tells his auditors that the priests bless Cleopatra in her sacred, leaky state, when she is 'riggish' (II. ii. 246), slimy and wet with desire. Every performance of this play, like those clouds returning to the highlands, travels back to the source in Shakespeare's style.

The same visionary conviction of seeing things at the source, the source of poetry and the source of life, occurs when Cleopatra enters into that dreamlike state in which she imagines, or dreams, the Antony she knew. The high style of her speech is not, however, as in early Shakespeare, a poem leaking from the stage through a character one can hardly imagine speaking this way. Cleopatra so owns her speech it comes upon us that what she's asking about Antony may also be asked about her. Was she, is she real?

> CLEOPATRA   I dreamt there was an Emperor Antony.
>   O, such another sleep, that I might see
>   But such another man!
> DOLABELLA   If it might please ye—
> CLEOPATRA   His face was as the heav'ns, and therein stuck
>   A sun and moon, which kept their course and lighted
>   This little O o'th' earth.
> DOLABELLA   Most sovereign creature—
> CLEOPATRA   His legs bestrid the ocean; his reared arm
>   Crested the world. His voice was propertied
>   As all the tunèd spheres ...
>   His delights
>   Were dolphin-like; they showed his back above
>   The element they lived in. In his livery
>   Walked crowns and crownets. Realms and islands were
>   As plates dropped from his pocket.
>
>   (V. ii. 75–91)

The Antony Cleopatra imagines is literally false, as Dolabella tells her, except, perhaps, for the islands dropping from Antony's pocket, a major annoyance to Octavian and the Roman Senate:

> CLEOPATRA   Think you there was, or might be, such a man |
>   As this I dreamt of?
> DOLABELLA   Gentle madam, no
>
>   (V. ii. 92–3)

From Dolabella's point of view she is temporizing, although he does feel the power of the being that gives her this power of speech. That power seems now to be leaking away, a receding flood, the purest residue of saturated mimesis. The effect—of a flood that momentarily swells even as it recedes—is sublime. 'You lie, up to the hearing of the gods', Cleopatra exclaims,

> But if there be, or ever were one such,
> It's past the size of dreaming. Nature wants stuff
> To vie strange forms with fancy; yet t'imagine
> An Anthony were nature's piece 'gainst fancy,
> Condemning shadows quite.

(V. ii. 94–9)

The alternative, *if there be* and *if there ever were*, implies the question, can we say things in the past exist now? What she is seeing is beyond anything mere dreams could produce. But such fancies have one advantage over the reality that is nature, which has limited 'stuff' to embody its strangest forms. Nature cannot 'vie' or weigh its 'strange forms' against those made by fancy because these are not limited by material embodiment, and so may vastly exceed in number and size the totality of things in the world.

Cleopatra says the Antony she calls to mind isn't a dream in this sense, however, a disembodied fancy. That is because she's slept with the man. At this moment, memory and imagination come together in her speech. She is recalling someone real, and his body, colossal and cosmic, is calling her home. But she has not forgotten the competition between fancy and nature. Antony is nature's *piece* against fancy, a chess move executed so well that all fancies that would 'vie' with it fall into its shadow, condemned to become shadows themselves. Cleopatra's ontological discourse, mixing fantasy and logical rigour, follows at a distance Anselm's argument for the existence of God. God is a being than which no greater can be conceived. If a being than which no greater can be conceived did not exist, that being would be lesser than the being that exists. An inexistent God is therefore a contradiction, because it is lesser and greater at once. Therefore, God exists, condemning shadows quite. Substitute *Antony* for *God* in this argument and you get close to what Cleopatra means.

It is a most Graeco-Roman colossus Cleopatra imagines. Antony has the heavens in his face and a voice like the music of the spheres. His pleasures leap like dolphins and his bounty knows no limits, dropping realms and islands from his pocket. Yet we feel behind this complex image the presence of something closer to what Cleopatra is herself, a supersaturated Antony, like the silt hanging in the waters of the Nile. And like Cleopatra, he will need constant renewal by mimetic performance, which is the continual, pulsating release of the energies that belong to Shakespeare's radiant style.

The final category is the *evacuated mimesis* of the plays we have learned to call the romances. All the mess is gone. There is almost no noise in the signal, no complex *timbre*, such as we hear in everything Cleopatra says. The characters ring clear as bells and never talk aside from the purpose. In *Pericles* we hear of the sweat and infected lungs of the brothel, but these are just words. Marina, that evacuated girl—she's perfectly empty, but empty as a cello is empty—has all but purged the brothels of Tyre with singing, dancing, sewing, and philosophy: 'Deep clerks she dumbs' (xx: 5). By her power she seems almost to make the halyards and stays of Pericles' ship resonate with the music of the spheres (xxi: 210).

Miranda, in *The Tempest*, is likewise a *tabula rasa*. She is prompt but vacuous, not unlike her magician father, Prospero, who for all his studies has a little rage in him and not much else, so that the rage may amplify and re-echo in his inner, empty spaces. He inhabits a cave and he is one. Prospero does show forgiveness, as it happens, although the forgiveness appears when required by the logic of the plot—'I do forgive thee, | Unnatural though thou art' (V. i. 78–9)—not from any great effort on Shakespeare's part to show psychological depth. Nor is this missed. The villains in the romances are villains because they are, as long as they are, but there is no motivation, as there is in Iago, and no constancy to them. In *Cymbeline*, Iachimo repents. Posthumus, with much noble reverberation, hardly does even that as he forgives his deceiver. 'Pardon's the word to all' (V. vi. 423) says King Cymbeline, who cheerfully pays up to the Romans, having just beaten them in a battle, the occasion of which was refusal of this payment. Spinelessness rules.

Yet somehow, oddly, we like the characters in the romances for this, because they belong more purely to art as the truth of appearing, of shining forth; they show style and are the style they show. The imitation of life in these plays is not a *mimesis* in the traditional sense of a modeling from without. It is an invitation to contemplate the characters' shining forth at an aesthetic distance, and this distance has its own truth to tell. To shine is perfect style.

We have passed in this survey of Shakespeare's mimetic styles from elevated to evacuated mimesis. What last example might be given for this last, this most evanescent of Shakespeare's styles, in which the faintness of the illumination has its own beauty, like starlight? I would choose Florizell's vision of Perdita as a wave of the sea, always in the moment and always the same:

> When you do dance, I wish you
> A wave o'th' sea, that you might ever do
> Nothing but that, move still, still so,
> And own no other function.
>
> *The Winter's Tale* (IV. iv. 140–3)

'Own no other function': not even thought.

SELECT BIBLIOGRAPHY

Abrams, M. H. (1999) 'Style' and 'Stylistics', in *A Glossary of Literary Terms*, 7th edn (Fort Worth, Texas: Harcourt Brace) 303–7.

Barton, Anne (1980) 'Leontes and the Spider: Language and the Speaker in Shakespeare's Last Plays', in Philip Edwards, Inga-Stina Ewebank, and G. K. Hunter (eds) *Shakespeare's Styles: Essays in Honour of Kenneth Muir* (Cambridge: Cambridge University Press) 131–50.

Catano, James V. (2005) 'Stylistics.' *The Johns Hopkins Guide to Literary Theory and Criticism*, 2nd edn, Michael Groden, Martin Kreiswirth, and Imre Szeman (eds), (Baltimore: The Johns Hopkins University Press) 895–9 (with bibliography).

Danson, Lawrence (2000) *Shakespeare's Dramatic Genres* (Oxford: Oxford University Press).

De Grazia, Margreta (2001) 'Shakespeare and the Craft of Language', in Margreta de Grazia and Stanley Wells (eds) *The Cambridge Companion to Shakespeare* (Cambridge: Cambridge University Press) 49–64.

Dolven, J. (2012) 'Style', in *The Princeton Encyclopedia of Poetry and Poetics*, 4th edn, Roland Greene (Editor in Chief), Stephen Cushman (gen. ed.), Clare Cavanagh, Jahan Ramazani, Paul Rouzer, Harris Feinsod, David Marno, and Alexander Slessarev (eds), (Princeton: Princeton University Press), 1369–70 (with bibliography).

Erne, Lucas (2003) *Shakespeare as Literary Dramatist* (Cambridge: Cambridge University Press).

Greer, Germaine (1986) *Shakespeare: A Very Short Introduction* (Oxford: Oxford University Press).

Hardison, O. B. (1989) *Prosody and Purpose in the English Renaissance* (Baltimore: Johns Hopkins University Press).

Holland, Peter (2004) 'Shakespeare', in H. G. C. Matthew and Brian Harrison (eds) *Oxford Dictionary of National Biography*, (Oxford: Oxford University Press) 49: 939–76

Kermode, Frank (2000) *Shakespeare's Language* (New York: Farrar, Strauss, Giroux).

McDonald, Russ (2001) *Shakespeare and the Arts of Language* (Oxford: Oxford University Press).

——(2006) *Shakespeare's Late Style* (Cambridge: Cambridge University Press).

Palfrey, Simon, and Tiffany Stern (2007) *Shakespeare in Parts* (Oxford: Oxford University Press).

Parker, Patricia (1996) *Shakespeare from the Margins: Language, Culture, Context* (Chicago: University of Chicago Press).

Poole, William (2003) 'Unpointed Words: Shakespearean Syntax in Action', *Cambridge Quarterly* 32: 27–48.

Stern, Tiffany (2004) *Making Shakespeare: From Stage to Page* (London: Routledge, 2004)

Stern, Tiffany (1997) 'Was Totus Mundus Agit Histrionem ever the Motto of the Globe Theatre?', *Theatre Notebook* 51: 122–7.

Vickers, Brian (1968) *The Artistry of Shakespeare's Prose* (London: Methuen).

Winslow, R. (2012) 'Stylistics', in *The Princeton Encyclopedia of Poetry and Poetics*, Fourth Edition, eds. Roland Greene (Editor in Chief), Stephen Cushman (gen. ed.), Clare Cavanagh, Jahan Ramazani, Paul Rouzer, Harris Feinsod, David Marno, and Alexander Slessarev (eds.), (Princeton: Princeton University Press) 1370–2 (with bibliography).

Wright, George T. (1988) *Shakespeare's Metrical Art* (Berkeley: University of California Press).

CHAPTER 2

....

SHAKESPEARE'S STYLE IN THE 1590S

....

GORAN STANIVUKOVIC

2.1 STYLE IN THEORY

....

The last decade of the 16th century shaped not only England's history and politics but also left a mark on the style through which the 1590s expressed themselves. Yet materialist and historicist criticism have neglected to study formal properties of style and have showed no interest in the analysis of language of the 1590s, as if neither style nor language is a materialist practice in its own right. The fact that some of the most popular playwrights in this period—Shakespeare, Marlowe, Jonson—were also major poets is evidence that the 1590s placed a greater importance on language than on the stories and characters, and that the innovations of the Elizabethan world spoke primarily through language.

Two distinctive features of the style of 1590s are ornament and symmetry. These two stylistic properties provide a general aesthetic framework within which different stylistic strategies gave form to literature and other fields of artistic expression. From architecture to garden design, from paintings to tapestries, from music to poetry and prose, and from interior design to embroidery in clothing, ornament and symmetry shape the aesthetics of the 1590s. In the process of crafting meaning in poetry, through formal devices of language, ornament features not only as an embellishment of syntax or an utterance, but also as an acoustic unit of 'great force', according to George Puttenham, a theorist of poetry whose writing on the art of ornamentation is a key text of the 1590s ideas about style as a rhetorically produced practice of expression in speech and writing.[1]

Puttenham defines ornament in the following way:

---

[1] George Puttenham, *The Art of English Poesy*, Frank Whigham and Wayne A. Rebhorn (eds), (Ithaca: Cornell University Press, 2007) 226.

The ornament we speak of is given to it by figures and figurative speeches, which be the flowers, as it were, and colors that a poet setteth upon his language by art, as the embroiderer doth his stone and pearl of passements of gold upon the stuff of a princely garment, or as the excellent painter bestowed the rich orient colors upon his table of portrait.[2]

Puttenham writes at the time when the expansion of the semantic field of the English language occurred alongside literary influences which came largely from Italy and France, and which provided writers of the 1590s with an opportunity not only to compete with one another, but also to develop new strategies for creating meaning. Rhetorical tropes and figures, which Puttenham and his contemporaries consider principal vehicles of ornamentation, became tools with which the new semantic and acoustic potential of language expressed the two stylistic properties most powerfully. Shakespeare's writing of the 1590s consistently registers these main features of 1590s aesthetics.

The earlier phase of Shakespeare's writing, the decade of the 1590s, was a highly productive period. He wrote twenty-two plays, two popular narrative poems, and some of the Sonnets. In the earliest part of this rich decade, up to 1595, Shakespeare adheres more closely to the rhetorical and stylistic norms of his age. By the end of this decade, in the years 1595–1600, the style of Shakespeare's writing becomes more flexible and rhetorically subtler, and he questions the limits of style to shape meaning in more obvious ways. The boundary that separates these chronological segments in the development of Shakespeare's earlier style is not firm; some stylistic features are prominent throughout this earlier phase, others change or cease to be prominent only in one of the temporal segments. Some of the earliest works, like *Titus Andronicus* (1592), *The Comedy of Errors* (1594), *Venus and Adonis* (1592–3), *The Rape of Lucrece* (1593–4), and some of the Sonnets, mix rhetorical sophistication, characteristic of his later phase, with rhetorical repetitiveness which stands out in his earlier works. And this earlier phase already shows that in using even the smallest of poetic devices, such as epithets and metaphor, Shakespeare is aware of the limits, potential, and dangers produced by ornaments: he treats figures and tropes as vehicles through which the material world is invoked in order to search for meanings that transcend these objects and that question how reason processes reality, or nature, in the formation of meaning in poetry. The style of earlier Shakespeare is far from being coherent and consistently rhetorical. There are variations in the subtlety and purpose of using tropes to achieve symmetry. Those variations are especially evident in the difference between the lyricism of the early comedies, the figurative language of the narrative poems, and the rhetorical 'declamation' of the early history plays.[3]

In the earlier phase of writing, Shakespeare complements his emulation of symmetry and ornamentation with his fondness for hyperbole and bombast, two closely related

---

[2] Whigham and Rebhorn (2007) 222.
[3] F. E. Halliday, *The Poetry of Shakespeare's Plays* (London: Gerald Duckworth, 1964) 60.

but not identical forms of stylistic excess. Hyperbole is a trope inextricable from the notion of bombast. As a trope, hyperbole is a formal unit of style, a figure of thought, described in rhetorical and poetic treatises from Graeco-Roman times to Shakespeare's age. In the pages of rhetorical manuals published at the end of the 16th century, hyperbole features as one of the few most elaborately described tropes, alongside metaphor, irony, metonymy, and synecdoche. This suggests that the trope was considered particularly crucial to rhetorical composition and effective persuasion. Thus Gabriel Harvey considers hyperbole one of the 'most spirited formulas of exaggeration', alluding to the large creative potential of this trope.[4] Judging by the attentiveness to detail of theoretical explication and the amount of hyperbole and bombast in literature in the 1590s, this decade could be called an age of excess. While theatre practitioners of the 1590s generally treated bombast as a derogatory feature of style, in the same period, theorists of style remained silent on the subject of bombast, focusing instead on describing the variety of ways in which exaggeration produced by hyperbole shapes the fictions of reality.

The contrast in their treatment of bombast, which was often viewed in pejorative terms, and hyperbole, which was typically recommended as a good stylistic device, suggests that, in the 1590s, there was a marked difference in judging bombast when it is delivered on stage and when it is executed in writing. Any assessment of Shakespeare's style of the 1590s has to take into account the fact that symmetry often includes repetitions and parallelism which may or may not turn into bombast, and that bombast and hyperbole have their roots in both aesthetic and cultural developments and transformations in this decade. The bombast and hyperbole of the 1590s dominate Shakespeare's earlier style, not only because Shakespeare is engaged in the creative imitation of other forms of bombastic and excessive writing which preceded him, the Euphuistic writing of John Lyly's prose, the bombast of Senecan tragedies, and the extravagant rhetoric of Ovidian poetry of desire, but because social excess and individual ambition of the 1590s set the tone for how individuals expressed themselves in politics and culture.

Bombast and hyperbole, however, are not interchangeable terms. Hyperbole is a figure of thought and one of the devices used to achieve bombast. Bombast is a stylistic mode, a manner of speaking and writing characterized by turgid and inflated language. The Elizabethans seem to have understood bombast to be more of an acoustic and an almost renegade quality of language, in contrast to rhetoric which was generally organized into a system. They considered hyperbole a cognitive device whose purpose is to communicate reason through a specific verbal form and to shape judgement by manipulating truth. Hyperbole shares with bombast the force of exaggeration, but not necessarily its lexical limitlessness and inelegance. The Greek etymology of hyperbole, 'to throw beyond', links this trope to the dynamism of upward movement, beyond the credible and the probable. This makes hyperbole a trope that forces thinking, whereas bombast is the cumulative effect created either by heaping of hyperboles or through

---

[4] Gabriel Harvey, *Ciceronianus*, C. A. Forbes (trans.), H. S. Wilson (ed.), University of Nebraska Studies: Studies in the Humanities 4 (Lincoln: University of Nebraska Press, 1945) 53.

linguistic inflation, or by the mixture of these two ways of creating excess. In a world which started to reach beyond the boundaries of its geography and politics, hyperbole became a convenient vehicle to carry newfangled ambitions further than before. And Shakespeare turns the propensity of hyperbole to capture the incredible into the virtue of his style.

Contemporary definitions of hyperbole explore this trope precisely in relation to truth. In the second, expanded edition of his rhetorical manual, *The Garden of Eloquence* (1593), Henry Peacham defines hyperbole as a 'sentence or saying surmounting the truth onely for the cause of increasing or diminishing, not with purpose to deceiue by speaking untruly'.[5] In this formulation, the purpose of hyperbole lies in the interplay between truth and deception. For George Puttenham, however, the work of hyperbole lies in 'great dissimulation', which does not make the hearer believe or not believe what is being said. Rather, the purpose is to mean 'nothing less' than what has been spoken.[6] In hyperbole, Puttenham suggests, the route to truth leads through falsehood, or the dissimulation of truth. And this kind of paradox, involving a game between truth and dissimulation, becomes a flexible and frequently employed instrument of creative imagination in Shakespeare's earlier style.

The situation with bombast is different. Since bombast is not a subject of theoretical attention it does not share the same fate as hyperbole in the critical writing of Shakespeare's contemporaries. Yet even the derision with which bombast is met in that writing is not a simple and clear-cut matter of dislike. Among the earliest references to Shakespeare's presence in London, Robert Greene's vehement attack on players, *Groatsworth of Wit Bought with a Million of Repentance*, published in 1592, picks fault with 'an upstart Crow', who thinks of himself as a 'Shake-scene', steals style from others and 'supposes he is as well able to bombast out a blank verse as the best' of poets, and in the process writes a critique of both the style of acting and the new style of writing dramatic poetry.[7] Katherine Duncan-Jones interprets Greene's phrase 'bombast out' as conceivably alluding to 'Shakespeare adding extemporized blank verse lines to a part *in performance*, rather than to his having composed such lines in advance for himself or others to deliver', especially since 'bombast', stuffing or padding, suggest addition or inflation'.[8] Yet Greene directs his own inflated rhetoric, not so much at Shakespeare's use of bombast itself, but at the fact that Shakespeare may use it better than his contemporaries. It is a matter not of the quality of style but of the success in competition that is the subject of Greene's critique. Similarly, Greene's contemporary, William Scott (*b.* ?1579), the great-grandson of Sir Thomas Wyatt, says in his treatise 'The Model of Poesy or the Arte of Poesye', written most certainly in 1599, that 'Soe many self-pleasing writers cover their shalowe concepted Berths in glorious style, and peace out their want

---

[5] Henry Peacham, *The Garden of Eloquence* (London: Richard Field for H. Jackson, 1593) sig. F4^r.

[6] Whigham and Rebhorn (2007) 276.

[7] *Greene's Groatsworth of Wit Bought with a Million of Repentance*, D. Allen Carroll (ed.), (Binghampton, NY: Medieval and Renaissance Texts and Studies, 1994) 84–5.

[8] Katherine Duncan-Jones, *Shakespeare: Upstart Crow to Sweet Swan, 1592–1623* (London: A & C Black, 2011) 39, italics Duncan-Jones'.

of matter with store of Idle words and fustian terms'.[9] Since Scott's treatise contains references to productions of some of Shakespeare's plays and to the narrative poetry, one wonders whether one of the 'self-pleasing writers' using 'fustian terms' (inflated language) may be a reference to Shakespeare. Like Greene, Scott is less concerned by the fact that bombast and fustian terms are used than by the fact that they are used by writers without the social status to claim poetic fame. The distinction is crucial because it suggests that the target of Greene's and Scott's attacks is not bombastic style itself, but a factor external to the text or the performance.

2.2 STYLE IN PRACTICE

Because Greene's and Scott's dismissals of bombast are motivated by a combination of social and artistic factors, they leave the question of the actual appropriateness of bombast in the 1590s open for debate. Literary and cultural backgrounds for the period's critique shed a different light on bombast as an unwelcome stylistic mode—despite Thomas Nashe's warning directed at 'better pens' to protect themselves against 'the swelling bombast of a bragging blank verse', which he writes in the 'Epistle to Students' in Robert Greene's *Menaphon*.[10] In *Love's Labour's Lost*, a play probably written in 1594 or 1595 and thus belonging to the earliest phase of Shakespeare's career, the Queen mocks Biron's 'letters full of love' as 'bombast and lining to the time' (V. ii. 773). I will return to Biron's love rhetoric later. Now I want to use a later reference to bombast, made in *Othello*, written in 1603 or 1604, to illustrate how context determines both the meaning and interpretative judgement used to assess a derisory qualification of bombast. Iago describes Othello's rhetorical performance to the 'great ones of the city' of Venice, as 'a bombast circumstance | Horribly stuffed with epithets of war' (I. i. 13–14). No doubt, Othello's language suffers from too much stuffing because, often in Shakespeare, bombast is the stylistic medium that fits the language of war and by which heroic bravado produced by war is captured at a time when the Hundred Years' War with France and the Wars of the Roses are still alive in the historical memory and on the stage in 1590s England. But bombast is also a medium by which a critique of war itself is offered in an age which witnessed a shift in the conceptualization of masculine virtue, from militant and chivalric towards civic virtue. Nowhere in his earlier works does Shakespeare stuff bombast circumstance with epithets of war as much as he does in the *Henry VI* trilogy. Here is Gloucester in *1 Henry VI*, a 1592 play, reflecting on the heroism of Henry V:

> His brandished sword did blind men with his beams.
> His arms spread wider than a dragon's wings.
> His sparkling eyes, replete with wrathful fire,

---

[9] British Library MS Add 81083, f. 27ᵛ.
[10] Thomas Nashe, 'Epistle to Students', Robert Greene, *Menaphon* (London: T[homas] O[rwin] for Sampson Clarke, 1589) sig. **.

> More dazzled and drove back his enemies
> Than midday sun, fierce bent against their faces
> What should I say? His deeds exceed all speech.
>
> (I. i. 10–15)

The idea in each line of this bombast speech, in which hyperboles are strung together in a parallel fashion, is intensified in the line that follows. The clamour of arms and the glitter of swords are produced by bombast which, cumulatively, sounds like linguistic artillery. And the king himself, whose militant vigour produces bombast circumstances, is rendered in exaggerated terms: he is 'too famous to live long' (I. i. 6) and he is a 'king blest of the King of Kings'. (I. i. 28). Gloucester's bombastic peroration is a sign of Shakespeare's deep interest in England's heroic past. There is a sense that, too, in this example, bombast serves two purposes: one is the critique of war as an undertaking; the other, a vivid and nostalgic memory of a popular monarch from England's chivalric past. Shakespeare's bombast may be a subject of critique and bombast itself the target of derisory criticism, but Shakespeare is conscious of both the limits and potential of this stylistic strategy to serve just the kind of purpose called for by the dramatic situation.

In his earlier style, Shakespeare works around and through the delicate line which separates the horribly stuffed language of bombast as linguistic inflation, from hyperbole, an elegant trope (as Gabriel Harvey implies) which has more advantages than disadvantages in poetic composition. If we take Greene's attack as an indicator that the earliest works of Shakespeare already strive, not toward a flat-out imitation of others but toward a new creation that threatens to outdo the original, than we can think of the rhetoric of *Titus Andronicus* as reaching beyond Senecan bombast, not emulating it without a critical distance. One of the recurrent criticisms of this earliest tragedy is that its style is highly bombastic. It is. But the bombast in this play complements, integrates, and enhances the symmetrical forms which make up the stylistic grandeur of this play. This is evident in the scene which shows a gruesome banquet, in which Titus is about to mince into a pie the bodies of the lecherous young Goths, Lavinia's two sons; their mother is present and about to witness the event:

> I will grind your bones to dust,
> And with your blood and it I'll make a *paste,*
> And of the *paste* a coffin I will rear,
> And make two *pasties* of your shameful heads,
> And bid that strumpet, your unhallowed dam,
> Like to the earth swallow her own increase.
>
> (V. ii. 185–90)

Several kinds of symmetry are interlaced here in order to produce harmony at both visual and acoustic levels: the repetitive parallelism of clauses beginning with And ... and the repetition of paste/pasties, prepare the parallelism achieved by the successive use of the words 'unhallowed' and 'swallow', whose acoustic force comes from the doubling of the core syllable—allow-. To modern readers and critics, the banquet speech illustrates Shakespearean bombast at its most extreme, even ridiculous. But this is because modern audiences *hear* bombast differently from their early modern predecessors. The highly aural Elizabethan culture audience would have appreciated the variety of verbal harmonies achieved through repetitions, because the culture was accustomed to consider repetition as a sign of elegance and harmony. Elizabethan listeners, as Puttenham suggests, expected to find 'good symmetry' in a speech, a symmetry made up of ornaments 'which … showeth not only more art, but serveth also much better for briefness and subtlety of device'.[11] Analysed against the background of Puttenham's idea of pleasing style, the verbal excess from the end of *Titus* suggests that the Elizabethans found enjoyment, or 'delight',[12] in what comes across as turgid language to modern recipients of this poetry.

If bombast is produced by symmetry, hyperbole enhances it. William Scott associates 'hyperbolicall speaches' with symmetry, considering them one the particulars of 'agreablenes in the corespondency of the invention, so as it be still proportionable in it selfe'.[13] For Scott such exaggerated speeches constitute a kind of symmetry 'in it selfe'. So Titus says: 'I tell my sorrows to the stones', and continues: '*A stone is soft as wax*, <u>tribunes more hard than stones</u>. | *A stone is silent and offendeth not*', (III. i. 36, 44–5, italics added). Hyperbole ('tribunes more hard than stones') bridges two symmetrical clauses ('<u>A stone</u> is soft …' | '<u>A stone</u> is silent'), enhancing the property of stones by drawing attention to their realism (they are hard) in contrast to their metaphoric quality (they are silent). Repetition as a form of symmetry is a stylistic strategy to which Shakespeare frequently resorts in his earlier work where he uses it to new ends. What the modern ear hears as repetition resulting in bombast, the early modern ear would have heard as 'garnishing'; that is, as Dudley Fenner says, as a speech that 'itself is beautified and made fine' by the choice of ornament used to create beauty through harmony.[14]

Since Shakespeare lived and worked in the language environment which held the 'linguistic expressiveness involving wit and sound'[15] in high regard, the style of his works written and performed in the 1590s reflects the variety of ways in which these two properties of language enhanced ornamentation, especially in the ways in which he employs figures of repetition as tools for achieving symmetry. Rhetorical theories of the 1590s do not describe repetition as ornament in itself. But repetition is a form of lexical excess through which Shakespeare frames meaning by working on, and enhancing, the acoustic (and visual) quality of language. As such, repetition is a kind of syntactic ornament rooted in symmetry. In the early 1590s, when Shakespeare is building his reputation in the public theatre, he relies on the figures of repetition as vehicles of meaning particularly crucial to the sonic effect of his plays since the audiences went to the theatre to

---

[11] Whigham and Rebhorn (2007) 179.

[12] Whigham and Rebhorn (2007) 221.

[13] William Scott, 'The Model of Poesy or the Art of Poesy drawn into a short summary discourse', BL MS Add 81083, f. 20ʳ.

[14] Dudley Fenner, *Art of Logike and Rhetorike* (Middleburg: R. Schilders, 1984) sig. D1ʳ.

[15] N. F. Blake, *Shakespeare's Language: An Introduction* (London: Macmillan, 1983) 28.

'hear' plays, not just watch them. The earlier comedies abound with this kind of syntactic ornament.

Love's Labour's Lost (1594–5), a play which employs and questions rhetoric, heavily relies on repetition and parallelism. Shakespeare not only employs such devices, but often doubles them within a single sonic unit, as he does in the doubly woven anaphora in the following speech:

> BIRON   For wisdom's sake—a word that all men love—
> Or for love's sake—a word that loves all men—
> Or for man's sake—the author of these women—
> Or women's sake—by whom we men are men—
> Let us once lose our oaths to find ourselves.
>
> (IV. iii. 333–7)

The stylistic vigour of these lines depends on the cumulative acoustic effect created by the interlacing of several figures of repetition. In the first four lines, anaphora, a figure based on the repetition of the last word in successive clauses,[16] is interlaced with anadiplosis,[17] a figure in which the last word of one line begins the next. The effect of this combined sonic unit is further enhanced by the interlacing of the sounds /s/ and /z/, which seal the last line of this sentence in verse. Isocolon, 'A lover's eyes will gaze an eagle blind. | A lover's ear will hear the lowest sound' (IV. iii. 310–11) and 'Love's feeling is more soft and sensible ... | Love's tongue proves dainty Bacchus gross in taste' (IV. iii. 313; 315), prepares the ear for the acoustic symmetries that follow these lines. Isocolon, a figure in which phrases of roughly equal length and corresponding structure are repeated,[18] enhances the idea of the transformative power of love—only to question it immediately by completing the speech with hyperbole (IV. iii. 310; 313). The cumulative effect of this acoustic unit of lines enhances what the play has been about thus far: a call to the lovers to free themselves from the bonds of duty and cultural habits in order to give themselves to women and pleasure.

Figures of repetition especially dominate *The Tragedy of King Richard the Third* (1592–3), a highly rhetorical play. From Richard's anaphora in the opening speech— 'Our bruised arms ... | Our stern alarums ... | Our dreadful marches ...' (I. i. 6–8)—to Queen Margaret's speech rich with interlaced *commoratio* ('Where is thy husband ... | Where be the thronging troops', lines 92–6)[19] and isocolon—('For happy wife ... | For she commanding', lines 98–104)—a range of emotions is enhanced through repetition

---

[16] Lanham, *A Handlist of Rhetorical Terms: A Guide for Students of English Literature* (Berkeley and Los Angeles: The University of California Press, 1969), 'repetition of the last word at the beginning of successive clauses' 124.

[17] Lanham (1969) 124.

[18] Lanham (1969) 125.

[19] Lanham defines *commoratio* as 'emphasizing a strong point by repeating it several times in different words' (1969) 125.

whose acoustic intensity matches the rattle of arms, the extremes of sorrow, and verbal violence. Critics have often remarked that the rhetoric of this play is highly schematic.[20] Repetition is both a form of stylistic aggression and a sign of verbal virtuosity, but Shakespeare exposes the matter of his play in which repeated violence has its stylistic correlative in figures of repetition. Stylistic excess produced in this way represents a kind of acoustic bombast aimed not so much at manipulating thought as augmenting the sound of thought, in turn illustrating that repetition is the basis of symmetry in Elizabethan aesthetics.

In Shakespeare's earlier style, parallelism and the balance of words are complemented by other stylistic properties which intensify meaning through heaping. An example of this strategy is the use of compound epithets.[21] Especially rich with this device are Shakespeare's earliest works. *Venus and Adonis* has no shortage of the constructions in which a double qualifier expands the meaning of a noun, like 'hard-favoured' and 'wrinkled-old' (133), 'ill-nurtured' (134), 'flap-mouthed' (920), and 'shrill-tongued' (849). *The Rape of Lucrece* (1593–4) matches *Venus* in the use of the same form: 'fleet-winged' (1216), 'black-faced' (547), 'sour-faced' (1334), or 'low-declinèd' (1705). And in the linguistically and rhetorically rich and playful *Love's Labour's Lost*, compound epithets, such as 'curious-knotted' (1.1.241), 'strong-jointed' (I. ii. 71), and 'slow-gaited' (III. i. 53) are the most frequently used vehicles for achieving acoustic harmony and verbal witticism. By 1595, Shakespeare's experimentation with this form of ornamental lexical doubling has peaked. *Richard II* (1595) contains an abundance of such two-partite adjectives, like 'time-bewasted' (I. iii. 214), 'oil-dried' (I. iii. 214), 'new-delivered' (II. ii. 65), 'pale-faced' (II. iii. 93), 'heavy-gaited' (III. ii. 15), and 'ill-erected' (V. i. 2). And *A Midsummer Night's Dream* (1595) matches *Richard II*, in this instance, offering examples like 'hoary-headed' (II. i. 107), 'russet-pated' (III. ii. 21), and 'crook-kneed' (IV. i. 121). As complements to nouns, with which compound epithets often form an unpredictable pair—'heavy-gaited' are 'toads' and 'slow-gaited' is a 'horse'—adjectival pairing sounds like bombast. Compound epithets have the effect of a softened bombast, because the excess they produce is limited by the small number of lexical parts involved in them. As a marker of Shakespeare's earlier style, compound epithets show us Shakespeare at his most playful and ingenious at the level of poetic semantics. The semantic pairs he creates draw their expressive vigour from experimentation with the expansion of meaning.

The expansion of meaning through poetic grammar and the experimentation with rhetorical forms used to create symmetry suggest that Shakespeare's earlier style is highly rhetorical not because he is beginning as a writer but because he is responding to a specific moment in the development of rhetorical tradition in 1590s England. Rhetorical theory of the 1590s pays considerable attention to ornamentation and devotes

---

[20] For example, Robert Ornstein, *A Kingdom for a Stage: The Achievement of Shakespeare's History Plays* (Cambridge, MA: Harvard University Press, 1972) and Nicholas Brooke, *Shakespeare's Early Tragedies* (London: Methuen, 1968).
[21] See also Halliday (1964) 55.

ample space to detailed descriptions, definitions, and illustrations of the use of figures and tropes. Shakespeare of the 1590s is particularly keen on experimentation with both ornamentation and symmetry because these properties of style produce harmony and balance, the defining features of Elizabethan aesthetics. Within this general aesthetics that calls for a harmony of parts involved in ornamentation, the weaving of sonnets into dramatic dialogues, as in *Romeo and Juliet* (1595), and inserting sonnets between blocks of a dramatic text, at a 'reasonable distance',[22] as in *Much Ado About Nothing* (1598–9), represent a compositional strategy which illustrates Shakespeare's use of texts as well as rhetorical devices as vehicles for achieving symmetry and playing with ornament.

The sonnet with which Shakespeare interlaces Romeo's courtship of Juliet is itself an ornament, differentiated by its verse form, embroidered rhetorically onto the larger surface of dialogues and longer speeches. But it also carries within itself forms of patterning, or ornaments within an ornament.

> ROMEO   If I profane with my unworthiest hand   92
>   This holy shrine, the gentler sin is this: 93
>   My lips, two blushing pilgrims, ready stand   94
>   To smooth that rough touch with a tender kiss.   95
> JULIET   Good pilgrim, you do wrong your hand too much,   96
>   Which mannerly devotion shows in this.   97
>   For saints have hands that pilgrims' hands do touch,   98
>   And palm to palm is holy palmers' kiss.   99
> ROMEO   Have not saints lips, and holy palmers, too?   100
> JULIET   Ay, palmer, lips that they must use in prayer.   101
> ROMEO   O then, dear saint, let lips do what hands do: 102
>   They pray; grant thou, lest faith turn to despair.   103
> JULIET   Saints do not move, though grant for prayers' sake.   104
> ROMEO   Then move not while my prayer's effect I take.   105
>
>   (I. v. 92–105)

This Shakespearean sonnet, consisting of three quatrains and a rhyming couplet, encapsulates different levels of symmetry. Parallel arrangement of the words *pilgrims /pilgrim* (94, 96) and *hand /hands* (96, 98), and the parallel break of one line separating each of the two lines containing symmetry, are linked with the phrasal parallelism of *palm to palm* (99) and with the parallelism of *holy palmers* (99–100) in two successive lines. In turn, this symmetry is followed by the successive repetition of the word *lips* in three successive lines (100–2). Then, the symmetry achieved by the repetition of the word *prayers'/prayer's* is acoustically enhanced by the parallelism of rhyme in the closing couplet (104–5). The cumulative effect of these parallel structures and repetitions make of this sonnet a masterpiece of symmetry and parallelism as ornaments. The sonnet is an example of poetry 'as a skill to speak and write harmoniously', as Puttenham advises.[23]

---

[22] Whigham and Rebhorn (2007) 174.
[23] Whigham and Rebhorn (2007) 154.

The sonnet also interconnects two kinds of proportions in the stylistic taxonomy of the period: 'proportion of figure' and 'proportion poetical'.[24] The first kind of proportion (of figures) works on both the eye and the ear, and it is manifested in the almost geometrical figures created by the successive parallelisms of words *holy palmers*, *lips*, and *prayers*. The second kind of proportion (poetical) involves the arrangement of lines into stanzas with the usual sonnet rhyming structure in three quatrains and a couplet (*abab, cdcd, efef, gg*). Playing with the conventional vocabulary of Petrarchan courtship, this sonnet becomes a source of new rhetorical invention for an exercise with the main virtues of Elizabethan style.

Later in the 1590s Shakespeare will repeat the same technique of weaving sonnets into drama. In *Much Ado About Nothing*, a play full of lexical eccentricity, Shakespeare inserts an incomplete sonnet. In the hands of Beatrice, alone on the stage reciting, the sonnet reads:

> What fire is in mine ears? Can this be true?
> Stand I condemned for pride and scorn so much?
> Contempt, fairwell; and maiden pride, adieu.
> No glory lives behind the back of such.
> And, Benedick, love on. I will requite thee,
> Taming my wild heart to thy loving hand.
> If thou dost love, my kindness shall incite thee
> To bind our loves up in a holy band.
> For others say thou dost deserve, and I
> Believe it better than reportingly.
>
> (III. i. 107–16).

The focus in these lines is not on verbal patterns woven into the sonnet, itself an ornament within the play, but on using the sonnet as a lyrical poem to enhance a block of dramatic text. The parallelism is less formal and more conceptual, in that the sonnet encapsulates much of the amorous behaviour and belief hitherto displayed in action and rhetoric. Shakespeare plays with some of the sonnet conventions, like Beatrice's admission that she will requite Benedict's love ('And, Benedict, love on. I will requite thee'). Hardly a detached and silent Petrarchan lady who rejects the lover, Beatrice embodies that beloved's obverse, a desiring woman of flesh and words. This imperfect sonnet (it misses one quatrain) suggests that Shakespeare's attention here is on using patterns of lines as ornaments in their own right, and with questioning the style of the Petrarchan sonnet to capture the full meaning of love.

In his earlier style, Shakespeare's love of rhetorical display and ornamentation often produces symmetries through the combination of verbal heaping and 'proportion poeticall'; that is, an arrangement of lines within a stanza.[25] The effect of this stylistic strategy

---

[24] Whigham and Rebhorn (2007) 175.
[25] Whigham and Rebhorn (2007) 179.

comes close to, but does not become, bombast. Words that are piled up are mostly adjectives, alone or as qualifiers of nouns. The technique of heaping, or of accumulation, is prominent in *Venus and Adonis*, but it also stands out in the two lines for which Sonnet 129 is remembered.[26] While in the sonnet, 'lust in action' (129, l. 2) is rendered as 'perjured, murd'rous, bloody, full of blame, | Savage, extreme, rude, cruel (lines 3–4), in *Venus and Adonis*, lust embodied as a horse in heat is imagined in the similar lexical register and form as 'Broad breast, full eye, small head, and nostril wide, | High crest, short ears, straight legs, … | Thin mane, thick tail, broad buttock, tender hide–' (lines 296–8). In her game of seduction, Venus 'hath learned to sport and dance, | to toy, to wanton, dally, smile, and jest' (lines 105–6) and in Venus' self-deprecatory rhetorical playing, Shakespeare's toying with the style of accumulation climaxes into bombast: 'Were I hard-favoured, foul, or wrinkled-old, | Ill-natured, crooked, churlish, harsh in voice, | O'er-worn, despisèd, rheumatic, and cold, | Thick-sighted, barren, lean, and lacking juice' (lines 133–6). The examples from the sonnet and the narrative poem illustrate that accumulation ends up sounding bombastic. But bombast produced in such a way is shaped syntactically by repetitions of parallel structures whose cumulative force creates both verbal harmony, within a line, and syntactic harmonies through the repetition of several lines. While in the sonnet, the piled-up adjectives appear after the noun they qualify and spill over two lines, enhancing the phrase 'lust in action', in the narrative poem the combination of verbs and adjectives are organized in the lines which produce harmony through repetition. In both the sonnet and the narrative poem, lust in action or lust which reason cannot control results in the language that cannot control itself; the disorientating excess of yearning for the object of desire, that is slipping away, finds its most suitable expression in bombast whose own stylistic excess captures such unbridled energies of libido.

Shakespeare exploits the same technique in *Romeo and Juliet*, too. When he shows us Romeo piling up syntactic clichés, he does so not so much to show that Romeo has not experienced true love yet (as criticism has argued for a long time) but in order to illustrate that literary love is primarily a stylistic construct removed from the metaphysical meaning of love: 'Feather of lead, bright smoke, cold fire, sick health' (I. i. 177). Shakespeare compresses, in one line, the familiar formula from the Petrarchan vocabulary of love, creating bombast out of a series of accumulated oxymora, as if questioning the usefulness of such vocabulary to speak about love as anything but style. In a play which questions precisely the notions of love as ornament and emotion, *Love's Labour's Lost*, verbal heaping appears in abundance, as if suggesting that no amount and volume of ornament is enough to capture the definition of love as affect. As if commenting on Romeo's habit of heaping-up clichés from the Petrarchan lexicon of love, Biron says: 'When shall you hear that I | Will praise a hand, a foot, a face, an eye, | A gait, a state, a brow, a breast, a waist, | A leg, a limb?' (IV. iii. 181–4).

---

[26] Richard Lanham (1969) defines *accumulatio* as 'Heaping up praise or accusation to emphasize or summarize points or inferences already made', 1.

Here Shakespeare questions the usefulness of Petrarchan stylistics, using the figure of *congeris*, a figure of verbal heaping, in the context of an extended debate about the nature of love, felt and written about in a sonnet. Accumulation is never an end in itself, but a stylistic device through which either praise or accusation is displayed.[27] Shakespeare's earlier style brims with the examples of what I call *congeric* style, because *congeris* captures that early style based on the heaping of words. Through this kind of syntactic ornamentation, Shakespeare achieves what the rhetorician Thomas Wilson recommends as one of the purposes of verbal heaping: to force and stir 'the mind either to desire or else to detest and loathe anything more vehemently than by nature we are commonly wont to do'.[28]

2.3 STYLE IN HISTORY

The vogue for stylistic expansion as a general stylistic strategy developed alongside the geographical expansion across the seas on which England embarked in the 1590s vigorously. Writers captured the enthusiasm for such ventures, turning the ambitious prospects which such voyages inspired and the promises of wealth that came with those enterprises, into the subject of poetry where such undertakings are most often stylized in hyperbole. Thus John Donne, in the elegy 'To his Mistress Going to Bed', transforms the idea of geographical discovery into erotic discovery of the female body:

> O my America, my new found land,
> My kingdom, safeliest when with one man manned,
> My mine of precious stones, my empery,
> How blessed am I in this discovering thee.
> To enter in these bonds is to be free,
> Then where my hand is set my seal shall be.[29]

In the imperial rhetoric of these lines, limitless freedom in accumulating pleasure juxtaposes the exploitation of wealth with an unbridled liberty in sex, as if pleasure were gems brought from the newly discovered America. Hyperbole which frames this idea of expansion and exploitation articulates both socio-cultural and political aspirations of a society beginning to establish itself on the European models of political power gained by colonialism, but also in a robust competition with the colonial precursors from Europe, especially Spain

Similarly, Shakespeare turns the rhetoric of long-distance travel into several corners of the world, into hyperbole and into a comically inflated language about the discovery

---

[27] Lanham (1969) 1.

[28] Thomas Wilson (1569), *The Arte of Rhetoric*, Peter Medine (ed.), (University Park, PA: The Pennsylvania State University Press, 1994) 153.

[29] John Donne, *The Major Works*, John Carey (ed.), (Oxford: Oxford University Press, 1990) 13.

of love, in *Much Ado About Nothing*. Speaking to Don Pedro about Beatrice, on stage, Benedick says:

> I will go on the slightest errand now to the Antipodes that you can devise to send me on. I will fetch you a tooth-picker now from the furthest inch of Asia, bring you the length of Prester John's foot, fetch you a hair off the Great Cham's beard, do you any embassage to the pigmies, rather than hold three words' conference with this harpy.
>
> (II. i. 247–54)

Benedick's hyperbole shows that by 1599 Shakespeare has continued to use hyperbole to shape meaning, as he did in his earliest works, except that he now employs hyperbole with more subtlety. If the hyperbole in 'To his Mistress' sounds like an endorsement of the pleasures of erotic and colonial exploitation, Shakespeare's hyperbole parodies both geographical and amorous conquests as excessive enterprises, inviting the audience to question the validity of exaggeration to convey truth, since the plot will bring Beatrice and Benedick together as lovers. Even when he comes up with the kind of language which is ridiculously inflated as Benedick's version of imperial undertakings is, Shakespeare remains devoted to symmetry as a virtue of stylistic modeling: Benedick's bombast is constructed of five parallel hyperboles based on geographical expansion and the legends it produced. When Puttenham calls hyperbole a 'Loud Liar',[30] he does not refer to the acoustic effect of this ornament (hyperbole is not loud) but draws attention to its capacity to alter reality in unexpected ways—yoking together eroticism and colonial travels. In these instances of verbal grandeur we see how the language of poetry captures the potential of hyperbole as a trope that 'is uniquely suited to represent extraordinary things, experience and events'.[31]

Shakespeare penned his geographical bombast in *Much Ado* only several years after the publication of Richard Hakluyt's collection of travel narratives, *Principal nauigations, voyages, traffiques and discoueris of the English nation*, first published in 1589 and reprinted in 1599. The first edition of this important book, detailing the opening of the English overseas travel on a grand scale, opens with an epistle which Hakluyt dedicates to Francis Walsingham, the Queen's Secretary. In the epistle, Hakluyt, motivated by the discoveries already undertaken, urges the Queen to encourage further voyages by 'men full of activity, stirrers abroad, and searchers of the remote parts of the world', in order to overtake the Spanish in the race for colonial territories and resources. Hakluyt says:

> in searching the most opposite corners and quarters of the world and, to speak plainly, in compassing the vast globe of the earth more than once, [merchant-adventurers] have excelled all the nations and peoples of the earth. For which of the kings of this land before Her Majesty had their banner ever seen in the Caspian Sea? Which of them hath ever dealt with the Emperor of Persia as Her Majesty hath done, and

---

[30] Whigham and Rebhorn (2007) 276.
[31] Christopher J. Johnson, *Hyperboles: The Rhetoric of Excess in Baroque Literature and Thought* (Cambridge, MA and London: Harvard University Press, 2010) 4.

obtained for Her merchants large and loving privileges? Who ever saw before this regiment at English ligier in the stately porch of the Grand Signior at Constantinople? Who ever found English consuls and agents in Tripoli in Syria, at Aleppo, at Babylon, at Balsara, and, which is more, who ever heard of Englishmen at Goa before now? What English ships did heretofore ever anchor in the mighty River Plate, pass and repass the unpassable … Strait of Magellan, range along the coast of Chile, Peru, and all the backside of Nova Hispania further than any Christian ever passed, traverse the mighty breadth of the South Sea, land upon the Luzons [Phillippines] in despite of the enemy enter into alliance, amity and traffic with the Princess of Moluccas and the Isle of Java, double the famous Cape of Bona Speranza, arrive at the Isle of St Helena, and, last of all, return home most richly laden with the commodities of China, as the subjects of this now flourishing Monarchy have done?[32]

I quote this segment of text in full in order to draw attention to the fact that the rhetorical style, in which both the piling up of geographical locations drawn from all corners of the world (from the Caspian Sea to Chile and from the Cape of Good Hope to China) in the form of parallel rhetorical questions, and syntax which occasionally comes close to hyperbolic exaggeration (e.g. the merchant-travellers 'have excelled all the nations and peoples of the earth'), feature as the prose correlative to Shakespeare's bombast encompassing different corners of the globe and including the legends that came out of long-distance travels. Since Hakluyt's text focuses on the zeal for exploration and the exploitation of commodities, and since the tone and language of this excerpt capture the restlessness and ambition of these entrepreneurial subjects of the Queen's 'most famous and peerless Government' (sig. *2ʳ), in Shakespeare's version of overseas discoveries, the language of travel and expansion, stuffed with superlatives and bolstered with a catalogue of geographical names which create an exotic effect, ends up being the target of criticism and mockery. Yet read alongside Hakluyt's appeal to the Queen, the language of Benedick's bombast sounds more infused with politics than it first appears, except that the politics of this speech is now reversed. By parodying imperial voyages of discovery, Shakespeare offers us the critical obverse of the enthusiasm for geographical expansion voiced eloquently and hyperbolically by Hakluyt. The examples from Donne and Shakespeare, in which hyperbole and bombast in imaginative literature are juxtaposed with hyperbolic ambitions of merchant-adventurers embarking on geographical expansion in search of more and more resources, represent a good illustration of the fact that style neither transcends nor subsumes cultural practices but exposes them, reconfigures them, in order to make visible and heard something which may otherwise have remained removed from poetry and theatre. Style, then, is a glimpse into history.

The most difficult 'balancing trick'[33] in assessing the earlier style of Shakespeare's career, and the greatest difficulty in understanding what Shakespeare does with

---

[32] Richard Hakluyt, 'The Epistle Dedicatory', *The principal nauigations, voyages, traffiques and discoueries of the English nationa made by sea or ouer-land, to the remote and farthest distant quarters of the earth* (London: by George Bishop, Ralph Newberie, and Robert Barber, 1598–1600) sig. *2ʳ.

[33] N. F. Blake, *Shakespeare's Language: An Introduction* (London: Macmillan, 1983) 24.

language, lies in estimating the measure between his use of rhetorical ornaments within the general aesthetic culture which loved harmony, repetition, and balance, and his period's criticism of bombast and grand style which also abound in the 1590s.[34] In the decade of pronounced literary competition, the grand style of Shakespeare's poetic composition is founded on a balance achieved between his use of 'fustian terms', bombast and hyperbole, and various other forms of lexical ornamentation at the moment when the expansion of the semantic potential of the English language occurs alongside ornamentation and symmetry as dominant features of style. This earlier style, therefore, is not a single phenomenon. Rather, Shakespeare's style involves bringing together—by reconciling or colliding—the stylistic ornaments and rhetorical strategies which create, rather than disturb, symmetry.

Given the complexity of the idea of style of the 1590s, it is worth pausing over the flexible, even arbitrary and ambiguous, meaning of the concept *early* and its derivatives *earliest* and *earlier*, here used as operative terms, since *early* suggests both undeveloped and premature, both unskilled and emerging.[35] Since style itself is a historical category, Shakespeare's earlier style is both highly rhetorical and rhetorically adaptable to the time, and the cultural, political, and historical contexts within which that style originates. One of the best tests of the endurance and transformation of Shakespeare's earlier style in his later writing appears in *Antony and Cleopatra*, a play written in 1606, some thirteen years after *Venus and Adonis*. The Roman tragedy is no less rhetorical than the Ovidian narrative poem, and it is more bombastic than *Romeo and Juliet*, one of the most hyperbolic of early plays. If Antony and Cleopatra represent the mature obverse of the young lovers from Verona, then the verbal grandeur through which they express love is also the obverse of the vehement style through which maturing youth articulates its emotional excess. In the 1590s, Shakespeare is an artist learning his craft and a rhetorical craftsman who plays with and tests the ornaments available to him, and invents new verbal ornament, in a style that stretches and metamorphoses beyond the 1590s. The endurance of some of its most distinct forms is the sign of its rich creative potential and flexibility.

SELECT BIBLIOGRAPHY

Adamson, Sylvia (2001) 'The Grand Style', in S. Adamson, S. Hunter, L. Magnusson, L. Thompson, A. Thompson, and K. Wales (eds) *Reading Shakespeare's Dramatic Language: A Guide* (London: Arden Shakespeare) 31–50.

——, Gavin Alexander, and Katherine Ettenhuber (2007) (eds) *Renaissance Figures of Speech* (Cambridge: Cambridge University Press).

Blake, N. F. (1983) *Shakespeare's Language: An Introduction* (London: Macmillan).

---

[34] Blake (1983) 24.

[35] My use of the word *early* is opposite to Michael Wood's use of the word *late*, which he uses to qualify the notion of style in music and literature. See Michael Wood, 'Introduction', Edward W. Said, *On Late Style: Music and Literature Against the Grain* (London: Bloomsbury, 2006) xi.

Duncan-Jones, Katherine (2011) *Shakespeare: Upstart Crow to Sweet Swan, 1592–1623* (London: A&C Black).

Fenner, Dudley (1584) *The Arte of Logike and Rhetorike* (Middleburg: R. Schilders).

Halliday, F. E. (1964) *The Poetry of Shakespeare's Plays* (London: Gerald Duckworth).

Hope, Jonathan (2010) *Shakespeare's Language: Reason, Eloquence and Artifice in the Renaissance* (London: Methuen).

Johnson, Christopher D. (2010) *Hyperboles: The Rhetoric of Excess in Baroque Literature and Thought* (Cambridge, MA and London: Harvard University Press for Harvard University Department of Comparative Literature)

Peacham, Henry (1593) *The Garden of Eloqvence, Conteining the Most Excellent Ornaments, Exornations, Lightes, Flowers, and forms of speech, commonly called the Figures of Rhetorike* (London: R. F. for H. Iackson).

Puttenham, George (2007) *The Art of English Poesy, A Critical Edition*, Frank Whigham and Wayne A. Rebhorn (eds) (Ithaca and London: Cornell University Press).

Scott, William, 'The Model of Poesy or the Art of Poesy drawn into a short summary discourse', BL MS Add 81083.

Shuger, Debora (2006) 'Conceptions of Style', in Glyn P. Norton (ed.) *The Cambridge History of Literary Criticism*, vol. 3, *The Renaissance* (Cambridge: Cambridge University Press), 176–86.

Turner, Robert Y. (1974) *Shakespeare's Apprenticeship* (Chicago and London: The University of Chicago Press).

Wilson, Thomas (1560) *The Arte of Rhetoric*, Peter E. Medine (1994) (ed.) (University Park, Pennsylvania: The Pennsylvania State University Press).

CHAPTER 3

....

SHAKESPEARE'S LATE STYLE

....

A. R. BRAUNMULLER

In 1853, Matthew Arnold defended Shakespeare's 'over-curiousness of expression' and quoted a witty French swipe:

> This over-curiousness of expression is indeed but the excessive employment of a wonderful gift—of the powers of saying a thing in a happier way than any other man; nevertheless, it is carried so far that one understands what M. Guizot meant, when he said that Shakespeare appears in his language to have tried all styles except that of simplicity.[1]

'Curiousness' is an obsolete word meaning 'carefulness ... skillfulness; scrupulosity, fastidiousness' (*OED*), and it describes a highly prized feature of Tudor artistry in every field from the literary to the fine arts and architecture.

Shakespeare's contemporaries and immediate successors left few comments on his style, and the few tend to be vague and general praise. Those who admired his style called it 'mellifluous & hony-tongued' and (for the Sonnets) 'sugred' (Francis Meres) or, just as unhelpfully, 'language exquisite' (Leonard Digges), which might be an anticipation of Arnold's 'over-curiousness'. The hostile and envious Robert Greene accused Shakespeare of plagiarism and of believing he could 'bombast [stuff] out a blanke verse' as well as any contemporary. Ben Jonson characteristically mixed praise and blame when he complained of Shakespeare's stylistic fecundity: Shakespeare 'had ... brave notions, and gentle expressions: wherein he flow'd with that facility, that sometime it was necessary he should be stop'd'. Writing from within the utterly changed theatrical and literary circumstances of the Restoration, John Dryden reached a masterly and sympathetic

---

[1] Matthew Arnold, Preface to *Poems: a new edition* (London: Longman, Brown, Green, and Longmans, 1853) xxiv. Guizot was prime minister of France, 1847–8.

summary. He begins his discussion of Shakespeare in *An Essay of Dramatick Poesie* (1668) grandly:

> he was the man who of all the Modern, and perhaps Ancient Poets, had the largest and most comprehensive soul. All the images of Nature were still [always] present to him, and he drew them not laboriously, but luckily, when he describes any thing, you more than see it, you feel it too ... he needed not the spectacles of Books to read Nature; he look'd inwards, and found her there.

Conceding that Shakespeare 'is many times flat, insipid; his Comick wit degenerating into clenches [puns, quibbles], his serious swelling into Bombast', Dryden immediately asserts 'But he is always great, when some great occasion is presented to him'. More tellingly but without any authentication, Dryden tells an anecdote about Ben Jonson: 'In reading some bombast speeches of *Macbeth*, which are not to be understood, he used to say that it was horror; and I am very much afraid that this is so'.[2] A possible candidate for a 'bombast' speech in *Macbeth* is the hero's soliloquy considering the murder of Duncan. The speech begins with a general proposition—if the assassination is an act complete in itself, then speed is best—which is then explored and tested through a series of metaphors: *trammel* and *catch* can both refer to controlling or capturing animals, and the latter may lead to the river metaphor in 'bank and shoal of time':

> If it were done when 'tis done, then 'twere well
> It were done quickly. If the assassination
> Could trammel up the consequence, and catch
> With his surcease success: that but this blow
> Might be the be-all and the end-all, here,
> But here, upon this bank and shoal of time,
> We'd jump the life to come.
>
> (*Macbeth* I. vii. 1–7)

Macbeth has already used 'but' in the sense of 'only'; now he repeats it as a contrastive conjunction introducing a series of objections and qualifications to his very opening *if* clause, seven lines earlier; another meaning of 'bank'—judicial bench—helps introduce the 'judgement' and 'justice' meanings that now appear:

> But in these cases
> We still have judgement here, that we but teach
> Bloody instructions which, being taught, return
> To plague th'inventor. This even-handed justice
> Commends th'ingredience of our poisoned chalice
> To our own lips.
>
> (I. vii. 7–12)

---

[2] 'Defence of the epilogue' in George Watson (ed.), John Dryden, *Of Dramatic Poesy and other critical essays*, 2 vols. (London: J. M. Dent, 1962) i, 173.

Macbeth then finds personal reasons not to commit the murder, but his arithmetic is oddly weak:

> He's here in double trust:
> First, as I am his kinsman and his subject,
> Strong both against the deed; then, as his host,
> Who should against his murderer shut the door,
> Not bear the knife myself.
>
> (I. vii. 12–16)

The speech does not end or conclude—it is interrupted by Lady Macbeth's agitated entrance—rather, it explodes into a series of striking metaphors tumbling upon one another.

> Besides, this Duncan
> Hath borne his faculties so meek, hath been
> So clear in his great office, that his virtues
> Will plead like angels, trumpet-tongued against
> The deep damnation of his taking-off,
> And pity, like a naked new-born babe,
> Striding the blast, or heaven's cherubin, horsed
> Upon the sightless couriers of the air,
> Shall blow the horrid deed in every eye
> That tears shall drown the wind. I have no spur
> To prick the sides of my intent, but only
> Vaulting ambition, which o'erleaps itself
> And falls on th' other.
>
> (I. vii. 16–28)

Dryden also acknowledged changes in language and taste:

> Yet it must be allow'd to the present Age, that the tongue in general is so much refin'd since *Shakespear*'s time, that many of his words, and more of his Phrases, are scarce intelligible ... and his whole stile is so pester'd with Figurative expressions, that it is as affected as it is obscure ... I will not say of so great a Poet, that he distinguish'd not the blown puffy stile, from true sublimity ... but to use 'em [metaphors] at every word, to say nothing without a Metaphor, a Simile, an Image, or description, is I doubt [fear] to smell a little strongly of the Buskin [i.e. high-flown tragic discourse].

Suavely phrased, these sympathetic analyses and criticisms have truth. To our purposes, Dryden comments, "'Tis true, that in his later plays he had worn off somewhat of the rust'.[3] Thus prompted by recognizing how the language had changed since Shakespeare's

---

[3] With the exception of the text cited in n. 2, these selections from contemporary and near-contemporary comments on Shakespeare's style are drawn from excerpts collected by G. B. Evans and J. J. M. Tobin in the *Riverside Shakespeare* rev. edn (Boston: Houghton Mifflin, 1997) 1970–5.

day, Dryden seems to be the first writer to understand that Shakespeare's own style changed over time.

By 'rust' and its loss in Shakespeare's 'later plays', Dryden evidently means whatever stylistic features distinguish Shakespeare's earlier from his later theatrical writing, and it is the purpose of this chapter to identify the features of Shakespeare's style in the second half of his professional career, to explore the imaginative effects of those features, and to speculate on why these changes from his earlier plays might have occurred. Discussions of Shakespeare's late style typically proceed through comparison, either of his earlier with his later styles or with the styles of his contemporaries. Charles Lamb's excellent early effort contrasts Shakespeare with John Fletcher in their collaborative play, *The Two Noble Kinsmen*:

> His [Fletcher's] ideas moved slow; his versification, though sweet, is tedious, it stops every moment; he lays line upon line, making up one after the other, adding image to image so deliberately that we see where they join: Shakspeare [*sic*] mingles every thing, he runs line into line, embarrasses sentences and metaphors; before one idea has burst its shell, another is clamorous for disclosure.[4]

In the last phrase, Lamb may be slyly importing allusions to support his case: Horatio recalls the proverb about the lapwing and its shell (*Hamlet* V. ii. 146–7) where deceptive clamour accompanies partial disclosure, and Lennox remarks on yesternight's

> … prophesying with accents terrible
> Of dire combustion and confused events,
> New hatched to th' woeful time. The obscure bird
> Clamoured the livelong night.
>
> (*Macbeth* II. iii. 56–9)

Dryden, remember, might have been temperamentally and cultural predisposed to find the tragic and the heightened in Shakespeare's style 'blown [a flower in full bloom]' and 'puffy' and 'pestered with Figurative expressions', but the extraordinary richness, to some writers an *over*-richness, of Shakespeare's figurative language has long been noticed, eloquently by Coleridge:

> At first sight, Shakespeare and his contemporary dramatists seem to write in styles much alike: nothing so easy as to fall into that of Massinger and the others; whilst no-one has ever yet produced one scene conceived and expressed in the Shakespearian idiom. I suppose it is because Shakespeare is universal, and, in fact, has no *manner*; just as you can so much more readily copy a picture than nature herself.[5]

[4] Charles Lamb, *Specimens of English Dramatic Poets* (London: Longman, Hurst, Rees, and Orme, 1808) 419, n. 103.
[5] S. T. Coleridge, from *Table-Talk*, 17 February 1833, in *Coleridge's criticism of Shakespeare: a selection*, R. A. Foakes (ed.), (London: Athlone, 1989) 186.

Less elliptically, by A. C. Bradley:

> After *Hamlet* the style, in the more emotional passages, is heightened. It becomes grander, sometimes wilder, sometimes more swelling, even tumid. It is also more concentrated, more rapid, varied, and, in construction, less regular, not seldom twisted or elliptical. It is, therefore, not so easy and lucid, and in the more ordinary dialogue it is sometimes involved and obscure, and from these and other causes deficient in charm. On the other hand, it is always full of life and movement, and in great passages produces sudden, strange, electrifying effects which are rarely found in earlier plays, and not so often even in *Hamlet*. The more pervading effect of beauty gives place to what may almost be called explosions of sublimity or pathos.[6]

Here, Bradley succinctly outlines still widely held convictions about Shakespeare's style post-*Hamlet* (i.e. post-1601 or thereabouts): a grandeur verging on tumidity (= swollenness); diminished grammatical and metrical regularity; elliptical phrasing; liveliness; less 'beauty' and more jagged eruptions of 'sublimity or pathos'. Persuasive or not, Bradley's formulations are strongly qualitative and impressionistic: how does one tell when grandeur becomes tumidity, for example, or when does sublimity leak smoke rather than explode?

Finally, writing of *The Winter's Tale*, but in terms easily transferred to other late plays, an expert editor summarizes:

> It is syntactically and lexically often baffling, though this is an aspect of the text that has been generally ignored by editors and critics since the middle of … [the nineteenth] century. But if we consider the editorial debates over … [various passages are listed] … it is clear that even where a consensus has been reached, it is based on no real linguistic evidence.[7]

Consider a few passages that might illustrate and ground these claims. Critics often notice what Gordon McMullan calls 'digression and deferral' in Shakespeare's later writing.[8] For instances, we might look at Posthumus' response to his vision of his family ghosts and Jupiter:

> 'Tis still a dream, or else such stuff as madmen
> Tongue, and brain not; either both, or nothing,
> Or senseless speaking, or a speaking such
> As sense cannot untie. Be what it is,

---

[6] A. C. Bradley, *Shakespearean Tragedy* (1903; New York: Meridian, 1955) 77–8 (Third Lecture).

[7] Stephen Orgel (ed.), *The Winter's Tale*, Oxford Shakespeare (Oxford: Oxford University Press, 1996) 7.

[8] Gordon McMullan, *Shakespeare and the idea of late writing* (Cambridge: Cambridge University Press, 2007) 113; McMullan here writes about *Cymbeline* III. ii. 49–68, where the deferrals and digressions are matters of plot and geography.

>   The action of my life is like it, which I'll keep,
>   If but for sympathy.
>
>   (*Cymbeline* V. iii. 239–44)

In the first half of Shakespeare's career, this dramatic moment would occasion a deliberative soliloquy which would divide possible responses into categories, list arguments for and against both or all, and draw a balance leading to action. Examples range from Proteus' debate over jilting Julia (*The Two Gentlemen of Verona*, II. iv), to Richard III's meditation after his dream on the eve of Bosworth Field (*Richard III*, V, iii), to (a fairly late example) Macbeth's response to being named Thane of Cawdor—'This supernatural soliciting | Cannot be ill, cannot be good. If ill | ... If good ... ' (*Macbeth*, I. iii).

Again, had it appeared earlier in Shakespeare's canon, Posthumus' speech would be read psychologically—a mimetic record of his confusion—and criticized as imprecise, almost imageless, but perhaps justified as an attempt to convey an unsettled mental state. Yet the vague language, the contradictory abstractions, the frequent comparisons so frail they muddle rather than clarify: these features all point to Shakespeare's later style, as does the implied mental effort at definition (dream, mad speech spoken but not understood, both, nothing, 'senseless speech' or speech sense cannot understand) that first collapses ('Be what it is') and is then quasi-defined through a comparison of something undefined—'dream', etc.—with something else undefined (the 'action of my life') which 'is *like* it'. That final failure to specify tempts one to hear the speech as a meditation on the failure of analogical thinking and definition, both staples of argument in Shakespeare's earlier plays. Beyond that humble failure, the speech creates wonder at an experience defeating both language and thought and yet, of course, conveyed both as thought and in language. Indeed, the language itself is invented to meet a new expressive occasion: *brain* and *tongue* are typical Shakespearean conversions of nouns to verbs.[9]

Neologism is not the only form of variety the late style embraces. Posthumus' awakening has been preceded by his family ghosts and their petitions to Jupiter, expressed in fourteener triplets, a rare form in Shakespeare and completely antiquated by the moment of *Cymbeline*'s composition (1609). First Marlowe and then Shakespeare had long ago forced the fourteener couplet and triplet offstage in favour of iambic pentameter, but it had once been regarded as an English equivalent of the most serious and high Greek and Latin metre, the dactylic hexameter of Homer's epics, Virgil's *Aeneid*, and Ovid's *Metamorphoses*. Hence it was that George Chapman translated the *Iliad* and Arthur Golding *The Metamorphoses* into fourteener couplets.[10] That the ghosts use the metre marks them as classical and venerable and, perhaps, old-

---

[9] This passage is the earliest citation for the words' respective definitions in the *OED*. See, in general, Vivian Salmon, 'Some Functions of Shakespearian word-formation' in V. Salmon and E. Burness (eds), *Reader in the language of Shakespearean drama* (Amsterdam: Benjamins, 1987) 205–6.

[10] Arthur Hall's translation of ten books of the *Iliad* (1581) was in alexandrines (hexameter couplets), another form largely superseded by 1609.

fashioned and ineffective because Jupiter soon interrupts to berate them in vigorous blank verse:

> No more, you petty spirits of region low,
> Offend our hearing …
>
> ….
>
> Be not with mortal accidents oppressed;
> No care of yours it is; you know 'tis ours.
> Whom best I love, I cross, to make my gift,
> The more delayed, delighted. Be content.
>
> (*Cymbeline*, V. iii. 183–8, 193–6)

These last four lines are lapidary and elliptical, full of authority and monosyllables, and deeply memorable. Again, there is linguistic invention or torsion: Jupiter's gift will not be 'delighted', as the grammar seems to say, but its recipient will be. The principle that a joy delayed is enjoyed all the more intensely, compressed into a two-line aphorism here, is examined at length and critically in the last acts of *Measure for Measure*.

Various techniques in the first passage from *Cymbeline* force us away from a fused, individuated speaker and speech and toward a place where the speech is almost characterless or uncharacterizing, where the speech takes part in an evolving set of ideas and feelings more play-centred than character-centred. Shakespeare's 1590s-long effort to anchor distinctive styles in distinct characters (part of his effort both to escape and excel Marlowe) climaxes in the psychologically based agonies of *Lear* and *Macbeth* and then gradually yields to the dominance of event and atmosphere, especially in the last plays, but heard, too, in the late tragedies. For example, after Cleopatra's great elegiac aria ending

> … His [Antony's] delights
> Were dolphin-like; they showed his back above
> The element they lived in. In his livery
> Walked crowns and crownets. Realms and islands were
> As plates dropped from his pocket …
>
> (*Antony and Cleopatra*, V. ii. 89–91)

she turns to Dolabella, 'Think you there was, or might be, such a man | As this I dreamt of?' and he replies, 'Gentle madam, no' (V. ii. 92–3). Cleopatra's question may have or may be given a psychological explanation—'was, or might be' is a debilitating emotional tremor—but question and reply firmly establish the heroic, almost magical Antony the play now requires. (See, for example, the synecdoche of 'crowns and crownets' followed immediately by the metonymy of 'realms and islands' = 'plates'.) Dolabella then speaks for what Cleopatra calls 'the dung, | The beggar's nurse and Caesar's' (V. ii. 7–8).[11] These

---

[11] G. R. Hibbard describes this effect as 'an astonishing union of the hyperbolical with the simple, the downright, and the direct' ('Feliciter audax: *Antony and Cleopatra*, I, i, 1–24' in Philip Edwards, Inga-Stina Ewbank, and G. K. Hunter (eds), *Shakespeare's Styles: essays in honour of Kenneth Muir* (Cambridge: Cambridge University Press, 1980) 100.

violent intersections of almost untethered magniloquence with daily grit are mature and more effective versions of the self-parody Shakespeare can rarely resist, early or late.

This magniloquence can be expressed quite simply, with a plainness and abstraction both powerful and mysterious and often with sly double meanings too fine to be called puns:

> HERMIONE   My life stands in the level of your dreams,
>   WHICH I'LL LAY DOWN.
> LEONTES   Your actions are my 'dreams'.
>
>   (*The Winter's Tale*, III. ii. 80–1)

Of course Hermione's 'actions' are dreamed up by Leontes, not real; similarly, he dreams, jealously, of her imagined actions. Even finer is Leontes' satisfied horror (in the 'I have drunk, and seen the spider' speech) that his suspicions are true: 'All's true that is mistrusted' (*The Winter's Tale*, II. i. 50) which has a semantic flex worthy of an oracle or riddle: those characters who are mistrusted are, in fact, loyal; everyone and everything under suspicion is true.[12]

Combine knotty lexical choices with the late style's tendency to stray into seeming irrelevances or hard-to-harness digressions, and we have the following exchange between Camillo and Polixenes. Camillo hints,

>   There is a sickness
>   Which puts some of us in distemper, but
>   I cannot name th' disease, and it is caught
>   Of you that are yet well.
>
>   (*The Winter's Tale*, I. ii. 384–7)

And Polixenes catches at the hint:

>   Camillo,
>   As you are certainly a gentleman, thereto
>   Clerk-like experienced, which no less adorns
>   Our gentry than our parents' noble names,
>   In whose success we are gentle: I beseech you,
>   If you know aught which does behove my knowledge
>   Thereof to be informed, imprison't not
>   In ignorant concealment.
>
>   (*The Winter's Tale*, I. ii. 390–7)

While Camillo's reluctance to share Leontes' suspicions with Polixenes is certainly honourable (and therefore gentlemanly), his only slightly evasive and paradoxical remarks—semi-quibbling on 'sickness' | 'well'—elicit an oddly extended version of a

---

[12] See Anne Barton, 'Leontes and the spider: Language and speaker in Shakespeare's last plays' in Edwards et al. (1980) 144.

standard Shakespearean response when a social equal or superior demands the truth. In an early comedy, a slightly extended version would be the Duke's to Valentine: 'as thou art a gentleman of blood' (*The Two Gentlemen of Verona*, III. i. 121), but many characters are satisfied with 'as I am a gentleman' and even mildly verbose Hamlet is satisfied to abjure Horatio and the guard with 'As you are friends, scholars and soldiers' (*Hamlet*, I. v. 145).

Leontes first cites Camillo's status as a gentleman who is 'clerk-like experienced' (that is, one who is a scholar ('clerk') of worldly behavior or of the mysterious 'sickness', presumably). Already this is more speech than the formulaic moment requires, but Leontes now takes three lines to parse the relative importance of clerk-like experience and noble descent and add the tautology that noble descent is what makes successors 'gentle'. As conversation or dialogue, this is unnecessary matter, especially since Polixenes repeats the charge and the prolixity in his next speech—'I conjure thee by all the parts of man | Which honour doth acknowledge ... ' (I. ii. 400–1)— and Camillo capitulates at once. If we ask not 'is this good, persuasive, necessary dialogue?' but instead ask, 'do this dialogue and its subjects link to larger concerns in the play?' then an explanation may be proposed. Of course Camillo's social standing and royal intimacy must be established, especially since what he now does might be considered treason by a king considerably more balanced than Leontes. Likewise, the audience. The elaborate unfolding of what it means to be gentle, noble, etc.—realistically redundant here—is part-preparation for the marvellous turn the play makes in Act IV, where precisely what constitutes nobility and royalty is at stake and where, technically, Camillo betrays his master again, only in the geographically opposite direction this time.

Of the plays just mentioned, *Antony* is the earliest (1606?) and *Cymbeline* (1610–11) and *The Winter's Tale* (1609–10) are among the latest unaided plays in the canon. All three, and the passages from them considered here, show signs of the weakening of 'the link between speech and speaker' in Shakespeare's later tragedies and final plays dating to 'about 1607'.[13] If there seems to be a growing skepticism or suspicion about words alongside this weakening link, what remains? As early as *King Lear*, Anne Barton diagnoses 'a broken, a dislocated speech that is offered. All Cordelia can do [as reported in *Lear*, IV. iii] is repeat proper and generic names, tangible things which weigh like coins in the hand, without verbs to link them, without sentence structure ... Words define the gap between individuals; they do not bridge it'.[14] In tandem with the severing of 'character' from distinctive speech, although often proceeding at different rates, there come changes to the language and rhetoric themselves.

[13] Russ McDonald, *Shakespeare's Late Style* (Cambridge: Cambridge University Press, 2006) 34; see also at 99 on consistency of character, and 'language ... in the service of characterisation' (Frank Kermode, *Shakespeare's Language*, New York: Farrar, Straus and Giroux, 2000, 46).

[14] Anne Barton, 'Shakespeare and the limits of language' (1971) in Barton, *Essays, mainly Shakespearean* (Cambridge: Cambridge University Press, 1994) 61–2.

A small example of the linguistic oddity found in Shakespeare's later plays appears at the end of Polixenes' speech we have just considered. He concludes:

> If you know aught which does behove my knowledge
> Thereof to be informed, imprison't not
> In ignorant concealment.

> *(The Winter's Tale, I. ii. 395–7)*

Again, there are far more words than strictly' necessary here and a very strange use of 'ignorant', which must, as the *OED* says, be a nonce-use meaning, 'That keeps one in ignorance'. This explanation in turn means that Shakespeare has added an agentive suffix, *-ant*, to 'ignore' making 'ignorant' (on the model of *tenant*, or *servant*), but it must have been difficult to catch that nonce-meaning in the theatre rather than to hear the common adjective and think of a personified Concealment serving as prison or gaoler to 'aught'.[15] Psychological explanations for this abstract, unanchored language and frequently knotty syntax are hard to find. Better to explain the phenomena as a generalized royal or court speech combined with minds grappling with the outlandish accusation against Hermione.

As elsewhere, this conversation also exemplifies the contrasts of simplicity with over-elaboration Shakespeare's late style can embrace. Polixenes contributes this to a bout of courtly afflatus,

> O, then, my best blood turn
> To an infected jelly, and my name
> Be yoked with his that did betray the Best!
> Turn then my freshest reputation to
> A savour that may strike the dullest nostril
> Where I arrive, and my approach be shunned,
> Nay hated, too, worse than the great'st infection
> That e'er was heard or read!

> *(The Winter's Tale, I. ii. 417–24)*

After Camillo's equally heightened response, Polixenes asks, simply, 'How should this grow?' And Camillo answers with equal simplicity, 'I know not: but I am sure 'tis safer to | Avoid what's grown than question how 'tis born' (*The Winter's Tale*, I. ii. 432–3). Slowed by monosyllables into solemnity, this exchange encapsulates the difference between tragedy and romance: Shakespearean tragedy always looks to origins—'How should this grow?'—romance strives to avoid evil consequences and looks to a better future,

---

[15] Compare 'Alas, what ignorant sin have I committed?' (*Othello* IV. ii. 72), cited in *OED adj* and *n* 3a for 'showing absence of knowledge'.

however contrived.[16] Simple monosyllables can convey great emotion, and humble alliteration can become a form of violence. Leontes attacks Paulina:

> A callat
> Of boundless tongue, who late hath beat her husband,
> And now baits me! This brat is none of mine,
> It is the issue of Polixenes.
>
> (*The Winter's Tale*, II. iii. 91–4)

Historically, the vowels of 'beat' | 'baits' are a true rhyme, and the openness of 'boundless' and the snap of 'brat' elegantly frame the alliterating series. It is also difficult not to hear the hiss of 'issue' echoed in 'Polixenes', at least as the actor of Leontes is likely to speak it.

As Polonius and Osric in *Hamlet*, not to mention a dozen speakers in the history plays, neatly show, court speech frequently attracted Shakespeare's parodic blade. The charges are severe: a ballooning of trifles, language pretentious and circumlocutionary, wrought tropes and schemes indulged for their own sake, categories seized upon as sources of sub-categories, verbal preening. For example, someone must have found Polonius' blustery generic codification funny because the theatrically derived Folio text expands the list in the second Quarto: 'Pastoricall-Comicall-Historicall-Pastoral: Tragicall-Historicall: Tragicall-Comicall-Historicall-Pastorall'. This is the germ of a Gilbert and Sullivan patter song where sound trumps sense. The habit of listing is one of Polonius' favorite and most ridiculed devices:

> And he [Hamlet], repulsed—a short tale to make—
> Fell into a sadness, then into a fast,
> Thence to a watch, thence into a weakness,
> Thence to a lightness, and, by this declension,
> Into the madness wherein now he raves,
> And we all mourn for.
>
> (*Hamlet* II. ii. 147–52)

As the final, abrupt half-line of sympathy makes clear, the joy of the 'declension' has almost completely displaced the emotional content of the speech and the speaker's awareness of his audience. What is perhaps Polonius' masterpiece of egoism starts rather like Polixenes' digressive remarks to Camillo and ends with a rebuke:

> My liege, and madam, to expostulate
> What majesty should be, what duty is,
> Why day is day, night night, and time is time,

---

[16] '[T]he capacity to accept the world-as-it-is has had to be bought by a sacrifice of heroic pretensions, by a loss of confidence in the heroic individual. In reading the Last Plays, we should feel the sense of this loss even as we rejoice in the sweetness of their reconciliations'. See G. K. Hunter, 'The last tragic heroes' in J. R. Brown and B. Morris, (eds), *Later Shakespeare* (London: Arnold, 1966) 28.

> Were nothing but to waste night, day, and time.
> Therefore, since brevity is the soul of wit,
> And tediousness the limbs and outward flourishes,
> I will be brief. Your noble son is mad—
> 'Mad' call I it, for to define true madness,
> What is't but to be nothing else but mad?
> But let that go.
> QUEEN   More matter with less art.
>
> (*Hamlet* II. ii. 87–96)

Superficial productions of *Hamlet* find merely the buffoon in Polonius, or the tedious old fool; more considered productions often see the tediousness and apparent folly as shield and mask at a court run by a cunning king and populated by some intricately deceitful folk.

Polonius is principally mocked for losing himself and his listeners in the sort of patterned speech especially obvious in Shakespeare's first tetralogy of history plays and his early comedies. Fools and clowns display continuing interest in highly decorated rhetorical figures, and those patterns—the schemes and tropes Shakespeare learned in school—never disappear, but they do become more subtle and conform less and less with the metre and the disposition of words within the line, the phrase, and the sentence.[17]

On many occasions, Shakespearean characters profess their verbal inadequacies in self-deprecating eloquence, but then there are occasions when the profession of inadequacy is demonstrably true—consider Quince as Prologue in *A Midsummer Night's Dream* or Moth's attempts to introduce the Muscovites in *Love's Labour's Lost* or the 'dyer's hand' sonnet (111). What do we make of 'the rhetoric of discursive incompetence' when it drowns in plain incompetence?[18] For example, Archidamus to Camillo: 'Verily, I speak it in the freedom of my knowledge. We cannot with such magnificence—in so rare—I know not what to say.—We will give you sleepy drinks, that your senses, unintelligent of our insufficience, may, though they cannot praise us, as little accuse us' (*The Winter's Tale*, I. i. 11–16). The last feeble, contradictory antistrophe—praise *us*, accuse *us*—may turn us back to what looks like a verbal and therefore possibly an expressive antithesis, 'unintelligent' | 'insufficience', that proves purely auditory (*un-*, *in-*) and includes a neologism, *unintelligent of* for 'having no knowledge of'. These syntactical, lexical, and rhetorical bits and pieces are awash in unmeaning verbiage like once-meaningful rhetorical wreckage in an unfathomable sea.

Superb, two-faced examples of court speech come from the mouths of Gonoril and Regan in *King Lear*. Here, Gonoril protests her love for her father: with a self-deprecatory preface and coda surrounding a highly skilled piece of flattery,

---

[17] See George T. Wright, *Shakespeare's Metrical Art* (Berkeley: University of California Press, 1988) *passim*.

[18] See Kier Elam, 'Early modern syntax and late Shakespearean rhetoric' in Carmela Nocera Avila, Nicola Pantaleo, and D. Pezzini (eds), *Early Modern English: trends, forms and texts* (Fasano: Schena, 1992) 79.

> Sir, I do love you more than words can wield the matter;
> Dearer than eyesight, space, or liberty;
> Beyond what can be valued, rich or rare;
> No less than life; with grace, health, beauty, honour,
> As much as child e'er loved, or father, friend;
> A love that makes breath poor and speech unable.
> Beyond all manner of so much I love you.
>
> (*King Lear* Q 1.50–6)

The speech depends on both apparent modesty and masterly use of comparison-as-measure (in a way anticipating *Measure for Measure* itself). The speech leaves Regan a difficult task which she fulfils by out-comparing her sister:

> Sir, I am made
> Of the self-same mettle that my sister is,
> And prize me at her worth. In my true heart
> I find she names my very deed of love—
> Only she came short, that I profess
> Myself an enemy to all other joys
> Which the most precious square of sense possesses,
> And find I am alone felicitate
> In your dear highness' love.
>
> (*King Lear,* Q 1.63–71)

Regan first asserts equality with her sister, then inflates her claim of naming the 'very deed of love' by claiming Gonoril has come 'short'. Comparison heaped upon comparison: where Gonoril specified child, parent, and friend as persons whose love is outweighed by hers for her father, Regan retorts she is 'an enemy to all other joys' than love for her father, whose reciprocal love makes her 'felicitate', a rare word meant to ornament and perhaps exoticize her claim.[19]

However non-current, 'felicitate' is, at least, no comparative, although one could complicate the moment by asking what would contrast with it. More often than not, Shakespeare's understanding of figurative language or figuration itself seems to have arisen from comparison explicit or implied, simile or metaphor. Unsurprisingly, then, attempts to talk about the changes in Shakespeare's imaginative language and rhetoric that appear toward the end of his professional career resort to imagery themselves: 'tumid', 'twisted or elliptical', 'sublimity or pathos' have been mentioned. To these, add: 'intensity, vagueness, and obscurity'; 'grammatical and formal instability ... an expressionistic, or perhaps manneristic, poetics'.[20]

---

[19] The only citation in the *OED* for the adjectival use of 'felicitate'.

[20] Respectively, Stephen Orgel (ed.), *The Winter's Tale* (Oxford: Oxford University Press, 1996) 12, and Elam (1992) 70.

For 'formal instability' consider the syntax of two stringent moments in *The Tempest*, moments when clarity and authority would seem to be paramount in both the dramatized situations and for the audience's grasp of the play's direction. The first is Ariel's address, as harpy, to Prospero's usurpers and enemies:

> You are three men of sin, whom destiny—
> That hath to instrument this lower world
> And what is in't—the never-surfeited sea
> Hath caused to belch up you, and on this island
> Where man doth not inhabit, you 'mongst men
> Being most unfit to live. I have made you mad,
> And even with suchlike valour men hang and drown
> Their proper selves.

(*The Tempest*, III. iii. 53–60)

The speech certainly conveys deep threat—destiny, the sea, madness, suicide—but its thought is discontinuous, rushing from one threat to another before the first has been fully expressed. What exactly is the ocean's place? It has belched these men up, no doubt, but has Destiny 'caused' the sea's behaviour and is the sea therefore one of Destiny's 'instruments'? Or is Destiny simply the authorizing entity allowing Ariel's (or the harpy's or Prospero's) actions with the sea an independent, hostile actor? The phrase 'never-surfeited sea' seems both in apposition with 'it'—one of the lower world's instruments—and either the object or the subject of the following verb, 'hath caused'. Ariel hurries on with the oddly bland 'and' to specify the island's claimed lack of inhabitants as an explanation for why this uninhabited place suits men unworthy of life. Now it may become clear that ' 'mongst men | Being unfit to live' refers not to this group as selected from all humankind—you three sinners among all other men—but rather 'you are unfit to live in human society'. And now a new threat appears—madness—which will drive the listeners to suicide because they are fit neither to live among men nor in an uninhabited island. These swirling possibilities are not the rush of metaphor upon metaphor that worried Dryden and, for him, seemed especially characteristic of such a play as *Macbeth*; rather, the grammar and syntax have collapsed, or almost collapsed, under the weight of imagined punishments, punishments so fierce and irresistible they tumble out any which way.

Perhaps it is especially characteristic of Prospero's complexly derived authority (duke, ex-duke, father, colonist, future father-in-law) that he should soon mingle a blessing with a curse. Having affirmed 'I | Have given you here a third of mine own life— | Or that for which I live', he demands Ferdinand delay consummating his union with Miranda:

> If thou dost break her virgin-knot before
> All sanctimonious ceremonies may
> With full and holy rite be ministered,
> No sweet aspersion shall the heavens let fall
> To make this contract grow; but barren hate,

Sour-eyed disdain, and discord, shall bestrew
The union of your bed with weeds so loathly
That you shall hate it both.

(*The Tempest*, IV. i. 15–22)

Pompous, latinate diction—'sanctimonious ceremonies', 'sweet aspersion'—mingles with half-hearted personification—'barren hate', 'sour-eyed disdain'—and a tired pun on 'weeds' as both detested plants and loathsome garments.[21] As we have seen in earlier examples, a psychological explanation is available: Prospero has difficulty relinquishing authority; he mourns giving up a third of his life; he stresses his remaining powers and their future terrors. Yet the tone is unsteady, neither consistently ducal and mage-like nor grimly violent in a manner reminiscent of earlier plays like *King John*.[22] Lurking within the speech there lies an almost unexpressed reference to the product of Miranda and Ferdinand's 'contract' and 'union of your bed', their not-yet-conceived child or children. Even more than the soon-to-be ritualized marriage, a child will unite the warring families and assure the future of the play's societies. Genre, we might say, requires this comic token lest the future be sterile vengeance and all Prospero's exigent magic wasted.

This hint of a comic ending needs to be made more explicit through Prospero's self-knowledge, or what might be self-knowledge if the play proceeded by the protocols of Shakespeare's earlier great tragedies. Here the *Tempest* proceeds differently, first with Ariel's status report and then, putting an extreme twist on Lady Macbeth's tactics, his sly hint of what Prospero might lack. Ariel's catalogue of prisoners ends with

Him you termed, sir, the good old lord, Gonzalo:
His tears run down his beard like winter's drops
From eaves of reeds. Your charm so strongly works 'em
That if you now beheld them your affections
Would become tender.

(V. i. 15–19)

To which Prospero replies, 'Dost thou think so, spirit?' And Ariel famously replies, 'Mine would, sir, were I human'. By this moment, we do not need to be reminded of Ariel's status as 'spirit'; the word occurs purely to elicit its antithesis, 'human'. As in the many short repetitions of *Lear* or Dolabella's 'Gentle madam, no', we recognize a long-standing and growing habit of mixing polysyllabic and /or image-heavy and emotive lines with lines largely monosyllabic, simple in diction. That simplicity may make the oddity of Ariel's qualification stand out the more: 'Mine would, sir, were I human'. Of course, Ariel iterates the island's fantastic qualities and cast, but he also gently invokes Lady Macbeth's humiliation-by-hypothesis: 'When you durst do it, then you were a man ... Had I so sworn | As you have done ...' (*Macbeth*, I. vii. 49, 58–9). Prospero's response,

---

[21] This passage is the earliest citation for 'aspersion' in *OED n.*2.
[22] See, for example, Constance's curses in Act III, Scene i.

a long, slightly repetitive meditation on the differences between the human and the non-human, prepares the audience for the extraordinary abjuration of his art—'Ye elves of hills, brooks, standing lakes, and groves. . . . ' (*The Tempest*, V. i. 33ff.)—and arraignment of the 'men of sin' that immediately follow Ariel's exit. All this descends from Ariel's pointed counterfactual, 'Mine would . . . were I human'.

A section of the latter part of the speech illustrates much about Shakespeare's later style:

> Holy Gonzalo, honourable man,
> Mine eyes, ev'n sociable to the show of thine
> Fall fellowly drops. [*Aside*] The charm dissolves apace;
> And as the morning steals upon the night,
> Melting the darkness, so their rising senses
> Begin to chase the ignorant fumes that mantle
> Their clearer reason.—O good Gonzalo,
> My true preserver, and a loyal sir
> To him thou follow'st, I will pay thy graces
> Home both in word and deed.—Most cruelly
> Didst thou, Alonso, use me and my daughter.
> Thy brother was a furtherer in the act.
> Thou art pinched for't now, Sebastian. [*To Antonio*] Flesh and blood,
> You, brother mine, that entertained ambition,
> Expelled remorse and nature, whom, with Sebastian—
> Whose inward pinches therefore, are most strong,—
> Would here have killed your king, I do forgive thee,
> Unnatural though thou art. [*Aside*] Their understanding
> Begins to swell, and the approaching tide
> Will shortly fill the reasonable shores,
> That now lie foul and muddy.
>
> (V. i. 62–82)

This portion of the speech is a series of addresses to the Milanese and Neapolitan would-be regicides-usurpers and (twice) to the good and loyal Gonzalo. Recapitulating what happens before their arrival on the island and after, this segment serves as a minia-turized version of *The Tempest*, Act 1, Scene 2. Interspersed among the direct addresses are generalizing, near-choric comments that seem to arise not from the embodied actor of Prospero but from some less precisely defined psyche: 'The charm dissolves apace . . . '; 'Whose inward pinches therefor, are most strong'; 'Their understanding | Begins to swell . . . '. As is the case here, editors have sometimes been tempted to insert asides or changes of address or both in the speech because Prospero's focus, not to mention his composure and his moralizing vary so much. Note that most of the moments when Prospero changes addressees or when he seems closest to losing his temper do not begin iambic lines but interrupt them (see lines 68, 72, 74, 75).

Just before the first address to Gonzalo, Prospero has stage-managed and narrated the party's entrance:

> [*To Alonso*] A solemn air [music], and the best comforter
> To an unsettled fancy, cure thy brains,
> Now useless, boiled within thy skull. [*To Sebastian and Antonio*] There
>   stand,
> For you are spell-stopped.
>
> > (*The Tempest* V. i. 58–61)

After a series of not quite disjointed phrases comes a command all in monosyllables, 'stopp'd' before it can fill the pentameter. Now follow the regular beats, feet, and phrases matched with line-endings of 'Holy Gonzalo … '—two and a half lines so regular and orderly they might come from *Romeo and Juliet* or *Julius Caesar*. It would be unusual, however, to find in *Romeo* or *Caesar* a full stop after the first two feet or so of a line and then a sentence (itself a grammatical interruption) that runs for three lines, ending in the middle of another pentameter with a full stop before a renewed speech, with vocative, to Gonzalo.[23] Once more, we find Shakespeare's particular understanding of a familiar word: 'ignorant fumes that mantle | Their clearer reason' must mean 'fumes that replace clear reason with ignorance'. Again, a recessive set of personifications appears faintly: flesh and blood expelled remorse and nature, the latter apparently guests entertained as a consequence of Antonio's ambition.[24] Traditional rhetorical schemes are certainly audible and visible—anaphora-like, two successive clauses begin with quasi-alliterating past-tense verbs, 'entertained … expelled … ', though the clauses they introduce are not quite of the same length and thus form only a near-isocolon. The speech's most memorable set of metaphors (also running mid-line to mid-line) makes a humble analogy between the group's dawning awareness and the tide, presumably in the Thames, returning to cleanse the excrement and refuse exposed by its ebb. While found much earlier in the canon, the grammatical twist in 'reasonable shore'—not a shore that reasons but Reason's riverine boundary—recalls the earlier metamorphoses of 'ignorant' through varied parts of speech. These features and others all testify to the generally agreed sense that Shakespeare's late style is one where rule-following has largely disappeared and a surge of rule-bending if not rule-breaking has occurred.

A final question concerns what Dryden called 'the other harmony of prose'.[25] How does Shakespeare's later prose compare with his earlier? One response: '[i]n Shakespeare's late work, both [verse, prose] are constructed out of the same peculiar intensity and … sleeplessness, of metaphor'.[26] However similar the late prose and verse may seem at first, there are many differences, especially in their respective degrees and speed of evolution. Shakespeare's prose was a magnificent instrument from the first,

---

[23] Again, see Wright (1988) esp. ch. 14, 'The Play of Phrase and Line' 207–28.

[24] The passage has been debated since the 18th century; Frank Kermode glosses 'you, my brother, my own flesh and blood, who entertained ambition and expelled remorse'; see Kermode (ed.) *The Tempest*, Arden Shakespeare, rev. edn (1954; London: Methuen, 1961) V. i. 74–76 n.

[25] Dryden, ed. Watson (1962) ii, 272.

[26] Simon Palfrey, *Late Shakespeare: a new world of words* (Oxford: Clarendon Press, 1997) 18.

it 'matured early, but then changed relatively little ... that such change as can be perceived consists mainly in a widening of range, in the use of prose for increasingly serious and powerful effects ... ';[27] that is, techniques changed relatively little, deployment did. The prose of Falstaff in *1 Henry IV*, Pistol's orgies of quotation and the invective of Doll Tearsheet in *2 Henry IV*, the old men reminiscing in Gloucestershire in the same play—all these are highly developed artistry.

What of application? One intriguing comparison is between the unfortunate Clown Titus dispatches to Saturninus in *Titus Andronicus* (1592?) and the asp-bearing Clown of the last scene in *Antony and Cleopatra*. In both cases, the rustic intrudes upon the aristocratic and the royal; in both examples the intruding, humble folk do not understand, or do not seem to understand, their circumstances. And after a few jokes at his mistaking speech (Jupiter/'gibbet-maker'), the Clown in *Titus* is sent off to see the Empress (small joke, 'Emperial') and Emperor. Illiterate, the Clown delivers a presumably insulting or threatening letter, with a knife wrapped inside, and is sent off to hanging with a final joke, 'Then I have brought up a neck to a fair end' (*Titus Andronicus*, IV. iv. 48–9).

The analogous, slightly longer, episode in *Antony and Cleopatra* comes approximately fourteen years later in Shakespeare's career. It includes more and less-laboured malapropisms—'his biting is immortal' is quite fine as a preface to the illogic of 'those that do die of it do seldom or never recover', and 'this is most fallible, the worm's an odd worm' is close enough to metaphor to make the diagnosis of malapropism questionable (*Antony and Cleopatra*, V. ii. 241–2, 242–3, 252–3). Unlike the Clown of *Titus*, the later character gets the opportunity to contribute, unwittingly as may be, to larger issues: 'You must think this, look you, that the worm will do his kind' (V. ii. 257–8), where doing one's kind—performing behaviour characteristic of individual or species—has immense resonance for the play's three central characters and their actions. He continues in a passage that teeters on reductive parody, but hews just close enough to a persuasive earthiness to broaden the play's emotional reach at this moment: 'You must not think I am so simple but I know the devil himself will not eat a woman. I know that a woman is a dish for the gods, if the devil dress her not' (V. ii. 267–9). The imagery, and its contending morals, embrace the play: what kind of 'dish' was Cleopatra, 'cold upon | Dead Caesar's trencher' (III. xiii. 117–18)?

Witty as M. Guizot was—and in truth he was writing about Shakespeare's Sonnets, not his plays—Matthew Arnold was closer to the truth when he described 'over-curiousness of expression' as 'excessive employment of a wonderful gift'. Even so tempered, the account would also require an acknowledgement of how much use, and how powerful, Shakespeare's style early and late makes of simplicity. Indeed the wider range of Shakespeare's style as he matures—his growing willingness to mix different registers and different vocabularies—makes the contrasts between the simplest and the most 'curious'

---

[27] Jonas A. Barish, 'Continuities and discontinuities in Shakespearian Prose' in Clifford Leech and J. M. R. Margeson (eds), *Shakespeare 1971* (Toronto: University of Toronto Press, 1972) 59.

writing stronger. Simplicity's power appears often in brief exchanges such as the one we examined between Prospero and Ariel at the beginning of Act 5. Consider further:

> When did you lose your daughter? | In this last tempest
> (*The Tempest*, V. i. 154)
>
> O brave new world
> That has such people in't! | 'Tis new to thee.
> (*The Tempest*, V. i. 186–7)

Or in more epigrammatic or lapidary contexts: 'This thing of darkness I | Acknowledge mine'; 'Every third thought shall be my grave' (*The Tempest*, V. i. 278–9, 315). The emotional effects of these passages are complex and strong; the language, the syntax, the figuration are simple, almost stripped.

SELECT BIBLIOGRAPHY

Barton, Anne (1994) *Essays, mainly Shakespearean* (Cambridge: Cambridge University Press).

Bradley, A. C. (1955) *Shakespearean Tragedy* (New York: Meridian).

Edwards, Philip, Inga-Stina Ewbank, and G. K. Huntger (1980) (eds) *Shakespeare's Styles: essays in honour of Kenneth Muir* (Cambridge: Cambridge University Press).

Houston, John Porter (1988) *Shakespearean Sentences: a study in style and syntax* (Baton Rouge: Louisiana State University Press).

Kermode, Frank (2000) *Shakespeare's Language* (New York: Farrar, Straus and Giroux).

Lamb, Charles (1808) *Specimens of English Dramatic Poets* (London: Longman, Hurst, Rees, and Orme).

McDonald, Russ (2006) *Shakespeare's Late Style* (Cambridge: Cambridge University Press).

McMullan, Gordon (2007) *Shakespeare and the idea of late writing* (Cambridge: Cambridge University Press).

Palfrey, Simon (1997) *Late Shakespeare: a new world of words* (Oxford: Clarendon Press).

Salmon, V. and E. Burness (1987) (eds) *Reader in the language of Shakespearean drama* (Amsterdam: Benjamins).

Vickers, Brian (1979) *The Artistry of Shakespeare's prose* (London: Methuen).

Wright, George T. (1988) *Shakespeare's Metrical Art* (Berkeley: University of California Press).

CHAPTER 4

··

SHAKESPEARE AND THE
ARTS OF COGNITION

··

SOPHIE READ

Hamlet, with its meditative temper and deep interest in the limits of the intellect, might seem the most natural place in Shakespeare's works to begin thinking about thinking. Its protagonist is famous for it: hours of real time, weeks of stage time pass, in which he does little else; the action of revenge that we await is long-delayed and happens, when it comes, in a messy convulsion that renders the preceding stratagems and deliberations quite absurd. It is this very emphasis on thought as divorced from action, however, that makes the cerebral prince less interesting from a cognitive point of view than a character almost directly his opposite: the rashly impulsive regicide, Macbeth. If *Hamlet* drags in the most fascinating of ways until its high-speed ending, *Macbeth* traces the reverse trajectory of temporal extremes: it starts off at breakneck pace, and slows almost unendurably towards the final moments, with the drawn-out fulfilment of a fate that has been inevitable since the first scene. The play dramatizes the dilation and contraction of time, imagines it experienced subjectively, and part of the way it does this is through the arts of rhetoric.

Many crucial passages in *Macbeth* demand unthinkably swift apprehension, or rather a dual process of mind—a fast understanding that is succeeded by the slow reconstructions of frame-by-frame replay. Our perception of duration is affected by figurative complexity: we sense the speed of the character's thought, and behind that the writer's, leaping from word to image and back again with completely intuitive contingency: this is what Coleridge meant when he said that 'In Shakespeare one sentence begets the next naturally; the meaning is all inwoven. He goes on kindling like a meteor through the dark atmosphere'.[1] Because so much is conveyed in these elliptical moments, however,

---

[1] Samuel Taylor Coleridge, quoted in *The Romantics on Shakespeare*, Jonathan Bate (ed.), (Harmondsworth: Penguin, 1992) 162–3; the reference is to *Specimens of the Table Talk of Samuel Taylor Coleridge*, 2 vols, 2nd edn, H. N. Coleridge (ed.), (London: J. Murray, 1836) 7 April 1833 and 5 March 1834.

they feel simultaneously and paradoxically slow, as if they are happening underwater. This quality—not unique in Shakespeare's drama but given here an exceptionally intense expression—is one reason why so many accounts of the phenomenon of illogical comprehension that is the chief interest of this chapter, the mind outdistancing itself in understanding, start with *Macbeth*.[2] *Hamlet* is no less temporally confused or figuratively complex, but its picture of an unquiet mind is intriguing rather than compelling. The prince's oblique words 'unpack' his heart and eddy around his strange stasis:[3] they do not, as Macbeth's do, short-circuit the processes of reason to offer decisions magnificently, precariously dependent on a self-generating logic. Macbeth's thought is active and urgent: we follow, as critics have consistently remarked, without really knowing how, and without minding or even noticing the lag between comprehension and construction.

Not all of these attempts to explain *Macbeth*'s stylistic signature are explicitly cognitive in the terms of their arguments, but they all confront a phenomenon of staggered comprehension that reveals the way the mind works: 'No matter how challenging the syntax or the metrical pattern becomes', Russ McDonald notices, '*what* the lines mean is considerably easier to discern than *how* they deliver their meanings. [...] Intuitive understanding precedes grammatical cognition'.[4] This temporal dysmorphia is particularly acute in those passages which concentrate, as many of the most complex ones do, on the nature and experience of time itself. Before Macbeth kills Duncan he fantasizes about its complete collapse; action and consequence are comprehended in the same moment: then 'here, | But here upon this bank and shoal of time, | We'd jump the life to come' (1.7.6–7). By 'jump' Macbeth might mean hazard his chance at eternity, or accelerate to it, or beyond: what should be an important distinction is effaced, as time becomes the vast unknowable abyss of ocean, Macbeth a man at the mercy of its capricious tides.

Again, near the end of the play, he reflects upon odd folds in the temporal fabric. Lady Macbeth is dead.

> She should have died hereafter.
> There would have been a time for such a word.
> Tomorrow, and tomorrow, and tomorrow,
> Creeps in this petty pace from day to day
> To the last syllable of recorded time,
> And all our yesterdays have lighted fools
> The way to dusty death. Out, out, brief candle.

---

[2] Instances over the last few years include Russ McDonald, *Shakespeare's Late Style* (Cambridge: Cambridge University Press, 2006), Brian Cummings, 'Metalepsis: The Boundaries of Metaphor', in *Renaissance Figures of Speech*, Sylvia Adamson, Gavin Alexander, and Katrin Ettenhuber (eds), (Cambridge: Cambridge University Press, 2007), 217–33, and Raphael Lyne, *Shakespeare, Rhetoric and Cognition* (Cambridge: Cambridge University Press, 2011).
[3] *Hamlet*, III. i. 588. Future references to Shakespeare's works will be to this edition, and will be given as Act, Scene, and line numbers (where appropriate) in the text.
[4] McDonald (2006) 31, 46.

> Life's but a walking shadow, a poor player
> That struts and frets his hour upon the stage,
> And then is heard no more. It is a tale
> Told by an idiot, full of sound and fury,
> Signifying nothing.
>
> (V. v. 16–27)

The idea is difficult, and its expression in a series of obliquely connected images commensurately complex. A thought comes into focus and is held for a moment before giving way to another, and the conceptual overlap between them is perceptible but not luminously logical; the unit of the line orders but does not contain the progression. Macbeth's meditation is deeply embedded in the play's action, but still apart from it: time moves slowly and is gone in an instant, the individual lifespan as nothing against the stretch of eternity, and these very words measure the shock of apprehension against the process of intellection. Time is protean, quicksilver: it creeps, becomes a book ('recorded'), a path; somewhere in here the expired moment is imagined as producing enough energy in its passing to illuminate the long lives of others in a kind of apocalyptic funeral procession: 'all our yesterdays have lighted fools | The way to dusty death'. Macbeth's words catch another sense, as the latent image here ignites the 'brief candle' of a life whose relative insignificance is figured reflexively as a performance; the very performance, perhaps, that he is in this moment in the act of giving. This progression, characteristically, hinges on the contingency of a word: the candle's shadow breeds its secondary sense of 'actor', and that figure animates the comparison of dramatic time, with its faults and fluctuations, to the span of a human life.[5] Brian Cummings identifies in this passage the figure of *metalepsis*, the far-fetched conceit, and he registers its brilliance and its daring: 'this sentence takes risks with its own meaning, risks indeed that it will emerge as meaningless'.[6] That this breakdown does not in fact happen has as much to do with a reader's process of cognition as with Shakespeare's rhetorical control.

There is no space here to do more than touch on the complexity of lines fraught with intersecting and self-spawning metaphors, and compounded by accretions of allusion (the 'dust' of the burial service, shadows, and candles from Job and the Psalms); I want, though, to notice particularly two things about this passage. One is how easily and how powerfully we understand what is being said, despite the missing pieces, and how willing we are to defer or even dispense with complete elucidation in favour of this experience of construction: we take the dynamic process over its static conclusion, and achieve a richly attenuated perception. This is a moment of crux, as Macbeth sublimates shock and grief into these knotty, measured lines, and we struggle with their meaning because he does: a moment of such intellectual and emotional difficulty demands a form of expression whose triumph is in its closeness to failure, and that his words here threaten

---

[5] See *OED*, 'shadow', *n.*, senses 4(a), 6(b).
[6] Cummings (2007) 218.

to dismantle themselves under their shifting and compound signification is part of the way in which they signify. The other is how this passage itself attempts to confront the processes of comprehension as both temporal and contingent. Macbeth's labour to make sense of what has happened is matched by the strain of his metalepses, and these are importantly underwritten by a sense of understanding as driven by verbal construction. Death is a 'word', time is measured in 'syllables', the poor player risks, as Macbeth does, utterance lost to 'sound and fury'. As Raphael Lyne recognizes in an important new study, *Shakespeare, Rhetoric and Cognition*, 'a cognitive rhetoric is a means of addressing the challenges of complex experiences': the moments when words threaten to fail, in the face of love, and death, and time, they assume shapes of complex figuration.[7] Places where the meaning is difficult, occluded, and resistant to resolution are, Lyne goes on to say, 'the best indications that poetic thinking is ongoing, and struggling to culminate [...]; the efficacy of the trope in capturing the predicament is discovered in its collapse as much as in its construction'.[8]

That lengthy preamble was designed to introduce some of the ideas on which this argument is predicated where they can most clearly be seen: in the wild, as it were, of the dramatic moment, a character surprised mid-thought. In what follows I intend to extend this way of reading to Shakespeare's lyric verse, primarily the Sonnets, and to suggest that its confrontations with the almost inexpressible phenomena of love, death, and time—although they occur in a very different context—might be facilitated by just such feats of cognitive rhetoric as those that appear in *Macbeth*. But before I do that I need to backtrack a little and explain briefly what precisely I mean by 'cognitive rhetoric', and where this kind of thinking fits in with existing research. It is, first, important to establish that while the terminology might be new, the effects and experiences it describes certainly are not: 'I neer found so many beauties in the sonnets—they seem to be full of fine things said unintentionally—in the intensity of working out conceits—Is this to be borne?'[9] This is Keats in 1817 confronting with a characteristically forthright subtlety a sensation experienced by many readers of Shakespeare's verse before and after him: the impression of a serious disjunction between swiftness of composition and speed of comprehension. A reader labours in the wake of a connection so slender, so glancing, and so brilliant that it might be suspected of contingency—of luck. Meanings and ghosts of meanings proliferate, often in a single word or turn: this lightning intuition we follow falteringly, when we do it consciously, and so can scarcely credit as considered and meant. Keats' response is to try to establish a distinction between the intentionally and the unintentionally figurative; he calls Shakespeare 'the Whim King', and thinks of some of his most astonishing verbal feats as accidental, ancillary to the governing conceit.[10] Keats' interest in 'fine things said unintentionally', half-shaped half-thoughts,

---

[7] Lyne (2011) 75.

[8] Lyne (2011) 199–200.

[9] John Keats to J. H. Reynolds, 22 November 1817, in *Selected Letters*, Robert Gittings (ed.), (Oxford: Oxford University Press, 2002) 38–40 (39).

[10] Gittings (2002) 40.

the mental by-blow, anticipates by a couple of centuries a recent trend in Shakespeare criticism: the investigation of a cognitive rhetoric. The wrought and complex rhetorical structures, of the poems as much as the plays, lend themselves to a kind of psychological archaeology that tries to recover both their shades of significance within the text and the impulse of composition as something personal, interior, and communicable.

The title of this chapter intends to recall Russ McDonald's fine work, *Shakespeare and the Arts of Language*; this itself alludes to the seminal study by Sister Miriam Joseph, *Shakespeare's Use of the Arts of Language*, which first appeared in 1947.[11] Both of these have a foundational interest in rhetoric, and so do I, although my argument might at times be couched in terms that seem unfamiliar—even alien—to that discipline as it is understood in its classical and renaissance guises. The attempt, however, is to reintroduce the relatively recent insights of cognitive linguistics to the theories of thinking and meaning that underpin traditional accounts of the arts of language: not necessarily to oversee the trans-historical shotgun marriage of Aristotle and Gilles Fauconnier, but to point out that they have much strangely in common. Both are, at root, interested in how patterns of figuration might map on to patterns of thought—how figuration, in fact, might be importantly anterior to thought. Identifying a cognitive rhetoric at work is neither as newfangled nor as iconoclastic as it might sound; the intention is rather to deepen and shift the terms of a discourse about passion and intellection that has characterized readers' experience of Shakespeare's verse at least since the time of Coleridge and Keats.

The lines of sympathy between the disciplines of rhetoric and cognitive neuroscience have been persuasively drawn by Mark Turner and Michael Billig, among others, and they are given a pioneering application to literary criticism in new work by Lyne already mentioned in connection with *Macbeth*. 'The cognitive study of art, language, and literature is concerned with patterns of thought and patterns of expression and the nature of their relationship', Turner explains; 'In this way it has a basis, intellectually and sometimes wittingly, in the work of Greek rhetoricians on patterns of thought and of expression'.[12] Lyne thinks about things the other way around, and calls the study of rhetoric 'in effect a kind of proleptic cognitive science'.[13] Developments in our understanding of how the brain and the mind work, and particularly in how language relates to thought, offer a modern scientific rationale for the primacy of rhetoric as a form of conceptual organization and understanding. The art of rhetoric, before it ossified into arid taxonomy, was a dynamic instrument of composition and analysis, interested in

[11] Russ McDonald, *Shakespeare and the Arts of Language* (Oxford: Oxford University Press, 2001); Sister Miriam Joseph, *Shakespeare's Use of the Arts of Language* (New York: Columbia University Press, 1947).

[12] Mark Turner, *Reading Minds: The Study of English in the Age of Cognitive Science* (Princeton: Princeton University Press, 1991) 9. See also Michael Billig, 'Psychology, Rhetoric, and Cognition', in *The Recovery of Rhetoric: Persuasive Discourse and Disciplinarity in the Human Sciences*, R. H. Roberts and James M. M. Good (eds), (London: Bristol Classical Press, 1993) 119–36.

[13] Lyne (2011) 50.

codification only insofar as that might aid the study of the emotional and intellectual processes that were constituted in writing and speech. Both classical and Renaissance rhetoricians understood that the arrangement of words might control meaning, as well as vice versa, and in this they intuitively recognize that language is a faculty not separate and apart, but one intimately involved with other conceptual and cognitive frameworks. As Raymond Gibbs explains, 'human cognition is fundamentally shaped by various poetic or figurative processes. Metaphor, metonymy, irony, and other tropes are not linguistic distortions of literal mental thought but constitute basic schemes by which people conceptualize their experience and the external world'.[14] Poetic expression, in other words, is not aberrant or ornamental—the translation of something literal and anterior into different, more difficult terms—but a representation of ordinary structures of thought. We think in metaphors, and they structure our inner lives. It is not just metaphors, however. A peculiarity of the state of the discipline, if cognitive rhetoric is sufficiently established to warrant that appellation, is the degree of attention that has been given to metaphor at the expense of almost every other figure and trope. It is not difficult to see why this is the case, and metaphor is clearly of central importance to any account; its dominance is, nevertheless, distorting. One of the subsidiary aims of this argument, and one of the points of foregrounding a connection with classical traditions, is to assist in the rehabilitation of the discourse of rhetoric in all its intricate particularity: to suggest how the arts of rhetoric less frequently regarded, tropes like *synecdoche* and *metalepsis*, figures like *chiasmus* and *polyptoton*, might also trace cognitive patterns in the verse they shape.[15]

In broad terms then, the conceptual intersection represented by cognitive rhetoric offers a major insight. Understanding language, particularly poetic language, as constituting a mental process, might in principle allow for the recuperation of that process: not the reconstruction of the neural impulses of any particular historical individual, but the sympathetic reimagining of the thought and feeling of the creative, mediated, written voice. Lines of verse and their complex rhetorical patternings have a double influence: first, on the lives of the characters whose thought and speech is constrained into those patterns; and, second, on the readers who follow their stories with such intimate attention. Cognitive rhetoric offers a way of explaining why we find ourselves compelled to obscure understanding, as we are by *Macbeth*, or moved to curious recognition, as when we are worked on by the centuries-old sufferings of the Sonnets. Because what we have in every case is the words and only the words, it matters little for this compassionate identification whether its subject is real or imaginary; what is important is the action of the mind—both as it is found in the text, and in the answering empathic movement it demands.

---

[14] Raymond Gibbs, *The Poetics of Mind: Figurative Thought, Language, and Understanding* (Cambridge: Cambridge University Press, 1994) 1.

[15] I take my cue from Lyne, who also challenges the hegemony of metaphor in this discourse: 'Other figures, which can be very different from metaphor, might also map out ways in which thinking works'. Lyne (2011) 69.

There is something particular in Shakespeare's dramatic and lyric verse that fits him as a subject, perhaps even the preeminent subject, for this kind of study.[16] Cognitive accounts exist of many kinds of writing, but there is least strain, least stretch with Shakespeare, whose work has, almost from the beginning, been described in terms of the thought it catches, transcribes, embodies—or fails to catch, transcribe, embody. The attempt to separate thought from figure has a long and distinguished history of failure. An early example is Dryden trying to adapt for the Restoration stage, forever puzzled about where the greatness is, as he refines and rewrites in order to trap an idea that eludes him in its re-expression. He imagines himself smelting down the ornate and unwieldy filigree of trope and figuration and imagery to find the pure silver at its core, but he has hold of the wrong metaphor, and thought and feeling are gone with the very structures he believed were impeding their apprehension and tarnishing their shine. This is from the preface to his rewritten *Troilus and Cressida*:

> If *Shakespear* were stript of all the Bombast in the passions, and dress'd in the most vulgar words, we should find the beauties of his thoughts remaining; if his embroideries were burnt down, there would still be silver at the bottom of the melting-pot: but I fear (at least, let me fear it for my self) that we who Ape his sounding words, have nothing of his thought, but are all out-side; there is not so much as a dwarf within our Giants cloaths.[17]

That play was not a popular success; for all his contempt for a style 'so pester'd with Figurative expressions, that it is as affected as it is obscure', Dryden does best when he tries to trust in the phrases themselves as if they are talismans.[18] *All for Love*, produced frequently throughout the 18th century, extracts as freely from *Twelfth Night*, *As You Like It*, *Richard II*, *Othello*, *Hamlet*, *Macbeth*, and countless others as it does from its ostensible source, *Antony and Cleopatra*; its magpie borrowings are awkward and sterile, though, in their new setting, cheap glitter without the animating intention of true allusion.[19] Although he did not like the fact, Dryden's early and instinctive understanding that in Shakespearean verse the thought inheres in the words was sound; it is this property that makes both the plays and the poetry so susceptible to a cognitively inflected interpretation.

---

[16] Stephen Booth describes 'a defining peculiarity of Shakespeare's sonnets: as the line in which it appears is read, any given word is likely to slide imperceptibly from one system of relationship to another. [...] [I]n making the shifts from one context to another', he concludes, 'the reader's mind is required constantly to act', Booth, *Essay on Shakespeare's Sonnets*, (New Haven: Yale University Press, 1969) 120.

[17] John Dryden, *Troilus and Cressida: Or, Truth Found too Late* (A. Small and J. Tonson: London, 1697) xx.

[18] Dryden (1697) vi.

[19] See the introduction to Dryden, *All for Love*, David M. Vieth (ed.), (London: Edward Arnold, 1973) xix–xx.

Another important feature—one that came out of the reading of *Macbeth* that started this chapter—is swiftness, both of initial thought and of receiving apprehension. This characteristic speed gives rise to the kinds of metaleptic leaps that defy sense and coherence but nonetheless have a perfectly comprehensible, felt logic of their own; slowed down, it is difficult to bridge the figurative gaps, to get from candle to actor, say, in fewer than three moves. Mary Thomas Crane ascribes this to a particular kind of verbal dexterity: 'Shakespeare's tendency to play on and with the mental links between words (which most writers efface)', she writes, 'means that his texts are marked by particularly evident traces of cognitive process'.[20] Philip Davis goes further. In his short but seminal work, *Shakespeare Thinking*, he describes the poetry as forging neural pathways, itself generating as well as exploiting links, the 'hints and secrets of creation, things half-lost to us or half-forgotten'.[21] 'Shakespeare's [mind]' Davis writes, 'was essentially non-linear: he saw everything acting and reacting together, and co-existing at once, the mutual interactions of dialogue and of metaphor being characteristic of the mind'.[22] Ghosting this account is the notion, familiar from Coleridge's kindling meteor, of the powerfully originary imagination lighting on word after word and using their juxtapositional energy to fuse distant thoughts; for Davis, this process is not confined to the theatre or the text, but finds its proper referent in the world. Rhetorical structures preserve and convey experience almost before we are aware they have done so, and in this lies something dangerous: an involuntary sympathy for the man whose motives and mind we are intimate with, the king-killing Macbeth. It seems there may, too, be an ethical imperative for recognizing a cognitive rhetoric at work and acknowledging the power of its suasive force.[23]

I have returned briefly to *Macbeth*, instead of moving straight on to the discussion of the Sonnets that will constitute the second half of this chapter. That is because there is a real question here. It is easy to see why drama, which must portray characters experiencing moments of intellectual and emotional extremity, might provide a rich hunting ground for evidences of cognitive rhetoric: but can the same really be said of lyric poetry, which is not constrained to represent process in the same way? I believe it can, and that there is something at work here that an account based solely on the plays risks effacing. Traces of cognition are to be found in the patterns of verse, line breaks, and metrical rhythms, which shape and measure the process of apprehension. Verse demands concise, condensed expression, and provides the restraint that spurs the verbal acrobatics, the pregnant ellipses, the rhetorical leaps that constitute the kind of thought-in-motion that is the concern of this argument. 'Shakespeare's lines are Renaissance brain scanners', Davis goes on to assert, 'where scanning is to do both with poetic rhythm and with

---

[20] Mary Thomas Crane, *Shakespeare's Brain: Reading With Cognitive Theory* (Princeton: Princeton University Press, 2001) 28.

[21] Philip Davis, *Shakespeare Thinking* (London: Continuum, 2007) 3.

[22] Davis (2007) 11.

[23] This is an important strand of McDonald's argument: 'in responding to their poetry we place ourselves, unwittingly but certainly, in sympathy with them and their deeds. Shakespeare acknowledges—and fears—the physical effect of beguiling sounds', (McDonald, 2006, 50–1).

neurological patterning'.[24] Furthermore, the Sonnets are themselves centrally concerned with negotiating intense emotion and preserving its traces within their span, although the mediating role of writing is often occluded. Not always: Shakespeare once imagines a new notebook as a direct receptacle for thought; 'The vacant leaves', he tells his friend, 'thy mind's imprint will bear' (77). Another time, though the question leaves a fleeting space for scepticism, he offers the poem as a real representation of mental process: 'What's in the brain that ink may character | Which hath not figured to thee my true spirit?' (108). This is not of course to suggest that there is no significant generic distinction between play and poem, rather that the way we encounter textual difficulty and the methods by which we compass its meaning might not be so different; in each case, whether in the theatre or reading from a book ('an experience in time' as Booth reminds us),[25] our rhetorically structured minds make what sense they can of the words and the white spaces between as they flash past.

Lyric can be as quick as dramatic verse, and it can unite thought and its expression in the same way. The sonnet that starts 'Th'expense of spirit in a waste of shame | Is lust in action' (129) is a powerful instance of a quick poem (quick to read, that is, not necessarily to write). Grammatically, the first twelve lines are a single sentence, and urgent hurtling is encouraged by its paratactic listing ('perjured, murd'rous, bloody, full of blame, | Savage, extreme, rude, cruel, not to trust') and punning parallelism ('Past reason hunted', 'Past reason hated'). Syntax disregards line endings, and their breaks do not allow pause for breath. The experience of reading is mimetic of the compulsive instinct the lines describe: the opening thought is relatively leisured, but as the verse progresses, it picks up speed; eye and ear start to move rapidly through, careless of whether each clause is marked and understood, looking for a resolution to light on. There is much that is tangled or difficult, although figures of balance obscure this; 'A bliss in proof, and proved a very woe' offers a chiasmic shape far neater than the lurch from fervour to desolation it captures. Part of the way the sonnet achieves its affective meaning is in this sly coercion, in the seductive pairing of words and echoing of sounds that lends the lines irresistible momentum despite their complexity: that promises an order and clarity which turn out to be utterly illusory. The closing couplet is a triumphant mimesis: 'All this the world well knows, yet none knows well | To shun the heaven that leads men to this hell.' Again, the chiasmus ('well knows', 'knows well'), the tightly patterned repetitions of sounds and words, serve for an instant to disguise the fact that this ending is both abrupt and disappointing. Our experience of the verse in time, as with the example this chapter opened with, outstrips our ability to explain its effects; confusion is both what we read and how

---

[24] Davis (2007) 63.
[25] Booth (1969) 118; Ann Thompson and John O. Thompson have also put forward this view: 'The reader of a sonnet is able to look back and re-read in the light of later information: this is not possible in quite the same way in the theatre. However, there may not be as much difference between Shakespeare's practice in the two modes as one would expect', Shakespeare: Meaning and Metaphor, (Brighton: Harvester, 1987) 144.

we read it. Prosody is, or at least can be, a form of cognition, and this constitutes an important connection between lyric verse and its dramatic counterpart.[26]

In fact, *Macbeth* provides an interesting structural bridge across the divide. 'Shakespeare concludes more scenes with couplets than in any other play, both proportionately and abso-lutely', McDonald notices: 'this is a telling statistic in light of the play's unusual brevity'.[27] The concluding couplet is of course integral to the structure of a Shakespearean sonnet, and its particular function has long been noticed; as in *Macbeth*, the epigrammatic neatness of the rhyme offers a sense of completion often at odds with the preceding turmoil, as is the case in 129: it inclines to tidy away the unruly thoughts and emotions ready for their exercise in the next fourteen-line span. 'Most of the sonnets become decreasingly complex as they proceed', Booth observes; 'The couplet ordinarily presents a coincidence of formal, syntactical, and logical structure, and it ordinarily gives the impression that the experience of the preced-ing twelve lines has been a good deal simpler than in fact it has been'.[28] Consider as another example Sonnet 30, a complaint that begins by establishing an intricate internal temporality:

> When to the sessions of sweet silent thought
> I summon up remembrance of things past,
> I sigh the lack of many a thing I sought,
> And with old woes new wail my dear time's waste.

What is described here is the spontaneous regeneration of old griefs, which can be called to mind as witnesses before a judge. Initially savoured as a bittersweet spur to affective contemplation, the memories of things gone, friends dead, and lovers lost threaten to rupture an exercise in nostalgic indulgence with real distress. By the third quatrain, the emotional debt is to be paid anew, 'as if not paid before'. Careful phonetic patterning compounds the temporal collapse; not just the connective delicacy of the repeated 's' sounds, but the structural influence of the figure of polyptoton, which sets different constructions of the same word in relation. '[G]rieve at grievances foregone'; 'fore-bemoanèd moan'; 'new pay as if not paid before': the rhetorical pattern works to break down the distinctions between past memory and present emotion. So insistent is it that John Kerrigan, and Helen Vendler after him, have identified what might be thought of as a pseudo-polyptoton: 'sigh', 'sought', and 'sight'. These words do not share an etymological root, but Shakespeare makes them feel as if they should: in Vendler's words, 'A sigh is the eventual result of a sight sought'.[29] The sonnet is interested in the staging of an intimate psychological process which is, in its twelfth line, revealed to be

---

[26] See Simon Jarvis, 'Prosody as Cognition', *Critical Quarterly*, 40 (1998): 3–15; Clive Scott, *The Poetics of French Verse: Studies in Reading* (Oxford: Clarendon Press, 1998) 89 ff. Graham Bradshaw relates this explicitly to cognitive linguistics: 'I think metrical rhythm is or can be a constituent of meaning [...]; verse movement can work as a species of metaphor. This leads straight to the cognitive, anti-Cartesian conception of *embodied* thinking', Bradshaw, introduction to *Shakespeare Studies Today*, special issue: 'Shakespeare in the Age of Cognitive Science', (Aldershot, 2004): 108, 118.

[27] McDonald (2006) 48.

[28] Booth (1969) 130.

[29] Vendler, *The Art of Shakespeare's Sonnets* (Cambridge, MA: Harvard University Press, 1997) 167; see

unsustainable: grammatically and rhetorically, the necessary distinctions will not hold, and the old grief is acutely, too acutely, felt. Then comes the concluding couplet:

> But if the while I think on thee, dear friend,
> All losses are restored, and sorrows end.

It is not just that the reversal is so swift, and so complete; it strains credibility because it interferes with the elaborate temporal economy that has been set up. It is not 'when I think of you', or 'Haply I think on thee', as the previous sonnet in the sequence has it, but 'if the while I think on thee': a present thought makes restitution for remembered grief, but if that is really true, the grief—deliberately cultivated and dangerously indulged—cannot be real. The couplet seeks to interpolate inoculating thoughts of the friend among the same painful reflections that necessitate those thoughts, and that those thoughts negate; its logical failure points up the expressive triumph of the poem. The short-circuiting couplet is a way of crystallizing a comprehension hard-won from the dense preceding lines, just as it is in a play like *Macbeth*. With cognitively complex rhetoric, simplification can risk falsification, can 'seem to shrug off a poem's rhetorical convolutions', as Lyne remarks, but it can also offer a way of containing the emotional and intellectual upheaval of the experience of reading.[30]

There are, of course, particular challenges in interpreting a sequence predicated on a narrative it deliberately occludes, and much of the history of these poems remains obscure. Among the Sonnets' chief preoccupations, indeed primary begetting conceits, however, is an urgent compulsion to preserve and convey the processes of thought, apprehension, and emotion by which they are constituted: to model a fluid synaptic pulse into a shape from which it can be fully recuperated. Poem after poem struggles with the desire and the difficulty of the precise representation of inner impulse, the need to achieve a lasting emotional legibility through which the lover and the beloved can be perfectly known to one another, and to the witnesses of the world.[31] The Sonnets are not distinctive, even among Shakespeare's works, in their interest in what is after all a relatively commonplace conceit, 'writing understood as thinking on paper, [...] thought as writing in the mind'; but their concentrated and generative meditation on the idea gives it an unmatched vitality. Mark Turner, although he is not here talking specifically about the Sonnets, explains how significant this is: 'This sort of conceptual connection— between the mind and writing—and its systematic disclosure in the shape of language is a

---

also John Kerrigan (ed.) *William Shakespeare, The Sonnets and A Lover's Complaint* (Harmondsworth: Penguin, 1986) 212.

[30] Lyne (2011) 208.

[31] Although it finds its most acute expression here, the notion is not confined to this sequence: in some ways, the crisis of Lucrece arises from the gap between being and saying that the sonnets fight so hard to close. Her tragedy is one of unknowability, and she finds words inadequate surety for an inner virtue brought so violently into question; they present a surface, like the painted likeness of Achilles, that bears no necessary relation to what lies beneath. 'For much imaginary work was there', the narrative

topic whose analysis is at the centre of cognitive rhetoric'.[32] The poem becomes the poet's true emissary, both proof and earnest of his love; it distils and preserves his thought, and because that thought is all of the beloved, the poem becomes not just a tribute or a static monument, but a means of dynamic reanimation. 'So long as men can breathe or eyes can see, | So long lives this, and this gives life to thee' (18); 'Nor Mars his sword nor war's quick fire shall burn | The living record of your memory' (55); 'You still shall live—such virtue hath my pen— | Where breath most breathes, even in the mouths of men' (81). There are many such iterations of this central idea. Notice their emphasis on life and breath, as if articulation, saying over, could rehearse God's trick with the lump of clay, and resuscitate the scattered dust of the beloved. The Sonnets subscribe, obliquely but powerfully, to an idea of cognitive rhetoric which seeks to leave the mind's true traces in gift for the reader; even the little treacheries of love are couched in these terms: 'Accuse me thus', the poet confesses: 'That I have frequent been with unknown minds' (117).

This chapter has so far considered a dramatized moment of thought, and sonnets which concern themselves, to a greater or lesser degree, with thinking, and which there-fore provide an obvious purchase for this approach. I would like to draw this argument to a close in a more speculative vein, however, by testing the premises of a cognitive rhetoric against a sonnet which is not itself explicitly about mental process, but which displays some of the qualities of occluded thought and complex figuration that have characterized the other examples discussed here: Sonnet 94. This poem consistently trips up those who have attempted to understand it as having a fixed sense or a clear message, rather than allowing its meaning to be constituted by its incoherence, and to be modulated on every reading by the temporal experience of going through its motions.

> They that have power to hurt and will do none,
> That do not do the thing they most do show,
> Who moving others are themselves as stone,
> Unmovèd, cold, and to temptation slow—
> They rightly do inherit heaven's graces,
> And husband nature's riches from expense;
> They are the lords and owners of their faces,
> Others but stewards of their excellence.
> The summer's flower is to the summer sweet
> Though to itself it only live and die,
> But if that flower with base infection meet
> The basest weed outbraves his dignity;
>   For sweetest things turn sourest by their deeds:
>   Lilies that fester smell far worse than weeds.

voice pointedly remarks of the Trojan's image:

>   himself behind
> Was left unseen save to the eye of mind;
> A hand, a foot, a face, a leg, a head,
> Stood for the whole to be imaginèd.
>
>   (Lines 1425–8)

---

[32] Turner (1991) 246.

Its demanding obliqueness has over the years made this poem intimidatingly subject to interpretation, but while its general drift is relatively clear, it has in its detail resisted precise elucidation. In this it might perhaps be thought of as analogous to the kind of inscrutable figure it describes: rich in 'heaven's graces' and as beautiful, but unyieldingly hard to read. It seems at first to praise the restraint of one who will not exercise a 'power to hurt' conferred by considerable personal magnetism, but that capacity is ominously latent from the first line. To be as 'stone', to be 'cold', to be 'to temptation slow'— not immune, but slow—seem at best ambiguous attributes; as the poem progresses, the suggestion that this vaunted self-possession might mask an inner corruption, just as the poem's ostensible praise might conceal a lurking reproach, grows stronger. The subject modulates at l.9 to a 'sweet' flower, a lily it turns out, which is threatened with a canker at the core; the concluding couplet rewrites the proverbial notion that highest things fall furthest into an image of vivid aversion: 'Lilies that fester smell far worse than weeds'. Characteristically, the couplet's vicious neatness offers a welcome foothold, but does not quite manage to contain the ambivalent energies of the preceding lines.

Critics have consistently described this sonnet's intractability in cognitive terms: either the uncertainty and occlusion of the poet's thoughts, as he struggles to reconcile an admiration for the appearance of rectitude both with a conviction of its falsity and with the experience of its painful consequences for the human heart; or the reader's, as she follows these mental convolutions not to a complete apprehension of the poem's meaning, but to a rehearsed understanding of the emotional state it represents. Here are just two examples of such comments from accounts of the poem which are rather different, but both scrupulous and inspired: 'The lines exercise the reader's mind within the boundaries of their several artistic patterns', Booth writes. 'The reader's essential experience of the lines is the experience of his own mind in flux'. And J. H. Prynne in his *Specimen of a Commentary* identifies 'a struggle of mind about whether to admire or blame and exactly for what in either case'.[33] This resistance to unilinear interpretation stems in part from the uncertain relation between the poem's two dominant images— the impassive paragons of the octave, and the sestet's susceptible lily—which is symptomatic of the lines' general tendency towards logical gaps and unanchored referents. This is one of just three sonnets in the sequence in which the individuals of speaker and addressee remain implied throughout (5 and 129, which was discussed above, are the only others that don't feature an 'I' or a 'thee'). The levels of figuration here are complex

---

[33] Booth (1969) 165; J. H. Prynne, *They That Haue Powre to Hurt: A Specimen of a Commentary on Shake-speares Sonnets, 94* (Cambridge: Barque Press, 2001) 17. See also, Vendler (1997) 404 (she speaks of 'a process of thought in the speaker not overtly revealed') and Robert B. Pierce: 'It seems to me that the heart of this poem lies in the portrait of a tangle of human emotions and thoughts, and the poem is more real and more powerful because those feelings and thoughts are not neatly classifiable, not reducible to a set of ideas. Thus explicating this sonnet involves helping the reader to grasp an emotional and psychological condition; what matters is less to see how an ethic of withdrawal can be intellectually reconciled with the claims of human feeling than to see how one can be attracted to both ethics at the same time', 'How Does a Poem Mean?', *Philosophy and Literature*, 24 (2000) 280–93, at 289.

in a way that their confinement to the discrete constituent parts of the sonnet does not acknowledge; because of how we encounter them, we accept the transitions between quatrains, from the unmoved men to the prudent aristocrats and the fragile flower, much more smoothly than we might. These progressions are framed logically, as if one illustrative sententia seamlessly succeeds the next, but the sonnet is in fact riddled with what Prynne calls 'incessant small gaps'.[34] These fissures compel the reader to an understanding which is not so much warranted by the literal sense of the lines themselves, as extrapolated from an intuitive sympathy with the imagined speaker. The poem nowhere says that the flower that hides disease at its heart is like a man of enigmatic beauty, but we know nonetheless that it is. This is, in miniature, the same cognitive process as that witnessed and demanded by the yawning figurative gaps in Macbeth's great speech.

As in Sonnet 30, pairs of polyptotic repetitions—'moving, unmovèd', 'base, basest', 'sweet, sweetest', 'thing, things'—undermine rather than buttress any security of perspective. The little words in this poem—'they', 'that', 'who', 'his', 'do', 'thing', and so forth—carry much of the burden of its difficulty, partly in their refusal to do any such thing. Their indeterminacy (who are 'they'? 'do' what? which 'things'?) compounds the sense that there is a layer of meaning here submerged and implicit. Take as an example the sonnet's first word, whose necessary stress against the metrical template is a subtle but insistent indication of its significance. 'They' here is a carefully neutral pronoun that carries, perversely, a depth charge of private particularity. In this, it is like the same word, in the same position, in Wyatt's earlier lyric: 'They fle from me that sometyme did me seke'. That poem can keep up the pretence of careless generality only until the intrusion of intimate memory, when 'they', as we sort of knew all along, turns out to include, even to mean, 'she': the poet remembers 'ons in speciall [...] when her lose gowne from her shoulders did fall'.[35] Shakespeare's 'they' maintains its mortified distance, hinting at a specific referent—a 'he', even a 'you'—only in the slide from the general to the particular witnessed in the singular 'flower' of the sestet; when that flower risks the loss of 'his dignity' from some secret infection, it is hard not to read back to the allegedly plural, unmoved 'they' with whom it is structurally equated. We come to understand that 'they' might conceal an individual, and that the reason for this concealment might be an impulse of protectiveness, both towards the subject—so as not to shame him with a direct accusation—and towards the self. The creeping suspicion that some act has been committed, some event taken place that will falsify the beauty of the beloved, is kept at bay by 'they': that little word braces itself between the fear and the knowledge of betrayal.

It is my contention that the fact this is easier to understand than to explain, like so many moments across the corpus of Shakespeare's verse (both dramatic and lyric), is

---

[34] Prynne (2001) 20.

[35] Prynne (2001, 3–5) makes this connection; the first section of his commentary compares the two instances of 'they'. 'The initial "they"', in Wyatt's poem, as A. D. Nuttall points out, 'has the effect of neutralizing a painfully pointed reference by distancing it, or perhaps it would be more accurate to say, by spreading it out', *Overheard by God: Fiction and Prayer in Herbert, Milton, Dante and St John*. (London: Methuen, 1980) 55.

part of its strategy of meaning. The flinch that Sonnet 94 dramatizes is recognized and felt in spite of—perhaps because of—the obscurity and illogic of its patterns of figuration, and this I take to be an active achievement of cognitive rhetoric. As we read the lines they resolve themselves in an absolute clarity which, when we look again, is gone. It is not an illusion, however: it is importantly and permanently revelatory. Exposing ourselves to the patterns and pressures of such writing is not passively to experience, but actively to rethink, the catastrophes it describes. We are involved in the mental process of Macbeth's reflections and decisions by rhetoric that leaps with the same defiant ambition that he does; strange sympathy results from meeting his mind in its flights. The Sonnets offer a different kind of model, both more intimate and more obviously a rhetorical performance. Similarly, though, it is the triumphant transcendence of verbal control which marks moments of greatest affect; we are drawn into sympathy, into love, not by the achievement of expression but by its failure. Understanding rhetorical strategy in this way might have far-reaching effects, and not just for a reading of Shakespeare: this knowing in not-knowing has the ability to inflect our capacity of perception, if we can trust it enough not to privilege logical coherence and figurative consistency above the truth that is felt before it is thought.

SELECT BIBLIOGRAPHY

Booth, Stephen (1969) *An Essay on Shakespeare's Sonnets* (New Haven: Yale University Press).

Crane, Mary Thomas (2001) *Shakespeare's Brain: Reading With Cognitive Theory* (Princeton: Princeton University Press).

Cummings, Brian (2007) 'Metalepsis: The Boundaries of Metaphor', in Sylvia Adamson, Gavin Alexander, and Katrin Ettenhuber (eds) *Renaissance Figures of Speech* (Cambridge: Cambridge University Press) 217–33.

Davis, Philip (2007) *Shakespeare Thinking* (London: Continuum).

Gibbs, Raymond (1994) *The Poetics of Mind: Figurative Thought, Language, and Understanding* (Cambridge: Cambridge University Press).

Jarvis, Simon (1998) 'Prosody as Cognition', *Critical Quarterly*, 40: 3–15.

Lyne, Raphael (2011) *Shakespeare, Rhetoric and Cognition* (Cambridge: Cambridge University Press).

McDonald, Russ (2001) *Shakespeare and the Arts of Language* (Oxford: Oxford University Press).

——*Shakespeare's Late Style* (2006) (Cambridge: Cambridge University Press).

Prynne, J. H. (2001) *They That Haue Powre to Hurt: A Specimen of a Commentary on Shakespeares Sonnets, 94* (Cambridge: Barque Press).

Turner, Mark (1991) *Reading Minds: The Study of English in the Age of Cognitive Science* (Princeton: Princeton University Press).

CHAPTER 5

....

FATAL CLEOPATRAS AND GOLDEN APPLES

*Economies of Wordplay in Some
Shakespearean 'Numbers'*

....

MARGARET FERGUSON

5.1 A MATRIX FOR LOOKING AT SHAKESPEAREAN WORDPLAYS (IN POETRY)

....

Shakespeare's wordplay is no country for people committed to the idea that language should be a transparent and efficient medium of communication. Those who like their language plain tend to find wordplay an 'exercise of virtuosity to no profit, without economy of sense or knowledge'. That description comes from Jacques Derrida, who argues that wordplay (*jeu de mots*) is not a luxury or a 'diversion' but rather a necessity for all language users.[1] There have been and continue to be debates in many languages about whether wordplay, like poetry, is an ornamental phenomenon that, in a pinch or in a hurry, we could do without. Following Derrida, and Shakespeare as well, I suggest

I am grateful to Jonathan Post, David Simpson, Mary Anne Ferguson, Christopher Wallis, and Stephanie Elsky for their help with this chapter.

[1] Derrida, 'Proverb: 'He that would pun ...'", in John P. Leavey, Jr, *Glassary* (Lincoln, Nebraska: University of Nebraska Press, 1986) 17. Derrida's title, to the best of my knowledge his only use of the English word 'pun', alludes to the proverb 'He that would pun would pick a pocket', attributed to the Augustan critic John Dennis and cited by Pope in a note to Book IV of the *Dunciad*. For 18th-century critiques of the pun as a low form of 'diversion', see Simon J. Alderson, 'The Augustan Attack on the Pun', *Eighteenth-Century Life* 20, 3 (1996) 1–19. For a broad view of the pun's economy, see Jonathan Culler, 'The Call of the Phoneme', *On Puns: The Foundation of Letters*, Jonathan Culler (ed.) (Oxford: Basil Blackwell, 1988) 1–16, with further bibliography.

in this chapter that wordplay is integral to the work—or 'path'—of language; I also sug-gest, through a re-reading of Samuel Johnson's famous attack on Shakespeare's *exces-sive* love of 'quibbles', that we can usefully approach Shakespeare's practice of wordplay with specific reference to 'numbers': one of Shakespeare's most interesting synonyms for poetry.[2]

As a verbal practice marked both by a concern for 'measure' (as in syllable or line counting) and by a tendency toward 'license' (as in rule-breaking and a love for excess), poetry enacts and reflects on many meanings of 'numbers'. I have selected my main examples of poetic wordplay to illustrate, first, the range of Shakespeare's concern with the concept of numbers and, second, the different kinds—and tempos—of interpretive response he invites from his audience. Some wordplays come in many 'parts', requir-ing the interpreter to travel slowly, often through notes and translations consulted after a performance or during a re-reading. The main example I adduce here, suggested by Samuel Johnson's oblique reference to the myth of Atalanta, requires us to consider the place of classical allusion in Shakespeare's extended meditation on the relation between 'parts' and 'wholes' in both human and textual bodies. Another type of wordplay, fast cooking as opposed to slow, seems to hit the reader over the head, as it were, with an 'overplus' of plays on a single word: my main example involves the plays on '[W]ill' (as noun, verb, and proper name) from Sonnet 135.

Full of competing names and definitions for its many rhetorical types and/or parts, Shakespearean wordplay in poetry is not something that exists 'out there' for readers or auditors simply to discover.[3] On the contrary, Shakespearean wordplay arguably comes into existence only when two or more human agents meet with the text as a game board. The educated, historically situated writer and the auditor/reader in the past or present create meanings from the enormously unstable annotated text which shows signs of compositors and in some cases actors at work as well as the 'original' writer. As an object of attention that recalls Shakespeare's many puns on 'noting' as 'nothing', 'quibbling' can be compared to an unsettling kind of game in which the rules are not completely known: as Gregory Bateson suggests in his 'Theory of Play and Fantasy', some games are constructed 'not upon the premise "this is play" but rather around the question "is this play?"'[4]

Shakespearean wordplays are complex effects both of syntactic and lexical choices on the writer's, editor's, printer's, reader's, and actor's parts. In poetic texts, features of metre,

---

[2] For incisive discussions of Shakespeare's 'numbers' see Paula Blank, *Shakespeare and the Mismeasure of Renaissance Man* (Ithaca: Cornell University Press, 2006) 41–79; and Dympna Callaghan, *Shakespeare's Sonnets* (London: Blackwell, 2007) 74–88. For a methodological discussion of puns that anticipates parts of my argument, see Patricia Parker, 'The Merry Wives of Windsor and Shakespearean Translation', *Modern Language Quarterly* 52(3) (1991): 225–61.

[3] For a different view, see Sophie Read's fine essay 'Puns', in Sylvia Adamson, Gavin Alexander, and Katrin Ettenhuber (eds), *Renaissance Figures of Speech* (Cambridge: Cambridge University Press, 2007) 88.

[4] Gregory Bateson, *Steps to an Ecology of Mind* (New York: Chandler, 1972) 182.

rhyme, and line-shape also contribute to the wordplay's mode of existence. Shakespeare's wordplays rarely come singly; they come rather in battalions—or in groups and shapes more nebulous, intertwining different figures of rhetoric that often require the reader to decode inversions of 'normal' word order. Shakespeare's wordplays call attention to the opacity of their medium (or mixed media) of communication.

The ability to shuttle from ear to eye and back again is critical for students of Shakespeare's wordplay. The reading eye (I/ay), however, is often neglected in critical discussions of Shakespeare's wordplay. Theories about how Shakespeare and his contemporaries pronounced words are of course crucial to our appreciation of his many plays on words in different genres; some of these plays were clearly meant to be translated from page to stage. It is useful to recall, however, that our evidence of Shakespeare's acoustic world, brilliantly analyzed by Bruce R. Smith, comes largely from written sources, some accompanied by musical notation and others consisting of measured poetic lines, including those that end in rhymes close enough (in letters) to be debated as 'exact', 'near', or 'slant'.[5]

Some critics define Shakespeare's puns, his most famous species of wordplay, simply as 'acoustic knots'; and some believe that early modern 'speakers' saw puns in writing as 'a representation of language, not the thing itself'.[6] Both views arguably flatten the phenomenal complexity of Shakespeare's wordplays, which reflect a wide range of theories about what a 'word' is and how—and by whom—it may be 'mistaken'. Separations between words were not marked in the *scriptio continua* of ancient and early medieval manuscripts, but 'mistaking' distinctions between words and word-parts—syllables, endings, sounds, and letters—is considered a 'vice' in an ancient tradition of rhetorical discourse that continually had to modify its terms for, and conceptions of, linguistic error in relation to complex processes of cultural translation, including translations from speech to writing as well as from one language to another.[7] In his *Garden of Eloquence* of 1577, Henry Peacham finds an instance of dialectal variation (a northern versus a southern pronunciation/spelling—'wull' for 'will') to illustrate the vice 'antisoecon', or the 'replacing of one letter in a word by another'.[8] We shall later see examples of such

[5] See Bruce R. Smith, *The Acoustic World of Early Modern England: Attending to the O-Factor* (Chicago: The University of Chicago Press, 1999); see also Gina Bloom, *Voice in Motion: Staging Gender, Shaping Sound in Early Modern England* (Philadelphia: University of Pennsylvania Press, 2007), both with further bibliography.

[6] Many linguists define puns as soundplays; see for instance A. S. Partington, 'A linguistic account of wordplay: The lexical grammar of punning', *Journal of Pragmatics* 41 (2009): 1794–1809, quoting Arthur Koestler on the pun as 'two strings of thought tied together by an acoustic knot'. For the claim that 'early modern people' saw writing as a 'representation' of language, see Jonathan Hope, *Shakespeare and Language: Reason, Eloquence and Artifice in the Renaissance* (London: Methuen, 2010). For a counterview, see Terence Cave, *The Cornucopian Text: Problems of Writing in the French Renaissance* (Oxford: Oxford University Press, 1985).

[7] On *scripta continuo* see Peter Stallybrass, 'Introduction', in Jeffrey Masten, Peter Stallybrass, and Nancy J. Vickers (eds), *Language Machines: Technologies of Literary and Cultural Production* (New York: Routledge, 1997) 5.

[8] Peacham, *The Garden of Eloquence* (1577, rev. 1593), cited in William Poole , 'The vices of style', in Adamson et al. (2007) 236–51, at 239.

'vices' that could also be classified as 'virtuous' ornaments: how is the reader/auditor to draw the line between a 'proper' figure and an 'abuse'?

Fascinated by the border between licensed and unlicensed word use, Shakespeare often explores it by giving us communicative misfires between speakers of different social ranks and genders; both gender and rank affected one's access to grammar school education. Consider for example the moment in *Two Gentlemen of Verona* where the 'clownish servant' Speed asks another servant, Lance, 'what news with your mastership?' Lance fails to grasp the irony of Speed's address, which promotes the servant to the master's role, and thus Lance replies, 'With my master's ship? Why, it is at sea', to which Speed, who seems to have some acquaintance with grammar school rules of rhetoric, retorts, 'Well, your old vice still, mistake the word' (III.i .276–9).[9] Lance goes on to accuse Speed of being unable to read 'news' that's 'black as ink' on the page. Speed roundly denies being an 'illiterate loiterer'. The modern reader or auditor is invited to think about how discrepancies in linguistic 'wealth' can occur as one travels from hearing a word to reading it. Travels of all kinds affected early modern English readers' and auditors' understanding of specific words and of the 'word' as a concept. New words were entering the language constantly, sometimes as contraband ('low' French and Italian words for diseases, for instance), sometimes as imports of the kind Spenser's teacher Richard Mulcaster legitimates as 'enrichments' of the English tongue.[10] Shakespeare is credited with coining some 1700 new words, not all of which stayed in the language.

One that still exists according to the *Oxford English Dictionary* but that may well not look 'native' to most Anglophone readers today is 'dis-eate', as it is printed in the First Folio version of *Macbeth*, or, as it is printed in the Oxford Shakespeare, 'disseat': 'This push | Will cheer me ever or disseat me now' (V. iii. 22–3). For William Empson, the author of *Seven Types of Ambiguity*, this is a rich wordplay illustrating an 'intentional' creation of interpretive alternatives. Empson speculates that Shakespeare wrote 'something a little removed from any of the approximate homonyms, to set … reader[s] groping about their network'. We can translate 'disseat' most obviously as 'unseat' or 'dethrone'; Empson argues persuasively for additional associations to the words 'disease, disseizes, and defeat', with a further play on the word-part 'eate', suggesting both Macbeth's fear of the hostile army regarded as a hungry ogre and the remorse already 'gnawing' at Macbeth's entrails.[11] Empson allows, however, that the new-coined

[9] Renaissance readers might have classified this 'mistaking' as a 'barbarismus' (mispronunciation); see Richard Lanham, *A Handlist of Rhetorical Terms* (Berkeley: University of California Press, 1968) 18–19. Shakespeare is particularly interested in errors of 'hearing' caused by unevenly distributed alphabetic literacies in Latin and in English. On his rich puns on 'ear', 'air', 'hear', and 'heir', see Philippa Berry, 'Hamlet's Ear', in Catherine M. S. Alexander (ed.), *Shakespeare and Language* (Cambridge: Cambridge University Press, 2004) 201–12. See also Margreta de Grazia's discussion of malapropisms in 'Shakespeare and the Craft of Language', de Grazia and Stanley Wells (eds), *The Cambridge Companion to Shakespeare* (Cambridge: Cambridge University Press, 2001) 59–60.

[10] Richard Mulcaster, *The First Part of the Elementarie VVhich Entreateth Chefelie of the Right Writing of Our English Tung. 1582.* Facsimile edn (Menston, UK: Scolar Press, 1970) 168–9.

[11] William Empson, *Seven Types of Ambiguity* (New York: New Directions, 1930) 83.

verb—which Shakespeare perhaps used to spread our attention 'over a wide map of the ways in which [the word] may be justified'[12]—could look simply like a mistake to a printer or to later editors (or, I would add, to some among Shakespeare's first readers or auditors). How different is Shakespeare's coinage in *Macbeth* from Fluellen's inadvertent but politically rich Welsh-dialect deformation of a phrase describing Alexander the Great as 'Alexander the Pig' (for 'big'; *Henry V*, IV. vii. 12–13)?

As Margaret Tudeau-Clayton has astutely argued, 'the playwright-actor's stage and the translator's page "rhymed" in early modern English culture inasmuch as they both constituted sites for the production, regulation, and interrogation of the boundaries of "our English tongue"'.[13] Wordplays often arise in the territory between languages or dialects—two terms not distinguished in the Renaissance in the way they commonly are today.[14] This is a territory where speculative etymologies flourish and where George Puttenham finds many instances of 'mingle-mangle', his name for a broad category of 'vices' in ancient rhetoric that included both 'unnatural word coinage' and mistakes in pronunciation such as 'illiterate' males and females often perform in Shakespeare's plays; my favorite example occurs when Mistress Quickly hears 'nouns' as 'wounds' (*The Merry Wives of Windsor*, IV. i. 22).[15]

In zones between times, languages, cultures, and differently educated people, wordplays may easily be mistaken for something foreign and without value; they may also be simply missed, as no doubt continues to happen for Shakespeare's auditors and readers—including editors—today. The history of wordplay is tied up with the history of censorship: editors may deal with perceived 'mistakes' by cutting or emending them. The history of wordplay is also intertwined with differing modern understandings of the (linked) institutions of lexicography, of publishing, and of education. Samuel Johnson contributed to all three of those institutions in a passage that defines Shakespeare as an unthrifty 'traveller' in the world of words; I want to suggest, however, that the famous critique of Shakespeare's passion for the 'quibble' also shows Johnson himself travelling from trope to trope in a way that raises questions about the 'economy' of wordplay.[16]

---

[12] Empson (1930) 84.

[13] Margaret Tudeau-Clayton, 'Scenes of Translation in Jonson and Shakespeare: *Poetaster, Hamlet*, and *A Midsummer Night's Dream*', *Translation and Literature* 11 (March 2002): 3–4.

[14] On the Renaissance meanings of 'dialect', see Paula Blank, *Broken English: Dialects and the Politics of Language in Renaissance Writings* (London: Routledge, 1996); on the difficulty of distinguishing linguistic 'mistakes' from neologisms, see Sylvia Adamson, 'Literary Language', in Roger Lass (ed.), *The Cambridge History of the English Language: 1476–1776* (Cambridge; Cambridge University Press, 1999) 3: 539–653.

[15] See de Grazia (2001) 59. On 'mingle-mangle' as a term in rhetorical treatises and in antitheatrical tracts, see Margaret Tudeau-Clayton, 'Richard Carew, William Shakespeare and the Politics of Translating Virgil in Early Modern England and Scotland', *International Journal of the Classical Tradition*, 5 (1999) 507–27, esp. 525–6.

[16] In its earliest appearances in English, according to the *OED*, 'quibble', like 'pun', appears as a member of a sleazy group: 'We old men have our crotchets, our conundrums, / O[o]ur figaries, quirks and quibbles /A[a]s well as youth', says a comic character in 1611, illustrating *OED* 1. n. But 'quib', the word's short form, appears much earlier and in ways that support the *OED* editors' speculation that the word comes from the Latin *quibus,* a word associated with the 'quirks and quillets' of the law.

Johnson defines Shakespeare's love for quibbles in a way that pertains to concepts of number and measure; for Johnson, Shakespeare loves quibbles to excess: 'A quibble', Johnson writes,

> is to Shakespeare what luminous vapours are to the traveler; he follows it at all adventures; it is sure to lead him out of his way, and sure to engulf him in the mire. It has some malignant power over his mind, and its fascinations are irresistible. Whatever be the dignity or profundity of his disquisition, whether he be enlarging knowledge or exalting affection, whether he be amusing attention with incidents or enchaining it in suspense, let but a quibble spring up before him and he leaves his work unfinished. A quibble is the golden apple for which he will always turn aside from his career, or stoop from his elevation. A quibble, poor and barren as it is, gave him such delight, that he was content to purchase it, by the sacrifice of reason, propriety and truth. A quibble was for him the fatal Cleopatra for which he lost the world, and was content to lose it.[17]

William Empson sees Johnson here illustrating a typical 18th-century assessment of the pun as a 'petty' thing.[18] Ironically, however, Empson himself implies that there may be a significant similarity between Shakespeare the quibbler as Johnson describes him—pursuing 'luminous vapours' in a strange land—and the modern critic attempting to grasp the meaning of a pun in Shakespeare's (to us somewhat foreign) English. 'It is clear', Empson states, 'that we have to exercise a good deal of skill in cutting out implications that aren't wanted in reading poems.... [O]ne does not want merely irrelevant ambiguities.... [T]he question how far unintended or even unwanted extra meanings do in fact impose themselves, and thereby drag our minds out of their path ... is obviously a legitimate one'.[19] In the notion of 'unwanted' meanings beyond authorial 'intention', Empson allows for a certain blending of interpreter's and writer's dilemma: both grapple with an English language that Empson constructs here as potentially filled with spectres that may 'mislead' the critic trying to stay on his reasonable path through thickets of ambiguities; it is dangerous also, perhaps, to the critic's readers, especially if they are foreigners; 'as a teacher of English literature in foreign countries', Empson states, with irony, 'I have always tried to warn my students off [my] book'.[20]

The dangers of annotating or explicating Shakespeare's wordplay have long included the possibility of bringing sexual and scatological meanings into clear though not clean view from what Johnson vividly calls 'the mire'.[21] The dangers also include the possibility that the critic may be unable to defend an essential(ist) distinction between 'the puns

---

[17] Johnson, 'Preface to Shakespeare', in Arthur Sherbo (ed.) *Johnson on Shakespeare, The Yale Edition of the Works of Samuel Johnson* (New Haven: Yale University Press, 1966) 7:439.

[18] Empson (1930) 87–8.

[19] Empson (1930) xiii.

[20] Empson (1930) xii.

[21] This is a rhetorical territory brilliantly explored by Poole, 'The vices of style', in Adamson et al. (2007) 236–51.

that are under discussion and [the interpreter's] own discursive prose'.[22] Johnson himself offers a 'pregnant quibble' in his critique of Shakespeare: Cleopatra was 'fatal' in being 'both the death and destiny of Antony'.[23]

Johnson's pun initially seems safe from and indeed a bulwark against infection by the kind of quibbles he is critiquing. His use of 'fatal' is epistemologically manageable: it activates a witty pair of meanings, not a series stretching off into a vapourous twilight. Johnson's pun has a 'point' and performs closure, not openness, both in terms of rhetorical structure and in terms of semantic statement. By embedding his pun on 'fatal' in the third and last of three sentences that each begins with the phrase 'A quibble', Johnson builds toward a climax through the trope of anaphora—a 'repetition of the same word at the beginning of successive clauses or verses';[24] he then offers another series of three (but no more) in the daring metalepsis of the final period. (I use the Greek term 'metalepsis' here in the sense given in one early modern English treatise of rhetoric: the figure occurs when we 'goe by degrees to that which is shewed'.)[25] In Johnson's final sentence, we move from the nugatory little quibble to the big Egyptian queen to the whole 'world'. The steps of the series, rising in size and cultural value, come to an end and are neatly contained as a single enormous loss imputed to Shakespeare as an experience that made him 'content'. He is thus equated with his own character Mark Antony, but not the Antony hugely discontent with Cleopatra—and his loss of epic stature—after the battle of Actium; instead, the 'content' Johnson bestows upon Shakespeare is a state that Antony entered completely, we may surmise, only after his death; before then, his passion for Cleopatra '[o]'erflows the measure' (I. i. 2) without giving him—or her—full satisfaction.

Johnson captures Shakespeare both as a motionless Mark Antony inhabiting the timeless space of the infinitive 'to lose' and as a memorable lover yoked with his 'fatal' beloved. The author and his quibble are captured in prose that has some of the sonorous and measured qualities we expect from neo-classical poetry. Anaphora, like 'parison'— the balanced clauses of 'it is sure to lead him out of his way, and sure to engulf him in the mire'—are tropes that regularly cross the line between prose and poetry in classical and in English letters.

Posing a subtle threat to the economy of the quibble as Johnson defines it, however, and moving us closer to quibbles as they work in some selected passages of Shakespearan verse, is the figure of Atalanta. She is present in Johnson's passage only as a metonym, a 'golden apple'; the surmise that it is *her* apple—though bearing vapourous traces of other famous apples in classical, biblical, and perhaps even Norse literature—is supported by

---

[22] Catherine Bates discusses this distinction astutely in 'The Point of Puns', *Modern Philology* 96, 4 (May 1999): 421–38, quotation from 430.

[23] Molly Mahood, 'The Fatal Cleopatra', in *Shakespeare's Wordplay* (London: Methuen, 1957) 9.

[24] Lanham (1968) 8; other names for this trope are repetitio, iteration, epanaphora, epembasis, and, in Puttenham's English rendering, 'report'; see his *The Arte of English Poesie* (1589), facsimile edition with Introduction by Baxter Hathaway (Kent: Kent State University Press, 1970) 208.

[25] Peacham, *The Garden of Eloquence*, as cited in the epigraph of Brian Cummings, 'Metalepsis: the boundaries of metaphor', in *Renaissance Figures of Speech*, 216–33.

her brief appearance in Shakespeare's *As You Like It*, in a passage upon which Johnson comments. The apple that Johnson selects as the second of his three main images for Shakespeare's beloved quibble (first the 'vapours', third the 'fatal Cleopatra') is itself one of three distractions thrown in the virgin Atalanta's path by a suitor named Hippomenes in some versions of the story.[26] Her dispersed larger story—which has parallels to Cleopatra's and which has many more parts than Johnson mentions in his preface to his edition of Shakespeare—has significance for our understanding of Shakespeare's wordplay beyond the apparent boundaries of Johnson's preface. His allusion to Atalanta has not (to my knowledge) been much commented on; but she can arguably serve as a useful guide into one species of wordplay common in Shakespeare's poetry: a 'quiet' kind with dispersed riches that we can collect (in part) by the labour of interpretive tracking across textual and linguistic borders. Before illustrating such a labour by moving from Johnson's preface to his note on Atalanta in *As You Like It* to Ovid's two stories about a heroine who has a single proper name (from the Greek *atalantos,* meaning 'equal in weight') but two different fathers, possibly two husbands, and an illegitimate son, I want to pause to reflect on poetry as a mode of language formally and semantically concerned with 'numbers' and with the question of measure and thus of *limits* to one's erotic and verbal powers of play.

5.2 WORDPLAYS IN NUMBERED LINES

'These numbers will I tear, and write in prose', declares Longueville in *Love's Labour's Lost* (4.3.54). The line is delivered by a character whose name puns bilingually (in a promiscuous example of the trope 'mingle-mangle') on 'langue'—French for tongue and language—and on the English words 'long', 'town', and 'vile'. Despite expressing frustration with his poem—he fears that his 'stubborn lines' will fail to 'move' his even more stubborn lady—Longueville reads it aloud and sends it as a letter. It introduces two pun-clusters that are important to Shakespeare's theory and practice of love poetry, and of his parodies thereof. The first cluster—what Gregory Ulmer aptly names a 'puncept'—focuses our attention on the word 'lines'.[27] This, in its noun-forms, can signify not only the 'black lines' of poems on a page but also the male and female reproductive parts; scholars hypothesize a homophonic pun on 'lines' and 'loins' in Shakespeare's England.[28] In yet other shades of meaning, 'lines' can signify wrinkles on a face and, more generally, marks distinguishing some 'parts' of the human body, and/or of the world, from other

---

[26] For her different genealogies and appearances in classical sources, including as the 'virgin' mother of an illegitimate boy, see <http://www.theoi.com/Heroine/Atalanta.html>.

[27] See Ullmer, 'The Puncept in Grammatology', in Jonathan Culler (ed.), *On Puns: The Foundation of Letters.* (New York: Basil Blackwell, 1988) 164–89.

[28] See for instance Stephen Booth's astonishing comments on the phrase 'lines of life' in Sonnet 16.9 (*Shakespeare's Sonnets*, xi–xvii).

parts: Stefano in *The Tempest* bawdily conflates the terrestrial and female equator-lines, and King Lear shows Goneril her future lands as they appear on a map—'Of all these bounds even from this line to this' (I. i. 63).[29]

The second puncept to which Longueville introduces us centers (eccentrically) on the word 'tear'. This can morph from verb to noun in a way that transforms the sonnet—from the Italian word for 'little sound'—into an emission from the eye. In its noun form as a drop from an eye, 'tear' appears earlier in the same scene of *Love's Labour's Lost* in which Longueville promises to write henceforth in prose. Another amateur sonneteer, the King of Navarre, writes to his beloved, 'Thou shin'st in every tear that I do weep' (IV. iii. 31). His sonnet likens his tears both to water (in 'the deep' and as a 'drop'); and to glasses (as mirrors). A complex site for reflection on language itself as a far from 'transparent' medium, the King's sonnet goes beyond conventional limits of the form (it is sixteen rather than fourteen lines); it conveys sadness and frustration to its 'queen of queens' and offers her crafted lines like trembling liquid drops. These look forward to the bawdy pun on sexual orgasm in the iambic pentameter couplet that immediately follows the sonnet:

> How shall she know my griefs? I'll drop the paper.
> Sweet leaves, shade folly. Who is he comes here?
>
> (IV. iii. 40–1]

The end-rhyme on 'paper' and 'here' awkwardly pairs a feminine with a masculine final foot. Both formally and semantically, the couplet lacks closure. And, indeed, it opens wittily into the King's next line, in which he answers his own question with yet another rhyme conjuring up the 'tear' phoneme (also a grapheme): 'What, Longueville, and reading—listen ear!' (*Love's Labour's Lost*, IV. iii. 42). Both 'tears' and 'lines' emerge from this comic scene of writing and reading sonnets as sites of rich wordplay yoking sight and sound, seeing and reading, male and female—and also male and male.

Shakespeare's rhyming numbers here, as in the Sonnets, explore modes of 'increase' that both mirror and mock the 'reproductive marital economy of early modern England'.[30] I take that phrase from Mary Bly, whose study of bawdy wordplay and queer virgins in Jacobean drama helps me make my way back to Johnson's figure of Atalanta. She, as you will recall, is figured in Johnson's preface as a single golden apple. In Book 8 of Ovid's *Metamorphoses*, she is an Arcadian maiden whose father, Iasus, exposes her on a hillside because he wanted a son; suckled by a she-bear, Atalanta is protected by Diana (Artemis in Greek versions of the story) and is the first to wound a boar in the famous Calydonian hunt. In a better-known story, part of a monitory tale that

---

[29] For *The Tempest*'s play (IV. i. 235) on a 'jerkin' taken off a clothes 'line' that turns into a site of equinoctial venereal disease, see Gordon Williams, *A Glossary of Shakespeare's Sexual Language* (London: Athlone Press, 1997) 189.

[30] Mary Bly, *Queer Virgins and Virgin Queans on the Early Modern Stage* (Oxford: Oxford University Press, 2000) 9.

Ovid's Venus relates to Adonis in *Metamorphoses* 10, Atalanta the fleet-footed daughter of Schoenus loses a race to Hippomenes when he follows Venus' advice to distract Atalanta by means of three golden apples. Offended by Hippomenes' failure to thank her after winning Atalanta as his bride, Venus decides to 'make an example of them both' (Atalanta being guilty by marriage, as it were); the goddess fills Hippomenes with 'incontinent desire' as the couple is passing the temple of the mother goddess Cybele. They defile the temple with their lust and are about to be killed by Cybele when Venus decides that such a 'punishment was light'. Measurement of many kinds is important to the story. Venus turns the couple into savage lions of just the kind that her 'internal' auditor, Adonis, should avoid, lest 'your manly courage be the ruin of us both'.[31] When Shakespeare takes THAT story up in *Venus and Adonis*, he challenges the way Ovid's goddess metes out blame.

In *As You Like It,* Shakespeare groups Atalanta with three other ancient women who illustrate a fatal knot between love and death. The yoking, which I read as an intriguing poetic paratext for Johnson's prose critique of Shakespeare's 'barren' quibbles, occurs in a set of thirty rhyming lines praising Rosalind in Act III, Scene ii. Touchstone deems these lines 'bad fruit' and Rosalind herself judges them to be poorly measured; written in the seven-syllable tetrameter that Shakespeare uses in other riddling play-songs, the lines in Orlando's poem oscillate between being best construed as 'tailless' trochees or as 'headless' iambs; they have in them, Rosalind remarks, 'more feet than the verses would bear' (III. ii. 162–3).[32] The author of the verses bears a name that comes, as Longueville's does, from outside of England's borders: Orlando harks back to the love-mad hero of Ariosto's *Orlando Furioso*, and the English Orlando moves his comically uncertain poetic feet in a literary zone that is both mock epic and mock Petrarchan. Not yet a master of his medium, Orlando tries pastiche, and specifically, the method made famous by the Greek painter Zeuxis, who allegedly painted a beautiful woman by copying different parts of her body from different models. Orlando credits 'Nature', but we credit Shakespeare, for having 'distilled' Rosalind in these lines: [33]

> Helen's cheek, but not her heart,
> Cleopatra's majesty,
> Atalanta's better part,
> Sad Lucretia's modesty...
>
> (III. ii. 142–5)

---

[31] Ovid, *Metamorphoses* 10, 688–707, Frank Justus Miller (ed. and trans.), (Cambridge, MA: Harvard University Press, 1916) 112–15.

[32] Rosalind describes the metrically ambiguous poem's feet as 'lame' (III. ii. 163). Shakespeare uses seven syllable lines in other 'riddling' songs, for instance, 'Tell me, where is fancy bred' (*Merchant of Venice*). Puttenham discusses this phenomenon as 'catalecticke' and 'anacatalecticke' verse ('odde vnder and odde ouer the iust measure of their verse') in *The Arte*, 142.

[33] On the verb *distil* ('to drip or trickle down' [*OED*]) in Shakespeare's sonnets see Jeffrey Masten, 'Gee, Your Heir Smells Terrific: Response to [Richard Halpern's] "Shakespeare's Perfume"', *Early Modern Culture: An Electronic Seminar*, <http://emc.eserver.org/1–2/masten.html>.

What is Atalanta's 'better part'? Is there a play on 'part' as a part of 'partner' (as lover or husband)? Is there an allusion to Christ's praise of Mary (sister of Martha) for playing a 'good' part (or better or best part, depending on the translation) in Luke 10:42? There, 'part' is a woman's well-chosen role in a mini-drama that values an act of listening to Christ's words over toiling in the house. Johnson considers neither of these possibilities, but he does find the phrase more puzzling than modern editors do; whereas they usually gloss the phrase in a marginal word or two that presumes only one possible interpretive context ('beauty' and/or 'fleetness'), Johnson ponders (and constitutes) a larger problem, wondering whether Shakespeare perhaps knew more than one Atalanta composed of higher and lower parts; for him, the baffling word has both physical and moral connotations, though the former are present only by circumlocution:

> I know not well what could be the better part of Atalanta here ascribed to Rosalind. Of the Atalanta most celebrated, and who therefore must be intended here where she has no epithet of discrimination, the better part seems to have been her heels, and the worse part was so bad that Rosalind would not thank her lover for the comparison. There is a more obscure Atalanta, a huntress and a heroine, but of her nothing bad is recorded, and therefore I know not which was the better part. Shakespeare was no despicable mythologist, yet he seems here to have mistaken some other character for that of Atalanta.[34]

Johnson's tone is as puzzling to me as the Shakespearean phrase was (it seems) to him. Is he being ironic? Only a few lines earlier in this same scene, Touchstone gives us license to read Orlando's phrase 'better part' in terms of the 'worse part' Johnson mentions but disavows (as in the classic illustration of the presence of the negated phenomenon in language, 'do not mention white elephants'). Mocking Orlando's metre and his high Petrarchan register as well, Touchstone 'turns' Orlando's own apparently novel use of the word 'lined' as a past participle for an artistic act of 'outlining' or sketching—'All the pictures fairest lined | Are but black to Rosalind' (III. ii. 90–1)[35]—into a bawdy glimpse of a dark space inside a body likened both to a piece of 'wintered' clothing and to a female dog in the act of copulation: 'Wintered garments must be lined, | So must slender Rosalind' (III. ii. 103–4).[36] The couplet employs a comically close rhyme and sucks

---

[34] Cited from *As You Like It*, Variorum, Horace Howard Furness (ed.), 6th edn, (Philadelphia: J. & B. Lippencott, 1890) 8, 153. Alan Brissendon, in his 1994 Oxford edition of the play, glosses 'the better part' as 'Atalanta's beauty, compared with her swiftness'. Atalanta's son Parthenopaios, whose name stresses his birth to an unwedded female, is not mentioned in Ovid, but he is mentioned in many other classical sources that Shakespeare—and Johnson—could have known. Johnson sees that a 'worse' part of Atalanta is a logical corollary of Shakespeare's reference to her 'better part'; the 'worse' part belongs to a semantic web well analysed in *The Woman's Part: Feminist Criticism of Shakespeare*, Carolyn Ruth Swift Lenz, Gayle Greene, and Carol Thomas Neely (eds), (Urbana: University of Illinois Press, 1983) esp. 12–14.

[35] The *OED* finds this the earliest use of 'line' in this sense (v. 24).

[36] Touchstone's lines are often cut in production, and many editors do not gloss the two bawdy meanings of 'lined'; Frances Dolan does, and I draw on her Pelican edition (New York: Penguin, 2000).

the proper name into the vortex of the wordplay—as occurs elsewhere in Shakespeare's oeuvre. Given the labile eroticism of Touchstone's very name, and his closing ambiguous equation of 'sweetest rose' with 'love's prick', it seems likely that the entire passage plays with Rosalind's dual identity as boy and girl, 'master mistress' of passion, as Sonnet 20 famously puts it. As Rosalind and Ganymede both, s/he is transformed through Touchstone's punning couplet into a sexual container and, at the same time, a piece of winter clothing filled out from the inside. The couplet illustrates Debra Fried's argument that in many rhyming pairs, the second line gives a 'distorted memory of the first' that creates a pun-like wordplay; the verbal play has the potential to create a metamorphosis in our assessment of the situation or character.[37]

Atalanta, like Rosalind, at one time acted like a boy; she may have appealed to Shakespeare as a source for his meditation on Rosalind's multiple 'parts' because Atalanta's participation in a famous foot race conjures up questions about play-acting and bloodlines as well as about strange courtships. Moreover, as Angelo suggests in a complex wordplay in *Measure for Measure*—'And now I give my sensual race the rein' (II. iv. 160)—'race' may signify not only athletic competition but also 'blood' or passion. As the latter, it is something that needs checking, reining in, as a horse does, or as young women's bodies do—especially when they are far from their father's sight in wild forests with a 'heart' (rhymes with 'part') always threatening transgressive action. In Book 8 of the *Metamorphoses*, which is one of Johnson's likely sources for the 'more obscure' Atalanta he mentions in his note, Ovid depicts her as a skilled hunter who competes in a different competition pitting men against women: when she is 'first' to wound a boar, she shames her male competitors, among whom is Ancaeus. 'Armed with a two-headed axe', he is 'swollen with pride and with boastful lips'. The image reminds us that 'part' can also signify the male organ, here presented as the source of a primal competition: Ancaeus commands his audience to 'Learn now ... how far a man's weapons surpass a girl's'.[38] Ancaeus' boast leads directly to his death whereas Atalanta remains, for a time, in a comic romance that turns only at the very end to tragedy.

By comparing his beautiful Rosalind to 'parts' of stories about Atalanta, Cleopatra, Lucretia, and Helen, Orlando inadvertently leaves the reader/spectator with a chance to ponder different possible outcomes of Rosalind's and Orlando's story. The interpreter is in the middle of a riddling tale, part tragedy, part comedy; our situation is similar to Atalanta's at the moment when she consults an oracle and receives the usual opaque message: 'A husband will be your bane ... flee from the intercourse of husband; and yet you will not flee, and, though living, you will lose yourself' (564–66). Terrified of marriage, she devises the race-test for her suitors. Those who lose will die—and they do, until Hippomenes wins with the previously mentioned device of the three golden apples.

[37] Debra Fried, 'Rhyme Puns', in Culler (1988) 83–99.
[38] Ovid, *Metamorphoses* 8, 392, Miller (1961) 434–5.

The ball-like objects he throws sequentially on Atalanta's path arguably symbolize his masculine parts—perhaps even an 'excess' of them.[39] He symbolically sacrifices some portion of his masculine prowess in order to win her sexual favours. This mythological couple is thus an interesting analogue both for Antony and Cleopatra and for Orlando and Rosalind—and for a theory of wordplay as enabling potentially illicit crossings of boundaries between bodies and genders as well as languages.

By following Atalanta's figure out of Johnson's preface into the semantically and rhetorically fuzzier realm of the footnote and its Shakespearean and Ovidian 'paratext(s)', I have attempted to dramatize my chief concern in this essay, which is with those moments when the quibble's numbers, as I would like to call them, become too many to control with a single explanatory and/or evaluative net. Such moments create epistemological queasiness—what the French call *mise en abŷme*. Shakespeare's writing in numbered measures, especially but not only in metrical lines bonded by rhyme, makes aspects of poetic form cross dramatically with conceptual issues pertaining to the competition between artistic and bio-social forms of 'reproduction', and with concepts of keeping and losing control. In the final segment of this essay, I want to consider several Renaissance discussions of pun-like tropes as frames for thinking about Sonnet 135, an intensely puzzling small poem that seems to offer a type of fast-acting wordplay that contrasts with the slow, vapourish trail we have examined, with Johnson's help, in 'Atalanta's better part'. In both of my main examples, the question of parts and wholes is thematically as well as formally important.

5.3 WORDPLAYS IN OVERPLUS

In the Renaissance grammar school, pupils were repeatedly sent to Latin poetic texts to practice the art of 'double translation'.[40] Through this art, and its accompanying drilling in noting and judging rhetorical tropes as 'licit' or 'illicit', students became involved 'with the difficulties of rhetorical taxonomy'.[41] Those difficulties were dramatized in the terminological and evaluative slippages between multiple versions of an enterprise that involved both finding the 'same' terms across the English/Latin border and simultaneously distinguishing good tropes from 'improper' ones.[42] The rules were numerous,

---

[39] On 'ball' as testicle in early modern texts including Shakespeare's *Henry IV*, see Williams (1997) 34–5.

[40] On double translation, see Jeff Dolven, *Scenes of Instruction in Renaissance Romance* (Chicago: University of Chicago Press, 2007) 43–4. See also Martin Elsky, *Authorizing Words: Speech, Writing, and Print in the English Renaissance* (Ithaca: Cornell University Press, 1989) 54–6, 122–5.

[41] Poole, 'The vices of style' (2007) 243.

[42] For Cicero, metaphorical words are those 'which are transferred and placed, as it were, in an alien place' ('eis quae transferuntur et quasi alieno in loco collocantur'), *The Orator's Education* 3, 37, H. Rackham (ed. and trans.), (Cambridge, MA: Harvard University Press, 1942) 2, 118–19.

variably translated from different classical sources, and of course inconsistent; poetry, moreover, was typically a verbal zone where the rules were slackened, though not without repeated expressions of concern about how much poetic license was too much. This large discursive field about tropes (which spreads across discussions of logic, grammar, and poetry as well as rhetoric) provides a heuristic frame for thinking about wordplay in Sonnet 135, a poem that explores precisely the conceptual area where 'good figures' (if they exist at all) metamorphose into 'trespasses'.

Sophie Read offers a lucid analysis of the three classical tropes that she thinks come closest to corresponding to the wordplay-types known in English as 'quibble', 'clench', 'catch', and—after Shakespeare's death—as 'pun'.[43] Her choices are paronomasia (Puttenham's 'the nicknamer'); antanaclasis (Puttenham's 'the rebound'); and syllepsis (Puttenham's 'the double supply'). Read sees the difference between the 'nomenclature of the rhetoricians and the slang terms' (she doesn't mention Puttenham's more decorous English translations) as one of 'precision, and of prestige'.[44] Precision, perhaps, though the rhetorician's definitions, as I've been suggesting, can be baffling. Cultural prestige is also something hard to estimate in retrospect. While for modern readers 'antanaclasis' may carry more cultural capital than 'clench', we cannot be sure how readers in Shakespeare's time would have measured the phenomena. His texts are full of parodies of those whose small Latin and less Greek leads them into types of ornate diction considered 'vicious', and the cultural interest in rhetorical 'excess' could well have helped determine whether a wordplay under any particular name smelled sweet or weedy. The naming of tropes is clearly important to how modern critics select early modern examples; but the examples we choose in order to illustrate different tropes may in turn work to challenge and even in some cases erase the boundary lines drawn by the naming operations.

In Sonnet 135, 'Whoever hath her wish, thou hast thy Will', there are rich examples of paronomasia, antanaclasis, syllepsis, polyptoton, ploce, and a number of other pun-like wordplays as these are variously defined by some Renaissance rhetoricians and re-described by modern scholars. There are also (I would suggest) vivid illustrations of rhetorical 'vices' such as those William Poole categorizes under the rubric 'inordinate' and defines through phrases drawn from Richard Sherry's *A Treatise of Schemes and Tropes* (1550). Among those most relevant to Shakespeare's Sonnet 135 are 'aischrologia' (obscenity), 'as when the words be spoken, or joined together, that they may be

---

[43] The definitions Read (2007) selects for her tropes differ significantly from Puttenham's definitions—and from some modern critics' understandings of these words for operations in words. Margreta de Grazia, for instance, finds that *none* of the Renaissance tropes correspond to the 'simple definition of a pun as a single sound possessing multiple senses', 'Homonyms Before and After Lexical Standardization', *Shakespeare Jahrbuch* (1990), 154.

[44] Read (2007) 82. For Puttenham's terms, see *The Arte of English Poesie* (1589) 212 (in the index, he or his compositor calls this trope paronomasia but in the text, it is 'prosonomasia'); 216 (antanaclasis) and 176 (sillepsis).

wronge [wrung] into a fylthye sense'; and 'cacozelia' (affectation), 'as when affecting copy [copiousness], we fall into a vayne bablynge'.

Here is the Oxford version of the poem:

> Whoever hath her wish, thou hast thy Will,
> And Will to boot, and Will in overplus.
> More than enough am I that vex thee still,
> To thy sweet will making addition thus.
> Wilt thou, whose will is large and spacious,
> Not once vouchsafe to hide my will in thine?
> Shall will in others seem right gracious,
> And in my will no fair acceptance shine?
> The sea, all water, yet receives rain still,
> And in abundance addeth to his store;
> So thou, being rich in Will, add to thy Will
> One will of mine, to make thy large will more.
>   Let no unkind, no fair beseechers kill;
>   Think all but one, and me in that one Will.

In this sonnet's fourteen lines, the word 'will' appears twelve times—thirteen if you allow the verb form 'wilt' (by polyptoton, 'repetition of words from the same root but with different endings').[45] There are many more plays on 'will' if you count the parono-masias in the poem as including the rhyme words 'still' and 'kill'—and their many cous-ins from the associative matrix of the sonnet sequence as a whole: 'fulfill', for example, from the next sonnet, and of course 'ill'—the part-word repeated inside and outside the bounds of Sonnet 135; in 144, 'ill' rhymes with 'still' and also with 'evil' and 'devil', while there is a significant slant rhyme, here and elsewhere, on 'well' (as 'vagina') and 'will' in one of its senses. One definition of paronomasia is 'a figure which declineth into a contrarie by a likelihood of letters, either added, changed, or taken away'; that defini-tion certainly covers rhyming puns in which a single letter changes. The poem illus-trates 'syllepsis' in its definition of 'when … one word serveth to many sences'; and the sonnet also abundantly illustrates 'antanaclasis' as 'a figure which repeats a word that hath two significations, and the one of them contrary, or at least, unlike to the other'.[46] Intriguingly, antanaclasis as Puttenham illustrates it looks very like a paronomasia on 'will'/'kill'; Puttenham's example of antanaclasis, which Shakespeare borrows in at least two plays, consists in the subtraction of the letter 'i' in the word 'married': 'The maide that soone married is, soone marred is'.[47]

---

[45] Lanham (1968) 78; the trope is also named 'traductio' and 'adnominatio'.

[46] These definitions are from Peacham and Day, as cited in and selected by Read (2007) 80. Equally relevant to Sonnet 135 is 'ploce', from the Greek 'plaiting'; this trope is a 'repetition of a word with a new signification after the intervention of another word or words' (Lanham, 1968, 77–8).

[47] Puttenham (1589), 216. Cf. 'A young man married is a man that's marred', *All's Well that Ends Well*, II. iii. 298.

Our ideas about puns and kindred tropes—and the multitudinous discourse about them—are illuminated, and challenged, by this sonnet's formally bounded but semantically open reflection on 'will' and its mates. David Willburn, who himself participates in the sonnet's play on will as a 'proper' name belonging to many, offers this summary of the multiple meanings of that word 'in' the poem, or rather, as Willburn insists, 'potentially' in the poem's letters if a reader or speaker plays the game: 'The term occupies a densely over-determined semantic nexus within which notions of erotic appetite or desire, sexual and procreative organs, aggression (the will to power), wish, whim, inclination, volition, conscious intention, purpose, and bequest or testament co-exist at varying levels of potentiality'.[48]

A syllepsis or homonymic pun that is occluded by the modern-spelling edition of the sonnet but that can be readily seen in the original 1609 version sums up the nexus of concerns about verbal excess that I have been exploring in this essay. If I had to pick one word to stand in for my argument here, it would be 'abundance', in line nine of Sonnet 135: in the poem's 'original' version, which of course is not necessarily what was written by Shakespeare's hand, the word is 'aboundance'. The letter '0', also a number, paradoxically both restores and dissolves the idea of a *limit*; 'bound' lurks in the original spelling of 'aboundance', but noting that word-play—actualizing its potential—takes us to an aporia, a conceptual antinomy that we cannot master. 'Bound' is and is not a meaning licensed by this poem's image of 'abundance' as a rich and apparently limitless 'sea' (line 9) whose drops one cannot count.

This sea is a polyvalent and much discussed image; Eve Sedgwick reads it as a darkly funny and deeply misogynist insult to the addressee, signifying 'female sexuality as a great sociable melting pot' in which men, or their 'wills', seem to be reduced to the scale of homunculi, almost plankton, in a warm but unobservant sea';[49] Valerie Traub, citing but also swerving from Sedgwick, views the 'sea' as a homoerotic space composed of seminal fluid. For Traub, the sea signals an 'erasure of female reproductive power' that 'compensates defensively for the generative power accorded to male-male love' earlier in the sonnet sequence; but the sea is also the locus—or matrix, I would suggest—in which the female addressee's 'will' is transformed into an abiding threat to the social order. True, her abundant sea is not a cradle for biological reproduction; but it is a place that works, like the 'mother tongue', to remind the speaker that other wordsmiths who have

    [48] Willbern, *Poetic Will: Shakespeare and the Play of Language* (Philadelphia: University of Pennsylvania Press, 1997) xiv; see also Booth (ed.), with analytic commentary, *Shakespeare's Sonnets* (New Haven: Yale University Press, 1977) 466–7. See also Kathryn Schwarz, *What You Will: Gender, Contract, and Shakespearean Social Space* (Philadelphia: University of Pennsylvania Press, 2011), esp. ch. 5 and Valerie Traub, 'Sex Without Issue; Sodomy, Reproduction, and Signification in Shakespeare's Sonnet', in *Shakespeare's Sonnets: Critical Essays*, James Schiffer (ed.), (New York: Garland Publishing, 1999) 431–52, esp. 437–8. There has been an abundance of strong commentary on this poem; see Schwarz and Traub for further bibliography.
    [49] Eve Kosofsky Sedgwick, *Between Men: English Literature and Male Homosocial Desire* (New York: Columbia University Press, 1985) 38.

been there before him will be there still when he is gone. The sonnet's jocular misogyny spills into subtle fears of miscegeny, fears of mixing essences and of thereby losing the boundaries between self and other whether these are construed as separating fair from dark skins or 'male' from 'female' wills.[50] As Kathryn Schwarz justly observes of Sonnet 147, '[W]ill binds together what reason should hold apart'.[51] In Sonnet 135, the speaker argues that he should be allowed to add his liquid 'rain' to the addressee's 'store', her 'will', which can become 'more' without anyone noticing the 'addition'. The all-receiving pro-miscuous sea offers the speaker what Sedgwick calls the 'pleasure of amalgamation, not in the first place with the receptive woman but with the other men received ("Think all but one, and me in that one will")'. We cannot know, however, whether that 'one will' is a sign of the poet's vision of his phallic triumph, the godlike 'I am that I am' with which the speaker played in Sonnet 121.9;[52] or whether he is acknowledging the dark implications of the Renaissance proverb 'One is no number'[53]—a proverb with which he plays often and which, in an earlier sonnet to the fair young man, served as a warning against dying without 'proper' issue: 'Thou single wilt prove none' (Sonnet 8.14).

The conceptual 'ab[o]undance' of Sonnet 135 spills over its final line's 'one will' into the next sonnet, where the speaker's argument is repeated with a difference—as in line 8, 'Among a number one is reckoned none'. That line continues the sonnet sequence's larger line of inquiry into the meaning of 'none'—as the Arabic number and Roman alphabetic letter 0 signifying the female genitals: Hamlet's 'country matters' or, in the metaphor of Sonnet 136, 'thy store's account' [cunt](10). The 'O' also signifies the 'nothing' that the speaker strenuously protests he would never exchange for 'all thy sum of good' (109.12); and, at the beginning of that same sonnet, the 'O' signifies nothing except the letter or sound of addressing words to someone who evidently has reason to doubt the speaker's erotic and epistemological truth: 'O never say that I was false of heart' (109.1).

Counting and playing seriously in words leads Shakespeare often, as we have seen, to fantasies of sexual pleasure with both male and female bodies—and their parts. As Paula Blank observes, 'part' is a key word of the entire sonnet sequence;[54] moreover, in Sonnet 39, line 2, the poet refers to the young man as 'the better part of me', using the same phrase that Orlando used in his lines about Rosalind/Ganymede as Atalanta.[55] If wordplay in 'numbers' leads to thoughts about bodies joining and reproducing (in flesh and/or in poetic 'lines'), however, such wordplay also leads to thoughts about boundar-ies, including that 'bourn' that 'puzzles the will' (*Hamlet*, III. i. 81–2). Although Sonnet 135 seems to enact a defense against time's ravages by its circular play on 'will' at the end

[50] On the 'dark lady's' activation of 'the racialized tropes of Western aesthetics', see Traub, 'Sex without Issue', 446.

[51] Schwarz (2011) 134.

[52] Booth notes the allusion to Exodus 3.14 and also that the conjunction of 'wills' and 'I am that I am' contains the potential for a pun on 'William', 'Will-I-am' (*Shakespeare's Sonnets*, 410).

[53] For Shakespeare's iterations of this proverb, see Blank (2006) 51.

[54] See Blank (2006) 48.

[55] There are many other textual parallels; see Booth (1977) 198.

of the first and last lines, the last 'will' is not the same as the first. For a poet who shows even his dying heroes repeatedly succumbing to the lure of wordplay ('the *rest* is silence' [V. ii. 310], my emphasis), the lure is arguably not a deviation from the road of reason and propriety but instead (or also) a way of paying homage to the wordplay's generative power. We cannot name the 'nothing' of death without falsifying it as something. But that, perhaps, is one of the points of Shakespeare's exorbitant wordplay, whether in the quick moment of a witty homonym or in the longer, intertextual trails offered by a phrase like 'Atalanta's better part'—a phrase Johnson found himself pursuing despite his view that Shakespeare pursued 'luminous vapours' beyond the bounds of reason.

SELECT BIBLIOGRAPHY

Adamson, Sylvia, Gavin Alexander, and Katrin Ettenhuber (2007) (eds) *Renaissance Figures of Speech* (Cambridge: Cambridge University Press).

Bates, Catherine (1999) 'The Point of Puns', *Modern Philology* May: 421–38.

Booth, Stephen (1977) (ed.) *Shakespeare's Sonnets* (New Haven: Yale University Press).

Callaghan, Dympna (2007) *Shakespeare's Sonnets* (London: Blackwell).

Culler, Jonathan (1988) (ed.) *On Puns: The Foundation of Letters.* (New York: Basil Blackwell).

De Grazia, Margreta (1990) 'Homonyms Before and After Lexical Standardization', *Shakespeare Jahrbuch*, 143–56.

——(2001) 'Shakespeare and the Craft of Language', in Margareta de Grazia and Stanley Wells (eds) *The Cambridge Companion to Shakespeare* (Cambridge: Cambridge University Press) 49–64.

Derrida, Jacques (1986) 'Proverb: He that would pun ...', John P. Leavey, Jr. *Glassary* (Lincoln: The University of Nebraska Press).

Fried, Debra (1988) 'Rhyme Puns' in Culler (ed.) *On Puns*, 83–99.

Lanham, Richard A (1968) *A Handlist of Rhetorical Terms* (Berkeley: University of California Press).

McDonald, Russ (2001) *Shakespeare and the Arts of Language* (Oxford: Oxford University Press).

Parker, Patricia (2000) *Shakespeare from the Margins* (Chicago: University of Chicago Press).

Poole, William (2007) 'The vices of style', *Renaissance Figures of Speech*, in Sylvia Admanson, Gavin Alexander, and Katrin Ettenhuber (eds), (Cambridge: Cambridge University Press) 236–51.

Read, Sophie (2007) 'Puns, serious wordplay', *Renaissance Figures of Speech*, in Sylvia Admanson, Gavin Alexander, and Katrin Ettenhuber (eds), (Cambridge: Cambridge University Press) 81–94.

Schwarz, Kathryn (2011) *What You Will: Gender, Contract, and Shakespearean Social Space* (Philadelphia: University of Pennsylvania Press).

Willbern, David (1997) *Poetic Will: Shakespeare and the Play of Language* (Philadelphia: University of Philadelphia Press).

PART II

INHERITANCE AND INVENTION

CHAPTER 6

....

CLASSICAL INFLUENCES

....

COLIN BURROW

Once upon a time Shakespeare was regarded as a naturally English poet who needed no classical learning to be able, in John Milton's words, to 'Warble his native wood-notes wild'.[1] To many early critics Milton's description of Shakespeare seemed to chime with Ben Jonson's remarks about his 'small Latin and less Greek', which appeared in his elegy prefixed to the first Folio of Shakespeare's collected plays. By the 1640s the myth of Shakespeare as an English genius who needed no classical training was more or less established, and it lasted for years. Even in the mid-20th century it was still possible to argue that Shakespeare's classical learning consisted of rudiments poorly remembered from grammar school.[2]

This picture of Shakespeare as the native genius has been thoroughly dismantled.[3] Generations of scholars, stimulated by the indefatigable two-volume study of *William Shakespere's Small Latine and Lesse Greeke* by T. W. Baldwin, have shown how much Shakespeare learned about classical literature both from his grammar school and from his subsequent reading.[4] Even Ben Jonson's apparently disparaging remark about

---

[1] 'L'Allegro', line 134.

[2] J. A. K. Thomson, *Shakespeare and the Classics* (London: Allen and Unwin, 1952).

[3] General overviews are Charles Martindale and Michelle Martindale, *Shakespeare and the Uses of Antiquity: An Introductory Essay* (London and New York: Routledge, 1990), Charles Martindale and A. B. Taylor (eds), *Shakespeare and the Classics* (Cambridge: Cambridge University Press, 2004), Robert S. Miola, *Shakespeare's Reading* (Oxford: Oxford University Press, 2000). Specific studies of Shakespeare's relations to particular classical authors include Jonathan Bate, *Shakespeare and Ovid* (Oxford: Clarendon Press, 1993), Heather James, *Shakespeare's Troy* (Cambridge: Cambridge University Press, 1997), Margaret Tudeau-Clayton, *Jonson, Shakespeare and Early Modern Virgil* (Cambridge: Cambridge University Press, 1998).

[4] T. W. Baldwin, *William Shakespere's Small Latine and Lesse Greeke* (Urbana, IL: University of Illinois Press, 1944); developed especially in Emrys Jones, *The Origins of Shakespeare* (Oxford: Clarendon Press, 1977), Joel B. Altman, *The Tudor Play of Mind: Rhetorical Inquiry and the Development of Elizabethan Drama* (Berkeley and London: University of California Press, 1978). For some suggestions about Baldwin's limitations, see Colin Burrow, 'Shakespeare and Humanistic Culture', in Charles Martindale

Shakespeare's classical learning has been reinterpreted: 'though thou hadst small Latin and less Greek', it has been suggested, could be read as a hypothetical suggestion ('even if it were the case that you had …') rather than a statement of fact.[5] This chapter will seek to characterize the various 'classical' poetic styles that run through Shakespeare's writing. It will also attempt to explain a paradox: classical texts and classical training were vital to Shakespeare's poetry, and yet the critical tradition rapidly came to think of Shakespeare as an 'unlearned' poet. Why? The explanation lies, I will argue, in the particular way in which Shakespeare displayed his classical learning. But first we need to establish what he knew about the classics and how he learnt it.

6.1 LATIN LESSONS

Shakespeare's training at school in classical rhetoric and in Latin literature was a central foundation of his art. Like most Elizabethan grammar-school boys he would have read more Latin poetry by the age of sixteen than most classics undergraduates today will have done by the age of twenty. The playwright Terence (who was a favourite source of racy Latin phrases for schoolboys) would have shown him how much theatrical energy can be generated by a well-placed low-register word. Ovid and Virgil provided models of high poetic style, and textbooks by Desiderius Erasmus and his followers would have provided friendly guidance to classical style. Much has been written about the experiences of Elizabethan grammar-school boys, their early starts to the day, their heavy satchels borne down by classical grammars, and their daily exercises in the rote learning of classical texts. None of these experiences sound very poetic. Pupils at schools like the King Edward VI school at Stratford would be made to learn most of William Lily's *Latin Grammar* by heart, and were encouraged to memorize classical poems, to translate them, and to analyse their rhetorical structure. Without this educational system, strange as it may sound, we would not have had Shakespeare as we know him at all.

Nonetheless Shakespeare's relation to his schooling was often edgy and ironical. He gave his own unruly and comical representations of Latin lessons at two points in his plays. In *The Merry Wives of Windsor* a boy called William tries to memorize his Latin pronouns to comical effect (IV. i. 16–80). In *The Taming of the Shrew* (III. i. 26–44) a fraudulent Latin master attempts to seduce his pupil while failing to translate Ovid's *Heroides*. Representations of the processes of classical learning, and indeed of Latin

and A. B. Taylor, *Shakespeare and the Classics* (Cambridge: Cambridge University Press, 2004) 9–27 and Peter Mack, *Elizabethan Rhetoric: Theory and Practice* (Cambridge: Cambridge University Press, 2002). For more recent studies of the influence of early modern pedagogy, see Jeffrey A. Dolven, *Scenes of Instruction in Renaissance Romance* (Chicago and London: University of Chicago Press, 2007), and Lynn Enterline, *Shakespeare's Schoolroom: Rhetoric, Discipline, Emotion* (Philadelphia: University of Pennsylvania Press, 2012).

[5] Brian Vickers (ed.), *English Renaissance Literary Criticism* (Oxford: Clarendon Press, 1999) 539.

teachers, in Shakespeare tend to be deliberately unpoetic, and there are times when it even looks as though classical learning is an enemy of vernacular poetic skill. The pedant Holofernes in *Love's Labour's Lost* is unlearned enough to misquote from the first line of the *Eclogues* of Mantuan, a popular neo-Latin schoolroom text (IV. ii. 92–3). His attempts at vernacular poetry are painfully creaking:

> The preyful Princess pierced and pricked a pretty pleasing pricket.
> Some say a sore, but not a sore till now made sore with shooting.
> The dogs did yell; put 'l' to 'sore', then 'sorel' jumps from thicket ...
>
> (IV. ii. 56–8)

Although the records of Stratford grammar school are so patchy that we do not even know for sure if Shakespeare went there, it is likely that his actual schoolmasters would have encouraged him to look for three distinct kinds of things in his classical reading. They would have encouraged him to note the moral content of the first Latin texts he would have read; Leonhard Culmann's *Sententiae Pueriles* ('Moral Phrases for Boys'), the *Distichs* of Cato (which are not among the gems of Latin poetry), and the fables of Aesop. Grammar-school pupils were also encouraged to extract from their reading in Latin poetry the stories, myths, and exemplary tales with which they could lace their own exercises in composition. Above all Elizabethan grammar-school boys were encouraged to note how classical poets used the schemes and tropes of rhetoric, and to use the same techniques themselves.

This method of teaching gave Shakespeare, and many of his contemporaries too, a variety of ways of sounding 'classical', or of displaying learning in what were called 'polite letters'. They could quote from Latin poetry or cite classical phrases in support of an argument—as Holofernes tries to do, or as Titus Andronicus does when he sends weapons wrapped in *sententiae* from Horace to his enemies (IV. ii. 20–4). They could deploy a style which visibly or audibly displayed their knowledge of the schemes and tropes of rhetoric. Alternatively or additionally they could base a fiction on a classically derived narrative (either a myth or a piece of classical history). As a result, being 'classical' in the later 16th century was not one thing. A scene from English history could be treated in a 'classical' style, with speeches which displayed carefully controlled syntactic articulation and well-modulated use of the schemes and tropes of rhetoric, and which perhaps also drew on passages from Seneca's plays at emotional high points. Alternatively a fiction might be based on classical myth but without using a particularly learned style. These were just two of the ways of displaying 'classical' learning in this period. This was perhaps the principal reason why late Elizabethan and early Jacobean poets and playwrights were on the whole so happy to work with classical materials. They were not bound to replicate both the form and the content, the style and the narrative, of a classical work. They could mix and match.

It was argued long ago (in 1940) by the art historian Jean Seznec that the defining characteristic of Renaissance visual art was 'the reintegration of antique subject matter within the antique form: we can speak of a Renaissance from the day Hercules resumed his athletic breadth of shoulder, his club, and his lion's skin'.[6] It is difficult to transfer this view of 'the Renaissance' to the arts of poetry and drama, because 'form' and 'content' mean such different things in painting and poetry; but Seznec does nonetheless provide a suggestive formula for thinking about the relationship between Shakespeare's poetry and its classical origins. In some respects Shakespeare seems to have been entirely uninterested in classical poetic 'form'. Most of the Latin quotations in his writing are misquotations, and several of them do not scan properly. A few of his contemporaries were attempting to adapt classical metre (which is based on the notional length of syllables rather than on patterns of stress) to the English language.[7] Others, including Ben Jonson, were experimenting at the very end of the 16th century with the ways in which English stanza forms might replicate the complex metrical structures of classical odes and other poems. There is no sign that Shakespeare had any interest in these ways of recreating the 'form' of classical poetry in English. But that does not mean that he was not in his own way interested in reuniting classical content with something which he considered to be a version of classical form. It is just that his notion of 'classical form' was not the same as ours. The use of highly patterned rhetoric was, so far as he was concerned, a 'classical' form of expression, while his notion of classical 'content' comprised a large and elastic collection of historical and mythical stories culled from a wide range of authors, from Augustan poets such as Ovid and Virgil through to the Greek romances composed in the Hellenistic world of the 2nd century AD. That meant that for Shakespeare, as for most fashionable poets of the late 16th century, composing a poem that sounded 'classical' would not mean attempting to replicate in English the forms of Latin versification. It would mean taking a scenario or a story from the classical world and filling it with arguments shaped by the structures and clad in the tropes and figures of classical rhetoric.

It is easy, given this background, to see why Ovid's *Metamorphoses* was the greatest single classical influence on Shakespeare.[8] The *Metamorphoses* is a collection of myths and stories that could provide occasions for constructing emotionally charged speeches. It is also deeply and self-consciously rhetorical to the extent of being in love with its own art—a quality which was recognized by Ovid's very earliest critics.[9] The *Metamorphoses* provided both the things Shakespeare was trained to look for in classical poetry, and did so in spades: it provided an abundance of narratives, both short and long, and it layers rhetorical figures on top of tropes. It is therefore not surprising that Shakespeare started his career as a poet by audaciously recombining these two aspects of Ovid's poem in a

[6] Jean Seznec, *The Survival of the Pagan Gods: The Mythological Tradition and Its Place in Renaissance Humanism and Art* (Princeton: Princeton University Press, 1972) 211.

[7] Derek Attridge, *Well-Weighed Syllables: Elizabethan Verse in Classical Metres* (London: Cambridge University Press, 1974), Richard Helgerson, *Forms of Nationhood: The Elizabethan Writing of England* (Chicago: University of Chicago Press, 1992).

[8] Bate (1993), A. B. Taylor (ed.), *Shakespeare's Ovid: The Metamorphoses in the Plays and Poems* (Cambridge: Cambridge University Press, 2000).

[9] 'Ovid is a self-indulgent writer even in epic, and he was too fond of his own gifts', Quintilian, *The Orator's Education*, Donald A. Russell (ed.), (Cambridge, MA: Harvard University Press, 2001) 10.1.88; Cf. Seneca's *Controversiae*, 2.2.12.

way that produced works which looked quite different from their principal source. The first two published works to which Shakespeare's name was attached were the narrative poems *Venus and Adonis* (1593) and the 'graver labour' of *Lucrece* (1594). These two poems both take classical scenarios, both of which are found in poems by Ovid, and fill them with speeches artfully constructed to show the poet's mastery over rhetoric. *Venus and Adonis*, which is based on a story from Ovid's *Metamorphoses*, is Shakespeare's first printed exercise in his peculiar form of hybrid style. A classical narrative drawn from the *Metamorphoses* is filled, and ornamented, and drawn out, with 'classical' rhetoric. Its opening lets its readers know that fireworks are to come:

> Even as the sun with purple-coloured face
> Had ta'en his last leave of the weeping morn,
> Rose-cheeked Adonis hied him to the chase.
> Hunting he loved, but love he laughed to scorn.
>> Sick-thoughted Venus makes amain unto him,
>> And like a bold-faced suitor 'gins to woo him.
>
> (*Venus and Adonis*, 1–6)[10]

This was an invitation to learned readers in the summer of 1593 to get out their pens and begin to spot the 'classical' forms embedded in the writing. This description of morning is what rhetoricians would call a 'chronographia', 'when an orator describeth anie time for delectations sake'.[11] The turn on 'loved, but love', shifting from noun to verb, is a figure called *traductio*, 'which is when ye turn and tranlace a word into many sundry shapes'.[12] The compound adjectives declare that the poem is going to push plain English in new directions. The game of *Venus and Adonis*, though, is to make an artful counterpoint between an apparently endlessly copious variation of argument and rhetoric and its story drawn from Ovid. Venus cajoles, picks up, lies down on, talks to, banters, and argues with Adonis, and yet fails to persuade him to love her. Her speeches seem endlessly to display the kind of copious rhetoric which pedagogues such as Desiderius Erasmus sought to encourage among European schoolboys. But the narrative deriving from Ovid—Adonis scorns her, leaves, and dies—foregrounds the destructive power of time and the evanescence of life. 'Classical' style and 'classical' story are consequently made dynamically to pull in different directions, towards the pleasure principle of endlessly rhetorical ornamentation on the one hand, and towards death on the other. *Venus and Adonis* is a re-synthesis of different elements from Ovid, which generates enormous internal friction between classical *narratio* and classical *oratio*. It may not have been the reunification of classical form and classical content that Seznec described in the world

---

[10] Quotations from Shakespeare's poetry are taken from William Shakespeare, *The Complete Sonnets and Poems*, Colin Burrow (ed.), (Oxford: Oxford University Press, 2002).

[11] Henry Peacham, *The Garden of Eloquence Conteining the Figures of Grammer and Rhetorick* (London: Richard Field for H. Jackson, 1593) 142.

[12] George Puttenham, *The Art of English Poesy: A Critical Edition*, Frank Whigham and Wayne A. Rebhorn (eds), (Ithaca and London: Cornell University Press, 2007) 288.

of art and iconography, but it was sufficient to prompt Francis Meres in 1598 to regard Shakespeare as a kind of reincarnation of Ovid: 'as the soule of *Euphorbus* was thought to liue in *Pythagoras*: so the sweet wittie soule of Ovid lives in mellifluous & honytongued Shakespeare.'[13]

Lucrece is presumably the 'graver labour' promised in the dedication to *Venus and Adonis*. It takes a historical event, the rape of the chaste Lucretia by Tarquin, which Shakespeare found in Ovid's *Fasti* and in Livy's history of Rome—or more probably in an annotated edition of Ovid which included both texts.[14] It expands this brief tale by using the narrative as a pretext for all but endless eloquence, as Lucrece vainly argues against Tarquin's assault and then complains at length after her violation. This pairing of two poems, one based on a historical story and the other on a mythical tale, may well owe something to the schoolroom, since the classical rhetorician Aphthonius, whose rhetorical exercises or *Progymnasmata* were frequently reprinted and used in schools in the period, divided narrative matter into 'fiction' and 'history', and said his trainee orators should attempt both kinds.[15] The 'gravity' of the 'historical' poem *Lucrece* lies in its darker subject-matter and more complex stanzaic form, but it also draws far more deliberate attention than *Venus and Adonis* does to allusions to classical epic. After her violation, Lucrece sees 'a piece | Of skilful painting' (1366–7) which represents that central event of the early books of Virgil's *Aeneid*: the sack of Troy. In this painting Lucrece seeks out the figure of Hecuba:

> In her the painter had anatomised
> Time's ruin, beauty's wrack, and grim care's reign.
> Her cheeks with chaps and wrinkles were disguised:
> Of what she was no semblance did remain.
> Her blue blood changed to black in every vein,
>   Wanting the spring that those shrunk pipes had fed,
>   Showed life imprisoned in a body dead.
>
> (*Lucrece*, 1450–6)

This allusion to a classical narrative, which is 'framed' as an ecphrasis, or verbal description of a work of art, again is a kind of reassembly of classical forms and classical content in a new relationship. In Book 1 of the *Aeneid* the hero Aeneas sees a representation of the fall of Troy on the new buildings in Dido's Carthage, and weeps (1. 453–63). Lucrece re-enacts this moment of epic sorrow. Her focus on the figure of Hecuba pulls female grief to the centre of the Troy story, but it also creates an air of antiquity and apparent historical distance between the two women. The story of the sack of Troy, like Hecuba, seems to be 'time's ruin', a fragment of antiquity from which the observer is historically

[13] Francis Meres, *Palladis Tamia* (London: P. Short for C. Burbie, 1598) fol. 281v.
[14] Burrow (2002) 48–50.
[15] Aphthonius, *Aphthonii Sophistae Progymnasmata*, Rodolphus Agricola, Giovanni Maria Cattaneo, and Reinhardus Lorichius (eds), (London: Thomas Marsh, 1580) fol. 16v.

detached. The way the allusion to this 'classical' passage is 'framed' as a picture in order to draw attention to an allusion to the *Aeneid* is very different from anything in *Venus and Adonis*. But it does mark a vital stage in the development of Shakespeare's ways of indicating allusions to classical texts, as the next section will show.

6.2 'CLASSICAL' DRAMA?

One of the best things to have happened to the study of Shakespeare over the past twenty years is that the traditional distinction between the poems and the plays has broken down, and critics are willing to think about the two bodies of work as part of the same oeuvre.[16] Classical learning and a range of skills learned at grammar school run through all of Shakespeare's works in all genres. Henry IV's meditation on the sleeplessness of monarchs (*2 Henry IV*, III. i. 4–31), for instance, a speech clearly designed as a set-piece meditation from which *sententiae*, or memorable phrases, could be written down and quoted by its readers and audience, is directly indebted to exercises recommended in early modern grammatical textbooks: Renaissance editions of Aphthonius discuss a variety of different *sententiae* which contrast the sleeplessness of princes with the comfortable dozing of their subjects.[17] Classical texts as well as 'classical' methods of constructing speeches run throughout the plays: the violent threats and rages of *King Lear*, as well as the way in which his actions resonate with the world around them, are more or less unimaginable without the direct and indirect influence of the plays of Seneca, in which violent rhetoric is matched by violent ructions in the fabric of the universe.[18]

Although the poems and plays derive from substantially the same body of classical reading, they are in some obvious ways very different in the way they relate to classical literature. The narrative poems were immediately recognizable as classically derived works by the way in which they were printed. *Venus* has a Latin epigraph, and both poems were printed by Richard Field, who had inherited his press from a printer who enjoyed a monopoly on the publication of texts of Ovid in England. Even if Shakespeare, as Lukas Erne has argued, regarded his play texts as 'poems' to be read,[19] there is an intrinsic difficulty in marking 'classical' passages in a performed drama. This is perhaps best thought of as a problem of virtual footnoting. How does a dramatist say to his audience 'think

---

[16] Colin Burrow, 'Life and Work in Shakespeare's Poems', *Proceedings of the British Academy* 97 (1997) 15–50, Lukas Erne, *Shakespeare as Literary Dramatist* (Cambridge: Cambridge University Press, 2003), Patrick Cheney, *Shakespeare, National Poet-Playwright* (Cambridge: Cambridge University Press, 2004), Patrick Cheney (ed.), *The Cambridge Companion to Shakespeare's Poetry* (Cambridge: Cambridge University Press, 2007).

[17] Aphthonius (1580) fol. 16v.

[18] Gordon Braden, *Renaissance Tragedy and the Senecan Tradition: Anger's Privilege* (New Haven and London: Yale University Press, 1985).

[19] Erne (2003).

about Virgil here', or 'notice this clever adaptation of Ovid'? This problem is exacerbated by writing for audiences in the public stage, which would include both highly literate readers, who knew large sections of Virgil by heart, and barely literate apprentices. And it is one to which Shakespeare provided a variety of different answers at different stages in his career. With surprising frequency (although by no means invariably) he made passages which are directly related to classical sources sound, look, or feel different from the surrounding drama in ways which are analogous to the 'framing' of the Troy story in *Lucrece*. Shakespeare's classicism in the plays could therefore be called 'emic' classicism:[20] that is, classical moments are often audibly or visibly distinguished from the surrounding drama, although the ways of marking those distinctions vary from play to play and change throughout his career. The most clear and comic example is the rude mechanicals' play in *A Midsummer Night's Dream*. This is a play based on the story of Pyramus and Thisbe from Ovid, but the style in which it is written and performed is comically English and quite deliberately lacking in 'poise' or 'balance' or any of the other features of verse which by the late 17th century came to be regarded as distinctive features of classical verse. Pyramus certainly does not sound like a rhetorically skilled grammar-school boy when he believes Thisbe to be dead:

> O dainty duck, O dear!
>   Thy mantle good,
>   What, stained with blood?
> Approach, ye furies fell.
>
>   (V. i. 276–9)

The 'Ovidian' play within Shakespeare's own sophisticated drama is written in a style that seems several decades out of date, and is associated with a social register several strata below that of the courtly characters who witness the performance onstage. The play of Pyramus and Thisbe is consequently not simply a 'classical' drama: its style effectively puts quotation marks around a 'classical drama'. It draws attention to the comic difficulty of adapting Ovid for the modern stage, and also perhaps to the difficulty of extracting simple 'moral' readings from the poem in the way that a schoolmaster might like.[21] The 'tragical mirth' (V. i. 57) of the play has sometimes been seen as poking fun at the idiom of Arthur Golding, whose translation of the *Metamorphoses* appeared in 1567, when Shakespeare was only three-years old, or at earlier 16th-century attempts at classical drama.[22] This may or may not be correct. But the more significant fact about

---

[20] On the distinction between 'emic' and 'etic' approaches to a culture, see Kenneth L. Pike, *Language in Relation to a Unified Theory of the Structure of Human Behavior* (The Hague: Mouton, 1967) 37–72.

[21] Aphthonius (1580) fol. 19r-21v cites Ovid's story as an example of the value of obedience to parents and the avoidance of lust.

[22] On the relationship to Golding, see Madeleine Forey, "'Bless Thee, Bottom, Bless Thee! Thou Art Translated!'": Ovid, Golding, and *A Midsummer Night's Dream*', *Modern Language Review* 93 (1998): 321–9; Taylor (2000).

the mechanicals' play in the larger context of Shakespeare's career is that it marks a direct allusion to a classical narrative by deliberate stylistic clumsiness, and a style which appears, as it were, socially distinct from the surrounding drama and theatrically archaic.

We might set this beside one of the most perplexing 'classical' moments in Shakespeare's plays. When the players arrive at Elsinore, Hamlet tries to remember 'Aeneas's tale to Dido'. He stumbles his way into a speech which the first player has to complete for him. This classically derived speech is Shakespeare's most extended engagement with the subject-matter of Virgil's *Aeneid*. It is presented as a declamation—as a 'speech' for which the performer has to take a deep breath and brace his legs—and it is also in a quite different style from the surrounding drama:

> 'But who, O who had seen the mobbled queen'—
> HAMLET 'The mobbled queen'?
> POLONIUS That's good; 'mobbled queen' is good.
> FIRST PLAYER 'Run barefoot up and down, threat'ning the flames
> With bisson rheum; a clout upon that head
> Where late the diadem stood, and for a robe,
> About her lank and all o'er-teemèd loins,
> A blanket in th'alarm of fear caught up—
> Who had this had seen, with tongue in venom steeped,
> 'Gainst Fortune's state would treason have pronounced.
> But if the gods themselves did see her then,
> When she saw Pyrrhus make malicious sport
> In mincing with his sword her husband's limbs,
> The instant burst of clamour that she made—
> Unless things mortal move them not at all—
> Would have made milch the burning eyes of heaven,
> And passion in the gods.'
> POLONIUS Look whe'er he has not turned his colour, and has tears
> in 's eyes. Prithee, no more.

(Hamlet, II. ii. 504–21)

John Dryden said that this passage showed that Shakespeare could not distinguish 'the blown puffy stile, from true sublimity', and thought the speech was 'written by some other Poet'.[23] He did not like the notion that Hecuba's passion could 'milch' (or milk) the eyes of the gods, and objected that it didn't make sense that these eyes were at once producing milk and burning. The speech contains many words which Shakespeare's audience would not have heard before. Strikingly and surprisingly none of these has classical origins. That strange word 'mobbled', on which Hamlet and Polonius both remark, is

[23] John Dryden, *The Works*, Edward Niles Hooker, H. T. Swedenberg, and Vinton A. Dearing (eds), (Berkeley: University of California Press, 1956–2000) 13.244. See further Eric Griffiths, 'Dryden's Past', *Proceedings of the British Academy* 84 (1993) 113–49.

perhaps a dialect version of 'muffled'. Hecuba's 'bisson rheum' is her blinding tears: 'bisson' derives from an Old English word for short-sightedness. Yet this is a speech based on one of the best-known sections of Virgil's *Aeneid*.

What is going on here is in its way quite as curious as the rude mechanicals' simultaneously Ovidian and clumsy vernacular drama. The way that Shakespeare indicates to his audience that a passage of narrative broadly corresponds to a passage in Virgil is to deploy a vocabulary and poetic style which would strike its audience as just a little beyond their ken. He augments that effect by making the Player's speech into something Hamlet learned long ago and which he has partially forgotten, thereby making it within the context of the play seem like an 'antiquity', something old and almost forgotten. There has been much discussion about the sources and origins of this speech. It may be a pastiche of the play based on the *Aeneid* by Christopher Marlowe and Thomas Nashe, called *Dido Queen of Carthage*.[24] It could be sending up or evoking the style of the earlier Tudor translation of the *Aeneid* by Thomas Phaer and Thomas Twyne, which, like Golding's translation of Ovid, was by the very late 1590s sounding extremely old-fashioned. The speech also again owes something to the schoolroom. The *Progymnasmata* of Aphthonius encouraged students to attempt what was called 'ethopoeia', or a speech evoking character and emotion. One example of such an exercise was to write in a way that would 'show the commotion of the mind, like the words that Hecuba uttered after Troy was overturned'.[25]

The chances are, though, that Shakespeare was not here either trying to evoke a schoolroom exercise from Hamlet's past or to parody earlier English responses to Virgil. He is rather evoking a 'classical' style by writing a speech based on a classical source which *sounds* distinct from the surrounding drama. It is in that respect an extremely knowing and even learned move on the part of the playwright: the speech in its theatrical setting, with its audience of verbally sensitive and slightly pedantic listeners, says 'we know about Virgil, about the perhaps by now slightly rough and ready sounding ways of translating Virgil over the past decades, and we have all written exercises voicing the grief of Hecuba'. Gabriel Harvey described both *Lucrece* and *Hamlet* as 'pleasing the wiser sort'.[26] He probably did so partly because of the way in which both these works contain 'framed' passages which allude to major classical works. These do not simply assimilate classical texts into the surrounding texture of Shakespeare's drama. In a way they 'de-assimilate' them, since they draw the attention of readers and audiences to the presence of those classical texts by marking them as belonging to a different stylistic register from the rest of the play.

---

[24] George L. Geckle, 'The Wind or the Wound: Marlowe's *Dido Queen of Carthage*, II. i, 253–54', *Papers of the Bibliographical Society of America* 71 (1977) 194–9; Margaret Tudeau-Clayton, 'Scenes of Translation in Jonson and Shakespeare: *Poetaster, Hamlet*, and *a Midsummer Night's Dream*', *Translation and Literature* 11 (2002): 1–23.

[25] Aphthonius (1580) 177.

[26] G. C. Moore Smith (ed.), *Gabriel Harvey's Marginalia* (Stratford-upon-Avon: Shakespeare Head Press, 1913) 232.

Dryden would certainly have thought of himself as one of the 'wiser sort', yet he clearly was far from pleased by the speech about Hecuba. This tells us something vital. Shakespeare's highly idiosyncratic methods of marking allusions to classical writers were misunderstood by later generations of learned playwrights and poets. They thought he was just clumsy. This fact helps explain why generations of critics from the second decade of the 17th century onwards described Shakespeare as 'unlearned' or 'native' rather than 'classical' in his style. Shakespeare's ways of marking extended allusions to classical texts in his dramas were unusual, and they rapidly seemed outdated. His contemporary Ben Jonson—who was friends with the classical editors and schoolmasters John Bond and Thomas Farnaby, and a pupil of the antiquarian William Camden—tended to adopt what would have appeared much more 'modern' and 'learned' ways of marking classical allusions. When Jonson included an extended translation from Virgil's *Aeneid* in *Poetaster* (which was composed within a year or so of *Hamlet*), he had Virgil himself come onstage to recite the translation to the Emperor Augustus. He sought to create the illusion of direct quotation, as though the player was speaking with Virgil's own voice. In the printed texts of his masques, Jonson marked classical quotations with elaborate marginalia and citations. These practices distinguished him from the much less overtly citational style of his contemporaries, and in particular they made Shakespeare's tendency at the turn of the 16th century to mark classical allusions by an antiquated or *outré* style seem itself to be antiquated. By the 1620s it would have seemed as though 'native' Shakespeare became clumsy and obtrusively vernacular when he attempted to imitate a classical text, while 'learned' Jonson anticipates the age of both the footnoted allusion and the artful assimilation of a classical voice into the present.

Shakespeare's later plays (which Jonson was particularly keen to present as old-fashioned) treat the 'classical' in rather different ways, but they also tend to tag 'classical' moments by a range of theatrical or stylistic markers. Some of the classically derived passages that are most clearly designed to be noticed in the late plays are set within tableaux or plays within plays, and some are associated with magic. Paulina's highly stage-managed reawakening of the statue of Hermione at the end of *The Winter's Tale* (V. iii) is closely related to the tale of Pygmalion and the statue in Ovid's *Metamorphoses*. It uses magic and a strong dose of theatrical self-consciousness as virtual quotation marks, to create a 'frame' around a passage which derives from and transforms a classical episode.[27] Sometimes less self-conscious forms of stage-business can be used to alert an audience to a classical presence: Prospero dismisses Ariel in *The Tempest*, V. i. 32 and presumably shifts his position on the stage before he invokes 'Ye elves of hills, brooks, standing lakes and groves' (V. i. 33–57) in a speech which is strikingly close to one made by Ovid's Medea.[28] Slight onstage movements can alert an audience to expect a 'speech',

---

[27] Leonard Barkan, '"Living Sculptures": Ovid, Michelangelo, and *the Winter's Tale*', *ELH* 48 (1981): 639–67; A. D. Nuttall, '*The Winter's Tale*: Ovid Transformed', in Taylor (2000) 135–49.

[28] On the relationship, see Raphael Lyne, 'Ovid, Golding, and the 'Rough Magic' of *The Tempest*', in Taylor (2000) 150–64.

and to listen out for the signs of a classical performance to follow. Even in the late plays, however, Shakespeare still can tag a 'classical' voice with a distinctive poetic style or form. Jupiter, king of the classical gods, in Posthumus' dream vision in *Cymbeline* (V. v. 123–216) speaks quatrains laden with compound adjectives, while Posthumus' parents (who are contrasted with the 'modern' Roman, the Italianate Iachimo) in the same dream vision speak in the poetically old-fashioned form of fourteeners. As a result they sound as though they belong to a 'different, more primitive universe'.[29] Rhymed verse can also be used in the later plays to create an aura around classical deities, as when the goddesses in the masque in *The Tempest* speak in trim decasyllabic couplets (IV. i. 60–138). Curiously enough these lines had a massive influence on the young John Milton, who was so keen to claim that Shakespeare 'warbled his native woodnotes wild'. What Milton regarded as 'native woodnotes' was very close to one of Shakespeare's versions of a 'classical' style.

There are few stylistic markers of ancient Roman-ness in the plays explicitly set in Rome. *Julius Caesar* has some features which seem designed to characterize Roman-ness (a crisp preference for sententious remarks, which swells into Asiatic oratorical fullness in the speeches of Mark Antony), and *Antony and Cleopatra* is interwoven with allusions to the story of Dido and Aeneas.[30] But the 'Roman' plays on the whole do not distinguish a 'classical' idiom by creating a distinct poetic style. This is of course exactly what one would expect from what I have termed Shakespeare's 'emic' classicism: in an environment where everyone is imagined to be an ancient Roman there is no need to mark a distinction between those who are and those who are not 'classical'. There is one moment in *Timon of Athens* (which, like the Roman plays, has its origins in Plutarch's *Lives*), however, which does interestingly, but perhaps not very successfully, attempt to create an antiquated 'classical' style. This is at the end of the play, when an epitaph on the misanthropic hero Timon of Athens is discovered by an illiterate soldier. Since he can't read, he takes an impression of the epitaph in wax, and carries it to the Greek general Alcibiades. Alcibiades reads the wax impression aloud. It contains two couplets, one in 'poulter's measure' (a twelve-syllable line followed by a fourteen-syllable line) and one in fourteeners:

> Here lies a wretched corpse, of wretched soul bereft.
> Seek not my name. A plague consume you wicked caitiffs left!
> Here lie I, Timon, who alive all living men did hate.
> Pass by and curse thy fill, but pass and stay not here thy gait.

> (*Timon of Athens*, V. v. 71–8)[31]

---

[29] William Shakespeare, *Cymbeline*, Martin Butler (ed.), (Cambridge: Cambridge University Press, 2005) 216.

[30] See Barbara Bono, *Literary Transvaluation: From Vergilian Epic to Shakespearean Tragicomedy* (Berkeley: University of California Press, 1984).

[31] The Folio text (followed by the Oxford editors) breaks each line of these couplets at the caesura. I have followed the lineation of William Shakespeare, *The Life of Timon of Athens*, John Jowett (ed.), (Oxford: Oxford University Press, 2004).

Oddly enough this very bad piece of versification has some claims to be regarded as the most 'classical' piece of poetry in Shakespeare, since it is a close transcription of Sir Thomas North's translation (via the French of Jacques Amyot) of the Greek historian Plutarch's reproduction of two Greek epitaphs on Timon, which appear in his 'Life of Marcus Antonius'. North's poetic form by around 1606, when Shakespeare probably wrote *Timon of Athens*, was extremely old-fashioned, harking back as it did to the poetic idiom of the Earl of Surrey from the 1530s and 1540s. Despite this, Shakespeare only lightly modifies this piece of 'ancient' verse: he substituted the word 'caitiffs' for 'wretches' in the original (perhaps because with two occurrences of 'wretched' already he recognized the danger of overkill), and he merged together what were two poems in his source. After the first two lines North says, 'It is reported that Timon him selfe when he lived made this epitaph: for that which is commonly rehearsed was not his, but made by the Poet Callimachus',[32] and he goes on to quote the next two lines. Shakespeare reproduces these fragments of 'ancient' poetry almost with veneration, as though they were an authentic classical antiquity to be preserved—despite the fact that the two epitaphs contradict each other, since one of them urges the reader to 'Seek not my name', while the other names Timon directly.

There is, though, a typical self-consciousness about the whole sequence. Shakespeare invents the idea that a soldier carries a wax impression of the lines to his commanding officer perhaps in order to register the way that he is himself directly holding up a quotation of a 'classical' source to his audience. And the apparently illiterate soldier is also mysteriously able to read yet a third epitaph, which is not in Plutarch at all. When he first arrives at the tomb he says 'What is this? | 'Timon is dead, who hath outstretched his span. | Some beast read this; there does not live a man'. The Oxford editors excise this passage from the text, on the grounds that it is a false start and makes no sense given that the soldier cannot read.[33] This epitaph read aloud by a person who cannot read is indeed a curious moment. It may well indicate partially complete revision, or perhaps even Shakespeare's unease with the chiselled finality of the classical epitaph. Several of his contemporaries, including notably Ben Jonson, excelled at imitating this classical tradition. A handful of epitaphs came in the 17th century to be ascribed to Shakespeare (including, most convincingly, the verses carved on the Stanley tombs at Tong in Shropshire), but on the whole these ascriptions are implausible.[34] Epitaphs in his plays often function in ironic and unsettling ways.[35] And yet, as John Kerrigan has shown in Chapter 13, the

---

[32] Plutarch, *Plutarch's Lives of the Noble Grecians and Romans*, ed. George Wyndham (London: D. Nutt, 1895) 6.74.

[33] See the discussion in *Timon of Athens*, Jowett (2004) 317–18.

[34] See Burrow (2002) 146–8, 723–8; *Shakespeare's Poems*, Katherine Duncan-Jones and H. R. Woudhuysen (eds), (London: Arden Shakespeare, 2007) 438–63.

[35] See Joseph Quincy Adams, 'Shakespeare as a Writer of Epitaphs', in John Mathews Manly, *The Manly Anniversary Studies in Language and Literature* (Chicago: University of Chicago Press, 1923) 79–89, and Scott L. Newstok, *Quoting Death in Early Modern England: The Poetics of Epitaphs Beyond the Tomb* (Basingstoke: Palgrave Macmillan, 2009) 161–8.

conventions of epitaph do often weave in and out of Shakespeare's Sonnets. That fact is intimately connected, as the next section will show, with the quizzical and experimental nature of Shakespeare's classicism.

6.3 CLASSICAL SONNETS?

Surprisingly little has been written about classical elements in Shakespeare's Sonnets.[36] This is because in these poems Shakespeare's debts to classical poetry are elusive and diffusive rather than overtly displayed, and partly because, as we have already seen, 'classical' passages tend to be stylistically marked in his writings for the stage more prominently than they are in the poems. Many of the major themes of the sequence have classical origins (time the destroyer, poems as monuments for eternity), but, as with the narrative poems, classical theme and style do not come at once from any single source, but flow into these poems separately from the poetic and the rhetorical tradition. The form of the sonnet—fourteen lines, linked by a variety of rhyming patterns—is of course completely post-classical. Its artful foregrounding of rhyme was indeed associated in Shakespeare's lifetime with an aspiration to break free from the example of classical unrhymed verse. The sonneteer Samuel Daniel in his *Defence of Rhyme* (1603) condemned those who sought to bring classical metres to English verse: 'we should not so soone yeeld our consents captiue to the authoritie of Antiquitie'. He found a kind of native liberty in the sonnet form: 'wee are no longer the slaues of Rymes, but we make it [rhyme] a most excellent instrument to serue vs. Nor is this certaine limit obserued in Sonnets, any tyrannicall bounding of the forme, neither too long for the shortest proiect, nor too short for the longest, being but onely imployed for a present passion'.[37] Rhyming verse, Daniel argued, was a legacy from the Goths who liberated Europe from enslavement to Rome: it freed later European writers from classical tyranny.[38] As Daniel would have known well, the history of the sonnet form was in fact closely tied up in the complex arguments and interrelationships between vernacular and classical learning which ran back to the 14th century. After its first emergence in 13th-century Sicily, the sonnet was brought to prominence by Dante and Petrarch. They were simultaneously committed imitators of classical writing and eloquent defenders of the power of the vernacular.

---

[36] J. B. Leishman, *Themes and Variations in Shakespeare's Sonnets* (London: Hutchinson, 1961) remains valuable. See also Gordon Braden, 'Ovid, Petrarch, and Shakespeare's *Sonnets*', in Taylor (2000) 96–112, and A. D. Cousins, *Shakespeare's Sonnets and Narrative Poems* (Harlow: Longman, 2000) 121–46 for the presence of Narcissus and Adonis in the sequence. On Latinity generally, see Bradin Cormack, 'Tender Distance: Latinity and Desire in Shakespeare's Sonnets', in Michael Schoenfeldt, *A Companion to Shakespeare's Sonnets* (Oxford: Blackwell, 2007) 242–60.

[37] Samuel Daniel, *Poems and a Defence of Rhyme*, Arthur Colby Sprague (ed.), (Chicago and London: Chicago University Press, 1965) 138.

[38] See further Helgerson (1992) ch.1.

The sonnet in the form we now call 'Shakespearean', consisting of three quatrains rhyming *abab* and a final couplet, began to be deployed in England in the second and third decades of the 16th century by the imitators of Petrarch, Sir Thomas Wyatt, and the Earl of Surrey, both of whom also wrote poems derived in one way or another from Virgil. Its history therefore made the sonnet a culturally aspirational form, suitable for writers who wanted to ground themselves in classical example but who also wished to insist on the strength and vitality of the vernacular.

The kinds of classicism on display in Shakespeare's Sonnets are in many respects very similar to those in the narrative poems. The rhythms, thoughts, and topoi of classical verse repeatedly swirl through them. Individual poems are bound together by rhetorical structures, compounded by the vernacular artifice of rhyme. An individual quatrain can be united by structured repetitions, or an entire sonnet can be integrated by the sudden return in the couplet of a word or a thought that had been casually offered earlier in the poem, and which is given a new turn. Rhyme and rhetoric are therefore particularly richly interconnected in the form of the Shakespearean sonnet. And yet individual poems rarely seem to be 'sourced' in the conventional sense—where a book is on the desk or directly in the mind of the author—in classical poetry. The most overtly classical poem in the sequence is Sonnet 60. This owes a great deal to the end of Ovid's *Metamorphoses*, in which his great ironical epic of change winds itself up to consider the process of life and transformation as akin to the movement of the sea:

> Like as the waves make towards the pebbled shore,
> So do our minutes hasten to their end,
> Each changing place with that which goes before,
> In sequent toil all forwards do contend.
> Nativity, once in the main of light,
> Crawls to maturity, wherewith being crowned
> Crookèd eclipses 'gainst his glory fight,
> And Time that gave doth now his gift confound.
> Time doth transfix the flourish set on youth,
> And delves the parallels in beauty's brow,
> Feeds on the rarities of nature's truth,
> And nothing stands but for his scythe to mow.
>   And yet to times in hope my verse shall stand,
>   Praising thy worth, despite his cruel hand.

Part of the force of this poem, and part of what it is trying to do with Ovid, is a consequence of the compression of the sonnet form. Ovid's poem expounds in hexameter verse the movement of the sea:

> The time itself continually is fleeting like a brook,
> For neither brook nor lightsome time can tarry still. But look
> As every wave drives other forth, and that that comes behind
> Both thrusteth and is thrust itself; even so the times by kind

>Do fly and follow both at once and evermore renew.
>For that that was before is left, and straight there doth ensue
>Another that was never erst. Each twinkling of an eye
>Doth change.

(15. 199–206)[39]

Sonnet 60 edits onto this passage from the discourse of Pythagoras in the final book of Ovid's *Metamorphosis* Ovid's final vision of his qualified triumph over time, in which the poet imagines himself creating a poetic corpus that can spread as wide and live as long as the Roman Empire (with a dark suggestion that this might not last for ever):

>and all the world shall never
>Be able for too quench my name. For look how far so ever
>The Roman empire by the right of conquest shall extend,
>So far shall all folk read this work. And time without all end
>(If poets as by prophecy about the truth may ame)
>My life shall everlastingly be lengthened still by fame.

(15. 990–5)

Shakespeare's poem seems to crush Ovid's extended argument into fourteen lines in a way that is almost aggressive. It is a kind of triumph over the classical, where the metaphorical and rhetorical energy of Shakespeare, 'changing place with that which goes before', transforming and renewing the earlier work, supplants the classical poem to which he looks back, just as the young man may provide a kind of biological permanence which goes beyond the time-bound political control offered at the end of Ovid's poem. As Anne Prescott has shown in Chapter 8, one subject explored in both du Bellay's *Antiquitez de Rome* and in Spenser's sonnets on *The Ruines of Rome* was the destruction of the Roman Empire, whose impermanence Ovid ironically anticipates. The sonnet form owes its being to the collapse of Rome, and to the sequent cultural changes which follow that great event.

Shakespeare's is not a simply confident performance, however: the partial separation of the couplet in Sonnet 60 from the argument that has gone before (it seems less a sequent wave than a sudden turn in the tide) leaves it seeming almost beached, looking forward to 'times in hope'—a phrase which no-one else in the period seems to have used, but which suggests a wistful and anxious futurity—in which the poem will make the young man live. But Sonnet 60 also incorporates something like an epitaph into the sonnet form in a way that is characteristic of Shakespeare's unease with the point and finality of that particular classical poetic form. Can a rhyme really confound time? Can a poem in a vernacular tongue really hope to outlive Ovid, and outstretch in time and space the reach of the Roman Empire? One (negative) answer to this question comes from the

---

[39] Quotations from *Ovid's Metamorphoses Translated by Arthur Golding*, Madeleine Forey (ed.), (London: Penguin, 2002).

word 'rhyme' itself. Every single time the word 'rhyme' appears in a rhyming position in Shakespeare's *Sonnets*, that marker of a style of poetry distinct from the unrhymed verse of the classical tradition is rhymed with the word 'time'. Every time the poet writes 'rhyme' the reader expects, knows, that even the most 'powerful rhyme' will encounter 'Time' with his sickle or his 'antic pen', and that it will be forced to do so by its own sonic logic. This means that in a way Shakespeare's Sonnets are his greatest attempt to create a native rhyming version of the classical epitaph, and to grasp those great Horatian and Ovidian themes of the relationship between poetry, civilization, and permanence. But at every point that grand project is quizzically undercut:

> Or I shall live your epitaph to make,
> Or you survive when I in earth am rotten,
> From hence your memory death cannot take,
> Although in me each part will be forgotten.

(Sonnet 81. 1–4)

The movement here is profoundly restless: either the poet will outlive the addressee he seeks to immortalize, or else he will die first; either way 'From hence your memory death cannot take'. But where exactly *is* 'from hence'? The poem? The poet's mind? And it is each part 'in me' rather than 'of me' which is forgotten, almost as though the poet is imagining death as a kind of total amnesia of the young man, whose memory is lost in every single part of his body. The celebration of a young man who is never named, who may live on through biological reproduction, or whom time may transfix with his truant pen, is Shakespeare's most unsettling attempt to write an epitaph which is not quite an epitaph. In *Timon of Athens* he combined three different and incompatible epitaphs for the hero, two of which more or less quote a 'classical' source exactly. In the Sonnets a parallel attempt to reimagine a post-classical form of epitaph generates a great surging energy, in which poem after poem considers and reconsiders the nature of immortality, of poetic permanence, of monuments, and of living energies, and yet no one poem seems itself sufficient to stand alone as a definitive statement in which rhyme conquers its rhyme-word Time. Sometimes the young man seems to be remade as an antiquity from the classical past ('Describe Adonis, and the counterfeit | Is poorly imitated after you. | On Helen's cheek all art of beauty set, | And you in Grecian tires are painted new'. Sonnet 53. 5–8). At other moments he seems to be grass, flesh for Time's sickle to mow, as particularly in the ten-line truncated 'sonnet' 126, which seems to end the group of poems to the young man. The poems that comprise the Sonnets are not in any simple sense classical poems, but their endlessly copious iterations of a desire to retrieve and prolong the life of a mortal being are Shakespeare's deepest meditations on the classical tradition. Can a *rhymer* enjoy a permanent influence in the way that Horace, Ovid, and Virgil did in their august unrhymed metre? Can a post-classical writer revivify classical works? These questions were partly so vital for Shakespeare because in his lifetime the word 'classical' was only just coming to have the sense 'Of or relating to the ancient Greek or Latin writers whose works form a canon of acknowledged excellence' (*OED* 1).

As a result he did not have a simple word for describing the coincidence of antiquity and value which it is now so easy to unite in the word 'classic'. Instead he had words of dubious sense in which to celebrate his own future fame:

> If I could write the beauty of your eyes,
> And in fresh numbers number all your graces,
> The age to come would say 'This poet lies:
> Such heavenly touches ne'er touched earthly faces.'
> So should my papers (yellowed with their age)
> Be scorned, like old men of less truth than tongue,
> And your true rights be termed a poet's rage,
> And stretchèd metre of an antique song.
>   But were some child of yours alive that time,
>   You should live twice, in it, and in my rhyme.

(Sonnet 17. 5–14)

His own papers are imagined as yellow with age. They are not 'classics', but are 'old' like a garrulous old man, or 'antique'—a word which might suggest the deliberate archaisms of the poet Spenser, the medieval vocabulary of Chaucer, the madness of an 'antic' or lunatic, or the archaic style in which Shakespeare had himself sometimes marked allusions to poems from classical antiquity. The biological reproduction of the young man is consequently a far less slippery thing than the aspiration of a poem to live on into the future and to become 'antique': old, perhaps venerated, or perhaps (like the old king Lear) even mad. It is easy for us to see Shakespeare's relation to the classics as triumphant. He is now read and remembered throughout the world, and is a classic of our age as Ovid was of Shakespeare's. But he would not have known that. Indeed he did not even quite have the vocabulary to be able to imagine an English vernacular poet enjoying that degree of celebrity. Much of the excitement and drama of Shakespeare's poetry derives from his repeated and restless efforts to address the problem of how to become a 'classic' in a language and a poetic idiom which is profoundly unclassical.

SELECT BIBLIOGRAPHY

Baldwin, T. W. (1944) *William Shakespere's Small Latine and Lesse Greeke* (Urbana, IL: University of Illinois Press).

Barkan, Leonard (1981) '"Living Sculptures": Ovid, Michelangelo, and *the Winter's Tale*', *ELH*, 48: 639–67.

Bate, Jonathan (1993) *Shakespeare and Ovid* (Oxford: Clarendon Press).

Braden, Gordon (1985) *Renaissance Tragedy and the Senecan Tradition: Anger's Privilege* (New Haven and London: Yale University Press).

Burrow, C. (2002) (ed.) *The Complete Sonnets and Poems* (Oxford: Oxford University Press).

Enterline, Lynn (2012) *Shakespeare's Schoolroom: Rhetoric, Discipline, Emotion* (Philadelphia, PA: University of Pennsylvania Press).

James, Heather (1997) *Shakespeare's Troy* (Cambridge: Cambridge University Press).

Martindale, Charles and Martindale, Michelle (1990) *Shakespeare and the Uses of Antiquity: An Introductory Essay* (London and New York: Routledge).

——and Taylor, A. B. (2004) *Shakespeare and the Classics* (Cambridge: Cambridge University Press).

Miola, Robert S. (2000) *Shakespeare's Reading* (Oxford: Oxford University Press)

Taylor, A. B. (2000) *Shakespeare's Ovid: The Metamorphoses in the Plays and Poems* (Cambridge: Cambridge University Press).

CHAPTER 7

··

SHAKESPEARE AND
ITALIAN POETRY

··

ANTHONY MORTIMER

If not much attention has been paid to the relevance of Italian models to Shakespeare's poetry, the reason is perfectly obvious: there is no firm evidence that Shakespeare knew enough Italian to read those models in the original. As for translations, he probably knew the Wyatt versions of Petrarch that were being republished in *Tottel's Miscellany* well into the 1580s, and during his career he may well have read the epics of Ariosto and Tasso in translations by Harington and Fairfax, although they leave little or no trace in his work. What is certain, however, is that he would have been acutely aware of the prestige of Italian as the first modern vernacular to possess a literature with something like classical status. He would also have known that both major genres of his own poetic production, the Ovidian verse narrative and the sonnet sequence, had deep Italian roots. The purpose of this chapter is not to argue for a Shakespeare who is constantly or consciously engaged with Italian predecessors, but rather to examine the ways in which a knowledge of Italian poetry can shed light on how Shakespeare handles the genres he inherits. And it is a two-way process, for our understanding of the Italian texts benefits, in its turn, from a sharper awareness of those generic potentialities that Shakespeare exploits and reveals.

Fifty years ago, in the introduction to his Arden edition of Shakespeare's narrative poems, F. T. Prince acknowledged that 'the tradition of this witty and sensuous retelling of mythological stories went back through Italian literature to Ovid',[1] but neither he nor subsequent editors have found the Italian mediation worthy of much attention. This is regrettable because *Venus and Adonis* is by far the most Italianate thing that Shakespeare ever wrote and its resemblance to Italian models goes far beyond a common debt to Ovid. The Italian fashion for Ovidian adaptations had started in the

---

[1] *Shakespeare: The Poems*, F. T. Prince (London: Methuen, 1960) xxx.

early 15th century with Niccolò degli Agostini (*Tutti i libri di Ovidio Metamorphoseos*, 1522) and reached a wide audience with the influential *Metamorfosi d'Ovidio* (1561) of Giovanni Andrea dell'Anguillara where the Adonis story is enriched and expanded by a variety of non-Ovidian elements.[2] For our purposes, however, the major figure is the prolific humanist Lodovico Dolce who in 1539 began to translate the *Metamorphoses* into unrhymed verse but was eventually converted to stanzaic form. Even before his complete version, *Le trasformationi*, appeared in 1553, he had made the crucial move to the short Ovidian narrative and singled out the Adonis myth for special treatment in his *Stanze nella favola d'Adone* (1545). This *favola* or *idillio* (the usual Italian terms for what we have come to call the epyllion) set off a fashion for Adonis poems that lasted eighty years and culminated in the vast sprawling *Adone* (1623) of Giambattista Marino. Taken together with the Dolce version, the Adonis poems of Giovanni Tarcagnota (1550) and Girolamo Parabosco (1553) share most of their basic features with Shakespeare's poem. The original concise story, a mere seventy-six lines in Ovid (*Met.* X. 519–59, 705–39) is expanded into anything between fifty and eighty stanzas of ottava rima and is clearly divided into two almost autonomous sections, the first an erotic idyll in a faintly sinister *locus amoenus* and the second a female complaint owing more to the *Heroides* than to the *Metamorphoses*. The lovemaking tends to be both comic and erotic, and Parabosco especially makes much of the contrast between an aggressive Venus who is experienced in the arts of love and an initially timid and ignorant Adonis. Shakespeare's crucial innovation is to take this contrast a stage further and create an Adonis who simply refuses the advances of the goddess. As a result, the sexual consummation of the Italian versions is replaced by episodes of shared physical indignity ('She sinketh down, still hanging by his neck. | He on her belly falls, she on her back' 593–4)[3] which punctuate a debate where both protagonists demonstrate an extraordinary rhetorical self-consciousness. Venus' metaphorical exuberance and confidence in her own persuasive powers ('Bid me discourse, I will enchant thine ear', 145) is played off against Adonis' aphoristic moralizing and recognition of his own limitations ('The text is old, the orator too green', 806). The juxtaposition of rhetorical virtuosity with crude physical gesture is in itself an implied criticism of the Petrarchan ethos. Heather Dubrow is right to say of Shakespeare's narrative poems that 'the decision to write an epyllion is in important ways a decision not to write a Petrarchan love poem',[4] but it is worth remembering that, to use her own terms, the Italian tradition provides both the discourse and the counter-discourse.

One comes back to Petrarch simply because the 16th century considered him the pre-eminent vernacular poet. In the year when *Venus and Adonis* was published (1593)

---

[2] Versions of the Adonis story by Dolce, Tarcagnota, Parabosco, and Dell'Aguillara are to be found in Andrea Torre(ed.) *Variazioni su Adone I, favole, lettere, idilli* (Lucca: Maria Pacini Fazzi, 2009). The relation between Shakespeare's poem and the Italian Adonis texts is discussed at length in Anthony Mortimer, *Variable Passions: A Reading of 'Venus and Adonis'* (New York: AMS Press, 2000) 171–96.

[3] All Shakespeare citations are to Wells and Taylor (Oxford: Clarendon Press, 2005).

[4] Heather Dubrow, *Echoes of Desire: English Petrarchism and its Counter-Discourses* (Ithaca and London: Cornell University Press, 1995) 7.

Gabriel Harvey hailed Petrarch as 'the harmony of heaven, the life of poetry, the grace of art', and ten years later Samuel Daniel could still claim that 'all the wits of posterity have not yet much over-matched him in all kinds to this day'.[5] No other Italian poet is mentioned so often or in such glowing terms in English critical discourse of the period. Part of his popularity, no doubt, resulted from his limitations. The restricted vocabulary, the narrow subject matter, the fact that he works best in short forms; all these factors made Petrarch eminently readable and imitable. That he should be the only Italian poet named by Shakespeare and that this should occur in *Romeo and Juliet* is hardly surprising. Mercutio, mocking Romeo's infatuation with Rosaline, comments: 'Now is he for the numbers that Petrarch flowed in. Laura to his lady was a kitchen wench—marry, she had a better love to berhyme her' (2.3.36–8). The tone is typical of the period's attitude to a model that was already becoming over-familiar. If, on the one hand, it recalls Sidney's gibe at those who sing 'poor Petrarch's long-deceasèd woes' (*Astrophil and Stella*, 15), on the other it recognizes that the original has a prestige that cannot be diminished by inferior imitations. The use of Petrarchism in the early part of the play confirms this ambivalence. Romeo's first speech is an anthology of the antitheses, paradoxes, and oxymora that Shakespeare and his contemporaries could have learned from those two hoary and much-translated old favourites, *S'amor non è* ('If it is not love', RVF 132) and *Pace non trovo* (Peace I do not find, 134):[6]

> Why then, O brawling love, O loving hate,
> O anything of nothing first create;
> O heavy lightness, serious vanity,
> Misshapen chaos of well-seeming forms,
> Feather of lead, bright smoke, cold fire, sick health,
> Still-waking sleep, that is not what it is!
> This love feel I, that feel no love in this.
>
> (I. i. 173–9)

One can hardly read this as anything but a piece of deliberately debased Petrarchism, underlining the shallowness of a self-induced passion. Its parodic aspect becomes even clearer when we contrast it with the freshness of the deft two-voiced sonnet 'If I profane with my unworthiest hand' (I. v. 92–105) that marks the first meeting of Romeo and Juliet. Here Shakespeare blends the standard Petrarchan celebration of the hand with the pilgrim motif that so often signals the complex correspondences between sacred and

[5] Gabriel Harvey, *Pierce's Supererogation* (1593) in G. Gregory Smith (ed.), *Elizabethan Critical Essays* II (Oxford: Clarendon Press, 1904) 260; Samuel Daniel, *A Defence of Ryme* (1603) in Smith (1904) 368.

[6] All citations and translations from Petrarch's *Canzoniere* are indicated according to Italian practice by RVF (*Rerum vulgarium fragmenta*) and are to *Petrarch's Lyric Poems, the 'Rime sparse' and Other Lyrics*, Robert Durling (trans. and ed.), (Cambridge, MA: Harvard University Press, 1976). Durling's volume also includes Dante's *Rime Petrose*. For selected English translations of RVF 132 and 134 see Anthony Mortimer (ed.), *Petrarch's Canzoniere in the English Renaissance* (Amsterdam and New York: Rodopi, 2005) 75–82.

profane love. For all the bustle of the feast, we are reminded that here, as in Dante and Petrarch, the birth of love is a solemn occasion. In a perceptive analysis of the scene, Ronald Martinez links Romeo via Surrey with Chaucer's Troilus and thus with the earliest translation of a Petrarch poem into English,[7] but he also stresses the modifications that Petrarchism undergoes when it passes from a lyric to a dramatic situation. For one thing this sonnet is a dialogue in which the woman has a voice, and for another it marks the initial physical contact that foreshadows a consummated marriage. Both the continuities and the discontinuities support his argument that *Romeo and Juliet* can be read as 'a site of Shakespeare's confrontation with Petrarch and Petrarchism'.[8]

It has long been accepted that if we want to see how the Sonnets relates significantly to the Italian lyric tradition, we need to look beyond the stylistic surface of individual poems to the idea of the poetic sequence as such—its process of composition, its underlying structural principles, its varying relations to the confessional mode, as they emerge in the *Canzoniere*. What has been less often noted is that the same approach needs to be applied to the *Canzoniere* itself in its relation to Dante's *Vita Nuova*. Michael Spiller claims that the *Vita Nuova* was not particularly influential in the history of the sonnet and that 'Petrarch seems not to have paid it any special attention',[9] but Petrarch's attitude to Dante was notoriously tense and his silences are eloquent. Recent Italian criticism has argued that the *Canzoniere* engages seriously with the earlier text as a model that it attempts to emulate and supplant. The *Vita Nuova*, strictly speaking, should be described not as a poetic sequence, but as a *prosimetrum*, a mixture of prose and verse. The most celebrated precedent is Boethius' *Consolation of Philosophy* which, like Dante's text, also blends strong autobiographical elements with visions of personified abstractions. The *Vita Nuova* is, however, very much *sui generis* and involves three distinct components: a selection of poems about Beatrice that Dante composed between 1283 and 1292; a prose narrative dating from 1293–95 explaining and linking the occasions of these poems; and structural analyses or 'divisions' of the poems. Whereas in Boethius the poems are merely illustrative of themes presented in the prose, here they constitute the primary material of Dante's 'book of memory' whose overall purpose is not to present an autobiographical narrative embellished by verse, but to show the true nature and genesis of a certain kind of poetry. In other words, the *Vita Nuova* involves the definition and demonstration of a new poetics.

The essence of the poetic sequence—what distinguishes it from the long poem or from the collection of miscellaneous lyrics—is the double perspective that it forces upon the reader who experiences each single poem both as a self-sufficient unit and as part of a larger developing whole. In the *Vita Nuova* this is underlined by the prose that frames poems that were written years earlier: the reader is constantly reminded of the difference

---

[7] 'If no love is, O God, what fele I so?', *Troylus and Criseyde*, I. 400–20.

[8] Ronald L. Martinez, 'Francis, Thou Art Translated: Petrarch Metamorphosed in English', *Humanist Studies and the Digital Age*, 1.1 (2011): 96, <http://journals.oregondigital.org/hsda>.

[9] Michael R. G. Spiller, *The Development of the Sonnet* (London: Routledge, 1992) 39.

between what an event seemed to mean at the time of its occurrence and what it now means to the retrospective understanding of the prose narrator whose hindsight we are privileged to share. Thus, for example, after the first dream poem, *A ciascun' alma presa e gentil core* ('To every captive soul and gentle heart', III), we are told that none of its original poet-readers understood it 'though now its meaning is clear to the simplest'.[10] Dante presumably includes himself in the initial failure of understanding, since the true meaning is only available in the light of what the prose tells us about the subsequent death of Beatrice and her assumption into glory. The tensions involved in the double perspective are compounded by the way Dante draws attention to the unreliability of short-term memory. Poems that purport to be written almost immediately after the events they recount abound in terms like *pareva, pareami* ('it seemed', 'it seemed to me'). The gap between the speaker of the poems and the prose narrator will be closed only in the final sonnet with its vision of Beatrice in Heaven.

The *Vita Nuova* is an account of how Dante learned to understand the true nature of his own early work, but we must recognize that we are not reading those early poems exactly as they were first written, for they have been subjected to an elaborate process of ordering, selection, and revision. The symmetrical disposition of the book's three canzoni and twenty-eight shorter poems (10|+|canzone|+|4|+|canzone|+|4|+ |canzone|+|10) is intrinsically unlikely to reflect the chronological order of composition, and, in any case, we know that not all the poems written for or about Beatrice are included in the volume. It is possible that something like the prophetic canzone *Donna pietosa* ('A lady moved by pity', XXIII) was actually written before the death of Beatrice, but if so, the details leave little doubt that it was radically revised after the event. The poems of the *Vita Nuova* are at least partly ordered according to a fictional chronology.

The significance of all this for the future of the sonnet sequence can hardly be over-estimated. Already we have a text where narrative and lyric elements are played off against each other and where poems written over a number of years are re-ordered and revised within a retrospectively imposed frame. But this frame is, as we shall see, deceptive. The two-part structure that we are tempted to find in the *Vita Nuova*, the *Canzoniere*, and Shakespeare's Sonnets is not what it appears at first sight, and closure tends to be illusory. Even the sense of finality conveyed by the final sonnet of the *Vita Nuova*, with its vision of Beatrice in glory, *Oltre la spera che più larga gira* ('Beyond the circling of the widest sphere', XLI), is undermined by the prose passage that follows where Dante resolves 'to write no more about this blessed lady' until he can 'do so in a more worthy manner' and 'write of her what has never been written of any woman' (XLII). It used to be conventional to see this as an anticipation of the *Divine Comedy*, but it also conveys a sense of incompletion that will become typical of the great son-

---

[10] Citations from the *Vita Nuova* are to *Dante Alighieri: Vita Nuova*, tr. Anthony Mortimer (Richmond: Oneworld Classics, 2011). Chapters are indicated by Latin numerals in parenthesis.

net sequences which, precisely because they purport to be autobiographical, are nearly always work in progress.

One cannot, of course, speak of a connection between autobiography and the sonnet sequence without conjuring up the monumental amount of energy wasted on trying to discover the historical identity of the Fair Youth and the Dark Lady in Shakespeare's Sonnets. But the problem has, in fact, been around since the very beginnings of the genre. As early as 1336, when the *Canzoniere* had hardly begun to take shape, we find Petrarch replying to a letter from Giacomo Colonna that had apparently cast doubt on the real existence of Laura:

> But what are you saying? That I have invented the lovely name of Laura so that I could speak of her and that through her many might speak of me; but that in fact there is no Laura in my heart unless it be the laurel of the poets to which I obviously aspire with long and unstinting study, and that of this living Laura whom I feign to love, all is artifice, feigned my verses and simulated my sighs. In this alone I could wish your joking were true and that it really were simulation and not madness.[11]

Both the accusation and the indignant rebuttal were to become fairly conventional aspects of Petrarchism, but it is worth noting that, in the most popular 16th-century edition of the *Canzoniere*, Alessandro Vellutello (1525) goes to extraordinary lengths to fill in what seem to be gaps in the narrative, seeking the *picciol borgo* ('small village', *RVF* 4) that Petrarch mentions as Laura's birthplace, poring over parish records until he finds a Laura baptized at the right time, and providing a guide-map for readers who might want to follow the Petrarch heritage trail.[12] Moreover, he anticipates the treatment that would later be dished out to Shakespeare's Sonnets by tampering with the established order of the sequence in order to make it tell a more coherent love-story. Thomas Roche may be right to argue that Vellutello's approach combined with the linguistic concerns of his contemporary Bembo 'to kill off the the old scholarship of allegorical reading' and diminish our awareness of the 'moral implications of the love described in the *Canzoniere*',[13] but that does not mean that autobiography and allegory must be mutually exclusive. In the *Vita Nuova* Dante tells us that Beatrice's extraordinary association with the number nine proves that 'she was herself a nine—that is, a miracle whose root is none other than the wondrous Trinity', but he goes on to insist that he is 'speaking of an analogy' (*similitudine* XXIX), and the term is crucial because it warns us that Beatrice is not allegorical in the same way as the figure of Love who appears in his dreams or as Spenser's Red Cross Knight and Bunyan's Christian, who exist only in function of the abstractions they represent. When, in his letter to Cangrande della Scala, Dante

---

[11] *Familiarum rerum libri* 2.9. in *Francesco Petrarca: Prose*, G. Martellotti, P. G. Ricci, E. Carrara, and E. Bianchi (eds), (Milan and Naples: Ricciardi, 1955) 824. My translation.

[12] *Le volgari opere del Petrarcha con la espositione di Alessandro Vellutello* (Venice: Giovanniantonio & Fratelli di Sabbio, 1525).

[13] Thomas P. Roche, *Petrarch and the English Sonnet Sequences* (New York: AMS Press, 1989) 74.

outlines the various levels of scriptural interpretation, he begins with the literal, with the assumption that the events of the Old Testament are not allegorical fictions, but attested historical events that demand an allegorical reading. Whatever its real degree of fictionality, there can be no doubt that we are expected to read the *Vita Nuova* in the same way.

That the genre arises from an autobiographical impulse is confirmed by what we know about the genesis of the *Canzoniere*. It was in the decade 1340–50 that a series of personal bereavements and disappointments culminating in the death of Laura (1348) led Petrarch to take stock of his life so far in a large autobiographical project that included the revision, re-ordering, and amplification of his letters (the *Familiares*) and the application of a similar operation to the vernacular poems. The most immediate product of this period is the *Secretum*, an imaginary Latin dialogue between the poet 'Franciscus' and St Augustine. Augustine condemns the poet's love both for Laura and for the poetic laurel, while Franciscus argues in favour of the nobility of love as a means towards sanctification. There is no solution, but Franciscus concludes by promising 'I will be as present to myself as I can and I will gather together the scattered fragments of my soul.'[14] The image echoes not only Augustine's own declaration of intention in the *Confessions* ('recollecting myself out of that broken condition of mine, wherein I was piecemeal shattered asunder')[15] but also the Latin title that Petrarch chose for the vernacular poetic sequence that we now call the *Canzoniere—Rerum Vulgarium Fragmenta* ('Fragments in the vulgar tongue').

The *Canzoniere*, therefore, takes shape under the influence of two conflicting autobiographical models, the *Vita Nuova* and the *Confessions* of St Augustine. This is not an argument in favour of reading the great sonnet sequences as strictly autobiographical narratives, nor need we assume that the original audiences did so. But the fact remains that the genre, even as it progressively abandons any firm narrative dynamic, continues to play with the expectation of autobiographical revelation. *Astrophil and Stella* can hardly be taken as a factual account of the relations between Sir Philip Sidney and Lady Penelope Devereux, later wife to Robert, third Baron Rich; but when the speaker of the poems is called Astrophil and tells us that Stella 'hath no misfortune, but that Rich she is' (*Astrophil and Stella*, 27), then surely we are being provoked into speculation about what events lie behind the poetic fiction. In the same way whoever composed the puzzling dedication to Shakespeare's Sonnets was surely counting on the reader's curiosity about the identity of Mr. W. H.—a curiosity both stimulated and frustrated by a text that vows 'Your name from hence immortal life shall have' (81) and then abstains from yielding that name. And even if we settle for a fictional beloved, we are still provoked into narrative. The *Canzoniere* lacks the prose frame of the *Vita Nuova*, but there is enough allusion to presumed events to make the reconstruction of a rudimentary narrative seem possible. It is, perhaps, too simple to say that we should not try to transform

---

[14] Secretum III in *Francesco Petrarca, Prose*, 214
[15] *St Augustine's Confessions*, William Watts (trans.) (Cambridge, MA: Loeb-Harvard-Heinemann, 1968) I, 64.

sonnet sequences into narratives. In Petrarch's *Canzoniere*, Sidney's *Astrophil and Stella*, Spenser's *Amoretti,* and Shakespeare's Sonnets, what matters is that we should try ... and fail. The frustration of narrative is an essential part of our experience of the genre.

The *Vita Nuova* faces a problem that had occupied Italian lyric poetry from its very beginnings in the Sicilian school—how to reconcile the love of God which belongs to the spirit with the love of a woman which, however chaste or ennobling it may seem, is still rooted in the flesh. Giacomo da Lentini (the presumed inventor of the sonnet form) fears that he will find no pleasure in Heaven if his lady is not there; Guido Guinizzelli in a poem that is usually considered as a manifesto for the *dolce stil novo* ('sweet new style') claims that *Al cor gentil rempaira sempre amore* ('Love always comes to the noble heart') but concludes with a half-apology to God for placing the two loves on the same level: *Tenne d'angel sembianza | che fosse del Tuo regno ; | non mi fu fallo, s'in lei posi amanza* ('She seemed an angel from your kingdom; I was not at fault if I loved her'). Dante's solution was to allegorize this angelic woman into a vehicle of divine grace in a process that involves a conversion both of the self and of the poetry. At a first reading it would be easy to think of the *Vita Nuova* in terms of a before and an after, with the death of Beatrice as the pivotal episode. But once we recognize that Dante is, in fact, announcing a new poetics, it becomes clear that if anything divides the book into two parts, it is not the death of Beatrice but the poet's discovery, in the great canzone, *Donne ch'avete intelligenza d'amore* ('Ladies that have intelligence of love'), that his subject-matter lies not in anguished introspection after the manner of his early master Cavalcanti, but in the praise of Beatrice where he finds all his beatitude. There is plenty of evidence, especially in the second part of the *Canzoniere*, that Petrarch attempted a similar shift. In a number of dream sonnets, for example, Laura is seen being received into Heaven, reaching down to comfort the poet, assuring him of his ultimate salvation. And yet the resemblance remains superficial, and Laura as *donna angelicata* lacks the theological resonance that Dante confers on his beloved.

Laura in heaven embodies the same essentially aesthetic vision as Laura on earth. It should be remembered that, though the division of the *Canzoniere* into two parts is clearly marked in the Vatican MS 3195 prepared under the supervision of Petrarch himself, the titles *In Vita* and *In Morte* were added by a later hand. In fact, the formal division occurs not with the poem that announces the death of Laura but with the long self-lacerating canzone *I' vo pensando* ('I go thinking', RVF 264), in which Petrarch atttempts to renounce his two great passions, love of fame and love of Laura. As with the *Vita Nuova*, the loss of the beloved is ultimately less important than the thematic change of direction. But although Petrarch's intention is to signal a conversion, a turning away from profane love, this is not what actually happens. The oscillation between *Vita Nuova* and *Confessions* continues almost to the end of the sequence and helps to create its characteristic blend of instability and paralysis.

The absence of an accompanying prose commentary means that in the *Canzoniere* the double perspective has to be embodied in the poems themselves. In this context, the opening sonnet may be seen as giving precise instructions as to how to read the sequence:

> Voi ch'ascoltate in rime sparse il suono
> di quei sospiri ond'io nudriva 'l core
> in sul mio primo giovenile errore,
> quand'era in parte altr'uom da quel ch' i' sono:
>
> del vario stile in ch' io piango et ragiono
> fra le vane speranze e 'l van dolore,
> ove sia chi per prova intenda amore
> spero trovar pietà, non che perdono.
>
> Ma ben veggio or sì come al popol tutto
> favola fui gran tempo, onde sovente
> di me medesmo meco mi vergogno;
>
> e del mio vaneggiar vergogna è 'l frutto,
> e 'l pentersi, e 'l conoscer chiaramente
> che quanto piace al mondo è breve sogno.

You who hear in scattered rhymes the sound of those sighs with which I nourished my heart during my first youthful error, when I was in part another man from what I am now:

for the varied style in which I weep and speak between vain hopes and vain sorrow, where there is anyone who understands love through experience, I hope to find pity, not only pardon.

But now I see well how for a long time I was the talk of the crowd, for which often I am ashamed of myself within;

and of my raving, shame is the fruit, and repentance, and the clear knowledge that what pleases in the world is a brief dream.

This is a recantation that anticipates Sidney's 'Leave me, O love, which reachest but to dust' and Shakespeare's 'Th'expense of spirit' (129) or 'Poor soul, the centre of my sinful earth' (146), but it does a great deal more than that: it clarifies Petrarch's purposes in creating a sequence. The 'scattered rhymes' recall the *Rerum vulgarium fragmenta* and the sense of fragmentation and dispersion that such a title conjures up, reminding us that the act of gathering together a body of once-autonomous lyrics is part of a desperate attempt to repair the disintegration of the self. In this light the phrase *vario stile* ('varied style') is less an artistic boast than a confession of chronic instability and lack of direction, a point underlined by the alliteration *vario–vane–van* and, perhaps, by the etymological sense of *errore*. In *altr'uom da quel ch' i' sono* the gap between past and present merges into the difference between false and true—'another man from what I am now', but also 'other than what I truly am'. The anguished self-examination that makes the *Canzoniere* such a milestone of subjectivity is sharply conveyed by the tortuous polyptoton of *di me medesmo meco mi vergogno* (literally something like 'of me myself within myself I feel ashamed'). And the shame derives not so much from his love for Laura as from the poems themselves and the ambition that has created them.

The adjective *sparse* ('scattered'), might well allude to another kind of dispersion: the fact that the poems of the *Canzoniere* have become widely known. The fame, however, is not of the kind that he has counted on, since he has made himself a common laughing stock (*al popol tutto favola fui gran tempo*). We remember Shakespeare's 'Alas, 'tis true, I have gone here and there | And made myself a motley to the view' (110). For both Petrarch and Shakespeare the poetry does not simply *describe* a process of moral decline; it is itself a prominent agent in that process, only to be redeemed by being framed in a way that stimulates moral discrimination. *Era il giorno* (*RVF* 3), for example, gives us a speaker who is culpably ignorant of the implications of his own words.

> Era il giorno ch' al sol si scoloraro
> per la pietà del suo fattore i rai
> quando i' fui preso, et non me ne guardai,
> ché i be' vostr' occhi, Donna, mi legaro.
>
> Tempo non mi parea da far riparo
> contr' a' colpi d'Amor; però m'andai
> secur, senza sospetto, onde i miei guai
> nel comune dolor s'incominciaro.
>
> Trovommi Amor del tutto disarmato,
> et aperta la via per gli occhi al core
> che di lagrime son fatti uscio et varco.
>
> Però al mio parer non li fu onore
> ferir me de saetta in quello stato,
> a voi armata non mostrar pur l'arco.

It was the day when the sun's rays turned pale with grief for his Maker when I was taken, and I did not defend myself against it, for your lovely eyes, Lady, bound me.

It did not seem to me a time for being on guard against Love's blows; therefore I went confident and without fear, and so my misfortunes began in the midst of the universal woe.

Love found me altogether disarmed, and the way open though my eyes to my heart, my eyes which are now the portal and passageway of tears.

Therefore, as it seems to me, it got him no honour to strike me with an arrow in that state, and not even to show his bow to you, who were armed.

This might, on a first reading, be taken as a light, witty, and faintly blasphemous version of Ovid's *nec tibi laus armis victus inermis ero* ('Nor will it be praise for your arms to conquer me unarmed', *Amores* 1.2.22), but the implications are profound and far-reaching. Petrarch's first meeting with Laura, as he tells us elsewhere, took place in the church of St Clare in Avignon on 6 April 1327 at the hour of prime. Here, in order to stress the sequence's exemplary religious significance, that date is made to coincide with Good Friday. The speaker pleads the coincidence as an excuse for his infatuation, but for the attentive reader it can only work to his condemnation. The lover complains of 'Love's blows' when he should be thinking of the blows inflicted on Christ; he is bound by the eyes of Laura on the day when Christ was bound and delivered up to crucifixion; he falls victim to the arrows of Cupid, the false God of Love who delights in wounding men, precisely because he forgets the true God of Love who was wounded *for* man. On the day of 'universal woe' he isolates himself from the human family by retreating into a selfish personal grief.

In *Era il giorno* Christ is replaced by Cupid, but in the celebrated pilgrim sonnet, *Movesi il vecchierel canuto et bianco* ('The little white-haired pale old man', *RVF* 16), it is Laura herself who poses the same threat:

> et viene a Roma, seguendo 'l desio,
> per mirar la sembianza di colui
> ch'ancor lassù nel ciel vedere spera.
>
> Così, lasso, talor vo cercand'io,
> Donna, quanto è possibile in altrui
> la disiata vostra forma vera.

and he [the pilgrim] comes to Rome, following his desire, to gaze on the likeness of Him whom he hopes to see again up there in Heaven.

Thus, alas, at times, I go searching in others, Lady, as much as is possible, for your longed-for true form.

The speaker, seeking the likeness of Laura in other women, is compared to the pilgrim who goes to Rome to see the miraculous image of Christ known as the Veronica. The 16th-century commentator Ludovico Beccadelli was moved to revise the conclusion because he found it *troppo ardita e quasi impia* ('too daring and almost impious').[16] What he failed to acknowledge was the profoundly moral intention of Petrarch's irony when he makes the besotted youthful speaker replace a heavenly quest by an earthly one and the image of Christ by the image of Laura. Petrarch's irony is not always as clear as this, but one cannot do justice to the complexity of the *Canzoniere* without a constant awareness of the religious counterpoint that accompanies and undermines the discourse of secular love.

The central problem of the *Secretum* and the *Canzoniere* is that Petrarch or his speaker cannot really follow St Augustine's injunction to renounce profane love as the source of moral disorder without simultaneously reflecting negatively upon Laura. The last sonnet of the sequence, *I' vo piangendo* ('I go weeping', *RVF* 365), regrets the time spent *in amar cosa mortale* ('in loving a mortal thing'), but stops short of naming or condemning the loved object. Elsewhere in the sequence, indications of guilt on Laura's part are so rare as to be easily overlooked. In *RVF* 45 and 125 there is some suggestion that, like the Fair Youth of the Sonnets, she takes a narcissistic pleasure in her own beauty, although only the crucial canzone that opens the second part (*RVF* 264) makes the accusation explicit: *quella che sol per farmi morir nacque, | perch' a me troppo et a se stessa piacque* ('she who was born to make me die, since she pleased me and herself too much'). On the

---

[16]   Cited in *Francesco Petrarca: Canzoniere*, ed. Marco Santagata (Milan: Mondadori, 1997) 71.

whole, however, Laura is, as it were, exempted from moral judgement by being trans-formed into plant as the laurel or animal as the white hind of *RVF* 190 and the cruel wild creature of *RVF* 23. Or else, as in *RVF* 3, the blame is transferred to a malevolent and deceptive personified Love, replete with bait and snares. Dante might have provided the model for a less evasive approach with his so-called *Rime petrose* ('stony rhymes'), and at times the aloofness of Laura does indeed recall the icy sadism of Dante's stony woman; but there is really nothing in the *Canzoniere* to compare with the raw violence and sensuality of *Così nel mio parlar voglio esser aspro* ('So in my speech I would be harsh', *Petrose* 4), although Petrarch actually does quote the poem in *RVF* 70. The *Vita Nuova* and the *Petrose* offered Petrarch two extremes that could not be accommodated in the *Canzoniere*, although Petrarch is tempted by both of them.

This preamble should have established three essential and related characteristics of the genre that Shakespeare inherits from Petrarch and develops in the Sonnets:

1) The sequence relies on some kind of putative autobiography, constructed as an exemplary narrative which it adumbrates but ultimately fails to deliver.

2) It involves a constant double perspective where each poem has a different weight depending on whether it is read as an autonomous utterance or in the light of the sequence as a whole.

3) A sequence can always be reordered, revised, and augmented. As a result, structural and/or thematic divisions turn out to be deceptive and closure provisory: beneath what looks like narrative progression we find paralysis and repetition.

The first point need not be laboured here. A recognition of the lyrical 'I' of early modern poetry as a literary construct need not lead us to doubt that Shakespeare was working with the genre's inherent confessional assumptions. One need only think of the extraordinarily unconventional situations that the Sonnets evokes—a youth who is urged to marry and who also inspires a scarcely veiled homoerotic passion, a mis-tress who is in every way the opposite of the pure Petrarchan heroine; enforced chas-tity in the former relationship and unbridled indulgence in the latter; the complex triangular relationship between the three protagonists. All this would suggest that Shakespeare, if he was not actually writing confessional poetry, went out of his way to make his readers think that he was. Giacomo Colonna's gibe about Petrarch inventing Laura so that he could pursue the poetic laurel could have been feasibly addressed to a dozen Elizabethan sonneteers, but hardly to Shakespeare. Katherine Duncan-Jones has remarked that Shakespeare 'may be seen as overturning the conventions of more than two hundred years of "Petrarchism"'[17], but she does well to place the term within inverted commas, for it is not in the notorious Petrarchan conventions, conceived as a fairly limited range of situations, rhetorical figures, and imagery, that we should seek the relevence of the *Canzoniere* to the Sonnets. It has been said often enough that Petrarch's invention of the poetic sequence is a milestone in the history of subjectivity:

[17] *Shakespeare's Sonnets*, Katherine Duncan-Jones (ed.) (London: Nelson, Arden Shakespeare, 1997) 47.

in that sense, at least, Shakespeare makes full use of the resources that Petrarch made available and is more faithful than any of his contemporaries to the lesson and spirit of the *Canzoniere*.

The second major characteristic of the sequence, the double perspective, comes into play above all in the poetry of praise which continues to be a major feature of sonnet sequences even when it degenerates into the mechanical itemization of body parts as it often tends to do in the 16th century. In Shakespeare's Sonnets the poet's praise of the Fair Youth comes across both as the convincing expression of emotions and as a mature criticism of those emotions. Readers are left to find their own balance between empathy and assessment.

> Let not my love be called idolatry,
> Nor my belovèd as an idol show,
> Since all alike my songs and praises be
> To one, of one, still such, and ever so.
> Kind is my love today, tomorrow kind,
> Still constant in a wondrous excellence.
> Therefore my verse, to constancy confined,
> One thing expressing, leaves out difference.
> 'Fair, kind, and true' is all my argument,
> 'Fair, kind, and true' varying to other words,
> And in this change is my invention spent,
> Three themes in one, which wondrous scope affords.
>   Fair, kind, and true have often lived alone,
>   Which three till now never kept seat in one.
>
> (105)

The panegyric remains moving even as it is undermined by its own hyperbole. Idolatry, according to Dr. Johnson, is 'the worship of images' or 'the worship of any thing as God which is not God'. Both definitions function here, but the second line, with its emphasis on appearance ('show') makes it clear that image-worship is the more operative sense. One could almost read the poem as Petrarch's pilgrim sonnet (*Movesi il vecchierel*) updated to a Reformation context. Petrarch's lover replaces the image of Christ with the image of Laura; Shakespeare's speaker replaces God with an image—that of the beloved youth. In both poems the tone is rather hard to pin down—moving, yes, but at the same time one suspects that there is something queasily jocular about the echoes of the *Gloria*, the insistent trinitarian imagery, and the patently false assumption that monotheism and idolatry are mutually exclusive. It is as if the speaker were attempting to treat as a piece of light-hearted banter an accusation that he fears could be made in all seriousness. Indeed, in the theological climate of the times, hyperbolic praise couched in religious terms could not always be shrugged off as poetic licence. When the *Vita Nuova* was first printed in 1576, even Dante's impeccable Catholic orthodoxy could not prevent the censors or the nervous editor from replacing such loaded terms as *beatitudine* and *salute* into the bland and inoffensive *felicità* and *quiete*.

Sonnet 84 also plays with fire and the implications are no less extreme.

Who is it that says most which can say more
Than this rich praise: that you alone are you,
In whose confine immurèd is the store
Which should example where your equal grew?
Lean penury within that pen doth dwell
That to his subject lends not some small glory;
But he that writes of you, if he can tell
That you are you, so dignifies his story.
Let him but copy what in you is writ,
Not making worse what nature made so clear,
And such a counterpart shall fame his wit,
Making his style admirèd everywhere.
    You to your bounteous blessings add a curse,
    Being fond on praise, which makes your praises worse.

In the *Canzoniere* we are told that Laura is the perfect work of God and Nature (*RVF* 248), the ultimate and the proximate cause. Here we have Nature alone since the young man is seen in terms that render God superfluous. The key phrase is the repeated tautology 'you are you' which is far more than an emphatic way of saying that the beloved is unique. Tautological definition is properly reserved for the Deity who declares 'I am that I am' (Exodus 3.14). All creatures are defined in relation to something else: only the creator God is self-defining. The hyperbole is made more not less monstrous by the final couplet where we see that the lover has not yet lost all capacity for moral perception; and the crowning irony is that the worst of praises is indeed the tautology which the speaker recommends as an example of plain speaking.

The major vehicle of praise is, of course, comparison, and it is the validity of comparison that the double perspective repeatedly calls into question. The phrase 'false compare' occurs at the end of a sonnet ('My mistress' eyes are nothing like the sun', 130) which is significantly the only one in the sequence that may depend directly on a Petrarchan original (*Erano i capei d'oro a l'aura sparsi*, 'Her golden hair was loosed to the breeze', *RVF* 90). 'My mistress' eyes' may be the kind of iconoclastic squib that had become a standard feature of late Petrarchism since Du Bellay's 'Contre les pétrarquistes' (1553), but Shakespeare's anxiety about comparison is pervasive and cannot be divorced from the broader issue of true and false perception.[18] Prominent among the negative effects of love in both Petrarch and Shakespeare is the lover's growing incapacity to distinguish between the real and the imaginary. In *RVF* 90 Laura's physical presence is remembered with a cluster of literary allusions (mostly Virgilian) that endow her with mythic status. The living Laura, whose eyes have lost their old radiance, is simultaneously recognized and dismissed: *piaga per allentar d'arco non sana* ('a wound is not healed by the loosening of the bow'). Here as elsewhere, the aesthetic stasis induced by the vision of Laura is both compelling and dangerous. In the canzone *Chiare fresche et dolci acque* ('Clear, fresh, sweet waters', *RVF* 126) it brings the lover to a state where, *carco d'oblio* ('laden

---

[18] For a discussion of 'false compare' see *Shakespeare: The Sonnets and A Lover's Complaint*, John Kerrigan (ed.), (London: Penguin, New Penguin Shakespeare, 1986) 18–33.

with forgetfulness'), he loses contact with *l'imagine vera* ('the true image'). Or again, in *Di pensier in pensier* ('From thought to thought' *RVF* 129), Laura's absence allows the poet to see her features in the water, the grass, the clouds, and the trees until at last *il vero sgombra | quel dolce error* ('the truth dispels that sweet deception'). And one thinks inevitably of the sonnet that Wyatt translated as 'My galley chargèd with forgetfulness' (*Passa la nave mia colma d'oblio, RVF* 189). *Oblio* is a key term in the *Canzoniere* precisely because it links aesthetic stasis with moral failure.

In the Sonnets also the power of the poetic imagination to create its own object is seen as a moral danger. Like the lover of *RVF* 129, the speaker of Sonnet 113, 'Since I left you mine eye is in my mind', transforms all that he sees into the features of his beloved, but the nature of the antitheses suggests a deeper level of corruption:

> For if it see the rud'st or gentlest sight,
> The most sweet favour or deformèd'st creature,
> The mountain or the sea, the day or night,
> The crow or dove, it shapes them to your feature.
> Incapable of more, replete with you,
> My most true mind thus makes mine eye untrue.

> (ll. 9–14)

Quarto reads 'My most true mind thus maketh mine untrue', but the emendation adopted by most modern editors preserves the eye–mind association of the opening and stresses the moral dilemma of the text with its use of the popular 'eye–I' pun to indicate that the speaker's truth (constancy) to his beloved has made him untrue to his real or better self—not unlike the lover of *RVF* 1. Even if we agree with Malone that 'untrue' should be read as a substantive meaning 'untruth',[19] the wordplay on 'true' still functions and its implications are made clear in the subsequent sonnet, 'Or whether doth my mind' (114) where the imagination that transforms reality is likened to a palate that has acquired a taste for poison or to an alchemy that has taught the lover

> To make of monsters and things indigest
> Such cherubins as your sweet self resemble,
> Creating every bad a perfect best.

A beloved who teaches one to see monsters as cherubins may well be something of a monster himself; he is certainly not the angel that he resembles. The sonnet's conclusion (''tis the lesser sin | That mine eye loves it and doth first begin') creates what is, in effect, a typically Petrarchan vicious circle: love of the youth induces a false vision of reality, but it was, in the first place, a false vision of reality that allowed the speaker to love someone so unworthy of his affections.

That sense of a vicious circle brings us to what I have suggested is the third aspect of continuity between the *Canzoniere* and the Sonnets: the deceptive nature of apparent

---

[19] Cited by Duncan-Jones (1997) 336.

divisions. The poem that opens the second part of the *Canzoniere* announces a change of direction, *vorre' 'l ver abbracciar, lassando l'ombre* ('I wish to embrace the truth, to abandon shadows', *RVF 264*), but, as we have seen, the radical Augustinian surgery that this would seem to promise is never, in fact, fully applied, challenged as it is by sporadic attempts to emulate the *Vita Nuova* scheme of human love as a redemptive force. Rapt visions of Laura in heaven surrounded by the admiring ranks of saints and angels (*RVF 345*) or basking in the delighted regard of God (*RVF 348*) have the same effect of aesthetic stasis that her presence produced on earth while the last penitential sonnet, *I' vo piangendo i miei passati tempi* ('I go weeping for my past time', *RVF 365*), provides no convincing conclusion since the same sentiments have been expressed at regular intervals throughout the sequence. In short, our experience of the *Canzoniere* ends by frustrating the expectations of an exemplary conversion narrative that the two-part structure seemed designed to create.

To speak of a two-part structure in Shakespeare's Sonnets would involve accepting the placing of the six-couplet non-sonnet 'O thou my lovely boy' (126) as a formal marker. At the thematic level, no doubt, there would seem to be a clear contrast between the idealizing and sublimated passion for a noble young man that has been prominent up to this point and the degrading physical lust for a loose female that will occupy the rest of the sequence. Yet in the long run the continuity is no less obvious than the contrast. We see that both loves are linked by the speaker's perverse indulgence in self-abasement, by his chronic inability to escape from domination by a moral inferior. The physical corruption through venereal disease caught from the Dark Lady mirrors the spiritual corruption brought on by the Fair Youth. The lover who announces 'Two loves have I, of comfort and despair' (144) is forced, in the same sonnet, to recognize that he is deceiving himself for they are 'both to each friend', both ultimately equally corrupting.

In both sequences apparently clear divisions are undermined and narrative expectations are frustrated in favour of an incessant probing meditation on a given subjective condition, conveyed by an array of juxtapositions, contrasts, repetitions, echoes, anticipations, symmetries, and so forth. There is no forward movement, only a constant unsettling of the reader who is forced into reconsideration and re-evaluation of poems already read in a potentially endless process. It has often been noted that many of the major English sonnet sequences either end abruptly like Sidney's *Astrophil and Stella* and Spenser's *Amoretti*, or become subject to the kind of revision, re-ordering, and expansion that marks the successive editions of Drayton's *Idea's Mirrour*, Daniel's *Delia*, and, in a later age, Rossetti's *House of Life*. That open-endedness, that flexibility is inherent in the genre that Petrarch developed out of Dante's *Vita Nuova* and St Augustine's *Confessions*—a genre that remains a fitting vehicle for our modern sense of the self with its aspiration towards coherence, its fear of dissolution, its transitory victories, and its inconclusive defeats.

It used to be fashionable to see Petrarchism as a stultifying international idiom to which poets as different as Wyatt, Sidney, Shakespeare, and Donne offered a succession of challenges that defined the independence of English poetry. Recent criticism has put us in position where we can see Shakespeare's Sonnets as part of the larger canvas of late

Renaissance Petrarchism. In the Italian context the most obvious point of reference is the poetry of Michelangelo, now seen as having a literary value in its own right, independent of the light it casts on the great sculptor's personality. There are obvious limits to any comparison with Shakespeare's Sonnets. Michelangelo's poetry does not constitute a sequence and it embraces a wider variety of forms and themes. Moreover, the woman (Vittoria Colonna) and the noble youth (Tommaso dei Cavalieri) are both thoroughly idealized in neo-Platonic fashion and subjected to none of the critical irony that marks Shakespeare's treatment of his two loves. But Michelangelo shares with Shakespeare a thematic extension of Petrarchism that crosses and blurs the boundaries of gender. *Un uomo in una donna, anzi un dio | per la sua bocca parla* ('It is a man, indeed a god, whose speech | Is in the mouth of a woman', 235) he proclaims of Vittoria Colonna, while his passion for Tommaso dei Cavalieri, however sublimated, is still homoerotic enough to generate a deep anxiety about how it might be seen by others:[20]

> E se 'l vulgo malvaggio, isciocco e rio,
> di quel che sente, altrui segna e addita,
> non è l'intensa voglia men gradita,
> l'amor, la fede e l'onesto desio.
>
> And if the foolish, fell, malevolent crowd
> Point others out as sharing their own ill,
> I do not cherish less this yearning will,
> The love, the faith, the chaste desire of good.
>
> (83)

As with Shakespeare, the problem is compounded by a jagged nervous awareness of the noble youth's social superiority:

> Tu sa' ch'i' so, signor mie, che tu sai
> ch'i' vengo per goderti più da presso,
> e sai ch'i' so che tu sa' ch'i' son desso:
> a che più indugio a salutarci omai?
>
> You know, my lord, that I know that you know
> That here I come more closely to enjoy you,
> And who I am you know I know you know:
> What keeps us from exchanging greetings then?
>
> (60)

All told, it is not surprising that when Michelangelo's poems were first published by his great-nephew in 1623 they were subjected to the same kind of gender normalization that was sporadically imposed on Shakespeare's Sonnets in the 1640 Benson edition. Finally, in a century that was learning to doubt the value of analogy as a mode of

---

[20] Italian citations are to *Michelangiolo Buonarroti: Rime*, Enzo Noè Girardi (ed.), (Bari: Laterza, 1967). Translations are from *Michelangelo: Poems and Letters*, Anthony Mortimer (trans.), (London: Penguin, 2007). Numbering of poems follows Girardi.

argument, Michelangelo shares some of Shakespeare's suspicion of 'false compare'. The famous sonnet *Non ha l'ottimo artista alcun concetto | c'un marmo solo in sé non circonscriva* ('The best of artists can no subject find | That is not in a single block of stone', 151) begins by comparing Vittoria Colonna to the stone from which the sculptor removes what is superfluous in order to reveal the form within. But the comparison breaks down as the poet draws from her both *Il mal ch'io fuggo, e 'l ben ch'io mi prometto* ('The evil that I flee and good I crave'). Plurality takes over. Michelangelo the sculptor may uncover a single form within the block of stone; Michelangelo the poet cannot escape from his own contradictions. The points of contact between Shakespeare and Michelangelo are not numerous enough to warrant a lengthy comparison, but they are nonetheless significant in that they show how Petrarchism could evolve in response to far-reaching cultural shifts and how far it enabled rather than hindered some of the most seminal achievements of European poetry in the 16th century.

SELECT BIBLIOGRAPHY

Braden, Gordon (2000) 'Shakespeare's Petrarchism' in James Schiffer (ed.) *Shakespeare's Sonnets: Critical Essays* (New York and London: Garland) 163–83.

Dubrow, Heather (1995) *Echoes of Desire: English Petrarchism and its Counter-Discourses* (Ithaca and London: Cornell University Press).

Durling, Robert (1976) (trans. and ed.) *Petrarch's Lyric Poems: the 'Rime sparse' and Other Lyrics* (Cambridge, MA and London: Harvard University Press).

Kennedy, William J. (1989) 'Commentary into Narrative: Shakespeare's Sonnets and Vellutello's Commentary on Petrarch', *Allegorica* 10, 119–33.

Kerrigan, John (1986) (ed.) *Sonnets and A Lover's Complaint* (London: Penguin, New Penguin Shakespeare).

Leishman, J. B. (1961) *Themes and Variations in Shakespeare's Sonnets* (London: Hutchinson).

Martellotti, G., P.G. Ricci, E. Carrara, and E. Bianchi (1955) (eds), *Prose* (Milan and Naples: Ricciardi).

Mortimer, Anthony (2000) *Variable Passions: A Reading of Shakespeare's 'Venus and Adonis'* (New York: AMS Press).

——— (2011) (trans. and ed.) *Vita Nuova* (Richmond: Oneworld Classics).

Roche, Thomas P. (1989) *Petrarch and the English Sonnet Sequences* (New York, AMS Press).

Spiller, Michael R. G. (1992) *The Development of the Sonnet: An Introduction* (London, Routledge).

Torre, Andrea (2009) (ed.) *Variazioni su Adone I, favole, lettere, idilli* (Lucca: Maria Pacini Fazzi).

Wolf, Max (1916) 'Petrarkismus und Antipetrarkismus in Shakespeares Sonetten', *Englische Studien* 49: 161–89.

CHAPTER 8

···

DU BELLAY AND SHAKESPEARE'S SONNETS

···

ANNE LAKE PRESCOTT

Despite significant exceptions, scholarship on the Sonnets usually ignores how its poetry relates, if at all, to that of France.[1] It seems clear, though, that Shakespeare knew Joachim Du Bellay's *Antiquitez*, a sonnet sequence on the pride, fall, and remnants of the

---

[1] Much relevant scholarship cannot here receive its due. *Shakespeare longus, ars brevis.* See, first of all, Hassan Melehy, *Poetics of Literary Transfer in Early Modern France and England* (Farnham: Ashgate, 2010), who explores English writers' ambivalence toward the ruins that make room for them and is eloquent on how mutability shakes words loose from meaning (211). Also crucial: A. E. B. Coldiron, 'How Spenser Excavates Du Bellay's *Antiquitez*; or, The Role of the Poet, Lyric Historiography, and the English Sonnet', *JEGP* 101.1 (2002) 41–67; Tom Muir's heavily theorized 'Without remainder: ruins and tombs in Shakespeare's *Sonnets*', *Textual Practice* 24.1 (2010) 21–49 (which to my ear exaggerates the 'anxiety' of those contemplating Rome's past); Muir's 'Specters of Spenser: Translating the *Antiquitez*', *Spenser Studies* 25 (2010) 327–61; and Michael Haldane's website (<http://www.michaelhaldane.com/TranslationandRuinContents.htm>). For background, see Anne Janowitz, *England's Ruins: Poetic Purpose and the National Landscape* (Oxford: Basil Blackwell, 1990). I quote *Antiquitez* from *Oeuvres poétiques*, Henri Chamard (ed.), (Paris: Didier, 1961) II, also consulting the edition by Françoise Joukovsky (Paris: Garnier, 2009), and Spenser from *Shorter Poems*, Richard A. McCabe (ed.), (London: Penguin, 1999). Richard Helgerson's *Joachim du Bellay* (Philadelphia: University of Pennsylvania Press, 2006) offers a fine translation. Malcolm Smith's edition of the *Antiquitez* and *Ruines of Rome* (Binghamton, NY: Medieval & Renaissance Texts and Studies, 1994) has useful notes, although what Smith calls errors others might call revisions. *A Companion to Shakespeare's* Sonnets, Michael Schoenfeldt (ed.), (Oxford: Blackwell, 2007) ignores Du Bellay/Spenser but has good bibliographies and essays on time by Dympna Callaghan and Amanda Watson. Schoenfeldt's otherwise helpful *Cambridge Introduction to Shakespeare's Poetry* (Cambridge: Cambridge University Press, 2010) condescends to Spenser and ignores France. See also Warren Chernaik's *Myth of Rome in Shakespeare and his Contemporaries* (Cambridge: Cambridge University Press, 2011); *Roman Images*, Annabel Patterson (ed.), (Baltimore: Johns Hopkins University Press, 1984); and *Rome in the Renaissance*, P. A. Ramsey (ed.), (Binghamton NY: Medieval & Renaissance Texts & Studies, 1982), particularly George Pigman on Du Bellay's ambivalence. Clifford Ronan's well-illustrated '*Antike Roman*': *Power Symbology and the Roman Play in Early Modern England, 1585–1635* (Athens, GA: University of Georgia Press, 1995), quotes Du Bellay, 43.

Eternal City that a homesick Du Bellay wrote in Rome while secretary to his cousin Jean, Cardinal Du Bellay. True, Shakespeare probably relied on Spenser's *Ruines of Rome*, included in the latter's *Complaints* (1591), a volume perhaps all the more enticing for having been called in by the authorities. In addition to Du Bellay's tumbled walls and the nothing into which Rome dwindled, in this essay I also offer a Roman prostitute, some anti-Petrarchism, and a coda on *Titus Andronicus*. Juxtaposing Shakespeare and Du Bellay himself is tricky, for the degree to which Shakespeare read French remains unclear. One can, moreover, be influenced by unopened books. I once bought some madeleines from a saleswoman who said brightly that if I ate one I might think I remember reading Proust. But you don't need a madeleine if you can remember talking to someone who has read Proust. Perhaps Shakespeare found his Holofernes, for example, not in Rabelais but in a chat over a tankard at the Mermaid. We can forget the role in our cultural memory of *viva voce* witnesses to paradoxes, resonant names, or narrative twists in books we have not opened.

8.1 EXPLOITING 'RUINISH'

The Sonnets and *The Ruines of Rome*, however, share so much phrasing that Kent Hieatt could plausibly argue that Shakespeare read the latter.[2] Kent and I, together with his brother Charles Hieatt, planned a book describing the impact on England of what we called 'RR' or 'Ruinish'—a lexical force-field made of walls, *tempus edax*, bloody foundations, civil broils, 'ruinate', 'injurious', 'of yore', prideful self-containment, giants, maps, 'wear', 'outworn', 'map', and more. The Hieatts focused on using this vocabulary to date the sonnets. My assignment was to search older texts to make sure our claims held up. I found far more Ruinish than Kent had thought was there, but we agreed that only in Spenser's Roman poetry and the sonnets is it so densely packed. We also agreed that some writers, such as Daniel and Drayton, used Ruinish extensively, whereas others, such as Jonson and Donne, avoided it. Philip Sidney, writing before *Complaints* saw print, has virtually none; his sister Mary has a great deal.[3]

We never wrote that book. But I was left with piles of texts exploiting Ruinish, a dialect deployed with especial relish by those lamenting Time's teeth or scythe, urging a beloved to bed, grieving a death, meditating on a painful yet satisfying *translatio imperii* or *studii* from ruinated Rome, warning of what civil war can do to proud sky-reaching empires,

---

[2] A. Kent Hieatt, 'The Genesis of Shakespeare's *Sonnets*: Spenser's *Ruins of Rome: by Bellay*' (*PMLA* 98, 1983) 800–14.

[3] On Mary Sidney, see my 'The Countess of Pembroke's Ruins of Rome', *The Sidney Journal* 23.1–2 (2005) 1–17. My chapter on Du Bellay in *French Poets and Renaissance France* (New Haven: Yale University Press, 1978) is updated in 'Du Bellay in Renaissance England: Recent Work on Translation and Response', *Oeuvres & Critiques* 20 (1995) 121–8 and again in 'Spenser and French Literature', in *The Oxford Handbook of Edmund Spenser*, Richard McCabe (ed.), (Oxford: Oxford University Press, 2010) 620–34.

or imagining the collapse of modern Rome with its giants, many-hilled or -headed Beast, its papal Whore, and its future replacement by the New Jerusalem, probably in England's green and pleasant land.

True, English application of Ruinish to Rome itself left important matters unresolved. Du Bellay himself cannot settle on the cause of Rome's fall and neither, collectively, could the English. Titanic arrogance? Of course. Northern barbarians (our ancestors, Du Bellay and Shakespeare might reflect)? No question. War? Yes. There is also a chronological problem. One of Du Bellay's explanations for Rome's fall was its civil broils, its self-murder—and yet even though the Republic fell after civil violence, Rome itself did not fall for some centuries after the events and corruption that Lucan and Petronius had described. Du Bellay died before France slid into not one civil war but several, intestine conflicts suggesting the split self that the Sonnets can express. Indeed, to have a *triple* civil war with each side led by an Henri seems beyond schizoid—Gaul was once again divided *in partes tres*. English readers of the stories in Jacques Yver's 1572 *Courtlie controversy of Cupids Cautels* would have found echoes of Du Bellay in one lady's dismay over such domestic war: France had shown a Roman-like willingness to arm its 'mightie hande' against its own greatness, wreck its 'auncient myghtie walles', and bury itself (trans. 1578, C3-C4). Robert Garnier's plays, well known in England, can talk Ruinish while glancing out of the corners of their eyes at the destruction wracking France (and the Low Countries). In sum, as Ingrid Daemmrich wrote some years ago, '[French] Renaissance writers were attracted to ruins not only because they respected the monuments of antiquity but also because the religious and civil wars of the period resulted in the destruction of many French buildings'.[4] Neither the *Sonnets* (1609) nor *The Rape of Lucrece* (1594) is 'about' such modern European violence, but their fascination with ruin, with bare ruined choirs, surely looks not just to the past or future but across the Channel.

Such words haunt many Elizabethan texts published before or while Shakespeare worked on the Sonnets. George Turberville edges into proto-Ruinish in the verse preface to the *Tragicall Tales* (1587) he translated from Italian when he says, with many references to Lucan, that 'the civill swords of Rome | and mischiefes done thereby, | May be a myrrour unto us, | the like mishappes to flye' (B2). Thomas Churchyard, whose poetry often incorporates phrases in Ruinish, is closer to Du Bellay when he has Flanders (Spenser's 'Belge') grieve in his *Lamentable Description* that she will be another Troy, that her pillars have sunk and her 'former fame, and bright renowme, | in darknesse now lyes hid'. Once she was great, but 'My members must give place to time, | and I therewith decay' (1578; B2ᵛ-B4). Thomas Lodge has a good pun in his *Wounds of Civil War* (1594; a sort of homage to Lucan): 'Rome shall rue' says his Scilla (Sulla, the Roman general), in a line recalling one in the *Ruines of Time*.[5] Daniel's *Civil Wars*? Of course: it is the 1590s,

---

⁴ Ingrid G. Daemmrich, 'The Ruins Motif as Artistic Device in French Literature', Part I, *Journal of Aesthetics and Art Criticism* 30 (1971/2): 449–547. Richard Cooper, 'Poetry in Ruins: the Literary Context of du Bellay's Cycles on Rome', *Renaissance Studies* 3.2 (1989): 156–66.

⁵ H3ᵛ; *Ruines of Time*: 'O Rome thy ruine I lament and rue' (McCabe, line 78).

and so too Kyd's 1594 *Cornelia* (from Garnier) has 'civill furie' and a Rome that 'Could never have been curb'd but by itselfe' (A2). I spare the reader further examples, but there are many, many others both before and after *Complaints*.

That Shakespeare adopted phrases from Spenser's Du Bellay, and possibly looked at Du Bellay is, I think, close to certainty, but what are the implications of his Ruinish? Are we to remember, as forty winters besiege his young man's brow, or as Shakespeare urges him to 'Make war upon this bloody tyrant time | And fortify yourself in your decay' (Sonnets 2, 16), that in the *Antiquitez* such temporal assault had merged, however illogically, with anguish over civil war? Are we to recall Rome's arrogant self-absorption, its conviction that it was sufficient unto itself, was the whole world, was all there is, when the young man apparently refuses to beget offspring? His cheek will be a 'map of days outworn' (Sonnet 68); are there overtones to 'map' and its suggestion of a world—a crumpled Mercator projection or a shrunken globe? Rome lies buried in itself—self-love's punishment and perhaps its perverse aim. The youth is a modern English aristocrat, but he should remember Roman glory even as Time dines on him when it isn't wearing him away or letting temporal waves lap at his being or crumbling his walls. Self-isolating pride almost invites besieging and even battering. ('Who builds a palace and rams up the gate, | Shall see it ruinous and desolate', Marlowe's Leander warns Hero, perhaps remembering where virtue got Lucrece.)[6]

As Shakespeare worked, off and on, writing and revising his Sonnets, and also—although this is not the place to cite the Ruinish in his plays—as he wrote about the hollow crown, favoritism, and regicide, more than we remember to stress, a mere twenty-two miles away there were savage civil wars on the Continent that ended (for a time) only in the late 1590s and that involved the murder of two dukes of Guise, one Cardinal of Guise, and one Valois king (the year after the Sonnets appeared yet another king, Henri IV, would be killed). To write of ruins, bodies, bloody walls, siege warfare, and the like could not help but recall what was happening, or had recently happened, on the other side of England's moat. How unlike England—at least for now, and thus far. No wonder that Ralph Norris called his one-page broadside on such conflicts *A Warning to London by the fall of Antwerp* (1585?); that rich city's fall 'Thy wrack and ruine dooth foretel. | Make not a gibing jest therat: | Lest stately Troy be beaten flat'. Not quite Ruinish, but a reminder that events on the Continent contributed to English poetry on ruination, on topics that could invite Du Bellay's and Spenser's vocabulary and phrasing.

So too, Robert Humston's 1588 sermon preached after the Armada's defeat (for Ruinish can figure in the Armada discourse) warns of bloody fields in England, 'Bloudie fieldes, bloudie vinyardes, bloudie cities, bloudie houses, bloudie Majestrates, bloudie Ministers and bloudie platters, and the price of bloud within our walles' (C5^v, citing Habakkuk 2.11; Rome's bloody foundation has biblical parallels). In 1589 Lambert Daneau's polemical *Treatise, touching antichrist* often adapts phrases from the *Antiquitez*

---

[6] *Hero and Leander*, 11.239–40, in *The Collected Poems of Christopher Marlowe*, Patrick Cheney and Brian J. Striar (eds), (Oxford: Oxford University Press, 2006).

to describe the Rome that he claims is Revelation's Babylon (e.g. Rome raised 'her courage to the skie'; K1ᵛ-K3; cf. *Antiquitez* 6's 'courage au cieux'). Daneau then explains that since Jews write backward, 'Armageddon' must be 'Geddon-Harma', meaning that a 'high place was cut down: as if ye should terme it, the Ruine of Rome'. So true is this that 'such as are not well acquainted with the Citie, might seeke for Rome, beeing in the middest of her' (K4). Yes; see *Antquitez* 3. In sum, the Antichrist Rome is 'built upon the grave, ruines, and ashes of that auncient and famous Rome, which was layde in the dust by the Gothes: that is, which is seene to be re-edified and inhabited againe', but which is the opposite of the New Jerusalem. Or, as E. L. says in his 1596 *Romes monarchie, entituled The globe of renowned glorie*, with clear echoes of Du Bellay or Spenser, 'So worketh time in everything the change ... Whom Time hath rais'de, and likewise made to fall' (B1ᵛ). Remember the towers of Carthage, too, 'Whose toppes high mounted, seem'de to touch the ayre' (B2). Be warned: 'Flye civill discord, bringing woes and spoyles: | Most foule are fowles their owne nests that defiles' (K4ᵛ). Rome fell to divisions, ambition, and rebellion, we read, but its arrogance lives on with the Popes (G4ᵛ).

Indeed, Ruinish or its close cousins can enliven assaults on modern Rome. This would not have entirely displeased the Gallican Du Bellay, although it is hard to imagine him happy to see ruined by civil war any French choirs where sweet monks still sang. In England such language had become so associated with hopes for a New Jerusalem built on the rubble of Rome that it is hard to imagine Shakespeare reading Spenser's Roman poetry, especially the *Visions of Bellay*, without hearing such echoes. Whether in Mary Sidney's psalms or in post-Armada bravado, Ruinish had geopolitical resonance. Did it still have any in 1609? By the time Sonnets saw print they had perhaps faded, and the young man's one day 'tombed' beauty (Sonnet 4) was now a more private matter. It had been some years since the compiler of a manuscript wrote '*spes altera*' above a version of Sonnet 2—remembering how Aeneas' son Ascanius was the 'second hope of Rome'.[7]

8.2 WHORES, CITIES, TIME

I turn now to a poem by Du Bellay that travelled to England, certainly in translation and perhaps before that in French: *La vieille courtisanne*, published in *Divers jeux rustiques* (1558).[8] In the absence of evidence that Shakespeare read the original, one can resort to comparative literature, not reception history, or at least not with Shakespeare as receiver. The poem at least added to the lexical cluster generated by the *Antiquitez*, and

---

[7] In *The Times Literary Supplement* 19 April 1985, 45, Gary Taylor describes a manuscript with 'spes altera' written above Sonnet 2; cf. *Aeneid* XII, 168.

[8] *Divers jeux rustiques*, Henri Chamard (ed.), (Paris: Didier, 1947) 148–81; Joukovsky edition, II 240–55. Barbara Welch notes a mix of Ovid and Aretino; see 'La "courtisanne" de Du Bellay: Défense et Acte de Contrition', in *Du Bellay: Actes du Colloque International d'Angers du 26 au 29 Mai 1989*, Georges Cesbron (ed.), (Angers: Presses de l'Université d'Angers, 1990) II, 559–68.

Shakespeare may well have known the poem as published in 1609 (without mention of Du Bellay) by Gervase Markham, cousin to John Harington and expert on horses.[9] *The Famous Whore*'s relish in describing decay recalls the swagger with which some poets, including Du Bellay, praised ugly beauty, often with a glance at Horace's obscene epodes on old women repellent with wrinkled breasts and discouragingly desiccated nether parts.[10] But the poem also suggests the melancholy we can feel when looking at decayed cities, at ruined walls and forever-open gates. This aged whore, once as corrupt as the church dignitaries who draped her in riches, is as physically fallen as ancient Rome and as morally fallen as its papal successor.

In *Divers jeux* the old courtesan's monologue had followed two shorter ones translated from now lost Latin originals by Pierre Gillebert.[11] The first, 'La Courtisanne Repentie', bids farewell to the Roman flock that follows the Great Wolf. 'Wolf' (*lupa*) was Latin slang for 'prostitute', but it was a real she-wolf, they say, who suckled Romulus and Remus, those twins whose fratricidal conflict foreshadowed Rome's civil wars and bloodied its foundation, giving us another way to explain the empire's collapse. After all, as Shakespeare's King John says, the play's author conceivably thinking of modern France as well as of medieval England, 'There is no sure foundation set on blood' (IV. ii. 104). John must have foreseen *Antiquitez* 24, which asks, in Spenser's words, if the Romans perhaps 'embrew' their 'blades' in their 'owne bowels' because of 'brothers blood, the which at first was spilt | Upon your walls, that God might not endure, | Upon the same to set foundation sure'?[12] In any case, Du Bellay's speaker now foreswears her lute, her abortificant medications, her deodorants, even her Petrarch and Ariosto. But now comes the 'Counter-Repentant', spoken by a woman 'buried in herself' (line 15)—a temporal recursiveness not unlike the self-entombing Rome of *Antiquitez* 28 or the 'fond' youth of Sonnet 3 who may become the sterile 'tomb | Of his self-love'.[13] This freshly sinful courtesan boasts that more so than the monuments devoured by time, we whores are the ruin-filled city's remaining ornaments; and if Rome, which once knew how to conquer the world, can no longer do so by arms, it can now do so by sex and syphilis (lines 69–76, a boast that gives new meaning to the old palindrome, *Roma summus amor*). The more vigorous Protestant polemicists would agree with her and then

---

[9] See my '*Translatio Lupae*: Du Bellay's Roman Whore Goes North', *RQ* 42.3 (1989): 397–419.

[10] Horace, *Odes and Epodes*, C. E. Bennett (ed.), (Cambridge, MA: Harvard University Press, 1964) 416–17, tastefully left untranslated. Cf. Du Bellay's Horatian 'Antérotique' (1549).

[11] *Divers jeux*, ed. Henri Chamard (Paris: Didier, 1947) 136–41.

[12] *Antiquitez* 24: 'Ne permettant des Dieux le juste jugement, /Voz murs ensanglantez par la main fraternelle/Se pouvoir asseurer d'un ferme fondement'. Spenser changes 'gods' to God. See also Charles Hieatt, 'Dating *King John*: The Implications of the Influence of Edmund Spenser's *Ruins of Rome* on Shakespeare's Text', *N&Q* 35.4 (1988): 458–63. Shakespeare can parody walls: if Rome's walls could be breached, the one between Pyramis and Thisbe in *Midsummer* has an actor playing it, and with a chink for whispers that lead to a gently roaring lion and death.

[13] *Divers jeux* 142–7. Might one hear in 'Or who is he so fond will be the tomb' an embedded 'fond will', a fond [foolish, loving] will [desire, intention, maybe Will]? A fond will is one explanation for Rome's collapse.

ask what we might plausibly call such a contagion-spreading, conquest-hungry Roman whore? Obvious—she wears a triple crown and presses on us a chalice of abominations. If she were prettied up, we could call her Duessa.

The 'Vieille courtisanne' returns us to remorse.[14] Paulina, as Markham names her, imparts some trade secrets, advising us to avoid Spaniards, for example, because the French pay better. She is aged, although Rome's executioner has enjoyed her flesh—after all, he's a *carnifex*. Now she is disintegrating and in English is *rheumy* (E3; Du Bellay merely gives her eye trouble). Markham's word may be a quasi-pun on Rome/rheum, one with overtones recalling the paradox Du Bellay borrowed from the neo-latin poet Janus Vitalis for *Antiquitez* 3 about a perpetually running Tiber and a time-halted city.[15] After all, the city-crowned Cybele, 'Berecynthian Goddesse bright' (*Ruines of Rome* 6), who also haunted Spenser's imagination, is also 'Rhea'. The goddess of the built world means 'Flowing'. Toward the end of her lament Du Bellay turns to the language of the *Antiquitez*—and also, with a tinge of irony, of Virgil, for 'Oh that I am different from her that I was once' adapts 'quantum mutatus ab illo | Hectore' (Markham has, 'so much changd am I from what I was').[16] As the poem closes, the connections with ancient Rome tighten. Was it not enough that civil broils made you, Rome, the world's prey? Do you not lament your lost liberty even more than the antique palaces of which you see 'les poudreuses reliques'? (Markham has 'antient monuments which now to dust | Are turned' [F1], banishing the 'relics'.) That her 'lost liberty' refers to the Pope's stringent new laws governing prostitution may diminish her situation's pathos. The low-lifes in *Measure for Measure* would sympathize with her, though (as would *2 Henry IV*'s Doll Tearsheet), even if the play's initially reformist Angelo would not. Although I have not found quotations from Markham's poem in polemics using Ruinish, somewhere behind it flickers a more darkly anti-Catholic allegory than the one the Gallican Du Bellay probably intended.

One way to give an old courtesan more pathos—if not more usefulness for Reformation polemics—would be to turn her into the ghost of a faded royal mistress or some other once beautiful but somewhat less sullied victim of Time. Du Bellay's poem is a cousin of the female laments that in England can follow a sonnet sequence.[17] Indeed some such complaints, especially those by Michael Drayton, Thomas Lodge, and not least Samuel Daniel, incorporate allusions to ruins and echoes of Du Bellay or Spenser. Daniel's now aged Rosamond, for example, remembers herself as a Minotaur of sin in her own labyrinth, a beauty whose brow once tyrannized over the whole world but whose very monuments Time is now eating.[18] 'Time', she says, has

---

[14] *Divers jeux* 148–80; a perhaps unauthorized Lyon edition by Nicolas Edoard added notes.

[15] And *Rome* has *room* for only one man says Cassius (*Julius Caesar* I. ii. 157).

[16] *Aeneid* II 274–5; 'Vieille courtisanne' ll. 501–2 and note; Markham E3.

[17] *Ant.* 13. Thomas Middleton's *Ghost of Lucrece* (1600), which connects ancient to Papal Rome, says 'So Beauty's blot drops from the pen of Time' (C2ᵛ); Robert Parry's *Sinetes passions* (1597) tells Robert Cecil that Parry will make him famous despite 'Devouring time', 'steling time', and 'time with cutting Sithe'.

[18] 'The Complaint of Rosamond', soon attached to *Delia*, in Samuel Daniel, *Poems and a Defence of Ryme*, A. C. Sprague (ed.), (Chicago: University of Chicago Press, 1965).

'long since worne out the memorie' of her life (l. 17). We see 'the ruine of my youth' even though once she had known how to 'tyrannize, | And make the world do homage' (lines 64, 104–5). Do not let her name be entombed, she asks the poet (line 319), an issue not without parallels in *Antiquitez* and Du Bellay's fascination, shared by Shakespeare and many others, with surviving *names* and lost *things*. Then, near the poem's end, she shows her linguistic and imaginative cousinship with Shakespeare's Spenser and maybe his Du Bellay:

> For those walles which the credulous devout,
> And apt-beleeving ignorant did found:
> With willing zeale that never call'd in doubt,
> That time theyr works should ever so confound,
> Lye like confused heapes as under-ground.
>> And what their ignorance esteem'd so holy,
>> The wiser ages doe account as folly.
>
> And were it not thy favourable lynes,
> Reedified the wracke of my decayes:
> And that thy accents willingly assignes,
> Some farther date, and give me longer daies,
> Few in this age had knowne my beauties praise.
>> But thus renewd, my fame redeemes some time,
>> Till other ages shall neglect thy rime . . .
>>> (lines 708–21)

Rosamond's doubt concerning poetry's lasting strength against time has parallels in the *Antiquitez*. At least, if those shades that in *Antiquitez* 1 Du Bellay tries to summon do not answer forcefully enough, French and English poets can move on past the likes of Virgil (whom Du Bellay ostentatiously, with a glance at Ronsard, refuses to imitate when writing the *Regrets*). Nor does Rome have a monopoly on the ruins that recall antiquity. Later poets can sing of them, too. In *Musophilus*, Daniel almost boasts of England's Stonehenge in a then not infrequent gesture of *translatio ruinarum*: if Rome can boast of ruins we can too.[19] Thus Richard Carew reports in *The Survey of Cornwall* (1602) that 'Tintogel in his ruines vauntes, | Sometime the seate of Kings' (Ii1ᵛ). But for how long? Ruins also disappear. The narrator of *The Ruines of Time* even declares that of Verlame—the city, not its spectre—nothing remains, a degree zero of ruination, with perhaps the same 'grandeur' that Du Bellay's *Antiquitez* 13 had found in 'rien'. There is pleasure in thinking of Verlame as a (not) ruined city, but when Time hangs up his hourglass and scythe, will words persist? Shakespeare insists that his words will last, but words can age too.

---

[19] Lines. 337–60; Daniel grieves that 'nothing should remain' to tell us what the stones meant (line 353), although some seemed to have relished the thought of ruination as what one might call 'zeroification'. Spenser's Verlame in *Ruines of Time* 'lies' in her 'owne ashes' (line 40), 'buried' in her 'ruines' (line 172).

The chief relevance of Du Bellay's courtesan to Shakespeare's Sonnets, though, like that to Spenser's ghost of Verlame, is also the connection the poem makes explicit toward the end between a ruined female body and a ruined city. If the young man will be 'besieged' by the 'bloody tyrant, time' (Sonnets 2, 16), if 'broils' will 'root out the work of masonry' (55), if time will 'transfix the flourish set on youth' (60) and age ply his 'cruel knife' (63), then 'Ruin hath taught me thus to ruminate, | That time will come and take my love away' (64). To describe the ravished protagonist of his *Lucrece*, Shakespeare likewise adopts some of the *Antiquitez* | *Ruines* lexicon, exploiting an ancient analogy that treats the body as a city, nation, or microcosm: as a 'ruined' woman, Lucrece has civic meaning. One English printer, Thomas Berthelet, even had a decorative image showing her against a background of ruins (see FIGURE 8.1).[20] Why ruins? Are they proleptic? Or are they ruins of the Tarquin monarchy? Do they suggest, as we remember the Roman republic founded thanks to Tarquin's crime, that there is no sure foundation set on a raped female? Her head when her rapist enters the bedroom, where she lies 'like a virtuous monument', is 'entombed' between pillows (lines 390–1), phrasing with some resonance when we recall both the old story that the 'Capitol' was named for a head found in the earth under its foundations and Rome's pride in being the head of the world on its seven hills. After calling on 'injurious, shifting Time' (line 930), Lucrece says in good Ruinish:

> Time's glory is to calm contending kings,
> To unmask falsehood and bring truth to light,
> To stamp the seal of time in agèd things,
> To wake the morn and sentinel the night,
> To wrong the wronger till he render right,
>   To ruinate proud buildings with thy hours
>   And smear with dust their glitt'ring golden towers;
>
> To fill with worm-holes stately monuments,
> To feed oblivion with decay of things,
> To blot old books and alter their contents,
> To pluck the quills from ancient ravens' wings,
> To dry the old oak's sap and cherish springs,
>   To spoil antiquities of hammered steel
>   And turn the giddy round of fortune's wheel ...

(lines 939–52)

Herself a ruinated building, Lucrece will grieve that her soul's house 'is sacked, her quiet interrupted, | Her mansion battered by the enemy; | Her sacred temple spotted, spoiled,

[20] Illustrations for Daniel and Hosea in the 1568 *Bishops Bible* have ruins; those in Ezekiel go well with 'Songe'/'Visions of Bellay' 13. Spenser remembers *translatio imperii*: when writing on Lewis Lewkenor's translation of Contarini's *Commonwealth and Government of Venice* (1599; McCabe 502): Babel's 'upreard' buildings yielded to the 'Second *Babell tyrant of the West*', and 'under the weight of their own surquedry' both 'buried in their own ashes ly, | Yet shewing by their heapes how great they were'. Perhaps Shakespeare, gathering material for *Merchant*, enjoyed this.

FIGURE 8.1. A 'Roman' Lucrece in Front of the Ruins of Ancient Troy or Future Rome (Thomas Berthelet's printer's mark on the final leaf of Sir Thomas Elyot's 1545 *A preservative agaynste deth*). Reprinted with the kind permission of the British Library Board: shelfmark C.124.aaa.19.(1).

corrupted' (lines 1170–2). No wonder she takes a dagger to 'make a hole' in her soul's 'blemished fort' (line 1175). Her body is a sacked military structure, and the long section on the taking of Troy makes the urban connection clearer. Nor is Lucrece alone: the Bible's Jerusalem is sometimes a ruined wife, Babylon a to-be-ruined whore whom Revelation clearly reads as a future Rome.[21]

I have no space here to explore a fuller range of the often allegorical connections between urban and female ruination, but they might, in a gender-bending way, further illuminate Shakespeare's self-enclosed, walled-in youth who risks self-burial. He is not whorish like Du Bellay's city/courtesan (indeed he is the opposite), but, subject to the same ruination as Rome, he is another example of the metaphoric connections

---

[21] Cf. Lawrence Manley, 'Spenser and the City: The Minor Poems', *MLQ* 43 (1982): 203–27, although I do not hear 'youthful apocalyptic hysteria'.

between cities and ruined ... women. No, he is not a woman, even if for the moment he is very, very pretty. In Sonnet 20, of course, Nature had designed him as one, so perhaps there's enough of the female left in him to make a good city, or at least somebody to whom not only Du Bellay's *Antiquitez* are relevant but also his old ruined Roman whore and her overused lower naught. And yet women's unfillable 'will', as Shakespeare calls the Dark Lady's nothing in Sonnet 135, is vital to humankind. Abraham Fraunce, slipping into Ruinish for a moment in his *Third Part of The Countesse of Pembrokes Yvychurch* (1592), says that Saturn spared his daughter because the 'devouring continuance of outwearing time consumeth all things'—but only '*individua*, this thing, and that thing, but not the roote and ground of things figured by the femall sex' (C1).

8.3 BEING (ANTI) PETRARCHAN

Du Bellay's satire on Rome and courtesans is further evidence, if in reverse, for Wayne Rebhorn's argument that the *Antiquitez* offers translated Petrarchism—from the untouchable lady Laura to unreachable Roman antiquity with shades that do not reply, or not audibly, to the observer's prayers.[22] Laura speaks to Petrarch more than some critics think she does, but she does not say what he wants to hear, any more than do the ashy ghosts and pale spirits when Du Bellay tries to magic them upward. The courtesan poems and Markham's *Famous Whore* seem in their own way not-Petrarchan: if ladies who say 'no' will someday, as Samuel Daniel warns his Delia, bend their wrinkles homeward to the earth or if, as Ronsard tells his own beloved, ladies who say 'non' should study rose petals that fall before they can be plucked, then in this poem ladies who say 'yes' too often will someday beg in the streets, their bodies ruined like any Roman arch or forum.[23] Shakespeare himself gives such warnings to the still beautiful young man, not to the Dark Lady (she is hardly the refusing type), because it is the youth who says no. And, like any good Petrarchist, Shakespeare's poet can associate the stance of upright refusal with collapse into ruins, even if his overt answer to time's effect on the beloved is son-making and not leaping into bed with the poet. In an essay on Du Bellay, François Rigolot has said that to 'Petrarquize' is to make oneself prisoner of a perpetual refusal.[24] Yes, and yet (to repeat) one who like the young man perpetually refuses may be buried in the jail of self: a virtuous or even stoic self, but still providing house arrest. Here may

[22] Wayne Rebhorn, 'Du Bellay's Imperial Mistress: *Les Antiquitez de Rome* as Petrarchist Sonnet Sequence', *RQ* 33.4 (1980): 609–22. Cf. Heather Dubrow, *Captive Victors: Shakespeare's Narrative Poems and Sonnets* (Ithaca: Cornell University Press, 1987), and Jason Leubner's 'Temporal Distance. Antiquity, and the Beloved in Petrarch's *Rime sparse* and Du Bellay's *Les Antiquitez de Rome*', *MLN* 122 (2007): 1079–1104.

[23] See Daniel, *Delia*, Sonnet 42 (1592), in a sequence owing much to Du Bellay, and Pierre de Ronsard, 'Mignonne, allons voir si la rose', in *Oeuvres complètes*, Jean Céard, Daniel Ménager, and Michel Simonin (eds), (Paris: Gallimard, 1993) I, 667.

[24] François Rigolot, 'Du Bellay et la poésie du refus', *BHR* 36 (1974): 489–502, at 493.

be another place where we can perceive if not a debt to Du Bellay or Spenser then at least a pair of resonant parallels: self-enclosure, proud identity, the 'I' with no 'you', is a self-conquest in more than a stoic sense. To be the whole world is to risk being not an 'I' but a tomb.

Du Bellay's courtesan poetry thus serves a discourse in which erotic over-compliance is the obverse of Petrarchism. But what of Petrarchism itself?[25] Du Bellay's *Olive* (1549, 1550) is a sonnet sequence so abjectly indebted to Petrarch that in the enlarged second edition Du Bellay thought he should explain: I read a lot, he says, and have a good memory. English poets sometimes imitated *Olive's* sonnets, although I find little trace in Shakespeare. Du Bellay wrote one poem, however, that I suspect entertained the man who said his own mistress' eyes were absolutely non-solar. 'J'ai oublié l'art de petrarquizer', revised for inclusion in the *Jeux rustiques*, renounces the style of *Olive*, with maybe an implied renunciation of alien Italianate fanciness.[26] Did Shakespeare read it? He could, possibly, have known the condensed version by Sir Arthur Gorges, translator of Lucan, friend of Spenser, and fan of Du Bellay.[27]

In a paradoxical palinode a recovering Petrarchist explains that he now prefers to be *frank*, without flattery, disguise, forced sobs, without covering 'rotten weedes with flowers', as Gorges puts it. No more saying your fair looks 'represent the lofty Skies | And frame too stares of your too eyes'. No comparing of your hair to gold, your hands to ivory. You a goddess? What a world of fictions! One poet makes a heaven of his affections, another a hell of his passions; some feign an ocean of tumultuous waves in their hearts. No more 'paintede shewes to bleare the eyne | And make off mortall things devyne'. The lover cannot 'reache soe hye'. He has 'volonté franche', frank desire, honest will. He is earthy, 'terrestre'. If you love me back, that's my true Androgyne (like the young man of Sonnet 20?). And, seriously: 'Nor tyme itt selfe awaye shall weare | The honour that I owe your face'. Believe those lying Petrarchists if you will, but 'in my selfe in truthe I finde | ... To lyve to love and serve yow still'. Du Bellay had said more: when you are old, the gold turned to silver, your ivory and lilies faded, who will love you? Do not wait for the great scythe of time (Shakespeare's 'bending sickle') to mow the flower of your spring. The years leave only regrets and sighs, winging away our wills and pleasures.

Then the kicker: 'If nevertheless Petrarch pleases you more, then I will take up again my melodious song and fly to the heavens to find a thousand novelties with which I will paint your beauties on the most beautiful idea'. The joke is obvious: Du Bellay is doing what he says he has forgotten how to do. Does the lady prefer Petrarch? He has been Petrarch all along. Perhaps Shakespeare knew this witty *recusatio* (not 'I will not write an epic', but rather 'I will not write love poetry'), for some related vocabulary encourages

[25] For that matter, Roger Kuin reminds me, Cicero never replied to Petrarch's letters.
[26] Bernard Weinberg, 'Du Bellay's "Contre les Pétrarquistes"'. *L'Esprit créateur* 12.3 (1972): 159–77, gives an analysis.
[27] Sir Arthur Gorges, *Poems*, ed. Helen E. Sandison (Oxford: Clarendon Press, 1953) 50–2. Cf. David Klein 'Foreign Influence on Shakespeare's Sonnets', *Sewanee Review*, 13.4 (1905): 454–74.

the thought. He certainly performs the same joke, if more briefly: mistress, eyes, sun—
not. This is also *not*, of course, how to forget Petrarch. It is, though, a reminder that such
parallels might encourage us to recall yet more often that the snarky style of clever young
men about London in the late 1590s had precedent, and in this case a poem by one who
had not merely imitated Petrarch but grovelled at his feet, and indeed borrowed those
feet to walk in.

8.4 WHEN ALL IS NOTHING

Du Bellay and Spenser both liked circles: *Olive* hints at a liturgical olive wreath and
Spenser's *Amoretti* is even more clearly calendrical. A circle, though, can be a zero.
Rome claimed, says Du Bellay, to be an *all* but is now a nothing, *rien*. In the paradoxical
sonnet that I cited earlier (*Antiquitez* 3), Rome is gone but the Tiber remains. A reader
knows that rivers, unlike the waves in Shakespeare's Sonnet 60 that make for the pebbled
shore, flow downward into oblivion, into the devouring sea. But here the Tiber remains
and Rome is nothing. (A Greek sceptic might say the *name* Tiber remains—or can you
give the same name to the same river twice?) Over and over in the *Antiquitez* Du Bellay
returns to *rien*, if also to nothing's 'grandeur', its all, its 'rondeur', and to the identity that
nothing might erase or the nothing to which Rome's effort to be the globe brought it.
In Spenser's translation the word is more commonly 'nought'—as in 'nought of *Rome*
in *Rome* perceiv'st at all' (*Ruines of Rome* 3; the text's juxtaposition of 'all. O' is clever).[28]
Rome's spires in *Ruines of Rome* 7 are the verticals juxtaposing the 'nothing' to which
the city 'flie[s]'. The sequence is filled with nothings, with the knowledge that 'this whole
shall one day come to nought' (*Ruines of Rome* 9). This is not just the work of time, civil
strife, and Goths, the sequence makes clear, but of pride, of being the whole world when
all the world was Rome before becoming the tomb of the whole world. And yet 'this
nothing' makes 'the world wonder' (the 'grandeur du rien ... face encor' emerveiller le
monde', *Antiquitez* 13). The zeros add up, and Rome is now an impressive 'nought' where
'all this worlds pride once was situate' (*Ruines of Rome* 31). Even the *translatio imperii*
that brought power to Rome will not move on, argues Yvonne Bellenger, for this imperial circle devolves to nothing.[29] At the end of this sequence Spenser gives Du Bellay
himself a circle ('first garland of free Poësie'), but the same sonnet gives a spire to Du
Bartas, who raises his 'heavenlie' muse to adore the Almighty. Rome's circle offers no
such vertical movement.

Shakespeare was hardly the only author of love sonnets to exploit this nothingness.
Robert Tofte's 1598 *Alba*, for example, which uses Ruinish and mentions a production
of *Love's Labour's Lost* (sig. G5), not only remembers Rome's 'stately Hils' and 'princelike

---

[28] So, perhaps, is '*Rome* is no more' (*RR*5): 'more' is Rome's anagram.
[29] *Le Temps et les jours dans quelques recueils poétiques du XVIe siècle* (Paris: Champion, 2002) 181–8.

Ruins olde' but says of Alba's beauty: 'All this doth Time consume and bring to nought, | And all what ere into this world is brought' (H8). But English writers also enjoyed making something of the very sign for 'nothing', a sign still fairly new in Europe and usually called 'cipher'; how exciting to make a number ten times as big by adding such a nought! (Stephen Gosson's 1582 *Playes Confuted in Five Actions* even calls actors ciphers to the playwright's 1, a suggestion not without ambiguity).[30] And the puns ... *Much Ado About Nothing* indeed, and with a heroine named Hero. Sonnets has similar puns, of course, and not just play with the dark lady's nothing. In Sonnet 20 what Nature has added to the young man is to the speaker's purpose 'nothing', although in fact her addition is shaped like a '1'. (At least the 1 thing and the 0 together make him a 10.) There is something haunting, something relevant to the young man, about the similarity of zero and enclosure, of the walled self that characterizes a Coriolanus and the love-resistant youth. Stoics and zero have something in common. Rome is no more, and if you imagine a bird's-eye view of its remains, then the Coliseum, that largely circular ruin that often appears in English images (such as that for Spenser's 'Januarie' in *The Shepheardes Calender*), would appear a zero. So would Shakespeare's 'wooden O' of a theater, or the great '[G]lobe' that *The Tempest*'s Prospero says will one day fade and leave not a rack behind. To make Rome a zero, *rien* may make room for the once-barbarian France and England, but they advance themselves, still, in terms of the city Du Bellay calls nothing. If it is a nothing it is still, to our purpose, something—and ten times over. We are the ones to its zero.

In his Sonnets and Roman plays, then, Shakespeare would have learned from Du Bellay, or had his thoughts reinforced, that to be a whole, to be an 'I'—a mere one and mere ego, is to bury oneself and be nothing. Somehow Rome's 'allness', its self-enclosure encircled by seven hills, by giants of arrogance, by the claim to be all the world, the very map of the world, leads to nonentity. The young man will be less of a zero if he uses that little straight line with which Nature pricked him out and pays emotional and physical attention to others.

8.5 Coda: Ruination in *Titus Andronicus*

Apparently written not too long after *The Ruines of Rome* saw print, *Titus Andronicus* does not have quite enough Ruinish to show that Shakespeare had already been impressed by Du Bellay's (or Spenser's) thoughts on devouring time, walls, worn monuments, bloody foundations, and suicidal civil embroilments. It does, though, have an unnamed Goth who reports that when looking at 'a ruinous monastery' he had 'heard

---

[30] A8ᵛ. John D. Barrow, *The Book of Nothing* (London: Vintage, 2001), wittily discusses Shakespeare (87–91).

a child cry underneath a wall' of the 'wasted building'.[31] Like a clown swearing by St Stephen (IV. iv. 42), or Titus' reference to 'hermits in their holy prayers' (III. ii. 40), or like a 'castle' (III. i. 170) that sounds a little medieval, this monastery is a puzzle. What ruined it? Time? Goths? Nero and Diocletian did not ruin *monasteries*, just Christians.[32] And why would the villain Aaron fear 'popish tricks and ceremonies' (V. i. 76)? *Popish*? This play is to chronology as Cubism is to a photograph.

Titus had opened with a question of succession—just the issue in the civil wars still going on in France and speaking to unease over who or what would follow Elizabeth. We hear of 'city walls', 'barbarous Goths', and lovely Lavinia as 'Rome's rich ornament', words recalling Spenser's *Ruines of Rome* if not definitive proof that Shakespeare had yet read it. Both works, moreover, bear witness to forces that can destroy an arrogant city/ self. Castles and monasteries are both enclosed (and although Stephen—with a name meaning 'wreath'—was not built of stone, it was stones that killed him). I suspect that in Shakespeare's imagination the ruination of Rome has merged with the ruined choirs of England. This need not show Catholic sympathies, even if it allows the thought, because Protestants too could believe that Henry VIII's reformation and the recycling of abbey stones had been needlessly destructive.[33]

In the Sonnets the young man faces a destruction that Shakespeare's lexicon relates to that of Rome. In the poets' analogies he does not always fade, dropping his remaining yellow leaves as most of us do. He is more often a victim of force, of something metallic and swift: Time undermines him, carves him, besieges him, digs in him, harvests him (bristly white beard and all, in Sonnet 12). *Tempus edax* has chewed up much of Rome, but Du Bellay/Spenser also ascribes much of the desolation to civil war and barbarian or civic violence—and to divine anger at its Titan complex. England's ruined monasteries, perhaps including the one that has travelled through space–time to this fictional Rome, were likewise victims not of time but of human force. Yet there is something else at work. Some have noted Shakespeare's implied connection between the play's embattled Rome and the body of its soon mutilated and ravished Lavinia.[34]

---

[31] The final scene recalls Du Bellay: beware lest 'she whom mighty kingdoms curtsy to … Do shameful execution on herself' (V. iii. 73–6), and the last line hopes that events 'may ne'er it ruinate'. Helga L. Duncan, '"Sumptuously Re-edified": The Reformation of Sacred Space in *Titus Andronicus*', *Comparative Drama* 43.4 (2009): 425–53, touches on city and female body (426); cf. Raria Del Sapio Garbero, Nancy Isenberg, and Maddalena Pennacchia (eds), *Questioning Bodies in Shakespeare's Rome* (Goettingen: V&R Press, 2010). Aparna Khastgir, 'Ending as *Concordia Discors*: *Titus Andronicus*', *Studia Neophilologica* 73 (2001): 36–47, discusses the anachronisms' implications for space, burial, and Reformation, remarking that 'Shakespeare's Goths are as civilised and humane as Roman letters can make them' (39). Like Goths, I would add, Du Bellay and Spenser look from the north.

[32] I thank Lauren Silberman for sharing work in progress on *Titus'* biblical and Augustinian subtexts.

[33] Margaret Aston, 'English Ruins and English History: The Dissolution and the Sense of the Past', *Journal of the Warburg and Courtauld Institutes* 36 (1973): 231–55.

[34] For Vernon Guy Dickson, in '"A pattern, precedent, and lively warrant": Emulation, Rhetoric, and Cruel Propriety in *Titus Andronicus*', *RQ* 6.2 (2009): 376–409, Shakespeare links 'The chaos of the political state' to 'vying over Lavinia' and 'political ruin to sexual transgression' (406). Chernaik's chapter on *Titus* sees a comment on Rome's self-contradictory imperial ideology.

She is another Lucrece, if more savagely hurt. Even if the traces of Ruinish are fewer than in the Sonnets, here too Shakespeare exploits the ancient imaginary in which a city is a woman. *La Vieille Courtisanne* and Lucrece are cities, are Rome—and in Lucrece's view, also Troy. The play's audience knows that what happens to Lavinia will happen to Rome. Rome will even, like Lavinia, have not only the hands of its power cut off but its tongue torn out, for although several times used in this play, and although still read by the educated, Latin will cease to be a living language, unlike French and English. The poetry produced by that tongue will haunt Du Bellay and Spenser, for of course they had no need to summon the poets' shades. Virgil and Ovid are and are not ashy ghosts.

In the *Antiquitez* and *Ruines of Rome* the intellectual contradictions of implying that Roman culture is over even while lifting lines from its writers, and the ambiguities/ambivalences of mourning and satisfaction, of weeping over a grave even while surreptitiously dancing on it, are not wholly unlike the irresolution of a Shakespeare not quite able to decide if poetry really bestows immortality despite that inevitable 'edge of doom' and the effect of Time's scythe on words, on names. In sum, to have a ruined abbey, which must recall to the mind the Gothic architecture of the future and not the arches and pillars of ancient Rome, can summon up—for the author if not for his audience—Du Bellay's (or Spenser's) linguistic complex involving a fallen city, fallen woman, civil violence, and barbarian cruelty. And where is Time? Not for nothing is an emperor in *Titus* named Saturninus. Saturn once ruled an Age of Gold that will, one reads, someday return.[35] In the meantime—thanks to a confusion of Kronos with Chronos—he is Father Time, castrator of his father and wielder of a scythe, and yet thrown a party during the time of year that the coming age of monasteries will call Christmas. That the ruined abbey in *Titus* is anachronistic and out of place (anatopic?) shows a playwright's power over time. As a poet, if not as a Renaissance humanist, Du Bellay might applaud. So might Spenser. Granted Renaissance writers' mixed feelings toward Roman ruins it seems fitting, even touching, that in this play Shakespeare has Saturn stumble on his forward path.

SELECT BIBLIOGRAPHY

Aston, Margaret (1973) 'English Ruins and English History: The Dissolution and the Sense of the Past,' *Journal of the Warburg and Courtauld Institutes* 36: 231–55.

Bellenger, Yvonne (2009) (ed.) *Du Bellay et ses sonnets romains: Études sur les Regrets et les Antiquitez de Rome réunies par Yvonne Bellenger* (Paris: Champion).

Cesbron, Georges (1990) (ed.) *Du Bellay: Actes du Colloque International d'Angers du 26 au 29 Mai 1989*, 2 vols (Angers: Presses de l'Université d'Angers).

Chernaik, Warren (2011) *Myth of Rome in Shakespeare and his Contemporaries* (Cambridge: Cambridge University Press).

---

[35] On Saturn's appetite, see Roland Derche, 'J. Du Bellay: les Antiquitez de Rome, III', *L'Information littéraire* 25 (1973): 232–8.

Du Bellay, Joachim (2009) (ed.) *Œuvres poétiques*, 2 vols (Paris: Garnier).

Helgerson, Richard (2006) *Joachim Du Bellay* (Philadelphia: University of Pennsylvania Press).

Hieatt, A. Kent (1983) 'The Genesis of Shakespeare's *Sonnets*: Spenser's *Ruines of Rome: by Bellay*,' PMLA 98: 800–14.

Klein, David (1905) 'Foreign Influence on Shakespeare's Sonnets,' Sewanee Review 13.4: 454–74.

Melehy, Hassan (2010) *Poetics of Literary Transfer in Early Modern France and England* (Farnham: Ashgate).

Muir, Thomas (2010) 'Without remainder: ruins and tombs in Shakespeare's *Sonnets*,' *Textual Practice* 24.1: 21–49.

CHAPTER 9

....

OPEN VOICING

Wyatt and Shakespeare

....

LINDA GREGERSON

9.1

In the transit from Petrarch to Petrarch-as-Englished-by-Thomas-Wyatt, we see the birth of a rhetorical proposition that will come to be of considerable importance for 16th-century English poetry. Wyatt cultivates a kind of vocal gesture—fugitive, erratic, deliberately discontinuous—we have since come to regard as the hallmark of personality. Experimenting with voice as a symptom of character, he conjures the figment of an individuated speaking persona, one who is biased, irritable, and rhetorically unstable. The innovation lies not in the quality of strong feeling—to speak of and with strong feeling is as old as poetry itself—nor in the reference to biographical and social circumstance: this too is old. The innovation lies in method, the symptom-effect or vocal signature that suggests, by way of back-formation, a socially embedded, distinctive personality. Wyatt's contribution is consequential precisely because his method is at odds with the fully contextualized monologue that will reach its apotheosis in the work of Robert Browning, and is also distinct from personation on the early modern English stage. It left its mark upon that stage, as I shall hope to describe below. But first I should like to focus on the 16th-century lyric itself, on the supple movement into and out of implied character, on the porousness of limned persona that makes that lyric such a limbre and profound instrument. I propose we think of this phenomenon as open voicing.

The most conspicuous example I can adduce is also, and not by accident, the most frequently anthologized of Wyatt's lyrics, his adaptation of poem 190 from Petrarch's *Rime sparse*. Here is Robert Durling's prose translation of the Petrarch:

> A white doe on the green grass appeared to me, with two golden horns, between two rivers, in the shade of a laurel, when the sun was rising in the unripe season.
>
> Her look was so sweet and proud that to follow her I left every task, like the miser who as he seeks treasure sweetens his trouble with delight.

'Let no one touch me', she bore written with diamonds and topazes around her lovely neck. 'It has pleased my Caesar to make me free'.

And the sun had already turned at midday; my eyes were tired by looking but not sated, when I fell into the water, and she disappeared.[1]

The poem narrates a vision: the speaker beholds a white doe with golden horns; he follows her; he reads a warning in the collar she wears around her neck; he falls into the water; the vision disappears. Or rather, these things have happened at some point in the past: the time of speaking is distinct from the time of action. The poem is spoken to everyone and no one; the moment of speaking is undifferentiated except by backward longing. We are told the duration of the vision—it has lasted from sunrise to midday—and yet, as befits the poet's chronic inclination toward transcendence, it is bathed in an aura of timelessness.

Wyatt's version is deliberately pitched at the opposite end of the rhetorical spectrum:

> Whoso list to hunt, I know where is an hind,
> But as for me, helas, I may no more.
> The vain travail hath wearied me so sore,
> I am of them that farthest cometh behind.
> Yet may I by no means my wearied mind
> Draw from the deer, but as she fleeth afore
> Fainting I follow. I leave off therefore
> Sithens in a net I seek to hold the wind.
> Who list her hunt, I put him out of doubt,
> As well as I may spend his time in vain.
> And graven with diamonds in letters plain
> There is written her fair neck round about:

---

[1] Robert Durling (trans. and ed.), *Petrarch's Lyric Poems: The* Rime sparse *and Other Lyrics* (Cambridge, MA: Harvard University Press, 1976). All citations of Petrarch, in English and Italian, derive from this dual language edition.

> *Una candida cerva sopra l'erba*
> *verde m'apparve con duo corna d'oro,*
> *fra due riviere all'ombra d'un alloro,*
> *levando 'l sole a la stagione acerba.*
>
> *Era sua vista sì dolce superba*
> *ch' i' i' lasciai per seguirla ogni lavoro,*
> *come l'avaro che'n cercar tesoro*
> *con diletto l'affanno disacerba.*
>
> *'Nessun mi tocchi', al bel collo d'intorno*
> *scritto avea di diamanti et di topazi.*
> *'Libera farmi al mio Cesare parve'.*
>
> *Et era 'l sol già vòlto al mezzo giorno,*
> *gli occhi miei stanchi di mirar, non sazi,*
> *quand' io caddi ne l'acqua et elle sparve.*

'*Noli me tangere* for Caesar's I am,
And wild for to hold though I seem tame'.[2]

'Whoso list to hunt, I know where is an hind'. Grounded, demotic, shot through with grievance and insinuation, the poem begins by conjuring not only a speaker with an axe to grind but also an implied inner audience. And this audience, like the speaker, has attributes. It is gendered; it is 'interested'. Wyatt's poem begins in a kind of locker-room vernacular, male. You want to try your luck? he says; I can point you in the right direction. In another era, he'd be scrawling the woman's telephone number on a public wall or posting her picture on Facebook. 'Whoso list to hunt, I know where is an hind'. And almost immediately, the first of several turnings: 'But as for me, helas, I may no more'. This modulates, almost, to the more orthodox Petrarchan lover's complaint. Almost, but not quite. For the speaker is pointedly not alone with his suffering, not even in the special sense of lyric complaint, which always inhabits the paradoxical public/private domain of that-which-is-written-to-be-read. This speaker has hunted with others who are in the game: 'The vain travail hath wearied me so sore, | I am of them that farthest cometh behind'. The deprivation of which he complains, in other words, is relative as well as absolute; the problem is not merely the beloved's coldness or inaccessibility but the social insult of a poor competitive showing.

The instabilities of renunciation and continued entanglement have been amply noted in this sonnet before, but for my purposes, the key point is that they both solicit and evade a psychological reading. On one level, the inconsistent push and pull ('I may no more', 'I follow', 'I leave off') suggests the turmoil of captive desire and thus the symptoms of a psyche under pressure. And the haunting image with which the octave concludes ('Sithens in a net I seek to hold the wind') is drawn directly from a second Petrarchan poem, *Rime sparse* 239,[3] whose very form—the perpetual reshufflings of the sestina—enacts the persona's tortured buffetings between hope and despair. The symptom-effect again. But this is one level only: we do not find ourselves inside a single, coherent subjectivity in 'Whoso List to Hunt'. Producing the effects of psychological instability, and exceeding them as well, is something else: an instability of rhetorical proposition. From the leering pseudo-confidentiality of line one, which conjures an inner audience of fellow cynics, the speaker segues to a complaint mode in which that audience is vaporized. The bluff companions so deftly granted shadow-existence by 'whoso list to hunt' might be imagined as sticking around for 'vain

---

[2] For this and subsequent citations of Wyatt's poems, I have relied upon R. A. Rebholz (ed.), *Sir Thomas Wyatt: The Complete Poems*, (New Haven: Yale University Press, 1978).

[3] The image appears in the final tercet of Petrarch's sestina:

> In a net I catch the breeze and on ice flowers,
> and in verses I woo a deaf and rigid soul
> who esteems neither the power of Love nor his notes.

> In rete accolgo l'aura e'n ghiaccio i fiori,
> e'n versi tento sorda et rigida alma
> che né forza d'Amor prezza né note.

travail' and 'may no more', but surely they would have no patience for the second quatrain, which inhabits a different speaking and listening cosmos altogether. We have moved from a quasi-dramatic mode to lyric complaint. Even within that lyric mode, the speaking persona seems to waver between personal and social grievance, which wavering is temporarily 'solved' by the abrupt and bitter return to the mockeries of public auction: 'Who list her hunt, I put him out of doubt, | As well as I may spend his time in vain'.

Let me confess at once that these 'slow readings'[4] are by nature both ungainly and distorting. I do not for a minute mean to propose that the reader of the poem on the page, or, in ordinary circumstances, 'on the voice', will consciously pause to contemplate the blow by blow vicissitudes of the inner audience I have described: now he's got their attention, now he's losing it, etc. Nor even: now they're vividly invoked, now they're fading into something else, etc. Much less do I mean to suggest that Wyatt's compositional method involved the minute pre-plotting of local transitions. This is not, as I understand it, how poems get written. It is the speed and economy with which Wyatt limns the ever-changing social circumstance of lyric speech, it's the radical provisionality of speaking voice, the overlap and permeability and cross-fades of rhetorical propositions, that make his work so thrilling and so new and also so decisive for later lyricists like Sidney and Shakespeare. Instability is the method, mobility the key effect. And when I insist that all this is deliberate, I mean chiefly to counter the interpretive tradition that construes Wyatt's vocal 'intermittence' as a technical failure, 'the inadequacies of a poetic technique still in the early stages of development'.[5] Experimental he certainly is, but Wyatt's 'intermittence' is his genius.

It is deliberate, for example, that in the poem we have been considering, Wyatt turns the structure of Petrarch's sestet on its head. In the Italian original, the interpolated speaking voice—the deer as rendered by words on the collar around her neck—occupies the first half of the sestet only: it is fully bounded by the voice of lyric narration. In Wyatt's poem, the words on the collar are granted the privileged, final place. Furthermore, the distance between citation and citation-within-the-citation is heightened when the words of the risen Christ (*Noli me tangere*) are transposed from Petrarch's Italian back to the Latin of the Vulgate.[6] In the *Rime sparse*, the shimmering visitations of transcendence are wholly consistent with Petrarch's larger frame of reference. In Wyatt's poem, they are jarring and provocative. Petrarch invokes and manifests, through the whole long evolution of his sequence to Laura, a philosophical system in which the paradox of freedom and prior possession, untouchability and stamp of ownership, makes sense. Wyatt invokes and dramatizes a social and political system in which that paradox is dangerously demystified.

[4] For a recent consideration of 'reading in slow motion' (the phrase is Reuben Brower's), see Marjorie Garber, 'Shakespeare in Slow Motion,' *Profession* (2010): 151–64.

[5] Stephen Greenblatt, 'Power, Sexuality, and Inwardness in Wyatt's Poetry,' *Renaissance Self-Fashioning: From More to Shakespeare* (Chicago: University of Chicago Press, 1980) 115–56, 276–83; passage cited 278, fn.13. Greenblatt's larger, and impeccable, point is that the effect of 'inwardness' in Wyatt's poetry does not exist *in spite of* inherited literary convention but *by means of* its negotiated deployment.

[6] John 20:17.

In the wilfully secularized world of Wyatt's poem, Caesar's claims and God's claims are restored to their foundational irreconcilability, and the scriptural citation becomes conspicuously gratuitous, which is to say, it acquires the faintest whiff of blasphemy. Whose blasphemy? Not the poet's: the outer citation, the ostensible transcription of words on a collar, gives him a built-in disclaimer. And not, or not wholly, the lady's blasphemy either, she who is so thinly disguised as a hind. The trespass, and the overreaching, must partly belong to Caesar, whoever that powerful claimant may be;[7] he who has caused the words to be worn around her neck—which means in turn that the disappointed poet/rival has not entirely retired from the field. He has simply altered the terms of the hunt. What was originally cast as pursuit of sexual conquest has now become pursuit of something like armchair revenge, which is still very much an erotic field. The couplet is both disclaimer (It is not I who speak; it is 'they'.) and coup, designed to expose both lady and lady's lord. It is also a highly impacted instance of multi-vocality. Caesar speaks his power through the lady; the lady speaks resistance through her 'wildness'. Caesar's vanity speaks the words of Christ. The players speak their privilege in diamonds. The system speaks its ultimate triumph, and the ultimate entrapment of everyone else, in a collar. The poet speaks his mastery, and also his collusion, in an inherited piece of fourteen-line machinery.

9.2

The changeable silk of personality, and the radical predication of self upon the interlocutory other, is thematized in another of Wyatt's sonnets, the poem that in Tottel is called 'Of change in minde':[8]

> Each man me telleth I change most my device,
> And on my faith me think it good reason
> To change purpose like after the season.
> For in every case to keep still one guise
> Is meet for them that would be taken wise;
> And I am not of such manner condition
> But treated after a diverse fashion,
> And thereupon my diverseness doth rise.
> But you that blame this diverseness most,
> Change you no more, but still after one rate

[7] On the widespread habit of writing about Wyatt's poems as evidence of specific erotic intrigues in the Henrician court, Catherine Bates has recently interjected some very sensible cautionary words. See Catherine Bates, 'Wyatt, Surrey, and the Henrician Court', Patrick Cheney, Andrew Hadfield, and Garret A. Sullivan (eds), *Early Modern English Poetry: A Critical Companion* (Oxford: Oxford University Press, 2007) 38–47.
[8] *Tottel's Miscellany* (Exeter: Shearsman Books, 2010) 44. Rpt. of Richard Tottel (ed.), *Songes and Sonettes Written by the Ryght Honorable Lorde Henry Haward Late Earle of Surrey, and Other* (London: 1557). The text that follows is taken, once again, from Rebholz (1978).

> Treat ye me well and keep ye in the same state;
> And while with me doth dwell this wearied ghost,
> My word nor I shall not be variable
> But always one, your own both firm and stable.

The poem's chief currency is the quibble. 'Device' may refer to inclination, opinion, or 'purpose', as in line three, and thus potentially to an authentic manifestation of character. But it may also refer to the outward badge of essence or allegiance, as in heraldry. Honour demands that badges speak truth, but badges may be taken on and off and honour disappointed. The poem does not much credit honour, and it quickly multiplies the species of equivocation. Constancy, the implicit standard that governs the accusatory force of 'change' in line one, is, just a few lines later, granted no more than the calculated plausibility of 'keep[ing] still one guise'. Attributes are revealed to be precisely that: qualities conferred by someone else, attributed or simulated, for the purpose of swaying opinion—signifying gestures in a volatile hall of mirrors. The very units of syntax and poetic lineation mimic the speaker's strategy of non-coincidence. Their quarrel, interestingly, is not conducted in the ordinary way, by means of enjambment, but rather by a succession of sliding resolutions. The relative boundedness of end-stopped and end-paused lines keeps promising an imminent tying up of meaning, but syntactical continuance defeats the expectations deliberately aroused. Ought that first sentence to end with line three? Line five? Line seven? With each continuance, the speaker contrives a shuffling-off of meaning and, by the way, of blame. The octave is a series of ducks and feints.

In the sestet, the rhetorical proposition alters. The unlocalized, impersonal, default audience conjured in the octave becomes a localized 'you'. At first, that you ('and you that blame … ') might simply be another version of the third-person chorus of critics so combatively engaged in the octave. But progressively, the you assumes more definite contours, emerging from the shadows of the vaguely plural to the light of the decidedly singular. In the octave, the circle of detractors exists in undefined proximity to the circle of readers or listeners: they may or may not coincide. In the sestet, the one who blames and the one who is spoken to are singular and coincident. He (or she?)—this 'one'—has no attributes, except the one: diverseness, which, oddly, makes the one a sort of many too. So again, the hall of mirrors and the shuffling off of blame. The remedial proposition—if you become constant, so shall I—sounds less like a petition than like a dare or challenge. In other words: you first. Yet the speaker confesses to a 'wearied ghost'. The first person, who tellingly enters the poem in the accusative case—the one who is acted upon by others—makes its one ostensibly confessional gesture in the accusative as well. It is not 'I' who am weary; it is the weary ghost that dwells 'with me'. Feeling is outsourced. Prior to and apart from changeable practice, the self is a divided thing. As is the couplet,

> My word nor I shall not be variable
> But always one, your own both firm and stable.

Disputes about Wyatt's metric and Wyatt's pronunciation quickly become quite intricate,[9] but of the final couplet in the present poem, suffice it to say that the instabilities of Kentish and courtly dialects in the early 16th century, combined with a more lenient attitude toward opportunistic 'promotions' of an unstressed syllable, may mean that the rhyme is more than the eye-rhyme it seems to modern readers to be. In other words, vári-áble might have sounded a bit less ghastly to Wyatt's early readers than it does to us. But we needn't go so far to feel the sting of Wyatt's final quibble. The pull between plain váriable and the rhyming back-formation of very-áble, whether we actually pronounce the word according to this forced symmetry or not, enacts in miniature the selfsame instability that is the subject, and the larger method, of this poem. As does, of course, the feminine rhyme. The speaker's word, proffered in this final couplet very nearly in the form of a contractual undertaking, sits on a slightly dubious, hendecasyllabic foundation, without the resounding closure of a final stressed syllable. The speaker's 'firm and stable' is anything but.

Wyatt has moved a long way from the proposition of Petrarchan subject formation. In Petrarch, the derivation of self from the other, or rather, from longing for the other, who must, by definition, be withheld, is a tension-riddled but integrated system of vocation and faith as well as erotic desire. Wyatt's reading of Petrarchan system is a much more jagged thing: worldlier, deliberately demystified, naked in its machinations. It is also, as par excellence in 'Whoso List to Hunt', deliberately equivocal: tautly divided between conflicting vocal pitches that the poet refuses to resolve. In Wyatt's system of open voicing, no one voice subsumes the others; brazenly, maddeningly, productively, all are kept in play. Sidney will combine this knowing gamesmanship with the duration and suggestive ligature of Petrarchan sequence, albeit a much altered one. Shakespeare will confer upon the project of provisional subject formation an emotional capaciousness that alters it forever. But the rhetorical breakthrough was Wyatt's.

9.3

No field more richly occasions and aggravates the instabilities of lyric voicing than the field of social blame. Whose is the fault? And whose the injury? And who is it who judges? The inconstancies of 'purpose' and 'device' that are the ground of reproach in Wyatt's poem above assume a specifically erotic cast in Shakespeare's Sonnet 94. Paradoxically, this narrowed resonance seems to fracture the ground of possible trespass: the sonnet is shot through with ambiguity about the ideal from which an ambiguous third-person plural has or may have or may in future lapse. 'Oneness', whatever that difficult fidelity to self and others might actually entail, was a locus of value in Wyatt's poem. But where is the locus here?

---

[9] See R. A. Rebholz (1978), 'A Note on Wyatt's Language' and 'A Note on Wyatt's Metres' 33–55.

> They that have pow'r to hurt, and will do none,
> That do not do the thing they most do show,
> Who moving others are themselves as stone,
> Unmovèd, cold, and to temptation slow—
> They rightly do inherit heaven's graces,
> And husband nature's riches from expense;
> They are the lords and owners of their faces,
> Others but stewards of their excellence.
> The summer's flow'r is to the summer sweet,
> Though to itself it only live and die;
> But if that flow'r with base infection meet,
> The basest weed outbraves his dignity.
>   For sweetest things turn sourest by their deeds;
>   Lilies that fester smell far worse than weeds.[10]

'To hurt' is transitive: we are in the realm of the interpersonal. To hurt another, one imagines, is bad. But the 'power to hurt' appears to be good, a kind of qualifying aptitude. One who uses it well, which is to say, refrains from using it at all, will 'rightly' garner rich reward, nothing less than 'heaven's graces'. The power to move, also transitive in the present case, is not quite parallel: one may apparently move others without incurring blame, provided one is oneself immune to being moved. To husband, an action commended in the second quatrain, appears to consist in a kind of hoarding, conservation of resources taken to a stern extreme. All in all, the precepts advanced in the octave appear to be wholly negative: 'they' are counselled not to do, not to be moved, not to spend. Although the governing imagery shifts in the sestet—we appear now to be in the realm of flowers—the governing logic stays roughly the same, at least for a time: self-containment is commended; looseness is blamed. All of this quite reverses, of course, the homiletic thrust of the earliest sonnets, where husbandry meant propagation (Sonnet 13), 'beauty's use' (Sonnet 2) was actively encouraged, and hoarding was condemned as an abuse (Sonnet 4).

In a rather wicked moment, William Empson once suggested that the internal logic of this sonnet alone suggests '4096 possible movements of thought'.[11] His point was that we need something more than ingenuity to read a poem: 'one has honestly to consider what seems important' (89). But where is such an anchor to be found? I will defer, for a moment, the rich and necessary question of (implied) narrative context (for that, see Section 9.4). Even in isolation, Sonnet 94 is a fascinating feeling-machine, vibrating around two poles. The octave moves with considerable dignity of cadence; its well-balanced end-paused lines are subtly varied, seeming to exemplify the very poise and self-containment they recommend. The undertow—our sense that the generalized

---

[10] Citations from Shakespeare's sonnets will be drawn from Stephen Booth (ed.), *Shakespeare's Sonnets* (New Haven: Yale University Press, 1977).

[11] William Empson, *Some Versions of Pastoral* (New York: New Directions, 1974) 89. Empson's deadpan logic went like this: if there are four loci of value in the poem—flower, lily, 'owner', and person addressed—the number of possible alignments among them—like, like, unlike, etc.—will be 4096.

third-person discourse harbours a more specific address—does little to disturb the general lordliness. The surface eddyings—the imperfect parallelisms described above, the conundrum of 'do' and 'show'—do not much alter the sense of a general logic at work. The sestet moves with a difference, however: the units of sense are shorter and require a more athletic working-out. And the hinge between octave and sestet shows an odd, recursive power to disturb the equilibrium of that which has gone before. If a flower confers the benefit of sweetness (fragrance)[12] to the season, has it not dispersed a portion of itself? How then can it be said to live and die 'to itself' alone? Does the proprietary ambiguity of giving-away and retaining call attention to a troubling ambiguity, hitherto dormant, in the earlier distinction between stewardship and ownership? To 'husband heaven's riches' is precisely to steward them, is it not? And isn't this what Christianity has told the faithful they ought to do? How then can the one act be praised and the other censured? And now that one thinks of it, what could it possibly mean to be 'lord and owner' of something so public as a face? Does this not imply too much cunning to be wholly admirable? Such musings begin to be too curious by half; we are well on our way to the thicket of perplexity that Empson warned against. Perhaps the kind of tonal shifts or vocal signatures we found in Wyatt can offer better guidance than can imagery or argument.

Throughout its first ten lines, the poem has largely maintained decorum, mapping the ethics and entailments of personal beauty, casting its principles as general ones. The descent to 'base' and 'basest', 'weed' and 'sourest' marks a rupture in that decorum, culminating in the vehemence of the final line: 'Lilies that fester smell far worse than weeds'. Here, to answer Empson's challenge, is a moment that honestly feels important. Something deeply unlovely has burst its bounds, and the proprietary question assumes an even greater urgency: to whom does the unloveliness belong? Whose is the affliction? And whose the deeper self-betrayal?

The difficulty of attribution betrays the radical interdependence that constitutes the subject of the poem. The clues to social circumstance are thick and contradictory. The speaker who scorns the subordinate status of stewardship reveals his own subordination to be something considerably more abject. Beneath the cover of shifting persons, 'they' and 'others', 'flower' and 'weed', he sends a shifting and conflicted message: I will thrive on your indifference, provided you are indifferent to others as well; I will love your coldness if it keeps you from debauchery; I measure your power by your power to hurt; I fear I shall have to measure your worth by your foulness. The central formulation is Petrarchan—the constitution of a self by means of longing for the other—but overlaid with Wyatt's agitation and Wyatt's refusal of transcendence. Shakespeare has embraced the symptom-effect, has become a master of vocal signature. This is Petrarch with a vengeance.

---

[12] For the semantic specificity of floral 'sweetness', see Andrew Marvell, 'The Picture of Little T. C. in a Prospect of Flowers': 'Make that the tulips may have share | Of sweetness, seeing they are fair'. Frank Kermode and Keith Walker, eds, *Andrew Marvell: A Critical Edition of the Major Works* (Oxford: Oxford University Press, 1990) 37.

9.4

In an interesting reversal of figure and ground, Shakespeare's Sonnet 116 is regularly tapped for duty in modern wedding ceremonies.

> Let me not to the marriage of true minds
> Admit impediments. Love is not love
> Which alters when it alteration finds,
> Or bends with the remover to remove.
> O no, it is an ever-fixèd mark
> That looks on tempests and is never shaken;
> It is the star to every wand'ring bark,
> Whose worth's unknown, although his height be taken.
> Love's not time's fool, though rosy lips and cheeks
> Within his bending sickle's compass come.
> Love alters not with his brief hours and weeks,
> But bears it out ev'n to th'edge of doom.
>   If this be error and upon me proved,
>   I never writ, nor no man ever loved.

What in the 16th-century poem is the shadow presence of the Anglican marriage service is reinvested in the later, often secular, context with the force of sacrament: it comes full circle. The poem is ravishing, one of the best-loved and most frequently cited sonnets in the language. Its argument appears to be abstract or philosophical, not personal at all, not 'interested' in the narrow sense, thus ripe for general adoption and redeployment. But this is to ignore the vocal instabilities.

'Let me not': the poem begins in the imperative mood. Its internal action is semantic—it aims to delineate the allowable parameters of love—and its goal appears to be air-tightness. I will not grant, the poet asserts, that love can be thwarted by impediment. If it falters, it is not love. The love I have in mind is a beacon; it is the North star. Like that star, it exceeds all narrow comprehension (its 'worth's unknown'); its height alone (the navigator's basis for calculation) is sufficient to guide us. The poem's ideal is unwavering faith, and it purports to perform its own ideal. Odd then, isn't it, how much of the argument proceeds by means of negation: 'let me not', 'love is not', 'O no', and so forth. Perhaps the speaker is less confident than he appears to be.

And there are other signs of faltering confidence. The poem has been written to refute certain concepts (alteration, removal) that it relegates, at the start, to the realm of abstraction. But in the third quatrain, abstraction begins to break down. Time, it seems, has something to do with change and threatened removal. The poet argues back: time is paltry compared to love. Time may alter loveliness, but love will not flinch. Time may be measured in petty hours and weeks; love's only proper measure begins where time leaves off ('the edge of doom'). Quite apart from the continued heaping up of negation (two more 'not's'), this quatrain registers increasing strain. Line ten (the ominous sickle) is all but unpronounceable: the consonants come fast and thick; the hissing alliterations deform the line as surely as time deforms the beauties of the flesh. 'Doom' was capable of a neutral meaning in Shakespeare's day—it could refer to judgement of any sort, good or bad—but it was always a gloomy syllable, especially in the context of final judgement (again, 'the edge of doom'). 'Bears it out' rings with defiance, which ironically tends to direct the reader's attention to that which faith defies. That something else, that deliberately unnamed enemy to love has, in other words, begun to assume palpable presence. What the poem has gained in vehemence, it has lost in genuine assurance. Quatrain by quatrain, line by line, despite, or rather by means of its brave resistance, the sonnet has been taken over by that which it has tried to write out of existence: by faithlessness.

In the context of Shakespeare's sequence, moreover, this poem is not wholly unprompted. The spectre of impediment has not risen out of thin air. The layering and multivalence that Wyatt achieves in 'Whoso List to Hunt' by means of a broken rhetorical surface, and, quite possibly for his original readers, by means of shifting, deniable allusions to contemporary court intrigue, Shakespeare achieves by means of a broken and shifting narrative frame. Well before the stirring manifesto of 116, the sonnet sequence has signalled trouble in paradise: unspecified 'sins' (35), specific infidelities (41, 42) and rivals (78–86), and, worst of all, incipient corruption of character (94, 95). So the reader who encounters 116 in context encounters it as an assertion in the face of all evidence. This oppositional momentum contributes mightily to its power.

It is worth distinguishing my point from one that, on the surface, it resembles. Helen Vendler has argued, quite justly, that 116 does not bear scrutiny as an impersonal testament to constancy in love; we must construe it, she says, as one in a sequence of 'situationally motivated speech-acts'.[13] This seems to me to be right. My quarrel is with the nature of the speech-act she envisions, which is so fully consolidated, so firmly embedded in a fleshed-out narrative as to misrepresent both the poem and the nature of the lyric sequence. In Vendler's reading, Sonnet 116 stages itself as the explicit refutation of an anterior speech whose contours we can know in some detail. She imagines this anterior speech as having been spoken by the young man; she posits its assertions blow-by-blow; she summons prosody to support her reading, proposing, for example, that we hear the first line thus: 'Let *me* not to the marriage of true minds'.[14] Like the forced iambic scansion, the forced explicitness of dramatic antecedent obscures important elements of Shakespeare's lyric method. Quite apart from the fact that faithlessness is likelier to be 'argued' in actions than in words, the sonnet sequence consistently refuses to provide a fully consolidated back story: narrative fragmentation and indirection are essential to its effects. The vocal gestures that seem to manifest a suffering subjectivity in Shakespeare's Sonnets, the tantalizing hints of prior history and action in the margins, work precisely by means of their insufficiency.[15] Voicing is unstable. One rhetorical proposition will

---

[13] Helen Vendler, *The Art of Shakespeare's Sonnets* (Cambridge, MA: Harvard University Press, 1997) 492.

[14] Vendler (1997) 488.

[15] For an excellent overview of narrative technique in the sonnets, see James Schiffer, 'The Incomplete Narrative of Shakespeare's Sonnets', in Michael Schoenfeldt (ed.), *A Companion to Shakespeare's Sonnets* (Chichester: Wiley-Blackwell, 2010) 45–56.

begin to infect or strain the contours of another. Bleed-through effects are common and constituent.

We may grant some justice, for example, to the lovers who choose to speak lines from 'the marriage of true minds' before their wedding guests. They pay tribute to something that is authentically part of Shakespeare's poem. In context, we may construe the straining after lofty principle as a sign of tension in Shakespeare's speaking persona, but the lofty principle is there, and eloquent. The objective voice is something reached for, something tried on for size and solace. It recruits the powers of figuration much as, later on, it recruits the formal contours of logic. Witness the couplet. Having conceded and defied the depredations of time, having used the universal affliction of time to displace and obscure a series of less savoury fallings off, the lover turns to buried syllogism: I am obviously a writer (witness this poem!); I assert that love is constant; therefore love must be constant. As any schoolboy could testify, however, these premises have no necessary relationship to one another or to their conclusion. The couplet seems designed to shut down all opposition, to secure the thing (unchanging love) on which the poem has staked its heart. It is sheer bravado, an attempt to secure control of fickle fate by sheer force of assertion, and, as such, of course it fails. Fate was never subdued by argument, nor was a loved one's faltering faith.

This is not to say that disillusion triumphs. The sonnet moves through time, yes. It mounts a vocal proposition—the proposition of transpersonal speech—at some expense, as registered in a launching division of self: 'Let me not'. That proposition is sustained for a time and then breaks down. That breaking down, that quasi-dramatized failure, is one of the principle means by which Shakespeare achieves the effect of emotional depth. And yet, a lyric poem is not a plot. Its action is of a different sort; 'what happens' is only one of meaning's tributary streams. And in the present poem, a portion of speaking falls out of dramatic solution. That is the portion the Shakespeare-quoting newly-weds have heard, the stirring profession of faith. The poem *in situ* partakes of what has gone before; its very abstractions appear, in part, to derive from dramatic and psychological siting; it invites us to imagine the pressures that impel a mind toward abstract manifesto, embracing whatever can be put to use along the way: truism, consolatory formulation, logical paradox, sonic closures that cover for lack of emotional closure. At the same time, the poem and the sequence of which it is a part resolutely relegate the dramatic field to a fragmentary and intermittent presence. Shakespeare, like Wyatt before him, refuses to endorse a single voice.

9.5

When the glories of the Elizabethan drama are linked at all to lyric poetry from the earlier part of the 16th century, it is Surrey's development of blank verse that is most often invoked. When the phenomenon of character-based 'depth' and its distinctive evolution in the Shakespearean corpus is to be accounted for, it is the soliloquy that is most often adduced and analysed as the telling example.[16] With all deference to these important linkages and unfoldings, I would like to propose another line of transmission, one which credits Wyatt for the revolution he well and truly started, and an alternate focus, one I take to be a signal achievement of character-based innovation in the Shakespearean drama. Soliloquy in Shakespeare's hands is the culmination of a tradition that can be traced, in English, to the medieval drama. The vocal gestures that mark a more radical break with the past, and with contemporary developments on the European continent, are something very different: fleeting, discontinuous, fragmentary eruptions of irrelevance that seem to impede or 'forget' the forward movement of the plot. They constitute a kind of open voicing of their own: non sequiturs and throw-aways, misprisions and deflections, ruptures in the ordinary fabric of conversation. Their power is irreducibly synedochal: the world they conjure into being depends upon an insufficiency of explanation; its contours are not and must not be filled in. These moments do not surface in the solitude of private reflection or in the showcase of consolidated public speech; their origin lies neither in meditative tradition nor in the classical rhetoric that contributes so much else to early modern literature; they exemplify a new thing altogether: a gratuitous or purely supplemental symptom-effect. Three instances will have to stand for the whole: brief passages from a comedy (*Twelfth Night*), a history play (*1 Henry 4*), and a tragedy (*Othello*). Without occluding the very real distinction between lyric voicing and speeches written for the stage, I wish to argue that one crucial feature of Shakespeare's dramaturgy—the distillate superfluity that conjures the impression of character-based depth in a single, ostensibly gratuitous gesture—is deeply indebted to Wyatt's innovation in the lyric poem.

Example one: 'I was adored once, too' (*Twelfth Night*, II. iii. 175). Sir Andrew Aguecheek belongs to the genus *gull*: he serves as a source of funding and amusement for other, smarter, and more ruthless characters. He is perpetually missing the point; the failure of understanding that constitutes the ground of all his other failures of understanding is a hopeless misapprehension of his own real and potential standing in the eyes of others. When he praises Maria as 'a good wench' (II. iii. 173), we do not credit him with more than a superficial apprehension of her real worth. When he praises her as 'a good wench' to Sir Toby, we know him to be oblivious to the awkward and conflicted circumstances Feste has had the wit to see: 'If Sir Toby would leave drinking thou wert as witty a piece of Eve's flesh as any in Illyria' (I. v. 24–6). When Sir Andrew praises Maria to the man with whom she shares an occluded and hitherto thwarted understanding, in other words, he knows neither to whom nor of whom he speaks. In every sense that matters most, he does not know what he is saying. We may assume, therefore, that the full import of Sir Toby's rejoinder—'She's a beagle true-bred, and one that adores me. What o' that?' (II. iii. 173–4)—is lost on his interlocutor. Telling

---

[16] I am speaking here chiefly about aesthetic and formal analysis of the dramatic texts. There is also, of course, a rich arena of cultural and historical analysis which has contributed immensely to our understanding of precedents and implications. See especially Katherine Maus, *Inwardness and Theater in the English Renaissance* (Chicago: University of Chicago Press, 1995).

enough, but that rejoinder is in its turn a triggering speech: 'I was adored once too', says the gull. Against a background of missed connections, Toby with Maria, Maria with Toby, Toby with his drinking friend Sir Andrew, the gull misfires again. And yet, of course, his ostensible tangent is no tangent at all but the shortest route from one heart (his) to another (ours). Sir Andrew may be as deluded about the past as he is about the present—we have no way of judging that—but with five bare, poignant words he acquires a third dimension, which is to say, a soul.

Example two: 'In Richard's time—what d'ye call the place? | A plague upon't, it is in Gloucestershire' (*1 Henry IV*, I. iii. 240–1). Hotspur, blunt soldier, is capable of eloquence as stirring as any in Shakespeare, as when, for example, he describes the battle between his kinsman Mortimer and the Welshman Owen Glendower.

> Revolted Mortimer?
> He never did fall off, my sovereign liege,
> But by the chance of war. To prove that true
> Needs no more but one tongue for all those wounds,
> Those mouthèd wounds, which valiantly he took
> When on the gentle Severn's sedgy bank,
> In single opposition, hand to hand,
> He did confound the best part of an hour
> In changing hardiment with great Glyndŵr.
> Three times they breathed, and three times did they drink,
> Upon agreement, of swift Severn's flood,
> Who, then affrighted with their bloody looks,
> Ran fearfully among the trembling reeds,
> And hid his crisp head in the hollow bank,
> Bloodstainèd with these valiant combatants.
>
> (I. iii. 92–106)

For momentum, image, sonic echo, and balancing cadence, the speech is a prosodic and rhetorical masterpiece, not least because the playwright makes it seem to be the work of passion rather than art. And yet it is not proportioned cadence at all, nor force of eloquence, that makes the decisive impression in this scene; it is rather the young man's repeated tendency to run off the rails. The scene is a crucial one: Worcester and Northumberland must lay the groundwork for dangerous insurrection; the audience must be made to understand the conspirators' motives as well as their plans; exposition alone is dauntingly complex. It is also perpetually thwarted, because Hotspur cannot hold his peace: he interrupts, he expostulates, he misconstrues, he drives his uncle and his father to distraction. And at one point, he simply cannot bring to mind a missing word:

HOTSPUR   In Richard's time—what d'ye call the place?—
    A plague upon't, it is in Gloucestershire.
    'Twas where the madcap duke his uncle kept—

His uncle York—where I first bowed my knee
Unto this king of smiles, this Bolingbroke.
'Sblood, when you and he came back from Ravenspurgh.
NORTH   At Berkeley castle.

(I. iii. 240–6)

Waylaid by his own wild temper, Hotspur cannot put his finger on the place. A small moment, but like the small moment in *Richard III* when the beleaguered usurper botches instructions to his own messengers (IV. iv. 432–56), it resonates with portent: the fault that opens up in words betrays the fault that opens up in fate. In Hotspur's case, the moment is also a decisive one for establishing his place in the hearts of theatrical spectators. 'At Berkeley castle'. A father's deadpan reply: all hope for expedition lost, he must ride out the son's digression. In the crossed dynamics of urgency and derailment, common purpose and familial abrasion, conspiracy assumes the contours of domestic comedy. This is the plot that will threaten the kingdom, Hotspur the man who will challenge the prince; the play will have to expunge them both. But first, so we feel what it costs when the crisis comes, the play will make us love the man. The decisive conjuring of individuated presence, of presence worth the treasuring and worth our grief when it is gone, comes not from fine speeches but from goings-astray. The Hotspur whose death is the mortar of a kingdom is born of an impertinence: a by-blow in an irreducibly social field.

Example three: 'This Lodovico is a proper man' (*Othello*, IV. iii. 33). When Shakespeare's play of tragic jealousy is poised on the very brink of irreparable calamity, when Othello has resolved upon violence and Desdemona foresees her death, the action pauses in its precipitous momentum for a scene of rare intimacy between two women. Desdemona recalls her mother's maid, who died for love; Emilia helps her mistress prepare for bed; the scene is saturated with equal parts tenderness and dread. At which point, with the abruptness of non sequitur, the conversation turns for five brief lines to the man who has just that day arrived from Venice with a message from the Duke.

DESDEMONA   This Lodovico is a proper man.
EMILIA   A very handsome man.
DESDEMONA   He speaks well.
EMILIA   I know a lady in Venice would have walked barefoot to Palestine
     for a touch of his nether lip.

(IV. iii. 33–7)

What can the playwright have had in mind? Desdemona's place in the drama depends upon her unimpeachable fidelity in marriage. Othello's tragedy depends upon the chasm between that fidelity and his own false suspicions. Iago's villainy depends upon a casual misogyny that presumes and exploits the cultural fear of woman's wandering eye. Yet Shakespeare allows his paragon of virtue, at the very crisis of her entrapment in a hostile ideological system, to confess—or seem to confess—a wandering eye.

A fuller reading of this moment would address the very structure of that hostile ideological system—we may call it for short the cuckold's dilemma—and the playwright's explication of its workings. My immediate purpose, however, is narrower: I wish only to point, once again, to the power of superfluity for opening up a world of depth. The resonant space, in this instance, is a space between: Desdemona and Emilia acknowledging between them a shared noticing of male beauty, the lady in Venice allowing between them a sensuous elaboration of that noticing. Emilia will later argue that women 'have their palates both for sweet and sour, | As husbands have' (IV. iii. 94–5). Desdmona has earlier argued for her rights to the rites of marriage (I. ii. 257). But, argued for, a woman's appetite is still a rather abstract thing. The 'touch of his nether lip', by contrast, is as sensuous as anything the playwright ever wrote and opens up a space where, fleetingly, feminine appetite may be palpable and also palpably benign. Were it not that 'barefoot to Palestine' sounds less like suffering than like extravagance, the lady in Venice might come a shade too close to Desdemona's mother's maid. As it is, she lends delight and colour to a small exchange between Desdemona and Emilia, which in turn suggests an alternate world in which women too might participate in the economies of pleasure and do so at no one's expense. The moment is not useful to plot; if anything, it disorders plot's trajectory. It is purely value added.

In the lyric poem, the impression of access to an individuated locus of thought and feeling is irreducibly provisional, an epiphenomenal matter of 'voice'. In the drama, the impression of access is both intensified and destabilized by the paradox of bodily presence: actor and character at once, imperfectly aligned with either. Writing for the page, Shakespeare preserves the license of intermittence, or open voicing, as practised and proposed by Wyatt. Writing for the stage, he uses the instabilities of voice and purpose to create a present/absence: the sense of psychic depth as rendered by words that work by means of insufficiency. In an era like our own, which is sceptical about the a priori status of the self, the conceptual power of the back-formation, the inwardness produced by means of symptom, affords real opportunities for thinking through. The collaborative nature of this thinking through is familiar to every theatre-goer. Instabilities of voice and rhetorical proposition promote the lyric reader to a position of comparable collaborative scope, where the act of reading and the act of composition bear joint responsibility for the performative discovery of point-to-point and part-to-whole connection, what the actor calls a through-line. This was Wyatt's gift to Shakespeare, and to us.

SELECT BIBLIOGRAPHY

Bates, Catherine (2007) 'Wyatt, Surrey, and the Henrician Court,' in Patrick Cheney, Andrew Hadfield, and Garrett A. Sullivan, Jr. (eds), *Early Modern English Poetry: A Companion* (New York: Oxford University Press) 38–47.
Booth, Stephen (1977) (ed.) *Shakespeare's Sonnets* (New Haven: Yale University Press).
Durling, Robert M. (1976) (trans. and ed.) *Petrarch's Lyric Poems: The Rime sparse and Other Lyrics* (Cambridge, MA: Harvard University Press).

Empson, William (1974) 'They That Have Power,' in *Some Versions of Pastoral* (New York: New Directions) 89–118.

Garber, Marjorie (2010) 'Shakespeare in Slow Motion,' *Profession*: 151–64.

Greenblatt, Stephen (1980) 'Power, Sexuality, and Inwardness in Wyatt's Poetry,' in Stephen Greenblatt, *Renaissance Self-Fashioning: From More to Shakespeare* (Chicago: University of Chicago Press) 115–56.

Maus, Katherine (1995) *Inwardness and Theater in the English Renaissance* (Chicago: University of Chicago Press).

Rebholz, R. A. (1978) (ed.) *Sir Thomas Wyatt: The Compete Poems* (New Haven: Yale University Press).

Schiffer, James (2010) 'The Incomplete Narrative of Shakespeare's Sonnets,' in Michael Schoenfeldt (ed) *A Companion to Shakespeare's Sonnets* (Chichester: Wiley-Blackwell) 45–56.

Tottel, Richard (2010) (ed.) *Songes and Sonettes Written by the Right Honorable Lorde Henry Haward Late Earle of Surrey, and Other* (London, 1557) rpt. as Tottel's Miscellany (Exeter: Shearesman Books).

Vendler, Helen (1997) *The Art of Shakespeare's Sonnets* (Cambridge, MA: Harvard University Press).

CHAPTER 10

'GRAMMAR RULES' IN THE SONNETS

Sidney and Shakespeare

ALYSIA KOLENTSIS

The final decades of the 16th century represent an epoch in the development of the English language. In many respects, the English used by late-century writers was a language on the cusp: it was engaged in the process of written standardization, and its global status was on the rise.[1] The concerns with eloquence reflected in manuals of rhetoric from the mid-16th century onward were extended, by century's end, to questions of proper usage and codification. Debates about the relative merits of Latin and English, and the potential of the vernacular as a sophisticated, profitable, and unifying language, were flourishing. In addition, the structure of the language itself was in flux, transforming into what is recognized as 'modern' English and gradually shedding many of its earlier lexical and syntactic forms. These factors converged to produce a varied pool of linguistic resources, ideal fodder for writers, whose craft depended on sharp attunement to the language of the age, and who often acted as vociferous participants in the debates surrounding language use and standardization. In this chapter, I consider how the shifting linguistic terrain that characterized the closing decades of the 16th century informed the literary culture of the period. In what ways did the changing status and structure of English, and new attention to the rules governing its use, inform the literature of the late century? How might poets engage with these changes? Here, I consider Sidney and Shakespeare, whose sonnet sequences represent two of the most prominent examples of a definitive English genre of the period. I focus specifically on the broad category of 'grammar', and explore various ways that Sidney

---

[1] Jonathan Hope, 'Shakespeare's "Native English"', *A Companion to Shakespeare*, ed. David Scott Kastan (Oxford: Blackwell, 1999) 243.

and Shakespeare play with aspects of grammar in their sonnets. I suggest that Sidney's witty appeals to the rules of grammar, and his experimentation on the border between classical and vernacular language, highlight the changing linguistic resources available to late-century writers. Similarly, Shakespeare's engagement with the changing structure of the language—an aspect of grammar that was ripe for exploitation during the period—points to a recognition of the rhetorical possibilities opened up by the distinctive linguistic climate of the age.

In this chapter, I am taking a broad view of grammar, considering at once its significant history as a humanist cornerstone and pedagogical tool in Tudor classrooms, as well as its injunctions about the rules of usage for both Latin and English, as exemplified in texts such as William Lily's *Shorte Introduction of Grammar* (first published in 1540) and William Bullokar's *Pamphlet for Grammar* (1586). In this sense, 'grammar' represents a foundational ideal of humanist education, a means of codifying and structuring a language and offering concrete rules for proper usage. However, in addition to this institutional notion of grammar, I am also using 'grammar' to designate transitions in the language itself, linguistic details such as syntax and verb morphology that were undergoing changes during the period that Tudor schoolboys like Sidney and Shakespeare were learning to read and write. 'Grammar', then, is an umbrella term that encompasses the public face of language, the prescriptive rules of usage, as well as the internal structure of the language, the gradual shifts in actual usage that are most evident in retrospect, but that form part of the ambient context of language use in practice. In a sense, this chapter considers two different but intricately related stories of grammar: one about the teaching of language (both classical and vernacular), and the ways in which grammar is learned, reinforced, and deployed rhetorically, and another about the English language itself, and the ways that the variation that characterizes a swiftly changing language opens up a wealth of linguistic resources to writers of the age.

It is not unusual for the category of 'grammar', one of the most ambiguous terms in the lexicon of linguistics, to cover such broad ground. In early modern England, 'grammar' was a shifting and elastic concept, subject to 'riotous diversity' in its definitions, and used to refer to everything from the study of Latin, the vernacular, or foreign languages, to translation, etymology, language use, and the language itself. [2] Indeed, there is a strong correlation between linguistic change and innovation and debates about grammar, and because the early modern period featured such remarkable linguistic change, the age was characterized by 'numerous conflicts over what is called "grammar".[3] Disputes were fed, in part, by changing perceptions about Latin and English, for in the late sixteenth-century,

---

[2] Linda C. Mitchell, *Grammar Wars: Language as Cultural Battlefield in 17th and 18th Century England* (Aldershot: Ashgate, 2001) 1–2. For a discussion of shifting and elusive definitions of 'grammar' over the centuries, see Dick Leith, *A Social History of English* (London: Routledge, 1983). See Jonathan Hope's *Shakespeare and Language: Reason, Eloquence, and Artifice in the Renaissance* (London: Methuen, 2010), especially 98–137, for an excellent account of competing ideas about grammar in the early modern period.

[3] Mitchell (2001) 1.

English was only just beginning to be thought of as a language that, like Latin, had a structure, order, and grammar of its own. Vestiges of older beliefs—that systematized grammar rules were exclusive to Latin, and that English was a vulgar and disordered tongue—coexisted with burgeoning ideas about the capacity of English to have its own set of rules, different from but equal to those of Latin.[4] In its broader sense, too, 'grammar' in early modern England held a more prominent place in literary culture than in its present-day incarnations. From the Middle Ages, *grammatica* was at the heart of literacy and learning. It was the first part of the *trivium*, followed by logic (*dialectica*) and rhetoric (*rhetorica*), and together these disciplines comprised the three essential components of medieval education, and subsequently formed the cornerstones of humanist pedagogy.[5] However, grammar alone transcended the role of mere scholarly discipline. As Brian Cummings explains, the scope and influence of grammar in the Middle Ages was wide; it 'was the *ars* before and within every other *ars*', a concept which 'covered the full range of the linguistic and the literary, the semantic and the semiotic'. This legacy persisted into the early modern period, as 'grammar continued to encompass not only the acquisition of basic language skills and the engendering of literary "eloquence", but also the interpretation of linguistic meaning or of literary theory'.[6] In short, in the period that Sidney and Shakespeare were composing their sonnets, 'grammar' could be associated with language in all of its guises. In this unusually rich and dynamic linguistic age, the term could effectively refer to any aspect of language use, including writing, speaking, learning, and analysis. Early modern poets such as Sidney and Shakespeare, who traded in the currency of words, had good reason to be attuned to the various aspects of grammar, for they defined the parameters for eloquence, play, and possibility within their language.

In several respects, English sonnets provide an exemplary case study for an investigation of grammar play and linguistic inventiveness. Timing is one important factor, for the crest of the sonnet wave in England, during the years 1580–1610, coincided with significant transitional decades for the English language. Form is also significant, since the brevity and formal constraints of the sonnet grant exceptional weight to individual words. In the prescribed structure of the sonnet, arguably to a greater extent than in more flexible poetic forms such as odes or epics, there is an emphasis on accuracy and precision: each word must be exactly right in terms of connotation, nuance, rhythm, and metre. Indeed, there are suggestions of a dynamic relationship between sonnet form and sonnet language, and we might find traces of an interchange between the structure of the sonnet and the words that comprise it. This is evident even in the pre-English history of the sonnet; in his treatise *De vulgari eloquentia*, Dante suggests that the sonnet

---

    [4] Manfred Görlach, 'Regional and Social Variation', *The Cambridge History of the English Language (CHEL)*, vol. 3, Roger Lass (ed.), (Cambridge: Cambridge University Press, 1999) 482.
    [5] Brian Cummings, *The Literary Culture of the Reformation: Grammar and Grace* (Oxford: Oxford University Press, 2002) 112.
    [6] Cummings (2002) 21–2.

was particularly suited to the idiosyncrasies of the Italian vernacular, even more so than the classical Latin.[7] When the sonnet was introduced to England in the early sixteenth century, Thomas Wyatt famously altered the form, making the rigid structure more flexible in terms of rhyme, and establishing the couplet ending. While there are several possible explanations for this structural shift, the influence of the particular properties of English should not be ignored; as I shall discuss further, the epigrammatic couplet is perfectly designed to showcase terse English words. Additionally, the sonnet presents a complex and telling picture of the culture from which it emerges, 'rendering formal, courtly, and political messages through verse "play".[8] The sonnet skirts the boundary of private reflection and social commentary, with contexts both erotic and political, and polysemy and linguistic experimentation are vital to its multiple resonances.

Composed around 1582, and circulated in manuscript before its first publication in 1591, Sir Philip Sidney's *Astrophil and Stella* was a popularly received addition to the crush of Elizabethan sonnet sequences. Thomas Nashe, in a laudatory preface to the unauthorized 1591 edition, praises *Astrophil and Stella* as the antidote to years of stale verse: '*Tempus adust plausus aurea pompa venit*, so endes the Sceane of Idiots, and enter *Astrophel* in pompe'.[9] True to Nashe's endorsement, the sequence is refreshingly inventive on many fronts. It announces its difference immediately with the formal and stylistic departures of the opening sonnet, which is written in alexandrines (twelve-syllable lines) rather than iambic pentameter, and alters the traditional Petrarchan rhyme scheme to favour a closing rhyming couplet. Furthermore, the poems that follow set up the dynamic between the speaking subject and the admired object so that the reader's gaze rests squarely on the speaker, one who is winkingly aware of his own linguistic ingenuity, and who claims to expose frankly the contents of his soul. The speaker, Astrophil, is the self-styled 'Fool' who follows his Muse's injunction to 'look in thy heart and write' (1. 14) rejecting the models of his predecessors and painting himself as a truth-teller who forgoes ornamentation to lay bare his heart: 'I can speak what I feel, and feel as much as they' (6. 12).[10] These bold claims hint at the slipperiness of the speaking subject who emerges in these poems: he is evasive, self-aware, and alert to the advantages of inhabiting the roles of plain-speaking confessor and rebuffed admirer. Astrophil recognizes that the pose of subjugation provides an opportunity to exercise a countering type of control: linguistic mastery. The innovative language of *Astrophil and Stella* has frequently been noted, and Sidney's attention to rhetorical figures helped to establish some of the characteristic wordplay associated with the English sonnet

---

[7] Michael R. G. Spiller, *The Development of the Sonnet* (London: Routledge, 1992) 8.

[8] Diana Henderson, *Passion Made Public: Elizabethan Lyric, Gender, and Performance* (Urbana: Illinois University Press, 1995) 171.

[9] 'Now is the time for applause; the golden procession is coming', 'Somewhat to reade for them that list', *Syr P. S. His Astrophel and Stella Wherein the Excellence of Sweete Poesie is Concluded* (London: Thomas Newman, 1591) sig. A3r.

[10] These and all subsequent quotations from *Astrophil and Stella* are taken from *Sir Philip Sidney: The Major Works*, ed. Katherine Duncan-Jones (Oxford: Oxford University Press, 2002).

tradition. His rhetorical flourishes include the ostentatious figure of *antanaclasis*, where a word is repeated in different senses—'Of touch they are that without touch doth touch' (9. 12)[11]—and *epanalepsis*, where a line begins and ends with the same word: 'Fly, fly, my friends, I have my death wound, fly' (20. 1).

In addition to these flamboyant gestures, Sidney also demonstrates a more subtle kind of linguistic showmanship by presenting Astrophil as a cunning scholar, capable of invoking both the apprehension and peculiar comfort offered by the regimen of the Tudor grammar school. Indeed, the experience of the classroom provides a vital intertext for *Astrophil and Stella;* the sonnets regularly allude to 'schools' and 'scholars,' while interactions are frequently framed 'in terms of "spelling," "reading," "learning," "lessons," and "teaching".[12] In his invocation of the Tudor grammar school, Sidney conjures a place of control and discipline. Boys began their grammar-school education at age seven, and spent each day of their early years in the classroom engaged in long hours of rote memorization and drills in the basics of Latin grammar.[13] As Mary Ellen Lamb notes, such an environment promoted a rapid entrée into adulthood, as schoolboys were taught to surrender 'the simple, sensual pleasures of early childhood' in favour of the virtues of renunciation and restraint.[14] Sidney himself was intimately familiar with the early relinquishment of boyhood; at age nine, he left home to attend the elite Shrewsbury grammar school, a move that reflected a shift in standard approaches to education, and that placed him 'in the vanguard of aristocratic sons whose parents abandoned traditional household rearing for humanist education in the public schools'.[15] In the transition from childhood nursery to regimented classroom, pupils were swiftly inculcated into the virtues of order and obedience, subject to the paternal control and magisterial authority of the schoolmaster.[16] This early experience evidently left a deep impression on Sidney, for *Astrophil and Stella* is rife with recollections of the classroom as a place where awe and wonder coexist with peril and tyranny. On the one hand, school is held up as a place to be revered and respected: the Seventh Song pays tribute to the 'sweet tunes' to be learned in 'wonder's schools' (2, 5); Sonnet 79 imagines a kiss as a 'schoolmaster of delight' (8); and other sonnets suggest strong affinities between 'virtue' and the classroom (9, 25). Yet these schools, however virtuous and honourable as models of authority, also instil

---

[11] As Duncan-Jones explains, this 'elaborate punning metaphor' plays on various senses of 'touch': Stella's eyes are of touch-stone (black marble), which without 'touching' 'touch', or move, those who see them (2002, 386, n.156).

[12] Andrew Strycharski, 'Literacy, Education, and Affect in *Astrophil and Stella*', *SEL: Studies in English Literature, 1500–1900* 48.1 (2008) 48.

[13] Ursula Potter, 'Performing Arts in the Tudor Classroom', *Tudor Drama Before Shakespeare 1485–1590,* Lloyd Kermode, Jason Scott-Warren, and Martine van Elk (eds), (New York: Palgrave, 2004) 145.

[14] Mary Ellen Lamb, 'Apologizing for Pleasure in Sidney's 'Apology for Poetry': The Nurse of Abuse Meets the Tudor Grammar School', *Criticism* 36:4 (1994): 505.

[15] Strycharski (2008) 48.

[16] Lynn Enterline, 'Rhetoric, Discipline, and the Theatricality of Everyday Life in Elizabethan Grammar Schools,' *From Performance to Print in Shakespeare's England,* ed. Peter Holland and Stephen Orgel (New York: Palgrave, 2006) 176.

darker fears. 'Schools' can just as easily figure as the domain of 'tyrants, just in cruelty' (42. 4, 6), while the whims of teachers can be capricious and punishing: 'Alas poor wag, that now a scholar art | To such a school-mistress, whose lessons new | Thou needs must miss, and so thou needs must smart' (46. 9–11).[17]

While Astrophil recognizes the jeopardy in being subject to the authority of the schoolmaster, he is also eager to challenge this sovereign power. He assumes the persona of a 'truant' (1. 13), a rebellious scholar who can fashion his own lessons according to his needs. In particular, he is sensitive to the power of the teacher's tools, and proves himself eager to expropriate them. Grammar offers an especially enticing source of authority. In Sonnet 63, Astrophil pays remarkable attention to its details and deftly manipulates its rules:

> O grammar rules, O now your virtues show:
>   So children still read you with awful eyes,
>   As my young dove may in your precepts wise,
> Her grant to me, by her own virtue, know.
> For late, with heart most high, with eyes most low,
>   I craved the thing, which ever she denies:
>   She, lightning love, displaying Venus' skies,
> Lest once should not be heard, twice said, 'No, no.'
> Sing then, my muse, now Io Pæn sing;
>   Heavens, envy not at my high triumphing,
> But grammar's force with sweet success confirm.
> For grammar says (O this, dear Stella, weigh),
> For grammar says (to grammar who says nay?)
> That in one speech two negatives affirm.
>
> (63. 1–14)

The poem's charming wit risks obfuscating an underlying plea: if there is order to be had in the fraught arena of romantic exchange, it is to be found in lessons well-remembered from boyhood, the logical and rule-bound avenues of Latin grammar. Astrophil's wry appeal here is for control, and he petitions the authority of a familiar schema that has commanded the 'awful eyes' of legions of schoolboys. The apostrophized idol of grammar, here figured as the arbiter of Astrophil's desire, represents the indomitable enforcer of order and compliance. It is through the force of grammar's unassailable pronouncements, to which no canny pupil says 'nay,' that Astrophil will claim dominion over the denied 'thing' of his craving. The large-scale grammar system, with its entrenched and universal rules, boasts an authority that Astrophil lacks, and offers a salve for his vulnerability.

Some critics have suggested that the appeal to grammar heightens the playfulness of the sonnet; the notion that Astrophil can successfully exert control only in the realm of

---

[17] Interestingly, in this case the paternal control of the schoolmaster is manifested in the persona of Stella's 'school-mistress', a shift that emphasizes the singular authority accorded to Stella.

language perhaps hints at his ineptitude in other more vital arenas.[18] Yet the legacy of many formative years spent in grammar lessons is a profound appreciation of the power of words, and in the broader context of *Astrophil and Stella*, the conflation of linguistic mastery and erotic conquest is far from hollow. Consider the sentiment behind some of the sequence's most renowned lines: 'Then think, my dear, that you in me do read | Of lover's ruin some sad tragedy: | I am not I, pity the tale of me' (45. 12–14). This passage has often been read as an assertion of self-created identity, featuring dissembling words that use the tropes of lamentation to encode an assertive self who is firmly in control of his own persona. While Astrophil's cunning manipulation is clearly in play, the underlying image of an 'I' that can no longer recognize itself is rather chilling. The unrecognizable self, transformed by an alien and uncontrollable world, is at the heart of the genre of 'sad tragedy'. In *Astrophil and Stella*, the remedy for this destabilized self lies in the skills that befit an attentive scholar of language and its rules; Astrophil's sole assurance is his words, and he revels in his subtle manipulation of their finer details. The bitter contention of the Fifth Song—'But I in me am changed' (76)—is softened by the mastery demonstrated in the Fourth Song, wherein Stella's reiterated refusals—'No, no, no, no, my dear, let be'—are ultimately turned against her with the final twist of 'Soon with my death I will please thee' (53). As in Sonnet 63, here the muse of grammar offers a promise to override Stella's injurious negatives, shifting the target of her refusal so that ultimately she denies not Astrophil's entreaties but his death. Stella's repeated 'no's provide a chorus of rejection—vocal reminders of the despair and loss that lie in wait in any romantic entanglement—and it is only Astrophil's linguistic manipulation that offers the promise of rescue.

If the 'grammar rules' learned in Tudor classrooms by students such as Sidney were emblematic of control and mastery, they were also flashpoints for the tensions between classical and vernacular language, one of the most pressing language-related issues of the day. While the emphasis on Latin was a fundamental tenet of humanist pedagogy, it was subject to increasing scrutiny by the closing decades of the sixteenth century. Some began to criticize a curriculum that promoted classical languages at the expense of the vernacular, and pedagogical treatises lamenting the lack of English in the classroom began to proliferate. Reformers, who supported the nationalistic idea that English speakers should celebrate the eloquence inherent to their native tongue, pointed to the rising commercial and diplomatic significance of English, and also suggested that the practical aims of education were changing. The majority of boys who attended grammar schools did not proceed to university, but instead worked in areas where skill in English took precedence over Latin fluency.[19] It is not surprising that early modern

---

[18] Cf. Joseph Loewenstein, who maintains that 'only a schoolboy, indulging in the joys of pedantry, will invest "Grammer" with preemptive authority', 'Sidney's Truant Pen', *Modern Language Quarterly* 46.2 (June 1985): 135.

[19] Ursula Potter, 'To school or not to school: Tudor views on education in drama and literature', *Parergon* 25.1 (2008): 116.

schoolmasters—many of whom moonlighted as grammarians—were at the forefront of this push for a more English-focused curriculum.

Perhaps the most prominent advocate was Richard Mulcaster, headmaster at the distinguished Merchant Taylors' and St Paul's schools, whose broad aim was to see English eclipse Latin as the language of learning. In his 1582 work *The First Part of the Elementarie*, Mulcaster derided the 'bondage' that saw English speakers become servants to Latin, while neglecting the 'treasur in our own tung': 'I loue *Rome*, but *London* better, I fauor *Italie*, but England more, I honor the Latin, but I worship the *English*'.[20] During the school days of Sidney and Shakespeare, the slowly rising tide of English was making small but pervasive incursions against the dominant force of Latin. Curiously, the very methods by which Latin was taught in grammar schools encouraged an awareness of the power and effectiveness of English. Latin and English were set alongside one another in textbooks and in exercises, a practice that invited comparison. On the surface of things, this arrangement seemed to confirm the superior nature of Latin: it appeared elegant and organized where English was chaotic, a confirmation of the widely held belief that grammar was the exclusive purview of Latin, while English, 'lacking norms in spelling, pronunciation, morphology and syntax, was considered to be largely irregular and, many would have claimed, incapable of being reduced to a proper system and orderliness'.[21]

Yet even in the orthodox Lily's *Grammar*, it is English, the familiar mother-tongue, that has the authoritative final word: 'English is given a peculiar form of subservient ascendency over its erstwhile master. Latin meaning is verified through the vernacular, and tested in the mind of the schoolboy by reference to vernacular forms'.[22] In addition, a cursory comparison of Latin and English reveals that they are not always in accord; rules that are correct in Latin do not apply in English, a reality that undermined the sacred notion that Latin grammar provided an *ur*-model for the grammars of other languages. Indeed, the acknowledgement that English possessed a grammar of its own set the stage for its recognition as an estimable language: 'To endow the vulgar tongue with its own grammatical apparatus was to deliver to it a newfound and a potentially divisive power'.[23] And just as the schoolbooks designed to exalt Latin inadvertently hinted at the power of English, the pedagogical drills used to instil Latin rules paradoxically served to expose the creative potential of the vernacular. One of the most striking of these exercises, used with even the youngest of schoolboys, was the practice of double translation, which required students to translate a passage of Latin into English, and then convert the English back into Latin without the benefit of the original. Such a practice, while surely vexing, encouraged an intimate awareness of the nuances of grammar, and at the same time introduced a sense of creativity and play into an ostensibly rigid framework: 'students keep inventing as they travel across the language barrier until they achieve a text

---

[20] Richard Mulcaster, *The First Part of the Elementary* 1582 (Menston: Scolar Press, 1970) 254.
[21] Görlach (1999) 482.
[22] Cummings (2002) 25.
[23] Cummings (2002) 25.

that is at once their own voice and the re-creation of a pre-existing model'.[24] Interestingly, then, the experience of learning Latin in school improbably served to accent the creative possibilities of English.

The expressive potential of English and the latent friction between Latin and English are realized in various ways in *Astrophil and Stella*, offering another illustration of how the 'rules' of grammar inform these poems. Specifically, we can trace a tension between Latinate and English word choices that illustrates how Sidney might be responding to the shifting linguistic allegiances of his age. In these sonnets, the English language emerges as a compelling force, often at the expense of Latin. Sonnet 55, which takes as its subject the inadequacy of classical literary forerunners, provides a good example:

> Muses, I oft invoked your holy aid,
>   With choicest flowers my speech to engarland so
>   That it, despised in true but naked show,
>   Might win some grace in your sweet skill arrayed;
> And oft whole troops of saddest words I stayed,
>   Striving abroad a-foraging to go,
>   Until by your inspiring I might know
> How their black banner might be best displayed.
>   But now I mean no more your help to try,
> Nor other sugaring of my speech to prove,
> But on her name incessantly to cry:
> For let me but name her, whom I do love,
>   So sweet sounds straight mine ear and heart do hit
> That I well find no eloquence like it.
>
> (55. 1–14)

The sonnet exemplifies a tension between Latin and English, ostensibly celebrating—yet conspicuously omitting—the Latinate name 'Stella', while at the same time implicitly promoting the potential of English. Its underlying theme, that ornamented, classically influenced words ultimately fall short in their expressive function, is reinforced in its lexical fabric. When set beside the terse English-based words, the ostentatious Latinate words used to describe the 'Muses' and their language—'invoked', 'engarland', 'inspiring'—seem to be merely superfluous ornaments, both excessive and inadequate. The point is subtly made early in the poem: '... despised in true, but naked show, | Might win some grace in your sweet skill arrayed' (3–4). Here, the negatively inflected, Latinate 'despised' is followed by a string of native Saxon words that suggest—both in connotation and cadence—a purity and directness not found in their Latin-derived counterparts. 'True', 'win', 'sweet', and 'skill' are powerful English monosyllables that demonstrate the surprising power of un-'sugar[ed]' speech, while 'naked' might be read as the touchstone

---

[24] Leonard Barkan, 'What did Shakespeare read?' *The Cambridge Companion to Shakespeare*, Margreta de Grazia and Stanley Wells (eds), (Cambridge: Cambridge University Press, 2001) 35.

for the entire sonnet. True 'eloquence' is achieved not through showy Latinate language, that distant province of the Muses, but rather through a pared-down form of expression. As the lexical composition of the sonnet implicitly suggests, this eloquence might be found in a return to English. The thudding and unusual closing rhyme of 'hit' and 'it' reinforces the message; 'it', the decidedly unadorned Saxon stand-in for the name 'Stella', provides the poem's final, resounding note.

In taking a closer look at the word choices in this poem, I am suggesting that Sidney is engaging in another type of grammar play in *Astrophil and Stella*, more subtle than his exuberant apostrophe to 'grammar rules' but still suggestive of the distinctive linguistic terrain of his age. Because the gap between Latin and English had particular currency during the period that coincided with the composition of *Astrophil and Stella*, the technique of drawing attention to the differences between Latin and English within a single poem offers significant insight into this debate.[25] And while 'no Elizabethan possessed technical lexicographical skills, there was, as Sylvia Adamson has argued, "a general awareness of the etymological origins of words"',[26] and English speakers were accustomed to register-switching between Latinate and native Saxon, or Germanic, words. Adamson notes that some of these choices were predetermined, since many 'function' words in English—prepositions, articles, conjunctions—are exclusively Germanic. In the 'open class' of words, however—nouns, verbs, and adjectives—'significant choice can be made'.[27] Writers such as Sidney, tuned in to changing linguistic resources and at the forefront of language reform, had the creative advantage of a context in which multiple languages were available, and the choices that they make are telling. In the *Defence of Poesy*, a work contemporaneous with *Astrophil and Stella*, Sidney makes an impassioned case for why 'the Englishe before any Vulgare language I know' is uniquely suited to 'versifyeing', famously concluding that 'our tongue is most fitt to honor Poesi and to be honnored by Poesie'.[28] We might view *Astrophil and Stella* as a sort of companion piece to the *Defence*, a forum in which the rich possibilities for English identified by Sidney in his work of criticism are demonstrated. By deliberately highlighting English words, as he does in Sonnet 55, Sidney offers a tangible illustration of the potential of English as a rich literary language.

As Adamson observes, many nuts-and-bolts elements of the English language are Saxon, and it is to be expected that a sonnet sequence, with its focus on the speaker's actions and perspective, will feature a high proportion of personal pronouns and other function words. Yet very often, even in cases where many Latinate synonyms are

---

[25] Cf. Bradin Cormack, who provides an elegant and thorough discussion of the tension between Latin and English in Shakespeare's sonnets in 'Tender Distance: Latinity and Desire in Shakespeare's Sonnets', *A Companion to Shakespeare's Sonnets*, ed. Michael Schoenfeldt (Oxford: Wiley-Blackwell, 2010).

[26] Cormack (2010) 244.

[27] Sylvia Adamson, 'Literary Language', in *The Cambridge History of the English Language*, vol. 3, Roger Lass (ed.), (Cambridge: Cambridge University Press, 1999) 573.

[28] Sir Philip Sidney, *The Norwich Sidney Manuscript: The Apology for Poetry*, Mary R. Mahl (ed.), (Northridge: San Fernando Valley State College, 1969) 49–50.

available, lexical choices skew in favour of native English words. Indeed, many of the most forceful lines of *Astrophil and Stella* are emphatically English-based: 'Even those sad words in sad me did breed' (58.14); 'I can speak what I feel, and feel as much as they' (6.12). The powerful words that anchor these lines—adjectives and verbs such as 'sad', 'breed', 'speak', and 'feel'—are decisively English, and these choices suggest that Sidney is actively demonstrating the force and eloquence of English. Consider, as well, the arresting core of Sonnet 47, a poem which offers succinct expression of the anguished process of self-loss and reassessment: 'What, have I thus betrayed my liberty? … I may, I must, I can, I will, I do | Leave following that, which it is gain to miss' (1, 10–11). Line 10's heady catalogue of English monosyllables, a series of desperate vows that draw attention to Astrophil's successive attempts to force himself out of his fettered state, reads like an excerpt from a grammar textbook. In fact, this declaration strikingly accents the modal verbs, an English grammatical category that has no counterpart in Latin, and hence was an infamous source of discordance in grammar textbooks and an ongoing challenge in the teaching of grammar. Moreover, the modal verbs codify a system that allows speakers to articulate the actions of 'promising, threatening, commanding, predicting, and questioning',[29] impulses central to the negotiation of relationships in the sonnets. As I shall discuss further in terms of Shakespeare's sonnets, the modal verbs are powerful and quintessentially English words, and the fact that Sidney holds them up for display here suggests that he was sensitive to English's nuances. Responding in his sonnets to the changes that were taking place in both the structure and the status of his native tongue, Sidney engages with the peculiar dynamics of his linguistic environment, drawing on his experience learning Latin and English as a schoolboy, and implicitly commenting on shifting social attitudes toward English.

Like Sidney, Shakespeare had the experience of Tudor grammar school behind him, and the context of a language in flux around him. His sonnets followed Sidney's by at least ten years; the precise dates of their composition are unknown, but it is thought that they were written and revised over a period that extended from the early 1590s until well into the first decade of the seventeenth century. While they demonstrate a keen grasp of the distinctive linguistic climate of the age, as well as an attunement to the 'grammar rules' celebrated by Astrophil, their engagement with the details of grammar is more understated. The metaphor of schooling so evident in *Astrophil and Stella* is muted in Shakespeare's sonnets, where references to the experience of learning are glancing and self-conscious. While Astrophil's 'truant pen' conjures notions of rebellion and self-determination, the 'pupil pen' of Shakespeare's sonnet speaker (16. 10) suggests youthful inexperience and insecurity. Elsewhere, the speaker points to the illumination of a reluctantly learned lesson—'But thence I learn, and find the lesson true' (118. 13)—to demonstrate the hard-won virtues of learning, an idea which is

---

[29] Leslie K. Arnovick, *The Development of Future Constructions in English* (New York: Peter Lang, 1990) 1.

supported by the repeated warnings of the perils of being 'untutored' and 'unlearned' (138. 3,4).

Anxiety about one's perceived learning is perhaps not surprising in Shakespeare, who, despite his ample instruction in the classics at the King's Free Grammar School in Stratford-Upon-Avon, has often been cast as under-educated.[30] Shakespeare regularly mines his memories of the classroom in his drama, where references to grammar school are played to memorable comic effect in works such as *The Merry Wives of Windsor* and *Love's Labour's Lost*. In the Sonnets though, the speaker's relationship to schooling is less playful and more tentative. Whereas Astrophil fancies himself an apt pupil, Shakespeare's speaker seems more like an underdog, self-deprecating and overlooked, but subversively skillful:

> Why is my verse so barren of new pride,
> So far from variation or quick change?
> Why, with the time, do I not glance aside
> To new-found methods and to compounds strange?
> Why write I still all one, ever the same,
> And keep invention in a noted weed,
> That every word doth almost tell my name,
> Showing their birth and where they did proceed?
> O know, sweet love, I always write of you,
> And you and love are still my argument;
> So all my best is dressing old words new,
> Spending again what is already spent;
> > For as the sun is daily new and old,
> > So is my love, still telling what is told.

(76)

The speaker professes anxiety about his ostensibly staid verse, his inability or reluctance to adopt the 'new-found methods' and 'compounds strange' of his contemporaries. Yet he locates the beauty and novelty of his verse in its relentless capacity to remake itself from existing methods, the very 'same' tools that create at the same time that they reveal. In this sense, the student has learned his lessons well; he recognizes the potential inherent in unsuspecting little words and phrases. Unlike Sidney's sonnets, which in their overt allusions to schooling and lessons tend to highlight cultural and social elements of grammar, Shakespeare's sonnets deal more thoroughly with a less obvious aspect of grammar, the functional and structural features of the language. In Shakespeare's Sonnets, the speaker's innovative engagement with grammar provides a means for him to be stealthily creative with compounds 'familiar', the resources at hand. An excellent example of this understated sort of invention can be found in the word 'will' (which does indeed 'tell' the author's 'name'): a proper name, common noun, and modal verb, it

---

[30] Colin Burrow, 'Shakespeare and humanistic culture', *Shakespeare and the Classics*, Charles Martindale and A. B. Taylor (eds.), (Cambridge: Cambridge University Press, 2004) 11.

represents a seemingly banal grammatical building-block, and it is precisely the type of word that seems particularly 'spent' but is perpetually made new by the speaker.

Sonnets 135 and 136 are especially conspicuous platforms from which the speaker promotes his linguistic aptitude, notoriously unfolding around the possibilities for ribald wordplay offered by the various meanings of 'will':

> Whoever hath her wish, thou hast thy Will,
> And Will to boot, and Will in overplus ...
> Shall will in others seem right gracious,
> And in my will no fair acceptance shine? ...
>
> (135. 1–2, 7–8)

> If thy soul check thee that I come so near,
> Swear to thy blind soul that I was thy Will,
> And will, thy soul knows, is admitted there;
> Thus far for love my love-suit, sweet, fulfil.
> Will will fulfil the treasure of thy love,
> Ay, fill it full with wills, and my will one.
>
> (136. 1–6)

While these sonnets are cheekily suggestive, darker undertones are apparent beneath the salaciousness. Critics who have attempted non-bawdy readings often concentrate on the onomastic effects of a speaker creating a persona for an author who shares that name. It is possible to catch echoes of discontent in lines such as 'Swear to thy blind soul that I was thy Will' (136. 2), where the past tense 'was'—with its implication that the speaker is no longer in any sense the 'will' of the beloved—suggests a cynicism at odds with the playfulness of the poem. Indeed, this intimation of rupture is eventually borne out when, in later sonnets, the lover and the speaker are both 'forsworn' (152. 1–2). The word 'will' also hints at a gravity beyond the ecstatic antanaclasis of the sonnet. By holding up a word so rich in possibility, the speaker is 'dressing' an old word 'new', for 'will' unfolds in its expected senses as well as unexpected ones. In using a word that is both noun and verb, that can signal desire and intention, and that provides one of the standard means of conceptualizing and articulating future time, the speaker subtly draws on the conditions of grammar to create a multiply resonant type of polysemy. The 'will' sonnets highlight the speaker's attention to a particular version of the future, one which is desired and sought but is by no means assured. The fraught interaction in which Shakespeare's speaker is involved ensures that future outcomes are not entirely in his hands, and his expressions of a future that is 'willed' are implicated in claims of desire and control.

Moreover, the exhaustive attention to 'will' returns us to the sort of grammar play suggested by Astrophil's grammar-text excerpt: 'I may, I must, I can, I will, I do'. Modal verbs such as 'will' were emblematic of the diverse and shifting grammatical terrain of the late century, and they were ripe for rhetorical experimentation. These words represent a locus of linguistic change, and act as exemplars for the transitional nature of English at the end of the sixteenth century. They constitute a distinctive category in that they were originally main verbs which could occur alone in a clause; however, they gradually moved away from their position as primary verbs to act as auxiliaries (verbs used only in conjunction with other verbs). The period concurrent with Shakespeare's career witnessed a significant evolution in the semantic and grammatical application of modal verbs. During this transition period, these words were more fluid than their contemporary counterparts; they had lingering 'non-auxiliary features', and so retained remnants of their lexical meanings while simultaneously fulfilling a grammatical function.[31] In the late 16th century, the use of 'will' was never a simple marker of the future; it was semantically linked to volition even in its modal sense, so its use in expressions about the future pointed to an outcome that is particularly desired. The present-day tendencies of 'will'—'used where there is reference to a general envisaged, planned, intended, hoped for, etc. state of affairs, as opposed to a statement that a specific event or specific events will in fact take place'[32]—were in Shakespeare's English even more pronounced. In addition to their specialized and transitional function and meaning, the modal verbs encapsulated the tension between Latin and English that was playing out in grammar books and schools across the country. They provide one of the more striking examples of forms that are specific to English, and consequently they posed a problem for grammarians struggling to have them conform to Latin paradigms. In textbooks such as Lily's *Grammar*, and later in Bullokar's *Shorte Introduction*, there is 'a dim realization … that the modal auxiliaries behave according to their own pattern of rules, independent of Latin'.[33] In their own small way, these puzzling words thus lay bare some fundamental differences between Latin and English, and they stand as examples of powerful and uniquely English words.

The resonant 'wills' so prominently displayed in Sonnets 135 and 136 reverberate throughout Shakespeare's sonnets. For example, Sonnet 89 also draws attention to 'will', but with a markedly different tenor: 'Say that thou didst forsake me for some fault, | And I will comment upon that offence; | Speak of my lameness, and I straight will halt | … As I'll myself disgrace, knowing thy will. | I will acquaintance strangle and look strange …' (89. 1–3, 6–7). As in Sonnets 135 and 136, various senses of 'will' are employed to powerful effect, but here the playfulness is absent. The word is used as a noun only in the phrase 'thy will', a choice that highlights the beloved's desire. Yet this sense of desire is echoed in the repeated modal use of 'will': 'I will comment', 'I'll myself disgrace', 'straight will halt', 'I will acquaintance'. Because 'will' is semantically linked to volition even in its grammatical capacity as a modal auxiliary, the sense is that the speaker is aligning his own desire with that of the beloved, even if the result is a sort of self-betrayal. Here, as in the case of Astrophil's 'I am not I', we see the threat of a self destabilized, but the twist in this case is that the speaker makes himself complicit in this process by tailoring his desire to

[31] Matti Rissanen, 'Syntax', in *The Cambridge History of the English Language*, vol. 3, Roger Lass (ed.), (Cambridge: Cambridge University Press, 1999) 232.
[32] F. R. Palmer, *Modality and the English Modals* (London: Longman, 1979) 115.
[33] Cummings (2002) 212.

that of the beloved. The 'wills' of this sonnet trace a process of self-abnegation, and at the same time they highlight a word that was particularly evocative, and strikingly English. I do not mean to suggest that Shakespeare approached 'will' as a grammarian would, keen to demonstrate and exemplify all of its possible usages. However, as a poet attuned to the possibilities contained in individual words, he appears particularly alert to the special resonance of 'will', and often brings together its disparate forms in suggestive ways. With this subtle form of grammar play, Shakespeare taps the linguistic resources of his age to capture a number of tensions, and to exploit the possibilities of his native language, in one succinct and expressive word.

The implicit commentary on the riches of English suggested by the highlighting of the word 'will' extends to other aspects of Shakespeare's sonnets. Like *Astrophil and Stella*, these poems regularly demonstrate their concerns with etymology, and display a particular interest in the tensions between Latinate and native words. Often, this Latin-English play is exemplified in a specialized type of antanaclasis, imbued with a cross-etymological flavour, so that the wordplay is enriched by the disparate origins of the word's variants. In one sense, this play on the boundary between Latin and English reflects what Bradin Cormack calls Shakespeare's 'experimental philology', his acute attunement to the meanings, contexts, and associations of individual words, and his eagerness to exploit distinct etymological origins.[34] But there is also the sense that, as in *Astrophil and Stella*, special attention is paid to the unique impact of English, and forceful English words often seem to be held up for display, especially in the dramatic closing lines. For example, in the bitter penultimate line of Sonnet 92—'But what's so blessèd fair that fears no blot?' (13)—the arresting 'blessèd' and 'blot', with their hard, voiced consonants, are both distinctively English words, each with no corresponding form outside of English, even in other Germanic languages.[35] In a sonnet that reflects on the precariousness of 'love' that should endure 'For term of life' (2–3)—the Saxon 'love' and 'life' are repeated in the poem—these words act as anchors. 'Blessèd', rooted in the Old English *bloedsian* and cognate with 'blood', suggests a natural and inviolable bond, but it is uncomfortably close to its antithesis, the homophonic 'blot', which undoes the sanctity of this union. 'Blessèd', 'blot', and their shared undercurrent 'blood' all encapsulate the conflict at the heart of this sonnet: the potential for betrayal is inherent in all bonds, no matter how consecrated or apparently secure.

Similarly, in Sonnet 5, English words provide the subtle engine of the poem: 'A liquid prisoner pent in walls of glass, | Beauty's effect with beauty were bereft, | Nor it nor no remembrance what it was. | But flowers distilled, though they with winter meet, | [Leese] but their show; their substance still lives sweet' (10–14). The sonnet illustrates Shakespeare's characteristic ear for the idiosyncrasies of English; its effective use of rare regional variants such as 'pent' (10) and 'leese' (14)[36] hints at the rich

---

[34] Cormack (2010) 244.

[35] *OED*, 'blessed'; 'blot'.

[36] Most modern editors emend this word to 'lose', but the Quarto has 'leese', a variant Shakespeare uses only here.

stores, and surprising potential for variation and eloquence, of the English language. The closing couplet features the antanaclastic echo of 'distill'/'still,' a trick that, by drawing out the impact of the word 'still,' deepens its association with endurance. At the same time, the repetition highlights the differences between the two words, particularly in terms of their origins. The Latinate 'distill' is transformed into the English 'still', which is paired with two other brief English words, 'lives sweet.' The sonnet thus closes with the concise, resonant impact of native words, a feature that seems significant in a poem that draws attention to unusual English words in its word choices while thematically (like *Astrophil and Stella*'s Sonnet 55) it celebrates liberation from adornment, and the beauty inherent in bareness. Another telling instance of Latin–English antanaclasis can be found in 'Thou art all my art' (78. 13), a formulation in which 'the first "art" is native in origin, the second Roman'.[37] By coupling the English-based verb 'art' with a derivation of the Latin *ars*, Shakespeare shrewdly hints at the rich possibilities for English. It is not merely an uncouth tongue fit only for function, set against the Latin capacity for style and eloquence; rather, its 'art' can stand richly and rightfully alongside that of Latin. In examples such as this, Shakespeare demonstrates that the 'common' words of English 'are not simply the inert residue or the thread' undergirding the 'great' words of Latin.[38] Their creative deployment in Shakespeare's sonnets reflects the emergent idea that the singular qualities of English have a fundamental place in literary language.

Sidney and Shakespeare, like all great poets, are connoisseurs of language, remarkably cognizant of its shades of meanings, its idiosyncrasies, and its rules. They absorb and transmute lexicons from all sorts of communities: the court, the church, the grammar school. Most of all, though, they are attuned to the ambient language of their age, the specific features and resources available in a given social and historical context. By attending to the undertows of this cultural and linguistic moment—the unique experience of grammar school, the latent tension between classical and vernacular language, and the transitional status and structure of English—I hope to have suggested some ways that the dynamic linguistic climate of the late sixteenth century informed the poetry of the time. Sidney's *Astrophil and Stella* compellingly alludes to the broad social aspects of grammar, including the institutionalized methods of language teaching and learning, and the influence of a creative environment wherein various forms of language clash and compete. Shakespeare also taps into this varied linguistic environment, exploring in his sonnets the smaller-scale elements of structure and function, and exploiting the nuances of a language in transition. Together, the sonnets of Sidney and Shakespeare grant us a window into the unique linguistic and literary culture of the age, and equip us with a new appreciation for the 'grammar' that was so salient and encompassing.

---

[37] Cormack (2010) 243.
[38] Adamson (1999) 583.

SELECT BIBLIOGRAPHY

Barkan, Leonard (2001) 'What did Shakespeare read?' in Margreta de Grazia and Stanley Wells (eds) *The Cambridge Companion to Shakespeare* (Cambridge: Cambridge University Press, 2001) 31–47.

Cormack, Bradin (2010) 'Tender Distance: Latinity and Desire in Shakespeare's Sonnets' in Michael Schoenfeldt (ed.) *A Companion to Shakespeare's Sonnets* (Oxford: Wiley-Blackwell) 242–60.

Crane, Mary Thomas (1993) *Framing Authority* (Princeton: Princeton University Press).

Cummings, Brian (2002) *The Literary Culture of the Reformation: Grammar and Grace* (Oxford: Oxford University Press).

Grantley, Darryll (2000) *Wit's Pilgrimage: Drama and the Social Impact of Education in Early Modern England* (Aldershot: Ashgate).

Hope, Jonathan (2010) *Shakespeare and Language: Reason, Eloquence, and Artifice in the Renaissance* (London: Methuen).

Jones, R. F. (1953) *The Triumph of the English Language* (Stanford: Stanford University Press).

Lass, Roger (1999) (ed.) *The Cambridge History of the English Language*, vol. 3 (Cambridge: Cambridge University Press).

Mitchell, Linda C. (2001) *Grammar Wars: Language as Cultural Battleground in 17th and 18th Century England* (Aldershot: Ashgate).

Palmer, F. R. (1979) *Modality and the English Modals* (London: Longman).

CHAPTER 11

....

COMMONPLACE SHAKESPEARE

Value, Vulgarity, and the Poetics of Increase in Shake-Speares Sonnets *and* Troilus and Cressida

....

CATHERINE NICHOLSON

11.1 SHAKESPEARE FOR SALE

....

In 1609, London printer George Eld embarked on the production of two Shakespearean quartos: a 'new play' titled *The Famous History of Troilus and Cressida*, and a collection of poems titled *Shake-speares Sonnets*. Today we know—and care—far more about the latter: the first (and, for a good while, the only) printed edition of a sequence of poems that now stands as the fascinating and frustrating center of Shakespeare's *oeuvre* and, by extension, the corpus of Renaissance poetry, the canon of English literature, and, by some accounts, the history of modern Western subjectivity. The 1609 *Troilus*, by contrast, slumps at the margins of literary history, a 'bad quarto' of a distinctly minor work, distinguished, if at all, as the quintessential 'problem play'. In 1609, however, the relative value of the two texts would have been calculated rather differently. In printing Shakespeare's collection of sonnets, Eld and his collaborator Thomas Thorpe gambled— unwisely, perhaps—on the public's waning interest in a somewhat outmoded form; three decades would pass before John Benson attempted a new edition, and a full century elapsed before literary critics took notice. In *Troilus*, by contrast, Eld possessed a dramatic work by one of the most popular playwrights of the day, featuring a plot derived from the most prestigious classical and vernacular literature—as close to a sure thing as one could imagine.

Eld's involvement in both projects is a coincidence, but an illuminating one. It isn't simply that the shifting fortunes of the two texts offer an object lesson in the mutability of popular taste and scholarly judgement; read alongside the Sonnets, *Troilus and Cressida* underscores and glosses the poems' ambivalent theorizing of their own literary value. Like the Sonnets, the 1609 quarto of *Troilus* confronts readers with overtly incommensurate standards of aesthetic and moral value, asking us to reckon the worth of what we read in terms that threaten to undo the very notions of textual property and personal propriety. In these texts Shakespeare reveals himself as a consummate practitioner of rhetorical and poetic strategies that take commonness as the paradoxical ground of excellence; he also reveals himself as a sharp-eyed critic of the contradictions—and flat impossibilities—on which those strategies, the Erasmian poetics of 'increase', depend.

What makes the Sonnets and *Troilus* still more interesting is the degree to which the ambivalence about value within each text gets communicated to those who seek to establish their value from without—beginning with George Eld and his collaborators. *Shakes-speares Sonnets* are a notorious market failure; the survival of two distinct versions or 'states' of the 1609 *Troilus* indicates that securing readers for that text was no simple matter, either. The first version advertises the play in what was, in 1609, the usual manner: 'The Historie of Troylus and Cresseida. As it was acted by the Kings Maiesties seruants at the Globe'.[1] But an epistle to readers prefixed to the quarto's second state, titled 'The Famous Historie of Troylus and Cresseyd',[2] disavows any link to the theatre, advertising instead 'a new play, neuer stal'd with the Stage, neuer clapper-clawd with the palmes of the vulgar'.[3] However, having emphatically rejected the conventional association between dramatic success and print appeal, the epistle's author struggles to

---

[1] *The historie of Troilus and Cresseida. As it was acted by the Kings Maiesties seruants at the Globe. Written by William Shakespeare* (London: G. Eld for R. Bonian and H. Walley, 1609). The late 16th- and early 17th-century market for printed play-texts assumed a more or less intimate connection to the world of performance: Richard Jones' 1590 edition of the two parts of Marlowe's *Tamburlaine the Great* set the marketing precedent by assuring potential customers of the identity between its text and the dramatic spectacle that had 'bene (lately) delightfull for many of you to see, when the same were shewed in London vpon stages' ('To the Gentleman Readers'). Of course, in the next breath, Jones famously acknowledges that he has 'omitted' some portions of the performance text that he has judged unworthy of his gentleman readers: the market for printed plays may constitute itself as an offshoot of the theatrical economy, but that dependency is rivalrous from the start, as Lukas Erne has argued (*Shakespeare as Literary Dramatist*, Cambridge: Cambridge University Press, 2003, 47–50). For more on the pivotal role played by publishers like Jones in creating the play-text as a saleable commodity, see Zachary Lesser, *Renaissance Drama and the Politics of Publication: Readings in the English Book Trade* (Cambridge: Cambridge University Press, 2004).

[2] *The Famous Historie of Troylus and Cresseid. Excellently expressing the beginning of their loues, with the conceited wooing of Pandarus Prince of Licia. Written by William Shakespeare* (London: G. Eld for R. Bonian and H. Walley, 1609).

[3] For more on the revision of this prefatory material see Lesser, *Renaissance Drama*, 1–4. See also David J. Baker, *On Demand: Writing for the Market in Early Modern England* (Stanford: Stanford University Press, 2010) 69–74, for a discussion of the play's commercial failure in relation to the 'market-world' it stages.

define an alternate measure of value for his play text—or, more accurately, he invokes a confusing multiplicity of standards. On the one hand, the epistle heralds *Troilus* for its accessibility, being the work of an author whose inventions 'are so fram'd to the life that they serue for the most common Commentaries, of all the actions of our liues', and so broadly appealing that 'the most displeased with Playes, are pleasd with his Commedies'. On the other hand, it identifies Troilus as part of an elite canon, 'deseru[ing]' the labour of learned commentators 'as well as the best Commedy in *Terence* or *Plautus*', and as a soon-to-be-rare commodity: 'beleeue this', the epistle declares, 'when he is gone, and his Commedies out of sale, you will scramble for them'. Readers are urged not to conflate popularity with merit—'refuse not, nor like this the lesse, for not being sullied, with the smoaky breath of the multitude'—but also advised to regard *Troilus* as a near-victim of obscurity, 'thank[ing] fortune for the scape it hath made amongst you', since 'by the grand possessors wills' it might never have seen print at all.[4]

Troilus' value as printed text thus inheres in paradox: it is both 'a new play' and a '*Famous Historie*', 'most common' and yet 'neuer stal'd', liberated from the clutches of its 'grand possessors' but also in imminent danger of going 'out of sale'. Such rhetorical confusion is perhaps compensatory: the epistle works (too) hard to make good on *Troilus*' most obvious commercial defect, citing its apparent failure to secure an audience in the theatre as an emblem of literary prestige.[5] But the mutual exclusivity of the positions adopted by the epistle's author—that value inheres in novelty and rarity and that value accrues through use and circulation—correspond as well to a tension within the central positive strategy by which he seeks to establish the value of his text: by offering it both as the distinctive offspring of a particular genius—'a birth of your braine, that neuer vnder-tooke any thing comicall, vainely'—and as a work that communicates its brilliance to even the dullest readers, who will find 'that witte there, that they neuer found in them selues', and part 'better wittied than they came'. According to the printer, this paradoxical union of particularity and commonality elevates *Troilus* to the level of a classic: Shakespeare's play is like 'the best Commedy in *Terence* or *Plautus*' not simply because it is identified with its superlative author—'when hee is gone, and his Commedies out of sale, you will scramble for them'—but also because it is at the disposal of a much broader (indeed, universally inclusive) group. *Troilus* belongs, that is, to a corpus of literary works whose prestige inheres precisely in their ability to 'serue for the most common Commentaries, of all the actions of our liues'.

The design of the printed text facilitates this latter claim. Together with the 1603 first quarto of *Hamlet*, the 1609 *Troilus* is the only first-edition Shakespearean quarto to be 'commonplaced': adorned with typographical markers identifying particular passages as especially apt for extraction and reuse by readers.[6] Unlike the modern quotation

---

[4] *The Famous Historie of Troylus and Cresseid*, sig. ¶2ʳ.
[5] See Baker (2010) 69–70.
[6] For an analysis of Q1 Hamlet and the emergent practice of commonplacing vernacular playtexts, see Zachary Lesser and Peter Stallybrass, 'The First Literary Hamlet and the Commonplacing of Professional Plays', *Shakespeare Quarterly* 59:4 (Winter 2008): 371–420.

marks they closely resemble, the inverted commas placed to the left of certain lines in the play signal to the 17th-century reader that they are commonplaces—not, that is, expressions proper to Shakespeare or his characters, but conventional formulas available and adaptable to any speaker, anywhere, and at any time. From our own perspective, such marks, and the practices of reading and writing they promote, might seem to diminish the status of the author and his work, but from the perspective of an early 17th-century reader, they also testify to that status. In the case of the 1609 quarto of *Troilus*, this seemingly minor—literally marginal—textual feature reinforces the dedicatory epistle's claims for the play's quasi-classical status, by encouraging the reader to digest and assimilate Shakespeare's language using the same techniques he would have learned to apply to Greek and Latin texts in the grammar-school classroom.[7] Commonplace marks thus secure the value of the play-text by *not* insisting on its integrity as a complete work, or, to put it more precisely, the value of the whole depends upon the dispersal of its component parts into the hands and mouths of the multitude.[8] For as Erasmus, Renaissance Europe's foremost theorist and practitioner of the art of commonplacing, explains in the preface to his *Adagia*, commonplaces acquire distinction by being 'passed around': like 'a road … well polished in use and circulating',[9] the commonplace proves its singular merit by spreading itself as widely as possible.

The conception of literary value inhering in such textual artefacts is peculiarly resistant to post-17th-century notions of literary property and propriety. Even the typography of commonplacing is likely to mislead us: for a modern reader, as Margreta de Grazia observes, quotation marks 'mark off private property'—to quote without attribution is to devalue textual property—while, in the Renaissance the identical feature 'signaled communal ground[,] … mark[ing] material to be copied …, thereby assuring that the

[7] We have evidence of at least one Renaissance reader—the owner of a First Folio of Shakespeare's plays now at Meisei University—who did just that, diligently noting in the margins of each play the topoi under which he might distribute various passages in his own commonplace book. See Akihiro Yamada, *The First Folio of Shakespeare: A Transcript of Contemporary Marginalia in a Copy of the Kodama Memorial Library of Meisei University* (Tokyo: Yushodo Press, 1998).

[8] Here my reading of the print presentation of the 1609 quarto of *Troilus and Cressida* departs from Erne's thesis about the invention of Shakespeare as 'literary dramatist' in one important respect: Erne emphasizes that when plays are imagined predominantly as performance texts, 'their realization [was] by nature collaborative and subject to constant change'; the transfer from playhouse to print shop moves the text in the direction of textual stability and proprietary authorship (34). In a broad sense this is surely true, but if we take the use of commonplace markers as a pre-eminent contemporary sign of literary textuality, the shift away from collaboration and change is much less clear. Peter Stallybrass and Roger Chartier discuss the particular implications of such a reading practice for our notion of Shakespearean authorship and authority in the seventeenth century in 'Reading and Authorship: The Circulation of Shakespeare 1590–1619', *A Concise Companion to Shakespeare and the Text*, Andrew Murphy (ed.), (Oxford: Blackwell, 2007).

[9] These phrases are Erasmus' literal translation of, respectively, the Greek *paroemia*, or proverb, and the Latin *adagium*. See *The Adages of Erasmus*, ed. William Barker (Toronto: University of Toronto Press, 2001) xxix; see also *The Collected Works of Erasmus* (hereafter: CWE) vol. 31, Margaret Mann Phillips (trans.), (Toronto: University of Toronto Press, 1982) 4–5.

commonplaces would become more common still'.[10] In the essay that follows I want to suggest, first of all, that that very disjunction between Renaissance and modern conceptions of literary value makes commonplacing an essential framework for thinking about value in (and the value of) the Shakespearean text. To think of Shakespeare's own poetics as commonplace—that is, as kin to an extremely widespread set of literary practices *and* as overtly committed to the value of use and reuse—prevents us from moving too quickly or thoughtlessly to our preferred metrics of originality, novelty, and radical inventiveness.[11] That isn't to say that Shakespeare's poems and plays place no premium on rarity or novelty—*Troilus* is, after all, advertised as a 'new play'; the 1609 Sonnets are advertised as 'Neuer before imprinted'[12]—or that there is nothing rare or novel in them, but rather that, within the texts, the values of rarity and novelty are attenuated by, and often subordinated to, a prior commitment to abundance and commonality.

For us, readers and critics of Shakespeare in the 21st century, attending to those Erasmian values means resisting our impulse to identify Shakespeare either as origin or, alternatively, as *telos* of a literary tradition: according to the terms of Shakespeare's own poetic practice, it may be that the middle is a far more valuable and productive place to be. This is true in a particular way of the 1609 quarto of *Troilus*, a text that gives both the first and last word to an unrepentant middleman, opening with an acerbic speech by Cressida's cousin Pandarus and concluding with an epilogue spoken by that 'broker-lacky', a mock-plangent lament rebuking the world for its undervaluation of his kind: 'poore agent[s]', 'traitors and bawds', 'traiders in the flesh', and all those whose vigorous efforts to cross the boundaries of property and propriety are so 'ill requited' by the world they serve.[13] To that company we might add Shakespeare himself—the Shakespeare who claims a narrative passed down from Homer to Caxton, depleted and replenished along the way by countless intermediary retellings, as his own, but also the poet of *Shake-speares Sonnets*. For, to a degree that unsettles many of our assumptions about their unique value, those poems invoke commonplacing as the guarantor of textual—and personal—virtue; nonetheless, as we shall see, they also identify the commonplace

[10] Margreta de Grazia, 'Shakespeare in Quotation Marks', *The Appropriation of Shakespeare: Post-Renaissance Constructions of the Works and the Myths*, ed. Jean I. Marsden (New York: St. Martin's Press, 1991) 58–9.

[11] This rhetoric is itself so pervasive as to warrant the appellation 'commonplace', but the most influential such account of the Sonnets is clearly Joel Fineman's *Shakespeare's Perjured Eye: The Invention of Poetic Subjectivity in the Sonnets* (Berkeley: University of California Press, 1986). Fineman doesn't deny the familiarity of Shakespeare's conceits in the *Sonnets*, but he insists nonetheless that a radically personal disclosure is encoded even in the most outworn tropes.

[12] Shakespeare, William. *Shake-speares Sonnets, Neuer before Imprinted* (London: G. Eld for T[homas] T[horpe], 1609). All subsequent citations refer to this edition.

[13] *The Famous Historie of Troylus and Cresseid*, sig. M[1]ᵛ. In the Oxford Shakespeare, these lines appear in the 'Additional Passages' collected at the end of the play (Wells and Taylor (2005) 766). For ease of reference I will provide act, scene, and line references to this edition alongside the page-signature references to the 1609 Quarto. The 1623 Folio text mitigates Pandarus' satiric influence, cutting the reference to him on the quarto's title page, relocating his final speech to a moment earlier in the play, and displacing his jesting opening speech with a Prologue that decorously situates the action in the midst of Homeric marital strife.

as the natural habitation of the bawd, the pimp, and the whore, Pandarus' 'brethren and sisters of the hold-dore trade' (sig. M[1]ᵛ; 'Additional Passages', 776). This divided perspective on the literary technique that inaugurates and sustains the poems themselves instantiates within the sequence a debate very like those that so often disrupt the action in *Troilus*: on the one side, commonality stands as the ultimate proof of value; on the other, commonness threatens to dissolve value into a promiscuous lack of distinction.

11.2 DESIRING INCREASE

The opening two lines of Shakespeare's first sonnet offer a bracingly straightforward, indeed quasi-mathematical, formula for the calculation of worth:

> From fairest creatures we desire increase,
> That thereby beauties *Rose* might neuer die.
>
> (lines 1–2)

What we seek from beautiful persons or objects, the poet proposes at the outset, is, precisely, more of the same, an eternity founded on the virtues of resemblance, familiarity, and plenitude: as Sonnet 6 calculates, if 'an other thee' is good, then 'ten times happier be it ten for one' (lines 7–8). The early sonnets to the fair youth in fact consist entirely of elaborations, dilations, and variations of the expression of this conviction: 'Thou single wilt prove none' (8, l. 14); 'Be not selfe-wild'—that is, do not be the sole heir of your own bequest—'for thou art much too faire' (6, l. 13); 'Look in thy glasse and tell the face thou vewest | Now is the time that face should forme an other, … But if thou liue remembred not to be, | Die single and thine Image dies with thee' (3, lines 1–2, 13–14).

A century after those lines first appeared in print, however, this very premise—that singleness is nullity—appeared to deprive the Sonnets of their own claim to literary value. For, taking 'increase' as the fundamental standard and guarantor of worth—as Sonnet 11 does when urging the young man to 'print more, not let that coppy die' (line 14)—Shakespeare's Sonnets were demonstrably the *least* worthy of his literary efforts. In 1710, when Charles Gildon sought to rescue the Sonnets from obscurity by gathering Shakespeare's poems into a single printed volume (meant to ride in the successful wake of Nicholas Rowe's six-volume edition of the plays), he was keenly aware of this fact. As he acknowledged to readers, the merit of the poems could not be anchored to their success in the marketplace: even the editors of the first folio edition of Shakespeare's *Works* had excluded the Sonnets from their volume (or—perhaps more damningly—had not known of their existence). Some, Gildon conceded, might conclude that the poems themselves 'are not valuable enough to be reprinted, as was plain by the first Editors of his Work, who would otherwise have join'd them together'.

Gildon resists this conclusion by anchoring the merit of his text in relation to an alternate—and emphatically private—standard of value. In an ingenious, if highly speculative move, he argues that the very fact that the Sonnets did not circulate widely testifies to their proximity to the experiences and feelings—the person—of Shakespeare himself. The plays might be more widely appreciated, he writes, but the poems—and, above all, the Sonnets—offer a more distinctive pleasure, the distillation of the author's own style:

> I am confident that tho' the Poems this Volume contains are extreamly distinguish'd in their Excellence, and Value, yet there is not one of them, that does not carry its Author's Mark, and Stamp upon it. ... [W]hoever knows any thing of Shakespear will find his Genius in every epigram of these Poems in every particular I have mention'd.

Far from casting doubt on the merit of the Sonnets, he continues, their exclusion from the First Folio testified to their intimate significance: 'Besides these poems being most to his Mistress', Gildon speculated, 'it is not at all unlikely, that she kept them by her till they fell into her Executors Hands or some Friend, who would not let them be any longer conceal'd'.[14] The shift proposed by Gildon—from assessing the value of Shakespearean text not in terms of its popularity in print but rather by reference to its ability to perpetuate the dead author's unique sensibility—fuelled the 19th-century revival of interest in the Sonnets, culminating in the Romantic conviction that, as Wordsworth puts it, in these lyrics 'Shakespeare unlock'd his heart'.[15]

This critical turn was abetted by the rediscovery of the 1609 quarto, with its tantalizingly oblique dedication to 'Mr. W. H.', the poems' 'onlie begetter' and the presumed object of the poet's—that is, of Shakespeare's own—heartfelt pleas.[16] Gildon worked from what was, in 1710, the only available edition of the Sonnets, John Benson's 1640 edition of *Poems: Written by Wil. Shakes-peare, Gent.*, a volume that treats the poems not as a narrative 'sequence' but as texts to be collated and conflated under general topical headings—changing, when necessary, masculine pronouns to feminine. As de Grazia notes, this treatment earned Benson the opprobrium of later editors and scholars—he has been accused of everything from piracy to homophobia—but she urges that we consider him

---

[14] 'Remarks on the Poems of Shakespear', in *Poems. The Works of Mr. William Shakespear*, vol. 7, Nicholas Rowe (ed.), (London, 1710); excerpted in Bloom's *Shakespeare Through the Ages: The Sonnets*, ed. Brett Foster (New York: Bloom's Literary Criticism, 2008) 57.

[15] William Wordsworth, 'Scorn not the sonnet', line 3.

[16] The reinvestment of value in the 1609 Quarto by editors like Edmond Malone thus created a fresh set of difficulties: as Peter Stallybrass observes, 'in returning to the 1609 Quarto of the Sonnets, Malone was intent upon rescripting Shakespeare's poems to show the contours of the man behind them.... [But] having created the "authentic" character of Shakespeare, that character steps into the spotlight as a potential sodomite' ('Editing as Cultural Formation: The Sexing of Shakespeare's Sonnets', *Modern Language Quarterly* 54 (March 1993): 91–103.) Following Stallybrass, de Grazia argues that this 'scandal' is a backformation of modern sexual anxieties; it has obscured, in her view, the poems' own preoccupation with the far more serious threat posed by the mistress' indiscriminate sexuality ('The Scandal of Shakespeare's Sonnets', *Shakespeare Survey* 46 (1996): 35–49).

instead as 'the first reader' of the 1609 Sonnets, one who ensures the poems' survival by shaping them into 'a volume that promised to make sense to its projected readership'.[17] Indeed, Benson's chief concern seems not to be the concealment of secret passions but accessibility: the identification and promotion of common sentiments in poems that might otherwise frustrate readers with their opacity. His grouping of the poems thematically, under more or less generic titles ('The glory of beautie', 'Injurious time', 'Loves crueltie', 'Good Admonition'), works incidentally to obscure the figure of the fair youth, but it is his particularity rather than his gender that Benson seems most eager to efface.[18] His edition encourages readers to approach the sonnets not as the private outpourings of one heart to another, but as meditations on conventional themes, a commonplace book of verses—and it invites them, by copying extracts or individual poems into the blank spaces of their own commonplace books, to dissolve Shakespeare's text into the currents of earlier and later literary history.

In this regard, Benson is not simply the 'first reader', he is also a responsive one: his editorial instincts are exactly in line with the poet's own rhetorical purposes so far as the young man is concerned. For poems that are now treated as working through a set of intensely (perhaps embarrassingly) private erotic concerns—the poems to the 'fair youth'—would have been readily intelligible to early 17th-century readers as examples of and meditations on a literary practice that was the reverse of private, a literary practice that defined 'increase' as its highest virtue and its central strategy. As those readers would have recognized, the first seventeen sonnets in the 1609 quarto are not exactly personal or, indeed, original: on the contrary, they conspicuously and ingeniously rework a text borrowed from one of the most widely used volumes in the 16th-century English grammar school, Erasmus' *De Conscribendis Epistolis*. As part of his theoretical disquisition on the art of letter-writing—a textual practice he identified as essential to the development of literary skill—Erasmus supplied schoolboy readers with an array of sample letters, including a long epistle urging a youthful male acquaintance to overcome his reluctance to marry and shoulder the privileges and responsibilities of continuing the family line.[19] In adapting the tropes and logic of Erasmus' well-known epistle for the opening of his own sonnet sequence, Shakespeare hardly risked exposing himself as an impoverished or dependent wit; on the contrary, his refashioning of the epistle into verse advertises his mastery of the very literary values Erasmus espouses in *De Conscribendis Epistolis*: 'A letter's style will not only conform to the topic', Erasmus writes in his prefatory remarks, 'but, as befits any good go-between (for a letter performs the function of a messenger), it will take account of times and persons, ... play[ing] the part of a Mercury,

[17] Margreta de Grazia, 'The First Reader of *Shake-speares Sonnets*', *The Forms of Renaissance Thought*, Leonard Barkan, Bradin Cormack, and Sean Keilen (eds), (New York: Palgrave Macmillan, 2009) 86–106.

[18] *Poems: written by Wil. Shake-speare. Gent.* (London: Thomas Coates for John Benson, 1640), sigs. A2ʳ, A3ʳ, [A5]ᵛ, [A7]ʳ.

[19] *De Conscribendis Epistolis*, CWE 25, Charles Fantazzi (trans.) 129–45. In addition to encountering Erasmus' epistle in *De Conscribendis*, a full translation of the epistle takes up several pages in the first fully fledged English art of rhetoric, Thomas Wilson's *Arte of Rhetorique* (1560, 1563).

as it were, transforming itself into every shape required by the topic at hand, yet in such a way that amid great variety it retains one feature unaltered, namely that of being refined, learned, and sane'.[20]

This marvellous play of mutability and constancy is the selfsame feat Shakespeare achieves in reworking Erasmus' famous epistle into sonnet form, and in the reshaping of the conceits of the argument from one sonnet to the next: indeed, in his handling of Erasmus' epistle on marriage, Shakespeare might simply be said to have combined a number of Erasmus' own favorite classroom exercises—translating a passage from prose into verse; translating a text from one language to another; illustrating an idea with as many different figures and tropes as possible—into a sustained, bravura performance. Recognizing this broader pedagogical context for the sonnets to the fair youth has interpretive consequences: to take just one example, readers schooled in Erasmian techniques of amplification would likely have had a very different response to 'beauties *Rose*' than did those 19th- and 20th-century critics who sought in the phrase a coded allusion to the young Earl of Southampton (Henry 'Roseley' = Henry Wriothesley = Mr H. W. = the dedicatory epistle's mysterious Mr. W. H.?). For the products of 16th-century rhetorical training, the rhetorical force of the image may well have inhered in its very conventionality, its familiar—indeed generic—power. For as Erasmus suggests about the epistolary form itself, familiarity is the mother of rhetorical inventiveness, and variety is the engine of continuity: the rose that blooms in Sonnet 1 begets the mirror image reflected in Sonnet 3, the perfume distilled in Sonnet 5, the musical notes that sound in Sonnet 8, the seal impressed in Sonnet 11, the counterfeit painted in Sonnet 16, while the argument these figures illustrate remains—like the genealogical succession it is meant to inspire—constant.

Like Erasmus' epistle, then, the opening sonnets of Shakespeare's sequence offer a practical demonstration of that greatest of rhetorical and aesthetic achievements, what Erasmus dubs *copia* and Shakespeare Anglicizes as 'increase'. Both Erasmus and Shakespeare have self-conscious fun with the fact that their literary efforts model the very virtue to which they call their youthful addressees: like a fruitful marriage, the capacity to fashion a single line of argument into infinitely varied metaphors, examples, and proofs is the test of—and testament to—a generative power that is as conservative as it is transformative. As Erasmus emphasizes in his master-treatise on rhetorical and poetic skill, *De Copia*, the theory and practice of *copia* take as their founding assumption that 'Nature above all delights in variety', but the cultivation of this variety depends, paradoxically, on a willingness to repeat. In Erasmus' ideal schoolroom, to write is invariably to rewrite.[21] This is true not simply because the spurs to composition are examples and adages taken from elsewhere, but also because the writing done in the classroom is so often an exercise of the capacity to say something again, again, and yet again. Although *De Copia* and *De Ratione Studii* offer countless variations of schoolroom exercises

---

[20] *CWE* 25: 19.
[21] For detailed instructions concerning the maintenance of classroom commonplace books see *CWE* 24: 672.

to keep young minds from chafing at the monotony of that process,[22] the underlying method is always the same: 'we should frequently take a group of sentences and deliberately set out to express each of them in as many versions as possible, as Quintilian advises, using the analogy of a piece of wax which can be molded into one shape after another'.[23]

Needless to say, novelty and originality of thought are not the literary values at which such a practice chiefly aims—or, at least, not the kind of novelty and originality we often ascribe to poems like Shakespeare's Sonnets, when we credit them with inaugurating or departing radically from some literary or cultural tradition. Erasmus implies as much when he likens rhetorical invention to the modelling and re-modelling of a piece of wax. The figure of the wax is valuable here not simply because it aptly embodies the union of continuity and change on which *copia*—which is to say, the literary and philosophical traditions—depends, but also because the figure itself had proved so malleable: behind the overt allusion to Quintilian's *Institutio Oratoria*, we must also hear the implicit allusions to Ovid's *Metamorphoses*, where wax represents for Pythagoras the constancy of the soul and the mutability of form, while it supplies Pygmalion and Daedalus with the substance of artistic creation, to Aristotle's theory of sensory impressions in *De Anima*, to Plato's philosophy of memory in the *Theaetetas*.

And if having the first word is not the point, neither is having the final say: 'It is not my intention to write a book dealing exhaustively with the whole subject', Erasmus declares, 'but rather a short treatise in which I hope to open up the way for teachers and students and provide the raw material for future work'.[24] Some of this deprecation, of course, is itself conventional, the modesty *topos* invoked prophylactically by any writer at the start of a frankly ambitious undertaking, but a good portion of it also reflects the ethos of *copia* itself, a rhetorical virtue inhering in openness to what has been written before and what remains to be written in the future.

It is this same openness that the initial poems of Shakespeare's Sonnets both enact—in their reworking of Erasmus' epistle, itself a compilation of older themes and tropes—and celebrate—in their pleas to the fair youth, who is enjoined to participate in the genealogical equivalent of *copia*. This call requires a thoroughgoing re-signification of the lexicon of property, such that exclusive ownership becomes a form of poverty: 'hauing traffike with thy selfe alone', warns Sonnet 4, 'Thou of thy selfe thy sweet selfe dost deceaue' (lines 9–10). 'That vse is not forbidden vsery | Which happies those that pay the willing lone', insists Sonnet 6, eliding singleness (a 'willing' or wilful 'lone') into shared value (a 'willing loan'). Sonnet 10 turns 'possession' itself into loss: 'For thou art so possest with murdrous hate | That gainst thy selfe thou stickst not to conspire' (lines 5–6); 'that fresh bloud which yongly thou bestow'st | Thou maist call thine, when thou from youth convertest', promises Sonnet 11 (lines 3–4). The injunction with which that sonnet ends, to 'print more, not let that copy die', reminds the youth that 'copy'—like its

---

[22] See *CWE* 24: 679.
[23] *CWE* 24: 302–3.
[24] *CWE* 24: 297.

Latin antecedent, *copia*—refers both to the original from which further iterations are derived (*OED* 8a) and to the successive versions which are as perfectly preserved in one as in the other. Sonnet 13 thus invites the fair youth to position himself neither as first word nor as last word, but as the crucial conjunction in an ongoing, repetitive dialogue of past with future: 'You had a Father, let your Son say so' (line 14).

When the poet finally inserts himself into this conversation, in Sonnet 15, it is to promise his beloved a form of renovation firmly grounded in actual commonplaces:

> When I consider euery thing that growes
> Holds in perfection but a little moment;
> That this huge stage presenteth nought but showes,
> Whereon the Stars in secret influence comment.
> When I perceiue that men as plants increase,
> Cheared and checkt euen by the selfe-same skie,
> Vaunt in their youthfull sap, at height decrease,
> And wear their braue state out of memory;
> Then the conceit of this inconstant stay
> Sets you most rich in youth before my sight,
> Where wastfull time debateth with decay
> To change your day of youth to sullied night,
> > And all in war with Time for loue of you,
> > As he takes from you, I ingraft you new.

The first eight lines of the poem enlarge upon the fact of mutability, but the images invoked—the world as stage, the uncertain stars, withered plants, outmoded or threadbare garments—are themselves perennial: all changes, but the language of change proves remarkably durable. The poet gestures at this paradox with what Colin Burrow calls the 'deliberately unsettling' phrase *unconstant stay*, a formula that forces inconstancy into conjunction with persistence and delay.[25] The poet's proposed defense against the ravages of time is suspended equally between metamorphosis and conservation: engrafting, the technique by which the poet will make the fair youth 'new', works by dissolving the distinction between the established stem and the fresh offshoot. The plant that grows is simultaneously old and new, the same and not the same. In a similar fashion within the sonnet, the singular beloved—as Helen Vendler notes, the repeated puns on 'you' and 'youth' turn 'youth' into 'you-ness': the beloved is 'most rich' in his own unique selfhood[26]—is grafted onto, written into, a more durable corpus of rhetorical conceits. To identify the fair youth with the most banal expressions of a conventional truth might seem to diminish his rich selfhood—and, indeed, the sonnet works to remind him that he is *not* ultimately exempt from that truth—but it also creates for him a poetic refuge grounded in the assurance of repetition and plenty.

---

[25] Burrow, *Complete Sonnets and Poems*, (Oxford: Oxford University Press, 2002) 410, n. 9.
[26] Helen Vendler, *The Art of Shakespeare's Sonnets* (Cambridge, MA: Harvard University Press, 1997) 110.

The Sonnets themselves found a similar sort of refuge within 17th-century commonplace books. Indeed, to say that the 18th-century editions of Charles Gildon and Edmund Malone rescued the poems from obscurity is true enough if we mean the sequence as a published whole, especially (in Malone's case) in the form of the 1609 quarto, but less accurate if we consider that individual sonnets (and especially Sonnet 2) survived in manuscript miscellanies and printed commonplace books, with or without attribution to Shakespeare, often under emblematic titles emphasizing their conventional wit and wisdom, and at times in fragments, recombinations, or wholly modified versions.[27] Acting in accordance with the most widespread and elementary practices of reading, then, and responding too, perhaps, to the promptings of the sequence's own opening verses, 17th-century readers seem to have treated the Sonnets not as a coherent poetic narrative, nor as the outpourings of a private passion, nor even as the property of William Shakespeare, but as an aggregation of items available for excerption, citation, and reuse. In other words, the Sonnets' earliest readers valued Shakespeare as Shakespeare valued Erasmus, and as the poet of the sonnets values the fair youth: as an endlessly renewable source of inspiration and material for general use.

11.3 SWEETS GROWN COMMON

Here, however, it must be admitted that reading the Sonnets in this fashion—partially and selectively, with one's own rhetorical agenda in mind—is the only way to maintain the impression that Shakespeare wholeheartedly embraces the poetics of the commonplace book. For if we read past the opening sonnets to the fair youth, the poet's faith in the virtues of abundance and accessibility undergoes a series of stressful trials: the incursion of his mistress into his relationship with the fair youth, followed by the competitive advances of the rival poet, precipitates a yearning for a more proprietary model of erotic and literary value. The young man's status as an abstract and general source of value, 'beauties *Rose*'—once regarded as the essence and the guarantee of his perfection—becomes instead the locus of anxiety and resentment. Commonplacing offers a genuinely useful theoretical lens for interpreting the poetic and rhetorical strategies by which the Sonnets define and promote 'increase', but to adopt commonplacing as the solution to critical anxieties about the Sonnets' literary value is to ignore the poems' evident—increasingly evident—qualms about the strategies of use and reuse on which their own creative energies depend.

These qualms circle around two features of *copia* that Erasmus himself takes for granted: first, that the cultivation of *copia* is a fundamentally collaborative

---

[27] See Gary Taylor, *Bulletin of the John Rylands University Library of Manchester* (68:1) 1985 Autumn: 210–46, and Arthur F. Marotti, 'Shakespeare's Sonnets and the Manuscript Circulation of Texts in Early Modern England', in *A Companion to Shakespeare's Sonnets*, Michael Shoenfeldt (ed.), (Oxford: Blackwell, 2007) 185–203.

enterprise—when assigning students a topic for elaboration, he suggests, it 'will be more profitable if a group of students competes together orally or in writing on a common theme', for 'they will all be helped individually by the suggestions made by other members of the group, and each of them will have his imagination stimulated by being given a starting point'[28]—and second, that the achievement of *copia* is an act of successful commodification: '[T]o take something that can be expressed in brief and general terms, and expand it and separate it into its constituent parts', he writes, 'is just like displaying some object for sale first of all through a grill or inside a wrapping, and then unwrapping it and opening it out and displaying it fully to the gaze'.[29] The first claim assumes that value accrues not to individuals but to a collective: what is 'profitable' for the group is profitable for the individual. The second claim implies a more proprietary system of value: if *copia* enables participation in a rhetorical marketplace, the worth of an idea or expression depends more intimately on its belonging to a particular speaker or writer; if an object or argument is for sale, it is not, by definition, free for the asking.

Within Erasmus' writing, this tension between *copia* as collaboration and *copia* as wealth remains implicit, but the sample sentence he supplies to illustrate the analogy between *copia* and merchandizing is, given the context, a bit jarring: 'He wasted all his substance in riotous living'. A similar irony eats away at the sonnets to the fair youth: the very facility with which the youth supplies the poet with fuel for his desire and material for his craft starts to seem less like abundance than like profligacy, a morally suspect failure of discrimination. 'How can my Muse want subiect to inuent', asks Sonnet 38, 'While thou dost breath, that poor'st ino my verse | Thine own sweet argument, to excellent | For euery vulgar paper to rehearse?' (lines 1–4). But the assurance offered in lines 3 and 4 can't be sustained: if the fair youth can inspire even the speaker's self, what's to keep him from inspiring others: 'For who's so dumbe that cannot write to thee, | When thou thy selfe dost giue inuention light?' (lines 7–8). The poet hesitates to blame the young man for the very qualities he had earlier urged upon him—'Those pretty wrongs that liberty commits, | When I am some-time absent from thy heart, | Thy beautie, and thy yeares full well befits', temporizes Sonnet 41 (lines 1–3)—but 'liberty' here veers away from liberality toward licentiousness, from 'pouring' to 'pooring': 'He wasted all his substance in riotous living'.

With increasing frequency, the poet has recourse to the language of ownership. 'Aye me, but yet thou mightst *my* seate forbeare', he wails in Sonnet 41 (line 9, emphasis added). Despite claiming in Sonnet 40 that 'All mine was thine, before thou hadst this more' (line 4), he nonetheless registers an injury: 'I doe forgiue thy robb'rie, gentle theefe | Although thou steale thee all my pouerty' (lines 9–10). Sonnet 86, a complaint against the rival poet, abandons any pretence of shared or communal value: 'But when your countinance fild vp his line, | Then lackt I matter, that infeebled mine' (lines 13–14). Instead, the youth's ability to dissolve the boundaries between 'mine' and 'thine'

[28] *De Copia*, CWE 24: 303.
[29] *De Copia*, CWE 24: 572.

becomes a failure to distinguish between 'thine' and 'theirs', his own singular perfection and the claims of intrusive outsiders. Oddly, this failure seeps into the very printed text of the 1609 quarto: according to the majority of modern editors, a peculiar manuscript ambiguity throughout the middle section of the Sonnets caused a compositor to repeatedly read 'their' in lines where 'thy' makes better sense. Without entering into the debate over the merits of this particular emendation,[30] I would suggest that it's worth pausing over the fact that the confusion of possessive pronouns proliferates in poems that are themselves preoccupied with the problem of ownership. By the time we arrive at Sonnet 69, the fact that 'All toungs' give the young man praise has become bitterly ironic, and whether it is 'thy outward' (as most modern editions read) or 'their outward' (as the 1609 Quarto suggests) that 'thus with outward praise is crownd' hardly seems to matter, for the end result is the same: 'The soyle is this, that thou doest common grow' (lines 3, 5, 14).

Now it is envy, not beauty, that is 'euermore inlarged' (Sonnet 70, line 12) by the copious outpourings of praise for the young man. Correspondingly, within these later poems to the fair youth adages and proverbs resurface, not as the agents of aesthetic preservation, but as the emblematic language of overuse, depletion, and devaluation. Beauty's rose was enriched by spreading itself abroad; in Sonnet 94, by contrast, 'The sommers flowre is to the sommer sweet, | Though to it selfe, it onely liue and die' (the 'sommer' here figuring both the season and the 'owner' of excellence who measures and 'husbands' his own worth in the previous lines), while what spreads is assumed to contaminate: 'But if that flowre with base infection meete, | The basest weed outbraues his dignity' (lines 9–12). 'Take heed (deare heart) of this large priuiledge', cautions Sonnet 95: 'The hardest knife ill vsd doth loose his edge' (lines 13–14). Sonnet 102 takes the turn against *copia* to its logical extreme, insisting that silence alone is truly eloquent: 'That love is marchandiz'd, whose ritch esteeming, | The owners tongue doth publish euery where', and 'sweets growne common loose their deare delight' (lines 3–4, 12). This latter, by virtue of its sententious phrasing, masquerades as a commonplace against commonplacing: amplitude or 'looseness' has now become synonymous with loss. Thus *copia* undoes itself: 'O blame me not if I no more can write!' the poet protests in Sonnet 103, for the fair youth's own abundant graces have impoverished him: 'And more, much more then in my verse can sit, | Your owne glasse showes you, when you looke in it' (lines 5, 13–14).

In the sonnets addressed to the poet's mistress, the speaker's mingled anxieties about erotic and poetic integrity are manifest in an emphatic prejudice against the very kind of language once used to valorize the fair youth. Sonnet 130 famously casts aside the trove of commonplaces the poet drew upon in his opening sonnets to the fair youth. Sun,

---

[30]   Burrow summarizes the controversy in his notes to Sonnets 26 and 35 (*Complete Sonnets and Poems*, 432, 450), coming down on the side of emendation. In a paper given at the April 2011 meeting of the Shakespeare Association of America ('Q: A Love Story'), however, Bradin Cormack argued convincingly for restoring 'their', attributing the editorial preference for 'thy' in part to a desire to make the Sonnets speak in a more personal and intimate voice.

roses, perfumes, music are all rejected as figures for his mistress' value, which inheres in novelty, rarity, and—above all—in belonging to him: '*My* Mistres eyes are nothing like the Sunne' (line 1, emphasis added). In fact, of course, the poet suspects that his mistress is not exclusively his, and his own efforts to invent for her a distinctive—indeed, aggressively uncommon—language of beauty and desire founder in the face of her indiscriminate appetites and too-general appeal. Sonnets 135 and 136 attempt to make a virtue of this abundance—the mistress' 'will is large and spatious' (135, line 5) and she is urged to 'fill it full with wils, and my will one' (136, line 6)—but Sonnet 137 collapses in anguished protest: 'Why should my heart thinke that a severall plot, | Which my heart knowes the wide worlds common place?' (lines 9–10). The crudely misogynist pun lays bare the sexual and textual anxieties that bedevil the poet's investment in the Erasmian poetics of increase: what, finally, is a commonplace if not the site of radical devaluation, the figure embraced by those who have nothing to call their own?

It is at this juncture—with commonplacing resurfacing as the emblem of sexual promiscuity and linguistic exhaustion—that the Sonnets intersects most directly with *Troilus and Cressida*, a play in which 'anxiety about assessment amount[s] almost to vertigo'.[31] In many ways, *Troilus* affirms an Erasmian conception of literary value: its main characters are inveterate purveyors of proverbs and the most sententious of them all, Ulysses, marshals his commonplace wisdom to make an explicit case for the essentially public, shared character of personal worth. In his appeal to Achilles, who has retreated stubbornly to his tent, Ulysses argues that seclusion is the enemy of value: '[N] o man is the Lord of any thing, | Though in and of him there be much consisting, | Till he communicate his parts to others' (sig. G[1]ᵛ; III. iii. 110–12). But when it comes to Cressida, Ulysses deploys the analogy between person and text to very different ends. In a grotesquely literal test of Erasmus' contention that rhetorical value inheres in what can be found 'on every man's lips', Ulysses protests when Cressida arrives at the Greek camp and is welcomed with a kiss from Agamemnon himself: 'Yet is the kindnesse but perticular, 'twere better shee were kist in general' (sig. I[1]ʳ; IV. vi. 21–2). Cressida is passed around the group accordingly, but when she comes to Ulysses, he spurns her cruelly:

> Fie, fie vpon her,
> Theres language in her eye, her cheeke her lip,
> Nay her foote speakes, her wanton spirits looke out
> At euery ioynt and motiue of her body,
> Oh these encounterers so glib of tongue,
> That giue accosting welcome ere it comes,
> And wide vnclaspe the tables of their thoughts,
> To euery ticklish reader, set them downe,
> For sluttish spoiles of opportunity:
> And daughters of the game.
>
> (sig. I[1]ᵛ; IV. vi. 55–64)

---

[31] Lars Engle, *Shakespearean Pragmatism: Market of His Time* (Chicago: University of Chicago Press, 1993) 151.

If masculine virtue depends on communication to others, its female counterpart is exhausted by use: Cressida's worth is anchored absolutely and tragically to her ability to keep her person out of general circulation.

Of course, we as readers already know this: we know it because Cressida herself has told us so, and because what she says is marked within the 1609 Quarto as already common knowledge. In fact, all four of the lines marked as commonplaces for extraction in the 1609 text belong to Cressida. The first three comprise her effort to 'teach a *maxim* out of love' at the conclusion of her first scene in the play: 'Things won are done; joy's soul lies in the doing'; 'Men prize the thing ungained more than it is'; 'Achieuement is command; ungained, beseech' (sig. B3ʳ; I. ii. 283–9)—thus Cressida rebuffs her uncle's incitements to accept Troilus as a lover. Much later, having given herself not only to Troilus but also to his rival, Diomedes, she laments, 'Minds swayed by eyes are full of turpitude' (sig. K3ᵛ; V. ii. 114). An unmistakable irony attends the commonplacing of such remarks. As in the 1611 Q3 *Hamlet* (another Eld production), where the lines marked for general use are Laertes' cautions to Ophelia against giving herself to Hamlet ('The chariest maid is prodigall enough | If she vnmaske her beauty to the Moone | Vertue it selfe scapes not calumnious strokes | The canker gaules the infant of the spring | Too oft before their buttons be disclos'd'),[32] Cressida's commonplaces emphasize the cost of accessibility, the tendency of sexual commerce to devalue a woman. But such calculations are profoundly at odds with the assumptions governing the use of commonplaces themselves: if women are desirable only so long as they resist use by men, commonplaces are valuable insofar as they are used by as many men as possible. The textual accessibility promised and promoted by the inverted commas that mark Cressida's claims to sexual integrity in the play's first act thus serve as ironic signals of her eventual degradation to the status of wide-open book, 'unclasp[ed] … to every ticklish reader'.

Here, as in the 1609 Sonnets, a sharp contrast emerges between the proprietary notion of sexual value that governs *what* is said (especially about and to women) and the distinctly non-proprietary notion of rhetorical value that governs *how* it is said (and read). To urge critics of these texts to frame their readings in terms of the theory and practice of commonplacing is *not*, therefore, to rebuke those who have understood them in terms of erotic desires and anxieties. On the contrary, my point is that, for Renaissance readers and writers—for Shakespeare himself—conceptions of literary value are so thoroughly entangled with conceptions of sexual propriety that to talk about one is necessarily to talk about both. In Sonnets and *Troilus*, the mistress and Cressida bear the brunt of the anxiety of increase, but Shakespeare's own language is not spared the perils of overuse. The persistence and ubiquity of certain rhetorical formulas may prove their value, but even truth is, as Troilus complains, 'tyrd with

---

[32] *The Tragedie of Hamlet Prince of Denmarke* (London: [George Eld], 1611), sig. C3v; I. iii. 36–40 in Wells and Taylor. Margreta de Grazia discusses the marking of these lines, and Ophelia as a kind of commonplace book or *florilegium* of received wisdom, as part of a rich exploration of the play's disgusted fascination with female sexuality, in which abundance is always in danger of running to excess (*Hamlet without Hamlet*, Cambridge: Cambridge University Press, 2007, 102–11).

iteration' (sig. F3ᵛ; III. ii. 172). Certainly this is the case with the similes he mocks in his courtship of Cressida—'As true as steele, as plantage to the moon, | As sunne to day, as turtle to her mate, | As Iron to Adamant: as Earth to th' Center' (III. ii. 173–5)—phrases whose commonness belies the singularity and integrity of devotion they are meant to express. But eschewing such hackneyed comparisons leaves Troilus with nothing but tautologies: 'I am as true as truths simplicity' (III. ii. 165), he boasts, and so 'As true as *Troylus*, shall croune vp the verse' (III. ii. 178). Such claims escape the charge of overuse, but they also offer no firm ground for comparison, and their emptiness forces Troilus to fall back on mechanical self-quotation: 'Be thou but true of heart' (sig. H3ᵛ; IV. v. 57); 'I speak … be thou true' (IV. v. 61); 'But bee thou true say I' (IV. v. 64); 'My sequent protestation; bee thou true' (sig. [H4]ʳ; IV. v. 65); 'But yet be true' (IV. v. 73). Who can blame Cressida for her impatient response to this litany—'O heauens be true againe?' (IV. v. 74)?

It is precisely to avoid this gravest of all rhetorical sins—mere repetition, *tautalogia*—that Erasmus promotes his theory of *copia*, but *Troilus and Cressida* and the Sonnets suggest that, in actual practice, increase invariably tends to exhaustion. What troubles both texts, finally, is an unresolved tension within the Erasmian discourse of *copia*, which is itself haunted by the spectre of a literary tradition depleted by overuse (*De Copia* begins with a commonplace referencing the ruinously expensive whores of ancient Corinth).[33] Thus Troilus identifies Cressida's willingness to give herself to Diomedes with a false and easy eloquence that rings endless changes on stale ideas and expressions: her actions, he protests, will 'giue aduantage' to uninspired orators who, 'without a theme | For deprauation', will prove 'apt … to square the generall sex | By *Cresseids* rule' (sig. [K4]ʳ; V. ii. 132–5).[34]

Not coincidentally, the turn of the 17th century sees the publication of the first printed vernacular commonplace books: contemporary English analogues to Erasmus' (massively profitable) gathering of antiquity in the *Adagia*. Peter Stallybrass and Roger Chartier identify the appearance of such texts as a moment of 'radical' revaluation of past and present literary traditions, of antiquity and currency: within collections like Nicholas Ling's *Politeuphuia: Wit's Commonwealth* (1597) and Francis Meres' *Palladis Tamia: Wit's Treasury* (1598), the words of still-living vernacular authors mingled

---

[33] 'The speech of man is a magnificent and impressive thing when it surges along like a golden river, with thoughts and words pouring out in rich abundance', the *De Copia* begins. 'Yet the pursuit of speech like this involves considerable risk. … As the proverb says, "Not every man has the means to visit the city of Corinth"' (*CWE*, 24: 295). Erasmus glosses the proverb in his *Adagia*: 'In this city there was a temple dedicated to Venus, so rich that it had over a thousand girls whom the Corinthians had consecrated to Venus as prostitutes in her honour. And so for their sake a large multitude crowded into the city, with the result that the public funds became enriched on a vast scale; but the traders, visitors and sailors were drained of resources by the extravagance to which the city's luxury and voluptuousness led them' (*Adagia* I. iv. 1; *CWE*, 31: 317–19).

[34] Here he seems almost to anticipate the response of the Meisei Folio reader, who notes in the margins of this scene a reminder to copy Cressida's lines into his copy-book under the heading 'villainie of vild women' (see Yamada's *Transcript at Troilus and Cressida*, sig. sig. ¶¶5v).

promiscuously with the sayings of the ancients—indeed, Meres joins to his collection an essay that attempts to define a literary canon for Renaissance England.[35] That essay also contains the earliest surviving reference to Shakespeare's 'sugred Sonnets'. In keeping with his practice throughout the essay—which confers prestige on English poets and playwrights by pairing their names with those of classical authors—Meres doesn't commend those poems for their novelty or originality; on the contrary, he calls them to 'witnes' the fact that 'the sweete wittie soule of *Ouid* liues in mellifluous & honytongued *Shakespeare*'.[36] The *Sonnets* thus make their way into the English canon not as Shakespeare's own creation, but as the precious transmission of a long-dead poetic spirit, and Shakespeare himself enters the critical tradition in the pander-like guise of the medium.

From Meres' perspective, of course, identification with Ovid can only augment Shakespeare's value as a poet—but here, as in the Sonnets themselves, augmentation starts to look a lot like depletion: if Ovid's soul lives in Shakespeare, who possesses whom? In the Sonnets and in *Troilus and Cressida*, Shakespeare puts a very similar question to his own poetic practice, an art of increase whose hidden costs are laid so richly bare.

SELECT BIBLIOGRAPHY

Baker, David J. (2010) *On Demand: Writing for the Market in Early Modern England* (Stanford: Stanford University Press).

Chartier, Roger, and Peter Stallybrass (2010) 'Reading and Authorship: The Circulation of Shakespeare 1590–1619', in Andrew Murphy (ed.) *A Concise Companion to Shakespeare and the Text* (Oxford: Blackwell) 35–56.

Eden, Kathy (2001) *Friends Hold All Things in Common: Tradition, Intellectual Property, and the Adages of Erasmus* (New Haven: Yale University Press).

Engle, Lars (1993) 'Always Already in the Market: The Politics of Evaluation in Troilus and Cressida', in Lars Engle, *Shakespearean Pragmatism: Market of His Time* (Chicago: University of Chicago Press, 1993) 147–63.

Erne, Lukas (2003) *Shakespeare as Literary Dramatist* (Cambridge: Cambridge University Press).

De Grazia, Margreta (1991) 'Shakespeare in Quotation Marks' in Jean I. Marsden (ed.) *The Appropriation of Shakespeare: Post-Renaissance Constructions of the Works and the Myths* (New York: St. Martin's Press) 57–71.

——(1996) 'The Scandal of Shakespeare's Sonnets', *Shakespeare Survey* 46: 35–49.

Hunter, G. K. (1951–1952) 'The Marking of Sententiae in Elizabethan Printed Plays, Poems, and Romances', *The Library*, 5th series, 6: 171–88.

Lesser, Zachary, and Peter Stallybrass (2008) 'The First Literary Hamlet and the Commonplacing of Professional Plays', *Shakespeare Quarterly* 59:4: 371–420.

Marotti, Arthur F. (1990) 'Shakespeare's Sonnets as Literary Property', in Elizabeth D. Harvey

---

[35] Chartier and Stallybrass (2010), 9–10; see also Lesser and Stallybrass (2008), 383–7.

[36] Francis Meres, *Palladis Tamia* (London: P. Short for Cuthbert Barbie, 1598), sig. Oo[1]ᵛ, 281ᵛ.

and Katharine Eisaman Maus (eds) *Soliciting Interpretation: Literary Theory and Seventeenth-Century English Poetry* (Chicago: University of Chicago Press) 143–73.

——(2007) 'Shakespeare's Sonnets and the Manuscript Circulation of Texts in Early Modern England', in Michael Schoenfeldt (ed.) *A Companion to Shakespeare's Sonnets* (Oxford: Blackwell) 185–203.

CHAPTER 12

PHILOMELA'S MARKS

*Ekphrasis and Gender in Shakespeare's
Poems and Plays*

MARION WELLS

In a recent issue of *Classical Philology* devoted to the subject of ekphrasis, Valentine Cunningham begins answering his own question ('why ekphrasis?') by putting forward the following hypothesis: 'Writing is always tormented by the question of real presence, by challenges to knowability, by the problematics of truth and validity ... The ekphrastic encounter seeks, I think, to resolve this ancient and continuing doubting by pointing at an allegedly touchable, fingerable, *thisness*.'[1] Whether one accepts the broad classical view of ekphrasis as denoting any detailed description, or restricts the definition to a verbal description of a work of art, ekphrasis does clearly interrogate the relation between a visually present 'real' object and the words that can discursively evoke it.[2] A number of influential earlier discussions of ekphrasis anticipate Cunningham's interest in its gestures towards materiality. Discussing ekphrasis as a theoretically charged site of contestation between image and word, mimetic and arbitrary signs, Murray Krieger writes: 'we are to use the free play in our minds of the words' *intelligible* character to allow us to indulge the illusion that they create a *sensible* object'.[3] But recent critics have also emphasized the ideologically motivated construction of these differences, particularly insofar as the division between intelligible and sensible, verbal and pictorial also promotes, in Bryan Wolf's terms, the projection onto the latter category of 'an aura of

---

[1] Valentine Cunningham, 'Why Ekphrasis?', *Classical Philology* 102:1 (2007): 61.

[2] Stephen Cheeke discusses the broad use of the term in classical rhetoric to denote 'any elaborate digressive description embedded within rhetorical discourse.' *Writing For Art: The Aesthetics of Ekphrasis* (Manchester: Manchester University Press, 2008) 19.

[3] Murray Krieger, *Ekphrasis: The Illusion of the Natural Sign* (Baltimore and London: Johns Hopkins University Press, 1992) 12. The entire first chapter of this book is relevant for my argument here.

nonverbal immediacy'.[4] According to Wolf, ekphrasis itself has contributed to the myth of a 'silent' visual art by 'withdrawing [art's] rhetorical license'.[5] In a similar vein, Grant F. Scott writes that 'ekphrasis... is not only a form of mimesis but a cunning attempt to transform and master the image by inscribing it'.[6]

Given the contribution of feminist and psychoanalytic criticism to the study of the image, both in painting and cinema, it is hard not to see this debate between word and image as importantly implicated in the question of gender, although this aspect of the cultural work of ekphrasis is missing from studies of the topic surprisingly often.[7] In his book-length study of ekphrasis, James Heffernan does immediately acknowledge the gendering of ekphrasis: 'the contest it stages [i.e. between the 'silent image' and the 'rival authority of language'] is often powerfully gendered: the expression of a duel between male and female gazes'.[8] Drawing on the story of Philomela, who constructs a tapestry to convey the details of her rape and mutilation to her sister Procne, Heffernan argues that ekphrasis can give voice to the silenced woman: 'In talking back to and looking back at the male viewer, the images envoiced by ekphrasis challenge at once the controlling authority of the male gaze and the power of the male word'.[9] Taking my cue from Heffernan's reorientation of the critical debate and from the Philomela story itself, I will interrogate the ways in which Shakespeare's work makes unavoidably manifest the crucial role of gender in the fiction of *materiality* that ekphrasis undertakes to create. As Judith Butler has amply demonstrated, *matter* has long been associated in the Western philosophical tradition both with femininity and with what she calls 'a problematic of reproduction'.[10] When Heffernan remarks that 'ekphrasis is dynamic and obstetric; it typically delivers from the pregnant moment of visual art its embryonically narrative impulse', he is, I believe, using the term 'pregnant' entirely metaphorically.[11] However, this culturally overdetermined reproductive nexus constitutes the thematic centre of Shakespeare's most vivid experiments in the genre of ekphrasis, suggesting that in these texts the 'obstetric' poetic power of ekphrasis is deeply connected to its verbal representation of female sexual power.

Cunningham argues (rightly, of course) that 'the agonies of women are only a part—a large part, but still only a part—of what the ekphrastic moment direly confronts us with',

[4] Bryan Wolf, 'Confessions of a Closet Ekphrastic: Literature, Painting and Other Unnatural Relations', *Yale Journal of Criticism* 3: 2 (1990): 185. See also Don Fowler's discussion of the role of ekphrasis as figure in *Roman Constructions: Readings in Postmodern Latin* (Oxford: Oxford University Press, 2000) chs 3 and 4.

[5] Wolf (1990) 185.

[6] Grant F. Scott, 'The Rhetoric of Dilation: ekphrasis and ideology', *Word and Image: A Journal of Verbal/Visual Enquiry* 7:4 (1991): 302.

[7] The *locus classicus* for feminist discussion of the image is Laura Mulvey, 'Visual Pleasure and Narrative Cinema', *Screen* 16: 3 (1975): 6–18.

[8] James Heffernan, *Museum of Words: The Poetics of Ekphrasis from Homer to Ashbery* (Chicago and London: University of Chicago Press, 1993) 1.

[9] Heffernan (1993) 7.

[10] Judith Butler, *Bodies that Matter: On the Discursive Limits of Sex* (New York and London: Routledge, 1993) 31.

[11] Heffernan (1993) 5.

pointing to (among other examples) the shields of Achilles and Aeneas.[12] But it is also true that in a significant ekphrastic tradition (beginning at least with Virgil and continuing strongly in Ovid) the 'bodily suffering' that Cunningham does take to be the unifying ekphrastic theme is frequently figured in the body of a *woman*—we need think only of Cleopatra 'pallentem futura morte' (*Aeneid*, 8.609; 'pale at her future death') on the shield of Aeneas, or the multiple variations on the theme of the raped woman on Arachne's tapestry.[13] It is precisely this kind of ideologically motivated *organization* of the image in these examples that calls for interpretation. Tracing the impact of Ovid's account of Philomela's tapestry on *Titus Andronicus*, *The Rape of Lucrece*, *Cymbeline*, and *The Winter's Tale*, I will argue that Shakespearean ekphrasis typically stages not a speaking out of the silenced female image, as Heffernan suggests, but instead an abjection and appropriation of feminine sexual power.[14] The 'fingerable *thisness*' of ekphrasis seems to be predicated first on the representation of female reproductive power as radically 'other' to the masculine culture of the play or poem; this threatening otherness is then rendered intelligible by its translation into verbal form—what we might call drawing on W. T. J. Mitchell's term an 'imagetext'—in the ekphrasis.[15] The shift from the unintelligible sexual matter of the female body into the writerly matter of the imagetext suggests that ekphrasis both figures a kind of cultural disciplining of the unruly potential of the womb (*matrix*) and at the same time derives its power from an occluded source of inspiration beyond the texts' ostensible alignment with reason and discourse.

12.1 'PURPUREAE NOTAE': BEYOND THE NAME OF THE FATHER

When Tereus hacks out Philomela's tongue in a brutal reprise of the rape, it seems important to remember that we have just seen Philomela use highly effective and articulate language to respond to her violation; she threatens Tereus with the open revelation of what he has done, calling on a kind of Orphic power to move her hearers:

> si silvis clausa tenebor,
> inplebo silvas et conscia saxa movebo;
> audit haec aether et si dues ullus in illo est!

---

[12] Cunningham (2007) 68.

[13] On bodily suffering as a unifying ekphrastic theme, see Cunningham (2007) 68.

[14] I am drawing here on Butler's exploration of the necessity for 'unthinkable, abject, unlivable bodies' for what she calls the 'phallogocentric economy' of sex. See Butler (1993) xi.

[15] Mitchell writes that he tries to replace the 'predominantly binary theory of that relation [between pictures and discourse] with a dialectical picture, the figure of the "imagetext"'. W. J. T. Mitchell, *Picture Theory: Essays on Verbal and Visual Representation* (Chicago and London: University of Chicago Press, 1994) 9.

> If I am kept shut up in these woods, I will fill the woods with
> my story and move the very rocks to pity.
>
> (*Metamorphosis*, 6.546–7, Loeb, ed.)

Her tongue continues to call on the name of the father ('nomen patris') even as it is violently torn out. Once this patriarchal language is denied her, however, Philomela finds a substitute: the ambiguously described 'pupureae notae' that she weaves on her loom:

> grande doloris
> ingenium est, miserisque venit sollertia rebus:
> stamina barbarica suspendit callida tela
> purpureasque notas filis intexuit albis,
> indicium sceleris; perfectaque tradidit uni,
> utque ferat dominae, gestu rogat; illa rogata
> pertulit ad Procnen nec scit, quid tradat in illis.
> evolvit vestes saevi matrona tyranni
> germanaeque suae carmen miserabile legit
> et (mirum potuisse) silet: dolor ora repressit,
> verbaque quaerenti satis indignantia linguae
> defuerunt, nec flere vacat, sed fasque nefasque
> confusura ruit poenaeque in imagine tota est.

> But grief has sharp wits, and in trouble cunning comes. She hangs a
> Thracian web on her loom, and skillfully weaving purple signs on a
> white background, she thus tells the story of her wrongs. This web, when
> completed, she gives to her one attendant and begs her with gestures to
> carry it to the queen. The old woman, as she was bid, takes the web to
> Procne, not knowing what she bears in it. The savage tyrant's wife unrolls
> the cloth, reads the pitiable fate of her sister, and (a miracle that she could!)
> says not a word. Grief chokes the words that rise to her lips, and her
> questing tongue can find no words strong enough to express her outraged
> feelings. Here is no room for tears, but she hurries on to confound right
> and wrong, her whole soul bent on the thought of vengeance.
>
> (*Metamorphosis*, 6.576–86, Loeb, ed.)

Heffernan proposes that the 'notae' on this tapestry are intended to be pictorial, 'a picture of her mutilated body', although he acknowledges the fact that 'nota' can denote either a written or graphic sign.[16] Ann Bergren notes a similar ambiguity in the earlier version of the story by Apollodorus, who writes that Philomela wove 'grammata' (pictures or writing) on a robe.[17] Bergren also explores the significance of the fact that women in Greek texts 'do not speak, they weave', pointing out that weaving is intimately connected in the Greek tradition with the utterance of poetry or

---

[16] Heffernan (1993) 47.
[17] Ann Bergren, 'Language and the Female in Early Greek Thought', *Arethusa* 16 (1983): 72.

prophecy.[18] Given this connection between weaving and extraordinary elocutionary power, the salient point in these depictions of Philomela's craft is perhaps not that the tapestry contains *either* words *or* pictures, but rather that the weaving transcends this binary opposition, operating in a rhetorically powerful register that conveys experience in a non-discursive and physically immediate way. In any case, it is highly significant that this tapestry does *not* receive an elaborate ekphrastic description of the kind that Ovid includes in Arachne's story; the 'purple marks' may be read by Procne but they are not translated for us, since Procne's silence mirrors Philomela's own.

What Procne actually reads ('legit') on the tapestry is a 'carmen miserabile', meaning a mournful song or magical charm, and its effect on her is powerful: she is silenced by grief ('dolor ora repressit') and instead of speaking she leaps immediately ('ruit') into the enactment of a desperate revenge.[19] The tapestry seems to 'speak' to Procne at the level of dreams, hallucinations, and psychotic states rather than of rational discursive thought, driving her literally into frenzy ('furiisque agitata doloris'). Significantly, the utterance that accompanies her breaking down of Philomela's prison is the ecstatic cry of the Bacchante ('euhoe'), a vocalization of emotional and bodily experience rather than a discursive utterance: 'exululatque euhoeque sonat' ('she shrieks aloud and cries Euhoe!' 6.597). Because Procne's reactions have so closely mirrored Philomela's own (her mouth suppressed with grief, her tongue questing but unable to speak, her focus on vengeance), one feels in this moment as though the breaking through of Philomela's prison and the ecstatic cry of 'Euhoe!' permit the release of the bodily, non-discursive vocality figured by the tapestry—it is Philomela's cry as much as her sister's.[20]

The extraordinary rhetorical power of these purple marks in the context of a violently sexualized conflation of mouth and womb authorizes a suggestive connection between Philomela and the figure of the sibyl. A significant body of literature represents the inspiration of the sibyl by Apollo as a form of sexual penetration, often, as in Virgil's account, of a violently coercive kind. There is considerable related evidence that the prophetic utterance of the sibyl was connected to pregnancy—she is, in Ovid's words, 'plena dei' ('full of the god').[21] Like Philomela, the sibyl in Virgil's account inscribes 'notae' and 'carmina in foliis' (verses on leaves), and like Philomela's 'notae' these mysterious markings are at the limits of what is intelligible, as indicated by their propensity to blow away and vanish altogether.[22] In Virgil's text the sibyl, like Procne and Philomela in their

---

[18] Bergren (1983) 71.

[19] R. J. Tarrant's recent *Oxford Classical Texts* edition of Ovid's *Metamorphoses* (2004) supports the emendation from 'fatum' to 'carmen' in line 582.

[20] I disagree, therefore, with Elissa Marder's contention that 'the language with which she communicates her body's silence is a language that is no longer bound to the body.' 'Disarticulated Voices: Feminism and Philomela', *Hypatia* 7: 2 (1992): 100.

[21] Susan Skulsky refers to Ovid's prophetess and several other crucial sources in 'The Sibyl's Rage and the Marpessan Rock', *American Journal of Philology* 108, 1 (Spring 1987): 58.

[22] 'insanam vatem aspicies, quae rupe sub ima | fata canit *foliisque notas* et nomina mandat. | Quaecumque in *foliis descripsit carmina* virgo | digerit in numerum atque antro seclusa relinquit.' *Aeneid* 3.443–6, italics mine.

'revenge' phase, displays wild maenadic behaviour during her possession. This suggestive connection between Philomela and the sibyl (which as we shall see extends into Shakespeare's plays) imbues Philomela's tapestry not merely with the magical power of a 'charm' but also with a special kind of truth-status. As a liminal inscription falling somewhere between words and painting, body and art, speaking and writing, the tapestry seems to represent the possibility of immediate communication between interior worlds of artist and audience. It is, in tragic form, the vehicle of inspiration. The story of Philomela's tapestry clearly exemplifies what Ann Bergren has described in the context of Greek literature as the attribution of ungraspable truth to an often-victimized female figure (the Muse, the Pythia, Cassandra, Diotima, etc.).[23]

Because we receive no description of this artwork beyond the highly schematic and ambiguous 'purpureae notae', the translation of power from silent or silenced artwork to expressive ekphrasis that perturbs Bryan Wolf is interrupted.[24] The expressive power of the tapestry remains embodied in the women, who, turned murderous bacchants, commit their own version of a gruesome 'nefas' and bear the bloody marks of the crime on their bodies thereafter: 'And even now their breasts have not lost the marks ['notae'] of their murderous deed, their feathers stained with blood ['signata sanguine']'(*Metamorphosis*, 6.669–70).[25] I will argue in what follows that Shakespeare repeatedly supplies the missing ekphrasis to this Ovidian template, crucially transforming the trajectory of Ovid's unique account of female revenge even as he taps into the immense rhetorical power figured by the tapestry.

12.2 'SHALL I SPEAK FOR THEE?': EKPHRASTIC TRANSFORMATION IN *TITUS ANDRONICUS*

In *Titus Andronicus* Demetrius literally and symbolically marks Lavinia's assimilation to the Philomela myth by cutting off Lavinia's flow of rhetoric with the brutal line: 'Nay then, I'll stop your mouth' (II. iii. 184).[26] Lavinia herself has already referred to her imminent rape as an unspeakable event when she tries to persuade the merciless Tamora to take pity on her (looking backwards, perhaps, to Ovid's 'nefas'): ''Tis present death I beg, and one thing more | That womanhood denies my tongue to tell' (II. iii.

---

[23] Bergren (1983) 70.

[24] Wolf (1990) 185.

[25] I am indebted for this observation to Charles Segal, who writes: 'At the end [of the story]…the *notae*, still of the same bloody color, are the "marks" left in the world of nature as the "signs" of the crime.' Segal, 'Philomela's Web and the Pleasures of the text: Reader and Violence in the Metamorphoses of Ovid', in *Modern Critical Theory and Classical Literature*, I. J. F. de Jong and J. P. Sullivan (eds.), (Leiden: Brill, 1994) 257–80, 266.

[26] I am indebted to my colleague James Berg for helpful conversation about ekphrasis in Titus Andronicus, and especially for pointing out the ekphrastic nature of Marcus's description of Lavinia.

173–4). Immediately following this exchange the action turns to the pit, which is metaphorically connected to both mouth and womb. 'What subtle hole is this', asks Quintus, 'Whose mouth is covered with rude-growing briers | Upon whose leaves are drops of new-shed blood | As fresh as morning dew distilled on flowers?' (II. iii. 198–201). This 'unhallowed and blood-stained hole' is also called a 'swallowing womb' by Quintus a few lines later (239). The grisly evocation of the mouth of the pit stained with 'new-shed blood' also prefigures Marcus' disturbing ekphrastic depiction of Lavinia's body after the rape, a 'crimson river of warm blood … ris[ing] and fall[ing] between [her] rosèd lips' (II. iv. 22–4). As a displaced figure for Lavinia's violated body, the pit emphasizes the brutal reduction of Lavinia's body to mouth and womb.[27]

As in Philomela's case, this conflation of mouth, womb, and sexual violence invokes the figure of the sibyl, whose shadowy presence is made explicit in Act 4:

> Let alone,
> And come, I will go get a leaf of brass
> And with a gad of steel will write these words,
> And lay it by. The angry northern wind
> Will blow these sands like Sibyl's leaves abroad,
> And where's our lesson then?
>
> (IV. i. 101–5)

Like the sibyl Lavinia seems somewhat possessed or maddened at the beginning of Act 4, running after young Lucius 'in fury'; like the sibyl her communication is a forced and difficult one, her 'lesson' verging on the unintelligible.[28] Lavinia's 'lesson' is Ovidian rather than Apollonian—she 'quotes' from Ovid's *Metamorphoses*: 'See, brother, see. Note how she quotes the leaves' (IV. i. 50.) But instead of placing purple 'notes' or marks on a tapestry that is a surrogate for the material voice, Lavinia produces the text in which those 'notes' were first inscribed. One lesson that Lavinia appears to tell is the forced renunciation of her own story for one already written—she gives up the lively tapestry for the written and quotable text.

The most vivid account of Lavinia's fate is provided not by the female weaver but by Marcus, who offers an elaborate description of her physical appearance—a digressive and detailed description that certainly would have qualified as ekphrasis in classical usage.

> Speak, gentle niece, what stern ungentle hands
> Hath lopped and hewed and made thy body bare
> Of her two branches, those sweet ornaments
> Whose circling shadows kings have sought to sleep in,

---

[27] Heather James argues that the pit represents 'the perverse conflation of Lavinia's rape and Tamora's sexual pleasures', *Shakespeare's Troy: Drama, Politics, and the Translation of Empire* (Cambridge: Cambridge University Press, 1997) 59. My sense of this pit, especially given Lavinia's plea to be 'tumble[d] into some loathsome pit' (II. iii. 176), is that it is more closely and importantly associated with Lavinia's body.

[28] See Jessica Malay, *Prophecy and Sibylline Imagery in the Renaissance* (New York and London: Routledge, 2010) 117–18 for a discussion of the significance of the sibylline imagery in the play.

And might not gain so great a happiness
As half thy love. Why dost not speak to me?
Alas, a crimson river of warm blood,
Like to a bubbling fountain stirred with wind,
Doth rise and fall between thy rosèd lips,
Coming and going with thy honey breath.
But sure some Tereus hath deflowered thee
And, lest thou shouldst detect him, cut thy tongue.
Ah, now thou turn'st away thy face for shame,
And notwithstanding all this loss of blood,
As from a conduit with three issuing spouts,
Yet do thy cheeks look red as Titan's face
Blushing to be encountered with a cloud.
Shall I speak for thee? Shall I say 'tis so?

(II. iv. 16–33)

As James and others have noted, this digressive and bizarrely ornamental description reworks a Petrarchan blazon to create a grotesque portrait of the violence that has been done to Philomela's body.[29] The lips are now rosy with blood, mixed in with the 'honey breath' more suitable to a love lyric, and her arms, compared to branches that recall the consistent rendering of Laura as laurel tree, are literally 'lopped and hewed.'[30] The ekphrasis seems to dramatize the implicit violence of the blazon, and to suggest that the violence done to her body is the precondition for its materialization as poetry. Lavinia herself becomes a kind of 'imagetext', but rather than overcoming the binary relation of picture and discourse, this imagetext seems to insist on the primacy of the word as Lavinia's displaced body recedes into the background.[31] She herself ceases to speak as her body materializes in new form in Marcus' ekphrasis.[32]

Speaking the ekphrasis that replaces the tapestry sent to Procne, Marcus already knows exactly what has happened to Lavinia ('some Tereus hath deflowered thee'). But the 'purpureae notae' are no longer woven by the woman herself into a material record to convey her own experience but instead constitute the elaborate rhetorical digression of an observing male figure. Unlike Procne, who receives the gift of the tapestry with a silenced mouth and an overwhelming bodily experience of grief, Marcus transforms Lavinia's experience, and then Lavinia herself, into the text of an ekphrasis that he then conveys to a coterie of male relatives. She becomes a sign in another's discourse, subjected to a linguistic process that will ultimately transform her into a kind of emblem of the suffering Andronici. The force of this transformation is especially clear in the 'sibyl'

---

[29] See James (1997) 64–5
[30] See James (1997) 64.
[31] I am drawing here on Mitchell's terminology and in particular his exploration of the picture-discourse binary: see n. 15 above.
[32] Grant F. Scott's observations on the ambivalence of ekphrastic description apply here: while helping the 'silent' picture or statue speak, ekphrasis is 'also a way of demonstrating dominance and power'. Scott (1991) 302.

scene. The desire expressed in this scene for Lavinia to 'give signs' as to what has happened to her seems oddly superfluous in light of Marcus' earlier interpretation of her appearance, but the scene seems thus especially important symbolically as a dramatization of Lavinia's increasing subjection to a language not entirely her own. Encouraged by the men around her to write in the dust, Lavinia inscribes the Latin word 'stuprum' and the names of her assailants. She does so, moreover, with the distinctly phallic instrument of the staff. As Craig Williams has noted, the term 'stuprum' in its Roman context was used to denote the kind of sexual disgrace damaging to the bloodline of the family, and thus to support 'the proprietary claims of the *paterfamilias*'; certainly part of Tamora's goal in permitting the violation of Lavinia is to attack Titus himself.[33] Lavinia's words, then, express primarily her own inscription within and subjection to this patriarchal territory. It is as though Marcus' ekphrastic description of Lavinia displaces the power of Philomela's own 'purpureae notae' by transforming them into the signs of a paternal discourse—precisely the 'nomen patriae' that fails Philomela.

Shakespeare's response to the crisis of Lavinia/Philomela's 'fury' is to return the ambiguously graphic purple notes back into text, and in doing so to forestall the transformation of his sibylline figure into her Bacchic alter ego, the figure capable of producing in her sister the vocalization ('euhoe') mysteriously contained within her tapestry. It is at this moment, I would argue, that the Bacchic potential of Lavinia's story drains away from her and passes to her father, who styles himself as a kind of scribe, 'wrest[ing] an alphabet' (III. ii. 44) from her bodily gestures and writing 'with a gad of steel' the lesson that her body tells. This shift from the vocalizing power of the tapestry to the literary ekphrasis in *Titus Andronicus* seems to dramatize the same violent disciplining of the body that the rape itself more brutally enacts. The fact that Titus ultimately kills Lavinia (as though with this same 'gad of steel') into the part he has written for her merely underscores the traumatic sacrifice of her own body into its role in a patriarchal narrative.

12.3 'SOME NATURAL NOTES ABOUT HER BODY': EKPHRASIS AND SEXUAL VIOLATION IN *CYMBELINE*

The use of the story of Philomela in *Cymbeline* reinforces the idea that ekphrasis facilitates a transfer of power from a rhetorically powerful female form to a masculine scribe who contains and appropriates that power. Like Lavinia, Innogen is represented as an intense reader of Ovid's *Metamorphoses*, and like Lavinia she undergoes a transformation into an

---

[33] Craig Williams, *Roman Homosexuality: Ideologies of Masculinity in Classical Antiquity* (Oxford: Oxford University Press, 1999) 97.

imagetext by means of an ekphrastic process.[34] Her body, like Lavinia's, is displaced by its description. This time, however, the ekphrastic process is itself represented as a violation, and the circulation of the ekphrastic text among men emerges as a central concern.[35]

As the work of Eve Sanders and others has shown, early modern women were expected to read primarily devotional, improving works. Sanders writes: 'Humanists did advocate educating women so that they ... would be able to read moral and religious texts to their children. Yet the same writers argued vociferously against allowing women to read secular texts, in particular the erotic poems of Ovid, as Lavinia has done.'[36] The fact that Innogen has been reading Ovid for three hours and has 'noted' the story of Philomela and Tereus suggests that she is far removed from the ideal reading woman. If there is something transgressive about Innogen's Ovidian literacy, it seems connected to the rhetorical power that she displays earlier in the play (and in this she looks forward to Hermione). She counters her father's rage about her clandestine marriage to Posthumus with forceful retorts: 'I am senseless of your wrath. A touch more rare | Subdues all pangs, all fears' (I. i. 136–7). Her voice, like Hermione's in *The Winter's Tale*, seems more powerful than the patriarchal apparatus that seeks to contain it.

The scene in Innogen's bedroom seems to constitute a kind of response to Innogen's verbal fearlessness. Although there is no literal rape in this text, Giacomo himself invokes the rapist Tarquin as he emerges from the trunk into Innogen's chamber, and Cloten's grotesquely sexual remarks the following morning as he stakes out Innogen's room prefigure his later transformation into a Tereus figure: 'Come on, tune. If you can penetrate her with your fingering, so; we'll try with tongue too' (II. iii. 13–14). This desire on the part of both men to 'finger' the woman's body recalls Cunningham's view of the 'fingerable *thisness*' that the ekphrasis attempts to invoke as a bridge between signifier and signified in poetic discourse. Since Shakespeare clearly wishes us to understand the scene as a figurative rape, the 'noting' of Innogen's sleeping body vividly illustrates the troubling imbrication of artistic and sexual motives in the transformation of the female body into the matter of an ekphrastic narrative.

Giacomo launches into a highly eroticized Petrarchan blazon of Innogen's sleeping body that seems to threaten, as in Tarquin's case, to facilitate a movement towards rape. Instead he redirects his attention to collecting 'notes' from her chamber and her body to 'prove' his own sexual knowledge of Innogen to Posthumus:

> That I might touch,
> But kiss, one kiss! Rubies unparagoned,
> How dearly they do't! 'Tis her breathing that
> Perfumes the chamber thus. The flame o'th' taper

---

[34] See n. 12.

[35] Rebecca Olson suggests that in Cymbeline we might understand ekphrasis as 'a discourse motivated by an overtly literary 'contention' between two male speakers'. 'Before the Arras: Textile Description and Innogen's Translation in Cymbeline', *Modern Philology* 108 (August 2010): 46.

[36] Eve Rachele Sanders, *Gender and Literacy On Stage in Early Modern England* (Cambridge: Cambridge University Press, 1998) 63.

Bows toward her, and would underpeep her lids,
To see th' enclosèd lights, now canopied
Under these windows, white and azure-laced
With blue of heaven's own tinct. But my design—
To note the chamber. I will write all down.
Such and such pictures, there the window, such
Th' adornment of her bed, the arras, figures,
Why, such and such; and the contents o'th' story.
Ah, but some natural notes about her body
Above ten thousand meaner movables
Would testify t' enrich mine inventory.
                              … On her left breast
A mole cinque-spotted, like the crimson drops
I'th' bottom of a cowslip. Here's a voucher
Stronger than ever law could make. This secret
Will force him think I have picked the lock and ta' en
The treasure of her honour. No more. To what end?

                              (II. ii. 16–30, 37–42)

The final piece of Giacomo's noting of Innogen's chamber and her body includes the 'noting' of the text she has been reading: 'She hath been reading late, | The tale of Tereus. Here the leaf's turned down | Where Philomel gave up' (II. iii. 44–6).

The repeated reference to 'notes' in this passage recalls and perhaps alludes to Philomela's 'purpureae notae.' In this instance the violating masculine figure rather than his female victim commits 'notes' of the event to some kind of graphic memorialization; as before Shakespeare disambiguates the complexity of the Ovidian passage by making it clear that Giacomo *writes down* his observations. The importance of this writerly observation, this 'noting' of the woman's body, seems to be that Giacomo is invading her body at the level of its meaning, its signification. He will transform her body into a signifier in his own narrative, dividing it entirely from the voice that should be the material vehicle (like the tapestry) of its meaning for Posthumus.

Within this ekphrastic narrative, the odd description of the mole on her breast as 'cinque-spotted, like the crimson drops | I'th' bottom of a cowslip' seems overdetermined in a number of ways. The reference to *crimson* drops seems suggestive of drops of blood; this in turn suggests that Shakespeare is conflating his most immediate source, Boccaccio's *Decameron*, in which the lady has a wart on her breast, with his more distant one in Ovid, in which the purple marks that begin on Philomela's tapestry have, by the end of the story, been transferred to the bloody marks on the breasts of the sisters. In his reading of Innogen asleep in her room, then, Giacomo turns down the page, like Innogen herself, at the story of Philomela; but unlike Innogen he removes the focus from the moment at which 'Philomel gave up' to the end of the story, when the sisters have taken a bloody revenge on Tereus that will mark their bodies forever (*signata sanguine*). In Shakespeare's other possible source for this moment, *Frederyke of Jennen* (a translation of a German tale similar to Boccaccio's), the husband, believing (as Posthumus will) that his wife has deceived him, demands her tongue and a lock of hair from his servant as tokens of her death. Although the source does nothing with the Ovidian overtones of the tongue here, it resonates with Shakespeare's allusion to the Philomela story, and perhaps suggests the ways in which Shakespeare figuratively deprives Innogen of her tongue through the embassy of the ekphrastic description of her body just as he literally deprives Lavinia of hers.

If, as Aristotle's reference to the 'voice of the shuttle' suggests, the act of weaving is a substitute for female speech, Philomela regains her voice through her weaving, as do the women who appear in Chrétien's and Chaucer's versions of the story.[37] But in *Cymbeline*, the tapestries are not woven by the woman but by the ekphrastic gazer, Giacomo. The discrepancies between the first scene of viewing and 'noting' and the second ekphrastic portrayal of the chamber are suggestive in this regard, and clearly emphasize the transfer of authorship from Innogen to Giacomo. In the first scene, Giacomo quickly passes over the details of the tapestries:

> Such and such pictures, there the window, such
> Th' adornment of her bed, the arras, figures,
> Why, such and such; and the contents *o'th' story*.
>
> (II. ii. 25–7, italics mine)

When he returns with his 'notes' to the male coterie of listeners he elaborates upon this 'story' considerably:

> First, her bedchamber—
> ... it was hanged
> With tapestry of silk and silver; *the story*
> Proud Cleopatra when she met her Roman,
> And Cydnus swelled above the banks, or for
> The press of boats or pride: a piece of work
> So bravely done, so rich, that it did strive
> In workmanship and value; which I wondered
> Could be so rarely and exactly wrought,
> Such the true life on't was.
>
> (II. iv. 66, 68–76, italics mine)

Not only does this ekphrastic 'story' refer back to a story that Shakespeare has himself told, in his *Antony and Cleopatra*, it also refers to an *already* ekphrastic description of Cleopatra in that play. Reporting that the figure of Cleopatra 'beggared all description', Enobarbus claims that she 'O'er pictur[ed] that Venus where we see | The fancy outwork nature'(*Antony and Cleopatra*, II. ii. 207–8). In a reverse form of *enargeia*, where the liveliness of the description is confirmed by its ability to turn something living into a painting, Enobarbus conjures up a Cleopatra whose only activity is to lie in state to be gazed upon.

37 Aristotle, *Poetics* (16.4).

The tapestry of silk and silver that contains the story in Innogen's bedroom refigures the 'cloth of gold, of tissue' that encompasses Cleopatra in her pavilion, but its self-referentiality renders it also a figure for the 'tissue' of the poet's own artistry. If it is true, as Bryan Wolf suggests, that the ekphrastic is 'one who would charm art into silence' in order to empower the poet, that charm in Shakespeare's text seems conjoined with the power of sexual domination.[38] Because Giacomo's ekphrastic narrative reduces Innogen from the speaking, reading subject that she so clearly is at the beginning of the play to a silent signifier in a tapestry of his own linguistic weaving, the external matter of the body becomes a text whose meaning (rendered by the ekphrasis) is dangerously adrift from the voice that could and should authenticate its meaning. The dematerialization of the woman's voice is dramatized by the translation of an actual woven cloth (both in the original story and in Innogen's bedroom) into a literary ekphrasis written (and then spoken) by a man.

As an allusion to the bloody sign on the breasts of the transformed bird-sisters, the 'crimson' stain on Innogen's breast seems to refer obliquely to what Jane O. Newman calls 'the counter-tradition of vengeful and violent women associated with the Bacchic legend.'[39] But just as Marcus undertakes an ekphrastic description of Lavinia that replaces Philomela's 'purpureae notae', so Giacomo steals the equivalent of the purple mark and reproduces it within an ekphrasis that is a substitute for the tapestry itself; the revenge will be turned against the true (female) bearer of Philomela's marks. The recipient of this intercepted female tapestry is not a sister or female figure but Posthumus, who immediately internalizes it as what he calls the 'testimonies [i.e. of her alleged strumpetry that] lies bleeding in [him]' (III. iv. 22–3) and thus as motive for revenge. This substitution suggests that the distinctively female sign of Philomela's 'purpureae notae' and of Innogen's crimson-spotted mole has, via the ekphrastic portrait, been sutured within Posthumus in a violently appropriative action symbolized in the text's Ovidian matrix as rape.

When Posthumus reappears in the play bearing the bloody cloth (the supposed sign of Innogen's death), we seem to witness the uncanny re-emergence of Philomela's tapestry, suppressed entirely in *Titus Andronicus*, translated into an ekphrastic tableau in the earlier part of this play, and now materialized in this 'bloody sign' of revenge. Janet Adelman writes:

> The bloody cloth that is the 'sign' of revenge alludes, like Othello's handkerchief, to the bloodied wedding sheets, but it reverses the act that left Posthumus's testimonies bleeding there: in effect, it signals the excision of the woman's part in him and the punitive re-inscription of it in Imogen.[40]

But since the bloody cloth is profoundly concerned with Ovid's story of Philomela, it alludes not just to the conventional *topos* of the wedding sheets but also, and more

[38] Wolf (1990) 186.

[39] Jane Newman, 'And Let Mild Women to Him Lost Their Mildness: Philomela, Female Violence, and Shakespeare's Rape of Lucrece', *Shakespeare Quarterly* 45: 3 (1994): 305.

[40] Janet Adelman, *Suffocating Mothers: Fantasies of Maternal Origin in Shakespeare's Plays, Hamlet to the Tempest* (New York and London: Routledge, 1992) 214.

pertinently, to the bloody tapestry that Philomela fabricates after the rape that doubly silences her. It alludes thus not just to sexuality *per se*, though I of course concur with Adelman's reading to this extent, but also and more importantly to the mutual imbrication of sexuality, power, and *art* in Shakespearean ekphrasis. As Rebecca Olson observes: 'as much as Giacomo's pleasure at the sight of Innogen ... is sexual pleasure at the sight of Innogen's sleeping form ... it is also pleasure in participating in the tradition of masculine descriptions of the feminine'.[41] The scene therefore offers a deeply unsettling exploration of the uncomfortable connection between violation and artistic power. Just as in *Titus* the male figure takes on the role of both scribe and revenger through an ekphrastic appropriation of Lavinia's grief, so in this play Posthumus receives (like Procne) the inspiring message of revenge inscribed within Giacomo's ekphrasis. In both cases the female body's capacity for a vivid and vocal materiality is swiftly transformed into a silent textuality that submits itself to linguistic reorganization within the ekphrasis. The focus on the 'signs' of the body testifies to the reduction of Innogen's subjectivity to a pictorial surface that is ominously juxtaposed with the 'story' of the glorious but doomed Cleopatra. As Adelman points out, *Cymbeline* is the 'undoing of that story [of proud Cleopatra], the unmaking of female authority, the curtailing of female pride'.[42] That this paradigmatic 'unmaking' is fabricated through an ekphrasis offers a striking commentary on the violence implicit in the attempt to reproduce the 'fingerable *this-ness*' of the female body not in but *as* art through the mediation of ekphrasis.

12.4 'COME PHILOMEL, THAT SING'ST OF RAVISHMENT': EKPHRASIS AND RAPE IN *LUCRECE*

We seem at first to find a different treatment of ekphrasis in the third and final rape narrative that I will consider in this essay. While the ekphrastic passage clearly does advertise its connection to the sexual violence that precedes it, it is Lucrece herself who speaks the ekphrasis rather than a male intruder or relative. Lucrece explicitly turns to the 'piece | Of skilful painting made for Priam's Troy' as a means to 'mourn some newer way' (1366–7; 1365). The focal point of the painting from Lucrece's point of view is Hecuba, whose face seems to epitomize sorrow itself:

> To this well painted piece is Lucrece come,
> To find a face where all distress is stelled.
> Many she sees where cares have carvèd some,

---

[41] Olson (2010) 57.
[42] Adelman (1992) 211.

> But none where all distress and dolour dwelled
> Till she despairing Hecuba beheld
>   Staring on Priam's wounds with her old eyes
>   Which bleeding under Pyrrhus' proud foot lies.
>
> In her the painter had anatomized
> Time's ruin, beauty's wreck, and grim care's reign.
> Her cheeks with chaps and wrinkles were disguised;
> Of what she was no semblance did remain.
> Her blue blood changed to black in every vein,
>   Wanting the spring that shoes shrunk pipes had fed,
>   Showed life imprisoned in a body dead.
>
> On this sad shadow Lucrece spends her eyes,
> And shapes her sorrow to the beldame's woes,
> Who nothing wants to answer her but cries
> And bitter words to ban her cruel foes.
> The painter was no god to lend her those,
>   And therefore Lucrece swears he did her wrong
>   To give her so much grief, and not a tongue.
>
> (ll. 1443–63)

This tongueless Hecuba is an apt emblem of the female figures who appear in Shakespearean ekphrasis; she is a signifier of grief (hence her usefulness to Lucrece at this moment) but with no 'cries' or 'bitter words' of her own to express that grief. This voiceless image that gains meaning only through the translation work of ekphrasis illustrates especially clearly the displacement of the female speaker by the description of her body.

Although Lucrece seems to introduce a complicating female agency into the story of ekphrasis we have told thus far, the presence of the story of Philomela conditions our reading of this shift in useful ways. Before turning to the painting of Troy's sorrows, Lucrece calls upon Philomela to act as a model for her:

> Come, Philomel, that sing'st of ravishment,
> Make thy sad grove in my disheveled hair.
> As the dank earth weeps at thy languishment,
> So I at each sad strain will strain a tear,
> And with deep groans the diapason bear;
>   For burden-wise I'll hum on Tarquin still,
>   While thou on Tereus descants better skill.
>
> And whiles against a thorn thou bear'st thy part
> To keep thy sharp woes waking, wretched I,
> To imitate thee well, against my heart
> Will fix a sharp knife to affright mine eye,
> Who if it wink shall thereon fall and die.
>   These means, as frets upon an instrument,
>   Shall tune our heart-strings to true languishment.
>
> (ll. 1128–41)

When Lucrece turns to the painting as '*means* to mourn some newer way', offering to '*tune* [Hecuba's] woes with [her] lamenting tongue', she echoes her earlier language about Philomela, and suggests that the painting itself—and implicitly the ekphrasis she will construct around it—will constitute the metaphorical 'thorn' that continues to inflict pain. The knife that is the ostensible tenor of the metaphor will of course ultimately kill Lucrece in a quite literal way, but because of the underlying association between thorn and painting as the 'means' for mourning, the knife itself seems to become a metaphor for the wounding rhetorical structure that positions Lucrece both as a suicide and as the object of her own ekphrasis.

As Jane O. Newman has argued, Shakespeare chooses to elide from his references to Philomela the ferocious ending of her story in Ovid's text, choosing instead a self-wounding Philomela who does not appear in Ovid's text at all.[43] Rather than express her sufferings in an authentic voice/text of her own, as Philomela does, Lucrece steps into the masculine role of the ekphrastic, a choice that showcases what Newman calls her 'almost obsessive compliance with the phallogocentric logic of reading and writing'.[44] For it is not only that the ekphrastic viewer/rhetorician happens to be male in the other texts we have considered. The clear intertext for this ekphrastic description of the painting of Troy is Virgil's description (focalized through Aeneas) of the murals depicting the fall of Troy in Dido's temple to Juno.[45] Lucrece stands in for Aeneas as she views this painting, and although her absorption in it differs in kind from his absorption in Dido's murals, this allusive substitution indicates that her gaze is profoundly conditioned by the patriarchal structure that contains her from the beginning of the poem.

When Lucrece 'tunes' her woes to Hecuba's, she also begins to adopt the Trojan queen's posture in Euripides' play: 'Pity me:—Like a painter so draw back, | Scan me, pore on my portraiture of woes'(Loeb, ed. 807–8). Like Hecuba in this moment, Lucrece turns herself into the object of a pitying gaze, and ultimately into the material for the ekphrastic rendering of her 'bleeding body' that occurs at the poem's end. Unsurprisingly, rather than acting as a source of power over a traumatic occurrence, this ekphrasis constitutes a painful re-application of Tarquin's objectifying violence—itself produced by the vivid *enargeia* of Lucrece's beauty by her husband, Collatine.[46] The scene confirms the centrality of pain in this transformation of the gazing woman into the gazed-upon object.[47] For this reason, this ekphrastic figure is not—or not for long—an artist figure. She is well on her way to becoming the silent muse figure who will inspire others, and her absorption

---

[43] See Newman (1994).

[44] Newman (1994) 310.

[45] I discuss the intertextuality of this moment in more detail in my article 'To Find a Face where all Distress is Stell'd: Enargeia, Ekphrasis, and Mourning in *The Rape of Lucrece* and the *Aeneid*', *Comparative Literature* 54: 2 (2002): 97–126.

[46] See Nancy Vickers' influential discussion of the triangulation of desire through description in this poem, 'The Blazon of Sweet Beauty's Best: Shakespeare's Lucrece', in Patricia Parker and Geoffrey Hartman eds, *Shakespeare and the Question of Theory* (New York: Methuen, 1985) 95–115.

[47] For a more detailed discussion of the role of pain, see Katherine Eisaman Maus, 'Taking Tropes Seriously: Language and Violence in Shakespeare's Rape of Lucrece', *Shakespeare Quarterly* 37: 1 (1986): 73

in Hecuba signals precisely the transformation of her own pain into a signifier in this new Roman narrative. Her 'bleeding body' is the sign of 'Tarquin's foul offence' to be shown throughout Rome.

12.5 'I'll Make the Statue Move Indeed': *The Winter's Tale* as Epigraph

Although *The Winter's Tale* is not literally a rape narrative, it certainly mobilizes the original meaning of 'raptus' as theft; Hermione is robbed of her two children, one permanently, the other for sixteen years (the years, not coincidentally, of her own fertility).[48] She herself appears to have died of grief at the news of her son's death, only to be reanimated in statue form in the closing scene. The play forms an apt epilogue to our exploration of ekphrasis in Shakespeare's work because it seems both to reflect on and to attempt to undo the violent appropriation of female sexual and rhetorical power so central to these ekphrastic narratives. Hermione survives, in the mysterious story of the play, as a statue; she is not dead, exactly, just stilled (or 'stell'd', like Hecuba) into art.

The play revolves around Leontes' attack on Hermione's maternal body in response to his sexual jealousy of her relationship with his friend Polixenes. Importantly, this jealousy only materializes in the context of Hermione's display of rhetorical power. Having failed to persuade Polixenes to lengthen his stay in Sicilia, Leontes turns to his heavily pregnant wife, and urges her to add her voice to his: 'Tongue-tied, our queen? Speak you' (I. ii. 27). It is a command, even a somewhat peremptory one, opening a space for Hermione to try some variations on the theme that Leontes has already established. But Hermione's speech proves explosively powerful; she cajoles and ridicules and finally, offering Polixenes the Hobson's choice of 'prisoner' or 'guest', she succeeds in gaining his acquiescence. She seems quite consciously to eroticize her speech, mocking what she calls Polixenes' limber (flaccid or impotent) vows and mercilessly reworking them into her own commands: 'Verily, | You shall not go. A lady's "verily" 's | As potent as a lord's' (I. ii. 51–2). Although Hermione was supposed to intercede with Polixenes on Leontes' behalf, and as it were in his place, she seems to have succeeded in winning Polixenes over only by exceeding this circumscribed place and speaking, precisely, as a *lady*.[49]

The conjunction of her almost at-term pregnancy and her rhetorical power seems deliberate and suggestive. As I have argued elsewhere, early modern medical writers tended to associate voice in women with her reproductive organs.[50] Galen developed

---

[48] See for instance Corinne J. Saunders, *Rape and Ravishment in the Literature of Medieval England* (Suffolk: D. S. Brewer, 2001) 79.

[49] I benefit in particular from David Schalkwyk's reading of the eroticization of this scene in '"A Lady's 'Verily' is as Potent as a Lord's": Women, Word, and Witchcraft in *The Winter's Tale*', ELR (1992) 248–9.

[50] 'Full of Rapture: Maternal Vocality and Melancholy in Webster's *Duchess of Malfi*,' forthcoming in *Intersections*, ed. Manfred Horstmanshoff and Helen King.

an analogy between the uterus and the mouth that makes itself felt in much later descriptions of the womb as 'greedy', while Helkiah Crooke emphasizes what he calls the 'sympathy and consent' between 'the chest, the paps, the seede, and the voice'.[51] The articulation of pneuma as voice in the mouth and throat mimics the articulation of related pneumatic substances in the reproductive organs—a dangerously literal analogy that helps to motivate Leontes' extreme suspicion of the power of 'whispering' in this play.[52] Hermione's rhetorical success suggests that in this scene her voice is 'pregnant' with meaning in more than the usual sense; just as the timbre of the voice was believed to betray sexual activity, so Hermione's voice seems 'full' of her maternal power.

We find attention to this mutual imbrication of sexual and vocal pneuma in classical treatments of the sibyl, as Susan Skulsky has observed.[53] The play's depiction of Hermione's rhetorical power draws on this material more explicitly later in the play, when Hermione's figure, robed in white 'like very sanctity', appears to Antigonus in a dream:

> I never saw a vessel of like sorrow,
> So filled, and so becoming ...
>   ... thrice bow'd before me,
> And, gasping to begin some speech, her eyes
> Became two spouts. The fury spent, anon
> Did this break from her.
>
>   (III. iii. 20–1, 23–6)

This description of Hermione as a 'fill'd' vessel overcome with 'fury' resonates with many descriptions of the Pythia as a labouring figure filled with an alien spirit, and her attitude of 'gasping to begin some speech' evokes the struggles typical of the priestess as she begins her utterance. She seems, like Ovid's sibyl, 'plena dei', although her full speech has in this play come into tragic conflict with her literal, maternal fullness.

In the pivotal scene of the play, Leontes denies the truth of the oracle that exculpates her, whereupon their son Mamillius is immediately reported dead. It is as though Leontes attempts to disown and even kill his children in order to rob his wife's voice of its extraordinary elocutionary power. He appears to succeed: Paulina reports the queen's death: 'This news is mortal to the Queen. Look down | And see what death is doing' (III. ii. 147–8). As far as Leontes or the audience knows, Hermione is dead, just as Mamillius is certainly and irrevocably dead. Although she has not exactly had her tongue cut out like Philomela or Lavinia, Hermione has been found guilty of too much rhetorical (and sexual) power, and has accordingly been silenced. What is important for the purposes of this essay is

---

[51] Helkiah Crooke, *Microcosmographia. A Description of the Body of man* (1615) 207.

[52] I benefit here from Gina Bloom's discussion of early modern voice in *Voice in Motion: Staging Gender, Shaping Sound in Early Modern England* (Philadelphia: University of Pennsylvania Press, 2007) esp. ch. 1. See also Bonnie Gordon's work on the eroticization of voice in the pneumatic system of the body and soul, in *Monteverdi's Unruly Women: The Power of Song in Early Modern Italy* (Cambridge: Cambridge University Press, 2004) 32: 'The deflowering of the lady manifests itself in the sonically less pure—thus deflowered—voice'.

[53] Skulsky (1987) 57–8.

that she is in fact mysteriously 'kept' in life by Paulina for sixteen years—only to emerge as (apparently) a marvellously verisimilar statue. Like both Lavinia and Lucrece, she has been stilled (or stelled) into an art form that effectively silences her own words.

The scene in which this 'statue' appears to come to life both reflects on and transforms the dark ekphrastic trajectory that we have traced thus far. Unlike the previous texts we have considered, *The Winter's Tale* does not glorify the transformation of woman into art; on the contrary, the play seems to deconstruct the dynamics of the transformation, dramatizing the theft and deprivation involved—the loss of fertility, children, and the sixteen years of life that elapses between the two halves of the play. The statue itself bespeaks the same kind of confusion that we saw in *Cymbeline* between a virtuosic *enargeia* that makes the verisimilar appear real, and the real that miraculously passes as verisimilar:

> The Princess, hearing of her mother's statue, which is in the keeping of Paulina, a piece many years in doing, and now newly performed by that rare Italian master Giulio Romano, who, had he himself eternity and could put breath into his work, would beguile nature of her custom, so perfectly he is her ape. He so near Hermione hath done Hermione that they say one would speak to her and stand in hope of answer.
>
> (V. ii. 92–101)

The gradual reanimation of Hermione into a living—and, importantly, *speaking* woman—seems to correct the irrevocable inscription of Lucrece or Lavinia into emblematic form. But at the same time, Shakespeare still uses the body of Hermione as a signifier of something else—this time the extraordinary power of the dramatic artist. For the dramatic statue appears in a paragonal relationship with the narrative description of the statue in the previous scene, and 'Giulio Romano' is the true mastermind behind the statue's marvelous power, in spite of Paulina's role as stage director. As Richard Meek points out: 'Seeing Hermione's supposed statue becoming 'real' after hearing this description of Romano's perfect mimetic skills has the effect of making Shakespeare's dramatic art appear even more authentic than what was already a work of art that perfectly 'ape[s]' reality'.[54] It is as though Hermione's fertility has been brutally emptied out in the course of the play and returned here *as a trope* for art.[55] Her bodily capacity to create a child, thematized powerfully from the very beginning of the play, has returned not as childbearing power (she is wrinkled and 'aged' now), but as a figure for the playwright's power to animate the figures in a narrative, to bring the 'sad tale' of winter to life. But if the playwright has drawn upon the mysterious sibylline powers of the maternal body into order to demonstrate the miraculous materiality of his own art, the costs of this transaction are still palpable: the dead, too-knowing child Mamillius,

---

[54] Richard Meek, 'Ekphrasis in *The Rape of Lucrece* and *The Winter's Tale*', *Studies in English Literature 1500–1900* 46: 2 (2006): 401.

[55] I am drawing here on Bryan Wolf's reading of Dürer's 'Man Drawing a Reclining Woman.' He writes that the woman in the image is present to the artist 'only as represented: she has been abstracted into language, transformed into a symbol, voided out as nature and returned as trope'. Wolf (1990) 198.

whose attempt to whisper the 'tale of winter' into his mother's ear places him at the play's symbolic center, remains a signifier of Hermione's enduring loss.

This exploration of ekphrasis in Shakespeare's poetry and plays illustrates its function as a gendered site of contestation between image and word in which the feminine image is organized and contained by the masculine 'noting' of an artist figure, whether Marcus, Giacomo, Lucrece herself, or the stand-in for the playwright, Giulio Romano. In each case this ekphrastic noting effects a translation of the female body into a stilled or 'stelled' form that seems to figure the subjection of female sexual and rhetorical power to the discipline of literary, linguistic form. The ekphrastic translation is paradoxically both an act of mastery (as in Apollo's mastery of the sibyl) and a gesture towards the aspect of voice that escapes analysis—a source of power at the edge of what is intelligible. This analysis dovetails to some extent with Mitchell's view of ekphrasis as an exercise in encountering and 'overcoming otherness': 'ekphrastic poetry is the genre in which texts encounter their own semiotic 'others', those rival, alien modes of representation called the visual, graphic, plastic, or 'spatial' arts.'[56] As Mitchell makes clear, this construction of otherness is a function of a power structure in which 'the self is understood to be an active, speaking, seeing subject, while the 'other' is projected as a passive, seen, and (usually) silent object.'[57] But as we have seen, the feminine other in Shakespearean ekphrasis also possesses the mysterious sibylline power to communicate a message beyond the usual discursive limits; the semiotic 'other' in these texts is not exactly silent—although she is eventually *silenced*. In this respect again Philomela is a pivotal figure—silenced but still rhetorically active. Her importance to Shakespearean ekphrasis indicates Shakespeare's own recognition that the encounter with the 'other' in ekphrasis is a violently appropriative one. Only in *The Winter's Tale* does this pattern change, when Paulina emerges as a central controlling figure; but the redemptive aspects of this shift are narrowly conditioned by the use of Hermione as a signifier of dramatic representation. Thus although Mitchell is surely right that 'gender is not the unique key to the workings of ekphrasis, but only one among many figures of differences that energize the dialectic of the imagetext', the fact that Shakespeare uses gender as a central trope for difference nonetheless takes us deeply into the imaginative sources of his poetry. The materialization of words as *things in the world* is predicated in these exemplary ekphrastic moments on the abjection of the sexual matter of the female body, inscribed and stilled within the verbal frame of ekphrasis.

SELECT BIBLIOGRAPHY

Bergren, Ann (1983) 'Language and the Female in Early Greek Thought,' *Arethusa* 16: 69–95.

Cheeke, Stephen (2008) *Writing For Art: The Aesthetics of Ekphrasis* (Manchester: Manchester University Press).

Cunningham, Valentine (2007) 'Why Ekphrasis?' *Classical Philology* 102: 1: 57–71.

[56] Mitchell (1994) 156.
[57] Mitchell (1994) 157.

Heffernan, James (1993) *Museum of Words: The Poetics of Ekphrasis from Homer to Ashbery* (Chicago and London: Chicago University Press).

Krieger, Murray (1992) *Ekphrasis: The Illusion of the Natural Sign* (Baltimore and London: Johns Hopkins University Press).

Meek, Richard (2006) 'Ekphrasis in *The Rape of Lucrece and The Winter's Tale*', *Studies in English Literature 1500–1900* 46: 2, 389–414.

Mitchell, W. J. T. (1994) *Picture Theory: Essays on Verbal and Visual Representation* (Chicago and London: Chicago University Press).

Olson, Rebecca (2010) 'Before the Arras: Textile Description and Innogen's Translation in Cymbeline', *Modern Philology* 108: 45–64.

Scott, Grant F. (1991) 'The Rhetoric of Dilation: ekphrasis and ideology', *Word and Image: A Journal of Verbal/Visual Enquiry* 7:4, 301–10

Wells, Marion (2002), 'To Find a Face where all Distress is Stell'd: Enargeia, Ekphrasis, and Mourning in *The Rape of Lucrece* and *The Aeneid*', *Comparative Literature* 54: 2, 97–126.

Wells, Stanley and Taylor, Gary (2005) (eds), *The Complete Works* (Oxford: Oxford University Press).

Wolf, Bryan (1990) 'Confessions of a Closet Ekphrastic: Literature, Painting and Other Unnatural Relations', *Yale Journal of Criticism* 3: 2, 181–203.

CHAPTER 13

···

SHAKESPEARE, ELEGY, AND EPITAPH

1557–1640

···

JOHN KERRIGAN

On 21 October 1601, the market town of Wrexham, a few miles into Denbighshire on the Welsh side of the border with England, was the site of a contested election. The court's preferred candidate for the last parliament that would be held during the long reign of Elizabeth I was Sir John Salusbury, a county magnate, poet, and patron, squire of the body in the royal bedchamber, who had been knighted a few months earlier, in part, it may be assumed, because of his loyalty to the crown during the Essex Rebellion. His election was bitterly opposed by Sir Richard Trevor, Sir John Lloyd, and others, who declared, according to Salusbury, in a complaint addressed to the Queen, 'That since they could not cary the said Eleccion by voyces They would wyn it with blades'.[1] Wrexham, in the east of Denbighshire, far from Salusbury's estate at Lleweni, had probably been chosen for the election because Trevor's followers were strong there. They allegedly brought into the town 'Troopes of wilfull & disordered persones...armed & weaponed with pykes forest bills & other like vlawfull weapons'. These 'troopes of armed persones flocking vp & downe the streetes'—pluming themselves like unruly birds—ignored proclamations imposing order and greatly alarmed the people.

The showdown came in a graveyard. As Sir John made his way to church, to walk inside it with his friends, he ran into Trevor and his men. Unable to escape into the building, which, as Salusbury reminded the Queen, doubled as a gunpowder store for the entire county, because it was 'locked against him with new lockes at & by the appointment & direction of the said Sr Richard Trevor', he was forced to face his enemies. As a good subject, Sir John knew his duty. 'He willed them in your maiesties name to keep your highnes

---

[1] 'A Complaint Addressed to Queen Elizabeth ... ', *Poems by Sir John Salusbury and Robert Chester*, Carleton Brown (ed.), Early English Texts Society, extra series 113 (London: Kegan Paul and Oxford University Press, 1914) 81–6.

Peace and praying god to preserve your Maiestie aduized them … to remember the place they were in'. Before he could draw his sword, however, 'they had persued & driven him vnto the Church wall and their swordes about his eares'. At the sound of a warning shot, two hundred of Trevor's supporters poured into the churchyard, and, in the ensuing mayhem, Sir John escaped being 'murdred' only 'by godes good providence'.

When framing his complaint, Sir John's primary tactic was to accuse his opponents of riot verging on rebellion—why else would they commandeer the gunpowder? But he also knew that he could use the location of the brawl against them. This is why he told Trevor and his men 'to remember the place they were in'. Despite the radical post-Reformation belief that salvation did not depend on where you were buried, churchyards remained holy ground. They were thought of as places of sanctuary, where Sir John should have been safe. Protestant commentators played down the superstitions associated with graveyards, where the dead were believed to haunt the living, but they regarded them as serious places, where reminders of mortality should turn people's minds to repentance. The increased erection of gravestones, the spread of epitaphs within churches and beyond, and the establishment of individual and family plots for burial were held to encourage piety. Yet, the more these phenomena took hold, the more competition and status-seeking of the sort that drove Trevor and Salusbury to violence was installed in the physical fabric of church and graveyard. The size of a vault or monument, the degree of heraldic elaboration and quality of the inscriptions, became a measure of a family's status, whether inherited or (more worryingly, for some) purchased.

Shakespeare was alert to competition and its interplay with eschatology in graveyards. There is the funeral procession for Henry V at the start of *1 Henry VI*, disrupted by quarrelling between the bishops and Gloucester, and by bad news from France. Paris and Romeo fight in the loose, dug-over ground of the graveyard, rivals who want to break into the monument of the Capulets.[2] Shakespeare knew that burials involved the frequently conflicting interests of church and state. In the 'maimèd rites' of Ophelia, the lack of a sung requiem and other ceremonies marks her death as 'doubtful' (V. i. 212–37). She may have committed the sin of suicide. Laertes is distraught, and he compensates for his own, typically social sense of damaged status by denouncing the priest as 'churlish'. The crown has prevailed so far as to allow burial in sanctified ground, but the church maintains the grip that its control of death rites gives it over the fears and consciences of believers by restricting the rites allowed. Then the grave itself is violated when Hamlet leaps into it to compete with Laertes. For the latter, the permitted ceremonies do not console and confirm. They do not match his vision of Ophelia as a ministering angel, but their deficiencies are also degrading. Her burial painfully recalls that of Polonius, put away hugger mugger, as Laertes complains to the king, 'No trophy, sword, nor hatchment o'er his bones' (IV. v. 211).

After the Reformation there was a shift in emotional and financial expenditure away from the iconography of saints and prayers for souls in purgatory towards memorials of the dead, which asserted and preserved their fame. One consequence was a heightened

---

[2] *Romeo and Juliet*, V. iii.

anxiety about defacement. The tombs were subject to iconoclasm by hot Protestants and spoliation by thieves. They were defaced, pillaged, and neglected. They were also moved about, demoted by others willing to pay for prime spots in and around the church.[3] Shakespeare's sonnets make much of the inadequacy of tombs in the face of active destruction and the damage inflicted by neglect. They turn this, conventionally enough, with Ovid and Horace behind them, into a source of poetic strength, by declaring the superior ability of verse to give immortality to the noble young man:

> Not marble nor the gilded monuments
> Of princes shall outlive this powerful rhyme,
> But you shall shine more bright in these contents
> Than unswept stone besmeared with sluttish time.
> When wasteful war shall statues overturn,
> And broils root out the work of masonry,
> Nor Mars his sword nor war's quick fire shall burn
> The living record of your memory ....
>
> (55)

The poet can readily imagine himself writing the young man's epitaph; that is a natural extension of the love-and-patronage relationship. When he reflects, however, 'Or I shall live your epitaph to make, | Or you survive when I in earth am rotten', the assumption, at least in the earlier and middle-period sonnets, is that the verse of the poem itself will keep memory alive: 'Your name from hence immortal life shall have', and 'Your monument shall be my gentle verse' (81).

How would reflections such as these feed back into epitaphs? Up to a point, they inform the epigraphy that Shakespeare seems to have prepared for the Stanley family, c. 1600–03. These inscriptions are recorded in several of the verse collections and treatises—compiled by heralds and antiquarians such as John Stow, William Camden, and John Weever—that gathered up epitaphs and elegies, during and after the poet's lifetime. But they also survive in situ, in St Bartholomew's Church, Tong, Shropshire. In situ, yet predictably, not quite. As a result of competition for places in the church, the Stanley tomb (which is depicted in all its 17th-century splendour in FIGURE 13.1) has been moved from its initial location on the north side of the altar at Tong to a position in the south transept, and reconfigured.[4] This sort of fragility is anticipated by the first set of verses (east end):

> Ask who lies here, but do not weep.
> He is not dead; he doth but sleep.

---

[3] For an overview of doctrine and practice, see Peter Marshall, *Beliefs and the Dead in Reformation England* (Oxford: Oxford University Press, 2002) esp. chs 4 and 7.

[4] On the orders of George Durant II (1776–1844), to make way for a memorial to his father, George Durant I (d. 1780). See Robert Jeffery, *Discovering Tong: Its History, Myths and Curiosities* (Robert Jeffery/Tong Parochial Church Council: Tong, 2007) 89.

FIGURE 13.1. Seventeenth-century drawing, by Francis Sandford, of the Stanley tomb, St Bartholomew's Church, Tong. By permission of the College of Arms.

> This stony register is for his bones;
> His fame is more perpetual than these stones,
> And his own goodness, with himself being gone,
> Shall live when earthly monument is none.

The monument will be rooted out, the epitaph we are reading lost. In the absence of a book of sonnets, the memory of the dead man and his goodness must survive through common fame.

Even closer to Sonnets 55 and 81 are the verses at the west end:

> Not monumental stone preserves our fame,
> Nor sky-aspiring pyramids our name.
> The memory of him for whom this stands
> Shall outlive marble and defacers' hands.
> When all to time's consumption shall be given,
> Stanley for whom this stands shall stand in heaven.

The memory of this Stanley's virtue is more conducive to fame than marble cerements or high pyramids (like the obelisks on the tomb at Tong).[5] Stone memorials are not safe from time nor the iconoclasm and pillage of defacers. Weever thought monuments socially as well as historically valuable. They provided a living record of virtuous deeds and ancient lineages. But he knew, at the same time, that 'It is a vanitie for a man to thinke to perpetuate his name and memory by strange and costly great Edifices', including 'sumptuous

---

[5] At this date, 'pyramid' could be used of any triangular, pointed structure, including spires, pinnacles, and obelisks.

Pyramids'.[6] The copying and printing of epitaphs makes the Stanley line more lasting—durable through their virtue, although an ability to 'stand' the test of time is already audible in the family name, and is for the witty poet a matter of language.

For all that, we do not know *which* Stanleys are remembered in these epitaphs, any more than we know the identity of the young man immortalized by Sonnet 55. Virtue may not be its own reward, exactly, in this writing, but it must spread, we might conclude, its own renown. This is a train of thought that follows readily from the widespread early modern belief that epigraphy is socially valuable because it makes the dead exemplary. In Shakespeare, it draws strength from the equally familiar awareness that monumental stone is fragile, to move towards the perception that there is an anonymity about the dead—about their dust, but also the praise that is rendered them—which makes virtue their best hope of immortality. Most likely, the Tong epitaphs were written to memorialize, respectively, Sir Thomas Stanley (*d.* 1576) and his son Edward, whose late death, in 1632, is a salutary indication that elegies and epitaphs can be written ahead of the loss that they mark, that their generic connection with panegyrics on the living can be close.[7]

We should recall Shakespeare's own struggle for status and how this manifested itself in funeral rites and memorials. In 1596, he purchased for his father the heraldic device of jousting spear and falcon shaking its feathers that is affixed to his own memorial in the chancel of Holy Trinity Church, Stratford-upon-Avon. Beneath it lies his grave, side by side with that of his wife, Anne. Whatever else his plays and poems did, they got him out of the graveyard and the anonymity of the charnel house, up close to the altar. And there he has stayed, not moved about like the Stanleys, partly due to his cultural authority. But partly also, we can assume, due to his sharp understanding (evident in his characterization of the gravediggers in *Hamlet*) of how the mind of a sexton would work. On the stone over his grave is inscribed what FIGURE 13.2 shows more directly:

> GOOD FREND FOR IESVS SAKE FORBEARE,
> TO DIGG THE DVST ENCLOASED HEARE.
> BLESTE BE YE MAN YT SPARES THES STONES,
> AND CVSRT BE HE YT MOVES MY BONES.[8]

The consensus is that these lines were written by Shakespeare himself—a simplistic claim, theoretically speaking, given the formulaic language in which epitaphs are couched, and the extent to which this particular text depends for its impact on the abrupt, impersonal skill of stone-carver, but nonetheless a ponderable one. It points, not least, to the likelihood of this being another epitaph written before its subject was dead.

---

[6] John Weever, *Ancient Funerall Monuments* (1631) 3, quoting Propertius.

[7] See e.g. O. B. Hardison, *The Enduring Monument: A Study of the Idea of Praise in Renaissance Literary Theory and Practice* (Chapel Hill: University of North Carolina Press, 1962).

[8] Further quotations from the 'Epitaph on Himself', as it is often called, are taken from Wells and Taylor, 811.

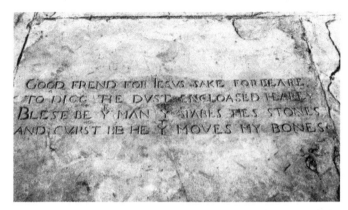

FIGURE 13.2. Inscription on Shakespeare's grave, Holy Trinity Church, Stratford-upon-Avon. By permission of the Shakespeare Birthplace Trust.

It is plain but discreetly forceful; the construction of a block of text out of a pair of couplets creates a minimally monumental structure without losing energy and point. 'Good friend' is both a low-key, affable greeting and a moral judgement that urges cooperation. 'For Jesus' sake', likewise, is a coercive, even profane locution which is steadied by 'forbear' then takes on the intonation of a prayer. This adds a religious register that is not just appropriate to its location but gives metaphysical weight to the curse. The alliterative patterning is firm, if not chiselled: 'dig the dust … spares these stones'. And this combines with a judicious stepping-up and contrast between 'Blessed' and 'cursed'. Who now utters and so wrote 'my bones'? Shakespeare, in his study or the next world, and if not him, 'Shakespeare'. So 'my bones' suddenly implies that the speaker is *hence*; that within the Christian context of his words, he has immortality. And there his bones remain, but not those of Susanna, his favoured daughter, initially buried a few feet away from her father. Her bones, unprotected by family name or curse were dug up and cast into the charnel to make way for the remains of a Mr. Watts in 1707.

All this brings perspectives to bear on Shakespeare's most exquisite, unexpected poem about death, those lines on the phoenix and turtle dove that were published in a group of 'Poeticall Essaies' by 'Ignoto', Shakespeare, Marston, Chapman, and Jonson as an appendix to Robert Chester's *Loves Martyr* (1601). This book is dedicated to Sir John Salusbury, who was married to Ursula Stanley, an acknowledged, illegitimate scion of the dynasty celebrated at Tong. The prefatory matter makes it clear that Chester's book was published after (and in celebration of) Salusbury's knighthood in June 1601, quite likely during the period when he was dealing with the fallout from the Wrexham brawl. Was it designed to enhance his profile in London, as that long-running local feud—there had been earlier complaints on both sides—came to a head? If so, it did him no harm. He kept his place at court and represented Denbighshire in the House of Commons. This puts Shakespeare's poem, which has been known since 1807 as 'The Phoenix and the Turtle' or 'The Phoenix and Turtle' (it was first published without a title) into the same time-frame as the Stanley inscriptions. It concerns a double death, a double cremation, burial, and enurnment—like the burial of Shakespeare next to Anne, a conventional husband-and-wife arrangement. In *Loves Martyr*, a turtle dove leaps into a funeral pyre and is followed by his beloved phoenix. In Shakespeare, the mutual intensity of the birds' love burns them up. But still, in this ode-like, Latinate poem, as in the equally clipped, alliterative lines on Shakespeare's grave, we hear of 'dust enclosèd here' ('here enclosed in cinders lie').

The poem has been variously interpreted, in the light or semi-obscurity of Chester's story of the Phoenix and the Turtle, as being about Elizabeth and the Earl of Essex, Elizabeth and the English people, the execution of recusants, and Elizabeth and Sir John Salusbury. That last coupling cannot be ignored. Elizabeth was too strongly associated with the iconography of the phoenix to be kept out of an Elizabethan reader's mind. And the details in *Loves Martyr*, as I'll show in a moment, quite often link the Turtle with Salusbury. This is not confined to Chester's parts of the book. When Shakespeare writes, 'Distance and no space was seen, | 'Twixt this turtle and his queen' (11. 30–1), it is hard not to register, in the context of 1601, the geographical mileage and difference of rank, but also political intimacy, that obtained, or was hoped for, between Salusbury with his estate at Lleweni and the Queen at court.

We can go archipelagically further, and, remembering the geopolitics caught up in the relationship, find new overtones in the paradoxes at the core of 'The Phoenix and Turtle'. 'Single Nature's double name | Neither two nor one was called.... "How true a twain | Seemeth this concordant one!"' (11. 39–40; 45–6). If the 'threeness' of the witches in *Macbeth* parodies the unity-in-triplicity of James' three kingdoms after 1603,[9] the twainness of the Phoenix–Turtle is an abstracted, oblique reflection of the Anglo-Welsh union under Elizabeth inaugurated by Henry VIII, a union that secured the claims of Welsh magnates to access and influence. But allegorical poetry in this period is never merely topical. We can read Book V of *The Faerie Queene* as romance and moral allegory without reducing Artegal to Lord Grey and Grantorto to Spain. Topical allegory does not predominate in *Loves Martyr*, whose title-page, probably drafted by Chester, points up the theme of fidelity: '*Allegorically shadowing the truth of Loue*, in the constant Fate of the Phoenix and Turtle'. Shakespeare's own lines, as we shall see, are even more tied to the truth of love, and less biographical, than Chester's contribution to the book.

Indeed, if we are thinking about biography, we should recall the last illness and burial of the apparently Catholic John Shakespeare on 8 September 1601, which is generally agreed to have influenced the composition of *Hamlet* during the preceding eighteen months or so. Order is called for in 'The Phoenix and Turtle', 'Lest the requiem lack his rite' (1. 16). The traces of unreformed ritual in the poem, along with echoes of the *Dies Irae*, and, it may be, of the Roman Catholic poetry of Southwell, might owe something to this circumstance, as well as to the currents of pre-Reformation belief and practice that persisted in North Wales (a notoriously recusant area) around and within Salusbury's

⁹ See John Kerrigan, *Archipelagic English: Literature, History, and Politics 1603–1707* (Oxford: Oxford University Press, 2008) 97–8, 104.

circle. Thomas, Salusbury's elder brother, had been executed in 1586 for his part in the 'Babington plot' to assassinate the Queen; he reaffirmed his Roman Catholicism on the scaffold. It was only as a result of his death that Sir John inherited the family estate. That Sir John was loyal, ostensibly anti-Catholic, and concerned (*Loves Martyr* suggests) to stress his obedience to the Queen, does not necessarily make him Protestant all the way down. All this makes the survivalist, pre-Reformation elements in Shakespeare's poem the more tantalizing. It does not fully account for these features to notice the quasi-medieval, archaizing quality which the poem artfully combines with neo-classicism. But we are passing beyond allegory and biography here, into the broader reaches of cultural history.

For 'The Phoenix and Turtle', like *Hamlet* and the Sonnets, engages with widespread, late 16th-century concerns about memorials, prayers for the dead, and seemliness in mortuary ritual. It starts with a funeral procession of birds which abstracts from, and reflects on, the social bases, the logic, and the consolation of ritual in ways that would not be possible if it were directly about human beings. We are not dealing here with anything as specific as Ophelia's burial rites, but with the wondrous properties of birds where the heraldic becomes the totemic. Yet religion and the law impinge; the swan is a priest in a surplice, the black crow a parish clerk, merging into a flock of mourners. As we cross a threshold in the poem, into something like ecclesiastical space, the 'requiem' proper begins and an 'anthem' is said or sung. In a metaphysical discussion of love, identity, and death, Christian beliefs are penetrated by Neoplatonic speculation. The dyadic unity of the Phoenix–Turtle is associated, through scholastic language, with the Trinitarian mysteries of the Divine. The final section of the poem is subtitled '*Threnos*'; it is an epitaph composed by Reason, which ends, no doubt surprisingly, by calling for prayers for the dead. These triplets lay the remains of the birds to rest in an urn that is beyond defacement.

'The Phoenix and Turtle' most immediately draws on a semi-parodic line of poems about bird-funerals that goes back to antiquity: Ovid's elegy on Corinna's dead parrot (in *Amores* II), Skelton's *Phillip Sparow*, and Matthew Roydon's elegy for Sir Philip Sidney in *The Phoenix Nest* (1593). But I see it as more deeply involved with a broad, multiply motivated shift in early modern attitudes to memorials and monuments, a shift which left its impression on Shakespeare's plays (on Timon's tomb, for instance)[10] as well as on his Sonnets and the Stanley epitaphs, and which ultimately had as much to do with life-writing as with the rituals of death. For this is a story, a story with a Welsh accent, that can be followed, as I shall show, beyond *Loves Martyr* into the gatherings of memorial poetry that shaped Shakespeare's image and creative biography after his death, from the preliminary pages of the First Folio (1623) to the elegies and epitaphs that are published in the first full-scale collection of his *Poems* (1640).

The tomb of the Salusburys in St Marcella's Church, Denbigh (FIGURE 13.3), is almost as impressive as that of the Stanleys at Tong. It tells us much about the status of Anglo-

---

[10]   See the contradictory inscriptions at *Timon of Athens*, V. v. 71–8.

FIGURE 13.3. Salusbury tomb (showing Sir John, *d.* 1578, grandfather of the poet-patron of Lleweni, with his wife and children) in St Marcella's Church, Denbigh. Photograph by Su Gillespie. By permission of the Parish Treasurer.

Welsh magnates under the Tudors. We can get closer to the life of Sir John, however, and to the valency of elegies and epitaphs, by turning to the family manuscripts associated with Lleweni. Two of these, held at Christ Church, Oxford, are as miscellaneous as one would expect. Manuscript 183 starts with 'Sundrie necessarie obseruations, meete for a Christian' and the printed text of a poem, written by Sir John himself, called 'Certaine necessarie obseruations for Health'. There are recipes, weights, and measures, the formula for an oil that will heal any wound, the family crest and motto, and copies of letters. There are more than a score of poems in Welsh in praise of Sir John, and others on his son Henry. Affectingly, however, there are elegies on two sons who died young, John and Ferdinando. Manuscript 184 includes a handwritten text of 'Certaine necessarie obseruations', epigrams and acrostic verses by Sir John, his wife, and others, including (at length) Robert Chester, but also fourteen elegies in Latin, Welsh, and English on his mother, Catherine of Berain, and a note, in Sir John's own hand, on the death of 'my deare syster Jane'.

Those manuscripts are well known. Edited by Carleton Brown, almost a century ago, in the hope of shedding light on *Loves Martyr*,[11] they have recently been placed in a fuller context by research into the cultural milieu of Lleweni. Under Sir John there was an attachment to traditional Welsh harping, but also, partly through the Stanley connection, contact with English song, the London playhouse, and it may be with Shakespeare.[12]

[11] Brown (ed.), (1914) esp. xxvii–xl.
[12] Sally Harper, 'An Elizabethan Tune List from Lleweni Hall, North Wales', *Royal Musical Association Research Chronicle*, 38 (2005): 1–98. Against Tom Lloyd-Roberts, 'Bard of Lleweni? Shakespeare's Welsh Connection', *New Welsh Review*, 23 (1993): 11–18 see Jeremy Griffiths, '"Loose Sheets and Idle Scribblings": The Case against Shakespeare's Lleweni Connection', *New Welsh Review*, 25 (1994): 52–7.

Less familiar is a third manuscript, which carries the history of Lleweni forward into a later, more Anglicized period. Like the Christ Church volumes, National Library of Wales MS 5390D is rich in literary material. It includes lines, probably by Sir John's son, Sir Henry, congratulating the actors John Heminges and Henry Condell for seeing the Shakespeare First Folio into print.[13] It gives us a detailed picture of the abilities of Sir John's grandson, Sir Thomas, as a poet and dramatist.[14] But it is also strikingly abundant in elegies and epitaphs—not just 'Lord Stranfords Elegie', 'Sr Philip Syddneys Epitaph', Thomas Salusbury's 'Elegie meant vpon the death of Ben Johnson', and 'An Epitaph on the Duke of Buckingham made by Dr Corbet', but several handfuls of poems on deaths in the extended Salusbury circle.

Towards the end of the manuscript we find 'An Epitaph vpon the death of ... Sr John Salusbury who died the XXVth of July 1612', by John Davy of Caermeradin. This long, rhetorically basic poem does more than give us a sympathetic depiction of the dedicatee of *Love's Martyr*. It shows what the stock elegiac mode was like in the early 17th century. An exercise in celebration, dealing only conventionally with grief ('Yee hardiest rockes yeeld foorth your watrie dropps | yee driest eyes lett gush your brinest teares'), it displays the extent of its respect for the dead by being so copious. It lacks the epigrammatic pithiness that classically inspired writers and rhetoricians, such as Puttenham,[15] advocated (but rarely achieved) in epitaphs. It also begins with a reminder that, despite his career at court, Salusbury was a Welshman:

> What gl[oomie] shades and clouds of duskie night
> obscures the climate of faire *Brittaine's* Coast
> the shininge sonne hath lost his wonted lyght
> and to an other *Horizon* did poast
> behould a breach in *Brittaines* brason wall
> and darkening of her *Sonne* great *Salusberies* fall.

It is not that 'faire *Brittaine's* Coast' has to be, exclusively, that of North Wales, but that talking about Wales brings in train Britishness. This is a very Welsh view of country and identity under the Tudors. It reflects a strongly held conception of Britain as England/Wales which persisted for many despite the success of Anglo-Scottish regal union.

Salusbury, in Davy's epitaph, is a warrior. With his 'steelie hands' and 'undaunted spirit', he resembles Hercules, or one of the ancient British, proto-Welsh knights of 'Arthur's Table'. Like them, and like Shakespeare's Glendower, with his 'couching lion' and 'ramping cat', he is associated with elaborate heraldry.[16] Davy describes 'His white undied lion and sangwine crose | in signe of mercie & in signe of blood'. This 'Lion rampant in the bloodie field' is the emblem of Lleweni (which means, 'the place of the

---

[13] Israel Gollancz, 'Contemporary Lines to Heminge and Condell', *TLS*, 26 January 1922: 56.

[14] David Klausner, 'Family Entertainments among the Salusburys of Lleweni and their Circle, 1595–1641', *Welsh Music History*, 6 (2004): 129–42.

[15] George Puttenham, *The Arte of English Poesie* (1589) Bk. 1, ch. 28.

[16] *1 Henry IV*, III. i. 149.

Lion'). Like Glendower, also, Salusbury was a scholar, an erudite poet. 'But man cannot the power of death with stand | nor learned bookes' preserve him. Despite 'His Genious good', Sir John was brought 'vnto his graue'. As so often, it is what is not said that catches attention. The emphasis on valour and loyalty is orthodox for a Tudor lord, but it is the more assertive here because the poem must simplify the history of a family involved in local, and national, tumult. Given the execution of his brother, Sir John's devotion to the crown was necessary as well as ennobling. His appointment to an office of trust in the bedchamber and his knighthood in 1601 were steps in the rehabilitation of a family as well as the rise of an individual.

It would be rewarding to investigate more fully all three Salusbury family manuscripts because their connection with *Loves Martyr* has not been exhausted by scholars. Poems by and in J. S.'s hand about male wantonness and female 'fickel waveringe', in MS 184, although commonplace in themselves, help suggest why Chester might have thought that the story of the Phoenix and Turtle as an allegory of the truth of love might have appealed to his patron. Equally striking are the poems and biblical quotations and jottings about Salusbury's 'enimies'. They gloss the animal fables and bird poems by means of which Chester and Sir John deal with the conflicts with Trevor and others before they came to a climax at Wrexham. In one of these, by J. S., a rival wins favour from 'the Imperious eagle' (i.e. Elizabeth); not being able to overcome his nature, this 'base bread haggard' will fall into scorn and beggary. But there are plenty of birds in MS 184. Another poem, welcoming Salusbury back to Lleweni, says that, although, in London, the nightingale and swans have sung to him, now he must make do with the 'hoarse-throat rauens song' of Chester. Yet again, the poet denounces the crafty beasts of Denbighshire, who are powerless against the Welsh-British Lion who enjoys the favour of the English queen:

> ffor yf the Lyon rore by sea or land
> The craftie forrest beasts Amazd will stand
> Long liue thow milkwhight terror to thy ffoes
> With the great Lyones of Brytania
> Whose verie name her foemen overthrowes
> As subiugate to royall Anglia: ... [17]

The text ends 'Yours in all duty: etc. R Chest'. Who this writer was remains unclear. The Arden 3 editors, in the course of a valuable reassessment of Shakespeare's Welsh connections, contend that he was Robert Chester of Royston (a town between Cambridge and London), but I share the older view that he was a local poet, based in North Wales.[18] The sensitivity to Welsh distinctions between 'Brytania' and 'royall Anglia' is indicative. So is the inclusion in *Loves Martyr* of what the title-page calls 'the true legend of famous King

[17] Brown (1914) xxxiii, 22, 23–6.
[18] *Shakespeare's Poems*, Katherine Duncan-Jones and H. R. Woudhuysen (ed.), (London: Arden Shakespeare, 2007) 106–7; for the North Wales view see e.g. *The Complete Sonnets and Poems*, Colin Burrow (ed.), (Oxford: Oxford University Press, 2002) 84 and Brown (1914), xlvii–liv.

Arthur, … being the first *Essay* of a new *Brytish* Poet'. The British poet, who appears to be Chester himself, gives an account of Arthur's life which does not play down his wars with the Saxons, and, in a recognizably Welsh way, stresses the duplicity of the Picts up in Scotland. If the Welsh version of 'Britain' was losing ground, in 1601, to the prospect of Anglo-Scottish union, the poets of Wales could only welcome that development in qualified terms. This telling of Arthur's story makes much of death and burial. The simplicity of his interment is contrasted with the competitiveness of today. He is not buried with sumptuous royalty nor under curiously wrought marble but in a simple, hollow tree trunk. Like the 'dead birds' in Shakespeare's poem, he is buried jointly with his Guinevere.

The central deaths in *Loves Martyr*, however, are those of the Phoenix and the Turtle. Death becomes the test of how true (faithful) love can be and how that is the only true (for real) love. Chester's refashioning of the phoenix myth to make it an allegory of fidelity has attracted critical condescension. Rather than add to this, it seems worth noting that, although Shakespeare has been accused of writing elegies in the manner of the 'Epitaph vpon … Sr John Salusbury'—notably, a couple of decades ago, 'A Funeral Elegy for Master William Peter'—the charge has never stuck, whereas he was stimulated into creativity by Chester's very different sort of emblematic love-death. By the end of this chapter, and Chapter 30, some reasons for that will be apparent.

For now, a sketch is in order. *Loves Martyr* starts with Dame Nature complaining to a parliament of the gods (a resonant enough opening for 1601) that the Phoenix is in decline. She blazons the bird as a woman (which is appropriate, in its slightly tasteless way, to a poem dedicated to a squire of the royal body). Jove agrees to help and commands Nature to escort the Phoenix from Arabia to Paphos. There is some satire in the allegory. Arabia is equated with 'the plaines of white *Brytania*', a place that is fruitless, base, and lacking redemptive fire. This is Elizabeth's court, not far from the white cliffs of Dover, and it contrasts with Paphos 'Ouer the mountaine tops', a location which suggests Lleweni.[19] Paphos is the seat of 'true *Honors* louely *Squire*, | That for this *Phoenix* keepes *Prometheus* fire'. As in the manuscript 'Epitaph', white and red are united in the heraldry of the Turtle's face ('Bloud and sweete Mercie hand in hand'). The handsome bird's devotion is, riskily, almost that of a lover. He does not just hold an office in the royal bedchamber but will come 'to this *Phoenix* bed'. It is, though, a bed of death. 'On a high hill', Jove declares, the Turtle will meet the Phoenix, 'And of their Ashes by my doome shal rise, | Another *Phoenix* her to equalize' (1–12).

Despite its apparent simplicity of purpose, *Loves Martyr* is a patchwork. It has something of the overlapping miscelleneity that one finds in the family manuscripts. Next, for instance, comes a prayer for the Phoenix, reminiscent of the loyal prayer for Elizabeth in Christ Church MS 184.[20] There is then a Dialogue between Nature and the Phoenix (16–34). Once Nature has promised to protect the Turtle against 'foule *Enuy*' (Denbighshire

[19] Cf. Brown (1914) lxv–lxviii; Thomas P. Harrison, '*Loves Martyr*, by Robert Chester: A New Interpretation', *Studies in English*, 30 (1951): 66–85, 75–6.
[20] Brown (1914) 19.

enemies at court), the Phoenix agrees to favour him and the main narrative begins. Nature flies with the Phoenix from Arabia, but they land, abandoning allegory, not in Paphos but in 'this large Ile of sweete *Britania*'. Something of an antiquarian, Nature tells the Phoenix about the cities and worthies of England and Wales. One of these is Arthur, and we hear quite a lot about him even before the poem is interrupted by 'the Birth, *Life* and Death of honourable Arthur, *King of Brittaine*'. This has been dismissed as a huge irrelevance, but it is salient in a book about Anglo-Welsh queen/magnate relations, and the Britishness of the Tudors. It also bears on the question of succession that, in various ways, haunts *Loves Martyr*: the revenant Phoenix, the once-and-future king who is buried deep with Guinevere (34–77).

Arrival in Paphos prompts a listing of the many plants that grow there, with their properties, then precious stones, then animals. It has been said that Paphos must be Ireland,[21] where Essex led a campaign against Tyrone in 1599, but that cannot be the case because there are 'Serpents', as there are not in Ireland, albeit in 'a little corner towards the East' (113)—which might suggest, to an enthusiast for topical allegory, the eastern part of Derbyshire, the Wrexham area. After another catalogue, of birds, the Turtle appears. Initially, he is disappointing. He droops with despondency at the loss of his mate, another dove, but in the logic of the allegory this makes him an appropriate coupler with the Phoenix: he represents fidelity, not a disloyal widower, when he chastely pairs up again. Nature can now fall out of the narrative (we are on a higher plane of love), and the Phoenix and Turtle withdraw into a mutuality that is close to the core of Shakespeare's poem: 'We are all one, thy sorrow shall be mine', says the Phoenix, 'thou shalt be my self'.

Chester's narrative takes a clumsy turn as the birds gather firewood for their pyre, but the scene of conflagration, which boldly varies traditional phoenix iconography, gave Shakespeare a vital emblem. The Phoenix wonders whether her rebirth could be achieved without the death of the Turtle, but the dove will not accept this. Two into one must go. Witnessed by a Pelican, who is lurking behind nearby foliage, the Turtle leaps into the pyre, which has been ignited by the sun, and is followed by the Phoenix. Here are love's martyrs. The Pelican reassures the reader that the presence in the Phoenix' heart of 'a perpetuall loue, | Sprong from the bosome of the Turtle-Doue', makes the new bird even more perfect than the old. 'Long may the new vprising bird increase', he adds (123–34). It is, we may assume, another prayer on behalf of the Queen.

It is also, at least allegorically, the consummation that Salusbury must have wished for. Like Sir Edward Stanley, buried at Tong under lines composed before his death, his epitaph was proleptic. The poetry written by Chester but also by Chapman, Jonson, and others in *Loves Martyr* constitutes his living monument eleven or so years before the poem by John Davy. The long effort at reinstatement for the Salusbury family at court is brought in the death of the Turtle to a climax of obedience and devotion. Sir John's self-sacrificing service will reinvigorate the Queen's rule. Alternatively, or moreover—and

---

[21] William H. Matchett, *The Phoenix and the Turtle: Shakespeare's Poem and Chester's 'Loues Martyr'* (The Hague: Mouton, 1965) 135.

this is where the fascination with succession in *Loves Martyr* comes into play—he will recur in the heart of whichever phoenix replaces the Queen. It is a fantasy of political survival, of success in a court which looks likely to be handed over to King James. The idea that James was a phoenix is, of course, prominent in the panegyrical literature that greeted his accession—as in the account of the Tudor–Stuart succession in Cranmer's prophecy at the end of *Henry VIII*.

But the epitaph-ending of 'The Phoenix and Turtle' was closer to the mark, politically, than Chester's allegory of revival: 'For these dead birds sigh a prayer' (1. 67). When the Queen died, Salusbury slipped out of the picture. The relationship in the royal bedchamber left what Shakespeare's poem calls 'no posterity' (1. 59). Sir John retired from court hoping to be recalled but he was not. A letter from him to Cecil, written a few weeks after the Queen's death, asks 'whyther yt ys your pleasure that I shulde make my repayre to attend your honor'.[22] The summons never came. He declined into a long illness. The reprint of *Loves Martyr* with a new title-page in 1611 may not be accidental. Was it a last call for favour? The epitaph of a dying man? If so, with what hope of influence? Interestingly, the title page draws attention to exactly the sorts of Welsh-British historical matter that we find in Shakespeare's late romance, *Cymbeline*: 'The Anuals of Great Brittaine. Or, A Most Excellent Monument, wherein may be seene all the antiquities of this Kingdome'. The closest analogue to this book in Shakespeare's plays can be found, indeed, in the funeral rites for Innogen, and the dirge (in 'Phoenix and Turtle' metre) that is uttered over her body ('Fear no more the heat o'th' sun') by the Welsh-bred, British princes, Guiderius and Arviragus. 'The bird is dead', Arviragus cries, 'That we have made so much on' (IV. ii. 198–9, 259–82). Both the 'Monument' which is the reprint and the play owe something to the accession of Prince Henry as Prince of Wales and Great Britain in 1610. This must have created an environment in which the interests of Salusbury seemed ready for revival. The prince's death on 6 November 1612 (which generated reams of memorial poetry), like that of Salusbury a few months earlier, brought to an end a certain Elizabethan and in Henry's case neo-Elizabethan, neo-Arthurian view of the matter of Wales, and the position of Welsh magnates, in the emergent Britishness.

The Salusbury family manuscripts are not unique in their inclination to elegy and epitaph. Both genres are well represented in Elizabethan miscellanies and verse collections from Tottel's *Songes and Sonettes* (1557), through Googe's *Eglogs, Epytaphes, and Sonettes* (1563), George Turberville's *Epitaphes, Epigrams* (1567), and Timothy Kendall's *Flowers of Epigrammes* (1577). These set a long-range precedent for the 'Poeticall Essaies' in the sense that the verses by Shakespeare, Jonson, and the rest are not exclusively elegiac but use the occasion of Chester's allegory to place the death of the Phoenix and Turtle in a varied scene of Platonic love, mythology, satire, and mock-heroic. A closer analogue can be found in the books of memorial verse that began to appear after the death of Sidney in 1586.[23]

[22] Brown (1914) xxv.
[23] For a helpful survey see Raphael Falco, 'Instant Artifacts: Vernacular Elegies for Sir Philip Sidney', *Studies in Philology*, 89 (1992): 1–19.

It was one of those books, *The Phoenix Nest*, that includes the bird-funeral poem by Roydon ('An Elegie, or Friends Passion, for his Astrophill') which has been seen as linking Shakespeare's poem with Sidneyan elegy, and with the hard, lyrical, trochaic metre of the Eighth Song of *Astrophil and Stella*.[24] These were not the first English elegies on poets (think of Surrey on Wyatt), but they did create an arena for affiliation, rivalry, and display, as well as appreciative tribute. They pioneered a species of 'critical elegy' which became widespread in the 17th century.[25] In elegies of this sort, poets conventionally declare that the work of an admired predecessor will be their living monument. They go with the grain of Sonnet 74, where Shakespeare tells the young man: 'My life hath in this line some interest, | Which for memorial still with thee shall stay'. They assess the qualities that make for such immortality (as part of a critical debate), they at least implicitly situate their own work in relation to the dead poet's achievement, and they advance their own reputations while crying up the merits of the deceased. It is another version, we might feel, of competitiveness among the tombs.

Shakespeare, by 1601, was no stranger to appearing in an assemblage of works by several hands. In 1599, *The Passionate Pilgrim* was attributed to him on its title-page even though it includes, in addition to versions of Sonnets 138 and 144, and sonneteering poems from *Love's Labour's Lost*, fifteen texts by Marlowe, Bartholomew Griffin, and others. Scholars cannot decide whether the publisher, William Jaggard, put '*By W. Shakespeare*' on his title page because he was under-informed about what he had, wanted to associate his book with a 'Shakespearean' style of writing, or was simply being dishonest. That Shakespeare was unhappy about this blurring of authorial identity can be inferred from his annoyance—reported by Thomas Heywood—when an enlarged edition of *The Passionate Pilgrim* was published, with an unchanged attribution, including material by Heywood.[26] As the playhouse and the printing press became viable sources of income for writers, towards the end of the 16th century, the building of authorial identities became a more important element in literary careers. This led poets, on the one hand, to manage their reputations more jealously, and commentators, on the other, to indulge in the sorts of critical ranking and lineage-building that Francis Meres pioneered in 1598 when he classed Shakespeare with Sidney, Spenser, Daniel, and others, and declared that 'the sweete wittie soule of *Ouid* liues in melliflous & honytongued *Shakespeare*, witnes his *Venus* and *Adonis*, his *Lucrece*, his sugred Sonnets'.[27] All of which helps explain the explicitness of the attributions in the 'Poeticall Essaies'. As the title page of *Loves Martyr* puts it: '*To [Chester's poems] are added some new compositions, of severall moderne Writers, whose names are subscribed to their severall workes*'. We may not be finally sure of the allegorical identity of the dead birds, but we are told, in large letters,

---

[24] E.g. Shakespeare, *The Poems*, rev. edn, John Roe (ed.), (Cambridge: Cambridge University Press, 2006) 47–50; Barbara Everett, 'Set Upon a Golden Bough to Sing: Shakespeare's Debt to Sidney in "The Phoenix and Turtle"', *T L S*, 16 February 2001): 13–15.

[25] Avon Jack Murphy, 'The Critical Elegy of Earlier Seventeenth-Century England', *Genre*, 5:1 (1972): 75–105.

[26] Thomas Heywood, *An Apology for Actors* (1612) G4r-v.

[27] Francis Meres, *Palladis Tamia* (1598) 281.

that 'The Phoenix and Turtle' was written by *'William Shake-speare'*. The poem's defunctive music gives him a memorial.

There is another difference from *The Passionate Pilgrim*. Jaggard's collection is backward-looking; readers are given Marlowe, Raleigh, early Shakespeare, and other pieces of high-Elizabethan eloquence. The 'Poeticall Essaies' are, by contrast, the work of *'moderne Writers'* (the word 'essaies' is itself novel and fashionable, imported from Montaigne's French). The well-established Shakespeare is surrounded in *Loves Martyr* by a set of rivals, young and up-to-date. In the Sonnets, the poet apologizes for his old-fashioned style, and forgives the lovely youth for seeking out 'Some fresher stamp of these time-bettering days' (82). We need not assume that one of the contributors to the 'Poeticall Essaies' is the rival praised and mocked in Sonnet 86 (although Chapman fits the description). The whole scenario in the middle-numbered sonnets about rival, 'alien pens' is based on the contest for patrons and readers in the late-Elizabethan period. In the 'Poeticall Essaies' we see this rivalry going on in actuality. Is it any wonder that, invited into the company of a rising generation of metaphysically ambitious, Latinate poets, Shakespeare should have struck out in new ways, and written a poem which combines with unique, luminous ease the antiquated, the philosophical, and the neo-classical.

The 'Poeticall Essaies' were 'consecrated … *to the loue and merite of the true-noble Knight*, Sir Iohn Salisburie'. Two decades later, in their dedication to the First Folio (1623), Heminges and Condell 'consecrate to' another pair of Welsh magnates, the Earls of Pembroke and Montgomeryshire, 'these remaines of your seruant *Shakespeare*'. The mortuary implication of this ('remaines' meaning corpse as well as corpus) is not accidental. Earlier, the actors say that they have 'done an office to the dead, … onely to keepe the memory of so worthy a Frend, and Fellow aliue, as was our SHAKESPEARE'.[28] It has not been sufficiently recognized that the Folio, like *Loves Martyr*, is a memorial volume, is itself, indeed, a memorial; the prefatory poems combine the idea from Ovid, Horace, and the Sonnets that verse can be a monument with literary-critical constructions of 'our Shakespeare'. In this, Jonson's great poem, 'To the memory of my beloued, The AVTHOR Mr. WILLIAM SHAKESPEARE', gives a lead. William Basse's widely read but inept early elegy had urged Spenser, Chaucer, and Beaumont to shift across in their graves in Westminster Abbey to make room for Shakespeare. Mocking this morbid conceit, Jonson assures his dead friend that 'Thou art a Moniment, without a tombe, | And art aliue still, while thy Booke doth liue'. At the end of his elegy-panegyric, there is more than a hint of the climax of 'The Phoenix and Turtle', where the dead birds become 'Co-supremes and stars of love' (1. 51). Shakespeare is hailed as 'Sweet Swan of *Auon!*', a 'Constellation' and 'Starre of *Poets*'.

This is not the only time that Jonson praised a contemporary as a glorious, eloquent swan. In prefatory verses to Hugh Holland's *Pancharis* (1603), he calls the author 'a

---

[28] An 'office' is a duty, but the phrasing also glances at the prayers or divine service said for one deceased ('Office for the Dead').

blacke Swan …. A gentler bird, then this;' he goes on, using an adjective that he would later apply to Shakespeare, 'Did neuer dint the breast of *Tamisis*'. Who was this bird-like prodigy? Holland returns us to the Anglo-Welsh axis that produced *Loves Martyr* and its appendix. Born in Denbigh in 1563, he became a pupil of Camden, who called him one of the 'most pregnant witts of these our times'.[29] Although based in London, beside the Thames, Holland retained an attachment to North Wales. He was there in 1601, the year of the showdown in Wrexham, 'probably in connection with the disturbances surrounding the Denbighshire elections in that year'.[30] He was certainly, at that time, perhaps to dissociate himself from Essex's supporters in his home county, drawing Anglo-Welsh themes into his loyal, unfinished epic about the courtship of Owen Tudor and Queen Katherine, *Pancharis*. Holland was not a courtier, but he moved in court-related circles, as well as among the literary men associated with the Mitre tavern. Like others in that milieu, he sought to develop his connections with the court by marking royal deaths: there is an epitaph on Elizabeth and an elegy on Prince Henry, while his *Cypres Garland* (1625) lamented the death of King James.

Did Holland have a direct role in the compilation of *Loves Martyr*? It has been plausibly suggested that he 'introduced Ben Jonson'—often seen as the moving spirit of the 'Poeticall Essaies'—'to his near neighbour in Wales, Sir John Salusbury'.[31] His association with Jonson and Shakespeare is more demonstrable in the Folio, where he adds to the Welshness of the enterprise,[32] because immediately after Jonson's elegy comes Holland's 'Vpon the Lines and Life of the Famous Scenicke Poet, Master WILLIAM SHAKESPEARE'.

Those hands, which you so clapt, go now, and wring
You *Britaines* braue; for done are *Shakespeares* dayes:
His dayes are done, that made the dainty Playes,
Which made the Globe of heau'n and earth to ring.
Dry'de is that veine, dry'd is the *Thespian* Spring,
Turn'd all to teares, and *Phoebus* clouds his rayes:
That corp's, that coffin now besticke those bayes,
Which crown'd him *Poet* first, then *Poets* King.
If *Tragedies* might any *Prologue* haue,
All those he made, would scarce make one to this:
Where *Fame*, now that he gone is to the graue
(Deaths publique tyring-house) the *Nuncius* is.
    For though his line of life went soone about,
    The life yet of his lines shall neuer out.

---

[29] Camden, *Remaines* (1605), 'Certaine Poemes', 8.

[30] Colin Burrow, 'Hugh Holland', *Oxford Dictionary of National Biography* (Oxford: Oxford University Press, 2004).

[31] Burrow (2004).

[32] Cf. D. Lleufer Thomas, 'Welshmen and the First Folio of Shakespeare's Plays (1623)', *Transactions of the Honourable Society of Cymmrodorion*, Session 1940 (1941) 101–14, 101–2.

Presumably as a tribute to Shakespeare, this is written, unfashionably, in sonnet form, with a decisive couplet. It draws on the play between poetry, genealogy, and immortality—the 'lines to time' motif—that runs through the sonnets to the young man. It has an Anglo-Welsh aspect in its address to 'You *Britaines* braue'. And it is, of course, a memorial poem, focused on, and seeking to redeem, the author's 'corp's' and 'coffin'. The level of critical analysis may not be high, but again we find a conjunction between elegiac writing and the attribution of particular qualities to Shakespeare's 'dainty Playes'.

The 17th-century construction of 'William Shake-speare' drew on a variety of utterances and artefacts, from anecdotes told in taverns to the tribute of literary imitation. To judge from what we have seen in *Loves Martyr* and the Folio, however, the image was partly generated by his own writing of elegies and epitaphs, and reinforced by memorial verses doing literary-critical work. We find this, for instance, in Milton's 'Epitaph on the admirable Dramaticke Poet, W. SHAKESPEARE', added to the Second Folio (1632):

> What neede my *Shakespeare* for his honour'd bones,
> The labour of an Age, in piled stones
> Or that his hallow'd Reliques should be hid
> Under a starre-ypointing Pyramid?
> Dear Sonne of Memory, great Heire of *Fame*,
> What need'st thou such dull witnesse of thy Name?
> Thou in our wonder and astonishment
> Hast built thy selfe a lasting Monument:
> For whilst to th' shame of slow-endevouring Art,
> Thy easie numbers flow, ...

What is striking is not just the echo of the Stanley epitaphs, plainly part of the Shakespeare corpus for Milton,[33] but the rebuttal of Jonson's insistence that his friend should be commended for 'slow-endevouring Art' rather than—as Heminges and Condell claimed—his facility and flow. By 1632, a critical discourse had been articulated. Jonson's elegy in the First Folio set the terms of debate. His less than warm remark about Shakespeare's 'small *Latine*, and lesse *Greeke*', and his emphasis on Jonsonian labour, on 'a good *Poet*' being 'made, as well as borne', were echoed, but also, as in Milton's poem, turned against the elegist. Here, then, are the beginnings of what Ian Donaldson has noticed, the growth of arguments about the qualities of Shakespeare that were defined against the self-definition implicit in Jonson's critique.[34] How quickly did this debate develop, and how far did Shakespeare's non-dramatic poetry provide an arena for argument?

The distance covered within a couple of decades can be gauged from two poems written by Shakespeare's fellow-Stratfordian, Leonard Digges. In the First Folio, he

---

[33] Cf. Gordon Campbell, 'Shakespeare and the Youth of Milton', *Milton Quarterly*, 33:4 (1999): 95–105.
[34] Ian Donaldson, *Jonson's Magic Houses: Essays in Interpretation* (Oxford: Clarendon, 1997) chs 2 and 11.

compliments the author within the memorial conventions inherited from Ovid, Horace, and the Sonnets:

> TO THE MEMORIE of the deceased Authour Maister W. SHAKESPEARE
>
> Shake-speare, at length thy pious fellowes giue
> The world thy Workes: thy Workes, by which, out-liue
> Thy Tombe, thy name must when that stone is rent,
> And Time dissolues thy *Stratford* Moniment,
> Here we aliue shall view thee still. This Booke,
> When Brasse and Marble fade, shall make thee looke
> Fresh to all Ages: . . .

The monument in Holy Trinity, topped by the family coat of arms, is not merely an exemplar of decay. The locally secured awareness of the material impressiveness of the tomb, as a prestigiously situated marker of Shakespeare's worldly success, allows Digges the more grandly to assert the immortalizing power of 'This Booke'. Jonson's reservations about his friend, already current as table-talk,[35] are not yet a challenge to be met. In John Benson's landmark edition of Shakespeare's *Poems* (1640),[36] by contrast, Digges takes on Jonson directly. His verses, at the front of the book, 'Vpon Master WILLIAM SHAKESPEARE, the Deceased Author, and his POEMS' start with the bold rebuttal, 'Poets are borne not made', and he goes on on to make a virtue of Shakespeare's small Latin and less Greek: 'thou shalt find he doth not borrow, | One phrase from Greekes, nor Latines imitate'. That this is untrue is hardly the point; a misleading assertion of Jonson's sets up a polarized, argumentative reaction, within the panegyrical dynamics of elegy—which is how debate advances. Audiences, Digges defiantly observes, would rather watch *Julius Caesar* than Jonson's 'tedious (though well laboured)' *Catiline*, while Falstaff, Beatrice, Benedick, and Malvolio are more reliable theatre-fillers even than *Volpone* and *The Alchemist*.

Ending with these poems by Digges highlights what is often forgotten, that the First Folio was not the only major collection of Shakespeare's work made in the 17th century. Benson's *Poems* became the basis of every gathering of the non-dramatic poetry[37] until Malone. Significantly, although this book appeared twenty-four years after Shakespeare's death, it is still presented as a memorial volume, as though the prefatory poems, which are largely independent from those included in the Folios, could not do the critical work of introducing the long-dead poet if they did not at least ostensibly have an elegiac role in their dealings with 'the Deceased Author'.[38] It is an effect enhanced by the way the 1640

[35] See the 'Conversations with William Drummond of Hawthornden', in e.g. Ben Jonson, *The Complete Poems*, George Parfitt (ed.), (Harmondsworth: Penguin, 1975) Appendix II.

[36] For different views of Benson see Margreta de Grazia, *Shakespeare Verbatim: The Reproduction of Authenticity and the 1790 Apparatus* (Oxford: Clarendon Press, 1991), 166–73, and Patrick Cheney, *Shakespeare, National Poet-Playwright* (Cambridge: Cambridge University Press, 2004) 1–12.

[37] Omitted by Benson, *Venus and Adonis* and *Lucrece* had their own histories until they were added by Charles Gildon (1710) to Rowe's 1709 edition of Shakespeare.

[38] Contrast such relatively prompt, commemorating volumes as John Donne, *Poems, by J. D. with Elegies on the Authors Death* (1633), *Ionsonus Virbius: Or, The Memorie of Ben: Johnson* (1638), William Cartwright, *Comedies, Tragi-Comedies, with Other Poems* (1651).

collection is not just prefaced but rounded off by a run of elegiac verses, from 'The Phoenix and Turtle', through Milton's 'Epitaph' and Basse's 'On the death of *William Shakespeare*', to an anonymous 'Elegie' which initially declares that it wants 'learned *Iohnson*' to 'sing a Dirge for thee' but then decides that 'we neede no Remembrancer' because, in this monumental volume, 'we have | So much of thee redeemed from the grave'.

SELECT BIBLIOGRAPHY

Brady, Andrea (2006) *English Funeral Elegy in the Seventeenth Century: Laws in Mourning* (Basingstoke: Palgrave).

Brown, Carleton (1914) (ed.) *Poems by Sir John Salusbury and Robert Chester*, Early English Texts Society, extra series 113 (London: Kegan Paul and Oxford University Press).

Chester, Robert (1601) *Loves Martyr: Or, Rosalins Complaint* (London).

Houlbrooke, Ralph (1998) *Death, Religion, and the Family in England, 1480–1750* (Oxford: Clarendon Press).

Marshall, Peter (2002) *Beliefs and the Dead in Reformation England* (Oxford: Oxford University Press).

Pigman, G. W. III (1985) *Grief and English Renaissance Elegy* (Cambridge: Cambridge University Press).

Weever, John (1631) *Ancient Funerall Monuments*. (London).

PART III

SONGS, LYRICS, AND BALLADS

CHAPTER 14

....

SONG IN SHAKESPEARE

Rhetoric, Identity, Agency

....

GAVIN ALEXANDER

We may think of lyric as a mode of poetry in which a poet talks to him- or herself, and we are simply meant to be interested in what that poet has to say. But this is a mode that only became the norm for lyric with the Romantics, as W. R. Johnson has shown. A first-person lyric voice in Shakespeare's day is more likely to be addressing a second person, and with an ambiguity of situation that will make us ask questions. Is the first person the poet or just a mask he is wearing? Who is the addressee—a real person, a fiction, or something in between? Is the poem written for us or are we snooping? The listener (or reader), Johnson argues, can identify with the poem's 'I' or its 'you', or with both; 'he becomes … part of the lyrical moment': 'witnessing this compressed, dramatic instant, listening to the words and the rhythms that illumine it, he is moved to ponder himself in relation to it.'[1] But let us imagine a lyric in which the poem's first-person voice is framed by a narrator; and then, further, a performance of such a lyric within a play by a character on stage. There are now many more persons, real and imaginary, with a stake in what is being said and between whose different identities and intentions the lyric must operate: the members of the audience, the actor, the character being acted, the character narrating in the poem, the character being narrated in the poem, the poet, the dramatist, and perhaps also the composer of the music, or the performers of that music.

I want in this chapter to think more about the place of lyric poetry within Shakespeare's plays, about where such poems come from, what uses are made of them, and how we are to respond to them, and especially about what difference it makes when they are performed

---

[1] *The Idea of Lyric: Lyric Modes in Ancient and Modern Poetry* (Berkeley and Los Angeles: University of California Press, 1982) 72. Johnson is describing ancient lyric, but his model can be readily transplanted to the Renaissance, since this 'older, classical, universal lyric form' (7) was, he argues, the dominant mode before the Romantics.

as songs. I also want to think about them as texts—in the way that an editor would—because what very soon emerges when one looks at Shakespeare's songs is that their onto-logical oddity—the way they raise questions about what they are doing in that dramatic setting—is bound up with various kinds of textual oddity, both in the routes they take into their printed texts and in the appearance they are given when they get there.

Thanks to Tiffany Stern's work in *Documents of Performance in Early Modern England* we now know a great deal more about dramatic texts and about songs within them. Song texts circulated in different material forms from play texts. They may never have appeared in prompt copies or even in authorial drafts: some songs were so well known as never to need writing down; others might have started life on separate pieces of paper sent directly to the performers (if to already-known music) or composer (if new music was required), and then have continued their existence in musical scores. For this reason songs are often missing from printed play texts, or are textually suspect. But they were also the first thing to go when a play had to be cut and the easiest thing to add when a play needed expan-sion, and they could be substituted as fashion, personnel, or performance conditions changed. They therefore 'always present a major line of textual uncertainty'. Because there are often questions hanging over their role in a play, questions raised by their status in a scene and often reinforced by textual evidence, they 'should always be regarded as poten-tially cohabitants of the play they are in, rather than as elements of that play'.[2]

There are dozens of songs in Shakespeare's plays, and once his company had taken on the indoor playhouse at Blackfriars in 1608 we start in the late plays to see something which is almost musical drama, culminating in *The Tempest*.[3] Shakespeare and The King's Men were responding to a rising interest in dramatic music and song fostered by the Jacobean court masque and influenced by French practices as well as by the Italian humanist experiments which ultimately led to opera.[4] But Shakespeare was also pursu-ing an interest in the dramatic uses of song developed in an earlier phase of his career, between around 1599 and 1604, a phase which gave us Ophelia, of course, as well as all of the examples that I shall discuss below. I shall return very briefly to *The Tempest* at the end of this chapter, but what interests me about these earlier plays is that—both in the material appearance of their play texts and in the nature of their earliest performances—they represent a more uneasy integration of song into drama.

---

[2] Tiffany Stern, *Documents of Performance in Early Modern England* (Cambridge: Cambridge University Press, 2009), ch. 5 ('Songs and masques') 120–73 (145 and 160, respectively). For Stern's survey of lost songs in Shakespeare, noting that his texts 'preserve more songs than most', see 122–4. There may of course have been other songs whose loss has left no textual trace.

[3] On the musical implications of this move see Andrew Gurr, *The Shakespeare Company, 1594–1642* (Cambridge: Cambridge University Press, 2004) 80–4.

[4] On the musical backgrounds to Shakespeare see works by Doughtie and Maynard in the bibliography, and, most recently, David Lindley, *Shakespeare and Music* (London: Thomson, 2006). For a useful concise survey of Shakespeare's uses of music see John Stevens, 'Shakespeare and the Music of the Elizabethan Stage', in John Stevens, Charles Cudworth, Winton Dean, and Roger Fiske, *Shakespeare in Music* (London: Macmillan, 1964) 3–48, and for a full account of his songs see Peter J. Seng, *The Vocal Songs in the Plays of Shakespeare: A Critical History* (Cambridge, MA: Harvard University Press, 1967).

14.1 *As You Like It*

In Shakespeare's earlier plays, a single song (occasionally two) had become the norm in the comedies alone. But the inclusion for the first time of a song in a tragedy, *Julius Caesar* (*c*. 1599), heralded an explosion of song in comedy and its more habitual inclusion in tragedy. *Hamlet* (*c*. 1600–1) and *Twelfth Night* (*c*. 1601–2) are the leading examples here, but it starts with *As You Like It*, written in 1599 or 1600 and including five songs. In Act V, Scene iii, two of the Duke's pages sing a song to Touchstone and Audrey in what is a scene created as a vehicle for that performance. My composite text below uses for the first two stanzas the text as it appears in a contemporary musical setting by Thomas Morley, printed in 1600 (FIGURE 14.1), then for stanzas 3 and 4 the text as given when the play was first printed, in the 1623 Folio:

> It was a louer and his lasse, With a haye with a hoe and a haye nonie no and a haye nonie nonie no, That o're the green corne fields did passe in spring time, in spring time, in spring time, the only pretiring time when birds do sing, hay ding ading ading, hay ding ading ading, hay ding ading ading, sweete louers loue the springe in spring time, in spring time, The onely pretiring time when birds do sing, Haye ding ading ading, Haye ding ading ading, Haye ding ading ading, sweete louers loue the spring.

> Betweene the Akers of the rie,
> With a hay, with a ho and a hay nonie no,
> These prettie Countrie fooles would lie,
> In spring time, the onely prettie ring time,
> When Birds doe sing, hay ding a ding a ding,
> Sweete louers loue the spring.

> *This Carroll they began that houre,*
> *With a hey and a ho, & a hey nonino:*
> *How that a life was but a Flower,*
>   *In spring time, &c.*

> *And therefore take the present time,*
> *With a hey, & a ho, and a hey nonino,*
> *For love is crowned with the prime.*
>   *In spring time, &c.*[5]

The Folio heads the song 'Song' and sets it in italics—both common features in printed plays. The effect is to acknowledge in its appearance that the song belongs to a different medium—requires a different kind of performance—from the dialogue around it, and

---

[5] Thomas Morley, *The First Booke of Ayres* (1600) B4v-C1r; text of stanza 1 is extracted from the music, with contractions (including 'ditto' marks) expanded. *Mr. William Shakespeares Comedies, Histories, & Tragedies* (1623) S1r (= 5.3.15–38).

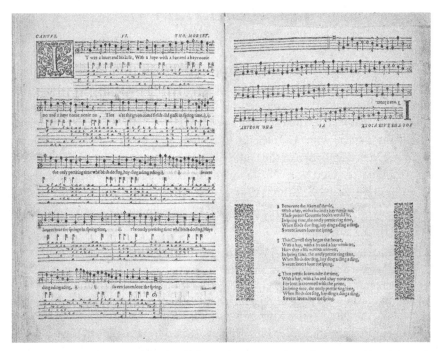

FIGURE 14.1. 'It was a louer and his lasse', from Thomas Morley, *The First Booke of Ayres* (1600) B4v-C1r. By permission of the Folger Shakespeare Library. Printed in round-the-table format: lute and voice sit/stand on one side of the music book and (optional) bass violist on the other.

also to set the song apart textually, as if to register the possibility that it may have found its way into the Folio text via a different route from the other parts of the play.

It is a strange song. It has refrain (or 'undersong') elements with which both poem and setting get rather carried away, so that very little in the way of narrative is actually delivered. After the scene has been set for 'This Carol' we get virtually nothing that is clearly in the voice of the lovers: their song is reported indirectly ('How that a life was but a Flower') and the final stanza could be their conclusion or that of the narrator framing the song. The undersong elements belong simultaneously inside and outside this framework—we can imagine them sung by the lovers and reported by the narrator or interjected by the narrator as his own commentary. Is something missing? Poems like this can go on for many more than four stanzas, so perhaps this is a cut-down version of a much longer poem where the ratio of framework to inset song was less off-kilter and in which the lovers' voices emerged more clearly. (It is worth noting that the stanza order 1, 4, 2, 3 in the Folio suggests that at one point in the play's production history the song was cut even further, with only the outer two stanzas being performed.)[6]

---

[6] See *Lyrics from English Airs, 1596–1622*, Edward Doughtie (ed.), (Cambridge, MA: Harvard University Press, 1970) 496–7.

This is in fact one of the few songs in Shakespeare to survive in a setting that appears to be its original one. Whether play or song came first, though, we cannot know. Nor can we even be certain that the song's words are by Shakespeare. Printed songbooks do not commonly attribute their lyrics; that Morley's book tells us nothing about the poem's authorship is therefore unremarkable. Perhaps this setting was composed by Morley for an early production of the play, or perhaps the players, or Shakespeare, decided to use the song as already composed by Morley. These are alternatives that the evidence will not allow us definitively to choose between, and it remains possible that another setting than Morley's was originally used.

The song neither obviously belongs nor obviously does not belong in its position in the play. It is ambiguous and ambivalent. Two pages sing the song, probably splitting the varying and constant elements between them. The scene that contains the song also unfolds by twos. Touchstone and Audrey discuss their marriage. The two pages enter. Touchstone calls for a song, and they oblige, as the second page says, 'both in a tune, like two gipsies on a horse' (V. iii. 13–14). They sing their song and Touchstone criticizes it; the banter that follows jokes its way through various binaries: although the pages' performance is tuneless, they keep time (39–43). Touchstone and Audrey, first page and second page, lover and lass, verse and refrain, song and inset song, tune and time, words and music, Shakespeare and Morley perhaps. Or some other poet and some other musical setting. If we ask straightforward questions like 'where has this song come from?', 'why is it being performed?', and 'whom does it address and how does it affect them?' we get at least two answers in each case. This is because a song within a play is like a play within a play: it is one performance to the characters and another to us, and to us it is also *about* performance, is metatheatrical. And it is also because of the equivocations about the song's nature and performance written into this scene and also preserved in the documentary record. The song is a site of duplications and collaborations, alternating possibilities, multiple voices.

Among *As You Like It*'s various songs is another of which the same can be said. Act II, Scene v opens with Amiens singing a first stanza of 'Under the greenwood tree'. Has he made this song up or is it well known? Is it well known to us but new in the world of the play? Or, vice versa, is it new to us but apparently an established part of the oral culture within the play? As he starts to sing, are we meant to think, 'Oh, that old song' or 'He is saying something spontaneous, about that moment and that place'?

> *Enter, Amyens, Iaques, & others.*
> Song.
> *Vnder the greene wood tree,*
>   *who loues to lye with mee,*
> *And turne his merrie Note,*
>   *vnto the sweet Birds throte:*
> *Come hither, come hither, come hither:*
>   *Heere shall he see no enemie,*
> *But Winter and rough Weather.*[7]

---

[7] Text from Folio, Q6v (= 2.5.1–8); the penultimate line is split in two in modern editions.

Amiens then engages in some banter with Jaques before we get a second stanza:

> *Song.   Altogether heere.*
> *Who doth ambition shunne,*
> *   and loues to liue i'th Sunne:*
> *Seeking the food he eates,*
> *   and pleas'd with what he gets:*
> *Come hither, come hither, come hither,*
> *   Heere shall he see. &c.*

Nothing in the dialogue makes clear that this second stanza will be a chorus. 'Song' in printed play texts can mean that a gap in the prompt copy or authorial papers marked only 'Song' has been filled out from another source by the words of that song. This should make us ask questions of the authority of the stage direction 'Altogether heere' that turns the solo song into an ensemble piece. But it works well enough as such because the song is all about creating a community, as Duke Senior and his exiles are trying to do, and as what follows makes ironically clear:

> IAQ.   Ile giue you a verse to this note,
> That I made yesterday in despight of my Inuention.
> AMY.   And Ile sing it.
> AMY.   Thus it goes.
> *   If it do come to passe, that any man turne Asse:*
> *   Leauing his wealth and ease,*
> *   A stubborne will to please,*
> *   Ducdame, ducdame, ducdame:*
> *   Heere shall he see, grosse fooles as he,*
> *   And if he will come to me.*
> AMY.   What's that Ducdame?
> IAQ.   'Tis a Greeke inuocation, to call fools into a circle.

Jaques has written a contrafactum—a new lyric to pre-existing music—or parody, which establishes that the song new to us is not new to him. It is not marked 'Song' in Folio and is not indented like the two stanzas of 'Under the greenwood tree', even though it exactly copies their form. Indeed the first two lines are run into one, something editors are only too happy to correct. But it is—like the song—in italics. Is its textual difference a sign that Jaques has written it down, perhaps even that the printed text incorporates the scroll or piece of paper used on stage (the text of which might then be omitted from the prompt copy)?[8] Is it sung? Editors correct the Folio's apparently duplicated speech headings by transferring 'Thus it goes' from Amiens to Jaques, and they do not direct that the song should be sung, presumably because Jaques' contrafactum isn't headed 'Song'. But these textual wrinkles allow all sorts of interpretations, including perhaps the thought that how this scene was staged might have changed depending on which

---

[8] See Stern (2009) 142 and, on scrolls, ch. 6.

members of the cast could sing, and that is why the text is confused. The options include: (i) Jaques hands Amiens the text and Amiens sings it; (ii) Jaques sings his stanza; (iii) Jaques recites his stanza, perhaps by reading from a piece of paper (and perhaps Amiens, having been taught the words, then sings it). The recent RSC production directed by Michael Boyd (2010–11) featured in Forbes Masson a sardonic folk-rock god of a Jaques who could sing brilliantly to the guitar, so Amiens was got rid of here altogether and the scene became a dialogue with the audience. Does it matter who sings or speaks the words? Are they any less Jaques' if Amiens sings them? Are they meant to be heard as if their singer or speaker is expressing something of what he feels? Is he being himself or someone else as he performs?

The song and its parody represent a rose-tinted and a jaundiced view respectively of the play's community of pastoral exiles, and of ideas of community itself. Jaques comes together with his fellows in order to set himself apart from them, as his song's words do with its source music. In being both like and unlike its source, Jaques' parody uses likeness to assert difference, something which defines Jaques' relation to those around him throughout the play. Both lyrics are about leaving behind one identity, finding another, and then seeing that it is shared with others. The two performers and their songs speak to and for each other and those around them. How they speak (or sing) and what it is they are saying is confused for us by the textual record. That confusion most likely derives from variations in how the scene was performed in the play's early history on stage, variations which in their turn are enabled and encouraged by how the scene and its songs were written and the view of song and its performance that they offer. Songs mean different things to different people on different occasions: our understanding of a song depends on who is performing, what they think of what they are singing, and what we think of them. That is one of the things that we learn from this scene and others like it. And it is the reason for the oddities of textual and dramatic form that they display.

14.2 THE WILLOW SONG

When I leave the theatre or the cinema, I often do so singing to myself one of the tunes or songs I have just heard. It is not just that music is more memorable than speech, but that we like to use songs and tunes as metonymic hooks to call up our memories of their contexts. The song in my head helps me take the play with me as I leave, in the same way that 'I don't like Mondays' by The Boomtown Rats pretty much transports me to the summer of 1979. It is a key to all my other memories of a particular time and place.

Shakespeare understood this. He gives us Desdemona, full of premonitions of her death, looking forward to when she will be a memory, and getting a tune stuck in her head. I quote from the Oxford *Complete Works*:

DESDEMONA
If I do die before thee, prithee shroud me

In one of these same sheets.

EMILIA   Come, come, you talk.

DESDEMONA

My mother had a maid called Barbary.
She was in love, and he she loved proved mad
And did forsake her. She had a song of willow.
An old thing 'twas, but it expressed her fortune,
And she died singing it. That song tonight
Will not go from my mind. I have much to do
But to go hang my head all at one side
And sing it, like poor Barbary. Prithee, dispatch.

EMILIA

Shall I go fetch your nightgown?

DESDEMONA   No. Unpin me here.
This Lodovico is a proper man.

EMILIA

A very handsome man.

DESDEMONA   He speaks well.

EMILIA I know a lady in Venice would have walked barefoot to Palestine
for a touch of his nether lip.

DESDEMONA (*sings*)
    'The poor soul sat sighing by a sycamore tree,
        Sing all a green willow.
    Her hand on her bosom, her head on her knee,
        Sing willow, willow, willow.
    The fresh streams ran by her and murmured her moans,
        Sing willow, willow, willow.
    Her salt tears fell from her and softened the stones,
        Sing willow'—
Lay by these.—
                    'willow, willow.'
Prithee, hie thee. He'll come anon.
    'Sing all a green willow must be my garland.

    'Let nobody blame him, his scorn I approve'—
Nay, that's not next. Hark, who is't that knocks?

EMILIA It's the wind.

DESDEMONA (*sings*)
    'I called my love false love, but what said he then?
        Sing willow, willow, willow.
    If I court more women, you'll couch with more men.'
So, get thee gone. Good night.

(*Othello*, IV. iii. 23–56)

'Nay, that's not next'. Desdemona's song seems to be an old ballad, although Elizabethan
evidence only takes us to fragments of the refrain in other lyrics or to textless versions of

FIGURE 14.2. *A Louers complaint being forsaken of his Loue. To a pleasant new tune.* Printed broadside in two parts, Pepys 1.358–9, © The Pepys Library, Magdalene College, Cambridge.

the music in manuscript music books.[9] The words Desdemona recalls are found in two printed broadsides from the early 17th century (FIGURE 14.2), probably both printed after the play had been first performed.[10] The text of these, Ross Duffin notes, 'is similar enough to Shakespeare's to show that he based Desdemona's singing on it or a closely related text—with a few omissions calculated to show her distraction',[11] We should at least ask if some of the distraction might be Shakespeare's.

Does the Oxford text given above represent more or less than Shakespeare originally wrote? This question, it turns out, is even more complicated than it might first appear, but let us just compare that text to some other texts of the ballad. The first we must look at is the Oxford edition's sole source, the 1623 Folio:

> *Des. The poore Soule sat singing, by a Sicamour tree.*
> *Sing all a greene Willough:*
> *Her hand on her bosome her head on her knee,*
> *Sing Willough, Willough, Willough.*

---

[9] Substantial research on sources and analogues is summarized briefly in Ross W. Duffin, *Shakespeare's Songbook* (New York: Norton, 2004) 469–70. See in particular F. W. Sternfeld, *Music in Shakespearean Tragedy* (London: Routledge and Kegan Paul, 1963) 23–52, and Seng (1967) 191–9.

[10] See Claude M. Simpson, *The British Broadside Ballad and Its Music* (New Brunswick and New Jersey: Rutgers University Press, 1966) 788–91.

[11] Duffin (2004) 469.

The fresh Streames ran by her, and murmur'd her moanes
Sing Willough, &c.
Her salt teares fell from her, and softned the stones,
Sing Willough, &c.   (Lay by these)
Willough, Willough. (Prythee high thee: he'le come anon)
Sing all a greene Willough must be my Garland.
Let no body blame him, his scorne I approue.
(Nay that's not next. Harke, who is't that knocks?
    Æmil. It's the wind.
    Des. I call'd my Loue false Loue: but what said he then?
Sing Willough, &c.
If I court mo women, you'le couch with mo men.
So get thee gone, good night:

                                        (2V3r-v)

We should notice the italics for the song and how the abbreviated refrains with their '&c's have been fleshed out to give all the words that the Oxford editors think are implied. Next is the opening stanza as it is found in a musical setting in a manuscript dating from 1614–16. The text found in this manuscript has only eight stanzas of the twenty-three in the printed broadsides. The most obvious difference from Desdemona's version is key and is shared with the broadsides—the 'poor soul' is in these versions not a woman but a man:

        The poore soule sate sighinge by a Sickamore tree
        Singe willo, willo, willo
        wth his hand in his bosom & his heade vpon his knee
        o willo willo willo willo
        O willo willo willo willo,
        shalbe my gareland
        Singe all agreene willo,
        willo, willo willo,
        Aye me the greene willo must be my gareland.[12]

This version is not so much a transcription of the bare form of the popular ballad as a working up of it into an art song (that is to say, something composed, scored, and faithfully performed), so it may introduce some elaboration. Nevertheless, we might want to imagine that Shakespeare or Desdemona is recalling the song in something like this form, and that this is what we should hear. Here, though, is the less elaborate opening of the ballad in its printed broadside form:

        A Poore soule sat sighing by a Sicamore tree,
            O willow, willow willow,

---

[12] British Library Add. MS 15117, 18r, with 'ditto' marks expanded. The manuscript is reproduced in facsimile in *English Song 1600–1675*, Elise Bickford Jorgens (ed.), 12 vols (New York: Garland, 1986) vol. 1. See also John P. Cutts, 'A Reconsideration of the "Willow Song"', *Journal of the American Musicological Society*, 10 (1957): 14–24 (transcription, 15), and for a reproduction Sternfeld (1963) 38–9.

With his hand on his bosome, his head on his knee,
> *O willow, willow, willow,*
> *O willow, willow, willow,*
> *Sing O the greene willow shall be my garland.*[13]

The '&c's found in the Folio text and in subsequent stanzas of these other versions are common in texts of refrain poems. Shakespeare, or the compositor, or a manuscript copyist, might have employed such conventions, or they might be faithfully copied from a text of the song. Perhaps a prior printed version of the ballad was in front of Shakespeare as he wrote, and gave him the materials for his bricolage. The Folio text's '&c's seem clearly to indicate something rather different from what the Oxford editors have given us at lines 45–7 ('Sing willow'— | Lay by these.— | 'willow, willow'). But that is only to read an '&c.' in more intelligent relation to convention and to the other sources for this song,[14] The Folio text remains in many respects unclear. It is not an exact transcription of what Desdemona will sing; rather, it is an indication of what she might sing, upon which we can expand depending on how we think about song texts—as sketches or as transcripts; as prior to song or mere echo of it. We are used by now to the idea that the texts of early modern plays—and Shakespeare's in particular—are unstable, that they are inexact witnesses of such different things as original authorial intention or final authorial intention or original theatrical performance or subsequent theatrical performance, because they are often tessellations of those different occasions and intentions. The songs in Shakespeare are especially concentrated instances of such instability: it is often quite impossible to deduce where exactly a song has come from and how much Shakespeare has had to do with it.

Let us for a moment imagine that Shakespeare and Desdemona know the words more or less as they are found in the printed ballad,[15] as opposed to the shorter and differently ordered selection in the surviving manuscript version. What can we deduce from the selection we are given in *Othello*? The first thing we notice is that Desdemona prefers the narrative sections of the ballad to those (by far the majority) that give the words of the complaining lover. It is as if Desdemona has difficulty singing anything in the lover's voice apart from the refrain. Perhaps she is uneasy about any more precise applicability to her than of the narrated situation and the melancholy refrain; perhaps she knows that the lover's voice was originally a man's; or perhaps the unease was Barbary's, whose voice Desdemona is happier to borrow. We are of course limited in all these speculations

---

[13] *A Louers complaint being forsaken of his Loue. To a pleasant new tune* (London: for I. W.) STC 5610.5, replacing 'vnder' in l. 1 with 'by', the reading in the later *The Complaint of a Lover forsaken of his Love* (Roxburghe 1.54–5; see Simpson, *British Broadside Ballad*, 788), and rendering the broadside's black letter and roman fonts as roman and italic respectively. The STC dating of this ballad as *c.* 1615 is presumably based on the dating of Add. MS 15117 and is therefore to misunderstand the relation between printed and manuscript ballads. A lost printed ballad probably preceded both Add. MS 15117 and *Othello*, and was the ancestor of the surviving broadsides.

[14] Cf. Cutts (1957), for the suggestion that Shakespeare's text should be expanded to include full versions of the refrains as found in the manuscript setting.

[15] For a modernized text see Duffin (2004) 468–9.

about what Shakespeare or Desdemona did to their source because we do not know what exactly it was like—how long? the stanzas in what order? about a man or about a woman? oral culture or text?—let alone what contemporary audiences thought it was like and how much variation there was in their different understandings. That refrain, as so often in songs of this kind, is poised with a kind of serene vagueness between the many voices and subject positions who might speak or sing it. Is it what the lover sings? Is it what the narrator interjects? Is it—as will often be the case in performance—for us to sing? It is all of these, of course. As such a song develops we often feel that the boundaries between reported voice, narrating voice, and auditor are being erased as they become a single chorus; even the 'fresh streams' join in this song.

That the scenario I describe has a certain fuzziness to it is in fact typical of the genre to which this ballad belongs. I want at this point to raise the useful distinction between popular song and art song only to insist that it might mislead in a case like this.[16] Popular song need not mean a lack of sophisticated connection to high literary genres. The Willow Song is found in manuscript among a collection of art songs and songs composed especially for the theatre; it is flanked by settings of poems by Jonson and Sidney. The printed ballad, however popular in form, is carefully wrought. It belongs to the genre of pastoral elegy or complaint and shares tropes with poems by the likes of Petrarch, Sidney, and Montemayor: the overheard lover, the definite and yet dream-like setting, the material tokens of memory, the pathetic fallacies in every rock, bird, and stream—all these, indeed, it shares with that other 'Lover's Complaint' printed with *Shake-speares Sonnets* in 1609. Behind them all lies the communal, willowy complaint of Psalm 137, 'By the rivers of Babylon'.

Desdemona's identity in this scene thus bleeds into a generic one shared with others. She is struggling not to reenact her mother's maid's love-lorn reenactment of the scenario in the ballad itself. And this memory of the song that Barbary died singing begins a pattern which will end with Emilia's death, a moment where the layers of performance, of mask laid over mask, reach an extraordinary pitch. An actor plays Emilia, who borrows Desdemona's voice, which had been given her by another actor so that she could borrow Barbary's voice and give life to the voice of a female lover based on the voice of a male lover in this converted, adapted, half-forgotten, remembered, revised ballad:

> EMILIA   What did thy song bode, lady?
> Hark, canst thou hear me? I will play the swan,
> And die in music. (*Sings*) 'Willow, willow, willow'.—
>
> (V. ii. 253–5)[17]

Emilia is not given these lines in the 1622 quarto, because Desdemona does not sing in the first place in that version of the text ('. . . that Song to night, | Will not goe from my mind—harke, who's that knocks?').[18] Scholars differ over whether the Folio expands

[16] Cf. Lindley (2006) 141.
[17] Sternfeld (1963) 37: 'the only instance where Shakespeare quotes a melody that had been sung earlier in the play'.
[18] *The Tragœdy of Othello* (1622) L2v.

on the Quarto or Quarto cuts Folio.[19] Because it makes little sense to mention the song in Act IV, Scene iii only to change the subject, it seems most likely that the song was not added to the original but cut from it—perhaps as Stern suggests because the voice of the boy actor who had played Ophelia and Desdemona had finally broken.[20] But it is important to acknowledge that internal evidence will not decide this for us. The Willow Song may have been added in to expand this scene or cut from it to shrink it; it might be regarded as something lost from the scene or found for it. And we cannot decide which, in part at least, because the song, and its performance, is all about the lost and the found; it enacts and exploits the very textual instability that has confused editors.

This is because it is a song. The texts of songs take editors away from their hypothesized prompt copies and authorial papers to other documents and imagined sources: to collective memories, to musical scores, or to loose sheets of paper on which the lyric would be written and sent to the composer or to the musician charged with coaching the actor. Their textual discrepancy witnesses that they are sites of collaboration—between words and tune, theatre and music, poet and composer, text and oral culture, actor and singer, singer and audience, Desdemona and Barbary, and so forth. And songs as they are dramatically performed do something similar. They take us away from the play's present moment and into a shared and less determinate time and space where we can all, to some extent, sing these words. Just as they are sites of collaboration, so they are places where personal identity shifts and blurs. When the actor sings, his mask slips: he might put on another, become someone else for a moment; or we might stop seeing Desdemona and listen to the adolescent boy with the squeaking voice doing his party piece. Because song is a different kind of performance, it draws our attention to it.

Shakespeare's play with the Willow Song shows us how interested he was in the ways song performs personal identity, and enables one person to identify with another. By its conceit of Desdemona-as-Barbary this scene in *Othello* draws attention to how any song involves a collaboration between the identity of the singer and that of the character created by the song. I now want to put this observation into terms that Shakespeare and his contemporaries would recognize: the terms of classical rhetoric.

14.2 SONG AND PERSONA

In *The Complete Gentleman* (1622) Henry Peacham makes the point that music can be understood as rhetoric:

> Yea, in my opinion no rhetoric more persuadeth or hath greater power over the mind; nay, hath not music her figures, the same which rhetoric? What is a revert

[19] Earlier arguments are summarized by Sternfeld (1963) 25–6. See also Wells and Taylor, *William Shakespeare: A Textual Companion* (Oxford: Clarendon Press, 1987) 476–8, and E. A. J. Honigmann, *The Texts of 'Othello' and Shakespearian Revision* (London and New York: Routledge, 1996).

[20] Stern (2009) 147.

but her antistrophe? her reports, but sweet anaphoras? her counterchange of points, antimetaboles? her passionate airs, but prosopopoeias? with infinite other of the same nature?[21]

Prosopopoeia is the rhetorical figure of creating a character and performing another's voice; it is a key term in a Renaissance literary rhetoric and poetics that had not yet developed our way of talking about character.[22] Within the paradigm of the oration, the term would describe a moment when the orator would suggest what might be said by an absent or dead person, or even the defendant himself, or what might be said by something inanimate or abstract, like a city, or by something mute, like an animal. It is a catch-all for various rhetorical acts of ventriloquy. That *prosopopoeia* was seen as a fundamental rhetorical skill is indicated by its inclusion among the late classical school exercises or *progymnasmata* that were to be resurrected in the Renaissance schoolroom: pupils would be set the task of writing a speech in the character of a mythical or historical person. And because rhetoric is an art not only of composition but also of delivery, *prosopopoeia* as a figure is to be seen as issuing not in text but in vocal performance. Where that performance divides—as the oration does not—the performer from the author, *prosopopoeia* becomes the job of both, which is why Peacham should be understood as talking not just about the poet or composer who writes the song but about the singer who performs it. This is how, as Mark W. Booth describes it, we come as listeners of song to be 'drawn into the state, the pose, the attitude, the self offered by the song':[23] not by the fact that the song has been written, but by the fact that it is being performed.

It is to the rhetorical theory of *prosopopoeia* that we must look for a Renaissance poetics of character, since literary theory itself had little to say on the subject. The points I want to make about *prosopopoeia* and its relation to Shakespearean song can best be introduced by some attention to etymology. The Greek term means the making of a mask, from *prosōpon*, mask. The Latin equivalent is *fictio personae*, which is why Puttenham calls *prosopopoeia* 'the Counterfait in personation'.[24] Those two words for mask, Greek *prosōpon* and Latin *persona*, nicely divide up the point of masks, since one has an etymology concerned with what we look at (*prosōpon* means something like *aspect*), and the other is concerned with what we hear (*persona* names the mask as something through which sound passes, *per-sono*).[25] A remarkable fact about both terms is that they came in later classical usage to fill a gap in their respective lexicons for a term equivalent to our *person* or *self*. Selfhood, identity, subjectivity were articulated by analogy to theatre. To talk about one's own person is to use a dramatic metaphor.

---

[21] *Source Readings in Music History: Volume 3, The Renaissance*, Gary Tomlinson (ed.), (New York and London: Norton, 1998) 73.

[22] For more detailed consideration see my 'Prosopopoeia: The Speaking Figure', in Sylvia Adamson, Gavin Alexander, and Katrin Ettenhuber (eds), *Renaissance Figures of Speech* (Cambridge: Cambridge University Press, 2007) 96–112.

[23] *The Experience of Songs* (New Haven: Yale University Press, 1981) 15.

[24] Puttenham (1589) 2D2v.

[25] An etymology available to Shakespeare's contemporaries. See the *Attic Nights* of the Roman philologist Aulus Gellius, 5.7.

Prosopopoeia helps us to think about how language creates semblances of personhood which are performed rhetorically, on particular occasions, and aimed at particular audiences. Rhetoric insists that language is purposive—it aims to teach, delight, or move. The song as *prosopopoeia* is therefore expected to *do* something, to its performer and its audience, both within the play and without. This framework demands that we think of any song as the creating of a persona (or mask) and the performing of that song as a further act of personation. It shows us that personhood in dramatic song is always a complex product—of the prior voices whispering in the generic background, of the associations the tune might have with other words or remembered performances of these words, of the needs of this performer and that auditor.

14.3 *MEASURE FOR MEASURE AND TWELFTH NIGHT*

I want to turn next to a much more straightforward incorporation of what Peacham calls a 'passionate air' within one of Shakespeare's plays. It is another play printed only post-humously, in the 1623 Folio, and where the song has something of the lost and found about it. At the start of Act IV of *Measure for Measure* we are introduced to Mariana, Angelo's jilted ex; she is discovered listening to a boy singing:

> BOY
>> Take, O take those lips away
>>> That so sweetly were forsworn,
>> And those eyes, the break of day,
>>> Lights that do mislead the morn;
>> But my kisses bring again, bring again,
>> Seals of love, though sealed in vain, sealed in vain.
>>> *Enter the Duke, disguised as a friar*
> MARIANA
> Break off thy song, and haste thee quick away. [...]
> I cry you mercy, sir, and well could wish
> You had not found me here so musical.
> Let me excuse me, and believe me so:
> My mirth it much displeased, but pleased my woe.
> DUKE
> 'Tis good; though music oft hath such a charm
> To make bad good, and good provoke to harm.

(IV. i. 1–7; 10–15)

The orthodox view nowadays is that Shakespeare did not write the lyric or even this part of the play as it was printed, but that it is one of several signs that the play as written by Shakespeare and first performed around 1604 was later revised, perhaps by

Middleton.[26] Part of the evidence is that the same song, with a second stanza that it clearly needs, is found within a play by Fletcher and others first performed around 1617 and printed in 1639 as *The Bloody Brother,* and in 1640 as *Rollo, Duke of Normandy.*[27]

It is important not to let hypothesis ossify into fact. We cannot know if *The Bloody Brother* took the song from *Measure for Measure* or gave it to it.[28] What we know about songs in play texts and in non-dramatic manuscripts tells us that the presence of a stanza is no proof that it belongs there, just as its absence is no proof that it does not. That the song survives in a wonderful setting by John Wilson, who was only born in 1595 and only started working for The King's Men in around 1617, may be significant.[29] But the repetitions in lines 5 and 6 of the Shakespearean version are not found in *The Bloody Brother* version or in Wilson's setting. Since they wreck the poem's catalectic trochaic tetrameter they are clearly the work not of the poet but of the composer of a different setting, and the Folio text probably derives from that source: it could easily have lost a stanza in transmission (single-stanza copies of strophic songs are not uncommon in manuscript songbooks). Arguments that the second stanza does not suit *Measure for Measure* because it makes clear that the song is about a woman are absurd.[30] We do not only listen to songs that seem to be about us, and we can choose to listen to songs that make us put ourselves in another's shoes. There is no reason that Shakespeare would recognize, I think, why Mariana should not listen to a song sung by a boy giving voice to a jilted man still stuck on a frosty woman. It might even be good for her. There is nothing in the evidence that forces us to conclude that Shakespeare did not write both stanzas of the lyric or that both stanzas were not sung to Mariana in or around 1604.

The balanced paradoxes which Mariana and the Duke trade at the end of the excerpt above, shortly before he sends her and Isabella offstage so that the one can coach the other in how to take her place, remind us that this play is built in every way on patterns of inversion and exchange. Mariana has summoned up a voice to be performed for her, a *prosopopoeia* that is collaborative—the result of multiple agencies including hers, the boy's, the poet's, the composer's, and perhaps also an accompanying lutenist or violist. That *prosopopoeia* expresses something of her, something for her, something to her. She can relate to and identify with its first person or its second person. Its performed self—its persona—is not hers, or the boy's, or the composer's, or the poet's. (Imagine, if you like, that Mariana wrote this lyric herself, and composed its setting: it makes no difference.) That self exists only in the moment of this performance by these players of this song in this production to this audience. But where *Othello* works to conflate and overlay these *prosopopoeias*, the brutal algebra of *Measure for Measure* must always articulate and distinguish them. This

[26] See Wells and Taylor (1987) 468–9; *Complete Works,* 870–1 for the 'conjectured reconstruction of Shakespeare's original version' (843) of this section; and John Jowett's 'genetic text' of *Measure for Measure* in Thomas Middleton, *The Collected Works,* Gary Taylor and John Lavagnino (eds), (Oxford: Clarendon Press, 2007) 1542–85 (1570–2 for this section).

[27] John Fletcher (attrib.), *The Bloody Brother* (1639) H4v.

[28] Cf. Stern (2009) 133–4.

[29] See Duffin (2004) 379n.

[30] See e.g. Taylor and Lavagnino (2007) 1570 n.

moment in the play as printed in 1623 has much to do with the way Angelo deputizes for the Duke and Mariana for Isabella, Ragozine's head for Barnardine's for Claudio's, with the way Lucio coaches Isabella, or the Duke eavesdrops, or Angelo soliloquizes to us about the discrepancy between selfhood and performance. Song as *prosopopoeia* has much to tell us about a play which is all about characters who wear masks.

For another example of this idea we might look at *Twelfth Night*, again a play first printed in the 1623 Folio but showing the signs of theatrical revision. We see the character of Shakespeare's Viola changing under pressure from musical exigencies. She is already a complicated case—a boy playing a girl playing a boy. In Act II, Scene iv Orsino asks Viola/Cesario to sing a song s/he had apparently sung just the previous evening, only for Curio to interject oddly that 'He is not here, so please your lordship, that should sing it' (II. iv. 8–9). Feste then turns up and sings a song, 'Come away death' (II. iv. 50–65). Here is Stern:

> This entire exchange is a surprise and for three reasons: it is a surprise that Feste, Olivia's jester, should be in Orsino's house at all; it is a surprise that Orsino misremembers who sang the song the night before; and it is a surprise that the song finally produced in no way accords with Orsino's description of it … [T]his play, too, has been updated along song lines, perhaps to showcase the company's new singing clown, Armin; and perhaps, as elsewhere, to rescue the boy-player of Viola from a vocal challenge he could no longer meet. (148)

Viola, we remember, had described herself as a singer at the play's start: 'I'll serve this duke […] for I can sing, | And speak to him in many sorts of music' (I. ii. 51; 53–4). Among the things taken from her in the version of the play that survives, then, is the ability to express herself as Feste does, through the personations of song. Her various masks and personae, therefore, evolve and alter under pressure from various directions and agencies—author, players, composers—and most especially under pressure from the demands of music. The performer of musical *prosopopoeias* becomes a listener to them; Feste's gain is her loss.

14.4 CONCLUSION

Shakespeare's most metatheatrical play features his most advanced singing role: Ariel. Ariel is made to use music with a kind of multi-layered purposiveness that we should recognize by now. A song like 'Full fathom five' intends a particular response from Ferdinand, another from us. As David Lindley observes, it is late in the play—only once promised freedom by Prospero—that Ariel gets a song ('Where the bee sucks') that simply speaks in his (or her) own person.[31] This fact is connected to what is clearest about Ariel: for all his extraordinary musical power and the rhetorical efficacy of the songs he

---

[31] Lindley (2006) 230–2.

sings, he is singing on Prospero's behalf and we must decide for ourselves to what extent and in what senses his words are his own. Song is used by Shakespeare to explore the ways we understand and perform identity. The characters in a song, the characters in a play, the actors who played them, the writers and musicians, the scribes and printers, the oral and literary traditions that produced the plays as written, as variously performed in Shakespeare's day, and as printed—all determine and inflect the words of Shakespeare's songs. We must situate the personae that speak or sing in his songs between all these various agencies. In recognizing that these songs therefore emerge as particularly rich collaborations, we are better able to hear them, to respond to them in performance, and to interpret them as text. Ariel is Shakespeare's way of reminding us that song straddles many thresholds, blurs many categories, and stops us thinking too simplistically about our own identities and those of others. He is named for the airy element he inhabits and for the 'passionate airs' he sings. Like a song, he is insubstantial, un-pin-downable, in-between, ambiguous, hard to trace, an exquisite thing which is there and not there, found and lost again, breath, spirit, melting into air, into thin air.

SELECT BIBLIOGRAPHY

Doughtie, Edward (1986) *English Renaissance Song* (Boston: G.K. Hall).

Duffin, Ross W. (2004) *Shakespeare's Songbook* (New York: Norton).

Gurr, Andrew (2004) *The Shakespeare Company, 1594–1642* (Cambridge: Cambridge University Press).

Johnson, W. R. (1982) *The Idea of Lyric: Lyric Modes in Ancient and Modern Poetry* (Berkeley and Los Angeles: University of California Press).

Lindley, David (2006) *Shakespeare and Music*, Arden Critical Companions (London: Thomson).

Marsh, Christopher (2010) *Music and Society in Early Modern England* (Cambridge: Cambridge University Press).

Maynard, Winifred (1986) *Elizabethan Lyric Poetry and its Music* (Oxford: Clarendon Press).

Seng, Peter J. (1967) *The Vocal Songs in the Plays of Shakespeare: A Critical History* (Cambridge, MA: Harvard University Press).

Stern, Tiffany (2009) *Documents of Performance in Early Modern England* (Cambridge: Cambridge University Press).

Sternfeld, F. W. (1963) *Music in Shakespearean Tragedy* (London: Routledge and Kegan Paul).

....

CHAPTER 15

SHAKESPEARE'S POPULAR SONGS AND THE GREAT TEMPTATIONS OF LESSER LYRIC

....

STEVE NEWMAN

It is not easy for scholars, performers, and audiences to know what to do with Shakespeare's songs because he does so many things with them. In his works there are 160 songs sung in full or part, quoted in passing, or alluded to in other ways.[1] He uses songs throughout his career and across genres, and he does so in all sorts of situations and to various effects. To limit ourselves just to *Hamlet,* he puts songs in the mouths of a prince pretending to be mad, a court lady who is actually mad, and a gravedigger whose singing underscores his clownish sanity. Add to this the heterogeneity of their sources (from lyrics by Sidney and well-known court composers to anonymous broadside ballads), their refusal to respect current disciplinary boundaries by combining music and text, and their ontological instability, and they seem even more elusive and changeable than the play texts in which they (sometimes) appear.[2] These elements make it a challenge to say anything about the songs as a whole without merely describing their variety or either making a stronger claim that can be undermined by a counter example or a claim that relies on ungrounded assumptions about authorship, textual situation, or performance.

---

[1] See Ross W. Duffin's *Shakespeare's Songbook* (New York: W. W. Norton, 2004). Although the topic, frame, and conclusions differ, this essay draws significantly from my entry on oral tradition in *The Cambridge World Shakespeare Encyclopedia*, Bruce Smith (gen. ed.), (Cambridge University Press, forthcoming). Thanks to the editor for permission to use this essay.

[2] On ontological instability, see Tiffany Stern, *Documents of Performance in Early Modern England* (Cambridge: Cambridge University Press, 2009) 120–68.

Yet the very ubiquity of songs in Shakespeare's works and their centrality to the plays (what is *Othello* without The Willow Song?) entice us to make sense of them. I give in to that temptation here, not by presuming to explain all of the songs, but by showing how Shakespeare uses them to exemplify the powerful temptations of a genre through which the songs can be productively viewed—lyric. More specifically, I show how Shakespeare exploits the possibilities of popular song as lesser lyric, commanded by aristocrats and performed for less-distinguished characters who often buy them from a ballad-hawker. In various ways, Shakespeare uses the freedom of this unassuming genre to stage moments of absorption allying it with the Orphic power of the greater lyric of the ode. As Jaques puts it in his parody of Amiens' 'Greenwood' song in *As You Like It*, the 'Ducdame, ducdame, ducdame' of the refrain is merely 'a Greek invocation to call fools into a circle' (II. v. 51; 56), and among the fools are the audience outside of the play *and* the anhedonic Jaques himself: 'I do desire you to sing' (II. v. 15–16).

Turning to lyric is not so much a solution as a useful complication. Grasping Early modern lyric and especially the role of Shakespearean song within it is not easy, even if we properly set aside the equation of lyric with the authorial 'I' as a post-Romantic anachronism that itself ignores the 'communitarian' elements vital to Romantic lyric.[3] Consider Heather Dubrow's important *The Challenges of Orpheus*. It almost always succeeds in avoiding anachronistic and reductive conceptualizations of early modern English lyric. Yet when she takes up Shakespeare's songs, her argument that they 'grant a voice to otherwise marginalized Others' depends on her ruling out certain songs as 'not lyrics' without sufficiently defending the claim—for instance, what is 'unlyrical' about the 'mood' of Autolycus' 'When daffodils begin to peer'?—or depends on invoking a distinction between narrative and lyric that she explicitly challenges elsewhere.[4]

A more capacious approach to popular songs in Shakespeare reveals how they foreground lyric's capacity to condense affect, and how the absorption of the singer in the song models the absorption of the audience. But to a greater extent than songs with a higher pedigree, the lyric absorption triggered by popular song brings with it enlivening conflicts over 'the common'. Gavin Alexander ably shows in Chapter 14 how Shakespearean songs provide opportunities to inhabit and perform personae; I would add the truism that not all personae are created equal in the eyes of Shakespeare's world (or in the eyes of most worlds since). This means that thinking about songs

---

[3] On 'communitarian lyric', see Anne Janowitz, *Lyric and Labour in the Romantic Tradition* (Cambridge: Cambridge University Press, 1998); on 'The Ballad Revival' and lyric, see Steve Newman, *Ballad Collection, Lyric and the Canon* (Philadelphia: University of Pennsylvania Press, 2007) and Maureen N. McLane, *Balladeering, Minstrelsy, and the Making of Romantic Poetry* (Cambridge: Cambridge University Press, 2008).

[4] *The Challenges of Orpheus: Lyric Poetry and Early Modern Lyric* (Baltimore: The Johns Hopkins University Press, 2008) 216; 220; 224. For another productive reading of Shakespearean song in terms of lyric that also overlooks ballads—in this case, 'King Cophetua' in *Love's Labour's Lost*—see Diane Henderson, *Passion Made Public: Elizabethan Lyric, Gender, and Performance* (Urbana, IL: University of Illinois Press, 1995) 167–213.

brings us up against the boundaries between high and low—permeable and shifting and subject to parody, but present nonetheless. Songs offer up the possibility of a common-as-universal participation that levels distinction and can even lend agency to marginalized characters. They invite the audience to sympathize with low characters and with a genre often associated with forms of 'common culture' bound together by 'passion' that pre-exist their performance on a stage 'and will continue to exist … long after the present moment has passed'.[5] Yet they often elicit a countervailing reaction against the common-as-vulgar, associated with a debased print ephemerality, and as such position the audience to distance themselves from these same characters, who in their balladry make themselves the object of derision. Just as the collections of the time are attempting to sort out elite lyric from low broadside, Shakespeare repeatedly draws on them to ask what his audiences should and should not feel they have in common with these singers and each other, and how lyric, lesser lyric included, triggers those identifications.[6] This strategy is most apparent in the comedies, and I first take up a pair of them, one relatively early and another relatively late (*A Midsummer Night's Dream* and *Twelfth Night*); but to acknowledge the important work they do in other genres, I also look at a history (*2 Henry IV*) and a tragedy (*Hamlet*), before ending with Shakespeare's richest meditation on the place of lyric high and low, *The Winter's Tale*.

15.1 *A MIDSUMMER NIGHT'S DREAM*: LYRIC, MOONSHINE, AND OTHER DRUGS

In *A Midsummer Night's Dream*, we know that the potion Oberon has squeezed into Titania's eyes has worked when she hears as angelic a low song likely set to a ballad tune and performed by a would-be actor in an amateur troupe of 'mechanicals' whose musical taste is for the rough 'tongs and the bones' (IV. i. 29):

> BOTTOM I see their knavery. This is to make an ass of me, to fright me, if they could; but I will not stir from this place, do what they can. I will walk up and down here, and I will sing, that they shall hear I am not afraid.

---

[5] Bruce R. Smith, 'Shakespeare's Residuals: The Circulation of Ballads in Cultural Memory', *Shakespeare and Elizabethan Popular Culture*, Stuart Gillespie and Neil Rhodes (ed.), (London: Arden Shakespeare, 2006) 197; 200.

[6] Eric Nebeker, 'Broadside Ballads, Miscellanies, and the Lyric in Print', *ELH* 76, no. 4 (Winter 2009): 989–1013; Christopher Marsh, *Music and Society in Early Modern England* (Cambridge: Cambridge University Press, 2010) 263–6. For an account of Shakespeare's use of broadside ballads and the ballad market's use of Shakespeare that shows how '[t]he play and the poem, the stage and the street, are symbiotic', see Simone Chess, 'Shakespeare's Plays and Broadside Ballads', *Literature Compass* 7, 9 (September 2010): 773–85.

(*Sings*)

> The ousel cock so black of hue,
>   With orange-tawny bill;
> The throstle with his note so true,
>   The wren with little quill.
>
> TITANIA (*awaking*)
> What angel wakes me from my flow'ry bed?

(III. i. 114–22)

Behind this elevation of the ballad is a tale that encompasses more exalted lyric modes. After Titania angrily refuses Oberon's demand to give him the Indian 'changeling', he tells Puck of how he discovered the substance that will allow him to overcome her resistance:

> OBERON
> My gentle puck, come hither. Thou rememb'rest
> Since once I sat upon a promontory
> And heard a mermaid on a dolphin's back
> Uttering such dulcet and harmonious breath
> That the rude sea grew civil at her song
> And certain stars shot madly from their spheres
> To hear the sea-maid's music?

(II. i. 148–54)

What Hugh Grady calls the 'lush lyric intensity of the verses' fittingly echoes an Orphic moment, the myth of Arion the bard on a dolphin's back; like Orpheus, her singing has power over nature, though instead of wringing tears from stones, it calms 'the 'rude sea'.[7] This is in contrast to the disharmony within nature and between humankind and nature due to the 'distemperature' between the Fairy King and Queen (II. i. 88–117). To set things right and revenge himself on his willful consort, Oberon then explains how he will take advantage of what happened next; he saw 'Cupid, all armed' shoot but fail to hit 'a fair vestal thronèd by the west' because the 'fiery shaft [was] [q]uenched in the chaste beams of the wat'ry moon', his arrow instead lodging in a flower now called 'love-in-idleness' (II. i. 155–68). Picking the flower, Oberon exploits the erotic desire that animates a lyric of a kind less grand than the world-making energies of Orphic lyric but nonetheless potent. It proves more powerful than the protective lullaby sung by Titania's servants (II. ii. 9–30), rendering her unable to distinguish between it and Bottom's ruder song. It moves her to utter a command to see to Bottom's needs that rhymes so thickly it takes on the character of a spell empowering the asinine object of her intoxicated desire to order her servants around (III. i. 144–53). The same love-juice also elicits the amatory poetic stylings of Demetrius and Lysander as they pursue their new object of desire, Helena, whose bewildered resistance activates the Petrarchan discourse of the cruel mistress.

---

[7] Hugh Grady, 'Shakespeare and Impure Aesthetics: The Case of *A Midsummer Night's Dream*', *Shakespeare Quarterly* 59: 3 (2008): 285.

In keeping with the foregrounding of artifice in the play, this scenario exposes the artificiality and arbitrariness of Petrarchan lyric yet also shows how natural its conventions can seem. The audience knows that the two men have been drugged, and Helena and Hermia sense something is not right; but those under the spell of 'love-in-idleness' view their sudden change in desire as the height of 'reason', as Lysander repeatedly protests (II. ii. 117–28). So they eagerly reach for the lyric genre that seems to fit the occasion. Triggering both Titania's warped hearing of Bottom's song and the courtly effusions of Demetrius and Lysander, 'love-in-idleness' thus levels the distinctions between elite lyric and popular song.

By the play's end, order seems to be re-established. Oberon uses 'Dian's bud' (IV. i. 72) as an antidote in order to pair the Athenian lovers properly and to restore Titania's vision now that she has agreed to give up the changeling. Oberon's antidote is part of the moonshine that suffuses the play, but it also gestures at the sociopolitical world that informs the restoration of order. Diana's deflection of Cupid's arrow from the 'fair vestal thronèd' is itself predicated on the myth of another Fairy Queen, the chaste huntress Elizabeth. This at once makes her the unknowing licenser of the play's erotic hi-jinks while keeping her safe from it, and the players safe from any political trouble. Within the frame of the play, political order is upheld by Theseus, who sanctions the marriage of the two pairs of lovers, and, to pass the time until his wedding night, selects 'Pyramus and Thisbe' starring a re-translated Bottom after rejecting the tale of Orpheus' death among other possibilities. This play-within-a-play is subject to the derisive commentary of the courtiers, and the status distinctions between actors and audience is even more marked.

However, the lines separating high and low are not as bright as they may appear, a blurriness that again reveals itself through the lesser lyric of the ballad. Hoping to explain his 'rare vision', Bottom declares: 'I will get Peter Quince to write a ballad of this dream. It shall be called "Bottom's Dream", because it hath no bottom, and I will sing it in the latter end of a play, before the Duke. Peradventure, to make it the more gracious, I shall sing it at her death' (IV. i. 211–15). Although this ballad never gets composed, it points to the difficulty in writing off Bottom and the mechanicals. On the level of textual production and circulation, it raises questions about the proximity of ballads to genres with higher aspirations. 'Pyramus and Thisbe' has many potential sources, but its metre 'matches the version in *A Handefull of Pleasant Delites*' (Duffin 320). *A Handefull*, dating to a lost copy of 1566 and re-issued in 1575 and 1584, is unlike *Tottel's Miscellany* (1557), *A Gorgeous Gallery of Gallant Inventions* (1577), and other collections of the era in consisting entirely of already printed broadsides. Similarly, while other collections downplay their inclusion of broadsides, *A Handefull* makes no apology for inviting its readers to '[p]eruse it wel ere you passe by' if targeting the casual consumer.[8] I mention this potential link not to insist that the ballad is Shakespeare's source but rather that the possibility reminds us of the fluidity of the literary field at the time and the uncertain status of the theatre itself.

---

[8] Qtd. in Nebeker (2009) 997.

That fluidity is matched by the place of 'Pyramus' within the themes and structures of the play. Bottom puts his 'Dream' forth as a jig, the conventional song-and-dance to end 'Pyramus', which, as C. L. Barber long ago observed, acts like a jig for Shakespeare's play. Drawing on Barber to nuance recent readings emphasizing the carnivalesque energies of the play, Peter Holland notes, 'If the jig is a form of inversion then "Pyramus and Thisbe" offers inversion both of the matter of the rest of the play (into tragedy) and the manner (into farce). To perceive only one side of this inversion is to lose the force of the jig'.[9] Theseus perceives only one side: He views it merely as an expression of 'simpleness and duty' (V. i. 83), but the mechanicals perform it in strategic hopes of patronage, and however misplaced those hopes, the 'seriousness of purpose' with which they approach imaginative metamorphosis survives Theseus' famous dismissal of the 'fine frenzy' of '[t]he poet's eye'. (Holland 95; V. i. 2–22). The dream may have no bottom, but it has a Bottom in it as well as ballads.

This double vision is carried through to the actual end of the play. After more singing and dancing by the fairies, Puck excuses any offense by instructing the audience to treat the play as they would a dream. Although Puck tries to separate himself from the 'hempen homespuns' (III. i. 71), he appears in the epilogue carrying a broom, 'evok[ing] his coarse folk origins', and his concluding suggestion places the audience not so very far from Bottom's ballad, underlining the play's 'impure aesthetics'.[10] This impurity emerges out of an interplay of various ranks, including various strands of lyric, from Orphic 'frenzy' to Petrarchan lyric to ballads associated with but not limited to mechanicals, that, like Bottom in his moment of feigned courage, 'walk up and down'.

15.2 'WHO CAN SING BOTH HIGH AND LOW': SONGS, SERVANTS, AND MASTERS IN *TWELFTH NIGHT*

In *Twelfth Night*, Viola does not sing, and it is strange on many counts that she does not. First, she asks the captain to introduce her to Orsino 'as an eunuch … for I can sing, | And speak to him in many sorts of music | That will allow me very worth his service' (I. ii. 52–5). She cannot know it at this point, but this talent should fit her particularly well for serving Orsino, since the play's first lines have him famously calling for his servants to play music, 'the food of love' he hopes will cure him of his melancholy by 'surfeiting' his appetite. The song closest to Viola in the play, 'Come Away Death', also seems well-made for her, since it is sung by women: 'The spinsters, and the knitters in the sun, | And the free

[9] Peter Holland, 'Introduction', *A Midsummer Night's Dream* (Oxford: Oxford University Press, 1998) 93.
[10] Mary Ellen Lamb, *The Popular Culture of Shakespeare, Spenser, and Jonson* (New York: Routledge, 2006) 124; Grady (2008) esp. 299–302.

maids that weave their thread with bones, | Do use to chant it' (II. iv. 43–5). Moreover, its piteous love lament matches well the 'loyal cantons of contemnèd love' Viola-as-Cesario vividly imagines singing to Olivia from 'his' 'willow cabin' (I. v. 257; 259). Indeed, at one point, Orsino does call on her to perform it if the line is read in a particular way: 'Now good Cesario, but that piece of song' (II. iv. 2). And yet she does not.

Why not? One theory holds that 'the scene was revised in response to theatrical circumstances, perhaps the breaking of a boy-actor's voice'.[11] Warren and Wells claim that this Occam's razor cuts too neatly, arguing instead that not allowing Viola to vent her love for Orsino in a song intensifies the effect of her suppressing her desire and that giving it to Feste instead adds to 'its bittersweet mood' through his arch commentary on Orsino's passionate instability (75). I suggest an alternate though not exclusive explanation. With two exceptions, Shakespeare does not have women sing in his plays except when they are near death (Desdemona and Ophelia), and this is in keeping with a wider concern over women singing.[12] Even in disguise, for Viola/Cesario to sing a song of erotic longing in a public setting to a character so susceptible to music as Orsino, a character whom she longs for, would put her in dangerous proximity to the figure of the siren who frequently appears in early modern literature.[13] She may imagine doing him service through her song, but the fiction that would enable it (being a eunuch) involves a perilous feint. It would pretend that the phallic guarantor of masculinity that was never there has been taken away, made more dangerous by the fact that what *is* there within the fiction of the play, a female body, is prone to stimulate desire—and, behind this, yet another dangerous body, the homoerotically seductive one of the young male actor.

Assigning the song to Feste is more appropriate by way of a related but different logic. To sing for Orsino appears to be a sign of servitude not proper for someone of Viola's rank, whatever service she renders him as Cesario and will render him as his wife. There is a hint of rivalry between Feste and Viola at the beginning of Act III, Scene i, as they sound each other out, beginning with her observation that his fool's occupation involves music: 'Save thee, friend, and thy music. Dost thou live by thy tabor?' This initiates a series of witty exchanges in which Feste twice wrings money from his fellow 'servant', perhaps by penetrating her disguise. That she pays him and then again is not only about her place as a woman but as his social superior; this scene reminds us that if Viola has a double it is not Feste, an actual servant, but her twin brother, although the difference in their gender makes for a difference in rank, too. In other words, the agency reflected in Feste's singing, which Alexander cannily observes in Chapter 14, p. 263 is at Viola's expense paradoxically founded on his being a servant in general and in particular an 'allowed fool' (I. v. 90).

This licenses him to sing a song like 'Come Away Death' to Orsino. It appears to be the *sine qua non* of lyric solitude: The speaker's only addressee is death, and he demands no

---

[11] Roger Warren and Stanley Wells, 'Introduction', *Twelfth Night* (Oxford: Oxford University Press, 1994) 75.

[12] The two exceptions are Mariana singing (along with her boy), 'Take, O Take Those Lips Away' (*Measure for Measure*, IV. i) and the Welsh Lady's song in *1 Henry IV* (III. i).

[13] See Linda Phyllis Austern, '"Sing Againe Syren": The Female Musician and Sexual Enchantment in Elizabethan Life and Literature', *Renaissance Quarterly* 42: 3 (1989): 440–8.

flowers for his coffin, no friends to mourn him, and no monument where a heart-sick lover might repair. Yet this self-dramatizing song of the Petrarchan lover's solitary pain comes to Orsino's ears via a surprisingly low and communal medium, plebeian women who 'chant it' as they spin, knit, and weave (II. iv. 41–5). Orsino describes this imagined work song as 'old and antic', a welcome alternative to the 'light airs and recollected terms | Of these most brisk and giddy-pacèd times' (II. iv. 3, 5–6). By doing so, Orsino (if not Shakespeare) betrays an ignorance of how women's work conditions had recently changed, one of the earliest cases we have of an elite song-catcher casting a rosy glow on the laborious life-world of his source.[14] But however much women's actual work-lives appear in this song, it is presented as a lyric that turns the potential vulgarity of the work song into a universal and timeless sentiment that bridges the solitary and social and stands in contrast to merely fashionable songs.

Having sung it, Feste is rewarded as a servant should be. But as a 'licensed fool' he also has a particular sort of freedom. First, he objects to Orsino's characterization of his performance as 'pains': 'No pains, sir. I take pleasure in singing, sir' (II. iv. 67). Feste may be insisting on his own autonomy or the value of art; he sings because it pleases him. But, of course, he would not have sung this song then if not ordered to, and he makes his living in part from giving pleasure by skillfully impersonating the figures in his songs, including those who are in pain. On accepting Orsino's gratuity, he then turns on various proverbs that sum up the intersecting economies of courtship and service that structure the play: 'Truly, sir, and pleasure will be paid, one time or another' (II. iv. 69–70).

The latitude Feste enjoys is also on display in the prior scene, where he entertains Sir Toby and Sir Andrew. Paid beforehand by the pair and directed to sing a 'love song' rather than a moral one, he sings 'O Mistress Mine' (II. iii. 38–43). Its tone differs profoundly from 'Come away death'. Rather than staging a figure locked into solitude, it plays with address, as the persona tells his mistress to stop 'roaming' because 'your true love's coming', referring to himself in the third person. It turns out he's already there, 'sing[ing] both high and low', as the melody itself shows, and inviting his lover to embrace the fleeting pleasures of the present. From here, the singing becomes more participatory, as Feste, Toby, and Andrew join in on the catch 'Hold thy peace, thou knave'. It levels distinctions between fool and knight as each tells the other 'knave' to be quiet, but the reaction it catalyses also shows how songs reveal the limits of that leveling. When Maria comes to warn them that their 'caterwauling' will move Olivia to send for Malvolio to 'turn you out of doors', Toby replies with a medley of songs to put Malvolio in his place and to confirm Toby's own status as 'consanguineous' with Olivia. He uses one popular song, which survives only in a fragment, to dismiss Malvolio as a 'Peg-o'-Ramsey', quotes a popular refrain to praise himself and his fellow singers as 'merry men', and sings the first line of the broadside ballad of 'Constant Susannah' perhaps to mock Olivia's or Maria's concern (II. iii. 72–81). Feste is impressed by Sir Toby's 'admirable fooling', and joins in to insult Malvolio to his

---

[14] Fiona McNeill, 'Free and Bound Maids: Women's Work Songs and Industrial Change in the Age of Shakespeare', *Oral Traditions and Gender in Early Modern Literary Texts*, Mary Ellen Lamb and Karen Bamford (eds.), (Burlington, VT: Ashgate, 2008) 102–4.

face, adapting a ballad that appears in Robert Jones' *First Book of Airs* (II. iii. 99–108). Then the challenge from Toby: 'Art any more than a steward?' (II. iii. 109–10)

As Maria's gambit reveals, Malvolio *would* be more, and he expresses his desire to vault upwards into Olivia's bed in his coy answers to her confused queries by alluding to three popular songs, two of them bawdy: 'Please one, and please all', 'Black and Yellow', and 'To bed? Ay, sweetheart, and I'll come to thee' (III. iv. 22–9). The problem here is not that Malvolio likes smutty songs but that he is a Puritanical hypocrite who condemns others' singing but who is happy to use songs in his deluded bid to climb too high, too fast. Feste, who has no such pretensions to morality or social mobility and who is much more attuned to his audiences, is free to use song as he sees fit even when commanded to sing, often commenting wryly on the follies of the great and the would-be great, as in the songs he aims at Malvolio after the Sir Topaz scene (IV. ii).[15] He continues in that role in the curious song that ends the play. Feste follows Orsino's joyous embrace of the lovers' 'golden time'—Viola now no longer a domestic servant but a duchess-to-be—with an obscure tale of knavery, thievery, swaggering, and drunkenness, its darkness leavened with the refrains, 'With hey, ho, the wind and the rain ... the rain it raineth every day'. Having been left on stage alone, Feste turns in conclusion to acknowledge the masters who have been there all along: 'But that's all one, our play is done, | And we'll strive to please you every day (V. i. 403–4)'. Whether those in attendance find their own ugly reflections in what Roger Warren and Stanley Wells call a 'Lecher's Progress' and yet are pleased with the play is in part a test of the wily and pleasing power of Feste's songs.[16]

15.3 HISTORY, LYRIC, AND BALLAD IN 2 *HENRY IV*

Hotspur would not be pleased with Feste's songs. Out to make history, he has no time for the frivolities of lyric. When Glendower defensively observes that Percy lacks his courtly ability to 'fram[e] to the harp | Many an English ditty lovely well', he scornfully replies: 'Marry, and I am glad of it, with all my heart. | I had rather be a kitten and cry "mew" | Than one of these same metre ballad-mongers' (*1 Henry 4*, III. i. 120–1; 124–6). But Percy's anti-lyric stance, which tars it with the dirt of ballads sung and sold in the streets, actually suggests that he lacks historical vision, and this is confirmed by his failure to make history as he wishes. The joke is that he cannot be aware of his own starring role as the valiant loser in those ballad-mongers' favorites, 'The Battle of Otterbourn' and 'Chevy Chase'.

[15] For a reading that shows how various characters are judged in terms of their ability to sing and play and the contrast between these modes of communication and the elite forms of letter and emissary, see Thomas A. DuBois, '"That Strain Again!" or, *Twelfth Night*, A Folkloristic Approach', *Arv* 56 (2000): 35–56. See also ch. 5 of his *Lyric, Meaning, and Audience in the Oral Tradition of Northern Europe* (Notre Dame, IN: University of Notre Dame Press, 2006).

[16] Warren and Wells (1994) 70, 73.

More attuned to lyric's role in shaping history is Hotspur's opposite, Falstaff. In *2 Henry IV* he threatens to write a ballad if Prince John does not record his 'valor' in taking Sir John Coleville prisoner: '[L]et it be booked with the rest of this day's deeds; or, by the Lord, I will have it in a particular ballad else, with mine own picture on the top on't, Coleville kissing my foot' (IV. ii. 45–8). Like Bottom, Falstaff plans to have a ballad produced; but, slyer and more aware of the relationship between texts and political power, he uses the ballad as a weapon. It would, he threatens, make everyone else engaged in the battle seem like counterfeits ('gilt twopences') compared to him, just as he threatens in *1 Henry IV* to have ballads 'sung to filthy tunes' made on Hal and everyone else who does not do their part in the mischief at Gadshill (II. ii. 44–6).[17] Prince John does not seem exactly fearful of Falstaff's threat, but he does promise to 'better speak of you than you deserve' (*2 Henry IV*, IV. ii. 82). This seems only right, since we would be hard-pressed to rank Falstaff's happening upon Coleville as less valorous than John's imprisoning and then executing the rebels after promising that their grievances will be redressed. Sir John, then, has a right to claim a place in Prince John's 'book' of the battle, and here the ballad once again marks the wavering line between mere travesty of the high and revealing parody of it. It also shows Falstaff's awareness of the way history can be made by Rumour, who opens the play with an allegorical self-explication that includes the observation that even 'the still-discordant wav'ring multitude, | Can play upon it' (Induction 19–20). Falstaff knows that cheap print and catchy tunes help to spread musical/historical discord.

Of course, he is hoping for more than a brief mention in Prince John's report; he aims for the sort of license that comes with being an intimate of John's brother, the heir to the throne. Ballads help to articulate this dream. They appear first as Falstaff begins his assignation with Doll Tearsheet, coupling lines from 'When Arthur first in court'—a ballad celebrating the valour of Lancelot written by the 'professional' ballad-writer Thomas Deloney (first printed *c.* 1592)—with a command that a servant empty a pisspot (II. iv. 32–3). This dream of a promiscuous, grossly-embodied monarchy seems to be confirmed with the appearance of another ballad, 'King Cophetua and The Beggar Maid', which Shakespeare draws on more frequently than any other:

> PISTOL   A foutre for the world and worldlings base!
> I speak of Africa and golden joys.
> FALSTAFF   O base Assyrian knight, what is thy news?
> Let King Cophetua know the truth thereof.
> SILENCE   (*singing*)
> 'And Robin Hood, Scarlet, and John.'[18]
>
> (V. iii. 100–4)

---

[17] For other examples of the ballad as threat, see *Antony and Cleopatra* (V. ii.210–12). The threat is realized in Marlow's *Edward II* (VI. 174–5).

[18] In addition to *Love's Labour's Lost* and *2 Henry IV*, Duffin locates allusions to 'King Cophetua' in *Romeo and Juliet* and *Much Ado About Nothing* (235–6).

First published in Richard Johnson's *A Crowne Garland of Golden Roses* (1612) but clearly older than that, 'King Cophetua' tells of an African king who, scorning women, is shot by Cupid and falls in love with the first woman he sees, a beggar maid. (We might read the Titania–Bottom romance as a variation of this plot, with Oberon redirecting Cupid's arrow through his potion.) Just prior to this, Falstaff has been enjoying the country hospitality of his old acquaintance, Master Shallow, whom Falstaff privately sneers (in the Quarto of 1600) at 'as ever in the rearward of fashion', swearing to the 'overscutched' objects of his amours that 'the carmen[s'] whistle ... were his fancies or his good-nights' (III. ii. 303–4).[19] If his commentary reminds us that history can be charted by popular songs as well as by decisive battles or the machinations of great men, it is Falstaff who is left behind by the mirror of his own era's fashion, the soon-to-be Henry V. That Falstaff casts himself in the role of King Cophetua is a sign of the larger mistake he is soon to be painfully made aware of when the newly crowned Hal snubs him. In fact, he is at best the Beggar Maid in this story, the lowly favourite of an irrational monarch. But an old song can carry you only so far. Here, 'King Cophetua' indicates the limits of Falstaff's ascendance, a rough equivalent to the popular songs that Shakespeare draws on. They may please the audience and even offer the possibility of identification with low characters, but they never quite rise to the highest level.

15.4 MAD SONGS (REAL AND FEIGNED) AND JIGS IN *HAMLET*

Correction: Popular songs never rise to this level except when brought to court by a distracted maid. Ophelia's songs have for decades been a critical touchstone, and for good reason. Unusual, perhaps unique, in bringing popular songs into the exalted precincts of tragedy, Shakespeare puts his high characters in touch with the unruly energies of these songs, never to more powerful effect than in *Hamlet* as Ophelia's songs attest to her madness, the elusiveness of her character, and the corruption of the Danish court. But her songs sound different when we acknowledge that the first person to sing (or say) a ballad in the play is a man, not a maid. Ophelia's distracted singing is prefigured when Hamlet flatters Polonius' view that his madness is caused by love for his daughter by citing 'Jepha, Judge of Israel', as the broadside is titled:

HAMLET   O Jephthah, judge of Israel, what a treasure hadst thou!
POLONIUS   What a treasure had he, my lord?
HAMLET   Why,
            'One fair daughter and no more,
            The which he lovèd passing well'.

---

[19] *Henry IV, Part 2*, René Weis (ed.), (Oxford: Oxford University Press, 1998).

POLONIUS   (*aside*) Still on my daughter.
HAMLET   Am I not i'th' right, old Jephthah?
POLONIUS   If you call me Jephthah, my lord, I have a daughter that
I love passing well.
HAMLET   Nay, that follows not.
POLONIUS   What follows then, my lord?
HAMLET   Why

> 'As by lot
> God wot',

and then you know

> 'It came to pass
> As most like it was'—

the first row of the pious chanson will show you more, for look where
my abridgements come.

(II. ii. 404–23)

This is not the first lyric attached to Hamlet. Earlier in this long scene, Polonius reads to the King and Queen a stilted, brief love poem Hamlet has addressed to Ophelia in a letter as proof of his love-madness. Laertes has warned Ophelia that she must not 'with too credent ear … list his songs' (I. iii. 30) for Hamlet's importance to the state and Ophelia's relatively low status make a marriage impossible and thus any romance between them dangerous to her honour. Then, because of the very reasons Laertes adduces, one of his 'songs' is exposed to the king and queen through their chief councillor. It is impossible to tell whether he has written these lines with the knowledge that his interactions with Ophelia are being actively monitored—she reports that she has, at her father's command, refused to receive any new letters—but in either case, his poem becomes an exhibit in how the fiction of lyric privacy is subject to the prying eyes of a court ruled by a king with a guilty conscience and thus prone even more than most monarchs to using surveillance. The quatrain in question is thoroughly conventional down to its protestations of sincerity, but there is a difference between the publicity of convention and the publicity of exposure.

Subject to surveillance but needing to conceal his motives even as he temporizes about what action to take, Hamlet changes genres. He moves from love lyric to the more public orientation of the ballad, and he shifts his audience from the beloved (whether or not he imagines a paternal reader over her shoulder) to her father as well as Rosencrantz and Guildenstern, all agents of the king he aims to dethrone. The ballad in question, 'The songe of Jesphas Dowghter at his death', was registered in 1567–68; its print version is now lost but 'A proper new Ballad, intituled When Jepha Judge of Israell' is preserved in the Shirburn Manuscript.[20] The story is from Judges 11: Jephtha makes the mistake of promising that if God will grant him a victory, he will sacrifice 'the first quicke thing | Should meete with him'. That 'first quicke thing' is his daughter, and so she is sacrificed

---

[20]   *The Shirburn Ballads, 1585–1616*, ed. Andrew Clark (ed.), (Oxford: Clarendon Press, 1907) 175–6.

after bewailing her virginity for two months. Here, Hamlet appears caught up not only in his love for Ophelia but also in the ballad itself; when Polonius tries to connect himself and his daughter to the story, Hamlet bats away this clumsy attempt to pluck out the heart of his mystery by telling him 'that follows not'. Polonius takes this as an objection to his logic, but Hamlet insists instead on following the song, quoting the next lines of 'the pious chanson' to which he refers Polonius for further instruction as he greets the players. By doing so, he feeds Polonius' view of his madness while modelling the way lyric can absorb its audience, though the lyric is in this case not a love poem but a ballad about affairs of state that Hamlet cites to further the hypothesis that his mind is unfit for such affairs.

By way of 'The Mousetrap', Hamlet switches genres again to the most public of all, the staging of a tragedy, and accordingly switches audience to a more direct targeting of the king. But we are not yet done with popular song; we still need the jig. Having confirmed the Ghost's allegation through the King's appropriate identification with the regicidal villain and having earlier joked to Ophelia that he is 'your only jig-maker' (III. ii. 119), Hamlet celebrates his dress-rehearsal for revenge by properly marking the end of this embedded play with a jig of sorts, 'Why, let the stricken deer go weep' (III. ii. 259–72), and citing it as evidence of his fitness to 'get me a fellowship in a cry of players' (265–6). So the play-within-the-play is book-ended by popular songs that show how they are at once a conventional and yet disruptive element in the rough margins of the stage as a cultural institution.

The ballad's disruptive power is highlighted by the way the plot of 'Jephthah' exceeds Hamlet's intent in citing it, absorbing its analogues in a mortal coil. Unable to grasp the balladic hint, the father (Polonius) dies first after Hamlet mistakes him for Claudius, and the grief caused by this and the identity of the slayer drives the virginal Ophelia to unfeigned madness and then death. The comedic antics of Hamlet's jig are famously transformed to melancholy by the songs Ophelia sings in the wreckage generated by his strategies, as she, like Jephthah's daughter, bewails her lot. Commenting on Ophelia's songs Stephen Buhler has observed that their 'astonishing power ... derives, in part, from her ability to retrieve the ballad from the conventions of the jig'.[21] Yet if Ophelia's heartbreaking songs cut against the comedic mischief of the jig, they also carry with them some of the jig's disturbing lowness, shocking the courtly figures with songs not only mourning her father's death but also telling of maids being 'tumbled' (IV. v. 62). Their uncanny power is attested to by the unnamed gentleman who reports on them before Ophelia comes on stage: 'Her speech is nothing, | Yet the unshapèd use of it doth move | The hearers to collection' (IV. v. 7–9). Gertrude immediately picks up on the threat portended by this solicitation for her hearers to complete her fragmentary songs according to 'their own thoughts'(IV. v. 10): it will produce '[d]angerous conjectures in ill-breeding minds' (IV. v. 15). In the upending of amatory lyric and the growing danger

[21] Stephen Buhler, 'Musical Shakespeares: Attending to Ophelia, Juliet, and Desdemona', *The Cambridge Companion to Shakespeare and Popular Culture*, Robert Shaughnessy (ed.), (Cambridge: Cambridge University Press, 2007) 162.

to Claudius' rule, the 'nothing' of Ophelia's utterance, which contains within it the musical pun 'noting', might unwittingly stimulate (or wittingly exploit?) the associative power of song to multiply discontent, a lyric parallel to the restive 'rabble' who put Laertes forth as their choice for king (IV. v. 100–6). She drafts her hearers into her songs, telling them, 'pray you mark', enjoining them to answer others by repeating 'Tomorrow is Saint Valentine's Day', and finally instructing Laertes to sing 'Down, a-down' (IV. v. 28; 45–6; 171). They are 'nothing sure', a provocation to sympathy and even conspiracy, punctuated by 'her winks and nods and gestures' (IV. v. 13; 11).

But if the songs echo to some degree Hamlet's political machinations, they signify primarily in terms of pathos. Unlike Hamlet, Ophelia does not seem to be feigning madness, and unlike Hamlet she does not have other genres at her command. Plucked from a tide of popular song by a mind not quite itself, her fragments travesty the fiction of lyric privacy more completely than Hamlet's earlier lines to her, giving vent to her agonies in a barely coded way, a pain ultimately caused by the sins, at once familial and political, at the heart of the Danish court. In the end, her image is sanitized by Gertrude's lyric tableau, which pictures her 'chant[ing] snatches of old tunes' (IV. vii. 149) as she drowns. Here, the violence and death of the songs we hear directly from Ophelia's lips are absent—the Second Quarto has 'laudes' instead of 'tunes', which turns her into a hymn-singer—as she becomes a *genius loci* of the brook alongside which she once gathered poetic and floral garlands, 'a creature native and indued | Unto that element' (151–2). This, however, does not erase what the audience has already seen and heard.

As for Hamlet, his fate is foreshadowed by the play's last song. Sung by the grave-digger, it is a work-song that reverses Orsino's appropriation. Where the duke brings an 'old and antic' piece sung by 'spinsters and knitters' into the court, the grave-digger sings his mangled version of an aristocrat's concession to the ravages of time (V. i. 61–4; 71–4; 91–4)—Lord Vaux's 'The Aged Lover Renounceth Love', first printed in *Tottel's Miscellany* and shortly thereafter as a broadside (1563–4). There is no sense that the gravedigger is aware of his socially elevated source, and this seems in keeping with Hamlet's shock that he would sing while he digs graves, an insensitivity unthinkable to 'the daintier sense' of 'the hand of little employment' (65–70). A daintier ear would catch the pathos of Vaux's speaker as he appears to muse lyrically to himself about the defalcations of old age. But, despite these more refined thoughts, the levelling force of the clown's performance is in keeping with Vaux's sentiments, which in the end are turned epitaphically outward to the universal 'ye' made of 'clay'. As it turns out, the gravedigger's song prefigures Hamlet's own sententious couplets about the mortality of Caesar and everyone else (208–11). What Hamlet does not yet know is that his own death is soon to come, when he will be lamented with dignified oratory far removed from the demotic accents of the clown. But in a possibility that would scandalize an audience today: 'It is tempting to ask whether the three corpses [left on stage at the end of the play] might not have sprung back to life to dance a final jig'.[22]

---

[22] Andrew Gurr, *The Shakespeare Company, 1594–1642* (Cambridge: Cambridge University Press, 2004) 75.

15.5 THE SEDUCTIONS OF PASTORAL AND AUTOLYCUS' LYRIC WARES IN *THE WINTER'S TALE*

Where popular songs presage and punctuate the tragedy in *Hamlet*, in *The Winter's Tale* they help to transform tragedy into renewal but also to complicate pastoral structures and lyric temptations. In the sheep-shearing scene (IV. iv), Camillo and Polixenes have disguised themselves as shepherds in order to spy on Florizel, who in his pursuit of Perdita seems to have forgotten that aristocrats should only play at pastoral. Or, to cite William Empson's *aperçu*, Florizel has forgotten that pastoral is 'about' 'the people' but neither 'by' nor 'for' them.[23] His infatuation is clear from his forays into love lyric, here refreshed by a pastoral landscape that makes his praise appear unpremeditated: 'When you do dance, I wish you | A wave o'th' sea …'. (IV. iv. 135–46). Of course, 'covert pastoral' (Empson again) goes the aristocratic men one better, since Perdita turns out to be a princess who, unbeknownst to everybody, is also disguised as a shepherdess. At stake in this scene, then, is the fate of both kingdoms—in pastoral terms, whether the breach can be healed between the 'twinned lambs' (I. ii. 69), Polixenes and Leontes. Added to this is the often noted debate over the relationship between nature and art that encapsulates the desires of pastoral; Polixenes defends art as a supplement of nature that itself springs from nature, and Perdita, even while she resists his assertion out of concern for the suspect morality of 'painting', embodies the marriage of the two in the cultivated innocence of her reply.

After the rural sport of the satyr dance, Autolycus makes his appearance and challenges these pastoral assumptions on multiple levels through his ballads. These are not the quaint, 'antic song[s]' sung by 'the spinsters and the knitters in the sun' as fondly recalled by Orsino. We already know that Autolycus' 'traffic is sheets' (IV. iii. 23), which associates the clothes lines he pilfers with the linen-based sheets on which broadsides are printed. We know, too, that he was once Florizel's servant. Unlike Feste, he is no longer part of any household, a move into the dangerous freedom of vagabondage, as he, like his ballads, circulates swiftly and enters into fugitive exchanges with those he happens to meet. His entrance in the sheep-shearing scene is preceded by the breathless report of a servant who praises the rapidity of his singing—'faster than you'll tell money' (IV. iv. 185)—a phrase that allies him with a commercial world that would seem alien to pastoral. His songs are also tied to a 'bawdry' unlike the innocence of Perdita or the more straightforward sexuality of the satyr dance, encoded in the 'delicate burdens of dildos and fadings, "jump her and thump her"' and 'Whoop, do me no harm, good man' that the servant naively takes as avoiding licentiousness rather than winking at it (192–201). His songs match up well with this advertisement and in so doing also show

---

[23] William Empson, *Some Versions of Pastoral* (1935; Norfolk, CT: New Directions, 1960) 6.

that they are not particularly interested in categories constructed by the pastoral debate over art and nature. One testifies to 'how a usurer's wife was brought to bed of twenty money-bags at a burden' and another tells of an enormous fish that sings a song against cold-hearted maids (260–79). When Mopsa and Dorcas ask if they are true, Autolycus insists that the latter has been attested to by the signatures of five justices and the former by the midwife, 'one Mistress Taleporter' (267–9), thereby supplementing print with the 'authority' of handwriting and oral gossip, as the midwife's name richly combines feminine tale-telling with bawdry, marketing female as 'tail'.

Although Autolycus' songs are presented in part as jokes on the credulity of peasants who, to cite an oft-quoted phrase, 'love a ballad in print, alife, for then we are sure they are true' (258–9), they cannot be confined so easily to simple country folk. As Aaron Kitch has shown, the ballad on the usurer's wife, which is part of a sub-genre of 'monstrous birth broadsides', speaks to the play's central concern with the threat of bastardry to political and representational stability.[24] An analogous interpenetration of high and low on the level of text is revealed in the ballad actually performed by Autolycus, Mopsa, and Dorcas, 'Get You Hence'. It has been attributed to Robert Johnson, lutenist to George Carey, the Lord Chamberlain, and then to King James and Prince Henry; Johnson is also the author of 'Full Fathom Five' and 'Where the Bee Sucks'. Autolycus seeks to hook his would-be purchasers by observing that 'There's scarce a maid westward but she sings it', and Dorcas replies that '[W]e had the tune on't a month ago' (287–92). Shakespeare thus takes a song written by a professional court musician, perhaps for the play itself, and imagines the tune already familiar in the countryside. So in their textual ontology, their themes, and their mode of circulation, these songs refuse the bifurcations typically woven into pastoral, introducing a third, unmoored social identity into the dyad of aristocrat and peasant, and subtended by an unpictured but nonetheless present urban world of commodified textual exchange that complicates the opposition of court and country.

At the end of the play, Shakespeare attempts again to separate his idea of art and his own work from the broadside. Autolycus is now off stage, having promised to 'amend [his] life' to Perdita's newly elevated but still boorish foster-father and foster-brother (V. ii. 152–3). His favored genre is also explicitly set aside and surpassed: Perdita's return and the reconciliation of Polixenes and Leontes are so remarkable, according to an unnamed gentleman, 'that ballad-makers cannot be able to express it' (V. ii. 24–5). Then we have the ocular proof of Hermione's statue come to life, a 'true' wonder sanctioned by the patriarchal state that sets aside the unstable legitimacy of the printing press for 'the institution of the theater itself' (Kitch 64). By this theatrical magic, king and queen are reconciled as are 'the twinned lambs', royal shepherd and shepherdess are married, and art is confirmed again as the powerful supplement of nature.

Yet the difficulty in effecting this complete separation is indicated by the very line that precedes the attempt to set the play beyond the expressive powers of ballad-makers. One gentleman asks another, 'The news, Ruggiero!' (V. ii. 20–1), and Duffin has persuasively

---

[24] Aaron Kitch, 'Bastards and Broadsides in The Winter's Tale', *Renaissance Drama* (2001): 43–71.

linked this line to a broadside ballad on jealousy sung to the tune 'Rogero' (342–5). The persistence of ballads in Shakespeare, whether loudly sung, referred to in passing, or silently drawn on for plots, shows that it is not at all obvious that one can distinguish definitively the mediations of high art from the Clown's taste for a ballad 'if it be doleful matter merrily set down, or a very pleasant thing indeed and sung lamentably' (IV. iv. 188–91) or that one can separate the awestruck courtly audience of Hermione's revivification from the peasants absorbed in the song Autolycus has sold, making them prime targets for thievery—'No hearing, no feeling but my sir's song, and admiring the nothing of it' (IV. iv. 613–14). Those who have attended Shakespeare's plays for the last four hundred and more years have not, we hope, felt that they have had their pockets picked. But in this last figure of the great temptations of lesser lyric and its 'nothing'/ noting of an audience enraptured by the performance of a popular song cheaply (and dearly) bought, we can see why Shakespeare turns to this vital genre so often and why he also seeks at once to draw on and to distance himself from its dangerous commonality.

Select Bibliography

Buhler, Stephen (2007) 'Musical Shakespeares: Attending to Ophelia, Juliet, and Desdemona' In Robert Shaughnessy (ed.) *The Cambridge Companion to Shakespeare and Popular Culture* (Cambridge: Cambridge University Press, 2007) 150–74.

Chess, Simone (2010) 'Shakespeare's Plays and Broadside Ballads'. *Literature Compass* 7: 9, 773–85.

Dubois, Thomas A. (2006) *Lyric, Meaning, and Audience in the Oral Tradition of Northern Europe.* (South Bend, IN: University of Notre Dame Press).

DuBrow, Heather (2008) *The Challenges of Orpheus: Lyric Poetry and Early Modern Lyric.* (Baltimore: The Johns Hopkins University Press).

Duffin, Ross W. (2004) *Shakespeare's Songbook.* (New York: W. W. Norton).

Fox, Adam (2000) *Oral and Literate Culture in England, 1500–1700.* (Oxford: Clarendon Press).

Henderson, Diane E. (1995) *Passion Made Public: Elizabethan Lyric, Gender, and Performance.* (Urbana, IL: University of Illinois Press).

Lamb, Mary Ellen (2006) *The Popular Culture of Shakespeare, Spenser, and Jonson.* (New York: Routledge).

Marsh, Christopher (2010) *Music and Society in Early Modern England.* (Cambridge: Cambridge University Press).

Nebeker, Eric (2009) 'Broadside Ballads, Miscellanies, and the Lyric in Print'. *ELH* 76, 4: 989–1013.

Smith, Bruce R. (2006) 'Shakespeare's Residuals: The Circulation of Ballads in Cultural Memory', in Stuart Gillespie and Neil Rhodes (eds) *Shakespeare and Elizabethan Popular Culture* (London: Arden Shakespeare) 193–217.

PART IV

SPEAKING ON STAGE

CHAPTER 16

....

SHAKESPEARE'S
DRAMATIC VERSE LINE

....

ABIGAIL ROKISON

In *As You Like It,* Jaques, having partaken in a prose exchange with Rosalind, disdainfully greets Orlando:

ORLANDO   Good day and happiness, dear Rosalind.
JAQUES   Nay, then, God b'wi'you, an you talk in blank
           verse. (*As You Like It*, IV. i. 28–30)

This exchange seems pertinent in a discussion of Shakespeare's dramatic verse line, since the humour inherent in Jaques' response is dependent on the ability of an audience to distinguish between a line of verse and a line of prose. It thus presupposes an understanding on the part of a Renaissance audience of the use of the two different mediums in drama; their capacity to hear the changes from verse to prose and vice-versa, and the actors' ability to distinguish between the two forms in their delivery.

What distinguishes blank verse from prose in Shakespeare's work is its division into lines—often blank verse lines, of which Orlando's is a suitably regular example. Using examples from Shakespeare's early, middle, and late plays (those written pre-1600, between 1600 and 1606, and from 1607 onwards) and from his tragedies, comedies, and histories, this chapter charts developments and establishes patterns in Shakespeare's verse line across the duration and genres of his dramatic writing. Looking at incidences of end-stopping and enjambment, mid-line breaks, shared lines, short lines, and long lines, I consider the potential dramatic function of these various forms. In doing so, I look at assertions made by modern theatre practitioners about the way in which Shakespeare's lineation and punctuation provide actors with clues as to the interpretation of characters or scenes.

16.1 END STOPPING, ENJAMBMENT, AND MID-LINE BREAKS

In Shakespeare's early dramatic verse there is a regular correspondence between verse-line and phrase. As Russ McDonald notes—'the lines are mostly end-stopped' and 'some form of terminal punctuation ends the lines':[1]

> PROTEUS   He after honour hunts, I after love.
> He leaves his friends to dignify them more,
> I leave myself, my friends, and all, for love.
> Thou, Julia, thou hast metamorphosed me,
> Made me neglect my studies, lose my time,
> War with good counsel, set the world at naught;
> Made wit with musing weak, heart sick with thought.
>
> (*The Two Gentlemen of Verona*, I. i. 63–9)

This is the poetic structure that Shakespeare inherited from his predecessors in Tudor poetry, which 'treated the iambic pentameter as the sum of two phrases, the first of four syllables, the second of six'.[2] As George T. Wright notes, even as poets began to recognize in the early 1590s that 'the line need not pause after the fourth syllable', creating more syntactically varied verse, they continued to use enjambment with 'considerable restraint'.[3] The example cited above from *The Two Gentlemen of Verona* (probably Shakespeare's earliest play, dating from 1589–91),[4] corresponds with this tendency, containing some variation in line breaks (although most occur at the mid-line point, after either the fourth, fifth, or sixth syllable) and a high preponderance of end-stopping.

It is notoriously difficult to establish precise statistics for the incidence of enjambment in Shakespeare's work, since, as illustrated by E. K. Chambers, critics disagree over what precisely constitutes an overflow of sense. The percentage of overflowing lines in *Coriolanus*, for example, is given by G. König as 46 per cent and H. Conrad as 37 per cent—a quite substantial difference.[5] However, irrespective of their slightly differing criteria and the resulting differences in some of their percentages, the statistics presented by both critics indicate a marked increase in overflows from *The Two Gentlemen of Verona* (12 per cent König; 9 per cent Conrad) to *Measure for Measure* (23 per cent König and Conrad) to *The Tempest* (42 per cent König; 37 per cent

---

[1] Russ McDonald, *Shakespeare and the Arts of Language* (Oxford: Oxford University Press, 2001) 91.
[2] George T. Wright, *Shakespeare's Metrical Art* (Berkeley: University of California Press, 1988) 207.
[3] Wright (1988) 208–9.
[4] Wells and Taylor, (2005) ix.
[5] E. K. Chambers, *William Shakespeare: A Study of Facts and Problems*, 2 vols (Oxford: Clarendon Press, 1930) i.401.

Conrad),[6] enjambment gradually becoming, as Wright notes, 'the rule rather than the exception'.[7]

Along with an increase in enjambment, we find in Shakespeare's verse an increasing tendency, as noted by Ants Oras, to introduce multiple and late line breaks, the number of strong pauses increasing, according to Oras' tables, from 118 in *The Comedy of Errors* to 642 in *Hamlet* to 1227 in *The Winter's Tale*.[8] Oras cites as 'strong pauses' those that are 'shown by punctuation marks other than commas'.[9] There is, however, as with enjambment, some complication over the precise identification of such 'strong pauses', since their perception is largely dependent on punctuation, which varies from edition to edition.

Although it is true that the early verse tends to exhibit a 'lineal regularity' and 'aural uniformity', and the later verse a 'metrical variety' and subordination of 'the regular beat to the semantic energies of the sentence',[10] there is, within these general patterns, significant variation in the incidence of enjambment, end-stopping, and inter-lineal pauses within speeches of differing mood and tone.[11] In public orations and measured summations one frequently finds a high incidence of end-stopping, and infrequency of line-breaks, even in the later plays such as *Coriolanus*, in which Aufidius' final summation is mostly end-stopped and the lines divided no more than once, and often at the mid-line point:

> AUFIDIUS   Take him up.
> Help three o'th' chiefest soldiers; I'll be one.
> Beat thou the drum, that it speak mournfully.
> Trail your steel pikes. Though in this city he
> Hath widowed and unchilded many a one,
> Which to this hour bewail the injury,
> Yet he shall have a noble memory. Assist.
>
> (V. vi. 147–54)

By contrast, in speeches in which characters are distressed, highly emotional, or uncertain, there is a greater tendency towards enjambment and more frequent and varied internal line-breaks, which, whilst not as extreme as in the later plays, is certainly visible from as early as *Romeo and Juliet* as evidenced in Juliet's highly agitated 'potion' speech:

> O, look! Methinks I see my cousin's ghost
> Seeking out Romeo that did spit his body
> Upon a rapier's point. Stay, Tybalt, Stay!
> Romeo, Romeo, Romeo! Here's drink. I drink to thee.
>
> (IV. iii. 54–7)

---

[6] Chambers (1930) i.401.

[7] Wright (1988) 213.

[8] Ants Oras, *Pause Patterns in Elizabethan and Jacobean Drama: An Experiment in Prosody* (Gainesville: U of Florida Press, 1960) 74–5.

[9] Oras (1960) 3.

[10] McDonald (2001) 92,104.

[11] Abigail Rokison, *Shakespearean Verse Speaking: Text and Theatre Practice* (Cambridge: Cambridge University Press, 2010) 168–9.

The dramatic function of end-stopping, enjambment, preservation, or fracturing of the verse-line is, of course, only fully discernible in performance, and is dependent on the actors' methods of delivery. There are two main theories regarding the speaking of the verse-line current in the modern British theatre. The first, of which the most famous advocate is director Peter Hall, is that the verse structure provides the phrasing. Hall insists on 'the integrity of the single line of Shakespearean verse',[12] and based on this makes two principal assertions: that each line should be spoken without a break, and that the actor must take 'a tiny sense break (*not* a stop) at the end of each line'.[13] The second theory, advocated by influential voice practitioner Patsy Rodenburg, amongst others, is that the grammatical sense takes precedence over the verse line in terms of phrasing a speech. Rodenburg bemoans the 'tendency to stop at the end of a line regardless of whether the end of the thought has been reached', asserting that the actor should phrase with the 'thought' as opposed to the verse, the thought being, according to Rodenburg, 'signposted by punctuation'.[14] This is, as already mentioned, immediately problematic, since much of the punctuation, even of the earliest printed texts—the quartos published during Shakespeare's lifetime—is likely to have been compositorially or editorially imposed and is unlikely to be indicative of authorial practice.

Despite the absence of any complete extant theatrical manuscript in Shakespeare's hand, the three sheets of *The Book of Sir Thomas More* known as Hand D are widely believed to be a Shakespearean holograph.[15] The punctuation of Hand D is extremely sparse. In sixty-nine lines of iambic pentameter speeches assigned to More on Fols. 8b and 9a,[16] there are only twenty-four commas, three semicolons, and six full stops, an average of 0.5 marks of punctuation per line. If these pages are Shakespeare's, then it seems reasonable to assume that a similarly scant method of punctuation might have been found in his other manuscripts. Even if Hand D is not the work of Shakespeare, it remains of interest in providing some indication of styles of punctuation found in Elizabethan manuscripts, particularly when considered alongside the work of the writers known as Hands A, B, and C in *The Book of Sir Thomas More*, in which the punctuation is similarly sparse.[17]

However, although the punctuation of Shakespeare's manuscripts is likely to have been far scarcer than that of any of the printed texts, there are also problems with Hall's assertion that punctuation internal to a verse line should be completely disregarded. Comments in Renaissance grammars and prosodic treatises provide an indication of the perceived function of punctuation as a guide to breathing and

---

[12] Ron Rosenbaum, 'Peter Hall Unveils "The Naked Shakespeare"', *New York Observer*, 2 April 2001, <http://www.observer.com/node/44209>.

[13] Peter Hall, *Shakespeare's Advice to the Players* (London: Oberon, 2003) 29.

[14] Patsy Rodenburg, *Speaking Shakespeare* (London: Methuen, 2002) 119.

[15] Vittorio Gabrieli and Giorgio Melchiori (eds), *Sir Thomas More* (Manchester University Press, 1990) 23.

[16] W. W. Greg (ed.), *The Book of Sir Thomas More* (Oxford: Malone Society, 1911) 76–7.

[17] Greg (1911) 66–93 (*passim*).

pausing when reading or speaking a text aloud, and thus, a playwright, or indeed scribe, transcribing lines for an actor to speak, might expect them to observe the marks included, however sparse. In the earliest grammar in English—John Hart's *An Orthographie* (1569)—Hart asserts that the purpose of 'pointing' (punctuation) is 'to give the reader knowledge the nearest a man may to pronounce the writing, as the writer would speake it'.[18] In the Elizabethan period, punctuation was, as Anthony Graham-White explains, 'primarily rhetorical', becoming increasingly grammatical 'with the development of printing', the punctuation of the Shakespeare Folio (1623) being 'noticeably fuller and more grammatical than that of the quartos of some twenty years earlier'.[19] However, even in Ben Jonson's *The English Grammar*, written in 1623, emphasis is placed on the rhetorical role of punctuation. Jonson describes punctuation as a 'meanes, whereby men pausing a pretty while, the whole speech might never the worse be understood'.[20]

George Puttenham's comments in his *Art of English Poesie* are of particular interest, not only for their discussion of punctuation, but also of caesural pauses and line integrity in verse. Puttenham defines the three marks of punctuation—comma, colon, and full stop—as 'three maner of pauses' indicative of where the speaker should breathe. Drawing parallels between these three marks and the 'staies or easements' on a traveller's journey, he relates the comma to a quick break on horseback for 'a cup of beere or wine', the colon to an hour long stop for refreshment at noon, and the full stop to a break at night for rest before the next day. Particularly significant for this study is Puttenham's next comment that 'our Poet when he hath made one verse, hath as it were finished one dayes iourney, & the while easeth him selfe with one baite at the least, which is a *Comma* or *Cesure* in the mid way'.[21] This indicates Puttenham's perception of the end of the verse line as a break equivalent to a full stop, and the caesura, or mid-line break, as equivalent to a comma. Puttenham was writing in 1589, towards the beginning of Shakespeare's writing career, and it is perhaps not surprising to find him insisting on the integrity of the verse line; however, in 1610 Dudley North, in the dedication to his *A Forest of Varieties*, writes that 'it cannot bee good in limited lines, which are a purposed pause to the voice, to carry with a counter-time the period of the sense to the body of the next line',[22] suggesting an ongoing perception of the line-ending as indicative of a pause, even if by the 17th century many poets were, contrary to North's recommendations, running the grammatical phrase across the line-endings.

If then, the line-ending was regarded as indicative of some form of punctuation, the question arises as to how Shakespeare exploits this tension between line-ending and

[18] John Hart, *An Orthographie* (London: W. Serres, 1569) Gi v.
[19] Anthony Graham-White, 'Elizabethan Punctuation and the Actor: *Gammer Gurton's Needle* as a Case Study', *Theatre Journal* 34, 1 (March 1982): 96.
[20] Ben Jonson, *The English Grammar* (London, 1640) 74–5.
[21] George Puttenham, *The Arte of English Poesie* (London, Richard Field, 1589) Book 2, ch. 4, 61–2.
[22] Dudley North, *A Forest of Varieties*, Part 1 (London: R. Coates, 1645) 3.

phrase-ending and to what dramatic effect. If we take Juliet's 'potion' speech, as cited above, if the actor takes a breath or observes a small break after 'ghost' and 'body', the ungrammatical pauses may give the impression of breathlessness and panic as Juliet sees the ghost of her cousin Tybalt. A pause at the end of a verse line throws emphasis onto the words that follow, and, in the case of 'spit his body | Upon a rapier's point', may be used to emphasize the method of Tybalt's death, and suggest Juliet's horror at it. Clearly the consistent observation of line-endings with a pause would become monotonous; however, in places, an ungrammatical pause created by a line-ending might prove a useful tool of characterization. Equally, the short phrases in this speech, if marked with a breath or pause, may add effectively to the sense of Juliet's breathless agitation; however, an exclusive adherence to the punctuation over the line-ending is in danger of making the speech sound like prose, a form which Shakespeare uses in deliberate contrast to verse for specific dramatic effect.

16.2 SHARED LINES

One of the most common variations in Shakespeare's dramatic line is the shared verse line, in which the line is divided between two or more characters. There is a notable increase in the number of shared lines from Shakespeare's early to late work,[23] although once again, precise statistics are difficult to establish. The indentation of the second part of a shared line in order to indicate metrical continuity originated with George Steevens' 1793 edition of Shakespeare's work, and whilst the presence of many shared lines is uncontroversial, there are instances of editorial dispute, particularly in cases where two short lines when linked would form a line of more than eleven syllables or, as will be discussed, when three short lines succeed one another.

The most common assertion made by theatre practitioners in relation to shared lines is that they demand metrical continuity in performance, with the second actor coming in on cue, an assertion that makes sense in terms of maintaining the aural perception of the verse. According to John Barton, the structure functions 'as if Shakespeare had written in the stage direction, "don't pause here"'.[24] Theatre practitioners also make assertions about the intended dramatic effect of shared lines, invariably asserting that they are indicative of a 'sharpness of verbal exchange'—'heated' or 'frantic' conversation in which 'the speakers jump in almost interrupting each other'.[25]

There is, of course, a precedent for the use of stichomythia (alternating half-line exchanges) 'to render intense debate ... or interrogation' in Classical Greek and

[23] Rokison (2010) 128.
[24] John Barton, *Playing Shakespeare* (London: Methuen, 1984) 32.
[25] Cicely Berry, *The Actor and his Text* (London: Harrap, 1987) 68; Patsy Rodenburg, *The Actor*

Roman drama.[26] However, in Shakespeare's plays, the dramatic function of shared lines is largely dependent on the period of composition, the context of the passage, and the structure of the verse. In Shakespeare's early plays, where end-stopped pentameters are the norm, shared lines have a more obvious aural impact, creating the impression of increased rapidity, particularly when coinciding with urgent or confrontational dialogue. For example in *The Taming of the Shrew,* where most of the speeches are comprised of full pentameters, the sudden preponderance of shared lines in Petruccio and Katherine's first encounter adds to the combative tone of the exchange:

PETRUCCIO   What, you mean my face?
KATHERINE   Well aimed of such a young one.
PETRUCCIO   Now, by Saint George, I am too young for you.
KATHERINE   Yet you are withered.
PETRUCCIO   'Tis with cares.
KATHERINE   I care not.

(*The Taming of the Shrew,* II. i. 232–4)

In the later plays, however, where shared verse lines become the norm, for most speeches ending in a half line completed by the next speaker, the aural impact of the structure is perhaps less evident.

Three distinct types of shared line are discernible in Shakespeare's work—those composed of individual short lines, those that link a single short line with a longer speech, and those that link two longer speeches—and a clear distinction may be drawn between the aural, and hence dramatic, effect of these different forms. Shared lines consisting of single short lines are often formed of questions and answers, commands, and exclamations, frequently producing an impression of terseness or urgency, an impression intensified when shared lines are formed of more than two parts as in the final line of the Katherine and Petruccio exchange, above, or when multiple shared lines occur in swift succession, as in this example from *Coriolanus*:

AUFIDIUS   Insolent villain!
ALL THE CONSPIRATORS   Kill, kill, kill, kill, kill him!
LORDS   Hold, hold, hold, hold!
AUFIDIUS   My noble masters, hear me speak.
FIRST LORD   O Tullus!
SECOND LORD   Thou hast done a deed whereat
Valour will weep.

(*Coriolanus*, V. vi. 130–3)

Speaks (London: Methuen, 1997) 201; Kristin Linklater, *Freeing Shakespeare's Voice* (New York: Theatre Communications, 1992) 166.
 [26] Alex Preminger and T. V. F. Brogan (eds), *The New Princeton Encyclopedia of Poetry and Poetics* (Princeton: Princeton University Press, 1993) 1214.

When a single short line links with a longer speech, it is similarly frequently exclamatory, interrogatory, or imperative, and often appears interjectory, as in Cymbeline's angry outburst in the midst of Innogen's self-defence:

INNOGEN   No, I rather added
     A lustre to it.
CYMBELINE   O thou vile one!
INNOGEN   Sir,
     It is your fault that I have loved Posthumus.

(*Cymbeline*, I. i. 143–5)

However, the aural effect of shared lines formed by the linking of two longer speeches is quite different, particularly in the later plays, like *The Winter's Tale*, in which over 90 per cent of speeches consist of or end in a half-line.[27] The division of a line between two characters seems more frequently designed to maintain a fluidity to the dialogue than to indicate brusque or aggressive conversation:

POLIXINES   Your guest then, madam.
     To be your prisoner should import offending,
     Which is for me less easy to commit
     Than you to punish.
HERMIONE   Not your jailer then,
     But your kind hostess. Come. I'll question you
     Of my lord's tricks and yours when you were boys.
     You were pretty lordlings then?
POLIXINES   We were, fair Queen[.]

(*The Winter's Tale*, I. ii. 57–63)

16.3 SHORT LINES

The most common assertion made about short lines, by theatre practitioners, editors, and critics, is that they imply a pause in the dialogue, roughly equivalent to the number of missing syllables. According to Hall, 'if a pause is wanted, Shakespeare leaves the pentameter incomplete. The silence is written as surely as it is in Pinter'.[28] Similarly, Simon Palfrey and Tiffany Stern assert that 'short speech units are always prompts for action', and 'a rule of thumb can be identified whereby any 'missing' stress or syllable in the actor's iambic line implies a pause of roughly equal length'.[29]

---

[27] Rokison (2010) 131.
[28] Hall, *Exposed by the Mask* (London: Oberon, 2000) 54–5.
[29] Simon Palfrey and Tiffany Stern, *Shakespeare in Parts* (Oxford: Oxford University Press, 2007) 346.

This commonly held assumption is one which I contest in relation to most forms of short line, based on evidence from Renaissance theatre practice and an analysis of the context of short lines in Shakespeare's work.[30] Although Wright makes some distinction between short lines 'that come at the end of a verse speech' and 'the anomalous short line, either within a speech, or at its beginning, or as a separate spoken line',[31] I would argue that there are in fact four distinct types of short line: the single, isolated short line, the final short line that ends a speech, the initial short line that begins a speech, and the internal short line that comes in the middle of a speech, all of which can be seen in this passage from Act II, Scene iv, *Measure for Measure*:

```
SERVANT    One Isabella, a sister, desires access to you.
ANGELO     Teach her the way. O heavens,              [ INITIAL SHORT LINE]
     Why does my blood thus muster to my heart,
     Making both it unable for itself,
     And dispossessing all my other parts
     Of necessary fitness?                            [ INTERNAL SHORT LINE]
     So play the foolish throngs with one that swoons—
     Come all to help him, and so stop the air
     By which he should revive—and even so
     The general subject to a well-wished king
     Quit their own part and, in obsequious fondness,
     Crowd to his presence, where their untaught love
     Must needs appear offence.
     How now, fair maid?                Enter Isabella.
ISABELLA    I am come to know your pleasure.          [ SINGLE SHORT LINE]
ANGELO     That you might know it would much better please me
     Than to demand what 'tis. Your brother cannot live.
ISABELLA    Even so. Heaven keep your honour.         [ SINGLE SHORT LINE]
ANGELO     Yet may he live a while, and it may be
     As long as you or I. Yet he must die.
ISABELLA    Under your sentence?                      [ SINGLE SHORT LINE]
ANGELO     Yea.                                       [ SINGLE SHORT LINE]
ISABELLA    When, I beseech you?—that in his reprieve,
     Longer, or shorter, he may be so fitted
     That his soul sicken not.                        [ FINAL SHORT LINE]
ANGELO     Ha, fie, these filthy vices! …
```

(II. iv. 18–42)

Of major significance in considering the dramatic function of the various types of short line is the Renaissance practice of working from cue-parts. Although Edward Alleyn's part for the role of 'Orlando' in *Orlando Furioso* is famously the only extant professional Renaissance actor's part, the Harvard manuscript Thr. MS 10.1, contains four parts from

[30] Rokison (2010) 181–3.
[31] Wright (1988) 121–2.

academic plays thought to have been performed at Oxford in around 1616–18, all of which are similar in format to Alleyn's. All five parts consist of the speeches for the actor concerned, each preceded by a brief cue consisting of a horizontal stroke followed by the last few words spoken by the previous speaker.

The practice of working from parts has significant implications for the delivery of the verse. For modern actors, working from complete texts, the metrical connection of their lines to those of others in a scene is easily visible. However, the metrical structure of a scene becomes extremely difficult to discern when working from a part. If we return to the section from *Measure for Measure*, cited above, this is what the cue part for the actor playing Angelo might have looked like:

SERVANT ——— access to you.
ANGELO ——— Teach her the way. O heavens,
    Why does my blood thus muster to my heart,
    Making both it unable for itself,
    And dispossessing all my other parts
    Of necessary fitness?
    So play the foolish throngs with one that swoons—
    Come all to help him, and so stop the air
    By which he should revive——and even so
    The general subject to a well-wished king
    Quit their own part and, in obsequious fondness,
    Crowd to his presence, where their untaught love
    Must needs appear offence. How now, fair maid.
ISABELLA ——— your pleasure.
ANGELO ——— That you might know it would much better please me
    Than to demand what 'tis. Your brother cannot live.
ISABELLA ——— your honour.
ANGELO ——— Yet may he live a while, and it may be
    As long as you, or I. Yet he must die.
ISABELLA ——— your sentence?
ANGELO ——— Yea.
ISABELLA ——— sicken not.
ANGELO ——— Ha, fie, these filthy vices! [...]

(*Measure for Measure*, II. iv. 18–42)

There is, as we can see, no way for the actor playing Angelo to distinguish between a full cue line such as the Servant's 'access to you', and short cue lines such Isabella's 'your pleasure', 'your sentence', and 'sicken not', and hence no way for him to make a decision where to leave a metrical pause. The only short line clearly visible to him from looking at his part is the internal short line—'of necessary fitness'. Although it is possible that the actor might have recognized the distinctions between long and short cues once he began to perform the scene, given the limited rehearsal time afforded actors in the Renaissance theatre, and the fact that by the time the actor came to perform with his fellow actors he would have already committed the role to memory,[32] it seems unlikely that he would then have begun altering his delivery accordingly.

Evidence from cue-parts, suggesting that single and final short lines are unlikely to be indicative of a pause, is confirmed most convincingly by the nature of many of the lines that follow them. Whilst the placement of a pause in delivery is always a matter for the actor or director's discretion, in a number of instances these lines are followed by what are clearly immediate responses, where the insertion of a pause makes no dramatic sense:

> BOLINGBROKE   My gracious uncle—
> YORK   Tut, tut, grace me no grace, nor uncle me no uncle,
>
> (*Richard II*, II. iii. 85–6)

Here, the second speaker seems to cut off the first, York's hexameter enhancing the impression of urgency, and possibly even indicating an overlap between speakers, which would have been possible to indicate to actors working from cue parts by giving the actor playing York the cue 'gracious' rather than 'Uncle'. The highest proportion of such short lines can be found in the middle tragedies and problem plays, in which the verse tends to be more fractured than in the early plays or the late Romances, a metrical form which seems appropriate to the often troubled subject matter of the plays.

With initial short lines, the impression is less frequently of interruption by another speaker, and more often of self-interruption or a change of focus. This speech of Helena's from *All's Well That Ends Well*, which has been the subject of contention amongst editors, may be one such instance of an initial short line coinciding with, and enhancing, the rhetorical figure of *aposiopesis*, defined by Puttenham as—'when we begin to speake a thing and breake in the middle way, as if either it needed no further to be spoken of, or that we were ashamed, or afraide to speake it out':[33]

> HELEN   Not my virginity, yet ...
> There shall your master have a thousand loves,
>
> (*All's Well that Ends Well*, I. i. 161–2)

The Oxford editors' choice of punctuation (ellipsis) suggests their perception of Helena's first line as broken off. Susan Snyder (Oxford edition), choosing a dash rather than ellipsis, writes that 'the incomplete line and the sudden shift in subject may be functional', the 'radical rupture' serving to 'convey Helena's inability to go on with the game',[34] whilst Russell Fraser (Cambridge edition), although punctuating with a colon at the end of the line, asserts that 'a moment of meditative silence is often found appropriate in

---

[32] Tiffany Stern, *Rehearsal from Shakespeare to Sheridan* (Oxford: Clarendon Press, 2000) 46–123.
[33] Puttenham (1589) 139.
[34] Susan Snyder (ed.) *All's Well That Ends Well*, (Oxford: Oxford University Press, 1993) 87.

performance'.[35] However, as Fraser also suggests, a number of editors 'conjecture that something has dropped out here',[36] finding the line not deliberately short, but caused by an error in transmission.[37]

Irrespective of whether this particular example is regarded as deliberate or erroneous, the possibility that some short lines are not deliberate metrical devices but the result of corruption must be entertained. The most common instance of corruption to the text resulting in apparent initial short lines is that of the division of the first line of a speech by the Folio compositors, due to the fact that whilst each page in the early quartos contains a single column of approximately 11.5 cm, each Folio page contains two columns of approximately 9 cm, meaning that there was often insufficient space for both the line and the preceding speech prefix. Thus, whilst in all three quarto texts of *Titus Andronicus* Bassianus' line reads:

> BASSIANUS   Romaines, friends, followers, fauourers of my right,
>
> > (*Titus Andronicus*, I. i. 9; Q3 A2r)

In the Folio text, widely acknowledged to have been printed from a copy of Q3, the line is printed:

> BASSIANUS   Romaines, Friends, Followers,
>   Fauourers of my Right:
>
> (*Titus Andronicus*, I. i. 9; F.cc4r, TLN.15–16)

The Folio lineation, separating the address from the remainder of the line, can thus only have originated in the printing house, and cannot therefore be claimed to have any rhetorical purpose.

It is, of course, the case that some single, final, and initial short lines are followed by entrances, exits, sound effects, or business which may reasonably be seen to suggest a pause in the dialogue. However, I would argue that whilst the action may create a natural hiatus in the dialogue, which in coinciding with the short line enhances the impression of curtailment, the fact remains that an actor would not have been able to distinguish a full-line cue from a short-line cue when working from a part, and hence the deliberate insertion of a pause seems untenable.

One further dramatically effective use of final short lines merits discussion here, since it counters the common assertion that Shakespeare, throughout his career, often finishes

---

[35] Russell Fraser (ed.) *All's Well That Ends Well* (Cambridge: Cambridge University Press, 2003, updated edn) 53.

[36] Fraser (2003) 53.

[37] Thomas Hanmer proposed the emendation 'Not my virginity yet. You're for the Court' (*The Works of Shakespear in nine volumes* (London, 1743–1744) 337); Samuel Johnson wrote that 'some such clause has, I think, dropped out' (*The Plays of William Shakespeare in eight volumes*. vol. 3 (London 1765), 285); W. G. Clark, J. Glover, and W. A. Wright assert that 'It cannot be doubted that there is some omission here' (*The Works of William Shakespeare*. vol. 3, London: Macmillan (1863) 215).

a scene on a rhyming couplet. McDonald, for example, comments that as Shakespeare 'matures poetically, he relies on rhyme to create certain special effects … most often to close off a scene, to indicate with a rhymed couplet that the episode is over'.[38] However, whilst this is true of many scenes in his early plays, Shakespeare shows an increasing tendency throughout his work to end a scene on a short line. Indeed, in *The Winter's Tale* over 40 per cent of verse scenes end with a short line, whilst only one scene—that of Time's choric speech—ends on a rhyming couplet. The effect of ending a speech on a short line is to provide, rather than a neat summation, an abrupt finish, which drives the action onwards into the next scene, as in Martius' urging of his soldiers to battle at the end of 1.4 *Coriolanus*:

> Come on, my fellows.
> He that retires, I'll take him for a Volsce,
> And he shall feel mine edge.   [*Exeunt*]

> (*Coriolanus*, I. iv. 27–9)

As mentioned above, internal short lines can be distinguished from other forms of short lines since they would have been readily identifiable to actors working from a cue part, and it is possible that they may, in a number of instances, be perceived as indicative of a break, often preceding sound effects or implied action, or occurring where a rhetorical or emotional pause seems appropriate. In this example from *The Tempest*, for example, the short line marks the point where Prospero casts his spell, making the men freeze, a point at which a pause seems appropriate:

> […]   There stand,
> For you are spell-stopped.—
> Holy Gonzalo, honourable man,
> Mine eyes, ev'n sociable to the show of thine,
> Fall fellowly drops.

> (*The Tempest*, V. i. 60–4)

Shakespeare would, as J. C. Maxwell suggests, have found a precedent for the use of internal short lines in Virgil's *Aeneid*, in which a number of short verse-lines can be found amid the dactylic hexameter. John Sparrow comments on the 'dramatic' effects of these Virgilian short lines—creating a pause, marking a sigh, replicating disjointed speech, terminating the dialogue in mid-speech due to the emotional content, suspending a climax, preceding an imperative, and indicating an interruption.[39]

It is possible that Shakespeare was influenced by his Classical education into using such metrical devices to similar effect, examples matching Sparrow's criteria being identifiable in Shakespeare's dramatic writing.

---

[38] Russ McDonald, *The Bedford Companion to Shakespeare* (Boston: Bedford, 1996) 50.
[39] John Sparrow, *Half lines and Repetition in Virgil* (Oxford: Clarendon Press, 1931) 18, 26, 42–5.

A further type of metrically deficient line which merits discussion is that which has an omitted syllable, most frequently at the beginning of the line or at the mid-line point. Although these lines are relatively rare—Wright estimating that they average 'fewer than four appearances in each play and about six in the later plays'[40]—this is another form of short line which may be deemed to indicate a pause, particularly when coinciding with a strong rhetorical break:

Under my battlements. ^ Come, you spirits

(*Macbeth*, I. v. 39)

Carol M. Sicherman, asserting that in the case of missing syllables, 'metrical pauses serve endless expressive purposes' cites the above example as marking 'a midline shift of mood',[41] a typical function of the mid-line pause. A different, but equally dramatically effective use of the missing mid-line syllable can be seen in the scene from *Measure for Measure*, cited above:

Even so. ^ Heaven keep your honour.

(*Measure for Measure*, II. iv. 34)

Here the pause seems designed to give Isabella a moment to take in the enormity of Angelo's statement before resuming a civil tone and making the decision to leave. The aural effect of the missing syllable is, in each case, to throw emphasis onto the succeeding word, thereby marking the beginning of the new thought.

With a headless line, in which the first unstressed syllable is missing, the impression is similarly one of emphasis, giving a sense of a decisive verbal attack. These lines often coincide with monosyllabic orders, adding force to the command as in this example from *Richard II*:

Lord Marshall ^ Stay, the King hath thrown his warder down.

(*Richard II*, I. iii. 118)

Although less frequent than at the start or mid-line point, missing syllables can occur at other points in the line, again seeming mostly designed to give emphasis, often to a monosyllabic word. In the following speech of Horatio's, for example, there are missing syllables before not only the first command—'Stay!'—but before both of the first two charges to 'speak':

^ Stay! ^ Speak, ^ speak, I charge thee speak!

(*Hamlet*, I. i. 49)

---

[40] Wright (1988) 174.
[41] Carol M. Sicherman, 'Meter and Meaning in Shakespeare', *Language and Style* 15 (1982): 175.

These implied pauses give weight to each of the orders, and may, as Sicherman suggests, provide a sense of 'Horatio's terror impeding then permitting speech'.[42]

Finally, but quite rarely, some missing syllables occur at the ends of lines, as in line 364 of Miranda's speech in Act I, Scene ii, *The Tempest*:

> [...] therefore wast thou
> Deservedly confined into this rock,
> Who hadst deserved more than a prison.
>
> (*Tempest*, I. ii. 362–4)

However, many apparently nine syllable lines can be explained by the practice of pronouncing what are now considered three-syllable words as four:

> ULYSSES   I do not strain at the position –
> (*Troilus and Cressida*, III. iii. 107)

In addition, Wright suggests that many appear as 'random, perhaps mistaken, violations of the norm', suggesting only tentatively that 'possible explanations can be found' for some.[43] Wright's caution is, perhaps, worth reiterating in relation to short lines as a whole. Whilst, as outlined here, patterns can certainly be discerned and in many cases an effective dramatic explanation for a line can be found, we should be wary of assuming that all metrical variants have a dramatic purpose, and cautious of trying to find plausible explanations for metrical deficiency which may well have resulted from authorial, scribal, or compositorial error.

16.4 THREE OR MORE CONSECUTIVE SHORT LINES

The discussion relating to the inability of an actor working from a cue part to identify any form of short line other than the internal variety is of equal significance to the consideration of the dramatic function of three consecutive short lines, a metrical structure which, like single short lines, is most common in plays from around 1600–1608, another feature of their more varied metrical style and uneven verse form. In accordance with Steevens' method, modern editors encountering three consecutive short lines (the Oxford and RSC *Complete Works* being notable exceptions) have tended to link one pair of lines in favour of the other, with substantial variation occurring in the linkages as a

---

[42] Sicherman (1982) 175.
[43] Wright (1988) 182.

result of the different principles used to make such decisions.[44] Most theatre practitioners, presumably influenced by this form of lineation, have thus tended to assume that the device is indicative of a shared line, a short line, and a pause.[45] However, as discussed above, the metrical connections of their lines to those of other characters would not have been visible to Renaissance actors working from a cue part, and hence, like short lines, the dramatic function of this structure requires reconsideration.

The possibility of deliberate metrical ambiguity in the case of three consecutive short lines was first raised by E. A. Abbott in his *A Shakespearean Grammar* (1869) in which he suggested that this metrical structure might be regarded as a single structure, the middle line of which might either be seen as an 'amphibious section' linking with both the lines on either side, or constitute an overlap with the first and third lines forming a single verse line.[46] A possible example of the use of the structure to indicate an overlap may be found in Act II, Scene ii, *Measure for Measure*:

> ISABELLA   [...] Oh, it is excellent
> To have a giant's strength, but it is tyrannous
> To use it like a giant.
> LUCIO   That's well said.
> ISABELLA   Could great men thunder
> As Jove himself does, *Jove* would never be quiet.
>
>   (II. ii. 109–14)

Here, Lucio's line may be seen to interject into Isabella's otherwise continuous pentameter.

In addition to appearing designed, at points, to indicate overlapping dialogue, there is a clear pattern in the use of three consecutive short lines in Shakespeare's work at points of conflict, urgency, and excitement. A particularly high incidence of these structures is evident in Act IV, Scene i, *Othello*, in the altercation between Othello and Desdemona:

> DESDEMONA
> By my troth, I am glad on't.
> OTHELLO   Indeed!
> DESDEMONA   My lord?
> OTHELLO   I am glad to see you mad.
> DESDEMONA   Why, sweet Othello!
> OTHELLO   Devil!
> DESDEMONA   I have not deserved this.
>
>   (*Othello*, IV. i. 235–41)

---

[44] See Fredson Bowers, 'Establishing Shakespeare's Text: Notes on Short Lines and the Problem of Verse Division', *SB* 33 (1980) and Paul Werstine, 'Line Division in Shakespeare's Verse: An Editorial Problem', *AEB* 8 (1984).

[45] Rokison (2010) 70–5.

[46] E. A. Abbott, *A Shakespearian Grammar* (London: Macmillan & Co., 1869) 426.

This example contains seven short lines, the metrical connection of which is ambiguous. Editors seek to connect these lines in various ways to form pentameters or short lines. Norman Sanders, for example, in the Cambridge edition, creates two shared lines followed by two short lines, inserting a stage direction following Othello's 'Devil!':

DESDEMONA
    By my troth, I am glad on't.
OTHELLO   Indeed!
DESDEMONA   My lord?
OTHELLO   I am glad to see you mad.
DESDEMONA   Why, sweet Othello!
OTHELLO   Devil!   [*He strikes her*]
DESDEMONA   I have not deserved this.[47]

Michael Neill, in the Oxford edition, creates, by contrast, two shared lines and one short line:

DESDEMONA   By my troth, I am glad on't.
OTHELLO   Indeed?
DESDEMONA   My lord?
OTHELLO   I am glad to see you mad.
DESDEMONA   Why, sweet Othello!
OTHELLO   Devil!
DESDEMONA   I have not deserved this.[48]

Whilst these editorial emendations may not seem problematic in themselves, to actors taught to observe the 'rule' that a short line is indicative of a pause, the first may imply a pause after both 'Devil!' and 'I have not deserved this' and the second after 'I have not deserved this'. I would argue, however, that the metrical ambiguity is a deliberate means of creating an increase in pace. If the lines are spoken with continuity, the urgent questions, answers, and exclamations seem almost to overlap as the listener hears two pentameters in the space of one and a half lines. The loss of a sense of metrical control thus mirrors the characters' loss of emotional control.

16.5 LONG LINES

After the short verse line, whether linked to form a shared line, or left to stand alone, the next most common variation on the pentameter line is the long verse line. This variation manifests itself either in the form of hexameters (lines of twelve syllables), epic caesuras (in which an additional syllable appears at the mid-line point) or feminine endings

---

[47] Norman Sanders (ed.) *Othello* (Cambridge: Cambridge University Press) 150–1.
[48] Michael Neill (ed.) *Othello* (Oxford: Oxford University Press, 2006) 338–9.

(in which the additional syllable comes at the end of the line). Each of these forms of line, the incidence of which, like other metrical deviations, increases in the process of Shakespeare's writing career, not only provides metrical variety, but may be seen to serve a dramatic purpose within a scene.

Two main forms of hexameter line can be identified: that which is divided into two equal parts, either shared between two speakers or spoken by a single character, and that which begins with a brief address or exclamation. The former, Wright suggests, is used predominantly to create an 'antiphonal balance between echoing three-foot line-segments':

> PETRUCHIO   I say it is the moon.
> KATHERINE   I know it is the moon.
>   (*The Taming of the Shrew*, IV. v. 16)
>
>   None that I know will be, much that I fear may chance
>   (*Julius Caesar*, II. iv. 34)

The hexameter permits two segments of equal length, thus balancing the two halves of the line and creating an aural equanimity particularly appropriate in instances of antithesis. Abbott asserts of the latter form that the address or exclamation with which it begins may be seen as 'not part of the verse'. Citing the following line from *Macbeth*, printed as a single verse line in the Folio, he argues that 'Sirrah' might be regarded as an extra-metrical address:

>   *Sirrah,*
>   A word with you. Attend those men our pleasure?
>   (*Macbeth*, III. i. 46–7)[49]

A similar example, also printed as a single verse line in the Folio, can be found in Act II, Scene iii, *All's Well That Ends Well*, in which Helena addresses the court of the King of France:

>   Gentlemen,
>   Heaven hath through me restored the King to health.
>   (*All's Well that Ends Well*, II. iii. 64–5)

In these cases, the aural effect of the extra syllables is the same irrespective of whether the lines are perceived as a hexameter or a pentameter with a preceding extra-metrical foot. However, as the discussion on short lines has shown, the common editorial practice of printing the first foot on a separate line of text (as above) to indicate its perceived extra-metrical nature, is in danger of leading actors, following common theatrical

---

[49] Abbott (1869) *A Shakespearian Grammar* 425.

practice, to leave a pause after the address, a practice which obscures the sense of impor-
tunity often inherent in such lines.

In addition to hexameters, which contain an extra foot, we also find, increasingly in
Shakespeare's work, a propensity for the inclusion of extra unstressed syllables, either
at the mid-line point or at the end of the line, the former given the name 'epic caesura'
and the latter 'feminine ending'. Again there is some variation in the perception of the
presence of these structures, based on notions of pronunciation. In terms of feminine
endings, once again we see a steady increase in the percentage of such metrically devi-
ant lines in the process of Shakespeare's writing career, with some variation in the early
plays. The fewest feminine endings, according to Chambers' statistics, are in *Love's
Labour's Lost* (1594–5) which he cites as having only twenty-six instances, and the most
in *Cymbeline* (1610–11), which, according to his statistics, has 799.[50]

Wright describes the effect of the feminine ending as 'soft, haunting, yearning, pliant,
seductive'.[51] In finishing on an unstressed beat, it also replicates the aural effect of the
upward inflection of a question. It can be no coincidence that one of the most famously
'questioning' speeches in Shakespeare—Hamlet's 'To be or not to be'—begins with four
lines all of which have feminine endings:

> To be, or not to be; that is the question:
> Whether 'tis nobler in the mind to suffer
> The slings and arrows of outrageous fortune,
> Or to take arms against a sea of troubles,
> And, by opposing, end them.
>
> (*Hamlet*, III. i. 58–62)

Wright tells us that, as well as additional syllables at the ends of lines, 'Shakespeare's
plays include more than sixteen hundred lines with an extra syllable before a mid-line
pause',[52] almost always followed by some form of syntactic break. This metrical device,
the 'epic caesura', was 'a standard variation' in 15th-century poetry, but generally less
common in that of the 16th century.[53] Although Shakespeare rarely uses such a device
in his non-dramatic poetry, he uses it particularly regularly in the middle and late tragedies and the problem plays.[54] As with missing syllables at the mid-line caesura, the effect
is of some form of hiatus, often coinciding with a change of tack. As Wright notes, 'the
extra syllable is almost always followed by punctuation':

> That my youth suffered. My story being done
> (*Othello*, I. iii. 158)[55]

[50] Chambers (1930) ii, 400.
[51] Wright (1988) 164.
[52] Wright (1988) 165.
[53] Michael Dobson and Stanley Wells (eds), *The Oxford Companion to Shakespeare* (Oxford: Oxford
University Press, 2001) 61.
[54] Chambers (1930) ii, 400.
[55] Wright (1988) 165.

The device is sometimes referred to as a 'feminine caesura', and may take on a similarly questioning tone to the feminine ending, as in Macbeth's interrogation of the witches:

> But how of Cawdor? The Thane of Cawdor lives
>
> *(Macbeth*, I. iii. 70)

Theatre practitioners seem to have less to say about the long line than the short—presumably because the delivery is not perceived as having as profound an effect on the structure of a scene or its characterization. Hall states that it is important for actors to 'start by scanning the speech', and that 'every line that … has too few or too many syllables, needs to be registered and pondered over';[56] however, he does not elucidate as to what such pondering might reveal in the case of feminine endings or epic caesuras. However, Cicely Berry makes some comment on feminine endings, suggesting that they 'often give a quality of working through the thought, sometimes giving it a haunted and unfinished sound as though leaving thoughts in the air'.[57] She cites Katherine's lines from *The Taming of the Shrew*, stating of the three consecutive feminine endings that 'they seem to point up the discovery and consideration of her thought: as the speech goes on she becomes surer and these endings become scarcer':[58]

> A woman moved is like a fountain troubled,
> Muddy, ill-seeming, thick, bereft of beauty,
> And while it is so, none so dry or thirsty
> Will deign to sip or touch one drop of it.
>
> *(The Taming of the Shrew*, V. ii. 147–50)

However, as Berry acknowledges of the feminine ending 'the effects are different' depending on the context of the lines.[59] In Richard III's first speech, the two feminine endings, amid the regular end-stopped lines, lend a contemptuous tone to Richard's description of flippant activities—'merry meetings', 'delightful measures', and capering in a 'Lady's chamber':

> Now are our brows bound with victorious wreaths,
> Our bruised arms hung up for monuments,
> Our stern alarums changed to merry meetings,
> Our dreadful marches to delightful measures.
> Grim-visaged war hath smoothed his wrinkled front,
> And now—instead of mounting barbed steeds
> To fright the souls of fearful adversaries –
> He capers nimbly in a lady's chamber
> To the lascivious pleasing of a lute.
>
> *(Richard III*, I. i. 5–13)

[56] Hall (2003) 30.
[57] Berry (1987) 62.
[58] Berry (1987) 63.
[59] Berry (1987) 62.

Such disparity in the employment of a metrical variant is, of course, the case with most of the variations to the dramatic verse line discussed here. It therefore seems worth ending by saying that despite efforts to produce statistics and tables which allow a neat summation of the increase in variations in Shakespeare's dramatic line from the plays of the late sixteenth to those of the early 17th century, within this general movement we find great variety in Shakespeare's use of devices such as the shared line, short line, long line, enjambment, and end-stopping depending on subject matter and characterization. To try to establish a single 'rule' for the delivery and dramatic function of a particular structure can thus only prove reductive and obscure Shakespeare's 'infinite variety'.

SELECT BIBLIOGRAPHY

Abbott, E. A. (1869) *A Shakespearian Grammar* (London: Macmillan & Co.).

Berry, Cicely (1987) *The Actor and his Text* (London: Harrap).

Chambers, E. K. (1930) *William Shakespeare: A Study of Facts and Problems*. 2 vols (Oxford: Clarendon Press).

Hall, Peter (2003) *Shakespeare's Advice to the Players* (London: Oberon).

McDonald, Russ (2001) *Shakespeare and the Arts of Language* (Oxford: Oxford University Press).

Oras, Ants (1960) *Pause Patterns in Elizabethan and Jacobean Drama: An Experiment in Prosody* (Gainsville: University of Florida Press).

Rokison, Abigail (2010) *Shakespearean Verse Speaking: Text and Theatre Practice* (Cambridge: Cambridge University Press).

Sicherman, Carol M. (1982) 'Meter and Meaning in Shakespeare', *Language and Style* 15: 169–92

Wells, Stanley and Taylor, Gary (2005) (eds) *William Shakespeare: The Complete Works*, 2nd edn (Oxford: Oxford University Press).

Wright, George T. (1988) *Shakespeare's Metrical Art* (Berkeley: University of California Press).

CHAPTER 17

....

SHAKESPEARE'S
WORD MUSIC

....

PAUL EDMONDSON

I begin with the desire to hear the music of Shakespeare's poetry, its rich and varied sounds, for it is this that makes my heart sing and my mind dance. I would like to enable the readers of my chapter to find this music for themselves in Shakespeare, to carry around with them ears that are hungry for it, eyes that can recognize it, minds that know it to be an important Shakespearian attribute, and bodies which can be stirred and warmed by it.

The banished Valentine imagines a world without his beloved:

> Except I be by Silvia in the night
> There is no music in the nightingale.
> Unless I look on Silvia in the day
> There is no day for me to look upon.
>
> (*The Two Gentlemen of Verona*, III. i. 178–81)

Lord Biron convinces his King and friends that no abstinence, however virtuous, can make up for the absence of love:

> And when love speaks, the voice of all the gods
> Make heaven drowsy with the harmony.
>
> (*Love's Labour's Lost*, IV. iii. 320–1)

The Queen of the fairy kingdom, Titania, remembers the captivating and intimate friendship of a mortal mother:

> His mother was a vot'ress of my order,
> And in the spicèd Indian air by night
> Full often hath she gossiped by my side.
>
> (*A Midsummer Night's Dream*, II. i. 123–5)

Prince Florizel sees in his lover's movements something as powerful as the ocean:

> When you do dance, I wish you
> A wave o'th' sea, that you might ever do
> Nothing but that, move still, still so,
> And own no other function.
>
> (*The Winter's Tale*, IV. iv. 140–3)

Richard II implores our pity with an ingratiating pizzicato of monosyllables:

> I live with bread, like you; feel want,
> Taste grief, need friends. Subjected thus,
> How can you say to me I am a king?
>
> (*Richard II*, III. ii. 171–3)

The unstoppable and loquacious Rosalind spills her words across highly shaped sentences and comic sounds:

> I drave my suitor from his mad humour of love to a living humour of madness, which
> was to forswear the full stream of the world and to live in a nook merely monastic.
>
> (*As You Like It*, III. ii. 402–5)

Cleopatra captures something of her own inevitable future oblivion in her response to the death of Antony:

> The odds is gone,
> And there is nothing left remarkable
> Beneath the visiting moon.
>
> (*Antony and Cleopatra*, IV. xvi. 68–70)

Prospero tells Miranda the magical story of her life, the story of a sea adventure:

> Sit still, and hear the last of our sea-sorrow.
>
> (*The Tempest*, I. ii. 171)

By 'music', I mean the *sound* of Shakespeare's poetry, something more than, but inextricably related to, verbal communication. Music even more than spoken words has a physical effect on us; word music is the essence of Shakespeare's poetic drama and his dramatic poetry. Shakespeare's sounds require us to be close readers of and close listeners to the text. Since all acting begins by reading, I make no distinction between an armchair reader or student of Shakespeare and the highly experienced professional actor preparing for or performing a role. The difference lies only in experience, intention, and skill. The starting point for each is a reading, and all readings and readers can potentially find sound and share Shakespeare's musicality.

This chapter considers some of the rewards of being attentive to Shakespeare's word music through 'sound' readings of two different Shakespearean moments, one verse, the other prose. How can we as readers of Shakespeare 'mark the music' (as Lorenzo says to Jessica, *The Merchant of Venice*, V. i. 88) and how might this translate itself into practice, either in private readings of Shakespeare or into a live performance on stage?

There is a strong dramatic relationship between Shakespeare's words and their music, a relationship often lacking in modern Shakespearian productions. The examples I began with are moments when the sounds of Shakespeare are connected to their meaning. Writing about reading Shakespeare's sonnets aloud, David Fuller reminds us that 'meaning in poetry is never wholly independent of sound'.[1] We might open a copy of Shakespeare's Complete Works randomly and hear the music immediately (when Virginia Woolf did this on Sunday 13 April 1930 she came across 'upon a gather'd lily, almost withered' from *Titus Andronicus*, III. i. 113).[2] Shakespeare's word music can be found in his prose as well as his verse. Both forms seem equally flexible in the patterning they make available for sound as well as sense. The literary critic and clergyman, Francis Meres, writing in 1598 referred to the 'mellifluous and honey-tongued Shakespeare',[3] but it requires a musical sensibility to recognize this quality and to enliven it into spoken sound.

We are more likely to be able to do this if we take with us a desire to hear the word music in the first place. By this I do not mean delivering the lines with a particular timbre of the voice—vibrato, tremolo, *sotto voce*, still less an 'actorly' voice—I mean the music that can be released from (and brought to) the words when they are spoken with sensitivity and with an ear attentive to their individual sounds, shapes, and dramatic effects. My interest does not lie in trying to re-imagine the sounds that Shakespeare himself heard, so-called 'original pronunciation'. This pursuit is worthy and distinguished in and of itself but requires that we learn a different set of sounds in order to practice it. We are 21st century readers and need only to use the sounds available through our contemporary voices in order to hear and make dramatic Shakespeare's word music. We can do this by being hypersensitive to the shape, sound, and dramatic quality of each word, phrase, and line.

It is not surprising that a discussion about Shakespeare's word music should be haunted by several modernist voices. Virginia Woolf has already been mentioned and will appear again. The second modernist voice is Edith Sitwell's, who in *A Notebook on William Shakespeare* (1948) shares her own insights as an aural poet on Shakespeare's poetry. Her account of the plays is uneven; she has sometimes been mocked for it, but she remains an engagingly close reader of Shakespeare's sound. She is interested in assonance (internal vowel rhyme) and dissonance (different vowel sounds in close proximity); she is

[1] David Fuller, *The Life in the Sonnets* (London: Continuum International Publishing Group, 2011) 76.
[2] Virginia Woolf, *A Writer's Diary* (London: Grafton, 1978) 197.
[3] William Shakespeare, *The Complete Poems and Sonnets*, Colin Burrow (ed.), (Oxford: Oxford University Press, 2002) 74.

acutely sensitive to the fine balances of rhythm and sound she hears progressing through each line, a sensitivity which, for instance, notices the effect of multisyllabic words when set amongst monosyllabic ones. So, at the end of her notes on the moments leading up to Cleopatra's suicide in *Antony and Cleopatra*, she can step back and observe that 'the whole play is one of the greatest miracles of sound that has ever come into this world'.[4] But we do not read entirely for sound. The third modernist is Clemens Krauss, the librettist with Richard Strauss for Strauss' last opera, *Capriccio* (1942), 'a conversation piece in music', and a work which poses the question: which is the most important artistically in the theatre, words or music? We are invited to see the debate from the lead soprano the Countess' point of view, for in her person the question becomes one of romantic intention: whose affection shall she requite, Olivier's the poet, or Flamand's the musician? I shall return to *Capriccio* and to the Countess' decision at the end.

Although actors often have to focus more on the primary, literal meaning of Shakespeare's words, the actor who only focuses on the intellectual shape of Shakespeare's language will very likely miss its poetry and musicality. Some famous and contrasting examples among actors would be the difference between John Gielgud or Judi Dench and Laurence Olivier or Ian McKellen. Gielgud and Dench allow the sounds of words to help convey meaning. One of Dench's favourite techniques is to allow Shakespeare's words to rest on her breath. Olivier and McKellen are mainly interested in the rhetorical impact and meaning of the words. It is a question of balance, and this, as many theatre practitioners will testify, is difficult to strike.

Take, for instance, the director John Barton's *Playing Shakespeare* (1984; reissued 2009). The book accompanied a television series that featured prominent British actors. Barton's last chapter, 'Poetry and Hidden Poetry', conveys a struggle with the musicality of Shakespeare's language. He makes the distinction between 'where the text is *obvious* poetry' and 'text which is poetic and yet not obviously heightened'.[5] Barton can hear the words as he reads them to himself, but resists explaining to the actors how they might sound. By way of a summation he makes the following admission: 'some actors have a feel for poetry and some don't, and if they don't have that feel nothing I say can release it'.[6] If they do then the experience is enriched since, 'in Shakespeare the character and the poetry go together. More than that, they are one'.[7]

Another influential practitioner is the voice coach Cicely Berry. Writing in 1973, she shares some of Barton's anxieties about actors

> feeling that there is some sort of mystique about [poetry], some way of doing it. If this is the case, one of two things may happen: either you are over-reverent about it, and the 'poetry voice' happens; or, in rebelling against the 'poetry voice' you ignore the form and go only for the logical sense, and the poetry then sounds like prose.

---

[4] Edith Sitwell, *A Notebook on William Shakespeare* (London: Macmillan, 1948) 142.
[5] John Barton, *Playing Shakespeare* (London: Methuen, 1984; repr. 2009) 194.
[6] Barton (2009) 205.
[7] Barton (2009) 208.

Of course, neither need happen. It is a question of finding the balance between the formal and the informal, the colloquial and the heightened language.[8]

Berry contextualizes these remarks with her own small anthology of poems by Robert Herrick, John Donne, Gerard Manley Hopkins, W. B. Yeats, Thomas Hardy, and D. H. Lawrence, a selection aimed at helping actors feel more comfortable about speaking poetry. She recommends rooting the text 'in the need to speak it, and speak it in that particular fashion and in those particular words'.[9] Berry's advice was amplified a decade later in *The Actor and His Text*:

> There is a pleasure in the music; there is often humour in the interplay of sounds, assonance and alliteration, and a meaning beyond the grammatical sense which audiences pick up on, and which is not far removed from our pleasure in nursery rhymes. And, most important, we should not explain—this reduces it, and the audience has too many signals to pick up. So the thought and feeling must seem instinctive and must be let go unambiguously with the words, for there is no time for naturalistic consideration: it is always explicit.[10]

What Berry here refers to as 'a pleasure in the music' can sometimes conjure up unfortunate comparisons with an acting style often characterized as either a 'booming' or 'sing-song' delivery. Adrian Noble, like many others, associates this with actors of the past (it applies to some but by no means all) when he observes, 'the main aim is to make the verse sound beautiful rather than to reflect character or situation'.[11] However, he then goes on to express caution in approaches which ignore the musicality of the language: 'it's not enough to just overlay Shakespeare with the rhythms of modern speech—it probably won't make much sense and will certainly be very boring to listen to'.[12] Importantly, Noble was initially excited about the sound of Shakespeare. He was given a copy of the complete works for his twelfth birthday:

> After I watched Laurence Olivier's films of *Henry V* and *Hamlet*, I caught the bug and began to speak some of the speeches aloud in the privacy of my own bedroom. I became intoxicated by the sound of the language—it gave me a voice and a private reality.[13]

Barton's, Berry's, and Noble's accounts all acknowledge that Shakespeare's language is heightened and comes to life with a true connection between sound and sense. Writing in 2008, Berry expresses '[her] long-held belief that we do not, we cannot, cannot understand Shakespeare in all its complexity fully [...] until we have spoken it aloud and

---

[8] Cicely Berry, *Voice and the Actor* (London: Harrap, 1973; new edn Virgin Books, 2000; repr. 2009) 101.
[9] Berry (2009) 121.
[10] Cicely Berry, *The Actor and His Text* (London: Virgin Publishing, 1987) 47.
[11] Adrian Noble, *How to do Shakespeare* (London: Routledge, 2010) 3.
[12] Noble (2010) 3.
[13] Noble (2010) 7.

heard where the sound takes us'.[14] When this happens in performance, or when a private reader discovers it for him or herself, the results can indeed intoxicate.

I offer no rules in this chapter, only encouragement for the reader to discover Shakespeare's word music. The sound of the language itself is performative. We will all sound different, but we can all be conscious of the word music as an imperative dimension in our understanding and enjoyment of Shakespeare. It is good, when we read Shakespeare alone, always to read him aloud.

Two theatre reviews, written more than a hundred years apart, help to set a goal for the effect that Shakespeare's word music can produce. The first is by John Keats writing about the actor Edmund Kean's

> elegance, gracefulness, and music of elocution. A melodious passage in poetry is full of pleasures both sensual and spiritual. [...] Surely this intense power of anatomizing the passion of every syllable—of taking to himself the wings of verse, is the means by which he becomes a storm with such fiery decision; and by which, with a still deeper charm, he 'does his spiriting gently.' Other actors are continually thinking of their sum-total effect throughout the play. Kean delivers himself up to the instant feeling, without a shadow of a thought about anything else. He feels his being as deeply as Wordsworth ... We will say no more. Kean! Kean! Have a carefulness of thy health, an innursed respect for thy own genius, a pity for us in these cold and enfeebling times! Cheer us a little in the failure of our days! For romance lives but in books. The goblin is driven from the heath, and the rainbow is robbed of its mystery.[15]

Keats' account crackles with his own poetic sensibility. He appreciates the sensuality of Kean's speaking, a 'music of elocution' which combines with the spiritual. Every syllable counts for Kean; each one can give him wings; he encounters and delivers the language with 'instant feeling'; he is alive in each moment. And then Keats compares the great actor to the great poet (Wordsworth), and the musicality which he hears in Kean becomes something transformative and alchemical 'in these cold and enfeebling times'. The ways in which Kean performs—including the music he finds in and brings to the words—are the stuff of which mythical creatures and rainbows are born.

The second review comes from Herbert Farjeon's account of Edith Evans as Mistress Page in Nigel Playfair's 1923 production of *The Merry Wives of Windsor*:

> The honors of the performance fell to Miss Edith Evans. She is that rare thing, an actress with both breadth and subtlety. She is that equally rare thing, an actress who can bring out the full literary flavor of every word. [...] Miss Evans quickens every syllable, recognizes in a choice epithet something as three dimensional as a living being, reveals new wonders unsuspected and never to be forgotten.[16]

[14] Cicely Berry, *From Word to Play* (London: Oberon Books, 2008) 6.
[15] Jonathan Bate (ed.), *The Romantics on Shakespeare* (London: Penguin, 1992) 201–2.
[16] Stanley Wells (ed.), *Shakespeare in the Theatre: An Anthology of Criticism* (Oxford: Clarendon Press, 1997) 202.

Imagine waking up to a press notice like that! Evans seems successfully to have combined meaning with musicality in what for Farjeon was no less than a master-class in how to speak Shakespeare. Evans, we learn, did not shy away from the complexities of the language, but found life in its difficulty. Her quickening of 'every syllable' conjures an image of her breathing new life into old words, and she brought forth 'wonders unsuspected'. This praise for Evans' masterly delivery is for a part written entirely in prose, in a play which is 87 per cent prose.[17] Prose can be every bit as musical and life-giving as verse.

Any close, performance-focused reading of Shakespeare will involve at least three dimensions: the literal (what do the words actually mean?), the sub-textual (what is implied but not said and how might this be discerned?), and the imaginative (where do the images and metaphors lead us visually and emotionally?). To this I would add a fourth dimension: the musicality of the words (how do the words sound, and what effect does this have on their overall meaning and dramatic function?).

Suppose one started with this fourth dimension, with the sound of the words themselves? Here the advice of the French poet Paul Valéry is relevant:

> In studying a piece of poetry to be spoken aloud, one should never take as a beginning or point of departure ordinary discourse or current speech, and then rise from the level of prose to the desired poetic tone; on the contrary, I believe one should start from the song, put oneself in the attitude of the singer, tune one's voice to the fullness of musical sound, and from that point descend to the slightly less vibrant state suitable to verse. [...] The first condition for speaking verse well is an understanding of what it is not, and of how great a difference separates it from ordinary language. [...] Above all, do not be in a hurry to reach the meaning. Approach it without forcing and, as it were, imperceptibly. Attain the tenderness and the violence only by the music and through it [...] Remain in this purely musical state until the moment the meaning, having gradually supervened, can no longer mar the musical form. You will gradually introduce it as the supreme nuance which will transfigure your piece without altering it.[18]

Valéry's directions are best tried out by the solitary reader getting to know the text for the first time. He advises the reader to start with a heightened sense of sound and then to allow the meaning to supervene by which time the original sounds which brought life to the text will have become a real and lasting part of the sound experience. In reading and experiencing Shakespeare's language as closely as possible for its sound, the poetry resonates dramatically and powerfully. Close readings reveal what Valéry calls the 'supreme nuance' and, in so doing, close 'sound' readings 'transfigure' the text.

---

[17] Brian Vickers, *The Artistry of Shakespeare's Prose* (London: Methuen, 1968) 433.
[18] Cited by David Fuller (2011) 87–8.

17.1

Twelfth Night, or what you will (c. 1601) comes around the midpoint in Shakespeare's career. He has moved away from the formal, rhetorical shaping which characterized some of his earlier works (especially the two history tetralogies) and has begun to move on from his approximately five-year intense interest in the use of prose. His explorations of prose and his mastery of it have a demonstrable affect on his versification. The rhythms in the iambic line become, from the mid- to late 1590s onwards, much looser and more flexible—Hamlet's soliloquies are perhaps the first fully fledged example. *Twelfth Night, or what you will* is two-thirds prose, but in performance can achieve distinctive lyrical effects. Songs from Feste (and a couple of bursts from the drunken midnight revellers) punctuate the action. Reviewing a 1933 production, which she had not really enjoyed, Virginia Woolf explored reading the play for its word music, and wondered at the

> queer jingles like 'live in her; when liver, brain, and heart' … 'and of a foolish knight that you brought in one night' and to ask oneself whether it was from them that was born the lovely, 'And what should I do in Illyria? My brother he is in Elysium' […] From the echo of one word is born another word, for which reason, perhaps, the play seems as we read it to tremble perpetually on the brink of music.[19]

In appreciating Shakespeare's linguistic music, the more comprehensive the initial reading the likelier is the possibility that its sound and resonance will move forward into the lively action of word on stage.

Take, for example, the moment that Countess Olivia and Viola share in Act I, Scene v. Viola is disguised as Cesario and has been pleading with Olivia on behalf of her master, Duke Orsino. Placing a single speech under a microscope like this reveals attributes that are not normally apparent (some more relevant to performance than others) and illustrates the process of how to read closely for Shakespeare's musicality.

> 1 Make me a willow cabin at your gate
> 2 And call upon my soul within the house,
> 3 Write loyal cantons of contemnèd love,
> 4 And sing them loud even in the dead of night;
> 5 Halloo your name to the reverberate hills,
> 6 And make the babbling gossip of the air
> 7 Cry out 'Olivia!' O, you should not rest
> 8 Between the elements of air and earth
> 9 But you should pity me.

(*Twelfth Night, or what you will*, I. v. 257–65)

---

[19] Virginia Woolf, *The Death of the Moth and Other Essays* (London: Hogarth Press, 1942; new edn Penguin, 1961) 43.

1 'Make me a willow cabin at your gate': I hear an imperative command at the start of this speech. The double 'm' sound of 'Make me' offers the opportunity for two strong alliterative stresses. Could this be Viola herself momentarily breaking through the disguise of Cesario with hitherto uncharacteristic self-assertion? The phrase 'a willow cabin' makes the shape of the mouth look as though it is caressing the words as they trip out, pouting, momentarily for the beginning of the labial 'willow', then perhaps moving into an almost half smile for 'cabin'. A mild or restrained flirtation could be apparent. The 'w' of 'willow' is another strong beat; the word 'at' carries forward the first syllable of 'cabin'. 'Your' is prominent because it introduces a new person and vowel sound to the line; 'gate' echoes the vowel sound of 'make', a 'gate' which swings open, in invitation, with a definite stress, at the end of the line.

2 'And call upon my soul within the house': This is a regular line of iambic pentameter (arguably the only one in the speech), giving due prominence to 'call', 'soul', and 'house' on the major beats. The long vowels in the words 'And call upon my soul' seem naturally to slow the speaker down, imitating the calling that Cesario imagines enacting from the willow cabin at the end of the drive to the manor house, to 'my soul' Olivia. The endings of 'call' and 'soul' tie them together as sounds. Visually, the words 'willow cabin' are printed above 'my soul' connecting together the two romantic images by their central positions in their respective lines. 'Within' echoes the sound and mouth position of 'willow'. The 's' sound at the end of 'house', connects it to 'soul' and continues the musical linkage through the line on its major beats: 'call', 'soul', and 'house'. Just as a 'willow cabin' was built in the first line, a house appears at the end of the second: two physical structures between which Cesario's imagined sound can travel.

3 'Write loyal cantons of contemnèd love': This is another imperative command (like line 1). 'Write' directs the line with its major beat, followed by the major beat of the first syllable of 'loyal'. This line about writing evokes a Latinate vocabulary—'cantons of contemnèd' ('cantons' means 'verses'; 'contemnèd' means 'rejected')—in contrast to the Anglo-Saxon simplicity of 'love' itself. There is a chiasmic quality to the alliterative patterning and sound of 'loyal cantons of contemnèd love'; the end of 'cantons' runs through the vowel sound of 'of' and into the beginning of 'contemnèd'. But the words also convey a sense of struggle and conflict with the clash of those hard, alliterative 'c's (which echo the sound of 'cabin') and the awkwardness of the trisyllabic 'contemnèd'. 'Love' echoes the softer sound of 'loyal', and makes 'love' the end much to be desired, as well as the end of the line. Here the meaning of 'contemnèd' tempers 'love' and makes it unrequited, a sentiment that harks back to the 'willow cabin' and its associations with melancholy lovers.

4 'And sing them loud even in the dead of night': This line about singing again slows the speaker down because it is made up almost entirely of monosyllables; 'even' could be pronounced fully (rather than elided to 'e' en') in order to emphasize 'night'. There are long vowel sounds through every major word. 'And' slows the speaker down, if it is pronounced fully with its hard consonant. An internal vowel rhyme connects the 'them' to the word 'dead'. There is an implied retrospective pun on the word 'even' when we arrive at 'night': 'even' turns to night, and still Cesario is singing. 'Loud', 'dead', and 'night' have

hard, consonantal endings, like 'gate' and 'write', and attract special emphases as sounds in this line. The phrase 'dead of night', the end of this line's journey, tempers 'sing' with dissonance; there is only failing endeavour—with a falling vowel sound—in the middle of a night like the one being imagined and evoked here.

5 'Halloo your name to the reverberate hills': 'Halloo' or 'Hallow' (as in the Folio)? The words have different meanings (the first is a fox-hunting call, the latter is a blessing) and different stresses. To cry 'halloo' would wake someone up in the middle of the night; to 'hallow' them suggests something prayerful and quieter ('Hallow your name' is even an allusion to the Lord's Prayer). Both words make sense, but the interpretation 'Halloo' is more evocative of the sound that the speaker imagines invoking over the next couple of lines. 'Halloo' is so strong a sound to occur at the beginning of the line that it dominates what follows, easily creating an arc of sense and sound across to 'the reverberate hills'. The prolonged sound of 'halloo' is broken and fractured into echoes by the stuttering sound of 'reverberate'. The musical arc of 'halloo' is end-stopped by the ending of 'reverber*ate*', and seems to trickle away with the long vowel sound and gentle ending of 'hills', its 'h' echoing the 'h' of 'halloo' at the beginning of the line. Viola takes the indicative command onto a new and deeper level. And traveling through this extraordinary changing arc of sound is 'your name', written in those cantons, and already sung during the night from the gate.

6 'And make the babbling gossip of the air': With 'And', it is possible to sound major stresses at the start of this line (like three of the five preceding lines: 'Make me', 'Write loyal', 'And sing'). Here the sound is one of something being forged, created, moulded. The hard endings of 'ma*ke*', 'babbling', and 'gossi*p*' convey a sense of an arrested flow of sound. The hard 'g' at the beginning of 'gossip' automatically prevents 'babbling' from eliding with it. Viola's echoing 'Halloo' is doing its best to metamorphose the air; 'babbling gossip' describes what the air is already doing as it echoes 'halloo', as well as what Viola is trying to make that same air do—to form itself into intelligible sound and speak with a definite purpose and aim. The vowel sound of the first syllable of 'gos-sip' internally rhymes with 'of', pushing that process of metamorphosis forward into the open vowel sound of 'air', a note which the speaker can hold for as long as the speaker wishes. 'Air', though, cannot last too long, as it spills into the sense of the next line.

7 'Cry out "Olivia!" O, you should not rest': Again, two major stresses to start the line—'Cry out', the final, hard consonant of 'out' demands a slight pause before the name is sounded, and contributes to the sense of climax (whether cried out loudly or spoken softly) "Olivia!" The sound of the name caresses the mouth; the shape of the mouth caresses the name. There is a culmination of passion and commitment at this point in the speech, signaled by both its sound and its meaning. The name explodes a succession of vowel sounds across four syllables, 'O-li-vi-a', making it the longest word in the speech, a status it significantly shares with 'reverberate' (as Oscar Wilde's Gwendolen says about the name Ernest: 'It is a divine name. It has a music of its own. It produces vibrations').[20]

---

[20] Oscar Wilde, *The Complete Works of Oscar Wilde*, J. B. Foreman (ed.), (London: Collins, 1948; repr. 1990) 330.

A small breath after this exclamation is required. This might coincide with the word 'O' by sounding it as a sigh rather than a vocative, or, more musically, there might be a tiny pause as the speaker fills the lungs quickly to sound the word 'O'—a dying fall—a moment of recollection and renewed self-consciousness. In spite of the exclamation and the break it involves, this line is connected musically by the vowel sounds made by 'o': 'out', 'Olivia', 'O', 'you', 'should', and 'not'. The word 'rest' is the journey's end of the line and much to be desired, but it breaks the assonance. The hard 't' at the end of 'rest' underlines that word 'not' immediately before it, and carries the sound and the sense immediately through into the next line.

8 'Between the elements of air and earth': The long vowel sound of the second syllable of 'Between' starts the line musically (like line 260's 'And sing') and connects the vowel sound of its first syllable 'Bet' with the quick staccato sound of the trisyllabic 'el-em-ents'. The line slows down after this with monosyllables. 'Air' is a key word and experience in this speech and conveys associative meanings with music (like Caliban's 'sounds, and sweet airs, that give delight and hurt not', The Tempest, III. ii. 139). The long vowel sound of a repeated 'air' sinks gradually down through 'and' to land with a gentle thud in the short sounding 'earth'. The speaker has come back to the ground after having taken flight, but is still in motion, as the sound and sense continue to flow over into the next line.

9 'But you should pity me': The descent of vowel sounds continues to couple with a slowing down through the monosyllabic 'But you should'. The disyllabic 'pi-ty' now sounds gently and humbly, a final flicker of variation after seven monosyllabic words. Finally, we arrive at the object of the second sentence of the speech, a sentence which has flowed over three lines: 'me'. This harks back to the beginning of this personal, imaginative, emotional, and distinctively musical journey which started eight lines ago. It is an aria in verse. We have travelled from 'Make me' to 'pity me' with a strong sense that the speaker and the hearers—Olivia and the audience—have been changed and charged by both the music and the sense of what has been spoken. This is a speech about sound and its effects—'call', 'sing', 'loud', 'halloo', 'gossip', 'cry out'—sound which can be understood as music.

A few further reflections. Readers will scan the rhythm of any line in Shakespeare differently. Line 262, for example, can be read as a regular line of iambic pentameter (like line 258), but the word 'make' might be stressed especially firmly and slow the reader down; 'babbling' can easily sound trisyllabic. Whilst rhythm is important, and is one of Shakespeare's guiding and grounding principles in the verse line, the sound of the words and their meaning will come first for the reader; these should be guided but not governed by the rhythm. Who is making music in this passage? One answer is Viola's persona Cesario. She has just begun to imagine how she would feel if she loved Olivia in her 'master's flame' (I. v. 253). Olivia then asks the page before her what he would do (I. v. 256). The speech is Viola's response as Cesario and as such is self-consciously wrought as poetic music. Thus, the dramatic context allows the reader/actor to bring as much music to these words as might be appropriate. But whereas the moment's self-awareness of its own musicality is important dramatically, the way the words sound and work together as music is quintessentially Shakespearian and, as such, the principles of close reading here can be transferred to many other similarly lyrical passages.

Ways of reading word music include: an attentiveness to internal vowel sounds and their patterning through a single line; an awareness of the words' interconnectedness through alliteration, hard or open endings; special attention to the key words in each line which carry the bulk of the sound, as well as the words at the ends of lines; and a willingness to give each word its due stress. Here I think it is best to be guided by how we would pronounce a word in our own modern speech. Worrying too much about rhythm can sometimes lead to the occasional word sounding clipped, or being wrongly emphasized to the modern ear. But an awareness of metre can show how some words are being given special emphasis. The 20th-century Shakespeare director and Cambridge don, George 'Dadie' Rylands (another modernist voice, friend of Lytton Strachey, E. M. Forster, and Virginia Woolf, and tutor to John Barton, Peter Hall, Trevor Nunn, Derek Jacobi, and Ian McKellen), notes that 'meter enables the poet to underline a word as it were'.[21] It is useful to be sensitive to the contrast between Latinate words and simpler, Anglo-Saxon ones; how monosyllabic words (which are usually Anglo-Saxon in origin) slow the sound down, and how the word music of multisyllabic words agitates and stirs up.

17.2

What about the music of Shakespeare's prose? A contrasting example, from a later play, would be Lady Macbeth's sleepwalking scene (*c.* 1605).

> [*Enter Lady Macbeth with a taper*]
> GENTLEWOMAN   Lo you, here she comes.
>   This is her very guise, and, upon my life, fast
>   asleep. Observe her. Stand close.
> DOCTOR   How came she by that light?
> GENTLEWOMAN   Why, it stood by her. She   5
>   has light by her continually. 'Tis her command.
> DOCTOR   You see her eyes are open.
> GENTLEWOMAN   Ay, but their sense are shut.
> DOCTOR   What is it she does now? Look
>   how she rubs her hands.   10
> GENTLEWOMAN   It is an accustomed action
>   with her, to seem thus washing her hands. I
>   have known her continue in this a quarter
>   of an hour.
> LADY MACBETH   Yet here's a spot.   15
> DOCTOR   Hark, she speaks. I will set down
>   what comes from her to satisfy my remembrance the more strongly.

---

[21] George Rylands, *Words and Poetry* (London: Hogarth Press, 1928) 41.

LADY MACBETH   Out, damned spot; out, I
say. One, two—why, then 'tis time to do't.   20
Hell is murky. Fie, my lord, fie, a soldier
and afeard? What need we fear who knows
it when none can call our power to account?
Yet who would have thought the old man to
have had so much blood in him?   25
DOCTOR   Do you mark that?
LADY MACBETH   The Thane of Fife had a
wife. Where is she now? What, will these
hands ne'er be clean? No more o'that, my
lord, no more o'that. You mar all with this starting.   30
DOCTOR   Go to, go to. You have known what you should not.
GENTLEWOMAN   She has spoke what
she should not, I am sure of that. Heaven
knows what she has known.   35
LADY MACBETH   Here's the smell of the
blood still. All the perfumes of Arabia will
not sweeten this little hand. O, O, O!
DOCTOR   What a sigh is there! The heart
is sorely charged.   40
GENTLEWOMAN   I would have not have such
a heart in my bosom for the dignity of the
whole body.
DOCTOR   Well, well, well.
GENTLEWOMAN   Pray God it be, sir.   45
DOCTOR   This disease is beyond my
practice. Yet I have known those which
have walked in their sleep who have died holily
in their beds.
LADY MACBETH   Wash your hands, put on   50
your nightgown, look not so pale. I tell you
yet again, Banquo's buried. He cannot come
out on's grave.
DOCTOR   Even so?
LADY MACBETH   To bed, to bed.   55
There's knocking at the gate. Come, come,
come, come, give me your hand. What's
done cannot be undone. To bed, to bed,
to bed. [*Exit*

(*Macbeth*, V. i. 18–65)

Unlike the extract from *Twelfth Night, or what you will* this is not a lyrical passage, but the sounds of the words help to convey the dramatic effect. The ordinary and loyal duty of the Doctor and Gentlewoman provide a directness and openness of dialogue in prose which frames an extraordinary scene of breakdown and insight. The two observers create a bridge from Lady Macbeth's nightmare to the audience. Their language is crisp and matter of fact. They draw the audience's attention to Lady Macbeth's light. The Gentlewoman's word 'continually' sounds long and confidentially, and is quickly backed up by the sudden hard alliterative 'c' of 'command' (line 6). Then we are directed to look at Lady Macbeth's face. Her eyes are 'open' and 'shut' (lines 7 and 8); the sense of feeling moves from the eyes to her hands. 'Rubs' (line 10) sounds ordinary and direct, but the movement, as it unfolds before us, becomes elongated, fascinating, and more precisely defined with the emphatically sounding 'accustomed action' (line 11) and the onomato-poeic 'washing' (line 12). This whole scene is an exploration of the five senses. We are asked to see the spot of imaginary blood: all of the spectators' eyes will be focusing on the actor's hand at line 19. We are then immediately invited to hear the sound of the bell that Lady Macbeth rang to prompt Macbeth to go and murder King Duncan (line 20). We are asked to imagine the smell of the blood itself (lines 36–7), the perfumes of Arabia (line 37), and we might see Lady Macbeth tasting the blood as she rubs and touches her hands.

The scene is full of monosyllables and can almost be read as an exploration of Shakespeare's versatile use of this particular style. When Lady Macbeth first speaks we hear monosyllables. Their resonance is emphatic. They serve to slow the speaker down, and help to depict a mood of precision, understatement, and disarming naivety. 'Yet here's a spot' (line 15) focuses the dramatic attention on the movement of her hands in a sudden and particularized way. The Doctor's reply is made of contrasting, longer, mul-tisyllabic words (lines 16–18). Lady Macbeth then recalls the sound of the bell that she rang to signal to Macbeth that it was time for him to murder King Duncan. The sound of its striking is evoked with the internal vowel sounds of 'out', 'spot', and the repeated 'out', clipped, measured, tolling ominously—'Out, damned spot; out, I say. One, two—', and then the pace quickens, becomes urgent, with 'why then 'tis time to do't' (lines 19–20). 'Murky' (line 21) is the first word of more than one syllable she speaks in this scene, and the first in the last seventeen words. Its sound pulls the lips forward to make the long first syllable, 'mur' (the first syllable of 'murder'). As a description of hell it resonates with a childish sense of horror and understatement. The slow sound of 'murky' sounds from the depths and evokes Lady Macbeth's own sense of murkiness within. Apart from 'soldier', 'afeard', 'power', and 'account' (lines 21–3), the rest of the speech provides one of the most effective uses of monosyllables in all of Shakespeare. Here Lady Macbeth refers to an imagined, off-stage reality that only she was privy to when she returned with the daggers and smeared Duncan's blood over the sleeping grooms. Her eyewitness account patters out in monosyllables which, however quickly the actor might try to speak, seem to demand an elongated and painful emphasis with the internally similar long vowel sounds of 'old man to have had so much blood in him'. (lines 24–5). There is something elemental and basic in the phrase 'old man', conveying a sense of universal pity which, for example, 'old King' would not. Taking the bloody daggers back to the scene of the crime was Lady Macbeth's significant mistake. What she saw there started to destroy her and now haunts her dreams. Her sleep as well as Macbeth's has been murdered. The sound of childish fear is again evoked with the nursery rhyme-like fragment, 'The Thane of Fife had a wife. Where is she now?' (lines 27–8). These few words might evoke the sound of the murdered son of Macduff, as well as his mother. The focus then shifts again to the washing of the hands (more blood), and a change of tone as she recalls more direct speech with Macbeth.

The Doctor's 'go to, go to' echoes Lady Macbeth's 'one, two', and exposes again the underlying pulse beat and heart-thumping rhythm of the moment. Lines 31–5 repeat similar sounds and sense: 'what you should not' and 'what she should not' and, importantly, the long, fateful vowel sound of 'known' which occurs twice (and a half with 'knows'). 'Heaven' provides an antithesis to Lady Macbeth's earlier mentioned 'Hell'. In context, the sonorous yet sibilant 'Heaven knows what she has known' (lines 34–5) is in stark opposition to the hell which is being experienced by Lady Macbeth in front of us.

There are more monosyllables from Lady Macbeth, who implores us to smell as well as see the blood. The word 'smell' is tied with its long, labial ending to 'still' (lines 36–7), and offers the opportunity for Lady Macbeth's shocked disgust to linger in our ears.

Suddenly there is an outpouring of lyricism. The long vowel sound of 'all' (closely tied because of its ending to 'smell' and 'still') gives way to the two-and-a-half syllables of the Latinized 'per-fume-s' and the long, exotic sound of 'Ar-a-bi-a' (line 37). Its elongated and surprising sound conveys Lady Macbeth's longing to escape. There is the sound of much lyrical self-pity in 'will not sweeten this little hand', the assonance of the internal vowel sounds of 'will', the squeezed sound of 'sweeten', 'this', and 'little' (tied closely with the labial sounds of in 'will' and 'little' and the hard 'ts' in 'sweeten' and 'little') are finally contrasted by the short and definite dissonance of 'hand' (lines 37–8).

Lady Macbeth's sound reiterates how impossible any escape is for her and her language breaks down. All we hear is 'O, O, O!' (line 38). This sigh might be as gently pathetic, exclamatory, or as terrible as the actor chooses. One of the most shattering of all sighs at this point was made by Judi Dench when she played the role for Trevor Nunn in 1976, opposite Ian McKellen as Macbeth. The production was filmed for television. You can hear the sigh start somewhere down in her boots until she gradually allows it to work its way up through her body, finally throwing her head back to let out a terrifyingly slow scream which Dench makes last for twenty-five seconds. Dench explained to me that she wanted to give a reason for Lady Macbeth's suicide and that once Macbeth has effectively left her on her own it destroys her. The scream was part of that slow destruction. Lady Macbeth's 'O, O, O!' is a Shakespearian way of requiring an extreme emotion to be articulated by the actor. Lady Macbeth's scream is the most significant sound in the entire scene.

The response of the Doctor sounds tenderly with its open vowel sounds and measured sibilance: 'What a sigh is there! The heart is sorely charged' (lines 39–40). The Gentlewoman's reaction 'I would not have such a heart in my bosom for the dignity of the whole body' (lines 41–2) half echoes the rhythm of Lady Macbeth's realization a few seconds earlier, 'yet who would have thought the old man to have had so much blood in him' (lines 24–5). But whereas Lady Macbeth's earlier locution was one of profound and lonely regret, the Gentlewoman's sounds softly and sympathetically with the gentle resonance of 'bosom', 'dignity', and 'whole body'. The Doctor's 'well, well, well' (line 44) echoes and balances Lady Macbeth's 'O, O, O!'. The Gentlewoman's 'Pray God it be, sir' (line 45) conjures up memories of one of the sleeping grooms crying out 'God bless us' just after Macbeth has murdered King Duncan (II. i. 46). The Doctor's next speech is measured and resigned (lines 47–9), matter-of-fact, and lyrically balanced, those 'which have walked in their sleep' arriving finally at a holy death 'in their beds'.

Lady Macbeth, though, seems to undercut the Doctor's wisdom, impressionistically re-enacting her relationship with Macbeth (lines 50–3). Her lines are rhythmically measured and balanced, too, and give three direct instructions, followed by three emphatic, interdependent clauses. In finding language again, she has retrieved something of her former self. The Doctor's interjection 'Even so?' lifts the moment briefly for a heightened emphasis, and then the sound of the knocking on the south entry (II. i. 63–4) echoes through the castle into Lady Macbeth's nightmares from two Acts earlier, like an irregular heart-beat. Nearly every word thumps in lines 55–9, like the way blood pulsates in the ears during moments of extreme anxiety. As Lady Macbeth reaches out for Macbeth's hand, the monotonous inevitability of 'what's done cannot be undone' turns into the gentle limping iambic of 'to bed, to bed, to bed'. Her memory of going to bed after King Duncan's murder coincides here with the sounds of her steps as she exits to her present bed. The end of the repeated phrase 'to bed' could be followed by a step in performance.

<h1 style="text-align:center">17.3</h1>

The kinds of treatment I have brought to bear on Viola's verse and Lady Macbeth's prose speeches will, I hope, prove to be transferable to Shakespeare's 'great variety of readers' and how we experience the sound of his word music throughout the canon.

To return to Strauss' *Capriccio*. In the final moments of the opera, the Countess sings Olivier's sonnet to herself, set to Flamand's music, and realizes that neither the words nor the music alone can satisfy. She needs both, and holds both in creative tension within herself. I can think of no better metaphor for the work required of Shakespearian readers—enthusiasts, students, actors—than the Countess at the end of Strauss' *Capriccio*. We, like the Countess, must decide on the creative effect for ourselves, but the words and their music are interdependent. She sings:

> In vain do I try to keep them apart, for words and music are blended together to form a single creation. Mysterious experience—finding one art restored by the other.[22]

In Strauss' *Capriccio* there is indeed a unification of what Richard Barnfield calls 'music and sweet poetry' in a sonnet attributed to Shakespeare in *The Passionate Pilgrim* of 1599:

> One god is god of both (as poets feign)
> One knight loves both, and both in thee remain.[23]

---

[22] Richard Strauss and Clemens Krauss, *Capriccio*, conducted by Karl Böhm (Munich, 1971), Deutsche Grammophon, CD booklet, translated by Maria Massey (London: Boosey and Hawkes, 1963) 111.

[23] Burrow (2002) 348.

The approach I am encouraging slows us down as readers, rather like a musician practising individual bars of music, and is a reminder that Shakespeare is never writing naturalistic dialogue. A hypersensitivity towards Shakespeare's word music will, I hope, put the mystery back into the rainbow that so inspired Keats when writing about Edmund Kean and will bring to the language an energy and life which quickens every syllable and reveals, as Edith Evans did, 'new wonders unsuspected and never to be forgotten'.

SELECT BIBLIOGRAPHY

To read

Foakes, R. A. (1980) 'Poetic Language and Dramatic Significance in Shakespeare', in *Shakespeare's Styles: Essays in Honor of Kenneth Muir*, Philip Edwards (ed.), Inga-Stina Ewbank, and G. K. Hunter (Cambridge: Cambridge University Press) 79–93.
Fuller, David (2011) *The Life in the Sonnets* (London: Continuum International Publishing Group).
McDonald, Russ (2001) *Shakespeare and the Arts of Language* (Oxford: Oxford University Press).
Noble, Adrian (2010) *How to do Shakespeare* (London: Routledge).
Rokison, Abigail (2010) *Shakespearean Verse Speaking: Text and Theatre Practice* (Cambridge: Cambridge University Press).
Rylands, George (1928) *Words and Poetry* (London: Hogarth Press).
Wright, George T. (1988) *Shakespeare's Metrical Art* (Berkeley and Los Angeles: University of California Press; repr. 1991).

To listen to

Edith Evans (1959?) *Twenty Shakespeare Sonnets and Scenes from 'As You Like It'* (London: Columbia Records); available to download from i-Tunes.
Mendelssohn, Felix (1994) *A Midsummer Night's Dream*, CD, including readings from the play read by Judi Dench (Hamburg: Deutsche Grammaphon).
Shakespeare, William (2003) *Antony and Cleopatra*, The Complete Arkangel Shakespeare, CD, Cairon Hinds as Antony, Estelle Kohler as Cleopatra (North Kingstown: BBC Audiobooks America).

To watch

Macbeth, dir. for television by Philip Casson, DVD, Ian McKellen as Macbeth, Judi Dench as Lady Macbeth (London: Thames Television, 1979).
Twelfth Night, dir. by Trevor Nunn, 1996.

CHAPTER 18

FINDING YOUR FOOTING IN SHAKESPEARE'S VERSE

BRUCE R. SMITH

How to do that? Let me suggest five ways:

- Ride a horse.
- Run a foot race.
- Dance a round.
- Walk the talk.
- Hear with your eyes.

One by one, here's how.

18.1 RIDE A HORSE

The late 16th-century manuscript of Sir Philip Sidney's *A Defence of Poesie* discovered in the Norfolk County Record Office in 1967 lay undetected so long for a simple reason: an 18th-century owner, Francis Blomefield, had interleaved it in his manuscript collection under the heading 'A Treatise of Horsman Shipp'.[1] It is indeed with the management of horses that the *Defence* begins. Sidney and his friend Sir Edward Wotton have learned all about horses, horseman, and horsemanship at the court of the Holy Roman Emperor

---

[1] Mary R. Mahl's identification of the text as Sidney's was announced in 'A Treatise of Horsman Shipp', *The Times Literary Supplement* no. 3434 (21 December 1967) 1245. The manuscript is catalogued as one of two surviving 16th-century manuscripts of the *Defence* in Sir Philip Sidney, *Miscellaneous Prose*, Katherine Duncan-Jones and Jan van Dorsten (eds), (Oxford: Clarendon Press, 1973) 65.

Maximilian II. Their instructor, Jon Pietro Pugliano, a squire of the emperor's stable, said so much in praise of horses and horsemanship that Sidney confesses, 'if I had not beene a peece of a Logician before I came to him, I thinke he would have perswaded me to have wished myselfe a horse'.[2]

You don't need to *be* a horse to find your footing in Shakespeare's verse; you just need to ride one. Let us not underestimate the importance of horses' three gaits—walk (four beats), trot (two beats), canter (three beats)—for most people's experience of rhythm before the advent of the steam engine and railroads.[3] From the back of a horse the difference between the quantitative metres of Greek and Latin verse and the stress metres of English verse might not feel so great. The thumps of the hooves mark the stresses of English verse; the intervals between, the times of classical verse.

Stresses and times are, after all, both species of rhythm. And so is rhyme. The English words 'rhyme' and 'rhythm' are derived alike from the Greek *rhythmos* and the Latin *rhythmus*. According to the *OED*, the distinction between them ('rhythm' as metre, 'rhyme' as syllables that sound similar) emerged in the early 14th century, after the structural principle of verse being written in Latin had shifted from the duration of vowel sounds to the like-soundedness of whole words.[4] Both of the major Latin-to-English dictionaries of the 16th century—Thomas Eliot's *Bibliotheca* (1542) and Thomas Cooper's *Thesaurus* (1578)—define *rhythmus* in terms that embrace both rhyme and metre. Eliot translates the word as 'numbre or armony in speakyng', and notes that 'it is also callyd a ryme', while Cooper defines *rhythmus* as 'Number or harmonie in speaking: meeter: rhime'.[5] William Webbe, Graduate (as he is styled on the title page), may set out in *A*

---

[2] Sir Philip Sidney, *A Defence of Poesie* (London: William Ponsonby, 1595) sig. B1v.

[3] The three gaits are described by Elisabeth LeGuin, 'Man and Horse in Harmony', in Karen Raber and Treva J. Tucker (eds), *The Culture of the Horse: Status, Discipline, and Identity in the Early Modern World* (New York: Palgrave Macmillan, 2005) 175–96. LeGuin contrasts the range of possibilities that four legs makes possible (a horse's two pairs of legs can move in tandem laterally or diagonally) with the two-beat trot to which human beings are limited by having only two legs. Although horses were expensive to buy and to maintain, the late 16th and early 17th centuries witnessed increases in the use of horses for transportation and agriculture (Peter Edwards, *The Horse Trade of Tudor and Stuart England,* Cambridge: Cambridge University Press, 1988, 1–20) and a demystification of the horse as an index of aristocratic status (Bruce Boehrer, 'Shakespeare and the Social Devaluation of the Horse', in *The Culture of the Horse*, 91–111). Wolfgang Schivelbusch, *The Railway Journey: The industrialization and perception of time and space* (Berkeley: University of California Press, 1987) quotes James Adamson, writing in 1825 and comparing travel on horseback with travel by railroad: 'The animal advances not with a continued progressive motion, but with a sort of irregular hobbling, which raises and sinks its body at every alternate motion of the limbs. This is distinctly felt on horseback, and it is the same when an animal draws a load. Even in walking and running one does not move regularly forward. The body is raised and depressed at every step of our progress; it is this incessant lifting of the mass which constitutes that drag on our motions which checks their speed, and confines it within such moderate limits' (8–9).

[4] *Oxford English Dictionary Online*, 'rhyme', *n.*, etymology, 1.†a, 1.b, <http://www. www.oed.com>, accessed at various times in April and May 2011. Further quotations from the *OED* are cited in the text.

[5] Thomas Eliot, *Bibliotheca Eliotæ: Eliotis librarie* (London: Thomas Bertholet, 1542) sig. 2G3v; Thomas Cooper, *Thesaurus linguæ Romanæ & Britannicæ* (London: Henry Denham, 1578) sig. 5S5v.

Discourse of English Poetrie (1586) to persuade English poets to eschew rhyme as a patterning device and to adopt instead the quantitative metres of Greek and Latin verse, but he recognizes that rhythm and rhyme are, at bottom, both versions of the same thing: 'measurable or tunable speaking'.[6] Speaking, *rhythmus* exists not on the page but in speech, not in poems but in persons.[7]

'I was never so berhymed since Pythagoras'[s] time that I was an Irish rat, which I can hardly remember': Rosalind's response to the verses that Orlando has been hanging on Arden's trees in *As You Like It* (III. ii. 172–4) parodies Orlando's defective tetrameter even as it redresses his feeble wit by executing a turn on the transmigration of souls and the fame of the Irish for enchanting rats and killing them with rhymes.[8] (I will 'Rime' hem to death, as they doe *Irish* rats, | In drumming tunes', Jonson threatens his detractors in the 'apologeticall Dialogue' appended to *Poetaster*).[9] Poor (quasi-)dumbstruck Orlando! The verses he hangs on Arden's trees are perfect illustrations of the mindless rhyming that Webbe excoriates in *A Discourse of English Poetrie*. Orlando may make every line of his love-poem rhyme with—*ind* ('From the east to western Ind | No jewel is like Rosalind', III. ii. 86–7, etc.), but he can't manage time.

Sometimes Orlando comes up with only seven syllables (as in the first line), not the eight that the verse asks and his readers crave (as in the second). Hence Touchstone, after improvising twelve more lines in this vein, can exclaim, 'This is the very false gallop of verses' (III. ii. 111)—a gallop because a rhyme every seven or eight syllables makes the verse move along rapidly, false because Orlando's four hooves don't mount the air as they would in a true gallop (*OED*, 'gallop', *n*., 1.a) but hit the ground with a clump when a syllable is wanting or there is one too many. This is the effect Rosalind describes when she says that some of Orlando's verses 'had in them more feet than the verses would bear' (III. ii. 162–3). Celia's return of this verbal serve, and Rosalind's after that, continue the conceit of a galloping horse:

CELIA   That's no matter; the feet might bear the verses.
ROSALIND   Ay, but the feet were lame, and could not bear themselves without the
    verse, and therefore stood lamely in the verse

(III. ii. 164–7).

Not for nothing does Sidney's *The Defence of Poesie* begin with a story about horsemanship.

---

[6] William Webbe, *A Discourse of English Poetrie* (London: Robert Walley, 1586) sig. B2v. Further quotations are cited in the text.

[7] I allude to Norman Holland's *Poems in Persons: An introduction to the psychoanalysis of literature* (New York: Norton, 1973), even as I insist on the primary early modern sense of 'person' as physical body.

[8] Wells and Taylor, (2005) 668. I have added the [s] after the apostrophe to give the two lines in Rosalind's rhyme seven syllables each. Further quotations from Shakespeare's plays and poems are taken from the Oxford edition and are cited in the text by Act, Scene, and line numbers (plays) and line numbers (poems.)

[9] Ben Jonson, *Poetaster*, 'To the Reader', in *The Workes* (London: Will Stansby, 1616) sigs. 2G2v.

18.2 RUN A FOOT RACE

'More feet than the verses would bear': Rosalind is speaking prose here, but her words exemplify Webbe's alternative definition of *rhythmus*, 'iust proportion of a clause or sentence, whether it be in prose or méeter, aptly comprised together' (sig. F2). Rosalind's words have a rhythmic cadence that enacts the semantic sense:

more *feet* than the **vers**-es would *bear*.

(The system of notation I use throughout this chapter is that proposed by Martin J. Duffell in *A New History of English Metre* [2008]. Primary stresses are indicated in bold face, secondary stresses by underlining; caesuras by ||, and missing beats or voids, with [V]).[10] Those extra feet in Orlando's lame gallop impede the phrase's beginning before the phrase picks up speed and clips along to its expedient close. 'More *feet*' (or perhaps '*more feet*') quite literally 'shackles the feet' (*im*|+|*pedes*), while the anapestic canter of 'than the **vers**-es would *bear*' serves to 'free the feet' (*ex*|+|*pedes*) (*OED* 'impede', *v.*, etymology; 'expedite', *v.*, etymology).

According to George Puttenham in *The Art of English Poesie* (1589), it is the monosyllabic nature of the English language that makes it unfit for the 'measures' of Greek and Latin verse. The classical languages, Puttenham observes, are made up of polysyllabic words—hence their susceptiblity to 'diversity of motion and times in the pronunciation of their words'. By contrast,

> because our natural and primitive language of the Saxon English bears not any words (at least very few) of more syllables than one (for whatsoever we see exceed cometh to us by the alterations of our language grown upon many conquests and otherwise), there could be no such observation of times in the sound of our words, and for that cause we could not have the feet which the Greeks and Latins have in their meters.[11]

Puttenham has more profound reasons, however, for regretting that 'feet' in 16th-century English verse are not the feet (no need for quotation marks) in Greek and Latin verse. According to Puttenham, English 'feet' are just metaphors, while Greek and Latin feet are the real thing. Drawing ultimately on a pun in Horace's satires ('*Nempe composito dixi pede currere versus/Lucili*', 'To be sure I did say that the verses of Lucilius run on with

---

[10]   Martin J. Duffell, *A New History of English Metre* (London: Modern Humanities Research Association, 2008). Duffell's system takes into account elements from four approaches to metre: the traditional stress-syllabic approach, Derek Attridge's rhythmic approach, Kristin Hanson and Paul Kiparsky's parametric approach, and the Russian statistical approach (20–6).

[11]   George Puttenham, *The Art of English Poesy*, Frank Whigham and Wayne A. Rebhorn (eds), (Ithaca: Cornell University Press, 2007) 158.

halting foot'),[12] Puttenham follows Julius Caesar Scaliger's *Poetics* (Lyons 1561, Leyden 1581), in explaining why English 'feet' are just metaphors. By counting syllables,

> ye may say we have feet in our vulgar rhymes, but that is improperly, for a foot by his sense natural is a member of office and function, and serveth to three purposes, that is to say, to go, to run, and to stand still; so as he must sometimes be swift, sometimes slow, sometime unequally marching or peradventure steady. And if our feet poetical want these qualities, it cannot be said a foot in sense translative as here.[13]

Doesn't Rosalind's phrase 'more feet than the verses would bear' put the lie to such a statement? '*More feet*' sounds slow, and 'than the **vers**-es would *bear*' fast. Spondaic rhythm by nature is slow and anapestic rhythm is fast. If it seems so to us, the reason is that we have naturalized the names of Greek and Latin feet (spondee, pyrrhic, iamb, trochee, anapest, dactyl) and think of them in terms of stresses, not durations. Puttenham and his contemporaries, well trained in Latin if not in Greek, understood that a spondee was a measure of time (so many fractions of a second), just as pyrrhics, trochees, iambs, anapests, and dactyls were, and that, generally speaking, classical verse moved in just one rhythm, with only occasional variations.

The situation is easy enough to appreciate in musical scores. A time signature at the beginning of a piece (4/4, say) indicates the number of beats per measure and what kind of note gets one beat. Within a given measure those beats can be realized as a whole-note (perceived as slow), four quarter-notes (faster), eight eighth-notes (faster still), sixteen sixteenth-notes (fastest of all), or any combination thereof that adds up to four beats where a quarter-note equals one beat. (It is no accident that Thomas Campion, a composer as well as a poet, argued for classical metres in English. But of course Campion, like all composers of Shakespeare's time, did not use time signatures or mark measures; a singer or a player performed with a rhythmic pattern that was *felt*, not counted out precisely.) By contrast with the measured pace of classical verse, the stresses of English verse must have seemed haphazard. But the differences between classical metres and English stresses are not as profound as they seemed at the time. Common to both systems was the idea that rhythm is fundamentally a matter of motion. Puttenham's word for the effect is 'stir'. Greek and Latin have it; so, in its own way, does English.

For his objection that English feet don't really *move*, Puttenham's authority is impeccable: 'by the Philosopher's definition, stir is the true measure of time' (157). Aristotle's inquiry into the nature of time in *Physics*, Book 4, Chapters 10 to 14, gave Scaliger and Puttenham their cue. Aristotle's fundamental proposition is simple enough: 'we

---

[12] Satires 1.10.1–2 in Horace, *Satires, Epistles and Ars Poetica*, H. Rushton Fairclough (trans.), Loeb Library (Cambridge, MA: Harvard University Press, 1991) 114–15.

[13] Wigham and Rebhorn (2007) 157. Compare Julius Caesar Scaliger, *Poetices* (Lyons: Antonius Vicentius, 1561) 2.2: 'officium pedis motus est, vt laxè dicam. Nam videtur vox in diction quaedam celeries absolui, in alia tardius. Quare ab Horatio quoque tum *sententiam*, tum *versum currere* dictum est' (sig. f2).

apprehend time only when we have marked motion, marking it by before and after; and it is only when we have perceived before and after in motion that we say that time has lapsed'.[14] This and other passages from Aristotle's *Physics* are likely the inspiration for Augustine's observation in *Confessions* Book 6, Chapter 14, that we apprehend the world in a perpetual 'now'—'Presentism' with a vengeance.[15] To mark time, to demarcate that 'now', Aristotle requires four things: (1) a soul to do the counting, (2) a unit in which the counting can be done, (3) a thing that changes by moving, and (4) a space within which it moves. For counting horses, the unit is a horse; for counting dogs, a dog; for counting sounds in poetry, a foot. Why a foot? Perhaps because listeners are apt to beat rhythm with their feet (*OED* 'foot', n.1, II. 6). Perhaps because poetry started out as choreography. 'Dance is, perhaps, an even better analogy for metre than percussion', Duffell observes, 'because *rhythm* is a term derived from the Greek word for *balanced movement*. The earliest comparison between dance and verse rhythm was made by Plato ..., and Greek metrics borrowed its most basic terms, *podes, arsis,* and *thesis,* from dancing'.[16] More on dance in a moment. One can imagine that a human soul could mark time by watching an object move—a galloping horse, say—but the thing that changes most often in Aristotle's discussion of time is the human body, and the space of change is measured by movement: 'the "now" corresponds to the body that is carried along, as time corresponds to the motion. For it is by means of the body that is carried along that we come aware of the before and after in the motion, and if we regard these as countable we get the "now"' (219.b.23–5). This distinction between motion and *loco*-motion (literally 'motion-in-place') is crucial to Aristotle's understanding of time. In terms of motion, the measure of time in which two things change may be the same—three seconds, say. But *loco*-motion, the motion within that space of three seconds, can vary. It can be fast or slow: a horse might walk (four beats), or trot (two beats), or canter (three beats) at varying speeds.[17] In an hour a jogging horse can cover four miles; trotting, eight miles; cantering, ten miles; galloping, twenty-five.[18] Thus, 'movements that have simultaneous limits have the same time, yet the one may in fact be fast and the other not' (223.b.6–7). Within the confines of a verse of six feet a pyrrhic happens more rapidly than a spondee.

---

[14] Aristotle, *Physics* 219.a.22–5, in *Complete Works*, Jonathan Barnes (ed.), 2 vols (Princeton: Princeton University Press, 1984) 1:371. Further quotations are taken from this edition and are cited in the text by reference number.

[15] Augustine, 'What is Time?' in Ernâni Magalhães and L. Nathan Oaklander, eds, *Presentism: Essential readings* (Lanham, MD: Lexington Books, 2010), 27–34. Augustine's essential idea is this: 'If we can think of some bit of time which cannot be divided into even the smallest instantaneous moments, that alone is what we can call "present". And this time flies so quickly from future into past that it is an interval with no duration. If it has duration, it is divisible into past and future. But the present occupies no space' (28).

[16] Duffell (2008) 28, n. 20.

[17] 'Now the change or movement of each thing is only *in* the thing which changes or *where* the thing itself which moves or change[s] may chance to be. But time is present equally everywhere and with all things. Again, change is always faster or slower, whereas time is not; for fast and slow are defined by time—fast is what moves much in a short time, slow what moves little in a long time; but time is not defined by time, by being either a certain amount or a certain kind of it' (218.b.12–18).

[18] 'Horse gait', <http://en.wikipedia.org/wiki/Horse_gait>, accessed 17 April 2011.

Is it, though, 'feet' that we hear when we hear verse? Do we hear spondees and ana-pests? Do we somehow recognize '*more feet*' as one entity and 'than the **vers-**' as another? I accept Puttenham's scepticism about the 'feet' of English verse even as I insist that English verse has feet with no quotation marks. When we trot with our two limbs, we don't think, 'Now I'm putting the right foot down, now the left, and now I've completed a trochee'. No, we feel the rhythm more diffusely, especially when we're moving rapidly. This is also the case in dramatic verse. Duffell, drawing on work by Kristen Hanson, has demonstrated through statistical analysis that Shakespeare's non-dramatic verse tends to move in feet, with a discrete sense of the line as an organizational unit of ten syllables and five stresses, while his dramatic verse tends to move in beats that may or may not coincide with iambic pentameter as a template.[19]

We can hear that effect in Menenius' attempt to hold back the rage of the Roman mob in *Coriolanus*, Act III, Scene i. Slow trochaic rhythm arrests the crowd's momentum before rapid anapestic rhythm in the next line and enjambment of the second line with the third enacting the tiger's leap:

> *One* word **more**, one *word*!
> This *ti*-ger-foot-ed **rage**, when it shall *find*
> The *harm* of un-scanned **swift**-ness, will *too late*
> Tie *lead*-en **pounds** to's *heels*. Pro-*ceed* by **pro**-cess ...

(III. 1. 312–15)

In this acoustic context, 'unscanned' suggests not only unexamined or not discussed (*OED* 'scan', *v.*, 3.a) but unanalysed with respect to syllables (*OED* 'scan', *v.*, 1.a). The tiger's swiftness is not, technically speaking, 'unscanned', just scanned very differently from iambic measures. The anapestic leap is arrested in '*too late*' before due deliberation is achieved in the iambic regularity (albeit with an extra final syllable) of 'Proceed by process'. Aristotle's point is this: each line in Menenius' speech can be measured in pre-cisely equal units of five feet, but the speed of locomotion within each foot is different. The spondees ('word more, one word', 'too late') take longer than the pyrrhics ('when it', 'of un-', '-ness will'). Duffell's point, and mine, is this: we don't hear spondees or pyrrhics at all but beats that move now in spondaic rhythm, now in anapestic rhythm, now slow, now fast.

The differences in the sense of line that Duffell draws between Shakespeare's dramatic verse and his non-dramatic verse can be witnessed in Sonnet 19 ('Devouring time, blunt thou the lion's paws'). This time the feet are not a tiger's but a lion's:

> And *do* what-*e'er* thou **wilt**, *swift*-foot-ed *time*,
> To the *wide* **world** and *all* her *fad*-ing *sweets*.
> But I for-*bid* thee *one* most **hein**-ous *crime*:
> O, *carve* **not** with thy hours my **love's** fair *brow*

(19. 6–9)

---

[19] Duffell (2008) 131–5, 142–4.

Anapestic swiftness with 'footed time' and 'To the wide' reaches an abrupt halt in the spondaic slowness of 'O, carve not'. The measure of time (five feet per line) remains the same; locomotion within that measure varies in speed. What is different here from similar phenomena in Menenius' speech is the integrity of the line, the persistence of just five stresses per line, the weakness of the enjambment between lines 6 and 7.

Scaliger and Puttenham take Aristotle at his word: for them, a *metrical* foot is a *human* foot. It is not the poem that moves, it is the human body that moves, and it moves within the temporal boundaries marked out by the metrical pattern. *Rhythmus* is physiological. Puttenham imagines the pyrrhics, spondees, iambs, etc. of Greek and Latin verse as operating like a foot race:

> of this stir and motion of their devised feet, nothing can better show the quality than these runners at common games, who, setting forth from the first goal, one giveth the start speedily and perhaps before he come halfway to the other goal, decayeth his pace, as a man weary and fainting; another is slow at the start, but by amending his pace keeps even with his fellow or perchance gets before him; another one while gets ground, another while loseth it again, either in the beginning or middle of his race, and so proceeds unequally, sometimes swift, sometimes slow, as his breath or forces serve him; another sort there be that plod on, and will never change their pace, whether they win or lose the game.[20]

Modern cognitive science confirms the intuitions of Aristotle, Scaliger, and Puttenham. Experiments summarized in Vyvyan Evans' *The Structure of Time* (2005) suggest that acts of perception involve an oscillation of neurons within a range of time from fractions of one second to an outer limit of three seconds. Music, poetry, and language seem to be apprehended in 'perceptual moments' lasting two to three seconds.[21] By my calculation, three seconds is exactly the time it takes me to pronounce aloud, at a slow trot, the regular iambics of the opening line of Shakespeare's Sonnet 12: 'When I do count the clock that tells the time' (12. 1). One line of verse, one perceptual moment. Does six-tenths of a second (the time it takes me to pronounce an iamb) dictate the pace at which I run this particular race? If so, Puttenham assures me that I can certainly keep up with my competitors—and perhaps outpace them. At every stride, I start slow and pick up speed. Because I am speaking English, not Greek or Latin, the pace that I run must be reckoned in units of five feet, not in units of a single foot.

In the 'stir' of *1 Henry IV*, there are three characters who compete for space and time: Falstaff, Hotspur, and Prince Harry. Each runs the race at a different pace. The irregularities of prose keep Falstaff from getting very far very fast. Waiting for his comrades on Gads Hill, for example, Falstaff measures out an aural space that is no less delimited than the physical space he occupies:

---

[20] Wigham and Rebhorn (2007) 159.
[21] Vyvyan Evans, *The Structure of Time: Language, meaning and temporal cognition* (Amsterdam: John Benjamins, 2005) 23–7.

Poins! *Hal*! A *plague* upon you **both**! *Rus*-sell! *Harv*-ey! I'll **starve** ere I'll rob a *foot*
furth-er.... *Eight* **yards** of un-*ev*-en *ground* is *three*-score and *ten* **miles** a-foot with
me, and the *ston*-y-heart-ed *vil*-lains **know** it well e-*nough*

(II. ii. 21–2, 25–7)

Uneven ground indeed. Falstaff exemplifies the last of Puttenham's competitors, those
who 'plod on, and will never change their pace, whether they win or lose the game'.[22]

From his very name, you might know that Hotspur's pace is a gallop. Instead of attending to Lady Percy's complaints in Act II, Scene iv, Hotspur is chomping at the bit, thinking about the horse that will carry him off to battle. Has Butler brought that crop-ear
roan from the Sheriff, Hotspur asks his servant. He has.

That *roan* shall be my **throne**.
[V] *Well*, I will **back** him *straight*.—O, *Es*-pe-rance!—
Bid But-ler lead him **forth** in-to the *park*

(II. iv. 70–2)

Pyrrhic and trochaic rhythms here keep the verse moving forward at a headlong
clip. Line 71, at least in my hearing, exemplifies Duffell's calculation that Shakespeare's
lines of dramatic verse often contain more than ten syllables: I hear a pause before '*Well*'
(a void that functions as a silent syllable) and a trailing off on '*Es*-pe-rance' (giving the
line a feminine ending that pushes the pace along). Ultimately, Hotspur proves to be the
kind of racer who starts off speedily but before the finish line 'decayeth his pace, as a man
weary and fainting'.[23] At his death he is cut off in mid-sentence.

Between these extremes, in rhythm as in so much else, Prince Harry strikes a mean.
Hotspur may refer to him as 'The *nim*-ble-footed *mad*-cap *Prince* of **Wales**' (IV. i. 95),
with a typical rush on 'nimble-footed', but Prince Harry shows his hand—and his footing skills—early in the play when he leaves the uneven ground of his prose exchanges
with Falstaff and Poins in Act I, Scene ii, and walks confidently onto centre stage in the
underlying iambic rhythm of his soliloquy:

So when this *loose* be-*hav*-iour I **throw** *off*
And *pay* the **debt** I nev-er *pro*-mis-èd,
By *how* much *bet*-ter than my **word** I am,
By **so** *much* shall I **fal**-si-fy men's *hopes* …

(I. ii. 205–8)

Prince Harry is the sort of runner who may be 'slow at the start, but by amending his
pace keeps even with his fellow or perchance gets before him'.[24] His metrical dexterity is

[22] Wigham and Rebhorn (2007) 159.
[23] Wigham and Rebhorn (2007) 159.
[24] Wigham and Rebhorn (2007) 159.

an advantage—now speaking in prose, now in verse—but it is his iambic steadiness that wins the day.

18.3 DANCE A ROUND

Among actions scripted to be done with feet in Shakespeare's plays, four are cued most often: falling prostrate at someone else's feet, marching, walking, and dancing.[25] (These might be distinguished from foot work alluded to in speeches but not actually performed: stomping a cardinal's hat under foot, standing foot to foot against an enemy, stepping from shore to land.) Dance, though it would seem to have the least to do with speech, can help us attune our ears to the tongued feet in marching, walking, and falling. Many of the major terms in metrics, let us recall, have their origins in Greek words associated with dancing.[26] Among the scenes in Shakespeare's scripts where dancing is cued—the Russian maskers' scene in *Love's Labour's Lost*, Capulet's inauguration of the ball in *Romeo and Juliet*, Act I, Scene v, the multiple dances in *A Midsummer Night's Dream*, the rustic revelry that Duke Senior initiates in *As You Like It*, Act V, Scene iv, the after-supper dance in *Much Ado About Nothing*, Act II, Scene i, the shepherds' festival in *The Winter's Tale*, Act IV, Scene iv, the wedding masque in *The Tempest*, Act IV, Scene i, the mummers' crashing of Wolsey's banquet in *Henry VIII*, Act I, Scene iv—speech is implicated into dance and dance into speech in varied ways. We can distinguish three scenarios. In the first, verbal invitations to the dance set up the rhythms of the dancing that follows. In the second, verse and dance happen simultaneously. In the third, verse and dance diverge in thematically significant ways.

On occasion, words of invitation to the dance establish the rhythm of the dance. '*Wel*-come, *gentle*-men': Capulet repeats that phrase three times, like a musical motif, as he greets the maskers at his ball (*Romeo and Juliet*, I, v, 16, 21, 25). Reminiscing about his own dancing days, Capulet falls into a triple iambic rhythm just before he calls for the music to play:

> *Wel*-come, *gentle*-men. I have *seen* the **day**
> That I have *worn* a **vis**-or, and could *tell*
> A *whisp*-er-ing *tale* in a *fair* **la**-dy's *ear*
> Such as would *please*. 'Tis *gone*, 'tis *gone*, 'tis **gone**.
> You are *wel*-come, *gentle*-men. *Come*, mu-*sic*-ians, **play**.
>   *Musicke plays: and the dance.*
> A *hall*, a *hall*! Give *room*, and **foot** it, *girls*
>
>   (I. v. 21–6)[27]

---

[25] I base these numbers on my search for 'foot', 'feet', and 'footing' at OpenSourceShakespeare, <http://www.opensourceshakespeare.org>, accessed 10 April 2011.

[26] Duffell (2008) 28, n. 20.

[27] The original stage direction has been supplied from Charlton Hinman (ed.), *The First Folio of Shakespeare*, Norton Facsimile edition (New York: Norton, 1968) 673 (sig. ee5).

The placement of the stage direction in the Folio text, in the midst of Capulet's speech, suggests the way rhythms of speech are enjambed with rhythms of dance.

So, too, does the dance provide the rhythmic matrix in which Romeo and Juliet declare their love in exchanges of rhymed lines. Romeo and Juliet do not dance, but their *words* do, in almost perfectly regular iambic rhythm. Romeo begins the verbal choreography that moves from an exchange of quatrains to a quatrain shared between them, to a couplet spoken one line each to a final shared quatrain that ends in a symmetrical half-line each. Juliet is remembering this concatenation of speech and dance when, later in the scene, the Nurse asks what she has just said in an aside and Juliet replies, 'A rhyme I learnt even now/Of one I danced withal' (I. v. 141–2). Dance she did, but not with her physical feet. In its coordination of speech with dance this scene in *Romeo and Juliet* exemplifies the second scenario, in which verse and dance occur together, either in alternation or simultaneously. In this respect it reprises the Russian maskers' scene in *Love's Labour's Lost* and anticipates the after-supper dance in *Much Ado About Nothing*, II. i, and the shepherd maskers' scene in *Henry VIII*, I. iv.

Tybalt's unsuccessful attempt to expose Romeo and persuade Capulet to throw him out happens as a kind of aside while the dance is in progress—an instance of the third scenario, in which words and dance diverge. The most surprising of these instances occurs during the wooing rite in *Much Ado About Nothing*, II. i. Unlike Romeo and Juliet, the couples on this occasion banter in prose *before* the music sounds and they exit the stage to dance elsewhere, in another chamber as it were, while during the music, in jarring prose, Don John and Borachio gull Claudio, a man left out of the dance.[28] The synchrony of speech rhythm and dance rhythm that is witnessed in *Romeo and Juliet* is thus broken, but in the comedy's closing moments Benedick restores the connection by calling for a dance *before* the multiple weddings, 'that we may lighten our own hearts and our wives' heels' (V. iv. 117–18). This time Claudio is included.

Before the dance begins in Act II, Scene I, Beatrice provides a handy catalogue of the dances the couples might do. As Leonato gives Hero her last-minute instructions vis-à-vis the attentions of Don Pedro, Beatrice advises her cousin to 'tell him there is measure in everything, and so dance out the answer' (II. i. 64–5). Beatrice goes on to choreograph the entire round of courtship: wooing is a Scotch jig, 'hot and hasty' (67), wedding is a 'measure', 'mannerly modest, … full of state and ancientry' (68–9), repenting is a cinquepace, forcing the dancer to go 'faster and faster until he sink into his grave' (71–2). In the event, the couples 'walk about' (II. i. 78, the reading in both the 1600 quarto and the 1623 folio texts)—or, as the Oxford edition would have it, even in the 2nd edition, 'walk a bout'. The lovers do spar with one another.

The dances in Beatrice's catalogue, despite the vigorous pace of some of them and the ethnic hipness suggested by 'a Scotch jig', were court dances. They may have had their

---

[28] Only after Balthasar and Margaret, Antonio and Ursula, and Benedick and Beatrice have exchanged speeches—in prose—as they 'walk a bout' do stage directions actually call for music and dancing: '*Dance*' in the 1600 quarto and '*Musicke for the dance*' in the Folio are both accompanied by an '*Exeunt*' that leaves the stage to Don John, Borachio, and Claudio vizarded as Benedick. In the Folio the '*Exeunt*' comes *before* the cue for '*Musicke*', clearly indicating that the couples do their dancing off stage.

origins in popular dances on the green or in the barn or (God forbid) in the churchyard, but all of them had been appropriated by gentle folk for showing off their dancing skills to their peers. Christopher Marsh's distinction between 'social dancing' on the green, in the barn, or in the churchyard and 'performative dancing' in the great hall directs us to a tension that is played out in the dances scripted to be performed in Shakespeare's plays.[29] That tension is realized in rhythm. The courtly dances that Beatrice mentions, along with others, are allied with specific poetic metres in Sir John Davies' *Orchestra or A poeme of dauncing. Iudicially proouing the true obseruation of time and measure* (1596). In Davies' etiology it is Love who invents the seven basic movements performed on the dance floor as in the sky: '*Upward*, and *downward, forth*, and *back againe*, / *To this side*, and *to that*, and *turning round*'.[30] '*Rounds* and *winding Heyes*' were the first dances that Love invented. Davies' verse suggests the trochaic rhythm ('*up*-ward', '*down*-ward', '*forth* and', '*back* a-') that many linguistics take to be the fundamental rhythm of the English language. More complicated movements were then invented by Love. Each of the court dances current in the late 1590s is identified by Davies with a particular metrical foot: measures with spondees, the cinquepace with pentameter, the curanto with dactyls, the volta with anapests. In Davies' conceit, *every* poem is a poem of dancing.

The question of popular versus courtly rhythms becomes critical at the end of *As You Like It*. Duke Senior has just assured the exiles in Arden that each of them 'Shall share the good of our returnèd fortune/According to the measure of their states' (V. iv. 172–3) before he issues an invitation to dancing:

> *Play, mus*-ic, and you **brides** and **bride**-grooms *all*,
> With *mea*-sure **heap**ed in **joy** to th'*mea*-sures *fall*
>
> (V. IV. 176–7)

(The Folio text marks the iambic elision thus: 'to'th measures'.)[31] If it was one of 'the measures' (rather than dance-measures more generally) to which Duke Senior invites the couples, then the 1599 audience at the Globe would have seen, not a rollicking hand-in-hand round dance of the sort often staged in modern productions, but a sequence of stately movements that the inns-of-court men in that audience would have known from first-hand—make that first-*foot*—experience.[32]

But what does Duke Senior mean when he invites his listeners to forget their newly acquired social dignity (for which 'the measures' would be appropriate) and instead 'fall

[29] Christopher Marsh, '"The Skipping Art": Dance and society', in *Music and Society in Early Modern England* (Cambridge: Cambridge University Press, 2010) 328–90. Skiles Howard's classic study, *The Politics of Courtly Dancing in Early Modern England* (Amherst: University of Massachusetts Press, 1998), depends on the same distinction.

[30] Sir John Davies, *Orchestra or A poeme of dauncing*, in *The Poems of Sir John Davies*, Robert Krueger (ed.), (Oxford: Clarendon Press, 1975) 106.

[31] Hinman (1968) 225.

[32] On 'the measures' see Barbara Ravelhofer, *The Early Stuart Masque: Dance, Costume, and Music* (Oxford: Oxford University Press, 2006) 38–41; Alan Brissenden, *Shakespeare and the Dance* (Atlantic Highlands, NJ: Humanities Press, 1981) 9–10, 54–6; and Skiles Howard (1998) 9–10, 83–5, 99–100.

into our rustic revelry'? Are there rhythmic cues to be found in his words? If so, those cues are ambiguous. The almost perfect iambic *gravitas* of 'According to the measure of their states' yields to trochaic rhythms in Duke Senior's immediate cue to the music—but not before he has returned to regular iambic rhythm in the line that clearly is intended to strike up the band. Before the music and the dancers can take up Duke Senior's rhythm, however, Jaques interrupts with an emphatic trochee ('*Sir*, by your **pa**-tience')—or is that a spondee ('*Sir*, **by** your *pa*-tience')? After his interchange with Jaques, Duke Senior again cues the dance, this time with a perfectly regular iambic pulse and again a gesture of circular closure: 'Pro-*ceed*, pro-*ceed*. We'll *so* be-**gin** these *rites*/As we do *trust* they'll **end**, in *true* de-*lights*' (V. iv. 195–6). Just what kind of dance took up the rhythm in 1599? A pavane, or a country round? Perhaps, as sometimes was the case with 'the old measures', a pavane gave way to something livelier, a brawl perhaps or a cinquepace. Duke Senior's alternation of walking rhythm with tripping rhythm suggests either possibility, or both.

Whatever the steps may have been, the verbal gesture that cues the final dance is circular: may we end where we began, in true delights. In this regard Duke Senior speaks true to time. If time can be apprehended only through movement, as Aristotle argues, if the movement in question is locomotion (a body or bodies moving within a certain space), if the marking is being done over and over again in the same units (in this case feet), then a circle is the commonest spatialization of time. 'Regular circulation motion', Aristotle observes in *Physics*, 'is above all else the measure, because the number of this is best known. Now neither alteration nor increase nor coming into being can be regular, but locomotion can be. This also is why time is thought to be the movement of the sphere, viz. because the other movements are measured by this, and time by this movement' (223.b.23–4). Recall Davies' report that the original dance was a round or winding hey.

18.4 WALK THE TALK

To accommodate the variety of dances called for in *A Midsummer Night's Dream*— the fairies' 'roundel' at II. ii. 9–32, the hand-in-hand turn by Oberon and Titania that rocks the ground at IV. i. 84–5, the 'bergamask' by Flute and Bottom that rounds off the mechanicals' play at V. i. 355, the hopping, tripping dance that the fairies perform to charm the sleeping household in Act V, Scene ii—Skiles Howard has proposed the term 'kinetic economy'.[33] The script cues the actors to move their limbs, torsos, hands, and feet to the sounds of music in a variety of rhythms. Some of the schemes may have been recognized social dances—the hand-in-hand turn by Oberon and Titania, for example—while others, like the sleeping charm, may have been performance dances, choreography specific to this particular fiction.

---

[33] Howard (1998) 70.

It is not just the rhythms of music that cue body movement in *A Midsummer Night's Dream*; speech rhythms do the same. Take, for example, the speech by Theseus that opens the play:

> *Now*, fair Hip-*pol*-y-ta, our **nupt**-ial *hour*
> Draws *on* a-*pace*. **Four** hap-py *days* bring in
> An-**oth**-er *moon*—but *O*, me-thinks *how* **slow**
> This **old** moon *wanes*!
>
> (I. I. 1–4)

No music is scripted to sound (although fanfare would have been possible), but here, in Theseus' speech rhythms, are Beatrice's 'measures' of state and ancientry. Davies' spondees, solemn, grave, and slow, determine the pace at which the actor playing Theseus speaks—and the pace at which he walks. If Burbage or whoever personated Theseus spoke these lines at the rate of six-tenths of a second, it would have taken him a little more than ten seconds to speak the lines just quoted. If Burbage covered the same amount of ground per line that I do when I speak pentameter at a deliberate pace—about eight linear feet per five metric feet—then he would have covered twenty-eight feet from the tiring-house door to a more central place on the platform, enough to put him in the position of visual and aural power that he attempts to maintain throughout the scene.

The shift in the verse at this point, spondaic rhythm giving way to anapestic rhythm, perhaps indicates not just that Theseus undergoes an increase in passion but that he stops walking:

> She *ling*-ers my de-**sires**
> Like to a *step*-dame or a **dow**-ager
> *Long wither*-ing *out* a *young* man's **rev**-en-ue
>
> (I. I. 4–6)

For her part, for now, Hippolyta takes up Theseus' second, more passionate rhythm.

When Egeus, Hermia, Lysander, and Demetrius enter, the kinetic economy shifts, in Davies' terms, from spondaic measures (a pavane, perhaps) to a dactylic curanto. Certainly Egeus continues the measures established by Theseus and Hippolyta, but Hermia, Lysander, and Demetrius break out into a dactylic rhythm that continues in the forest scenes, where true love is not the only thing that does not 'run smooth' (I. i. 134). The words 'run' and 'running' figure frequently in the lovers' speeches, and Act II, Scene ii contains the explicit stage direction '*Enter Demetrius and Helena, running*' (stage direction before II. ii. 90). The lovers may not actually use their feet to run in Act I, Scene I, but the rhythm of their verse betrays a chomping at the bit. Hermia begins her speaking in the mode of her elders ('I do entreat your grace to pardon me', I. i. 58), but she soon breaks out into the impetuosness that drives the lovers' speeches when they are on their own:

> *So* will I *grow*, so *live*, so **die**, my *lord*,
> Ere I will **yield** my *virg*-in *pa*-tent up

Unto his *lord*-ship whose un-*wish*-èd **yoke**
My *soul* con-*tents not* to give **sov**-ereign-ty

(I. I. 79–82)

No actual running here, not just yet.

The kinetic economy shifts yet again in Act I, Scene ii, when Bottom and his fellows gather for their rehearsal. The rhythms of their prose speech lack the solemn measures of Theseus, Hippolyta, and Egeus as well as the running impetuosity of the lovers. What we hear instead is the randomness of everyday speech:

QUINCE   Is *all* our **com**-pan-y *here*?
BOTTOM   You were *best* to **call** them *gen*-erally, *man* by *man*, ac-*cord*-ing to the **scrip**

(I. II. 1–3)

What movements of feet, of torsos, limbs, hands, and heads, are suggested by these rhythms? Something casual, something that looks uncoordinated and uncalculated. (One thinks of the gait and the postures implied in Touchstone's admonition to his prose-speaking wife: 'Bear your body more seeming, Audrey', *As You Like It,* V. iv. 67–8.) All the greater is the contrast with the footwork implied when Bottom tears into the part of Hercules, with absolute iambic regularity that is accentuated by alliteration: 'The *rag*-ing **rocks**/And *shiv*-ering **shocks** …' (I. ii. 27–8). In Bottom, if in anyone in Shakespeare, is to be found the 'strutting player' described by Ulysses in *Troilus and Cressida,*

whose conceit
Lies in his hamstring and doth think it rich
To hear the wooden dialogue and sound
'Twixt his stretched footing and the scaffoldage

(I. III. 153–6)

Hercules' alliterating iambic dimeter, if Ulysses is to be believed, would have thudded on the floorboards as well as in the air.

Yet another regime of footing is introduced by the fairies' entrance in *A Midsummer Night's Dream*, Act II, Scene i:

ROBIN How *now*, spi-rit, *whith*-er **wand**-er *you*?
FAIRY Ov-er *hill*, ov-er **dale**,
Tho-rough *bush*, tho-rough **brier**,
Ov-er *park*, ov-er **pale**,
Tho-rough *flood*, tho-rough **fire**:
I do *wan*-der **ev**-ery-*where*,
Swift-er than the **moon**-ës *sphere* …

(II. I. 1–7)

The anapestic rhythm here, as well as the visual images, cue a very different kind of footwork than anything the audience has witnessed so far in the play: an up-and-down, back-and-forth movement not unlike the volta as Davies describes it. The rhythmic shift in the last two lines—a trochaic beat against the iambic beat—introduces a syncopation that continues until the end of the speech, a syncopation that implies a forward foot in some measures where a back-step would be expected. In speech rhythms as well as in dance rhythms, *A Midsummer Night's Dream* operates within a kinetic economy that accommodates bodily movements that can be ranged along a continuum from the ambling of the mechanicals to the stately measures of the royals to the running of the lovers to the scampering of the fairies. To discern the locomotions implicit in Shakespeare's locutions a special skill is required. That particular skill can be cultivated, even in an age of visual culture.

18.5 HEAR WITH YOUR EYES

Duke Senior may find tongues in trees and books in the running brooks, but the only time the tongues are heard and the books are read is when Orlando takes to his feet and uses his hands: 'Run, run, Orlando,' he exhorts himself; 'carve on every tree | The fair, the chaste, and unexpressive she' (*As You Like It*, III. ii. 9–10); that is, 'not-to-be-expressed' (*OED*, 'unexpressive', *adj.*, †1). In this speech, a truncated sonnet, Orlando claims tree-bark as his medium, but later in the scene Celia is directed to enter 'with a writing' (stage direction before III. ii. 121). Has Celia copied down verses from the bark, or is Orlando also affixing to the trees pieces of paper that can be taken down and collected? 'Hang there, my verse', he has apostrophized in the scene's first line (III. ii. 1). Most modern productions opt for the second possibility. Either way, it is 'writing' that occasions Rosalind, Celia, and Touchstone's wordplay on verses as feet. In general, this is true in all of Shakespeare's verse: the disposition of verse into lines is explicitly mentioned only when the verse is written down, when it is seen before it is heard. Four hundred years later, that is our situation exactly, with *all* of Shakespeare's verse, dramatic and non-dramatic alike.

As Duffell has demonstrated by the numbers, Shakespeare in his sonnets and narrative poems seems to have been keenly conscious of the line as the measure of verse. The 'lines of life' in Sonnet 16.9 cancel the lines etched by Time on the beloved's brow. Death's defeat 'When in eternal lines to time thou grow'st' in Sonnet 18.12 shackles eternity in a pentameter line. The demonstratives in the final line of Sonnet 18, 'So long lives this, and this gives life to thee', refer specifically to the lines on the page, as confirmed by the demonstratives in Sonnets 32.4 ('These poor rude lines'), 63.13 ('in these black lines'), 71.5 ('read this line'), 74.3 ('in this line'), 86.13 ('filled up his line'), 103.8 ('Dulling my lines'), and 115.1 ('Those lines that I before have writ').

For a demonstrative to function, there has to be something *there* to be gestured towards. When the verse is *not* written down, as it is not when a script is being performed, 'feet' become *feet*. In performance the medium for the verse is not bark or paper but the performer's body. Our challenge, confronted with bark or paper or a virtual window, is to find our footing, through *hearing* what we *see*. For this feat (the pun is Shakespeare's)[34] a particular kind of bodily coordination is required. To do well at many pursuits—drawing, say, or playing baseball—hand–eye coordination is crucial. In appreciating Shakespeare's verse something more complicated is required: three-way coordination among eye and ear—and *foot*. Rosalind, Celia, and Touchstone point the way. Reading the writing in Celia's hands, they hear with their eyes, and they move what they hear as they speak. So should we. Let us heed Samuel Daniel's admonition in *The Defence of Ryme* that we not regard a particular culture from a far-off vantage point— from the top of a high mountain, say, or from a map in an atlas. Nor should we castigate a culture (Daniel has in mind his own) for not conforming to the mores of Greece and Rome (in this case the failure of English poets to use the unrhymed quantitative metres of classical verse). No, 'the best measure of man is to bee taken by his owne foote, bearing euer the nearest proportion to himself'.[35]

SELECT BIBLIOGRAPHY

Dubrow, Heather (2008) *The Challenges of Orpheus: Lyric poetry and early modern England.* (Baltimore: Johns Hopkins University Press).

Duffell, Martin J. (2008) *A New History of English Metre.* (London: Modern Humanities Research Association).

Evans, Vyvyan (2005) *The Structure of Time: Language, meaning and temporal cognition.* (Amsterdam: John Benjamins).

Fussell, Paul (1979) *Poetic Meter and Poetic Form.* (New York: McGraw Hill).

Howard, Skiles (1998) *The Politics of Courtly Dancing in Early Modern England.* (Amherst: University of Massachusetts Press).

Marsh, Christopher (2010) *Music and Society in Early Modern England.* (Cambridge: Cambridge University Press).

Oliver, Mary (1998) *Rules for the Dance: A Handbook for writing and reading metrical verse.* (New York: Houghton Mifflin).

Pinsky, Robert (1999) *The Sounds of Poetry: A brief guide.* (New York: Farrar, Straus and Giroux).

Raber, Karen, and Treva J. Tucker (2005) (eds) *The Culture of the Horse: Status, Discipline, and Identity in the Early Modern World.* (New York: Palgrave Macmillan).

Rokison, Abigail (2009) *Shakespearean Verse Speaking: Text and theatre practice.* (Cambridge: Cambridge University Press).

[34] Polixines observing Perdita, 'She dances featly' (*The Winter's Tale*, IV. iv. 177); Ariel singing 'Come unto these yellow sands', 'Foot it featly here and there' (*The Tempest*, I. ii. 381).
[35] Samuel Daniel, *A Panegyrike Congratvlatorie ... with A Defence of Ryme* (London: Edward Blount, 1603) sigs. G4-G4v.

CHAPTER 19

FROM BAD TO VERSE

Poetry and Spectacle on the Modern Shakespearean Stage

JEREMY LOPEZ

Is it possible to hear blank pentameter verse during a theatrical performance? Can an audience perceive the difference between verse and prose, get a sense of the shape of a line of poetry, hear when the playwright is altering the iambic rhythm? Is blank pentameter verse in fact a constitutive element of the performance event, a medium for theatrical meaning and, therefore, something whose handling by the actors can be used as a measure of a production's aesthetic success? If blank verse is inaudible as such to an audience, and is susceptible to significant alteration by actors, what is its status with respect to things like characterization and narrative? Does poetry encode or create character? Is the poetry the actors speak in fact more important than the visual and narrative experience they work to create?

In this chapter I examine some of the answers that have been provided to these questions by historical scholarship, modern performance, and critical reactions to modern performance. The chapter is in three parts. Part 19.1 discusses some scholarly conceptions of dramatic blank verse as an historical phenomenon. Part 19.2 discusses the place 'Shakespeare's poetry' has held in post-Renaissance engagements with Shakespeare's plays in performance. Part 19.3 focuses on the particular case of *Othello* in order to draw some conclusions about the historical and ideological stakes of speaking, experiencing, and criticizing dramatic poetry in live performance.

19.1 PERSISTENTLY PATTERNED SPEECH

Scholars generally agree that a heightened perception of blank verse during live theatrical performance *was* possible for early modern audiences. Coburn Freer wrote in 1981:

> At the heart of the interest in dramatic poetry is a concern for the line itself. Audiences could hear the blank verse line emerge and take shape, and their ability to do this gives the point to literally hundreds of speeches and scenes in English renaissance drama.[1]

The crucial thing about Freer's argument is its situation of this perceptivity firmly in a culture of the past: while he says that 'we still can share' early modern methods of verse-speaking and verse-hearing 'if we wish' (61), the larger thrust of his argument suggests that cultural and technological developments since the 18th century have permanently affected our ability both to create and to experience poetic drama:

> [D]ramatic poetry changed because the wider contexts of human action and possibility changed; these conceptions shifted in such a way as to encourage certain forms of poetic discovery and to discourage certain others. (216)

More recently, Robert Miola, Russ McDonald, and Abigail Rokison have all made the similar claim that the 'major difference between the early modern and the modern ear' is that 'Shakespeare's first audiences seem to have been more sensitive to verbal structures than their modern counterparts'.[2]

Arguments for the continued efficacy of early modern dramatic verse *as such* must rely on a certain impressionism. Thus George T. Wright's influential assessment of Shakespeare's metrical art speaks of its effects on 'us', but without requiring that 'we' be conscious of those effects:

> To be sure, most of us do not follow the verse lines consciously. Iambic pentameter—especially when it is blank—is too subtle and variable to encourage us to stamp our feet in obedience to the beat, but if the actors will keep the meter, our nervous systems can

[1] Coburn Freer, *The Poetics of Jacobean Drama* (Baltimore: Johns Hopkins University Press, 1981) 33.
[2] The quotation is from Russ McDonald, *Shakespeare and the Arts of Language* (Oxford: Oxford University Press, 2001) 108. Robert Miola, *Shakespeare's Reading* (Oxford: Oxford University Press, 2000), argues that early modern playwrights and audiences 'could appreciate sonic effects which are lost on moderns' (2–3). Abigail Rokison, *Shakespearean Verse Speaking: Text and Theatre Practice* (Cambridge: Cambridge University Press, 2009) says that actors 'accustomed to performing blank verse and audiences accustomed to hearing it are likely to have been more attuned to the pentameter line than is the case in the modern theatre'. While not concerned specifically with pentameter verse, Bruce R. Smith and Wes Folkerth have both written about the particular aural sensitivity of the early modern playwright and playgoer. See Smith, *The Acoustic World of Early Modern England* (Chicago: University of Chicago Press, 1999) and Folkerth, *The Sound of Shakespeare* (New York: Routledge, 2002).

register the continuing metrical pattern even while our more conscious attention is being directed to the action, the characters, and the substance of their words and sentences.[3]

And while Wright suggests that Shakespeare's poetic art might continue to register with late modern audiences, he also suggests that it was an art that ran its course in its own time: Shakespeare's subtle variations on the iambic-pentameter form were 'tempered and finally abandoned by most Jacobean and Caroline dramatists and by every later poet without exception' (101). Sensuous metrical experience in the theatre is, and almost always has been, a thing of the past.

Conceiving sensuous metrical experience in historical terms still obliges a critic to make distinctions between levels and kinds of perception, and these distinctions have important ramifications for the kinds of possibilities for verse which we admit to modern theatrical experience. One means by which critics express the efficacy of early modern dramatic poetry is by hypothesizing an unsophisticated audience, or an incompetent playwright or acting company. Discussing the antecedent form to blank verse, the rhymed fourteeners of the late Tudor period, Wright says:

> For unsophisticated spectators, the rhymes must have come down with a pounce. Much of this verse [...] has the same effect as clowns tumbling at a circus. The first rhyme sets up a pratfall, and the second meets this expectation with mindless good nature. Experienced readers or viewers may tire of such an empty-headed game. But for an illiterate or barely literate audience, the rhymes make it possible to take pleasure in persistently patterned speech. (95)

In this argument, the barely literate audience provides the very mechanism by which patterned speech becomes the basis of the greatest English drama. Freer differs from Wright somewhat, arguing that poetry suffused the very texture of everyday life: even the 'most rudimentary education for future tradesmen', for example, 'began with verse lessons of the names of the implements' (37). Persistently, even subtly patterned speech would have been something that any spectator was prepared to appreciate, and the important distinction to be made was among playing companies and their actors. 'Then, as now, better companies got the better plays ... [and] in the process they also got the better poetry' (33); but even 'the sorriest company must have felt there was a minimum standard that had to be met' (40). In these negative examples, the importance of blank verse as a marker of high art is demonstrated by its connection with formal education; and the power of verse as a tool of artistic communication is demonstrated by its heightened development in and for a theatre whose spectators could by no means be guaranteed to have a formal education.[4]

---

[3] George T. Wright, *Shakespeare's Metrical Art* (Berkeley: University of California Press, 1988) 92. Miola (2000) makes, in passing, a similar physiological argument about early modern audiences: 'The practice of reading aloud and of reciting verse developed acute inner ears' in Elizabethans, allowing them to appreciate, perhaps unconsciously, the subtlest poetic effects (2).

[4] Rokison (2009) also discusses the importance of Elizabethan education, which 'would have equipped Shakespeare and his fellow writers with the ability to understand verse structure and its expressive and dramatic potential' (81).

Another means by which critics express the efficacy of early modern dramatic poetry is by hypothesizing a community of auditors linked by their thorough understanding of, or heightened sensitivity to, theatrical conventions. Both Freer and McDonald call attention to the moment in *As You Like It* (IV. i) where Rosalind has been speaking in prose to Jaques when Orlando enters:

> ORLANDO   Good day and happiness, dear Rosalind.
> JAQUES   Nay, then God b' wi' you an you talk in blank verse.
>
> (IV. i. 28–9)

Freer says that the audience must have had 'an instant grasp of Orlando's line as a rhythmic unit' in order for the joke to work (34), and McDonald says that the line is 'historical proof' of the particularly sensitive nature of the early modern ear (108). Neither critic accounts for the possibility that Orlando, whose tree-poem in Act III, Scene ii features many lines ending with 'Rosalind', might speak his line with deliberate artificiality— that the actor might comically call attention to it *as* a rhythmic unit in order to make a joke about the character. Both Freer and McDonald seem to think about this moment in terms of the line's textual identity (ten syllables) rather than its verbal identity (five stresses), and to imagine an audience's response to the joke being precipitated by the poet's intention, whether or not the actor telegraphs it. In this positive example, the presumed subtlety of blank verse as a poetic device is at the heart of its theatrical effects: blank verse is a kind of textual code whose meaning is to be knowingly perceived but not explicitly spelled out.[5]

A third element in historical considerations of theatrical blank verse which draws together the question of education with the importance of subtlety is the element of acting style. In 1951, B. L. Joseph made a systematic and influential argument about the relation between Elizabethan rhetorical, and oratorical, training and the conventions of early modern acting and verse-speaking.[6] Working from educational and rhetorical manuals, Joseph imagined a declamatory style of verse-speaking, and a conventional repertory of gesture that accompanied it. This 'was a highly formal art', as Richard David said a decade later, in an essay on Elizabethan acting which was explicitly indebted to Joseph:

> The orator was trained not only to modulate his voice according to the nature of the sentiments he was expressing, but to accompany his words with appropriate movements of the body and especially of the hands.[7]

Both David and Joseph cited Hamlet's injunction against 'mouthing' lines (III. ii. 2) as evidence that 'correct modulation' of the voice involved the observance of (in Joseph's

[5] For a related discussion of the quoted lines from *As You Like It*, and the textuality of the verse 'line', see Chapter 16 in this volume. See also Paul Menzer, 'Lines', in *Twenty-first Century Approaches to Early Modern Theatricality*, Henry S. Turner (ed.), (Oxford, forthcoming). I am grateful to Professor Menzer for letting me read a draft of his work, and for his careful reading of mine.

[6] B. L. Joseph, *Elizabethan Acting* (Oxford: Oxford University Press, 1951).

[7] Richard David, 'Shakespeare and the Players', *Proceedings of the British Academy* 47 (1961): 139–59, 152.

phrase) 'meaningful inflexions … according to the metre' (79). In this argument metrical language is itself, even as it is also bodied forth by, a physical gesture—a constitutive element of *both* the visual and verbal experience a play provides.

Theatre-historical scholarship has gradually moved away from more rigid applications of Joseph's argument, correctly perceiving that insistence upon a declamatory or gestural style can have the anachronistic effect of suggesting, contrary to all available evidence, that Elizabethan acting seemed artificial to Elizabethans. Thus McDonald's discussion of Orlando's blank-verse intrusion appropriately hedges the question whether 'dramatic verse was declaimed in an oratorical and perhaps sing-song manner' (108).[8] But to some extent the hedge had already been made by Joseph, who tackled the question of 'how far the Elizabethan audience was capable of appreciating all [these] refinements of technique' (80) by suggesting that the refinements were primarily important as resources for playwrights and actors. Making an analogy with musically illiterate modern concert-goers who can nevertheless enjoy a composer's and an orchestra's technical proficiency, Joseph argued that the rhetorical techniques of early modern acting were

> designed traditionally to evoke an adequate response from people who were not capable of analysing an oration or a play…. [A]n Elizabethan audience responded to the dramatist's knowledge of prosody, however ignorant the individual groundlings may have been of that art. (81)

Thus, much as with Wright's argument, even as Joseph's anatomization of a formal system for declaiming theatrical meaning makes rhetorical and prosodic techniques highly visible, his conception of the theatre as an instrument of mass artistic communication suggests that those techniques are effective precisely because they need not be seen.

Historical conceptions of early modern poetry in performance thus construe blank pentameter verse as the sign of a unique and lost moment in popular theatrical culture where literate and non-literate experience were harmonized around a shared understanding of formal conventions—where, indeed, non-literate experience provided the impetus for formal conventions that would later seem to require a high degree of literacy to be appreciated as such. In this argument, blank verse is a highly artificial code for the ordering of theatrical language, and a code that is most meaningful if it doesn't have to be fully translated—if its meaning is experienced at the level of sensation or intuition. Blank verse is on one hand, a technical skill that requires specialized training and education both to speak and to understand, and on the other hand, a ubiquitous medium whose maximal theatrical efficacy is somehow independent of, or necessarily works to obscure, the specialized technical skill required for its production. These interrelated and conflicting historical ideas, which above all share an anxiety about the role of specialized academic knowledge in the evaluation of popular theatrical experience, provide

---

[8] For a revisionist discussion of early modern actorly gesture, see also Paul Menzer, 'That old saw: Elizabethan acting and the infinite regress', *Shakespeare Bulletin* 22:4 (2004): 27–44.

the necessary background for examining how blank verse is and has been used and perceived in the modern Shakespearean theatre.

19.2 POEL, PYTHON, AND PENTAMETER

The engine that drove Shakespearean theatrical production at the beginning of the 20th century was William Poel's 'Elizabethan revival', an ostensibly uncompromising reaction against overwrought Victorian scenography and acting style whose goal was to achieve a more transparent mediation between modern and early modern theatrical experience. It would be nearly a century before Poel's interest in reconstructed early modern theatres really took hold, but he had an immediate and far-reaching influence in his insistence upon the primary importance of verse-speaking in the production of early modern drama. As Stephen C. Schultz puts it, if 'the actor possessed a voice capable of characterising the role, other qualities—gesture, facial expression, personal appearance—mattered little'. Indeed, for Poel, who believed that the modern stage depended upon visual effects and the early modern upon aural, one 'could not substitute "a stage-picture for a word-picture" without destroying the play's "reality"'.[9] It was in order to realize the primacy of verbal and aural experience in practice that Poel laboured to develop 'a principle which has since become almost universally acknowledged: that classical acting requires mastery of special techniques' (343)—a rigorous mental, vocal, and physical method for bringing forth the characterizations and theatrical effects encoded in the poetry.

Poel's method was not, however, based in metrical analysis—or, rather, he was never able to harmonize his idea about poetry as the source of characterization and meaning with a method for realizing poetry's prosodic character. Although he was famously tyrannical in his insistence upon proper accent and modulation, forcing actors to repeat a single line, phrase, or word until it had lost all meaning, he nevertheless failed to explain how to read metrically structured language in a 'natural intonation' while simultaneously preserving some auditory experience of the metre. He hinted at the possibility of such a combination, but as far as one can tell from his writings, he assumed (1) that metre is divorced from meaning, and (2) that a reading which obeys scansion will fall into chanted alteration between two extremes of stressed and unstressed syllables. (348)

---

[9] Stephen C. Schultz, 'William Poel on the Speaking of Shakespearean Verse: A Reevaluation', *Shakespeare Quarterly* 28 (1977): 334–50, 336. The quotations within my second quotation are from William Poel, 'Poetry in Drama', *Contemporary Review* (November 1913) 705–6. Schultz provides an extraordinarily efficient and thorough digest of Poel's views on verse-speaking, much of which is drawn from the director's voluminous correspondence. See also William Poel, *Shakespeare and the Theatre* (London: Sidgwick & Jackson, 1913); Robert Speaight, *William Poel and the Elizabethan Theatre Revival* (London: Heinemann, 1954); Claris Glick, 'William Poel: His Theories and Influence', *Shakespeare Quarterly* 15.1 (1964): 15–25; and Edward M. Moore, 'William Poel', *Shakespeare Quarterly* 23.1 (1972): 21–36. For a bracing and unsympathetic treatment of the divergence between theory and practice in Poel's experiments, see Peter Thomson, 'William Poel', in *The Routledge Companion to Directors' Shakespeare*, John Russell Brown (ed.), (London: Routledge, 2008) 356–73.

Instead of metre and scansion, Poel's approach to poetic language was based upon 'key words' and 'tones': each line has a limited number of words that should be emphasized for the sake of meaning, and every character and every speech has a certain sonic quality that can be orchestrated with every other. Since, Poel said, dialogue written in verse always contains more words 'than are needed to convey the actual thought that is uppermost in the speaker's mind', the important thing for an actor to do was to arrest the attention of the listener by the accentuation of those words which convey the central idea [... and] keep in the background, by means of modulation and deflection of voice, the words with which that thought is ornamented.[10]

To master the special techniques that Poel thought essential for the speaking of verse was not, then, to discover theatrical meaning in the predetermined metrical character of the text. Rather, it was to develop an idiosyncratic and impressionistic method of critical interpretation which, in its strategic emphases and occlusions, would reshape the text.

A polemicist and a visionary, Poel was nevertheless also an amateur, and most of his theatrical work was undertaken with amateur actors under straitened circumstances; what overarching coherence there might have been in his passionate but conflicted ideas about verse-speaking had little chance to be realized in his own productions, where the actors were frequently unequal to his demands as well as the demands of the Shakespearean text. Just as B. L. Joseph's theory of Elizabethan acting became most important for subsequent theatre history by means of its continual dilution and diffusion, so Poel's ideas about the primacy of poetry would gain most traction through the work of his less uncompromising disciples—first Harley Granville-Barker, and then George Rylands. The latter is most important for the purposes of this essay. As Abigail Rokison has shown, it was through the filter at Cambridge in the 1950s and 1960s that the seeds Poel had planted were really able to flourish—with the help of, on the one hand, Rylands' practice-based historical scholarship and, on the other, F. R. Leavis' highly textual close reading. Subjected to these two apparently antithetical approaches to the Shakespearean text, generations of future British directors, many of whom are still working today—including Peter Hall, Trevor Nunn, Richard Eyre, Nicholas Hytner, and Sam Mendes[11]—began to develop an idea of both production and reception in which an understanding of the playwright's theatrical intentions was to be merged with a meticulous appreciation of his verse forms and the verbal texture of his poetry.

The period in which Poel's ideas were being gradually disseminated into mainstream theatrical practice was also a period of titanic virtuoso performers who cultivated particular styles of verse-speaking: Ralph Richardson, John Gielgud, Anthony Quayle, and Laurence Olivier. The explosive combination of practical, historical, and literary-critical work being fired in the crucible of Cambridge University during the 1950s and 1960s might in some respect be seen as an attempt to replicate—and make replicable—in the academy what these great performers seemed to make possible in the theatre: an

---

[10]   Poel (1913) 58.
[11]   This list comes from Peter Hall's *Shakespeare's Advice to the Players* (London: Theatre Communications Group, 2003) as cited in Rokison (2009) 33.

apparent synthesis between word and action, present and past. It was directly out of this academic endeavour that the work of J. L. Styan and the field of performance criticism arose, and with it the increasing consensus that theatrical performance should be considered an interpretive practice in its own right. These developments, so important for the systematization and institutionalization of historically based performance practices—and for the creation of audiences and practitioners capable of appreciating them—occurred alongside crucial changes in the essential character of Shakespearean acting and production: the huge increase in Shakespeare productions from the mid-1960s on; the increasing importance to actors' careers of 'naturalistic' media such as television and film; the corresponding disappearance of virtuoso actors such as Gielgud and Olivier whose identities were tied up with a particular physical and vocal realization of the Shakespearean text; and—corresponding to *that*—the increasingly widespread idea that the speaking of Shakespearean verse is a specialized technical skill that can nevertheless be taught to and learned by any actor.

It is this last development that has finally resulted in the codification of verse-speaking techniques which Poel's theory of theatrical practice implied but could not realize. Since the huge proliferation of Shakespearean productions in the latter half of the 20th century resulted (somewhat paradoxically) in an increasing number of actors without any training in verse-speaking, as well as an ever-expanding audience with little experience of Shakespearean language, there has been a corresponding proliferation of technical courses and published manuals dedicated to teaching verse-speaking techniques. These courses and manuals—the origins of which are traceable primarily to the work of the RSC's voice director Cicely Berry, whose *Voice and the Actor* appeared in 1973—use some combination of theatre history, textual analysis, and physiology to provide actors with rules or guidelines for approaching Shakespearean language. Through them, actors are given ways of discovering rhetorical emphases and aspects of character in (rather than using those things to determine) metrical emphases, elongated or truncated lines, punctuation, and the like.

Rokison provides a good analytical history of these manuals,[12] and convincingly demonstrates that the stringency of a given vocal method is generally in direct proportion to its historical contingency. Drawing upon the work of theatre historians like Tiffany Stern, Rokison argues that

> The modern tendency to view the metrical structure of a scene not only as indicative of pace and rhythm but of character and motivation and interaction as well, is unhistorical .... [A]n actor working from an individual part would have had little

[12] Texts she discusses include Patsy Rodenburg's *The Actor Speaks* (London: Methuen, 1997), Kristin Linklater's *Freeing Shakespeare's Voice* (London: Theatre Communications Group, 1993), Patrick Tucker's *Secrets of Acting Shakespeare* (London: Routledge, 2001), Wesley Van Tassel's *Clues to Acting Shakespeare* (New York: Allworth, 2000), Declan Donnelan's *The Actor and the Target* (London: Theatre Communications Group, 2002), and Don Weingust's *Acting from Shakespeare's First Folio* (London: Routledge, 2006). For a rigorous critique of vocal techniques deriving from Berry, see Sarah Werner, 'Performing Shakespeare: Voice Training and the Feminist Actor', *New Theatre Quarterly* 12 (1996): 249–58.

idea of the metrical relationship of his lines to those of the other characters .... He would not have been able to use such information in the initial stages of preparation for a role, when he would have committed the part to memory and presumably made some of his decisions about characterisation and delivery. (183)

In her discussion of shared verse lines—a favourite site for vocal technicians to locate ostensibly encoded theatrical meanings—Rokison also demonstrates the way in which specialized vocal techniques can be applied quite arbitrarily in practice: over and above the fact that lineation is often the product of compositors and editors rather than the playwright, it is as easy to say, depending on the dramatic context, that a pentameter line shared between two or more actors is meant to be slowed by a series of obvious pauses, as it is to say that such a line should be spoken more rapidly. What these manuals provide is not a reliable rubric for realizing theatrical meaning in its final, textually, and historically grounded form. Rather, they create a system for imagining that meaning in an early modern dramatic text is essentially technological, that it can be realized through a systematic approach to the poetry; the flexibility of this system arises out of a belief in the *possibility* of inflexible rules.[13]

The difficulty, dramatized in these manuals, of sorting out the priority of verse-speaking as technique and verse-speaking as the communication of sense is the same difficulty that vexes historical considerations of Elizabethan acting, and helps to explain why even critics with specialized training in verse construction frequently find it hard to describe what proper verse-speaking sounded like or should sound like on the stage. This is Richard David on Anthony Quayle's 1954 production of *Othello* at Stratford, in which Quayle played the title role:

The Desdemona of Barbara Jefford was particularly disappointing. She is one of those rare actresses who can phrase verse like music, but to fashion the artless, the even-tempered, the subservient Desdemona she had so lightened and pinched her speech that it lost all character. She was certainly a 'picture out of doors', and a handsome one; but one need not go all the way with Iago in his catalogue of women's qualities to believe that the mere façade is too thin a slice of personality for drama, or the audience's sympathies, to take hold upon.[14]

It is hard to tell, from this analysis, whether Jefford did not in fact phrase Desdemona's verse 'like music', or whether the music she came up with simply didn't appeal to David's ear. He suggests that Jefford's manner of speaking verse *did* do the work of providing a characterization for Desdemona, but he also suggests that this was not the characterization encoded by the verse in the text. David does not assume that Desdemona's character

---

[13] For a related analysis of the way actors make use of historical information, see W. B. Worthen, 'Invisible Bullets, Violet Beards: Reading Actors Reading', in Edward Pechter (ed.), *Textual and Theatrical Shakespeare: Questions of Evidence* (Iowa City: University of Iowa Press, 1996) 210–29.

[14] Richard David, 'Stratford 1954', *Shakespeare Quarterly* 5 (1954): 384–94, 387.

is the product of the spectator's temporal, evolving interpretation of what she says (and how she says it) in the moment of performance. Rather, as we also saw in Freer's and McDonald's historical arguments, verse-speaking is conceived as a textual rather than a verbal phenomenon, or, perhaps more precisely, the quality of verse-speaking on stage can be evaluated only with reference to the text. But even in this return to the text, a non-metrical form of analysis—that is, an interpretation of Desdemona's character— precedes and predetermines any metrical analysis.[15]

Attempts to evaluate or describe Shakespearean theatrical experience by positing a logical or empirical separation between textually encoded form and subjectively deter- mined meaning turn inexorably in upon themselves largely because Shakespearean the- atrical forms are never new: they come to each interpreter with a built-in theatrical and critical history that helps to determine the pulse of a given production as much as even the most strictly observed verse-speaking might. A similar problem of priority con- fronts the interpreter who would separate verse-speaking and spectacle as essential con- stitutive elements of theatrical experience. Robyn Heales and Dennis Bartholomeusz, reviewing Shakespeare productions in Australia in 1984, complained of an *Antony and Cleopatra* that used a 'slim four-foot infant of a python' in its climactic scene. This was more spectacle than the play required, and at the expense of the play's language:

> The audience, both thrilled and horrified by the realism, paid little attention to Shakespeare's verbal poetry. When Lindy Davies, who played a passionately maternal Cleopatra, said 'Dost thou not see the baby at my breast', the business threatened the intensity and emotional depth of the moment. The artistic problem here is that both the business and the words must be given due weight.[16]

The reviewers seem to be working at cross-purposes with themselves here. The fact that the spectators were noticeably 'thrilled and horrified' by the snake would seem in at least some respect to show how caught up they were in the 'intensity and emotional depth of the moment'. The reviewers' desire to mitigate, through an appreciation of 'Shakespeare's verbal poetry,' the theatre's particular ability to create intense mimetic experience seems decidedly non-theatrical.

The opposition of verbal and visual matter is, then, to some degree an arbitrary means by which to express dissatisfaction with a production that might have been (and prob- ably was) unsatisfying for all sorts of unquantifiable reasons. We can get some sense of what lies beneath this arbitrariness by looking at what would seem to be an example of the exact opposite form of criticism to that of the python production. Reviewing Peter Hall's 2003 touring production of *As You Like It*, Michael Dobson complained of the

---

[15] For an analogue in historical criticism, see Miola (2000), which begins by locating both the creation and the aural experience of dramatic verse in the act of reading: grammar-school education, training in Latin rhetoric and composition, etc., 'fostered certain habits of reading, thinking, and writing. Students acquired extraordinary sensitivity to language, especially its sound' (2).

[16] 'Shakespeare in Sydney and Melbourne', *Shakespeare Quarterly* 35 (1984): 479–84, 484.

director's 'pedantic insistence that all the cast should pause audibly at the end of every line of verse, regardless of the demands of the syntax, as though Shakespeare had never discovered enjambment'.[17] Although Dobson reviewed it alongside Gregory Thompson's too-elaborately scenic *As You Like It* at the RSC the same year, he had little to say about the visual quality of Hall's production, noting only that Rebecca Callard's Celia 'looked dumpy in the half-Elizabethan formal dress she wore in the opening court scenes' (267). What is similar about Dobson's response to Hall's pentameter on the one hand, and Heales and Bartholomeusz's response to the python on the other, is that each arises out of a production's desire to give its audience a close-up view (my cinematic metaphor is deliberate) of an essential element of the play, and in each case the close-up provides a somewhat alienating experience of the play. In each case the jaded reviewer sees or hears the play in a new way. In each case the play provides an intense experience of something an audience is supposed to want or value—and, at least in the case of the python production, the audience did in fact seem to value it. Dobson does not describe the audience's reaction to Hall's end-stopping. But as tedious as the verse-speaking likely was, Dobson's criticism is necessarily based upon an idea that the audience already knows what the poetry is going to say, and is waiting to hear the sense realized, rather than an idea that the audience is (as an early modern audience might have been) listening for the sense to develop out of the evolving shape of each successive line. In the case of both python and pentameter, the ideal of properly balanced, and proper attention to, verse-speaking functions to mark the difference between two kinds of spectator, those who have the special training to appreciate verse construction and those who do not. What the reviewer wants is to feel as though that difference does not exist.

   To privilege subtlety in verse-speaking, as well as in stagecraft, in evaluations of modern performance is to fantasize a maximally expressive text directed at a maximally receptive historical audience, where neither ostentatious actorly craft nor pictorial scenery were required to mediate prosodic structure or thematic meaning. The modern actor who is most frequently said, or remembered, to have embodied the possibility of realizing this fantasy is John Gielgud. As Gareth Lloyd Evans said in a 1968 article on the different vocal styles of Gielgud, Olivier, Paul Scofield, and Ian Richardson, Gielgud 'brings the art of vocal music to serve the art of impersonation'. His particular form of impersonation was a heroic one, 'which satisfies an urge in audiences to see Gods stride the world again'.[18] Evans' retrospective assessment of Gielgud's verbal art was based on the actor's very popular *Ages of Man* recital, a performance of select speeches from Shakespeare plays organized under the headings 'Youth', 'Manhood', and 'Old Age'. Gielgud originated the show in 1956 and toured it regularly through 1967. An audio recording was made in 1959, and Gielgud did a broadcast performance for CBS in 1966.

[17] Michael Dobson, 'Shakespeare Performances in England, 2003', *Shakespeare Survey* 57 (2004): 258–89, 267. For a more detailed discussion of Peter Hall's approach to metre, see Rokison (2009), ch. 1, especially 23–4, where Hall is quoted as saying that 'the over-marking of the end of the lines ... is monotonous and sends an audience to sleep'.
[18] 'Shakespeare and the Actors: Notes Towards Interpretations', *Shakespeare Survey* 21 (1968): 115–25, 116.

Working from the memory of Gielgud's live performance a number of years before, as well as the audio recording, Evans attempted to quantify, and to record graphically, the manner in which Gielgud balanced the speaking of poetry as such with the representation of character: the way he 'reached for, and attained, the poetry of character' (116).

For Evans as for Poel, however, the essential quality of the poetry was not its metre so much as its key words. Thus he gives a passage from *Richard II* which Gielgud recited, and uses italic type to indicate where the rhetorical emphases came:

> I'll give my jewels for a set of *beads*,
> My gorgeous palace for a *hermitage*,
> My gay apparel for an almsman's *gown*,
> My figured goblets for a dish of *wood*,
> My sceptre for a palmer's *walking-staff*,
> My subjects for a pair of carved saints,
> And my *large kingdom* for a *little grave*.
>
> (III. iii. 147–53)

Evans is not concerned with the fact that Gielgud's lines generally do not scan as pentameter—that, for example, he tends to run together short words (e.g. 'for a' in each of the lines quoted here), so that lines like 'My gay apparel for an almsman's gown' sound almost like Anglo-Saxon tetrameter. Indeed, he finds that Gielgud's 'shrewd' but counterintuitive phrasing, where balanced pairs such as *figured goblets—dish of wood* are not given corresponding balanced stress, usefully avoids 'an over-regular rhythm, a tum-ti-tum … Such regularity takes the attention away from the mood that is being created' (116). In this analysis, as in Dobson's, regular pentameter itself is conceived almost in the same terms as the Australian python, as something that distracts one from the poetry. This is less surprising, however, if we understand that any critical, graphical representation of metrical speech is preceded by an aural recreation on the part of the critic, and that no one critic's recreation will be identical to any other's. When I listened to the Gielgud recording and attempted to mark the emphases according to Evans' scheme, I corresponded with Evans on many points, but differed on many others. In general, I tended to hear the very balancing that Evans thought was left out: I thought *gorgeous palace* and *gay apparel*, and *goblets* and *sceptre* received equal emphasis. This is likely because I brought to the act of listening an interpretation of Richard's character which imagines him striving to achieve a kind of control in poetry which he is losing in politics; this is a somewhat different interpretation from that which informs (but is presented as though it were the result of) Evans' metrical analysis, namely that Richard is concerned with 'what he is turning *to*' more than with 'what he is rejecting' (116–17).

There is also the problem, as Evans notes, echoing Poel, that 'italics and notices of stress cannot convey' the 'tonal qualities' of a given speech (117). For Evans, who was working both with a sound recording and the memory of a live performance, these tonal qualities were 'superb' and 'musical'. For me, on the other hand, listening to the fifty-year-old recording on my laptop computer in a library basement, there was often not much difference between Gielgud's expository introductions of passages and his recitation of those passages; this somewhat numbing quality of sameness was exacerbated by the fact that the passages Gielgud recites from *Richard II* are all from different parts of the play, but are arranged to suggest that they are from the single scene of Richard's deposition. The soul of poetry is in performance, not only in the temporal movement and development of each successive line—which registers a series of rhetorical rather than metrical emphases—but also in the movement of the language away from and back toward the preconceived, textualized idea of character and play which each spectator (or auditor) has brought into the theatre. Requiring specialized knowledge for technical evaluation as metrical art, dramatic poetry in live performance nevertheless stands and falls upon idiosyncratic and impressionistic modes of textual interpretation.

19.3 FROM BAD TO VERSE

John Gielgud's final appearance at the Shakespeare Memorial Theatre in Stratford-upon-Avon took place in 1961, when he played the title role in Franco Zeffirelli's disastrous production of *Othello*. By all accounts the main problem with this production was its overwhelming scenic design. Peter Hall, interviewed for Sheridan Morley's biography of Gielgud, said that the 'realistic Italian sets [were] more suited to Verdi than Shakespeare, [and] took forever to change' (311–12). Due to the time required to change the sets, the opening night production ran for over four hours; Gielgud, Hall said, attempted to bring out 'the simple naïveté of Othello', but ended up seeming 'swamped in the enormous, misplaced splendour of the production' (312).

But evaluations of this production do not stop at the opposition between Gielgud's novel characterization and Zeffirelli's ill-judged spectacle. The real failure of the production is seen to be a failure of language, and to originate in the deliberately cultivated verse-speaking style of the great Gielgud himself. While J. C. Trewin felt that Zeffirelli was defeated by his own scenic ambitions, he also said that the director had 'the help of Sir John Gielgud's voice, which could be like a storm in silver'.[19] Yet Gielgud ultimately succumbed to the same problem as the director, namely too much of a good thing—too much of his own signature style.

> There must be more in *Othello* than verbal majesty. It was something the artist in Gielgud understood but could not fully express: the temperament of the man . . . . His nobility was absolute: he used the glory of the *Othello* music. Withal, Gielgud could not present the primitive side; he seldom got us to credit the racial division, the racial inflammability. (Trwein, 512–13)

---

[19] J. C. Trewin, 'The Old Vic and Stratford-upon-Avon 1961–1962', *Shakespeare Quarterly* 13.4 (1962): 505–19, 512. See also Sheridan Morley, *John G.: The Authorized Biography* (London: Hodder and Stoughton, 2001) 312, where Peggy Ashcroft is quoted as expressing frustration with Gielgud's inability to 'register any kind of jealousy'.

The something 'more' which Trewin thinks essential to *Othello* is, in a manner of speaking, something less: there must be less majesty, less music, less of the imperious verbal control for which Gielgud was famous, and which Gareth Lloyd Evans suggested might be pinned down for observation through italic type. Although it might easily be argued, based on an analysis of the text, that Othello is far and away one of Shakespeare's most controlled speakers, the performance event brings to the surface a viewer's prior assumptions about the way the character should violate any control that might be encoded in the text. What is meant to provide control in *Othello* is Iago whom, played by Ian Bannen in this production, Trewin found inadequate for the inverse reason: Bannen provided 'a gabbled, prickly-heat performance of a demi-devil turned to a gnat. Subtlety was dispersed in restlessness and vocal mannerism' (513). Against the backdrop of Zeffirelli's enormous operatic sets, which insist upon a particular form of high-culture identity for the theatrical event,[20] Gielgud's patrician inflections, his ear for 'the *Othello* music', seem simply like a further extension of modern culture's neutralizing power over the authentic form of early modern drama. What is wanted is 'the primitive side'. Or, as Peter Hall said to Sheridan Morley: 'the poetry was extraordinary, but the animal wasn't there' (312).

The Gielgud *Othello* is significant because it represents both the pinnacle and the passing of an age. Gielgud was, as Lois Potter says, 'at the peak of his career' in 1961:[21] he toured his *Ages of Man* recital in North America and the United Kingdom in 1958–9, opened a successful production of Peter Shaffer's *Five Finger Exercise* in London in 1958 and New York in 1959, and won a Tony award for his direction of Hugh Wheeler's *Big Fish Little Fish* in 1961. He was tempted back to Stratford by Peter Hall for the inaugural season of the new Royal Shakespeare Company on the promise of getting to work with the up-and-coming Zeffirelli, whose *Romeo and Juliet* had taken London by storm in 1960. There was no reason to think the Gielgud *Othello* would be anything less than a great success, a momentum-generating sign of the direction of classical theatrical production in the second half of the 20th century. In the event, it was hastily removed from the RSC repertory, Zeffirelli turned to film, John Barton and Peter Hall swept any last vestiges of operatic staging out of Stratford-upon-Avon, and Gielgud took only two more Shakespearean roles on the stage for the remainder of his career: Prospero at the Old Vic in 1974 and Julius Caesar at the National in 1977. As a speaker of verse, Gielgud turned out to be an embodiment of theatrical conventions from the modern past, rather than a semi-mystical conduit, through the music of Shakespeare's poetry, by which the early modern past was recreated in the present. The nature of the change theatrical culture was undergoing is made clear at the end of Potter's very brief treatment of the Gielgud *Othello*, when she begins talking about the most famous modern production of that play:

---

[20] Hall told Zeffirelli that people would be frustrated with a 40-minute interval; the director responded that 'audiences would not mind the wait if what they saw, finally, was beautiful'. '[N]othing could be that beautiful', Hall replied. See Morley (2001) 312.

[21] Lois Potter, *Shakespeare in Performance: Othello* (Manchester: Manchester University Press, 2002) 147.

Three years later Gielgud saw Laurence Olivier walk on to the stage of the National Theatre at the Old Vic, dressed like an African, barefoot, smiling with half-closed eyes, and radiating complete, self-contained self-satisfaction. 'Staggered,' he suddenly remembered that in rehearsals Zeffirelli had tried unsuccessfully to convince him that 'this man is very vain'. (147)[22]

Speech has been replaced by spectacle, the *Othello* music by Othello's body, and out of the meticulous recovery of the primitive arises a form that is distinctly modern. Alan Seymour found that the production blew away all the artifice that had heretofore made the play a mere 'romantic charade' for modern audiences, and brought it 'firmly into a world of reality'.[23]

But as awed as Seymour was by the production's naturalistic grandeur, he was unimpressed with the verse-speaking, which he found to be plagued by the same problems as verse-speaking in other modern productions.

> It is right to eschew the making of beautiful sounds—which is anyway a bastardized idea of what poetry in the theatre is meant to be. It is not right to allow a bluntly prosaic, realistic method to throw out the making of beautiful sense. (17)

Like so much discussion of Shakespeare's poetry in performance, it is hard to see what would actually satisfy the critic. Indeed, it may be that the critic's construction of an impossibly paradoxical wish arises out of the desire not to speak like a critic—not to be worried that Olivier's astonishing physical transformation (positively fetishized in later accounts, including Olivier's own, of the play) might stand in for the unrecoverable skill of early modern verse-speaking. To bring *Othello*, indeed any Shakespeare play, firmly into a world of modern reality is inevitably to lose something as well. From our perspective, of course, a black-face *Othello* must necessarily look like a relic, and yet, unsurpisingly, Ray Fearon's 1999 rendition of the role at the RSC—the first by a black actor in the main house for forty years—was haunted by the ghost of Olivier: while the relatively soft-spoken actor was admired for a moving naturalness, he was also found to be lacking both 'emotionally and musically'.[24] The ever more powerful or precise images

---

[22] Potter is quoting Gielgud in John Gielgud (with John Miller), *Shakespeare: Hit or Miss* (London: Sidgwick and Jackson, 1991) 82–3.

[23] Alan Seymour, 'A View from the Stalls', in *Othello: The National Theatre Production*, Kenneth Tynan (ed.), (The National Theatre, 1966) 13–26, 13. For a further discussion of the modernity of Zeffirelli's production—with a particular focus on what critics at the time perceived as Ian Bannen's 'neurotic' interpretation of Iago—see Russell Jackson, '"An *Othello* to Forget": Zeffirelli's Stratford *Othello* and its Reputation', *Shakespeare Bulletin* 25.4 (2007): 11–21.

[24] The quotation is from the review in the *Independent on Sunday*, 25 April 1999, quoted in Julie Hankey, *Shakespeare in Production: Othello* (Cambridge: Cambridge University Press, 2005) 104. Pages 103–5 discuss the reception of the Fearon *Othello* (directed by Michael Attenborough). See also Russell Jackson's review of this production in *Shakespeare Quarterly* 51.2 (2000): 217–29, which attributed the 'diminishment in Othello himself from the customary heroic ideal' both to the 'excellent ensemble work' (221) and to the fact that Fearon was 'perhaps a little quieter than he could have afforded to be in the more grandiloquent passages of the part . . . . [T]he valuable quality of danger may have been lacking in this Othello' (220).

of the modern theatre, which erupt longingly in the gap between Shakespeare's language and our experience, remind us that the past is always on the verge of fading into oblivion—or, perhaps, becoming indistinguishable from the present. Invoking the power of Shakespeare's poetry, we call up an image of the past, and listen for its animal heart.

Select Bibliography

Berry, Cicely (1973) *Voice and the Actor* (New York: Wiley).

Evans, Gareth Lloyd (1968) 'Shakespeare and the Actors: Notes Towards Interpretations', *Shakespeare Survey* 21: 115–25.

Freer, Coburn (1981) *The Poetics of Jacobean Drama* (Baltimore: Johns Hopkins University Press).

Hankey, Julie (2005) *Shakespeare in Production: Othello* (Cambridge: Cambridge University Press)

Joseph, B. L. (1951) *Elizabethan Acting* (Oxford: Oxford University Press).

Potter, Lois (2002) *Shakespeare in Performance: Othello* (Manchester: Manchester University Press).

Rokison, Abigail (2009) *Shakespearean Verse Speaking: Text and Theatre Practice* (Cambridge: Cambridge University Press).

Schultz, Stephen C. (1977) 'William Poel on the Speaking of Shakespearean Verse: A Reevaluation', *Shakespeare Quarterly* 28: 334–50.

Seymour, Alan (1966) 'A View from the Stalls', in Kenneth Tynan (ed.), *Othello: The National Theatre Production* (London: The National Theatre) 13–26.

Werner, Sarah (1996) 'Performing Shakespeare: Voice Training and the Feminist Actor', *New Theatre Quarterly* 12: 249–58.

Wright, George T. (1988) *Shakespeare's Metrical Art* (Berkeley: University of California Press).

CHAPTER 20

....

'MAKE MY IMAGE BUT AN ALEHOUSE SIGN'

The Poetry of Women in Shakespeare's Dramatic Verse

....

ALISON FINDLAY

Queen Margaret's words 'make my image but an alehouse sign' in *2 Henry VI* (III. ii. 81) offer an appropriate metaphor for the female voice in Shakespeare's texts because they advertise the ways female characters strive to speak in a discursive environment that silences them as images and objectifies them as commodities. In the same play, the Duke of Somerset's political ambitions (including the 3rd Duke's building of the palace of Somerset House) are mocked when he is murdered 'underneath an alehouse paltry sign, | The Castle in Saint Albans, Somerset' (*2 Henry IV*, V. ii. 2–3).[1] For the Duke, the alehouse sign means abjection and death; for Margaret, as for other female characters, its commercial display of the female image connotes prostitution. How do women in Shakespeare negotiate a space to speak within a poetic discourse that repeatedly defines them as objects? The texts offer some blatant examples of this reductive practice: Hero is 'but the sign and semblance of her honour' (*Much Ado About Nothing*, IV. i. 33), while Innogen is 'a good sign' (a beautiful appearance) with little wit (*Cymbeline*, I. ii. 29). Posthumus' need for 'some corporal sign' to identify her as unchaste is a perverse reworking of the blason tradition in which a woman is anatomized as a series of body parts. In *Love's Labour's Lost*, the French Princess and her ladies throw scorn on the men who woo using this technique and, 'Following the signs, wooed but the sign of she' (V. ii. 470).

---

[1] The dangers of aligning oneself with a sign for male characters are shown in *Richard III*, where a publican citizen of London is executed for declaring his son heir to the Crown 'meaning indeed his house | Which, by the sign thereof was termed so' (III. v. 76–7).

A later French Princess, Catherine, engages more fully and discursively with the blason tradition in *Henry V*. As feminist criticism has argued, her English language lesson in Act III, Scene iv, which immediately follows Henry's threats to rape the daughters of Harfleur (III. iii. 103–4), identifies Catherine's body with France as the object of imperialist expansion. Learning the English names for the parts of her body leads to the dynastic marriage that will sanction Henry's project to prove his manhood via sexual and military possession. Catherine's naming of parts thus prefigures Henry Reed's Second World War poem of the same name by enlisting the body in the mechanized process of military conquest.[2] Moreover, 'Anglicizing' her body translates it into the bawdy signs that characterize the speech of Mistress Quickly, the brothel keeper. Quickly's malapropisms and double entendres in advertising her bawdy house of gentlewomen 'that live honestly by the prick of their needles' (II. i. 32–3) acts as prologue to Princess Catherine's self-anatomization.[3] Ann Kaegi observes that 'by figuratively undressing and sexualising parts of her anatomy' Catherine unwittingly engages 'in a titillating striptease conducted in the presence of male playgoers' in the English theatre.[4]

To read Catherine's part in Anglo-centric terms ignores the fact that most of it is in French so, despite the lesson, she is still linguistically marked off from the conquering English. The three English words in the top fifteen she uses most are, significantly, 'hand' (that which she anticipates giving to Henry in marriage); 'de' (meaning 'of' in French but translating into the definite article 'the' in English: thirty-eight of the forty-one uses are of this kind) and 'dat' for that, a pronoun which registers the objectification of her body parts as English goods. French offers no safe haven for Catherine, though. What commentaries on this scene have ignored, to date, is the way it draws on a specifically French form of the blason tradition, exemplified in *Sensvivent: Les Blasons Anatomiques du corps feminin* (1543) a collection of blasons and counterblasons on different parts of the female body by a group of rival male poets, competing in wit rather than love.[5] The collection starts with the hair and moves downwards to the foot, taking in all the body parts in between, most beginning with a header illustrating the 'part'. This popular book (running to ten editions in 16th-century France) was probably familiar to Shakespeare since Jaques' satiric portrait of the youthful lover 'with a woeful ballad/Made to his mistress eyebrow' in *As You Like It* (II. vii. 148–9), alludes to Scève's poem 'Blason du Sourcil'.[6] In *Henry V*, Catherine's naming of parts covers similar territory to *Sensvivent*

---

[2] Henry Reed, *Lessons of the War*: 'Naming of Parts', in *The Oxford Book of Twentieth Century English Verse*, Philip Larkin (ed.), (Oxford: Oxford University Press, 1973) 478–9.

[3] See, for example, Jean E. Howard and Phyllis Rackin, *Engendering a Nation: A Feminist Account of Shakespeare's English Histories* (London: Routledge, 1997) 209–15.

[4] Ann Kaegi, 'Introduction' to *Henry V*, A. R. Humphreys (ed.), (Harmondsworth: Penguin, 2010) lxxiv.

[5] *Sensvivent Les Blasons Anatomique de corps femenin, ensemble les contreblasons de nouveau composée & additionez, avec les figures, les tout par ordre: composez par plusieurs poetes contemporains. Avec la table desdictz Blasons & contreblasons, Imprimez en ceste Année pour Charles Langelier*, 1543.

[6] Scève's poem 'Blason du Sourcil' is on A5r-A5v of the *Sensvivent*. David Scott Kastan and Nancy J. Vickers noticed Shakespeare's allusion to the poem in their note 'Shakespeare, Scève and 'A Woeful Ballad', *Notes and Queries*, n.s. 27 (1980): 165–6.

Les Blasons Anatomique. The 'blason de la main', for example, praises the hand as having the power to bind and unbind hearts ('Main qui les cueurs fait lier & deslie,' sig 23v), which is presumably what Catherine is thinking about as she anticipates a match with Henry. Less attractively the nails in the counterblason have scratched the body and are black with muck 'au bout noir et tres ordz' (sig 69v). The neck is a divine creator on whose ivory altar the lover has expressed his devotion by sacrificing his heart in eternal flames (C3v).[7] By cataloguing her body in French, Catherine advertises how she is already defined by the blason at home.

When the last two items in her list, 'les pieds et la robe', are translated into English as 'de foot' and 'de cown', the bawdy nature of the original French blasons is revealed, signalling the cross-channel complicity of patriarchal literary language. Catherine hears 'foutre' (to fuck) and 'con' (cunt), terms which pun on intercourse as the ultimate goal of Henry as English aggressor. In *Sensvivent*, a series of blasons praise 'le con'. (FIGURE 20.1) Under the alehouse-type sign which displays it on the page, the 'petit con' is celebrated as plump and fearless, agile as a lion in battle or playful as a monkey or kitten, clothed with its flirtatious covering of hair, richer than the golden fleece. The 'Blason du Con de la Pucelle' describes the virgin's as 'mon plaisir, mon gentil jardinet' (27r) which anticipates the alignment of Catherine with 'this best garden of the world, | Our fertile France' in Burgundy's speech (V. ii. 36–7). Bouchetel's 'blason du con' emphasizes fertility, pointing out 'Con est la forge de quoy nature humaine | Faict ses devins & excellens ouvraiges'.[8] While the eye attracts the lover, this is the site of action: 'Con est la fin dont amours se couronne | Con est le pris dont amour se guerdonne.'[9] Spectators are reminded of how bawdy blasoning effectively prostitutes Catherine's body as a prize of war by the banter amongst the French nobles on the night before Agincourt. They tease the Dauphin for writing a sonnet to his horse, the pun on horse/whores, mistresses and jades (prostitutes) quickly inflecting the whole conversation with innuendo as in the tradition of competitive blasoning (III. vii. 38–66). The French nobles speak in English, erasing differences between men on opposing sides of the battle and demonstrating complicity in the process of constructing women poetically, culturally, and economically as objects of exchange. Catherine may speak with a difference, but uses French only to alienate the anatomization of her body, not to invent a poetic voice of her own.

Dramatic roles such as the Jailer's Daughter in the co-authored *Two Noble Kinsmen* or Ophelia in *Hamlet* suggest that madness may free the female voice to express itself through verse. The Jailer's Daughter speaks with a distinctive idiolect, all in monologues after her first scene (II. i) and although she is driven mad by her unrequited love for Palamon, for the early modern actor who received and performed the part, it has a

---

[7] La ou l'ay faict par grand devotion | Maint sacrifice, & mainte oblation | De ce mien cueur, qui ard sur son autel En feu quie est a jamais immortel. (19, sig. c3r-v).

[8] 'Cunt is the forge in which human nature's divine works are wrought' (27v-28r).

[9] 'Cunt is the end to which all desires run | Cunt is the prize which love wins' (28r).

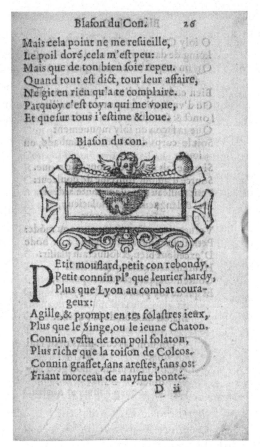

FIGURE 20.1. Clement Marot, *Blasons du corps feminin* (1543), 26 r,sig. D2 (Gordon 1543. B53), courtesy of Special Collections, University of Virginia Library, digitized with funding from the National Endowment for the Humanities and the Florence Gould Foundation.

strong internal coherence. The consistency is especially remarkable in a joint-authored play, running across scenes generally agreed to be by Fletcher (II. iv., II. vi., III. ii., III. iv., III. v., IV. i., and V. ii) and those by Shakespeare (II. i. and IV. iii). Perhaps this woman's part was constructed by and around the boy actor, possibly the talented Edmund Robinson who joined The King's Men in 1611 and was praised by Ben Jonson for his ability to 'talke bawdy'.[10] At the end of *Two Noble Kinsmen*, listeners are reminded that 'smallness' of voice identifies the singer as 'A boy or woman' (IV. i. 59).

Free association and striking metaphor make the Jailer's Daughter's poetry sound spontaneous. In Act III, Scene iv, for example, she translates her experience of being

[10] Ben Jonson, *The Devil is An Ass* (1616), Anthony Parr (ed.), in *The Works of Ben Jonson*, David Bevington, Martin Butler, and Ian Donaldson (eds), (Cambridge: Cambridge University Press, 2012), vol. 4, 465–609 (II. viii. 69–73)

hungry, cold, and lonely into a vision of being shipwrecked at sea: 'Yonder's the sea and there's a ship—how't tumbles! | And there's a rock lies watching under water—| Now, now, it beats upon it' (III. iv. 5–7). Her image of the rock watching beneath the water is unique amongst the collection of 12,284 texts currently transcribed from Early English Books Online. The character's bizarre juxtaposition of images and her address to the sailors 'Good night, good night' (III. iv. 11) does sound like madness, recalling something of Ophelia's voice. However, when the Jailer's Daughter shifts into lines from the ballad 'Child Waters' (III. iv. 19–24), she makes explicit what has been implicit all along: her poetic voice and thoughts are held together by the popular discourse of ballads. Douglas Bruster perceptively reads the ballads as the emotional 'unconscious' of the text, reminding listeners of a lost rural, organic community.[11] For the character, lyrics are a way to pursue her fantasy of a relationship with Palamon independently of him. Taking a cue from his own singing of sad songs (II. iv. 19–20), she styles herself as the heroine of 'The Fair Flower of Northumberland' (1597), a ballad in which a jailer's daughter frees a Scots' prisoner. The folklore fantasy of cross-class romance in the ballad is tragic since he rejects her and sends her home. This reminds us that the autonomy in lyrics sung by an independent female voice is just as fictional, fantastic, and short-lived as the lyrics themselves. The refrain of the song, 'Oh but her love was easy won,' haunts the dramatic character of the Jailer's Daughter. Broken echoes of ballad form—rhythm, repetition, half-rhyme run through her first soliloquy:

> 'Tis odds
> He never will affect me. I am base.
> My father the mean keeper of his prison,
> And he a prince. To marry him is hopeless,
> To be his whore is witless …
>
> (II. iv. 1–5)

Even in the apparent spontaneity of the character's words, her images are like alehouse signs since she recycles popular folkore (a tradition of which Ophelia, the young woman in 'A Lover's Complaint', and Lucrece in *The Rape of Lucrece* are also aware). Carol Thomas Neely has noted that Shakespeare's dramatizations of madness are characterized by 'quotation' or 'italicization' and that such characters' discourse is not their own.[12]

For the Jailer's Daughter, the art of quotation is dangerous because the tragic lyric has power to invade the bodies of both singers and listeners in performance.[13] The Jailer's Daughter seems, like Mopsa and Dorcas in *The Winter's Tale*, to be an eager consumer

---

[11] Douglas Bruster, 'The Jailer's Daughter and The Politics of Madwomen's Language', *SQ*, 46 (1995): 277–300.
[12] Carol Thomas Neely, 'Documents in Madness: Reading Madness and gender in Shakespeare's tragedies and early modern culture', *SQ* 42: 3 (1991): 315–38.
[13] See Bruce R. Smith, 'Shakespeare's Residuals: The Circulation of Ballads in Cultural Memory', in *Shakespeare and Elizabethan Popular Culture*, Stuart Gillespie and Neil Rhodes (eds), (London: Cengage Learning, 2006) 193–217 (198).

of ballads. She has listened, learned, and now recreates the experiences of suffering they express through her own bodily and vocal performances. Her part exemplifies Stuart Gillespie's point that 'Old ballads reflect the way things are, or possibly *vice versa*'.[14] Her part is shaped by the songs she knows. Fully aware of the tragic plot and the moral that 'maids will not so easily | Trust men again' (II. vi. 20–1), she still cannot avoid it. Her descent into madness follows folksong tradition, in particular the fate of Mad Bess in 'Love's Lunacy', though the parallels with this ballad have gone unremarked by critics.[15] Mad Bess admits 'I'm metamorphozed; | Strange sights and visions I doe see,' and recounts being led over hills, through valleys and water, complaining that 'Tom was the cause of all my woe'. The Jailer's Daughter likewise admits she loves Palamon 'beyond love and beyond reason | Or wit or safety' (II. vi. 11–12). Both heroines' fantasies of embracing or kissing their men are succeeded by a bitter (but again fantastic) sense of sexual exploitation. Mad Bess feels emotionally raped:

> I'm like to faire Philomela,
> by Tereus basely ravished;
> Yet when his burning lust did thaw,
> he closely her imprisoned:
> even so I'm quite defloured
> by Tom of all my senses
> My love and meanes he hath devowred
> Making no recompenses.

The Jailer's Daughter, likewise, takes Philomel as her model: 'for a prick now, like a nightingale | To put my breast against' (III. iv. 25–6). Her despair transforms her environment with poetic intensity: 'would it were perpetual night, | And darkness lord o'th' world' (III. ii. 3–4). The emotional darkness contrasts starkly with her appearance as '*She-fool*' in the country Morris dance. By now, the voice of the Jailer's Daughter is drowned out by the ballads 'The George Alow' and 'The Choice of Inventions' (III. v. 59–71) as her tragedy is transformed into a spectacle of 'rarest gambols' (III. v. 74–6).

Since 'Love's Lunacy' was sung to the tune of 'Mad man's morris', its depiction of Bedlam may lurk behind the fate of the Jailer's Daughter in the play. In the ballad Mad Bess ends with a dark vision of incarceration:

> The day is past, and night is come
> and here comes our commander;
> Hee'l locke me into a darke roome,
> 'tis sorrowes chiefest chamber.

In *The Two Noble Kinsmen,* the Jailer's daughter continues to weep and sing of neglected love, including the lyric 'May you never more enjoy the light …' (IV. i. 80 and 104). In

---

[14] Stuart Gillespie, 'Shakespeare and Popular Song', in Gillespie and Rhodes (2006) 174–92 (190).
[15] *Roxburghe Ballads,* Charles Hindley (ed.), (London: Reeves and Turner, 1874) vol. II, 286–90.

a positive reading, her acceptance of the faithful wooer follows yet another ballad tradition in which the forsaken maid is rescued from despair. In 'The Honest Wooer', for example, the maid transfers her desires to the 'constant lover' eagerly, declaring 'Love is a thing that ought to be done'.[16] For the Jailer's Daughter, the happy ending is less secure. Although the wooer is obviously devoted to her, she still sees him as the cruel lover, Palamon, who might reject her for her poverty (V. iv. 85–6). The Doctor wants to 'confine her to a place where the light may rather seem to steal in than be permitted' (IV. iii. 71–2) and her fears that the wooer will hurt her and make her cry (V. iv. 112–14) suggest that she is still mentally confined like Mad Bess.

The plots and metaphors of folk song are thus a form of poetry that allows the female voice to plot, to express pain and desire autonomously, but they are not effective forms of social interaction. The tragic ballad has a dangerously masochistic appeal. By offering an immediate means to accommodate traumas of abjection and loss, it seduces the performer into living within these scripts. For characters like the Jailer's Daughter and Ophelia, the ballad translates loss into self-dissolution. The metaphor of the willow garland is a noose that leads to muddy death or darkness as the voice of possibility is drowned. The status of the ballad form also cheapens the poetry of these female characters. As popular texts sold for pennies, ballads were, as Thomas Lodge put it, 'odd rhymes which runnes in every rascales mouth, savouring of ribaldry'.[17] To articulate oneself through ballads, as the mad Ophelia and the Jailer's Daughter do, is thus to advertise oneself, once more, as an alehouse sign.

The poetic voice of Lady Macbeth displays a more complex type of fragmentation. Linguistic analysis supports the critical view that Lady Macbeth mimics the language of phallocratic power so well that the part becomes suffocated by this dominant discourse. Having read out Macbeth's letter (I. v. 1–12), Lady Macbeth conjures military metaphors by 'the valour of my tongue' (I. v. 26) to conquer more feminine images such as the 'milk of human kindness' (I. v. 16), in pursuit of 'the golden round' (I. v. 27). Mikhail Morozov noted as early as 1949 that Lady Macbeth's images, which are 'much more concrete and substantial' than Macbeth's dreamlike fantasies, are characterized by 'courageous militancy'.[18] She assesses the 'fitness' of Duncan's arrival 'under my battlements' (I. v. 39), imagines her household as a military camp with the owl as 'bellman' (II. ii. 3) to sound lights out, and describes the memory as 'the warder [soldier or guardsman] of the brain' (I. vii. 65–70). Her language transforms her household into a battlefield where she, as general, will dispatch the 'night's great business' and thereby implicitly hold power to give 'solely sovereign sway and masterdom' in the days to come (I. v. 67–8).

---

[16] Hindley (1874) 89–93 (92–3).

[17] Thomas Lodge, *Protogenes Can Know Apelles by His Line though he se him not* (London, 1579) 20. On the commercial nature of ballads see Natasha Wurzbach, *The rise of the English Street Ballad 1550–1650* Gayna Walls (trans.), (Cambridge University Press, 1990).

[18] Mikhail Morozov, 'The Individualization of Shakespeare's Characters Through Imagery', *Shakespeare Survey*, 2 (1949): 83–106 (92).

Such imagery supports Christina Alfar's view that Lady Macbeth speaks as the phallus to support her husband in a parodic performance of wifely duty.[19] Linguistic analysis of Lady Macbeth's part using *Wmatrix*, a statistical method and software tool for corpus comparison, created by Paul Rayson,[20] confirms the direction of Lady Macbeth's aggressive desires. Among her most common words are second person pronouns: 'you', 'your', 'thou', addressed to men: Duncan, the community of nobles, and her husband.[21] Linguistically, Lady Macbeth is utterly different from the weird sisters, whose equivocal language is matched by equivocal gender. They 'should be women' but their beards 'forbid me to interpret | That you are so', Banquo points out (I. iii. 43–4). Supernatural status allows them to play much more freely with the language of power, bandying ceremonial titles as they address Banquo and Macbeth in a shower of greater and lesser 'All hail' (I. iii. 46–67). They shift effortlessly between the voyages of merchant shipmen and the domestic arena of the sailor's wife.

By contrast, Lady Macbeth's appropriation of masculine speech entails a warlike subjection of images of domestic nurture. Comparing her lines to those of Lady Macduff exposes the absence of words like 'harm', 'fly', 'father', 'poor', 'wit', 'wisdom', and 'flight', which characterize Lady Macduff's image of herself as the protective 'poor wren' guarding her chicks (IV. ii. 9).[22] In Lady Macbeth's appeal to the spirits to invade and impregnate her with cruelty (I. v. 39–42), followed by the vision of plucking away her suckling child to dash its brains out (I. vii. 55–9), her poetry constructs her as both a conqueror *and* a victim. Her military trope reworks that of Henry V at Harfleur warning that soldiers will rape maidens and impale infants upon pikes to the confused howls of 'mad mothers' (*Henry V*, III. iii. 121–2). It is not surprising that Lady Macbeth's speech collapses under the pressure of this concatenation of domestic and military metaphors. She ends the play by quoting fragments of herself: both the conquering commands of

---

[19] Christina Leon Alfar, *Fantasies of Female Evil* (London: Associated University Presses, 2003) 116.

[20] Scripts of characters' speeches and complete play texts from the First Folio were tagged by Mike Scott (Lancaster University) to exclude stage directions and speech prefixes. They were then analysed comparatively using Paul Rayson's tool *Wmatrix*. This can produce a list of most frequently used words and, more sophisticatedly, it can conduct a statistical comparison between the words of a corpus (or word list) such as a part spoken by an individual character (and performer) and a bigger reference corpus such as the whole script, in order to identify keywords: words that are unusually frequent or unusually infrequent. See Paul Rayson, 'From key words to key semantic domains' *International Journal of Corpus Linguistics* 13:4 (2008): 519–49 and, online, Paul Rayson, 'Wmatrix: a web-based corpus processing environment', UCREL, Lancaster University (2011), <http://ucrel.lancs.ac.uk/wmatrix/>.

[21] Discounting 'the', and 'and', 'to', 'of', these pronouns are the most common words in the part: 'you' is used thirty-nine times, 'your' twenty-six times, 'thou' thirteen times, and 'thou'd'st' once, with relative frequencies of 2.02 per cent, 1.35 per cent, and 0.67 per cent. She uses 'I' twenty-four times (1.24 per cent frequency), and 'me' sixteen times (0.83 per cent frequency), whereas 'I' is the word used most frequently by Macbeth (besides 'the', 'and', and, 'of') occurring 306 times (a relative frequency of 2.32 per cent).

[22] In addition to listing the differences, *Wmatrix* produces a 'log likelihood' percentage which shows statistically how significant the difference is between the character's use of a word and its occurrence in other parts of the text (in this case, Lady Macbeth's part). Comparison reveals a log likelihood of 11.48 per cent for 'harm' and 'fly'; 10.63 per cent for 'father'; 8.31 per cent for 'poor' and 7.66 per cent for 'wit', 'wisdom', 'wilt', and 'flight' in Lady Macduff's speeches.

pragmatic strategy and the suffocated words of pity, fear, and corporeal vulnerability that have been sacrificed in the pursuit of success but still cling to her like blood. In the part received by the early modern actor, the two registers bleed into one another:

> Fie, my lord, fie, a soldier and afeared? What need we fear? Who knows it when none can call our power to account? Yet, who would have thought the old man to have had so much blood in him? ...
> The Thane of Fife had a wife. Where is she now? What, will those hands ne' er be clean? No more o' that, my lord, no more o' that. You mar all with this starting....
> Here's the smell of the blood still. All the perfumes of Arabia will not sweeten this little hand. O, O, O!
>
> (V. i. 34–8, 40–3, 48–50)

Acknowledgement is a key feature of the scene.[23] Lady Macbeth's urgent denial of 'knowledge' of her guilt is fractured by her mad speech, spotted with the 'compunctious visitings of nature' that she had tried to 'stop up' (another melding of aggression and defence), but which continue to pollute her body, now from the outside.[24] Susan Zimmerman observes that Duncan's blood is the 'metaphoric life' of *Macbeth* because it deconstructs representation, overflowing the discursive structures through which humans make sense of the world.[25] Blood signifies both the hyper-masculinity of absolute kingship and the feminine weakness of the victim. Lady Macbeth's obsessive focus on it acknowledges that her masculine campaign has set her at war against herself, murderer against victim. 'Self-murder', in which men and women sinned by 'laying violent hands upon ... themselves', as John Sym put it, is thus an appropriate exit for her.[26] Since Lady Macbeth tried to silence 'human kindness', her suicide, which releases a 'cry of women' (V. v. 8), constitutes a perverse poetic justice.

In the case of dramatic characters, the repetition of a male-dominated poetic is echoed by the boy actors who speak for woman on the commercial stage. Lady Macbeth's struggle to suppress the woman's part by employing images of war may have been shadowed by a boy actor's striving to reach maturity and achieve a manhood he fantasizes as 'perfect, | Whole as the marble, founded as rock' instead of being 'confined' in female roles, 'bound in | To saucy doubts and fears' (III. iv. 20–1). While many of Shakespeare's dramatic texts

[23] T. G. Bishop 'Reconsidering a Folio Reading in *Macbeth* 5.1', *SQ* 46:1 (1995): 76–80, argues that the Folio's punctuation draws attention to knowing and acknowledgement, 78.

[24] On Lady Macbeth's inability to suppress the woman's part in her see, for example, Joan Larsen Klein, 'Lady Macbeth: "Infirm of Purpose"', in *The Woman's Part: Feminist Criticism of Shakespeare*, Carolyn Ruth Swift Lenz, Gayle Greene, and Carol Thomas Neely (eds), (Urbana: University of Illinois Press, 1983) 240–55, and Kay Stockholder, *Dream Works: Lovers and Families in Shakespeare's Plays* (Toronto: University of Toronto Press, 1987) 100–17.

[25] Susan Zimmerman, *The Early Modern Corpse and Shakespeare's Theatre* (Edinburgh: Edinburgh University Press, 2005) 174.

[26] John Sym, *Lifes Preservative Against Self-Killing* (London, 1637) Michael MacDonald (ed.), (London: Routledge, 1988) B1v.

exploit the double voice of female character and boy performer, the remainder of this essay will consider how the plays succeed in giving women verse-speakers distinctive poetic voices, in spite of a tradition that seems to cabin, crib, or confine them as objects or alehouse signs.

Jonathan Culpeper has shown how corpus linguistics can draw attention to a character's idiolect as 'a foregrounded style,' created specifically for that character (and, one could add, performer). Comparative analysis of the parts can thus show how the character's style 'may deviate from or be parallel to the idiolectal styles of other characters.' *Wmatrix* produces statistical data about a character's keywords (the words her part uses most frequently in comparison to the rest of the play) from which theories about her ideolect can be drawn. Culpeper argues, for example, that Juliet's most frequent keyword 'if' demonstrates that she 'is in a state of anxiety for much of the play.'[27] Its provisionality also brilliantly pinpoints Juliet's liminal quality: poised on the threshold between childhood and womanhood and catapulted through it by the tragic plot. Grammatical keywords and pronouns can reveal much, as here and in the case of Lady Macbeth's top keywords 'you', 'your', and 'thou'. Particular attention to keywords related to content (which Mike Scott defines as 'aboutness' keywords) and word clusters helps to identify a character's distinctive poetic style.[28] Cognitive metaphor theory has moved away from traditional rhetorical definitions to see different figures as members of the same cognitive category, which helps to build a more rounded picture of female poetry in Shakespeare's dramatic texts.[29]

The part of Cleopatra, for example, reveals a carefully crafted poetic style designed to sustain sovereignty in the face of subjection to Rome. Cleopatra's most frequently used word is 'I', suggesting her self-assertion, while her 'aboutness' keywords in the top forty-five betoken an equally strong assertion of sovereignty (gold; crown; resolution; kingdom) alongside terms of abjection (help; forgotten; shackles; bolts; desolation; villain; slave; beggar). A third group of aboutness keywords relate to female identity (Charmian; Iras; women; girls; nurse; dug). Cleopatra melds the contradictions of majesty, subjection, and corporeal womanhood much more successfully than Lady Macbeth. Indeed, Freeman notes that Cleopatra's propensity to link metaphors is encapsulated by her metaphoric description of life as a 'knot intrinsicate'.[30] It is her iconic status as an Egyptian queen that gives her the power to speak and act metaphorically, to translate her experience and that of Antony into the register of myth. Janet Adelman's excellent analysis of hyperbole and scepticism in

[27] Jonathan Culpeper, 'Keywords and characterization: An analysis of six characters in *Romeo and Juliet*' in David Hoover, Jonathan Culpeper, and Keiran O'Halloran, *Approaches to Corpus Stylistics* (London: Routledge, forthcoming).

[28] See M. R. Scott, 'Focusing on the Text and Its Key Words,' in *Rethinking Language Pedagogy from a Corpus Perspective*, L. Burnard and T. McEnery (eds), vol. 2 (Frankfurt: Peter Lang, 2000) 103–22, and Scott, *WordSmith Tools Help Manual*, Version 5.0. (Liverpool: Lexical Analysis Software, 2008).

[29] See Monika Fludernik, Donald C. Freeman, and Margaret H. Freeman, 'Metaphor and Beyond: An Introduction,' *Poetics Today*, 20:3, Metaphor and Beyond: New Cognitive Developments (1999): 383–96.

[30] Donald C. Freeman, '"The Rack Dislimns": Schema and Metaphorical Pattern in *Antony and Cleopatra*', *Poetics Today*, 20:3 (1999): 443–60

the play focused on Antony as the object of Cleopatra's speech.[31] My approach is to define Cleopatra's technique as a speaking subject, a poet tasked with transforming both protagonists from abjection to heroic transcendence as 'a race of heaven' (I. iii. 37). She tells Alexas that Antony's presence, 'that great medicine', has 'with his tinct gilded thee' (I. v. 36–7). Cleopatra's poetry works in just this way, like alchemy.

Like alchemy, it is dangerously explosive, as evidenced by the messenger who reports Antony's marriage. Cleopatra's display of majesty changes in a flash to an instrument of torture: 'The gold I give thee will I melt and pour | Down thy ill-uttering throat' (II. v. 33–4). Gold is an unstable, tyrannical signifier because it betrays Cleopatra's insecurity as queen and colonized subject. Her fear that Egypt could be 'submerged and made | A cistern for foul snakes' (II. v. 95–6) informs many images of traps and dissolution.[32] For Cleopatra the traps are ideological rather than physical: the temptation to betray her national identity and her female identity. She recognizes the dangers of masquerade or 'excellent dissembling' (I. iii. 79) even as she pursues this tactic with Caesar's messengers. She rejects objectification as a jewel in his triumph, determining that his 'imperious show' will never 'Be brooched with me' (IV. xvi. 24, 26). She would rather ruin the 'mortal house' (V. ii. 50) of her body than become a decorative object of display. In spite of Caesar's superior material power, Cleopatra's poetic style (unlike Lady Macbeth's) vigorously conceives majesty in female terms. She refers to commanding female personifications: 'a Fury crown'd with snakes' (II. v .40) or Fortune with her wheel of destiny (IV. xvi. 46; V. ii.3 and 29). The one notable exception is in the field of military action, where she enters the Battle of Actium 'as the president of my kingdom' to 'Appear there for a man' (III. vii. 17–18). The disastrous consequences of her masquerade make it clear that she does not have the heart and stomach of a king. It is as a poet queen that she can defeat Caesar. She reminds herself 'Not being Fortune, he's but Fortune's knave, | A minister of her will' (V. ii. 3–4).

Cleopatra maintains her integrity as a woman by moving from the simile of masquerade to a metaphoric embodiment of queenship. Her poetry prioritizes her own body parts animated by emotion. To be cold-hearted would be to engender a hailstorm that would destroy her dynasty and lay waste her kingdom:

> Till by degrees the memory of my womb
> Together with my brave Egyptians all,
> By the discandying of this pelleted storm
> Lie graveless, till the flies and gnats of Nile
> Have buried them for prey!
>
> (III. xiii. 166–9)

The lines are spoken to assure Antony, yet they advertise a much broader scope of love. By making others know feelingly 'there were a heart in Egypt' (I. iii. 41), Cleopatra puts

---

[31] Janet Adelman, *The Common Liar* (New Haven: Yale University Press, 1973) 102–21.
[32] These are also noted by Freeman as part of the play's metaphoric schemae of 'container' and 'liquefaction' metaphors.

emotions at the heart of the kingdom rather than trying to block them up in pursuit of power, as Lady Macbeth does. Cleopatra's skill in articulating emotion is shared by other female speakers such as Viola in *Twelfth Night*. Orsino is surprised and annoyed when his role as laureate is outmatched by Viola who 'dost speak masterly' (*Twelfth Night*, II. iv. 21) and wins Olivia's love by articulating her own. Her male disguise allows a glimpse of the passion and poetry that is usually buried by conventions of female modesty, silenced and fossilized 'like patience on a monument' (II. iv. 114). As Queen of Egypt, Cleopatra has much more freedom to speak what she feels when on and in the monument. Faced with the tragedy of Antony's death, she emphatically defines herself in emotional terms, as 'no more but e' en a woman' (IV. xvi.75). By claiming she is commanded 'By such poor passion as the maid that milks | And does the meanest chores', she uses a simile that erases class differences, inviting the empathy of sisterly spectators or readers (IV. xvi. 76–7). Cleopatra shows that passion, the woman's part, is not mean or poor but transcendent, powerful, and transformative.

Although she is subject to Rome and the object of male passion, Cleopatra recreates herself as a consuming subject by imitating Isis, the Egyptian goddess of resurrection whose written name betokened the power of the throne.[33] The detail of Cleopatra 'In th' habiliments of the goddess Isis' (III. vi. 16–19) draws on the more extensive description in Plutarch's *Lives* which says Cleopatra appeared thus 'as a new Isis' at 'all other times els when she came abroad' suggesting a costume style for the Egyptian queen that would have created a three-dimensional poetry in and of performance.[34] Plutarch's account of Isis and her murdered brother Osiris, whose limbs she recovered from the Nile to revivify his generative power, commented on the symbolic significance of Isis' robes. Their 'different tinctures and colours' reflect her infinite variety 'to wit, light, darknesse, day, night, fire, water, life, death, beginning and end'.[35] The contradictions of Isis lie beneath Cleopatra's references to the moon, the Nile, the sun as lamp, and finally the passion of fire and air 'my other elements | I give to baser life' (V. ii. 284–5). The 'serpent of old Nile' who is 'wrinkled deep in time' with the cultural legacy of Isis, is thus not merely a 'morsel for a monarch' (I. v. 25–31). Cleopatra, like her predecessor, has the power to dismember and remember male subjects. Her face draws in Pompey's eyes to 'anchor his aspect and die | With looking on his life' (I. v. 33–4). She imitates the supernatural goddess in order to remember Antony in embodied mythic terms. Cleopatra's love poetry of mourning makes Antony 'dolphin-like' by magnifying his body parts 'above | The element they lived in' (V. ii. 88–9). In her blason, his face is as the heavens, with eyes like the sun and moon, his limbs reach across earth and sea like a Colossus and his voice resonates through the atmosphere (V. ii. 81–5).

[33] See Alison Findlay, *Women in Shakespeare: A Dictionary* (London: Continuum, 2010) 205, and Michael Lloyd, 'Cleopatra as Isis,' *Shakespeare Survey*, 12 (1959): 89–94.

[34] Alison Thorne, *Vision and Rhetoric in Shakespeare: Looking Through Language* (Basingstoke: Macmillan, 2000) 166–97, draws attention to the spatial and optical dimensions that have been largely neglected in critical accounts of the play's hyperbolic discourse.

[35] Plutarch, *The Philosophie, commonlie called the Morals*, Philemon Holland (trans.), (London, 1603) 1318.

Cleopatra's suicide is performance poetry that amalgamates supernatural, regal, and womanly qualities in a spectacle of infinite richness within the little room of the monument. The 'best attires' which show her 'like a queen' (V. ii. 223–4) and the 'worm of Nilus' that brings liberty (V. ii. 239) invest her with the regenerative power of Isis. Cleopatra's 'immortal longings' (V. ii. 276) for Antony collapse the boundaries between sex and death in a 'lover's pinch' (V. ii. 290). Catherine Belsey memorably claimed that the early modern woman had no unified subject position from which to speak in tragedy.[36] Nevertheless, Cleopatra's triumphant transcendence of tragedy is precisely as an embodied woman with 'my baby at my breast | That sucks the nurse asleep' (V. ii. 303–4). Woman is the living flesh or matrix in which the contradictions of majesty and subjection, passion and loss, death and rebirth are held together in a 'knot intrinsicate' (V. ii. 299).

Cleopatra's sensitivity to the border-crossings of life and death is shared by other female characters in Shakespeare. In particular, they inform the poetic voices of female protagonists from comedies, histories, and tragedies who, in spite of coming from different contextual fields, share common ground as widows. Their proximity to experiences of birth and mortality opens up space for a peculiarly intense poetry that looks beyond the immediate world. Widows personify the borderline position typically occupied by women, at the margins of official discourse, yet their independence from patriarchal control also gives them freedom of expression. In *King John* Elinor warns that Constance's speech has 'kindled France and all the world | Upon the right and party of her son' (I. i. 33–4). Constance relies on the stereotypes 'A widow, husbandless and subject to fears; | A woman naturally born to fears' (II. ii. 14–15), to invoke feelings of guilt in those around her, using the most powerful poetry in the play (as actors such as Sarah Siddons have recognized). The widow's independence gives her licence to speak out against the 'perfect wrong' of masculine policy (III. i. 115). She has no fear of slandering the French and English monarchs when she rails at length against the strumpet Fortune for 'adulterat[ing] hourly' with King John (II. ii. 54–61), or points out the hypocrisy of the wedding.

Pandulph objects that 'you utter madness and not sorrow' (III. iv. 43), but there is a candid emotional truth in Constance's laments. She manages her experiences as a widow and mother via the poetic technique of personification, peopling her poetry to express her loss. 'Grief fills up the room of my absent child' she remarks, giving a detailed account of the emptiness of daily life without Arthur in which grief 'stuffs out his vacant garments with his form' (III. iv. 93–6). The poignancy of such details carries emotional resonance for anyone who has lost a child through death or simply because the child has grown up and left home. The absence articulated by words is, paradoxically, full of emotion. Like Cleopatra's, this is a sustaining poetry of love: 'My life, my joy, my food, my all the world, | My widow-comfort and my sorrow's cure' (III. iv. 104–5). Widowhood has

[36] Catherine Belsey, *The Subject of Tragedy: Identity and Difference in Renaissance Drama* (London: Routledge, 1985) 121.

already familiarized Constance with death; her personification of it in erotic terms is a remarkable gothic cameo:

> Arise forth from the couch of lasting night,
> Thou hate and terror to prosperity,
> And I will kiss thy detestable bones,
> And put my eyeballs in thy vaulty brows,
> And ring these fingers with thy household worms,
> And stop this gap of breath with fulsome dust,
> And be a carrion monster like thyself.
> Come, grin on me, and I will think thou smil'st,
> And buss thee as thy wife. Misery's love,
> O, come to me!
>
> (III. iv. 27–36)

For spectators and readers, the vividness of these corporeal images makes the invocation curiously seductive. Constance's passion is dramatically attractive, her desire transgressing all conventions of female modesty. Her poetry of love stands out from the rhetorically precise yet heartless political negotiations in the rest of the play.

Constance is an exceptional figure. However, by looking at the group of female protagonists in *Richard III*, who are all widows, it is possible to identify a poetic ideolect in this generic type. Statistical analysis of the parts of Queen Margaret, Queen Elizabeth, Queen Anne, and the Duchess of York in comparison with the full script reveals that their top 'aboutness' keywords are, unsurprisingly, 'hell', 'sorrow', 'curse', 'death' (and dead). The widows in *Richard III* use 'o' and 'ah' much more frequently than other characters in the script. These expressions mark off their apostrophes of grief in the poetic tradition of female complaint. A proximity with the borderlines of human life inspires Queen Elizabeth to redefine her reproductive power as plentiful poetry of sorrow at Edward's death. Widowed for the second time, 'I am not barren to bring forth complaints' she insists: 'All springs reduce their currents to mine eyes,' so that she can 'send forth plenteous tears to drown the world' (II. ii. 66–72). The Duchess of York, whose grief stretches back even further, appoints herself a 'mother of these griefs' and 'your sorrow's nurse,' who promises to 'pamper it with lamentation' (II. ii. 80–8).

By Act IV, the widows' chorus of complaint has swelled to three with Anne's lamentations, and then to four with Margaret's entry. Proximity to death appears to have stretched time for the widows, lengthening their earthly existence beyond the normal span. The Duchess of York's reminder, 'Eighty odd years of sorrow have I seen' (IV. i. 95), is upstaged by Margaret's insistence on the 'benefit of seniory' in 'ancient sorrow' (IV. iv. 35–6). Margaret takes over as tragic bard, cataloguing their losses in lines that make extensive use of epiphora (the repetition of phrases) to create a ritualistic chant that draws the widows together:

> If sorrow can admit society
> Tell o' er your woes again by viewing mine.

> I had an Edward, till a Richard killed him;
> I had a husband, till a Richard killed him.
> [*To Elizabeth*] Thou hadst an Edward, till a Richard killed him;
> Thou hadst a Richard, till a Richard killed him.
> *Duchess of York*: I had a Richard too, and thou didst kill him;
> I had a Rutland too, thou holpst to kill him.
>
> (IV. iv. 38–45)

The interactive relationships between the widows are evidenced by their three most common keywords: 'thou', 'thy', and 'thee' (Constance's top keyword is also 'thou').[37] The preponderance of second person pronouns (in comparison to first person pronouns for the whole play's script) is indicative of a relational sense of identity on the part of the speakers, something that feminist theory has argued is typical of women's self-construction.[38] The familiar form 'thou' as opposed to 'you' also suggests the authority of the speaker in relation to the addressee.[39] While the widows speak from outside patriarchal social structures and their poetry is thus culturally 'invisible', it still exerts a powerful effect on listeners. Like old wives' tales, their riddling verse of curse and prophesy circles back on itself like a chant, the form imitating the cyclical sense of time that apprehends past, present, and future simultaneously. For Anne, who fulfils the stereotype of the remarrying widow, the repetitions of 'my husband' (IV. i. 65–8) and her prophetic curse on Richard's future wife, which turns out to be herself (IV. i. 71–6), make a tragic closed circle like the wedding ring and the crown that lead to her death.

By contrast, Elizabeth, who learns from Margaret how to curse and prophesy, becomes an expert riddler by the end of the play when she is interviewed by Richard. Her verse employs antithesis to express the inversion of order in his reign of terror. Her enigmatic references to time, meanwhile, hint that her tight control of language gives her power over 'the time to come':

> That thou hast wrongèd in the time o' erpast,
> For I myself have many tears to wash
> Hereafter time for time past wronged by thee.
> The children live, whose fathers thou hast slaughtered—
> Ungoverned youth, to wail it in their age.
> The parents live, whose children thou hast butchered—
> Old barren plants, to wail it with their age.
> Swear not by time to come, for that thou hast
> Misused ere used, by times ill-used o' erpast.
>
> (IV. iv. 319–27)

[37] 'Thou' (log likelihood 43.73), 'thy' (log likelihood 33.24), and 'thee' (log likelihood 16.37). The log likelihood for 'thou' in Constance's part is 19.84.

[38] 'We' and 'our' are the top keywords in the playscript. 'I' is used 695 times in the playscript, a relative frequency of 2.52 while in the combined scripts of the widows there are 136 uses, producing a lower relative frequency of 2.16, and a differential log likelihood of 2.72.

[39] Your and you are used more in the playscript than by the widows. Relative frequencies for 'your' are 0.95 (playscript) compared to 0.60 (widows), a log likelihood of 7.42. Relative frequencies for 'you' are 1.33 (playscript) compared to 0.95 (widows), a log likelihood of 6.14.

When Richard raises the possibility of Princess Elizabeth as a bride, Queen Elizabeth refers to herself as 'My daughter's mother' (IV. iv. 243) marking a division of speaking and acting self. At one level, this responds to Richard's tactic of 'confounding the integrity' of the women's titles and identities as mothers, daughters, wives.[40] Its enigmatic, depersonalizing form also warns him that, like a sybil, she holds the power to deceive, to outwit Richard by marrying Elizabeth to Richmond. In the present, controlled by Richard, Elizabeth mourns as a victim, but it is she who will fashion the 'time to come'.

Margaret is nearly trapped by Richard's deft trick of turning her curse back on her (I. iii. 231). However, her strong poetic persona transcends his chronological form of self-construction even more powerfully than Elizabeth's. The Lancastrian French Queen is, paradoxically, the immortal bard of Tudor history. Her presence in the England of *Richard III* is choric rather than historical since the real Margaret had retired to France. The character's unnerving power as bard is developed across the tetralogy. Besides Mistress Quickly, she has the longest theatrical life, which perhaps explains her curious omnipresence in *Richard III*. There is no stage direction to mark her entrance in Act I, Scene iii; it is as though she has always been there. As a monument without a tomb, she offers an ironic commentary on Shakespeare's growing sense of his own identity as national bard.

Margaret's successive parts across the four plays also constitute Shakespeare's most extensive treatment of the growth of an independent, poetic female voice. In *2 Henry VI*, the character complains that Henry cheapens her to 'make my image but an alehouse sign' (III. ii. 81). Margaret repeatedly rejects identity as a passive image. She does not remain silent even as the object of Suffolk's admiring gaze in *1 Henry VI*. As a quid pro quo for his attempt to imprison her 'fairest beauty' (V. v. 2), she remarks that he is mad, using asides to the audience (a technique she has perfected by Act I, Scene iii of *Richard III*). After Gloucester's death in *2 Henry VI*, she styles herself a mistress-poet rather than the object of male invention, distracting Henry's grief and suspicions with an epic narrative that describes her journey to England. This scene's portrait of the artist as a young woman shows Margaret's deft manipulation of image and emotion, albeit with rather crude sentimental effects.

> The pretty vaulting sea refused to drown me,
> Knowing that thou wouldst have me drowned on shore
> With tears as salt as sea through thy unkindness.
> The splitting rocks cow'red in the sinking sands,
> And would not dash me with their ragged sides
> Because thy flinty heart, more hard than they,
> Might in thy palace perish Margaret.
>
> (III. ii. 94–100)

Margaret writes herself as a tragic heroine, drawing on classical allusion (and probably Marlowe's *Dido Queen of Carthage*, published in 1594)[41] to compare herself to Dido,

---

[40] Madonne M. Miner, 'The Roles of Women in *Richard III*', in Lenz et al. (1983) 35–55 (44).

[41] Marlowe, *Dido, Queen of Carthage* (London: Thomas Woodcocke, 1594).

Henry to the faithless Aeneas, and concluding melodramatically 'Die, Margaret | For Henry weeps that thou dost live so long' (III. ii. 120–1). In case Henry should miss the point, the heart-rending experience is made literal in a jewel—'A heart it was, bound with diamonds'—which the heroine takes from her neck and casts into the sea in the hopes it will reach England (III. ii. 106–13). The diamond-hard object reminds the off-stage audience or readership that Margaret's epic is an empty fiction to deceive Henry, while her living heart beats for Suffolk.

In affective terms, the banishment and death of Suffolk widows Margaret. Stylistically, she matures; her verse becomes less schematic, her metaphors more organic. Words are accompanied by physical gestures as she strives to wash his hand with tears and imprint his palm, as though it were a letter, with a kiss 'That thou might'st think upon these lips by the seal | Through whom a thousand sighs are breathed for thee' (III. ii. 348–9). The suspended moment of painful separation when she looks on him 'as one that surfeits thinking on a want' is amplified by verbal antithesis: 'even now be gone! | O, go not yet' and 'yet now farewell, and farewell life with thee' (III. ii. 356–7, 360). As their bodies embrace and part, Margaret's condensed phrases testify that this is loving in truth and fain in verse her love to show.

She moves politically from incoming queen in *2 Henry VI*, to effective head of state in *3 Henry VI*, and at Tewksbury reworks her earlier sea narrative. She adapts the trope of the ship of state (V. iv. 1–38), peopling it with members of the Lancastrian army to unite them against the Yorkists: 'And what is Edward but a ruthless sea? | What Clarence but a quicksand of deceit? | And Richard but a raggèd fatal rock?' (V. iv. 25–7).

By the time Margaret bids farewell in Act IV, Scene iv of *Richard III*, she has come a long way from the young Queen who was so angered by the thought of being reduced to a cheap image on an alehouse sign. Her thirty-eight lines to Elizabeth are a testament to her poetic maturity. This chronicle of their mirrored lives blends passion and tight rhetorical control, personal anger with a deeper political outrage at the masculine historical project. It is studded with metaphors that critique the marginalization of female experience. To play the part of 'painted queen' is to continue that history, to be merely the 'flattering index of a direful pageant' (IV. iv. 85) in which women are 'garish flag[s]' of themselves, without dignity. Margaret's stunning poetic performance cautions her successor about that tragic legacy and simultaneously triumphs in her own escape from it: 'Farewell, York's wife, and queen of sad mischance' she concludes, 'These English woes will make me smile in France' (IV. iv. 114–15). For Princess Catherine in *Henry V* France offers no safe haven from the gaze of the male poet, but for Queen Margaret it represents another country from which her poetic voice, crafted in England, can comment freely.

SELECT BIBLIOGRAPHY

Belsey, Catherine (1985) *The Subject of Tragedy: Identity and Difference in Renaissance Drama* (London: Routledge).

Bloom, Gina (2007) *Voice in Motion: Shaping Gender, Shaping Sound in Early Modern England* (Philadelphia: University of Pennsylvania Press).

Bruster, Douglas (1995) 'The Jailer's Daughter and The Politics of Madwomen's Language,' *SQ*, 46: 277–300.

Callaghan, Dympna (2000) (ed.), *A Feminist Companion to Shakespeare* (Oxford: Blackwell).

Findlay, Alison (2010) *Women in Shakespeare: A Dictionary* (London: Continuum).

Howard, Jean E. and Phyllis Rackin (1997) *Engendering a Nation: A Feminist Account of Shakespeare's English Histories* (London: Routledge).

Lenz, Carolyn Ruth Swift, Gayle Greene, and Carol Thomas Neely (1983) (eds), *The Woman's Part: Feminist Criticism of Shakespeare* (Urbana: University of Illinois Press).

Rackin, Phyllis (2005) *Shakespeare and Women* (Oxford: Oxford University Press).

PART V

READING SHAKESPEARE'S POEMS

CHAPTER 21

‘TO SHOW ... AND
SO TO PUBLISH’

*Reading, Writing, and Performing in
the Narrative Poems*

CHARLOTTE SCOTT

At the close of Shakespeare's *The Rape of Lucrece*, the narrator tells us how the Romans will present the heroine's death:

> They did conclude to bear dead Lucrece thence,
> To show her bleeding body thorough Rome,
> And so to publish Tarquin's foul offence;
> Which being done with speedy diligence,
> The Romans plausibly did give consent
> To Tarquin's everlasting banishment.
>
> (lines 1850–5)

The public spectacle of Lucrece's body is also an act of publication, simultaneously writing the history of the oppressor and the oppressed.[1] Central to this act of publication is the unrestricted access to her body; within the public arena her dead body becomes a site of record. Marked and visible the physical body *shows* the narrative of her ordeal. The Romans, responding to Tarquin's punishment, applaud ('plausibly'), concluding the narrative as though it were a dramatic event. At the centre of this language of

---

[1] Andrew Zurcher gives a fascinating analysis of the relationship between the oppressed and oppressor in the context of Tudor law. Using an Augustinian model, he explores the ways in which suicide can be read as guilt, *Shakespeare and the Law* (London: Methuen, 2010) 155–69.

representation and reception—showing, publishing, and applause—is the importance of audience in the creation of meaning.[2] This is a public event in which a personal history is being performed through the staged interpretation of specific images.

Whilst Shakespeare is writing to an oratorical Roman tradition, he is also evoking a powerful dynamic between the written and the performed that has underpinned the poem as a whole:

> To see sad sights moves more than hear them told,
> For then the eye interprets to the ear
> The heavy motion that it doth behold,
> When every part a part of woe doth bear.

(lines 1324–7)

The heavy lesson that Lucrece learns is that her eye alone failed to 'interpret' Tarquin's intentions. The interpretive relationship between the eye and the ear is central to the narrative of the poem. For Shakespeare, and for Lucrece, looking and listening, reading and performing provide a powerful semantic landscape in the poem's exploration of meaning. Central to these forms of meaning are the roles of interpretation, the necessity of audience, and the instability of perception. Shakespeare's investment in methods of interpretation is especially significant if we consider the context of the narrative poems and the point at which they emerge in his career as a playwright, as well as a poet.

There are two dominant, and not unrelated, critical commonplaces regarding the understanding of Shakespeare's narrative poems: that they emerged as a result of the closure of the public theatres during a particularly virulent episode of the plague (1593–4), and that they express a definitive form of *literariness* not present in the drama. Both these perceptions present Shakespeare's poetry as distinct from his plays.[3] They seek to expose Shakespeare as a reluctant author, forced into publishing his poetry because his major source of income was compromised, and as a man who was both expedient and industrious, but not necessarily fulfilled. History makes this a plausible argument, since the theatre closures would have certainly affected Shakespeare's dramatic writing. However, as Patrick Cheney observes: 'Shakespeare did not abandon poetry for the stage but wrote poems during the whole of his professional life'.[4]

---

[2] Andrew Gurr, in *The Shakespeare Stage 1574–1642*, 3rd edn (Cambridge: Cambridge University Press, 1992), explores the question of audiences and 'audience behaviour'; see particularly 226–31.

[3] Patrick Cheney, 'Shakespeare's Literary Career and Narrative Poetry', in *Early Modern English Poetry: A Critical Companion*, Patrick Cheney, Andrew Hadfield, and Garrett A. Sullivan (eds), (Oxford and New York: Oxford University Press, 2007) 160–71, tackles this distinction head on. He explores this question further, including an in-depth study of the narrative poems, in *Shakespeare, National Poet-Playwright* (Cambridge: Cambridge University Press, 2004). See also Katherine Duncan-Jones, *Shakespeare Upstart Crow to Sweet Swan 1592–1623* (London: Methuen, 2010) for an analysis of the ongoing role of the theatre in Shakespeare's poetic mind.

[4] Cheney (2007) 162. Cheney's chapter addresses Shakespeare's poetry within the context of his identity as an 'author' and the long-held assumption that Shakespeare was not interested in a 'literary career'.

For Cheney, Shakespeare is not a poet or a playwright, but an author who 'interleaves poems with plays from beginning to end'.[5] Central to Shakespeare's evolution as an author is his profound investment in questions of representation. Through both poetry and drama Shakespeare explores the printed word and the theatrical body for their representational capacities: from the silent gesture, through the static image, to the polyphonic voice, it is the relationship between theatre and text, I shall suggest, that gives Shakespeare his greatest mimetic range.

The boundaries between printed poetry and public theatre are not as distinct as most 20th-century criticism would imply.[6] Whilst the presentation (and dissemination) of forms can appear idiosyncratic, the methods of representation, the constructions of character, and the images of motion frequently coincide. For Shakespeare, writing itself is dramatic, dependent as it is on the creation of competing voices, the representation of the expressive body, and the creation of an audience.[7] Recent scholarship has tried to reunite poetry and drama, not only through a widened understanding of the oral traditions through which both forms emerge, but also through a heightened attention to print culture and the multiple ways in which readers and audiences were being created.[8] The period in which these poems were published is now emerging as particularly important since, as Zachery Lesser and Alan Farmer have shown, it marks a turning point in the history of the book trade. Published in 1593, *Venus and Adonis* is Shakespeare's first work to appear in print. Not long after, in 1594, *The Rape of Lucrece* appears, both under the auspice of his fellow Stratfordian, Richard Field. As Shakespeare's poems appear in print for the first time, so the book market changes and there is a decided shift towards the publication of plays alongside the publication of poetry: 'In 1594 publishers brought out eighteen new playbooks, almost as many as in the previous two decades of professional playing combined'.[9] This apparently sudden interest in the published play might in part be explained by the creation of a readership that was also an audience. Whilst the

---

[5] Cheney (2007) 162.

[6] Describing words as 'actors' in lyric, Helen Vendler goes on to suggest that 'The art of seeing drama in linguistic action proper ... is an art that has lapsed, even in interpreters whose criteria appears to be literary rather than political or psychological'. *The Art of Shakespeare's Sonnets* (Cambridge, MA: Harvard University Press, 1997) 4.

[7] David Schalkwyk, '"She never told her love": Embodiment, Textuality, and Silence in Shakespeare's Sonnets and Plays', *Shakespeare Quarterly* 45 (1994): 381–407, aims to move beyond, what he calls, the 'internal moral and poetic symbolism of the texts conceived in a formalistically disembodied way': 398.

[8] For questions of professional authorship see Patrick Cheney (2004) and Lukas Erne, *Shakespeare as Literary Dramatist* (Cambridge: Cambridge University Press, 2003). On the subject of the relationship between the theatre and the book, see Julie Stone Peters, *The Theatre of the Book, 1480–1880* (Oxford: Oxford University Press, 2000), and Robert Knapp, *Shakespeare, the Theater and the Book* (Princeton, NJ: Princeton University Press, 1989). For a recent evaluation of the publication of playbooks see Zachary Lesser, *Renaissance Drama and the Politics of Publication* (Cambridge: Cambridge University Press, 2004). And for an, as yet, unparalleled account of the publication of plays, see Peter Blayney, 'The Publication of Playbooks', in *A New History of Early English Drama*, John D. Cox and David Scott Kastan (eds), (New York: Columbia University Press, 1997).

[9] Zachary Lesser, 'Playbooks', in *The Oxford History of Popular Print Culture, vol 1: Britain and Ireland to 1660*, Joan Raymond (ed.), (Oxford: Oxford University Press, 2010).

increasingly professionalized nature of London's public theatres allowed for the development of 'audience', so the publication of plays supported the idea of multiple 'readers'. The relationship between showing and publishing speaks as much for Elizabethan media as it does for Lucrece's ordeal.[10] In what follows, I will explore Shakespeare's narrative poems within the context of this media and the developing culture of print as well as performance. Above all, I would like to suggest, Shakespeare is interested in exploring the limits of representation—authorial, literary, dramatic, and interpretative.

To publish means, of course, to make public or declare (formally and informally) as well as 'to prepare and issue copies of a book'. The nature of being made public remains central to the latter meaning, and at the heart of the semantics of publishing is the anxiety of, or desire for, an audience.[11] Like the term 'publish', 'show' suggests a form of spectacle, as it denotes something being made visible. The emphasis on the visual is clear but even within this sphere there are multiple ways in which the visual can take shape.[12] Whilst traditionally Shakespeare has been understood as responding to a humanist tradition of *ekphrasis*, in which the 'speaking picture' is celebrated as a powerful poetic device, there is also a more complex interplay of the language of representation that seeks to explode the limits of poetic form as well as to describe them. As *Lucrece* ends with a reliance on the reading Roman public, so it also defers to the theatrical body, but the language of the visual also reacts against the painting, rejecting the inanimate or 'lifeless' qualities of the plastic arts. Instead what both *Venus* and *Lucrece* search for as the most heightened means of expression is drama: the animated body and the expressive heart. Shakespeare's interest in the dramatic body is audible in the strength of the characters' voices, but it is also present in the active language of revelation and animation: to show, to publish, to print, to act, to authorize.

Both poems discussed here tell a version of a well-known story and yet despite their classical or mythical pre-histories, Shakespeare re-presents history within the context of instant human drama. Like William Baldwin's resuscitation of kings in *The Mirror for Magistrates*, the immediate voices of the characters speak in a present tense that is inherently dramatic, rehearsing an ethical dialogue with the audience/reader. Given the relatively recent advent of a 'culture of print', as well as the development of public theatres, the critical language of showing or publishing is still in development.[13] The multiple ways of representing matter,

---

[10] I use the term 'Elizabethan media' to refer to the collective means of communication available at this time which are, primarily, the printed book and the public stage.

[11] At the centre of any claim to 'publish' or to 'show' is the awareness of an audience, public or private; the act of revelation requires a reception. Initially, of course, the word 'audience' emerged from the French *audire*, meaning to *hear*. Despite the words' assimilation into the language of visual arts, its primary meaning remains auditory. As we listen in public, so the language of oral culture takes root in the visual imagination to become comprehensive in its representational range.

[12] John Kerrigan, *Motives of Woe: Shakespeare and the 'Female Complaint': A Critical Anthology*, John Kerrigan (ed.), (Oxford: Oxford University Press, 1991), Stephanie H. Jed, *Chaste Thinking: The Rape of Lucretia and the Birth of Humanism* (Bloomington and Indianapolis: Indiana University Press, 1989), and Ian Donaldson, *The Rapes of Lucretia: a myth and its transformations* (Oxford: Clarendon Press, 1982).

[13] Roger Chartier and Alan Boureau coined this term in their seminal book, *The Culture of Print: Power and the Uses of Print in Early Modern Europe* (Cambridge: Polity Press, 1989).

both visual and aural, to a public audience became rapidly more complex as it evolved through an ever-increasing network of diction. In Shakespeare's narrative poems the idea of performance is never far from the writing hand. Schematically both poems depend upon a narrative action in which events and emotions must fall hard upon each other.[14] In both cases we are supplied with a narrator who directs our attention and governs our response: from the strained pity of *Venus'* 'She's Love, she loves, and yet she is not loved' (line 610) to the agonized empathy of *Lucrece's* 'O deeper sin than bottomless conceit | Can comprehend in still imagination!' (lines 701–2). Central to the poems' success is their attention to action, and the ways in which action can precipitate questions of interpretation and expression.

Towards the end of the poem Venus, having seen the bloody boar and imagined Adonis is dead, suddenly hears a hunting cry and changes her mind, thinking it is Adonis alive and well. Ashamed of her apparently false accusation of Death, she attempts to apologize to the figure explaining that it was the boar that was at fault:

> 'Tis not my fault: the boar provoked my tongue.
> Be wreaked on him, invisible commander.
> 'Tis he, foul creature, that hath done thee wrong.
> I did but act; he's author of thy slander.

> (lines 1003–6)

The distinction that Venus makes between the 'author' and the 'act' is based upon interpretation and performance. The author, it seems, provides the information; the actor performs it. Within the context of the poem, the boar is the author of such 'slander' because he represents a circumstantial image on the basis of which Venus acts. Shakespeare creates an apparently simple distinction between authorship and acting that would be both humorous and resonant to anybody who worked in the theatre, knowing that there were times when an actor might well want to separate himself from the playwright.[15] But such a distinction is spurious, however, since Venus is right: Adonis is dead and the boar is both the author and the actor of the deed. The dramatic irony here allows Shakespeare to make more of this comment than a straightforward truism would have done. Understanding action as response, Venus exposes the vertiginous space between information and interpretation; a space that is fundamental to the development of Shakespeare's art. Venus'

---

[14] Although David Schalkwyk observes 'emotion' as anachronistic, and it is in the modern day sense, for the Tudors 'emotion' meant a public display of agitation or feeling; 'civil unrest' or 'political agitation'(*OED*). Here, however, I use the word to convey the human's ability to experience sensations and feeling, which is in use from the beginning of the 16th century. For Schalkwyk's analysis of the difference between interiority and behaviour, see *Twelfth Night: New Critical Essays*, James Schiffer (ed.), (Abingdon and New York: Routledge, 2011) 81–98.

[15] In *The Comedy of Errors*, the relationship between writing and performing is presented in another key when Dromio of Ephesus, confronting his master, compares his beaten body to a marked page: 'If the skin were parchment, and the blows you gave were ink, | Your own handwriting would tell you what I think' (III. i. 13–14).

attempt to disengage herself from what she believes is misinformation locates a discourse that runs deep in Shakespeare's plays. Interpretation, whether it is construed as misprision or manipulation, comes to represent one of the most creative spaces in Shakespeare's work.[16] The sight of the boar stages a complex moment of interpretation as Venus construes and then reconsiders the information in front of her. Her language of action and authorship allows her to open up the space to competing definitions that come to reflect her subjective desires rather than her objective experience.

In any conversation about writing or performing, the relationship between subjective experience and objective action is always present. Part of the duty of the creative process (textual or theatrical) is to take a position on this relationship. The prefatory dedications that accompany these poems are suggestive of Shakespeare's posture towards the written text. Whilst *Venus* is an unstable yield from his harvest, *Lucrece* is a 'pamphlet', representing a 'superfluous moiety' of the poet's love for his patron, Henry Wriothesley. The oxymoronic 'superfluous moiety' (an abundant part) suggests how the text is both excessive and deficient, representing a version of its author's aspirations but only a part of its readers' desires. To read, we are told, is to accept inadequate information; 'untutored' and 'unpolished', the text is imperfect yet suggestive of a greater hope, ambition, or whole. In this way the ambiguity of the written word begins our journey into the dramatic worlds of these stories. Whilst Venus may distance herself from the 'author' of her feelings, Lucrece 'would not blot the letter | With words, till action might become them better' (lines 1322–3). For both poems, as this essay explores, the language of action is intricately bound up with the language of writing, so that the dramatic body is always in contest with the written text.

From the outset, the poem's status as a form of narrative action is constantly under scrutiny. Whilst the narrator repeatedly insists that we 'look' on a 'show', the goddess Venus is rendered in distinctly vital terms: she 'sweats', she 'blushes', she falls over, and she makes mistakes. Adonis, on the other hand, equally capable of sweating, vanity, and distraction, is relatively silent, obstinately refusing to succumb to seduction. Central to Adonis' characterization in the poem is his inability to respond; whilst on one hand this is part of the humour that the young vain boy could turn away the beautiful older woman, on the other it is reflective of Venus' insistence on an audience. Turning on him for his lack of physical or verbal responses to her, she declares:

> Fie, lifeless picture, cold and senseless stone,
> Well painted idol, image dull and dead,
> Statue contenting but the eye alone,
> Thing like a man, but of no woman bred:
>   Thou art no man, though of a man's complexion,
>   For men will kiss even by their own direction . . .
>
>   (lines 11–16)

---

[16] Whether it is Hamlet's use of the play, Richard's II's use of the mirror, or Maria's abuse of the letter in *Twelfth Night*, the interpretative space is a catalyst for both action and resolution.

Venus' rejection of the plastic arts, her contempt for inanimate representation, finds its most acute expression in this portrait of Adonis. Here the idol, painting, or statue is rejected on the basis of its inanimation, its *lifelessness*. [17] Venus craves a response, an effect, an audience. Pleasing the eye alone is of no virtue, she tells us; he must *act* the feelings of the body and the mind. In contrast to this image of the mute and narcissistic boy stands Venus, frenzied with frustration at her silent witness:

> This said, impatience chokes her pleading tongue,
> And swelling passion doth provoke a pause.
> Red cheeks and fiery eyes blaze forth her wrong.
> Being judge in love, she cannot right her cause;
> And now she weeps, and now she fain would speak,
> And now her sobs do her intendments break.

> (lines 217–22)

Unlike the muted demeanour of the 'lifeless picture', Venus' silence is powerfully physical, paradoxically audible, and capacious in its scope for affect. Her choked tongue, her swelling pause, and her blazing face set her body alight with the drama of feeling.

The intense noise of silence is similarly explored by Shakespeare in Sonnet 23. Like the narrative poem, the sonnet explores the tension between expression and representation through the image of the actor:

> As an unperfect actor on the stage
> Who with his fear is put besides his part,
> Or some fierce thing replete with too much rage
> Whose strength's abundance weakens his own heart,
> So I, for fear of trust, forget to say
> The perfect ceremony of love's rite,
> And in mine own love's strength seem to decay,
> O'er-charged with burden of mine own love's might.

> (lines 1–8)

Invoking the powerful emotions of love, fear, or rage, Sonnet 23 recognizes the power of repression or suppression; of enforced silence and bodily betrayal.[18] What becomes expressive here is not what is said but what is felt, and the registers for feeling are chaotic, unpredictable, and opaque.

---

[17] See Cheney (2004) 81–95.

[18] See also G. T. Wright on silence in the sonnets, 'The Silent Speech of Shakespeare's Sonnets', *Shakespeare and the Twentieth Century*, Jill A. Levenson and Jonathan Bate (eds), (Newark: University of Delaware Press, 1998) 314–35.

For Venus, Adonis' lifelessness is so profound that she is forced to set both their bodies in motion:

> Sometime she shakes her head, and then his hand;
> Now gazeth she on him, now on the ground.
> Sometime her arms enfold him like a band.

(lines 223–5)

Animating him like a puppet, she moves between the actor and the audience, playing both simultaneously. Her frustration is articulated through bodily gestures that are expressive in their relationship to each other: the head shaken in disapproval to the hand shaken in irritation; the eyes that gaze in devotion and then in annihilation. Venus involves Adonis in her dramatic space in the hope of making him perform. The poem's attention to animation continually reminds us of the interpretative roles of the body over and above speech. As the public theatre developed, so it became naturally more sophisticated in its interest in forms of expression; and alongside the development of theatrical representations the expanding book trade encouraged a more self-conscious exploration of the written word.

This combined investment in communicative forms supported increasingly thoughtful responses to human expression. On the continent, for example, Michel de Montaigne had become an important figure in the development of a literary consciousness. Whilst his *Essais* precipitated a shift in the representation of subjective experience, his 'Apology for Raymond Sebond' tackles the necessity of gesture in our social world:

What doe we with our hands? Doe we not sue and entreate, promise and performe, call men vnto vs, and discharge them, bid them farwell, and be gone, threaten, pray, beseech, deny, refuse, demaund, admire, number, confesse, repent, feare, be ashamed, doubt, instruct, command, encite, encourage, sweare, witnes, accuse, condemne, absolve, injurie, despise, defie, despight, flatter, applaude, blesse, humble, mocke, reconcile, recommend, exalt, shew gladnes, reioyce, complaine, waile, sorrowe, discomfort, dispaire, cry-out, forbid, declare silence and astonishment? And what not? With so great variation, and amplifying, as if they would contend with the tongue. And with our head, doe we not envite and call to-vs, discharge and send away, avowe, disavowe, be-lie, welcome, honour, worship, disdaine, demaund, direct, rejoyce, affirme, deny, complaine, cherish, blandish, chide, yeeld, submit, brag, boast, threaten, exhort, warrant, assure, and enquire? What doe we with our eye-lids? And with our shoulders? To conclude, there is no motion, nor jesture, that doth not speake, and speakes in a language, very easie, and without any teaching to be vnderstoode: nay, which is more, it is a language common and publike to all: whereby it followeth (seeing the varietie, and severall vse it hath from others) that this must rather be deemed the proper and peculiar speech of humane nature.[19]

---

[19] Michel de Montaigne, *Essays Written in French ... done into English, according to the last edition*, by John Florio (London, 1613), 'An Apology of Raymond Sebond', 251.

Montaigne's comprehensive list of the body's expressive functions recognizes that it 'speakes in a language … [which is] common and publike to all'. This common language becomes a powerful site of expression in the drama of the written word. The army of emotions that can accompany gesticulation provides access to the 'peculiar speech of human nature' which is both 'very easie, and without any teaching'. In this way, 'motion' or 'jesture' become central to the interpretative space between word and performance. As the stage must learn to articulate silence, so the page must learn to perform the body.

Despite the insistent presence of Venus' voice in the poem, it is her body that becomes the dominant form of expression. When she initially lays siege to her lover, she proposes herself as something organic and edible: 'Graze on my lips, and if those hills be dry, | Stray lower, where the pleasant fountains lie' (lines 233–4). Briefly metamorphosing into vegetative matter, Venus' earthy sexuality becomes central to her characterization. Yet despite her powerfully articulate sexuality she remains caught in an endless struggle between lucidity and frustration that the text must accommodate. Focusing on the expressive body, Shakespeare uses theatrical metaphors to develop the tension between the lovers:

> O, what a war of looks was then between them,
> Her eyes petitioners to his eyes suing!
> His eyes saw her eyes as they had not seen them;
> Her eyes wooed still; his eyes disdained the wooing;
>   And all this dumb play had his acts made plain
>   With tears which, chorus-like, her eyes did rain …
>
> (lines 355–60)

Conflating the public nature of the legal court as well as the stage, the textual body once again requires interpreting in its silent form. The drama of the human body is foregrounded through both gesture and expression so that the lovers can play actor and audience simultaneously. Whilst Adonis 'acts', Venus reacts responding to the action in its purest physical form. The heightened way in which Shakespeare moves in and out of the theatrical body in this poem centralizes the various ways in which he is exploring forms of representation. Recognizing that all acts of communication are also acts of interpretation, he treats Venus' body as a theatrical form as well as a textual act.

The physical gesture as a readable sign exposes the mobility of textual metaphors as well as opening up the interpretive possibilities of the theatrical text. In *The Rape of Lucrece* the idea of the text and questions of reading (or misreading) become central tropes in the expressions of both innocence and experience, action and impotence.[20] Published in the same year that printed plays began to take hold of the market, Shakespeare's tale of 'rape and republicanism' has often been understood as his

---

[20] See also John Kerrigan, 'Keats and Lucrece', *Shakespeare Survey* 41 (1989): 103–18.

'literary' exploration of Virgilian epic and Ovidian imperialism.[21] This critical tradition tends to read Lucrece as a figure of mediation through which acts of violence can become acts of regeneration. For Patrick Cheney, however, this 'is also a story about authorship': as Lucrece writes her history to her husband and then turns to the marketplace to enact her suicide, so she takes control of both the written text and the theatrical space 'in a new way, channelling art into political action through religious sanction'.[22] The poem's increasing dependence on the language of text and performance reveals Shakespeare's investment in exploring multiple forms of representation. The idea or image of the word—spoken, written, read—becomes a mobile metaphor in the pursuit of meaning. Central to a poem about rape is the body: whether it is the body as a form of incitement in which 'beauty' is read as an invitation for desire; or the body as a mode of betrayal in which it is appropriated, misused, or destroyed; or the body as an agent of violence in which the lines of responsibility are blurred as a conflict of needs is articulated.

However the bodies within the poem may be presented, their performance and legibility is crucial to the narrative. Shakespeare first confronts the legible body through an idea of beauty:

> Beauty itself doth of itself persuade
> The eyes of men without an orator.
> What needeth then apology be made
> To set forth that which is so singular?
> Or why is Collatine the publisher
>   Of that rich jewel he should keep unknown
>   From thievish ears, because it is his own?
>
> (lines 29–35)

Beauty performs itself simply by existing—it needs no language and no defence, it is indivisible and contained. Why then should Collatine publish Lucrece's qualities when he should in fact conceal them? The complex interplay between public performance and private responsibility is created through the precise terms of acting and writing. Beauty performs in silence; it needs no publication and no voice. The power of the physical body is defined here by its unique independence from audible means of expression. In this construction of beauty there is an intense distrust of the public arena in which the 'rich jewel' becomes interpreted or exposed. This distrust of the public space is reiterated in another key through the image of the book. Like her beauty, Lucrece is shown to be 'singular' or isolated in a way that makes her especially inexperienced in human behaviour:

---

[21] See Cheney (2007) 116. Heather Dubrow, *Captive Victors: Shakespeare's Narrative Poems and Sonnets* (Ithaca: Cornell University Press, 1987), and Catherine Belsey 'Tarquin Dispossessd: Expropriation and Consent in *The Rape of Lucrece*', *Shakespeare Quarterly* 52 (2001): 315–35.

[22] Cheney (2007) 116.

> But she that never coped with stranger eyes
> Could pick no meaning from their parling looks,
> Nor read the subtle shining secrecies
> Writ in the glassy margins of such books ...
>
> (lines 99–102)

'Coped' is an unusual word in this context: usually glossed as some form of 'encounter', the term is suggestive of meeting or coming together. In its literal form, however, it means to wear a cape—literally to be cape-d—yet it can also appear in early modern usage within the context of conflict. In Thomas Thomas' Latin English (1587) dictionary, for example, he explains *conflictus* as:

> To goe with another, to fight, and cope with, to encounter, to dispute with: to go in hand, to talke with: to haunte, or be in companie withone: to ioyne with one in, & c.[23]

Lucrece's encounter with Tarquin's alien eyes is instantly construed as aggressive and discursive. The idea of 'dispute' inherent in Thomas' description of 'cop[ing] with' is picked up in Tarquin's 'parling' eyes. Unlike Lucrece's silent beauty, Tarquin's face is animated; his eyes challenge her with their desire as well as their unfamiliarity. The language of motion puts their bodies into a dynamic that will be explained through the language of reading.

As we are told that Lucrece could not decipher Tarquin's eyes, so we are also told that she could not read his face either. Tarquin's body is set up as a text that is at once discursive (parling) and arcane (secretive). It is suggestive yet opaque, and the combination of the two exposes Lucrece's vulnerability. The vitreous surface that Shakespeare attributes to 'such books' as Tarquin resembles amplifies the confusing image he presents. Through the dense network of ideas that are simultaneously confrontational and discursive, arcane and transparent, Shakespeare presents Lucrece's reading experience as both fraught and isolating. The perfomative text of Tarquin's body reproduces forms of representation not as enabling and educative but as exclusive and threatening:

> Nor could she moralize his wanton sight
> More than his eyes were opened to the light ...
>
> (lines 104–5)

The use of 'moralize' to mean 'morally interpret' discloses Lucrece's inability to read Tarquin's body for his sinful mind. The textual metaphor becomes a profoundly important language in the expression of human relations since it supports the power to deceive as well as to know. On the stage, of course, the tension between knowing and not knowing is presented as dramatic irony, as it creates parallel spaces of inclusion and exclusion. In *Lucrece*, however, this tension is sustained over a relatively long period of time

---

[23] Thomas Thomas, *Dictionarium linguae Latinae et Anglicanae* (London, 1578) 212.

through the semantics of reading. Having established Lucrece's social illiteracy the narrator tells us how Tarquin lures her into a false sense of security:

> He stories to her ears her husband's fame,
> Won in the fields of fruitful Italy.
> …
> Her joy with heaved-up hand she doth express,
> And wordless so greets heaven for his success …
>
> (lines 106–7, 111–12)

Turning story into a verb, the narrator describes a process by which Tarquin both deceives and entertains Lucrece, inducing her to perform a partial dumb-show, partial genuflection in honour of her husband's glory. The method of Tarquin's approach and the representation of Lucrece's response synthesizes the story and the play in such a way as to invite suspicion. We know that Lucrece is not equipped for this human drama and yet she has now become its main player. The dense networks of images that direct the moral fabric of the poem also define our reactions to it. Whilst dark and light, for example, expose the symbolic constructions of sin and virtue, or violation and redemption, the textual and theatrical metaphors work to build up a portrait of expression and action that is, at times, profoundly ambiguous.[24] Had Lucrece been able to read she might have understood Tarquin's parling eyes. This apparently fragile distance between preservation and devastation is construed as interpretation, as 'moralizing' denotes right reading.

Once the narrator has established the instability of perception, he goes on to describe the multiple ways in which Tarquin rehearses 'in his inward mind' (line 185) the consequences and pleasure of his deed. Much of the power of these stanzas lies in the tension that has already been established by Lucrece's illiteracy. The legibility of Tarquin's face remains central to the significance that Shakespeare affords images of textuality. Imagining the dishonour that his rape would bring to his status as a knight he declares: 'Then my digression is so vile, so base, | That it will live engraven in my face' (lines 202–3). Once again Tarquin's face becomes a theatrical site of expression as it performs both his actions and their interpretation. How mimetic that site is, however, depends upon the literacy of its audience. As Lucrece reminds us, the dynamic between the audience and the image, or the text and the reader, is central to the moral transparency of human actions. When Tarquin confronts the strength of his desire he thinks about how such moral boundaries are defined: 'Who fears a sentence or an old man's saw | Shall by a

---

[24] Light is constantly associated with revelation and virtue whilst dark is symbolically attached to sin and concealment: 'And therefore would they still in darkness be, | To have their unseen sin remain untold', (lines 752–3). Colour is equally powerful in the poem's creation of its moral fabric, as Lucrece's face changes between white and red as she moves through her multiple stages of innocence, shame, fear, and death.

painted cloth be kept in awe' (lines 244–5). The static vision of the 'painted cloth' cannot withstand the energy of Tarquin's passion.[25]

The battle that Tarquin stages between his 'frozen conscience and hot-burning will' (line 247) is also a battle between animation and stasis: where his conscience stands still his will forges ahead, reflecting a similar conflict of energies in the representation of human expression. Like Venus' rejection of Adonis' 'lifeless[ness]', the inanimate becomes emotionally redundant in the depiction of human behaviour. The constant motion at the centre of Tarquin's 'inward mind' and Lucrece's predicament is constructed through the lively ways in which the characters' thoughts are presented. Tarquin's rejection of anything static reflects the gathering pace of his commitment to rape her; that his conscience is 'frozen' is clear in the semantics of action. Having declared that 'affection is my captain' (line 271), he goes on to use a theatrical metaphor to amplify the vigour of his attitude:

> Then childish fear avaunt, debating die,
> Respect and reason wait on wrinkled age!
> My heart shall never countermand mine eye,
> Sad pause and deep regard beseems the sage.
> My part is Youth, and beats these from the stage.
>
> (lines 274–8)

Here Tarquin takes centre-stage, beating off the reasonable and the old. The lively intemperance of youth becomes the central image, equating theatre with action and action with affect. As Tarquin's 'inward mind' moves towards the commitment to his deed, he steadily rejects anything inert. The poem's amplification of motion is highly provocative in its representation of human feeling, since it seeks to expose animation as the pre-eminent form of expression. Later Lucrece will also take this position as she rejects the 'painting made for Priam's Troy' (line 1367). Having examined it in empathy and identification and rehearsed her feelings through 'Conceit deceitful, so compact, so kind' (line 1423), she then denies its mimetic status. Recalling her fatal misreading of Tarquin, she draws attention to the 'fair' representation of Sinon:

> Such signs of truth in his plain face she spied
> That she concludes the picture was belied ...
>
> (lines 1532–3)

The painted cloth was nothing more than a brief diversion, 'That she with painted images hath spent, ...| Losing her woes in shows of discontent' (lines 1577, 1580). Lucrece's frustration with her ambiguous world in which characters are not clear, intentions are obscured, and emotions are suppressed leads her to a search for a composite

---

[25] Clark Hulse, in *Metamorphic Verse: the Elizabethan Minor Epic* (Princeton NJ: Princeton University Press, 1981), examines the 'painted cloth' as a composite form, something that can be simultaneously cloth, painting, and tapestry.

form of representation. Yet the representational world that the poem constructs is fraught with interpretive possibilities that the characters persistently deny or obscure.

Tarquin's aberrance, for example, is explored through multiple metaphors of attack and resistance, as we witness his dogged attempts to reach Lucrece irrespective of the world's displeasure:

> As each unwilling portal yields him way,
> Through little vents and crannies of the place
> The wind wars with his torch to make him stay,
> And blows the smoke of it into his face …
>
> (lines 309–12)

The detailed images of animation that the poem presents creates a theatre of morality in which each object engages with another to set an ethical stage. Yet where Tarquin's 'hot will' projects him lucidly through the poem, Lucrece's body is less legible, constrained as it is by the conflict between passive innocence and irrepressible destiny:

> Her hair like golden threads played with her breath—
> O modest wantons, wanton modesty!—
> Showing life's triumph in the map of death,
> And death's dim look in life's mortality …
>
> (lines 400–4)

The co-existence of movement and stasis stages a war between life and death, at once representing her active sleep and proleptic death.

The constant tension between stillness and motion drives the moral fabric of the poem and its dominant mode of expression is the text and the stage. Having set himself upon the theatre of 'Youth', Tarquin moves into Lucrece's bedroom to visually consume her:

> What could he see but mightly he noted?
> What did he note but strongly he desired?
> What he beheld, on that he firmly doted,
> And in his will his wilful eye he tired …
>
> (lines 414–17)

The movement from the outward image to the inward mind by way of the 'note' uses the idea of the text to establish the irrevocability of Lucrece's ordeal. Tarquin's note anticipates his action and the dynamic here between narrative and performance gives way to an electrifying representation of authorial authority. As Tarquin writes her, so he will also rape her.[26]

---

[26] Jocelyn Catty's *Writing Rape, Writing Women in Early Modern England* (Basingstoke: Palgrave Macmillan, 2010) is the most recent book to tackle the question of the formation of gender roles in the representation of rape.

Through the power of the textual metaphor to both mark and create, the idea of the author becomes a free-floating image of responsibility. As Tarquin threatens to destroy her family's honour if she does not concede, he transfers the authority of the rape onto Lucrece:

> And thou, the author of their obloquy,
>   Shalt have thy trespass cited up in rhymes
>   And sung by children in succeeding times …
>
> (lines 523–5)

In a grotesquely ironic image, the illiterate Lucrece becomes the quoted author, written into ballads as a morality tale and bandied about in a childish game. Tarquin anticipates Lucrece's history through the written word that not only memorializes her but registers the profound shift she has made from negligent reader to infamous author.

The text here becomes an irrepressible marker of human history, but like the book of Tarquin's face it has the power to deceive as well as destroy. Set against the written word, however, is the performance which is construed as sympathetic, responsive, and utilitarian:

> But if thou yield, I rest thy secret friend.
>   The fault unknown is as a thought unacted.
>   A little harm done to a great good end
>   For lawful policy remains enacted.
>
> (lines 526–9)

If the sexual act is enacted, he will let it be thought unacted 'to a great good end'. The play on the word 'act' opens up a vast space between reality and performance which is here understood as a 'good' 'secret'. The performative metaphors which have driven Tarquin to the brink of this rape now protect him in their flexible representations of reality. Enlisting dissimulation as a friend to sin, Tarquin declares that something unknown is something undone. Once again it is the audience that defines his reality: just as he had declared that 'Thoughts are but dreams till their effects be tried' (line 353), so he admits that acts are not acts if they remain unknown.

In *Venus and Adonis* the goddess's sense of audience defined her reality; her frustration with her lover was created by his lack of response, his inability to physically recognize her sexuality. For Tarquin, however, the audience is a more powerful site of equivocation; he will define its presence according to the demands of his will. In both poems, however, Shakespeare explores the interpretive relationship between cause and effect through the presence of an audience. In either watching or reading, the sign becomes a critical image in the poem's exploration of moral accountability. When Lucrece confronts Tarquin's iniquity she turns to the image of the book:

> For princes are the glass, the school, the book,
>   Where subjects' eyes do learn, do read, do look.

> And wilt thou be the school where lust must learn?
> Must he in thee read lectures of such shame?
>
> (lines 615–18)

Once again recalling the book she could not read, she now construes Tarquin's body as a comprehensive process of representation in which he is not only the text but the place of learning too. As Lucrece understands the profundity of Tarquin's sin, she rehearses her future of shame and ignominy:

> Where now I have no one to blush with me,
> To cross their arms and hang their heads with mine,
> To mask their brows and hide their infamy,
> But I alone, alone must sit and pine.
>
> (lines 792–5)

Imagining gestures of both empathy and dishonour, she locates her agony in isolation. Like Venus, Lucrece's affirmation of emotion comes only in company: the need for an audience is amplified here by her desire for a mimetic response to her feelings. Recognizing her isolation—or exclusion—Lucrece fears the 'tell-tale Day':

> The light will show charactered in my brow
> The story of sweet chastity's decay,
> The impious breach of holy wedlock vow.
> Yea, the illiterate that know not how
>   To cipher what is writ in learnèd books
>   Will quote my loathsome trespass in my looks.
>
> (lines 807–12)

The textual image has come full-circle: the charactered face, marked with its intentions as well as its history, emblazons the body for all to read; even the illiterate, she tells us, will discern her 'trespass'.

The bathetic relationship between the material and the metaphoric creates a powerful discourse of literacy: no longer dependent upon an ability to 'cipher what is writ in learned books', reading is a moral act of social interaction. The body or, specifically, the face, is a register not only of instant emotion but of personal history. Lucrece is marked by her ordeal in a way that shapes her future and dictates her image:

> The nurse to still her child will tell my story
> And fright her crying babe with Tarquin's name;
> The orator to deck his oratory
> Will couple my reproach to Tarquin's shame.
>
> (lines 813–16)

Memorialized as both a cautionary tale and a rhetorical trope, Lucrece becomes a public textual figure. The idea of the word—the charactered brow, the nurse's story, the parling eyes or the orator's speech—comes to define the irrepressible expressions of human emotion. Leaking out of the bodies that contain them, emotional experience enters the public word through the gesture, the trope, or the story.

Lucrece's awareness of her role in the textual history of Rome increasingly propels her towards this image. Having decided to write her story for her husband before she commits suicide, she explains:

> My stained blood to Tarquin I'll bequeath,
> Which by him tainted shall for him be spent,
> And as his due writ in my testament.
>
> (lines 1181–3)

Conflating the language of law and the language of the Bible, Lucrece's suicide will write her violation in blood on Tarquin's conscience. Charging him with her death, she writes her future as she also writes her past. Lucrece wrests control from Tarquin in this image of the text, no longer at the mercy of public interpretation, and in a moment which theatrically anticipates *The Duchess of Malfi*, she declares: 'I am the mistress of my fate' (line 1069). The dangerously equivocal nature of the written word now starts to shift as it becomes Lucrece's focus of control:

> Go, get me hither paper, ink, and pen;
> Yet save that labour, for I have them here.
> …
> This cause craves haste, and it will soon be writ …
>
> (lines 1289–90, 1295)

The unnecessary injunction to her servant to get writing instruments, since she has them next to her, amplifies the role of writing in Lucrece's appropriation of her fate. Her urgency and impassioned response mark this moment as a turning point in the history of her story:

> Her maid is gone, and she prepares to write,
> First hovering o'er the paper with her quill.
> Conceit and grief an eager combat fight;
> What wit sets down is blotted straight with will …
>
> (lines 1296–9)

Animating her mental conflict through the 'hovering pen', emotion takes precedent over reason in the representation of her ordeal. As Lucrece writes, she 'hoards' her 'sighs and groans' so that she can play them out when Collatine reads the letter.

Finally aware of the interpretive space between the reader and the text, Lucrece anticipates the role of action in the fulfilment of her story:

> To shun this blot, she would not blot the letter
> With words, till action might become them better ...

(lines 1322–3)

Having misread the intentions and body of her assailant she is now acutely aware of the
power of the articulate body. Intent on evoking her emotion as well as her narrative,
she explores the various ways in which she can tell her story in its most mimetic form.
What she comes up against is the limits, not the capacities, of representation: from the
'helpless smoke of words' (line 1027) to the 'short-schedule' she realizes that she can only
articulate 'her grief, but not her grief's true quality' (line 1313).

The search for the 'true quality' of experience is fundamental to the poem's exploration of both action and emotion. Intent on examining the conflicts of the human heart,
the characters within the poem are forced to confront the multiple ways in which action,
intention, and affect take shape. The textual metaphors become redundant as Lucrece
searches for a mimetic form that exceeds the limits of expectations: 'Besides, the life and
feeling of her passion | She hoards, to spend when he is by to hear them' (lines 1317–
18).[27] Perhaps part of her rejection of the text is that it is a tainted image, replete with the
irony of her own illiteracy, which comes to inhabit a space that is derogatory, feeble, and
dangerous: 'Though men can cover crimes with bold stern looks, | Poor women's faces
are their own faults' books' (lines 1252–3).

The rejection of the text is amplified through the extended attention to the 'painted
cloth', depicting the siege of Troy. Despite Lucrece's previous dissatisfaction with the
inanimate word she turns to the image as a static cue for the evolution of her iconic self:
'To pencilled pensiveness and coloured sorrow. | She lends them words, and she their
looks doth borrow' (lines 1497–8). This briefly reciprocal relationship between the image
and the word is articulated as one of sympathy but not efficacy. Lucrece can make her
history animate but not effective: 'It easeth some, though none it ever cured, | To think
their dolour others have endured' (lines 1581–2). As she performs her emotions alongside the text of her endurance, Lucrece brings together the limits of her experience:

> With this they all at once began to say
> Her body's stain her mind untainted clears,
> While with a joyless smile she turns away
> The face, that map which deep impression bears
> Of hard misfortune, carved in it with tears.

(lines 1709–13)

---

[27] Fatally aware that, as John Marston said, 'the life of these things consists in action', Lucrece holds
onto the life of her emotion until she can make it action. See John Marston, 'To the Reader', *The Fawn*
(1606).

Just as she feared, Lucrece is 'charactered', marked by a joyless smile and riven with tears. The complex face of profound emotion performs its final moments and is acquitted by its audience. Blood and tears plot the lines on her body, and it is now a readable image ready 'to show ... and so to publish' her history in an instant.

When the theatres closed in 1593, Shakespeare had only just begun to write for the stage. When he turned to the narrative poem and published his first work, he created one of the most popular and enduring publications of his lifetime. In the midst of a developing media Shakespeare began to explore questions of representation. From the animation of the physical body to the manipulation of textual interpretation, the page provided Shakespeare with a representational space on which 'much imaginary work was there' (line 1422). Often complex, always restless, the imaginary work of the written text went in search of the bodies to perform it. As Shakespeare's poetry and drama collide in the infancy of his writing career, so he developed a language that interrogates the capacities of representation as well as its limits.

SELECT BIBLIOGRAPHY

Catty, Jocelyn (2010), *Writing Rape, Writing Women in Early Modern England* (Basingstoke: Palgrave Macmillan).

Cheney, Patrick (2004), *Shakespeare National Poet-Playwright* (Cambridge: Cambridge University Press).

—— Andrew Hadfield, and Garret A. Sullivan (2007) (eds), *Early Modern English Poetry: A Critical Companion* (Oxford: Oxford University Press).

Fowler, Elizabeth (2002), *Literary Character: the Human Figure in Early English Writing* (Ithaca and London: Cornell University Press).

Gurr, Andrew (1992), *The Shakespearean Stage 1574–1642* (Cambridge: Cambridge University Press).

Jager, Eric (2000), *The Book of the Heart* (Chicago: University of Chicago Press).

Kerrigan, John (1989), 'Keats and Lucrece', *Shakespeare Survey 41*.

Lesser, Zachary (2004), *Renaissance Drama and the Politics of Publication* (Cambridge: Cambridge University Press).

Schalkwyk, David (2007), *Speech and Performance in Shakespeare's Sonnets and Plays* (Cambridge: Cambridge University Press).

Scott, Charlotte (2007), *Shakespeare and the Idea of the Book* (Oxford: Oxford University Press).

Zurcher Andrew, (2010), *Shakespeare and the Law* (London: Methuen).

CHAPTER 22

OUTGROWING ADONIS, OUTGROWING OVID

The Disorienting Narrative of Venus and Adonis

SUBHA MUKHERJI

This chapter will show how Shakespeare weaves his rhetorical engagement with Ovid with a sexual narrative to 'disorient' his readership, in the process critically re-orienting his own relationship with Ovid as early as his first attempt to emulate him. The narrator's evolving attitude to the figure of Adonis will emerge as a site for this metamorphosis, as readerly desire is set at variance with that of the inscribed subject(s). The discussion will be situated in relation to several plays and poems. But it is a brief, final digression into *Lucrece* that will illustrate most directly what is at stake in the Ovidian Shakespeare's redefinition of his poetic in his earliest poem, and the nature of its urgency at this juncture in his career.[1]

Venus and Adonis (1593), prefaced by a familiar quote from Ovid's *Amores*, and followed by a dedication of the 'first heir of [his] invention', sees Shakespeare looking for his own poetic myth of origin, and placing his poem explicitly in the tradition of what we now call the epyllion, an Ovidian erotic narrative poem.[2] Retelling a story told by Orpheus in Ovid reinforces this self-location in a specific literary genæalogy. But Orpheus

---

[1] I am grateful to Patrick Cheney for commenting on a draft of this essay.

[2] But see Patrick Cheney on the parallel Ovidian *and* Virgilian legacies that he sees Shakespeare signalling across the epigraph and the dedication, and negotiating and interweaving in the poem itself; and how this in turn shows him processing the poetic projects of Marlowe and Spenser, closer to home: 'Authorship and acting: plotting *Venus and Adonis* along the Virgilian path', in Cheney, *Shakespeare, National Poet-Playwright* (Cambridge: Cambridge University Press, 2004) 81–107.

was also, famously, the narrator who, after losing Euridyce, turned from marriage to 'tell of prettie boyes/That were the derlings of the Gods' (*Metamorphoses* X, 157–8).[3] Orpheus is the best known of a succession of Ovidian men who were all unresponsive to women, and, in one sense or another, grew unto themselves, like Shakespeare's Adonis. What was the intractable appeal of this curious human type in poetry? And where does it lead Shakespeare?

John Addington Symonds, the eminent Victorian scholar, had an epiphanic encounter with the poem, leading to self-discovery:

> Now the first English poem which affected me deeply—as it has, no doubt, impressed thousands of boys—was Shakespeare's 'Venus and Adonis'. I read it … before I was ten years old. It gave form, ideality and beauty to my previous erotic visions. Those adult males, the shaggy and brawny sailors, without entirely disappearing, began to be superseded in my fancy by an adolescent Adonis. The emotion they symbolised blent with a new kind of feeling. In some confused way I identified myself with Adonis; but at the same time I yearned after him as an adorable object of passionate love. Venus […] only expressed my own relation to the desirable male. She brought into relief the overwhelming attraction of masculine adolescence and its proud inaccessibility. Her hot wooing taught me what it was to woo with sexual ardour. I dreamed of falling back like her upon the grass, and folding the quick-panting lad in my embrace.[4]

This response could be one kind of gloss on the enticing adolescent froideur of Adonis. Besides anticipating the male, same-sex object of love in the Sonnets, Adonis is himself 'a lily prisoned in a jail of snow, | Or ivory in an alabaster band' (362–3), with shades of Ovid's Hermaphroditus. Like Narcissus, he 'himself himself' wooed (161). With a touch of postmodern camp, he cares more about sunburn than about the Goddess of love's rhetoric: 'Fie, no more of love! | The sun doth burn my face; I must remove' (185–6). Venus takes his unresponsiveness to be a sign of his androgyny, but we could see it otherwise: 'Thou art no man, though of a man's complexion, | For men will kiss even by their own direction' (215–16).

Nor is Adonis' alluring iciness merely a question of sexual disorientation. Shakespeare makes of it a particular aesthetic. The tantalizing unyieldingness of Adonis spills over into the poem itself. *Venus and Adonis* opens cleverly. Ovid was the newly discovered inventive writer who somehow managed to combine erotic appeal with respectability through an association with classical values and sophistication: 'Yett Ouid's wanton Muse did not offend. | He is the fountaine whence my streames do flowe', as

---

[3] All references are to *Ovid's Metamorphoses: The Arthur Golding Translation 1567*, John Frederick Nims (ed.), (Paul Dry Books: Philadelphia, 2000). There is not space here to reflect on the affinities and differences between Golding's style and Ovid's, but suffice it to say that Golding captures some of the elegant lightness of Ovid's verse.

[4] *The Memoirs of John Addington Symonds*, ed. Phyllis Grosskurth (London: Hutchinson, 1984) 62–3.

Nashe puts it, in presenting *his* epyllion, *A Choise of Valentines* (1592).[5] What better footsteps could a young unheard-of writer in 1593 tread? The epyllion had already become a trendy form—rhetorical, sellable, and sexy. But it would also arouse specific *erotic* expectations. The readership had been fed by such poems as Nashe's, where the mistress freely complains about premature ejaculation in the name of lamenting the impossibility of complete merger in love. Trying to beat the expense of spirit, she offers help: 'Vnhappie me, quoth shee, 'and wil't not stand? | Com, lett me rubb and chafe it with my hand' (131–2). When the lover finally rises to it, he bids her hold wide her lap '[a]nd entretaine the golden showre so free, | That trilling falles into thy treasurie' (194–5).[6] This over-elaboration of the body is present in Shakespeare's poem too— witness Venus' description of her hills and her dales, her brakes and her bushes. The generic signals would not have gone unnoticed: in Middleton's *A Mad World, My Masters*, the suspicious husband Hairbrain '[conveys] away all [his wife's] wanton pamphlets', as *Hero and Leander, Venus and Adonis* (I. ii. 44–5), 'stirring books best kept under one's skirt' (90–1). The poem inscribes a significant context. Newly revived from her feigned death, Venus wishes the 'verdure' of Adonis' crimson lips to 'drive infection from the dangerous year' and for star-gazers to say that 'the plague is banished by [his] breath' (505–10). This curiously placed allusion, bolstered by a later reference to 'life-poisoning pestilence' (740), is a reminder that the epyllion flourished in the plague years when the theatres were closed for fear of contagion. Narrative poetry opened up a chance of reaching readers in an intimate way, free of representational constraints affecting stage-plays. An epic reduced for easy consumption, the epyllion both catered to and generated a new kind of readership, and the erotics of private reading. *Venus and Adonis* sees Shakespeare discovering for himself the pleasures and excitement of this new, lucrative readerly site, and playing to it.[7]

But does he deliver? In *Hero and Leander* (written around 1593), arguably the best-known epyllion circulating at the time, Marlowe delivers the joy of consummation, and then Chapman turns it into a tragedy. In *Venus and Adonis*, however, sexual union never happens. In fact, the text's own relationship with the reader is brought into a curious parallel with the central relationship of the poem itself—that between Venus and Adonis. For all her rhetorically persuasive wooing of the unresponsive Adonis, Venus does not succeed. At the peak of sexual desire, the very posture of sexual enjoyment becomes an image of deep unfulfilment:

> Now is she in the very lists of love,
> Her champion mounted for the hot encounter.

[5] 'The Choise of Valentines', in *The Works of Thomas Nashe*, Ronald B. McKerrow (ed.), 5 vols (Oxford: Blackwell, 1958) vol. 3, 403–16 (415).

[6] McKerrow (1958) vol. 3, 409, 411.

[7] For suggestive explorations of the readership of the poems, see Sasha Roberts, *Reading Shakespeare's Poems in Early Modern England* (Basingstoke: Palgrave, 2003) chs 1 and 2. On the erotics of the epyllion in Elizabethan culture, see Georgia Brown, *Redefining Elizabethan Literature* (Cambridge: Cambridge University Press, 2004) ch. 3.

All is imaginary she doth prove.
He will not manage her, although he mount her,
    That worse than Tantalus' is her annoy,
    To clip Elysium, and to lack her joy.

(595–600)

Playing on the expectation of his readers buying and taking home his first self-declared epyllion, Shakespeare arouses them, but leaves them, like Venus, clipping Elysium but lacking its joys. It becomes a poem *about* erotic poetry, and the kind of desire it kindles in its readers but need not necessarily satisfy: 'But when her lips were ready for his pay, | He winks, and turns his lips another way' (89–90). The pleasure of Shakespeare's own text, its jouissance, lies in this sophisticated, almost mannerist treatment of sexual poetry.

But if the excitement of Shakespeare's narrative is premised on a tease, it operates at crosspurposes with Venus' narrative and its telos. The end of Venus' *suasoria* is to have sex with Adonis. But '[her] treatise makes [him] like [her] worse and worse' (774). It is, thus, a 'bootless chat' (422), a readerless text. Her words echo each other, '[ending] without audience' (846). The narratorial comment is brusque: 'Her song was tedious, and outwore the night' (841–2). Yet, the denial of her desire is the whetting of the reader's. Therein lies the secret of Shakespeare's play with *his* auditors. What is more, the deferral of the reader's expectation, or his 'pleasure', is assumed to be pleasurable, not painful, like Venus'—the poem, after all, was a hit. If we assume a largely male readership in the 1590s, this complicates the targeted reader's selective sympathy with Venus who is left unsatisfied. The identification, at this stage, does not lie in a sharing of her distress, but her desire. That the poem makes her a smothering mother swooping down and '[feeding]' on his breath 'as on a prey' (63) makes it possible to respond to Adonis' disdainful prettiness *with* her, but not feel her desperation. The narrative makes him attractive by contrast with Venus whom it does not desist from presenting in faintly repulsive terms: 'By this, the lovesick queen began to sweat' (175). Broad comedy is generated at her expense when she clutches on to Adonis on top of her—'My boding heart pants, beats, and takes no rest, | But like an earthquake shakes thee on my breast' (647–8). As Venus talks about the 'forceless flowers' that support her, the 'strengthless doves' that draw her through the sky (152–3), we feel the contrast between her professed 'lightness' and the smothering weight of her eroticism, between the sublimating, neoplatonic language of love and the substantiality of her sexualized body: 'Is love so light, sweet boy, and may it be | That thou should think it heavy unto thee?' (155–6). This earthy, over-the-top Goddess grabs and almost crushes Adonis, who, in his Shakespearian incarnation, is an inheritor not only of Orpheus but of a whole line of androgynous scorners of women's advances—Narcissus, Hermaphroditus, and Hippolytus, Ovidian characters all. Venus is a lust-driven, sweaty, panting, aggressive female wooer, like her mythological peers—Scylla, Oenone, Aurora, and Salmacis, also Ovidian figures. In the strife between 'rose-cheeked Adonis' (3) and 'sick-thoughted Venus' (5), the direction of readerly sympathy is predictable. Thus far, the particular erotics of the poem, not unlike the appeal of the elusive, unyielding Adonis, functions through a disengagement with Venus' subjectivity, even a feeding off it. Its aesthetic is complicit in the Adonic, which is also the Ovidian.

Yet this begins to change unexpectedly. Not only does the polarity of roles dissolve, so do the polarities in the reader's response. The means are twofold. First, Adonis begins to look less attractive and more callow as the poem goes on. The poetry registers this—although it often fails to be registered in critical writing. When Venus moralizes against her nature, he unceremoniously responds, 'leave me, and then the story aptly ends. | The night is spent'. 'Why, what of that?' quoth she. | 'I am', quoth he, 'expected of my friends' (716–18). This is an example of what I will call the 'callow couplet', increasingly used by Adonis. Here, the pat, easy rhyme suggests the uncomprehending nature of Adonis' urge—like an adolescent's restlessness to join his mates in the pub down the road, rather than a Hollinghurstian sense of cruisy excitement at the prospect of going off into the night to hunt! There is something pre-sexual about Adonis, something 'unripe' (524). And while he is, undoubtedly, 'the tender boy' (32) that he is not in Ovid, and 'more lovely than a man', he is also 'young, and so unkind' (187). The hint of something unnatural alludes to a wider spectrum of resistance or deviance than the specific suggestion of homosexuality, and embraces the entire mythic history of not only Adonis but also Venus.[8] Venus' words, 'Things growing unto themselves are growth's abuse' (166), echo beyond the immediate context of her vested interests to recall the history of inbreeding and unnatural sexuality in Adonis' Ovidian family history. Pygmalion fell in love with the statue he made and prayed to Venus to bring her alive. This done, Paphus was born out of the union of Pygmalion and Statue-woman. Paphus' son Cinyras was tricked by his daughter Myrrha into sleeping with him—Adonis was the 'misbegotten chyld' delivered by the tree into which Myrrha was turned by the Gods (*Metamorphosis* X, 577). This is where the excised history surfaces in Venus' narrative:

> Art thou a woman's son, and canst not feel
> What 'tis to love, how want of love tormenteth?
>   O, had thy mother borne so hard a mind,
>   She had not brought forth thee, but died unkind.
> …
>
> Fie, lifeless picture, cold and senseless stone,
> Well painted idol, image dull and dead,
> Statue contenting but the eye alone,
> Thing like a man, but of no woman bred [.]
>
> (201–4, 211–14)

To see Adonis as 'unkind', thus, is not necessarily to be heteronormative about his response to Venus. If any historical narrative of penalty is being evoked, it is Venus'

[8] I am using the term 'homosexuality' as shorthand for what was a less fully defined sense of identity in Shakespeare's time than what the modern word suggests, but nevertheless expressive of a perceived sexual orientation or preference relevant to the period.

rather than Adonis'.[9] She forgets that Paphus too, like his descendant Adonis, was of no woman born. Besides, she it was who once brought an artificial woman out of art into life, out of 'senseless stone' into live flesh.[10] Could Adonis' marmoreal unresponsiveness be Venus' punishment for her part in that originary act of unnatural union?

But 'unkind' suggests not only unnaturalness but also cruelty. Adonis is at his best at his rare moments of self-knowledge such as this:

> 'Fair queen', quoth he, 'if any love you owe me,
> Measure my strangeness with my unripe years.
> Before I know myself, seek not to know me'
>
> (523–5)

And later, 'More I could tell, but more I dare not say; | The text is old, the orator too green' (805–6). But his usual mode is petulance, altogether inadequate for love, and reflected in tritely tidy couplets:

> For all my mind, my thought, my busy care
> Is how to get my palfrey from the mare.
>
> (383–4)

> 'I know not love', quoth he, 'nor will not know it,
> Unless it be a boar, and then I chase it.
>
> (409–10)

The venereal rhetoric with which he condemns Venus' 'device in love', and distinguishes between Love and 'sweating Lust' is not to be confused with the poem's philosophy of love. He is professing a reductive and immature Platonism which Shakespeare's poem *places* in a young boy's mouth, as a piece of adolescent moralism:

> Love comforteth, like sunshine after rain,
> But lust's effect is tempest after sun....
>   Love surfeits not; lust like a glutton dies.
>   Love is all truth, lust full of forgèd lies.
>
> (799–800, 803–4)

---

[9] Cf. Ovid, *Metamorphosis* X, 605: 'He did revenge the outrage of his mother's villanye' through Venus' immoderate love.

[10] The revenge narratives of the *Metamorphoses* often translate into intertextual wit in Shakespeare, which, in this poem, finds its intra-textual vehicle in the desperately expedient Venus, in whom all moralizing is harnessed to her immediate goal. The dialogue even extends to other recent texts: witness Venus' blaming of the blight of all earthly beauty on Cynthia (727–50), a belated revenge on Luna/Cynthia's 'Astronomicall Description' in Greene's *Planetomachia* (1585) which had blamed some of these very afflictions on Venus (N. Das (ed.), *Robert Greene's Planetomachia*. Aldershot: Ashgate, 2007, 48–50). But Venus' forgetfulness of her personal history teeters between agency and its absence, for this also looks forward to her own curse at the end of the poem—an instrument of creating subjectivity, even agency, albeit affective rather than moral.

It is precisely this all-too-simple dualism that the Sonnets collapse—a binary that is here undermined by the closed contained, *young* rhymes of Adonis' speech. Think of Sonnet 144—'Two loves I have, of comfort and despair', where mind and body, heaven and hell, sexual and spiritual, are run together. The 'beams' of Venus' opening eyelids, for all their art, seem wasted on Adonis' 'hairless face' (487). At the poem's close, Venus' love is so complex and encompassing of the fluidities of desire, emotion, and orientations that it can even participate imaginatively in the act of her rival—the boar—penetrating Adonis' soft, white flanks. Adonis, remember, has spent most of his time straining at Venus' leash and wanting to go and hunt the boar—the very animal often envisioned in medieval and Renaissance literature as a figure for a male sexual rival, a threat to the devoted lover.[11] But the lover here is Venus. 'Disoriented' by this surprise, critics have often seen the boar in *Venus and Adonis* as a figure for Venus herself, even the male principle in her, driven by a fierce, destructive will to possess Adonis. But in fact at the first mention of the boar a sudden paleness 'usurps her cheek' (591)—intimating, perhaps, sexual usurpations the Queen of love is powerless to prevent. But even when Adonis' urge to go hunting for the boar with his friends represents the alternative world of male-bonding, and the boar itself 'the sour, unwelcome guest' (459), the only 'love' Adonis knows and chases (409–10),[12] Venus can feel *with* the boar rather than simply against it, as at first sight. She has known its sexual aggression; she has often, as she imagines it did, 'by a kiss thought to persuade him there' and nuzzle lovingly in his 'soft groin' (1114–16). This is no mere inversion of gender roles. It is, rather, a longing that contains the apparent polarities of sexual desire, even subsumes them in a 'solemn sympathy' (1057), which extends its own imaginative parameters to include not only same-sex longing but also the things of nature which 'seemed with him to bleed' (1056–7). Adonis, after all, lies exactly in the same position as she did earlier when he refused to 'manage her'. Why then should she not be able to feel with both Adonis and the boar, desire domination as well as subjection, be the deer as well as the park? Even what Adonis might be, or might become, is better comprehended in *her* erotic subjectivity than in Adonis' own inchoate, pre-erotic intimations of non-heterosexual urges. Ironically, she displaces Adonis as the figure who queers the reading experience, coming closer as she does to the polymorphousness of desire that is an instrument of the poem's own disorienting project.

By contrast with Adonis, then—and this is the second means of changing affect—the comic-grotesque element in Venus acquires depth, and pathos gradually overrides comedy. The lovesick queen 'is Love; she loves; and yet she is not loved' (610). For all her

---

[11] Witness Troilus' dream in Chaucer's *Troilus and Criseyde*, of a 'bor with tuskes grete', who, 'faste in his armes folde, | Lay kyssyng ay his lady bryght, Criseyde' (V. 1238–41) in F. N. Robinson (ed.), *The Riverside Chaucer* (Oxford: Oxford University Press, 1988, 1st pub. 1987) 576; or Posthumus' imagining, in *Cymbeline*, 'a full-acorned boar' mounting his unravished bride and crying 'O!' (II. v. 16–17).

[12] The hint of a male sexual object of desire here—though that hint seems to come from Venus' perception (and the narrator's) rather than Adonis'—may well have been picked up from Ovid, who describes the boar 'hyding in his codds [= Adonis' testicles] his tuskes as farre as he could thrust' (*Metamorphosis* X, 839).

manipulation of rhetoric, 'Being judge in love, she cannot right her cause' (220). Her comparison of herself to a deerpark (229–40) is eloquently suggestive of the vulnerability and impotence that is the other side of her apparent power over Adonis. What might have been a fairly conventional piece of Elizabethan body-writing—and bawdy writing too—becomes, in the poem's dramatic context, a passage about the pathos, paradox, and humiliation of self-blasoning, reinforced by the reversal not only of traditional gender roles and Petrarchan conventions but also of the divine–mortal hierarchy. Adonis is no doubt 'hemmed' in within the limit of her body; but the plea itself is premised on passivity and powerlessness, an offer of one's self as a pasture, rather than self-assertion as a predator. The feeding images turn out to stand not only for Adonis' vulnerability and Venus' appetitive desire, but also for his satiety and her starvation. Venus' offer is met by Adonis' disdain; but the narrative voice here is full of humour and empathy—'Poor queen of love, in thine own law forlorn' (251). When Adonis breaks free of the embrace she has procured through deceit—pretending to be dead—he 'Leaves Love upon her back, deeply distressed' (814). The other Venus begins to emerge, the Venus who embodies erotic pathos. The position of sexual enjoyment itself becomes one of deep deprivation.

One of the developments of this figure is the desperately scheming Helena in *All's Well*, who has to steal what by law is her claim; who, Venus-like, works through contracts and exchanges, tricks and strategies, but is poignantly aware of her self-effacement in the bed-trick: 'O my good lord, when I was like this maid/I found you wondrous kind' (V. iii. 311–12). Adonis, on the other hand, has shades of a slightly different type of character we encounter in later Shakespeare. He is not merely unresponsive and pre-sexual; he is 'flint-hearted' (95), 'frosty in desire' (36). The precise arguments Venus puts to him are indicative of the negative potential of his character, which prefigures characters less callow but more chilling than Bertram or Bassanio (one unresponsive to a woman's love, and the other blithely uncomprehending of the love of a man). He anticipates the chilling self-possession of Angelo before his fall (witness the Duke's near-admonition of his culpable self-containment and refusal to give of himself);[13] the young man of Sonnet 94, lord and owner of his face, 'Unmovèd, cold, and to temptation slow'; and the newly crowned Henry V in his steely self-possession and his denial of Falstaff. Falstaff, interestingly, has a quasi-paternal relationship to his sweet Harry. He too is made of flesh and of words, like Venus. Yet they are both devoted to the point of self-abasement, a sentiment that forms an integral part of Shakespeare's vision of love.[14]

Thus, when Venus lies on the ground in pretence of death, she embodies love in all its complexity, its half-truths and abjection. But '[t]he silly boy, believing she is dead, /Claps her pale cheek till clapping makes it red' (467–8). Adonis' callow couplets, note, have begun to spill over into the style of the narrative where the latter describes his actions.

---

[13] *Measure for Measure*, I. i. 26–40.
[14] Cp. Sonnet 88, or 57 and 58.

When Adonis rejects love, his declared immunity to it offers a less sinister, but more petty sense of careful self-enclosure than Sonnet 94:

> Lest the deceiving harmony should run
> Into the quiet closure of my breast,
> And then my little heart were quite undone,
> In his bedchamber to be barred of rest.
>   No, lady, no. My heart longs not to groan,
>   But soundly sleeps, while now it sleeps alone.
>
>   (781–6)

Shakespeare has always rendered suspect a certain self-sufficiency—the living principle of 'love-lacking vestals and self-loving nuns' (752). While Adonis is by no means condemned for turning down heterosexual love, his specific disinterest is linked up with a more generic, less gender-specific attitude of ungivingness. Venus' pathetic grief, in contrast, gains stature as Shakespeare gives her the nightmare mode, making of sexual unfulfilment almost a dark night of the soul (810–76). Her wails multiply and echo, like the abject plaints of the forsaken maiden in 'A Lover's Complaint'.

> For who hath she to spend the night withal
> But idle sounds resembling parasites,
> Like shrill-tongued tapsters answering every call
> Soothing the humour of fantastic wits?
>
>   (847–50)

A surreal atmosphere, compounded of desolation, non-reciprocity, and humiliation, produces a new poetic that both describes and gives voice to Venus and signals the emerging interface between Shakespeare's epyllion and the 'complaint'. The heaving, overbearing Goddess morphs, as the poem turns away from the purely and comically erotic. When Venus finds the gored Adonis, the neat, end-stopped, rhyming couplets containing each stanza up until this point open out and flow from one stanza into the other, as if to signal this expansion and fluidity (1027–54).[15] It is the perspectival effect of Venus' 'mangling eye' (1065) that the reader is invited to share, with its dazzling distortions and dynamic pluralities, as she becomes a protagonist of a wholly different order of tragedy—that of immurement, of the 'hollow cradle' and the 'empty skies' (1185–91). This switch produces a strange effect of narrative embarrassment, a generic tremor at the narrative's memory of its own earlier complicity with an aesthetic that worked at the cost of affect, at the cost of Venus. It marks at the same time a rupture of a different

---

[15] To my knowledge, the only critic who comments on the ongoing surge of these lines is Colin Burrow, in his Introduction to *William Shakespeare: The Complete Sonnets and Poems* (Oxford: Oxford University Press, 2002) 40.

complicity: that of the intellectual, intertextual, and coterie male authorship and reader-ship of the Elizabethan epyllion—a genre inaugurated by Lodge's *Scillaes Metamorphoses* (1589) written for Lincoln's Inn students.[16] Outgrowing Adonis is also, more specifically, an outgrowing of Ovid. While Venus, in her almost tragic stature at the end of the poem, grows out of the Ovidian into the Shakespearean, Adonis—exquisite in death as in life—remains pent up in his Ovidian walls of glass. There remains, however, the delicate irony of Shakespeare's persistent Ovidian allegiance in the variability of Venus herself.[17]

The final metamorphosis is at once Ovidian and turns Ovid on his head—at least the Ovid that the young Shakespeare set out dazzlingly to emulate in his epyllion. In *The Metamorphoses*, the dead Adonis is turned into a flower by Venus' own 'powre' (X, 853): she possesses and immortalizes him. This transformation is absorbed into a larger etiological narrative of comedic metamorphoses: evanescent forms transmut-ing into self-renewing, cyclical, or imperishable ones, through self-delighting artistic narration (the narrative equivalent of divine intervention). But there is no change of essence—rather, an ironically tragic continuity erased by cool, crystalline metamorphic poetry, with the exquisite material end-product of metamorphosis often emptied out. The dead Phaeton's grieving sisters, for instance, are turned into trees, still weeping, but their tears become 'things of price | To decke the daintie dames of Rome and make them fine and nice' (II, 457–8). In Shakespeare's poem, the flower springs prettily from the blood spilled on the ground, while Adonis melts like a vapour from Venus' sight: she has no choice but to treasure the flower which is not metonymically identified with Adonis, but represented as 'the next of blood': 'Sweet issue of a *more* sweet-smelling sire' (my italics) (1178). What is at stake here is presence, its absence, and its illusion. This takes one into the Ovidian domain of what Philip Hardie calls 'an illusionist poetics of pres-ence', the duplicity in Ovid's enargeic representation of persons and objects, his '[equiv-ocation] between absence and presence which delights in conjuring up illusions of presence'.[18] Hardie identifies this as a hallmark both of Ovidian ekphrasis and of Ovidian self-reflexiveness. The visualization of what is not really there as if it *were* is evident, for example, in the playful evocations of the beloved in the fiction of the *Amores* which becomes a medium for the desired woman to transit from the imagination, through the page, to the world (7).

Crucial here is the artist's role; hence Hardie's identification of Pythagoras and Orpheus as metafictional insets for the metamorphic poet himself. Indeed this function could be seen to extend to Ovid's Venus who aspires to Persephone's power of making 'rank sented Mints' out of 'womens limbes' (X, 851–3)—'and may I not like powre upon mee take | Without disdeine and spyght, to turne Adonis into a flowre?' (853–4). But Shakespeare's Venus serves as an odd semi-inset. A tuner of tales (74), teller of '[stories]' (716, 1013–14, 1125), singer of ditties (836), eloquent rhetor as well as 'chorus-like' actor

---

[16] See Brown (2004) 109–110, on the epyllion as an élite social activity.

[17] Burrow (2002), unlike most critics, notes that Venus is a 'mobile creation'. But 'so is his Adonis', he says (Introduction, 36)—and on this latter point, my reading differs.

[18] Philip Hardie, *Ovid's Poetics of Illusion* (Cambridge: Cambridge University Press, 2002) 15, 3.

(360), she is the would-be creator who is pathetically aware that her poetic power is ultimately limited to analogy. The new-sprung flower that Venus is left with '[resembles]' the red and white of Adonis' cheeks (1169), its scent is '[compared] … to her Adonis' breath' (1172); it takes its place in the 'hollow cradle' of Venus' breast as the child of Adonis, whose rightful place is in his father's bed (1183–5).[19] The self cannot be replicated or immortalized, either by breeding or by aesthetic transformation—'true sweet beauty lived and died with him' (1080). This transformation is also, of course, a culmination of the poem's series of conversions—mostly by Venus' rhetoric—of the grotesque into the dainty, sweaty breath into 'heavenly moisture' (64); the poem shares her habit when, for instance, it describes Adonis' mouth as a 'ruby-coloured portal', yielding 'honey passage' to his speech (451–2). But the form of Venus' ultimate possession of him, no matter how aestheticized, implies both a diminution and a death. We are made to feel the human cost at which art confers immortality, as she tucks the flower in her bosom and fades away, weary, into the empty skies—meaning to cloister herself now, and never to be seen. The etiology Venus' prophecy signals here is that of the origin of love's sorrows, and art's fated connection with it (1135–59), rather than that of the Adonis-flower, anemone or whatever it might be, as in Ovid, or a sheer celebration of the narrative inventiveness that explains it. Meanwhile, in the way that the climactic metamorphosis divests her of the power of the Ovidian Venus, Shakespeare also strips his own 'Ovidian' poetics of its illusionist potency. The failure, and fantasy, of identity in the creation of the flower is an inscription of the early Shakespeare's resistance of a poetic of *cultus*[20] or refinement that is more absorbed in its own illusionist virtuosity than in the affective dimension of its content.

Yet this narrative may be too simple, for there is a hint of something Ovidian in a wider sense in Shakespeare's intimation of a poetics of longing in the very emptiness of failed metamorphosis. Hardie places desire at the heart of Ovid's 'poetics of illusion'. He connects this with the vivid evocations of 'erotic absent presences', which are in turn correlated to the power that artefacts have to stimulate desire in their receivers (11). But the link between love and grief that he sees in Ovid (Ch. 3) is more explicit in the *Heroides* and *Tristia*, poems where the absent beloved, whether person or place, is the presence from which the speaker is exiled, so that the illusionism of those poems is premised on loss. The desire operative there includes a desire to commemorate, recreate, visualize, and believe in translated presence: hence the connection Hardie suggests between ekphrasis and exclusion in the context of exile (6).[21] But the Ovid of the 1590s, available through a

[19] The word 'hollow' carries an unmistakeable pathos in the narrative poems—cp. *Venus and Adonis*, 268: Venus' 'hollow womb'; or that image of stifling and impotent copia in *Lucrece*, 'the hollow-swelling feathered breast' of the birds with whom Lucrece identifies (1122).

[20] Ovid, *Ars Amatoria*, 3.127; cp. 3.113 for Ovid's claim of sophistication and elegance as the hallmark of his art, as opposed to the simple rusticity of the past which it has outmoded: '*simplicitas rudis ante fuit*', in *Ars Amatoria Book 3*, Roy K. Gibson (ed.), (Cambridge: Cambridge University Press, 2003) 54.

[21] See also Colin Burrow on exile and re-embodiment in Renaissance Ovids in 'Re-embodying Ovid: Renaissance Afterlives', in *The Cambridge Companion to Ovid*, Philip Hardie (ed.), (Cambridge: Cambridge University Press, 2002) 301–19.

predominantly amoral and eroticized reading, and through the associations of the love elegies and the *Metamorphoses*, is the Ovid who stood for narrative self-consciousness and aesthetic smoothness, and also for a pleasure somewhat wicked and dangerous. In *Venus and Adonis*, it is this Ovid who is gradually exhausted and outgrown, while the other Ovid is drawn on to change tone and affect, as Shakespeare's first experiment in tragicomedy is worked out. While Hardie sees the 'desire of the mourning lover' and the 'desire which works of art and texts stimulate in their viewers and readers' as collaborative and correlative in Ovid (11; see also 176), I see a split between readerly desire and the desire of the inscribed lover and mourner in Shakespeare's poem, an un-Ovidian distance that allows the reader to feel the pathos of Venus' palpably imperfect attempt at illusionism, collapsing no sooner than begun. The surrogate flower reflects not only on love's or desire's illusions, but art's too. Ovid, as Hardie says, 'elides fully the gap between ecphrastic image and narrative reality by producing a "work of art" that *is* the event that it depicts' (179). Shakespeare spells out that very gap. If 'the demiurge's power to call the real world into existence, and the poet's ability to conjure up his own world of illusion, are parts of a seamless whole' in Ovid's persuasive project (178), that continuum is translated by Shakespeare into a rupture between natural-philosophical process and poetic conjuration at the final moments of his first dramatic poem.

With this, Shakespeare's poem, and his career, move on from the realm of Ovidian *amor* to a 'graver' type of poetic and dramatic labour. But it is not merely in the promised future but within this very poem that, as Venus' prophecy unfolds, Shakespeare's own narrative gets detached from, and expands beyond, the point of mythic origin that it started out by locating. In the process, the cost and subjectivity that are written out of physical transformations by Ovid's self-contained art, are written back into the very idea of metamorphosis. Ovid, the source of erotic verse, becomes the source of a distinctly different idea. The interplay of narrative and erotic desire creates a poetic of unfulfilment out of the confrontation between heterosexual female desire and potentially homoerotic modes of being and reading; this is neither an undialectically homoerotic tease, nor the 'meelder style' in which Orpheus promises to tell his 'tale … of pretty boyes' (X, 157–8). The early, slightly adolescent thrill with the bizarre, the exquisite, the hyper-aesthetic, or the perverse ('sick-thoughted'), so brilliantly whetted in Shakespeare by Ovid, matures in its very act of realization into a questioning of its relation with its living material.

Several critics have noted that Shakespeare's relationship to Ovid changes by the time he comes back to his Ovidian preoccupations in his late plays.[22] As Burrow puts it, some of the same Ovidian episodes in the early works surface again, but 'reshaped by new preoccupations' associated with the power of the imagination.[23] Indeed, one may even find a translation of the pathos of poetic similitude in *Venus* into a textured awareness of the illusionism at the heart of theatre that Hermione's supposed statue, with all its

---

[22] Jonathan Bate, *Shakespeare and Ovid* (Oxford: Clarendon Press, 1993), esp. ch. 6, provides an influential model for Shakespeare's return to Ovid in the late plays.
[23] Burrow (2002), 310.

Ovidian associations, embodies; and indeed its imaginative rewards. Leontes' 'If this be magic, let it be an art/Lawful as eating' (*The Winter's Tale*, V. iii. 110–11), suggests that the identity between magic and eating, as between the lost and the restored, is at once a felt need, and, necessarily, a fantasy. Analogy offers him, and the audience, familiar cognitive parameters to make sense of the unintelligible but retains the mystery—and even a touch of the cognitive dissonance—created by Paulina's dramaturgical conceit of Hermione as a 'statue', resurrected: 'a natural perspective that is, and is not!' (*Twelfth Night* V. I. 214). A statue coming alive unmistakably evokes Pygmalion. All the potential kink of Ovid's Pygmalion fondling and pressing the ivory breasts of his statue, taking it to bed with him, and later, for a moment almost not knowing what to do with it when it comes alive, is translated into a single moment in Shakespeare—Leontes being held back by Paulina from kissing the statue, since the paint on her lips is still wet. The potential for 'sickness' is subtly evoked, and then averted. The metamorphosis, while less 'true' than Ovid's, is more healing. From death, 'dear life' redeems him (103).

Yet there remains in the later works a shadow of the aestheticist—as distinct from aesthetic—impulse associated with him in the early texts; only, in a new configuration. Burrow comments on the fact that in *Cymbeline* the story of Tereus and Philomel is relegated to a book but not physically enacted; on how 'the assault on Innogen becomes purely imaginary', the 'ravishing' description being enough, and suggests, memorably, that '[a]llusion to Ovid turns into illusion'.[24] But there is a further twist. The transference of the erotic energies to the aesthetic or narrative act—'the contents o'th' story' (2.2.27)—is precisely what makes the scene so peculiarly uneasy and perverse. The diversion (not just aversion) of the sexual potential of a proto-rape scene is oddly evocative of the particular erotics of the early part of *Venus and Adonis*, where the pleasure of the text is premised on withholding the delivery. But the agent is marked out differently here, and the theatrical medium contributes to a more immediately disturbing impact as the audience are themselves, in some senses, let into the vulnerably asleep Innogen's bedroom. Ovid's *Metamorphoses*, which figured so centrally and so materially in Shakespeare's early tragedy, *Titus Andronicus* (1594),[25] physically resurfaces: Innogen has been reading it at bedtime, and, if Iachimo is to be believed, reading specifically of the rape of Philomel by Tereus. She falls asleep, with the leaf 'turned down | Where Philomel gave up' (II. ii. 45–6)—and who should leap out of it (as it were) but Iachimo, the one figure explicitly associated with cool, self-delighting

---

[24] Burrow (2002) 310. Bate also reads this scene as innocuous (though he does not specifically connect it with the imagination): a 'sublimating of the image of rape', a mitigation of violence through metaphor and sibilance. He contrasts what he sees to be its 'tender' and 'gentle' effects with the 'brutal reality' of *Titus* (as well as *Lucrece*), suggesting that this '[makes] it easier for the theatre audience to put itself in the position of Iachimo. To note and to wonder at the beauty of the sleeping Innogen does not seem to do any harm …' (*Shakespeare and Ovid*, 216). My impression of the bedroom scene differs markedly from his.

[25] But see Brian Vickers, *Shakespeare, Co-Author: A Historical Study of Five Collaborative Plays* (Oxford: Oxford University Press, 2002) ch. 3, persuasively suggesting George Peele's collaboration with Shakespeare on *Titus*. The sections I touch on are among those where Shakespeare's dramaturgy, verse, and rhetorical application are easily distinguishable from Peele's, as Vickers shows, after Capell.

aesthetic narration? Physically, of course, the subtle Italian has popped out of a trunk in the English princess's bedroom.[26] What Burrow calls the 'ravishing detail of his description' keeps cropping up effortlessly at moments of suspense or anticipated knowledge, bringing artful but agonizing deferral in its wake: witness the relishing prolongation of his report of this very scene at the final disclosure ('O cunning, how I got it!'), when everyone else '[stands] on fire' (V. vi. 205, 168–9); or, earlier, when he sets about to narrate the scene in exquisite enargeic detail to Posthumus (II. iv. 66–104). The ravishment is all the narrator's, while the anguish is the inscribed listeners'. The extent to which Iachimo is 'placed' as an artificer is an index of Shakespeare's placing of the 1590s Ovid, and his distance from all that. Illusion is folded back into allusion. The association of Ovid with self-conscious, detached aesthetic sophistication does not disappear, but the writer's relationship with it changes. The 'mole cinque-spotted: like the crimson drops | I'th' bottom of a cowslip' (II. ii. 38–9) is the fluently metamorphic image-making of the designated aesthete, rather than the creation of a language variably shared by author and inset narrator, as with the transformations of physical attributes in *Venus and Adonis*: the 'purple tears' shed by Adonis' 'lily white' flanks (1053–4), or Venus' 'pearls in glass' tears (980).

I will end by looking at *Lucrece* (1594), Shakespeare's poetic tale about a woman struggling to tell her own story of violation, to reflect further on the outstripping of an aesthetic 'young and so unkind'—like Adonis himself—in *Venus and Adonis*. For here, as in its companion play *Titus*, it is not only the emotional tenor but the ethics of Ovidian representation that is interrogated. In Marcus' (in)famous forty-six-line address in *Titus*, lavishly describing the ravished and mutilated Lavinia in lyrically allusive, classicized diction, the horror of tonguelessness is met with the eloquence of poetry (II. iv. 11–57). This is not unlike those neat, trippingly light couplets that describe Philomel's tongue 'quivering on the ground' and '[wriggling] to and fro', in the source story where Tereus cuts off Philomel's tongue after raping her (*Metamorphosis* VI, 710–15). But while the visual is neatly contained in the aesthetics of the verbal in Ovid, it posits an immediate challenge to poetic language and Ovidian rhetorical control in Shakespeare's theatre.[27] At

---

[26] Innogen is staged as one of the earliest readers of Ovid, following on from Lucius and Lavinia. But could this be Shakespeare's joke about the erotics of Italy—'our Tarquin'—in the aesthetic imagination of English readers, and not just about the chaste English princess's bedtime pleasure in Ovidian rape-stories? Perhaps then, the readerly allusion glances at the erotics of private reading that I have connected to the epyllion, though the axis of male desire is complicated here: it becomes a scene about the male voyeuristic imagining of an eroticized female reader's closet-reading of Ovidian literature, as in several 17th-century texts alluding to *V&A*.

[27] Curiously, Marcus' metaphorical ornamentation of Lavinia's dismembered body as a tree from which the flower had been plucked and the limbs lopped includes what I think is a highly wrought allusion to literary ancestry through yet another intertext—a visual one. The image of 'her two branches, those sweet ornaments, | Whose circling shadows kings have sought to sleep in' (II. iv. 18–19), surely evokes a jesse tree—common in stained glass church windows in Elizabethan England—a genæalogical conceit which visually depicted prophets as well as the Kings of Judah under the branches of a tree that grew (often in a visibly phallic way) out of a sleeping Jesse, father of David. That this overtly Ovidian passage, rhetorically transforming a raped and mutilated woman into an *objet d'art*, weaves this image into its artifice focuses the associations and anxieties clustered around the Ovidian ancestry of the young Shakespeare.

this point in the play, Lavinia is turned into a mere theatrical sign, as Marcus speaks for her, pointing out that she is worse off than Philomel who 'but lost her tongue'. Not so that other Philomel, Shakespeare's Lucrece, a hypothetical Lavinia who has been spared her tools of communication. With her tongue, she can tell of her rape, with her hands, she can write. The trajectory from Lavinia to Lucrece might seem to be a release from dumbness into oratory, from silence into poetry. Yet is it really a liberation? When it comes to communicating her experience, her tongue is 'untuned' (1214). Unlike the female protagonists in the *Heriodes* whom the epistolary occasion moves into rhetorical fluency, all she ends up writing to her husband is 'a short schedule', for fear that her copia might misrepresent her feelings: the uncertainty is not in the emotion but in the writing and its reception—'her certain sorrow writ uncertainly' (1311). 'Much like a press of people at a door | Throng her inventions, which shall go before' (1301–2). 'Invention', the first part of rhetorical composition, suggests a covetable plenitude of ideas. But the image is also one of stampede and suffocation. The clue to the paradox lies in the Ovidian myth, where Philomel was transformed into a nightingale *after* being raped and silenced. Lucrece at first speaks the Marcus language: 'My tongue shall utter all; mine eyes, like sluices, | As from a mountain spring that feeds the dale | Shall gush pure streams to purge my impure tale' (1076–8). Her eloquence makes the narrator call her 'this, lamenting Philomel', singing her 'well-tuned warble' (1079–80). It would seem at this point that Lavinia is the raped, gagged woman of the Ovidian story, and Lucrece the metamorphosed bird singing in full-throated ease. But then the poem moves on to embody this duality, as Lucrece starts to vacillate between copious lament and choked silence: 'Sometime her grief is dumb and hath no word, | Sometime 'tis mad and too much talk affords' (1105–6). When she comes to identify herself with the nightingale eventually, it is the *prehistory* of the metamorphic myth that she addresses: 'Come, Philomel, that sing'st of ravishment'; 'For burden-wise I'll hum on Tarquin still, | While thou on Tereus descants better skill' (1128; 1133–4). Why is the nightingale so often associated in literary imagination with sweet melody, pleasing to the lover's ear? Is it because she sings so fully, freely, and fluently that we, and perhaps—briefly—the narrator in *Lucrece*, forget that she sings a 'sad strain' (1131)? Think of the chorus in *A Midsummer Night's Dream*: 'Philomel with melody/Sing in our sweet lullaby' (II. ii. 13–4).

It is no accident that two models meet in Lucrece: Ovid who deals with rape after rape with effortless elegance, and Seneca, who is into obtruded horror. Seneca was the source of the familiar tag, 'Curae leves loquuntur, ingentes stupent' [light griefs speak, huge griefs are silent] (*Phaedra*, 607). This is typical of articulations of anxiety within discursive cultures centred on rhetoric—an anxiety that laces early Shakespearean virtuosity. The main worry of the young Shakespeare is premature articulacy, confronted and foregrounded repeatedly in the narrative poems. There is only enough space to glance at one symptomatic word, which focuses a troubling discrepancy between the character's writing and Shakespeare's, which links it back to the dynamic of this relation in *Venus and Adonis*. I mean the rhetorical charge of the word and the concept of a 'let'.

Again and again in the course of the erotic combat between Lucrece and her rapist Tarquin, 'these lets attend the time, | Like little frosts that sometime threat the spring | To add a more rejoicing to the prime' (330–2)—'let' here is 'hindrance'. But there is another sense in which the word is used in the poem—flowing out. Ironically, Lucrece's pleading outpour ('lets' in that other sense) serves counter-productively as an obstacle that only inflames the passion it *seeks* to check: 'Have done', quoth he, 'my uncontrollèd tide/ Turns not, but swells the higher by this let' (645–6)—reminiscent of *Venus and Adonis'* comments on how '[an] oven that is stopped, or river stayed, | Burneth more hotly, swelleth with more rage' (331–2). Lucrece's 'let' is her eloquent plea which does exactly what a legal appeal is supposed to do—affect, persuade. But it is so eloquent that it has the opposite effect from the one intended.

Meanwhile, at Tarquin's end, the nature of the 'lets' operates on the level of sex and action. Lucrece's plea makes Tarquin's lust flow by providing a sexual obstacle. This brings Shakespeare's own narrative into dubious relation with Lucrece's. Her lament, rhetorically fluent and copious, is solitary and fruitless; her act of communication brief and choked, unlike Shakespeare's, woven eloquently out of her struggle for the power to tell. The letter over which Lucrece's 'quill' 'hovers', and her 'wit' fights what her 'will' blots (1296–1300)—as the language of erotic combat leaks from the inscribed story into the description of the act and mechanics of writing—is almost not written, except for six bald lines. Shakespeare's poem is a two thousand-line-long efflux. The hint of a perverse aesthetic that is set on fire by opposition links the outpouring of lust in Tarquin with that of rhetoric in Shakespeare, both a result of Lucrece's misfired resistance. But such parasitic artistic distance is questioned by the poem itself, by inscribing Shakespeare's discomfort with too much fluency. By presenting one kind of 'let' as the outcome of the other, Shakespeare not only writes *in* the communicative risks of facility but also suggests the importance of obstacles to strengthen an achievement or impact. There is a kind of obstacle which can be a dodgy aesthetic turn-on; there is another kind which stands in for the difficulty that needs to be inscribed to absolve the narrative of dubious complicities, especially in narrating extreme and subjective experience. Shakespeare's narrative teeters between the two a good while, but moves, with its focus on Lucrece's pain, towards the emergence of the unmistakably Shakespearean idea of the necessity of 'difficulty' in checking glibness.

In 1598, Francis Meres, in his *Palladis Tamia*, paid Shakespeare the highest compliment one could pay in the 1590s to a rising poet-playwright anxious to establish his credentials:

> As the soul of Euphorbus was thought to live in Pythagoras: so the sweete and wittie soul of Ovid lives in mellifluous and honey-tongued Shakespeare, witness his *Venus and Adonis*, his *Lucrece*, his sugred *Sonnets* among his private friends....[28]

Ovid is indeed at the heart of early Shakespearean poems; but it is the disengagement and aestheticism of his poetry that is confronted. No sooner does Shakespeare discover

---

[28] Francis Meres, *Palladis Tamia*, introduction, Don Cameron Allen (New York: Scholars Facsimiles & Reprints, 1938) 281–2.

his honey-tongued eloquence than he realizes the dangers of his tongue being untuned, even—and especially—when trying to narrate that most lucrative of narrative subjects: sex—desired, denied, or inflicted. No wonder, then, that Ovid, the archetypal source of tales of desire, comes to stand for an intimation of pain and violence. In that other early work, *Romeo and Juliet*, it is an Ovidian allusion that flickers like a stab of pain through Shakespearean poetry at its most absolute, which is also Juliet's unwitting liebestod: 'Bondage is hoarse, and may not speak aloud, | Else would I tear the cave where Echo lies, | And make her airy tongue more hoarse than mine | With repetition of my Romeo's name' (II. i. 205–8). This is one of many moments in that play where tragedy is intimated at moments of bliss, and vice versa. Does Ovid mark the precarious threshold between genres in early Shakespeare, as in that sublime sculpture by Bernini, depicting the very instant when Daphne is beginning to turn into a tree—capturing (and impeccably freezing) in one marmoreal moment both the comedic fluidity and the tragic fixity of metamorphosis, the expenses and achievements of translating sex (or pain or horror or death) into art?[29] Such generic disorientation is not unrelated to the affective re-orientations that begin in *Venus and Adonis*, Shakespeare's post-Ovidian Ovidian poem which outgrows its own tantalizing, self-loving artifice. What might have remained a young poet's bravura adoption of a trendy project becomes an exuberant yet confusing and responsible work that signals the beginning of a career that refuses to scrape poetic alchemy clean of its affective cost.

SELECT BIBLIOGRAPHY

Bate, Jonathan, (1993) *Shakespeare and Ovid* (Oxford: Clarendon Press).

Brown, Georgia (2004), *Redefining Elizabethan Literature* (Cambridge: Cambridge University Press).

Burrow, Colin (2002) (ed.) *William Shakespeare: The Complete Sonnets and Poems* (Oxford: Oxford University Press).

—— (2002) 'Re-embodying Ovid: Renaissance Afterlives', in *The Cambridge Companion to Ovid*, Philip Hardie (ed.), (Cambridge: Cambridge University Press), 301–19.

Cheney, Patrick (2004), *Shakespeare, National Poet-Playwright* (Cambridge: Cambridge University Press).

Hardie, Philip (2002), *Ovid's Poetics of Illusion* (Cambridge: Cambridge University Press).

Ovid, *Ars Amatoria Book 3*, ed. Roy K. Gibson (2003) (Cambridge: Cambridge University Press).

Ovid's Metamorphoses: The Arthur Golding Translation 1567, ed. John Frederick Nims (2000) (Philadelphia: Paul Dry Books).

Roberts, Sasha (2003), *Reading Shakespeare's Poems in Early Modern England* (Basingstoke: Palgrave).

Roe, John (1992) (ed.) *The Poems*, The New Cambridge Shakespeare (Cambridge: Cambridge University Press).

---

[29] Gian Lorenzo Bernini, 'Apollo and Daphne' (*c.* 1622–5), Galleria Borghese, Rome.

CHAPTER 23

....

SHAME, LOVE, FEAR, AND PRIDE IN *THE RAPE OF LUCRECE*

....

JOSHUA SCODEL

Shakespeare's *The Rape of Lucrece* (1594) is an ambitious, experimental, and surprising poem. Shakespeare re-imagines a famous story concerning Rome's mythic past told in his principal source, Ovid's poem on Roman festivals, the *Fasti* (2.685–856), as well as in two prose histories of Rome, Shakespeare's second major source, Livy's *Ab urbe condita* (Book 1, chapters 57–60), and Dionysius of Halicarnassus' *Roman Antiquities* (Book 4, chapters 64–85).[1] Excerpts of Livy and of Dionysius in Latin translation appear in the many *Fasti* editions with Paolo Marso's and Antonio Costanzo's commentaries, one of which Shakespeare undoubtedly used.[2] Drawing also on a variety of other classical and Renaissance texts, most notably Ovid's *Metamorphoses* and Edmund Spenser's *Faerie Queene*, Shakespeare turns Lucrece's story into a psychologically complex mini-epic.

Lucrece depicts a moral world based on classical conceptions of honour and shame. It does so not for antiquarian reconstruction but because these conceptions are very much part of Shakespeare's world. The poem explores the 'shame' of Lucrece's rape and the complex relationship of shame to other feelings such as love, fear, and pride. Lucrece, her rapist Tarquin, her ambiguous revenger Brutus, and even such minor characters as Lucrece's messenger, reveal themselves through their diverse responses to shame. By reimagining the role of shame and related passions in the Lucrece story, Shakespeare

---

[1] Citations and translations of classical texts and Augustine are from the Loeb Classical Library edition unless otherwise noted; citations follow the standard numbering system for each author.

[2] He may have also read William Painter's retelling of Livy's narrative in *The Palace of Pleasure* (1566) and the medieval retellings in John Gower's *Confessio amantis* and Chaucer's *Legend of Good Women*; see Colin Burrow's discussion of sources in Burrow (ed.), *Complete Sonnets and Poems*, by William Shakespeare (Oxford, 2002) 45–50.

challenges traditional gender and social roles and associated conceptions of proper ethical and political action.

23.1 TARQUIN'S YOUTHFUL LOVE, FEAR, AND SHAME

Shakespeare adds Tarquin's anguished debate with himself before raping Lucrece to his classical sources, in which Tarquin rapes without qualms. Shakespeare's Tarquin is torn between 'dread' and 'desire', 'honest' and 'heedful' 'fear', and 'lust' (lines 171, 173, 281–2).[3] What does he most fear? 'Shame' (lines 197, 223) and 'foul dishonour' to himself and his family (line 198).

As any reader familiar with the Lucrece story would immediately recognize, Shakespeare's Tarquin surprisingly shares Lucrece's core concern. In Shakespeare as in his sources, Tarquin seeks to overcome Lucrece's resistance by threatening her with what Livy calls 'disgrace' ('dedecus') (*Ab urbe condita* 1.58.4) and by cruelly exploiting what Ovid describes as her 'fear of [ill-]fame' ('famae ... metu') (*Fasti* 2.810). He threatens to kill her and make it appear as if she had been slain in flagrante delicto with a slave, thus destroying her 'honour' (line 516) and bringing 'shameful doom' (line 672) upon her, her husband, and her descendents. Yet only in Shakespeare does Tarquin exploit a fear of dishonour in Lucrece against which he himself has struggled.

Shakespeare draws upon ancient and Renaissance moral psychology, which ascribes 'hot' passions like lust to young men but claims that proper young men feel an inhibiting fear of reproach. Such fear of shame (Greek 'aidos', Latin 'pudor' and 'verecundia') has several common early modern English renderings, including 'shamefastness', 'bashfulness', or simply 'shame'. It is treated either as a moral virtue or as the closest that irrational youth can come to virtue. Aristotle's *Nicomachean Ethics* denies that 'aidos' or 'fear of ill-repute' is true virtue (which requires pursuing the good for its own sake) but argues that it is a suitable deterrent for youth who live by their emotions rather than reason (4.9).[4] Roman moralists commend 'pudor' and 'verecundia' in otherwise impetuous young men.[5] English Renaissance texts similarly praise such fear of reproach, sometimes without the Aristotelian disclaimer that such shame is not true virtue. Roger Ascham's *The Schoolmaster* (1570) praises 'bashfulness in youth' as 'fear to do ill'; Thomas Rogers' *Philosophical Discourse* (1576) claims 'bashfulnesse' or 'feare' of 'ignominie' is the best 'ruler of the Lustes' and 'becommeth yong men', and Pierre de

[3] All Shakespeare citations are from Wells and Taylor (2005).

[4] On 'aidos' in Aristotle, see Douglas L. Cairns, *Aidos: The Psychology and Ethics of Honour and Shame in Ancient Greek Literature* (Oxford: Clarendon Press, 1993) 393–431.

[5] Emiel Eyben, *Restless Youth in Ancient Rome*, Patrick Daly (trans.), (London: Routledge, 1993) 40–1.

La Primaudaye's *French Academy,* translated in 1586, declares 'vertuous shame' befits 'youth'.[6]

In Shakespeare, Tarquin's fear of the shame of rape pointedly challenges the gendering of virtues, common in both the ancient world and Renaissance England, which diminishes the heinousness of male sexual transgressions by associating male virtue with courage and only female virtue with sexual purity.[7] Shakespeare's portrayal of young Tarquin's Lucrece-like fear of shame foregrounds what classical and Renaissance moralists intermittently acknowledge, that the shamefast young man who controls his desires resembles the shamefast, chaste woman.[8] A 1547 English paraphrase of Aristotle's *Ethics* makes the resemblance explicit by claiming that 'shamefastness' is appropriate not only for young men but also for 'wenches' (i.e. young women). Edmund Tilney's marriage treatise of 1568 notes that 'shamefastnesse' is the 'defense' whereby women 'preserve their chastity' and 'honor'. A speaker in Baldasarre Castiglione's *Book of the Courtier,* translated by Thomas Hoby in 1561, opines that women need 'shame and feare of infamye' to guard their 'continency'. La Primaudaye claims that 'shame' is the 'defence' whereby women preserve 'chastitie, and honour' and compares women's shamefast self-regulation with young men's.[9]

Some moralists maintain gender divisions by associating young men's fear of reproach, unlike women's, with courage. Aristotle argues that fear of disgrace, though not inspiring true courage based on love of the good, inspires a lower form among soldiers (*Nicomachean Ethics* 3.8.1–3), while Plutarch's *Lives,* translated by Thomas North in 1579, notes that Spartans associate 'feare' of 'shame' with 'fortitude' in war. Primaudaye recounts Roman examples of such fear inspiring battlefield 'courage'.[10] Nevertheless, the celebration of inhibiting fear in young men is in tension with the traditional identification of courage as the quintessential male virtue. Ascham exposes this cultural conflict

[6] Roger Ascham, *The Schoolmaster* (1570), Lawrence V. Ryan (ed.), (Charlottesville, VA: University of Virginia Press, 1967) 42; Thomas Rogers, *A Philosophicall Discourse* (London, 1576) 29; Pierre de La Primaudaye, *The French Academie* (London, 1586) 257.

[7] See Curtis Brown Watson, *Shakespeare and the Renaissance Concept of Honor* (Princeton: Princeton University Press, 1960) 155–62; and Ian Maclean, *The Renaissance Notion of Woman: A Study in the Fortunes of Scholasticism and Medical Science in European Intellectual Life* (Cambridge: Cambridge University Press, 1980) 25, 51, 62. Praising Lucretia, Saint Jerome declares 'chastity' ('pudicitia') woman's special virtue (*Adversus Jovinianum* 1.49 in *Patrologia Latina,* vol. 23, J. P. Migne (ed.), (Paris, 1845), 282A).

[8] Robert A. White's argument for distinct Renaissance senses of 'shamefastness'—as a male or gender-neutral fear of dishonour and as an 'almost exclusively feminine' quality—is too rigid; see '"Shamefastnesse" as "Verecundia" and as "Pudicitia" in "The Faerie Queene"', *Studies in Philology* 78 (1981): 391–408 (quote on 403).

[9] Aristotle, *Ethiques* (London, 1547) ch. xxiii (no pagination); Edmund Tilney, *The Flower of Friendship: A Renaissance Dialogue Contesting Marriage,* Valerie Wayne (ed.), (Ithaca: Cornell University Press, 1992) 132; Baldassare Castiglione, *The Courtyer,* Thomas Hoby (trans.), (London, 1561), Ziii[vi]; Primaudaye (1586) 516.

[10] Plutarch, *The Lives of the Noble Grecians and Romaines,* Thomas North (trans.), (London, 1579) 860; Primaudaye (1586) 263–4.

when he complains that shameless youth at court deem it 'courage' to 'dare do any mischief'.[11]

Shakespeare's Tarquin reveals this felt tension in cultural codes by scorning his restraining fear of shame in the name of masculine daring. Disregarding his own contrast between a 'martial man' and 'soft fancy's slave' (line 200), he espouses erotic boldness:

> Who fears a sentence or an old man's saw
> Shall by a painted cloth be kept in awe
>
> (lines 244–5)

> Then childish fear avaunt, debating die,
> Respect and reason wait on wrinkled age! …
> My part is youth, and beats these from the stage.
> Desire my pilot is, beauty my prize.
> Then who fears sinking where such treasure lies?
>
> (lines 274–80)

Far from identifying fear of shame with youthful courage, Tarquin dismisses it as a timidity both immature and prematurely aged, as a childish subjection to elders' strictures.[12] Aggrandizing himself instead as an erotic soldier, he proceeds to imagine his attack upon Lucrece's chastity as a daring 'invasion' (line 287) of her 'never-conquered fort' (line 482).[13]

Shakespeare's Tarquin here recalls Ovid's, who compares his erotic daring to his boldness in conquering a city (*Fasti* 2.781–3). Yet other Ovidian echoes undercut the Shakespearean Tarquin's exculpatory, self-aggrandizing conception of rape as masculine daring. Throughout his career Shakespeare drew upon Ovid's *Metamorphoses*, both the Latin original and Arthur Golding's 1567 translation.[14] Shakespeare gives Tarquin's submission to his lust both a high epic tone and an ironizing gendered subtext by adapting the *Metamorphoses*' depictions of women whose illicit passions conquer their feminine 'pudor'. He recalls Medea, whose desire for her family's enemy Jason overcomes her 'pudor' (Golding's 'shamefastness') (*Metamorphoses* 7.72; Golding 7.102), and Myrrha, whose lust for her father conquers her

[11] Ascham (1967) 42.
[12] Compare Ascham's complaint that shameless young gentlemen misconstrue 'bashful' as 'babyish'; Ascham (1967) 41.
[13] On Tarquin as erotic soldier, see Heather Dubrow, *Captive Victors: Shakespeare's Narrative Poems and Sonnets* (Ithaca: Cornell University Press, 1987) 120–4; and Katharine Eisaman Maus, 'Taking Tropes Seriously: Language and Violence in Shakespeare's *Rape of Lucrece*', *Shakespeare Quarterly* 37 (1986): 67–8.
[14] See Leonard Barkan, *The Gods Made Flesh: Metamorphosis & the Pursuit of Paganism* (New Haven: Yale University Press, 1986) ch. 6; Jonathan Bate, *Shakespeare and Ovid* (Oxford: Clarendon Press, 1993). I cite Golding's book and line numbers from *Ovid's Metamorphoses*, Arthur Golding (trans.), Madeleine Forey (ed.), (Baltimore: Johns Hopkins University Press, 2002).

'shame' (*Metamorphoses* 10.371; Golding 10.418). Tarquin's rejection of elders' moral scruples specifically recalls Ovid's Byblis, in love with her brother. Rejecting 'pudor' or 'shame' for incestuous passion (*Metamorphoses* 9.515; Golding 9.613), Byblis celebrates youthful daring with an empty bravado anticipating Tarquin's. Here is Golding:

> Let agèd folks have skill in law; to age it doth belong
> To keep the rigour of the laws and search out right from wrong.
> Such youthful years as ours are yet rash folly doth beseem;
> ... Not dread of worldly shame
> ... nor fearfulness should let
> Our purpose. Only let all fear aside be wholly set
>
> (9.658–65)

In fashioning himself as a daring youth, Tarquin behaves like a shameless woman.

Shakespeare also undercuts Tarquin's daring by showing that his attempt to escape fear only causes him to embrace it. Vividly instantiating his youthful fear of reproach, Tarquin imagines his friend and kinsman, Lucrece's husband Collatine, discovering and rebuking him:

> O what excuse can my invention make
> When thou [Collatine] shalt charge me with so black a deed? ...
> The guilt being great, the fear doth still exceed,
>   And extreme fear can neither fight nor fly,
>   But coward-like with trembling terror die
>
> (lines 225–31)

Tarquin has fearfully adopted the procedure of imagining an audience to inhibit one from wrongdoing that Seneca advises after commending youthful 'pudor' (*Epistulae morales* 25.2, 5–6). Yet even as he testifies to his sense of shame by fearfully imagining both the guilt and greater fear he would feel in Collatine's presence, Tarquin's final image of 'extreme fear' as 'coward-like' provokes his subsequent dismissal of such fear as unworthy. The rape, however, brings back the very guilt and fear he dismisses: while in Shakespeare's classical sources Tarquin leaves the rape scene exultant with victory, Shakespeare's Tarquin 'creeps' from his deed with 'guilty fear' (lines 736, 740).

23.2 LUCRECE'S RESISTANT LOVE, FEAR, AND SHAME

The next major surprise after Tarquin's self-debate is Lucrece's long and forceful verbal resistance to Tarquin's threats (lines 561–666). In both Livy and Ovid, only Tarquin speaks during the rape scene; Livy's Tarquin commands Lucretia's silence, while Ovid describes her as mute with fear (*Fasti* 2.797–9). Both Livy and Ovid claim that until Tarquin threatens her with posthumous shame she resists, but without describing how she does so. Despite her 'trembling fear' (line 511), by contrast, Shakespeare's Lucrece reasons with Tarquin, continuing to plead after he bids her 'Have done' (line 645) and, after being gagged, uttering 'piteous clamours in her head' (line 681). Tarquin's previously described fear of being struck 'mute' (line 227) if confronted by Collatine makes fearful Lucrece's outspokenness all the more surprising.

Lucrece's extended speech counters traditional associations of women's modesty with saying little or nothing. Citing classical, Biblical, and patristic proof texts, numerous Renaissance writers contrast women's praiseworthy silence or brevity with men's eloquence.[15] Shakespeare associates 'modesty' with femininity by applying the terms 'modest', 'modesty', and 'modestly' only to 'modest Lucrece' (line 123; cf. 196, 401, 683, 1607) and to her devoted maid (line 1220), never to a male. Yet his praise of Lucrece's 'modest eloquence' (line 563), a probable Shakespeare coinage, overturns traditional conceptions of feminine modesty by playing off the more common phrase used in praise of women, 'modest silence'.[16]

Traditional notions of feminine decorum discouraged women from discussing other than household matters.[17] Starkly countering conventional understandings both of gender and of the occasion's presumed exigencies, terrified, 'modest' Lucrece adduces broad political arguments against her rape, advising Tarquin on proper governance with the rhetoric of a wise, presumptively male counselor.[18] Lucrece focuses on the shame Tarquin as rapist would inflict upon his royal status: 'Hast thou put on his [Tarquin's] shape to do him shame? ... | Thou wrong'st his honour, wound'st his princely name' (lines 597, 599); while Tarquin had identified himself with 'youth' against 'age', she warns him of the 'shame' that will come with 'age' when he becomes 'king' (lines 603, 606).[19] To do shame to a woman can mean to assault her sexually, as when Spenser in the 1590

---

[15] See Maclean (1980), 54–7, 62. In a work printed at least eight times from *ca.* 1529 to 1592, Ludovico Vives praises women who defended their 'chastity' with 'silence' rather than 'wordes' and denies women need 'eloquent orations' (*The Instruction of a Christen Woman*, Richard Hyrde (trans.), [*ca.* 1529], Virginia Walcott Beauchamp, Elizabeth H. Hageman, and Margaret Mikesell (eds), Urbana: University of Illinois Press, 2002, 63, 130).

[16] *Early English Books Online* yields no instance of the phrase 'modest eloquence' besides Shakespeare's, whereas 'modest silence' occurs in six texts (not including reprints) before *Lucrece* and in fifteen more from 1596 to 1640. Philip Sidney celebrates a bride's 'modest silence' (*The Countess of Pembroke's Arcadia (The New Arcadia)* [1593], Victor Skretkowicz, (ed.), Oxford: Clarendon Press, 1987, 48), Bartélemy Batt, a wife's (*The Christian Man's Closet*, London, 1579, 5ʳ). William Camden praises Elizabeth I's 'modesta eloquentia' (*Tomus Alter Annalium*, London, 1627, 139): Elizabeth as queen escaped traditional aspersions upon female eloquence.

[17] Vives (2002) cites Aristotle to argue that women should not discuss 'matters of the realme' (130).

[18] See Burrow (2002) 51–2.

[19] Stressing Tarquin's royal responsibilities, Lucrece sometimes collapses future into present, addressing him as if he were already king (lines 601, 652). 'Princely' is ambiguous, for it can mean a ruler's son or a ruler.

instalment of the *Faerie Queene* describes a brute's attempt at rape as 'the shame, he did' to a 'Damzell'.[20] Lucrece pleads that if Tarquin shames her with rape, he will also shame himself.

In stressing the implications of his rape for his future kingship, Lucrece redefines key terms in Tarquin's conception of erotic conquest, 'love' and 'fear': 'This deed will make thee only loved for fear, | But happy monarchs still are feared for love' (lines 610–11). Following Cicero, who noted that tyrants like Tarquin's father, Tarquin the Proud, were feared rather than loved (*De amicitia* 15.52–53), and Seneca, who distinguished beloved virtuous rulers from feared tyrants (*De clementia* 1.12.3–1.13.5), Renaissance humanists argued that rulers should seek to be loved, not feared. [21] Lucrece's more sinuous variant suggests that, by raping her, Tarquin will reveal himself as a future tyrant who will only be 'loved for fear' rather than as a just and therefore 'happy' king who will be 'feared for love'.

Lucrece adopts an antithesis already in Elizabethan circulation. A poem addressed to Queen Elizabeth first published in 1576, after counseling her to 'Embrace their love that willes you good' while avoiding flatterers and 'hollow hartes', advises: 'Geve faith to those that feare for love, and not that love for fear, | Regard not them that force compels to please you every where'.[22] Those that 'feare for love' are loving subjects who wish their monarch well. 'Fear' here has its positive sense of 'regard with reverence and awe; revere' (*OED* 6). Those that 'love for feare', by contrast, display the false, servile 'love' of 'hollow hartes', seeking to 'please' their queen for fear of her punitive 'force'.[23] The former treat Elizabeth as a beloved monarch, the latter as a feared tyrant.

Like the poem to Elizabeth, Lucrece, who compares 'kings' to 'gods' (line 602), applies to subjects' feelings for monarchs the reverence Christians were supposed to show God. Drawing on a dichotomy in Augustine and Calvin, English Protestants contrast 'servile' fear of God's punishment with reverential fear of displeasing Him. In 1562 James Pilkington opposes fear of God's wrath to 'feare for love', when we 'feare' God 'with love and reverence, & woulde not displease him for the love we beare him'.[24] But Lucrece's and the advice poem's 'feare(d) for love', applied to vulnerable earthly

[20] Edmund Spenser, *The Faerie Queene*, A. C. Hamilton (ed.), (London, 1977) 348 (3.5.13).

[21] See Quentin Skinner, *The Foundations of Modern Political Thought*, 2 vols (Cambridge: Cambridge University Press, 1978) 1:127–8.

[22] Richard Edwards published it, ascribed to 'D. S.', as 'A worthy dittie, song before the Queenes Majestie at Bristowe' in *The Paradise of Daintie Devises* (London, 1576) 23; Thomas Churchyard claimed the poem with the title 'Written of the Queene, when her highnesse was in trouble' in *A Pleasaunte Laborinth* (London, 1580) 27ᵛ-28ʳ. I cite Edwards' text.

[23] Compare Leonard Wright's claim that the 'common people' 'dread' the 'inferiour Magistrate', whom they 'love for feare', more than their 'Prince', whom they 'feare for love' (*A Display of Dutie* [London, 1589], f2ʳ). Commoners display 'love' born of fear toward the official who oversees (and punishes) them but feel loving awe for their remote ruler.

[24] James Pilkington, *Aggeus and Abdias, Prophetes* (London, 1562) M7ʳ·ᵛ. Compare Augustine, in *Patrologia Latina*, vol. 35, J. P. Migne (ed.), (Paris, 1841) 1708, and John Calvin, *Institutes of the Christian Religion*, John T. McNeill (ed.), Ford Lewis Battles (trans.), 2 vols (Philadelphia: The Westminster Press, 1960) 1:50, 573 (1.4.4, 3.2.27).

monarchs rather than almighty God, evokes not only subjects' loving fear of or reverence for their godlike just monarch but also their loving fear or anxiety about their monarch's well-being.[25]

Although breaching traditional female decorum, Lucrece's political advice responds directly to her threatened rape. Lucrece gives conventional antitheses new psychological pertinence. Tarquin the rapist will only be 'loved for fear' by subjects because he will have revealed himself to be a tyrant who has coerced 'love' (sex) from Lucrece's fear. In his self-debate Tarquin treated 'love' (really, lust) as antithetical to fear: 'Love thrives not in the heart that shadows dreadeth' (line 270). Yet both he and Lucrece know what her 'love for fear' would be. Both also know what the ideal of 'fear for love' or loving fear is. In his internal debate Tarquin recalls, as a perverse turn-on, Lucrece's 'fearing' for her 'belovèd' husband (lines 255–6), the 'loyal fear' (line 261) she displayed when inquiring about Collatine's safety. By threatening to inflict 'shame' upon her beloved husband, Tarquin seeks to turn Lucrece's spousal 'fear for love' into the 'love for fear' of coerced sex. Lucrece exhorts Tarquin instead to live up to royal ideals so that he will inspire among loyal subjects the 'fear for love' that Lucrece feels for her spouse and that she hopes Tarquin most deeply desires from her.

Lucrece further reveals her sense of the threatened rape's political implications when she argues that if Tarquin allows 'lust, dishonour, shame' (line 654) to control him,

> So shall these slaves be king, and thou their slave;
> Thou nobly base, they basely dignified;
> Thou their fair life, and they thy fouler grave;
> Thou loathèd in their shame, they in thy pride.
>
> (lines 659–62)

Tarquin himself had worried about becoming 'soft fancy's slave', and Lucrece here attempts to arouse Tarquin's royal dignity by adapting the Stoic doctrine that everyone, including a king, is a slave when ruled by passions rather than reason.[26] While Tarquin threatened to shame high-born Lucrece by joining her dead body to that of 'some worthless slave of thine' (line 515), Lucrece counters that Tarquin risks shaming himself more profoundly by abdicating his kingship to his own slaves, his vicious desires.

'Thou loathèd in their shame; they in thy pride' aggressively conjoins Tarquin's shame and pride. The narrator describes Tarquin's pride as well as lust motivating the rape: Collaltine's 'high-proud' estimation of his wife (line 19) incites Tarquin as 'proud issue of a king' (line 37) to compete with his friend; Tarquin approaches Lucrece with a 'proud' hand (line 437) and with his passions in their 'pride' (lines 298, 432). Tarquin

---

[25] 'Feared' in this sense is a passive construction of the Elizabethan transitive use of 'to fear' someone in the sense of 'to fear for, fear something happening to' someone. Compare 'The King is sickly, weak, and melancholy | And his physicians fear him mightily' (*Richard III*, I. i. 137–8).

[26] See Peter Garnsey, *Ideas of Slavery from Aristotle to Augustine* (Cambridge: Cambridge University Press, 1996) 129–33.

feels pride doing what he knows will bring him shame without acknowledging the paradox, but Lucrece asserts the inevitable joining of 'pride' to 'shame'. Editors have claimed that the elided word in 'Thou loathèd in their shame, they [] in thy pride' should be understood as an opposite of 'loathèd' like 'admired' in order to preserve the pride–shame antithesis. Yet Tarquin and his passions could be 'loathèd' alike in conjoined pride and shame. The elision's ambiguity underscores that shame and pride are not only antithetical but also complementary. Lucrece echoes Proverbs 11:2, much cited in Renaissance England: 'When pride cometh, then cometh shame' (Geneva Bible, 1587).

The narrator himself later connects pride and shame: 'proud lords, to blame, | Make weak-made women tenants to their shame' (lines 1259–60). 'Proud' lords like Tarquin possess 'shame' but make women like Lucrece the 'tenants' or occupiers of such 'shame'; 'to blame' implies both that 'proud' lords 'are to blame' for their own 'shame' and that they use women 'in order to blame' women instead. The raped Lucrece will, however, seek to return 'shame' to its 'proud' male owner.

23.3 LUCRECE'S SHAME AND HEROIC RESOLUTION

The rape itself is obliquely described as an act of 'shame': 'Shame folded up in blind concealing night | When most unseen, then most doth tyrannize' (lines 675–6). The personification 'Shame' strikingly becomes both perpetrator and victim. Shame as tyrant evokes Tarquin, who has reduced himself to the lustful 'shame' that has mastered him and tyrannizes over Lucrece. 'Shame' 'folded up' in night evokes Lucrece the shamed victim, especially since the stanza ends by describing how Tarquin's gagging of her mouth, a grim metonymy for his forced penetration, 'Entombs her outcry in her lips' sweet fold' (line 679).

The poem's long middle section (lines 736–1582) reveals the psychological process by which the violated Lucrece comes to a suicidal resolve that in Shakespeare's sources appears simply as a result. With psychologically plausible vacillation and obsessive backtracking, Lucrece laboriously works through her shame and anger. By casting off bodily contamination through suicide, revealing Tarquin's crime, and ensuring her revenge, she will 'murder shameful scorn', recover 'honour' and good 'fame' from 'shame's ashes' (lines 1184–90), and make her shame revert to Tarquin: 'My shame be his that did my fame confound' (1202).

Lucrece repeatedly affirms her mind's and soul's purity while expressing a visceral sense of bodily 'shame'. The narrator describes her 'bear[ing] the load of lust' that Tarquin 'left behind' (line 734). She feels that 'load' in her 'spotted, spoiled, corrupted' (line 1172) body, such that she 'shames herself to see' (line 1084). In the culminating suicide scene, although the summoned Collatine and his male companions assure her that 'her mind untainted' 'clears' her 'body's stain', she acts on her conviction that suicide is the only way to escape Tarquin's 'compellèd stain' (lines 1708, 1710).

As if anticipating Christian strictures against suicide, Lucrece wonders in soliloquy whether she should commit 'soul's pollution' because of bodily contamination but concludes it cannot be 'impiety' to 'convey' her soul from her 'blemished' body (lines 1157, 1174–6). Her response to bodily shame would have found sympathetic readers among many of Shakespeare's Christian, but highly honour—and—shame conscious, contemporaries. Augustine condemned Lucretia in *City of God* (book 1, ch. 19) for committing suicide out of 'weakness of shame' ('pudoris infirmitas') and pagan love of 'praise' ('laudis') rather than relying on God and her moral innocence. This negative view finds occasional direct or indirect echo in Elizabethan publications: William Bullein in 1579 warns against her fall from 'shame' to 'dampnacion', William Tyndale, in a treatise republished in 1573, attacks her sense of 'honour' as sinful 'pride', while a French work translated in 1586, invoking Augustine's viewpoint while undermining it with honour-based snobbery, condemns her concern for 'common' people's 'opinions'.[27] More 16th-century texts, however, extol her 'virtue', 'fame', 'praise', and 'renowne'.[28] Some echo pseudo-Quintilian's argument that through suicide she separated her 'chaste soul' ('pudicus animus') from her 'polluted body' ('polluto corpore') and Saint Jerome's declaration that she exemplified 'chastity' ('pudicitia') by destroying her bodily 'stain' ('maculam').[29] In his oft-reprinted guide to womanhood, Vives (citing 'Quintilian') admires Lucrece's separation of her 'pure mynde' from her 'defiled body'; noting her 'staine', Robert Greene in 1592 similarly praises her severing her 'pure soule' from a 'defiled body'.[30]

Shakespeare also sympathetically represents Lucrece's decision as an assertion of freedom that turns this victim of 'helpless shame' (line 756) into the 'mistress' of her 'fate' (line 1069). She recalls famous Roman celebrations of suicide as escape from oppression to freedom.[31] Lucrece seizes the freedom that she earlier accuses 'opportunity', complicit

---

[27] Wiliam Bullein, *Bulleins Bulwarke of Defence* (London, 1579) 29^r; *Whole Workes of W. Tyndall, John Frith, and Doct. Barnes* (London, 1573) 113; and Matthieu Coignet, *Politique Discourses upon Trueth and Lying*, Edward Hoby (trans.), (London, 1586) 78.

[28] Richard Rainolde, *The Foundation of Rhetorike* (London, 1563) xxvi^r; Ulpian Fulwell, *The Flower of Fame* (London, 1575) 39^r; John Merbecke, *A Booke of Notes* (London, 1581) 167; Nicholas Breton, *A Small Handfull of Fragrant Flowers* (London, 1579) Aiii^v; Thomas Salter, *The Mirrhor of Modesite* (London, 1579) Biii^r; and Philip Sidney, *An Apology for Poetry* (1595), Forrest G. Robinson (ed.), (Indianapolis: Bobbs-Merrill, 1970) 20.

[29] Quintilian, *Declamationes XIX Maiores*, Georg Lehnert (ed.), (Leipzig: Teubner, 1905), 50 (3.11 [trans. mine]); Jerome, *Adversus Jovinianum* 1.46, 1.49 in *Patrologia Latina*, vol. 23 (1845) 275B, 282A.

[30] Vives (2002), 34; Robert Greene, *Greene's Vision* (London, 1592) G2^v. Ian Donaldson's acute analysis of tensions between 'Augustinian' and 'Roman' values in *Lucrece* too readily equates Augustine's views with Christian values generally and insufficiently registers the vitality of 'Roman' values within syncretic Elizabethan culture; see *The Rapes of Lucretia: A Myth and its Transformations* (Oxford: Clarendon Press, 1982) 40–56.

[31] See Catharine Edwards, *Death in Ancient Rome* (New Haven: Yale University Press, 2007) 100–12.

in her rape, of not providing: 'free[ing] that soul which wretchedness hath chained' (line 900). In the suicide scene, Lucrece tells Collatine and his companions that, trapped in her defiled body, she is 'not free' from her rapist's 'foul enforcement' (lines 1623–4). Giving new resonance to the widespread classical and Christian image of the body as the soul's prison, the narrator describes her suicide as freeing her soul from its 'polluted prison' (line 1726).[32]

Suicide frees her not only from what Tarquin has done to her body but also from shame for what she feels she had failed to do. Even as she declares her moral inno-cence, Lucrece dwells with both shame and exculpatory rhetoric upon her initial trust in Tarquin and upon how 'fear' of death and posthumous shame had precluded physi-cal resistance. She recalls not her brave attempt to dissuade but that she was 'afeared to scratch her wicked foe' (lines 1035–6); her post-rape 'tear[ing]' of her 'flesh' with her 'nails' (line 739) seems self-punishment for failing physically to resist Tarquin. She tells her husband and his companions, 'Mine enemy was strong, my poor self weak, | And far the weaker with so strong a fear' (lines 1646–7). She even retrospectively reduces her lengthy speeches of 'modest eloquence' to a mere 'cry' (line 1639) silenced by Tarquin. As rape victim, she seems to have been shamed into self-blame.[33] Yet the narrator also retrospectively misdescribes the rape as inflicted upon a 'weak-made' (line 1260) woman overcome by fear of 'present death, and shame' (line 1263) and by a 'dying fear' (line 1266) that precluded effective resistance.[34] Recalling Ovid's and Livy's silent Lucretias, overcome with fear, he awkwardly forgets his own eloquently resistant Lucrece.

Yet these misleading retrospective accounts of her supposed female weakness pro-vide a foil and spur to Lucrece's counter-assertion of a traditionally masculine cour-age that 'stoutly' (bravely) embraces death (line 1209) rather than 'fear[s] to die' (line 1052). Elizabethan texts praise soldiers' battlefield 'resolution'.[35] In a 1582 defense of women, George Whetstone declares Lucrece's heroic 'resolution' to die greater than any man's.[36] Appropriating the term to aggrandize erotic conquest, Shakespeare's Tarquin had declared, 'My will is backed with resolution' (line 352). Appropriating the term for herself, Lucrece declares her suicidal 'resolution' will turn Collatine's shame to honour: 'My resolution, love, shall be thy boast' (line 1193; compare line 1200). 'Resolution' can also mean 'death' (*OED* 3a); the pun underscores that, for Lucrece, heroic 'resolution' and death are one.

---

[32] See Pierre Courcelle, 'Tradition platonicienne et traditions chrétiennes du corps-prison (*Phédon* 62b; *Cratyle* 400c)', *Revue des études latines* 43 (1966): 406–43.

[33] See Dubrow (1987) 105–14.

[34] See Coppélia Kahn, *Roman Shakespeare: Warriors, Wounds and Women* (London: Routledge, 1997) 40–1.

[35] See Francesco Guicciardini, *The Historie*, Geoffrey Fenton (trans.), (London, 1579) 999; François de La Noue, *Politicke and Militarie Discourses*, E.A. (trans.), (London, 1588) 411; Robert Greene, *The Spanish Masquerado* (London, 1589) D1ʳ.

[36] George Whetstone, *An Heptameron of Civill Discourses* (London, 1582) Oivᵛ.

23.4 BRUTUS' PRIDE AND SHAME

The poem's final section (lines 1730–1855), Shakespeare's account of L. Junius Brutus' famous expulsion of the Tarquins, is controversial. Critics disagree as to whether the poem endorses Brutus' mode of 'revenge' (line 1841) for Lucrece's rape.[37] In Livy, Lucretia lets the men determine how to avenge her, in Ovid her corpse (grotesquely) seems to approve Brutus' plan. Shakespeare's Lucrece, by contrast, makes Collatine and his companions swear that 'the traitor' will 'die' with 'swift' (lines 1686, 1691) revenge. When Brutus, after taking charge from lamenting Collatine and devising a new oath, shows Lucrece's bleeding body to the Roman people and obtains their 'consent' to 'banishment' (lines 1854–5), he breaks the oath to Lucrece. Shakespeare thus highlights the discrepancy between Brutus' political action and Lucrece's ethical code.

Lucrece's 16th-century text, lacking possessive apostrophes, concludes with 'Tarquins foul offense' (line 1852) punished with 'Tarquins everlasting banishment' (line 1855): most editors treat 'Tarquins' in both phrases as the singular 'Tarquin's', describing the individual's punishment for his crime. Yet as in Ovid's and Livy's well-known accounts, in the prose argument to *Lucrece*, Brutus had 'the whole hated family of the Tarquins … all exiled' and founded the Roman republic. It thus seems more likely that the poem concludes with the collective 'Tarquins' everlasting banishment'.[38] The possible shifting sense of 'Tarquins' from singular to plural within three lines underscores how Brutus as political innovator deviates from Lucrece's wishes.

The poem suggests that Brutus' unfaithfulness to Lucrece is an appropriate political response to a collective crisis. Lucrece works through shame and anger by contemplating a depiction of Troy's fall. As an ekphrasis (traditional in epic) concerning the quintessential epic story, this Troy tableau underscores *Lucrece*'s epic

---

[37] In support of Brutus, see Annabel Patterson, *Reading Between the Lines* (Madison: University of Wisconsin Press, 1993) 305–10; against Brutus, see Dubrow, (1987) 129–30, qualified in Heather Dubrow, *Shakespeare and Domestic Loss: Forms of Deprivation, Mourning, and Recuperation* (Cambridge: Cambridge University Press, 1999) 59–61; and Oliver Arnold, *The Third Citizen: Shakespeare's Theater and the Early Modern House of Commons* (Baltimore: Johns Hopkins University Press, 2007) 124–7. Andrew Hadfield argues the poem leaves 'open' whether Lucrece's demands went 'too far' or Brutus not 'far enough' in *Shakespeare and Republicanism* (Cambridge: Cambridge University Press, 2005) 151–2.

[38] See Katherine Duncan-Jones and H. R. Woudhuysen (eds), *Shakespeare's Poems* (London: Thomson Learning, 2007) 383 (line 1855 and note). The prose argument (of uncertain authorship) is not a conclusive gloss to the poem because they diverge in several details. Critics have noted contrasting emphases: while the elegiac, Ovidian poem dramatizes Lucrece's suffering and the passions surrounding it, the political, Livian prose argument stresses the transition from Tarquin tyranny to republican consuls; see Catherine Belsey, 'Tarquin Dispossessed: Expropriation and Consent in *The Rape of Lucrece*', *Shakespeare Quarterly* 52 (2001): 320–2; Dubrow (1987) 160–2; and Burrow (2002) 48. Nevertheless, the poem's description of Roman 'consent' to Tarquin 'banishment' suggestively echoes the argument's claim that 'with one consent' the men swear to root out the Tarquins and that 'with one consent' all the Tarquins were 'exiled'.

ambitions. Yet while Lucrece elegiacally analogizes captured Troy to her own violated body, which she calls 'my Troy' (line 1547), Brutus reverses this personalizing process and enacts epic's grand historical perspective by generalizing Lucrece's shame as an instance of how Troy's successor, 'Rome herself', has been 'disgraced' by 'abominations' that include, but are not necessarily limited to, Lucrece's 'wrongs' (lines 1832–3, 1840). Confronting the Troy picture, Lucrece wishes for individual punishment for individual crime when she laments that Paris' 'lust' destroyed Troy rather than himself 'alone': 'For one's offence why should so many fall?' (lines 1473, 1480, 1483). Yet Lucrece's own shifting responses undercut her individual focus. Before castigating Paris, Lucrece decries 'the strumpet that began this stir', Helen, and imagines tearing Helen's 'beauty' with her 'nails' (lines 1471–2) just as Lucrece tore her own flesh with her 'nails' after the rape. Lucrece thus first expresses displaced aggression against her own shamed body before shifting blame to Paris in a displaced version of her ongoing effort to shift shame back to Tarquin. Furthermore, her closely following complaint that 'doting' King Priam should have 'checked' his son (line 1490) suggests an analogous partial responsibility of Tarquin's royal father for his son's deed.[39]

Brutus' banishment of the Tarquins rather than killing of the rapist betrays not only the original oath but also Lucrece's belief in virtuous monarchy and associated conception of her rapist as one who 'shame[d]' his royal lineage with 'deeds degenerate' (line 1003). Yet far from being 'degenerate', Shakespeare's Tarquin resembles his royal father: the oft-mentioned 'pride' in erotic conquest of this 'proud issue of a king' closely links him and his deed to his father Tarquin Superbus ('the Proud'), whom the poem's argument begins by noting earned his surname from the 'excessive pride' he displayed as violent usurper. The poem thus recalls Ovid's claim that young Tarquin was 'proles manifesta Superbi' ('proven scion of [Tarquin] the Proud', *Fasti* 2.691). Several English Renaissance writers argued Tarquin Superbus' 'pride' was the real cause of the Tarquins' exile and that Brutus exploited Lucrece's rape as mere 'occasion' or 'meanes'.[40] Shakespeare, however, links the son's lustful 'occasion' to his father's tyrannical 'pride'. Brutus' new government of 'consent' is presumably closer than fearful Tarquin tyranny to Lucrece's ideal of love-inspiring monarchy.[41]

Nevertheless, Brutus' prudent political focus on collective shame and redress reveals indifference not only to Lucrece's oath but also to the personal honour and shame upon

[39] Shakespeare secularizes a Virgilian motif. The major model for *Lucrece*'s ekphrasis is *Aeneid* 2's account of Troy's fall, in which Aeneas similarly tries but fails to find a solitary culprit: intervening when Aeneas is about to kill Helen as punishment, Venus asserts that neither Helen's face nor Paris, but rather the gods, have destroyed Troy (2.601–3). (Renaissance editions treat this passage, deemed spurious by some modern commentators, as authentic.)

[40] See Thomas Elyot, *The Boke named the Governour* (London, 1537) 107^{r-v}; John Carr, *The Ruinous Fal of Prodigalitie* (London, 1573) E2^v; Richard Beacon, *Solon his Follie* (Oxford, 1594) 73.

[41] On 'consent', see Belsey (2001), 333–5.

which Lucrece stakes her life and death. Lines 1807–16 underscore his disregard for
Lucrece's code and resemblances to shameful-and-proud Tarquin:

> Brutus ...
> Began to clothe his wit in state and pride,
> Burying in Lucrece' wound his folly's show.
> He with the Romans was esteemèd so
>   As silly jeering idiots are with kings,
>   For sportive words and utt'ring foolish things.
>
> But now he throws that shallow habit by
> Wherein deep policy did him disguise,
> And armed his long-hid wits advisedly.

In having allowed himself to be 'esteemed' a fool, Brutus the pragmatic survivor
accepted what Lucrece heroically spurned, 'shameful scorn'. Following Livy and
Dionysius, Marso's Ovid commentary describes how Brutus feigned idiocy to escape
persecution and how Tarquin Superbus made Brutus his children's companion for
their amusement; Costanzo's commentary echoes Livy's description of Brutus as object
of ridicule ('ludibrium').[42] While similarly describing how Brutus made himself a
laughing-stock, Shakespeare adds the comparison to the hired fool, common in both
ancient Rome and Renaissance courts, who is not only the 'silly' object but also 'jeer-
ing' perpetrator of mocking shame. Renaissance humanists associate such fools with
shameful indifference to shame: Desiderius Erasmus' *Adages* describes one who plays
the fool because he 'has discarded his sense of shame' ('depuduerit'); Erasmus' *Praise
of Folly* claims (in Thomas Chaloner's 1549 translation) 'shameless' fools 'blousshe at
nothing'; Thomas More attacks fools who mock others because of their own shame
('obprobrium').[43] The narrator underscores the shamefulness of Brutus' 'foolish' and
'sportive' past by echoing Lucrece's bitter description of her rape as Tarquin's 'time of
folly' and 'time of sport' (line 992).

Brutus' having disguised himself with a 'show' of folly out of 'policy' also disconcert-
ingly recalls Tarquin the rapist. Lucrece likens Tarquin's appearance as a friendly guest
to a deceitful 'show' (line 1507), and Tarquin himself invokes ends-justify-the-means
'policy' when trying to persuade Lucrece to clandestine sex: 'A little harm done to a
great good end' was, he claimed, 'lawful policy' (lines 528–9). Brutus' recovered 'pride'
sounds morally ambiguous and raises the question of how different his republic will be

---

[42] Ovid, *De Fastis, cum duobus commentariis: Antonii de Fano et Pauli Marsi* (Venice, 1502) LXX^r.
Cf. Livy, *Ab urbe condita* 1.56.

[43] Desiderius Erasmus, *Adagiorum Chilias Secunda*, in *Opera Omnia*, vols. 2–3, M. Szymanski
(ed.), (Amsterdam: North-Holland Publishing Company, 2005) 326 (no. 1311, trans. mine); Desiderius
Erasmus, *The Praise of Folie*, Thomas Chaloner (trans.), Clarence H. Miller (ed.), (London: Oxford
University Press, 1965) 36–7; and Thomas More, *The Yale Edition of The Complete Works of St. Thomas
More: Volume 3, Part II, Latin Poems*, Clarence H. Miller (ed.), Leicester Bradner, and Charles A. Lynch
(New Haven: Yale University Press, 1984) 652–3.

from 'proud' Tarquin tyranny. The poem hints that Brutus as liberator is again using Tarquin-like ends-justify-the-means 'policy' by breaking his original oath and exploiting Lucrece's shame for political ends, however laudable.

23.5 GOLDEN-AGE BLUSHES

Brutus' pride and shame suggest that the emergent Roman republic, while superior to Tarquin tyranny, may be fundamentally flawed. Against this picture of a degraded masculine political sphere, two passages stand out as nostalgic laments for an ancient past of honourable shamefastness associated with feminine power. The narrator describes Tarquin's first glimpse of Lucrece's face as a mixture of beauty and virtue. Her red 'blushes' are initially associated with 'beauty', her 'white' skin with 'virtue' or sexual purity (lines 55–6), but

> Then virtue claims from beauty beauty's red,
> Which virtue gave the golden age to gild
> Their silver cheeks, and called it then their shield;
>> Teaching them thus to use it in the fight:
>> When shame assailed, the red should fence the white
>
> (lines 59–63)

This puzzling figurative passage describes Lucrece's virtuous blushing as a 'shield' or defense to 'fence' or protect her 'white' virtue whenever 'shame assailed'. In classical and Renaissance writing, women's blushes proclaim shamefastness. Whetstone in 1582 claims women are 'graced' with 'shamfast blushing', while Thomas Cooper's oft-reprinted Elizabethan Latin dictionary translates Virgilian and Ovidian descriptions of 'shamefast blushing in maydens' and a 'shamefaste' woman's 'blushynge cheekes'.[44] Shakespeare's description of such blushing as a 'shield' recalls the claims of moralists like Tilney and La Primaudaye that a woman's shamefastness provides the best defense of her sexual honour. In the context of Tarquin's lustful gaze, the phrase 'when shame assailed', suggests that virtuous blushing defends specifically against males' shameful assaults.

Shakespeare creatively re-imagines the myth of a golden age, however, to suggest that women's shamefastness protected them from sexual predation only in an ideal past. According to Ovid's *Metamorphoses,* golden-age humans behaved morally without law or fear of punishment, while in the current iron age 'pudor' (Golding's 'honest shame') has fled the earth (*Metamorphoses* 1.90–3, 129; Golding 1.147). Here 'pudor' or shamefastness apparently comes between a golden age of spontaneous virtue and a present of

---

[44] Whetstone (1582) E4ᵛ; Thomas Cooper, *Thesaurus Linguae Romanae et Brittanicae* (London, 1565) RRRtt4ᵛ, Hhh2ᵛ. See also White (1981) 405.

shameless vice. Shakespeare probably recalls, however, the less well-known description of the golden age in Ovid's *Fasti*, *Lucrece*'s major source. *Fasti* 1.251 draws on a traditional moral distinction to claim that people of the golden age were governed by 'pudor' rather than fear, that is, fear of shame rather than of punishment.[45] During the 'golden age' feminine blushing would have been an effective 'shield' against shameful advances because shamefastness governed both sexes. While Lucrece's face recalls this 'golden age', Shakespeare expects readers to realize immediately (as she does not) that her 'shield' will not protect her against Tarquin's violence.

After Lucrece's rape, Shakespeare introduces a second shamefast blushing figure as a 'pattern' (moral example) of the 'worn-out' (i.e. bygone) 'age' (line 1350). Four seemingly digressive stanzas describe Lucrece's interactions with the 'groom' (line 1345) who delivers her letter summoning Collatine home. 'Blushing on' Lucrece, the groom silently receives her missive and delivers it with 'bashful innocence' (lines 1339, 1341).

With blushes recalling the 'golden age' Lucrece of the opening, this groom challenges conventional gender roles. His lauded silence is an extreme version of the ideal of feminine silence and moderate speech. Shakespeare underscores the overturning of gender expectations by placing Lucrece's encounter with the groom immediately after her interactions with her maid, who gives Lucrece a 'demure' greeting, speaks with 'modesty', and humbly asks to 'be so bold' as to ask the cause of Lucrece's distress (lines 1219–20, 1282). The groom's silent deference outdoes even such exemplary feminine modesty.

The dutiful groom also challenges hierarchical social values. The narrator's praise ostentatiously overturns his ironic denigration of the groom as 'silly'—both 'humble' and 'foolish'—and of his blushing silence as a 'defect' (deficiency) of 'bold audacity' (lines 1345–6). Lack of boldness makes this lowly, quasi-feminized figure a positive counter to the royal rapist Tarquin. The groom's sense of duty, his 'true respect | To talk in deeds' rather than empty 'words' (lines 1347–8, 1351), pointedly contrasts with Tarquin's rejection of his own dictum that 'True valour' should have 'true respect' for the honourable and his consequent refusal to heed Lucrece's plea that such 'true respect' should bridle immoral 'desire' (lines 201, 642).

This groom also sharply differs from the 'rascal groom' (line 671; cf. line 1632) with whom royal Tarquin threatened to shame Lucrece on trumped-up charges of downwardly mobile adultery. While Tarquin imagines a 'worthless slave' (line 515), the narrator describes this 'groom' with pointed anachronism not as a Roman slave but as a 'duteous vassal' (line 1360) or faithful feudal retainer and deploys affective language that evokes a free but devoted servant. Classical and Renaissance authors regarded slaves as fearing punishment but devoid of shame, which was a privilege of free persons who could choose honourable or shameful action. Primaudaye cites Quintilian: 'shamefastnes is

---

[45] Marso glosses Ovid's 'fear' ('metu') as fear of punishment in Ovid (1502), XVIʳ. Aristotle's *Nicomachean Ethics* 10.9.4 influentially treats 'aidos' as nobler than fear of punishment; cf. Primaudaye (1586), 264–5. Cf. Horace's celebration of a new golden age of 'ancient' ('priscus') 'pudor' (*Carmen Saeculare*, lines 57–89).

the propertie of a free man, and feare of a bondman'.[46] Protestant attacks upon 'servile fear' of God's punishment underscore slavery's association with fear. The groom's silent blushing exhibits shamefastness, and his 'sour-faced' visage (suggesting non-flattering asperity) (line 1334), 'steadfast' eye (betokening a 'steadfast' spirit) (line 1339), and 'honest' (honourable, upright, candid) 'looks' (line 1351) all reveal him to be no cowering slave.

Lucrece's blushing interaction with her blushing gloom pointedly diverges from a model in Ovid's *Metamorphoses*:

> His kindled duty kindled her mistrust,
> That two red fires in both their faces blazed.
> She thought he blushed as knowing Tarquin's lust,
> And blushing with him, wistly on him gazed.
> Her earnest eye did make him more amazed.
>   The more she saw the blood his cheeks replenish,
>   The more she thought he spied in her some blemish.
>
> (lines 1352–8)

Lucrece recalls Byblis, who with shame ('pudibunda', *Metamorphoses* 9.568) gives a letter conveying her 'shame' (Golding 9.646) to a male domestic for delivery. As befits his servile status, the Ovidian slave is terrified ('pavidum', *Metamorphoses* 9.569) by his mistress's evident shame and what it might portend for him. Shakespeare's contrasting description of the groom's blushing as a 'kindled duty' that 'blazed' upon his face adapts the fire imagery used more conventionally earlier in the poem to figure the intensity of erotic love—Tarquin's 'hot-burning will' (line 247) and 'fire' (line 355) for Lucrece, Paris' 'heat of lust' that Helen 'kindled' (lines 1473, 1475)—in order to underscore that the groom feels not fear but an intense, loving, shamefast reverence for his mistress, what Lucrece earlier had celebrated as 'fear for love'. Yet Lucrece's blushing misconstrual of the groom's blushes—which makes him 'amazed' (bewildered), deepens his blush, and thus fuels her increasing shame—reveals his anachronism. The comedy and tragedy of errors in this scene of mutual blushing incomprehension is that the violated Lucrece, blushing with shame, comes face to face with, but no longer recognizes, a mirror of her former self, blushing with golden-age shamefastness.

A contemporaneous epic model-foil for this scene further underscores how shame prevents Lucrece from recognizing her former virtue: Guyon's gently humorous encounter with Shamefastness in Spenser's *Faerie Queen* (Book 2, canto 9, stanzas 40–44).[47] Guyon, the knight of temperance, encounters a silent, 'bashful' woman 'blushing' and 'abasht for shame' who is too modest to reply to Guyon's inquiry regarding her

---

[46] Primaudaye (1586), 265. See C. A. Barton, *Roman Honor: The Fire in the Bones* (Berkeley: University of California Press, 2001) 227; and Robert A. Kaster, *Emotion, Restraint, and Community in Ancient Rome* (Oxford: Oxford University Press, 2005) 23–4, 160 n3.

[47] Spenser (1977) 255.

identity. When he is informed by 'Alma' (the temperate soul) that 'You shamefast are, but *Shamefastnesse* it selfe is she', he blushes himself in modest 'privitie'. Spenser's blush-fest depicts Guyon's blushing, shamefast acquisition of self-knowledge; Shakespeare depicts Lucrece's blushing, shamed failure here to recognize the shamefastness she has lost.

While humbly fulfilling his social role, the loving, shamefast messenger challenges the moral validity of the elite male order of the Tarquins and Brutus alike, with its degraded coupling of pride and shame. He might partially be an allegory for Shakespeare as author, serving as Lucrece's respectful messenger to us. Yet he is such an anachronism of a 'worn-out age' that only the narrator, and the appreciative reader, can recognize his surprising worth.

SELECT BIBLIOGRAPHY

Arnold, Oliver (2007) *The Third Citizen: Shakespeare's Theater and the Early Modern House of Commons* (Baltimore: Johns Hopkins University Press).

Belsey, Catherine (2001) 'Tarquin Dispossessed: Expropriation and Consent in *The Rape of Lucrece*', *Shakespeare Quarterly* 52 : 315–35.

Burrow, Colin (2002) (ed.) William Shakespeare. *Complete Sonnets and Poems* (Oxford: Oxford University Press).

Donaldson, Ian (1982) *The Rapes of Lucretia: A Myth and its Transformations* (Oxford: Clarendon Press) 40–56.

Dubrow, Heather (1987) *Captive Victors: Shakespeare's Narrative Poems and Sonnets* (Ithaca: Cornell University Press).

—— (1999) *Shakespeare and Domestic Loss: Forms of Deprivation, Mourning, and Recuperation* (Cambridge: Cambridge University Press).

Duncan-Jones, Katherine, and H.R. Woodhuysen (2007) (eds) *Shakespeare's Poems* (London: Thomson Learning, 2007).

Hadfield, Andrew (2005) *Shakespeare and Republicanism* (Cambridge: Cambridge University Press).

Kahn, Coppélia (1997) *Roman Shakespeare: Warriors, Wounds and Women* (London: Routledge).

Maus, Katharine Eisaman (1986). 'Taking Tropes Seriously: Language and Violence in Shakespeare's *Rape of Lucrece*', *Shakespeare Quarterly* 37 : 66–82.

Patterson, Annabel (1993) *Reading Between the Lines* (Madison: University of Wisconsin Press).

Roe, John (2006) (ed.) William Shakespeare. *Complete Sonnets* (Cambridge: Cambridge University Press).

CHAPTER 24

....

THE SONNETS IN
THE CLASSROOM

*Student, Teacher, Editor-Annotator(s),
and Cruxes*[1]

....

DAVID SOFIELD

Remarking, unremarkably, that 'at least half of Shakespeare's allusions are unfamiliar, and many senses, puns and proverbial usages have been completely lost', Don Paterson states that it is 'far simpler to go in with a native guide' than to explore the Sonnets unaided. He offers his services. Helen Vendler's admonition is dire: 'Perhaps total immersion in the Sonnets—that is to say, in Shakespeare's mind—is a mildly deranging experience to anyone'.[2] Some readers of this chapter may have encountered a 'mildly deranged' student paper on the Sonnets, may, as undergraduates, have produced their own examples. The Sonnets do seem to lend themselves to critical make-believe.[3] It could be

---

[1] Apologies for the ungainly, but accurate, title. For wise counsel, thanks to Paul Alpers, Carl Atkins, Peter Berek, Anston Bosman, Ingrid Nelson, and William Pritchard.

[2] Don Paterson, *Reading Shakespeare's Sonnets: A New Commentary* (London: Faber and Faber, 2010) xviii; Helen Vendler, *The Art of Shakespeare's Sonnets* (Cambridge, MA: Harvard University Press, 1997) 1. Although both offer modernized texts of the poems, neither of these books is a critical edition; they command our attention by the usefulness of their commentaries. That usefulness has been challenged, Paterson himself—rising to climactic italics (as when emotion too far exceeds its cause)—contending that 'There is a hidden threshold in the poem, a point past which you go on insightfully identifying things *that are not there*, and *The Art of Shakespeare's Sonnets* saw Vendler cross it'. (Paterson, xx.) Alistair Fowler, in turn, has at Paterson's book in the *Times Literary Supplement* (14 January 2010); Paterson responds in kind in a 28 June 2010 letter in the *TLS*.

[3] And to over-confident assertion: as Jonathan Bate puts it, 'the sonnets have an extraordinary capacity to elicit categorical statements from their interpreters'. In Harold Bloom and Brett Foster (eds), *The Sonnets* (New York: Bloom's Literary Criticism, 2008) 309. *Caveat lector.*

argued that a student can best learn the difficult lessons that have to be learned about engaging early modern texts by proceeding *unguided*, or guided by no more than an instructor's preliminary map of the terrain, but experience has inclined me to endorse Paterson's advice.

There is no shortage of available cicerones. The rapidly multiplying editions of the Sonnets give one pause before choosing the reading text for a class. In the post-Rollins era alone, the list of modernized editions with extensive annotations is formidable: Ingram and Redpath (1964), Wilson (1966), Booth (extensive and then some, 1977), Kerrigan (1986), Evans (1996), Duncan-Jones (1997), and Burrow (2002).[4] These seven editions are the source of Michael Schoenfeldt's claim that 'the most significant and substantial scholarly engagements with the sonnets over the last several years have been editorial'. John Kerrigan takes that a step further: 'it is arguable that the sonnet as a form—with its densities and ellipses enforced by close patterning, and its structural modifications of ostensible meaning—most aptly finds resolution in a critical apparatus'.[5] Something like a consensus, handsomely articulated by Stephen Orgel,[6] may be settling for now on favouring Colin Burrow's Oxford World's Classics edition as the most balanced, indeed in its 'Introduction' and annotation the wisest, in print. Were I teaching in the near future a Shakespeare seminar for undergraduate majors (the 'classroom' posited in the title of this essay), one in which, say, the first three weeks would be devoted to the sonnets before moving on to three or four of the plays, Burrow would be the choice.[7]

In order to demonstrate what is at stake when editors modernize this or that sonnet differently, an hour or two could, I will argue should, be spent on examining a small handful of textual dilemmas. No-one now disagrees with a description of the 1609 Quarto as a reasonably 'good' text; compared with the quarto texts of a number

---

[4] A second group, published in the same decades, offers modernized texts and interpretive annotations while foregoing sustained textual commentary: Orgel, Mowat, and Werstine, and the Bate and Rasmussen RSC edition. Vendler and Paterson only occasionally address textual matters. The Wells and Taylor Oxford edition is the result of intensive textual study, although it is not annotated. Seymour-Smith's 1963 and Willen and Reed's 1964 editions present 1609, unemended, in modern typography and with abundant interpretive notes. Carl Atkins likewise prints 1609 but considers in detail selected textual problems. All in all, a rich, late harvest. For the proposed seminar, the choice lies among Booth's edition, in print from 1977, and the most recently published editions that, although not as comprehensively as Booth, address textual as well as interpretive matters: Evans, Duncan-Jones, and Burrow. (*See* Select Bibliography at the end of this chapter for full details of all references cited in this note).

[5] Michael Schoenfeldt (ed.), *A Companion to Shakespeare's Sonnets*. (Malden: Blackwell Publishing Ltd, 2007), 2; John Kerrigan (ed.), *The Sonnets and A Lover's Complaint* (Harmondsworth: Penguin Books, Ltd., 1986) 167. In another venue Schoenfeldt, speaking of the opacity of certain of the sonnets, writes, 'Perhaps this chronic inscrutability is why editing has proven to be such a rich area of inquiry for recent scholarly engagements with the sonnets'. (In Patrick Cheney (ed.), *The Cambridge Companion to Shakespeare's Poetry* (Cambridge: Cambridge University Press, 2007) 125.)

[6] In Schoenfeldt (2007) 137–44.

[7] A further word on the level of preparation desired (in some colleges, required): (1) a course in Shakespeare's plays and (2) an introductory course in reading lyric poetry.

of the plays, to say nothing of those of a contemporary 'manuscript poet' like John Donne, a better than good one. There remain, nonetheless, more than a few significant local problems. The suggestion here is that, selecting three poems for an eighty- or ninety-minute class, an instructor provides students with the textual and critical annotations of a range of editors. A course packet including that range would be in order. One recognizes that a single undergraduate class session on editorial problems is necessarily not what a graduate seminar solely devoted to textual editing would comprise.

Sonnets 16, 23, and 147 are candidates, each presenting a teachable representative crux. Yes, among the poems most frequently anthologized,[8] 129, 146, and a handful of others more famously contain cruxes (generously aired, all of them), the single insoluable one in the sequence occurring in 146. But because in a later class one might well choose to teach 129 and 146, both among the most important in the sequence, the specified three poems, each offering something more than merely bibliographical interest, should serve nicely. What is envisioned, then, is assigning as required reading *all* the sonnets, briefly noting such widely debated matters as (1) whether one should credit the 1609 order as authorial;[9] (2) the dating of sub-sequences on the stylometric evidence of vocabulary that overlaps the plays, themselves roughly datable; and (3) the belated moment, and radical substance, of Shakespeare's published contribution to the run of Elizabethan sonnet sequences that *Astrophil and Stella* began. (The avoidance of biographical questions is deliberate.) So, a first session introducing the sonnet, and then the Sonnets, centering on a close reading of one of the principal examples, followed by a class on such textual matters as are here explored, and then two weeks on whichever canonical, or non-canonical, sonnets the instructor chooses.[10]

24.1 SONNET 16

This poem may be best known for its ninth line. Eighty years ago, the virtuosic young William Empson convinced some of his readers that the phrase 'lines of life' could be

---

[8] For example, in *The Oxford Book of English Verse* (Oxford: Oxford University Press, 1999) Christopher Ricks, choosing eleven of the sonnets, omits all three. Offering fifty-two sonnets, *The Norton Anthology of English Literature* (Stephen Greenblatt and M H. Abrams (eds), New York: W. W. Norton, 2006.) prints 23 and 147, though not 16.

[9] Noting that an imposing team of recent editors—Kerrigan, Duncan-Jones, Vendler, and Burrow— agree, Margaret Healy is the latest to endorse the view that Shakespeare is responsible for the received order of the sonnets. (*Shakespeare, Alchemy and the Creative Imagination: The Sonnets and a Lover's Complaint,* Cambridge: Cambridge University Press, 2011, 5.)

[10] In 'Making the *Sonnets* Matter in the Classroom' Schoenfeldt sets out one sensible, unexceptionable outline of such classes. (In Patrick Cheney and Anne Lake Prescott, (eds), *Approaches to Teaching Shorter Elizabethan Poetry*. New York: Modern Language Association of America, 2000, 239–44.)

understood in seven distinct ways.[11] Ingram and Redpath rephrase Empson's contributions and proceed to add three more, citing first and subsequent occurrences in each instance.[12] Booth adds still another in the 1978 printing of his edition. Our recent annotators are more sparing, Orgel, who offers multiple glosses to many words and phrases, providing but one, 'family lineage'.

Notwithstanding this exuberance, it is not difficult to see why Sonnet 16 has been somewhat neglected. Vendler and Paterson alike hasten through it. No-one speaks of 16 the way Barbara Everett does of the more effective paired poem preceding it: 'Sonnet 15 begins with a new free and soaring flight, "When I consider everything that grows", and ends "I engraft you new", as if the poet were a gardening God Almighty, a maker of men in rhyme'.[13] (She might have added that the ringing iambic pentameter of the final line only heightens the effect.) Picking up 15's central horticultural metaphor—'everything that grows … men as plants increase … vaunt in their youthful sap'—16 in its second quatrain proceeds to belabour it in a way that to the modern ear sounds at best coy. Paul Hammond condemns the quatrain as 'in all respects bathetic'.[14] Acknowledging that such figures of speech must have been more attractive in the 1590s does not much help. Moreover, it has become commonplace to charge the first seventeen sonnets with 'casual misogyny'. Stephen Greenblatt, commenting on the conclusion of 15, writes that even as the poet presents the argument to marry and have children, he 'brings forth another, one that manifestly means more to him and that fulfills the fantasy of perfect, female-free reproduction'.[15] The reproduction that will thematically dominate the sonnets soon enough is of course the eternal youth that, as the poet correctly claims, his very poems will confer on the forever nameless fair young man. Compounding the patriarchalism here is the fact—at least for Andrew Gurr it is a fact—that 16 addresses its male auditor as the more intimate, less 'literary', 'you', rather than the 'thou' that prevails in the first twelve poems.[16]

---

[11] William Empson, *Seven Types of Ambiguity* 3rd edn (London: Chatto and Windus, 1953) 54–7. Duncan-Jones terms Empson's performance 'perhaps over-elaborate' (1997; 142). Referring to Robert Graves and Laura Riding, 'William Shakespeare and E. E. Cummings', in *A Survey of Modernist Poetry* (London: W. Heinemann Ltd, 1927), Empson himself credits Graves as 'the inventor of the method of analysis' he employs in *Seven Types* (xiv).

[12] W. G. Ingram and Theodore Redpath, (eds), *Shakepeare's Sonnets*. (London: University of London Press, 1964) 64.

[13] Barbara Everett, 'Shakespeare and the Elizabethan Sonnet', *London Review of Books* (8 May 2008): 15.

[14] Paul Hammond, *The Reader and Shakespeare's Young Man Sonnets* (Totowa, NJ: Barnes & Noble, 1981) 25. Sonnet 15 has been more than ably addressed in Booth's *An Essay on Shakespeare's Sonnets* (New Haven, CT: Yale University Press, 1969), Anne Ferry's *All in War with Time: Love Poetry of Shakespeare, Donne, Jonson, Marvell* (Cambridge, MA: Harvard University Press, 1975), and Patrick Cheney's *Shakespeare, National Poet-Playwright* (New York: Cambridge University Press, 2004).

[15] Stephen Greenblatt, *Will in the World* (New York: W.W. Norton, 2004) 237.

[16] Andrew Gurr, 'You and Thou in Shakespeare's Sonnets', *Essays in Criticism* 3 (1982): 9–25. Lynne Magnusson has a different take on matters pronominal in Sonnets 13–25. 'Surprisingly, this emerging "I" … shifts his pronoun of address, at least temporarily, to the more *deferential* "you" (Sonnets 13, 15, 16, and 17)'. (Italics added.) By sonnet 25 '"thou"—pretty clearly here the "thou" of intimacy—replaces the "you" of deference'. (Magnusson, in Mowat and Werstine (2009) 633–4.)

Here, unemended, is the poem as printed in 1609; the long 's' has been shortened.

> Bvt wherefore do not you a mightier waie
> Make warre vppon this bloudie tirant time?
> And fortifie your selfe in your decay
> With meanes more blessed then my barren rime?
> Now stand you on the top of happie houres,
> And many maiden gardens yet vnset,
> With virtuous wish would beare your liuing flowers,
> Much liker then your painted counterfeit:
> So should the lines of life that life repaire
> Which this (Times pensel or my pupill pen)
> Neither in inward worth nor outward faire
> Can make you liue your selfe in eies of men,
> > To giue away your selfe, keeps your selfe still,
> > And you must liue drawne by your owne sweet skill,[17]

Initial lessons are ready to hand: the many words, all common still, spelled differently; the rhetorical, rather than grammatical, comma at the end of line 6; the then-frequent colon rather than a modernizer's period or semi-colon closing the second quatrain; the sentence-ending comma concluding line 12; the careless compositorial comma closing, but not closing, the poem. Line 10 is another matter. Modernizers wrestle with it, and so they should, since a fundamental matter of interpretation is at stake.

Sonnet 16's third quatrain begins as a number of the sonnets' couplets do, with a confident 'So': so, given that these many maiden gardens, which I have just enjoyed imagining, wish (*virtuously* wish, a relief) only that you plant your seed in one of them, get to work. Doing that, having children, extending your lineage, will 'repair' your life, as nothing else could do. The first words of line 10, though, set in motion a lengthy discussion in the 'Preface' to Booth's edition. Although 'that life' appears to be the clear enough referent of 'which', as Booth acknowledges, he worries it for a paragraph. But that is nothing compared with the possibilities that lie in 'this'. Nearly every one of our editors addresses this 'this'. For them, it comes to a choice between *this poem* and *this time's pencil or my pupil pen*, the difference of course having a significant effect on how one reads the entire quatrain. For a reader in the 21st century, 'this time's pencil' offers immediately available sense—although Atkins argues that removing the parentheses 'tends to increase the ambiguity of the line rather than clarify it'.[18] A distinguished subset of our editors cancels the 1609 parentheses: Booth, not mentioning that as long ago as 1714 Charles Gildon had omitted them, is joined by Wells and Taylor, Kerrigan, Evans, Vendler, Mowat and Werstine, and, perhaps surprisingly, Burrow. Surprisingly because in his retrospective essay titled 'Editing the Sonnets'

---

[17] Booth (1977) and Vendler (1997) provide photographic reproductions of 1609. Except when reproducing 16, 23, and 147 in the 1609 text, I quote from Burrow's edition (2002).

[18] Atkins (2007) 63.

Burrow writes that he 'retained some of the more prominent aspects of Q's punctuation (brackets in particular) since I felt that these were less likely to be compositorial than the colons and stops which routinely fall at the end of quatrains and which may reflect mechanical compositorial expectations about the shape of the Shakespearean sonnet'.[19] Among our modernizing editors, Ingram and Redpath, Duncan-Jones (who, albeit to the same effect, replaces the parentheses with commas), Orgel, Bate and Rasmussen, and Paterson retain the 1609 parentheses. The emended punctuation—or lack of it, in this case—preferred by Booth changes the sense. For him and his descendents, 'this' is a demonstrative adjective, *this* time's pencil, not that of another time.

Macdonald Jackson observes that 'all but five of the forty-two parentheses in the Sonnets occur within numbers 26–98', from which one is tempted to infer that the brackets in 16 were likely in the copy text, whatever authority *it* may be said to have.[20] It has a great deal of authority, to be sure, for Duncan-Jones, who considers 1609 probably authorial, the punctuation, to an unspecified extent, apparently included.[21] But we may not be finished with line 10's 'this'. If one were inclined not to follow the modernizers who cancel the parentheses, the question of 'this' *what* remains. This sonnet? It has been thus glossed by many, and not unreasonably (*pace* Kerrigan). One hesitates to propose yet another reading, but it is not clear that 'this' does not refer to this *portrait*, the 'painted counterfeit' executed by one who wields a 'pencil', the kind of fine paintbrush used by Elizabethan portraitists. In his introductory paraphrase of the poem Wilson is explicit about the painting, calling it 'that portrait you have just had painted'.[22] Time, the bloody tyrant, as it were allows a contemporary artist to wield the pencil, but to wield it futilely, since time will incessantly decay 'you', *is* incessantly decaying you, thereby rendering the painter's effort constantly obsolete. The clock cannot be stopped. What is more, *my* means of keeping you alive in the eyes of men, these very poems written with my 'pupil pen'—which devises only barren rhyme—is equally ineffective, compared with your reproducing yourself biologically. This reading of line 10's 'or' as indicating, as usually in Shakespeare, an alternative, excludes the sense that here it means 'that is to say'.[23]

[19] In Schoenfeldt (2007) 159.
[20] Macdonald Jackson, 'Punctuation and the Compositors of Shakespeare's Sonnets, 1609', *The Library*. Fifth Series, 30: 1 (March 1975) 13.
[21] Her words: 'The "book" sold to Thorpe may have taken the form either of an autograph manuscript or of an authorially corrected scribal transcript' (41). 'In wording, format and punctuation, Q has been followed more closely than in any previous edition' (103).
[22] John Dover Wilson, (ed.), *The Sonnets*, 2nd edn (Cambridge: Cambridge University Press, 1967) 112. Defending his emendation of line 10—'Which this (Time's pencil) or my pupil pen'—Wilson writes, 'in Q the compositor has carelessly carried the second arm of the bracket to the end of the line' (113). An attractive notion, this, but the line makes good sense unchanged.
[23] See Atkins (2007) 64. Atkins also argues, with a handful of others, that the 'picture is a metaphor for the poem' (64). But why replace what may be understood directly and literally with a figurative sense? The poem gives us two representations of the young man: a painted counterfeit *and* a poem. Shakespeare reprises the vocabulary of art in the final line: 'And you must live *drawn* by your own sweet skill'. (Italics added.) As, in drawing you, the portraitist and I have both failed to bestow permanence on you, you must draw yourself by creating a child.

Two objections to this reading come to mind. First, the proposed referent of 'this', 'your painted counterfeit', rather than being what directly follows in appositional parentheses, is distanced by the intervening ninth line, even if line 9 contains nothing to which 'this' could refer. Second, that referent is at the end of the preceding closed quatrain; now we are in the second line of the next one. Nonetheless, because it may solve more problems than it raises, the reading here suggested may be worth the consideration of future editors and critics. What critics have taken pleasure in agreeing on is that Shakespeare enhances the reproductive argument by punning on 'pen'/penis, more than one of them naming as the 'sweet skill' that ends the poem the young man's (hetero)sexual prowess.

Although she will have been exposed to the issues and solutions here presented, a young student is likely to want to settle, however tentatively, on one of the available versions of a modernized Sonnet 16. Unlike Duncan-Jones, Burrow takes 1609 to be itself a text in its accidentals mediated (like the quarto texts and indeed the First Folio text of the plays) by both scribes and compositors, an early modern author commonly expecting that the punctuation and spelling would be supplied by the printing house.[24] Thus, Burrow states, 'there is nothing wicked in presenting a text which is mediated by modernized spelling and punctuation'.[25] Yet it does remain the responsibility of the instructor to set before a class the evident fact that, like critics, editors—those who modernize and those who do not, those whose annotations are textual or interpretive or both—shape and mean to shape one's experience of a poem. A student thereby begins to appreciate how particular to its historical moment any text necessarily is; in the process she also learns that what she might have assumed a four hundred-year-old poem to be, the words and punctuation she read in a high school textbook, both is and is not those words and punctuation. Proposing a possible new solution to a crux is a desirable, and inevitable, part of the ongoing effort to come to terms with an Elizabethan text.

24.2 SONNET 23

This poem presents a different kind of challenge, one arising not from punctuation but from a possible error caused by so small a matter as a single-letter foul-case substitution or a compositor misreading that letter in his copy text. From 1609 again:

> As an vnperfect actor on the stage,
> Who with his feare is put besides his part,
> Or some fierce thing repleat with too much rage,
> Whose strengths abondance weakens his owne heart;
> So I for feare of trust, forget to say,

---

[24] Ben Jonson's *Workes* (1616) is the most notable exception, the author having overseen its production.

[25] In Schoenfeldt (2007) 159.

> The perfect ceremony of loues right,
> And in mine owne loues strength seeme to decay,
> Ore-charg'd with burthen of mine owne loues might:
> O let my books be then the eloquence,
> And domb presagers of my speaking brest,
> Who pleade for loue, and look for recompence,
> More then that tonge that more hath more exprest.
>   O learne to read what silent loue hath writ,
>   To heare wit eies belongs to loues fine wiht.

Notwithstanding the weird, unconvincing 'fierce thing' of line 3—what Vendler calls Shakespeare's 'elated variety of invention'[26] gone awry?—this is a more effective poem than is Sonnet 16. After laying on an inoffensive example of what Orgel terms her 'occasional terrifying diagrams',[27] Vendler may overstate the quality of the octave—'one of Shakespeare's most memorable psychological summations'—but her reading of the couplet is masterful.

> The frustrating speechlessness of the lover ... has suddenly found a way of talking by deviating into the third person in the surprising and beautiful final line: *To hear with eyes belongs to love's fine wit.* This is a new-coined 'proverb' invented by the lover, impersonal in its third-person phraseology ... The conclusiveness of impersonal epigrammatic utterance has just that happiness of the *trouvaille* that enables the speaker to forget his shyness and cap his plea with his 'proverb'.[28]

The line, then, enacts the very wit it names, Vendler's response serving as a model of resourceful close reading for one's students.

Like 16, the poem is (eventually) directly addressed to the young man, but in a radically different tone. Where 16 attempts to advise, or at the least to reason with, the poem's 'you', in 23 the speaker, his heart too full for speech, pleads that the beloved recognize the authenticity of his love, an authenticity inherent in its stated desperation. Sonnet 23 is what Schoenfeldt calls a 'near-oxymoron', a love poem: 'there is a tension in all love poetry between the abandonment that emotional commitment requires and the self-conscious control that verse induces', metered and rhymed verse above all.[29] As a love poem, 23 deploys the well-worn, perhaps worn-through topos of claiming that being unable to speak one's love is the surest sign of its existence. Paul Edmondson and Stanley Wells direct us to the most memorable instance in literature. In 23, 'like Cordelia, Shakespeare points us to the "nothing" of his "silent love" (that is his inability to express love's inexpressibility) instead of some great

---

[26] Vendler (1997) 12.
[27] In Schoenfeldt (2007) 143.
[28] Vendler (1997) 138, 140.
[29] Michael Schoenfeldt, *The Cambridge Introduction to Shakespeare's Poetry* (Cambridge: Cambridge University Press, 2010) 17.

speech'.[30] The force of the poem, though, may lie less in this conventional thematic than in the way the speaker turns, in a volta with a vengeance, from the meditative third-person talking-to-himself octave to the prominently signalled vocatives that open both the third quatrain and the couplet. You *must* do what I ask of you because, in a word, my feeling is imperative. 'O let … O learn'. Gurr makes a fine point when he writes that 'the poem is the only sonnet which is clearly addressed to the young man … and which employs neither "thou" nor "you" nor any of their cognate forms. The perfect ceremony of love's right cannot make a choice between any of the intimate and the literary forms of address'.[31]

Editors and critics have enjoyed belaboring 'fear of trust' and 'presagers', but the real action lies in 'O let my books be then …' Or should it read, as Rollins, Evans, Vendler, Paterson, and Atkins argue, 'looks'? 'Looks' has a long and formidable set of advocates, beginning in the 18th century; reading through Rollins' painstaking compilation of its public defenders might, on the other hand, suggest that a degree of editorial humility is called for. One after another the commentators on this not-inconsequential debate declaim with utter certainty that *my* conclusion is the only possible one. But it isn't, almost needless to say. One ingenious argument after another is marshalled to defend the word, whichever word it may be. What, then, is the instructor to do?

The answer here proposed is to take a deep breath, then set the more persuasive annotations before her students. Again the course packet proves its worth. What it comes to is this: one weighs what is and should be a normal preference for the 1609 reading, if it can be shown to make tolerable sense, against an emendation that makes more than tolerable sense. In this case it can be shown that 'books' is defensible, despite the heated rhetoric of its nay-sayers. To cite the standard arguments, Shakespeare had published two very popular narrative poems, *books*, in which 'love'—or at least desire—is the subject, the 1593 *Venus and Adonis* and, in the following year, *The Rape of Lucrece*.[32] The Sonnets as well appear to have been drafted in the 1590s; Burrow's date for 23, and all of Sonnets 1–60, is 'composed c. 1595–6 (possibly revised thereafter)'.[33] Moreover, 'books', as editor after editor reminds us, could refer to single sheets, such as the ones on which these poems are written, not only to books that print and bind the autograph sheets. Case closed, therefore, for an editor as skilled as Burrow. Like Duncan-Jones, Kerrigan is so certain that 'books' rules that he chooses not to mention the alternative.

Others, though, do more than mention it. Among the look-ists, Evans and Paterson, editor and critic, devote a long paragraph each to promoting the alternative. 'Looks', expressions, are much more convincingly 'dumb presagers' of any man's

---

[30] Paul Edmondson and Stanley Wells, *Shakespeare's Sonnets* (Oxford: Oxford University Press, 2004) 84.
[31] Gurr (1982) 20.
[32] These narratives are written, perhaps not incidentally, in forms related to Shakespeare's handling of a sonnet sestet. The *Venus* stanza is normally a closed quatrain plus a couplet, while *Lucrece's* rhyme royal stanza adds a fifth line to the 'quatrain' before ending in a couplet. In the latter the line preceding the couplet is more frequently enjambed.
[33] Burrow (2002) 105.

'speaking breast', that is, of his heart. Paterson, who more than once pulls rank as a (highly regarded) poet, rightly notes that 'looks' results in 'superior lyricism, echoing the consonants of *eloquence*'. He acknowledges the awkwardness that 'look' in line 11 creates for his preference, but he excuses it on grounds of its being 'cleverly deliberate'.[34] Clever of him, one says.

I would be inclined to score this a draw, unsatisfactory as a draw invariably is. Foul-case substitutions do occur, but just how likely is it that the compositor misread 'l' as 'b'? Those who ask the question agree that it would not have been at all unlikely, given that in Elizabethan secretary hand the two miniscules closely resemble each other. And then there is the all-too obvious fact that this compositor did everything he could—was he nodding off, witless, like an occasional air-traffic controller, or merely flummoxed?—to botch the final line: 'wit' for 'with' and 'wiht' for 'wit'. One might recall,[35] too, that in *Henry V* IV. vii. 72 the identical confusion may have occurred. 'To book our dead' reads the Folio. T. W. Craik emends: 'to look our dead', that is, to seek out, citing *OED* sanction.[36] Craik notes that in the uncorrected Q1 of Beaumont and Fletcher's *The Maid's Tragedy* the same 'mistake' is made, the corrected Q1 and then Q2 getting it right. The conclusion? In 23 there is sufficient reason to prefer 'look' to 'book', but that reason is not sufficient to discredit fully 1609's 'book'. If one were editing the Sonnets one would indeed have to choose, fudging, or agonizing, to one's heart's content in the notes, but one is not editing the Sonnets. An instructor's responsibility is to put the issues on the table, thoroughly, and then to leave it to the enrolled future editors to wrestle with. Said editors will, one trusts, have a heightened sense of how perplexing the task of editing can be.

24.3 SONNET 147

It is not a single determinative letter this time, but, as in 16, a mark of punctuation, a mere comma in this case, that first occupies one's attention. 1609, again.

> My loue is as a feauer longing still,
> For that which longer nurseth the disease,
> Feeding on that which doth preserve the ill,
> Th' vncertaine sicklie appetite to please;
> My reason the Phisition to my loue,
> Angry that his prescriptions are not kept
> Hath left me, and I desperate now approoue,
> Desire is death, which Phisick did except.

---

[34] Paterson (2010) 72.

[35] Or, like the writer, one might not. I thank Carl Atkins for pointing it out.

[36] T. W. Craik, (ed.), *King Henry V* (London: Routledge, 1995) 316.

Past cure I am, now Reason is past care,
And frantick madde with euer-more vnrest,
My thoughts and my discourse as mad mens are,
At random from the truth vainely exprest.
  For I haue sworne thee faire, and thought thee bright,
  Who art as black as hell, as darke as night.

Although 147 has not received the attention given the poem with which it may be said to be paired, 146, it is one of the central, indeed climactic, sonnets in the sequence.[37] Despite the obvious sharing of diction and theme—146's 'fed' and 'feeds' anticipating 147's 'feeding', and death, the word and fact alike, lying at the heart of both poems—the pairing is not as direct as that of 16 with 15. Nor could it be, since 16, as readers immediately grasp, as much as continues the final sentence of 15, creating thereby a double sonnet: 'But wherefore do not you a mightier way … ?' Yet 146 is critical to a discussion of 147. Duncan-Jones flatly declares that 146 is 'Shakespeare's only explicitly religious poem', a statement with which all but all commentators agree.[38] The speaker addresses his soul—although the persistence of the four opening interrogatives might be said to cast some doubt on the imperatives and declaratives that attempt to answer—urging it to starve the body it inhabits. Noting that 'aggravate' means 'as usually in Shakespeare "augment, increase"', Burrow modernizes the volta of lines 9 and 10 thus:

Then, soul, live thou upon thy servant's loss,
And let that pine to aggravate thy store …

The reward for obeying this command—Schoenfeldt in a happy phrase terms it 'moralized anorexia'—will be nothing other than immortality.[39]

The final lines may have been in John Donne's ear when, combining as nearly always a Petrarchan octave with a Shakespearean sestet, he wrote 'Death be not proud'. The conclusion of 146 reads,

Within be fed, without be rich no more:
  So shalt thou feed on death, that feeds on men,
  And death once dead, there's no more dying then.

What 147 does with this conventional entreaty is startling. The poem proceeds as if quite deaf to the homiletic ending of 146, replying to it simply by defying it, that is, by demonstrating that the hunger of the flesh can render religious wisdom irrelevant. Assuming again that we can trust the order of the Sonnets to be the author's and not the publisher's

---

[37] Sonnet 147 may also be paired, thematically, with 148.

[38] Duncan-Jones (1997) 408. Paterson (2010), 447, is the dissenter: 'This sonnet is not religious at all. It's an angry poem …'. Unless one posits that by definition no 'religious poem' may be 'angry', this seems to exclude a poem like Herbert's 'The Collar'. True, 'The Collar' does not end in anger—quite the opposite—but anger is the first word that comes to mind when one names the tone of the body of the poem.

[39] Schoenfeldt, in Schiffer (1999) 308.

or a scribe's, by directly following 146 with 147, rather than reversing them, Shakespeare demonstrates that the body at times obeys and must obey its own compulsions. The poem may be said to carry the Petrarchan topos of love-sickness to an extraordinary extreme: I am sick because my love for you is sick; furthermore, I wish to remain sick in that I continue to reject my physician's prescriptions. I can curse and insult you but doing so only leaves me where I began, disillusioned, not to say disgusted, with you and with myself, yet fixed in this stasis of perpetual desire.

The crux arrives in line 10, but since the poem is the wrought and fraught performance that it is, the line—really the quatrain in which it is embedded—calls for a more detailed contextualization than has been required of the cruxes in 16 and 23. Substantial lyric energy is generated by the first quatrain, in part because, in a poem of particularly consistent metre, the opening trochee of line 3, 'Feeding', feeds the quasi-paradox that the line articulates: we move from nursing the disease that love is to nourishing it, thereby preserving rather than curing it. (Although the metre in 147 is regular, altered—in the standard manner—only by two initial trochees, the larger rhythms of the first seven lines are 'disturbed' by three febrile caesuras correctly placed, in Burrow's modernization, mid-foot, after unstressed syllables.)[40] The next line candidly identifies what is being fed: it is my 'appetite', as if explicitly tying 147 to 146. One registers that the entirety of 147 is declarative; there is no place for questioning anything in this poem. Greenblatt rises to the occasion when he states that the speaker 'cannot give her up … That he cannot do so has everything to do with the compulsions of "lust in action", the rhythm of tumescence and detumescence that defines him and what it means to be with her … This sexual rhythm, yoking vitality and death, pleasure and disgust, longing and loathing, is not a mere recreation or escape'.[41] We may not have been in danger of thinking it was. Reverting to the mundane, although the architecture of poetic argument is never mundane, one observes that the utterly conventional Petrarchan sentiment of the first line is instantly erased by the utterly unconventional second.

The next quatrain summons the doctor. Doctor Reason, a reader thinks for a second, until she thinks again, realizing that this physician is *my* (sick) reason, not that of the healthy world. Still, it is reason, not God or the sermonizing speaker of 146, that enters, only to be rejected. The rejection is quickly mutual: as 'I' refuse the 'prescriptions' of this potential healer, he in turn abandons me, distressed that his advice has not been followed. The consequence is dramatic: now I 'approve' (Duncan-Jones' gloss is solid:

---

[40] There is little dispute about these caesuras in lines 1, 5, and 7. Like most of our editors, Burrow marks all three by commas. The result is a rhythmic counterpoint, a slightly upsetting audible undertow, in these seven steadily iambic lines, of trochaic *words* (fever, longing, longer, nurseth, feeding, sickly, reason, angry, desperate).

[41] Greenblatt (2004) 255. Not every critic is convinced that this poem is addressed to the mistress. Expanding a conjecture by Heather Dubrow, Ilona Bell wonders if 147 might be spoken, by 'an unreliable narrator whose views we are "not to trust"', to the young man of 1–126. There appears to be no hurry to agree with this notion. For most readers, besides the weight of traditional reading that is inevitably brought to bear, the specific (female) gendering of 145 and 151, bracketing 146–7, reinforces one's sense that the same 'dark' mistress is the addressee here. (Bell, in Schoenfeldt (2007), 310.)

'discover by experience') that 'desire' is nothing less than 'death'. Beginning the line with this blunt phrasing, heavily alliterated, enforces the unignorability of the huge, hard truth, a truth that the mistress sub-sequence has been approaching and retreating from for a while. For all the devastation of these words that begin line 8, it is line 7 that sets it up. Its distinctly paused rhythm is telling—the off-placed caesura ('Hath left me, and I desperate …') puts unusual emphasis on the conjunction, as if to say that my reason's having left me is not enough, that it has the consequence of teaching me, desperate as I am, that in Romans 8:6 Paul had identified the inescapable truth of desire. It *is* death, nothing less, and certainly not the metaphorical 'little death' of orgasm that brightens or dulls the lines of dozens of early modern poems and many of Shakespeare's plays.

Sonnet 147 is a very good poem for eight lines, at which point it becomes more than that. *The Norton Shakespeare* glosses line 9's final word, 'care', 'medical care: inverting the proverb "Past cure, past care" (don't worry about what you can't control). In the proverb, you don't care because you can't cure; here, because you don't care, you can't cure'. The consequence of not caring about the love-fever—no, *my* love fever, as the first line insists—is drastic. The speaker claims that it turns him mad, indeed 'frantic-mad'. Sufficiently so that he repeats it in the next line, stating that both his thoughts and his 'discourse as madmen's are'. And yet one observes that the whole poem is never confused, its ideas following one after another in a fully rational manner. The intensity of feeling indeed increases quatrain by quatrain, as often in these sonnets, the very structure of their unvarying form—three closed quatrains followed by a couplet—encouraging just that sense of rational progression.[42] Consider what these three quatrains are saying step by step: I am sick; my physician has washed his hands of me; I cannot be cured, in fact I have become mad. One reason 147, like the entire sequence, keeps the reader reading is Shakespeare's insistence that the reader focus on what is being said, undistracted by the stylistic pyrotechnics of which the poet is clearly capable. Thus his rhyming in this poem never, and in the whole sequence rarely, strikes one as strained. It is made prominent by the fact that as noted the poet pauses, syntactically, after most lines: Burrow's modernizing of the punctuation produces in 147 but two enjambed lines, and, unsurprisingly, none at the ends of quatrains. We are compelled to hear the solid, full rhymes.[43]

[42] Our baker's dozen modernizers agree that in only two instances—Sonnets 63 and 154—must an editor omit end-punctuation at the conclusion of a quatrain. Clearly the sonneteering Shakespeare, like Samuel Daniel, *thought* in units of four lines, sometimes in two, less often in eight. (The apparently contemporaneous *Romeo and Juliet* contains three full sonnets that share precisely this undeviating 4–4–4–2 structure.) These even-numbered units are themselves composed of single lines the aural and phrasal integrity of which is unmistakable given the great frequency of rhetorical end-line pauses, marked by commas, in poem after poem. This practice produces what a twenty-first-century ear—trained on the varied conversational rhythms of, say, Robert Frost and Elizabeth Bishop—may hear as an overly predictable rhythmic flatness.

[43] It is worth noting that 1609 fully enjambs only two of its 154 line 12s, those in 24 and 121. Modernizers, undoubtedly suspecting compositorial incompetence, rectify these slips. Only 35 may be said to enjamb line 12; some recent editors, though, retain 1609's end-line comma.

The primary, and the logical, consequence of the speaker's madness is that he has been unable to apprehend 'truth'. But he retains his wits to this extent: turning to what feels like the long-delayed yet inevitable vocative, he pushes through to a certitude that his fever has been partially occluding.

> For I have sworn thee fair, and thought thee bright,
> Who art as black as hell, as dark as night.

The ironic rhyming of 'night' with 'bright' is superb in its finality, allowing no rejoinder. But what *kind* of 'finality' are we given in 147? Two of the most astute readers of the Sonnets in recent years, Heather Dubrow and Helen Vendler, have much to say about what Shakespeare is doing in the closed couplets (that is, not enjambed from line 12) with which he concludes nearly all of the sonnets. Dubrow, first in the field, writes, 'The sonnet is … one of the most orderly of literary forms; it is tightly structured and compact. Its couplet is the most orderly and ordering of its elements. No matter what the content of the couplet, in contrast to the syntactical and metrical complexities of the preceding quatrains it will often sound like an easily achieved truism'.[44] When Dubrow turns to 147's couplet she identifies 'the tension between the sense of order and stability implied by the couplet and the anarchic sentiments that Shakespeare's couplets so often express'. Anarchic indeed, for this beleaguered speaker, even if one slant on 147, and in particular its couplet, might be that the whole poem can be read as what poems sometimes are for their writers, an attempt at emotional relief, attained by the simple, but in practice not at all simple, confessionalism of speaking the whole truth about what most deeply troubles one.

Vendler writes that in his handling of the couplet Shakespeare's turn 'toward the proverbial always represents the speaker's despair at solving by himself, in personally formulated language, the conundrum presented by the sonnet. "*I don't know; what does the common wisdom say about this situation?*"' One may doubt that it is common wisdom we hear in 147, but Vendler's ensuing insight is smartly provocative: she describes 'a reader alert to the way boilerplate idiom, when it is found in the couplet (*as black as hell, as dark as night*, Sonnet 147), carries the speaker's despair of a solution'. Her attention to the poem's diction and rhythm are exemplary:

> After the elaborate Latinity of diagnosis and explanation [...] the predominantly Anglo-Saxon lexicon of the couplet comes as an enormous surprise [...] The direct second-person accusation of the last line departs from the self-diagnostic pose of the rest, while the perfect syllable balance—6, 4, 6, 4—of the closing two lines, coming after the irregular desperation of the diagnosis, suggests a complete and 'perfected' knowledge lying behind the 'madness' of thought and expression.[45]

---

[44] 'Shakespeare's Undramatic Monologues: Toward a Reading of the *Sonnets*'. In Orgel and Keilen (1999) 200. The next citation is from Dubrow's *Captive Victors: Shakespeare's Narrative Poems and Sonnets* (Ithaca, NY: Cornell University Press, 1987) 225.

[45] Vendler (1997) 26, 28, 618.

Even if one raises an eyebrow at Vendler's concluding 'suggestion' that this knowl-edge that lies behind madness is to be attributed to the speaker of 147, attributing it to Shakespeare, master-psychologist and master *of* psychologists, is not unreasonable. His speaker, in any case, is left face to face with what the poem has after all been about, the apprehension and statement of truth. The four symmetrical deployments of the unstressed 'as' in the final line nail the two adjectives and two nouns, monosyllables all, to the wall, the hard consonants of 'black' and the harder ones of 'dark' comprising the final blow. Most annotators find in 'hell' a ready allusion to the mistress's vagina, and the venereal disease it infects lovers with. We are not being let off the pain of 'truth' here, a 'truth' that Lear will fiercely restate: 'Beneath is all the fiend's: there's hell, there's darkness'. Ronald Levao writes that the sequence is 'increasingly explicit about the rough stuff of life', adding that in the late sonnets Shakespeare sets eros 'loose within the broadly skep-tical, Ovidian world of obsessive sexuality, dark wit, and epistemic labyrinths'.[46] Levao is not speaking explicitly of the end of 147, but his formulation strikes this writer as more persuasive than Vendler's to some degree redemptive one.

These paragraphs have responded to Burrow's modernized text of 147, ignoring the crux that he, like all modernizers save two, edits out. It is somewhat surprising that so many post-Rollins modernizers neglect Burrow's own thoughtful, and firm, advice: edi-tors must 'regularly [...] alert their readers to the quiet violence they may be perform-ing by modernizing the text'.[47] The 'violence' before us comes of the power of modern grammatical punctuation: we are taught, by example and even before we learn to read, that clarity of thought requires that ambiguity be avoided lest we muddy our heads when thinking about serious matters. Grammatical punctuation is what keeps things on track. Poetry, however, survives as the necessary antidote to the tyranny of this notion. One of its resources is the kind of double syntax that Sonnet 147 employs. Eleven of our mod-ernizers will have none of it.

Is line 10 to be construed with line 9 or with lines 11 and 12? The 1609 quatrain again:

> Past cure I am, now Reason is past care,
> And frantick madde with euer-more vnrest,
> My thoughts and my discourse as mad mens are,
> At random from the truth vainely exprest.

By replacing 1609's comma at the end of line 10 with a semi-colon, Ingram and Redpath, Kerrigan, Duncan-Jones, Orgel, Vendler, and Paterson elect option one. Wells and Taylor are still more insistent, preferring a full stop to the semi-colon. Perhaps this col-lective is exemplifying the fact that, as noted, Shakespeare often organizes his thought in units of two lines as well as units of four or eight. By contrast, Evans, Burrow, and Mowat and Werstine make 1609's 'And frantick madde with euer-more vnrest' a component of,

---

[46] "'Where Black is the Color, Where None is the Number": Something from Nothing in Shakespeare's Sonnets', *Literary Imagination*, 12: 3, (2010): 285.
[47] In Schoenfeldt (2007) 161.

and only of, the next lines. They accomplish that by retaining 1609's line-ending comma while inserting a medial comma after 'And'. Bate and Rasmussen achieve that result another way, closing line 9 with a semi-colon.

How, then, to choose? My answer is to defer deciding until one has paid attention to Booth's note on lines 9 through 11, a note that all post-Booth editors simply ignore. He writes: 'Line ten is both a continuation of the clause begun in line nine ("I am past cure and frantic mad"), and the first element of the clause that emerges in line eleven' (my thoughts and my discourse, which are 'frantic mad', are truly like a madman's). Such double syntax is not uncommon in early modern poems, a notion that our other editors presumably are not blind to, but must decide does not apply here.[48] The brilliant economy of applying a line-phrase to both preceding and following clauses only enriches the poem. No less an authority than Stanley Wells speaks the common wisdom about early modern syntax when he writes that 'the syntax of [Shakespeare's] time was in any case more fluid than ours; the imposition upon it of a precisely grammatical system of punctuation reduces the ambiguity and imposes definition on indefinition'.[49] That he and Taylor chose to ignore these words as well as Booth's example is curious.

Having, as I see it, simply carried the day by demonstrating how the double syntax functions here, Booth is not done with line 10, nor are we. Orgel, who praises Booth for having produced 'the enabling document for contemporary editorial practice', does note, accurately, that he 'worries every possible ambiguity at great length'.[50] Booth's note on line 10 offers three glosses on 'frantic mad'. The first states the obvious: 'frantic-mad as a result of, frantically mad as a result of'. The third is negligible. But the second gloss reads: 'made wild by (Q reads 'madde'; for the potential confusion between the words we spell 'mad' and 'made', see 129.9 and note)'. There we find a paragraph the concluding sentence of which remarks that 'although the evidence of rhymes does not suggest that Elizabethans pronounced "made" and "mad" alike, they do seem to have resembled each other enough for punning; Kökeritz gives several examples, including *TN* 3.4.50–53'. Why does this matter? Booth does not say, but it matters because many modernizing editors are wont to hyphenate—grammatical punctuation never tires of its work—'frantic' and 'mad': frantic-mad. Moreover, not one editor-annotator picks up on Booth's 'mad'/'made' ambiguity.

Without denying the undeniable 'mad' in line 9, to hear 'made' as a secondary, additional sense strengthens the quatrain. As an unemended line 10 invites the reader to

---

[48] Unlike Booth, the second editor (chronologically, the first) who leaves the quatrain's commas intact, Wilson, is silent on the effect of doing so. Another confirming, unmistakable example of double syntax in the Sonnets is found in the first quatrain of 60, where the third line may be construed both with the two preceding lines and the one following, thereby miming the wave-action metaphor itself. Booth terms the syntaxes here 'intermeshed'. Alpers in turn writes well about the syntactical 'shiftiness' of Sonnet 33. ('Learning from the New Criticism,' in Mark David Rasmussen, (ed.), *Renaissance Literature and Its Formal Engagements* (New York: Palgrave, 2002) 119–20.)

[49] Wells and Taylor (2005) xlii.

[50] In Schoenfeldt (2007) 142.

take the entire line with both the preceding and following lines, so 'mad' (frantic mad) yields one sense and 'made' yields another (made frantic). 'Made' rescues line 10 from an unwelcome anti-climax, since 'mad' makes line 11 not much more than a repetition of 10's claim of madness. If, as I argue, we also read *made frantic* in line 10, then line 11's move to 'My thoughts and my discourse as madmen's are' tells us that the speaker's mental state is getting progressively worse. Understood thus, the syntactical inversion—*frantic made* rather than *made frantic*—intensifies the speaker's anguished state. The principal objection to understanding 'madde' as *made* as well as *mad* is that 1609 only once confuses the spellings. That once, however, is striking. Sonnet 129, the other thoroughly disillusioned poem in the set, the poem that like 147 concludes in the mistress's 'hell', specifies the consequences of 'lust in action'. Lust is 'On purpose layd to make the taker mad. |Made in pursut and in possession so' If 'made' can be a modern's *mad*, 'madde' can be our *made*. The result, in any case, of being both 'frantic-mad' *and* 'frantic made' is, in a wonderful phrase, finding oneself 'random' from the truth. At which point, the bottom having been sounded, the untruth of swearing that black is fair and night is bright may allow a counter-movement toward saner life. That it does not happen in the final seven sonnets only confirms that the sequence, in the form that 1609 left to history, may be read, or must be read, as tragedy.

What generalizations are to be drawn from a look at these cruxes? One begins with the obvious: when engaging a crux it repays a student-reader of the Sonnets to think for herself as she encounters the proffered guidance of a host of editors and critics. It is equally clear that her thinking should not be applied to a crux as if it could be cleared up without the closest attention to the rest of the poem. Doing this work will, more often than not, heighten respect for the labours of those who in the last three-quarters of a century have brought the Sonnets out of the shadow of speculation about the many unresolved, apparently unresolvable matters of biography that long dominated sonnet criticism. Finally, the communal give-and-take that characterizes a seminar can sharpen and deepen a student's reading of the Sonnets. In time, this difficult sequence will begin to surrender some of its secrets.

SELECT BIBLIOGRAPHY

Editions

Atkins, Carl D. (2007) (ed.) *Shakespeare's Sonnets*. (Madison, NJ: Fairleigh Dickinson University Press).

Bate, Jonathan and Eric Rasmussen (2007) (eds.) *Shakespeare's Complete Works*. (New York: Modern Library).

Booth, Stephen (1977) (ed.) *Shakespeare's Sonnets*. (New Haven: Yale University Press).

Burrow, Colin (2002) (ed.) *The Complete Sonnets and Poems*. (Oxford: Oxford University Press).

Duncan-Jones, Katherine (1997) (ed.) *Shakespeare's Sonnets*. (London: The Arden Shakespeare).

Evans, G. Blakemore (2006) (ed.) *Shakespeare's Sonnets*. (Updated Edition) (Cambridge: Cambridge University Press).

Ingram, W.G. and Theodore Redpath (1964) (eds) *Shakespeare's Sonnets*. (London: University of London).

Kerrigan, John (1986) (ed.) *The Sonnets and A Lover's Complaint*. (Harmondsworth: Penguin Books, Ltd).

Mowat, Barbara A. and Paul Werstine (2009) (ed.) *Shakespeare's Sonnets and Poems*. (New York: Folger Shakespeare Library).

Orgel, Stephen (2001) (ed.) *The Sonnets*. (New York: Penguin Books).

Paterson, Don (2010) *Reading Shakespeare's Sonnets: a new commentary*. (London: Faber & Faber).

Rollins, Hyder Edward (1944) (ed.) *A New Variorum Edition of Shakespeare: The Sonnets*. 2 vols. (Philadelphia: J.B. Lippincott).

Vendler, Helen (1997) *The Art of Shakespeare's Sonnets*. (Cambridge, MA: Harvard University Press).

Wells, Stanley and Gary Taylor (2005) (eds.) *The Complete Works*. 2nd edn (Oxford: Oxford University Press).

Willen, Gerald and Victor B. Reed (1964) (eds) *A Casebook on Shakespeare's Sonnets*. (New York: Crowell).

Wilson, John Dover (1967) (ed.) *The Sonnets*. 2nd edn (Cambridge: Cambridge University Press).

Collections of Essays

Bloom, Harold and Brett Foster (2008) (eds.) *The Sonnets*. (New York: Bloom's Literary Criticsm).

Cheney, Patrick and Anne Lake Prescott (2000) (eds) *Approaches to Teaching Shorter Elizabethan Poetry*. (New York: Modern Language Association of America).

——(2007) (ed.) *The Cambridge Companion to Shakespeare's Poetry*. (Cambridge: Cambridge University Press).

Orgel, Stephen and Sean Keilen (1999) (eds) *Shakespeare's Poems*. (New York: Garland Publishing).

Schiffer, James (1999) (ed.) *Shakespeare's Sonnets: Critical Essays*. (New York: Garland Publishing).

Schoenfeldt, Michael (2007) (ed.) *A Companion to Shakespeare's Sonnets*. (Malden, MA: Blackwell Publishing Ltd.).

....

CHAPTER 25

'FORTIFY YOURSELF IN YOUR DECAY'

Sounding Rhyme and Rhyming Effects in Shakespeare's Sonnets

....

L. E. SEMLER

Rhyme is the unsung champion of mortality. It is a feat of control in the face of infinity. It is a fortification against decay (to modify a phrase from Sonnet 16) because it delivers forms of certainty that affirm or strive to affirm the integrity, persistence, and ambitions of the human. This is demonstrable not just in Shakespeare's Sonnets which *is* the focus of this chapter, but also in the plays, whether one glances at the use of end-rhyme by Iago or Hamlet, Romeo or Orlando, *Macbeth*'s weird sisters, Lear's Fool, or Bottom playing Pyramus.[1] A full consideration of Shakespearean rhyme would extend well beyond essay length, so this chapter is merely a brief sounding of rhyme and rhyming effects in the Sonnets. Early-modern theoretical accounts of rhyme in poetry, such as those by George Puttenham and Samuel Daniel, speak of its formal binding power and its patterns of sonic 'reply' and 'concord' that depend on memory's temporal capacity and deliver sensations of pleasure and control.[2] At the same time, rhyme models a principle

---

[1] Important explorations of rhyme in the plays and Sonnets include (respectively): Frederick Ness, *The Use of Rhyme in Shakespeare's Plays* (New Haven: Yale University Press, 1941), Lorna Flint, *Shakespeare's Third Keyboard: The Significance of Rime in Shakespeare's Plays* (Newark: University of Delaware Press, 2000), Simon Palfrey, *Doing Shakespeare* (London: Thomson, 2005) 92–105, Anne Ferry, 'The Sense of Rhyme: Sidney and Shakespeare', *Literary Imagination* 4.2 (2002): 163–89. Helen Vendler, *The Art of Shakespeare's Sonnets* (Cambridge, MA: Harvard University Press, 1997), and Philip C. McGuire, 'Shakespeare's Non-Shakespearean Sonnets', *Shakespeare Quarterly* 38.3 (1987): 304–19.

[2] Gavin Alexander, *Sidney's 'Defence of Poesy' and Selected Renaissance Literary Criticism* (London: Penguin, 2004) 119–29, 213, 216.

of difference unified that contributes to our understanding of the age-old conundrum of how aesthetic and semantic systems cooperate. Shakespeare's Sonnets exemplifies these concerns via end-rhyme and internal rhyming effects within an intricate weave of sound, rhetoric, and argument.

25.1 Rhyme And Early Modern Sonnets: Sounding Sonnet 18

Rhyme and rhyming effects, so essential to early modern poetry, find themselves peculiarly intensified in the constrained, aestheticized, and self-reflexive form that is the early modern sonnet. In his account of the sonnet in *A Defence of Rhyme* (1603) Daniel observes:

> For the body of our imagination being as an unformed chaos without fashion, without day, if by the divine power of the spirit it be wrought into an orb of order and form, is it not more pleasing to nature, that desires a certainty and comports not with that which is infinite, to have these closes, rather than not to know where to end or how far to go, especially seeing our passions are often without measure? ... Besides, is it not most delightful to see much excellently ordered in a small room....[3]

According to Daniel, sonneteering resembles world-making, and rhyme is a significant aspect of the 'orb of order and form' that disposes unruly imagination and passion into the pleasing certainty of circumscription. Rhyme is 'no impediment' to an able poet's 'conceit' or imagination, but rather 'gives him wings' for a 'far happier flight', and when well married to 'wit and industry' produces 'greater and worthier effects in our language' than 'loose measures'.[4]

A sonnet is a complex phonic event occurring through time as it is read aloud and, simultaneously, a rhetorical artefact ingeniously incorporating tropes and figures into its delivery of argument. It challenges the poet and rewards the reader with musical (sound and metre), rhetorical (tropes and figures), and logical (argument) arrangements that can be appreciated on their own terms and, ideally, as part of a sophisticated whole.

The prevalence within the sonnet of rhetorical figures specifically relating to repetition (and repetition with a difference) of words and sounds confirms the high importance of echoing and rhyming effects to this blend of aural pattern and rhetorical display. A short list of such figures abounding in Shakespeare's Sonnets would include: alliteration (repetition of initial consonant sounds); anaphora (repetition of same word

---

[3] Alexander (2004) 216.
[4] Alexander (2004) 216.

or phrase at start of consecutive clauses or lines); antimetabole or commutatio (repetition of words in reverse order); antistasis (repetition of a word in a different sense); assonance (resemblance of internal vowel sounds of words); chiasmus (repetition of ideas in reverse order); consonance (resemblance of consonant sounds of words); diacope (repetition of word with one or few words between); epizeuxis or subjunctio (repetition of a word with no words between); isocolon (repetition of phrases of similar structure and length); paronomasia or adnominatio (words of differing meaning but similar sounds brought close together); ploce (repetition of a word with a new meaning after intervening words); polyptoton (close proximity of different words with the same root); and pun.[5] The sheer density of phonically repetitive rhetorical figures in Shakespeare's Sonnets combines with pervasive end- and internal rhyming to prove that they are essentially sounded artefacts.

In his *Certain Notes of Instruction concerning the making of Verse or Rhyme in English* (1587), George Gascoigne states that while any short poem may be deemed a sonnet, 'I can best allow to call those sonnets which are of fourteen lines, every line containing ten syllables. The first twelve do rhyme in staves of four lines by cross metre, and the last two, rhyming together, do conclude the whole'.[6] Although he does not include mention of the iambic metre (opting instead for the more general 'ten syllables'), Gascoigne is describing the so-called 'English sonnet' with its characteristic structure of three cross-rhymed quatrains followed by a rhyming couplet. Rhyme is essential to this structure because the integrity of each quatrain is guaranteed by its two pairs of end-rhymes being arranged in 'cross metre' (thus: *abab*). He does not state that each quatrain must possess its own unique set of rhyming sounds, nor that the couplet's rhyme must be distinct also, thus giving a full set of seven aurally distinct rhyme pairs (*abab cdcd efef gg*). This is usually thought of as the basic early modern 'English' sonnet form, but it is important to note, as Philip McGuire does, that Shakespeare plays variations on this formula and other poets variously endorse or avoid it.[7]

End-rhyme acts as an aural binding agent in a sonnet and also as a divider because it usually gives discrete unity to each quatrain and also to the final two lines which hold to each other by being a rhyming couplet. The completion of an end-rhyme pair, in league with the emphasis that comes to the rhymed sound via iambic pentameter and a word's natural stress, delivers a concluding force that is relatively stronger in the couplet where the two end-rhyme words occur in close proximity to one another and no lines follow them, and relatively weaker in the quatrains where the second word in the end-rhyme pair is delayed by the intervention of a line that concludes with a word from another end-rhyme pair and further lines follow. The couplet gains additional concluding force because, usually, there is no other rhyming couplet in the poem to compete with its

---

[5] These terms and definitions come from Richard Lanham, *A Handlist of Rhetorical Terms*. 2nd edn (Berkeley: University of California Press, 1991) 182–96, and Brian Vickers, *In Defence of Rhetoric* (Oxford: Clarendon, 1998) 491–8.

[6] Alexander (2004) 245.

[7] McGuire (1987) 304–6.

emphatic power. Some of this power is derived from the couplet's delivery of a two-line concluding statement to the poem's argument which formally invokes the long tradition of aphorisms being expressed pithily in couplet form. The rhyming couplet delivers a tight sense of conceptual and aural completion by its swift return to a stressed sound that closes a rhyming pair and is coincidental with the end of a proverbial statement that is both a complete truth in itself and also an ingenious end to the sonnet's fourteen-line argument.

While many of Shakespeare's sonnets follow a continental pattern of argument where the octave (lines 1–8) presents a conceptual bloc and the sestet (lines 9–14) delivers a concluding section beginning with a conceptual turn (the volta), such as Sonnets 20 and 29, the additive effect of the English rhyme scheme allows a finer articulation of argument within each section as the octave is two quatrains and the sestet is a quatrain and a couplet. When the English rhyme scheme is blended, as it very often is, with the octave–sestet division of argument, a wider range of possibilities emerges for the poet who can foreground one or another set of divisions, or blend them, or set them in tension with each other as in Sonnets 3, 33, 49, 86, and 121. The English rhyme scheme can encourage the poet to create an argument that unfolds variations on itself through three stages of argument through the three quatrains with little heed to the octave–sestet split. This can delay the volta until the start of line 13 or 14, as in Sonnets 53, 60, 73, 116, and 144, which makes for an impressively condensed resolution.

The theses and rhetorical devices of most sonnets can be analyzed and appreciated through silent reading, but the soundscapes, including rhyme and rhyming effects, are significantly depleted by such an engagement regardless of how acute one's imaginative ear might be. Reading aloud involves the reader in the aural time of the sonnet during which sound patterns dependent on the reader's choices, echo, build, and vary in ways too complex to be predicted, but which must be experienced through the operations of vocalization, audition, and memory. Reading aloud forces one to commit to metrical, intonation, and pronunciation choices which involve assigning sounds as well as locations and degrees of emphasis, pause, and elision. The reader inhabits the aural time of the sonnet in which the current voicing of a line or syllable plays against the memory of recently heard sounds, and puts sonics and semantics into a living exchange.

Sonnet 18 is effective precisely because its thesis, rhetoric, and musicality are all characterized by moderation with no feature calling attention to itself for knotty obscurity, ostentatious display, or disruption of expectation. Shakespeare expressly limits the diversity of sound, vocabulary, and end-rhyme so that the poem holds together as a particularly strong sonic unity.

> Shall I compare thee to a summer's day?
> Thou art more lovely and more temperate.
> Rough winds do shake the darling buds of May,
> And summer's lease hath all too short a date.
> Sometime too hot the eye of heaven shines,
> And often is his gold complexion dimmed,
> And every fair from fair sometime declines,

By chance or nature's changing course untrimmed;
But thy eternal summer shall not fade
Nor lose possession of that fair thou ow'st,
Nor shall death brag thou wander'st in his shade
When in eternal lines to time thou grow'st.
   So long as men can breathe or eyes can see,
   So long lives this, and this gives life to thee.

Each of the quatrains is internally unified by the repetition of a keyword within it ('summer's', 'sometime', and 'eternal'). The quatrains are then unified with each other by the carriage of the keyword or its sound into the following quatrain(s). The word 'Sometime' phonically recalls the idea of 'summer' ('sum-'/'some-') from the preceding line and quatrain, while also blending this with the arch enemy of perfection, 'time', to capture the key idea of time-bound imperfection. The keywords of the first two quatrains are phonically recuperated in the third which brings 'summer' and 'time' into proximal relation with the keyword 'eternal' in clauses that envelope the quatrain and unify the friend's perfection with the poem's act of praise. Although the sonnet has the full complement of seven end-rhyme pairs, the aural distinction between quatrains is reduced by the fact that three of the pairs have almost identical stressed vowel sounds that are only finely distinguished by the effects of the following consonant ('day'/'May', 'temperate'/'date', 'fade'/'shade'). The notion of the sonnet delivering eternal 'life' to the friend, clearly introduced in the final line of the third quatrain, is consolidated in the couplet.

The couplet presents a beautifully controlled sound pattern that rhymes one line against the other, not just at the ends, but also at the beginnings. The internal arrangement of each line is self-echoing with the double pattern of line 13 ('men can breathe or eyes can see') and the assonant, consonant, and alliterative variation on antimetabole in line 14 ('long lives this, and this gives life'). If we follow the model of assigning keywords, then the keyword or phrase in the couplet should be, 'So long', which is repeated in the first and last lines of the couplet and suggestive of yet another modulation of the key concept of perfection in time. Just as 'summer's' and 'sometime' of quatrains one and two made room for the triumph of 'eternal' in quatrain three, so 'eternal' is subtly compromised by its own proxy status and softens to become a powerful residue of itself in the phrase, 'So long', which for all its optimism nevertheless falls short of eternalness.

The repetition of each section's keyword ('summer's', 'sometime', 'eternal', 'So long'), the closeness of the sounds of three of the end-rhyme pairs, and the internal echoing of the couplet, together suggest that the entire poem makes a virtue of sonic duplication. This is confirmed by the relentless recurrence of identical sounds rolling through the poem from start to finish: 'more ... and more'; 'too short ... / ... too hot'; 'And ... /And'; 'fair from fair'; 'Nor lose ... /Nor shall'; and 'thou ow'st/ ... thou wander'st ... / ... thou grow'st' (lines 2, 4–5, 6–7, 7, 10–11, 10–12). The poem also deploys a number of the literary figures relating to repetition, such as: ploce and antistasis (line 7: 'fair from fair'); diacope (1.2: 'more lovely and more temperate');

anaphora and isocolon (lines 10–11, 13–14: 'Nor ...: /Nor', 'So long ... /So long'); and assonance, consonance, and alliteration (line 14: 'So long lives this, and this gives life to thee').

Almost every line reaffirms the poet's commitment to a soundscape grounded in the weak end of the hierarchy of consonantal strength which is occupied by sonorant glides, liquids, and nasals ('l', 'r', 'm', 'n', 'ng'). When consonants from the stronger end of the hierarchy, with its voiceless fricatives and voiced and voiceless plosives, are clustered together—for example, 'do shake the darling buds', 'too short a date', 'By chance or nature's changing course untrimmed', and 'shall death brag thou wander'st in his shade' (lines 3, 4, 8, 11)—their sibilant, stopped, and obstruent sounds aurally foreground their words as disruptive terms. The essential phonetic stridency of these clustered sounds is made more emphatic via the alliteration and consonance built into the clusters and the greater oral effort and slower speed involved in their vocalization.

The dominant melody of the poem is achieved by the gentle remorselessness of its sonorants that push expressions of 'chance', 'changing', 'time', and 'death' into isolated knots of verbal resistance that, while strident and not fully dissolved, are disempowered by being enveloped in, or in some cases permeated by (e.g. line 6: 'gold complexion dimmed'), a melody 'more lovely and more temperate'. The aural stridency of time's articulation adds a tightly curtailed phonic disturbance to the poem that illustrates time's capture within the soft yet powerful amber of the poem's sonorants which carry the theme of adoring praise. This sonic contrast is an aspect of the poem's unique beauty and suggests that while time's impact may be poetically controlled, it is neither fully eradicable from, nor an entirely negative aspect of, human experience. Sonnet 18 suggests the importance of rhyme and rhyming effects to a poem's aesthetic integrity and to its orchestration of sound and meaning.

25.2 RHYME AS A DELIGHTFUL BINDER OF THE QUATRAIN

There is no question that to late-sixteenth- and early 17th-century theorists, rhyme acts as an aurally delightful binder in English poems. In his *The Arte of English Poesie* (1589), Puttenham gives a comprehensive account of this although, as his most recent editors note, he 'is essentially silent on the Elizabethan sonnet vogue' because its widespread take-up in England would not occur till the 1590s.[8] Nonetheless, Puttenham's remarks on stanzaic end-rhyme are evocative:

---

[8] Puttenham, *The Art of English Poesy: A Critical Edition*, ed., Frank Whigham and Wayne A. Rebhorn (Ithaca: Cornell University Press, 2007) 42.

there is a band to be given every verse in a staff, so as none fall out alone or uncoupled, and this band maketh that the staff is said fast and not loose: even as ye see in buildings of stone or brick the mason giveth a band, that is a length to two breadths, and upon necessity divers other sorts of bands to hold in the work fast and maintain the perpendicularity of the wall.[9]

Just as a mason uses band-stones set at right angles to the regular wall bricks in order to reinforce the strength of a wall and guarantee its trueness, so the poet deploys end-rhyme so that a poem's verses may be cross-fastened and the entire stanza given a robust unity and regularity. The sound system and semantic system of a poem, despite their inherently distinct values, both inhere in the same language as it is experienced through time. The poem needs a carefully integrated cross-bracing of these at least partially independent systems.

Rhyme's binding effects are probably limitless, but some insight into them may be gained by exploring their value for the quatrain, the poem, and the sequence. To begin with the quatrain, here is the opening of Sonnet 40:

> Take all my loves, my love, yea, take them all:
> What hast thou then more than thou hadst before?
> No love, my love, that thou mayst true love call–
> All mine was thine before thou hadst this more.

This quatrain reveals how reluctant Shakespeare is to isolate his end-rhymes, preferring instead to situate them as sonic prominences in a sympathetic phonic landscape. He explicitly pre-prepares the reader's ear for the end-rhymes so that when the first word in each end-rhyme pair is sounded ('all' and 'before') it immediately registers as a rhyme because of its assonance and consonance with words earlier in the line ('all' near the start of line 1, and 'more' in the middle of line 2). Although 'more' in line 2 is unstressed, it is aurally present enough to plant unobtrusively the sound that 'before' will emphasize, and it will find its fully stressed realization at the end of line 4. The end-rhymes of lines 1 and 2 ('all' and 'before') not only find their end-rhyme partners in lines 3 and 4 ('call' and 'more'), but are echoed verbatim in line 4 as well ('All' and 'before'). When one considers that the sounds of the two end-rhyme pairs ('-all' and '-ore'), although distinct, are phonetically not too distant from each other, that these sounds are repeated internally, and that line 4 repeats the first two end-rhyme words, the upshot is a powerfully cumulative sonic force in the final line of the quatrain.

The quatrain exemplifies how rhyme patterns are complemented by rhetorical figures dependent on repetition. Line 2 is a superb example of antimetabole or commutatio: the line can be folded in the middle at the word 'more' with the word order of the second half reversing that of the first. The nearly identical pronunciation of 'then' and 'than', and the almost elided distinction between 'hast' and 'hadst', facilitate the mirroring effect. Line

---

[9] Wigham and Rebhorn (2007) 178.

one delivers a rather less perfect version of the same figure in which 'Take all my loves' is reversed by 'my love, yea, take them all'. This figure creates neatly packed, indeed concentrically arranged, pairs of rhyme within each line as the second half delivers its series matching words to the first. This effect is distributed more widely by the recurrence of paronomasia, ploce, and diacope throughout the poem (including, 'No love, my love' and 'All mine was thine'), as well as the isocolon and antimetabole of the separated lines, 'more than thou hadst before' (line 2) and 'before thou hadst this more' (line 4).

The extensive use of rhetorical and sonic repetition within the lines reduces the diversity of sound, and this limited diversity along with the sonorants softens the aural starkness of the two end-rhyme pairs and absorbs them into the play of sound in the quatrain. The repetition of the intimate form of address, 'my love' (lines 1, 3), and the use of the colloquial 'yea' (line 1), give the quatrain an emotive edge that is maintained by the recurrence of the word 'love' throughout the poem. Affect is maintained by the poem's insistent use of personal pronouns which also keep alive a specific collection of sounds ('my', 'my'; 'thou', 'thou'; 'my', 'thou'; 'mine', 'thine', 'thou'; 'my', 'thou', 'my'; 'I', 'thee', 'my', 'thou'; 'thou'; 'thyself'; 'I', 'thy'; 'thou', 'thee', 'my'; 'me', 'we'). The poem attempts to absorb the friend's betrayal of the speaker's love into a larger and more resilient definition of their love. This larger definition depends on co-opting the divisive 'mine' and 'thine' into a 'we' (line 14) in which giving and taking are neutralized by an eternal sense of shared having that asserts no 'more' could be added to 'all'.

The speaker is under emotional strain and the poem does not resolve the act of betrayal or the pain it caused despite the reassuring, reflective harmonies of the first quatrain. Rhyming effects in lines 1–4 have given some comfort by their power to bind the speaker and his friend in a mirroring plenitude of love. Unfortunately, the very fact that this plenitude is figured as a mirroring effect of 'mine' and 'thine', means that it still reaches for the elusive unity of 'we' that is only projected, with urgent plaintiveness, in line 14.

25.3 END-RHYME WORDS AS A BINDER OF THE SONNET

Shakespeare's interest in building aesthetically unified quatrains that phonetically own their end-rhymes (a horizontal effect), is matched by his exploration of the possible effects of end-rhyme words as they cascade down the ends of all the lines in a sonnet (a vertical effect).[10] Sonnets 129 and 87 are suggestive in this connection.

In Sonnet 129, as surely as sound echo completes an end-rhyme unit, so lust is ever accompanied by its deleterious impact. A 'waste of shame' (line 1) is not just

---

[10] See Ferry's superb exposition of this effect (2002; 173–84).

phonetically, but also semantically, followed by 'blame' (line 3), as surely as 'lust' (line 2) is deemed 'not to trust' (line 4). Lust is 'despised straight' (line 5) as if a 'swallowed bait' (line 7), which as soon as 'had' (line 6) makes one 'mad' (line 8), and 'in possession so' (line 9) amounts to 'a very woe' (line 11). The trail of end-rhyme words asserts a unity of physiological impulsion and repulsion that rises to a crescendo with the word 'extreme' (line 10), and yet this word melts, via its rhyme partner, into the teasing aftertaste of a 'dream' (line 12). Lust is compellingly substantial and natural, yet somehow insubstantial and troubling. With 'dream' as a pointer to intellectual perplexity, the couplet then turns personal conundrum into universal human paradox. Well knowing clashes with knowing well (line 13) from which it separates irremediably, and heaven finds itself in league with hell (line 14). The reader is left with a final, end-rhyme paradox of 'well' and 'hell' (lines 13/14) which captures the poem's conceptual core and contains an ethical clash between the natural ('well') and the religious ('hell').

In Sonnet 87 the end-rhyme effect is more immediately obvious because it departs wholesale from the usual pattern:

> Farewell—thou art too dear for my possessing,
> And like enough thou know'st thy estimate.
> The charter of thy worth gives thee releasing;
> My bonds in thee are all determinate.
> For how do I hold thee but by thy granting,
> And for that riches where is my deserving?
> The cause of this fair gift in me is wanting,
> And so my patent back again is swerving.
> Thyself thou gav'st, thy own worth then not knowing,
> Or me to whom thou gav'st it else mistaking;
> So thy great gift, upon misprision growing,
> Comes home again, on better judgment making.
>   Thus have I had thee as a dream doth flatter:
>   In sleep a king, but waking no such matter.

Lines 2 and 4 of this poem function as regular iambic verses. This end-rhyme pair ('estimate'/'determinate') would be unexceptional in most sonnets, but has an aural prominence in Sonnet 87 because of the poem's unusual end-rhyme character. The remaining twelve lines all end with a hypermetrical, unstressed syllable, often called 'feminine rhyme'. In ten lines the extra syllable is '-ing', which usually drops the 'g' in original pronunciation to become '-in' (or the softer schwa sound plus 'n'). The couplet is also a feminine rhyme but, unlike the others, ends with the distinctive '-er'. The sonnet's rhyme scheme, if one considers only the stressed sound pairs of the tenth syllable, is regular (*abab cdcd efef gg*), but the twelve hypermetrical lines mean that the poem insistently delivers a soft, supplementary sound after the main rhyme sound and in ten instances this sound ('-in') rhymes widely.

In the first quatrain the speaker declares his friend 'too dear for my possessing' (line 1), which suggests primarily that the friend's higher status and inherent worth make the match between them unsustainable. For this reason the speaker declares the friend's obligation of love to him to be dissolved and his 'bonds'(line 4)—legal, emotional, intellectual—terminated. The curtness of line 4, with its end-rhyme closing on the strident word 'determinate' (line 4), affirms the speaker's certainty that began the quatrain with the emphatic 'Farewell' (line 1). Although the conceit of the friend's higher status or worth is maintained throughout the poem, the early phrase, 'too dear', can also suggest the friend is too dear to too many, that is, too much loved by another or by others, to be contracted in a faithful friendship with the speaker. This negative possibility shadows the more decorous and epideictic interpretation, and is activated again in line two ('And like enough thou know'st thy estimate') which suggests the friend could be secretly aware of his own failures in fidelity.

After the poem's conceptually and phonetically emphatic start (lines 1–4), the rest of it is overcome by hypermetric end-rhymes that spread their sound beyond the fitting end of each line. This failure of lines of verse to terminate firmly is complemented by the fact that almost all of these lingering syllables are part of present participles. Against the firm peg of 'determinate' there washes an endless ebbing and flowing of love and separation between the speaker and his friend: 'my possessing' and 'thee releasing' (lines 1–3); 'thy granting' and 'me is wanting' (lines 5–7); and 'deserving' and 'swerving' with its dark moral undertone (lines 6–8). The speaker's early decisiveness is overwhelmed by his indecisive second-guessing which aurally suggests both an interminable 'swerving' (line 8) of desire and its accompanying tedium via the list-like effect of the relentless termination, '-in'. The hypermetric, unstressed syllables that bind the poem together even while they weaken its limits, similarly hold the speaker and his friend in lingering togetherness that is uncertain and uncomfortable. Rhyme has adumbrated the troubling persistence and flux of desire.

25.4 END-RHYME WORDS AS A BINDER OF THE SONNET SEQUENCE

The binding power of end-rhyme reaches beyond the quatrain and individual sonnet to impact on the reader's sense of the pairing and sequencing of poems in Shakespeare's Sonnets. Within the subsequences of sonnets to the young man (1–126) and to the dark lady (127–52), there are pairs or clusters of sonnets that are thematically linked to one another such as: Sonnets 44–5 (on earth and water, and air and fire); 46–7 (the eye and heart at war and peace); 50–1 (the speaker's journeying to and from his friend on horseback); and 135–6 (the poems punning on 'Will'). In addition to such thematic clustering, some sonnets are bound together by their use of common end-rhyme words, such as Sonnets 95 and 96 which explore the beauty and moral faultiness of the friend.

In Sonnet 95 the speaker explains in an apostrophe to his friend how the telling of 'thy sport' (1. 6), rather than being mere dispraise, ends up as a sort of praise that 'blesses an ill report' (line 8). These uncommon rhyme-words ('sport'/'report') are redeployed in

Sonnet 96 in an emphatic way that enables the reader of both poems to experience their sonic relationship. Sonnet 96 begins by declaring that the friend's 'graces' and 'faults' are hard to distinguish from one another (lines 1–4) as his 'gentle sport' is a 'grace' (line 2). The first quatrain concludes: 'Thou mak'st faults graces that to thee resort' (line 4). The 'sport'/'resort' rhyme in Sonnet 96 reminds the reader of the 'sport'/'report' rhyme of Sonnet 95 and, so there can be no doubting the significance of this dual-poem rhyming effect, the couplet concluding Sonnet 96 restates the sounds again:

> But do not so: I love thee in such sort
> As, thou being mine, mine is thy good report.

It is exceptional that the two neighbouring and thematically paired poems give three end-rhyme pairs based on the one strident sound: '-ort'. The key rhyming words of these poems—the friend's 'sport' versus his 'report'—foreground the primary thematic axis of the poems which is the contradiction between internal (or moral) imperfection and external (physical or reputational) perfection. It is important, as the speaker is fully aware, that 'sport' and 'report' are terms that can accept positive or negative associations depending on how they are presented, and so graces and blemishes fade in and out of one another with unsettling fluidity.

In Shakespeare's day the word 'fault', so emphasized in the first quatrain of Sonnet 96 (mentioned three times), is sounded without the 'l' and so chimes roundly with the '-ort' sounds. The phonic match is very strong, but not identical, because the phonic and durational effect of the rhotic-r maintains a distinction. Thus the concept of 'fault' is evoked by the sounding of the words, 'sport' and 'report'. These two words simultaneously suggest and conceal, both semantically and phonetically, the friend's 'fault'. The couplet concluding Sonnet 96 and thus concluding the pair of poems, emphatically overwrites these moral concerns with a meta-poetic 'good report' arising from the speaker's desire for unity in love. The friend's 'fault' thereby finds its ultimate phonetic 'report' (to pun on Puttenham's word for the concluding sound in a rhyme pair that creates its 'concord') in the speaker's 'good report' (96. 14), which delivers aural and emotional closure that is effective, although not perfect.

It is one thing to argue for the carriage of identical rhyme sounds across two sonnets as a way of binding them together, but quite another to see such 'rhyme-links' connecting a longer series of sonnets in a structural chain. MacDonald P. Jackson argues that Sonnets 131 to 146 are a unique run of sixteen rhyme-linked sonnets in Shakespeare's sequence.[11] This means that at least one end-rhyme word from one end-rhyme pair in a sonnet finds itself repeated as an end-rhyme word in the next sonnet which introduces another end-rhyme pair from which at least one end-rhyme word finds itself recurring in the next sonnet and so on. So, to summarize the second half of Jackson's sequence, the end-rhyme word 'pain' in Sonnet 140 (line 4) is repeated as an end-rhyme word in

---

[11] Jackson, 'Shakespeare's Sonnets: Rhyme and Reason in the Dark Lady Series', *Notes and Queries* 46 (June 1999): 219–22.

Sonnet 141 (line 14), and 'thee'/'be' in 141 (lines 10/12) is repeated entirely in 142 (lines 10/12), and then 'thee' is repeated in 143 (line 9) which also introduces 'still' (line 14), which is repeated in 144 (line 2) which also introduces 'fiend' (line 9), which is repeated in 145 (line 11) which also introduces 'end' (line 9), which is repeated in 146 (line 8) and there, fittingly with the word 'end', the sequence ends.

Jackson argues that such a long sequence of rhyme-linked sonnets is so unusual in the entire collection, and so statistically improbable as a random occurrence, that it must be a deliberate arrangement, presumably by Shakespeare himself. If this is so, as Jackson points out, it helps respond to two complaints often made by critics about the collection: that the dark lady sonnets (127–52) in contrast to the sonnets to the young man (1–126) have little or no governing order, and that Sonnet 145, with its unique octosyllabic lines and unsophisticated conceit on Anne Hathaway's name, is out of place as a piece of juvenilia in a collection of otherwise mature verse. If the binding together of Sonnets 131–46 via a chain of recurring rhyme-words is a work of conscious artistry, and if this suggests Shakespearean authorship more than non-Shakespearean, then readers are encouraged to construct interpretive theses that incorporate a sense of this purposeful unity. Jackson attempts such a conclusion that presents Sonnet 145 as an authorially placed piece of thematically related 'comic relief' (though not trivial or without resonance) between the philosophically profound Sonnets 144 and 146.[12] Thematic and biographical reasons may be strong threads in the case for the careful positioning of Sonnet 145, but the forensic analysis of rhyme is valuable too, just as it is in the attempt to date the sonnets and attribute authorship to contested passages in the Shakespeare corpus.[13]

25.5 RHYME SOUNDING HUMAN CONCORD

Rhyme not only strengthens a poem's formal integrity, but in so doing gives pleasure. Puttenham joins with other early modern defenders of rhyme in thinking of it as a feature of English poetry that compensates for the absence of the pleasing metrical harmonies native to Greek and Latin verse:

> we make in the ends of our verses a certain tunable sound, which anon after with another verse reasonable distant we accord together in the last fall or cadence, the ear taking pleasure to hear the like tune reported, and to feel his return.[14]

---

[12] Jackson (1999) 221–2.

[13] See Jackson's arguments in 'Rhymes in Shakespeare's *Sonnets*': Evidence of Date of Composition', *Notes and Queries* 46 (June 1999): 213–19, and 'Rhymes and Authors: Shakespeare, Wilkins, and *Pericles*', *Notes and Queries* 58.2 (June 2011): 260–6.

[14] Wigham and Rebhorn (2007) 165–6.

The pleasure of poetry derives, at least in part, from the ear's perception of the recurrence of a distinct sound at the end of a verse after a certain gap of time: 'your verses answering each other by couples, or at larger distances in good cadence, is it that maketh your meter symphonical'.[15] Regardless of how regular one's metre or the gap between end-rhymes may be, without memory there can be no feeling of a 'return' and no sense of symphony. Memory is rhyme's unacknowledged *sine qua non* and the cause of its peculiar temporality in which the reader experiences both a recalling of the past and a sensation of present concord. Rhyme is beguiling because while it does deliver a 'symphonical' pleasure, half the experience is merely imagined. Rhyme, aided by memory, in a show of power, stages a collapse of time so that the temporally absent can sing with the aurally present in a harmony that is delightful, empowering, and always at least a little fraudulent.

It is no wonder, given this situation of difference unified, that rhyme has been associated by critics with the rich paradoxes of friendship where any friend's song of unity is always poised on the brink of real and imagined.[16] The association is inherent in Shakespeare's Sonnets as the analyses above have implicitly shown. Sonnet 8 takes the association further:

> Music to hear, why hear'st thou music sadly?
> Sweets with sweets war not, joy delights in joy.
> Why lov'st thou that which thou receiv'st not gladly,
> Or else receiv'st with pleasure thine annoy?
> If the true concord of well-tunèd sounds
> By unions married do offend thine ear,
> They do but sweetly chide thee, who confounds
> In singleness the parts that thou shouldst bear.
> Mark how one string, sweet husband to another,
> Strikes each in each by mutual ordering,
> Resembling sire and child and happy mother,
> Who all in one one pleasing note do sing;
>   Whose speechless song, being many, seeming one,
>   Sings this to thee: 'Thou single wilt prove none'.

The opening quatrain depends for its musicality on echoed sounds and repeated words within rhetorical figures of repetition, balance, and reversal. 'Music to hear' is balanced, echoed, and reversed in word and sense by 'hear'st thou music sadly' (line 1), and the ensuing three lines deliver variations on this effect. The quatrain manages to repeat, elegantly and in close succession, six significant words: 'music', 'hear'/'hear'st', 'sweets', 'joy', 'thou', and 'receiv'st'. Additionally, 'not', 'with', and 'why', are repeated; the '-st' suffix occurs four times (three being '-v'st'); and the end-rhyme

---

[15] Wigham and Rebhorn (2007) 169.
[16] Raymond N. MacKenzie, 'Rethinking Rhyme, Signifying Friendship: Milton's *Lycidas* and *Epitaphium Damonis*', *Modern Philology* 106.3 (2009): 531–6.

pairs, 'sadly'/'gladly' and 'joy'/'annoy', add to the unifying harmonics of the quatrain at the same time as they semantically underscore the paradox being described (sadness in gladness, annoy in joy).

What is so incredible about this opening is that it not only sets the fictive scene of the friend's melancholic experience of beautiful music which is developed into the conceit of sonic harmony (the sympathetic vibration of paired lute strings or human voices in chorus) chiding the friend for his barren 'singleness' (line 8), but also illustrates this conceit verbally via a dense tissue of echoes. The internal echoes and rhymes enable the reader to experience 'the true concord of well-tunèd sounds' (line 5) that signifies the perfection and desirability of marriage and family which condemn the friend's stubborn singleness. As the couplet, and also its end-rhymes taken as a pair, reveal: to be 'one' is to be 'none' (lines 13–14). This commonplace receives added point when one considers that 'one' was originally pronounced something like 'own' or 'awn' and this was an exact rhyme with the old pronunciation of 'none' which also preserved the long 'o'. This is a powerful sound that echoes through the poem's final three lines and culminates in a condemnation of the friend: 'one one', 'note', 'one', 'none'.

The speaker's lesson to the young man amounts to identifying the qualitative difference between 'being many, seeming one' (line 13), and being 'single' and therefore 'none' (line 14). The former is difference unified, like the rich fertility of the best sort of rhyme and love, while the latter is sameness repeated, like the poor and barren form called identical rhyme that dissolves instantly into mere self-echo. This sonnet comes closer than any other to collapsing time because it imagines the same-time sympathetic resonance of paired lute strings or a family's voices in chorus, and never forgets that 'true concord', like rhyme, is 'many, seeming one'.

25.6 RHYME SOUNDING TIME

It should come as no surprise, given the preceding discussion, that the word, 'rhyme', whether it means a specific poem, poems generally, or poetical skill, is always rhymed with the word, 'time', in the Sonnets. This end-rhyme pair in Sonnets 16, 17, 32, 55, 106, and 107 confirms that the speaker is a poet at war with time over his friend. In Sonnet 16 the speaker urges his young friend to procreate because it is a 'means more blessèd than my barren rhyme' to 'fortify yourself in your decay' (lines 3–4). The emphasis in the poem is on procreation's production of a truer reproduction of the self, and thus a 'mightier' (line 1) resistance to time, than poetry or painting could achieve. The theme is continued in the rhyme-linked Sonnet 17 where 'rhyme' is no longer suggestively 'barren' (16. 4), but has an opposite problem. The speaker declares his poetry will not be believed to reflect accurately the beauty of his friend 'in time to come' (line 1) because '[s]uch heavenly touches' (line 8) will be considered mere poetic exaggeration rather than 'true concord' (as Puttenham says of rhyme). The poet resolves the problem thus:

> But were some child of yours alive that time,
> You should live twice: in it, and in my rhyme.
>
> (lines 13–14)

In times to come the child's incarnation of the young man's beauty will be present evidence of the truth of the poet's poetic rhyme of the man's perfections. The rhyme will work and the poem be accepted only if time can be collapsed via 'some child of yours' who will function as a present memory of a past term (the dead friend) and thereby enable the reader's untroubled experience of symphony.

The sounding of time in the context of friendship reaches its astonishing climax in Sonnet 126, which of all Shakespeare's Sonnets is the most aesthetically unusual:

> O thou my lovely boy, who in thy power
> Dost hold time's fickle glass, his sickle-hour;
> Who hast by waning grown, and therein show'st
> Thy lovers withering as thy sweet self grow'st—
> If nature, sovereign mistress over wrack,
> As thou goest onwards still will pluck thee back,
> She keeps thee to this purpose: that her skill
> May time disgrace, and wretched minutes kill.
> Yet fear her, O thou minion of her pleasure!
> She may detain but not still keep her treasure.
>   Her audit, though delayed, answered must be,
>   And her quietus is to render thee.

The poem is the last of the large section of sonnets generally concerned with the young friend (1–126), and critics have noted how it functions as an envoi to that section. Oddly, Sonnet 126 comprises six rhyming couplets (*aabbccddeeff*) and omits lines 13–14. The poem, as originally printed in the quarto (FIGURE 25.1), has numerous other puzzling elements, three of which will be discussed here because of their relation to sound and rhyme.[17]

The first quatrain presents the friend as a controller of time, holding in his power 'times fickle glasse, his sickle, hower' (line 2, according to the quarto). The quarto's punctuation has made it difficult for readers to resolve the meaning and various editorial emendations are attempted. Time is traditionally associated with the hourglass, the sickle, and the hour, and one can easily imagine how time might be described as 'fickle', but how these evocative terms are meant to relate to one another grammatically is difficult to say. The quatrain is semantically compacted: in general terms, one could argue that the friend's youthful beauty resists time's effects and, as his lovers wither in their mortality and Petrarchan-style love-suffering, the friend grows in singular maturity and strength. At least part of the problem of line 2 is caused by rhyme because it would seem that the use of the word 'fickle' has phonetically provoked the appearance of its internal rhyme partner 'sickle'. These two words not only look identical because 'sickle' is printed

---

[17] I refer to the quarto text as reproduced in Vendler (1997).

SONNETS.

126

O Thou my louely Boy who in thy power,
   Doeft hould times fickle glaffe,his fickle,hower:
Who haft by wayning growne,and therein fhou'ft,
Thy louers withering,as thy fweet felfe grow'ft.
If Nature(foueraine mifteres ouer wrack)
As thou goeft onwards ftill will plucke thee backe,
She keepes thee to this purpofe,that her skill.
May time difgrace,and wretched mynuit kill.
Yet feare her O thou minnion of her pleafure,
She may detaine,but not ftill keepe her trefure!
Her *Audite*(though delayd)anfwer'd muft be,
And her *Quietus* is to render thee.
   (   )
   (   )

FIGURE 25.1 Sonnet 126, 'Shake-speares Sonnets. Neuer before imprinted' (1609), sig. H3r. By permission of the Folger Shakespeare Library.

with a long 's' (resembling identical eye-rhyme), but they have also separated the word 'hourglass' into its component parts, thereby opening up both 'hour' and 'glass' to further interpretive resonance related to time.[18] Add to this the fact that 'sickle' (along with 'waning' in line 3) suggests lunar inconstancy and change. Without denying its other resonances, the first quatrain is primarily about the friend holding time's hourglass in his power. Hours are sickle-like because they cut mortality down as they proceed, and the hourglass is sickle-like due to its curved profile. As the passage of time is measured by sand passing from one glass to the other, the friend grows in fullness like the lower glass while his lovers wither like the depleting contents of the upper glass.

While the first quatrain presents the friend's control of time's passage via the image of him holding an hourglass, the second introduces 'Nature' as a higher power that holds the friend in hand against the flow of time. Nature 'keepes' the friend, preserving his beauty, 'that her skill|May time disgrace, and wretched minutes kill' (lines 7–8). Here again the original quarto reading seems preferable: 'wretched mynuit kill'. Three important

[18] Shakespeare's Sonnets abound in rhyme-based provocation where the sound of one word seemingly causes the inclusion of another, phonically related word. In Sonnet 64 the speaker demonstrates and confesses this simultaneously: 'Ruin hath taught me thus to ruminate' (line 11).

qualities of the verse are lost when 'mynuit' is editorially transformed into 'minutes': first, the biting effect resulting from the strident, stopped consonants is weakened by the addition of the 's'; second, the singular absolute, 'mynuit', has far more abstract and sinister power as a cosmic force than the mundane progression of 'minutes' with which we are all familiar; and third, the addition of 's' to 'mynuit' risks the sounding of an identical rhyme between 'skill' and '–s kill' which is less desirable aesthetically than 'skill'/'kill' (lines 7–8).

The curtly bitten-off sounding of time in 'wretched mynuit kill' is suggestive of other evocations of time in the Sonnets. In the final line of Sonnet 100 we read of time's 'scythe and crookèd knife'. '[S]cythe' and 'knife' are near rhymes of each other and within them the word 'crookèd' almost rhymes on itself ('cru-cud'). In original pronunciation the vowel sound in 'scythe' approximates that in 'knife' so that both are short in duration, just as 'crookèd' sounds like two short sounds. The upshot is a quick, balanced, and phonically punctuated clause that seems to emphasize repeated abruptness via consonantal stoppages which the reader might associate with a cutting action. Interestingly, 'crookèd' appears only once more in the Sonnets, in Sonnet 60, where it again signifies time's malignity in a portentously clipped phrase: 'crookèd eclipses' (line 7).

Returning to Sonnet 126, in the third quatrain the quarto italicizes both '*Audite*' and '*Quietus*' (lines 11–12). This has a foregrounding effect because no other word in the poem is italicized and both suggest a subliminal context of sound for mortality. The primary meaning may be mercantile, aligning one's death with a final reckoning ('audit') that involves Nature's due payment ('quietus') of the friend to time's embrace, yet etymologically 'audit' relates to 'hearing' and 'quietus' to silence. It is as if mortality is a sonic event that ultimately concludes in silence. How fitting then that the quarto has this printed for lines 13–14:

$$(\hspace{8cm})$$
$$(\hspace{8cm})$$

As critics have noted, this unusual ending is suggestive of many things, not least including the profile of an empty hourglass (time run out), the dissolution of poetic praise (the poet's impotency), and the frame of an empty coffin (soon to hold the friend).[19]

The printed parentheses make this a sonnet rather than a defective twelve-line poem, and they create a regular sestet describing nature's ultimate handing over of the friend to death, if not now, then imminently. But more importantly, the parentheses, along with the poem's thorough commitment to couplets, strongly imply that this is also, somehow, a rhyming couplet. Up to this point, rhyme has represented difference unified and thereby underscored the troubling paradoxes of time-bound friendship. The desired symphony has always been a sleight of hand because time and place, and self and other,

---

[19] See Rayna Kalas, 'Fickle Glass' in *A Companion to Shakespeare's Sonnets,*' ed. Michael Schoenfeldt (Oxford: Blackwell, 2007) 261–76.

just like rhyme, will never resolve into singularity. And yet here, in the 'quietus' that will envelop the dead friend, the sounds of noisy mortality vanish and perfect silence ensues. Breathtakingly, in this final representation of defeat, Shakespeare's speaker reaches the zenith of ingenuity because his frail, wordless parentheses throw a net about eternity and steal a perfect rhyme from oblivion itself. In two miraculous lines Shakespeare has folded infinity on itself and delivered a rhyme that can neither be heard nor faulted.

Select Bibliography

Alexander, Gavin (2004) (ed.) *Sidney's 'Defence of Poesy' and Selected Renaissance Literary Criticism* (London: Penguin).

Ferry, Anne (2002) 'The Sense of Rhyme: Sidney and Shakespeare', *Literary Imagination* 4.2: 163–89.

Flint, Lorna (2000) *Shakespeare's Third Keyboard: The Significance of Rime in Shakespeare's Plays* (Newark: University of Delaware Press).

Jackson, MacDonald P. (1999) 'Rhymes in Shakespeare's Sonnets: Evidence of Date of Composition', *Notes and Queries* 46: 213–19.

—— (1999) 'Shakespeare's Sonnets: Rhyme and Reason in the Dark Lady Series', *Notes and Queries* 46: 219–22.

—— (2011) 'Rhymes and Authors: Shakespeare, Wilkins, and *Pericles*', *Notes and Queries* 58.2: 260–6.

Kalas, Rayna (2007) 'Fickle Glass', in Michael Schoenfeldt (ed.), *A Companion to Shakespeare's Sonnets* (Oxford: Blackwell) 261–76.

Lanham, Richard A. (1991) *A Handlist of Rhetorical Terms*. 2nd edn (Berkeley: University of California Press).

MacKenzie, Raymond N. (1009) 'Rethinking Rhyme, Signifying Friendship: Milton's *Lycidas* and *Epitaphium Damonis*', *Modern Philology* 106.3: 530–54.

McGuire, Philip C. (1987) 'Shakespeare's Non-Shakespearean Sonnets', *Shakespeare Quarterly* 38.3: 304–19.

Ness, Frederic W. (1941) *The Use of Rhyme in Shakespeare's Plays* (New Haven: Yale University Press).

Palfrey, Simon (2005) *Doing Shakespeare* (London: Thomson).

Vendler, Helen (1997) *The Art of Shakespeare's Sonnets* (Cambridge, MA: Harvard University Press).

Vickers, Brian (1998) *In Defence of Rhetoric* (Oxford: Clarendon Press).

Whigham, Frank, and Rebhorn, Wayne A. (2007) (eds) *George Puttenham, The Art of English Poesy: A Critical Edition* (Ithaca: Cornell University Press).

....

CHAPTER 26

THE CONCEPTUAL INVESTIGATIONS OF SHAKESPEARE'S SONNETS

....

DAVID SCHALKWYK

SHAKE-SPEARES SONNETS has been pursued for a number of elusive quarries: the identities of the Sonnets' putative addressees; whether or not through them Shakespeare 'unpacked his heart'; or their inauguration of a new form of poetic subjectivity. I tackle these issues via Samuel Beckett's question, 'What matter who's speaking?' (quoted by Michel Foucault in his pursuit of the question 'What is an Author?')[1] by arguing that the speaking voice and its situations of address reveal a conceptual mapping or investigations of the relation between love and desire.

26.1 WHO IS SPEAKING?

....

Who is speaking in Shakespeare's best-known sonnet?

> Let me not to the marriage of true mindes
> Admit impediments, loue is not loue
> Which alters when it alteration findes,
> Or bends with the remouer to remoue.
> O no, it is an euer fixed marke
> That lookes on tempests and is neuer shaken;
> It is the star to euery wandring barke,

---

[1] Michel Foucault, 'What is an Author?' in Michel Foucault, *Language, counter-memory, practice: selected essays and interviews* (Ithaca: Cornell University Press, 1980).

> Whose worths vnknowne, although his higth be taken.
> Lou's not Times foole, though rosie lips and cheeks
> Within his bending sickles compasse come,
> Loue alters not with his breefe houres and weekes,
> But beares it out euen to the edge of doome:
>   If this be error and vpon me proued,
>   I neuer writ, nor no man euer loued.[2]

(SONNET 116)

If we believe Helen Vendler, the speaker is whoever reads or recites it. The Sonnets, she declares, are 'scripted for repeated personal recitation. One is to utter them as one's own words, not as the words of another'.[3] But this is not quite right. The best man reciting this sonnet at a wedding is not presenting the thoughts entirely as his own. Rather than writing his own poem, or paraphrasing its views on love in his own words, he recites the sonnet in order, at least in part, to speak with *Shakespeare's* voice. But that is not quite right either, because *Shakespeare* is not the person speaking in these poems.[4] Conventionally, we say that it is Shakespeare's 'poet' who speaks. But the speaker of the Sonnets is not really the poet. Shakespeare is the poet. He writes the poems but, curiously, they do not speak in his voice. They speak with the voice of a *persona* or mask. This persona, among his many roles and attributes, happens on occasion to refer to himself as a poet. The speaker of Shakespeare's Sonnets is therefore whoever wears the mask that a sonnet makes available through its voice. Is the poem itself the mask, both hiding and providing a subjective space for whoever appropriates it? Or is the mask itself part of the performance of the sonnet: an aspect of its voice and structure rather than something that stands behind the poem? Either way, the sonnet is not just lyrical speech occupied or spoken by whoever reads it, but rather a performance, a set of actions, a tiny piece of theatre different, but not entirely separate, from both the person who reads or recites it and the one who wrote it.[5] They are joined by the mask of the sonnet.

Vendler concedes as much in her commentary on Sonnet 116 when she declares that it is not an 'impersonal' definition of love but rather a response to another, implied speaker: 'I read this poem as an example not of definition but of dramatic refutation or rebuttal' (489). Sonnet 116 is thus a fragment or continuation of an interrupted dialogue. In the face of an excuse offered by the young man that, while he still loves the speaker, he either vacillates in his affections or he has engaged in other affairs, the speaker responds that *he* certainly would not contemplate or engage in such vacillation and still call it

---

[2] Quotations from the Sonnets are all from the 1609 Quarto facsimile in Stephen Booth (ed.), *Shakespeare's Sonnets* (1977; rpt New Haven: Yale University Press, 2000).

[3] Helen Vendler, *The Art of Shakespeare's Sonnets* (Cambridge, MA: Harvard University Press, 1999) 18.

[4] See David Schalkwyk, 'Shakespeare's Speech', *Journal of Medieval and Early Modern Studies* 40, 2 (2010): 373–400.

[5] For a discussion of the perfomative language of the Sonnets in the negotiation of relationships, see David Schalkwyk, *Speech and Performance in Shakespeare's Sonnets and Plays* (Cambridge: Cambridge University Press, 2002).

love. *Love as such* does not allow for change or hesitancy. *If you insist on behaving in this way, don't call it love;* I *certainly won't be persuaded by your behavior or your excuses to do so.* The emphasis is initially on the first-person as respondent ('Let *me* not [even if *you* do]') and subsequently on the reason or justification of the response. Only then does it become a definition of love: 'Love is *not* love | Which alters when it alteration finds … | Oh *no* it is an ever fixed mark …'.[6]

Vendler's reading of the poem as a speech act in a dialogue is thus at odds with her earlier insistence that the lyric voice always belongs to the reader who appropriates it. To speak with the voice of this sonnet's speaker one has to extrapolate or imagine a different *persona* to whom the sonnet is responding (even if the final outcome is a general definition of love). One has to lose something of one's own character by assuming another voice. The poem is a mask through which one responds to other masks: the interlocutor, the bride and groom, the wedding guests, but also Shakespeare himself. This prompts two related questions: who is speaking in them, and what does it matter who speaks? Close attention to the language of the sonnet tells us that the speaker is engaging in a dialogue with an implied person; that an intimate relationship is at stake; and that the two personae differ in their respective stances towards their relationship in love. They thus differ in their understanding of the *concept* love.

As it is tossed about in Shakespeare's Sonnets, 'love' is the outcome of a variety of engagements among the voices that speak through the poems, to which they respond, that are embedded within them, and that they make available to the reader. Such voices are not abstractions, but phenomenologically and historically embodied, even if we need to recover those embodied voices through our reading them.[7] When one reads Sonnet 116, then, how does one embody its voices? Whose are they?

26.2 Two Voices: Master and Servant

Let us now turn to Sonnet 58, which, like Sonnet 116, also responds to a given situation and prior debate:

> That God forbid, that made me first your slaue,
> I should in thought controule your times of pleasure,
> Or at your hand th' account of houres to craue,
> Being your vassail bound to staie your leisure.
> Oh let me suffer (being at your beck)
> Th' imprison'd absence of your libertie,
> And patience tame, to sufferance bide each check,

---

[6] My emphasis here follows Vendler's analysis (1999; 489).
[7] Bruce R. Smith. 'How Should One Read a Shakespeare Sonnet?', *Early Modern Literary Studies* Special Issue 19 (2009): 2.1–39 <http://purl.oclc.org/emls/si-19/smitsonn.htm> (accessed 20 November 2011).

> Without accusing you of iniury.
> Be where you list, your charter is so strong,
> That you your selfe may priuiledge your time
> To what you will, to you it doth belong,
> Your selfe to pardon of selfe-doing crime.
>   I am to waite, though waiting so be hell,
>   Not blame your pleasure be it ill or well.

Almost all editors reduce the capital in 'God' of the first line to 'god'. They turn the appeal from an invocation of the Christian deity into an allusion to Cupid, the classical god of love. 'That' is read as a demonstrative pronoun, referring to a distant or removed figure—*that* god (not ours). This turns the poem into a game, a merely metaphorical or figurative evocation of an attenuated slavery, in which an excess of irrational passion makes the speaker the slave (in love) of the beloved.

There is indeed a long history of speaking of erotic relationships as if they involved master (or mistress) in relation to a servant (or slave). The lover devotes himself to his beloved, casting himself in terms of total servility, dedicated to her pleasure, desire, or whim without blame or complaint. That is precisely what this speaker seems to do. He ends with an apparent declaration of abject patience—he accepts that all power lies in the beloved: 'I am to waite … Not blame your pleasure be it ill or well'. The speaking lover is resigned to wait *at the pleasure* of the beloved. This phrase combines a general sense of the political prerogative of masters with a specific entitlement to one-sided sexual freedom and carnal enjoyment. There is no defiant 'Oh no' in this sonnet, as there is in 116. But the tone of resistance or rebuttal, however attenuated, remains. The very qualification, 'be it ill or well', suggests judgement.

The question is whether one can acknowledge the full complexity of the sonnet—involving the interaction of speakers and their relation—by reading the relationship between master and servant in a purely figurative way, as if it's about Cupid, not God. What if the sonnet involves both God and Cupid?

If we assume that the speaker appeals to the God who is supposed to govern not only human desire but also political and social relations, then the poem reveals a complex interweaving of subject positions. A servant acknowledges his ordained position of subservience to a master—his duty is to wait upon the pleasure of the master with no right of complaint or freedom of personal desire—while simultaneously tingeing that acknowledgement with a degree of ironic resentment. That resentment is specifically a *lover's* prerogative. Servants do not have the right to demand reciprocal dedication, and therefore to limit the 'pleasure' and 'libertie' of their masters. Lovers surely do. This sonnet thus crosses the discourse of service, which involves a hierarchical, asymmetrical kind of reciprocity, with a non-courtly language of erotic love, which demands the reciprocity of equality: 'mutuall render onely me for thee' (Sonnet 125).

Given a choice between reading a Shakespeare sonnet as a simple account of love as metaphor of service and one in which a real master-servant relationship is being renegotiated as an erotic entanglement, we should choose the more complex possibility, in which both the social rank and personal affection are engaged. For that begins to answer our two questions: who is speaking, and what does it matter who is speaking? The speaking persona in Sonnet 58 is a *real* servant who appeals to his God-ordained social station to affirm his duty—his lack of 'liberty' and 'pleasure', in the fullest sense of those words. But the speaker is also a lover who infuses his social powerlessness with the implicit demands of a lover. 'I am to waite—*though waiting so be hell*', he states, calling through his free, resentful confession for a response from the beloved that counters the explicit declaration of the speaker-as-servant. He points to a conflict between the two different kinds of reciprocity that exist between masters and servants, on one hand, and lovers, on the other.

This conflict lies at the heart of Shakespeare's Sonnets. They seek to move from one concept of love to another: from the reciprocal but unequal engagement of master and servant as an intimate or affective relation to the ethical equivalence of lovers as friends.

Two further Sonnets, 26 and 57, explicitly invoke the address of servant to master. In the first the speaker adopts a fairly straightforward discourse of abject duty. It takes an epistolary form in which its semi-feudal terms ('Lord', 'vassalage', 'thy merit ... my dutie', 'fair aspect', 'tottered louing'), like Shakespeare's dedicatory epistle to the Earl of Southampton to *Venus and Adonis*, attest to a love that respects an almost insurmountable separation of place and degree:

> Lord of my loue, to whome in vassalage
> Thy merrit hath my dutie strongly knit;
> To thee I send this written ambassage
> To witnesse duty, not to shew my wit.
> Duty so great, which wit so poore as mine
> May make seeme bare, in wanting words to shew it;
> But that I hope some good conceipt of thine
> In thy soules thought (all naked) will bestow it:
> Til whatsoeuer star that guides my mouing,
> Points on me gratiously with faire aspect,
> And puts apparrell on my tottered louing,
> To show me worthy of their sweet respect,
>> Then may I dare to boast how I doe loue thee,
>> Til then, not show my head where thou maist proue me

Why is *this* poem not recited at weddings? Because it is impossible to generalize, abstract, or appropriate its speaking voice, addressee, or its situation of address to a celebration of modern romantic love between two equals. Sonnet 116 contains the clues of a dialogical interaction, but those clues are neither overwhelming nor are they carried into the body of the poem. Sonnet 26 speaks from within a situation of love that is alien to the modern sensibility. It invokes an unequally reciprocal set of relations, as much public as private, in which 'duty' and 'merit' are informed by such obsolete notions as 'vassalage' and a deeply felt sense that whatever value the speaker might have is bestowed by the accommodating 'fair aspect' of the 'Lord of [his] love'. We like to think that we no longer inhabit the positions of such servants or masters. The 'tottered [or tattered] loving' that occupies its centre belongs to a radically different world from that in which we celebrate love as a lofty 'star to every wandering bark'. And yet Shakespeare wrote both poems.

If the speaker in Sonnet 26 is a servant speaking to a master, so is the speaker in Sonnet 57:

> Being your slaue what should I doe but tend,
> Vpon the houres, and times of your desire?
> I haue no precious time at al to spend;
> Nor seruices to doe til you require.
> Nor dare I chide the world without end houre,
> Whilst I (my soueraine) watch the clock for you,
> Nor thinke the bitternesse of absence sowre,
> VVhen you haue bid your seruant once adieue.
> Nor dare I question with my iealious thought,
> VVhere you may be, or your affaires suppose,
> But like a sad slaue stay and thinke of nought
> Saue where you are, how happy you make those.
>   So true a foole is loue, that in your Will,
>   (Though you doe any thing) he thinkes no ill.

'Being your slave …' Is this a literal or metaphorical claim? Coming immediately before Sonnet 58, it extends the master-servant discourse most evident in Sonnet 26, making it especially concrete in the autobiographical signal of the capitalized 'Will' in the penultimate line. But it also complicates it. The use of 'slave' (twice) moves the poem into the discourse of hyperbole (there were no slaves in England), as does 'my sovereign', for the addressee is not literally the speaker's king. The most recognizable form of that exaggeration is the discourse of courtly love, where desire enslaves the lover while elevating the beloved. In these Sonnets the language-games of social duty and subservience are crossed *afresh* with the discourse of abject desire, providing a simultaneously distinctive and traditional voice. And in contrast with Sonnet 26, which addresses the master as 'thou' and 'thee', these adopt the more familiar pronoun 'you'. What does this mean?

26.3 PRONOUNS

The use of second-person pronouns in Shakespeare's Sonnets is complicated.[8] The rule is that 'you' was used between equals or by inferiors to superiors, whereas 'thou' denoted either social superiority (master to servant) or special intimacy (between lovers). But in a rapidly changing language matters were not simple. Some scholars have suggested that

[8] See Ulrich Busse, *Linguistic Variation in the Shakespeare Corpus* (Amsterdam and Philadelphia: John Benjamins, 2002), esp. ch. 4, and Jonathan Hope, *Shakespeare's Grammar* (London: Arden Shakespeare, 2003) 67–103.

the otherwise unusual use of 'thou' by the commoner poet in early Sonnets to the noble young man is the residual effect of adopting an archaic 'high poetic style', and therefore a more distant relationship,[9] even if the use of 'thou' by a social inferior (poet to patron) would have been unacceptably familiar or insulting.[10] The move to 'you' thus may signal a more intimate and equal relationship. Lynne Magnusson, on the other hand, argues that the use of 'thou' in the Sonnets is derived from Erasmus' notion of 'aggressive familiarity'. In this mode 'the insistent use of the direct second-person address intensifies the immediacy ... with an in-your-face directness and familiarity that is surprising in address to a nobleman ... the dialogue script of the early Sonnets models the initial relationship not primarily as Petrarchan lover to beloved but instead as humanist poet-tutor offering precepts in a persuasive style of aggressive familiarity to a beautiful aristocratic patron'.[11]

Magnusson's argument makes the question of who actually *is* speaking in these Sonnets especially difficult in relation to the pronouns used in both enunciation and address. Is it a Petrarchan lover to a beloved, in which the invoked discourse of social difference is chiefly metaphorical? A real servant addressing a master, and declaring love by explicitly acknowledging accepted difference? A humanist servant-poet, engaged by the family of a narcissistic young aristocrat, who adopts the language-game of Erasmian 'aggressive familiarity' to persuade the young nobleman to marriage? Or is it simply whoever happens to read them? Let's deal with the last possibility first.

We have seen that it is extremely difficult, if not impossible, to inhabit the words of Sonnets 26, 57, and 58 as 'one's own' in the 21st century. *One* speaks, as Vendler puts it, but that speaker is never merely 'one'—the utterances are always crossed by the voices, and the subject positions, of many others, even when one is speaking in what one thinks is one's own voice.[12] Bruce Smith writes: 'With respect to the body, "I," "he," and "thou" merge into that useful but now rarely heard pronoun "one." "One" *purports to be* third person, but it *functions as* an amalgam of "I" and "you." It exists somewhere in between "I" and "you"'.[13] Already contained within Vendler's 'one', then, is a plurality. And that plurality is both synchronic and diachronic. It peoples the voice with the cross-accents

[9] Cf. the consistent use of *Thou* to address God in the King James Bible.

[10] Andrew Gurr, '*You* and *Thou* in Shakespeare's Sonnets', *Essays in Criticism* 32: 9 (1982): 9–25. The rule of thumb is that the T form is used by superiors to inferiors; and the Y form by equals or by inferiors to superiors. This is complicated by both the fact that early modern English was tending towards the exclusive you of T forms and an affective register in terms of which T forms could express intimacy, anger, or contempt. See Hope (2003) 77.

[11] Lynne Magnusson, 'A Pragmatics for Interpreting Shakespeare's Sonnets 1 to 20: Dialogue Scripts and Erasmian Intertexts', *Methods in Historical Pragmatics: Approaches to Negotiated Meaning in Historical Contexts*, Susan M. Fitzmaurice and Irma Taavitsainen (eds), (Berlin and New York: Mouton de Gruyter, 2007) 167–84 (174 and 176).

[12] This view is elaborated most fully in the now largely forgotten but nevertheless crucial philosophy of language of Mikhail Mikhaïlovich Bakhtin, *The Dialogic Imagination: Four Essays* (Austin: University of Texas Press, 1981) and V. N. Voloshinov, *Marxism and the Philosophy of Language* (Cambridge, MA: Harvard University Press, 1986).

[13] Smith (2009).

of one's immediate social world, but it is also haunted by the spectres of what language retains of those who have spoken and written in the past.

One of those ghosts is the pronoun 'thou' and its cognates. How does a modern reader give his own voice to the *thous, thees,* and *thines* of Shakespeare's Sonnets? And how does a female reader give her own voice to their *I's, me's,* and *mines,* especially in the Sonnets following 126? Émile Benveniste has shown that these pronouns are not merely short-hand names: they all act—but especially *I*—as shifters.[14] They designate different people or subject positions depending on the context in which they are used, but they derive their meanings relationally: *I* can designate only in contrast with *you, he,* or *they; I* can move to incorporate these *others* by turning itself into *we;* or *I* can negotiate a no-man's-land in between by merging itself and others as *one.* Anyone who speaks or reads Shakespeare's Sonnets has to negotiate—consciously or not—among these various subject positions, some of which are historically—and thus diachronically—strange, alien, uncomfortable, or inassimilable. *Thou* and its cognates are alien to any modern wedding guest trying to make it his or her own.

Shakespeare's Sonnets embody a complex experiment in the social, linguistic, and philosophical dimensions of English pronominal use, and therefore of the position of the reader and the possibilities of making different voices *one's own.* It is the nature of pronouns to be appropriated. It is the nature of poetry to use this possibility by working the aspectual mode: to speak *as if* with the voice of another. Shakespeare's early Sonnets might adopt the unusually familiar *thou* by speaking as if by a parent to a recalcitrant son. The 'familiarly aggressive' tone of Sonnet 4, for example, which contains such affectionate castigations as, 'Unthrifty lovelinesse, why dost thou spend | Upon thyself thy beauties legacy? | ... Profitles usurer ... | having traffike with thy selfe alone, | Thou of thy selfe thy sweet self dost deceave', might be a servant speaking with the voice of parental authority, which in turn becomes crossed with his own desires and emotions. The affection and authority characteristic of a parent are assumed as, and thereby to some degree become, his own subject position.

Sonnet 13 is the first to address the young man as *you:* it 'marks the momentous first instant in which the speaker first uses vocatives of love' (Vendler, 102). This switch from *thou* to *you* is underlined by the near manic re-iteration of the new pronoun in the opening lines: 'you ... your ... you ... yours ... you your'. They become a kind of mantra, a *'first hollowing of thy faire name',* which will, in the ideal at least, be 'to constancy confined ... To one, of one, still such, and euer so' (105). But here the directness of the unusual second person (as opposed to the somewhat impersonal *one* of 105), forges a special intimacy with the addressee that transforms the adoptive earlier voice of parental affection into that of intensely felt, loving friendship. Through the possessive vocative, 'dear *my* love', this affect is infused into the repeated *you* at the close as much as in the opening of the sonnet: '... deare my loue *you* know, | *You* had a Father, let *your* Son say so's (Sonnet 13, my italics).

[14] Émile Benveniste, 'Subjectivity in Language' in Émile Benveniste, *Problems in General Linguistics* (Coral Gables: University of Miami Press, 1973).

The speaker of Sonnet 13 does not so much abandon the parental voice as accommodate it to his own, new and daring, declaration of personal intimacy and affection. Personal desire uses the mask of parental authority in the early poems, but by the time we get to Sonnet 26 that mask will no longer suffice. The servant-poet who is commissioned to persuade a recalcitrant, narcissistic young noble to 'put on the destined livery' (*Measure for Measure*, II. iv. 138) by acceding to his parents' desire to marry, finds himself exposed once he begins to express his own affections and desires. Sonnet 26 replaces the mask of parental authority with the abject stance of a servant whose love finds itself transgressing the bounds of reciprocal social obligation. It helps that the discourse of such obligation has already infused that of erotic love through the courtly tradition, so that the poet can now speak with two voices at once, or through a double mask—the one (social obligation) acting as a front for the other (erotic devotion). By the time we get to Sonnets 57 and 58, the latter speaks much more forcefully, through its more intimate pronominal use and the irony that the third person makes available.

One needs to take care not to use the order of the Sonnets to construe a simple narrative of emotional development. Their voices are complex, and each poem may be an example of the speaker trying out different masks. But the cluster of Sonnets in the 20s do seem to attempt to negotiate a developing relationship between two related concepts of love: *eros* and *nomos*.[15] Although Sonnets 26 and 58 share a socially embedded discourse of master-servant relations, they use that discourse in different ways. Sonnet 26 reflects an abject love which dares not test the will of the master or assert his own; 57 and 58, in part through their shift of second-person pronoun from *thou* to *you*, revoice that relationship in terms of a more mutual, reciprocal concept of love.

26.4 AUTOBIOGRAPHY AND THE PLAYER'S MASKS

In Sonnet 23 a new dimension appears—the profession of actor, the social place of the theatre, and the relationship between public performance and private conversation:

> As an vnperfect actor on the stage,
> Who with his feare is put besides his part,
> Or some fierce thing repleat with too much rage,
> Whose strengths abondance weakens his owne heart;
> So I for feare of trust, forget to say,
> The perfect ceremony of loues right,
> And in mine owne loues strength seeme to decay,
> Ore-charg'd with burthen of mine owne loues might:

---

[15] See David Schalkwyk, *Shakespeare, Love and Service* (Cambridge: Cambridge University Press, 2008) ch. 1.

> O let my books be then the eloquence,
> And domb presagers of my speaking brest,
> Who pleade for loue, and look for recompence,
> More then that tonge that more hath more exprest.
>   O learne to read what silent loue hath writ,
>   To heare wit eies belongs to loues fine wiht [wit].

The speaking voice has now assumed the mask of an actor whose own mask has slipped—whose stage fright has caused him to forget his lines. The invocation of the player raises the perennial question of the autobiographical nature of the poems. And biography returns us to Foucault's essay, 'What is an Author?'

Foucault expresses the difference in the function between an author's name and the proper name of a person through the disparity between biographical information about the *man* Shakespeare (his place or date of birth, his marriage, his possession of the second-biggest house in Stratford, and so on), and information that would change the structural role of Shakespeare as the name of an *author*: it would make no difference if he hadn't married Anne Hathaway, but the discovery that 'Shakespeare did not write those sonnets which pass for his' would 'constitute a significant change and affect the manner in which the author's name functions' (Foucault, 122).

What would happen if we discovered that Shakespeare had nothing to do with the theatre? Shakespeare's biography would certainly be transformed if we found that he was not a member of any theatre company, but it would also make a difference to our conception of the texts that are collected under the 'name of the author' Shakespeare. The Sonnets stand between the two kinds of evidence. And when one (or more) of the Sonnets invokes the theatre, the question of Shakespeare's authorship becomes especially intractable. Do we thus read Sonnet 23 as evidence that Shakespeare's persona, as servant of the theatre, is 'subdu'd | To what it workes in, like the Dyers hand' (111)? Or is this reference to the theatre no more than a mask?

Rather than viewing Sonnet 23 as evidence of the autobiographical provenance of the Sonnets ('With this same key Shakespeare unlocked his heart'),[16] we should see Sonnet 23 as an instance of Shakespeare the poet (the author) adopting the mask of Shakespeare the player (the man). The sonnet is another exercise in the complex discourse of master and servant, in which the affective complexity of that relationship is pushed to its limits.[17] The speaker writes *as if* he were a player whose failure attests to his going beyond his social role. Precisely because of his personal engagement with his public audience the speaker cannot fulfil his duty to the master, who is now positioned between the private and the public. The Sonnets that begin as a (private) commission to persuade a young man to marriage turn into a struggle to wrest a properly private intimacy from a

---

[16] William Wordsworth, qtd. in William Shakespeare, *The sonnets of Shakespeare: from the quarto of 1609, with variorum readings and commentary* (London: Houghton Mifflin, 1916).

[17] Players in Elizabethan and Jacobean England were first and foremost servants, insofar as all actors' companies had to wear the livery of a nobleman, and subsequently, the king or queen.

world in which the declaration of love, as Philip Sidney declares, is incorrigibly public and treacherous.[18]

What Shakespeare's servant-player-poet pleads for, then, is to be permitted to move from a theatrical mode—the world of the player before an audience in whom the power of reception is invested—to one encapsulated by the intimate one-to-one relationship of the *book*:

> O let my *books* be then the eloquence,
> And domb presagers of my speaking brest,
> Who pleade for loue, and look for recompence,
> More then that tonge that more hath more exprest.
>
> (Emphasis added)

Many editors, wishing to retain the theatrical metaphor, change the Q 'books' of line 9 into 'looks', assuming that speaker asks the beloved to read the marks of love in the tongue-tied player's face rather than in his words. But the Sonnets originality lies in its demand that love's arena to be shifted from an exposed, vulnerable sphere of one-sided performance—here evoked by the public exposure of the theatre and the uncertain mask of verbal recitation—to the more enclosed intimacy of the sonnet, where a single reader responds to another in silence: 'To heare wit eies belongs to loues fine whit'. To put it in the words of Sonnet 125, what is sought is a 'mutuall render, onely me for thee', out of the public eye. Reading achieves a sympathetic, affective reciprocity that the public world, exemplified by the theatre, eschews.

By adopting the masks of different subject positions (poet, player, servant, lover, father) the speaker of Shakespeare's Sonnets tests conceptual relationships that are embedded in the social relations and language-games that give such concepts their life.[19] The general conceptual terrain they map is 1) the possibility of love between master and servant—in which reciprocity is logically necessary but unbalanced by hierarchy and *difference* of obligation and duty; 2) the love between friends—in which reciprocity is as necessary, but in which equality is paramount; 3) the love between lover and beloved—in which reciprocity, never guaranteed, is something to be *achieved*, and through which equality of obligation is the goal; and 4) erotic desire—in which mutuality is compulsive, fleeting, uncertain, and liable to produce reiterated feelings of self-loathing and disgust.

These concepts form a matrix; they are not identical, but they are also not absolutely distinct. Their relations are derived from who is speaking and to whom: servant to master; player to audience; tutor to pupil; father to son; lover to distant beloved; friend to friend; lover to lover; desire to object of desire; betrayed lover to betraying couple. Each of these relationships is tried and tested in Shakespeare's Sonnets. None of them can be reduced to any biographical facts; but as masks they inhabit a world haunted by

---

[18] 'What may words say, or what may words not say, | Where truth itself must speak like flattery?' (*Astrophil and Stella*, Sonnet 25).

[19] See Ludwig Wittgenstein, *Philosophical Investigations* (Oxford: Wiley-Blackwell, 1973).

biographical or historical figures in which that world is anchored. Shakespeare shadows them as servant, poet, dramatist, actor, father, husband, lover, ambitious member of the up-and-coming 'middling sort', ageing man overwhelmed by the fragility of human things and the inexorability of time.

26.5 WHAT MATTERS WHO IS BEING ADDRESSED?

If we have a fairly good idea of this 'Shakespeare' who speaks, what of those to whom the poems are addressed? I am not going to address the many historical candidates for the addressees or subjects of the Sonnets: the so-called 'fair youth', 'dark lady', or 'rival poet'. My point is this: if there is always someone (a mask) who speaks in the Sonnets, there is always concomitantly someone else (another mask) to whom the Sonnets are addressed. And it matters which of the possible masks of address we assume in our reading of any sonnet, although not, as I will show, in any traditionally biographical sense.

The usual assumption is that Sonnets 1–126 are addressed to a noble or well-born young man and 127–152 are to or about a promiscuous dark woman, with 40–3 and 133–4 and 144 about a triangular relationship involving all three. Furthermore this framework of differentiated addressees compels a narrative that structures the relationship among the three masks.[20]

Pursuing concepts rather than narrative, I am not concerned with what happened between whom, but rather how the Sonnets' *staged* situations of address embody and put pressure on the concepts in which they repeatedly trade: lust, desire, love, service, reciprocity, beauty, betrayal, singularity, repetition and decay, renewal through repetition. I argue that clarity about the identity of the addressees of the Sonnets shows that the concepts of love and desire are evenly distributed across all of them, rather than being divided across those usually considered homosexual and heterosexual. Furthermore, in the Sonnets to which I now turn, the syntactical movement of the poems begins to blur the distinctions between common nouns and pronouns.

Let us look at the concept of desire at work in Sonnet 147, a poem thought to be characteristic of the 'dark lady' Sonnets:

> My loue is as a feauer longing still,
> For that which longer nurseth the disease,

---

[20] Compare Heather Dubrow, who argues that 'often there is no way of being reasonably confident whether a given poem involves the friend, the dark Lady, or some third party, and this uncertainty has many implications for the imputed narrative of the sequence as a whole' ('"Incertainties now crown themselves assur'd": The Politics of Plotting Shakespeare's Sonnets', *Shakespeare Quarterly* 47: 3 (1996) 291–305).

> Feeding on that which doth preserue the ill,
> Th'vncertaine sicklie appetite to please:
> My reason the Phisition to my loue,
> Angry that his prescriptions are not kept
> Hath left me, and I desperate now approoue,
> Desire is death, which Phisick did except.
> Past cure I am, now Reason is past care,
> And frantick madde with euer-more vnrest,
> My thoughts and my discourse as mad mens are,
> At randon from the truth vainely exprest.
>   For I haue sworne thee faire, and thought thee bright,
>   Who art as black as hell, as darke as night.

In contrast to Sonnet 116, love is conceptualized not merely as a disease, but more darkly as an infection that desires its own destruction. Instead of *love's* being 'the star to every wandering bark', here '*desire* is death'. This is an instantiation of the general characterization of lust in Sonnet 129 ('Th'expence of Spirit in a waste of shame | Is lust in action'). Sonnets 129 and 147 are conjoined by a frantic sense of being trapped in a condition, akin to madness or fever, over which they are powerless, and, moreover, from which they *do not wish* to escape. What they desire is *in truth* undesirable, but they can't help it. This leads to one of the major conceptual issues of the Sonnets: the war between heart and eyes.

The Sonnets usually considered to be to or about the dark woman rehearse the intractable problem of love's 'perjured eye': as Helena declares in her feverish pursuit of Demetrius in *A Midsummer Night's Dream*: 'Love looks not with the eyes, but with the mind' (I. ii. 234). In his account of this problem, Joel Fineman argues that they inaugurate a new poetic subjectivity, whereby Shakespeare moves from a traditional ideal in which eye and object are in truthful agreement, to a more modern acceptance of the intractable nature of language, in which word and object are inevitably separated.[21] In this story, the Sonnets move from impossible ideal in their representation of the young man as being no different from himself or the words used to describe him to darker realism in their accommodation of themselves to a heterosexual desire torn between 'swearing someone fair' and seeing that she is *in fact* 'as black as hell, as dark as night'. In her revision of the 'scandal' of Shakespeare's Sonnets, Margreta de Grazia argues that it is not their same-sex love that is scandalous but rather their promiscuous heterosexual desires: 'nothing threatens the patriarchal and hierarchic social formation more than a promiscuous womb'.[22]

Both Fineman and de Grazia need to secure the person to whom the sonnet is addressed as male or female to sustain their respective arguments. So let's now take a pair of Sonnets frequently assumed to be addressed to the young man, 118 and 119:

---

[21] Joel Fineman, *Shakespeare's perjured eye: the invention of poetic subjectivity in the sonnets* (Berkeley: University of California Press, 1986).

[22] Margreta de Grazia, 'The Scandal of Shakespeare's Sonnets', *Shakespeare Survey* 46 (1994): 35–94.

Like as to make our appetites more keene
With eager compounds we our pallat vrge,
As to preuent our malladies vnseene,
We sicken to shun sicknesse when we purge.
Euen so being full of your nere cloying sweetnesse,
To bitter sawces did I frame my feeding;
And sicke of wel-fare found a kind of meetnesse,
To be diseas'd ere that there was true needing.
Thus pollicie in loue t'anticipate
The ills that were, not grew to faults assured,
And brought to medicine a healthfull state
Which rancke of goodnesse would by ill be cured.
  But thence I learne and find the lesson true,
  Drugs poyson him that so fell sicke of you.

What potions haue I drunke of *Syren* teares
Distil'd from Lymbecks foule as hell within,
Applying feares to hopes, and hopes to feares,
Still loosing when I saw my selfe to win?
What wretched errors hath my heart committed,
Whilst it hath thought it selfe so blessed neuer?
How haue mine eies out of their Spheares bene fitted
In the distraction of this madding feuer?
O benefit of ill, now I find true
That better is, by euil still made better.
And ruin'd loue when it is built anew
Growes fairer then at first, more strong, far greater.
  So I returne rebukt to my content,
  And gaine by ills thrise more then I haue spent.

On the face of it, Sonnets 118 and 119 entrench, internally, the external division of the poems between the 'fair, kind and true' love of the young man and the hellish, perverse, and false lust for the 'wide worlds common place'. These are exculpatory poems: the speaker offers excuses for his straying from the beloved. In the first, the traditional metaphor of love as a disease (the central conceit of 147) is mobilized to contrast 'sick' with 'healthy' love. But that contrast is complicated by two things: first, the identification of love as a kind of appetite ('like as to make our appetites more keen'), which undermines the notion that the speaker has had affairs with others (a kind of sickness or disease) in order to forestall his relationship with the young man becoming infected;[23] second, it is implied that his love for the young man has always been a kind of disease—the difference between poison and medicine is a matter of degree rather than kind, as in the Greek term *pharmakon*: 'Drugs poison him that so fell sicke of you'.

---

[23] Many assume that the poem contrasts heterosexual affairs with the love for the young man, but Booth correctly observes that the poem contains no evidence of the sex of the wayward partners (Booth, 1977; 400).

In addition to the abiding idea of love as a disease, 119 invokes the battle between eye and heart, a conceit that is distributed across all the Sonnets, although it is more intensely concentrated in the Sonnets after 126. This tension is set up in a sustained way in early Sonnets like 24 ('Mine eye hath play'd the painter and hath steeld, | Thy beauties forme in table of my heart'), 46 ('Mine eye and heart are at a mortall warre'), and 47 ('Betwixt mine eye and heart a league is tooke'), but it is intensified in all the Sonnets in which the uncertain character of the young man is entertained or his duplicity and inscrutability suggested, and it is the substance of love's perjured eye in the Sonnets after 126. Love's vision, which is essentially projective rather than reflective, turns the beloved into its own desired forms *throughout* the sequence.

26.6 PRONOUNS AND COMMON NOUNS

Sonnets 112 and 113 celebrate the capacity of the speaker's mind to convert even the worst things into the fair form of the young man. Sonnet 113 extends this variation on the common conceit, *you are all the world to me*:

> Since I left you, mine eye is in my minde,
> And that which gouernes me to goe about,
> Doth part his function, and is partly blind,
> Seemes seeing, but effectually is out:
> For it no forme deliuers to the heart
> Of bird, of flowre, or shape which it doth lack,
> Of his quick obiects hath the minde no part,
> Nor his owne vision houlds what it doth catch:
> For if it see the rud'st or gentlest sight,
> The most sweet-fauor or deformedst creature,
> The mountaine, or the sea, the day, or night:
> The Croe, or Doue, it shapes them to your feature.
>> Incapable of more repleat, with you,
>> My most true minde thus maketh mine vntrue.

Most editors supply a supposedly missing 'eye' after 'mine' in the last line, but Booth enriches the thought by conjuring 'm'eyene' from 'mine', so that the paradoxes of identity in love reveal themselves especially starkly. 'You' and 'I'; 'I', 'eye', 'mine', and 'minde'; 'see' and 'seemes'; 'you', 'true', and 'untrue' inhabit each other as barely distinguishable concepts.

Pronouns are now part of the common nouns (mind, eye, true) that define identity and personal relationships. What the speaker *sees* with the *eye* pertaining to the addressed *you*—which bears on the question of what is *true*—is hardly distinguishable from what *seems*, because the *eye* is determined by what is *mine* of the *mind*: the *I* speaking. Love is *essentially* projective: it shapes the beloved into the object of its own desires. This is not a gendered process. Projective love is not bad and reflective love good (the old distinction between 'appearance' and 'reality'); nor is love for the young man reflective (good, true), while that for the dark woman projective (bad, false).

Sonnet 114, in the 'young man' group, invokes the same discourse of poison, disease, gustatory desire, and transformative imagination as the 'perjur'd eye' invoked in the later poems:

> Or whether doth my minde being crown'd with you
> Drinke vp the monarks plague this flattery?
> Or whether shall I say mine eie saith true,
> And that your loue taught it this *Alcumie?*
> To make of monsters, and things indigest,
> Such cherubines as your sweet selfe resemble,
> Creating euery bad a perfect best
> As fast as obiects to his beames assemble:
> Oh 'tis the first, 'tis flatry in my seeing,
> And my great minde most kingly drinkes it vp,
> Mine eie well knowes what with his gust is greeing,
> And to his pallat doth prepare the cup.
> If it be poison'd, 'tis the lesser sinne,
> That mine eye loues it and doth first beginne.

In the face of the discursive similarity between the young man poems and those about the dark woman, we could either entertain the possibility that this poem is actually addressed to a woman, thereby unsettling the 'assured certainties' that Dubrow wishes to disrupt; or we could maintain the original, putative addressees, but now conclude that what the Sonnets offer via their speaking, listening, and reading masks is a set of conceptual investigations rather than biographical or ideological narratives.

26.7 CONCEPTUAL INVESTIGATIONS

In these investigations the speaking and listening/reading figures are masks. But so are the clearly performative and active entities to which they are related: eye and mind, hand and heart, palate and will. Reading across the sequence, no hard-and-fast differentiation of gender roles is apparent. Love for the young man involves as much of a contest between mind and eye as the unreliable woman. This means that the intractable imbrications of love and lust are as much at work in relation to the dark lord (Sonnet 43) as they are in relation to the fair woman (Sonnet 127). Moreover, the apparent contrast between the constancy of love and the feverish vacillation of lust encapsulated in Sonnets 116 and 129 is complicated in both cases by the Sonnets (assumed to be directed to the young man) in which love is essentially bound to repetition, and in which the possibility of falling off and change is always present along with the promise or hope of increase and enhancement.

If Sonnet 116 is often thought to exemplify the ideal of love or the young man, its complementary voice speaks through the earlier Sonnet 56:

> Sweet loue renew thy force, be it not said
> Thy edge should blunter be then apetite,
> Which but too daie by feeding is alaied,
> To morrow sharpned in his former might.
> So loue be thou, although too daie thou fill
> Thy hungrie eies, euen till they winck with fulnesse,
> Too morrow see againe, and doe not kill
> The spirit of Loue, with a perpetual dulnesse:
> Let this sad *Intrim* like the Ocean be
> Which parts the shore, where two contracted new,
> Come daily to the banckes, that when they see:
> Retun of loue, more blest may be the view.
>   As cal it Winter, which being ful of care,
>   Makes Somers welcome, thrice more wish'd, more rare.

The Sonnet addresses either the person of the beloved or the abstract figure or power of love, which may refer back to the speaker as a lover whose own affections have waned. In contrast to the traditional cliché in which love and appetite are morally differentiated, here love is urged to be no *worse* than appetite, in which the moment of satiety is inevitably followed by renewed desire. If love is *less* than appetite, it is nothing. Love is thus not merely recognized as being part of time: it is urged to follow the ebb and flow of the very things that other sonnets rage against for their inconstancy and fallibility: the sea, the seasons, appetite, and time itself. Indeed, this inconstancy enhances love by making it 'more wish'd, more rare'.

If this Sonnet's tone of desperation makes its argument unconvincing, Sonnet 115 (which comes just before 116) offers a more philosophically detached perspective on the way in which time is positively constitutive of love. It is a remarkable poem for its daring confession of having *lied* about the unchangeable constancy of love. It thus looks forward to the 'dark woman' Sonnets in which lying is constitutive of desire (especially Sonnet 138):

> Those lines that I before haue writ doe lie,
> Euen those that said I could not loue you deerer,
> Yet then my iudgement knew no reason why,
> My most full flame should afterwards burne cleerer.
> But reckening time, whose milliond accidents
> Creepe in twixt vowes, and change decrees of Kings,
> Tan sacred beautie, blunt the sharp'st intents,
> Diuert strong mindes to th'course of altring things:
> Alas why fearing of times tiranie,
> Might I not then say now I loue you best,
> When I was certaine ore in-certainty,
> Crowning the present, doubting of the rest:

> Loue is a Babe, then might I not say so
> To giue full growth to that which still doth grow.

In a sequence marked for its anxiety about the corrosive effects of time, this sonnet attributes to the mistaken fear of 'times tiranie' the projective distortions usually attributed to love itself. *Because I was afraid of what time might do to my/our love, I felt that I had to declare that I loved you best* then. Now, *however, I know that that was all a lie, because time has allowed me to love you even better. Through that lie I have discovered the truth that love is the child of time, not its enemy.* The sonnet moves radically away from the idea that love is not love that alters when it alteration finds to the insight that the change that inevitably comes from reiteration is in fact constitutive of love. In this thought, the defining conceptual difference between the dark woman and young man poems disappears.

Our final conceptual investigation concerns the singularity of the beloved. In each sequence the speaker of the Sonnets seeks to secure recognition from the beloved for his uniqueness—that he alone is desired or loved. In the case of the young man that is expressed by his re-iterated insistence of the *youth's* distinctiveness—'you alone are you' (84)—of which the concomitant fear is the suspicion that the youth 'doth common grow' (69). That word is strikingly present in Sonnet 137's characterization of the dark woman as the 'wide worlds common place'. But it is also offset by his celebration of her uniqueness as the unfashionable epitome of new beauty: 'euery toung saies beauty should looke so.' (128). The desire for the woman, in the shape of the multi-dimensional 'will' of Sonnets 135 and 136, appears to forego the insistence on singularity in the plea to be accommodated as merely one more 'Will' by and in *her* 'large will' (135). But the second of this pair of Sonnets focuses, finally, on the singularity of the speaker's proper name: 'Make but my name thy loue, and loue that still, | And then thou louest me for my name is Will' (136). What appears at first to be a plea for the accommodation of undifferentiated lust, turns to an urgent request not only to merge desire and the suitor's proper name ('Will'), but also to love that name without ceasing or variation: 'and loue that [i.e. me] *still*'.

The young man and the young woman Sonnets offer chiasmic representations of the same cluster of concepts related to love and desire—constancy and variation, fairness and blackness, disease and wellbeing, truth and lies—that are not distributed asymmetrically between the masks of the addressees. The Sonnets thus offer a conceptual account of love and its relation to desire *through* the specificities of their address—who is speaking to whom—in which three defining characteristics finally stand out: love's projective capacity ('love sees not with the eyes but with the mind'); its essential debt to time as a constitutive medium ('To giue full growth to that which still doth grow'); and its concern with the singularity or uniqueness of its object, which is itself a product of its projective imagination ('you alone are you').

It matters who is speaking in Shakespeare's Sonnets because as the subject of loving desire the speaking persona speaks from a position of singularity and seeks a reciprocal recognition of uniqueness from the other person. That such a position of singularity is offered as a series of masks should not bother us. Indeed, if the poems are to live on in the 'eyes of men' we should be able to adopt the masks of both speaker and addressee. Otherwise they would mean nothing to us. They would shrink into total solipsism. But happily we can inhabit the masks which Shakespeare gives us through our own singularity. In doing so, we acknowledge their insistent plea for the recognition of uniqueness in love, through the shared community of their singular language. That is simply, in these Sonnets, what love is, what it demands.

SELECT BIBLIOGRAPHY

Booth, Stephen (2000) (ed.) *Shakespeare's Sonnets*. (New Haven: Yale University Press).

Burrow, Colin (2002) 'Introduction', In William Shakespeare, *The Complete Sonnets and Poems*, Colin Burrow (ed.), (Oxford: Oxford University Press) 1–169.

Dubrow, Heather (1987) *Captive Victors: Shakespeare's Narrative Poems and Sonnets*. (Ithaca: Cornell University Press).

Duncan-Jones, Katherine (1983) 'Was the 1609 Shake-speares Sonnets Really Unauthorized?' *Review of English Studies*, 34: 151–71.

Fineman, Joel (1986) *Shakespeare's Perjured Eye: the Invention of Poetic Subjectivity in the Sonnets*. (Berkeley and Los Angeles: University of California Press).

Kerrigan, John (1986), 'Introduction', in William Shakespeare, *The Sonnets and A Lover's Complaint*, John Kerrigan (ed.), (Harmondsworth: Penguin) 7–64.

Schalkwyk, David (2002) *Speech and performance in Shakespeare's Sonnets and Plays*. (Cambridge: Cambridge University Press).

Schoenfeldt, Michael Carl (2007) *A Companion to Shakespeare's Sonnets*. (Oxford: Wiley Blackwell).

Vendler, Helen (1999) *The Art of Shakespeare's Sonnets*. (Cambridge: Harvard University Press).

CHAPTER 27

....

'PRETTY ROOMS'

Shakespeare's Sonnets,
Elizabethan Architecture, and
Early Modern Visual Design

....

RUSS MCDONALD

Recent commentary on the Sonnets has been preoccupied with implied narratives—
the young man, the dark lady, the rival poet—or has speculated about provenance and
authority—dates of composition, the authority of the 1609 collection, the organization
of the 1609 collection—or has related the poems to those broad contextual topics dear
to contemporary criticism—sexuality, class, race. The distance necessitated by these
approaches, with the reader positioned so as to be able to contemplate the whole collection, has mostly discouraged close inspection of particular poems, except as evidence
to be deployed in relation to the favoured topic, and has nearly proscribed attention to
formal concerns. In this chapter I first propose a new context for examining the Sonnets
and then scrutinize some verbal features of the poems with that context in mind. The
context is visual design in the second half of the 16th century: the cultural commitment
to arrangement in Tudor England is visible in furniture, textiles, gardening, and to a certain degree in painting, but especially in architecture, particularly Elizabethan domestic architecture. The feature I analyse is a species of poetic ornament: literal and lexical
forms of repetition.

   The 16th century saw the emergence of a new English architectural style, a practice
combining native preferences and traditions with a burgeoning attraction to classical
precedents. Analysis of this developing domestic style must be largely empirical, since
the critical discourse of architecture does not find an English voice until the beginning
of the 17th century. Acquaintance with this practice and such theory as there is proves
useful for studying the development of poetry in the period, particularly the sonnet.
Were there space I would approach Shakespeare's work by way of the early Tudor adaptations of Petrarch and then move through the sequences and individual poems by

Sidney, Spenser, Watson, Daniel, and others; I would address the poets' self-conscious attention to the architecture of the sonnet, particularly their exploitation of the octave/sestet structure of the Italian form and the quatrains and couplet of the English. Given practical limits, however, I move directly to Shakespeare's 1609 collection, confining attention to the poet's exploitation of a particular strain of poetic ornament. Notice of repetition illuminates anew the virtuosity with which Shakespeare exploits the possibilities of poetic artifice, helps to contextualize artistically his impulse to elaboration, and discloses his mixed attitude towards ornament itself.

One of my goals in placing the Sonnets of Shakespeare under this lens is to restore a sense of their poetic materiality, to reclaim the poems from the emphasis on narrative that has dominated recent critical discourse and to locate a major source of their appeal in their poetic ingenuity. The poet's irrepressible delight in pattern, similitude, correspondence, and playful alteration, and his concomitant desire to delight the reader with these ornamental effects, can be linked to the increasingly apparent devotion to formality and composition in Elizabethan visual design generally. The nature of this relation between the poetic and the visual needs to be clarified from the start, however. I do not urge a simple analogy between, on the one hand, the intricate visual decoration that becomes increasingly prominent in Tudor architecture over the course of the 16th century and, on the other, the extraordinary verbal patterning found in Shakespeare's collection of Sonnets. Rather, I propose that the visual pleasures of Elizabethan design and the acoustic delights of the Sonnets are both products of an increasing attraction, perceptible throughout the culture, to patterns of repetition and congruity; that objects manifesting such an inclination betoken the growing appreciation for order and harmony that we know to be one of the principal tenets of Renaissance humanism; and that the rhetoric of 16th-century design, both in its theoretical statements and material expressions, can furnish an appropriate and valuable historical framework for understanding the Sonnets of Shakespeare and his contemporaries.

My discussion modestly enlarges upon the implications of an observation made by Nikolaus Pevsner in his Inaugural Lecture at Birkbeck College, University of London, in 1960. Most of the printed text is given over to Pevsner's elegant survey of English architectural practice as it develops through the 16th century, his objective being to demonstrate the metamorphosis from almost pure functionalism to an architectural style based upon a 'composition'. Near the end of the piece the great observer turns his gaze from physical to verbal structures: 'And as, what we have seen, is really a process of ordering, can one not draw a parallel also with the tidying up of metre in poetry of the sixteenth century and especially the development of so highly contrived a form as the sonnet?'[1] The answer is 'yes', and profitably so.

---

[1] Nikolaus Pevsner, 'The Planning of the Elizabethan Country House: An Inaugural Lecture delivered at Birkbeck College 1960' (London: Birkbeck College, 1961) 24.

27.1

Hamlet's apology for his bad poetry, 'O dear Ophelia, I am ill at these numbers', is the most famous of many references to verse in mathematical terms. Literary scholars have neglected this intersection of the vocabularies of poetry with those of other disciplines, especially mathematics and geometry. To comprehend the growth of Tudor humanism is to observe an expanding interest in mathematics and related fields, notably the increase of what we might call geometrical literacy. Geographical expansion and technological progress gave the practice of measurement new significance. According to a recent study, 'surveying manuals', of which there was an outpouring in the 16th century, 'not only taught their readers how to measure the land: they directed their readers to perceive and to conceptualize the world in geometric terms'.[2] The basics of mathematics and geometry were articulated in the middle of the century by Robert Record in a series of 'how-to' books, effectively school texts, and in 1570 John Dee produced his 'Mathematical Preface' to Billingsley's translation of Euclid's *Elements of Geometrie*. The humanist schoolmasters often stress the connection between the two senses of *ratio*, its philosophical definition as 'reason' and its expression of the arithmetical relation between numbers.[3] Without speculating extensively on the cultural causes of this growing attraction to pattern and line, we might pause to note William Bouwsma's conviction that the comforts of proportion and the harmony implied in mathematical relations served the thoughtful, educated subject as a defense against the growing anxiety generated by the scientific uncertainties of early modernity.[4] In fact, these numerical relations were considered proof of the unity and meaning of human existence, as in Thomas Campion's *Observations in the Art of English Poesie*: 'The world is made by symmetry and proportion, and is in that respect compared to music, and music to poetry'.[5] The connection between geometrical and poetic lineation was a genuine, meaningful feature of humanist education and thought.

Such proportions as Campion describes find spatial articulation in the discipline of architecture. The metaphor of poem as monument is, of course, a classically sanctioned topos, the tradition to which Donne appeals in 'The Canonization' ('we'll build in sonnets pretty rooms') when he plays on the term *stanza*, Italian for 'room'. But this congruence between the poetic and the spatial is also implied in another term for stanza or

[2] Martin Brückner and Kirsten Poole, 'The Plot Thickens: Surveying Manuals, Drama, and the Materiality of Narrative Form in Early Modern England', *ELH*, 69 (2002): 625. See also Anthony Gerbino and Stephen Johnston, *Compass and Rule: Architecture as Mathematical Practice in England* (New Haven: Yale University Press, 2009) chs 2 and 3.

[3] See S. K. Heninger, Jr, *The Subtext of Form in the English Renaissance: Proportion Poetical* (University Park: Pennsylvania State University Press, 1994) 23.

[4] William J. Bouwsma, 'Anxiety and the Formation of Early Modern Culture', in *After the Reformation, Essays in Honor of J. H. Hexter*, Barbara C. Malament (ed.), (Manchester: Manchester University Press, 1980) 215–46.

[5] 'Observations in the Art of English Poesie', in *English Renaissance Literary Criticism*, Brian Vickers (ed.), (Oxford: Oxford University Press, 1999) 430.

verse in Renaissance poetic discourse, i.e. *stave*, a noun that means not only 'staff' but also refers to the rungs of a ladder (*OED* 2.a).[6] Shakespeare, of course, exploits this conventional trope with exceptional vividness in 'Not marble, nor the gilded monuments', among other Sonnets, but all early modern poets were aware of the tradition to a greater or lesser degree.

More interesting, for present purposes, is the parallel between the art of writing and the craft of building. Sidney, like almost everyone who takes up the topic, begins with the Greek etymology of the noun *poet*, meaning 'maker'. In the *Gorgias* Plato describes the successful orator as a builder who selects and arranges his materials into a useful and attractive structure, an analogy expanded by Horace and taken up by the Italian, French, and then the English humanists and rhetoricians. Samuel Daniel, justifying in *A Defence of Rhyme* (1603) the conventional forms of English poetry that had emerged in the 16th century, refers approvingly to the buildings he sees around him: 'Let vs go no further, but looke vpon the wonderfull Architecture of this state of *England*, and see whether they were deformed times, that could give it such a forme.'[7] In other words, native architecture of the recent past attests to the cultural health of the kingdom and thus provides a persuasive context for appreciating its recent poetic productions. The trope receives perhaps its most eloquent expression in George Chapman's dedication of his translation of Musaeus to Inigo Jones:

> Ancient Poesy, *and ancient* Architecture, *requiring to their excellence a like creating and proportionable Rapture, and being alike over-topt by the monstrous* Babels *of our Moderne* Barbarism; *their unjust obscurity, letting no glance of their truth and dignity appear, but to passing few, to passing few is their least appearance to be presented. Your selfe then being a Chiefe of that few, by whom Both are apprehended: & their beames worthily measur'd and valew'd.*[8]

Chapman's dedication represents an epitome of humanist thinking, especially his conception of an exalted group of intelligent beings for whom the mechanical and the literary go hand in hand, both grounded in noble ancient models, both constantly renewable despite the opposition of 'modern barbarism'.

But these cases are mostly metaphoric. To proceed more literally is to perceive an identity between the structural principles that govern the making of buildings and the making of poems. The artistic tastes of 16th-century England exhibit an increasing devotion to the decorative pleasures of ornament, most obviously in the form of symmetrical arrangement, and that preference for symmetry comes increasingly to characterize

---

[6] See also the notes to *The Art of English Poesy by George Puttenham: A Critical Edition*, ed. Frank Whigham and Wayne A. Rebhorn (Ithaca: Cornell University Press, 2007) 154–7.

[7] Samuel Daniel, *Poems and A Defence of Rhyme*, Arthur Colby Sprague (ed.), (Chicago: University of Chicago Press, 1930) 145.

[8] 'Epistle Dedicatory' to *The Divine Poem of Musaeus, translated according to the Originall, by George Chapman* (London: Isaac Jaggard, 1616) A3-A4.

Tudor domestic architecture. Describing the state of building at mid-century, William Harrison celebrates the advances in comfort and appearance characteristic of recent construction: 'If ever curious building did flourish in England, it is in these our years, wherein our workmen excel, and are in manner comparable in skill with old Vitruvius, Leon Battista, and Serlio.[9] The vital term is 'curious'—'made with care or art; skilfully, elaborately, or beautifully wrought' (*OED*, II.7.a)—which appears repeatedly as an absolute value in early modern descriptive writing. But the adjective is still rather general. What is notable is that Harrison implies the pleasures of geometric arrangement, as his reference to ancient and modern architects indicates. Pevsner documents this growing taste for similitude by contrasting the plans of buildings constructed or renovated in the early years of Henry VIII's reign with those of some of the great Elizabethan country houses, capping his proof with a model of Inigo Jones' plan for the Queen's House at Greenwich (1616).[10]

Architectural historians expend much energy disputing the relative strengths of the two main traditions influencing English construction in the 16th century, the native and the classical.[11] Without tarrying to identify origins, we can easily observe the results of these combined traditions: over the course of the 16th century there emerges a new cultural consciousness, a devotion to the general delights of form and to the specific satisfactions of balance, symmetry, and correspondence. Uniformity was the watchword, albeit with a generous allowance of internal variety, and one of the principal tools for achieving the desired uniformity was the repetitive pattern, whether linear, circular, or a combination of the two; whether simple or intricate; whether in stone or plaster or thread. When Sir William Cecil visited Holdenby, the great house that Sir Christopher Hatton had constructed for himself in Northamptonshire, Cecil wrote admiringly to his host about the pleasing concord of structural and decorative effects. 'Approaching to the house, being led by a large, long straight fairway, I found a great magnificence in the front or front pieces of the house, and so every part answerable to other, to allure liking'.[12] The key to this passage is the emphasis on correspondence, 'every part answerable to other, to allure liking'.

This passion for correspondence is often manifested not only in the house but in the garden. Anticipating the visit of the Queen in 1575, the Earl of Leicester undertook a series of improvements to Kenilworth that included a garden designed according to the most fashionable specifications. A famous letter by Robert Langham, a London mercer writing to a friend, lovingly depicts the result.

> Close to the wall is a beautiful terrace, ten feet high and twelve feet broad, quite level, and freshly covered with thick grass, which also grows on the slope. There are obelisks on the terrace at even distances, great balls, and white heraldic beasts, all made of

[9] William Harrison, *The Description of England*, Georges Edelen (ed.), (Washington: Folger Shakespeare Library, 1968) 199.

[10] Pevsner (1961) 3.

[11] Lucy Gent, '"The Rash Gazer": Economies of Vision in Britain, 1550–1660', in Gent, *Albion's Classicism* (New Haven: Yale University Press, 1995) 377–93.

[12] Quoted in Emily Sophia Hartshorne, *Memorials of Holdenby* (London: 1868) 15–16.

stone and perched on artistic posts, good to look at. At each end is a bower, smelling of sweet flowers and trees. The garden ground below is crossed by grassy avenues, in straight lines on both sides, some of the walks for a change, made of gravel, not too light and dusty, but soft and firm and pleasant to walk on, like sands by the sea when the tide has gone out. There are also four equal parterres, cut in regular proportions; in the middle of each is a post shaped like a cube, two feet high; on that a pyramid, accurately made, symmetrically carved, fifteen feet high; on the summit a ball ten inches in diameter, and the whole thing from top to bottom, pedestal and all hewn out of one solid block of porphyry, and then with much art and skill brought here and set up.[13]

The theme of Langham's description is layout, the rewards of arrangement. Colour and scent later get their proper treatment, but the primary consideration is the repetitive effect of the 'even distances', 'straight lines on both sides', 'equal parterres', symmetrical carving.

In expressing their taste for complement and balance, the politician, the courtier-poet, and the mercer all endorse Palladian principles: the *Four Books of Architecture*, published in Venice in 1570, were certainly known to a few Englishmen near the end of the century and would become well known through the work of Inigo Jones. But even in the sketchy Elizabethan records the same values find expression. For instance, Robert Stickells, a naval engineer and clerk in the Queen's Works, left some rather crude stipulations about proper and improper design, insisting that ancient models are superior to modern because the older structures are based on rectilinear, even-numbered plans: 'There is no more but Right & wronge in all things whatsoever, The squear Right the cirkell wronge'.[14]

A major goal of Elizabethan design, according to the architectural historian Christy Anderson, is that the composition should stimulate in the perceiver a sense of 'wonder, … a recognizable, if not clearly definable, quality of the English aesthetic experience and artistic creation'.[15] Keeping in mind Daniel's reference to 'the wonderful architecture of this state of England' and Chapman's contention that 'Ancient Poesie, and ancient Architecture' seek to create 'a proportionable Rapture', we can observe in some buildings of the age practical exhibitions of this aim. This principle is illustrated by some very famous dwellings, such as Longleat or Hardwick Hall, but the familiarity of those great houses means that many readers will already know them and will recognize their conformity to the theory. Instead, I introduce two structures that are perhaps less celebrated but make the point. One of the most gloriously 'curious' buildings of the century

[13] Robert Langham, *A Letter: Wherein, part of the entertainment unto the Queen's Majesty, at Kenilworth Castle, in Warwickshire, in this summer's progress, 1575, is signified: from a friend officer in attendant in court, unto his friend a citizen, and merchant of London*, R. J. P. Kuin (ed.), Medieval and Renaissance Texts, 2 (Leiden: Brill, 1983). The authorship of the letter is debated.

[14] Caroline van Eck (ed.), *British Architectural Theory, 1540–1750: An Anthology of Texts* (Aldershot: Ashgate, 2003) 21.

[15] Christy Anderson, 'Learning to Read Architecture in the English Renaissance', in Gent (1995) 267.

FIGURE 27.1 The Warrener's Lodge at Rushton represents Sir Thomas Tresham's effort to dazzle the viewer with ingenious patterning in a relatively small structure. Photograph by Chris Downer.

is the Warrener's Lodge at Rushton (FIGURE 27.1), a relatively small structure built in Northamptonshire in the 1590s by the mystical, evangelical Catholic convert, Sir Thomas Tresham. With his fierce Trinitarian bias—and with the bonus of *tre* in his surname—Tresham contrived a fantastic structure based entirely on the number three. The Lodge is a three-sided structure with multiple kinds of ornamental and functional triplets—three gables on each side, a triangular shield atop each of these, three windows on each of three levels, three windows on each level on each of the three sides, each designed in triplet configurations. Moreover, the frieze on each side is thirty-three feet long, and each of the three Latin inscriptions consists of thirty-three letters.[16] For my purposes the symbols are less meaningful than the dazzling ingenuity of the conception and the sense of likeness that informs the design of the whole. Anderson cites Tresham's Lodge as 'an exercise in producing a building of wonder, whose very complexity of symbolism seems intended more to encourage a lengthy experience of devotion in the viewer than to produce any clear analysis of the symbolic meaning'.[17]

---

[16] John Buxton, *Elizabethan Taste* (London: Macmillan, 1963) 59.
[17] Anderson (1995) 267.

FIGURE 27.2 This drawing of the south front of Burghley House was done for Sir William Cecil, by an unknown draftsman, ca. 1580. Courtesy RIBA.

FIGURE 27.3 The western front of Burghley House exhibits the Elizabethan passion for symmetrical arrangement and especially visual complement in its distribution of spatial units. Photo by Anthony Masi.

Equally illustrative, although at the other end of the scale, is Burghley House (FIGURE 27.2 and FIGURE 27.3), a building as grand as the Warrener's Lodge is miniature, but similarly calculated to impress, and by some of the same means and same materials. The house is especially striking in its combination of native English elements (e.g. the central gatehouse) with classical details, and especially the melding of all these features into strict uniformity. As Timothy Mowl puts it in *Elizabethan and Jacobean Style*, 'The whole composition is a test piece in aesthetic enjoyment of Elizabethan art. It endlessly diverts; it never rests; it demands response and elicits pleasure; there is no concession to simplicity or to order. It is the antithesis of Classicism yet it is wholly Renaissance in spirit'.[18] Such principles of patterning and symmetrical effect are visible not only in such specialized structures as the Warrener's Lodge or the prodigy homes like Burghley

[18] *Elizabethan and Jacobean Style* (London: Phaidon, 1993) 86–7.

House. Many of the smaller domestic projects undertaken in 16th-century England begin to embody some of the same tenets of design just described.[19]

In the pursuit of wonder and the growing attachment to repeated patterns, domestic architecture can serve as a synecdoche for such topics in other disciplines and sub-disciplines of Elizabethan art and design: funerary monuments, the detail in certain miniatures, objects such as the Gibbon Salt (now in the Victoria and Albert Museum), various portraits of Elizabeth I (particularly the Rainbow Portrait hanging at Hatfield), the fugal structure of much sacred music (e.g. motets of Thomas Tallis), and the Tudor versions of the court masque. Wonder receives a considerable degree of attention from the philosophers and rhetoricians in early modern Europe, as Stephen Greenblatt reminds us in his discussion of Columbus and his sense of the 'marvellous'.[20] And so it is with poetry, taking that noun in the broad sense that the Elizabethans used it, to refer to all imaginative writing, as in Sidney's title, *The Defence of Poesie.* The neo-Aristotelian and Platonist commentators assert the primacy of 'wonder' or 'astonishment' in the perceiver's response to the object of art, whether it be a building or a painting or a tragedy. According to Minturno, in his *De Poeta,* a work that influenced Sidney's *Defence,* 'No one can be called a poet who does not excel in the power of arousing wonder'.[21]

Evidence of this cultural commitment to induce wonder by means of ornamental complexity is that Sir Francis Bacon objected to it. In his essay on gardens, Bacon deplores efforts at visual delight based on antithesis and pattern: 'As for the making of knots or figures with divers coloured earths, that they may lie under the window of the house on that side which the garden stands, they be but toys: you may see as good sights many times in tarts'.[22] And in 'On Building' he declares bluntly and without apology: 'Houses are built to Live in, and not to Looke on: Therefore let Use bee preferred before Uniformitie; Except where both may be had: Leave the Goodly Fabricks of Houses, for Beautie only, to the enchanted Pallaces of the poets: Who build them with small Cost'.[23] Bacon's attitude here is consistent with his view of written expression, particularly the famous passage in which he assails the English Ciceronians, Ascham and Carr, as those who 'care more for words than for matter'.[24] In a variety of disciplines Bacon deplores this increasingly prominent pleasure in form: he doesn't like his prose style tarted up any more than he does his house or the garden behind it. But throughout the 16th century, many others did.

---

[19] Nicholas Cooper, *Houses of the Gentry, 1480–1680* (New Haven: Yale University Press, 1999) 74–107.

[20] *Marvelous Possessions* (Oxford: Clarendon Press, 1991) 79.

[21] Quoted in Greenblatt, (1991) 79; see also J. V. Cunningham, *Woe or Wonder* (Denver: Alan Swallow, 1960) 82.

[22] 'Of Gardens', *Francis Bacon: A Critical Edition of the Major Works,* Brian Vickers (ed.), (Oxford: Oxford University Press, 1996) 430–5, 432.

[23] 'Of Buildings', in Vickers (1996) 427–30, 427.

[24] *The Advancement of Learning,* in Vickers (1996), 120–68, 139.

27.2

It is axiomatic that the European humanists and their English counterparts thought of poetry and architecture as related disciplines. In both there is a paucity of theoretical writing in the 16th century, but the existing commentary indicates that the culture recognized a kinship between the eye and the ear. In articulating their understanding of poetics, Tudor writers describe this kinship and point out that both eye and ear respond to the harmonies implicit in fundamental mathematical relations. A persuasive example of this comparison appears in Henry Wotton's *Elements of Architecture,* essentially an English adaptation of Vitruvius. Praising Alberti's Pythagorean rules for windows and doors, Wotton speaks of 'the principall *Consonances*' in music (the fifth and the octave) and then moves to the visual: 'Now if we shall transport these proportions, from Audible to visible *Objects* ... there will indubitably result ... a gracefull and *harmonious* contentment to the Eye'.[25]

A full account of the place of artifice in Tudor poetry would begin with the Petrarchan translations and erotic plaints of Wyatt and Surrey and proceed through the growing canon of vernacular poetry to notice Spenser, Sidney, Marlowe, Drayton, and scores of minor figures. Instead of such a survey, I turn to George Puttenham, in *The Art of English Poesy,* invoking the visual to explain the poetic line. His commentary on the interweaving of rhymed lines constitutes one of the clearest endorsements in Elizabethan writing of the delights of similitude and of ingenuity generally:

> And so I set you down an ocular example, because ye may the better conceive it. Likewise, it so falleth out most times, your ocular proportion doth declare the nature of the audible, for if it please the ear well, the same represented by delineation to the view pleaseth the eye well, and *e converso*. And this is by a natural sympathy between the ear and the eye, and between tunes and colors, even as there is the like between the other senses and their objects...'.[26]

These claims come from Book II, entitled 'Of Proportion Poetical', where Puttenham takes up the topics of rhyme, rhythm, and other instruments of poetic music. Making much of the related derivation of the words rhyme (spelled *rime*) and rhythm, he connects them to the Greek original for *arithmos*, or number. A few lines earlier he describes the interplay between the senses and the imaginative faculty when contending that the proportional music of poetic lines 'breedeth a variable and strange harmony not only in the ear, but also in the conceit of them that hear it'. [27] The implicit identity between sight and sound informs those pages of the *Art* in which Puttenham illustrates the possibilities of rhyme with various visual patterns (FIGURE 27.4).

---

[25] Henry Wotton, *Elements of Architecture* (London, 1624) 54.
[26] Whigham and Rebhorn (2007) 174–5.
[27] Whigham and Rebhorn (2007) 174.

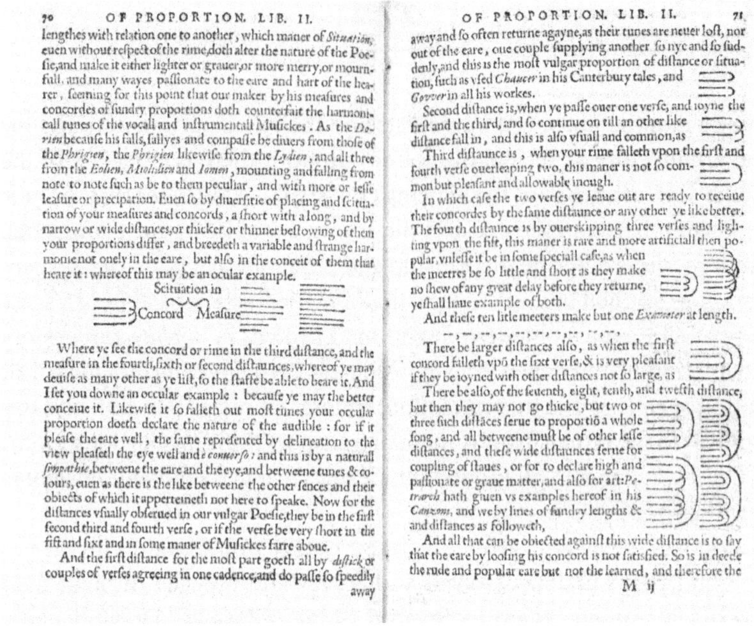

70 OF PROPORTION. LIB. II.

lengthes with relation one to another, which maner of *Situation*, euen without reſpect of the rime, doth alter the nature of the Poeſie, and make it either lighter or grauer, or more merry, or mournfull, and many wayes paſſionate to the eare and hart of the hearer, ſeeming for this point that our maker by his meaſures and concordes of ſundry proportions doth counterfait the harmonicall tunes of the vocall and inſtrumentall Muſickes. As the *Dorien* becauſe his falls, ſallyes and compaſſe be diuers from thoſe of the *Phrigien*, the *Phrigien* likewiſe from the *Lydien*, and all three from the *Eolien*, *Miolidien* and *Ionien*, mounting and falling from note to note ſuch as be to them peculiar, and with more or leſſe leaſure or precipation. Euen ſo by diuerſitie of placing and ſcituation of your meaſures and concords, a ſhort with a long, and by narrow or wide diſtances, or thicker or thinner beſtowing of them your proportions differ, and breedeth a variable and ſtrange harmonie not onely in the eare, but alſo in the conceit of them that heare it: whereof this may be an ocular example.

Where ye ſee the concord or rime in the third diſtance, and the meaſure in the fourth, ſixth or ſecond diſtaunces, whereof ye may deuiſe as many other as ye liſt, ſo the ſtaffe be able to beare it. And I ſet you downe an occular example: becauſe ye may the better conceiue it. Likewiſe it ſo falleth out moſt times your occular proportion doeth declare the nature of the audible: for if it pleaſe the eare well, the ſame repreſented by delineation to the view pleaſeth the eye well and *e conuerſo*: and this is by a naturall *ſimpathie*, betweene the eare and the eye, and betweene tunes & colours, euen as there is the like betweene the other ſences and their obiects of which it apperteineth not here to ſpeake. Now for the diſtances vſually obſerued in our vulgar Poeſie, they be in the firſt ſecond third and fourth verſe, or if the verſe be very ſhort in the fift and ſixt and in ſome maner of Muſickes farre aboue.

And the firſt diſtance for the moſt part goeth all by *diſtick* or couples of verſes agreeing in one cadence, and do paſſe ſo ſpeedily away

OF PROPORTION. LIB. II. 71

away and ſo often returne agayne, as their tunes are neuer loſt, nor out of the eare, one couple ſupplying another ſo nye and ſo ſuddenly, and this is the moſt vulgar proportion of diſtance or ſituation, ſuch as vſed *Chaucer* in his Canterbury tales, and *Gower* in all his workes.

Second diſtance is, when ye paſſe ouer one verſe, and ioyne the firſt and the third, and ſo continue on till an other like diſtance fall in, and this is alſo vſuall and common, as

Third diſtaunce is, when your rime falleth vpon the firſt and fourth verſe ouerleaping two, this maner is not ſo common but pleaſant and allowable inough.

In which caſe the two verſes ye leaue out are ready to receiue their concordes by the ſame diſtaunce or any other ye like better. The fourth diſtaunce is by ouerskipping three verſes and lighting vpon the fift, this maner is rare and more artificiall then popular, vnleſſe it be in ſome ſpeciall caſe, as when the meetres be ſo little and ſhort as they make no ſhew of any great delay before they returne, ye ſhall haue example of both.

And theſe ten litle meeters make but one *Exameter* at length.

There be larger diſtances alſo, as when the firſt concord falleth vpõ the ſixt verſe, & is very pleaſant if they be ioyned with other diſtances not ſo large, as

There be alſo, of the ſeuenth, eight, tenth, and twefth diſtance, but then they may not go thicke, but two or three ſuch diſtãces ſerue to proportiõ a whole ſong, and all betweene muſt be of other leſſe diſtances, and theſe wide diſtaunces ſerue for coupling of ſtaues, or for to declare high and paſſionate or graue matter, and alſo for art: *Petrarch* hath giuen vs examples hereof in his *Canzons*, and we by lines of ſundry lengths & and diſtances as followeth,

And all that can be obiected againſt this wide diſtance is to ſay that the eare by looſing his concord is not ſatisfied. So is in deede the rude and popular eare but not the learned, and therefore the

M ij

FIGURE 27.4 This page from Puttenham's *The Art of English Poesy* describes and illustrates various possibilities for rhyme and for creating aural delight with alternated lines of similar length. Photograph courtesy of Folger Shakespeare Library.

The Sonnets in the 1609 collection are valuable both as exemplars of early modern English artistic tastes and of the poet's own sophisticated, self-conscious response to that taste. For Shakespeare, delight in ornament and a simultaneous critique of it make for a tension that is essential to the meaning of the Sonnets. To read the poems in the context of the visual, especially in light of the emergence of English architecture, is to note his irrepressible desire to strike the reader with a sense of wonder. The Sonnets attest to Shakespeare's self-conscious virtuosity, specifically to his skill at exploiting the possibilities of poetic ornament and pattern and his relish at doing so. And yet this self-awareness includes concern at the potential speciousness of decoration. 'The world is still deceived with ornament', says Bassanio in *The Merchant of Venice* (III. ii. 74).[28] The lurking of the sinister in the beautiful is, of course, a major theme of those Sonnets written to the fair young man and even more obvious in those to the dark lady. The late appearance of Shakespeare's sequence, late in the poet's career and late in the cultural craze for sonnets, is relevant here. In many obvious ways these are quintessentially Elizabethan poems, and indeed for many years critics agreed that they seem to have been composed in the 1590s. But given that they were not published until six years after Elizabeth's death, some scholars have recently contended that many of the pieces were written late, in the first decade of the 17th century. Whatever the actual dates of composition, the point—a point extremely convenient for my analysis—is that they are both representative of and distanced from Elizabethan taste.

[28] All quotations from the plays and Sonnets are from Wells and Taylor (1988).

The affinity of the Sonnets with the structures and ideas surveyed here emerges clearly in the scrutiny of one species of lexical patterning, repetition of the same word or phrase in close proximity. This is a rhetorical or poetical strategy easily related to the correspondences and repetitive patterns—windows, columns, chimneys, types, galleries—of Elizabethan buildings. Puttenham defines several forms of repetition, including *anaphora, epanalepsis*, and *anadiplosis*, as well as the three that I consider here: '*Antimetabole*, or the Counterchange', also known as chiasmus, 'which takes a couple of words to play with in a verse, and by making them to change and shift one into other's place, they do very prettily exchange and shift the sense';[29] '*Epizeuxis*, the Underlay, or Cuckoo-Spell', when 'ye iterate one word without any intermission';[30] and '*Ploche*, or the Doubler', 'a speedy iteration of one word, but with some little intermission, by inserting one or two words between'.[31] These verbal patterns will already be familiar to many readers—'familiar to', but not necessarily 'favourites of'. Many of the literal and verbal configurations I identify are so extreme, so acoustically insistent as to be embarrassing to literary critics. This extravagance, both diverting and discomfiting, occupies the heart of my argument.[32] The prevalence and insistence of these patterns attest to Shakespeare's extraordinary playfulness, and yet the distaste acknowledged by some readers is not inappropriate because the poems also betray the ambivalent attitude of their creator.[33]

27.3

Each Shakespearean sonnet, and indeed each sonnet by Sidney, Spenser, Watson, Barnfield, Wroth, Drayton, Daniel, Greville, and everybody else, comprises multiple formal patterns that illustrate the taste for ingenuity and brilliance prevalent in the other arts.[34] Metaphor, wordplay, antithesis, rhyme—I will have occasion to refer to all these (and more) poetic and rhetorical schemes and figures in the ensuing analysis, but I shall concentrate on the simplest patterns of repetition. Antimetabole or chiasmus provides an instructive start because it constitutes a fairly obvious and playful instance of repetitive wordplay, as in the deadly opposition that begins Sonnet 46:

> Mine eye and heart are at a mortal war
> How to divide the conquest of thy sight.

---

[29] Whigham and Rebhorn (2007) 293.
[30] Whigham and Rebhorn (2007) 285.
[31] Whigham and Rebhorn (2007) 285.
[32] Pertinent here is Christopher Ricks' 2002 British Academy Lecture, 'Shakespeare and the Anagram', *Proceedings of the British Academy 121* (2002): 111–46.
[33] A recent book that brilliantly examines Shakespeare's playful virtuosity in the Sonnets is Brian Boyd, *Why Lyrics Last* (Cambridge, MA: Harvard University Press, 2012).
[34] The essential discussion of these coexisting patterns is Stephen Booth, *An Essay on Shakespeare's Sonnets* (New Haven: Yale University Press, 1968).

> Mine eye my heart thy picture's sight would bar,
> My heart, mine eye the freedom of that right.
>
> (46.1–4)

The pleasure of lines 3 and 4 springs from the reversal of the two nouns, with their accompanying possessive pronouns, but other forms of repetition magnify the obvious antithesis of *eye* and *heart*. In this case, the internal rhyming of the lines is extraordinary. The aural richness is created in part by the conventional substitution of *mine* for *my* to modify 'eye' since the noun begins with a vowel; this adds the 'n' sound, another repeated consonant to reinforce the multiple literal repetitions. Line 3 benefits from *thy* following the two nominal phrases, rhyming with *my* and *mine,* and then line four plays with that pronoun by almost but not quite repeating it, substituting 'the' for 'thy'. In addition, the repetition of *sight* in line 3 (from its terminal position in line 2) furnishes an internal echo for *right,* and another long *i* sound as well. Even the first line of the poem exploits the possibilities of echo: in lines 3 and 4 I have emphasized the sounds resembling *eye,* but the second half of the first line does much with the building-blocks inherent in *heart* (*are at, a mort, al, war*). Finally, this quatrain offers an implied parallelism, in that the verbal phrase *would bar,* present at the end of line 3, functions as a zeugma, absent from line 4 and yet understood to operate grammatically just as it does in line 3. The poem as a whole not only displays extravagant internal antitheses but by its position in the collection also participates in an antithetical grouping, an opposition of war and peace: the struggle conducted between heart and eye in 46 ends with a truce in the opening line of 47, 'Betwixt mine eye and heart a league is took'.

The chiasmic turns that assert themselves so blatantly in 46 and 47 strike the reader, I believe, both negatively and positively. There is, in the first place, the excessiveness of the sound patterns. As Stephen Booth puts it in his commentary on the first, 'The wit of this and the following sonnet is derived from extravagantly complex convolutions in the relationships between *eye* and *heart.* Both poems evoke a sense of futile waste, of barren ingenuity, and of neurotic diversion of energy on to trivia'.[35] In other words, the extravagant criss-crossing of *mine eye* and *my heart* contributes directly to the sense of desperation at the heart of the sonnet, and yet at the same time the intricate sounds of the chiasmus and the echoes supporting it create an irresistible music. Although the poet's ingenuity may be barren, it is nonetheless impressive and attractive to the reader or auditor. And of course many other poems illustrate this same worrying of antithetical units, notably 'They that have power to hurt and will do none' (Sonnet 94) and 'When my love swears that she is made of truth' (Sonnet 138).

Lexical repetition is perhaps the most insistent form of poetic echo. Sometimes words are repeated (and sometimes repeated again) in apparently random fashion; they may

---

[35] *Shakespeare's Sonnets,* edited with an analytic commentary by Stephen Booth (New Haven: Yale University Press, 1977) 208.

be configured into predictable patterns; sometimes the repetition can seem almost obsessive.

> To me, fair friend, you never can be old;
> For as you were when first your eye I eyed,
> Such seems your beauty still.

> (104.1–3)

Numerous tiny examples of patterned sounds animate these two and one-half lines, illustrating the configurations that make this poem memorable and that represent the intricacy characteristic of virtually all the Sonnets. 1) The opening establishes a rhythmic pattern: iamb, pause; iamb, pause. These two pairs of monosyllabic words afford a graceful beginning, after which the semantic force of the clause hustles to the end of the line. 2) The two main alliterative patterns in these lines differ strikingly: *fair friend* announces itself very plainly as an alliterative pattern; a slyer pattern is composed by the *s* words in the third line. 3) The internal rhymes and alliterative groupings in first part of the second line create an intense musical pattern: 'For as you were when first your' offers *you* and *your*, and then *for* creates a consonantal link with *were* and *first* and *your*. 4) The patterns created by these variously affiliated sounds, letters, and words are then capped by the final punning repetition, 'eye I eyed'. The phrase recalls Juliet's triple pun on *ay* (yes), *I* (first-person pronoun), and *eye* (ocular organ) in *Romeo and Juliet* (III. ii. 45–50). Here it is telling because the compression of all three sounds into the end of the line suggests a kind of joke. And yet the word-play is unequivocally serious. The attractions of the young man's eyes, the pleasures of beholding, the dangers of beholding, the guilt associated with looking (taking the sinister sense of 'eyed'), the self-disgust at merely playing with words so as to produce nonsense—all these nuances and themes stand at the heart of the 1609 Sonnets. Such self-conscious lexical repetition also dominates the first quatrain of Sonnet 8:

> Music to hear, why hear'st thou music sadly?
> Sweets with sweets war not, joy delights in joy.
> Why lov'st thou that which thou receiv'st not gladly,
> Or else receiv'st with pleasure thine annoy?

> (8.1–4)

This case is distinctive in that the terminal rhymes are semantically opposed, a scheme which makes the duplication seem necessary rather than almost parodic. It might be said that Shakespeare, observing the value of the patterned lines that Puttenham illustrates, adds colour to the rhyming frame by means of such semantic opposition.

Sonnet 40 begins with multiple repetitions of various kinds and then adds still more:

> Take all my loves, my love, yea, take them all:
> What hast thou then more than thou hadst before?

> No love, my love, that thou mayst true love call—
> All mine was thine before thou hadst this more.
> Then if for my love thou my love receivest,
> I cannot blame thee for my love thou usest;
> But yet be blamed, if thou this self deceivest
> By wilful taste of what thyself refusest.
> I do forgive thy robb'ry, gentle thief,
> Although thou steal thee all my poverty;
> And yet love knows it is a greater grief
> To bear love's wrong than hate's known injury.
>   Lascivious grace, in whom all ill well shows,
>   Kill me with spites, yet we must not be foes.

The poet accuses the young man of betrayal and humiliation, charging him with taking from the poet yet another lover. Divided over this act of theft, the poet is vexed at the loss and yet so powerfully attached to the beloved as to be willing to grant him rights to the third lover's person—whether body or mind we cannot be sure. That is a crude paraphrase of the content of the poem, but it is frustrating to try to summarize meaning in language other than the original because the verbal construction of the poem is the key to its effect.

As for patterns, we might just mention the rhyme scheme, which gives the poem its English shape, and we can also acknowledge the contribution of the metrical frame, working as it does in concert with the repeated sounds of the terminal rhymes. But we must linger over the passionate explosion of the opening, especially its extravagant repetition. Not only do we hear the echoing of *my loves* and *my love*, but the only slightly less insistent *Take all* at the beginning of the line and *take them all* at the end, bolstered by the emphatic and internally rhyming *yea*. The second line contains a similarly elaborate repetition of vowel and consonant sounds, but what is crucial to this line is that, loosely speaking, it is structured like a palindrome. This reversible structure is even more nearly precise when we note that in the Quarto printing of the Sonnets there is no difference between 'then' and 'than'—the sign 'then' stands for both. This palindromic structure is essentially symmetrical: the line moves towards its centre—'more'—and then moves away from it in exactly the same words.

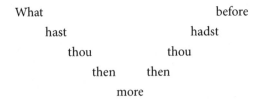

Aurally the line is equivalent to those visually repeated patterns visible in Elizabethan facades, structures with their parts distributed into an equivalent pairing and with an entrance gate or door as the centrepiece.

The remainder of the poem is no less inviting in its playing with aural echo. On close reading, simple lines become much more complex than they first appear. Line 3, 'No love, my love, that thou mayst true love call', for example, depends most obviously on the triply-spoken 'love', each with a monosyllabic modifier, *no love, my love, true love;* also on the metrical repetition at the head of the line, *No love,* pause, *my love,* pause; and then the alliterative **th**at **th**ou in the centre of the line. Next, 'All *mine* was *thine* before **th**ou hadst **th**is **m**ore' is similarly intricate, with the addition of the internally rhyming *mine* and *thine* and-*fore* and *more.* And the Elizabethan ear would probably have heard more assonance than we in line 10, 'Although thou steal thee all'. To break these lines down into their repeated constituent parts is to identify a major source of the musical attraction that the poems have continued to exert since their first appearance.

Apart from sounds, other kinds of repetition decorate and complicate the surface of the poem. Puns, of course, are inherently binary, offering at least two meanings, and in Sonnet 40 the complex signifier is the nominal phrase, 'my love', which bears at least three meanings. In order of significance (but not in order of usage in the poem), *my love* refers to the beloved, as a form of address. Second, it signifies the speaker's emotions, his passionate attachment to the beloved, my love for you. Third, it signifies another lover, *my love* who is stolen by *my love.* The overlapping of signifieds, the ambiguity inherent in these noun phrases, is the key to the kinky emotional content. Moreover, these puns provide a kind of narrative skeleton, forming the structure on which understanding of the poem depends. Less obvious puns arise also, as when the beloved is addressed as 'gentle thief'. Even such a simple phrase depends upon a series of inner contrasts. In the first place, the phrase is an oxymoron: thieves are criminal, outlaws, hardly 'gentle' or kindly. But 'gentle' has a further meaning than 'kindly', also connoting class, the aristocratic status of the beloved, and if so, this class marker also enforces the oxymoron of *gentle thief.* Moreover, thieves are not usually attracted to the poor: in this case, the aristocratic, gentle thief attacks the speaker's poverty. These paired contradictions are expanded in the couplet: 'Lascivious grace', for example, and also 'ill well'. And this last phrase, 'ill well', is part of a larger phrase, 'all ill well', another of those extravagant repetitions that seems almost laughable.

27.4

My attention to the reiterative aural figure in the Sonnets is hardly revelatory. Many other readers, from Empson to Booth to Vendler and beyond, have noticed and made interpretive use of this unusual degree of lexical repetition. What is new is my insistence on the affiliation between this kind of verbal patterning and the schemes of visual arrangement found in various forms of Elizabethan craft. Acquaintance with the forms of artifice in other disciplines teaches us how to appreciate the poetic artefact historically—that is, by entering into the cultural spirit that produced it. The popularity of the sonnet as a form is to some degree proof of the increasing devotion to the rewards of 'composition' and ornament throughout the second half of the 16th century. The sonnet, which reached its apex of popularity in just this period, is especially hospitable to interdisciplinary analysis because of its limits: its very restrictions invite ingenuity and invention. Samuel Daniel, himself a sonneteer, a writer not only of poetry but about poetry, helps to explain the satisfactions of limit in the following excerpt from the *Defence of Rhyme*: 'For the body of our imagination, being as an vnformed *Chaos* without fashion, without day, if by the diuine power of the spirit it be wrought into an Orbe of order and forme, is it not more pleasing to Nature, that desires a certaintie and comports not with that which is infinite, to haue these clozes, rather than, not to know where to end, or how farre to goe, especially seeing our passions are often without measure? … Besides, is it not most delightful to see much excellently ordred in a small roome … ?'[36] Daniel's use of the word 'close' is a critical detail thanks to its status as both a poetic and an architectural term: it means the end of the line, the close of the poetic measure, but it also suggests an enclosure, a contained space. In addition, the phrase 'much excellently ordered' captures the dynamic of concentrated poetic energy to which the extravagant repetitions contribute.

The 1609 collection of Sonnets indicates that Shakespeare maintains a mixed attitude towards the formal effects of reiteration. As I have tried to show, in many of the Sonnets such instances of repetition are so abundant and so highly wrought as almost to suggest a kind of playful or ironic use on the part of the poet. Schemes and figures such as these are the fundamental elements of poetic discourse, and Shakespeare's vigorous exploitation of parallels, opposites, doublings, and echoes not only places him in the tradition carried on by Sidney, Spenser, Drayton, and others but also attests to his sharing the Elizabethan taste for artifice and ornamentation. Sigurd Burckhardt argues that the function of the most important features of poetry—metre, rhyme, metaphor, and various kinds of repetition—is to 'release words in some measure from their bondage to meaning, their purely referential role, and to give or restore to them the corporeality which a true medium needs'.[37] This is precisely what Shakespeare does in the Sonnets, playing with words so dazzlingly that the reader can at first do little more than wonder at the poet's virtuosity. The Sonnets that I have examined are typical, but there are many others that might have been summoned to illustrate the argument: perhaps the most obvious omissions are the Will Sonnets, 135 and 136. The exuberance, the command, the delight in his own verbal powers exhibited by the poet are transferred to the reader so that we take part in this act of poetic exhilaration.

The obsessive repetition also exposes Shakespeare's underlying distrust of such patterning. Booth identifies this concern when he disparages the 'barren ingenuity' of the reiterated words and chiasmic play in Sonnet 46. Likewise, writing of *Romeo and Juliet*, Harry Levin identifies in the poetic surface of the play exactly the repetitions I have studied in the Sonnets; he contends that Shakespeare creates 'a running critique of

[36] Daniel (1930) 139–40.
[37] *Shakespearean Meanings* (Princeton: Princeton University Press, 1968) 24.

artificiality', that the exceptional number of lines containing a form of *ploce* establishes the baseline of the formal against which the lovers, with their 'authentic' less decorated speech, are able to react.[38] The pertinence of that analysis to the Sonnets is clear, in that the hyperbolic repetitions are a measure of the frustration experienced by the speaker. In other words, the extraordinary use of *epizeuxis* and other repetitive figures takes on a semantic dimension. The extravagant reiteration characteristic of the Sonnets I have treated suggests that the playing with words becomes a kind of erotic substitution for actual engagement, emotional or physical. One can sense beneath the decorated surface a kind of self-disgust on the part of the poet, a kind of mordant pleasure in the surrogacy of language for the real thing, whether intimacy, sexual engagement, emotional posses-sion, or other forms of love.

Such a response is articulated specifically in Francesco Colonna's 15th-century Latin romance, *Hypnerotomachia Poliphili*, translated as *Strife of Love in a Dream*, available to Londoners in a new translation in 1589. Throughout the work the narrator Poliphilus seeks his beloved Polia through a series of fantastic architectural settings. This being romance, of course, the lady is always just out of his reach, and so failing to find sexual satisfaction, he turns to admire the pretty rooms in which he finds himself. 'And I beeyng desirous and not satisfied, turned mee about towards the conspicuous Poarch, to beholde diligently the arti-ficious Pallaice, wonderfull and perfinite of the Art of building.... The subtiltie of which, no humane excogitation is able to imitate'.[39] The beauty of the architecture becomes a con-solation, a substitute for sex. For Shakespeare the sonneteer, so does the poem.

SELECT BIBLIOGRAPHY

Booth, Stephen (1968) *An Essay on Shakespeare's Sonnets* (New Haven: Yale University Press).
—— (1977) *Shakespeare's Sonnets, edited with an Analytic Commentary* (New Haven: Yale University Press).
Boyd, Brian (2012) *Why Lyrics Last: Evolution, Cognition, and Shakespeare's Sonnets* (Cambridge, MA: Harvard University Press).
Burckhardt, Sigurd (1968) *Shakespearean Meanings* (Princeton: Princeton University Press).
Cooper, Nicholas (1999) *Houses of the Gentry, 1480–1680* (New Haven: Yale University Press).
Eck, van, Caroline (2003) (ed.) *British Architectural Theory, 1540–1750: An Anthology of Texts* (Aldershot: Ashgate).
Gent, Lucy (1995) *Albion's Classicism* (New Haven: Yale University Press), 377–93.
Gerbino, Anthony, and Johnston, Stephen (2009) *Compass and Rule: Architecture as Mathematical Practice in England* (New Haven: Yale University Press)
Henderson, Paula (2005) *The Tudor House and Garden* (New Haven: Yale University Press).
Mowl, Timothy (1993) *Elizabethan and Jacobean Style* (London: Phaidon).
Pevsner, Nikolaus (1961) 'The Planning of the Elizabethan Country House: An Inaugural Lecture delivered at Birkbeck College 1960' (London: Birkbeck College).

---

[38] 'Form and Formality in *Romeo and Juliet*', in *Shakespeare and the Revolution of the Times* (Oxford: Oxford University Press, 1976) 114.

[39] Francesco Colonna, *Hypnerotomachia Poliphili, The Strife of Love in a Dream* (London, 1592) 66.

Puttenham, George, *The Art of English Poesy*, ed. Frank Whigham and Wayne A. Rebhorn (Ithaca: Cornell University Press, 2007).

Ricks, Christopher (2002) 'Shakespeare and the Anagram', *Proceedings of the British Academy* *121*: 111–46.

Schiffer, James (1999) (ed.) *Shakespeare's Sonnets: Critical Essays* (New York: Garland).

Schoenfeldt, Michael (2007) *The Blackwell Companion to Shakespeare's Sonnets* (Oxford: Blackwell).

Vendler, Helen (1997) *The Art of Shakespeare's Sonnets* (Cambridge, MA: Harvard University Press).

Wells, Stanley, and Paul Edmondson, *Shakespeare's Sonnets* (Oxford: Oxford University Press, 2004).

CHAPTER 28

THE POETICS OF FEMININE SUBJECTIVITY IN SHAKESPEARE'S SONNETS AND 'A LOVER'S COMPLAINT'

MELISSA E. SANCHEZ

Over the past few decades, scholars have discussed Shakespeare's Sonnets and 'A Lover's Complaint' from virtually every angle and have found little ground for agreement to questions they have posed. Some of the main questions that continue to generate controversy include: To what extent did Thomas Thorpe's, John Benson's, or Edmund Malone's editions distort subsequent readings of the poems' language, narrative, or representation of gender and sexuality? Can Shakespeare's Sonnets properly be called a sequence at all?[1] What type of love does the speaker feel for the young

---

[1] On these two related questions, see Stephen Booth, *Shakespeare's Sonnets* (New Haven: Yale University Press, 1977/2000) 543–50; John Kerrigan, *The Sonnets and A Lover's Complaint* (Harmondsworth: Penguin Books, 1986) 46–55; Katherine Duncan-Jones, 'Was the 1609 *Shake-speares Sonnets* Really Unauthorized?', *Review of English Studies* n.s., 34 (1993): 151–71; Margreta de Grazia, 'The Scandal of Shakespeare's Sonnets', in James Schiffer, *Shakespeare's Sonnets: Critical Essays* (New York: Garland, 1999) 89–112; Paul Edmondson and Stanley Wells, *Shakespeare's Sonnets* (Oxford: Oxford University Press, 2004) 3–21; Heather Dubrow, ''Incertainties Now Crown Themselves Assur'd': The Politics of Plotting Shakespeare's Sonnets', *Shakespeare Quarterly* 32 (1996): 291–305; Helen Vendler, *The Art of Shakespeare's Sonnets* (Cambridge, MA: Harvard University Press, 1997) 1–2; Colin Burrow, *The Complete Sonnets and Poems* (Oxford: Oxford University Press, 2002) 91–111; Valerie Traub, 'The Sonnets: Sequence, Sexuality, and Shakespeare's Two Loves', in Richard Dutton and Jean E. Howard, *A Companion to Shakespeare's Works, Vol. 4: The Poems, Problem Comedies, Late Plays*, (Malden: Blackwell, 2003) 275–301; Sasha Roberts, 'Shakespeare's *Sonnets* and the English Sonnet Sequence', in Patrick Cheney, Andrew Hadfield, and Garrett A. Sullivan, Jr, *Early Modern English Poetry: A Critical Companion* (Oxford: Oxford University Press, 2007) 172–83; and William Nelles, 'Sexing Shakespeare's Sonnets: Reading Beyond Sonnet 20', *ELR* (2009): 128–40.

man?[2] Does the lady's 'blackness' have racial meaning?[3] If so, is the 'real' scandal of the Sonnets about racial or class miscegenation rather than homoeroticism? How are we to understand the Sonnets' relation to the Petrarchan tradition? Did Shakespeare really write 'A Lover's Complaint'? If so, should it be read as part of the sonnet sequence (if it is a sequence) or as a separate work?[4]

All of these questions bear on this chapter in important ways, and I list them in order to demonstrate the impressive diversity of opinion that exists regarding virtually every aspect of Shakespeare's poetry. However, none of these questions is my primary focus here. Rather, I am going to discuss one of the few things that has *not* been a source of critical contention, with an eye towards showing how a shift in theoretical frameworks can transform our encounter with Shakespeare's verbal art. For amidst all the argument about the poems' editing, authorship and authorization, racial, gender, and sexual ideologies, Shakespeareans have found one point of consensus, a point so ingrained in our readings of the Sonnets that it appears to need no defence. This consensus is that sex without love and commitment is immoral, dangerous, degrading, indefensible—especially for women.[5] The maid of 'A Lover's Complaint' gets some degree of sympathy

---

[2] See Eve Sedgwick, *Between Men: English Literature and Male Homosocial Desire* (New York: Columbia University Press, 1985) 28–48; Joel Fineman, *Shakespeare's Perjured Eye: The Invention of Poetic Subjectivity in the Sonnets* (Berkeley and Los Angeles: University of California Press, 1986); Joseph Pequigney, *Such Is My Love: A Study of Shakespeare's Sonnets* (Chicago: University of Chicago Press, 1985); Bruce Smith, *Homosexual Desire in Shakespeare's England: A Cultural Poetics* (Chicago: University of Chicago Press, 1991) and 'I, You, He, She, and We: On the Sexual Politics of Shakespeare's Sonnets', in Schiffer (1999) 411–29; Peter Stallybrass, 'Editing as Cultural Formation: The Sexing of Shakespeare's Sonnets', *Modern Language Quarterly* 54 (1993): 91–145; Valerie Traub, 'Sex Without Issue: Sodomy, Reproduction, and Signification in Shakespeare's Sonnets', in Schiffer (1999) 431–52; and Jonathan Goldberg, 'Literary Criticism, Literary History, and the Place of Homoeroticism', in Cheney et al. (2007) 136–46.

[3] Kim F. Hall, *Things of Darkness: Economies of Race and Gender in Early Modern England* (Ithaca: Cornell University Press, 1996) 69–71 and 115–17, and '"These Bastard Signs of Fair": Literary Whiteness in Shakespeare's Sonnets', in Ania Loomba and Martin Orkin, *Post-Colonial Shakespeares* (London: Routledge, 1998) 170–82; and de Grazia (1999) 81–83.

[4] For the argument that 'A Lover's Complaint' completes a tripartite, Delian structure, see Kerrigan (1986) 112–17; Burrow (2002), 138–40; and Katherine Duncan-Jones (ed.), *Shakespeare's Sonnets* (London: Arden, 1997) 45. De Grazia treats 'A Lover's Complaint' as Shakespearean, but she rejects the Delian thesis; see 'Revolution in Shake-speare's Sonnets', in Michael Schoenfeldt, *A Companion to Shakespeare's Sonnets* (Malden: Blackwell, 2007) 57–70. For the complaint's thematic relation to the sonnets, see Ilona Bell, '"That Which Thou Hast Done": Shakespeare's Sonnets and A Lover's Complaint', in *Shakespeare's Sonnets*, ed. Schiffer (1999) 455–74. For the contrary opinion, see Dubrow, 'Incertainties' and, especially, Brian Vickers, *Shakespeare, 'A Lover's Complaint', and John Davies of Hereford* (Cambridge: Cambridge University Press, 2007). In the present essay, I treat "A Lover's Complaint" as a part of the context in which the Sonnets were initially presented and read in the 1609 Quarto. Drawing on Zachary Lesser's important insight that a work's publisher was also its first, and perhaps most interested reader, I consider what the pairing of the Sonnets and 'A Lover's Complaint' can tell us about both poems (see Lesser, *The Politics of Publication: Readings in the English Book Trade*, Cambridge: Cambridge University Press, 2004, 1–51).

[5] As Traub has observed, both male and female readers who align themselves with feminism tend to disavow any identification with the dark lady, while both male and female readers who align themselves with gay, lesbian, and queer studies tend to identify with the young man or the speaker's attachment to him (2003, 288).

from critics who see her as a victim of male aggression and deceit. David Bevington, for instance, argues that the presentation of the maid as 'weak, ashamed of herself, distraught about her moral collapse' makes the poem 'an indictment not of womanly frailty but of male thrusting aggression'.[6] But when it comes to the dark lady, several critics have followed the Sonnets' speaker at his most misogynistic of moments and seen her as, in Joel Fineman's analysis, 'black on the inside, as any orthodox Petrarchan would have known at first abhorrent sight', both 'corrupt and corrupting'; in Stephen Greenblatt's words, encompassing 'everything that should arouse revulsion'; or, in John Kerrigan's estimation, 'decidedly dark in the conduct of her love-life' to the extent that 'morally she inhabits, as she sexually enshrines, a "hell"'.[7] Most critics take the speaker's sexual slurs as a matter of misogynistic course, while those who have explicitly defended the dark lady have proceeded as though the best line of defence is to question the charge that she has—and likes having—multiple sex partners. In accepting the terms in which misogynist culture evaluates promiscuity, scholars have allowed to stand the more general assumption that such behaviour, if true, would indeed be blameworthy.[8]

I want to proceed from a different direction, asking what would happen to our reading of the Sonnets if we conceded that the dark lady is indeed promiscuous, but then followed up by asking, *and so what if she is?* This chapter is an attempt to explore what happens to our interpretive protocols if we borrow some of the rethinking of sexuality that queer theory has done with regards to same-sex desire and apply it to other non-normative sexualities—in this case, female promiscuity. Much as abandoning the belief that homoeroticism is indecent and unspeakable opened up previously unavailable readings of the Sonnets to the young man, so might explicitly challenging the view that sexual promiscuity is categorically immoral open up new readings of the dark lady poems.[9] In particular, I propose that if we set aside the notion that the best sex is that which occurs in loving and monogamous relationships, an ideal that has been widely critiqued by queer theorists, we can appreciate the ways in which the possibility of female promiscuity not only threatens but also enables patriarchal prerogative.[10] And

[6] Review of *Shakespeare, A Lover's Complaint, and John Davies of Hereford, Renaissance Quarterly* 60 (2007): 1463–66; 1465.

[7] Fineman, *Shakespeare's Perjured Eye* 56, 132; Greenblatt, *Will in the World* (New York: Norton, 2004) 244; and Kerrigan (1986) 59, 61.

[8] Ilona Bell, 'Rethinking Shakespeare's Dark Lady', in Schoenfeldt (2007) 293–313; Dympna Callaghan, *Shakespeare's Sonnets* (Malden: Blackwell, 2007), 146. Lorna Hutson examines the significance of ideals of female chastity and male husbandry to humanist education and criticism; see 'Why the Lady's Eyes are Nothing Like the Sun', in Clare Brant and Diane Purkiss, *Women, Texts, and Histories, 1575–1760* (London: Routledge, 1992) 13–38.

[9] See especially Stallybrass' analysis of the effects of homophobia on the editing and criticism of the Sonnets: 'the repeated act of putting straight appears as a form of cultural hysteria, but its excesses inscribe a crisis in the attempt to form a normative character and sexuality through Malone's Shakespeare' (1993) 96.

[10] Critics who have questioned the ideals of monogamy and romance include Leo Bersani, 'Is the Rectum a Grave?', *October* 43 (1987): 197–222; Michael Warner, *The Trouble With Normal: Sex, Politics, and the Ethics of Queer Life* (Cambridge, MA: Harvard University Press, 2000); and Leo Beransi and Adam Phillips, *Intimacies* (Chicago: University of Chicago Press) 2008.

Shakespeare's poetic language makes legible the cultural work of the stigma attached to women who desire non-monogamous sex—women who, as it were, desire like men.

Critics have long attributed early modern attacks on female promiscuity to male anxieties about dynastic legitimacy, homosocial order, and racial miscegenation.[11] As Jonathan Goldberg has observed, because early modern writers described female desire in the most stigmatized of ways as an excuse for exerting legal and institutional forms of control, feminist scholarship has generally responded by constructing a 'legend of good women' that denies imputations of excessive sexual appetite and, in the process, accords normative femininity only to women who are morally pure, suffering subjects.[12] To Goldberg's shrewd observation, I want to add that such a framework not only limits women's sexual choices but also serves to normalize and justify male sexual prerogative and violence. In other words, to suppose that women want love while men want sex (or that women want sex only as an expression of love) is to move uncomfortably close to pathologizing women's desire for sex *as* sex. Indeed, as Gayle Rubin has argued, the tendency of some feminists to treat heterosexual sex as 'dangerous and violent' is 'predicated on a Victorian model of distribution of libido in terms of male and female. There was the good woman who was not sexual. There is the man who is sexual. So whenever sex happens between a good woman and a man, it's a kind of violation of her'.[13] Moreover, if men are the only ones who naturally experience lust, who want sex as sex, male aggression and female passivity become naturalized. The stigmatization of female sexual appetite, then, not only seeks to shame women into protecting male genealogical interest but, in denying women the possibility of genuine consent, also denies them the possibility of genuine refusal. The imputation of promiscuity is a means of limiting female sexual subjectivity. For if the female libido can be described as indiscriminate and depersonalized, then the possibility of choice and agency disappear. The whore, no less than the virgin, is outside the economy of seduction and desire. Characterized less by appetite than by indifference, the promiscuous woman can be treated as a passively receptive object rather than a subject of sexual feeling. By rejecting the stigma attached to female promiscuity, we as critics can examine more objectively how this stigma works to sustain male prerogative as well as how it shapes the horizons of female identity.

Shakespeare's poetry dramatizes the power of a stigmatizing discourse of promiscuity to distort female sexual subjectivity, revealing in the process the contradictions of

---

[11] See, for instance, de Grazia (1999) 101–7; Jonathan Goldberg, 'Romeo and Juliet's Open R's', in *Queering the Renaissance* (Durham: Duke University Press, 1994); and Valerie Traub (1999) 431–52. For a more general treatment of early modern reactions to female promiscuity, see Laura Gowing, *Domestic Dangers: Women, Words, and Sex in Early Modern London* (Oxford: Clarendon Press, 1996). More recently, Johanna Rickman has argued that noble women were rarely punished or ostracized for promiscuity or adultery; see *Love, Lust, and License in Early Modern England: Illicit Sex and the Nobility* (Hampshire: Ashgate, 2008).

[12] *Desiring Women Writing: English Renaissance Examples* (Stanford: Stanford University Press, 1997) 12, 5.

[13] Deirdre English, Amber Hollibaugh, and Gayle Rubin. 'Talking Sex: A Conversation on Sexuality and Feminism', *Feminist Review* 11 (1982): 40–52.

the logic on which this distortion rests. By looking at the rhetorical constructions of the 'fickle maid' (5) of 'A Lover's Complaint' and the dark lady of the Sonnets, we can appreciate how strangely absent female sexual desire is from a pair of poems that feature fallen women as central characters.[14] I begin with 'A Lover's Complaint', a poem whose oft-noted dense and archaic language has obscured the curious lack of female pleasure at its centre. While critics have accorded the maid of this poem varying degrees of sympathy, they have generally agreed that her fall was a result of passion overcoming judgement. To take an example of two seemingly opposite views converging, when Bevington defends the maid against Brian Vickers' charge that she 'rejects the moral law and celebrates the pursuit of pleasure in libertine terms', Bevington does so on the grounds that the poem shows 'Shakespeare's generosity of Spirit and willingness to forgive a person who is truly sorry for what she or he has done'.[15] Ilona Bell similarly accepts the premise that it would be wrong to pursue 'pleasure in libertine terms' when she argues that the maid only consented to sex because she believed that the youth's '"lover's tokens" and "holy vows" constituted a legally binding, clandestine marriage contract'.[16] In other words, the question of the maid's culpability turns on the nature of her desire. What this debate fails to register is how consistently the maid insists on her own *lack* of passion— even the sense of compulsion with which her speech concludes paradoxically evacuates the possibility of physical desire. Kenneth Muir, I think, got it right when he argued that the maid is overcome not by the youth's words but by his tears, which cause her to pity him.[17] For the maid presents her loss of virtue as a sacrificial expression of love, and therefore a properly feminine, selfless act intended to assuage her seducer's own suffering. Nor does the maid's conspicuous misery bespeak the masochism that several critics have suggested.[18] Whatever pleasure the maid may or may not have experienced in the actual sexual encounter, her tale's rhetoric of pain seeks to deny pleasure, masochistic or otherwise, and to claim the more acceptable feeling of pity. Indeed, we might read her 'suffering ecstasy' (69) as a performance of what Wendy Brown has described as a 'wounded attachment', an identity and moral authority characterized by injury.[19] The

---

[14] All quotations of Shakespeare's poetry will be from John Jowett, William Montgomery, Gary Taylor, and Stanley Wells, *The Oxford Shakespeare: The Complete Works*, 2nd edn (New York: Oxford University Press, 2005).

[15] Bevington, Review, and Vickers, *Shakespeare*, 118.

[16] Bell (1999) 467.

[17] Muir, 'A Lover's Complaint A Reconsideration', in Edward A. Bloom, *Shakespeare 1564–1964*, (Providence: Brown University Press, 1964) 154–66; 163–4.

[18] See, for instance, Catherine Bates, 'The Enigma of *A Lover's Complaint*', in Schoenfeldt (2007) 426–40; and James Schiffer, '"Honey Words": *A Lover's Complaint* and the Fine Art of Seduction' and Shirley Sharon-Zisser, '"True to Bondage": The Rhetorical Forms of Female Masochism in *A Lover's Complaint*', both in Shirley Sharon-Zisser, *Critical Essays on Shakespeare's* A Lover's Complaint, ed. (Burlington: Ashgate, 2006) 137–48 and 179–90. Bell stresses the courtly background of the maid based on her education and rhetoric; she also reads the poem in the context of exculpatory rather than *de casibus* complaints ('Shakespeare's Exculpatory Complaint', in Sharon-Zisser, *Critical Essays*, 91–108).

[19] Brown, *States of Injury: Power and Freedom in Late Modernity* (Princeton: Princeton University Press, 1995) 52–76.

maid's *ecstasis* removes her from her body and its selfish desires into pure service to another. Yet this substitution of pity for pleasure is itself staged, and the poem's archaic language and convoluted syntax reveal the artificiality of both the maid's self-defence and the gender ideology on which its terms are premised.

The multilayered framework, or 'double voice' (3), through which we hear the maid's story has obscured the extent to which her tale of deceived innocence is a performance in the sense that Judith Butler has described. It is 'a ritualized production, a ritual reiterated under and through constraint, under and through the force of prohibition and taboo, with the threat of ostracism and even death controlling and compelling the shape of the production, but not … determining it fully in advance'.[20] As several critics have noted, we are not the direct audience of this production.[21] Rather, we hear the story from an unnamed narrator who himself (most critics, rightly I think, assume that it is a male) eavesdrops on the maid as she tells her tale, and rehearses the youth's words, to a 'reverend man' (59). This confessor, is also, moreover, a former courtier, himself 'Sometime a blusterer that the ruffle knew | Of court, of city' (58–9). Though now living the country life of *otium*, this courtier-confessor is specifically associated with the duplicitous rhetoric and performance of the world of *negotium*. Before she becomes aware of his presence, the maid virtually explodes in a fit of rage and sorrow, weeping and cursing over a pack of letters and love tokens:

> These often bathed she in her fluxive eyes,
> And often kissed, and often 'gan to tear;
> Cried 'O false blood, thou register of lies,
> What unapprovèd witness dost thou bear!
> Ink would have seemed more black and damnèd here!
> This said, in top of rage the lines she rents,
> Big discontent so breaking their contents.
>
> (50–6)

The maid's first word is less a word than an eruption of pain and fury: 'O' (50). This ecphonic cry not only articulates her helplessness before the youth's seductive lies but also, and more to the point, reveals the centrality of such a claim of helplessness to a speech that is as much self-defence as confession. Kerrigan has argued that ecphonesis, like the other stylistic features of apostrophe, antistrophe, epimone, echo, and anaphora that characterize the female complaint tradition, creates a female poetics of absence, emptiness, and abandonment.[22] The maid herself is quite conscious of this rhetorical tradition and its implications not only for love stories, but for the gendered morality to which she is subject. As George Puttenham's account of ecphonesis attests, such substitution of sound for articulate speech would itself have been recognized as a rhetorical

---

[20]   *Bodies that Matter: On the Discursive Limits of 'Sex'* (New York: Routledge, 1993) 95.

[21]   See, for instance, Kerrigan (1986), 16; and Bell (1999) 469–70.

[22]   Kerrigan, *Motives of Woe: Shakespeare and 'Female Complaint', A Critical Anthology* (Oxford: Clarendon Press, 1991) 8, 21–2.

calculation by attentive early modern readers. In *The Arte of English Poesie* Puttenham's defines 'Ecphonisis, or the Outcry', as 'the figure of exclamation', explaining that 'I call him *the outcrie* because it utters our mind by all such words as do show any extreme passion, whether it be by way of exclamation or crying out, admiration or wondering, imprecation or cursing, obtestation or taking God and the world to witness, or any such like as declare an impotent affection'.[23] The maid will register such 'impotent affection' by repeating the word 'O' ten more times when speaking for herself and four times in her direct report of the youth's speeches. This conspicuous use of ecphonesis performs the blurring of subjective boundaries. Such loss of will and agency may be as much a mark of proper femininity as is chastity insofar as both resist the pulls of self-serving carnal desire.

The youth's speeches, as others have pointed out, are typographically indistinguish-able from those of the maid in the 1609 Quarto, which uses no quotation marks. And even in modern editions that do set off the youth's speech from the maid's, it is easy to lose track of who is speaking. This blurring of voices certainly intimates the maid's complicity in her own seduction, but not quite in the way that critics have assumed. For the youth's appeals allow us to appreciate the suasiveness of vulnerability as a rhetori-cal ploy. The maid makes an easy and common mistake: she assumes that that which is helpless is also harmless. It is the youth's performance of suffering and subjection that both persuades the maid to take pity on him and provides a model for her own perfor-mance of victimization. In the youth's speeches, ecphonesis first appears in the plea 'O, then, advance of yours that phraseless hand', a line whose syntactical inversion and trope of inexpressibility ('phraseless') enact the youth's helplessness before the maid's beauty (225). The second instance occurs in his account of a nun who loved him, a story that seeks to establish the maid's power over him by citing his own power over others. These lines are even more opaque:

> Lo, this device was sent me from a nun,
> A sister sanctified of holiest note,
> Which late her noble suit in court did shun,
> Whose rarest havings made the blossoms dote;
> For she was sought by spirits of richest coat,
> But kept cold distance, and did thence remove,
> To spend her living in eternal love.
>
> But O, my sweet, what labor is't to leave,
> The thing we have not, mast'ring what not strives,
> Planing the place which did no form receive,
> Playing patient sports in unconstrainèd gyves!
> She that her fame so to herself contrives
> The scars of battle scapeth by the flight,
> And makes her absence valiant, not her might.

---

[23]   *The Arte of English Poesie*, 1589, ed. Edward Arber (London: Alex Murray and Son, 1869) 221.

O, pardon me, in that my boast is true!
The accident which brought me to her eye
Upon the moment did her force subdue,
And now she would the cagèd cloister fly.
Religious love put out religion's eye.
Not to be tempted would she be immured,
And now, to tempt, all liberty procured.

How mighty then you are, O hear me tell!
The broken bosoms that to me belong
Have emptied all their fountains in my well,
And mine I pour your ocean all among.
I strong o' er them, and you o' er me being strong,
Must for your victory us all congest,
As compound love to physic your cold breast.

(232–59)

The youth's speech here, like that of the conventional Petrarchan lover, insists on the tyrannical power that his helpless desire gives the maid. Yet he destabilizes the traditional gender roles of the sonnet by recalling a time when he himself was in a position of power over a nun who failed to sustain the maid's own strength of mind. Contrasting his own hot passion with a nun's 'cold distance' (237) from worldly temptations, the youth rhetorically asks 'But, O my sweet, what labor is't to leave | The thing we have not, mast'ring what not strives'. This elliptical statement is typically understood as meaning some version of Burrow's gloss: 'it is harder to overcome a love for someone who is not there than a love for someone who is present and resistant'.[24] But this does not seem quite right, particularly when read in the larger rhetorical context. For the youth's statement *denies* the praiseworthiness of the nun, who does not struggle against temptation but 'The scars of battle scapeth by the flight, | And makes her absence valiant, not her might' (245). Crucially, the youth's goal is to diminish the value of what John Milton in very different circumstances would call 'a fugitive and cloistered virtue'.[25] His accusation is also a form of persuasion, for it applies not just to the nun but to the maid, who has already told us that initially 'With safest distance I mine honour shielded' from the youth's seductions (151). A better paraphrase of lines 239–40, then, might be 'Is it really very hard to resist something that we have never known or enjoyed, to master a passion with which we have never struggled?' Having established the nun's avoidance of human suffering, the youth mimetically enacts his own brave struggle in his following two uses of 'O': 'O, pardon me, in that my boast is true!' (246) and 'How mighty then you are, O hear me tell!' (253). The maid is to the youth as he is to his previous lovers, so 'I strong o' er them, and you o' er me being strong, | Must for your victory us all congest, | As compound love to physic your cold breast'. The youth here appeals to the female 'homosociality' that

---

[24] Burrow (2002) 711 n. 240.
[25] *Areopagitica*, in *Complete Prose Works of John Milton*, 8 vols, Don M. Wolfe (ed.), (New Haven and London: Yale University Press, 1962) 2:516.

Catherine Bates has argued structures the poem.[26] But whereas Bates has seen identification with other women as the primary motive of the maid, I would argue that the maid here is invited to identify as much with the youth's own position of power as with the other women's positions of helplessness. For pity itself entails a hierarchal relation between its subject and its object. Since the youth has just insisted that he never desired the women who wooed him, he places the maid in the same benevolent position he himself has formerly occupied. Sex, he claims, will be an act of mutual compassion and charity, offering 'physic' not pleasure.

The youth's rhetoric of helplessness, of course, is 'but an art of craft', and since it so resembles the maid's we wonder if hers is 'an art of craft' too (293). Kerrigan has argued that the 'double voice' of 'A Lover's Complaint' casts suspicion on the maid, indicating her collusion in her seduction even as she herself seduces the audience by reenacting the youth's speeches.[27] It is true that the maid has been complicit in her own seduction and heartbreak, but in a different way than Kerrigan suggests. Rather, the maid participates in her own undoing precisely because such self-sacrifice is the mark of a *good woman*: she has neither the 'rocky heart' and 'breast so cold' of the immovably chaste Petrarchan mistress nor the selfish appetite for pleasure that characterizes the dark lady. In opposition to these archetypes of chastity and lust, the maid of 'A Lover's Complaint' repeatedly denies having a will (in all of the senses that Shakespeare's Sonnets exploit) of her own. In the final section of the poem, the maid's veritable explosion of ecphonic 'O's' works rhetorically to construct her fall as a result of her own naïve impulse to assuage the youth's agony.

Having recited the youth's seductive speeches, the maid not only describes but reenacts her own response. Crucially, this response is not one of reciprocal sexual desire, but of pity. And it is this performance of the distinction between the youth's and the maid's motivations—selfish lust versus selfless love—that aligns moral, sexual, and gendered subjectivity. The youth is culpable because he turned the specifically female virtue of instinctive sympathy against the maid, a process that she recreates in such lines as: 'O, how the channel to the stream gave grace' (285); 'O father, what a hell of witchcraft lies | In the small orb of one particular tear!' (288–9). Even as she recalls the youth's deceit, she stresses that it aroused her morally praiseworthy sympathies, not her morally culpable passions. The maid artfully translates the failure of chastity into the triumph of pity. The youth is particularly diabolical in that he has taken advantage of the maid's virtuous desire to relieve his pain:

> For lo, his passion, but an art of craft,
> Even there resolved my reason into tears.
> There my white stole of chastity I daffed,
> Shook off my sober guards and civil fears;
> Appear to him as he to me appears,
> All melting, though our drops this difference bore:
> His poisoned me, and mine did him restore.

> (295–301)

---

[26] Bates, 'Enigma' 431–2.
[27] See Kerrigan (1986) 15–16; and Bell (1999) 469–70.

The imagery is significant here: rather than inflaming her desire, the maid insists, the youth's appeal 'resolved my reason into tears'. Her tears here replace the involuntary bodily excretions of sexual arousal with a more innocent and ethically sound compassion. Insofar as virtuous female identity is defined by suffering—the most authentic sign of selflessness—the maid's identification with the young man, her choice to 'Appear to him as he to me appears, | All melting' becomes a performance of virtue. Removing the barrier of chastity, she melts into a formless extension of the youth's own will.

The maid notoriously concludes her tale by acknowledging that she would do it all again. This confession is typically understood to cast doubt on her virtue. Yet within a structure that equates female victimization with moral authority, we can read it as accentuating not continued desire for sex (as Kerrigan glosses it), and certainly not a celebration of libertine pleasure (as Vickers claims) but a selfless pity that is precisely the opposite of the pursuit of pleasure. For her final lines enact the same dissolution that characterized her first (and only?) sexual encounter with the youth: 'Ay me, I fell, and yet do question make | What I should do again for such a sake' (321–2). Kerrigan glosses line 322 as meaning either 'for the sake of falling in such a pleasant way' or 'for the sake of someone like the youth', and Burrow agrees with the latter reading. But if we treat the word 'sake' as an independent substantive, we come to a rather different reading. For while in the modern English of Shakespeare's day the phrase 'for the sake of' could certainly mean on account of, or out of desire for, something, it also retained the more archaic substantive meaning of 'charge', 'suit', or 'guilt'.[28] In light of the maid's emphasis on the youth's appeals to her pity, it makes more sense to read the line as 'I fell; and yet I wonder what I would do again when confronted with such pleas for pity'. Particularly given the legalistic etymology of 'sake', for the maid to have retained what she earlier calls her 'own fee-simple, not in part' (144) would have made her guilty of the coldness and cruelty with which chaste sonnet mistresses are invariably charged. In this economy either the maid or the youth must suffer, and in sacrificing herself the maid also proves her own virtue.

This focus on sex as a sign of pity rather than passion shifts the terms in which female virtue is expressed, replacing the self-discipline of chastity (etymologically related as it is to chastisement) with a self-sacrificial acceptance of shame and agony. The maid's final series of ecphoneses concludes the poem with howls of pain at the mere memory of youth's performance of suffering, and thereby rhetorically completes the mimetic circle of the poem:

> O that infected moisture of his eye,
> O that false fire which in his cheek so glowed,
> O that forced thunder from his heart did fly,
> O that sad breath his spongy lungs bestowed,
> O all that borrowed motion seeming owed
> Would yet again betray the fore-betrayed,
> And new pervert a reconcilèd maid.
>
> (323–9)

[28] *Oxford English Dictionary*, s.v. 'sake'.

The tension between corruption and repentance in the final line bespeaks the dilemma of female sexual subjectivity in a patriarchal economy. To remain a 'reconciled', or reformed, 'maid', to act *like* a virgin, is to accept sex as itself a form of perversion, a turn from the path of truth and virtue. Yet even as she admits her guilt, the maid mitigates it by denying her sexual agency. To fall again would confirm her willingness to sacrifice herself in order to assuage the youth's tears, flushes, cries of agony—a perverse demonstration of selflessness.

It is just such evacuation of subjectivity that the dark lady refuses when she presumes to occupy the male province of carnal desire. However, I want to propose that, contrary to critical consensus, it is not her promiscuity as such that so disturbs the speaker of the Sonnets. Rather, it is her assertion of sexual subjectivity, of agency and choice, which threatens the male prerogative he claims—the dark lady wants some men (maybe many men) but she does not want *all* of them. Kathryn Schwarz has brilliantly shown how the poet's attack on female 'will' exposes the contradictions within misogyny.[29] Schwarz focuses, however, only on the dark lady's will to say yes, whereas I am more interested in the poet's responses to her will to say no. Sonnets 135 and 136 dramatize the misogynistic attempt to deny female sexual choice by insisting that if a woman once says 'yes' she forever gives up the right to say 'no':

> Whoever hath her wish, thou hast thy Will,
> And Will to boot, and Will in overplus.
> More than enough am I that vex thee still,
> To thy sweet will making addition thus.
> Wilt thou, whose will is large and spacious,
> Not once vouchsafe to hide my will in thine?
> Shall will in others seem right gracious,
> And in my will no faire acceptance shine?
> The sea, all water, yet receives rain still,
> And in abundance addeth to his store;
> So thou, being rich in Will, add to thy Will
> One will of mine to make thy large Will more.
>   Let no unkind no fair beseechers kill;
>   Think all but one, and me in that one Will.

(135)

> If thy soul check thee that I come so near,
> Swear to thy blind soul that I was thy Will,
> And will, thy soul knows, is admitted there;
> Thus far for love, my love-suit, sweet, fulfil.
> Will will fulfil the treasure of thy love,
> Ay, fill it full with wills, and my will one.

[29] See Schwarz, 'Will in Overplus: Recasting Misogyny in Shakespeare's Sonnets', *ELH* 75, 3 (2008): 737–66.

> In things of great receipt with ease we prove
> Among a number one is reckoned none.
> Then in the number let me pass untold,
> Though in thy store's account I one must be;
> For nothing hold me, so it please thee hold
> That nothing me a something, sweet, to thee.
>> Make but my name thy love, and love that still,
>> And then thou lov'st me for my name is Will.

(136)

With all of the punning on the word 'will' in the two poems, it is easy to miss the fact that both are premised on the belief that by indulging or using her will in the past (in the sense of carnal desire and sex organs) the dark lady has forever relinquished the claim to a will of her own (in the sense of choice or agency). In the rhetorical situation on which the poem is premised, in which she has indeed said 'no' to our poet, such refusal appears perverse and unreasonable. In her 'large and spacious' 'will' (135.5), the speaker claims, his own 'will' can hardly register; amidst 'the number' of her partners he can 'pass untold' (136.9). Curiously, however, in attributing to the dark lady an uncontrolled, indiscriminate appetite, the poet also struggles to deny her active desire, indeed any feeling at all, for him or for anyone. So even as he claims that she has 'Will to boot, and Will in overplus', this excess depersonalizes sex, makes her indifferent to the speaker or any other man, like 'The sea', which, 'all water, yet receives rain still' (9)—and, significantly, has no choice about it.

This denial of female agency distorts the speaker's appeal: Sonnets 135 and 136 do not attempt to seduce the lady, but to badger her into compliance. The repetition of the word 'will' strives to enact the deadening, numbing experience of sex that the speaker attributes to the dark lady. Occurring thirteen times in Sonnet 135 and seven in Sonnet 136, this word almost loses meaning in the multiplication of its possible senses, much as the speaker insists that the lady has lost meaningful claim to the ability to distinguish between one man and another—or, indeed, even to notice that she is being penetrated. This sexual paralysis also appears in the poem's rhyme scheme. Rather than the traditional form of the Shakespearean sonnet (abab cdcd efef gg) we get an obsessive return back to the 'a' rhyme in both poems. In Sonnet 135 the scheme begins with what looks like standard progression from the first quatrain to the second, which rhyme, respectively, abab cdcd. But the third quatrain returns to the 'a' rhyme (aeae) as does the couplet (aa). In Sonnet 136 the rhyme scheme is, if anything, more perversely repetitive. We seem, in this case, to follow the standard pattern of abab cdcd efef up through the couplet, which concludes with a bb rhyme. Yet the internal 'b' rhymes of lines 5 and 6 stall the progression ('Will will fulfil the treasure of thy love, | Ay, fill it full with wills, and my will one'). So does the repetition of the word 'love' and its variants from its repetition in line 4, to placement as final rhyming word of line 5 to its triple appearance in the couplet—indeed, between these four lines the word 'love' appears in some form six times, the word 'will' 3. Similarly, the pair 'one' and 'none' forms not only the rhyme pattern in the second quatrain but its own internal rhyme in line 8, and for good measure 'one' is repeated again two lines later (136.10), even as 'number' appears in both lines 8 and 9, preventing a clean break between quatrain and quatrain, octave and sestet, the speaker and any other man.

What we might call a sputtering out of anticipated formal progression alerts us to what is perhaps the most striking thing about Sonnets 135 and 136: even though they are both focused on sex, and obsessively so, they are profoundly unsexy, unsatisfying. They call to mind Philip Sidney's verdict on an earlier age's sonnets: 'truly many of such writings as come under the banner of unresistible love, if I were a mistress, would never persuade me they were in love'.[30] In Sonnets 135 and 136, the poet does not even pretend to be dying of desire, nor does he bother to arouse it in his addressee. Rather, the argument of both 135 and 136 can be summed up, more or less, as: 'C'mon, you'll hardly know I'm here'.[31] And it is this argument for the *indifference* the dark lady might feel for sex that sets Sonnets 135 and 136 off from the rest of the sequence and from traditional antifeminist satires on uncontrolled female appetite. Even 129, for all its disgust, registers the intensity of the speaker's libido. It is only in the couplet of 135 that we get anything like the expression of intense longing that characterizes many other poems in Shakespeare's and other sonnet sequences: 'Let no unkind no fair beseechers kill' (13). Rather than imagine excessive female appetite, 135 and 136 project absolute female passivity, matched by a surprising male apathy. According to the logic of the poem, as what Sonnet 137 calls 'the bay where all men ride' and 'the wide world's common place' (137.6, 10), the dark lady has sacrificed the only agency allowed her by the logic of the traditional Petrarchan sequence: the choice to say 'no'. But, as Sonnets 135 and 136 reveal, 'no' and 'yes' are mutually constitutive. For the absence of desire in the poet's logic equally describes both chastity and promiscuity in that both indiscriminately accept or reject all 'fair beseechers', killing them with either privation or the *petit mort* of orgasm. Opposed to the simple rejection that characterizes the virgin or the utter submission that characterizes the whore is the unthinkable possibility that a woman may simultaneously desire many men without desiring *all* men, that she may fulfill every 'love-suit' but that of the poet. And insofar as sexuality is tied up with subjectivity, status as volitional subject rather than passive object, the dark lady's insistence on sexual choice threatens to undo a gendered binary that depends on the privileging of male 'will'—in all its senses—over female 'will'. By departing from the expected narrative, the dark lady has thrown into confusion the very logic by which desire, and the verse that attempts to capture it, sustains itself, a shortcoming manifested in the metrical irregularities and logical contradictions that characterize 135 and 136. The problem for the speaker is not, after all, that the lady is 'the bay where all men ride' or 'the wide world's common place'. The problem is that she is not common or accessible *enough*. Refusing to 'think all but one', she is having sex with *some* men, but not the speaker, at least not for now. The rejection hurts because it is personal, indicating a lack in him rather than the excess he projects onto her.

---

[30] *The Defence of Poetry*, in *Sir Philip Sidney: The Major Works*, Katherine Duncan-Jones (ed.), (Oxford: Oxford University Press, 1989).

[31] Indeed, this is how Callaghan, Kerrigan, and Burrow all gloss it.

Indeed, throughout Sonnets 135 and 136 the focus is less on any objective condem-nation of the dark lady's sexuality and more on the speaker's reactions to the fact that she—unlike most previous mistresses, at least in sonnets written by men—selectively indulges it. This aligns her even more with the young man than critics have recognized, and not just because both have been unfaithful to the speaker, but also because both have refused his advances. Unless we are to treat as accurate the speaker's earlier condemna-tion of *all* sexual desire as 'perjured, murd'rous, bloody, full of blame, | Savage, extreme, rude, cruel, not to trust', as 'a very woe', as 'hell' itself (129.3–4, 11, 14), the sequence gives us ample reason to question his perspective on promiscuity.

The situation depicted in the dark lady sequence would seem to divest the speaker of any claim to moral or ethical judgement: his anger, his sense of victimization, arises because he has hoped to be the exclusive lover of both the young man and the dark lady, and they have refused him this singularity. Their betrayals, that is, consist in refusing to let him have 'two loves' who, like the women enthralled to the youth in 'A Lover's Complaint', reward his promiscuity with singular devotion. The poet eschews the same monogamy he requires of others. His rage responds less to promiscuity as such than to the promiscuity of other peo-ple. He acknowledges as much in Sonnet 42 when he laments that 'Both find each other, and I lose both twain' (42.11), and, with far greater agitation, in Sonnet 144 where he com-plains that they 'being both from me, both to each friend' (144.11). He is fungible to 'both' of his lovers, and what he 'lose[s]' is not the possibility of a relation with the man or the lady, but the possibility of being either's exclusive object of affection or desire.

The careful division of male and female subjectivity for which the Sonnets strive, it turns out, does not—cannot—hold. As Helen Vendler has argued, even as the Sonnet 144 attempts to distinguish firmly between the male 'better angel' and the female 'worser spirit', this distinction repeatedly gives way (144.3, 4).[32] This confusion of gen-dered subjectivity was, of course, already anticipated by the poem that so scandalized Shakespeare's 18th- and 19th-century editors, Sonnet 20:

> A woman's face with nature's own hand painted
> Hast thou, the master-mistress of my passion;
> A woman's gentle heart, but not acquainted
> With shifting change as is false women's fashion;
> An eye more bright then theirs, less false in rolling,
> Gilding the object whereupon it gazeth;
> A man in hue, all hues in his controlling,
> Which steals men's eyes and women's souls amazeth.
> And for a woman wert thou first created,
> Till Nature as she wrought thee fell a-doting,
> And by addition me of thee defeated
> By adding one thing to my purpose nothing.
>   But since she pricked thee out for women's pleasure,
>   Mine be thy love, and thy love's use their treasure.

(20)

---

[32] Vendler (1997) 606.

Here it is precisely female desire—Nature's 'doting', 'women's pleasure'—that transforms the young man into a *man*, 'And by addition me of thee defeated | By adding one thing to my purpose nothing' (10, 13, 12). Critics have widely noted the use of 'nothing' to signify the female genitalia, both because there was 'nothing' to see and because, as Booth notes, the vaginal orifice formed the shape of a '0'.[33] We might therefore connect the poet's 'purpose nothing' to the prominent ecphonetic 'O's' of 'A Lover's Complaint' and the equation of excess and absence, infinity and nothingness, in Sonnets 135 and 136—a connection that begins to resolve one conundrum of Sonnet 20: if the poet dislikes women so much, why would he want the young man to be one? I want to propose that it is precisely *because* the poet dislikes women so much that he wants the young man to be one. I am not the first person to notice that the young man of the Sonnets bears a strong resemblance to the youth of 'A Lover's Complaint' in that the former 'steals men's eyes and women's souls amazeth' and the latter 'did in the general bosom reign | Of young, of old, and sexes both enchanted' (20.8; 127–8). Bell has read this affinity as suggesting the guilt of the young man for seducing the speaker, and I think there is something to that.[34] But what such a reading neglects is the association in both poems of masculinity with the ability to reduce others' wills to the 'nothing' signified equally by the passive female orifice and the maid's inarticulate outcries. The youth of 'A Lover's Complaint' and the young man of the Sonnets have a power that the Sonnets' speaker can himself exercise only in the space of poetry.

In making the 'Master Mistress' a man in Sonnet 20, the poet claims, Nature 'defeated' the poet's 'purpose' of absolute possession, of the superiority that the speaker performs in his misogynistic attacks on female duplicity. This may help explain why, as Bruce Smith has argued, the speaker's final gesture in Sonnet 126 is to turn the young *man* into a traditional object of homoerotic desire, a subordinate 'boy' who occupies the role of voiceless, powerless minion.[35] Female sexual subjectivity plays a similarly frustrating role in Sonnets 135 and 136, where the dark lady refuses the utter pliability, the nothingness, that the speaker would impose on her—and therefore her proper identity, what Angelo in *Measure for Measure* deems the 'destined livery', of a woman (II. iv. 138). The problem with the young man's promiscuous gender is the same as that of the dark lady's promiscuous desire: neither signifies the pliability and obedience that the speaker thinks they should. As Traub has argued, the 'convergence in Shakespeare's poems of male homoerotic desire and misogyny' certainly 'confronts (1) the desirability and significance of male desire for men; (2) the difficulties posed for male heteroeroticism in a society that systematically undervalues women; and (3) the necessity of insuring that women's desires accord with those of men, thus harnessing women to patriarchal reproduction'.[36] While Traub rightly describes the intersections between homoerotic

---

[33] Booth, *Sonnets* 164–5.

[34] Bell, 'Rethinking Shakespeare's Dark Lady', in Schoenfeldt (2007) 309–11.

[35] Smith, 'I, You, He, She, and We: On the Sexual Politics of Shakespeare's Sonnets', in James Schiffer, *Shakespeare's Sonnets: Critical Essays* (New York: Garland, 1999) 422.

[36] Traub, (1999) 432, 435.

ties, misogyny, and patriarchal privilege, her focus on reproduction as the central concern of patriarchy overlooks the ways in which patriarchy may be as invested in female promiscuity as female chastity. Insofar as the poetic speaker has no direct interest in the dark lady's reproductive capacities (she is, after all, not *his* wife, and the only mention of her maternal capacity, in 143, is metaphorical) I would argue that homoerotic desire and misogyny are even more intimately tied than Traub suggests.[37] For the desire that the poet feels for both of his loves is equally aggressive, even if the young man's masculinity—and therefore his claim to subjectivity and equality with the speaker—shields him from the full measure of vitriol directed at the dark lady.

As Shakespeare's 'A Lover's Complaint' and Sonnets indicate, the stigma attached to female promiscuity is not only prohibitive but also productive. And what it produces may be the possibility of hierarchy, dominance, and inequality that, for the speaker of the Sonnets at least, are precisely what make men men, women women, and sex sexy. The speaker of 'A Lover's Complaint' accepts this gendered definition of desire, which explains why her tale so relentlessly insists that she is a victim of pity rather than passion. The dark lady, by contrast, never speaks. Yet the sexual agency that we can infer from the speaker's pleas in Sonnets 135 and 136 also profoundly threatens the gendered binaries that he would uphold. In shifting our own evaluation of female promiscuity, I have sought to show how we can better appreciate the cultural logic that 'A Lover's Complaint' and the Sonnets perform, and thereby to contest the gendered hierarchies that they endorse.

SELECT BIBLIOGRAPHY

Bates, Catherine (2007) 'The Enigma of *A Lover's Complaint*', in Michael Schoenfeldt, *A Companion to Shakespeare's Sonnets* (Malden: Blackwell) 426–40.

Ilona Bell (2007) 'Rethinking Shakespeare's Dark Lady', in Michael Schoenfeldt, *A Companion to Shakespeare's Sonnets* (Malden: Blackwell) 293–313.

de Grazia, Margreta (1999) 'The Scandal of Shakespeare's Sonnets', in James Schiffer, *Shakespeare's Sonnets: Critical Essays* (New York: Garland) 89–112.

——(2007) 'Revolution in Shake-speare's Sonnets', in Michael Schoenfeldt, *A Companion to Shakespeare's Sonnets* (Malden: Blackwell) 57–70.

Dubrow, Heather (1996) '"Incertainties Now Crown Themselves Assur'd": The Politics of Plotting Shakespeare's Sonnets', *Shakespeare Quarterly* 32: 291–305.

Duncan-Jones, Katherine (1993) 'Was the 1609 Shake-speares Sonnets Really Unauthorized?', *Review of English Studies* n.s., 34: 151–71.

Fineman, Joel (1986), *Shakespeare's Perjured Eye: The Invention of Poetic Subjectivity in the Sonnets* (Berkeley and Los Angeles: University of California Press).

Schwarz, Kathryn (2008) 'Will in Overplus: Recasting Misogyny in Shakespeare's Sonnets', *ELH* 75: 3, 737–66.

---

[37] For a contrary argument, see de Grazia, who stresses the poet's 'uterine obsession' and fear of racial and class miscegenation (1999, 104).

Sharon-Zisser, Shirley (2006) '"True to Bondage": The Rhetorical Forms of Female Masochism in *A Lover's Complaint*', in Shirley Sharon-Zisser (ed.), *Critical Essays on Shakespeare's A Lover's Complaint* (Aldershot: Ashgate) 179–90.

Smith, Bruce (1999) 'I, You, He, She, and We: On the Sexual Politics of Shakespeare's Sonnets', in James Schiffer, *Shakespeare's Sonnets: Critical Essays* (New York: Garland) 411–29.

Stallybrass, Peter (1993) 'Editing as Cultural Formation: The Sexing of Shakespeare's Sonnets', *Modern Language Quarterly* 54: 91–145

Traub, Valerie (1999) 'Sex Without Issue: Sodomy, Reproduction, and Signification in Shakespeare's Sonnets', in James Schiffer, *Shakespeare's Sonnets: Critical Essays* (New York: Garland) 431–52.

——(2003) 'The Sonnets: Sequence, Sexuality, and Shakespeare's Two Loves', in Richard Dutton and Jean E. Howard, *A Companion to Shakespeare's Works, Vol. 4: The Poems, Problem Comedies, Late Plays*, (Malden: Blackwell) 275–301.

Vickers, Brian (2007) *Shakespeare, 'A Lover's Complaint', and John Davies of Hereford* (Cambridge: Cambridge University Press).

CHAPTER 29

....

POETRY AND COMPASSION IN SHAKESPEARE'S 'A LOVER'S COMPLAINT'

....

KATHARINE A. CRAIK

29.1

....

'A Lover's Complaint' occupies an uneasy place in Shakespeare's oeuvre. A haunting exploration of a woman's abandonment by an unscrupulous suitor, the poem has always stirred impassioned responses from its readers who have been both fascinated and perplexed by its strange beauty. The poem is linguistically and syntactically difficult, containing a strikingly large number of unfamiliar coinages and complex grammatical constructions.[1] Some regard 'A Lover's Complaint' as Shakespeare's best work, a fittingly virtuosic conclusion to the Sonnets. Others have expressed doubts about its authenticity and literary quality, and have argued for its exclusion from the canon.[2] The history of the poem's reception is indeed as unusual as the work itself, for although the maiden's

---

[1] For a survey of these, see A. K. Hieatt, T. G. Bishop, and E. A. Nicholson, 'Shakespeare's Rare Words: *A Lover's Complaint, Cymbeline*, and *Sonnets*' in *Notes and Queries*, 34.2 (1987): 219–24.

[2] William Hazlitt and C. S. Lewis were among the early doubters of the poem's attribution to Shakespeare, and J. W. Mackail argued in 1912 that the poem belonged to the Rival Poet of the Sonnets. Kenneth Muir and MacDonald P. Jackson restored the poem to Shakespeare in the 1960s and 1970s. See Muir, '*A Lover's Complaint*: A Reconsideration', in Edward A. Bloom, ed., *Shakespeare 1564–1964* (Providence: Brown University Press, 1964) 154–66; and Jackson, 'Shakespeare's *A Lover's Complaint*: its date and authenticity', *University of Auckland Bulletin*, 72 (1965). More recently, the debate was reopened by Ward E. Y. Elliott and Robert J. Valenza who used statistical analysis of style and language in order to argue the poem is unlikely to be Shakespeare's in 'Glass Slippers and Seven-League Boots: C-Prompted Doubts About Ascribing *A Funeral Elegy* and *A Lover's Complaint* to Shakespeare,' *Shakespeare Quarterly*, 48 (1997): 177–207 (198).

predicament has profoundly moved many people, it has embarrassed many more. This chapter suggests 'A Lover's Complaint' challenges readers in remarkably direct ways, inviting us to examine our own responses to poetry and grief. The young maiden's sadness is singularly difficult to imagine, and the justice of her complaint is hard to determine, but these difficulties may point to the poem's most important achievements. The fascination of 'A Lover's Complaint' lies in the problem of how—and indeed whether—to sympathize with the maiden whose regret seems incomplete and whose repentance looks only partial. This chapter aims to contextualize 'A Lover's Complaint' within the tradition of 'female complaint' and, through close attention to the poem's language, to explore Shakespeare's experimentation both within and beyond this mode. Shakespeare's exploration of early modern protocols of grief and consolation is also considered with the aim of reflecting upon the place of compassion in early modern theories of poetry.

Despite the formal complexity of 'A Lover's Complaint', its story is not difficult to summarize. An unidentified narrator overhears a maiden lamenting on a hillside and revealing her sorrows to a 'reverend man' (57). She describes her seduction by a beautiful aristocrat who has already taken and broken the hearts of many women. Graceful in appearance and accomplished in every aspect of life, the young man is also a treacherously persuasive orator. Nearly one-third of the poem's 329 lines are given to his artful seduction which the maiden reports verbatim. The young man describes the jewels, sonnets, and other love-tokens he has received from 'many a several fair' (206), and, insisting on his sincerity, he begs the maiden now to lend 'credent soul' (279) to his suit. She resists him for a time ('I mine honour shielded', 151), but his tearful performance finally overcomes her ('my white stole of chastity I daffed', 297). Devastated by her own naive failure to resist his advances, the maiden recognizes him, finally, as a 'conceald fiend' (317) with a seductive exterior. In the final stanza with its series of expostulations ('O, that infected moisture of his eye, | O that false fire that in his cheek so glowed', 323–4), she nevertheless insists that she would do the same thing all over again.

'A Lover's Complaint' was published for the first time by Thomas Thorpe at the end of *Shakespeare's Sonnets* (1609). Scholars cast aspersions on Thorpe's integrity as a publisher throughout the 1960s and 1970s, suggesting that 'A Lover's Complaint' may have been Thorpe's unauthorized addendum to the volume. As many others have since noted, however, the 1609 volume stands as an integrated whole.[3] Early modern sonnet sequences were often appended by a narrative complaint, and, moreover, the ruthless seducer of 'A Lover's Complaint' in many ways resembles the young man addressed in the first 126 of Shakespeare's Sonnets. 'A Lover's Complaint' may therefore have been designed to provide a commentary and conclusion to the poems which preceded it.[4] Questions about

---

[3] Katherine Duncan-Jones, 'Was the 1609 *Shake-speares Sonnets* really unauthorized?', *RES* 34 (1983): 151–71.

[4] See Ilona Bell, '"That which thou hast done": Shakespeare's Sonnets and *A Lover's Complaint*' in *Shakespeare's Sonnets: Critical Essays*, James Schiffer, ed. (New York and London: Garland, 1999) 455–74 (467). On the connection between sonnet sequences and complaints, see Kerrigan, *The Sonnets and A Lover's Complaint* (Harmondsworth: Penguin, 1986) 13–15; and Wendy Wall, *The Imprint of Gender: Authorship and Publication in the English Renaissance* (Ithaca: Cornell University Press, 1993) 250–69.

authorship nevertheless continue to bedevil its critical reception, and several contenders have been proposed including, most recently, John Davies of Hereford.[5] It is no coincidence that 'A Lover's Complaint' has consistently attracted debate about authorship for it is centrally preoccupied (as we will see) with questions of voice, authenticity, and origin.

Shakespeare returned at various moments in his career to the complaint mode and was surely familiar with the literature of complaint which flourished in the late 16th and early 17th centuries. Among his other grief-stricken maidens are Ophelia in Act IV, Scene v of *Hamlet*, Desdemona in Act IV, Scene iii of *Othello*, and the Jailer's daughter in *The Two Noble Kinsmen*. Complaint poems were remarkably wide-ranging in theme and style, encompassing penitent prayers, requests for patronage, and expressions of political or personal grievance as well as amatory poems in the voices of both ardent suitors and forsaken lovers.[6] Written in the form of lyrics, sonnets, ballads, and narrative poems, complaints are found in literary sources ranging from cheap printed broadsides to manuscript miscellanies compiled at the universities and Inns of Court. Some were written by men, some few by women, and many (like 'A Lover's Complaint') by men in the voices of women. This sub-group of laments known as 'female complaint' held a particular appeal for early modern readers and owed much to Ovid's *Heroides,* a series of letters written by royal and celebrated women to their absent husbands or lovers, and to Book 4 of Virgil's *Aeneid*, in which Dido, Queen of Carthage, laments the departure of Aeneas. The laments written by Shakespeare and others bring this classical inheritance together with Christian traditions of complaint, drawing in particular from the story of Mary Magdalen grieving for Christ. Among the other complaints written at this time are Samuel Daniel's *Delia* (1592), which concludes with *The Complaint of Rosamund*, and Thomas Lodge's *Phillis* (1593), which is followed by *The Tragical Complaint of Elstred*, as well as the plaints in the popular collection *A Mirror for Magistrates* (1559), particularly 'Shore's Wife' by Thomas Churchyard.[7] All of these laments draw in important ways on Petrarchan love poetry, as well as the contemporary literature of conduct dictating protocols for women's moral, emotional, and sexual behaviour.

'Female complaint' has always been associated with the fall of princes thanks to its association with *Heroides*, but the genre was flexible enough to accommodate the voices of commoners as well as queens. Early modern pastoral poems in the Virgilian and Theocritean tradition contain love laments in which shepherds and shepherdesses grieve for love lost or are otherwise forlorn. Elizabethan pastoral often introduces sophisticated rhetoric and noble sentiment into a bucolic setting, and many complainants are accordingly remarkably articulate. But readers also bought and read laments in the voices of

---

[5] See Brian Vickers, *Shakespeare, 'A Lover's Complaint' and John Davies of Hereford* (Cambridge: Cambridge University Press, 2007).

[6] On the variety of early modern complaint, see Kerrigan's introduction to *Motives of Woe* (Oxford: Clarendon Press, 1991) esp. 1–13; and Richard Allan Underwood, *Shakespeare on Love: The Poems and the Plays. Prolegomena to a Variorum Edition of A Lover's Complaint* (Salzburg: Institut für Anglistik und Amerikanistik, 1985) 1–3. The term 'female complaint' is also Kerrigan's.

[7] 'Shore's Wife' appeared in the 1563 edition. See Underwood (1985) 12.

women, both fictional and non-fictional, from lower social classes. Such laments borrow from traditional love lyric, including pastoral, but tend to be set in urban rather than rural spaces. Their speakers express franker forms of desire, and often dwell upon their own failure to temper overwhelming passion with reason or judgement. It is however difficult to place 'A Lover's Complaint' firmly within any of these various strands of the complaint tradition. Shakespeare's maiden is not quite the noble shepherdess familiar from pastoral poetry, nor the regretful subject of exculpatory lament, nor the morally ruined woman of urban complaint. Instead she is both rustic and cosmopolitan, both untutored and sophisticated. Shakespeare's equivocation about the maiden's estate serves an important purpose, allowing him to consider how love lament was coloured by social class. 'A Lover's Complaint' indeed enacts a class drama which explores how the experience and expression of sorrow is affected by social difference.

Complaint poetry articulates profound despair within a particular set of structural and narrative conventions, and its appeal lies partly in this fruitful combination of intimacy and formality. A unique resource for expressing (and organizing) intense emotion, complaint provides an unusual opportunity, like extended soliloquy, to explore emotional inwardness. This chapter thinks afresh about connections between narrative poetry and intense feeling, attending closely to the formal features of 'A Lover's Complaint' in order to reveal how the poem might have affected its first and subsequent audiences. As we will see, lament was designed to move readers in particular ways—especially by stirring up compassion or fellow-feeling. Sympathetic affect is dramatized within the fabric of 'A Lover's Complaint' through the reverend man and the narrator, who together comprise the maiden's double-layered audience. But the silence of these listeners at certain moments in the poem makes compassion seem elusive, and, in turn, casts into doubt the degree of sympathy readers themselves feel for the maiden's predicament. In order to explore the affective properties of lament at the time Shakespeare was writing, this chapter begins by exploring the place of compassion in early modern theories of poetry.

29.2

Theories of sympathy, or compassion, lie at the heart of George Puttenham's encyclopaedic treatise on the nature and function of poetry, *The Arte of English Poesie* (1589). In Book I, Puttenham describes the 'tunable sound' of rhyme and its suitability to the monosyllables of English vernacular. The cadence of verses whose lines all end with a repeated sound is delightful to hear, 'the ear taking pleasure to hear the like tune reported, and to feel his return'. More complicated is Puttenham's discussion of the generally harmonious, musical quality of spoken verse which he calls 'numerosity':

> that is to say, a certain flowing utterance by slipper words and syllables, such as
> the tongue easily utters, and the ear with pleasure receiveth, and which flowing of

words with much volubility smoothly proceeding from the mouth is in some sort harmonical and breedeth to the ear a great compassion.[8]

Puttenham here intends 'compassion' to mean 'harmony' rather than (as we might expect) fellow-feeling for suffering. Words which run easily and smoothly over the tongue are received with pleasure by the ear thanks to the agreeable sense of flow they create. Such compassion is central to Puttenham's theory of affect which hinges on proportion, or symmetry. The art of poetry, properly mastered, touches the reader with a delightful sense of harmony achieved through sonorous regularity and the careful numerical ordering of 'slipper words and syllables'. At the start of his second book, Puttenham suggests that this principle of proportion, or disciplined regularity, extends to nature and culture more generally. Not only poetry but all things 'stand by proportion, and [. . .] without it nothing could stand to be good or beautiful'.[9]

'A Lover's Complaint' is both good and beautiful, but few would describe it as well-proportioned. The poem is written in rhyme royal stanzas of seven decasyllabic lines rhyming *ababbcc*. This rhyme scheme was considered appropriate for serious subjects: George Gascoigne described it in *Certayne Notes of Instruction Concerning the Making of Verse* (1575) as 'a royall kinde of verse, seruing best for graue discourses'.[10] Despite the orderly structure and rhyme of 'A Lover's Complaint', J. M. Mackail deplored in 1912 its 'cramped, gritty, discontinuous quality' and objected to its 'stiffness, tortuousness, or cumbrousness ... [and] forcing of phrase'.[11] Recent readers have reacted similarly. MacDonald P. Jackson admits that 'A Lover's Complaint' is 'stylistically freakish' while John Roe describes it as 'ill-digested and infelicitous'.[12] The poem is indeed remarkable for its artfulness, freighted as it is with words designed to make the reader stop and think. Among its archaisms are 'eyne' for 'eyes', and 'enswathed' for 'wrapped'. The poem is also peppered with neologisms such as 'fluxive' for 'weeping', 'pensived' for 'altered by thought', and 'extincture' for 'extinguishing'; as well as words rarely found in Shakespeare, or indeed elsewhere in early modern poetry, such as 'commix', 'outwardly', 'slackly', and 'gyve'.[13] Shakespeare places a series of carefully wrought obstacles to the poem's easeful reception, hindering any sense of flowing utterance. This avoidance of sonorous regularity has left some readers with an impression of aloofness, but also affords Shakespeare an important opportunity. If Puttenham's temperate, well-proportioned verse proceeds smoothly from speaker to listener, or from author to reader, the stylized language of 'A

[8] Frank Whigham and Wayne A. Rebhorn (eds), *The Art of English Poesy by George Puttenham: A Critical Edition* (Ithaca: Cornell University Press, 2001) 166.

[9] Whigham and Rebhorn (2001) 153.

[10] *The Posies of George Gascoigne* (1575) sig. U1v.

[11] J. M. Mackail, 'A Lover's Complaint,' *Essays and Studies* 3 (1912) 51–70; quoted in Jackson, 'A Lover's Complaint Revisited,' *Shakespeare Studies*, 32 (2004): 267–94 (290).

[12] Jackson (2004) 290; John Roe (ed.), *The Poems* (Cambridge: Cambridge University Press, 1992) 73.

[13] A. Kent Hieatt surveys these unusual words in 'Cymbeline and the intrusion of lyric into romance narrative: Sonnets, A Lover's Complaint, Spenser's Ruins of Rome' in George M. Logan and Gordon Teskey (eds.), *Unfolded Tales: Essays on Renaissance Romance* (Ithaca: Cornell University Press, 1989) 98–118 (103).

Lover's Complaint' makes us aware instead of the fraught processes involved in receiving the words of others. The beauty and virtuosity of this poem do not reside in its easiness on the ear. Intemperate and unsettling, 'A Lover's Complaint' throws into doubt the idea that excellent poetry breeds harmonious compassion.

Compassion of a different sort is central to Puttenham's discussion in *The Art* of the cathartic usefulness of lament. Building on the rhetorical principle of *movere*, inherited from Aristotle, Puttenham understood the assimilation of good poetry, redeployed in informed practices of writing and speaking, profoundly to affect the passions (or emotions) and, through them, the moral and spiritual self. Lament engages the passions in particularly direct ways:

> Lamenting is altogether contrary to rejoicing: every man saith so, and yet is it a piece of joy to be able to lament with ease and freely to pour forth a man's inward sorrows and the griefs wherewith his mind is surcharged.[14]

The proper subjects for lament are the death of loved ones or allies, military defeats, loss of honour or reputation, and, finally, 'the travails and torments of love forlorn or ill-bestowed'. Love's sorrows give rise to the most complex and difficult laments, Puttenham argues, for love is 'the most puissant and passionate' of all emotions requiring 'a form of poesy ... most witty'. Poetry allows

> the many moods and pangs of lovers throughly to be discovered; the poor souls sometimes praying, beseeching; sometime honouring, advancing, praising; another while railing, reviling, and cursing; then sorrowing, weeping, lamenting; in the end laughing, rejoicing, and solacing the beloved again [...] moving one way and another to great compassion.[15]

Laments are best described not through their content, but through the feelings they arouse in those who encounter them—perhaps the beloved to whom the poem is addressed, or indeed the general reader. Just as the lover's emotions swing between longing, ambition, frustration, anger, and sorrow, the emotions of the addressee are moved 'one way and another' towards a sensation of compassion. Puttenham's suggestion that such affective sympathy is allied with solace, or rejoicing, again admits a kind of easeful pleasure no doubt drawn from Aristotle's observation in the *Poetics* that we delight in encountering representations of objects which would cause us sorrow if we actually saw them.[16]

In his *Apology for Poetry*, published in 1595, Sir Philip Sidney described in similar terms the power of 'the lamenting Elegiac; which in a kind heart would move rather pity

---

[14] Whigham and Rebhorn (2001) 135.
[15] Whigham and Rebhorn (2001) 136 and 134.
[16] Aristotle, *Poetics*, 4:1448b in *Rhetoric and Poetics of Aristotle*, W. Rhys Roberts and Ingram Bywater (trans.), (New York: Modern Library, 1954).

than blame'. Any writer able faithfully to paint suffering 'is to be praised, either for compassionate accompanying just causes of lamentations, or for rightly painting out how weak be the passions of woefulness'. Lament emerges here as collaborative or reciprocal, again in accordance with the principles of classical rhetoric. Skilful poets and orators know how to manipulate the emotions of readers and listeners, first by feeling passions themselves and then by arousing them in others. To compose lament is indeed to perfect a form of companionship, or sympathetic fellow-feeling, as the writer of lament 'bewails with' the complainant in a form of 'compassionate accompanying'.[17]

Such compassionate fellow-feeling is however difficult to find in 'A Lover's Complaint'. The poem begins with a series of embedded narratives, the male narrator reporting the words of the maiden who, in turn, reports the speech of the male aristocrat who seduced her. The introduction of the 'reverend man' who approaches the young maiden, and asks the 'motives of her woe' (63), adds another layer of listening, or receiving. The opening lines of the poem are among the most difficult to unravel:

> From off a hill whose concave womb re-worded
> A plaintful story from a sist'ring vale,
> My spirits t'attend this double voice accorded,
> And down I laid to list the sad-tuned tale.
>
> (1–4)

Here the narrator not only attends to the maiden's story, but also tries to align himself with her voice, anticipating a sense of accord, or companionate sympathy: 'My spirits t'attend this double voice accorded'. But this complaint is not easily uttered or smoothly received. Multiple and fractured, it is immediately reworded by the echo of a deep hillside and twice received by both the narrator and the reverend. The narrator is ready to 'list' (line 4), or harken, to the maiden's story—but the prospect of compassionate accord between them remains suspended. The narrator indeed seems doubtful about what he sees, or even what he thinks he sees: 'the thought might think sometime it saw | The carcass of a beauty spent and done' (lines 10–11). 'A Lover's Complaint' therefore immediately raises the difficulties involved in reporting and receiving facts without prejudice, and readers have consequently approached the poem from within various interpretive frameworks including legal witnessing, Catholic confession, and the conventions of amatory lyric and persuasion. But the opening lines of 'A Lover's Complaint' also present a dilemma of sympathy. For if questions of sympathy arise when readers (or indeed people in the world) encounter a spectacle of suffering, Shakespeare here considers how properly to recognize such a spectacle—and, in what follows, of how to feel a proper sense of accord with it.[18]

---

[17] *An Apology for Poetry*, Geoffrey Shepherd (ed.), (Manchester: Manchester University Press, 1973) 116.

[18] On theories of sympathy in art and literature, see David Marshall, *The Surprising Effects of Sympathy: Marivaux, Diderot, Rousseau, and Mary Shelley* (Chicago and London: University of Chicago Press, 1988).

Shakespeare therefore resists the compassion which Puttenham and Sidney regard as central to the affective power of lament. 'A Lover's Complaint' is not marked by easeful 'flowing of words' as the poem instead draws attention, from the very start, to the effort involved in accompanying others' sorrows. As Puttenham and Sidney make clear, however, the experience of reading lament should elicit more than spontaneous sympathy. Laments also invite their readers to judge, in a measured fashion, whether the sorrows expressed are truly pitiable. If there is indeed a good reason to grieve, the poet's art works as a therapy or antidote—for such sorrows are the ones that 'noble poets sought by their art to remove or appease'. Not all sorrows are equally pitiable, however, as Puttenham explains: 'Such of these griefs as might be refrained or helped by wisdom and the party's own good endeavour, the poet gave none order to sorrow them'. Compassion is due only when sorrow has 'just causes'; otherwise, the lament has the different function of pointing out 'how weak be the passions of woefulness'.[19] Central to lament, then, is the proper governance of passions. To express intense sorrow for a good reason confirms nobility of character, and the compassion felt by authors and readers in this case is powerfully curative. To bewail a preventable woe for which one has only oneself to blame, however, betokens shameful weakness.

Readers have found the 'undistinguished woe' (20) of Shakespeare's aggrieved maiden difficult to interpret, and the justice of her complaint peculiarly resistant to definition. Unlike many of the speakers of early modern 'female complaint', Shakespeare's is a fictional and modern figure drawn from neither legend nor history. She dwells on her plight with intense introspection, and her complaint resembles a confessional disclosure—not least because it is spoken to an attentive reverend.[20] Confession generally enjoys a privileged connection to truth and intimacy, but the maiden's at times seems reluctant. She is described from the outset as a 'fickle maid' (5) suggesting the inconstancy of her character. Among the love-tokens she carries are favours, jewels, and rings, as well as letters 'With sleided silk feat and affectedly | Enswathed and sealed to curious secrecy' (48–9). These suggest the clandestine nature of the liaison, but also—since the maiden now casts them into the 'weeping margin' of a river (39)—the impossibility of ever determining their full contents. This impression of mystery is compounded by the 'conceited characters' (16) embroidered on her napkin which imply a significance hidden to the beholder. When the maiden does make a frank confession, she immediately qualifies it in the stanza which follows:

> Yet did I not, as some my equals did,
> Demand of him, nor being desird yielded.

[19] Whigham and Rebhorn (2001) 136; Sidney, *Apology*, (Shepherd, 1973) 116.
[20] On the poem's confessional context, see Katharine A. Craik, 'Shakespeare's *A Lover's Complaint* and Early Modern Criminal Confession', *Shakespeare Quarterly* 53, 4 (2002): 437–59; Kerrigan (1991) esp. 39–41; and Paul Stegner, 'A Reconciled Maid: *A Lover's Complaint* and Confessional Practices in Early Modern England' in Shirley Sharon-Zisser (ed.), *Essays on Shakespeare's 'A Lover's Complaint'* (Aldershot: Ashgate, 2006) 79–90.

> Finding myself in honour so forbid,
> With safest distance I mine honour shielded.
>
> (148–51)

She did not go so far as to make importunate 'demand of him', she insists; and nor did she succumb without hesitation, guarding her honour instead 'with safest distance'. Most problematic of all, however, is the maiden's admission that she does not truly feel regret—despite the bitter recriminations she has already levelled against the man who deceitfully 'preached pure maid' (315): 'Ay me, I fell; and yet do question make | What I should do again for such a sake' (321–2). The maiden had declared that the young man's letters bore only 'unapprovd witness' (53) to his true character, although they were written in blood. This phrase also aptly describes her own testimony, for Shakespeare neither absolves the maiden of guilt by affirming (in Sidney's words) her 'just causes', nor quite suggests that her woes could possibly have been 'refrained or helped'.[21]

This problem of sympathy is compounded by the twofold dramatization in 'A Lover's Complaint' of the hazards of compassion. Firstly, the maiden is undone by her sympathy for the young man who begged her to '[h]ave of my suffering youth some feeling pity' (178). Against her better judgement, the maiden lent 'soft audience' (278) to his pleas; and Shakespeare's account of her surrender to the young man's persuasions is a description of compassion haplessly bestowed:

> But with the inundation of the eyes
> What rocky heart to water will not wear?
> What breast so cold that is not warmd here?
> O cleft effect! Cold modesty, hot wrath,
> Both fire from hence and chill extincture hath.
>
> (290–4)

The young man's tears wear the maiden's heart to water in an image which materializes the abstract notion of fellow-feeling. David Marshall has described compassion as 'a correspondence of feelings between people such as a mutual attraction or affinity'.[22] But if sympathy involves correspondence, it also here involves cleaving. For the seducer's tears are both fiery and chilly ('O cleft effect!', 293), and he remains separate from the maiden even when he appears most keenly at one with her. The maiden's fateful compassion here confirms her failure to discern the difference between mutuality and doubleness. Secondly, the young man's perfidy lies in his ability to foist his feelings into correspondence with others—or, to put it differently, to adopt a convincingly compassionate pose:

---

[21] Shepherd (1973) 116; Whigham and Rebhorn (2001) 136.
[22] Marshall (1988) 3.

In him a plenitude of subtle matter,
Applied to cautels, all strange forms receives,
Of burning blushes or of weeping water,
Or swooning paleness; and he takes and leaves,
In either's aptness, as it best deceives,
To blush at speeches rank, to weep at woes,
Or to turn white and swoon at tragic shows.

(302–8)

The seducer deceives people by adopting sympathy at will: 'he takes and leaves' different emotions, and grafts them onto events he witnesses according to their relative 'aptness'. This is a treacherous form of fellow-feeling, and his readiness 'to blush at speeches rank, to weep at woes' raises the quandary that sympathy, artfully assumed, may be that which 'best deceives'. For different reasons and with different consequences, the maiden and her seducer are both too compassionate. Compassion is perhaps the 'complaint' that they share, and for this reason, among others, the 'lover' in the poem's title aptly describes both the maiden and the young man.

'A Lover's Complaint' is an intensely dramatic poem full of theatrical references (including those quoted above) which reveal its author's immersion in stagecraft. Shakespeare was fascinated by theatre's ability to move or transport people into others' emotional worlds, the acts of sympathy performed publicly by actors giving rise in turn to sympathetic fellow-feeling among the audience members who see and hear them. 'A Lover's Complaint' explores the more intimate sympathies involved in privately turning our 'spirits t'attend' (3) the grief of others. We can only access others' sorrows by witnessing or imagining them, and 'A Lover's Complaint' vividly dramatizes this dynamic through the reverend man who listens—or struggles to listen—to the maiden. But he disappears from the poem after stanza 10 and the degree of sympathy he feels with the maiden is left unspoken. The narrator, too, expresses no sympathy in the opening fifty-six lines, and he does not return at the end of the poem to offer any words of consolation. The act of listening to this lament seems to involve no lessening of grief. Instead the narrative frame remains unclosed, and the maiden finishes the poem as aggrieved, sorrowful, and comfortless as she began.

This has important implications for readers since Shakespeare here undercuts the compassion described by Puttenham and Sidney as central to lament. 'A Lover's Complaint' questions the assumption that lament courts sympathy by presenting a demonstrably just grievance and by putting commensurate forms of sorrow into good order. The effect is disorienting, for Shakespeare here confounds our expectations of what lament should be and do. But 'A Lover's Complaint' emerges as an innovative experiment within the genre of early modern complaint poetry and, indeed, within the broader context of Renaissance lyric. For if the poem fails to live up to Puttenham and Sidney's description of lament, it succeeds spectacularly in other ways—not least its exploration of the moral, emotional, and aesthetic complexities involved in feeling sympathy for others.

29.3

The difficulties of sympathy raised by 'A Lover's Complaint' are, as we will see, closely bound up with Shakespeare's equivocation about the maiden's social standing. In many respects she resembles the eloquently woeful noblewomen of Ovidian lament. Her accoutrements look urban and courtly: her napkin is decorated with 'silken figures' (17) and she carries 'many a ring of posied gold and bone' (45). She has attended tournaments and knows the women who have been wealthy enough to bestow lavish gifts upon the young man.[23] Her assertion of emotional independence before her seduction again suggests her financial solvency, for she 'did in freedom stand, | And was my own fee-simple, not in part' (143–4). A 'fee-simple' is the absolute right to own a piece of land, and the maiden held this right herself rather than 'in part', or part-ownership.[24] Despite these confident assertions of independence, whether emotional or financial, the maiden's position in society remains as indeterminate at the end of the poem as it did at the beginning. There is no concluding revelation of her noble birth, such as might be found in one of Shakespeare's romances. At certain moments, indeed, she appears her seducer's clear inferior: she declares that she allowed herself to be seduced for socially ambitious reasons, for example, in order 'to gain my grace' (79). And when the narrator notices 'Upon her head a plaited hive of straw' (8), she resembles a rustic girl seduced by an urban, courtly suitor in accordance with the conventions of *pastourelle* which compares the virtues of the countryside to the city's decadence and moral bankruptcy.[25] These contradictory hints about the maiden's social standing are compounded when she gives voice to her grief in 'clamours of all size, both high and low' (21), for 'size' refers here not only to volume and pitch, but also to social status.[26] But how can the maiden—or, indeed, her woe—be both socially high and low? What sizes of lament were available to Shakespeare and his contemporaries, and how might these have accommodated different versions of sorrow? Reading the sorrowful maiden in 'A Lover's Complaint' alongside the grief-stricken women of Shakespearean drama, especially Ophelia in *Hamlet* and the Jailer's Daughter in *The Two Noble Kinsmen*, reveals how social class determined experiences of grief in early modern England—as well as the degree of sympathy such sorrows were thought to deserve.

Philosophers and physicians acknowledged that all men and women, regardless of their background, were vulnerable to the overwhelming sadness caused by disappointment in love. At the heart of their discussions lies the theory of the passions, drawn from Aristotle,

[23] For a survey of the maiden's social position, see Ilona Bell, 'Shakespeare's Exculpatory Complaint' in Shirley Sharon-Zisser (ed.), *Critical Essays on Shakespeare's 'A Lover's Complaint'* (Aldershot: Ashgate, 2006) 91–107 (93).
[24] Here I am indebted to Colin Burrow's gloss of these lines in his edition of *A Lover's Complaint* in *Complete Sonnets and Poems* (Oxford: Oxford University Press, 2002) 704.
[25] On *pastourelle*, see Kerrigan (1993) 396–7; and (1991) 14. The maiden's 'sheaved hat' is mentioned again at line 31.
[26] See Burrow (2002) 696.

Augustine, and Aquinas, which argued that extreme emotions, or perturbations, should be moderated using reason and the will. Love was regarded as one of the most complex emotions whose physical and mental symptoms could be either humiliating or ennobling.[27] The Hippocratic and Galenic theory of the humours described lovesickness as an imbalance with hot and cold symptoms which together gave rise to the 'freezing fire' imagery of Petrarchan love poetry. Sufferers were first consumed by burning desire characterized by the hot, moist humours of sanguinity, and secondly experienced the fear and sorrow characteristic of cold, dry melancholy. For maidens suffering from the related complaints of green sickness, hysteria, and uterine fury, the cures included coitus and blood-letting through which harmful humours were purged.[28] Medical accounts of the illnesses suffered by abandoned women suggest that such afflictions were common, and confirm that gynaecological problems were regarded as inseparable from emotional vulnerability.[29]

Everyone was vulnerable, then, to the perturbations caused by (in Puttenham's words) 'the travails and torments of love forlorn or ill-bestowed', and women's supposed passivity rendered them more susceptible than men to attendant physical infirmities.[30] But whereas highly literate women, like educated men, suffered from love melancholy and the related condition of erotomania, both of which were associated with creativity and the intellect, commoners were described as suffering from a dull, fruitless form of sadness known as 'mopishness' more akin to stupefaction or bewilderment than exaltation.[31] Although medical treatises, conduct books, and manuals of self-government take care to caution gentlewomen against the dangerous effects of love melancholy, they are generally reticent about their mopish inferiors. In a discussion of the afflictions caused by extreme passions, for instance, Nicholas Coeffeteau comments that 'Some the rich and mighty are subiect vnto, and others transport the poore and miserable' but fails in what follows to elaborate on the emotional lives of the lower estates, concentrating instead only on noblewomen.[32] Robert Burton's description in *The Anatomy of Melancholy* of maidenly lovesickness suggests that poor women simply feel less sorrow:

> seldom shall you see an hired servant, a poor handmaid, though ancient, that is kept hard to her work and bodily labour, a coarse country wench, troubled in this kind, but

---

[27] On the various interpretations of lovesickness in the period, see Lesal Dawson, *Lovesickness and Gender in Early Modern English Literature* (Oxford: Oxford University Press, 2008) 2.

[28] Dawson (2008) 20.

[29] See for example Edward Jorden, *A Briefe Discourse of a Disease Called the Suffocation of the Mother* (1603) sig. B4v.

[30] Whigham and Rebhorn (2001) 136.

[31] For a discussion of mopishness, see Michael MacDonald, *Mystical Bedlam: Madness, Anxiety, and Healing in Seventeenth-century England* (Cambridge: Cambridge University Press, 1981) 160–4. Lesal Dawson has argued that women (as well as men) experienced intellectual melancholy. See Dawson (2008) 96. The stock comic prototype of the lovesick 'coarse country wench' is familiar from Shakespearean comedy and Renaissance pastoral more generally. In Sir Philip Sidney's *Arcadia*, for example, the very name of the rustic shepherdess Mopsa suggests her dull mopishness.

[32] Coeffeteau, 'Of the diuerse Passions of men, according to their ages and conditions' in *A Table of Humane Passions. With their Causes and Effects* (1621) 654.

noble virgins, nice gentlewomen, such as are solitary and idle, live at ease, lead a life out of action and employment, that fare well, in great houses and jovial companies, ill-disposed peradventure of themselves, and not willing to make any resistance, discontented otherwise, of weak judgment, able bodies, and subject to passions [. . .] such for the most part are misaffected, and prone to this disease.[33]

Burton makes the pragmatic point that only those with leisure time have the opportunity to cultivate a fully nuanced emotional life, leaving working women subject to neither the infirmities nor the sublimities of lovesickness. Burton's account is striking now for its lack of compassion towards labouring women. The assumption that they were seldom subject to passions was indeed surely a useful means of keeping them immersed in 'work and bodily labour'. But the link Burton makes between gentility and melancholy—or between social 'coarseness' and poverty of feeling—remains tantalizingly underdeveloped.

Conduct books addressed to gentlewomen at this time emphasized the importance of cultivating emotional equilibrium through the avoidance of passionate excess. In *The English Gentlewoman* (1631), for example, Richard Braithwait extolled the virtues of chastity, cheerfulness, and constancy, arguing that noblewomen must exercise scrupulous restraint in order to avoid becoming 'enthralled to affection'. The experience of love presents particularly formidable challenges to emotional equanimity, and Braithwait insists that reason should hold sway at all times:

The Louer is euer blinded (saith wise *Plato*) with *affection* towards his beloued [. . .]. My Tenet is, *One cannot truely loue, and not be wise.* It is a Bedlam frenzy and no fancy, which giues way to fury, and admits not reason to haue soueraignty.

To love wisely involves neither frenzy, fancy, nor fury. A noblewoman's discretion and integrity are upheld only through her scrupulous policing of emotional disturbance, and her prompt replacement of inappropriately strong feelings with temperate judgement. Noble love assuredly does not involve lamenting or complaining, for true gentlewomen

scorne to paint out their passions in plaints, or vtter their thoughts in sighes, or shed one dispassionate teare for an incompassionate Louer [. . .]. Shee was neuer yet acquainted with a passionate *ah me*; nor a carelesse folding of her armes, as if the thought of a prevailing Lover had wrought in her thoughts some violent Distemper.

Each symptom of lovesickness ('a passionate *ah me*') betokens uncontrolled impulse and betrays moral weakness at odds with noble restraint. Inward chaos is the inevitable

---

[33] Burton, *The Anatomy of Melancholy*, Holbrook Jackson (ed.), (New York Review of Books: New York, 2001) 417.

and shameful consequence, Braithwait implies, of yielding to the emotional assaults of an 'incompassionate Louer'.[34]

The overwhelming grief expressed by Shakespeare's maiden ('Ay me!' 321) sits uneasily with Braithwait's remarks. Her noisy sorrow is indeed surely the most singular and memorable feature of 'A Lover's Complaint', as well as Shakespeare's most formidable challenge to our sympathies. Towards the start of the poem she is heard 'shrieking undistinguished woe' (20), and, later, in the profundity of her 'suffering ecstasy' (69), she describes the impossibility of assuaging her sadness with the tempering effects of reason:

> O appetite, from judgment stand aloof!
> The one a palate hath that needs will taste,
> Though Reason weep, and cry 'It is thy last'.
>
> (166–8)

The sensory appetite 'needs' to be indulged, and the governing forces of reason and judgement are accordingly overturned. It was indeed the maiden's unguarded emotions which made her seduction possible, for the young man's assault worked by 'Catching all passions in his craft of will' (126). The maiden goes on to describe how she abandoned all resistance, throwing instead her 'affections in his charmd power' (146). If Shakespeare's maiden is of noble stock, her frank abandonment of reason's sovereignty is irreconcilable with Braithwait's description of the constancy and resolve English noblewomen were expected to exercise in love.

The extremity of the maiden's grief, and her abandonment of reason, has more in common with contemporary ballad lament than with aristocratic complaint. The late 16th and early 17th centuries witnessed a dramatic increase in the number of laments written (by men) in the voices of ordinary women who suffered misfortune in love. Importantly for our purposes, this literature seldom appeals to readers' sympathies. Ballads were usually published in broadside, a cheap form of print comprising a single folded sheet of paper, and chronicled the lives of women from the lower social classes. Abandoned by suitors, some their social superiors, these women describe how they have been left pregnant, penniless, and 'comfortlesse alone'. Although spirited in their condemnation of the 'faithlesse false & forsworne wretch[es]' who have abandoned them, their own impetuousness and lack of judgement forms the substance of their laments.[35] In *The Distressed Virgin: or, The False Young Man* (1633), for example, a sorrowful maiden deplores her 'former follies'. She has acted hastily on her passion, and accepts her undoing: 'my life will soone be gone'.[36] Another ballad, *The Maiden's Complaint of her Loves Inconstancy* (1620), makes clear that the loss described deserves no compassionate sympathy:

> The Iewel's lost, the thiefe is fled,
> And I lie wounded in my bed:

---

[34] Braithwait, *The English Gentlewoman*, 32 and 4.
[35] *The Wofull Complaint of a Loue-sicke Mayde* (1630) stanza 1, line 8, and stanza 4, lines 1–2.
[36] *The Distressed Virgin: or, The False Young-man, and the Constant Maid* (1633), lines 5–8.

> If to repent I should begin,
> They'l say twas I that let him in.

To repent is useless, for everyone knows she is to blame for her loss of chastity. Her abandonment confirms her fault, and she swiftly declares herself ready to die: 'My dayes are short, my life not long'.[37] Ballad laments such as this are radically different in their scope and intent from aristocratic complaint where grief elevates the speaker and the virtues of candour and constancy are rewarded. Instead their intent is bluntly didactic towards the moral conscience of other 'Maides and wives and women kind'.[38]

The Jailer's daughter in *The Two Noble Kinsmen* has much in common with these women and with the maiden of 'A Lover's Complaint'. She suffers from mopishness rather than refined melancholia—'I am moped.—| Food took I none these two days' (III. ii. 25–6)—for she knows that her love for her social superior, Palamon, can never be requited. She has altogether abandoned the enobling faculty of reason, for her desire is overwhelming and irrational:

> I love him beyond love and beyond reason
> Or wit or safety. I have made him know it—
> I care not, I am desperate
>
> (II. vi. 11–13)

By the fourth act, she believes herself betrayed by Palamon, but her abandonment, like the affair itself, takes place only in her imagination. The snatches of filthy songs she sings suggest to her father and the Doctor that her senses are 'in a most extravagant vagary' (IV. iii. 70), but this vagary inspires scant pity among those who witness it. Urging those listening to 'by no means cross her' (IV. i. 118) for fear of worsening her condition, the Jailer's brother merely humours her delusions and praises her song as 'a very fine one' (IV. i. 105), shoring up her belief that she is soon to be Palamon's bride. The Doctor confirms 'It is a falsehood she is in, which is with falsehoods to be combated' (IV. iii. 90–1). His proposed cure is to make the Jailer's daughter believe, in her madness, that the wooer she takes to bed is actually Palamon. Her wildly unreasoned passion does not involve her listeners in companionate sympathy, but the comedy cannot conclude until a different remedy has been administered. As the Jailer reports in the final scene: 'she's well restored | And to be married shortly' (V. vi. 27–8).

There are also many similarities between 'A Lover's Complaint' and *Hamlet*, probably written several years previously and published for the first time in 1602.[39] Like the

---

[37] *The Maiden's Complaint of her Loves Inconstancy*, lines 37–40 and 73.
[38] *The Maiden's Complaint of her Loves Inconstancy*, line 1. See also *The Wofull Complaint of a Love-sicke mayde* (1630) which advises maidens to 'example take | By me that am in griefe' whilst *A Love-sick Maid's Song* concludes with a stark admonition: 'Ye maides be warnd by me'.
[39] For further discussion of the link with *Hamlet*, see John Roe, 'Unfinished Business: A Lover's Complaint and Hamlet, Romeo and Juliet and The Rape of Lucrece' in Sharon-Zisser (ed.), (2006) 109–20 (115–19).

favours of the young man in 'A Lover's Complaint', Hamlet's 'trifling … favour' is 'sweet, not lasting'. And like the seducer's false promises, Hamlet's vows turn out to be false 'brokers'.[40] Laertes admonishes his sister to guard her honour and chastity, the same prizes which the maiden in 'A Lover's Complaint' has yielded so disastrously. Most importantly for our purposes, the bawdy ballad which Ophelia sings in Act IV, about a maiden who yields to an importunate seducer, again does not receive a compassionate hearing:

> By Gis, and by Saint Charity,
>   Alack, and fie for shame!
> Young men will do't if they come to't,
>   By Cock, they are to blame.
> Quoth she 'Before you tumbled me,
>   You promised me to wed'.

He answers,

> 'So would I 'a' done, by yonder sun,
>   An thou hadst not come to my bed'.
>   (IV. v. 58–65)

As Gertrude remarks, Ophelia deserves sympathy: 'her mood will needs be pitied' (IV. v. 3). The poignancy of this scene resides, however, in the failure of Ophelia's listeners to react accordingly. As Horatio points out:

> Her speech is nothing,
> Yet the unshapd use of it doth move
> The hearers to collection. They aim at it
> And botch the words up fit to their own thoughts,
> Which, as her winks and nods and gestures yield them,
> Indeed would make one think there might be thought,
> Though nothing sure, yet much unhappily.
>   (IV. v. 4–13)

Ophelia's 'speech is nothing' because it is no longer her own. It is empty of significance, but its very emptiness, or 'unshapd use', breeds dangerous affect. Faced with the spectacle of Ophelia's suffering, her listeners feel themselves moved 'to collection'. But this process of collection, or identification, is not one of pity—for the listeners merely wrest Ophelia's words out of joint to make them 'fit to their own thoughts'. This is not the smooth, 'harmonical' process of listening which Puttenham described, nor does it resemble Sidney's 'compassionate accompanying' of sorrow. Instead the process is one of aiming and botching, an effortful interpretation which finds 'nothing sure'. Ophelia's winks, nods, and gestures 'would make one think there might be thought' a particular meaning, but this circumlocutory line (reminiscent of 'A Lover's Complaint') suggests

---

[40] *Hamlet*, I. iii. 5–8 and 127–9.

the impossibility of understanding Ophelia rightly. As Gertrude confirms, Ophelia's songs 'strew | Dangerous conjectures in ill-breeding minds' (IV. v. 14–5). Like the ballad laments explored above, especially *The Maiden's Complaint of her Loves Inconstancy*, Ophelia's own borrowed ballad serves (in the minds of her listeners) to display her unpitiable moral turpitude. A noblewoman turned coarse ballad-monger, Ophelia loses her claim to a compassionate hearing.

'A Lover's Complaint' is an extended exploration of the complex interplay between grief, class, and sympathetic fellow-feeling considered briefly in Act IV, Scene v of *Hamlet* and Act IV, Scene i of *The Two Noble Kinsmen*. Shakespeare's maiden is both 'high and low', as we have seen, and her sorrow is both sympathetic and estranging. Eloquent, articulate, and detached, she resembles in many ways the grieving aristocratic women of Ovidean lament whose exquisite sorrow affects the reader, in turn, with sorrowful compassion. Shakespeare's choice of metre, rhyme royal, serves to confirm her nobility of sentiment and gravity of purpose. At the same time, however, the maiden bluntly admits her failure to restrain passionate feeling with the tempering effects of reason, overturning the cultural expectation (articulated by writers such as Braithwait) that gentlewomen should exercise noble self-restraint; and refusing, finally, to offer unequivocal regret for her own part in her undoing. The poem's unclosed narrative frame, and the telling silence of the reverend man, further challenge the assumption, central to *de casibus* lament, that complaint arouses compassion among those who hear it. 'A Lover's Complaint' thus addresses some important cultural debates which were emerging at this time. How did social class affect the ways in which men and women arranged their inner lives, and disposed themselves in front of others? Was an aristocratic emotional landscape different from a 'common' one? In what ways were sympathetic responses calibrated according to the justice of a complainant's cause; or, to borrow Burton's terms, according to her social 'niceness' or 'coarseness'? Shakespeare used the complaint tradition (usually associated with the fall of princes) to deliberate how women of different social status might have experienced sorrow, and to explore their varying claims to compassion. A sophisticated and self-conscious exploration of affect and sympathy, 'A Lover's Complaint' nevertheless does justice, particularly in its final stanza, to the sublimity of grief and the incorrigibility of passion.

SELECT BIBLIOGRAPHY

Bates, Catherine (2010) 'The enigma of *A Lover's Complaint*' in Michael Schoenfeldt, ed., *A Companion to Shakespeare's Poems* (London: Blackwell) 405–25.

Bell, Ilona (2002) '"That which thou hast done": Shakespeare's *Sonnets* and *A Lover's Complaint*' in James Schiffer (ed.), *Shakespeare's Sonnets: Critical Essays* (New York: Garland) 455–74.

Craik, Katharine A. (2002) 'Shakespeare's A Lover's Complaint and Early Modern Criminal Confession', *Shakespeare Quarterly* 53, 4: 437–59.

Duncan-Jones, Katherine (1983) 'Was the 1609 Shake-speares Sonnets Really Unauthorized?', *Review of English Studies* n.s. 34: 151–71.

Elliott, Ward, E. Y. and Robert J. Valenza (1997) 'Glass Slippers and Seven-League Boots: C-Prompted Doubts About Ascribing *A Funeral Elegy* and *A Lover's Complaint* to Shakespeare,' *Shakespeare Quarterly*, 48: 177–207.

Healy, Margaret (2011) *Shakespeare, Alchemy and the Creative Imagination: The Sonnets and A Lover's Complaint* (Cambridge: Cambridge University Press).

Jackson, MacDonald P. (2004) '*A Lover's Complaint* Revisited', *Shakespeare Studies*, 32: 267–94.

Kerrigan, John (1991) *Motives of Woe: Shakespeare and 'Female Complaint': A Critical Anthology* (Oxford: Clarendon Press).

Muir, Kenneth (1964) '*A Lover's Complaint*: A Reconsideration', in Edward A. Bloom, ed., *Shakespeare 1564–1964* (Providence: Brown University Press), 154–66.

Sharon-Zisser, Shirley (2006) (ed.) *Essays on Shakespeare's 'A Lover's Complaint'* (Aldershot: Ashgate).

Underwood, Richard Allan (1985), *Shakespeare on Love: The Poems and the Plays. Prolegomena to a Variorum Edition of A Lover's Complaint* (Salzburg: Institut für Anglistik und Amerikanistik).

Vickers, Brian (2007), *Shakespeare, 'A Lover's Complaint' and John Davies of Hereford* (Cambridge: Cambridge University Press).

CHAPTER 30

....

READING 'THE PHOENIX AND TURTLE'

....

JOHN KERRIGAN

We have seen in Chapter 13 that the poem known since 1807 as 'The Phoenix and the Turtle'—or, with more appropriate, intense mutuality, 'The Phoenix and Turtle'—has behind it a substantial body of panegyrical and doleful verse, including a tradition of mock bird-funerals that goes back through Skelton to Ovid. But the poem also has immediate origins in the songs, charms, and dirges embedded in Shakespeare's plays. As early readers began to scan it, they would have detected a metrical signature. 'Let the bird of loudest lay' (1.1). Those catalectic trochaic tetrameters—strong–weak accents in four feet, minus a final syllable—are unusual in Elizabethan poetry. There may be a debt to Sidney's Eighth Song. But the metre is frequently used in Shakespeare's plays for incantation and epitaph:[1] the charms uttered by Puck, for example, in *A Midsummer Night's Dream*, or Hero's epitaph in *Much Ado*, 'Done to death by slanderous tongues' (V. iii. 3–10). That Hero is not really dead, but stages a reappearance, prompts the further thought that epitaphs in the plays are often false or riddling. 'The Phoenix and Turtle' similarly belies expectations because it laments the death of a bird that is famously supposed to regenerate from its ashes. This outcome is not unique. In Matthew Roydon's elegy on Sidney, for instance, in *The Phoenix Nest* (1593), which is a probable source for 'The Phoenix and Turtle', the poet finds it hard to believe that the Sidneyan phoenix will be replaced. But Shakespeare's conclusion is at odds with the revival of the phoenix both in Robert Chester's *Loves Martyr* (1601) and in the appendix of 'Poeticall Essaies' by Jonson, Marston, and others, in which 'The Phoenix and Turtle' first appeared. This chapter will ask, among other things, how terminal is the epitaph-like *'Threnos'* which ends the poem.

---

[1] Cf. Richard Allan Underwood, *Shakespeare's 'Phoenix and Turtle': A Survey of Scholarship* (Salzburg: University of Salzburg, 1974) 291–5.

The poem is not all threnody. In the little-discussed time-construction of this text, the 'Threnos' is set further into the past than the procession of birds which begins it, and which leads into the 'anthem' reporting the reaction of Reason to the birds' love when they were alive. Each section has a distinct verbal and syntactical manner. This is one reason why generalizations about the poem, which tend to be high-flown ('so elusive, so like music pitched just beyond the reach of hearing'),[2] can be unhelpful. It is a varied rhetorical performance. Overall, though, and especially in the opening stanzas, there is a fascination with ritual. To read it is to follow a funeral procession from the Phoenix' tree in Arabia to where a requiem is celebrated, then to be drawn from introit and anthem back to an account of the birds' love-death and the epigraphy of burial. This is the pattern of an early modern funeral: the coffin is led in procession from the dead person's home, to church, for a service, to the graveside, for more prayers, over a grave which will acquire an epitaph.

It would be narrow, however, to take 'The Phoenix and Turtle' as offering one variant or another on a set of funeral rites (more or less Catholic, more or less heraldic); it draws strength and complication from a general crisis in the status of ritual after the Reformation. The very existence of the poem owes something to the *invention* of ritual, not as an array of practices (those go back beyond the beginnings of the human) but as a category. 'It was during the Reformation that the generalized concept of *ritual* as a distinct kind of activity came into being'.[3] Was this an activity essential to Christian life, a contemptible sort of religious theatre, more superstitious than Godly, or one of the *adiaphora*, a practice that could be tolerated? For ordinary people, changes in ritual, and the counter-rituals of iconoclasm, brought reform into their lives in a way abstruse theology could not. The poem in this sense goes deep into the tissue of early modern experience. As a bird-funeral it inherits elements of comedy which are sometimes heightened by wordplay and a degree of reticent humour about the unlikely properties attributed to birds. But it is, for all that, a serious, sympathetic poem, at points an incantation that draws us into the consolations of ritual—a process that is the more perspicuous because detached here from human agency.

How anthropological an artefact is it? Shakespeare seems to have read Durkheim, not just in the sense that the order of ritual in the poem substantiates a larger social order, but because it starts from the primary act of separating the pure from the profane. The bird of loudest lay is admitted, the shrieking owl (almost as noisy) is excluded; the kingly eagle is in, birds of tyrant wing (also commanding) are out; the swan is allowed entry, and so on. 'All known religious beliefs', Durkheim wrote, 'whether simple or complex, present one common characteristic: they presuppose a classification of all things, real and ideal, of which men think, into two classes or opposed groups … *profane* and *sacred*'.[4] But the poet is also aware that, as some of Durkheim's successors (such as Max Gluckman) brought out, ritual participation is heterogeneous. It draws together those, such as

  [2] *The Complete Sonnets and Poems*, Colin Burrow (ed.), (Oxford: Oxford University Press, 2002) 90.
  [3] Edward Muir, *Ritual in Early Modern Europe* (Cambridge: Cambridge University Press, 1997) 7.
  [4] *The Elementary Forms of the Religious Life*, Joseph Ward Swain (trans.), (London: George Allen and Unwin, 1915) 37.

the swan and the eagle, who, in most circumstances, would be enemies. This is mostly about content. What of process and effect? Chester tries to persuade us narratively that he knows the truth about love; in the words of its title-page, *Loves Martyr 'Allegorically shadow[s] the truth of Loue*', in the constant Fate of the Phoenix and Turtle'. Shakespeare, by contrast, involves us in the structures and rhythms of a rite. We might think of later anthropologists: Radcliffe-Brown, who developed the Durkheimian perception that belief is not a cause but an effect of ritual, and Marc Bloch, who looks at how formal, archaic phrasing and the resources of repetition (both prominent in Shakespeare's opening stanzas) frame and characterize utterances and actions as ritualistic.

So the first phase of the poem analytically creates an *order*. The inclusions and exclusions of the birds require a classification, one which is cultural although posited on nature. Shakespeare, as so often, is interested in the possibility of a natural order but problematizes it by showing us its construction. When the Old Man says, in *Macbeth*, 'On Tuesday last, | A falcon, tow'ring in her pride of place, | Was by a mousing owl hawked at and killed' (II. iv. 11–13), we may want to believe that the murder of King Duncan by a thane creates or reflects disorder in the world of birds, but we are likely to conclude that an affront to social hierarchy is being projected, with hindsight and specious matter-of-factness ('On Tuesday last'), onto an unusual incident, which may not have occurred as described. The positing of an order is the more teasingly problematic in the poem because based on unlikely lore. We are told that the swan sings before its death and that crows breed by exchange of breath. Both species could be observed in the fields around Stratford-upon-Avon, and indeed around the Globe Theatre. Neither claim will have been taken as evidently true by early readers; they would, rather, have enjoyed the poet's playing of variations on a traditional catalogue of avian marvels. Yet all birds are actually possessed of extraordinary qualities. They fly, they lay eggs, they sing. Compared with what birds really do, what phoenixes are said to do is not much more. So there is an overlap between what Shakespeare was willing to take up and work with as legendary natural history (like 'The Anthropophagi, and men whose heads | Do grow beneath their shoulders', in *Othello* (I. iii. 143–4)) and a proto-scientific interest in animals.

You could go further and divine from the opening stanzas of 'The Phoenix and Turtle' a variety of proto-ethnology. By writing about birds, Shakespeare used creatures that could stand in for people not just allegorically but because they were known to have their own inclination to order—trooping, flocking, and conducting death rites. On funeral customs, here is Sir Thomas Browne: '*Civilians* make sepulture but of the Law of Nations, others doe naturally found it and discover it also in animals. They that are so thick skinned as still to credit the story of the *Phoenix*, may say something for animall burning: More serious conjectures finde some examples of sepulture in Elephants, Cranes, the Sepulchrall Cells of Pismires and practice of Bees; which civill society carrieth out their dead, and hath exequies, if not interrments'.[5] That said, Shakespeare's birds patently have symbolic

---

[5] *Hydriotaphia, Urne-Buriall* (1658) 13. '*Civilians*' are students and practioners of Roman law and the codes derived from it; 'Law of Nations' refers to man-made law. 'Others', Browne says, find the basis of sepulchral rites in the natural conduct of animals. 'Pismires' are ants.

associations; they are totemic, or, in early modern terms, heraldic. Recall the shaking falcon with the lance that is on the tomb of Shakespeare. Birds figured on the scutcheons carried at those funerals that were overseen by the herald's office, those funerals at which heralds (representing royal authority) were present as observing participants, while mourning feathers plumed the heads of horses in the cortege. To an imaginative onlooker, a noble funeral procession could have looked like a troop of birds.

So to begin, or begin again. But from where? Shakespeare's poem is unique among the 'Poeticall Essaies' in having no title. Since some of the titles seem to show the hand of Chester, the lack of one here looks the more deliberate. The poem starts from nowhere, then does not begin until it has already started. Until we are several stanzas in, we do not know what this avian procession is for, what we are heading towards:

> Let the bird of loudest lay
> On the sole Arabian tree
> Herald sad and trumpet be,
> To whose sound chaste wings obey.

$$(11.1-4)$$

Who is speaking? In noble funerals, the herald would advise on who walked where, what mourning would be worn, and so forth. But the poet's voice or something like it dictates even the identity of the herald, who is included in the division of sacred and profane. As we have seen, this is an unusual prosody, but the almost unique combination of trochaic tetrameters with the enclosed rhyme scheme makes the order of the poem even stranger. A haunting music, that contracts then expands, each stanza is audibly contained but open to the next, until the triplets of the 'Threnos' change the dynamics again. The effects created are various, but at this point commanding. The hanging rhyme, clinched at 'obey', requires the obedience it describes. Some think 'obey' an imperative, which is doubtful, but symptomatic. What should the reader make of the imperative that we do have? 'Let ... ' sounds like an absolute, almost Euclidean proposition. 'Let the line DC be equall to the line AB and draw the line BD'.[6] It is, however, a peculiar injunction, because although it sounds concessive, as though admitting a bird that wants to be included, it already contains something of the strictness of 'Let' as hindrance. The permission is not automatic. Exclusions are incipient.

Alliterative and metrical stress falls firmly on 'loudest' which is also the longest word in a line of monosyllables. Colin Burrow has a point when he notes in his Oxford edition, 'This is presumably "any bird, so long as it has a loud voice"'.[7] It is not the bird which matters so much as its property. But -est signifies in a poem that starts with a series of extremes: loudest, sole, Arabian (out there in the East, at the limits of the

---

[6] *The Elements of Geometrie of the Most Auncient Philosopher Euclide of Megara*, tr. H. Billingsley (1570) 27.

[7] Burrow (2002) 'Let the bird of loudest lay', line 1, n.

Christian/classical worlds). Nor is it necessarily a pedant's question, what *was* the loudest bird? The next stanza identifies the screech owl merely as a 'shrieking harbinger' (1.5). Yet it is not wrong to think of this as an owl. There is an elliptical potency in the naming that stems from the poem's knowing relationship with bird-funerals and parliaments. Compare 'The Crane with his trumpe' in Skelton, and Chaucer's 'Crane, the Geaunt, with his trompes soune'.[8] For Elizabethan readers who knew their poetry, this was bird of loudest lay.

'Loudest' is not the longest word in the stanza. That prize goes to *Arabian*, in 'On the sole Arabian tree'. With another touch of compression, its three syllables are elided into two. Unlike Chester (Chapter 13, p. 236 below), Shakespeare does not move the story of the Phoenix and Turtle from Arabia to Paphos. This has consequences we shall pursue. But the key locational word is 'sole'. Early readers would have found this a complex adjective. The *OED* definition starts from 'Having no husband or wife; single, unmarried; celibate … freq. of women'. This transfers to the tree qualities of the Phoenix before it met the Turtle; the Phoenix in its absolute condition. 'Sole' can also mean 'without companions, solitary, and lonely or secluded (of places), singular, unique and unrivalled'. All these ideas contribute metonymically to the thought that 'the bird of loudest lay' is the revived Phoenix, arranging the funeral of its dead predecessor. Several able scholars have argued this. But the likelihood is overruled by 'Herald sad and trumpet be'. Heralds at funerals were functionaries, not unique, majestic birds. And this one combines the role of heraldic organizer with ordinary trumpeter. Heralds, as bringers of messages, could come with trumpeters, as in Shakespeare's plays, but not act as trumpets. Trumpeters could herald, that is, announce a personage or a message, without being heralds.

Has Shakespeare become confused? More likely, given his dealings with heralds, when he secured his coat of arms, and (we may assume) went to noble funerals, he is not: this is another ellipsis. Why, then, the association between the 'grave', even 'truth-telling' (now-obsolete meanings of 'sad') bird and the Phoenix' perch? Compare the final line of the stanza: 'To whose sound chaste wings obey'. Is this the flutter of an approaching Turtle? The poem starts with an unnamed bird uniting two roles as it will end with two unnamed 'dead birds' joined in one. There is an imminence of Phoenix-like and Turtle-like qualities that continues as the procession is created for and by the reader. The birds in the opening stanzas are mostly one-offs, extreme or unique. Thus 'loudest', in relation to 'sole', then 'the' (definite article) 'eagle, feathered king'. Next we hear of the swan, with its solitary song—singular and Phoenix-like, white with purity, having mated, it was believed, for life. This procession is not just brought together by the Phoenix' and Turtle's rite but is shaped by the dead birds' qualities.

---

[8] John Skelton, *A Little Boke of Phillip Sparow* (1558), B3v, Chaucer, *The Assemblie of Foules* (*The Parlement of Foules*), *The Workes of Geffrey Chaucer* (1598) fols 244v-8r, 246r.

'Let … ', then, is conditional. The classification of the birds springs from the imposition of order that is so important in heraldic funerals, with their strict conventions, that affirmed privileges, 'the social nuances of placement' and the blight of rejection:[9]

> But thou shrieking harbinger,
> Foul precurrer of the fiend,
> Augur of the fever's end—
> To this troupe come thou not near.
>
> (11.5–8)

'Herald' is followed by 'harbinger', 'precurrer', and 'Augur'. Soon we shall be told about the 'death-divining swan'. The association of birds with divination is ancient (and it recurs in *Loves Martyr*),[10] but the closeness of 'sad' and 'augurs' might remind us, looking beyond Chester's book, of the 'sad augurs' who 'mock their own presage', in Sonnet 107, after the succession of 1603 proved peaceful. These are the first stirrings in 'The Phoenix and Turtle' of an issue that would have emerged tacitly but strongly for early readers, expecting, but not finding, a ritual acknowledgement of the element of succession which is still so important in many funerals (children of the deceased in the front row), and which is written into the processional form of the poem, with a train of birds leading to the glorious Phoenix and Turtle but not beyond.

This is not to say that early readers would have flatly identified Elizabeth I with the Phoenix and the dedicatee of *Loves Martyr*, Sir John Salusbury, with the Turtle. Traces of Chester's topical allegory (which is discussed on pp. 235–40) can be felt later in Shakespeare's poem, but it both more evidently and profoundly reads as 'Allegorically shadowing the truth of Loue'. The point is rather that, during the last years of the Queen's reign, anticipations of a phoenix' funeral would have been extensively and deeply inextricable from anxieties about continuity. There was much prophetic writing about the succession itself, some of it fearful. In the poem, the auguries are sifted and made safe by the power of the ordering voice to exclude the troublesome. Meanwhile, the build-up of anticipation reinforces the sense that the poem has not yet properly started. All is heralded. Yet there is a process afoot. The word 'troupe', in 1601 a variant of 'troop', although it now helpfully brings out the association between these birds and actors, perfectly catches how close order is to disorder.[11] A troop can be a disciplined rank and file, but

[9] Jennifer Woodward, *The Theatre of Death: The Ritual Management of Royal Funerals in Renaissance England, 1570–1625* (Woodbridge: Boydell, 1997) ch. 1, David Cressy, *Birth, Marriage, and Death: Ritual, Religion, and the Life-Cycle in Tudor and Stuart England* (Oxford: Oxford University Press, 1997) chs 17–20, quoting 437.
[10] e.g. 'The filthy messenger of ill to come | The sluggish *Owle* is', 'The vnsatiate *Sparrow* doth prognosticate, | And is held good for diuination', 'The sweet recording Swanne … Prognosticates to Sailers'; Robert Chester, *Loves Martyr* (1601) 116–23.
[11] Actors dressed as birds are not uncommon in masques and *commedia dell'arte*, and may have sung the songs of the Owl and the Cuckoo at the end of *Love's Labour's Lost*; players could also expect to troop in funeral and other processions associated with their patrons (see the opening lines of Sonnet 125).

also the makings of a rout, like the 'troopes of armed persones flocking vp & downe the streetes' in Wrexham, during the unrest around the contested election of Salusbury to the 1601 parliament (p. 225). As the poem evolves, the birds will play their parts and fall into line.

That requires more creatures to be excluded, most immediately, in stanza 3, 'Every fowl of tyrant wing'. The eagle is allowed entry, but we have now had two stanzas of exclusion versus one of inclusion. It might be called an exclusive event. Letting in and keeping out sets up a binary polarity which the Phoenix and Turtle will overcome because they are different species and of unequal status but combine. For now, the preponderance of exclusion enhances the effect of purification, of purging the profane. How unusual is all this? In Ovid, all birds mourn Corinna's parrot and can be trumpeters loud and sad: 'al-fowles her exequies frequent ... for long shrild trumpets let your notes resound'.[12] Skelton is catholic, in every sense, when he summons a huge list of birds to attend the funeral rites for Philip Sparrow:

> Lauda anima mea Dominum.
> To weep with me loke that ye come
> All maner of byrds in your kynd
> See none be left behind

Here are the goldfinch, the wagtail, the jay, and the magpie. Even 'the Owle that [is] so foule | Must helpe vs to houle'.[13] It is true that in Roydon's elegy for Sidney, the birds are arranged by degree. But there is no process of exclusion. Shakespeare's poem is exceptional in its self-conscious selectivity, in bird choice as well as word choice.

We start with heralds and harbingers, anticipators of the main event. The procession or requiem proper only starts now, four stanzas into the poem. So we have 'Let' again:

> Let the priest in surplice white,
> That defunctive music can,
> Be the death-divining swan,
> Lest the requiem lack his right.
>
> And thou treble-dated crow,
> That thy sable gender mak'st
> With the breath thou giv'st and tak'st,
> 'Mongst our mourners shalt thou go.
>
> (11.13–20)

After all the exclusions, there is an allocation of roles: white-surpliced minister and black-coated parish clerk, walking among the mourners (another pair of opposites which couple). 'Let ... But' gives way to 'Let ... And'. Why 'And', when the reader

---

[12] *Amores* II.6, in *Ouid's Elegies*, Christopher Marlowe (trans.), (1603).
[13] *Phillip Sparow*, B2r-3v.

expects 'But', especially given that the crow is so often classed as 'vncleane' in the early modern period? [14]

With its chaste reproductive habits, breeding by an exchange of breath, doubly giving and taking (like the antiphonal mode of requiem prayer), this crow is a 'natural' for inclusion. Because it is usually judged 'vncleane', the principles of classification are felt the more firmly to stem from resemblance to the Phoenix and Turtle. Yet the crow has no mate in the poem. Depictions of Elizabethan funerals often show the mourners walking two by two. Perhaps the crow and the swan are to be visualized as a pair. But birds will only pair in love when the Phoenix and Turtle are named, and the rite takes on a purpose. The crow is also a 'natural' for inclusion because black, a quintessential mourner. The greatest expense in many heraldic funerals was buying black mourning costumes. However appropriate the crow's presence, though, the poem still keeps the reader aware that decisions about classification are actively being made: "Mongst our mourners shalt thou go". This is the only use of 'our' in the poem. It does not sound participatory. The tone is even peremptory. Mourners in the period were easily brought in or bought (family retainers, the local poor). But the reader will still register the significance of the plural. We have reached the end of the processional section because we have arrived at *our*, the Durkheimian group.

'Here' is how the poem moves on: 'Here the anthem doth commence' (1.21). This sounds like a cue in a prayerbook, less a line in the poem than a gloss on what is said. As Burrow notes, the service for the burial of the dead (in at least one modern version of the Book of Common Prayer) begins: 'All stand while one or more of the following anthems are sung or said'. The effect, within the poem, is subtly to enhance our sense of how the ritual is being shaped. For if 'Here' is a place in the text, it is also a threshold or portal which the mourners have processed to, much as later 'Here' will be the place where the Phoenix and Turtle lie in their urn. This is what the locational becomes. What 'Here' is not, despite orientalist atmospherics, which will be heightened in the 'Threnos', is a place with the physical features of Arabia (whether actual or allegorical, as it represents the aridity of the court in *Loves Martyr*). The key shifts in the poem are provided by address, tone, and structure, not scenery. The transition marked by 'Here' is into another kind of music, not just sung, in prestigious funerals, but, characteristically, double. As the *OED* reminds us, anthems are 'sung antiphonally, or by two voices or choirs, responsively'. 'Let … But' and 'Let … And' now evolve into pairs of stanzas that are introduced 'Here … So' and 'Hearts …. So'.

The anthems in the service for the burial of the dead are about the resurrection of the body, and the promise of eternal life. The poem is less evidently Christian, as it moves towards Neoplatonic paradoxes:

> Love and constancy is dead,
> Phoenix and the turtle fled
> In a mutual flame from hence.
>
> (11.22–4)

---

[14] E.g. Raphael Holinshed, *The First and Second Volumes of Chronicles* (1587) 223.

By now the reader will be alert to the poem's doublings and fusions. 'Is dead' joins the qualities of the Phoenix and Turtle, but the next line separates them. A 'Phoenix' is by definition unique, and 'the turtle' uses the definite article to designate just that one. Now that turtle doves are so rare in England, we can miss the force of 'the', the need to identify a particular bird. Shakespeare inherits from Chester a myth in which the one-off Phoenix pairs with a lovely but everyday dove, an emblem of erotic devotion (sacred to Venus) that can be found in every hedge, pecking at fumitory. That the birds are of different species is just one of several contrasts between them, hooped into their union. The play of separateness and fusion is complex. 'Mutual', for instance, suggests total inclusivity, all-ness ('mutuall' is the 1601 spelling), only to shut that down into the self-burning of the dyad. Mutu-, meanwhile, in the Latinate intricacy of the poem, implies mutation (*mutare*) and motion (*mot-* from *movere*), a fleeing *hence*. 'From hence' is said by the *OED* to be the same as 'hence' ('with redundant from'). Since 'hence' can also mean 'in the next world', however, the idea that 'hence' is here is harder to be sure of. Where were, never mind are, these birds?

Dislocation enhances their purity, as does their flaming flight. Under early modern conditions the messiness of death could not be concealed: rot, smell, disfigurement. There was, as Browne painfully observes, a *shame* associated with death, 'that in a moment can so disfigure us that our nearest friends, Wife, & children stand afraid and stare at us'.[15] Cremation avoids that; it gives human control to disembodiment. The muck and mire and bones that the gravediggers churn through when they dig out a place for the corpse of Ophelia in sanctified ground are kept away from this poem. But cremation is a classical practice, not a Christian one. Early readers knew about it from Latin elegy, and from Stow and Camden, who describe the Roman funerary urns dug up in London.[16] The ritual of the poem refuses to be decoded in contemporary terms. Withdrawing even more decisively from the carnal squalor of the Elizabethan graveyard, it does not, strictly speaking, describe deaths leading to cremation but lovers consumed by their passion, prior to but entailing death. For Shakespeare, love's martyrs are not burned by their persecutors. They do not roast and sizzle before us, like Marian martyrs in front of a crowd. Already 'fled', they pass from epithalamion to epitaph without the intervening unpleasantness of mortality. This is more refined than the outcome of *Loves Martyr*, not just in the avoidance of a death-scene but in the fact that mutual combustion comes from flaming in each others sight rather than gathering firewood and depending on the sun to set the pyre alight.

The fantasy of love-death without the sin of suicide is a peculiarly Renaissance one, because it uses classical, ultimately Neoplatonic ideas to overcome prohibitions that were deeply installed in Christianity. Shakespeare must have been familiar with Cardinal Bembo in Castiglione's *Courtier*, reconciling religion with the *Symposium*: 'And therefore, as commune fire trieth golde and maketh it fyne, so this most holye fire

[15] Sir Thomas Browne, *Religio Medici* (1642) 76.
[16] John Stow, *A Suruay of London* (1598) 130–1; William Camden, *Britain*, Philemon Holland (trans.), (1610) 433–4.

in soules destroyeth and consumeth what so euer there is mortall in them, and relieueth and maketh beawtyfull the heauenlye part, whyche at the first by reason of the sense was dead and buried in them'. Love, in the manner of Chester, is for Bembo like 'the great fire in the whiche … *Hercule* was burned on the topp of the monntaigne *Oeta*'.[17] Yet the Platonism of 'The Phoenix and Turtle' is not that of Shelley's *Epipsychidion*. It is not fluid but tightly argued. The ardency of the mutual flame immediately gives way to a more scholastic account of the two-in-one, transcendental love advanced in the *Symposium*:

> So they loved as love in twain
> Had the essence but in one,
> Two distincts, division none.
> Number there in love was slain.
>
> (11.25–8)

Mid-20th century critics, schooled in 'metaphysical' poetry, took readily to this stanza, and the four or five that follow. They explicated the paradoxes, but did not sufficiently respond both to overtones of topicality and, more significantly, to the sense that, as the voice of Reason takes over, there is a decline into logical futility.

By topicality I mean the receptiveness of the poem to readers interested in the relationship between Salusbury and Elizabeth I:

> Hearts remote yet not asunder,
> Distance and no space was seen
> 'Twixt this turtle and his queen.
> But in them it were a wonder.
>
> (11.29–32)

The word 'remote' suggests the distance of the birds from us, but 'yet' pulls it back to the gap between the birds despite their being as close as man and wife ('Those whom God hath joined together let no one put asunder').[18] Almost all the *OED* examples (as well as the word's origin in *remotus*) imply a large, physical gap, as between London and the Salusbury estate at Lleweni.[19] 'Distance and no space' grows aurally out of 'distincts', but 'distance', like 'remote', carries relatively new implications of hierarchy and reserve. There was social as well as geographical distance between Sir John and his queen. Yet they were as one. As I have argued in Chapter 13, there would be geopolitical resonances here for readers in 1601. The Phoenix–Turtle dyad suggests not just Elizabeth and Salusbury, squire of the body in the royal bedchamber,[20] but what their intimacy manifested, the union of Wales and England in Tudor Britishness.

---

[17] *The Courtyer of Count Baldessar Castilio*, trans. Thomas Hoby (1561) X3v.
[18] Marriage service, noted in Burrow's edition.
[19] Cf. *Shakespeare's Poems*, Katherine Duncan-Jones and H. R. Woudhuysen (eds), (London: Arden Shakespeare, 2007) 118.
[20] See Chester's dedication to *Loves Martyr*, A3r.

The compliments come and go. We are now given an account of 'the truth of love' more intense and metaphysical than would be plausible for a courtier and his queen. Even here, there might be a glancing reference to Salusbury's 'right' at court.[21] But the tendency of the writing is more narrowly and strangely directed:

> So between them love did shine
> That the turtle saw his right
> Flaming in the Phoenix' sight.
> Either was the other's mine.
>
> Property was thus appalled
> That the self was not the same.
> Single nature's double name
> Neither two nor one was called.
>
> (11.33–40)

'Mine' is not just a possessive, nor only an excavation that yields up precious substances. It suggests, among other things, a military undermining or explosion, ignited by the flame of love. Philosophically, there is a violence to mutual possession, a threat adumbrated by the capacity of 'mine' to signify 'mind' in Elizabethan English.[22] The Phoenix and the Turtle were so mindful of one another, so mindingly of one another's mind, that they were given over to self-loss.

Shakespeare was fascinated by the non-identity of the self which such mutuality involved; but he was also, like 'Property',[23] 'appalled' by what it entailed ('rendered weak and pale', 'erecting a defensive paling around itself'). What he writes to the youth in the Sonnets, ''Tis thee, myself, that for my self I praise', is worldly and rueful. But the alienation can be more profound. When Desdemona is asked on her deathbed who killed her, and she replies, to protect Othello, 'Nobody, I myself', she unknowingly names 'Iago', the 'I/ego' who troublingly and accurately declares 'I am not what I am'.[24] In 'The Phoenix and Turtle', we have double-selving rather than self-doubling. But 'not the same' remains negative. The elegy laments the loss of self which was the making of the Phoenix-and-Turtle as well as the fiery death which followed.

Reason comes in aid, but fails. The reader hopes for lucidity, but finds elaborate confusion. 'Reason, in itself confounded, | Saw division grow together' (11.41–2). Reason in itself was confounded (inwardly collapsed, poured together) because, given 'it selfe' in the 1601 text, Reason in it (i.e. in this case of bird mutuality) was self-confounded by these paradoxes. Earlier we were told that there was 'division none'. Most likely Reason, whose prior composition of an epitaph is soon to be invoked, was there before the abolition of division was achieved. But there must already be a suggestion of the inadequacy

---

[21] Duncan-Jones and Woudhuysen (2007) 119.
[22] See *OED* spelling forms for *mine*, n and v.
[23] Senses range from 'ownership, of the self' to 'grammatical and ontological propriety'.
[24] Sonnet 62; *Othello* V. ii. 91, I. i. 65.

of Reason (supposedly pre-eminent in a Platonic system) to comprehend what it witnesses. In the Phoenix and Turtle, love and death forge a union that transcends number and implodes rationality, whereas Reason has to posit division before it can see a
union. The dryness that creeps into the self-doubling analysis becomes more oppres-
sive as Reason commands the poem: 'To themselves, yet either neither, | Simple were
so well compounded' (11.43–4). Is this inspiring, or faintly dessicated? The next stanza
begins, 'That it cried, "How true a twain"' (1.45). Is it unreasonable of Reason to cry out?
It gives up reasoning, we note, on the very point which, for Chester, was the message of
Loves Martyr: 'Allegorically shadowing the truth of Loue'. For Shakespeare, the truth of
the twain makes them truly one—a lively piece of wordplay, drawing on the capacity of
'twain' at this date to mean both distinct and double (i.e. 'the same thing, though twice').
The truth of love, Reason came to realize, is that 'Love hath reason, reason none'.
 So what did Reason do next?

> Whereupon it made this threne
> To the phoenix and the dove,
> Co-supremes and stars of love,
> As chorus to their tragic scene.

> (11.49–52)

'Whereupon' is unwieldy enough; it has the awkward consequentiality of Reason
doing its best. Like the Chorus of Romeo and Juliet, and the not-so-reliable Chorus of
Henry V, Reason can mediate what has happened only to a degree. The 'tragic scene'
belongs to the Phoenix and Turtle, though the birds do now hang over us like the stel-
lified heroes of antiquity (e.g. Castor and Pollux). In what sense is their scene tragic?
These lovers are not star-crossed, and the ecstasy of double-selving is far from wholly
destructive. The scene is tragic in the older, Elizabethan sense that it is deathly. As
Michael Neill has brought out, 'tragedy, … habitually dressed itself in the blacks
of funeral custom, incorporated episodes of funeral pageantry into its action'.[25] He
quotes Theodore Spencer: 'Death … was Tragedy' (30). This is not quite the limit of
tragedy though, because the poem now turns to the loss suffered by the world in the
death of the birds.
 At this point readers of Loves Martyr turned the page and found another form: five
three-lined stanzas, rhymed as triplets (FIGURE 30.1). The layout reflects the rhyme
scheme, and no doubt Shakespeare's intention. But some of the formal features were in
the hands of the printer, Richard Field. Even the stanza breaks, which do so much to
articulate the music of the poem, and to make the epitaph-like triplets, for many readers,
in some sense emblematic of the urn in which the birds' ashes end up, are not inevitable;
they are missing from John Benson's text in the first collected edition of Shakespeare's
Poems (1640), and in various later printings. The last page of 'The Phoenix and Turtle'

---

[25] Michael Neill, Issues of Death: Mortality and Identity in English Renaissance Tragedy (Oxford:
Oxford University Press, 1997) 47.

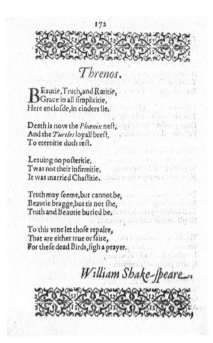

172

Threnos.

Beautie, Truth, and Raritie,
Grace in all simplicitie,
Here enclofde, in cinders lie.

Death is now the *Phænix* neft,
And the *Turtles* loyall breft,
To eternitie doth reft.

Leauing no pofteritie,
Twas not their infirmitie,
It was married Chaftitie.

Truth may feeme, but cannot be,
Beautie bragge, but tis not fhe,
Truth and Beautie buried be.

To this vrne let thofe repaire,
That are either true or faire,
For thefe dead Birds, figh a prayer.

William Shake-fpeare.

FIGURE 30.1. The *Threnos* of 'The Phoenix and Turtle', in *Loves Martyr* (1601). By permission of the Folger Shakespeare Library.

is also headed by the word 'Threnos', and framed by two lines of printers' vinets, lace, or flowers—patterns known in the period as *arabesques*, and deriving, like the Phoenix, from the orient, from the calligraphic-influenced designs of the Muslim world. Is this space-filler, inserted for the convenience of the printer, meant to stop blank sections of the page tearing or being spoiled with ink on the press, or is it a maze of ornate, semiotically charged lines, a continuation of the patterning of verse by other means?

Field was an experienced printer, whose relationship with Shakespeare was long-standing; a contemporary of the poet in Stratford-upon-Avon, he had produced the first editions of *Venus and Adonis* and *Lucrece* (1593–4). Here, if anywhere, was a situation in which authorial intentions could be realized by a printer. But does the evidence support this? Bands of flowers are sometimes used to mark thematically significant divisions in Elizabethan texts, but there are flowers elsewhere in *Loves Martyr*, and in many other books in the period, that seem functional for the printer and ornamental for the reader. That does not in principle stop them from having a meaningful effect in *this* case. The strip at the top of the page makes one poem two, in a Phoenix-and-Turtle fashion; the strip at the bottom, below the name '*William Shakes-speare*', adds to the urn-like effect of the 'Threnos'. What if, like Benson, or like Field himself later in *Loves Martyr*, when setting Jonson's imitation of Shakespeare, 'The Phoenix Analysde', Field had framed the 'Threnos' with straight lines. Do the arabesques mean more than lines, and differently? Juliet Fleming argues that to look for meaning in such markings is a mistake. Arabesques signify *nothing*, while disposing of a problem for the printer.[26] Yet the deep conjunction between the importation of the Arabian bird into Chester's book, and Shakespeare's poem, and the use by Field of an arabesque design must be culturally loaded. Like the densely arabesque title-page of *The Phoenix Nest* (which looks more like a Persian carpet than a frontispiece), Field's layout orientalizes, is expensive-looking, and exotic.

Many readers now find, as most probably did in 1601, the next word on the page, '*Threnos*', as opaque as the arabesque which frames it. Even more than the line 'Here the anthem doth commence', this is in the text but outside the poem (modern editions do not count it in the line numbering). That does not detract from its antiquity and authority. The word 'threne', already heard in 'The Phoenix and Turtle', can be found occasionally in vernacular writing after the mid-15th century, but '*Threnos*' is Ancient Greek enough to put Marston, Chapman, Jonson, and other early readers in mind of the many epitaphs in *The Greek Anthology*, some of them for animals, including birds. More immediately, it indicates that Shakespeare is following a relatively new convention (with precedents in Ovid's parrot-funeral poem and *Phillip Sparow*), that of adding to or ending an elegiac poem with an epitaph. Of this innovative, Renaissance practice, Scott L. Newstok interestingly observes:

> The epitaph, like a refrain, turns attention away from the previous composition, turning instead toward the end (death) of the work itself. An increasingly secular gesture of closure, the textual turn towards the epitaph displaces formulae of Christian consolation common to medieval lyrics and prayers. It thereby marks the advent of a new sense of *textualised* memory.[27]

As we saw in Chapter 13, that is the sort of memory that we find in Shakespeare's Sonnets and in a number of the 'critical elegies' written about him. Like many memories, we might add, it is not sound on names. We do not know the identity of the young man remembered by the Sonnets. And by the end of the 'Threnos', the Phoenix and Turtle are merely 'dead birds'. As strikingly, although the ending of the poem makes much of 'textualised memory', it does not rule out prayer.

The 'Threnos' is the work of Reason after ratiocination has been defeated. It has an air of clarity and acceptance that is in line with the advice about epitaphs given by Elizabethan commentators:

> Beauty, truth, and rarity,
> Grace in all simplicity,
> Here enclosed in cinders lie.
>
> (ll.53–5)

---

[26] 'How Not to Look at a Printer's Flower', *Journal of Medieval and Early Modern Studies*, 38 (2008): 345–71.

[27] Quoting *Death in Early Modern England: The Poetics of Epitaphs beyond the Tomb* (Basingstoke: Palgrave, 2009) 31.

As we read into the 'Threnos', we seem to find a reprise of the qualities of the Phoenix ('Beauty') and Turtle ('truth'), but the extension of the list confounds the expected duality. The birds have taken many virtues with them, or rather, left them 'enclosed in cinders'. The virtues now enclose each other (as the Phoenix and Turtle could not quite do) because they are ashes and can mingle, or they are intact but wrapped inside cinders. 'Cinders' are, in common usage, crunchy and irregular. This hints at the ungainliness of the body, which it is hard, even finally, to escape, much as, later in the 'Threnos', 'Truth and beauty buried be' has a grim touch of the grave. But it also preserves classical decorum, both by avoiding the Christian associations of dust and ashes (recall the 'dust enclosèd here' on Shakespeare's gravestone), and by evoking a false derivation (widely accepted in the period) from the word for ashes, *cineres*, in Latin elegy.

'Here' is now the here of an urn, not quite a place on the page, though the latter lingers, to reinforce the thought that the layout itself is urn-like. And 'lie' is magnificently terminal because free from the customary play on mendacity. This could easily have been elicited by the collocation with 'truth', but lying as deception is, as Christopher Ricks might put it, 'fended off'.[28] The experienced reader of poetry is sure to be aware on some level that, with so much beauty, truth, rarity, and simple grace said to 'lie', someone might be lying, yet the candour of the writing excludes this. The innocence of 'lie' is not naive; it rebukes our cynicism that we could think it deceptive about the virtues caught up in it. Yet it does mean less singly than it seems, because 'in cinders lie' could mean in cinders for a period rather than, euphemistically but usually, dead.

We know that traditionally the Phoenix revives or is replaced. It does so, with a difference, in *Loves Martyr*, and it is surprising how long the possibility is kept open in Shakespeare:

> Death is now the phoenix' nest,
> And the turtle's loyal breast
> To eternity doth rest.
>
> (11.56–8)

This could mean that the Phoenix dies but that death is her nest, from which rebirth will come. The Turtle's loyal breast is also the Phoenix' nest. But, as the triplet unfolds, that breast rests to eternity. 'Rest' is, typically for the poem's love of paradox, less definitely mortal sounding than 'Death', as though the Turtle, for a moment, seems more likely to revive than the Phoenix, but the Turtle is less death-defying, and 'to eternity' must point to an extinction for ever. The firm rhyme 'rest', after the feminine rhymes of the first triplet, carries weight. This outcome would be in line with *Loves Martyr*, where the Turtle's love is alive within the revived Phoenix' heart but the dove dies. As we shall see,

---

[28] See his classic discussion of lying and anti-punning in 'Lies', *The Force of Poetry* (Oxford: Clarendon Press, 1984) 369–91, 372.

the death of the birds' qualities is not final, though the subtlety with which they live on makes death/life not quite alternatives.

One reason for feeling that the birds are more dead than indeterminately fled comes in the next triplet:

> Leaving no posterity
> 'Twas not their infirmity,
> It was married chastity.
>
> (11.59–61)

As 'posterity' shifts from meaning 'futurity' in a general sense to 'offspring' in a particular, thanks to the bodily associations of 'infirmity', it is hard for the reader to take 'infirmity' merely as 'deficiency' ('it was no great loss to them not to have chicks'). Why does the threnodist raise the thought of 'infirmity' as 'physical impotence' in order awkwardly to dismiss it? The odds were never in favour of birds of different species breeding, even allegorically. Reason is still in search of explanations where only wonder is appropriate. It may be that the stanza reflects the scepticism of a poet in favour of breeding within marriage (as in Sonnets 1–17) about the programme handed down by *Loves Martyr*, where the Turtle is intimate with the Phoenix' bedchamber but has no sexual involvement. Ben Jonson's 'Epos', printed a few pages after 'The Phoenix and Turtle', has an equally willed passage on chastity being virtuous as the result of a positive choice, not when it is the fruit of incapacity. Perhaps this is an historical difficulty created by the conventions of compliment around any manifestation of the Virgin Queen as love object. But another consideration, sympathetic to Reason's difficulties, is that 'married' here means more than husband and wife. It signifies indissoluble union. The birds were so singularly combined that they could not be replicated; the union had a fullness so complete that it had to be unreproductive. It is a high point of condensation and paradox, seeking questionably, as is Reason's way, to elucidate a mystery.

The lack of children is one indicator that, in this bird funeral, there will be no ritual of succession. When John Shakespeare was buried, the coat of arms bought for him by his son descended to the playwright by inheritance. It was an important confirmation in the history of the Shakespeares. Was this handing-on part of the ritual of the father's funeral? It may have been, and in noble heraldic funerals it was. These rituals involved an offering at the altar and a handing over of knightly equipage and heraldry to the heir.[29] This brought out symbolically what is latent in most funerals, the passing on of status from an older generation to a younger. At a time when Elizabeth was ageing and the royal succession was in question, this has had to be a significant element in the envelope of a funeral poem that uses phoenix iconography. In 1601, as we have seen, it could not be anticipated that 1603 would be peaceful. The absence of a rite of succession is an indication,

---

[29] See e.g. Woodward (1997) ch. 1.

allegorically, of the sufficiency of the love between the birds, but also, especially for early readers, a measure of the limitation of their completeness.

The notion that this poem is an exercise in the higher French *symbolisme*, and sounds like Mallarmé,[30] takes a knock in the next triplet:

> Truth may seem but cannot be,
> Beauty brag, but 'tis not she.
> Truth and beauty buried be.
>
> (ll.62–4)

This is the language of satire. Seeming truth and bragging false beauty belong to *Measure for Measure*. As with the 'shrieking harbinger' (cf. *Macbeth*) and 'every bird of tyrant wing' (*Julius Caesar* or *Coriolanus*) expelled from the opening procession, we are reminded of the debased, threatening world from which the Phoenix and Turtle have fled. What we make of this depends largely on the next, the final stanza of the poem:

> To this urn let those repair
> That are either true or fair,
> For these dead birds sigh a prayer.
>
> (ll.65–7)

'Let … ' again. Another imperative, and another exclusion. Come to this urn if you are true or fair, much as, in the opening stanzas, only birds possessed of qualities shared with the Phoenix and Turtle are admitted to their procession.

A full-strength satirical account of this would say: that means no one can come, because truth 'cannot *be*' (so no use of 'are' applies) and beauty is not what it appears, is actually not 'fair'. Against this it should be held, on the grounds of both tone and philosophy, that lower-case 't' and 'b' (although 1601, by printer's convention, has 'T' and 'B') save the imperative from self-defeat. Absolute Truth and Beauty may no longer be extant, but truth and fairness survive. This, the reader might conclude, is the extent of the immortality granted by the poem to the Phoenix and the Turtle. They do not have posterity, but their achievement is not entirely vain. Why, though, 'true *or* fair'? Here a milder satirical implication could still be felt. Being true *and* fair is not now possible; the two do not go together. Or, more cynically, if a lover or a mistress is true s/he will not be fair and if s/he is fair, fidelity should not be expected. Before we run away with a mocking conclusion, however, remember (as critics have not) the injunction to 'repair'. The true and the fair are invited to repair to the urn in the sense of having recourse to something, going somewhere. If they repair in this sense, they will also *re-pair*, join up as they proceed—beauty meshing with truth—to where coupleness finds its shrine, and rhyme.

---

[30] E.g. Shakespeare, *The Poems*, ed. F. T. Prince, Arden Shakespeare (London: Methuen, 1960) xliv; Barbara Everett, 'Set upon a Golden Bough to Sing: Shakespeare's Debt to Sidney in "The Phoenix and Turtle"', *TLS*, 16 February 2001: 13–15, 15.

Perhaps, at a semantic limit, they will also begin to make reparation and/or repair the world in the image of the Beauty and Truth once combined in the Phoenix and Turtle.

What of the final line: 'For these dead birds sigh a prayer'. The reader is taken back to the anonymity of the birds in the opening stanza, reducing the wonderful creatures of legend and emblem to a tangle of dust and feathers. The birds almost take language with them. It is not just that they lose their Phoenix and Turtle names, but that those who are true or fair and who can be persuaded to take notice of the birds are left with prayers wreathed in wordless sighs. The balance of power between attraction and exclusion is starting to shift; couples may not repair to the urn, because, in this world, wonders will always cease. As they lose their Phoenix and Turtle aspect, the birds become more like us, mortal creatures. The epitaph arrives at its routine, early modern purpose, that of reminding readers that we resemble the dead ('as you are now, I was once, as I am, so you will be') and should not forget our mortality.

'Sigh a prayer' is another imperative. The reader is finally encouraged to be, not merely an observer, or initiate, but a participant. Just as exclusion returns, so does the injunction to wordless sound. The sigh is a muted version of the herald's invited trumpet-blast. But if we do sigh the prayer (and if the dead birds sigh one back?),[31] to whom or what is it uttered? Hardly to a Christian God, who would not be interested in the fate of a pair of birds, however drawn to beauty, truth, and grace. It is not just that these are animals, and so irredeemable, nor that they are perfect, so do not in that sense need our prayers (although 'dead birds' do not sound so perfect after all). An overarching point, which holds even allegorically, is that the dead cannot be in purgatory for Protestant readers. Prayers to assist the dead were discouraged after the Reformation (as in the 1552 prayerbook, or the homily 'Of Prayer'). They were still uttered, in practice, and one can imagine the human need. This is another way in which 'The Phoenix and Turtle' draws the rituals away from what could be the human situation and looks at them in a sparer but also more sceptical way. What could be more natural than to encourage prayers for the dead (Catholic). What could be more ineffectual than to pray for a couple of birds (Protestant).

And so we are left with the urn. Husband and wife burial was frequent in the period, and the motif of two-in-one union was commonplace in elegies and epitaphs.[32] Delayed to the final triplet, the urn carries more weight as an encloser, includer, and ender. It gives us a location, to which readers can return, but also a guarantee that the cinders are not scattered, but are held together, unsullied, in a terminal but womb-like vessel, a point of reference for others. The rebuilding of social bonds is a strong feature of many funerals, the only rebirth they can deliver. In the early modern period, a bell was rung to alert neighbours to the rites ('Who'll toll the bell?', in 'Cock Robin') and make them

---

[31] It is just possible, against the flow, to hear 'For' as meaning 'because' and 'sigh a prayer' as indicating that the dead birds pray for those left behind. Even some Protestant, early modern commentators believed that the virtuous dead prayed for the living; see e.g. Ralph Houlbrooke, *Death, Religion, and the Family in England, 1480–1750* (Oxford: Clarendon Press, 1998) 41–2.

[32] Cf. Newstok (2009) 55.

at least auditory participants. A dole was often paid, buying prayers from the poor. The funeral procession itself would represent family and society in miniature. Burial would be followed by a feast. But in 'The Phoenix and Turtle' these broader obligations are only met up to a point. The selection of birds for the procession is made in the image of the dead birds. The love of the birds is all-consuming, but for each other, not for anyone else, however their qualities devolve. They could be said to abscond, to flee the world. There are certainly no funeral baked meats. Only the true and the fair are summoned to the urn, to pair up as they repair. A community of such will never be as large as the world would wish.

Yet the Phoenix and the Turtle are *exemplary*. They fulfill in their '*Threnos*' the main generic requirement of the epitaph. Ralph Houlbrooke paraphrases the assumption: 'Virtuous life and good deeds are also (many inscriptions proclaim) the surest basis of lasting fame. They give the deceased a sort of immortality, and make them worthy of imitation.'[33] We can emulate the birds' fidelity, if not their beauty. They are exemplary, also, in the sense that their qualities create their fame, not an elaborate funeral monument. We are back with the Stanley tomb at Tong, or Shakespeare's Sonnets to the young man (pp. 226–30). Built memorials are of doubtful use. Think of Browne on the folly of those who 'subsist in bones, and be but Pyramidally extant'.[34] Or of Donne, whose memorial in St Paul's shows him rising from an urn, and who had clearly read 'The Phoenix and Turtle': 'As well a well wrought urne becomes | The greatest ashes, as half-acre tombes'.[35] This is a clue to understanding the modesty of the dead birds' urn. In one sense, it is the unexpected, logical outcome of the unseemly competition for memorial greatness that characterized the late Tudor period. As Nigel Llewelyn notes, after the Reformation tombs became bigger and more elaborate, until it became impossible for the Stuart monarchs to construct memorials grand enough to reflect their authority (they were never built).[36]

Remarkably, Shakespeare goes further. We have seen, in Chapter 13, how he invokes the poetically conventional but also actual vulnerability of funeral monuments in the face of war, time, and defacement in order to assert, by contrast, and at times vauntingly (as in Sonnet 55), the greater power of his own verse to grant immortality. Although the urn is from some points of view an emblem of what the poem becomes, the verse of 'The Phoenix and Turtle' does not announce its own durability. Immortality comes, not from proper names or 'half-acre tombes', but, if at all, from the dead birds' love, truth, and uniqueness. This characteristic of the poem may have been encouraged by the mission of *Loves Martyr* to shadow the truth of love. But there is a broader coincidence between this glowing reticence and the later, probably Jacobean, Sonnets to the young man, such as 123–5, in which what survives is not 'pyramids' (like those on the Stanley tomb) 'built

[33] Houlbrooke (1998) 353.
[34] *Hydriotaphia*, 72.
[35] 'The Canonization', in *Poems, by J. D.* (1633).
[36] Nigel Llewelyn, *Funeral Monuments in Post-Reformation England* (Cambridge: Cambridge University Press, 2000) 313.

up with newer might', not 'great bases' laid 'for eternity, | Which proves more short than waste or ruining', nor the 'powerful rhyme' that we are reading, but the poet's love for the fair youth, which 'all alone *stands* hugely politic' (the Stanley word, now free it seems of the impurity of flattering a patron). The background set out in Chapter 13 is consequently of great importance, though subsumed by the poem. 'The Phoenix and Turtle' is premised on but transcends the competitiveness among funeral monuments and memorial verses—for reputation, patronage, and survival in the face of mortality—that made the Elizabethan period so productive of elegies and epitaphs.

Select Bibliography

Alvarez, A. (1955) 'The Phoenix and the Turtle', in John Wain (ed.), *Interpretations: Essays on Twelve English Poems* (London: Routledge) 1–16.

Dronke, Peter (1968) 'The Phoenix and the Turtle', *Orbis Litterarum*, 23: 199–220.

Ellrodt, Robert (1962) 'An Anatomy of "The Phoenix and the Turtle"', *Shakespeare Survey*, 15: 99–110.

Enterline, Lynn (2007) '"The Phoenix and the Turtle", Renaissance Elegies, and the Language of Grief', in Patrick Cheney, Andrew Hadfield, and Garrett A. Sullivan (eds.), *Early Modern English Poetry: A Critical Companion* (New York: Oxford University Press) 147–59.

Everett, Barbara (2001) 'Set upon a Golden Bough to Sing: Shakespeare's Debt to Sidney in "The Phoenix and Turtle"', *TLS*, 16 February: 13–15.

Garber, Marjorie (1984) 'Two Birds with One Stone: Lapidary Re-Inscription in *The Phoenix and Turtle*', *The Upstart Crow*, 5 (Fall): 5–19.

Klause, John (2002) '*The Phoenix and Turtle* in Its Time', in Thomas Moisan and Douglas Bruster (eds.), *In the Company of Shakespeare* (Madison: Fairleigh Dickinson University Press) 206–30.

Underwood, Richard Allan (1974) *Shakespeare's 'Phoenix and Turtle': A Survey of Scholarship* (Salzburg: University of Salzburg).

PART VI

LATER REFLECTIONS

CHAPTER 31

SHAKESPEAREAN POETRY AND THE ROMANTICS

MICHAEL O'NEILL

31.1

The response of the major Romantic poets to Shakespeare is multifaceted. But recognition of Shakespearean vitality and suggestiveness is pervasive. A visual image intimates their capacity to respond to what Jonathan Bate calls the 'visionary power of imagination' embodied in Shakespeare's words. As Bate notes, awareness of this power is at work in William Blake's colour print, 'Pity'.[1] (FIGURE 31.1) Blake's divided view of 'Pity' as itself giving rise to inner division is expressed through his own highly idiosyncratic response to Shakespeare's lines in *Macbeth* about 'pity, like a naked new-born babe, | Striding the blast' (I. vii. 21–2). The horror of the purposed deed stings Macbeth's conscience and imagination into apocalyptic recoil. Blake shapes an image of tenderness, a maternal figure holding a small upright child and leaning down towards a sleeping young woman who may be dreaming the maternal figure into existence;[2] at the same time, there is a sense of potentially visionary energy as the 'sightless couriers of the air' head onwards.

The fact that their eyes are closed turns the horses into creatures that lack sight rather than being, as Shakespeare implies, invisible. Governing their direction, it seems, is a

---

[1] Jonathan Bate, *Shakespeare and the English Romantic Imagination* (Oxford: Clarendon Press, 1986) 125, 126.

[2] Compare the woman's posture, head back, eyes tilted upwards, with that of the Poet in the illustration to Dante: *The Circle of the Lustful: Francesca da Rimini*, where there is a strong suggestion that the image is part, even the product, of the Poet's dream or vision. Both images cited from *The William Blake Archive*, Morris Eaves, Robert N. Essick, and Joseph Viscomi (eds.), 22 May 2012. <http://www.blakearchive.org/>

FIGURE 31.1. Blake, 'Pity', by permission of Tate, London, 2012.

figure with his back to the viewer, arms stretched out, above the woman with the baby. The Shakespearean metaphoric tumult finds an answerable response in the Blakean image, even as it is simultaneously working within its own 'frame of reference'.[3] Without wholly agreeing with David L. Clark's post-De Manian reading—Clark sees the print as 'Suddenly rendering *Macbeth* uncannily opaque to itself'—one can assert that Blake's inspired literalism of illustrative focus ends up with an image that is a new creation.[4]

In so doing, he typifies, if in his own way, the imaginative responsiveness of the Romantics to Shakespeare. Yet this responsiveness does not arise from nowhere. When Dryden famously asserts of Shakespeare that 'When he describes any thing, you more than see it, you feel it too', he anticipates Keatsian and Hazlittean ideas and ideals.[5] For both those Romantic-era writers, Shakespeare embodied an outgoing capacity for sympathy, one that 'has as much delight in conceiving an Iago as an Imogen'.[6] They build in this respect on the admiration of Henry Mackenzie in 1780, author of that handbook to sensibility, *The Man of Feeling*. Though Mackenzie worries in neoclassical mode about the elements of 'licence' in Shakespeare's drama, he notes that this licence gave the dramatist 'an opportunity of delineating the passions and affections of the human mind as they exist in reality, with all the various colourings which they receive in the mixed

---

[3] Bate (1986) 125, to which my discussion is indebted.

[4] David L. Clark: 'How To Do Things with Shakespeare: Illustrative Theory and Practice in Blake's *Pity*', in *The Mind in Creation: Essays on English Romantic Literature in Honour of Ross G. Woodman*, J. Douglas Kneale (ed.), (Montreal: McGill-Queen's University Press, 1992) 108.

[5] John Dryden, 'An Essay of Dramatic Poetry', qtd from *Shakespeare: The Critical Heritage: Volume 5: 1765–1774*, Brian Vickers (ed.), (London: Routledge, 1979) 72.

[6] *The Letters of John Keats, 1814–1821*, 2 vols (Cambridge, MA: Harvard University Press, 1958) I. 387.

scenes of life'.[7] Mackenzie plays a variation on Samuel Johnson's praise for Shakespeare's ability to portray 'the real state of sublunary nature, which partakes of good and evil, joy and sorrow, mingled with endless variety of proportion and innumerable modes of combination' in 'compositions' that defy strict generic taxonomies of tragedy and comedy.[8]

Where Mackenzie differs from Johnson is that, like other critics of the half-century preceding Romanticism, he descends from generalization to particulars, showing himself to be a subtle critic of verbal effects. Commenting on Hamlet's lines, 'the Devil hath power | T'assume a pleasing shape; yea, and perhaps, | *Out of my weakness and my melancholy* | Abuses me to damn me' (quoted from Mackenzie; italics his), he writes: 'This doubt of the grounds on which our purpose is founded is as often the effect as the cause of irresolution, which first hesitates, and then seeks out an excuse for its hesitation'.[9] Johnson, by contrast, earns Keats' scorn for his 'patronizing' generalizations: 'lo fool again!' is the Romantic poet's derisive response to Johnson's assertion that *The Winter's Tale*, 'is, with all its absurdities, very entertaining'.[10] Keats' instinct, rather, was to underline phrases that showed the life of Shakespeare's language, such as Perdita's 'I'll blush you thanks' (IV. iv. 584).[11]

And yet Johnson's famous confession of his inability to re-read the last scenes of *King Lear*, 'so shocked' was he 'by *Cordelia*'s death', shows that he could respond to the affective impact of Shakespeare's drama with a force rivalling that of any of his successors.[12] Moreover, to read Mackenzie is to see that Coleridge's discernment of 'meditative excess' in Hamlet's character does not simply have a background in his reading of Schlegel for whom the play illustrates the fact that 'a calculating consideration, which exhausts all the relations and possible consequences of a deed, must cripple the power of acting'.[13] Coleridge clearly writes in a tradition of criticism closer to home, one that is attuned to the revelation of character through hesitations communicated through the diction and syntax of poetic speech. Gray, in sublime mode, writes of Shakespeare in not dissimilar terms in his 'The Progress of Poesy. A Pindaric Ode', where nature or 'the mighty Mother'(85) gives the young poet 'these golden keys': 'This can unlock the gates of joy; | Of horror that and thrilling fears, | Or ope the sacred source of sympathetic tears' (92–4).[14] Mark Akenside criticized 'opening a *source* with a *key*', but the metaphoric daring shows that Gray has caught something of Shakespeare's own manner, ready to mix

[7] *Shakespeare: The Critical Heritage: Volume 6: 1774–1801*, Brian Vickers (ed.), (London: Routledge, 1981) 280.

[8] See *Preface to Shakespeare*, in Samuel Johnson, *Rasselas, Poems, and Selected Prose*, Bertrand H. Bronson (ed.), 3rd edn enlarged (New York: Holt, Rinehart and Winston, 1971) 266.

[9] Vickers (1981) 276.

[10] Qtd from Caroline Spurgeon, *Keats's Shakespeare: A Descriptive Study Based on New Material* 2nd edn (London: Oxford University Press, 1929) 30.

[11] Qtd from R. S. White, *Keats as a Reader of Shakespeare* (Norman: University of Oklahoma Press, 1987) 83. See also Christopher Ricks, *Keats and Embarrassment* (London: Oxford University Press, 1976) 187, for discussion of Perdita's 'communicative blush'.

[12] Johnson (1971) 319.

[13] Jonathan Bate, ed., *The Romantics on Shakespeare* (London: Penguin, 1992) 323, 308.

[14] Qtd from *The Poems of Thomas Gray, William Collins, Oliver Goldsmith*, Roger Lonsdale (ed.), (London: Longmans, 1969).

figures in the interests of compressed revelations of feeling.[15] It took a major Romantic critic of Shakespeare fully to recognize and value this aspect of his style. Charles Lamb, in *Specimens of Dramatic Poetry*, writes that, by contrast with Fletcher who 'lays line upon line, making up one after the other, adding image to image so deliberately that we see where they join', 'Shakespeare mingles every thing, he runs line into line, embarrasses sentences and metaphors; before one idea has burst its shell, another is hatched and clamorous for disclosure'.[16] The description fits some of the finest writing by Romantic poets: Keats' figurative densities, Shelley's leaps from image to image.

31.2

That said, the diction employed by Gray rarely mingles the literary with the ordinary in the way that Shakespeare manages. The harbinger of Romantic concern with expressive feeling, he works within an Augustan idiom, with all its constraints of dignity and decorum. Wordsworth's turn to the daringly low and rustic in *Lyrical Ballads* draws on the Shakespeare who moves between registers. 'And never lifted up a single stone' (475): the climax of Wordsworth's *Michael* reminds us of Shakespeare's pervasiveness in the Romantic period.[17] Ghosting the line is Lear's trochaic wail of desolation over the body of his dead daughter: 'Thou'lt come no more. | Never, never, never, never, never' (V. iii. 283–4; the play is quoted from *The Tragedy of King Lear* text). Wordsworth plays down as well as up an intensity of feeling which, for all his poem's sub-title 'A pastoral poem', approaches the tragic. The reader is not brought face to face with the spectacle of raw grief, as is the viewer of Shakespeare's play; rather, he or she is both one with the village community and edging towards a glimpse of what remains private and virtually incommunicable; after all, the line in question is shaped as a possible belief rather than a hard fact, 'and 'tis believed by all', writes Wordsworth at his most narratively subtle, 'That many and many a day he thither went, | And never lifted up a single stone' (473–5).

Lear's grief is played out in the glare of dramatic revelation. The play's obsession with nothingness and need has involved hammering away at words associated with nullity, annulment, nothingness. 'Nothing' (I. i. 87), says Cordelia with faintly embittered crispness, when asked and indeed commanded by her over-demanding father: 'what can you say to draw | A third more opulent than your sisters? Speak' (I. i. 85–6). And yet even Cordelia's 'Nothing' has about it, as Coleridge noted, 'a something of disgust at the ruthless hypocrisy of her sisters, and some little faulty admixture of pride and sullenness'.[18]

---

[15] Lonsdale (1969), 173 n.

[16] Qtd from *Lamb as Critic*, Roy Park (ed.), (London: Routledge & Kegan Paul, 1980), 135–6.

[17] Unless indicated otherwise, Wordsworth's poetry is quoted from *21st-Century Oxford Authors: William Wordsworth*, Stephen Gill (ed.), (Oxford: Oxford University Press, 2010).

[18] Bate (1992) 389.

Lear on the heath will think that in Poor Tom he is encountering 'the thing itself' (III. iv. 100), man as a 'poor, bare, forked animal' (III. iv. 101–2), 'Unaccommodated' (III. iv. 100). The perception is ironical since Tom is not what he seems to be, being Edgar in disguise, and the difficulty of truly seeing into the depths of absolute nothing, complete devastation, haunts Shakespeare's tragedy and Wordsworth's poem. Both works investigate human suffering as though intent on tracing it to an absolute source; but in neither is such a source forthcoming: Lear dies, mistakenly thinking Cordelia still lives; exactly what Michael is feeling when 'seen | Sitting alone, with that his faithful Dog, | Then old, beside him, lying at his feet' (476–8) is never wholly disclosed.

Wordsworth's tactful dealings with Shakespeare show in an assimilation of one aspect of Shakespeare's practice, that of investing particular words with significance, making them magnets for a work's emotional and conceptual charge. Frank Kermode speaks about the 'awful deliberation' with which, in *King Lear*, Shakespeare will 'allow a word or set of words to occur almost obsessively'.[19] Wordsworth in *Michael* even repeats an earlier line and a half (43–4), in the climactic verse-paragraph describing Michael's response to Luke's disgrace: 'His bodily frame had been from youth to age | Of an unusual strength' (463–4). Echo only points up difference here; Michael may seek to carry on 'as before' (466), but his inability to work on the sheep-fold suggests his heart-broken endurance, another word that finds its way into *Michael* from the *King Lear* universe. At Lear's death, Kent says: 'The wonder is he hath endured so long' (V. iii. 292). The line has a bareness and tough music (supplied by the half-chime between the first syllables of 'wonder' and 'endured') for which Wordsworth finds his own equivalent, not least in lines which bring into our minds the idea of Michael's having to endure: 'There is a comfort in the strength of love; | 'Twill make a thing endurable, which else | Would break the heart' (457–9).[20] 'Break, heart, I prithee, break' (V. iii. 288) exclaims Kent at the spectacle of Lear's suffering and death; Wordsworth breaks his readers' hearts by showing Michael's refusal wholly to allow that his heart is broken.

Wordsworth draws on Shakespeare in indirect ways to help him produce his tragic narrative work. In so doing he typifies the creative interaction which marks the finest Romantic transactions with Shakespeare. Wordsworth's allusive practice with Shakespeare involves a simultaneous process of greeting and difference, saluting the Shakespearian original and wresting it into an altered context. He exploits the difference of changing genres. In 'Scorn not the Sonnet', he pays tribute to Shakespeare's handling of a brief lyric form through which he 'unlocked his heart' (3), where an allusion to Gray's lines quoted above may well be operative. Yet the fact that most of Shakespeare's work is drama means that when Wordsworth alludes to it he invokes and evokes a broader context of incident and event. In Wordsworth's lyric or narrative poetry such contexts of incident and events, with their accompanying words of power, find themselves subsumed within a changed literary form. When Macbeth says of the king he has murdered, 'Duncan is in his grave. | After life's fitful fever he sleeps well' (III. iii. 24–5), he speaks

[19] Frank Kermode, *Shakespeare's Language* (London: Allen Lane, 2000) 186 n.
[20] See Jonathan Wordsworth, *The Music of Humanity* (London: Nelson, 1969) 81.

with something close to envy of one who has escaped the mental terrors which his killer is experiencing. Duncan does not have to lie 'on the torture of the mind' (23), as Macbeth has just put it, where the phrasing turns the mind into its own rack. When Wordsworth's narrator concludes 'The Two April Mornings', with an echo of this passage in *Macbeth*:

> Matthew is in his grave, yet now
> Methinks I see him stand,
> As at that moment, with his bough
> Of wilding in his hand
>
> (57–60)

the poem subdues tragic horror into elegiac acceptance. Wordsworth imparts his own inflection to the verb 'is'; a word that speaks of the fact of existence takes on a transformed meaning when it applies to someone who 'is in his grave'. Lucy, too, in 'She dwelt among the untrodden ways', attracts a recollection of the passage in *Macbeth*, when the speaker says, 'But she is in her Grave, and Oh! | The difference to me' (11–12). In that poem, there is a glimmer of paradox, given that the lines immediately follow the apparent finality of 'When Lucy ceased to be' (10). Cessation of being ushers in a mode of existence, albeit 'in her grave', which does not so much imply any hope for an orthodox afterlife as suggest the uncanny way in which, though dead, Lucy is alive for the speaker. In 'Two April Mornings', the poem is less evidently paradoxical; the 'yet' follows 'is in the grave', whereas in the Lucy poem the 'But', more strangely, precedes the Shakespearean phrase. However, the reader is also taken into a virtual realm where 'Methinks I see him stand', a phrase that recalls Hamlet's 'methinks I see my father (I. ii. 183). For narrator and Hamlet, it is in the 'mind's eye', as Hamlet goes on to state, that the dead live again.

There are other allusions at work, their overall effect proving the truth of Bate's assertion that 'In the best of the *Lyrical Ballads*, Wordsworth is conscious of but unalarmed by Shakespeare', and proving, too, that the relations established through allusion involve a web of contrasts and connections.[21] Matthew echoes the posture of Dido as she is described in the duet which opens Act V of *The Merchant of Venice*: 'In such a night | Stood Dido with a willow in her hand' (V. i. 9–10). Dido's tragic fate resonates and contrasts with that of Matthew; he has lost a daughter; she her lover. Her emblematic willow speaks of sorrow; his 'bough | Of wilding' (the *OED*'s second meaning, 'A wild plant, flower, or fruit' is most applicable) suggests a freedom, a wildness. It is as though Wordsworth breathes a disconcerting reality into Lorenzo's and Jessica's exchanges, even as, in the confidence of love, they dare to compare their situation with that of a figure driven distraught by passion. Again, Matthew has just encountered a daughter-substitute, who 'seemed as happy as a wave | That dances on the sea' (51–2), an echo of Florizel's address to Perdita in *The Winter's Tale*: 'When you do dance, I wish you | A wave o'th' sea, that you might ever do | Nothing but that' (IV. iv. 140–2). Bate argues acutely that 'Perdita is in motion, is lost and found in a world where time is benevolent;

---

²¹ Bate (1986) 102.

the girl with the basket on her head is frozen in the past'.[22] Shakespeare's supple rhythms make the blank verse sway in line with Florizel's desire, yet it is 'desire' that speaks in the lines. Matthew sees the girl as being 'happy as a wave | That dances on the sea'; if the sight forces from him a sigh, it also confirms him in the irreducible value of his lost daughter, a confirmation that emerges in his use of 'wish': 'I looked at her and looked again; | —And did not wish her mine' (55–6). Both men may evince the 'princely nature' which Bate implicitly discerns in each.[23] However, Florizel wishes for an ideal of permanent change, where the dancer and dance are one; Matthew recognizes that, when the dancer dies, the dance cannot persist, not for him, even if it can for others. Wordsworth's ageing school-master teaches a lesson learned from suffering to Shakespeare's young man.

Shakespeare also serves as a yardstick by which Wordsworth measures his own change and development. At a critical moment in 'Lines Written a Few Miles above Tintern Abbey', he breaks away from his evocation of visionary insight in the following manner:

> If this
> Be but a vain belief, yet, oh! how oft,
> In darkness, and amid the many shapes
> Of joyless day-light; when the fretful stir
> Unprofitable, and the fever of the world,
> Have hung upon the beatings of my heart,
> How oft, in spirit, have I turned to thee
> O sylvan Wye! Thou wanderer through the woods,
> How often has my spirit turned to thee!
>
> (50–8)

The syntax is itself Shakespearean in its fidelity to the stops and starts of feeling. The long sentence never quite shapes a main clause of response to its opening conditional clause, continually dallying and finally accepting that exclamation will have to do the work of assertion in response to the original conditional. Hamlet's first soliloquy teems with exclamatory gestures that fail to go beyond themselves: 'O that this too too solid flesh would melt ...' (I. ii. 129); 'That it should come to this— ...' (I. ii. 137). It seems appropriate that, in addition to another allusion to Macbeth's 'life's fitful fever', Wordsworth summons the memory of Hamlet's lament: 'How weary, stale, flat, and unprofitable | Seem to me all the uses of this world' (I. ii. 133–4). Yet Wordsworth turns for release to the 'sylvan Wye', his spirit regaining its freedom through such thoughts; Hamlet will have to confront what he hopes is a 'spirit of health' (I. iv. 21) as he faces the unfolding truth that something is rotten in the state of Denmark. Wordsworth implies that he has his Hamlet-like moments of despair and won through to a post-tragic seren-ity, marked, among other things, by allusions to plays that have themselves inflections of calm and serenity.

[22] Bate (1986)102.
[23] Bate (1986) 102.

Thus, the concluding address to Dorothy draws on memories of *Antony and Cleopatra*, *As You Like It*, and *The Tempest* to reinforce its concluding mood of acceptance.[24] Octavius Caesar, contriving though he may be, says to Octavia: 'Farewell, my dearest sister, fare thee well. | The elements be kind to thee, and make | Thy spirits all of comfort' (III. ii. 39–41). Wordsworth, sometimes felt to be guilty of an Octavius-like use of Dorothy, not only addresses her with similar warmth ('My dear, dear Sister!', 122), but also seeks to release her imaginatively into her own life, in which the kindness of the elements will show itself as participating in her freedom: 'And let the misty mountain winds be free | To blow against thee' (137–8). Dorothy momentarily plays Ariel to her brother's Prospero, as we recall the latter's promise, 'Thou shalt be as free | As mountain winds' (*The Tempest*, I. ii. 495–6). In the same movement of feeling, an echo of *Romeo and Juliet* lends its own mixture of rapture and admonition to the Wordsworthian passage. When Romeo is leaving Juliet in the aubade scene in III. v, he asserts: 'Night's candles are burnt out, and jocund day | Stands tiptoe on the misty mountain tops. | I must be gone and live, or stay and die' (9–11). Wordsworth is conscious that no amount of natural beneficence can fend off the threat that 'solitude, or fear, or pain, or grief' (144) might be his sister's 'portion' (145). At the same time, there is the belief that nature's 'privilege' is 'Through all the years of this our life, to lead | From joy to joy' (125–6). Mason notes the echo of *As You Like It*, when Duke Senior says that 'this our life, exempt from public haunt, | Finds tongues in trees, books in the running brooks, | Sermons in stones, and good in everything' (II. i. 15–17): a celebration of pastoral that verges on the parodic.[25] Wordsworth redeems the Duke's nature-worship from facile optimism, incorporating it into his graver affirmation of 'joy'.

Shakespearean echo aids Wordsworthian expressiveness; it serves as a point towards which strength of feeling rushes and round which it gathers in the recollection and recreation in *The Prelude* X (1805) of the poet's nightmarish feelings in Paris just after the September Massacres. A number of allusions intensify the passage. Wordsworth writes, 'I thought of those September Massacres, | Divided from me by a little month' (64–5), echoing the Hamlet who in his first soliloquy laments that 'within a month … | A little month' after his father's death his mother was ready to marry, and 'post | … to incestuous sheets' with, his uncle (I. ii. 145, 147, 156–7). Both Hamlet and Wordsworth sense their proximity to catastrophic change; Hamlet is full of dismayed scorn; Wordsworth of a sense of near-apocalyptic and impending doom. Moreover, the poet is worked upon by feelings 'Until I seemed to hear a voice that cried, | To the whole City, "Sleep no more!"' (76–7). Stephen Gill writes that 'No reader is likely to miss the signalled quotation from *Macbeth* or the appropriateness of an allusion to another text which dramatizes the significance of power unleashed'.[26] This is so, yet Wordsworth manages to make the quotation seem his own; in context, even the fact that the words are English and from the

---

[24] The allusions are noted in Michael Mason (ed.), *Lyrical Ballads* (London: Longman, 1992) 213 n., 214 n.

[25] Hazlitt takes a more generous view: 'Never was there such beautiful moralising, equally free from pedantry or petulance', Bate (1992) 274.

[26] Stephen Gill, *William Wordsworth: The Prelude* (Cambridge: Cambridge University Press, 1991) 26.

most famous of English poets may speak of the vengeance which will be wreaked (to Wordsworth's dismay) by British forces upon the French. Moreover, he draws finely on Macbeth's own sense of self-division: 'Methought I heard a voice cry "Sleep no more; | Macbeth does murder sleep"' (II. ii. 34–5). Both voices, in play and poem, are internalized, yet appear to cry to character and poet as though they were external. Wordsworth extends the effects of guilt 'To the whole City', it and the poet complicit in the bloodbath licensed by the dreams of revolutionary reason.[27]

In 'Hart-Leap Well' Wordsworth uses Shakespearean tragic effects as a foil: 'The moving accident is not my trade, | To freeze the blood I have no ready arts' (97–8) is how the poem's 'Part Second' opens, alluding both to *Othello* and *Hamlet*. The allusions are meant, as Bate notes, to point up Wordsworth's own distinctness. [28] At the same time, they bring into play, in the act of warding off, ideas of adventure and terror that are functioning if subdued presences in the account of the hart's 'cruel leap' (140). When the shepherd remarks to the narrator, 'Some say that here a murder has been done, | And blood cries out for blood' (133–4), the echo of *Macbeth* III. iv. 121 ('Blood will have blood') develops the idea that the lyrical ballad and Shakespearean tragedy are threatening to occupy the same place: a threat kept in play even as it is exorcized by the natural piety of the poem's concluding exhortation 'Never to blend our pleasure or our pride | With sorrow of the meanest thing that feels' (175–6).[29] Again, in 'Ode: Intimations of Immortality', Wordsworth engages in difficult negotiation with Shakespearean tragedy when he speaks of valuing moments in childhood when the material world seemed to be 'not realized' (148), evidence of 'High instincts before which our mortal Nature | Did tremble like a guilty Thing surprized' (149–50). The language vibrates with an air of trembling awe, 'guilty' catching the attention with particular force. It is as though merely to be 'mortal' is to be 'guilty', a guilt that is of use in that it bears witness to our regard for 'High instincts'. Our 'mortal Nature' is 'surprized' by those 'High instincts' much as the ghost in *Hamlet* 'started like a guilty thing | Upon a fearful summons' when the 'cock crew' (I. i. 129–30, 128). Wordsworth enlists the idea of guilt from *Hamlet* as conducive to the discovery of deeper truths than are available in 'the light of common day' (76). In both cases the supernatural presses upon the natural with redefining power.

31.3

Coleridge's criticism of Shakespeare is famous for its responsive attention to detail, a responsiveness made possible by his fascination with larger issues. What he says about

[27] For valuable commentary, including the observation that the *Macbeth* allusion also occurs in William Godwin's *Caleb Williams*, see *The Prelude: The Four Texts (1798, 1799, 1805, 1850*, Jonathan Wordsworth (ed.), (London: Penguin, 1995)) 628.
[28] See the discussion in Bate (1986) 99.
[29] For the Shakespearean allusions in the poem, see Mason (1992) 218 n., 219 n.

Shakespeare warrants Charles Mahoney's praise for being uniquely 'at once abstract and particular, equal parts practical and speculative intervention'. It is concerned always, as Coleridge puts it, 'to prove that in all points from the most important to the most minute, the Judgement of Shakespeare is commensurate with his Genius'.[30] A few well-known examples must suffice to show his keenly appreciative antennae at work. He notes how in Marcellus' question from the opening scene of *Hamlet*, 'What, has *this thing* appear'd again to-night?', that 'Even the word "again" has its *credibilizing* effect'.[31] Not only do we engage in that 'willing suspension of disbelief for the moment, which constitutes poetic faith', but we also actively embrace Shakespeare's gift of a world we can enter.[32] Again, when Prospero tells Miranda of their expulsion from Milan, one involving 'Me & thy crying self', what is illustrated is 'The power of Poetry ... by a single word to produce that energy in the mind as compells the imagination to produce the picture'.[33]

His own poetry is comparatively restrained in its responsiveness to Shakespeare, and one can feel that Jonathan Bate's excellent study is at its most speculative in his attempt to find evidence of Shakespeare's presence in Coleridge. For example, Bate finds that '"Frost at Midnight" is like a Shakespearean soliloquy', and makes a decently persuasive case for a comparison between it and Bolingbroke's soliloquy in *2 Henry IV*, Act III, without doing very much more than suggesting potential likenesses and dissimilarities or dislodging Cowper from his position as the poem's presiding genius.[34] Coleridge alludes overtly to Shakespeare in a number of early poems, as when in the 1796 version of the 'Monody on Chatterton' he adapts a phrase from *King Lear* to would-be plangent lament over the fate of Thomas Otway who, as the Norton editors note, 'died in poverty': 'PITY hopeless hung her head, | While "mid the pelting of that merciless storm," | Sunk to the cold earth OTWAY's famish'd form!' (30–2).[35] This cadges an easy ride from the Shakespearean tragic chariot. More subtle, as Bate suggests, are the moments when Shakespeare appears as latent sponsor: the witches of *Macbeth* contributing their sorcery to the supernatural elements of *The Rime of the Ancient Mariner* and *Christabel*.

In the former work, the lines 'About, about, in reel and rout | The death-fires danced at night; | The water, like a witch's oils, | Burnt green, and blue and white' (127–30) recall the weird sisters' description of themselves as 'Posters of the sea and land' who 'do go about, about' (I. iii. 31, 32) and capture the mariner's (and the poem's) hidden sense of potentially sinister controlling forces at work in the universe. Significantly, the reference to one tragedy about a guilt-ridden hero follows a reference to a play in which the villainous hero ends up experiencing fear and remorse, *Richard III*. Here, though, the lines, 'Yea, slimy things did crawl with legs | Upon the slimy sea' (125–6), draw into

---

[30] Charles Mahoney, 'Coleridge and Shakespeare', in *The Oxford Handbook of Samuel Taylor Coleridge*, Frederick Burwick (ed.), (Oxford: Oxford University Press, 2009) 511, 513 (from where Coleridge is quoted).

[31] Bate (1992) 313.

[32] *Biographia Literaria*, ch. 14, in *Coleridge's Poetry and Prose*, Nicholas Halmi (ed.), Paul Magnuson, and Raimonda Modiano (New York: Norton, 2004) 490; hereafter *Coleridge Norton*.

[33] *Coleridge Norton*, 328

[34] Bate (1986) 65.

[35] Unless indicated otherwise, Coleridge's poetry is quoted from *Coleridge Norton*.

Coleridge's poetic reverie a recollection of Clarence's dream of drowning amid 'the slimy bottom of the deep' (I. iv. 32). Clarence is about to be murdered at Richard's behest, and the allusion establishes the mariner as a victim as well as some kind of latter-day Macbeth.[36] The poem orchestrates its Shakespearean echoes with tact; its shorter balladic lines refuse to compete with Shakespeare's iambic pentameters, even as they possess their own harmonies. And it orchestrates its echoes with affecting artistry. In the aftermath of the Albatross dropping from his neck, the mariner is simultaneously at his most piously Catholic and post-Shakespearean: 'To Mary Queen the praise be given! | She sent the gentle sleep from heaven, | That slid into my soul' (294–6). 'Mary Queen' pays a quasi-medieval homage, but what follows reworks Portia's description of mercy's gratuitous descent: 'It droppeth as the gentle rain from heaven' (IV. i. 185). 'She sent' makes the notion of a heavenly source even more securely stable than the Protestant inflection of 'It droppeth', with its refusal to rationalize a manifestation of grace. The detail of the echo plays a significant part in the poem's larger design. Portia's great speech brings into play an idea—that of divine mercy—which is more transcendent ideal than operative social principle. It is not an argument that wins the day, and she will fall back on legalistic technicality to outwit Shylock. Comparably the mariner may sense Mary's benign presence, but the poem will not leave us with the comforting conviction of living in a universe where a benevolent force watches over us.

In *Christabel* Geraldine suggests her evil nature and hints at some inner struggle when she switches from reinforcing Christabel's wish that her mother were present (196–7) to seeking to banish what in an unpublished annotation Coleridge calls 'The Mother of Christabel, who is now her Guardian Spirit'.[37] When 'with alter'd voice' (198) she says: 'Off, wandering mother! Peak and pine! | I have power to make thee flee' (199–200), she echoes the first witch's chant of destruction in *Macbeth* I. iii. describing how her afflicted victim shall 'dwindle, peak, and pine' (22).[38] Geraldine turns the last phrase into an imperative, an attempted increase in force that speaks of her 'alter'd' and, possibly, possessed state. The reference establishes both kinship and difference in Coleridge's treatment of evil. A similar conjunction of opposing vectors is operative at the close of 'Kubla Khan'. Coleridge enlists Theseus' description in *A Midsummer Night's Dream* of 'The poet's eye, in a fine frenzy rolling' (V. i. 12). The line finds an answerable correlative in Coleridge's depiction of the inspired Bard with 'flashing eyes' and 'floating hair'. Whereas Theseus is, at best, startled momentarily out of rationalist detachment, Coleridge brings us Romanticism's most potent image of the poet as ecstatic visionary, his syntax both confessing and overcoming that such an image is wished-for rather than confidently possessed.

At such moments, Coleridge affirms his ability to shape new narrative and lyrical structures out of various literary models and predecessors, especially Shakespeare, partly through his own possession of that musical power which he admired in *Venus*

---

[36] See Mason (1992) 184 n.
[37] *Coleridge Norton*, 168 n.
[38] *Coleridge Norton*, 168 n.

and Adonis. Coleridge praises as 'a gift of imagination' the presence in Shakespeare of 'the sense of musical delight, with the power of producing it', and his greatest poetry has an uncannily metapoetic dimension as it communicates such a sense and such a power.[39] It makes its readers aware of the workings of what in *Christabel* Coleridge calls 'figures strange and sweet, | All made out of the carver's brain' (173–4), often employing the trope of music, as though to assert the distinctiveness of its own poetic melody. 'That strain again!'(90), he exclaims towards the close of 'The Nightingale', after evoking with jubilant precision the 'choral minstrelsy' (80) of 'those wakeful Birds' (79). The allusion to Orsino's opening speech in *Twelfth Night*, with his longing for 'That strain again, it had a dying fall' (I. i. 4), is purposeful. It calls to mind a narcissistic indulgence from which it departs. Coleridge re-evokes the 'strain' to transmit to his son and his partners in the poem's 'conversation' (who include his readers) his wish to 'associate Joy' (109) with the night. Coleridge's new scenario writes itself with aplomb in the margins of Shakespeare's scene. On a smaller scale his brief unpublished quatrain, 'A Motto Adapted from *Love's Labour's Lost*', adapts its first two lines from the King's teasing question to Longueville (IV. iii. 131–4) and uses them as a springboard for a terse, affecting declaration of heartache:

> How oft I lay'd my wreathed arms athwart
> My bosom, to keep down my loving heart!
> And then the very pressure seem'd to make
> My loving Breast all heart; & heart-like, it would ake![40]

The King asks Longueville whether he 'never lay his wreathèd arms athwart | His loving bosom to keep down his heart' (IV. iii. 133–4). Coleridge first transfers 'loving' from 'bosom' to 'heart'; then, in a typical gesture of circularity (here wryly self-ironizing), he identifies 'loving Breast' and 'heart', suffusing rhyme and poem with a final recollection of how, in effect, his whole being 'would ake'.

Paradoxically, then, Coleridge's realization of the Shakespearean bequest results in some of the most assured and carefully differentiated Romantic responses to the writer he regarded as 'the Spinosistic deity—an omnipresent creativeness'.[41] Byron, as Jonathan Bate and Anne Barton bring out, couples detestation of Bardolatry with extensive allusive engagement with Shakespeare.[42] In a dialogue supposedly between Byron and Shelley about *Hamlet*, first published in 1830, he recalls neoclassical strictures, questioning the presence of conscious art in the plays: 'My dear fellow', the Byron figure says to 'Shelley', 'who can read this very play, and call Shakespeare a thoughtful artist?'[43] Whatever the authenticity of the dialogue, it succeeds in capturing that side of Byron

---

[39] Bate (1992) 148.

[40] Quoted from *Poetical Works: Poems (Reading Text)*, J. C. C. Mays (ed.), (Princeton: Princeton University Press, 2001).

[41] Bate (1992) 161.

[42] See Bate (1986) ch. 11 *passim*; Anne Barton, 'Byron and Shakespeare', in *The Cambridge Companion to Byron*, Drummond Bone (ed.), (Cambridge: Cambridge University Press, 2004) 224–35.

[43] Bate (1992) 339.

ventriloquized by Barton as akin to the person who 'only does it to annoy, because he knows it teases'.[44]

But Byron's own works bear witness against his supposed scepticism about Shakespeare's artistry. His practice of intertextual reference bespeaks admiration for Shakespeare's gift for the compelling phrase and image. 'Ode to Napoleon Buonaparte' uses its conflict-ridden, tortuous diction and rhythms to convey residual admiration, shock, baffled critique, and covert identification. Its ambivalences come to a focus in stanza 16 in which Byron sketches how Napoleon might respond to defeat: as a Promethean 'thief of fire' (136) whose conduct in 'that last act' (141), possibly 'a casual affair just before leaving for Elba', is said to be 'The very Fiend's arch mock' (142).[45] The last line echoes Othello's outcry against 'The fiend's arch mock, | To lip a wanton in a secure couch, | And to suppose her chaste' (IV. i. 69–70). Byron redirects the trajectory of emotional charge in his original. Othello curses what he feels to be the fiendish horror of sexual betrayal; he feels himself to be the butt of the fiend's mockery; Byron half-approves the Satanic pride evident in Napoleon's 'arch mock', going on to assert of the 'very Fiend' that 'He in his fall preserved his pride, | And, if a mortal, had as proudly died!' (143–4). The lines suggest a latent hope that Napoleon will have the haughty stamina to sustain a comparable 'pride'. It is as though Byron, Iago-like, turns Othello's words to his own purposes.

In this 'Ode', when he describes how Napoleon might 'trace with thine all idle hand | In loitering mood upon the sand | That Earth is now as free!' (122–4), Byron may also have been influenced, B. W. Procter suggested, by Edmund Kean's vividly dramatic portrayal of Richard III on the eve of Bosworth Field.[46] Here Shakespeare spurs a Byronic performative gesture, as is the case in many works from his pre-*ottava rima*, 'serious' career when he sat on the board of the Drury Lane theatre. The Byronic self in works such as the third canto of *Childe Harold's Pilgrimage* dons Shakespearean robes with tragic gusto. Thus, he concludes stanza 113, with its haughty, self-dramatizing contempt for 'the world' (1049), by claiming kinship with the Macbeth who regrets that 'For Banquo's issue have I *filed* my mind' (III. i. 66; Byron's emphasis in his noting of the echo). Byron converts regret into something closer to proud assertion, even boast: 'I stood | Among them, but not of them, in a shroud | Of thoughts which were not their thoughts, and still could, | Had I not filed my mind, which thus itself subdued' (1054–7).

Such self-defilement comes to seem like a mark of distinction. It is telling that Byron promotes Macbeth's use of the first person pronoun from an unstressed to a stressed syllabic position; telling, too, that the same stanza features Byron as a form of Coriolanus. 'I have not flatter'd its rank breath' (1050), he says of the world, as though rehearsing for an

[44] Barton (2004) 226.

[45] See *Byron's Poetry and Prose: Authoritative Texts, Criticism*, selected by Alice Levine (ed.), (New York: Norton, 2010) 161 n. Where possible, this edition is used for quotations from Byron's poetry; otherwise *Lord Byron: The Major Works*, Jerome McGann (ed.), (Oxford: Oxford University Press, 1986) is used, or McGann's multi-volume edition (see footnote 51).

[46] For this observation, see Bate (1986), 238. Byron seems also here to be remembering the account of Jesus writing on the ground in the episode narrated in John 8.

updated version of Shakespeare's truculent but impressive hero, with his contempt for 'the mutable rank-scented meinie' (III. i. 70) whom he will 'not flatter' (III. i. 71). Hazlitt views Byron in comparable terms, but with more hostility than admiration, in his essay on him in *The Spirit of the Age*, quoting from *Coriolanus* to capture the way in which the Noble Lord is 'the creature of his own will': 'He holds no communion with his kind', Hazlitt continues, 'but stands alone without mate or fellow—"As if a man were author of himself, | And knew no other kin"'.[47] This stance for Hazlitt is at one with a troubling dimension of Shakespeare's play itself, the fact that it appears to confirm how 'The language of poetry naturally falls in with the language of power'.[48]

This way of reworking Shakespeare confers glamour on Byron without seeming to pay more than indifferent homage to the earlier writer. Byron implies that his world-suffusing 'being more intense' (*Childe Harold's Pilgrimage*, 3. 47) subsumes previous examples of heroic suffering, so many adumbrations of his own potently dramatized anguish. In *Manfred*, his hero raids the Shakespearean word-hoard, notably that available in *Hamlet*, to assert his uniqueness in the act of conceding his ineluctable participation in the human condition:

> How beautiful is all this visible world!
> How glorious in action and itself!
> But we, who name ourselves its sovereigns, we,
> Half dust, half deity, alike unfit
> To sink or soar, with our mix'd essence make
> A conflict of its elements, and breathe
> The breath of degradation and of pride ...
>
> (I. ii. 37–43)

The echo of *Hamlet's* 'What a piece of work is a man!' (II. ii. 305) speech is evident.[49] Yet Manfred out-Hamlets Hamlet, soliloquizing in poetry where Hamlet converses in prose. Hamlet praises 'man' as 'the beauty of the world' (II. ii. 308–9); Manfred reserves his admiration for 'the visible world'. For Hamlet, it is man who is said to be 'in action ... like an angel' (II. ii. 307–8); for Manfred, nature is 'glorious in action and itself'. Hamlet, in despair, sees man as but 'a quintessence of dust' (II. ii.310); Manfred speaks of 'our mix'd essence', 'Half dust, half deity'. Byron does not so much paraphrase Shakespeare as build on his Renaissance sense of division to shape a Romantic image in which man is not just 'like a god', but is 'half deity'. Manfred captures a Romantic awareness of twinned possibility and self-destruction; he is able to see clearly our ironized capacity to misshape our ends and 'make/A conflict', where 'make' speaks of Manfred's existentialist sense of human responsibility.

---

[47] William Hazlitt, *The Spirit of the Age, Or, Contemporary Portraits*, ed. E. D. Mackerness (London: Collins, 1969) 113.
[48] William Hazlitt, *Characters of Shakespeare's Plays*, with introduction by Arthur Quiller-Couch (London: Oxford University Press, 1916) 56.
[49] Noted in Norton, 256 n.

By the time of *Don Juan* Byron has found a form that departs from romance travelogue or mental theatre in favour of 'epic satire' (14. 790). Here his relationship with Shakespeare is playful, even teasing, even as Bate is correct to assert that 'By writing in a form totally different from anything in Shakespeare, he avoided rivalry'.[50] Shakespeare is caught up in Byron's cavalierly intertextual net. When the elegiac spell cast by Haidée's death breaks on the rocks of Byron's cynically disruptive 'fear of seeming rather touched myself' (4. 588), the poem takes us back to 'Juan, left half-kill'd some stanzas back' (4. 592), whimsically glossing his 'Wounded and fetter'd' state with a tag from *Macbeth*, 'cabin'd, cribb'd, confined' (4. 593). The fun here lies in the gap between the tragic Macbeth, consumed by his own anxieties, and the picaresque Juan, at the mercy of pirates and poetical plotting.

Again, Donna Inez's power over her husband extends to all women, according to the narrator, who says of men, that 'you might "brain them with their lady's fan;"| And sometimes ladies hit exceeding hard, | And fans turn falchions in fair hands, | And why and wherefore no one understands' (I. 165–8). The quotation alludes to *I Henry IV*, II. iv, and Hotspur's scornful, '"Zounds, an I were now by this rascal, I could brain him with his lady's fan!"' (21–2). If the allusion suggests Byron's relish for Shakespeare's vigour, his own inspired reworking of the original, caught in spun-out rhymes that take the stanza in unpredictable directions, shows how the Shakespearean sparks his own creativity. There is surely a submerged reference to *King Lear* in the phrase 'And fans turn falchions', recalling, and lightly playing against, Lear's 'I have seen the day with my good biting falchion | I would have made them skip' (V. iii. 251–2). Byron and Shakespeare both deal with questions of gender struggle: an overbearing wife and hesitant husband in Byron, a near-despotic father in contention with his daughters in Shakespeare. But the principal point is the way in which Shakespeare is drawn to endorse, give texture to, and illustrate Byron's sense of life as exceeding taxonomy or generic category, except for the elastic, capacious form of his 'versified Aurora Borealis' (7. 11).

31.4

Byron, like Shelley, wrote plays under the Shakespearean shadow, clearly fighting to exorcize it in Byron's case. *Marino Faliero* deserves more than the label of 'lame imitation'. Even the most apparent of allusions use Shakespearean phrasing to convey a marked differentiation. The Doge asserting 'Farewell social memory! all thoughts in common! | And sweet bonds which link old friendships' (III. ii. 327–8) evokes the Othello who cries, 'Farewell the tranquil mind, farewell content' (III. ii. 353), only to point up difference: in the Doge's case, the farewell is to an idea of social community rather than to an ideal of military self-sufficiency.[51] One can apply to Byron Bate's justified praise for Shelley in

---

[50] Bate (1986) 239.
[51] Quoted from vol. IV (1986; 1992 corr.) of Lord Byron, *The Complete Poetical Works* Jerome J. McGann (ed.), 7 vols (Oxford: Clarendon Press, 1980–93).

The Cenci for the way in which, in its use of Shakespeare, 'similarity is compounded with difference'.[52] Shelley, for his part, manages to incorporate Shakespearean echoes and allusions into new wholes, guided by his instinct for what Jerrold E. Hogle calls 'trans-ference': a releasing of the original from its context so as it take on a changed and often corrective form.[53] Thus, when George III is depicted as 'An old, mad, blind, despised, and dying King' in the first line of the sonnet 'England in 1819' it is not only the form of the sonnet that is reversed (sestet proceeding octave), but also the sympathy elicited by Lear's description of himself as 'a very foolish, fond old man' (IV. vi. 53). Shelley's line is remarkable for its evocation of a figure who embodies what is worst about Lear, without any redemptive qualities, even if George is part of the world of 'graves from which a glo-rious Phantom may | Burst' (13–14).

Shakespeare participates in Shelley's project of world re-making. He sponsors the Romantic poet's revolutionary *Queen Mab*, which takes its title from the central fig-ure in Mercutio's brilliant flight of fancy in *Romeo and Juliet* (I. iv. 55–103). Whereas Mercutio is wry and fantastical about 'dreams, | Which are the children of an idle brain' (I. iv. 96–7), however, Shelley's poem depicts Mab as able to 'rend | The veil of mor-tal frailty' (I. 180–1) so that 'the spirit | ... may know | How soonest to accomplish the great end | For which it has its being' (181–4).[54] His engagement with Shakespeare takes its place in his sure sense of how allusion contributes to original creation: 'one great poet is a masterpiece of nature', he writes in the Preface to *Prometheus Unbound*, 'which another not only ought to study but must study' (p. 231). Aeschylus and Milton are reworked in Shelley's lyrical drama, but in his handling of genre, as he moves from near-tragic agon to final cosmic masque, he invokes a Shakespearean range; he not only 'touches both the sublimity of *Lear* and the ethereal music of *The Tempest*', but also the urgent dialectic of *Troilus and Cressida*.[55] When Shelley indicates that, in the renovated universe human beings will rule 'Over themselves', but remain 'man' (III. iv. 197), the affirmation refutes Achilles' realistically cynical view in *Troilus and Cressida* that 'not a man, for being simply man, | Hath any honour, but honour for those honours | That are without him' (III. iii. 74–6).

[52] Bate (1986) 211.

[53] See Jerrold E. Hogle, *Shelley's Process: Radical Transference and the Development of His Major Works* (New York: Oxford University Press, 1988). In analysing *Prometheus Unbound* 3.3, he asserts that 'quotations are not simply blended in the Promethean cave ... they remain "differences"', 203 (his allusions include one to *King Lear* V. iii). For the argument that Shelley wishes the reader to 'experience [*Prometheus Unbound*] as though it is autonomous, not allusive', see Earl R. Wasserman, *Shelley: A Critical Reading* (Baltimore: Johns Hopkins University Press, 1971) 274.

[54] For detail of Shelley's use of Shakespeare, see various editions of the poetry, including *The Poems of Shelley*, Kelvin Everest and others (eds.), 3 vols to-date (London: Longman, 1989–) and *The Complete Poetry of Percy Bysshe Shelley*, Donald, Reiman, Neil Fraistat, and Nora Crook (eds.), 3 vols to-date (Baltimore: Johns Hopkins University Press, 2000-); for relevant discussion, see also Bernard Beatty, 'Shelley, Shakespeare, and the Theatre', in *The Oxford Handbook of Percy Bysshe Shelley*, Michael O'Neill and Anthony Howe (eds), with the Assistance of Madeleine Callaghan (Oxford: Oxford University Press, 2012). Shelley is quoted from *Percy Bysshe Shelley: The Major Works*, Zachary Leader and Michael O'Neill (eds), (2003; Oxford: Oxford University Press, 2009).

[55] Bate (1986) 204.

Shelley's re-orchestration of Shakespeare in *The Cenci* is superbly sure-footed, despite F. R. Leavis' strictures in *Revaluation*. Often he ironizes the attempts of characters to strike a tragic pose by suggesting their strained assumption of a false rhetoric. Such is the case with Giacomo's attempt to win the upper hand in his debate with himself and the scheming Orsino after the news that Cenci has escaped: Shelley's replaying of *Othello* in 'And yet once quenched I cannot thus relume | My father's life' (III. ii. 51–2) brings to a focus the play's fascination with chance and choice, contingency and determined act, while coolly refusing to invest Giacomo with tragic status. It is as though Giacomo were quoting Shakespeare only to find his image deconstructed by Orsino's subsequent reference to 'Your own *extinguished* years of youth and hope' (III. ii. 55; emphasis added). Throughout, Shelley provokes recollection of a Shakespearean scenario in order to point up difference.

Shelley and Byron adapt Shakespeare to their lyric purposes, Byron alluding to the desolate Macbeth of the last act in his 'On This Day I Complete My Thirty-Sixth Year' ('My days are in the yellow leaf', 5); Shelley pointedly echoing *Hamlet* (Q version, IV. iv. 28) when in 'To a Skylark' he laments that human beings are condemned to 'look before and after, | And pine for what is not' (86–7), or adopting the role of an Ariel addressing Miranda in 'With a Guitar. To Jane', finding a voice through 'this silent token | Of more than ever can be spoken' (11–12). But it is Keats whose lyric poetry most demonstrably and deeply shows an absorption of Shakespearean influence. Even in a narrative poem such as 'The Eve of St. Agnes' Keats takes his bearings from Shakespeare in ways that lend themselves to lyric concentrations of feeling. Madeline has been told how, if they obey certain rites, 'Young virgins might have visions of delight, | And soft adorings from their loves receive | Upon the honeyed middle of the night' (47–9).[56] That last line calls to mind Isabella's description of how she will meet Angelo 'Upon the heavy middle of the night' (IV. i. 34). Christopher Ricks rightly notes that 'Keats' adaptation of the line converted its sombre pregnant physicality into a delighted physicality'.[57] One might add that Keats imbues heaviness with honeyed eroticism without surrendering Shakespeare's suggestion of unease: suggestions that, in Keats' case, hover, or might hover, round the phrase 'visions of delight', with its hint (in 'visions') of the impalpable and illusory.[58]

John Kerrigan argues helpfully that Keats' practice in 'The Eve of St. Agnes' differs from Shakespearean narrative in *The Rape of Lucrece* by allowing 'objects' (and, one might add, situations) to remain 'unglossed'.[59] Keats' delight in Shakespeare's 'fine things said unintentionally' comes close to capturing one aspect of his response to Shakespeare, the fineness of phrasing having no palpable design on the reader, but emerging through an 'intensity of working out conceits', where 'conceits' means 'conceptions' as well as 'fanciful, ingenious,

---

[56] Quoted from Miriam Allott (ed.), *The Poems of John Keats* (London: Longman, 1970).

[57] Ricks (1976) 136–7 (137).

[58] Paul Edmondson (in an email to the author) notes a possible echo of 'figures of delight', line 11 of Sonnet 98, which supports this point (about the potentially illusory nature of the 'visions').

[59] John Kerrigan, 'Keats and Lucrece', in *On Shakespeare and Early Modern Literature: Essays* (Oxford: Oxford University Press, 2001) 53.

or witty notions' (see *OED* 1 and 8).[60] The way in which Keats' odes and longer poems offer felicities of phrasing bears witness to an imagination prepared to relish each unfolding stage of an imaginative work, delighting in accumulated ramifications of meanings.

So, *Endymion* delights in *The Tempest*'s evocation of life's dream-like state (IV. i. 148–58), but turns Shakespearean dream into a source of endless creativity, 'The Morphean fount | Of that fine element that visions, dreams, | And fitful whims of sleep are made of' (I. 747–9).[61] Fine phrases do more than admire their aestheticized reflections; they speak of a Romantic pursuit of poetry itself. 'Shakespearean hieroglyphics', to use Keats' phrase from a review of Edmund Kean, allow for 'pleasures both sensual and spiritual' in Keats more than in any of the Romantics.[62] His markings, comments, and practice show him highly alert to Shakespeare's tragic vision; in 'On Sitting Down to Read *King Lear* Once More', for example, he speaks of setting himself to 'assay | The bitter-sweet of this Shakespearian fruit' (7–8). In harvesting such 'bitter-sweet' in and for his work, he created, in his great odes, a meditative art of turn and counterturn that bears witness to a 'knowledge of contrast, feeling for light and shade'.[63]

Influence runs deeply and alchemizes into new creation. Sonnet 31, with its image of the beloved as 'the grave where buried love doth live, | Hung with the trophies of my lovers gone' (9–10), assures the young man that 'thou, all they, hast all the all of me' (14). Keats' 'Ode on Melancholy' wrests a rich defeat out of the jaws of a difficult victory, when the quester who gains access to Melancholy's 'sovran shrine' (26) finds that his reward is to 'be among her cloudy trophies hung' (30).[64] Similarly, Edgar's admonition in *King Lear*, possibly contestable in context, that 'Ripeness is all' (V. ii. 11) flowers into the settled, equable vision of 'To Autumn', a poem able to accept both the arresting and arrested moment, and the fact of temporality, of living 'While barrèd clouds bloom the soft-dying day' (25) in a Shakespearean synthesis of glowing and expiration (see Sonnet 73, 9–11). Such moments pervade Keats' work. They are informed by a response to Shakespeare, even as, for Keats as for the other Romantics, Shakespeare is a stimulus to his own 'mental pursuit'.[65]

SELECT BIBLIOGRAPHY

Barton, Anne (2004) 'Byron and Shakespeare', in *The Cambridge Companion to Byron*, ed. Drummond Bone (Cambridge: Cambridge University Press), 224–35.
Bate, Jonathan (1986) *Shakespeare and the English Romantic Imagination* (Oxford: Clarendon Press).

---

[60] Keats, *Letters*, I. 89.
[61] For the suggested echo, see Allott (1970) 152 n.; see also the discussion in Christopher Ricks, 'Keats's Sources, Keats's Allusions', in *The Cambridge Companion to John Keats*, Susan Wolfson (ed.), (Cambridge: Cambridge University Press, 2001) 158–9.
[62] Quoted from White (1987) 89.
[63] Keats, *Letters*, 2. 360.
[64] For the suggested echo, see Allott (1970) 541 n.
[65] Keats, *Letters*, 1. 242.

—— (1989) *Shakepearean Constitutions: Politics, Theatre, Criticism 1730–1830* (Oxford: Clarendon Press).

——(1992) (ed.) *The Romantics on Shakespeare* (London: Penguin).

Beatty, Bernard (2012) 'Shelley, Shakespeare, and Theatre', in *The Oxford Handbook of Percy Bysshe Shelley*, Michael O'Neill and Anthony Howe (eds.), with the Assistance of Madeleine Callaghan (Oxford: Oxford University Press) 546–60 .

Clark, David L (1992) 'How To Do Things with Shakespeare: Illustrative Theory and Practice in Blake's *Pity*', in *The Mind in Creation: Essays on English Romantic Literature in Honour of Ross G. Woodman*, J. Douglas Kneale (ed.) (Montreal: McGill-Queen's University Press) 106–33.

Hogle, Jerrold E. (1988) *Shelley's Process: Radical Transference and the Development of His Major Works* (New York: Oxford University Press).

Kerrigan, John (2001) 'Keats and Lucrece', in *On Shakespeare and Early Modern Literature: Essays* (Oxford: Oxford University Press) 41–65.

Mahoney, Charles (2009) 'Coleridge and Shakespeare', in *The Oxford Handbook of Samuel Taylor Coleridge*, Frederick Burwick (ed.), (Oxford: Oxford University Press) 498–514.

Spurgeon, Caroline (1929) *Keats's Shakespeare: A Descriptive Study Based on New Material* 2nd edn (London: Oxford University Press).

White, R. S. (1987) *Keats as a Reader of Shakespeare* (Norman: University of Oklahoma Press).

....

CHAPTER 32

SHAKESPEAREAN BEING

The Victorian Bard

....

HERBERT F. TUCKER

32.1

....

'Who is it that can tell me who I am?' (*King Lear* I. iv. 225). Lear's question, shadowed by the abdication of political sovereignty he has just performed in public, savours already of the existentially involuted ordeal that gapes four long Acts ahead of him. The tone of the question accordingly hovers between angry indignation and pathetic modesty. In the mouth of a patriarchal king, it is flagrantly rhetorical: nobody tells Lear where to get off. Yet the question is also insistently genuine. The misgivings of unaccommodated man—suddenly vulnerable, stripped of his social lendings—whisper riddles of identity that Lear cannot solve, and that he begins to suspect nobody else can either. Two parallel clauses ('who is it', 'who I am') frame in a nutshell the play's central concern with what can or can't be said about the self in its wandering between two worlds: one dead (the realm of fixed hierarchy and role-prescription), the other powerless to be born (the modern condition of free self-actualization).

This no-man's-land charts a zone of cultural overlap to which Victorian poets' reception and transmission of a Shakespearean legacy consistently refers. During a long epoch that was defined by unstoppable if incremental Reform, and that in anxious cultural self-assessment regularly compared Victoria's reign to Elizabeth's back in the glory days of Reformation, the literature of the later 19th century placed poetry's prestige at the disposal of modern selfhood. Like the prose of bourgeois realism, which overtook verse as the century's medium of choice for continuous narratives of self-fashioning and its discontents, Victorian poetry bestowed on the ascendant ideology of individualism both enthusiastic articulation and austere critique. And it did so on terms distinct from the novel's. Discontinuity, instantaneous intimacy, sensation now abstractly elemental, now embodied with a stark directness: these were among the features that verse's charter to embody literary content, all the way down to the micro-levels of verbal structure, was with increasing urgency conscripted to enforce.

The Victorian was the last major literary period whose poets almost unanimously adhered to the accentual-syllabic prosody that English poetry had settled on just before Shakespeare began writing, and that Shakespeare's influence had done much to establish in its norms and, dialectically with those norms, its extremes of tolerance. In his Sonnets, his stanzaic and nonce song forms, and above all the athleticism of his dramatic blank verse, Shakespeare showed the Victorians, as he had shown generations of poets before them, how the tension between a fixed, recognized form and the insubordinate energies of passion or intellection or deceit might confer local habitation on contradictions roughly analogous to those Lear's question places before us.[1] In dramatic prosody the force of individuation wrestled with the discipline of circumstance—the givenness of the world in which the modern self must find itself—to build up and refine character. And it was the category of *character*, across a century of Shakespeare criticism inaugurated by Coleridge and Hazlitt and culminating in A. C. Bradley, that preeminently governed the Victorian literary appropriation of Shakespeare in general, and his poetic influence in particular.[2]

Each of the two most conspicuous Victorian initiatives in poetic genre was devoted to the development of literary character; each was manifestly, consciously, derived from a Shakespearean precedent. From the Sonnets, to which Romantic generic transvaluations had lately given new cachet within Shakespeare's oeuvre, there flowed by mid-century an impressive pageant of book-length lyric sequences. Some maintained the sonnet form, albeit seldom in its English or Shakespearean variant: Elizabeth Barrett Browning's *Sonnets from the Portuguese* (1850), Dante Gabriel Rossetti's *The House of Life* (1868–81), Augusta Webster's *Mother and Daughter* (1895), and, in briefer compass, George Eliot's *Brother and Sister* (1874) and Christina Rossetti's *Monna Innominata* (1881) are only the best-known exemplars of a Victorian renaissance in the composition of sequenced sonnets wherein, even for the Italianate Rossettis, Shakespeare loomed supreme. Love consistently furnishes the theme of these works, as the intimacies of dyadic interplay and self-analysis, which sonnet form famously facilitates, sustain moments of subjectivity

---

[1] Every stanzaic form employed in Shakespeare's narrative poetry found a Victorian imitator. The sesta rima of *Venus and Adonis* coldly furnished forth Bulwer-Lytton's epic *King Arthur* (1849), the rhyme royal of *Lucrece* occurs repeatedly in Morris' *The Earthly Paradise* (1868–70), and the 'abba' quatrain of 'The Phoenix and the Turtle' nearly anticipates that of Tennyson's *In Memoriam* (1850). On the nineteenth-century influence of Shakespeare's tetrameter song lyrics see Jonathan Bate, *Shakespeare and the English Romantic Imagination* (Oxford: Clarendon Press, 1986) 62.

[2] This topic is deftly opened and set in broad context by Jonathan Arac, 'Hamlet, Little Dorrit, and the History of Character', in Michael Hays (ed.), *Critical Conditions: Regarding the Historical Moment* (Minneapolis and London: University of Minnesota Press, 1992) 82–96, to whose focus on fiction may be added the emphasis on 'Action in Character, rather than Character in Action', which Browning signalled in the preface to his first play *Strafford* (1837). See also Gary Taylor, *Reinventing Shakespeare A Cultural History, from the Restoration to the Present* (New York: Weidenfeld and Nicolson, 1989) 221–3.

heightened by the effort to imagine the consciousness of the beloved. These moments of intense interiority are in turn strung like beads on a narrative line whose outcome, be it for better or worse, met the 19th-century's appetite for *Bildung*: the moving portraiture of a self matured and instructed by experience of the heart's events. The Shakespearean pattern of character-building persisted even into sequences that adapted or replaced sonnetry *per se*: George Meredith's sixteen-liners in *Modern Love* (1862), Coventry Patmore's blander quatrains from *The Angel in the House* (1863), and above all Tennyson's *In Memoriam* (1850), where the plangent central claim 'I loved thee, Spirit, and love, nor can | The soul of Shakspeare love thee more' (61.11–12) discloses the currency of feeling in which this Victorian genre trades, even where feeling proves bluntly embittered as in Meredith, or ironically wry as in so remote a congener as Arthur Hugh Clough's *Amours de Voyage* (1858).

In the poetic sequence, objective conditions ripen or chasten the core urgencies of internalized lyricism. Untold but insistently implied—and, like Shakespeare's Sonnets, ordinarily numbered so as, in part, to make this point—the emplotment that is sequence not only puts the constituent lyrics in each other's context but anchors the ensemble within a history whose shape accumulates an authority like fate's: an envelope of events outside the text and (what amounts to the same thing) beyond the lyric speaker's capacity to control. Barrett Browning's scrupulous defences against love are unavailing; in *Modern Love* the shipwreck of his marriage is something the husband can neither forfend nor repair. Imbalance between character and action—the surplus of explicit interior discourse in the text over implicit outward action in the world—owed more to Shakespeare than the example of his Sonnets. Tennyson implied as much when he subtitled his lyric sequence *Maud* (1855) a 'monodrama' and spoke of it as a miniature *Hamlet*: a drama that was all soliloquy, its constituent phases of passionate rumination informed at every turn by actions like a churchgoing, an arranged marriage, a duel that, while they occur off-page, exert an iron grip on the soliloquizing protagonist's evolving understanding of himself. The floor is his alone, by monodramatic design, yet the sobering truth of *Maud* is that it is the world that tells him who he is.

Thus the poetic sequence submitted lyric autonomy, that jewel in the Victorian ideological inheritance from Romanticism, to the test of time, which during the great age of literary serialization usually meant the test of history in its manifold cultural impingement on the self's postulated freedom. A test more strenuous, and more manifestly theatrical, was imposed by the second major generic innovation effected by Victorian poetry, the refinement of the dramatic monologue. Here again an individual speaker engrosses discourse; here again the discursive field proves to be criss-crossed with overdetermining constraints. First among these is the presence of a silent auditor, who in the full-dress Browning monologue serves as the world's delegate reinforcing class, gender, and other culturally specific norms (the police in 'Fra Lippo Lippi', 1855, offer a textbook example), and thereby transmuting poetic lyricism to more or less stagily rhetorical performance that suggests a spectrum of Shakespearean analogues from, say, Antony's funeral oration in *Julius Caesar* (III. ii) to the meditation on death that in *Richard II* makes a man of a king and, for a space, tongue-ties his attending nobles (III. ii. 140–73).

The auditor may, however, be omitted without loss to the essential generic effect, and the monologue be made a soliloquy indeed: the term occurs once ('Soliloquy of the Spanish Cloister'), the phenomenon often, in Browning's generically inaugural chapbooks from the 1840s. A fully developed instance of the soliloquy greets us, aptly enough, in 'Caliban upon Setebos' (1864). Although in Browning's monologue the aboriginal islander of *The Tempest* is discovered in total isolation, and loosens his tongue only after assuring himself that it is siesta time even in heaven, everything he freely goes on to utter confirms his mental confinement within manacles of primitive but unbreakable cultural manufacture: Caliban's leisure activities, from sado-masochistic child's play with flora and fauna up to higher-critical theological speculation, all reproduce the same grim structures of impotent resentment under discipline that regulate his working conditions as a colonial slave.

So it is across the board with the most cogently imagined Victorian free-standing verse soliloquies. Augusta Webster's kept, abandoned, or waiting women in *Dramatic Studies* (1866) and *Portraits* (1870) typically speak alone, but their solitude is so swiftly peopled with half-internalized, half-contested other voices that monologue verges on dialogue. When 'The Happiest Girl in the World' enjoys her recently declared fiancé's absence, so 'that I may think of him and tell myself | what to be his means, now that I am his' (lines 9–10), she has already begun performing scripts of Victorian womanhood dictated by others, laid to heart, and now told by herself to herself in a desperate, Lear-like effort at identity projection. The speaker's effort, and the more capable if more dismayed effort that Webster's poem exacts of the reader, belong on the same continuum of experiments in gender imagination where we also find Mary Cowden Clarke's *The Girlhood of Shakespeare's Heroines* and a shelf-ful of only less rash sister studies.[3] The explicit performativity of gender in Shakespeare's comedies, fed by lively awareness of the way femininity was necessarily impersonated on Shakespeare's stage, made the dramatic verse monologue an audition space even more eligible for gendered roles than for subject positions assigned, like Caliban's above, on the basis of race and class.

Only less striking, because more fully anticipated in earlier literary periods, was this Victorian genre's performances of masculinity. Browning's Duke ('My Last Duchess', 1842) and eponymous Andrea del Sarto (1855) tie themselves into rhetorical knots at a familiar Victorian nexus where marital dysfunction intersects the accumulation of prestige and profit in a man's world: definitively bourgeois concerns, which this poet repeatedly brought into burning focus by going back to the emergent urbane individualism of the Italian Renaissance where, among Englishmen, the author of *Othello* and *The Merchant of Venice* had found them first. It was from entanglements such as these—which are the very stuff of the Victorian dramatic monologue—that Tennyson undertook to disengage a pristine masculine ideal in 'Ulysses' (1842). Perhaps the best-known instance of its genre, this poem may be the most anomalous as well; for the speaker is a veritable generic Houdini, unravelling one by one the ties of kingship, marriage,

[3] *The Girlhood of Shakespeare's Heroines, in a Series of Fifteen Tales* (London: Smith, 1851).

paternity, fatherland, religion, and culture itself. Shedding as restrictive impediments every attribute that, according to the logic that confers on the dramatic agent his *persona*, defines the self, Ulysses emerges in the poem's infinitive finale ('To strive, to seek, to find, and not to yield') as sheer will: a Marlovian Faust or Tamburlaine, if not a Dantesque Ulysses; a figure pre-Shakespearean in his archetypal escape act, and to that extent negatively definitive of the statutes of limitation that identify Victorian poetic selves as essentially Shakespearean.[4]

32.2

I have outlined the genres of lyric sequence and dramatic monologue early, and at some length, because they constitute the widest and deepest aspects of Shakespeare's poetic bequest to Victorian literature. Admittedly a more impartial history than I am practising would start at a more obvious place: the steady barge traffic in pastiche verse drama (the majority closeted, some not) that floated its largely unregarded way down the 19th century towards oblivion. Given the insatiable Victorian appetite for time travel—the *succès d'estime* that knock-offs of manifestly Shakespearean dramaturgy by Henry Taylor, Serjeant Talfourd, and others enjoyed early in the period—ambitious poets up and down the scale of talent were tempted to try their hand at history plays too: Browning (who while young had an *entrée* with the actor-manager William Macready until it was forfeited by the oddity of his scripts); Tennyson (who in mellow Laureate years under command-performance conditions wrote frosty historical dramas attended by all the best people); Swinburne and the poetess-couple known as Michael Field (whose plays were meant for the study and have stayed there). These superior instances were tips of an iceberg of Elizabethan–Jacobean imitation. Like many aspects of Victorian theatrical production of Shakespeare's own plays, these examples expressed a depth of cryogenic reverence that held the Bard in a state of suspended animation, that should be acknowledged as part of our story here, but that should not be mistaken for living influence.[5] Writ large, Shakespearean designs did nourish robust contemporary work in the novel, whose generic distinctness from dramaturgy freed the likes of Dickens and George Eliot from the big chill that refrigerated poets seeking to engage Shakespeare at the macro level. Perhaps the best of the poetic lot was Browning's *Pippa Passes* (1841), an experimental script that, if it ominously lathers into soap-operatic melodrama when Scene 1 rewrites *Macbeth*, crackles into new literary life when it sets song against prose in a heteroglot modal medley.

---

    [4] See Adrian Poole, *Shakespeare and the Victorians* (London: Thomson, 2004) 53, 83, on aspects of Shakespearean character (Falstaff, Hamlet) that fed into this decontextualizing 'kind of drama'.
    [5] All this dramaturgical pomp found its confirmatory underside in pantomimic farce, e. g. W. S. Gilbert's *Rosencrantz and Guildenstern: A Tragic Episode in Three Tableaux, Founded on an Old Danish Legend* (1891).

Victorian poets found Shakespeare's influence much more congenial on a small rather than a large scale. Just this point sustains the gravamen of one of the canonical essays of Victorian poetics, Matthew Arnold's preface to *Poems* (1853). Arnold scolds modern poets for preferring superficial effects of phraseology to the architectural infra-structure of a significant 'poetical action', and he cinches his arguments with reference to Shakespeare. Like all great writers, Shakespeare knew a poetical action when he saw one, yet his gift for 'happy, abundant, and ingenious expression' tended 'to throw into comparative shade his other excellences as a poet. Here has been the mischief.'[6] One poet's mischief, of course, is another's opportunity. Is it any wonder when a writer even of Arnold's poise is obliged to introduce such a critique by an act of ritual genuflection ('Shakespeare: a name never to be mentioned without reverence')—when indeed the pretext for Arnold's preface is to explain the suppression of his own long verse drama *Empedocles on Etna* as unworthy—that poets in his day should take the main chance and imitate Shakespeare on the grounds of ad hoc ingenuity where they at least stood a chance of drawing even?

Arnold's immediate antagonists were poets of the Spasmodic school, a contemporary flash in the pan of mid-century literature whose genuine but brief glory seems foretold in the single-mindedness with which, in the person of J. Stanyan Bigg or Alexander Smith, they struck off similes like sparks from the forge of ostentatiously spontane-ous inspiration. Through these easy marks, however, Arnold meant to arraign bigger game: Keats and Byron, certain antinomian or luxuriating strains of Romanticism that these poets for him personified, and then back behind the Romantics the sponsor-ing word-wizardry of the Bard whenever he devolved 'into a fondness for curiosity of expression, into an irritability of fancy' (666). Here lay the bad early modern seed of a degenerative pathology that had fostered 'the dialogue of the mind with itself' and attended the 'doubts', 'the discouragement, of Hamlet and of Faust' (654). Hamlet's will-puzzled hesitancy at the prospect of action, and the modern poet's reluctance to embrace the wholesome action of a classically attested plot, seemed to Arnold two sides of one tinsel coin. Yet the poetic genius of the age ran along the very channels Arnold rejected. It was, after all, the mind's dialogue with itself that informed, along different axes but with a common purpose, the genres of lyric sequence and dramatic mono-logue with which we began.

In major Victorian poems time and again a Shakespearean 'curiosity of expression' germinates in fresh directions unforeseeable from the plotted contexts in which it ini-tially occurred. Tennyson's Mariana has little to do with her namesake in *Measure for Measure* beyond the stimulus to imagery and pathos that resides in the Victorian poet's adapted epigraph, 'Mariana in the moated grange'. The title of "'Childe Roland to the Dark Tower Came'" is, pointedly, a phrase in quotation caught wild from the already vagrant, threadbare context it has in *King Lear*. To this provenance Browning's Victorian,

---

    [6] Arnold, *The Complete Poems*, 2nd edn, Kenneth and Miriam Allott (London and New York: Longman, 1979) 663–4.

at least partially industrial hallucination of anomie stands in a strong if unforthcoming contrast, bred if ever poem was from the 'irritability of fancy'. For Christina Rossetti the prompt of a phrase from Lady Macbeth's mad scene cued new poems not once but twice. In 'Will These Hands Ne'er Be Clean?' (1846), a volubly irregular ode, the teenaged poet curses a murderer from the comparative security of righteous indignation, while in later years the bottomless guilt of '"Cannot sweeten"' (1866, the title another typically double-quoted Victorian ascription) derives not from homicide but from the speaker's anguished recognition that she murdered an innocent love when it was tendered long ago.[7] Within the terse balladic structure of Rossetti's later and better poem, initial stanzas of catechistic dialogue yield to monologue as self-inquest, thereby distilling at a formal remove from dramatic utterance something of the dazed affect of Shakespeare's Scottish queen.

Two of the 'terrible sonnets' that Gerard Manley Hopkins threshed out in the 1880s worry in different ways the resonance of phrases situated in plots from the tragedies. 'No worst, there is none' opens its untitled meditation on mental and spiritual torment by extrapolating from what Edgar has had to say on the subject in *King Lear* IV. i. 25–6: 'The worst is not | So long as we can say "This is the worst"'. The mind's power to articulate the soul's wretchedness draws an intellectual line beyond which there yawns an unknowable abyss. Hopkins figures this manifest infinitude as 'cliffs of fall | Frightful, sheer, no-man-fathomed' (lines 9–10), terms drawn again from Edgar's word-painting of an imagined scene for the benefit of his blinded father (IV. v. 11–24). That Gloucester in this scene commits his suicide and survives it too appears to have fascinated the Victorian poet who wrestled with *accidie* here and also in 'Carrion Comfort', which lurches into speech by groping after the most famous of Shakespearean formulae for entertaining the idea of self-slaughter:

> Not, I'll not, carrion comfort, Despair, not feast on thee;
> Not untwist—slack they may be—these last strands of man
> In me ór, most weary, cry *I can no more*. I can;
> Can something, hope, wish day come, not choose not to be.[8]

This sonnet again rehearses a Shakespeare phrase in pursuit of the poet's examination of the powers and limits of phraseology as such, what can and can't be said. The cadence that falls on 'not' in Hamlet's 'To be or not to be' comes back in Hopkins' fourth line with teeth clenched, by reason both of a caesura-cloven hexameter and of the obsessive iteration of 'not' four times across the first line and a half. The option 'not to be' evokes from Hamlet a contemplative poise; Hopkins avails himself of it as shorthand for an outcome whose seductiveness means it must be resisted. After three centuries the condition

[7] *The Complete Poems of Christina Rossetti*, R. W. Crump (ed.), (Baton Rouge and London: Louisiana State University Press, 1990) vol. 3, 96–7, 298–9.
[8] *The Poems of Gerard Manley Hopkins*, 4th edn, W. H. Gardner and N. H. MacKenzie (eds), (London: Oxford University Press, 1967) 99–100.

called not-to-be that Shakespeare lodged into the English language has grown so familiar that a conscientious Victorian in his hour of moral angst has to pitch all the stress
he can muster into the strenuous negation of that condition. For this contemporary of
Nietzsche's, one must *not* choose not-to-be. Or else.

So Arnold had it backwards: Shakespeare's allegedly bad influence on poets whom his
example reduced to mere verbalism repeatedly proved a force for good, not least where
allusion to his own words was at issue, even as dutiful imitation of his larger deployment
of mythic plots in structured dramatic action left Victorian poetry cold. Arnold himself
thought better of a young man's classicist dogmatism by the time he wrote 'The Study of
Poetry' (1880), best known for its brief anthology of 'touchstones' embodying literary
greatness in a phrase, two of the ten touchstone passages being forged by none other
than the meretricious wordsmith Shakespeare (*2 Henry IV* III. i. 18–20, *Hamlet* V. ii.
298–301). The authority Arnold vested in these passages, and others quarried from the
epics of Homer, Dante, and Milton, virtually confessed the migration of poetry's prestige
from longer into shorter modalities that had taken place in his lifetime. Of the two principal emphases that 19th-century lyricism assumed, one was textural and sensuous: the
lyre itself may have been out of earshot during the greatest of print centuries, but compensatory strategies of escape from print into acoustic air are hard at work on every good
page of Victorian poetry. And the melodious fluency and complexity of Shakespeare's
verse, which even those readers who turned up their noses at 19th-century stagecraft
had to concede was written for live oral interpretation, served Victorian poets in countless ways as an inventory of desired effects.[9]

Lyricism as assonant beauty had dimensions of aesthetic finesse, but these tended to
run only skin-deep; like the effects of phrasal citation and manifest allusion we have been
considering, and in keeping with the art-for-art's-sake ideology that gained momentum
as the century advanced, they lay open to appreciation by all who might cultivate a taste
for them. Victorian lyricism had another side, however, that was embroiled with deeper
mysteries arousing some of the period's strongest curiosities and defences. This was the
affiliation of lyric with subjectivity, and thus with those conundra of selfhood and character with which this chapter began. The heyday of the realist novel vouchsafed to lyric
poetry, as a kind of cultural consolation prize, a special privilege to expose the self—the
poet's self in the first instance, the reader's not far behind it. An anthology of lyrics was a
gymnasium where one's sensibility hung in the balance, where heartstrings and sinews
of intellect and fancy grappled with an imaginative greatness that was vested, not just
in the language, but in the soul. It was the Muse who could tell you who you were—so
ran one Victorian answer to Lear's question—and you knew it by the quality of your
encounter with who poetry reading showed you the poet was.

---

[9] Perhaps the most intensely practical reverence for Shakespeare's verbal artistry is to be found in the
prosody handbook by American poet Sidney Lanier, *The Science of English Verse* (New York: Scribner,
1880).

32.3

Right there of course was the rub, where Shakespeare was involved. Reading Shelley was one thing, reading Shakespeare quite another. Browning made this plain when he invoked the two authors as respective paradigms for 'subjective' and 'objective' poets in his 1852 'Essay on Shelley'.[10] And, to bring nearer to home the problem I wish to define here, so did Harold Bloom make it plain in the pages that inaugurated his remarkable 1970s studies of poetic influence, which in effect recast literary history as critically fraught episodes of interpersonal transaction.

> The greatest poet in our language is excluded from the argument of this book for several reasons. One is necessarily historical; Shakespeare belongs to the giant age before the flood, before the anxiety of influence became central to poetic consciousness. Another has to do with the contrast between dramatic and lyric form. As poetry has become more subjective, the shadow cast by the precursors has become more dominant.[11]

In other words, within a modern dispensation that apprehends 'lyric form' as a form of subjectivity and to that extent associates poetic power with personal charisma, the acknowledged pre-eminence of a poet who worked for the most part in forms other than lyric is something of an embarrassment. From our side, the near side of a reorientation of sensibility that conjoins our (Bloomian) literacy to the Victorians', the place Shakespeare occupies on the far side of history's modern watershed puzzles or blurs his influence by making it hard to know just where to have him.

In ways now both infamous and obscure, Victorian men and women of letters reacted to this anomaly with frenzies of crackpot scholarship. This was the golden age of the Shakespeare deniers who, in default of satisfactory evidence concerning the actor from Stratford, settled the works instead on Elizabethan eminences better known and, to that end, tortured what documents did exist into cryptogrammatic disclosures that Bacon or Marlowe or somebody, anybody, else had engineered the personality deficit into which the vacuum-abhorring energies of baulked individualism might now flow. Alternatively,

---

[10] 'Introductory Essay' to the *Letters of Percy Bysshe Shelley* (London: Moxon, 1852), in *The Poems*, John Pettigrew and Thomas J. Collins (eds), (New Haven and London: Yale University Press, 1981) vol. 1, 999–1013.

[11] Bloom, *The Anxiety of Influence: A Theory of Poetry* (New York: Oxford University Press, 1973), 11. Bloom goes on to allege it as 'the main cause' for Shakespeare's slender relevance to the poetic-influence project 'that Shakespeare's prime precursor was Marlowe, a poet very much smaller than his inheritor'; such 'absolute absorption of the precursor' left Shakespeare oddly frictionless, offering successor poets no points of purchase to grapple with. That this inspired student of Romanticism went on to beat the drum for the study of character in *Shakespeare: The Invention of the Human* (New York: Riverhead, 1998) reinforces—by the acclaim his book attracted as well as the obloquy—the cultural stamina of certain Victorian habits of reading. See *Harold Bloom's Shakespeare*, Christy Desmet and Robert Sawyer (eds), (New York: Palgrave, 2001) 6–10 and 145–209; also Neil Corcoran, *Shakespeare and the Modern Poet* (Cambridge: Cambridge University Press, 2010) 1–3.

for minds more philologically inclined, the matchless genius of dramatic psychology who set personal intimacy at defiance in regard to his own psyche might be made statistically knowable through oblique piecemeal analysis. The New Shakspere Society under Frederick Furnivall tabulated readily observable data like rhyme frequencies and the occurrence of end-stopped lines in order to index quantitatively the calculus of inspiration.[12] This hard-headed pursuit of fact ultimately partook of something softer, and more characteristic of the era: the Victorian need to know an author inwardly, the close identification of reading with personality profile.[13]

The eccentricity of these tunnel-visionary endeavours is obvious. Yet they centrally expressed something widely pertinent to 19th-century culture and to the increasingly lyricized place of poetry within it: the vulnerability to which the bourgeois self was exposed by its own unstoppable enfranchisement from traditional norms. The denial and dismemberment of Shakespeare were as furiously resented by Victorian champions of the Bard as they are amusedly condescended to nowadays. But in fact they, no less than the counterattacks they aroused, were large and remarkable acts of cultural homage that put Shakespeare in the very best of company: with Homer and Moses. For the foundational Greek epics and the testaments of Holy Writ were also treated in the 19th century to systematic deconstruction and rehabilitation. In each case a riddle of authorship posed so worrisome a challenge to lately embraced norms, which equated the experience of literary reading with deep inter-subjective exchange, that only radical solutions would do. The Wolfian hypothesis about the *Iliad*'s archaic collective minstrelsy, and the Higher Criticism that levelled scripture with other forms of writing ancient or recent, had shuffled and dealt the Western literary heritage into modern hands; it remained for the Baconian claimants and the prosodic analysts of Shakespeare to follow suit.

When poets tried their hand at this table, they gamed the Victorian literary system in ways that savoured of a spiritualist séance. Lyric's strong association with subjectivity obliged them, in the case of the curiously absent, absconded, or analytically dismantled Shakespeare, to hazard some compensatory necromancy. Any poet who meant not just to recall this or that Shakespearean phrase, but rather to have Shakespeare's living presence bless the creative spirit in new work, had to create that presence first, to cast the faceless dramaturge in a role suiting present purposes. The Bard famous for being all things to all people was not much use, interpoetically speaking, until—and this is to restate Bloom's point—he could be made some one thing to some one poet.[14]

---

[12] The lead mole in this scholarly tunnel was Furnivall's protégé F. G. Fleay: see 'On Metrical Tests as Applied to Dramatic Poetry: Part I, Shakspere', *Transactions of the New Shakspere Society Francis Bacon's Cipher in the So-called Shakespeare Plays* (Chicago: Peale, 1888). (1874) part 2. Among anti-Stratfordians the most notorious is Ignatius Donnelly, *The Great Cryptogram*: See on these matters Taylor, 162–230; Hugh Grady, *The Modernist Shakespeare: Critical Texts in a Material World* (Oxford: Clarendon Press, 1991) 47–51.

[13] The book that installed itself as the authoritative literary account of Shakespeare met this Victorian need in the priorities of its subtitle: Edward Dowden, *Shakspere: A Critical Study of his Mind and Art* (London: King, 1875).

[14] Poole (2004), 118, touches on the 'important questions about control, complicity and recognition' that in Victorian allusion haunt the gaps between Shakespeare and his characters.

Victorians often managed this by conscripting some other, earlier poet as straight man or fall guy, whose mediation stepped the superincumbent charge of Shakespeare down to more manageable currency. Such a pragmatic reduction went unremarked above in our last instance from Hopkins, 'Carrion Comfort', which gets its purchase on the dilemma of Hamlet through the opening stanza of Tennyson's 'The Two Voices' (1842): 'Were it not better not to be?' That, for Hopkins, was the question, an allusive lens whose double (k)not focused the diffuse radiance of Hamlet's much-disseminated line.

Tennyson may have shown Hopkins the way to such address when the great seventh lyric from *In Memoriam* enlisted, behind the mourner's pathetic ordeal at dawn outside the dead Hallam's house, the fraught simile 'like a guilty thing', which came from *Hamlet* by way of a textual crux in the 'Intimations' ode of Wordsworth. The latter's 'High instincts before which our mortal Nature | Did tremble like a guilty Thing surprised' reclaims for secular experience some portion of the otherworldly awe that attaches to Horatio's reporting how at daybreak old Hamlet's ghost 'started, like a guilty thing | Upon a fearful summons' (I . i. 129–30).[15] Tennyson at this point knows no more what he may be summoned to than what he may be guilty of; yet his double-jointed allusion recapitulates in epitome a history of the transformations in world-view that lie behind his encounter with a peculiarly Victorian liminality. Browning in bumptious contrast, and as always with a higher obliquity of angle, walked a like knife-edge at the finale to 'Master Hugues of Saxe-Gotha' (1855). 'Do I carry the moon in my pocket?': the loft-stranded organist's cry for light seems to come, with the flash of original genius, out of nowhere, while in fact it adapts a throwaway line from Cloten, of all characters, in *Cymbeline*, of all plays (III. i. 42–5), to mesh with a tissue of images deploring the embroilment of truth's natural light within webs of human artifice, 'our life's zigzags and dodges, | Ins and outs, weaving a new legislature' (lines 112–3). That last word 'legislature' clinches what has been riddling Browning's stanzas, the mediating presence of Shelley ('unacknowledged legislators of the World', *A Defence of Poetry*; the dome of life staining 'the white radiance of Eternity', *Adonais*), which burnishes the Shakespearean trouvaille to high gloss even as the implied fraternizing of Shelley with Cloten, rebellious scions whose politics went nowhere, keeps the Victorian poet's liberalism on a tight leash.[16] Thus Tennyson's third-party refraction of Shakespeare particularizes a perhaps too familiar text, Browning's generalizes a text perhaps too obscure; both allusions utilize an intervening poetic tradition so as to make of Shakespeare not a fetish but a renewable resource.

---

[15] *In Memoriam* 7.10, in *The Poems of Tennyson*, ed. Christopher Ricks (London: Longman, 1969), 870; Wordsworth, 'Ode: Intimations of Immortality', lines 140–51, in *Poetical Works*, Thomas Hutchinson and Ernest de Selincourt (eds), (1904; new edn, London: Oxford University Press, 1969) 461.

[16] 'Master Hugues of Saxe-Gotha', in *Poems* (1981) 1. 612–16. Shelley, *A Defence of Poetry* and *Adonais*, lines 460–64, in *Shelley's Poetry and Prose*, 2nd edn, Donald H. Reiman and Neil Fraistat (New York: Norton, 2002) 426 and 535.

32.4

Instances like these of local evocation and repurposing are scattered across the best Victorian poetry, yet they bear less freight as a cultural phenomenon than the quite different work of the Shakespeare fetishists. The friendliest way of approaching the Bardolatrous sonnets with which we shall conclude is to propose that they sought a viable alternative to spiritualist legerdemain, through a radically metapoetic acknowledgement of the scandal that Shakespearean objectivity posed to subjectivist canons of literary taste. Poets nonplussed by Shakespeare's impersonality could, and did, compose poems that were about Shakespeare's transcendence of the personhood in which poetic influence ordinarily took shape. Moreover, given the 19th-century tendency to regard the Sonnets as exceptions to Shakespeare's exceptionalism—dating at latest from the hour when 'with this key | Shakespeare unlocked his heart' to Wordsworth ('Scorn not the Sonnet', 1827, lines 2–3)—it is ironically appropriate that confessional meta-poems on this theme often materialized as sonnets themselves.[17] The best known is Arnold's, from 1849:

> Shakespeare
>
> Others abide our question. Thou art free.
> We ask and ask—Thou smilest and art still,
> Out-topping knowledge. For the loftiest hill,
> Who to the stars uncrowns his majesty,
>
> Planting his steadfast footsteps in the sea,
> Making the heaven of heavens his dwelling-place,
> Spares but the cloudy border of his base
> To the foiled searching of mortality;
>
> And thou, who didst the stars and sunbeams know,
> Self-schooled, self-scanned, self-honoured, self-secure,
> Didst tread on earth unguessed at.—Better so!
>
> All pains the immortal spirit must endure,
> All weakness which impairs, all griefs which bow,
> Find their sole speech in that victorious brow.[18]

It is not that Arnold, soon to become so acerbic a critic on the theme of poets' ignorance, knows *nothing* about Shakespeare. The encomium of epithets in line 10 recites with impressive confidence certain qualities of Shakespeare's inner aplomb amid a life of outward misrecognition; and the final tercet strongly infers that equipoise on this scale betokened a uniquely earned mastery of humanity's various pathos. All the same, there is a rogue ambiguity in the concluding deixis that exposes Arnold's large inference to a doubt larger still. For, while the 'brow' in question just may be the brainy forehead of William Shakespeare as handed down by Jacobean portraiture, such phrenology has no foundation within this sonnet, which instead properly looks back to the image of the

---

[17] Wordsworth (1969) 206.
[18] Arnold (1979) 39–40, which incorporates Arnold's revisions of this sonnet through 1877.

'loftiest hill' (3) whose slopes are visible but not—this being the whole point of the early conceit—its brow. If 'that' protuberance is the 'victorious brow', the one in the heavens hidden by clouds from human ken, then Arnold can have no share in its victory. The sonnet's concluding image thus unravels its argumentative conclusion, returning the foiled searcher to where he began, in the contemplation of a sublimity that overgoes mere knowledge. And that really is what a Victorian poem of this kind wants anyhow: to know that Shakespeare is as unknowable as the summit-dwelling God who, as Cowper had put it in a hymn to which (and not to any Shakespearean text) Arnold's sonnet alludes, moves in a mysterious way and 'plants his footsteps in the sea'.[19]

'Thou art free', at the end of line 1, deploys its adjective as a cipher that means, in effect, what Shelley told his divine, inhuman skylark: What thou art we know not. We should listen for a cognitive if not a vocal hitch just before the word 'free', a reluctance to predicate anything of the Hero as Poet (thus Carlyle's Shakespeare), who occupies the zenith, or nadir, of that chameleonic Negative Capability with which Keats famously associated him.[20] Swinburne, when he rewrote Arnold's act of poetic homage a generation later in 1882, outdid Arnold by making the reluctance to predicate an absolute show-stopper:

> William Shakespeare
>
> Not if men's tongues and angels' all in one
> Spake, might the word be said that might speak Thee.
> Streams, winds, woods, flowers, fields, mountains, yea, the sea,
> What power is in them all to praise the sun?
> His praise is this,—he can be praised of none.
> Man, woman, child, praise God for him; but he
> Exults not to be worshipped, but to be.
> He is; and, being, beholds his work well done.
> All joy, all glory, all sorrow, all strength, all mirth,
> Are his: without him, day were night on earth.
> Time knows not his from time's own period.
> All lutes, all harps, all viols, all flutes, all lyres,
> Fall dumb before him ere one string suspires.
> All stars are angels; but the sun is God.[21]

[19] 'Light Shining out of Darkness', lines 1–3, in Cowper, *Poetical Works*, H. S. Milford and Norma Russell (eds), (London: Oxford University Press, 1934) 455.

[20] Carlyle, *Of Heroes, Hero-Worship, and the Heroic in History* (London: Fraser, 1841). Reference to Shakespeare links two much-quoted passages from Keats' correspondence: 'At once it struck me, what quality went to form a Man of Achievement especially in Literature & which Shakespeare posessed [sic] so enormously—I mean *Negative Capability*, that is when man is capable of being in uncertainties, Mysteries, doubts, without any irritable reaching after fact & reason' (to George and Tom Keats, December 1817); 'As to the poetical Character itself … it is not itself—it has no self—it is every thing and nothing—It has no character … It has as much delight in conceiving an Iago as an Imogen' (to Richard Woodhouse, 27 October 1818). *Selected Letters*, Robert Gittings and John Mee (eds), (Oxford: Oxford University Press, 2002) 41–2, 147–8.

[21] Printed second (after Marlowe's) in a sequence of 'Sonnets on English Dramatic Poets', in *The Poems of Algernon Charles Swinburne* (London: Chatto and Windus, 1905) vol. 5, 298. Swinburne's *A Study of Shakespeare* (London: Chatto and Windus, 1880) offered the most spirited and rhapsodically insightful of Victorian rejoinders to the textual analysts discussed above. See Robert Sawyer, *Victorian*

There is delicate poignancy in this atheist's reverence for what does command his worship.[22] Although Swinburne ranks among the artists of excess, like the best of this school he is an adept in the opposite arts of curtailment as well. Here the apostrophic second-person address of which Arnold liberally availed himself is not used but disowned, subjunctively glanced at in the opening sentence—and then expressly declined. Swinburne refuses 'to speak Thee': he will not and does not say 'thou' to a being that transcends personhood, a being whose victory is, precisely, that 'he can be praised of none'. That Shakespeare for Swinburne is less a (mere) person than (a) mere being emerges towards the volta of this sonnet: 'He is'. Period. Full stop. Expressly retrenching from 'to be worshipped' to 'to be', Swinburne rebukes the presumption of contemporary undertakings, Arnold's included, to tell the king of poets who he is.

Swinburne's taboo on predication is a piece of that earnest commerce which the Victorians transacted between poetry and religion, and which culminated in the dying Tennyson's on-cue demand that he be given, not the Bible, but 'my Shakespeare', open to a beloved passage in *Cymbeline*.[23] For this traffic the border was opened in theory by Coleridge's definition of the imagination as 'a repetition in the finite mind of the eternal act of creation in the infinite I AM', and it was repeatedly crossed in practice when poets straining at the tether of orthodox belief reverted to basics and rekindled the unimaginable zero of the burning bush ('I am that I am', Exodus 3:14) in ritual celebration of the ontology of creation.[24] Shakespeare's inscrutability, like that of the more distant author-functions Homer and Moses—and Jehovah—served as a cultural absolute securing the freedom, even as it grounded the dilemma, of the modern individual, pledged to self-knowledge yet coiled against conceding any limit to the self. Hence the fascination of Victorian dramatic monologists with speech acts of truncated or pseudo predication: Ulysses' 'that which we are, we are' and the companion question framed by Webster's Circe, 'Why am I who I am?' (line 109), exemplify the extraction of their Victorian genre from such Shakespearean occasions as Hamlet's 'Seems, madam? Nay, it *is*. I know not "seems"' (I. ii. 76) and Iago's 'I am not what I am' (*Othello* I. i. 65). Comparison with properly dramatic originals draws out the shivering loneliness that inheres in Victorian poetry's isolation from the theatrical interchange of dialogue and action. 'This is I, | Hamlet the Dane' (V. i. 53–4); 'This is I, | *The Lady of Shalott*': the post-mortem greeting at the end of Tennyson's 1832 poem leaps, as it were, with pre-emptive literalness,

Appropriations of Shakespeare: George Eliot, A. C. Swinburne, Robert Browning, and Charles Dickens (Cranbury: Associated University Presses, 2003); also Nick Freeman, 'Swinburne's Shakespeare: The Verbal Whirlwind?', in *A. C. Swinburne and the Singing Word*, Yisrael Levin (ed.), (Farnham: Ashgate, 2010) 91–106.

[22] Grady finds that 'for Swinburne, God is, in effect, in the unquantifiable *je ne sais quoi* of Shakespeare's blank verse' (53).

[23] Hallam Tennyson, *Alfred Lord Tennyson: A Memoir by His Son* (London: Macmillan, 1897) vol. 2, 425–9.

[24] Chapter 13 of *Biographia Literaria*, J. Shawcross (ed.), (London: Oxford University Press, 1907) 1: 202. In succeeding chapters Coleridge exemplifies the operations of 'secondary' or poetic imagination through close analysis of *Lucrece* and *Venus and Adonis*.

into Ophelia's grave, eliding the interpersonal conflict staged there in the play and binding identity to mortality as a pair of non-negotiable absolutes. When the homely young woman who peers 'By the Looking-Glass' in Webster's monologue exclaims, 'Alas! it is I, I, I,' her cry collapses the mission statement heading *Richard III* ('I ... I ... I, that am curtail'd of this fair proportion, | Cheated of feature by dissembling nature', I. i. 14–19) into a textual impasse that corresponds to the generic and gendered constriction of her sphere of action.[25]

When Isabella J. Southern told Shakespeare, in yet another eponymous sonnet (1891), 'Impartial art thou, as the teeming earth, | On which swarm creatures vile and gay and good' (1–2), her care to distinguish impartiality in the Bard from moral indifference—'And yet far short of license dost thou stop' (8)—recruited Shakespeare, as a proxy god, in order to salve a Tennysonian angst lest the powers that be should prove to care for nothing.[26] A freer-thinking contemporary, Mathilde Blind, stood ready to go further and waive Southern's ethical scruple in favour of pure ontology, which we have seen emerging as the essential article of Victorian faith for those who swore by the Bard. Blind concludes her series of 'Shakespearean Sonnets' (1895) with a couplet that reaches back past Exodus to Genesis and the *Fiat lux*: 'For Shakespeare was, and at his touch, with light | Impartial as the sun's, revealed the All'.[27] The sovereign image of the sun and incantatory 'All' come to Blind's sonnet straight from that of Swinburne (in whose Shelleyan school she was a disciple); so does the tell-tale refusal to subscribe to anything beyond the proposition that 'Shakespeare was'. More was involved in the fashion for 'Shakespeare' sonnets, however, than lineal influence between one Victorian and another. With an indirection only less ambient than that of Shakespeare himself, by the fin-de-siècle these practices formed part of the cultic atmosphere enveloping poetry as such. Transcendentally abstaining from a predication that would profane the mysteries of creative identity, poets staking their claim on those mysteries practised a Bardolatry that dared not speak its name.

[25] Tennyson, 'Ulysses', line 66, and 'The Lady of Shalott', lines 170–1, in Ricks (1969) 361 and 565 n.; Webster, 'Circe', line 109, in *Portraits and Other Poems*, Christine Sutphin (ed.), (Peterborough: Broadview, 2000) 182, and 'By the Looking-Glass', line 25, in *Dramatic Studies* (London: Macmillan, 1866) 117. The way out of these melancholy generic self-predications lay through the contingencies of the world, although engagement with these contingencies required speakers to compromise their lyrical autonomy. 'Fra Lippo Lippi' (1855) strikes just this bargain the moment Browning's painter-monk opens his mouth: 'I am poor brother Lippo, by your leave!' (line 1, in Pettigrew and Collins (1981), vol. 1, 540).

[26] 'Shakespeare', in *Sonnets and Other Poems* (London: W. Scott, 1891) 61. Other late-century sonneteers of note include Constance Naden (1880) and Frances Kemble (1883); Eliza Cook contributed a 'Tercentenary Ode' (1864).

[27] 'Shakespeare', lines 13–14, in Blind, *Birds of Passage: Songs of the Orient and Occident* (London: Chatto and Windus, 1895) 117. Blind's 'Shakespearean Sonnets' were, true to Victorian form, in fact Petrarchan. This one also owed a trick or two to the epitaph Pope wrote for Newton, 'God said, *Let Newton be! and All was Light*': *Poems of Alexander Pope*, vol. 6, Norman Ault and John Butt (eds), (London: Methuen, 1964) 317. The Victorian installation of Shakespeare, rather than Darwin, in Newton's place tells in itself a tale of two centuries.

Calling the bluff of these pieties fell to the contrarian Browning, who paid them a whistleblower's respects in a late sonnet (1884) whose title—not, signally, 'Shakespeare' but 'The Names'—observed in a double sense the literary solemnities of the day. [28] That Browning took the full measure of Shakespeare's anomalous resistance to Romantic subjectivism—a resistance of which he himself was the most conspicuous Victorian imitator—is clear not only from the 'Essay on Shelley' mentioned above but also from the paradoxical riposte to Wordsworth that culminates the 1876 poem 'House': if Shakespeare did bare his soul in the Sonnets, Browning avers, then the Sonnets are *ipso facto* uncharacteristic of him, and unworthy too: 'the less Shakespeare he!'[29] At the same time, Browning could see that the reflexive Victorian reverence before Shakespeare's genius scanted his humanity, and thereby the influence of the very art his apotheosis was intended to glorify. By claiming too much for literature, the hyperbolical defence of poetry that was conducted in the Bard's name actually abetted everything in modern society that conspired to put literature in cultural quarantine. To interrupt this vicious circle called for the strongest medicine Browning knew, the name of God Almighty:

> The Names
>
> Shakespeare!—to such name's sounding, what succeeds
>   Fitly as silence? Falter forth the spell,—
>   Act follows word, the speaker knows full well,
> Nor tampers with its magic more than needs.
> Two names there are: That which the Hebrew reads
>   With his soul only; if from lips it fell,
>   Echo, back thundered by earth, heaven and hell,
> Would own 'Thou didst create us!' Naught impedes
> We voice the other name, man's most of might,
>   Awesomely, lovingly: let awe and love
> Mutely await their working, leave to sight
>   All of the issue as—below—above—
> Shakespeare's creation rises: one remove,
> Though dread—this finite from that infinite.

The distinction Browning draws between two orders of 'creation'—Shakespeare's of a richly compounded human diversity, God's of elemental humanity itself—rewinds the Victorian tradition to its theoretical point of origin and underscores, at the bottom line, the categorical divide supporting Coleridge's 'repetition in the *finite* mind of the eternal act of creation in the *infinite* I AM' (emphasis added). Shakespeare remains a name to

---

[28] Pettigrew and Collins (1981) 2. 964–5. First published 29 May 1884 in the *Pall Mall Gazette*, this sonnet was donated to a fundraising *Shaksperean Show Book* appearing on the same date; Browning wrote it with a lively sense of the company it would be keeping there. See the discussion by Danny Karlin in '"The Names": Robert Browning's "Shaksperean Show"', in Marshall and Poole (2003) 150–69. See also Browning's less prudent, and less successful, monologue for Shakespeare (also published 1876), 'At the "Mermaid"'.

[29] Pettigrew and Collins (1981), 2.438–9.

conjure with; but whoever 'tampers with its magic more than needs' is playing with fire: not blasphemy, exactly, but a corruption of the language that poets own a special duty to protect. This may be why Browning's sonnet uses the much-belabored verb *to be* so sparely, and in such as way as to shift the Shakespeare question from ontological to epistemological ground, from the language of transcendent being to the contingent being of language: 'Two names there are'. To know what's in a name, Browning suggests, is an occupation portioned to the hearts and minds of men and women, and it constitutes the beginning of wisdom for modern poets who would tell us who we are.

SELECT BIBLIOGRAPHY

Arac, Jonathan (1992) 'Hamlet, Little Dorrit, and the History of Character', in Michael Hays, ed., *Critical Conditions: Regarding the Historical Moment* (Minneapolis and London: University of Minnesota Press) 82–96.

Bate, Jonathan (1986) *Shakespeare and the English Romantic Imagination* (Oxford: Clarendon Press).

Foulkes, Richard (1986) *Shakespeare and the Victorian Stage* (Cambridge: Cambridge University Press).

Grady, Hugh (1991) *The Modernist Shakespeare: Critical Texts in a Material World* (Oxford: Clarendon Press).

Marsden, Jean I. (1991) (ed.) *The Appropriation of Shakespeare: Post-Renaissance Reconstructions of the Works and the Myth*, (New York: Harvester Wheatsheaf).

Marshall, Gail, and Adrian Poole (2003) *Victorian Shakespeare, Volume 2: Literature and Culture* (Houndmills: Palgrave Macmillan).

——(2009) *Shakespeare and Victorian Women* (Cambridge: Cambridge University Press).

Poole, Adrian (2004) *Shakespeare and the Victorians* (London: Thomson).

Sawyer, Robert (2003) *Victorian Appropriations of Shakespeare: George Eliot, A. C. Swinburne, Robert Browning, and Charles Dickens* (Cranbury: Associated University Presses).

Taylor, Gary (1989) *Reinventing Shakespeare A Cultural History, from the Restoration to the Present* (New York: Weidenfeld and Nicolson).

CHAPTER 33

SHAKESPEARE'S LOOSE ENDS AND THE CONTEMPORARY POET

PETER ROBINSON

33.1

Offering an argument for taking passages from plays out of context in an anthology of Shakespeare's poetry, Ted Hughes writes:

> if one specifies that 'To-morrow, and to-morrow, and to-morrow' is spoken by Macbeth as he faces the leafy army that will put an end to his spellbound, murderous career (having just heard that his wife, who prompted the course of action that converted him from the King's loyal champion to a regicidal tyrant, has died), it actually limits the use of the passage for a reader. Its relevance is then confined to Macbeth's unique predicament in a sacrosanct, old-fashioned play, rather than applied generally to the reader's own immediate plight, as an ephemeral creature, facing the abyss, on a spinning ball of self-delusion.[1]

Hughes makes the use of poetry a 'rather than' activity, the words either 'mine' or Macbeth's. Yet poetic uses depend on identifications where words remain a character's, or a lyric speaker's, while voicing predicament for us. Hughes compares Macbeth's speech (V. v. 18–27) to W. B. Yeats' 'Death' and 'Phlebas the Phoenician' in T. S. Eliot's *The Waste Land*, deciding that 'when the great speeches of the plays are taken out of context they are no more difficult to understand and appropriate than poems by other great

---

[1] Ted Hughes, Introduction to *William Shakespeare: Poetry selected by Ted Hughes* (London: Faber & Faber, 2000) vii–viii.

poets. In many cases they are very much easier'. If to find passages helpful is to 'appropriate' them, prior ownership remains implied, rendering 'inappropriate' processes essential to culture. He admits that 'by reading the passage out of context, one is missing the great imaginative experience of the drama—but one is missing that anyway'. Do we miss the drama in extracts when they're not taken out of context? Imagination and memory seem undervalued, the former notionally set free from the nourishment of the latter. I am supposing, then, that a quotation from Shakespeare will bring its dramatic narrative setting with it, prompting readers to ponder, question, and identify with both immediate and wider implications of its applied poetry. If this appears a later legacy of Shakespeare's canonicity, it is founded on his verse's being at the service of dramatized situation, a characteristic present even in the sugared sonnets for his private friends.

So when Hughes responds to lines from *Macbeth*, does his account illustrate such a preferred freeing of the poetry for reader use? The speech expresses a self-betrayed man's thoughts (one self-betrayed by listening to his wife's ambition) after learning she has died. If appropriating Shakespeare's lines to his own 'facing the abyss on a spinning ball of self-delusion', Hughes knows the drama in the words and identifies with the speech because of its plotted place, even while arguing for our benefit in disregarding them. He thus tacitly illustrates what poets actually do when alluding to Shakespeare's lyrically dramatic and dramatically lyrical verse. Making allusion so variously adaptable for later poets are Shakespeare's loose ends: the multiplicity of significance in his poetic language, whose ramifications he could not begin wholly to control, and the tangles of borrowed plots and scenes which inevitably and often significantly fail to catch all the hares they start running.[2]

When, after her violation, Lucrece tries to write a letter, Shakespeare describes a character with too much circumstance to narrate, too many emotions to articulate, and a plethora of figures with which to express them. It is as convincing a picture of the poet's compositional overcrowding, as of his heroine amid her fatal shame and woe:

> Her maid is gone, and she prepares to write,
> First hovering o' er the paper with her quill.
> Conceit and grief an eager combat fight;
> What wit sets down is blotted straight with will;
> This is too curious-good, this blunt and ill.
>   Much like a press of people at a door
>   Throng her inventions, which shall go before.

(lines 1296–1302)

This proffers an image for Shakespeare's figures of poetic speech, and his dramatized characters—each pressing at the door of the imagination. One difference between the poet and his heroine in *The Rape of Lucrece* is that her overwhelmed and self-thwarting

---

[2] For Hughes on 'Shakespeare's generosity of production' in such loose ends, see *Letters of Ted Hughes*, Christopher Reid (ed.), (London: Faber & Faber, 2007) 407–8.

invention, stymied by a search for the *mot juste*, results in a stanza-length note (lines 1303–9), while her creator was able to marshall his crowding thoughts through many a door onto parchment. A perceived mismatch between her inevitable fate and Shakespeare's baroque eloquence upon her predicament has focused critical debate over the poem.[3] Such a 'press of people' and throng of invention in his work can be noticed everywhere. No poet in English has left more for textual scholars to argue over, or whose meanings and implications critics can debate. The glory of his writings is in constituting an indeterminately extended texture everywhere liable to multifarious fraying.

The longevity of Shakespeare's phrasings could make anyone feel like 'an ephemeral creature, facing the abyss'; but what Hughes calls 'self-delusion' need not be attributed to the world, the 'spinning ball' on which we stand. It is Macbeth's or ours, figured for us by identifying with his fate. Hughes may take the speech out of the play, but he can't take the play out of the speech. Far from limiting reader use, Shakespeare's words trailing their clouds of dramatic circumstance facilitate it. If we do 'appropriate' Macbeth's lines to make them 'part of one's mental furnishings', as Hughes has it, his *appropriate* word 'appropriate' underlines that the speech *remains* Macbeth's, furnishing us with responses to such fatal errors of judgement. But when it comes to the 'all our yesterdays' phrase from his speech (which I first heard as the title to a British TV series showing old news-reels), it is not so much that I have appropriated Macbeth's words as that his have appro-priated me. 'Shakespeare has already exhausted the whole of human nature', Goethe said to Eckermann in 1824.[4] Hughes' attempt to spring passages from the plays illustrates a struggle that may have exaggerated rivalry at the expense of gratitude.[5]

W. B. Yeats wrote: 'I can never get out of my head that no man, even though he be Shakespeare, can write perfectly when his web is woven of threads that have been spun in many lands'.[6] The etymological heterogeneity of the English language would suggest, then, that *no-one writes perfectly* in it. Yet where Yeats hankers after an impossible per-fection of the work, the 'loose ends' kind stares him in the face. One Hughes version of Shakespeare's language, 'his famous pincer movement, where he contains an idea with a latinate word on one wing and an Anglo-Saxon on the other',[7] divides this verbal kingdom into just two language sources. Reductive of its etymology, this romance of the *Ivanhoe* variety, in which the honest Saxons struggle against Latinate Normans, struc-tures arguments such as Seamus Heaney's concerning Hopkins' language as resistant to

[3] See Peter Robinson, 'Talking Yourself to Death: *The Rape of Lucrece*', *Review of English Literature* [Kyoto], 61 (1991): 1–33.

[4] Johann Peter Eckermann, *Conversations of Goethe*, John Oxenford (trans.), (London: J. M. Dent, 1930) 31.

[5] Walter Jackson Bate cites Goethe in *The Burden of the Past and the English Poet* (London: Chatto & Windus, 1971) 5–6. Harold Bloom notes that the 'greatest poet in our language is excluded from the argument of this book'—a cause of, not subject to, influence anxiety. See *The Anxiety of Influence: A Theory of Poetry* (New York: Oxford University Press, 1973) 11.

[6] W. B. Yeats, *Essays and Introductions* (London: Macmillan, 1969) 109. See Neil Corcoran, *Shakespeare and the Modern Poet* (Cambridge: Cambridge University Press, 2010) 37.

[7] Ted Hughes, 'The Great Theme: Notes on Shakespeare', *Winter Pollen: Occasional Prose* William Scammell (ed.), (London: Faber & Faber, 1994) 104.

Keatsian mellifluousness—citing the Poet's words in *Timon of Athens* (I. i. 20–5) 'where Shakespeare seems to be glossing the abundance and naturalness of his own art', and recruiting him for the anti-mellifluous side.[8] So the poet's heterogeneous medium, to which Hughes and Heaney do respond warmly, is, notwithstanding, set analogically to figure civil war, class war, sex war, and other managerially reductive, constraining standoffs.

Boris Pasternak, caught in his time between the Cold War's mighty opposites, observed that Shakespeare's 'rhythm reflects the enviable laconicism of English speech, in which it is possible for one small iambic line to contain a whole statement consisting of one, two, or several propositions set against each other. It is the rhythm of a free historical personality'.[9] William Empson's trilogy, *Seven Types of Ambiguity* (1930), *Some Versions of Pastoral* (1935), and *The Structure of Complex Words* (1951), in constant dialogue with Shakespearean texts, explores such freedom, its resources and limits. Yet this 'rhythm of a free historical personality' speaks from amid the inevitabilities of the plays' plots, as Pasternak's Zhivago poem 'Hamlet' admits:

> I love your stubborn shaping of a theme.
> I have agreed to play this character.
> But now a different drama is in train.
> Leave me this once an unscripted actor.

'The time is out of joint', as Hamlet says, 'O cursèd spite | That ever I was born to set it right!' (I. v. 189–90)[10] and Pasternak notes of the play, as if a determinist march of history: 'But the scenes' sequence was thought out beforehand, | Not to be evaded is the theme they move to'.[11] As with Lucrece's complaints against Night, Time, and Opportunity, the superfluity of Shakespeare's poetry, its hybrid pidgin, heterogeneity of lexical stock and largely uninflected synthetic grammar, its additive syntax or terse directness, no less ambiguously suggestive, in brief exchange and aside, speak for his characters' drive to shape or resist their fates, offering readers and actors great fluidity of interpretation. Shakespeare presses the poetry of free historical personalities through the narrow door of his sequenced scenes. Hughes' account of the dramatist's medium, and his pursuit of Shakespeare's one great theme is unlike the loose ends he himself admired, as their variety makes for an inexhaustible polyphonic expressiveness, not a gorgon-petrified confrontation.

---

[8] Seamus Heaney, 'The Fire i' the Flint: Reflections on the Poetry of Gerard Manley Hopkins', *Preoccupations: Selected Prose 1968–1978* (London: Faber & Faber, 1980) 79.

[9] Boris Pasternak, 'Notes of a Translator', *Modern Russian Poets on Poetry*, ed. Carl Proffer (Ann Arbor: Ardis, 1976) 101.

[10] A study of *Hamlet* allusion could include Hood's 'The Bridge of Sighs', much Laforgue, Eliot's 'Prufrock', Luciano Erba's 'Una visita a Caleppio' or 'I piccioni in città', and many more.

[11] Boris Pasternak, *The Poems of Dr. Zhivago*, Donald Davie (trans.), (Manchester: Manchester University Press, 1963) 9, and 51–4 for the translator's note.

Such a gorgon-like encounter is what Geoffrey Hill evokes, in avowedly Shakespearean language, for his war-torn and carefully mended sequence 'Funeral Music' from *King Log* (1968):

> 'Prowess, vanity, mutual regard,
> It seemed I stared at them, they at me.
> That was the gorgon's true and mortal gaze:
> Averted conscience turned against itself'.
> A hawk and a hawk-shadow.[12]

Hill remarked that 'I found myself re-reading the *Henry VI* plays at exactly the right time; discovering the power of a certain kind of rhetoric which I'd been educated to think inferior to Shakespeare's later work',[13] and elsewhere 'I was attempting a florid grim music broken by grunts and shrieks'.[14] Here is Bedford from the opening of *I Henry VI*:

> Prosper this realm; keep it from civil broils;
> Combat with adverse planets in the heavens.
> A far more glorious star thy soul will make,
> Then Julius Caesar, or bright—
> *Enter a Messenger*
>
>   (I. I. 53–6)

Like Bedford interrupted here, Hill's sequence closes with one 'Crying to the end "I have not finished"'. It imitates and recomposes an abrupt style to evoke 'civil broils', using unattributed direct speech to dramatize conflicted circumstance.[15] Its high abstractions are cut with monosyllabic comments, as when historical figures mean things 'by | God', or 'delicate souls' are 'gasping "Jesus"', or when 'Soul' is said to be 'possibly | indestructible. That I can believe'.[16] Comparison of Hill's lines with Bedford's shows the difference between a later, carefully crafted poetic style and the busy efforts of a writer voicing calamity, conflict, and its consequences in dramatic action. Eliot perhaps overgeneralizes when stating that a poet 'fulfills once for all some possibility of the language, and so leaves one possibility less for his successors'.[17] Early work offers lines of development not exhausted by the subsequent elaborations of their poet. The finish of Hill's considered sequence is able to benefit from just such an unfulfilled possibility.

Attempting to free Shakespeare's poetry from its great drama for personal use in his anthology, Hughes discovered what he believed that drama to be, and defending an inkling of his theory in the following terms, saying it 'might be thought belittling and a disappointment, a pointless thing to do, to bring Shakespeare down to a single

---

[12] Geoffrey Hill, 'Funeral Music 7', *Collected Poems* (Harmondsworth: Penguin Books, 1985) 76.

[13] *Viewpoints: Poets in Conversation with John Haffenden* (London: Faber & Faber, 1981) 81.

[14] Hill, 'Funeral Music: An Essay' (1985) 199.

[15] That the lines may be Nashe's (or that Middleton adapted *Macbeth*) with other Shakespearean collaborations underline such loose ends traditionally attributed to a single author.

[16] Hill, 'Funeral Music' (1985) 72, 73, 77.

[17] T. S. Eliot, 'What is a Classic?' *Selected Prose*, ed. Frank Kermode (London: Faber & Faber, 1975) 125.

fundamental idea. However, singleness can be all-inclusive'.[18] The thread followed in this chapter avoids what Neil Corcoran calls the 'single identifiable myth' strand in Shakespearean interpretation, a 'devotedly relentless boar hunt'.[19] Corcoran's study outlines confrontations with the oeuvre by Yeats, Eliot, Auden, and Hughes, each differently measuring themselves against Shakespeare's copiousness. The later poets whose work I explore here evade or avoid such odious comparisons through oblique encounter, finding opportunity in ellipses. Yet disagreeing with Hughes' boar hunt by underlining the multiplicity in even one line of Shakespeare (such as Empson's reading of 'Bare ruined choirs where late the sweet birds sang' from Sonnet 73 or J. H. Prynne's book-length study of Sonnet 94, 'They that have power to hurt and will do none')[20] does not require us to discount his synthetic speculations on the one great theme. Their compulsive ingenuity also pays its topsy-turvy tribute to Shakespeare's loose-ended language, his mouldy tales, ghost characters, and gripping rhythmic patterns.

Reluctance to countenance a less determinate idea of Shakespeare's writings, one not so haunted by Romantic belief that myriad-mindedness resulted in organically unified works (with whose controlling originator aspirants may identify and struggle) appear too in comments on individual plays, as when Eliot first accuses Goethe and Coleridge of substituting 'their own Hamlet for Shakespeare's' only to do so with *Hamlet*, the play, accounting it an 'artistic failure' because 'Hamlet's bafflement at the absence of objective equivalent to his feelings is a prolongation of the bafflement of his creator in the face of his artistic problem'. Eliot is inversely correct, though, describing how *Hamlet* does not fully symbolize, hold, contain, or unify, the 'emotion'—because its unique complex of feeling is embodied in the innumerable implications of compounded words and textures. The indeterminate excess of meaning and reflection, contained *in* but not *by* the work's language and form, is essential to literary art, a cause of its interpretability, manifest in Shakespeare's poems and plays, not merely '*Hamlet*, like the sonnets' which 'is full of stuff that the writer could not drag to light, contemplate, or manipulate into art'. What we can know of that 'stuff' is what the work does, however incompletely, drag, contemplate, and manipulate, for, as Eliot admits, 'when we search for this feeling, we find it, as in the sonnets, very difficult to localize'.[21] Such loose ends of language in poetic and scenic form, such difficult to localize possibilities, implied but not fully followed out, enable allusion to Shakespeare in, for instance, *The Waste Land* and 'Marina'. In what follows I illustrate how relations with his poetry, implying its plotted contexts, contribute to poems by John Ashbery, Elizabeth Bishop, and Roy Fisher responding respectively to *Romeo and Juliet*, *Twelfth Night*, and *Measure for Measure*. These three must

---

[18] Hughes, 'The Great Theme: Notes on Shakespeare' (1994) 106.

[19] Corcoran, *Shakespeare and the Modern Poet*, 36, alluding to Hughes' *Shakespeare and the Goddess of Complete Being* (London: Faber & Faber, 1992) and the boar in *Venus and Adonis*.

[20] William Empson, *Seven Types of Ambiguity* (1930) 3rd edn. (Harmondsworth: Penguin Books, 1972) 21; J. H. Prynne, *They That Haue Powre To Hurt; A Specimen of a Commentary on Shake-speares Sonnets*, 94 (Cambridge: [No Publisher], 2001) 1–86.

[21] T. S. Eliot, 'Hamlet and his Problems', *The Sacred Wood: Essays on Poetry and Criticism* (London: Methuen, 1920) 95, 100, 101.

stand as representatives for innumerable other such poems, a few of which, by Thom Gunn, Ingeborg Bachmann, Derek Walcott, and Geoffrey Hill, I have space to glance at, as when concluding with an observation about Hill's section from *The Triumph of Love* occasioned by Cinna the poet's fate in *Julius Caesar*.

33.2

While a student at Harvard, John Ashbery wrote a poem called 'Friar Laurence's Cell' (composed 1948, published the following year), its title an allusion, as Mark Ford has pointed out, to the 'scene of Romeo and Juliet's secret marriage'.[22] The Friar's Cell is the setting for various key passages. Ashbery's poem explores identification with both characters and plot—characterizing present lives and loves in the terms of a narrative inevitability borrowed from *Romeo and Juliet*. He thus reflects upon attempts to live in the light of theatre and poetry:

> What accidental virtues they incur
> Talking in a quiet corner of the cell
> Is nothing to the pair of menaced lovers,
> Who make the most of each foreshortened minute.[23]

Beginning with a remark about romantic dialogue, Ashbery's poem evokes such moments as when the 'menaced lovers' exchange a few words in Friar Laurence's hearing:

> ROMEO Ah, Juliet, if the measure of thy joy
> Be heaped like mine, and that thy skill be more
> To blazon it, then sweeten with thy breath
> This neighbour air, and let rich music's tongue
> Unfold the imagined happiness that both
> Receive in either by this dear encounter.
> JULIET Conceit, more rich in matter than in words,
> Brags of his substance, not of ornament.
> They are but beggars that can count their worth,
> But my true love is grown to such excess
> I cannot sum up some of half my wealth.

(II. v. 24–34)

Moments before the Friar will marry them they are not so much expressing their mutual love as outdoing each other in views on disjunctions between true feeling and adequate expression—another means for expressing that feeling. They echo each other with compacted metaphors while announcing themselves unable to do any such thing. What is

---

[22] John Ashbery, *Collected Poems 1956–1987*, Mark Ford (ed.), (New York: Library of America, 2008) 1027.
[23] Ashbery (2008) 895–6.

to be expressed exceeds expression even as it is expressed, another way of turning an excess of figures to account, as in the stanza above from *The Rape of Lucrece*. Such verbal self-awareness may be among the 'accidental virtues they incur', as Romeo and Juliet show modesty, measure, and insight in their passion. How actors speak these lines will indicate whether Romeo and Juliet are thought to be aware of the virtues expressed, or leaking Shakespearean reflection through his figured language.

Ashbery's sentence asserts that the verbal excess of their articulation is 'nothing' to them, as, in acting, they 'make the most of each foreshortened minute' while the Friar will not let them 'stay alone | Till Holy Church incorporate two in one' (II. v. 36–7). The young Ashbery's 'nothing' might be indebted to the word's use by Romeo when rebuking Mercutio for his Queen Mab speech, one the poet also alludes to in his opening verse:

> Still, in the third act, peace is so near,
> It seems the curtain will not fall, the soul
> At last be free to do its famous dance,
> The players descend among us to perform
> Beautiful parables out of mind,
> And angels come to bless us in our love.

Friar Laurence's Cell is returned to after the secret marriage. Since 'the third act' begins with the killings of Mercutio and Tybalt, Romeo's flight for Mantua, leading to the mishaps that produce the lovers' deaths, it looks odd for Ashbery to write that 'peace is so near'. But the drama depends on this so-near-and-yet-so-far feeling, disaster occurring in the secret marriage's aftermath, dispersing felicity, the Friar calling Romeo 'wedded to calamity' (III. iii. 3). Alluding to Mercutio's Queen Mab speech, Ashbery sustains the memory of 'time' by substituting his 'parables', for 'Her chariot is an empty hazelnut | Made by the joiner squirrel or old grub, | Time out o' mind the fairies' coachmakers' (I. iv. 68–70). Contrasts of figure and matter are again at stake, Romeo silencing Mercutio with 'Thou talk'st of nothing' (I. iv. 95). Yeats too aptly uses the phrase to ponder on 'this house | Where passion and precision have been one | Time out of mind',[24] for 'passion and precision' of speech exercise the poet in *Romeo and Juliet*.

Ashbery's second verse pulls away from the setting of the play to compare its doomed lovers to the 'we' in the poem's present tense who are now introduced. It is as if the American poet foreshadowed Baz Luhrmann's film *Romeo + Juliet* (1996):

> Although we know such happiness is bound
> To a loss exclusively theirs, their violent world
> Is more our cluttered city than Verona.
> And if, some nights, our love seems almost whole,
> It is only so chance may make a grander entrance
> Later in the play. Not that suffering is all—

---

[24] W. B. Yeats, 'Upon a House Shaken by the Land Agitation', *The Collected Poems*, 2nd edn, Richard J. Finneran (ed.), (Basingstoke: Macmillan, 1991) 95.

> But love has very little time for us
> Until it must be leaving. Then, of course,
> Some horrible event is ready to claim the day,
> And sorrow triumphs easily, like a germ.

'Not that suffering is all', the poet writes, and we know it's not, because 'Ripeness is all' (*The Tragedy of King Lear*, V. ii. 11), although Edgar's words aren't all reassurance in their acknowledgement of temporal finitude: 'Men must endure | Their going hence even as their coming hither' (V. ii. 9–10). Poets have called upon this phrase, cited exactly by Empson in 'To an Old Lady'.[25] where, as his editor notes, 'it preserves a trace of its original context',[26] or have alluded to it in Italian ('maturità era tutto'), as Attilio Bertolucci does in 'I papaveri' (The Poppies).[27] Ashbery evokes by substituting words in garlic-like phrases, as 'parables' for 'time' and 'suffering' for 'ripeness', producing multiplied senses as substitution cannot efface reader recall of the seasoned words. Ashbery's lines urge 'our love' to seize its own youthful ripeness, as Shakespeare's lovers try to, even though we recognize suffering's sway in their miscarried fates.

'Friar Laurence's Cell' calls up 'time' and 'ripeness' to urge that 'Love should be put into action', as a phrase of Elizabeth Bishop's has it.[28] With these words, and the unlucky trajectory of *Romeo and Juliet*, he considers the role of figurative language in the managing of those loves:

> If poetry, by tempering these gothic
> Accidents, that at last appear quite sane,
> Might be allowed to ruin us herself—
> If even, below the Friar's painted window,
> Standing in the nameless street of real bricks,
> Some girl had suddenly sung: 'They are all gone,
> Those famous lovers, those sweet names,
> Lying under the sod so many winters …'
> —How happy then we could go home, to write
> Their elegies, and die to be with them!

Watching *Romeo and Juliet*, its outcome known in advance, can feel like a preemptive exercise in fatality and foresight, poetry being a way of allowing fore-experience of the future, with the risk that its prospect spoils us for life, as in the Pasternak epigraph from *Safe Conduct* (its closing words, prompted by Mayakovsky's suicide in 1930) which Ashbery attached to a poem he included in *Some Trees* (1956): 'He was spoiled from childhood by the future, which he mastered rather early and apparently without great

---

[25] William Empson, *The Complete Poems*, John Haffenden (ed.), (London: Allen Lane, 2000) 24.
[26] Empson (2000) 194.
[27] Attilio Bertolucci, *Opere*, Paolo Lagazzi and Gabriella Palli Baroni (ed.), (Milan: Mondadori, 1997) 173.
[28] Elizabeth Bishop, *Poems, Prose, and Letters*, Robert Giroux and Lloyd Schwartz (ed.), (New York: Library of America, 2008) 7.

difficulty.'[29] Poetry thus might 'be allowed to ruin us herself', inviting us to play at being in love with death—that of others so we can write their elegies, and of our own to be with Romeo and Juliet, or John Keats, or, differently, calling out for Pasternak's translation of Sonnet 66 ('Tired with all these, for restful death I cry'), as evoked in part CIV of Hill's *The Triumph of Love*: '*shestdesyat* | *shestoy*, they shout—give us the sixty- | sixth [sonnet, of Shakespeare—ED]. You could say | that to yourself in the darkness before sleep | and perhaps be reconciled.'[30] That poetry may ruin its readers after such fashions is not a bright idea, nor what Shakespeare's poetry need invite either, as the couplet of Sonnet 66 underlines: 'Tired with all these, from these would I be gone, | Save that to die I leave my love alone'. So love triumphs over toying with death, while Ashbery's conditional speculation in his third verse contemplates, but holds off, our dying to be with them— calling upon the Elizabethan play on 'die' meaning 'orgasm' for good measure. His young people take themselves and their feelings seriously enough, something one who had mastered the future early might find comical, as the poem also acknowledges with its concluding aside and exclamation mark. 'Friar Laurence's Cell' has the allusive insouciance of a youthful work. It flirts in imagination, long before the AIDS epidemic, with love embraced by death, and might be contrasted with Thom Gunn's late Shakespearean 'In a Wood near Athens', its asking 'who did get it right?' and offering, among unlikely examples, the serial sex-murderer Jeffrey Dahmer, and 'Tearaway Romeo and Juliet'.[31]

33.3

On 24 January 1964, Robert Lowell wrote to Elizabeth Bishop: 'The 12th Night poem is marvelous. It has the form, tightness and charm of some of your early poems, such as the one about the little horse and rider, but translated into nature and direct observation.'[32] Does Lowell link Bishop's 'Twelfth Morning; or What You Will'—sent him before its first publication in *The New York Review of Books* on 2 April in the 400th anniversary year—to Shakespeare's comedy, or only to the Feast of the Epiphany? Thomas J. Travisano assumes the latter, writing that the 'power of reticence could be no more directly illustrated'[33] in Bishop's poem, a power that she herself attributed to Marianne Moore in 'As We Like It', whose use of metaphor in description 'is one of the qualities that gives her poetry its steady aura of both reserve and having possibly more meanings, in

[29] Ashbery, 'The Picture of Little J. A. in a Prospect of Flowers', *Collected Poems 1956–1987* (Library of America, No. 187) 13.
[30] Geoffrey Hill, *The Triumph of Love* (Boston: Houghton Mifflin, 1998) 53–4.
[31] Thom Gunn, *Boss Cupid* (London: Faber & Faber, 2000) 106.
[32] Thomas Travisano with Saskia Hamilton (ed.), *Words in the Air: The Complete Correspondence Between Elizabeth Bishop and Robert Lowell* (New York: Farrar, Straus & Giroux, 2008) 517. Lowell has in mind 'Cirque d'Hiver' in Bishop, *Poems, Prose, and Letters*, 23–4.
[33] Thomas J. Travisano, *Elizabeth Bishop: her Artistic Development* (Charlottesville: University Press of Virginia, 1988) 156.

reserve'.[34] Travisano doesn't so much as mention Shakespeare's play. Yet her second title, 'or What You Will', intends an allusion with that pun, the one made in Sonnet 135 ('Whoever hath her wish, thou hast thy Will') meaning 'whatever you like' and 'what you wish for or intend', its innuendos aside. Neither writer indicates why Bishop gave it this title, and understandably so, for the poem makes no overt reference with its translation 'into nature and direct observation' to *Twelfth Night*, even if Bonnie Costello intuits 'a Shakespearean comparison of perspectives between classes'[35] and the *New York Review of Books* editors published it in the Bard's birth month for his anniversary year.

'Twelfth Morning; or What You Will' is set in Cabo Frio, Brazil. A note explains: 'Literally "cold cape", a coastal resort town approximately 100 miles from Rio de Janeiro'.[36] Critics have pointed to a possible 'background' of meanings in Bishop's views on the politics of its setting, though little can be teased from her letters referring to the place.[37] Writing to friends, Bishop emphasizes its holiday benefits. Composing a poem, she draws on its nondescript, exploited, and run-down look. The poem, one of her many littoral studies, states its topic foci as they emerge through morning mist. She then develops the last of them first:

> Like a first coat of whitewash when it's wet,
> the thin gray mist lets everything show through:
> the black boy Balthazár, a fence, a horse,
>   a foundered house,
>
> —cement and rafters sticking from a dune.
> (The Company passes off these white but shopworn
> dunes as lawns.) 'Shipwreck,' we say; perhaps
>   this is a housewreck.[38]

Twelfth Night begins with a shipwreck separating siblings. Their being washed up on the coast of Ilyria occasions the subsequent confusion and final resolution, playing out in comic key a gender-troubled triangle such as exercises, for instance, Sonnet 144 ('Two loves I have, of comfort and despair'). Perhaps the 'housewreck' is granted similar implications in Bishop's poem: it separates people, subjects them to confusing affective allegiance, requiring a star-guided intervention to resolve them. If this is the case, it appears between the lines of a poem admired by Lowell for its 'direct observation'. 'Twelfth Morning; or What You Will' might have helped give its author a reputation for

[34] Elizabeth Bishop, 'As We Like It', *Poems, Prose, and Letters*, 683. She criticizes 'our greatest poet' for descriptions 'full of preconceived notions and over-sentimental' (681) and for animals condescendingly moralized: 'regarding the deer as a man imprisoned in a "leathern coat"'. (686)

[35] Bonnie Costello, *Elizabeth Bishop: Questions of Mastery* (Cambridge, MA: Harvard University Press, 1991) 39.

[36] Elizabeth Bishop, *Poems, Prose, and Letters*, Robert Giroux and Lloyd Schwartz (ed.), (New York: Library of America, 2008) 935.

[37] See Elizabeth Bishop, *One Art: Letters*, Robert Giroux (ed.), (London: Chatto & Windus, 1994) 354, 369, 414.

[38] Bishop (1994) 89.

her 'famous eye', about which she joked in later life when putting on glasses to read in public—mocking not her descriptive powers, but the stopping at them for her work's significance. Bishop's calling upon readers' memories of *Twelfth Night* invites a more pointed reading of her poem's 'nature' and 'observation'.

'Twelfth Morning; or What You Will' was not the first poem of hers to allude to Shakespeare's most gender-disturbed comedy. In the third verse of 'Varick Street' she writes:

> Lights music of love
> work on. The presses
> print calendars
> I suppose; the moons
> make medicine
> or confectionery. Our bed
> shrinks from the soot
> and hapless odors
> hold us close.
> *And I shall sell you sell you*
> *sell you of course, my dear, and you'll sell me.*[39]

Anne Colwell reports that in 'earlier drafts of the poem, Bishop alludes more openly to *Twelfth Night*, beginning the stanza with 'If music be the food of love | play on' (Vassar Box 29)'.[40] The poet sensibly reduces this too-strong seasoning in revision. As happens in Shakespearean allusion especially, the whole context is called up by the briefest sampling of Orsino's start to the play with his much-cited instruction (I. i. 1). Bishop's revision-substitution from 'play on' to 'work on' refers to her invocation of industrial Varick Street: 'At night the factories | struggle awake, | wretched uneasy buildings | veined with pipes | attempt their work'.[41] From this and these, the domestic side 'shrinks' and 'hold us close': the factory 'odors' keep us together but won't let us escape their commerce. It is a loose end hanging from Orsino's speech, with his doubled terms ('quick and fresh', 'validity and pitch', 'abatement and low price'):

> O spirit of love, how quick and fresh art thou
> That, notwithstanding thy capacity
> Receiveth as the sea, nought enters there,
> Of what validity and pitch so e' er,
> But falls into abatement and low price
> Even in a minute! (I. i. 9–14)

Comparison with this cloyed 'love' in *Twelfth Night* suggests the lovers in 'Varick Street' will not only sell each other, they'll sell each other short. In the pre-gay-pride situation

[39] Bishop (2008) 58.
[40] Anne Colwell, *Inscrutable Houses: Metaphors of the Body in the Poems of Elizabeth Bishop* (Tuscaloosa: The University of Alabama Press, 1997) 78.
[41] Bishop (2008) 57.

of Bishop's poem, collected in *A Cold Spring* (1955), this play is allusively relevant to misjudged, mysteriously thwarted, and self-confusing attraction. Bishop's reticence in the poem regarding object choice points to its relevance to same-sex desire, understandable as heterosexuality in *Twelfth Night*, its frisson dissolved there by reuniting identical siblings from opposite sexes.

Of 'Twelfth Morning; or What You Will', the poet's biographer noted that 'Elizabeth was never at Cabo Frio on 6 January (Epiphany, or the Feast of the Magi, in the Christian calendar) of any year'. Pondering what's reported, what invented, Brett Millier adds: 'perhaps she wished to invoke the world of unexpected reversals, of things not what they seem, of Shakespeare's play'.[42] The allusion to *Twelfth Night* tacitly extends in its description what the 'unexpected reversals' can be, and how things being 'not what they seem' may reverberate in the poem:

> The sea's off somewhere, doing nothing. Listen.
> An expelled breath. And faint, faint, faint
> (or are you hearing things), the sandpipers'
>   heart-broken cries.

The *Twelfth Night* implications of an after-'Shipwreck' or 'housewreck' in her stanza two are extended to the 'expelled breath' or sigh that the waves make, and the sandpipers' cries may be or may be thought 'heart-broken'. 'The fence, three-strand, barbed-wire, all pure rust' comes forward 'hopefully | across the lots', but 'thinks better of it' and 'turns | a sort of corner ...'. It is anthropomorphized in seeming to make an amorous advance, as if Viola (Cesario) sent out in a proxy courting bid, or obliquely hinting at her love for Orsino; but the fence too shies away, as does the envoy acting against her own romantic interests in Shakespeare's play. The rusty fence invites thoughts about sexual or moral location, of where you're supposed to be, for the uncertainty of the weathered fence is taken up by 'the big white horse'. Bishop suggests it's not worth asking '*Are you supposed | to be inside the fence or out?*' The horse is 'still | asleep', but 'Even awake, he probably | remains in doubt'. Her poem finds possibility emerging from mist by allowing a sleeping perspective to influence the look and interpretation of things; but that viewpoint draws its background implications from the gender-confused encounters of *Twelfth Night*. So where's the comic ending? Well, from the 'pewter colored horse, an ancient mixture, | tin, lead, and silver' which 'gleams a bit' she conjures a more brightly gleaming object as an assertion of confident selfhood, even in poverty, which finesses the poem's close.[43]

Bishop's 'Twelfth Morning', in this light, compares with the Utopian yearnings and personal-life confusions in another work that, on one draft, is named as in homage to Shakespeare on his 400th anniversary,[44] Ingeborg Bachmann's 'Böhmen liegt am Meer'

[42] Brett C. Millier, *Elizabeth Bishop: Life and the Memory of It* (Berkeley and Los Angeles: University of California Press, 1993) 300.

[43] Bishop (2008) 89–90.

[44] See "'Böhmen liegt am Meer'—"das Gedicht, zu dem ich immer stehen werde"' in Ingeborg Bachmann, *Letzte, unveröffentlichte Gedichte*, Hans Höller (ed.), (Frankfurt am Main: Surkamp Verlag, 1998) 107 and 131 for the relevant typescript and comment.

('Bohemia Lies by the Sea'). Its title alludes to that notorious loose end—the Bohemian seacoast in *The Winter's Tale*, first noted by Ben Jonson in his conversations with Drummond of Hawthornden, but a likely joke of Shakespeare's. Bachmann contradicts Jonson, insisting with Oscar Wilde that a map which 'does not include Utopia is not worth even glancing at':[45] 'And I take Shakespeare to be right and not his great gain-sayer, the great scholar, Johnson [sic]. Rather, Shakespeare's got it right: Bohemia lies by the sea. And he'll always be right, as this is the land on which all of us rest our hopes'.[46] Bachmann's poem evokes various plays, including *Twelfth Night*, when inviting their casts to join her on that coast: 'Come here, all you Bohemians, seafarers, dock whores, and ships | unanchored. Don't you want to be Bohemians, all you Illyrians, | Veronese and Venetians'. She identifies comedies of errors, lost labours of love, and trials set for characters with romantic crises in her life: 'Play the comedies that make us laugh | until we cry. And err a hundred times, | as I erred and never withstood the trials, | though I did withstand them time after time'.[47] Bachmann voices a remorsefully utopian invitation to be reunited in a Shakespearean land, one not quite contiguous with the real place and its conflicted history, but providing a form of imaginative ground upon which she felt she could stand.

Bishop was never as optimistic through her desperations as Bachmann's poem tries to be. The conclusion of 'Twelfth Morning; or What You Will' shifts from tacit theatrical allusion to evocation of 6 January, although Balthazár (not the black Magi but 'the black boy' of Bishop's poem) is someone whose 'Will' represents the world trans-valued on his name-day with a gift in the shape of a 'four-gallon can' which 'keeps flashing that the world's a pearl, *and I,* | *I am'*

> *its highlight!* You can hear the water now,
> inside, slap-slapping. Balthazár is singing,
> 'Today's my Anniversary', he sings,
>   'the Day of Kings.'

Bishop's work, set in the Southern Hemisphere, ends with a song and the sound of water, as, differently, does Shakespeare's when Feste in an English January sings '*For the rain it raineth every day*'. Bishop allows one of the poor of Brazil to conceive that he is uniquely privileged, without wholly endorsing the idea. Such complexities of interpretation are equally Shakespearean, as Bishop also notes in 'As We Like It' when underlining the obligation not to condescend to animals, working class or peasant characters, to write 'without "pastoralizing" them, as William Empson might say, or drawing false analogies'.[48] 'Twelfth Morning; or What You Will' has a double plot where a hinted-at sexual drama is playing behind some

[45] Oscar Wilde, *The Soul of Man under Socialism and Selected Critical Prose*, Linda Dowling (ed.), (London: Penguin Books, 2001) 141.

[46] Cited from her Nachlaß in *Letzte, unveröffentliche Gedichte*, 131, n. 40.

[47] Ingeborg Bachmann, *Darkness Spoken: The Collected Poems*, Peter Filkins (trans.), (Brookline: Zephyr Press, 2006) 617.

[48] Bishop, 'As We Like It' (2008) 685.

emblematic narrative description, while a tragic-comic subplot emerges in which a local boy presents a symbol for a 'happy ending' which can be simultaneously (Malvolio- or Sir Andrew-fashion) proud, deluded, and yet acknowledged. Bishop knew racial and class complexities in Brazil.[49] Letting Balthazár play the Magi lets perspectives doze for political implications too, a use of Shakespeare in the Americas comparable with Derek Walcott's *Othello*-allusive 'Goats and Monkeys' where exogamous 'coupling still halves our world'.[50]

33.4

One of the loose ends in the 'problem' play *Measure for Measure* concerns the arrangements allowing Isabella's brother Claudio to escape execution. Misleading the provost by pretending that a Friar (himself) is his informant, the Duke decides to pardon Barnardine, a dissolute prisoner convicted of murder, and among the play's most marginal characters:

DUKE   Which is that Barnardine?
PROVOST   This, my lord.
DUKE   There was a friar told me of this man.
    (*To Barnardine*) Sirrah, thou art said to have a stubborn soul
    That apprehends no further than this world,
    And squar'st thy life according. Thou'rt condemned;
    But, for those earthly faults, I quit them all,
    And pray thee take this mercy to provide
    For better times to come.—Friar advise him.
    I leave him to your hand.

(V. I. 476–85)

In the Wells and Taylor edition no stage direction indicates Barnardine exiting at this point, but he's granted no more words. Indeed, his final speech has occurred in Act IV, and these *are* exit lines: 'Not a word. If you have anything to say to me, come to my ward, for thence will not I today' (IV. iii. 59–60). So he refuses death, the Duke still disguised as a Friar responding thus: 'Unfit to live or die. O gravel heart' (IV. iii. 61). This unlikely stalemate sets off a further oblique response to Shakespeare, from Roy Fisher in the form of 'Barnardine's Reply', written in 1975, first appearing as a pamphlet from Sceptre Press in 1977, then anthologized in *Poems for Shakespeare: A Selection* (1978). Fisher's poetic concern with other lives concentrates on survival far from the sources of power and will. Although for Fisher this distance from power is recalibrated by scepticism about

[49] See her comment on 'the black cook kissing the white mistress' in a Brazilian advert for stoves, Joelle Biele (ed.), *Elizabeth Bishop and The New Yorker* (New York: Farrar, Straus and Giroux, 2011) 269–10.
[50] Derek Walcott, *Collected Poems 1948–1984* (New York: Farrar, Straus and Giroux, 1986) 83–4.

the legitimacy of such authority, its tendency to simplify life from self-perpetuating self-interest, simultaneously the poet's laconic style disqualifies such subjects from a counteractive eloquence that has the power to shape lives. Not the expression of Pasternak's 'free historical personality', constrained within the exigencies of a plot, here language plots and a minor character's silence resists. Such reluctance in 'Barnardine's Reply' can thus appear a revulsion extending to Shakespeare's language itself:

> Barnardine, given his life back,
> is silent.
>
> With such conditions
> what can he say?
>
> The talk
> is all about mad arrangements, the owners
> counting on their fingers,
> calling it discourse, cheating,
> so long as the light increases,
> the prisms divided and subdivide,
> the caverns crystallise out into day.[51]

Driven by Shakespeare's twisting plot, and the Duke's role in it, Barnardine appears a plain-speaking victim of experience passed down by higher powers. He may not influence his fate by eloquent arrangement, but his staying drunk means a priest can't prepare him for death. His final silence is seen as a fitting response to such discourse 'all about mad arrangements', the owners of this discourse described by Fisher as 'counting on their fingers' perhaps because, unlike Barnardine's blunt prose, their speeches tend to be in blank-verse pentameters.

Instead of a directing discourse, there appear in Fisher's poem 'images without words | where armed men, shadows in pewter, | ride out of the air and vanish, | and never once stop to say what they mean'. It is as though the power of judicial speech that acts to arrange Barnardine's reprieve in *Measure for Measure* is so detached from the affairs being judged that anyone who experiences these, one such as 'Barnardine, | whose sole insight into time | is that the right day for being hanged on, | doesn't exist', is debarred from being able to describe or comment upon what happens, debarred thanks to a separation between the language which may arrange, and the silence of non-verbal experience linguistically implied or lightly sketched. This reinforces how Barnardine is a near powerless victim of experience, of perceptions afflicting the eyes, since the conditions that he must live through are given him as 'a free sample from the patentholders', authority figures in the play, which 'keeps him quiet for a while'.

Fisher's poem then engages in the inherently contradictory deployment of words to evoke 'images without words' and the actions performed by those who 'never once stop to say what they mean'. Perhaps they constitute Barnardine's reply, had he not been kept

---

[51] Roy Fisher, 'Barnardine's Reply', *The Long and the Short of It: Poems 1955–2005* (Tarset: Bloodaxe Book, 2005) 246–7.

'quiet'. The first is a Caravaggio-like depiction of a murder victim being toyed with by the killer:

> —thumb with a broken nail
> starts at the ear lobe,
> traces the artery down,
> crosses the clavicle, circles
> the veined breast with its risen nipple,
> goes down under the slope of the belly,
> stretching the skin after it—
>
>> butchered just for his stink,
>> and for the look in his eye—

The poem's penultimate passage gathers up a recollection of some reversed sexual power play in *Venus and Adonis* to add a brutish lust to the brutal violence:

> In the grey light of a deserted barn
> the Venus, bending to grip the stone sill,
> puts up no case for what she's after,
> not even a sigh,
> but flexes her back.
>> No choice for the Adonis
> but to mount her wordlessly, like a hunting dog—
>> just for her scent
>> and for the look in her eye.

'Barnardine's Reply' concludes with a set-piece image of a reduced power to understand and act ethically. Yet by characterizing this lack, the poem implies an ethical position, one with political and social implications of its own, rendering that image as a pointer towards values not articulated within it. Fisher's close tacitly comments on the disturbing opportunism in *Measure for Measure*, by representing Justice as suffering in the eyes and unable to speak:

> Somebody draws
> a Justice
> on the jail wall;
>
> gagged with its blindfold
> and wild about the eyes.

Geoffrey Hill's comments on the play in section CXX of *The Triumph of Love* find him revaluing its much-questioned means for producing a just outcome: 'in *Measure for Measure* moral uplift | is not the issue' he asserts, adding that 'Scrupulosity, diffidence, | shrill spirituality, conviction, free expression, | come off as poorly as deceit or lust'. Where Fisher explores the fate of one that, in the Duke's words, 'apprehends no further than this world', Hill aligns the play with a Christian message, hazarding that its 'ethical *motiv*' is 'opportunism, redemptive and redeemed'. *Measure for Measure* is also commented on in

Eliot's 'Hamlet and his Problems', where he attributes this 'profoundly interesting play of 'intractable' material and astonishing versification' to 'a period of crisis'[52] and aptly collocates the 'interesting' with the 'intractable' in the playwright's 'astonishing' verse. Arising perhaps from a crisis of his own, Shakespeare turns it into a permanent 'problem' for us—occasioning responses such as those by Fisher and Hill.

Let me conclude, then, with an emblematic instance of one more Shakespearean loose end, a brutally collateral effect of Mark Antony's eloquent poetry upon his Roman countrymen, one also alluded to by Hill. In *Julius Caesar* Act III Scene iii, Cinna the poet is accosted and set upon:

> THIRD PLEBIAN   Your name, sir, truly.
> CINNA   Truly, my name is Cinna.
> FIRST PLEBIAN   Tear him to pieces! He's a conspirator.
> CINNA   I am Cinna the poet, I am Cinna the poet.
> FOURTH PLEBIAN   Tear him for his bad verses, tear him for his bad verses.
> CINNA   I am not Cinna the conspirator.
> FOURTH PLEBIAN   It is no matter, his name's Cinna. Pluck but his name out of his heart, and turn him going.
> THIRD PLEBIAN   Tear him, tear him!
>   [*They set upon Cinna*]

(III. III. 26–35)

Section LXXIV of *The Triumph of Love* reads: 'For Cinna the Poet, see under *errata*'.[53] Hill praised Simone Weil for proposing 'a system whereby "anybody, no matter who, discovering an avoidable error in a printed text or radio broadcast, would be entitled to bring an action before [special] courts" empowered to condemn a convicted offender to prison or hard labour'[54] and he seems to call Cinna's killing 'an avoidable error' caused by confusion of persons, like a typo, for which the author has tried to make amends. Yet the Plebians who kill Cinna are not making a mistake, don't do it by an oversight, for the poet tells them they're mistaken. They don't care, and mock his verses into the bargain. That's a writer with errors pointed out before publication that won't stir to correct them, let alone press for an *errata* slip when it's too late. Hill's one-liner may, though, be sending us to his own *errata* or emblematic makings of amends. Shakespeare's scene is another irony at poetic language, a subtler instance than Romeo's 'nothing' in response to Mercutio's account of Queen Mab. The cruelty of eloquence and consequent responsibilities of speech and writing are themes that have much exercised Hill, as they differently exercise Fisher in 'Barnardine's Reply'. Yet it's an indication of Shakespeare's inexhaustibility that he drops in Cinna the poet's scene to mimic an incidental cost to the art from a compelling poetic speech, then moves his play on, without stopping to say what it means.

---

[52] Eliot (1920) 99.
[53] Hill (1998) 38.
[54] Geoffrey Hill, 'Poetry as "Menace" and "Atonement"' in *Collected Critical Writings*, Kenneth Haynes (ed.), (Oxford: Oxford University Press, 2008) 9–10.

SELECT BIBLIOGRAPHY

Corcoran, Neil (2010) *Shakespeare and the Modern Poet* (Cambridge: Cambridge University Press).

Haughton, Hugh (2011) 'Allusion: The Case of Shakespeare' in *T. S. Eliot in Context* Jason Harding (ed.), (Cambridge: Cambridge University Press).

Hill, Geoffrey (2008) '"The True Conduct of Human Judgment": Some Reflections on *Cymbeline*', *Collected Critical Writings* in Kenneth Hayes (ed.), (Oxford: Oxford University Press).

Hughes, Ted (1994) 'The Great Theme: Notes on Shakespeare' in *Winter Pollen: Occasional Prose* ed. William Scammell (London: Faber & Faber).

Paterson, Don (2010) *Reading Shakespeare's Sonnets: A New Commentary* (London: Faber & Faber).

Prynne, J. H. (2001) *They That Haue Powre To Hurt; A Specimen of a Commentary on Shake-speares Sonnets*, 94 (Cambridge: Barque Press).

Robinson, Peter (2002) 'Pretended Speech Acts in Shakespeare's Sonnets', *Essays in Criticism,* 51: 3, July 2001, and in *Poetry, Poets, Readers: Making Things Happen* (Oxford: Oxford University Press).

Roe, John (2011) 'Great Shakespeareans: John Berryman' in *Great Shakespeareans* vol. 8, Peter Rawlings (ed.), (London: Continuum).

Wilmer, Clive (2008) 'Thom Gunn, Shakespeare and Elizabethan Poetry', *PN Review* 182, 34: 6, July–Aug.

CHAPTER 34

....

THE SOUND OF
SHAKESPEARE THINKING

....

JAMES LONGENBACH

Near the end of *The Tempest*, when everything finally seems to be going well, the exiled magician Prospero stages a pageant, a play within the play, to celebrate the impending marriage of his daughter Miranda to Ferdinand, the Prince of Naples. 'Let me live here ever', says young Ferdinand, entranced by the performance (IV. i. 122). But suddenly the play stops—Prospero has had a thought, one that cannot be ignored: Caliban is still plotting Prospero's death.

Thinking in Shakespeare is what turns us, changes us, makes us move. This is why all the great speeches feel like dramatizations of the mind in motion. And this, in turn, is why we feel so acutely that we know Shakespeare's characters from the inside out, as if we were listening to their minds. 'Our revels now are ended', says Prospero to the startled Ferdinand.

> These our actors,
> As I foretold you, were all spirits, and
> Are melted into air, into thin air;
> And like the baseless fabric of this vision,
> The cloud-capped towers, the gorgeous palaces,
> The solemn temples, the great globe itself,
> Yea, all which it inherit, shall dissolve;
> And, like this insubstantial pageant faded,
> Leave not a rack behind. We are such stuff
> As dreams are made on, and our little life
> Is rounded with a sleep.
>
> (IV. I. 148–58)

What has happened to Prospero's alarm? Rather than running off to subvert Caliban's plot, he ruminates on the illusion he has created, the play itself, and his thoughts move

from the impermanence of artistic creation to the impermanence of human life. Then
another thought pierces him.

> Sir, I am vexed.
> Bear with my weakness. My old brain is troubled.
> Be not disturbed with my infirmity.
> If you be pleased, retire into my cell,
> And there repose. A turn or two I'll walk
> To still my beating mind.
>
> (IV. I. 158–63)

Does Prospero need to take a stroll because he's upset about Caliban? No, that once
urgent thought has passed, like the pageant it interrupted. Instead, Prospero has been
shaken by his unexpected thoughts about mortality. Who could have heard it coming?
In Shakespeare, all brains worth listening to are troubled. Prospero's thinking has been
undone by thinking itself, the unpredictably shifting process through which the beating
mind becomes audible to itself over time.

This sound is not often to be heard in the verse of Shakespeare's contemporaries, but it
echoes everywhere among Shakespeare's progeny. When did Shakespeare learn to produce it? *The Tempest* was the last play he wrote without a collaborator, and in his very
earliest plays no-one speaks his mind as Prospero does. Speaking here in *3 Henry VI* is
Richard, Duke of Gloucester, who will become Richard III and dominate the play subsequently named for him.

> Why, I can smile, and murder whiles I smile,
> And cry 'Content!' to that which grieves my heart,
> And wet my cheeks with artificial tears,
> And frame my face to all occasions.
> I'll drown more sailors than the mermaid shall;
> I'll slay more gazers than the basilisk;
> I'll play the orator as well as Nestor,
> Deceive more slily than Ulysses could,
> And, like a Sinon, take another Troy.
> I can add colors to the chameleon,
> Change shapes with Proteus for advantages,
> And set the murderous Machiavel to school.
> Can I do this, and cannot get a crown?
> Tut, were it farther off, I'll pluck it down.
>
> (III. II. 182–95)

Richard is touting his prowess as an actor, a role-player, a shape-changer. His language
registers the newfound power of selfhood that we associate with the Renaissance, when
the very word 'self' ceased to be merely a reflexive and took on the now familiar sense
(as the *OED* puts it) of a person who is 'really and intrinsically *he*'. Such a self immediately becomes capable of thinking of itself as other than itself, protean, a murderer who
smiles, a happy man who weeps.

But there is nothing protean about the way Richard speaks. The passage I've quoted from his speech is made of five sentences: the first three are from three to five lines long, and each begins with a clause that establishes the grammatical template for the parallel syntax to follow (*I can smile—I'll drown more sailors—I can add colors*). Then the speech concludes with two one-line sentences that have the gathering force of a sonnet's final couplet: 'Can I do this, and cannot get a crown? | Tut, were it farther off, I'll pluck it down'. Unlike Prospero's final words, which surprise him as much as they do us, this conclusion feels willed. Richard comprehends the power of metamorphosis, but his speech does not embody that power. This mind is standing still.

Part of the thrill of Richard's malevolence is due to the creepily static quality of his character. But none of Shakespeare's greatest characters speak the language of completed thought, not even his most conniving villains. *The Third Part of Henry the Sixth* was probably written around 1590, and just a few years later, in *King John*, we hear for the first time the kind of thinking we associate with Prospero, Hamlet, and Lear. Faulconbridge, called the Bastard, speaks here on the occasion of having discovered that his true father was Richard the Lionhearted, a revelation for which he is unexpectedly rewarded with a new identity; the king dubs him Sir Richard Plantagenet.

> Well, now can I make any Joan a lady.
> 'Good e' en, Sir Richard'—'God-a-mercy, fellow';
> And if his name be George I'll call him Peter,
> For new-made honour doth forget men's names;
> 'Tis too respective and too sociable
> For your conversion. Now your traveller,
> He and his toothpick at my worship's mess;
> And when my knightly stomach is sufficed,
> Why then I suck my teeth and catechize
> My pickèd man of countries: 'My dear sir',
> Thus leaning on mine elbow I begin,
> 'I shall beseech you—'. That is Question now;
> And then comes Answer like an Absey book.
> 'O, sir', says Answer, 'at your best command,
> At your employment, at your service, sir.'
> 'No sir', says Question, 'I, sweet sir, at yours.'
> And so, ere Answer knows what Question would,
> Saving in dialogue of compliment,
> And talking of the Alps and Apennines,
> The Pyrenean and the River Po,
> It draws toward supper in conclusion so.
> But this is worshipful society,
> And fits the mounting spirit like myself;
> For he is but a bastard to the time
> That doth not smack of observation;
> And so am I—whether I smack or no,
> And not alone in habit and device,
> Exterior form, outward accoutrement,

> But from the inward motion—to deliver
> Sweet, sweet, sweet poison for the age's tooth.
>
> (I. 1. 184–213)

As he speaks, the Bastard is discovering a power that the Richard of *Henry VI* assumes—the power of role-playing, of assuming a new name. The sentences I've quoted from his speech range in length from one to nine lines, and instead of following an established pattern, the syntax interrupts itself in unprecedented ways. At the same time, the structural logic of the passage is more associative than discursive. 'Well, now I can make any Joan a lady', begins the Bastard, imagining his newfound power to raise a woman's social status by marrying her. But in the second sentence he imagines being greeted by a fellow courtier ('Good e'en, Sir Richard') and then addressing his interlocutor by the wrong name ('And if his name be George, I'll call him Peter'), since a proper courtier displays his status by forgetting other people's names. A change of name, a conferral of a new identity, has provoked this speech, and the speech itself keeps altering its course as it progresses. The third sentence imagines a conversation with a fellow courtier over dinner, and while this scene follows logically enough from the meeting with George, called Peter, the turn from the end of the second sentence ('Tis too respective and too sociable/For your conversion') to the beginning of the third ('Now your traveller, | He and his toothpick at my worship's mess') is so swift that we may not heed the logic of the association. Instead, we register the sudden intrusion of the word 'toothpick' (with which a proper courtier would delicately pick his teeth), and then revel in the punning description of this interlocutor as the Bastard's 'pickèd man'.

As the speech continues, its direction feels as unconstrained as the conversation it recounts, veering with sound-driven authority from 'the Alps and Apennines' to 'the Pyrenean and the River Po'. But unlike the apparently arbitrary associations of the imagined conversation, the associations of the speech itself add up to something powerfully urgent. For when the Bastard declares in the final sentence that, whatever his outward appearance, he will 'deliver | Sweet, sweet, sweet poison for the age's tooth', we suddenly feel that the 'toothpick' that wandered so amiably into the speech has become part of an argument. While Richard seems to have known the conclusion to his speech all along, the Bastard's conclusion is extruded from the process of its own becoming. It happens to him. So while the language of the Bastard may seem more capricious than Richard's, the process of thought it embodies feels more robust. It happens to us.

In retrospect, Richard's speech sounds less like mature Shakespeare than like the more declamatory playwrights who were Shakespeare's contemporaries, particularly Christopher Marlowe. Coleridge observed that these playwrights 'see the totality of a sentence or passage, and then project it entire'. Their language represents completed thought, rather than the mind thinking. In contrast to them, said Coleridge, 'Shakespeare goes on creating, and evolving B. out of A., and C. out of B., and so on, just as a serpent moves, which makes a fulcrum of its own body, and seems for ever twisting and untwisting its own strength'.[1] This self-generating drama of discovery, simultaneously twisting and untwisting, at once wayward and inevitable, is what we feel not only in the speech of the Bastard but in the speech of all the great characters of Shakespeare's maturity—and in many of the minor characters too. It is also what we feel in the great lyric poems of our language.

'What has thou been', asks King Lear of Edgar, the unjustly reviled son of Gloucester, who plays the role of Tom o' Bedlam when he joins the outcast Lear on the heath (III. iv. 78). Like Richard, Edgar assumes the power of pretense, but he speaks with a rigorous charisma that Richard doesn't attain. His response to Lear's simple question feels larger than the scene provoking it, as if the individual will were as vast as language itself.

> A servingman, proud in heart and mind, that curled my hair, wore gloves in my cap, served the lust of my mistress' heart, and did the act of darkness with her; swore as many oaths as I spake words, and broke them in the sweet face of heaven; one that slept in the contriving of lust, and waked to do it. Wine loved I deeply, dice dearly, and in woman out-paramoured the Turk. False of heart, light of ear, bloody of hand; hog in sloth, fox in stealth, wolf in greediness, dog in madness, lion in prey. Let not the creaking of shoes nor the rustling of silks betray thy poor heart to woman. Keep thy foot out of brothels, thy hand out of plackets, thy pen from lenders' books, and defy the foul fiend. Still through the hawthorn blows the cold wind; says suum, mun, nonny. Dauphin my boy! Boy, *cessez*; let him trot by.

> (III. IV. 79–94, folio text)

Although it is cast in what might seem to be the looser decorum of prose, Edgar's speech is structured sturdily—as sturdily as Richard's is except that its repetitions do not consolidate but complicate the meaning as the speech unfolds, asking us to review and rethink. First the speech offers a paratactic list of all the bravura roles this role-player has played (servingman, hair-curler, glove-wearer, adulterer, defamer, wine-lover) that crests in a deliciously excessive second list of the animal qualities displayed in each of these performances: 'hog in sloth, fox in stealth, wolf in greediness, dog in madness, lion in prey'. Then the speech offers another list of parallel phrases, but the mood shifts from the declarative to the imperative ('Keep thy foot out of brothels, thy hand out of plackets'), as if suddenly to suggest that this wastrel's life is not to be glorified but condemned. Finally, out of these considered warnings erupts an unprecedented lyricism ('Still through the hawthorn blows the cold wind') that quickly segues into doggerel ('Dauphin, my boy') and pure sound ('suum, mun, nonny'). The whole speech

---

[1] *The Romantics on Shakespeare*, Jonathan Bate (ed.), (New York: Penguin, 1992) 163. See also Jonathan Bate, *Shakespeare and the English Romantic Imagination* (New York: Oxford University Press, 1986) and Theodore Leinwand, 'Shakespeare, Coleridge, Intellecturition', *Studies in Romanticism* 46 (Spring 2007): 77–104.

moves with the interlaced energy of surprise and inevitability that distinguishes alert conversation—

> FALSTAFF   'Sblood, I am as melancholy as a gib cat, or a lugged bear.
> PRINCE HAL   Or an old lion, or a lover's lute.
> FALSTAFF   Yea, or the drone of a Lincolnshire bagpipe.

(1 HENRY IV, I. II. 73–6)

—and, as a result, the speech consequently feels driven by forces larger than a single speaker's intention to express what he already knows. The language functions as the fulcrum of itself. It seems to be performing Edgar as much as Edgar is performing Tom. It embodies the kind of thinking that in *King Lear* gets things done.

Thinking, as Heidegger describes it in his *Discourse on Thinking*, may take one of two forms: calculative thinking, which is driven by the will, and meditative thinking, which enables and is enabled by an openness to the mystery of existence.[2] Richard is a calculative thinker, Edgar a meditative thinker—but only when he assumes the guise of Tom o' Bedlam. For when Edgar drops the guise he reverts to given wisdom: 'When we our betters see bearing our woes, | We scarcely think our miseries our foes', he says after his encounter with Lear on the heath.[3] This kind of willed language, based on the presupposition of justice and proportion in the universe, is precisely what *King Lear* beats to nothingness.

It is also the kind of language we first hear from the mouth of Lear himself, who begins the play as a calculative thinker—which is to say that, in a sense, he is not thinking at all. After he's exiled to the heath, Lear must go deeper than Edgar: he must learn truly to think—which is a way of saying that, in the narrowly prescribed psychic economy of the play, Lear goes mad.

> They flattered me like a dog, and told me I had the white hairs in my beard ere the black ones were there. To say 'ay' and 'no' to everything that I said 'ay' and 'no' to was no good divinity. When the rain came to wet me once, and the wind to make me chatter; when the thunder would not peace at my bidding, there I found 'em, there I smelt 'em out. Go to, they are not men o' their words. They told me I was everything; 'tis a lie, I am not ague-proof.

(IV. v. 96–105)

Lear's realization here is the same as Prospero's, and it is the simplest but most profound realization of all: he is mortal, he too can catch a cold. But Lear had to learn to sound like Tom o' Bedlam, to become a meditative thinker, in order to achieve this realization.

---

[2] See Martin Heidegger, *Discourse on Thinking*, trans. John M. Anderson and E. Hans Freund (New York: Harper and Row, 1966).

[3] These lines appear in the quarto text of *King Lear* (I. xiv. 95–6) but not in the folio text, from which I have been quoting elsewhere.

At the beginning of the play, Lear's language evinces very little interiority; he is simply walking through the role of the benignly despotic monarch. But by the middle of the third Act we feel, listening to Lear, that we are experiencing not only the outward drama of self-consciously performed language but the inward drama of a mind remaking itself by speaking itself.

This is why the conclusion of Lear's speech on the heath ('I am not ague-proof') does not feel merely ironic or paltry or funny; it feels truly like something the actor playing Lear does not know until he says it. The fourth sentence of his speech begins with a sequence of clauses delineating exterior actions (*when the rain came, when the wind blew, when the thunder clapped*), but the real action of the sentence is interior. And while the logic of such thinking may initially feel occluded, it never feels puzzling. For however disjunctive the movement of the sentences, conclusions arrive with an assurance that casts a retrospective sense of rigour over the process by which we've reached them. This is why the language gives us pleasure (we feel that something happens to us at the same time that we observe something happening to the character), and our pleasure depends not on mastery but submission: we feel something happen because we've trusted an utterance we cannot yet fully comprehend.

Which is to say that we come to trust ourselves. Thinking, as Freud conceives of it, begins as pre-conscious activity, an activity that we paradoxically become aware of only in consciousness: whatever we know of thinking is already a representation of thinking.[4] Listening to Shakespeare, we've learned to become conscious of what is more properly unavailable to consciousness; we have learned to imagine that his fluid enactments of interiority constitute interiority itself. And neither have we done this in isolation, for we have had other teachers who by listening to Shakespeare were themselves well taught. Milton, Wordsworth, Coleridge, Yeats, Stevens—between us and Shakespeare stands a long line of other poets who have trained our ears to listen for the sound of thinking. Reading poems from 'Tintern Abbey' through 'Sunday Morning' and beyond, we've come to expect a Shakespearean movement of mind, since, like the makers of these poems themselves, we've been taught by previous poems to imagine that our interiority is constituted in just that way.

---

[4] See Sigmund Freud, 'Regression', *The Interpretation of Dreams*, trans. James Strachey (New York: Avon Books, 1965) 571–88. Angus Fletcher summarizes the position elegantly in *Colors of the Mind: Conjectures on Thinking in Literature* (Cambridge, MA: Harvard University Press, 1991) 32: 'To wish to know thought absolutely, to be able to say it, to utter its *form* is finally impossible .... There cannot then be a stated thought, purely and as such, there can only be images and various icons of thoughts, that is, there can only be iconographies of thought'. In contrast, Helen Vendler, in *Poets Thinking: Pope, Whitman, Dickinson, Yeats* (Cambridge, MA: Harvard University Press, 2004), treats thinking as the conscious organization of ideas. Similarly focused on what rather than how Shakespeare thought, A. D. Nuttall's *Shakespeare the Thinker* (New Haven: Yale University Press, 2007) is nonetheless exemplary in its conclusions: 'His thought is never still' (24). While in *Shakespeare Thinking* (London: Continuum, 2007) Philip Davis is sensitive to the mobility of Shakespeare's thinking, his interest in cognitive processes as such leads him away from the language that must inevitably embody it: 'In Shakespeare it is not character that speaks, originally or finally, but a life-force' (9).

'My Brother Tom is getting stronger', wrote Keats with heartbreaking matter-of-factness in 1818, 'but his Spitting of blood continues—I sat down to read King Lear yesterday'.[5] Almost immediately Keats wrote the sonnet 'On Sitting Down to Read *King Lear* Once Again', but the more consequential impact of *King Lear* was registered in letters written over the subsequent year. Having absorbed the sound of Shakespeare thinking, he set out self-consciously in his letters to mimic and, through mimicry, inhabit that sound.

> Buy a girdle—put a pebble in your Mouth—loosen your Braces—for I am going among Scenery whence I intend to tip you the Damosel Radcliffe—I'll cavern you, and grotto you, and waterfall you, and wood you, and water you, and immense-rock you, and tremendous sound you, and solitude you. I'll make a lodgment on your glacis by a row of Pines, and storm your covered way with bramble Bushes.[6]

Keats described this kind of writing as wandering, running wild, or playing one's vagaries; yet however quixotic the energy, Keats' sentences are always as carefully constructed as Shakespeare's, the parallel syntax fuelling the alliteratively driven elaboration ('waterfall you, and wood you, and water you'). Keats can sound in his letters both like Shakespeare and like a writer of prose-poems from the early years of the 21st century. His greatest poems harness this apparently wayward energy without, given the elegance of their surface, advertising the fact that they do so.

Reading the 'Ode to a Nightingale', for instance, we don't feel that the stanzas follow one another in an orderly progression toward a foreseeable conclusion; instead, we feel the poem grappling with a variety of different attitudes toward mortality, oblivion, and transcendence. Sometimes the attitudes seem merely opposed to each other, but more often they seem partially overlapping, difficult completely to distinguish from one another. The nightingale is fraught with significance, made and unmade by the luxurious music of the poem itself.

For at first, the nightingale's song seems to promise a reprieve from the human world of mortality, a world

> Where palsy shakes a few, sad, last gray hairs,
> Where youth grows pale, and spectre-thin, and dies;
> Where but to think is to be full of sorrow.

But almost immediately the antidote to such suffering perpetuates the disease. 'I cannot see what flowers are at my feet', says Keats, impassioned by the nightingale's song, and the imagined flowers turn out to be as time-bound as the youth who grows pale and thin: 'Fast fading violets cover'd up in leaves'.

Yet the music of these lines says something else again. The gorgeous patterning of Keats' syntax, made more emphatic here by lineation (*where palsy shakes, where youth*

    [5] John Keats, *Letters*, Hyder Edward Rollins (ed.), 2 vols. (Cambridge, MA: Harvard University Press, 1958) 1:212.
    [6] Keats (1958) 1: 245.

grows pale, where but to think), invites us to take pleasure in this certain knowledge of our demise. And in no time, the very thing that the 'Ode to a Nightingale' sets out to evade becomes the poem's deepest wish: 'Now more than ever seems it rich to die'. But this wish fades as quickly as the violets that provoked it, since Keats quickly realizes that his death would not merge him with the ecstasy of the nightingale's song but sever him from it forever. The nightingale cannot perform simultaneously as a source of human pleasure and as an emblem of the obliteration of human pain. It continually eludes the function that the poem attempts to prescribe for it, and while the poem tries continually to catch up, its ultimate failure to do so feels the opposite of disheartening. The procedures of its thinking are more compelling than the conclusions, and were this not the case, the poem's final lines—

> Was it a vision, or a waking dream?
> Fled is that music:—Do I wake or sleep?

—would seem unbearably conclusive, even shallow, like the couplet rounding out Richard's speech in *Henry VI*. But any answer provoked by these questions is incapable of accounting for the tissue of equivocation which constitutes our experience of the poem. Offering to summarize our experience, the questions are everywhere surpassed by it. As a result, the poem seems freshly disorienting every time we read it again. Its thinking feels as elusive, therefore as alluring, as the song of the nightingale itself.[7]

Neither, in the world after Shakespeare, is this feeling restricted to poems.

> Mrs. Dalloway said she would buy the flowers herself.
> For Lucy had her work cut out for her. The doors would be taken off their hinges; Rumpelmayer's men were coming.[8]

The first three sentences of *Mrs. Dalloway* twist and turn against themselves as seductively as Edgar's, but since we're used to reading stories, we experience the opening of Virginia Woolf's novel with every expectation that our questions will be answered. As a result, we might not stop to register the extraordinary leaps in thinking which these sentences demand. Who is Mrs. Dalloway? Why is she buying flowers? Why can't Lucy buy the flowers? What is Lucy doing instead? Who is Rumpelmayer? Why are they taking the doors off their hinges? I'm feeling a little uneasy. I'm scared of Rumpelmayer's men.

Reading *Mrs. Dalloway*, we quickly deduce that Clarissa, wife of Richard Dalloway, is preparing to give a party. Flowers must be bought; access between the public rooms of her home must be made simpler. The tone here is one of practised, confident pleasure, and yet the sense of ominous discomfort unearthed by a slow reading of the novel's first three sentences is appropriate. The subsequent five sentences follow the thoughts of Clarissa as she moves from the morning air around her to the air she experienced as a young woman at her family's house at Bourton to the undeniable fact that something awful was about to happen.

---

[7] John Keats, *The Poems*, Jack Stillinger (ed.), (London: Heinemann, 1978) 369–72.
[8] Virginia Woolf, *Mrs. Dalloway* (New York: Harcourt, 1925) 3.

> Mrs. Dalloway said she would buy the flowers herself.
>
> For Lucy had her work cut out for her. The doors would be taken off their hinges; Rumpelmayer's men were coming. And then, thought Clarissa Dalloway, what a morning—fresh as if issued to children on a beach.
>
> What a lark! What a plunge! For so it had always seemed to her, when, with a little squeak on the hinges, which she could hear now, she had burst open the French windows and plunged at Bourton into the open air. How fresh, how calm, stiller than this of course, the air was in the early morning; like the flap of a wave; the kiss of a wave; chill and sharp and yet (for a girl of eighteen as she was then) solemn, feeling as she did, standing there at the open window, that something awful was about to happen.[9]

Something awful *will* happen. *Mrs. Dalloway* follows the structure of Shakespearean romance, and, like *The Tempest*, it is driven by the deepest wish: that the dead may be brought back to life. But like Prospero's pageant, Clarissa's party is interrupted by a suddenly unavoidable thought (the suicide of Septimus Smith), and like *The Tempest*, *Mrs. Dalloway* is driven by the simplest recognition: that everyone will die.

Despite her reputation as a socialite, Clarissa lives with this recognition more intimately than anyone; at Bourton, when she was a child, she saw her sister Sylvia crushed by a falling tree. But Clarissa's authority is established not through narrative information but through the quality of her thinking, which the initial movement of the novel's language embodies. The opening eight sentences have the shape and impact of a lyric poem because, like Keats' ode, they deliver us unexpectedly to a thought that seems at odds with the sequence of observations that has also produced it. The knowledge of impending mortality happens to Clarissa, as if for the first time. In the same way, it happens to us.

'The words drop so fast one can't pick them up', said Woolf of her experience of reading Shakespeare. 'This is not "writing" at all. Indeed, I could say that Shakespeare surpasses literature altogether, if I knew what I meant'.[10] What Woolf meant, I think, is that reading Shakespeare, she felt inexplicably intimate not with language but with pre-conscious activity, as if Shakespeare's language were providing unmediated access to the work of the mind, the work she herself aspired to capture in language on the page. To become intimate with Shakespeare is in this sense to become intimate with ourselves, and to do so at the moment when selfhood seems at once most powerful and most tenuous. It is to suffer the beautiful illusion of an inner life capable of full articulation at the same time that we're offered the terms of articulation—to exist viscerally in the process of change, to relinquish the will to fate.

This is why the great poems of thinking in our language are, like the 'Ode to a Nightingale', almost inevitably about what Heidegger called being-toward-death: to become a meditative thinker is to exist not in spite but because of the fact that one day we will have been.[11]

---

[9] Woolf (1925) 3.

[10] Virginia Woolf, *A Writer's Diary*, Leonard Woolf (ed.), (London: Hogarth Press, 1953) 155.

[11] See Martin Heidegger, *Being and Time*, John Macquarrie and Edward Robinson (trans.), (New York: Harper and Row, 1962) 304–11.

A full moon. Yesterday, a sheep escaped into the woods,
and not just any sheep—the ram, the whole future.
If we see him again, we'll see his bones.

The grass shudders a little; maybe the wind passed through it.
And the new leaves of the olives shudder in the same way.
Mice in the fields. Where the fox hunts,
tomorrow there'll be blood in the grass.
But the storm—the storm will wash it away.

In one window, there's a boy sitting.
He's been sent to bed—too early,
in his opinion. So he sits at the window—

Everything is settled now.
Where you are now is where you'll sleep, where you'll wake up in the morning.
The mountain stands like a beacon, to remind the night that the earth exists,
that it mustn't be forgotten.

Above the sea, the clouds form as the wind rises,
dispersing them, giving them a sense of purpose.

Tomorrow the dawn won't come.
The sky won't go back to being the sky of day; it will go on as night,
except the stars will fade and vanish as the storm arrives,
lasting perhaps ten hours altogether.
But the world as it was cannot return.[12]

Sentence by sentence, these stanzas from Louise Glück's 'Before the Storm' register their inhabitation of being-towards-death in their very syntax. Tense shifts constantly; the language of temporality is everywhere. 'Yesterday, a sheep escaped into the woods', and 'tomorrow, there'll be blood in the grass', but in no time even this evidence of prior existence will have been: 'the storm will wash it away'. The sheep is 'the whole future', but the future persists in this poem only by virtue of our recognition that it will someday be the past.

The choral speaker of 'Before the Storm' (a multiplicity of mortal beings speaking as one) is acutely aware of the inexorably forward motion of time, but like Prospero's or Lear's, the speaker's thinking darts in multiple directions at once, as if the poem were a conversation between multiple parties. Every new stanza sounds like the beginning of a new poem—

> A full moon. Yesterday a sheep escaped into the woods.
>
> In one window, there's a boy sitting.
>
> Above the sea, the clouds form as the wind rises.

—as if to suggest that our experience of the forward motion of time actually inheres in a constant movement back to a beginning, not to the point we first set out from but to a different starting point, one we couldn't have predicted. The poem moves not by projecting a totality out of a single sentence but by evolving (as Coleridge described Shakespearean

[12] Louise Glück, *A Village Life* (New York: Farrar, Straus and Giroux, 2009) 10–11.

utterance) B out of A and C out of B: tomorrow the rain will come, yesterday the ram escaped, tonight a boy's been sent to bed early. Quickly we braid these materials into a coherent sense of human mortality, but our incremental experience of the poem is seductively disorienting. For if we pay attention simply to what the poem is saying, the poem says everything is ending. But if we pay attention to how the poem dramatizes its thinking, the poem suggests that we're nonetheless free to recreate our beginning over and over again, turning back from the end. Like Shakespearean romance, the poem grants our deepest wish and at the same time denies it. Like the 'Ode to a Nightingale', it denies our deepest wish at the same time that it fulfills us. The ram will die, the boy will grow up, the flock will dwindle, the rain will fall, the dawn won't come, something awful will happen, the world will remain a mystery. 'Everything is settled now', says this poem, but the texture of the poem's thinking suggests that nothing is settled. 'A turn or two I'll walk', says Prospero, 'To still my beating mind', but we know that such turning can only make the mind's beat stronger, which is anyway what we crave.

Such turning has distinguished the manner of some of the most prominent poetry since modernism, allowing us to suffer the misapprehension that disjunctiveness is a characteristic feature of one school of poetry and not another. But the sound of thinking in our poetry has always been disjunctive, and whether we're reading Shakespeare or Keats, Ashbery or Glück, the best image for a poem's ultimate coherence is not the ouroborus, the serpent with its tail in its mouth, but the serpent making a fulcrum of its own body, moving relentlessly yet inexplicably forward. 'You seem to be *told* nothing', said Coleridge of the experience of reading Shakespeare, 'but to see and hear every thing', and what we hear is 'the rapid flow, the quick change, and the playful nature of the thoughts'.[13]

Shakespeare was primarily a dramatic poet, but the poetry of his plays has shaped the history of English-language poetry as powerfully as his lyrics, which were themselves shaped by the poetry of drama. Coleridge speculated that Shakespeare developed a purposefully meandering texture in his lyric poems as a way of compensating for the lack of the annotating presence of the actor—the voice and gesture that may transform even the most staid piece of writing into a visceral act of becoming. This seems plausible, except that Shakespeare's dramatic writing also offers this compensation, making his verse feel richly inward on the page and sometimes immune to the missteps of bungling actors.

The verse also keeps us open to missteps. The fact that Shakespeare was not only a poet but also one of the greatest prose writers in the language begs a larger argument, an argument that encompasses not only poetry but prose; an argument that encompasses not only prose but the metaphors we employ to represent thinking in most any circumstance; an argument that asks us to see that those metaphors have arisen not from an unmediated encounter with our own thinking but from our devotion to the makers of metaphors; an argument that demands, finally, to be raised to the level of hyperbole. But for Shakespeare, none of us would know what we imagine thinking to be.

[13] Samuel Taylor Coleridge, *Biographia Literaria*, James Engell and W. Jackson Bate (eds.), 2 vols. (Princeton: Princeton University Press, 1983) 2: 21–2.

SELECT BIBLIOGRAPHY

Bate, Jonathan (1992) (ed.) *The Romantics on Shakespeare.* (New York: Penguin).

Davis, Philip (2007) *Shakespeare Thinking.* (London: Continuum).

Fletcher, Angus (1991) *Colors of the Mind: Conjectures on Thinking in Literature.* (Cambridge, MA: Harvard University Press).

Heidegger, Martin (1966) *Discourse on Thinking,* trans. John M. Anderson and E. Hans Freund. (New York: Harper and Row).

Longenbach, James (2008) *The Art of the Poetic Line.* (Saint Paul: Graywolf Press).

Nuttall, A. D. (2007) *Shakespeare the Thinker.* (New Haven: Yale University Press).

Vendler, Helen (2004) *Poets Thinking: Pope, Whitman, Dickinson, Yeats.* (Cambridge: Cambridge University Press).

Voigt, Ellen Bryant (2009) *The Art of Syntax: Rhythm of Thought, Rhythm of Song.* (Saint Paul: Graywolf Press).

....

CHAPTER 35

MELTED IN AMERICAN AIR

....

JUDITH HALL

Induction: A chapter approaches below, dressed as a scene-shifting play but edited to be read in a handbook. The prologue, like an antiquated, ticklish hat, lends to the occasion a warm, but no more serious than comic, tone. Soon enough, you read, as if actually seeing, poets reading different Shakespeares in America. Walt Whitman first, then Emily Dickinson, T. S. Eliot, Gertrude Stein, and on to Cole Porter, Louis Zukofsky, to Frederick Seidel and Susan Howe, and others too. Such poets have done more with his texts than gild a single monologue with one of his admired characters. The chapter, imperiously, does no less than simply take his lines without acknowledgement.

35.1

....

[*Prologue*]: *Think, when we talk of* poetry, you see Shakespeare?[1] Here, in proud America? *Here and there, jumping o'er times?* His various treasures turned, generation by generation, into often contradictory practices? What spurs a poet?

Piece out our imperfections with your thoughts. If his name is now no more analogous to poetry than power, then? Then Shakespeare continues to figure in American poetry and how it is imagined.

Walt Whitman, reminiscing—about himself, naturally—wedded his apprentice days, his 'declamations and escapades' aboard an omnibus, in particular, to the 'gestation' of his *Leaves of Grass*.[2] No-one heard him, though, not passengers, not the drivers, men

---

[1] William Shakespeare, *The Life of Henry the Fifth*, Prologue, 26 in Wells and Taylor (2005) 597. Throughout the chapter, lines and phrases from Shakespeare's works are given in italics and taken without additional acknowledgement.

[2] Walt Whitman, 'Omnibus Jaunts and Drivers' *Specimen Days* in *Complete Poetry and Collected*

whose names he made a litany: 'Balky Bill, George Storms, Old Elephant, his brother Young Elephant … Tippy, Pop Rice, Big Frank …'; bus noise dominated, 'heavy, dense' instead. And bus noise protected—and the driver's 'animal' benevolence abetted—adolescent Walter's happiness, his pursuit of happiness in declamation: 'some stormy passage from … Richard'. ('The sound of the belched words of my voice … ').[3] 'You could roar as loudly as you chose', and still no-one heard his *Now is the winter of our discontent*.

He had seen *Richard III* more than once and considered John Wilkes Booth's performance 'wax' to his father's 'flesh'. When he was just sixteen, Whitman caught ('Booth *pere*') Junius Brutus' Richard at the Bowery Theatre, and he wrote on the performance repeatedly, mostly small exclamatory jottings, but also in unusual detail. The audience, like inadvertent supernumeraries, enlarged the show for him. '2000' men 'packed ceiling to pit'; 'alert, well-dressed, full-blooded'; 'full-sinewed'. This was a masculine vista, scanned with pride. And scanned again as men applauded, 'no dainty kid-glove business', but 'tempests of hand clapping', hands of workers: 'the best average of American-born mechanics'.

Booth's entrance seemed more silent after applause, and the audience in his happy memory swelled suddenly to 'perhaps 3000'. Stage business with a sword was analysed; Plato, cited to interpret Booth's 'insanity'. The actor fleshed force, 'fire, energy, *abandon*', and Whitman, among an overwhelmed audience, was enthralled. 'I never heard … such a sting to hauteur or the taunt'. (FIGURE 35.1A and B).

'The presence of the greatest poet conquers', Whitman wrote in his introduction to *Leaves of Grass* (1855). 'He is not one of the chorus'. 'He is', in the poem, a directing authority, projecting 'energy, *abandon*' at and over 'you'. And charismatic 'Walt', as a creation, is not unlike Shakespeare's king. Both are bodily defined and self-mocking and self-delighting. Richard's *delight to pass away the time* is tethered mockingly to self-regard in sunlight; Walt's is hyperbolic, *childish-foolish* in Richard's phrase: 'the song of me rising from bed and meeting the sun'. Personal charm triumphant!

Shakespeare's Richard III descended from the medieval figure Vice and then shared this progenitor with Falstaff. The brag, the glee: *I have a whole school of tongues in this belly of mine, and not a tongue of them all speaks any other word but my name.* Whitman's verse has been called 'Falstaffian' and, in the same breath, not 'Falstaffian' enough. Nevertheless, he wrote over and beyond lovable wickedness and 'wicked lovableness'.[4]

Prose (New York: Library of America, 1982), 702–3; also 'Plays and Operas Too' *Specimen Days*, 703–5; *Democratic Vistas*, 955; 'British Literature' *Notes Left Over*, 1058–60; 'A Thought on Shakespeare' and 'The Old Bowery' *November Boughs*, 1150–2, 1185–92.

  [3] Whitman, *Leaves of Grass (1855)* in *Complete Poetry* (1982) 27.

  [4] Harold Bloom, 'Shakespeare' in *Ruin the Sacred Truths* (Cambridge, MA: Harvard University Press, 1987); also Laurence Olivier, *Confessions of an Actor* (New York: Simon and Schuster, 1982) 147–8.

(B)

(A)

FIGURE 35.1. Duelling Flamboyancies: (A) Walt Whitman as Walt Whitman: Steel engraving of a daguerreotype, now lost, used as frontispiece for *Leaves of Grass*. 'The worst thing about this is, that I look so damned flamboyant—as if I was hurling bolts at somebody—full of mad oaths—saying defiantly, to hell with you!' (B) Junius Brutus Booth as Richard III. Photogravure of a painting, now lost, illustrating lines from Cibber's acting edition of Act IV, Scene iii: 'Hark! Murder's doing, princes, farewell! | To me there's music in your passing bell'.

Like Falstaff, like Richard, Walt's poses make even an apparently personal utterance extravagant. 'I lean and loafe at my ease …. observing a spear of summer grass'. And given the number and tenor of his brags ('I breathe the fragrance of myself, and know it and like it …'), a reader may hear directives in declarations; self-soothing; persuasions in reiterations.

An 'audience', so important to Walter on the omnibus and in the Bowery Theatre, served in *Leaves of Grass* as both scenery and 'you'. They offer by mere presence succor, not recognition. His 'you' is protean, now his soul, now self, now lover: perpetually ephemeral. The other audience—the crowds, images of tradesmen, labourers, women too, non-speaking bit parts—constitutes a quasi-democratic atmosphere. The crowds are named, evoked, and so combine his litany of bus drivers with the sense memories of his masculine vista. Walt then served as audience to the audience, watching his cavalcade of types with fellow-feeling for his vivid scenery.

Readers, an audience of readers, Whitman argued, finally figured the value of a poem, and the poem, for its part, should be grounded 'continually' in reader response. Better for a poem 'to arouse and initiate ... than to define or finish'. Such a fair exchange he considered 'modern' and democratic. The commerce between an actor's arousing performance and his audience he praised. Richard's words, though, the 'finish' of the Elizabethan's language, he opposed.

'Certainly some terrific mouthing in Shakspere!' Whitman wrote, but he 'belonged to the buried past'. He 'offended'; he was 'poison'; 'feudal'. 'He seems to me of astral genius, first class, entirely fit for feudalism. His contributions, especially to the literature of the passions, are immense ...'. A genius, but; praise, but: Shakespeare 'exhale[s] that principle of caste which we Americans have come on earth to destroy'.

Any contradiction between individual authority—an operatic dominating sound— and democratic vistas Whitman never did resolve. The privileges of personality epitomized his democracy. And the future of poetry would be democratic, by means of *Leaves of Grass*. A break with the past, a literature 'without debts', made exceptionalism easier to claim.[5]

And yet his *Leaves of Grass* was actually exceptional. Not just the character alone, 'Walt Whitman, an American, one of the roughs, a kosmos', and not just the imagery, the divine manifestations from *The Bhagavad Gita* stirred among the tavern brag.[6] ('Think of having that under your skin. All that!')[7] Unmetered, the poem sounded—exceptionally not English.

Cadenced enough to sound 'tremendous', sensual, majestic, Whitman called his 'rhythmed prose-verse'[8] a 'language experiment'. But was it free? Free verse? Not if readers hear more than two choices, more than merely metered (i.e. foreign) or American. Whitman wanted to give his country a purely American poem. Some readers assume that makes it free. Such readers, such assumptions, are part of our national tragedy or farce.

[*Additional Passages*]: *Flourish. For now sits expectation in the air* that what Whitman assumed, other poets, Americans, years later, also assume ... a license to dismiss Shakespeare, for example.

What mightst [they] *do* if Edgar Allan Poe, say, thrived in Whitman's stead? Would metre sound less English to American ears? Or English predecessors not promise— not seem to promise—*to divert* [American] *purposes? Linger your patience on, and we'll* digest | *Th'abuse of distance; force—perforce—a play.*

[*A Separate Scene*]: Emily Dickinson's faith in Shakespeare never softened. He was necessary; heaven: 'he has had his Future who has found Shakespeare'.[9] No other

[5] Leo Bersani, 'Incomparable America' in *The Culture of Redemption* (Cambridge, MA: Harvard University Press, 1990) 153.

[6] William Logan, 'Prisoner, Fancy-Man, Rowdy, Lawyer, Physician, Priest: Whitman's Brags' in *The Undiscovered Country* (New York: Columbia University Press, 2005).

[7] D. H. Lawrence, 'Whitman' in *Studies in Classic American Literature* (1923; available at <http://xroads.virginia.edu/~HYPER/LAWRENCE/dhlch12.htm>) 1.

[8] George Saintsbury, *Historical Manual of English Prosody* (1910; rpt. New York: Schocken, 1966) 33.

[9] Richard B. Sewall, *The Lyman Letters* (Amherst: Massachusetts, 1965) 75; for other letters cited, see Emily Dickinson, *Selected Letters*, Thomas H. Johnson (ed.), (Cambridge, MA: Belknap, 1971); for Emily

American poet so savoured, even venerated, his plays. Doubters persisted, at home, in school and Amherst, town and college, hopelessly preoccupied with morals, sin. They were unavoidable. Her father, for example, sent his children a magazine for 'genteel juveniles', and in it Shakespeare, 'worthless', ranked below Bunyan's *Pilgrim's Progress*.[10] To rear genteel juveniles was not such an uncommon ambition then.

And only single lines, like sweet temptations suddenly medicinal, were used in Ebenezer Porter's *Rhetorical Reader*. She learned, in a chapter on elocution, on rising and falling inflection: 'The fault, dear Brutus, is not in our *stárs*; | But in *oursèlves*, that we are underlings'. ('[Emphasis] is the most important principle, by which elocution is related to the operation of the mind'.)[11]

After school she belonged to a Shakespeare Club, 'a rare thing in those days', and during the first session, before anyone opened a book, a tutor offered to 'mark out the questionable passages'. Some dissenting whispers. Then a girl, a designated representative for girls, said, they 'did not want the strange things emphasized, nor their books spoiled with marks'. Debate, an exercise in reasoning, persuasion, ensued. 'Finally', the girls 'told the men to do as they liked—"we shall read everything"'. And they did, week after week, gather together, the 'men' using 'expurgated editions', the 'girls' reading 'everything', until the men surrendered, and 'the whole text was read out boldly'.

For the poet Dickinson, here were apprentice protocols in among 'a long foreground somewhere': multiple perspectives; aposiopesis; and then a memory of emphasis, grammar; a logic of dissection—speech extracted, isolated (as Shakespeare's was manipulated); memorized, owned. ('Paradise is that old mansion | Many owned before—Occupied by each an instant | Then reversed the Door—')[12]

Her poems do not flow forward but rather figure turbulence, all manner of it, from a merely neurological jolt, or a pun, to the 'wild grammar' of gratitude, madness, ecstasy.

> Unto my Books ...
>
> I thank these Kinsmen of the Shelf—
> Their Countenances Kid
> Enamor—in Prospective—
> And satisfy—obtained—

The final stanza disorients, as Dickinson suspends her poem's many animations between grammar and wonder. A reader absorbs more sound—over sense—when sense has been delayed by riddled syntax.

Fowler Ford on Shakespeare Club, see Mabel Loomis Todd (ed.), *Letters of Emily Dickinson* (New York: Grosset & Dunlap, 1951) 36–7.

[10] Alfred Habegger, *My Wars are Laid Away in Books* (New York: Random House, 2001) 99.

[11] Ebenezer Porter, *The Rhetorical Reader* (New York: Mark H. Newman, 1835) 39, 43.

[12] Emily Dickinson, *The Complete Poems*, Thomas H. Johnson (ed.), (Boston: Little, Brown, 1960) 503; poems cited are from this edition; for 'I greet you at the beginning of a great career, which yet must have had a long foreground somewhere, for such a start', see Ralph Waldo Emerson, letter to Walt Whitman, 21 July 1855.

And with the flow dashed, language halts, accelerates, 'jingling' too with rhyme—'Bells' needed, Dickinson wrote, in self-defense, to 'cool [her] Tramp'. 'Those short, quick probings at the very axis of reality', Melville wrote of Shakespeare, describing a comparably rapid kinetic effect. But 'reality'? 'The Brain—is wider than the Sky—' Speculation is her sustenance, and possibility—*might be the be-all and the end-all, here*—the joy.

This is not analogous to a character in Shakespeare finding through soliloquy distinctive form. A Macbeth, a Benedick might display among attractive mental convolutes, volutes of memory, conjecture, a progressive education, leading, as his time passes, to a 'self' whose limitations, because now known, are forgiven. Or not. Knowledge—of identity, mortality—may be of use, of course, to mortals, but possibility—as a play, a power—Shakespeare, like Dickinson, preferred. ('I dwell in Possibility—' and 'To be Alive—is Power'.) 'So the Eyes accost—and sunder | In an Audience'. Her tone can be, as here, oracular and intimate and intimate a metacognitive pulse (thought on thought on) that syncopates the 'operation of the mind'.

Some readers, though, prefer identity. Absorbed by virtuoso banter, foolish silence, 'sudden transitions and elliptical expressions',[13] however a jolt, they find in bits of Hamlet or Lear Shakespeare, the man himself, confessed. *O, reason not the need!* Dickinson too has been as earnestly possessed among her poems. Why hear her, for example, reading *Hamlet* (*You would play upon me, you would seem to know my stops, you would pluck out the heart of my mystery*), when you could see her pain?

> He fumbles at your Soul
> As Players at the Keys
> Before they drop full Music on—
> He stuns you by degrees—
> Prepares your brittle Nature
> For the Ethereal Blow
> By fainter Hammers—further heard—

Dickinson's choice of 'you' is uncharacteristic, a part of her borrowing from the calculated barrage on Guildenstern.

Her poems, even of acute release like this one, represent a language realm. 'When I state myself, as the Representative of the Verse—it does not mean—me—but a supposed person'. A poem tinted with 'personal history', as Emerson put it, 'remains prosaic'. Her sister reiterated more prosaically the terms: 'Her intense verses were no more personal expressions than Shakespeare's tragedies ...'. Intensity is not a frenzy but an effect of phrases jostled free of context, syntax, cause? Her procedure is then antic, very Hamlet.

To Dickinson, 'no part of the mind is permanent', not even its freedoms. Reading, not writing, brought the frenzy she admitted, befriended. 'How my blood bounded! Shakespear ... I flew to the shelves and devoured the luscious passages. I thought I

---

[13] William Hazlitt, 'The Plastic Imagination' (1818) in *Four Centuries of Shakespearian Criticism*, Frank Kermode (ed.), (New York: Avon, 1965) 127.

should tear the leaves out as I turned them'. She was not oppressed by his excellence, whether or not English, 'questionable', genteel.

35.2

Tradition and the Individual Talent: A Dialogue. Literature, the point of American literature, if conceived by Puritans and dedicated to democracy, is service. And the service will be small, technically proficient, useful as a pewter bowl. Printers, journalists were democratic; they would serve, inform. Sermons, religious tracts: Entertainment, any wit, should be welded to religious contemplation. 'A country of small adventures, short plans', Emerson said. 'Our books will be tents, not pyramids'.

No. Literature, a strictly utilitarian literature, will not accommodate manifest destinies, an insanely splendid wilderness. Democracy, too narrowly defined, fosters an 'incomplete' nation, 'a riot of mediocrities', Emerson observed.[14] Exit then in search of self-reliance, transcendence, individual talent.

Tradition and the Individual Talent: A Dialogue. Literature, in a democracy, is independent of class advantages, patrons, universities. A great American poem could surface anywhere in a field, and a great society serves the field, not chiefly the individual talent. Accomplishments—the pyramids, the poems—are aftermath, and a great society recognizes how long a 'foreground' may be. Individual talent thrives in a hodgepodge of literary enterprise, and a national endowment for the arts will fund writers' centres, societies, festivals; upstart quarterlies, letterpresses, kitchen-table presses; taped archives of poets reading; and translations in Austin, Boston, Brooklyn, Oakland, Portland, Cleveland, Kalamazoo; and distributors for the above and hundreds more.

No. Literature that is 'anti-Christian bigotry', 'elitist', or 'a riot of mediocrities' does not serve a democracy. 'A great nation deserves great art'[15] and might fund a few worthy, exceptional Americans; a master. Not the field.

Tradition and the Individual Talent: A Pedagogue. Literature, when handed down to students, is *altered when alteration find*, and teaching—another 'constant experiment'[16] 'obtain[ed] ... by great labor'—has no tradition in America but change.[17]

---

[14] Larzer Ziff, *Literary Democracy* (New York: Penguin, 1981) 42–57.

[15] Motto of National Endowment for the Arts, created in 1965 during the 'great society' era; also 'Dept. of Justice partnership supports Shakespeare projects for at-risk youth' press release, NEA, 23 April 2009; 'NEA brings Shakespeare to military bases' press release, 30 August 2004; 'NEA launches largest tour of Shakespeare in American history' press release, 23 April 2003.

[16] W. H. Auden, 'American Poetry' in *The Dyer's Hand* (New York: Random House, 1962) 361, on democracy as 'constant experiment'.

[17] T. S. Eliot, 'Tradition and the Individual Talent' in *American Literature 2*, Richard Poirier and William L. Vance (eds), (Boston: Little, Brown, 1970) 683–9; also '"Rhetoric" and Poetic Drama' in *The Sacred Wood* in *The Waste Land and Other Writings* (New York: Random House, 2001) 30; for 'The poet must become more and more comprehensive, more allusive, more indirect, in order to force, to dislocate

Shakespeare entered the American curriculum slowly, first a line or two, a turn of phrase, then as model oratory, more lines, samples from soliloquies, and finally, only with the end of the 19th century, plays were safely taught at Harvard and Yale. A hundred years later, as slowly, Shakespeare exited, is exiting, American curriculum, no longer required for a degree in literature. Literature, our tradition, is now American. Mongrel, polyglot, not English. Let English writers join the ranks of other world writers waiting our peripheral attentions.

Tradition and the Individual Talent: A Dialogue. Beyond an American literary field, world literature awaits our acknowledgement, our belated membership. Soon, all is foreign, local, familiar, peripheral, without a core. In that approaching, crowded future, our literature is not exceptional. A few poets, a line or two, a sample will be read. The hours for reading are not infinite, and none reserved automatically for America.

No. No-one is ready to be unexceptional. 'A great nation deserves great art'. If living talents will not serve, let Shakespeare be the great art the government supports: Fund performances in public schools; in 'economically disadvantaged schools'; for 'court-adjudicated youths'—the latter partly funded by the Department of Justice. And fund performances in time of war at Quantico Marine Base, Fort Leavenworth Army Base, Edwards Air Force Base, Pearl Harbor Naval Station, and many more. Mostly of *Macbeth*. Shakespeare may exit university curricula, departments of literature, but the Department of Defense recalls his authority.

Tradition and the Individual Talent: A Polliwog. 'There remains to define this process of depersonalization and its relation to the sense of tradition'. So T. S. Eliot choreographed the poet moving cautiously under his 'bewildering minute' reading; his surrenders, shuddering; and recovery from reading with laborious, concealed allusions.

'Trout-like', was Marianne Moore's positive review of Eliot's poetics: 'In his poetry, he seems to move trout-like through a multiplicity of foreign objects …'.[18] Some provocations can be navigated if considered foreign, an object, and Shakespeare was one among a multitude of foreigners. Messy, possibly ('the strained and mixed figments of speech in which Shakespeare indulged himself'), but all the same, the head boy: someone, if you cannot be, you surrender to. 'You don't really criticize any author to whom you have never surrendered yourself…'. A schoolboy enjoys a ragtime parody, a 'Shakespeherian Rag'. He labours with, against a gloom that cloys. Great poets 'steal', Eliot said, moving along Ben Jonson's sheen, 'forcing' it into a very American circumvention of indebtedness.[19]

---

if necessary, language into meaning', see 'Metaphysical Poets' in Poirier, 690; also Frank Kermode, 'Eliot and the Shudder' *London Review of Books*, 32, November 2009.

[18] Marianne Moore, 'Review of *The Sacred Wood*' (1921) in *The Complete Prose* (New York: Viking, 1986) 55.

[19] John Hollander, 'Ben Jonson and the Modality of Verse' in *Vision and Resonance* (New York: Oxford University Press, 1975) 168 for Eliot on Jonson: 'His poetry is of the surface'; and yet, one poet's sheen, his imitativeness, or polemic, could be another's objective correlative. Also Eliot on stealing ('Immature poets imitate, mature poets steal: bad poets deface what they take, and good poets make it into something better, or at least something different') steals—imitates? converts?—Jonson on the artist's prerogative ('to convert the substance, or riches, of another poet, to his own use'). *Timber, or Discoveries Made upon Men and Matter* (1640).

35.3

Gertrude Stein never considered the making of a composition labour. She chose writing, 'really writing', and would not have chosen it, if writing hurt. Her method is not speculative—responses to stimuli—but interrogative. She likes to ask and has a right to ask and takes it. 'And how do you like what you are | And how are you what you are | And has this to do with the human mind'.[20]

Reading is contiguous, not subordinate, to writing, not a tool. 'I have always been from my babyhood a liberal reader of all English literature'. Language surrounds and covers the reader, an immersion she treasures—'lost' in it. And it is 'inside me' as well.[21] 'It is nice that nobody writes as they talk and that the printed language is different from the spoken otherwise you could not lose yourself in books and of course you do, you completely do. I always do'. Her experiments with repetition as a 'continuous present' construct for her reader her pleasure reading.

When other people talk, she observed, their words, thoughts repeat 'the same thing over and over again', and the rhythm of personality is given neither by word nor thought but in the endless movement over minor 'infinite variations'. Collecting such data yields questions, all of which 'help me in my way'.

Field studies—hearing friends talk—inform material she assembles for early compositions. She also records in her 'Diagram Book' invented classifications of character types. When she groups herself in 'earthy boy, masculine in general outline' and delights in 'loving repeating is then in a way earth feeling', the methodology absorbs personal sentiment. Repetition is not then a nervous isolating solipsism but a determined initiation into art—a way to connect—only by rhythm. 'Must write the hymn of repetition'.[22]

Stein mentions Shakespeare's writings with affection not reverence, as if he were a better brother, companionable as Homer or the Bible. Name dropped, brought in to bear her glory, *Hamlet* acquiesces, as she jockeys with Charlie Chaplin over drinks: Nothing happens in 'Shakespeare's most interesting play', and this supports her excitement, her 'invention' of 'doing nothing' in *Four Saints in Three Acts: An Opera to be Sung* (1934).[23]

Hamlet plays a larger part in her lecture 'What Are Master-pieces and Why Are There so Few of Them' (1940). Here she distinguishes between entity writing, 'really writing'— that is, writing disentangled from prepositions (not writing *after* or *for*)—and 'identity'

[20] Gertrude Stein, 'Identity A Poem' (1935) in *A Primer for the Gradual Understanding of Gertrude Stein*, Robert Bartlett Haas (ed.), (Santa Barbara: Black Sparrow, 1971) 117–23; also 'A Transatlantic Interview' (1946) 15–35 and 'My Debt to Books' (1939) 113–14.

[21] Stein, 'What is English Literature' (1934) in *Writings and Lectures 1909–1945*, Patricia Meyerowitz (ed.), (Baltimore: Penguin, 1967) 31–58; also 'Plays' (1934) 59–83; 'The Gradual Making of *The Making of Americans*' (1934) 84–98; 'Poetry and Grammar' (1934) 125–47; 'What Are Master-pieces and Why Are There So Few of Them', 148–56; 'Henry James' in *Four in America*, 291–330.

[22] Brenda Wineapple, *Sister Brother* (Baltimore: Johns Hopkins University Press, 1997) 264, 294.

[23] Stein, *Everybody's Autobiography* (1937; rpt. New York: Random House, 1973) 282.

writing—*on* (*beyond, through, to*) human nature and time. The latter remembers and illustrates, has purpose and audience: 'I am I because my little dog knows me but, creatively speaking the little dog knowing that you are you and recognizing that he knows, that is what destroys creation'. Shakespeare's play may inherit a revenge, open *up* identity, psychology—human nature and time—but these do not determine a 'master-piece'. 'If it were the way a young man could react to the ghost of his father then that would be something anybody in any village would know they could talk about it talk about it endlessly but that would not make a master-piece ...'.

This formula, this understanding, key to Stein's immense enterprise, is viewed again in her portrait 'Henry James' (1947). Shakespeare she trusts to centre her prolegomenon, and she marches forward, back, looking at his plays and sonnets as examples of entity and identity writings. The sonnets sound to Stein prospective, too purposeful. Intent is felt. The future has implicitly entered the sonnets, and they become smoother, mere 'writing as it was going to be written'. Words then resonate less; they hesitate and only 'sound'. 'Shakespeare never expressed any feelings of his own in those sonnets.... If it is your own feeling, one's words have a fullness and violence'.

The plays though are 'writing as it is written'; their words—not muffled by hesitation, yesterday, tomorrow—are 'being' not 'doing'. Each word sounds and also mingles slightly with a neighbour sound. Intricate mingling adds a third bright sound. The music then combusts, becoming visible, beautiful.

'Does it sound different if the words used are the same or are the words used different when the emotion of writing, the intention in writing is different'. The question is rhetorical, of course, and Stein argues, and presents her argument as personal revelation, that the same word is altered by a writer's state of mind. Shakespeare's plays are not livelier than his sonnets because of form or 'substance' (characters or plot), but vitality. The difficulties of his language—the word choice, the placements, coinages, and microscopic harmonies and movement ('so exciting')—also prove he is 'writing as it is written'. 'Clarity is of no importance because nobody listens and nobody knows what you mean no matter what you mean ... it is not clarity that is desirable but force'.

All this precedes her witty, moving portrait of Henry James 'in general', as a general: 'I like to think what would he do if he had been a general'. James would have marshalled doing and being, identity and entity writings. His dense, gradual manoeuvres proceed, and yet, his hesitations are not 'prospective': 'He came not to begin but to have begun'. James overcomes her mutually exclusive categories. His success, though, casts no triumphant, retrospective shadow over Shakespeare's writings. They were 'always a passion' and remain a part of the 'intellectual recreation' of language.

35.4

Tradition and the Individual Talent: A Dialogue. Poetry, after the successes of modernists, needed no advocates, no apologists. America finally had a generation—a generation, not just a stray genius—worthy of international regard. Arrival could be construed as perpetuity, and perpetuity, importance. No need for a poet to argue any longer 'the fact that his art has importance'.[24]

Yes and no. Consider Cole Porter and his popular (commercial) songs—blithe, smart, assertively trivial. They were managed like crossword puzzles, with the metre the question the words answered. 'List' songs showed off rhymes that, by syllable count alone, were excessive and comically outré: 'You're Mahatma Gandhi | ... Napoleon Brandy' (1934). End-rhymes were punch lines. Hip-hop song writers made use of multisyllabic rhyme fifty years later for a comparably satiric, ostentatious effect.

Porter was hired to write songs for *Kiss Me Kate* (1948), an Americanization of *The Taming of the Shrew*. W. H. Auden considered the musical better than the original, but his opinion of the Shakespeare was low. One of Porter's list songs winks through a gangster's view of Shakespeare: 'to wow women', so 'they'll all kowtow':

> With the wife of the British embessida
> Try a crack out of 'Troilus and Cressida'.
> If she says she won't buy it or tike it
> Make her tike it, what's more, 'As You Like It'.
> If she says your behavior is heinous
> Kick her right in the 'Coriolanus'.

He considered this form, his most popular, 'the tinpantithesis of poetry'. On Broadway the 'splashy' musical gave Shakespeare's 'name' the longest run 'it' ever had, and in Hollywood, *Kiss Me Kate* (1953) was filmed in both technicolour and 3-D, one of the last big MGM musicals.[25]

[*Additional Passages*]: *Flourish. Thus ... our swift scene flies* among *the well-appointed* darlings of a visual culture—film, spectacle, thea-tah—humming *choice-drawn* Bard bits from Porter's 'great American songs'. Has American poetry any part of this, *either past or not arrived to pith and puissance*?

Well, the book design of Gertrude Stein's *The Making of Americans* (1925) could bring to mind 'early German engraving'.[26] Wallace Steven's *Ideas of Order* (1935)—on heavenly 'matte white Duca di Modena paper', handset in type 'which imitates the unical forms of early medieval manuscripts'[27]—could certainly cow a reader; and yet, how small these austere visual delights seem, compared to 'glorious Silver Screen ... amorous Cinemascope'.[28] Even 'in crisis', Hollywood, 'full of crumbling pyramids',[29] ('Elizabeth

[24] Louise Bogan, *Achievement in American Poetry* (Chicago: Gateway, 1951) 108.

[25] Bosley Crowther, 'Review of *Kiss Me Kate*' in *The New York Times*, 6 November 1953.

[26] Moore, 'Review' (1986) 128.

[27] Jerome McGann, *Black Riders* (Princeton: Princeton University Press, 1993) 24.

[28] Frank O'Hara, 'To the Film Industry in Crisis' in *Meditations in an Emergency* (New York: Grove, 1957) 3–5.

[29] David O. Selznick to Ben Hecht in Michael Wood, *America in the Movies* (New York: Columbia University Press, 1975) 173.

Taylor blossoming, yes, ...) was 'epic'. Poetry in an American field, sans 'great American song', sans epic, held fast to 'importance'.

Tradition and the Individual Talent: Agog. 'Anyone who explains William Shakespeare dreams in character',[30] and the character that dreamed Louis Zukofsky's four-hundred page 'explanation' could have been Rosalind's child, if she had chosen Jaques. His *Bottom: On Shakespeare* (1963) can be melancholy reading as it happily encompasses quotation, question, warm rebuttal, and then extends—as if an infinite dialectic were love—beyond love to philosophy (and 'a philosophy of suspecting philosophy'), until music intervenes, overtaking reason with a freely conjured love. *How bitter a thing it is to look into happiness through another man's eyes.* Eye images from all of Shakespeare are plucked out and used to contemplate 'when reason judges with eyes love and mind are one'.

Quotations dominate his commentary, and some readers find unadulterated material more true, objective—external to the mind. Others object, lost in an eagerly bottomless inquiry. ('The mind *stirred*, rarely or "happily" creates Bottom'.) In his poems, quotations are compressed, less extensive, pressed into service of a poem's music. 'Julia's Wild', for example, permutes only twenty times a single line from *The Two Gentlemen of Verona*: 'Come shadow, come, and take this shadow up, | Come shadow shadow, come and take this up'. Lorine Niedecker compared the ambition and the tone of his long poem 'A' to 'Lucretius as the creator of Hotspur might have read him':[31] 'River that must turn full after I stop dying | Song, my song, raise grief to music | Light as my loves' thought ... '.[32]

Any student looking for an introduction to his poems will find a different Zukofsky in the *Norton Anthology of Modern and Contemporary Poetry* (2003) than the one offered in 1973, an edition that conflated modern and contemporary. Shakespeare guided Zukofsky's poetry in the older anthology: His 'clear physical eye against the erring brain' foresaw 'the kind of poetry' Zukofsky 'tried' to write.[33] By 2003, Shakespeare's authority, no longer overstated, is unstated. He recedes, an image in a vacuum, something a boy watches in a Yiddish theatre in New York.

No mention of the adult poet reading Shakespeare. Zukofsky instead is positioned simply as a second-generation modernist, a hinge between Ezra Pound and later Black Mountain and Language poets. Much is made of his coinage 'Objectivists', a term he qualified with quotation marks and further qualified with a date in *Poetry* magazine— '"Objectivists" 1931'. He was not manifesto-inclined, but the chance to edit an issue came with a conviction that a 'standard', if not a rallying cry, for his contributors, would beef up the ballyhoo and then sales. 'Foolish—' he wrote at the time, 'but may excite the reading

[30] Louis Zukofsky, *Bottom* (Middletown: Wesleyan University Press, 2002) 9, 215, 325, 392–3.

[31] Lorine Niedecker, *From This Condensery*, Robert J. Bertholf (ed.), (Highlands: Jargon Society, 1985) 300.

[32] Zukofsky, '11' in 'A' (Baltimore: Johns Hopkins University Press, 1993) 380.

[33] Richard Ellmann and Robert O'Clair (eds), *The Norton Anthology of Modern Poetry* (New York, 1973) 657–8.

boob-like, hysterectomied & sterilized readers of "Poetry"...'.[34] And 'news'-minded editors to come ('Come, shadow, come, and take this shadow up'). No mention in these anthologies of his eccentric *Bottom*, an enormity he called an autobiography.

Tradition and the Individual Talent: A Dialogue. Poetry, after the successes of the Harlem Renaissance, needed no advocates, no apologists; America finally had a generation—a generation, not just a stray genius—worthy of international regard. Arrival could be construed as perpetuity, and perpetuity, importance. No need for a poet to argue any longer 'the fact that his art has importance'.

Yes and no. Consider Melvin B. Tolson and his 'curious art'—blithely, assertively intelligent. *Harlem Gallery: Book I, The Curator* (1965) is a bejewelled narrative poem on art: on makers, means, ends, and audience.[35] Art could uplift, be heroic or blue, joke, jazz, assimilate, or mask, resist, assist, or free. Or not. Characters glide in and out of fable-like scenes, 'in rococo synchronization', and represent contrasting possibilities.

> Hideho's voice
> jerked me out of my bird's-foot violet romanticism.
> He mixed Shakespeare's image with his own
> and caricatured me:
> 'Yonder Curator has a lean and hungry look;
> he thinks too much.
> Such blackamoors are dangerous to
> the Great White World!'

Tolson considered modernist orchestrations of extravagant conceits and allusions 'techniques of his time' that 'any artist must use'.[36] Like T. S. Eliot's poem, his moves 'through a multiplicity of foreign objects ...', Shakespeare—phrases, authority—included. When asked about a reviewer's compliment that he had 'out-Pounded Pound', Tolson said, 'Well, I did go to the Africans instead of the Chinese'. Eliot's 'multiplicity' throws into sharper relief a (white) wasteland; Tolson's catches more than a dialectic ('the racial ballad in the public domain/and the private poem in the modern vein'), as position after position, rendered, remains untenable.

By the time *Harlem Gallery* was published, modernism was not contemporary, and to the black literati, irrelevant, if not offensive. Poems that could be shored against a racist white culture seemed more urgently required. Langston Hughes defended Tolson to others but doubted the audience for an African American modernism. He questioned Tolson's rhyme, for example, of 'China' and 'orchestrina': 'Nobody knows what an orchestrina is (that is, nobody of the Race)'. Tolson could joke that his poetry was 'of the

---

[34] Zukofsky, letter to Carl Rakosi, 7 December 1930, in Mark Scoggins, *The Poem of a Life* (Emeryville: Shoemaker & Hoard, 2007) 112.

[35] Melvin B. Tolson, *'Harlem Gallery' and Other Poems*, Raymond Nelson (ed.), (Charlottesville: University of Virginia Press, 1999) 229.

[36] Tolson in Robert Farnsworth, *Melvin B. Tolson, 1898–1966* (Columbia: University of Missouri Press, 1984), 145, qtd. in Michael Bérubé, 'Masks, Margins, and African American Modernism' in *PMLA*, 105 (1990): 66.

proletariat, by the proletariat, and for the bourgeoisie', but he also mocked middlebrow gentility in his poem.[37] By the time the century ended, other definitions of poetry held sway. Tolson's poems were back in print, in the canon, and the part of his career devoted to debate was made into a major motion picture (*The Great Debaters* (2007), produced by Oprah Winfrey, distributed by MGM). 'Importance' for every audience! *Flourish.*

Tradition and the Individual Talent: A Travelogue. When Orson Welles wanted to film Shakespeare, bringing 'Shakespeare to everyone',[38] he told the president of Republic Pictures that his *Macbeth* would match the violence of *Wuthering Heights* (1939) and *Bride of Frankenstein* (1935). After the filming ended, a studio publicist echoed Welles' claim; Shakespeare was not merely—merely!—'highbrow' but also appealing to 'regular movie fans', even 'teen-agers': '*Macbeth* combines the thrills of Dick Tracy, Hopalong Cassidy, Roy Rogers, and Frankenstein'. So a text could be wrapped in familiar thrills and sweetened by a director's renown. 'Shakespeare speaks everybody's language', Welles wrote, 'but with an Elizabethan accent'—or a Scottish burr in his *Macbeth* (1948).

But if a text were not inviolate—had never really been inviolate—and a director, too *auteur* to tolerate, then an actor might conclude that cultural authority was actually, finally, high time too, hers. No need for a studio, a theatre; performance could be anywhere, for 'everyone'. Thus the allure mid-century of the monologue, the storyteller, and performance artist. Making a scene was suddenly performance: an artist talking, rush hour, New York; or talking in a bar; in someone's loft. A passing moment, so performed—happening—escaped—by ephemerality alone—becoming a commodity.[39]

Hannah Weiner's *RJ (Romeo & Juliet)* (1966) partook of this anti-capitalist, experimental tradition. Her poetry was found language, and she found for this playlet 19th century British editions of *The International Code of Signals for the Use of All Nations*. The code, drafted by the British Board of Trade, was 'a visual signal system for ships at sea'; flags hoisted signalled locations, warnings, requests, distress.[40] When Weiner read that designations for 'R' and 'J' were Romeo and Juliet, she wed the two authoritative structures.

SLD ROMEO	My name is
R	Romeo
EBQ JULIET	Your name is not on my list; spell it alphabetically
JG ROMEO	I wish to have personal communication with you
IJ JULIET	Unless your communication is very important, I must be excused

[37] Gary Lenhart, 'Caviar and Cabbage' in *The American Poetry Review* (March/April 2000): 38; also LeRoi Jones (Amiri Baraka), 'The Myth of a "Negro Literature"' (1962) in Poirier, 1134–9.

[38] Orson Welles, 'On Staging Shakespeare and on Shakespeare's Stage' in *The Mercury Shakespeare*, Welles and Roger Hill (eds), (New York: McGraw-Hill, 1939) 23; also Michael A. Anderegg, *Orson Welles, Shakespeare, and Popular Culture* (New York: Columbia University Press, 1999) 6; and Welles, Peter Bogdanovich, and Jonathan Rosenbaum, *This Is Orson Welles* (New York: DaCapo, 1998) 207.

[39] Richard Schechner, 'The Decline and Fall of the (American) Avant-Garde' in *PAJ*, 2 (1981): 48–63.

[40] Hannah Weiner [Note on Code Poems] in *Open Poetry*, Ronald Gross and George Quasha (eds), (New York: Simon and Schuster, 1973) 522; also Weiner, *RJ (Romeo & Juliet)* in *The Kenning Anthology of Poets Theater: 1945–1985*, Kevin Killian and David Brazil (eds), (Berkeley: Kenning Editions, 2010) 236–9.

Capital letters flush left transcribe the signal key, the sequence, and groupings of flags. The crisp, antiquated jargon sounds true and false as dialogue and then proudly amusing.

KZU ROMEO   I am in difficulties; direct me how to steer
OOX JULIET   You should swing and enter stern first
HBK ROMEO   What is the nature of the bottom or What kind of bottom have you?
HAY JULIET   Double bottom

Ships, passing in the night, pass a wedding night.

The playlet was performed, 'two people waving flags at each other from one end of West 26th Street to the other', and again in Central Park, 1968.[41] The latter, the one often remembered by poets in attendance, enlisted Coast Guard volunteers 'using alphabet flag hoists, semaphore signalmen, flashing light signals, megaphones, and flares'.

A brief diverting spectacle gives everyone a laugh. Victorian locutions ('I shall come off by and by. . .') are easier to mock for being foreign, old. The fun of it monopolizes meaning, for the playlet cannot signify without 'selling out'. Silliness disperses the aggression of absurdity. 'Romeo' and 'Juliet' are only flags, hoisting tragedy into a merry American air of willed innocence.

Shakespeare, to Orson Welles, remained 'the top', impossible to reach, and to make a film there by any means necessary was justified. Call *Macbeth* a sentimental melodrama; shoot the film in twenty-three days; don the cheapest costumes ('I looked like the Statue of Liberty...'); and expect, like a child, to be praised for trying. Innocence, as escape from experience, ruptures logic. 'It was almost as though', he wrote, 'America was discovered, Elizabeth made Queen, ... just so ... we could have William Shakespeare'.

35.5

Susan Howe's poems respond. They are not parthenogenetic or 'prolific'—formed of an excess of delights; rather, out of doubt ('We lack confidence in our authenticity'),[42] they 'devour'.[43] The poet, 'cutting this from that and that from this', savouring salvage, finds in marginalia, in the annotations of archival miscellany and minutiae, vision. The 'record of winners' is rejected. 'I wish I could tenderly lift from the dark side of history, voices that are anonymous, slighted—inarticulate'.[44] Humility is strategic, feminine, and

---

[41] John Perrault in Judith Goldman, 'Hannah=hannaH' in *differences,* 12.2 (2001); available at <http://epc.buffalo.edu/authors/weiner/goldman.html>.

[42] Jon Thompson, Susan Howe interview in *Free Verse,* Winter (2005) 4; also Lynn Keller, Howe interview cited in Paul Naylor, *Poetic Investigations* (Evanston: Northwestern, 1999) 56; and Tom Beckett, Howe interview rpt. in Howe, *The Birthmark* (Middletown: Wesleyan University Press, 1991) 46, 47.

[43] William Blake, *The Marriage of Heaven and Hell* (London: Oxford, 1975), xxiii; also Auden, *The Prolific and the Devourer* (Hopewell: Ecco, 1976) 1.

[44] Susan Howe, 'There Are Not Leaves Enough To Crown To Cover To Crown To Cover' her

valorizing failure involves an image of the poet as angel of history and house. 'Poetry shelters other voices'.

She looks past contemporaneous feminists whose poems could sound as confident, as doctrinaire in their confessions as 'winners'. And past their hortatory celebrations of the body too, she looks to sympathies, managed with the care of an Elizabeth Barrett Browning—the poet once considered the 'female Shakespeare'. In a preface to the first edition of *Casa Guidi Windows* (1851), a long poem in two parts on a failed Italian revolution, Barrett Browning offered her intention: 'no continuous narrative, not exposition of political philosophy', but 'personal impressions'.[45]

Howe also gentles the reader into her long, postmodern language experiments with prefatory, often personal, prose. *The Liberties* (1980), after a babyish epigraph by Jonathan Swift, opens with 'Fragments of a Liquidation' on Swift's muse Stella, prose tendered as fact, truth, both. The figure of Stella is then dislocated from history to art ('Stella's Portrait'), from art to language ('THEIR | Book of Stella'), a trajectory impressed with Howe's personal history (from visual to language artist).

Shakespeare's Cordelia is a second figure rescued by the poet's formulation from masculine vistas ('WHITE FOOLSCAP | Book of Cordelia'). Her title alludes to the practice of a single actor playing two parts, Cordelia and Fool. It also puns on 'foolscap', a fine, watermarked paper. Cordelia stands to the side of her father's script ('Wide of the mark'), as if asylum from King Lear and *King Lear* awaited her, along the margins and down a shadowy white paper gutter.

Is the liberation of Cordelia like some happy ending settled on Romeo and Juliet? (The woman not *the oldest hath borne most*?) Pathetic daughter-pawn (trying to be 'blind to the father's need') is meant to blind the reader to her father's tragedy. She does; at least, she did, when readers were taken by unchanging prejudice against women. Barrett Browning made her 'intensity' palatable by modesty; Howe, by abstraction (Cordelia as emblem, not character; pawned again?) and by stammering, stuttering ('the sounding of uncertainty') 'in a stammered place'. Repeated words, word bits, and ruptured syntax provide, in the silence of a slower reading and silence around words, an emancipative space.

Leafy I
      labyrinth am

lost in the woods (or hiding)
    Leafy I
      labyrinth am

  blind to

nothing.

introduction, *The Europe of Trusts* (New York: New Directions, 1990) 14; also Howe, *The Liberties* in *Europe*, 147–218.

[45] Elizabeth Barrett Browning, *The Poetical Works*, Cambridge Edition (Boston: Houghton Mifflin, 1974) 224.

'Strange translucencies:' Howe said, 'letters, phonemes, syllables, rhymes, shorthand segments, alliteration, assonance, meter, form a ladder to an outside state outside of States'. Not so strange the absences: grammar; the line. ('Poetry after the [second world] war has its psychic imperatives: to dismantle the grammar of control and the syntax of command').[46] Language splinters and then will not command:

love	tongue	milk	pasture	words
bare	arm	cause	cube	words
inherit		cause	willow	words

Meaning, in this context, stutters among possibilities, and possibility is meant to jolt a reader. (Howe: 'I wouldn't want the reader to be just a passive consumer. I would want my readers to play, to enter the mystery of language, and to follow words where they lead …'). Employ critics; toy with theorists. Explanation essays the poem.

Gertrude Stein said that explanation attaches to written phrases as empire expands. A phrase, however soothing, is not complete, like a sentence, or clear, like a word, and requires explanation. The pleasures of 'owning everything', inherent in explanation, enlarge the sentimental enterprise. The poet devours, and explanations proliferate with all the confidence of winners. Howe transports her poem and her readers 'to an outside state outside of States', and the benefits of moving offshore are supported by an industry of explanations.

[*A Separate Scene*]: Frederick Seidel creates in his character 'Frederick Seidel' an American, one of the smoothies, a cosmos turning on 'the glory of its hard, electric rage'.[47] ('Not that I care, being debonair'.)[48] The poet, born to rich Midwestern merchants, remembers luxury ('the best cars, the best clothes') as event and atmosphere, enchanting.[49] A life of pleasures, purchases (chauffeured, bespoke) makes a happy inadvertent mockery of the modernist argument 'No ideas but in things'.[50] Beloved liberal pieties too, our democratic vistas, dissolve, and a reader infers an easy distance from one ideal (freedom, prosperity) to another (ownership, wealth).

Some readers prefer that a poet resist the bourgeoisie—*épate*—it, howl or dive into a separate sphere and call the wreck a poem. Seidel's insult is his perspective (his perspective, his prerogative), above the bourgeoisie, above 'the celebretariat', above us all.

> Happy birthday to a *semper paratus* penis!
> His tiny Cartier wristwatch trumpets it!
> He dares to wear a tiny thing that French and feminine.
> Nose tilted up, arrogance, blue eyes.

[46] Charles Bernstein, 'The Second War and Postmodern Memory' in *A Poetics* (Cambridge, MA: Harvard University Press, 1992) 202.

[47] Robert Lowell, 'On Translating Phèdre' in *Racine's Phaedra* (New York: Farrar, Straus and Giroux, 1960) 8; also Bersani, 'Racine, Psychoanalysis and Oedipus' and 'Artaud, Defecation and Birth' in *A Future for Astyanax* (Boston: Little, Brown, 1976) 17–50, 259–72.

[48] Frederick Seidel, *Poems: 1959–2009* (New York: Farrar, Straus and Giroux, 2009).

[49] Jonathan Galassi, Seidel interview in *Paris Review* 190 (2009) available at <http://www.theparisreview.org/interviews/5952/the-art-of-poetry-no-95-frederick-seidel>.

[50] William Carlos Williams, 'A Sort of a Song' (1946) in *Collected Poems* 2 (New York: New Directions, 1991) 55.

No middle-class shame (á la John Berryman) or lower-brass (á la Charles Bukowski). No collusive wink at the reader either, who apprehends, as a voyeur, a display. Such a very naughty dandy amuses Seidel's friends who commission him to write poems for *The Wall Street Journal* and poems for a new planetarium at the Museum of Natural History in New York.

The delectations, the situations, the images, and lines repeat within poems and between them and then impale identity ('Frederick Seidel') in patterns of urbanity—an Astaire approaching Artaud. ('God rears and whinnies and gives a little wave. | He would rather be an owner than a slave.') To those outside the privileged circle, cruelty—racist humor, imperious misogyny—repels ('A naked woman my age is a total nightmare'). And yet, some readers do not fix on disgust but move on among his lines, mollified by language—harsh, rhythmic, witty ('You need a danger to be safe in'). And read again? A little revulsion serves, like a vaccination, to inoculate against abandoning the pattern. ('Ice cream for dessert | Is what Iraq is …'.)

Recurrent scenes from *Hamlet* further dramatize his rituals and formalize his vehemence. A young 'Seidel' plays Hamlet in tears, 'LSD tears', estranged from parents. In a poem published twenty years later (2001), a worldly Hamlet ('bombing Belgrade…'), stabbing Polonius ('like a man does a maid'), contemplates tears instead of shedding them. The prince ornaments Seidel's position as a poet of the ruling class and reorders, simultaneously, position and ornament, as a horsefly on his *Hamlet* is his Hamlet: 'Walking through words from left to right is rage'. Character is not coherent; desire is.

> And scream, 'This is I! Hamlet the Dane!' True—
> Too true—the lascivious iceberg you
> Are cruising to, *Titanic*, is a Jew
> Ophelia loved, a man she thought she knew.

An older Hamlet, in his recent 'In the Mirror' (2008), stands between performance and death. Again 'Seidel', a Jew, is acting English ('Superiority was English'), and again, additional figures (Fred Astaire, Baudelaire) cheer his solitude. The preparations needed to keep performance up add a poignancy to his familiar, now more clearly simulated insolence. ('I wouldn't dream of plastic surgery | Unless somehow it helps the poetry'.) Experience, even of decrepitude, that nightmare assigned to women, can be controlled, in a fantasy of desire and control.

[*Additional Passages*]: *Flourish. Then brook abridgment* … even of posterior traditions individuals, *tomorrow, and tomorrow, and tomorrow*, concoct and cancel; chase.

[*Epilogue*]: Shakespeare *in your fair minds* continues; but here, in proud America, in *mangl*[ed]-*by-starts-the-full-course-of*-[its]-*glory* America, find his language italicized, uncredited, *manag*[ed], *thus far*, and then mashed up—power cast in the role of ephemera—in the public domain.

Select Bibliography

Dickinson, Emily (1960) *The Complete Poems*. Thomas H. Johnson (ed.) (Boston: Little, Brown).

Eliot, T. S. (2003) *The Waste Land and Other Poems*. Frank Kermode (ed.) (New York: Penguin).

Howe, Susan (1990) *The Europe of Trusts* (New York: New Directions).

Kermode, Frank (2000) *Shakespeare's Language* (New York: Farrar, Straus and Giroux).

Porter, Cole, *Kiss Me Kate* (stage premiere) 1948; (film permiere) 1953.

Seidel, Frederick (2009) *Poems: 1959–2009* (New York: Farrar, Straus and Giroux).

Stein, Gertrude (1967) *Writings and Lectures 1909–1945*. Patricia Meyerowitz (ed.) (Baltimore: Penguin).

Tolson, Melvin B. (1999) *'Harlem Gallery' and Other Poems*. Raymond Nelson (ed.) (Charlottesville: Virginia).

Weiner, Hannah (2010) *RJ (Romeo & Juliet) in The Kenning Anthology of Poets Theater: 1945–1985*. Kevin Killian and David Brazil (eds) (Berkeley: Kenning Editions).

Whitman, Walt (1982) *Complete Poetry and Collected Prose* (New York: Library of America).

Wilde, Oscar (1969) 'The Portrait of Mr W. H.' (1921) *The Artist as Critic*. Richard Ellmann (ed.) (New York: Random House).

Zukofsky, Louis (2002) *Bottom: On Shakespeare* (Middletown: Wesleyan University Press).

PART VII

TRANSLATING SHAKESPEARE

CHAPTER 36

··

YVES BONNEFOY
AND SHAKESPEARE
AS A FRENCH POET

··

EFRAÍN KRISTAL

Yves Bonnefoy (b. 1923), France's most celebrated living poet and one of its premier critics of literature and the visual arts, is central to the contemporary French reception of
Shakespeare. Over six decades Bonnefoy developed a view of Shakespeare, inspired by
his own poetic vision, which in turn informs his interpretations of the works and even
the way in which he translated them. For Bonnefoy, the early plays are not particularly
strong, Shakespeare begins to find a poetic voice in the long poems, and he experiments
with an inferior, constraining form, the sonnet, which allows him to come to terms with
the fact that the stage would afford him a supreme platform to express his poetic genius.
Bonnefoy is not particularly interested in the histories or the comedies. Shakespeare
begins to come alive as a great poet for him in *As you Like It* and *Romeo and Juliet*, and
his supreme achievement is *The Winter's Tale*, a play which encompasses the scope of
the entire oeuvre while also summarizing a sophisticated view about the relationship
between art, nature, and existence. As it happens, the view that Bonnefoy identifies in
the play is very close to his own.

Bonnefoy translated eleven plays: *1 Henry IV* (1956), *Julius Caesar* (1957), *Hamlet*
(1961), *The Winter's Tale* (1961), *King Lear* (1965), *Romeo and Juliet* (1968), *Macbeth*
(1983), *The Tempest* (1997), *Antony and Cleopatra* (1999), *Othello* (2001), and *As you
like it* (2003). He translated *Venus and Adonis* and *The Rape of Lucrece* in 1961, and he
published the complete Sonnets in 2007.[1] As he has pointed out on several occasions, the

---

[1] For a bibliography of the Shakespeare translations and re-editions see Giovanni Dotoli, *Yves
Bonnefoy dans la fabrique de la traduction*, (Paris, Hermann, 2008) 144–6. All of my quotations from
Bonnefoy's translations come from the most recent editions. *Hamlet* (1978), *Jules César* (1995), *Le conte
d'hiver* (1996), *La Tempête* (1997), *Antoine et Cléopatre* (1999), *Roméo et Juliette* (2001), *Othello* (2001),

revisions of the poems and plays over six decades have been considerable in detail but not in substance.

Bonnefoy translated the long poems in prose, and after exploring other ways of translating the Sonnets, he settled for an approximation of the Elizabethan form, using three quatrains and a couplet in unrhymed lines of uneven length. He is persuaded that the plays must be translated freely with 'a language that is spoken today'.[2] In practice, his translations display a considerable amount of flexibility and the use of different kinds of prosody. He changes the linguistic register as he sees fit, and at times incorporates the vocabulary and forms of classical French theatre.

With the exception of *1 Henry IV*, all of his Shakespeare translations are available in popular editions and are frequently used in theatrical productions, and in high school and university courses. Bonnefoy's prologues, like most of his literary and art criticism, focus on central issues and presuppose a close acquaintance with the work. He is not interested in underscoring what others have had to say or the stage history of the plays, and does not summarize the plots. *Shakespeare and the French Poet* (2004) edited by John Naughton is the best available book in English to appreciate Bonnefoy's engagements with Shakespeare: it includes seven prologues, five essays on his approach to translating Shakespeare, and an interview with the editor.

There is evidence of Bonnefoy's engagements with Shakespeare in his own poetry. 'Les nouées' a poem from *Dans le leurre du seuil* (1975), for example, recreates the final scene of *The Winter's Tale*, and *L'heure présente* (2011) includes two prose poems inspired by *Hamlet*. That being said, his allusions to Shakespeare in these and other poems are not foreign to his poetic vision, since his understanding of Shakespeare is entirely informed by his general views on poetry.

36.1 BONNEFOY ON POETRY

Bonnefoy had a brief involvement with surrealism in the 1940s, and has always appreciated the surrealist impulse to dissolve those 'mirages that contaminate desire'.[3] He does not think, however, that the surrealist aesthetic—in particular the assumption that the unconscious ought to be liberated from the contingencies of everyday life—resolves the

Comme il vous plaira (2003). With the exception of the last one published by Livre de Poche, the others are the Gallimard Folio editions chosen because they are the most recent. The Shakespeare quotations in English come either from the English in the bilingual editions of *Antony and Cleopatra, Othello, The Tempest,* and *The Winter's Tale,* or from Wells and Taylor (Oxford: Oxford University Press, 2005) for the other plays.

² Bonnefoy, *La communauté des traducteurs,* (Strasbourg: Presses Universitaires de Strasbourg, 2000) 109. Note: All translations of Bonnefoy's works from texts in sources cited in French are mine, and in some cases I've modified the English translations of others, often to underscore Bonnefoy's technical vocabulary. I will not cite Bonnefoy's first name in the footnotes.

³ Bonnefoy, 'Breton à l'avant de soi', *Le siècle où la parole a été victime,* (Paris: Mercure de France, 2010) 91. This book will be referred to as *SPV*.

dilemmas posed by inauthentic human experience in the personal or social realm that André Breton and other surrealists purported to address. Bonnefoy would like poetry to reconnect with an everyday reality, rather than to shun it, in an encounter with what he calls 'presence', the most recurrent word in his vocabulary, even in his poetry, as one can appreciate in this fragment:

> Écoute-moi revivre, je te conduis
> Au jardin de présence
>
> (Hear me return to life, I take you
> To the garden of presence).[4]

Presence, for Bonnefoy, suggests an authentic, unmediated engagement with life and nature, with objects and other human beings. Bonnefoy is an atheist, but there is a spiritual element in his writings insofar as he speaks of presence in relation to the soul, of love as a force that moves the universe, and of reality as an indivisible unity that cannot be grasped with concepts. In Robert W. Greene's account: 'Elusive, skirting the ineffable, the notion of presence has haunted Bonnefoy for decades. Central to the notion for the poet is the fleeting experience of mutuality between self and other, of lighting transaction in the transient world, of a shared mortal destiny, hence a plenitude within finitude'.[5]

Experiencing presence, for Bonnefoy, is the opposite of self-alienation, the objectification of human beings, or the turn to lures such as religion or ideology, or attempts to grasp life without an awareness of our contingency, fragility, and mortality, which he often calls 'finitude'. Understanding through concepts or arbitrary images reduces the true scope of human experience in the sensory and sensual here and now to vacuous substitutes. Bonnefoy's main insight, informing his entire oeuvre, is that conceptual thought—inevitable, and necessary for many important human activities—is an obstacle to presence, but that true poetry is a means to connect with it: 'The function of poetry is to unsettle the web of conceptual relations that inform a limited image of reality precluding access to that unity which we sense is behind all of those partial, abstract representations'.[6]

Correcting Paul Valery's famous definition of poetry as a 'prolonged hesitation between sound and meaning',[7] Bonnefoy argues that a mysterious bond between sound and meaning can 'open into the unknown, into our consciousness of the world'.[8] According to Bonnefoy sound in poetry is presence itself and a solvent of conceptual thought.[9] He does not, however, offer insights into why certain combinations of sounds, but not others, can summon presence.

---

   [4] Bonnefoy (1958), 'Une voix', *Hier régnant désert*, (Paris Gallimard: *Poésies*) 166.
   [5] Robert, W. Greene, *Searching for Presence. Yves Bonnefoy's Writings on Art*, (Amsterdam and New York: Rodopi, 2004) 10.
   [6] Bonnefoy (2000) 49.
   [7] Paul Valéry, *Oeuvres II*, (Paris, Pléiade, 1960) 636.
   [8] Bonnefoy, *L'inachevable. Entretiens sur la poésie 1999–2010* (Paris: Albin Michel, 2010) 150.
   [9] 'Sound understood as sound confers to the thing associated with it the quality I call presence', Bonnefoy, 'Le degré zero de l'écriture', *SPV*, 183; '[the sounds of poetry] weakens the conceptual chains', Bonnefoy, 'Breton à l'avant de soi', 87.

Bonnefoy's views on poetry and presence are not unrelated to some Romantic longings for a lost unity, or to post-Kantian views on aesthetics, particularly those of Friedrich Schiller in his treatise on *Naïve and Sentimental Poetry* in which the German poet argues that modern man has become alienated from nature, Nietzsche's scepticism of reason's ability to account for life, or Heidegger's meditations on authenticity and being in the world. As with other French thinkers in the time of post-structuralism, Bonnefoy relies on distinctions from Saussurean linguistics, most notably on the difference between *langue* as a shared system of speech or signs (made up of signifiers and signifieds) and *parole* as the individual expression in language or speech, to anchor philosophical insights. Bonnefoy has expressed sympathy and some affinities with the deconstructive gestures of a French tradition aiming to 'undo the pseudo-evidences of collective discourse [to] combat ideologies, which use concepts in perverse and pernicious ways'.[10] That being said, Bonnefoy cautions that it is dangerous to limit critical thinking to discourse analysis, or to deny the psychic reality of poets when Barthes, Foucault, and others claim the death of the author.

Bonnefoy's interpretation of *Hamlet* is akin to his critique of French theory. The Hamlet who uses the play within the play as a tool to reveal Claudius' guilt would be the analogue of critical theory, but the Dane's inability to engage with the humanity of others is his limitation:

> The idea of a theatre that mirrors society could not do more than expose some of the most cynical or simpleminded misuses of appearances without ever resolving them or probing the depths of human existence (hence the failure of the 'play within the play' and the distress of its author, the prince of Denmark, at his inability to articulate the intuition that haunts him).[11]

Critical thinking, for Bonnefoy, is insufficient if not followed by an engagement with presence, and the greatest moments in Shakespeare's poetry are those in which he identifies presence, as in the following lines from Mark Antony's oration in *Julius Caesar*:

> If you have tears prepare to shed them now.
> You all do know this mantle. I remember
> The first time ever Caesar put it on.
> 'Twas on a summer's evening in his tent,
> That day he overcame the Nervii.
>
> (III. II. 167–71.)

Bonnefoy offers the following analysis to explain the role of presence in the speech: 'Caesar is there, before us, there as a presence. Because of the presence of Caesar's dead body, and because of Antony's affection for Caesar, the absoluteness of a person's being will irrigate Antony's words'.[12] Bonnefoy's translation is more apposite than the original

[10] Bonnefoy, 'Le degré zero de l'écriture', *SPV*, 169.
[11] Bonnefoy, 'Art and Nature', in *Shakespeare and the French Poet*, John Naughton, ed., (Chicago: University of Chicago Press, 2004a) 46. This book will be cited as *SFP*.
[12] Bonnefoy, 'Brutus, Appointment at Philippi', *SFP*, 115–16.

to his explanation of the lines. 'Look, in this place ran Cassius' dagger through', the lines that immediately follow the evocation of Caesar's past, poses no difficulty to a translator, and yet Bonnefoy renders them as 'Voyez-le, maintenant. Ici a penetré | La dague de Cassius' ('See him, now. Here is where Cassius' dagger penetrated'). He adds a stunning ambiguity, which is not in the original, when he renders 'Look' as 'Voyez-le, maintenant' ('See him, now'). 'Voyez-le maintenant' initially suggests the presence of a living Caesar brought back to life by the power of Antony's evocation of the man when he first wore the now bloodied robe. As such, 'Voyez-le, maintenant' is a summation reinforcing the suggestion that the previous five lines evoked Caesar's presence in the past. The second half of the line ('Ici a penetré' ['here has penetrated']) reorients the whole line as a return to the presence of Caesar's dead body in the present. 'Voyez-le, maintenant', therefore, suggests presence in poignant ways that the original does not. This sort of projection of his own views on poetry, this bold distortion, is common in Bonnefoy's translations.

36.2 BAUDELAIRE AND RIMBAUD

References to Baudelaire and to Rimbaud abound in Bonnefoy's explanations of Shakespeare because what matters to him in Shakespeare is also what matters to him in the two French poets he values above all others. Baudelaire was able to unearth 'the essence of poetry for the first time in the history of the French language'[13] because he grasped that 'in the heart of the visible and the lived, there is more to reality than the visible and lived. Not another world [but rather] the most natural of things'.[14] In signature poems, like 'Correspondances', Baudelaire addressed a reality 'which transcends our capacity to conceptualise allowing us to surmise a profundity in the relationship between two terms that eschews reductive interpretation'.[15] Bonnefoy also admires Baudelaire's celebration of evil in his poems as a provocation against repressive mores, his reckonings with human mortality and with death, and his celebration of sexuality not as an act of procreation, but as a shared experience with spiritual implications in a non-religious register, by beings who acknowledge each other's humanity.[16] Bonnefoy has not hesitated to call Baudelaire 'the greatest poet',[17] or to say that 'never has the truth of *parole*, a higher form of truth, shown its face so clearly'.[18] And yet, Bonnefoy thinks that Rimbaud reached greater heights because he showed 'decisively that poetry can survive the pitfalls of self-consciousness'.[19]

[13] Bonnefoy (2011) 277.
[14] Bonnefoy (2011) 267.
[15] Bonnefoy, 'Baudelaire', *Lieux et destins de l'image. Un cours de poétique au Collège de France, 1981–1993* (Paris: Seuil, 1999) 209.
[16] See for example his meditation on Baudelaire and sexuality in *Sous le signe de Baudelaire*, (2011) 269–72.
[17] Bonnefoy (1999) 234.
[18] Bonnefoy, 'Baudelaire's *Les Fleurs du mal*', *The Act and the Place of Poetry* (Chicago: University of Chicago Press, 1989) 44.
[19] Bonnefoy (2011) 7–8.

Bonnefoy's main insight regarding Rimbaud's contributions to poetry can be gleaned from his analysis of Rimbaud's famous dictum, 'Je est un autre' ('I is another'):

> underneath that 'me' ('le moi') is an 'I' (le 'je'), which keeps the speaking subject in contact with ways of being in the world lost on ordinary thought. When Rimbaud says 'Je est un autre' he is underscoring the transcendence of consciousness over the forms and the figures that the 'me' imposes on it.[20]

Bonnefoy's account of Rimbaud corresponds to John Naughton's summary of a guiding principle in Bonnefoy's own writings:

> He distinguishes between an 'I' in full relation to being, to 'itself' and to others, and an 'ego,' a 'me'—what Bonnefoy calls *le moi*—which is constituted by social and cultural codes and values, by language itself. This self will always exist more superficially, less authentically, than the 'I,' despite the moments of profound intensity—of *tragedy*—it may experience.[21]

Bonnefoy draws directly on his understanding of Rimbaud to explain the tragedy of *Othello*, which for him involves Iago's manipulation of the Moor's adherence to his 'moi', and his correlative inability to embrace his 'je' as represented by the possibility of true love with Desdemona. Citing several 'common points between Rimbaud and the Moor', Bonnefoy argues that in his desire to conform to the ideology of the Venetian state, Othello's 'moi' is in tension with his 'je' manifest in his desire to establish a true bond with Desdemona:

> [Othello's moi] revels in the unreal, and is therefore exposed to countless snares. But with Desdemona, in a private relationship in which the real elements of finite existence signify both an obligation and an abode, Othello would seem to have found a way to break away from his inevitably chimerical 'moi' for the sake of a now fundamental 'je' determined solely by the desire to go ever forward in the recognition of the Other, in sharing the essential.[22]

Bonnefoy's interpretations of Shakespeare are informed by a view of poetry he developed independently of his engagements with Shakespeare. Shakespeare is not essential to understand Bonnefoy's fundamental views about poetry, but his views about poetry are necessary to understand his interpretations and translations of Shakespeare.

36.3 JEAN MICHEL DÉPRATS AND BONNEFOY

Bonnefoy's main rival as a translator of Shakespeare into French is Jean Michel Déprats, the primary translator of the monumental Pléiade Edition, which has already issued two

---

[20] Bonnefoy, *Notre Besoin de Rimbaud* (Paris: Seuil, 2009) 28. The letter of 15 May 1871 to his friend Paul Demeny, is in Rimbaud, *Complete Works, Selected Letters*, Wallace Fowlie (trans.), (Chicago: University of Chicago Press, 1975) 304.

[21] John Naughton, 'Introduction', Bonnefoy, *SFP*, xiii.

[22] Bonnefoy, 'Desdemona Hangs Her Head', *SFP*, 181.

large volumes with the tragedies in 2002 and two equally large volumes with the history plays in 2008.

Déprats and Bonnefoy are both keen to render Shakespeare in an effective contemporary French idiom, although they do so in different registers and for different reasons. It is clear from their choices that they have studied the tradition of Shakespeare translation in French. Traces of the standard 19th-century translations by François-Victor Hugo (Victor Hugo's son) and François Guizot are evident in the work of both, and it is also clear that Déprats has studied Bonnefoy's translations. That being said, the attention the two have given to other translations, and even their borrowings from their antecedents, was in the service of their respective approaches to translation, which are hardly compatible: Bonnefoy is fundamentally committed to his own experiences of Shakespeare as a French poet whereas Déprats is committed to Shakespeare as an English dramatist.[23] In his translations, Bonnefoy projects onto Shakespeare a literary vision, sometimes identical to his own, deftly fitting, and sometimes forcing, Shakespeare's language, his characters and situations according to the same logic and arguments with which he has explained the meaning of poetry. Déprats, on the other hand, is concerned with the rendering of a language that will work on stage, facilitating the interpretive work of French actors: 'The process should favour the language being translated and not serve the target language', and this means trying to forge new forms, rather than manipulating existing expressions and standard turns of phrase.[24] Translation for the stage for Déprats 'does not mean twisting the text in favour of what one hopes to show, or the way it will be acted'.[25] Déprats is more interested in a translation that renders Shakespeare's images and the power of his language than one that interprets their meaning. His aim is to produce a Shakespeare translation that allows the French director and actor to be inventive in some of the ways that the English director and actor can be inventive with the original. His goal is 'to recreate, in an imaginative, energetic and spontaneous language, a language that speaks to today's spectator'.[26] Bonnefoy, on the other hand, is aware that his interpretations inform his translations, and thinks that interpretation is inevitable for anyone who engages seriously with the plays: 'everyone creates their own *Hamlet, Lear* or *Macbeth*, and the translator must do the same'.[27]

Déprats has expressed respect for Bonnefoy, but openly objects to his approach: 'the translator is the first interpreter of the work—more in the musical sense than in the hermeneutical sense—but he is neither a director nor a literary critic'.[28] Déprats is aware

---

[23] In a sense Bonnefoy is following in the footsteps of André Gide whose Shakespeare translations are also informed by a personal literary vision, and Déprats is more closely aligned to the work of a translators like Daniel Loayza, who is finely attuned to the imperatives of the stage in his brilliant versions that combine literary nuance with an attentiveness to contemporary speech, as per example, his magnificent version of *Lear: Le roi Lear* (Ivry-sur-Seine: Editions A propos, 2003).

[24] Jean-Michel Déprats, 'Translating Shakespeare's Stagecraft', in Ton Hoenselaars (ed.), *Shakespeare and the Language of Translation* (London, The Arden Shakespeare, 2004) 134

[25] Déprats in Hoenselaars (2004) 146.

[26] Déprats, 'Traduire Shakespeare', *Tragédies I*, (Paris: Pléiade, 2002) cxiii.

[27] Bonnefoy (2000) 127.

[28] Déprats (2002) cxiii.

that Bonnefoy's choices are informed by a vision, both poetic and interpretative, citing an example: 'the fact that Bonnefoy, in his version of *Hamlet*, often translates the word mind as 'âme' (soul) is a way through which he expresses his spiritual reading of the work.'[29] Bonnefoy was aware of Déprats' objection, but defends his choice arguing that his reading of the play is spiritual, to the extent that for the French poet, Hamlet's soul, and not his mind, is primarily at stake in a world in which it is no longer possible to rely on 'the will of God as the guarantor of our efforts [and] the protector of our meaning.'[30]

Bonnefoy's 'spiritual' Hamlet can be gleaned in the following four instances: in the 'To be or not to be' soliloquy Bonnefoy translates ''tis nobler for a mind to suffer' (III. i), as 'plus noble pour une âme de souffrir' ('nobler for a soul to suffer'); when Claudius speaks of Hamlet's 'mind impatient' (I. ii), Bonnefoy translates the phrase as 'un âme sans frein' ('a soul unchecked'); when Hamlet tells Horatio that he has seen his father 'in my mind's eye' (I. ii), Bonnefoy offers 'avec les yeux de l'âme' ('with the eyes of my soul'); and when Hamlet's ghost warns the young Hamlet: 'taint not thy mind, nor let thy soul contrive against thy mother' (I. v), Bonnefoy ventures 'ne souille pas ton âme, ne fais rien contre ta mere' (do not soil your soul, don't do anything against your mother'). Notice that in the last example Bonnefoy eliminates the contrast between mind and soul in the original by not translating the word 'mind' at all. Déprats does not take any liberties of this kind, and his own translation maintains the contrast between mind and soul.

Déprats' approach to the plays is premised on the assumption that in Shakespeare's language the theatrical and poetic dimensions coincide: 'its formal elements, its stylistics, its rhythm, its phrasing, its prosodic patterns constitute the very body of its theatricality.'[31] Bonnefoy, in contrast, is not interested in reproducing the formal elements, stylistics, rhythm, phrasing, or prosodic patterns of the original. He is committed, rather, to the creation of a poetic language that will work as French poetry, even if it does not reproduce Shakespeare's poetic effects. For Bonnefoy the raw material of the translator is his own experience of the original, and translation is *poetry* created in the target language while paying attention to the voice of another:

> My translation must be a poem: rhythm and sense each producing the other. But the rhythm must be mine. It will never be able to revive the rhythm of the original given the inevitable distance between what one is and what one admires. I did not attempt to render or trace Shakespeare's verbal music. One must make this sacrifice to enter, or at least to try to enter in this place of invention we call poetry.[32]

Bonnefoy's Shakespeare is a part of his own literary oeuvre, whereas Déprats' Shakespeare is an attempt to offer a window to a French reading public into the genius of another literary tradition. Bonnefoy's translations, therefore, offer a more instructive

---

[29] Déprats (2002) cxiv.
[30] Bonnefoy, 'Readiness, Ripeness: *Hamlet, Lear*', SFP, 19.
[31] Bonnefoy, SFP, 142.
[32] Bonnefoy, 'Traduire les *Sonnets* de Shakespeare', *L'Oeil de Boeuf, Revue littéraire trimestrale*, 1994 (4): 47.

window into an illuminating French distortion of Shakespeare precisely because they are informed by a poetic vision and a poetic language difficult to reconcile with the English reception of Shakespeare with roots in Coleridge, Hazlitt, and others. Bonnefoy's views on Shakespeare are often incompatible with those of Frank Kermode, Jonathan Bate, A. D. Nuttall, Stephen Greenblatt, Harold Bloom, and many other English language scholars.

36.4   THE CENTRAL PLACE OF THE SONNETS

Bonnefoy dislikes Shakespeare's Sonnets ('they were never particularly attractive to me'[33]), but he translated all of them, and sees them as the experience that allowed Shakespeare to become a true poet. Bonnefoy is not entirely averse to the genre, which he has practised himself, although not without a measure of irony and distance.[34] He has admired the sonnets of Petrarch, Spenser, and Sidney, but thinks the genre was rather stale by the time Shakespeare took it up.[35]

Bonnefoy's comments on Shakespeare's Sonnets are particularly disparaging. As poetry they amount to a 'triple murder: the murder of the other, man or woman; the murder of the self, who can not find himself among so many specious interpretations; and the murder of that simple transcendence which gives plain reality to the most fugitive moments of life'.[36] Bonnefoy's views are far from Colin Burrow's assessment that 'in their continual counterpointing of language against implied circumstance they are the culmination of Shakespeare's career as a poet'.[37] On the contrary, Bonnefoy sees in them 'the drama of a sublimation that is in fact nothing other than its own caricature'.[38]

There are many aspects of the Sonnets that 'distress and irritate'[39] Bonnefoy. They are 'too much on the side of rhetoric, and not enough on the side of poetry'.[40] They abound with 'sentiment unworthy of a great poet'.[41] Their main themes are prejudices of Shakespeare's time 'that implore the young man to procreate, or worse, those that insult a dark lady'.[42] For Bonnefoy there is too much idolatry in the representation of the beautiful young man, and too much prejudice against women in the assumptions that their

[33] Bonnefoy, 'Les sonnets de Shakespeare et la pensée de la poésie', in *Les Sonnets precedes de Vénus et Adonis et du Viol de Lucrèce* (Paris Gallimard, 2007a) 9.

[34] In the prologue to *Raturer outré*, (Paris: Galilée, 2010) Bonnefoy discusses his uneasy relationship to the sonnet as a form that takes him away from what he would normally want to express as a poet.

[35] Bonnefoy, *SFP*, 15.

[36] Bonnefoy, *SFP*, 27.

[37] Colin Burrow, 'Introduction', *The Complete Sonnets and Poems* (Oxford: Oxford University Press, 2002) 138.

[38] Bonnefoy, Yves, 'L'amitié et la réflexion', in Lançon, Daniel and Stephen Romer, eds, *Yves Bonnefoy. L'amitié et la réflexion* (Tours: Presses Universitaires François-Rabelais, 2007b) 71.

[39] Bonnefoy, *SFP*, 14.

[40] Bonnefoy, *SFP*, 7.

[41] Bonnefoy, *SFP*, 10.

[42] Bonnefoy, 'La decision de Shakespeare', Bonnefoy's prologue to his translation of *As You Like It*, Shakespeare, *Comme il vous plaira* (Paris: Livre de Poche, 2003) 9–10.

primary role is procreation, or in the assumption that sexual pleasure amounts to sin. The affirmation of love that informs the Sonnets 'transposes eros into a mystification of form, conceived as a deliverance which is nothing but to resume the great platonic dream'.[43] The reference to a 'platonic dream' amounts to a pointed criticism by the author of *Anti-Platon* (1947), a poetic appeal against Platonism, in which Bonnefoy's lyrical voice rejects Plato's presupposition that life in the here and now is an appearance. The idolatry of the object of love in the Sonnets is an expression of 'an exalted Platonism',[44] apposite to the slander against the dark lady of the poems because 'idolatry, as much as slander, is the denial of a real being'.[45] Bonnefoy reads the attacks on the dark lady as disparagement of female sexuality and the sexist expression of 'all the reservations that men have levelled against women'.[46]

Bonnefoy finds it incongruous that Shakespeare could have offered such a narrow-minded and superficial view of women in light of his nuanced and perceptive representation of female characters in the plays: 'One of the most surprising aspects of these poems is the obstinate attitude with respect to women. In his theatre Shakespeare is not afflicted by sexist prejudices, and it appears to me that he demonstrates a remarkable aptitude to perceive the alienation of the feminine in society and to combat it'.[47] In broader terms he is perplexed to find 'such astonishing superficiality by the author of Rosalind, Hamlet, and Perdita, which is so incompatible with the project and essential nature of poetry'.[48]

Given that Bonnefoy finds the Sonnets at odds with the plays, he has wondered if Shakespeare practised the popular form with cynicism to gain patronage or fame, or if there is anything in them more than 'ordinary mediocrity and hypocrisy'.[49] Bonnefoy's response to his own perplexities is the speculation that Shakespeare indulged in 'simplifications and distortions' in order to experience the 'illusory character' of an inauthentic poetic experience, so that he could then engage with a more authentic one which he had not yet developed: 'having exposed the hidden dialectic of a poetry committed to fixed forms, he can remember that on stage there exists another kind of poetry of existence and creation he had neglected to practice'.[50]

36.5 FROM THE SONNETS TO THE PLAYS

Bonnefoy is convinced that Shakespeare fleshed out his critique of the sonnet in *As You Like It* and *Romeo and Juliet* in a comic and a tragic register respectively. Orlando and Romeo are practitioners of the kind of poetry Bonnefoy loathes for being removed from

---

[43] Bonnefoy, *SFP*, 13.
[44] Bonnefoy, *SFP*, 30.
[45] Bonnefoy, *SFP*, 26.
[46] Bonnefoy, *SFP*, 13.
[47] Bonnefoy, *SFP*, 12.
[48] Bonnefoy, *SFP*, 70.
[49] Bonnefoy, *SFP*, 16.
[50] Bonnefoy, *SFP*, 29.

presence, which Rosalind seeks when she falls in love with Orlando and disabuses him of his idealizations of her in his doggerel. Bonnefoy is certain that Shakespeare changed the name of 'Rosader' in Thomas Lodge's *Rosalynde* to Orlando to refer to the protagonist of Ariosto's *Orlando Furioso* whose protagonist idealizes Angelica in the way that Shakespeare's lyrical voice had idealized the young man in the Sonnets:

> Rosalind refuses to be the object of idolatry, that is to say, she refuses to be abolished or assassinated. This is why she undermines her lover's discourse, identical to the rhetoric of Shakespeare's Sonnets. Rosalind disguises herself as a boy to liberate herself from the words that one expects of girls; of those words with which society traps women. And her disguise as a male is a denunciation of Lucrece's suicide as much as of the aspersion cast on the 'dark lady'.[51]

The suggestion that Rosalind is protecting herself from assassination and the reference to Lucrece's suicide are not intended as hyperbole, but rather as ways to connect the underlying theme in Rosalind's comedy with the tragedy of other plays in which women are either murdered like Desdemona or drawn to suicide like Cleopatra, in milieus in which they are either idealized or disparaged.

For Bonnefoy *Romeo and Juliet* is the tragic counterpart to *As You Like It* because it investigates the nefarious consequences of the idealization the Sonnets embodies. He sees a direct connection between Romeo's flaws and the pitfalls he identifies in the Sonnets: 'Who is Romeo? A *sonneteer*, a writer of poems in the style of Sidney dedicated to the idolatry of a figure who is obviously unreal'.[52] Bonnefoy does not distinguish Romeo's idealizations of Rosaline before he met Juliet, from his affections for Juliet. His expressions of love are nothing other than 'exalted devotion to that which is nothing but an image, and a denial of reality',[53] and the tragic events follow from Romeo's idolatry of women, which amounts to a death wish realized in the play: 'We must suspect, in he who idolises, a secret taste for death, which protects what is idealised from the cruel lessons of existence'.[54] Where others see the lovers as innocent victims of a family feud, Bonnefoy sees Romeo's behaviour as conducive to feuding: 'if Romeo had broken the circle of the family feud with the force and conviction of true love, something would have been set in motion in this social world, a bit of truth might have appeared'.[55]

For Bonnefoy, the play explores 'the rift between mind and world and the repudiation of life'.[56] Romeo's refusal to engage with life is an evil, which makes victims of others, and the same dynamic informs *Macbeth*, *Julius Caesar*, *King Lear*, and *Hamlet*. Indeed, for Bonnefoy, the main difference between Romeo and Hamlet is not their mode of behaviour, but their level of self-awareness: 'The prince of Denmark, melancholy, sceptical,

---

[51] Bonnefoy, *SFP*, 32–3.
[52] Bonnefoy, *SFP*, 17.
[53] Bonnefoy, *SFP*, 17.
[54] Bonnefoy, *SFP*, 19.
[55] 'Shakespeare et la poésie', in Daniel Lançon and Stephen Romer (éd.), *Yves Bonnefoy. L'amitié et la réflexion* (Tours: Presses universitaires François Rabelais, 2007) 74.
[56] Bonnefoy, 'Shakespeare's Uneasiness', *SFP* (Chicago: The University of Chicago Press, 2004b) 11–12.

sickened by life, is a more self-aware Romeo who knows the flaw in his love. Nonetheless, Ophelia will be as much a victim as Juliet. The most famous and modern of Shakespeare's tragedies openly tackles the problem that was only latent in his most romantic one'.[57]

36.6 BRUTUS AND HAMLET

Just as Bonnefoy considers the family feuds in *Romeo and Juliet* to be the context in which Romeo's death wish plays out, he thinks that the political dimension of *Julius Caesar* is also the context of Brutus' drama as a man unable to move from conceptual thought to presence: 'Shakespeare knew perfectly well he was not writing a political tragedy, but rather a study of the soul eternally torn between the intelligible and existence, between concept and presence'.[58] Brutus' flaw is 'his inclination to shut himself up in great abstract ideas out of aversion to actual existence'.[59]

Bonnefoy believes that the same aversion to 'actual existence' that spoils Brutus, is also at play in Hamlet, but in a Christian context in which the Dane is initially concerned with his soul. In his translation of *Hamlet*, Bonnefoy downplays the political dimension of the play, as in his rendering of Ophelia's response to Hamlet's violence against her: 'O what a noble mind is o' erthrown' becomes 'Helás, quelle âme noble voici détruite!' ('Alas, what a noble soul is here destroyed!'). Bonnefoy transforms 'mind' to 'soul' as he had done elsewhere, and eliminates the political connotation of 'o' erthrown'. The pattern of de-emphasizing the political in favour of the spiritual continues until the end of the play. In the original, Hamlet asks Horatio to remove himself from the joys of life to tell his story, but in Bonnefoy's translation Hamlet asks Horatio to remove himself from religious bliss to explain who he was. 'Absent thee from felicity a while' (V. ii) becomes 'Prive-toi un moment des joies du Ciel' ('Deprive yourself for a moment of the joys of heaven'), and 'To tell my story' becomes 'Pour dire ce que je fus' ('To say who I was').[60]

36.7 *OTHELLO*

Bonnefoy claims that *Othello* and *Hamlet* share the same central drama. In both,

a man is suspicious of the woman he both loves and does not love, insults her, threatens her, and brings about her death as well as his own. But the problematic of

---

[57] Bonnefoy, *SFP*, 12.
[58] Bonnefoy, 'Brutus, or Appointment at Philippi', *SFP*, 108.
[59] Bonnefoy, *SFP*, 121.
[60] For Bonnefoy's take on who Hamlet was, and on the implications of who he was, see '*Readiness, Ripeness*: Hamlet, Lear', in *SFP*. For Bonnefoy, Hamlet's soul is a void, and he King Lear's journey is Shakespeare's first attempt to fill a void of that kind.

'to be' and 'not to be' is better formulated in *Othello* than in *Hamlet*. Even though the desire to be will always be ensnared in the dreams of particular persons or of the social group as a whole, *Othello* tells us that following that desire is the only path to take.[61]

According to Bonnefoy the part of Othello Iago ensnares is his 'moi', his attachment to the values of Venetian society laden with bigotry and chauvinism: 'Othello is bound to the system of representations that make up Venice. He is bound to its noblest values, but doubtless also to its most dangerous prejudices'.[62]

Even before Iago interferes in his life Othello is already 'ensnared' by the values of Venice, and even before Desdemona becomes his victim she was vulnerable to the sexism and puritanism of her society, as well as the idealizations in Othello's language of his own life and of Desdemona's: 'Othello is a "poet" and, as such, is seductive. Yet, perhaps he is only superficially a poet, in a way that does not inquire into the real person, of whom we know almost nothing concerning the kind of life that might be shared with him'.[63]

Iago plays with Othello's attachments to the values of Venetian society in order to undermine the inclination of both Othello and Desdemona to experience presence, and he represents a puritan attitude that is relevant to Shakespeare's Elizabethan–Jacobean world: 'Much in Iago's way of thinking and acting was in fact the Puritans' own. Like Iago they feel disgust for the flesh, no appetite for pleasure, even the same need to accumulate profits in order to compensate for their lack of being'.[64] Bonnefoy understands Iago's 'I am not what I am' as the credo of someone devoid of presence: 'Iago simultaneously is and is not, since what he might consider his being, what he might hold and proclaim as his presence to himself is nothing more, in his eyes, than a heap of meaningless characteristics, as opaque and devoid of self as a dead animal'.[65]

In his translation, Bonnefoy is so keen to underscore the sexual prejudices in the Venetian society he represents that he significantly downplays the racial motifs of the play. For example, Iago casts aspersion on Othello, after he has eloped with Desdemona, hollering: 'an old black ram | Is tupping your white ewe' (I. i). Bonnefoy eliminates the adjective 'black' in favour of 'vieux bélier' ('old ram'). Bonnefoy also eliminates vestiges of racism in Desdemona's own language. For example, he translates 'black and witty' (II. i), Desdemona's description of a woman, as 'laide et futée' ('ugly and crafty'). Bonnefoy removes the racial overtones of Othello's insult to himself when he says 'O cursed slave!' (V. ii) by changing 'slave' to 'imbecile'. Bonnefoy's instinct is to erase most of the racist language in the play, until Othello suspects that Desdemona may have betrayed him, at which point the racist language from the original appears in the translation to poignant effect. Othello, in his humiliation, adopts the worst prejudices against his own

---

[61] Bonnefoy, *SFP*, 203.
[62] Bonnefoy, *SFP*, 184.
[63] Bonnefoy, *SFP*, 194.
[64] Bonnefoy, *SFP*, 201.
[65] Bonnefoy, *SFP*, 172.

race as Bonnefoy does translate the word 'black' in his translation of 'My name ... is now begrim'd and black | As mine own face' (III. iii).

36.8 ANTONY AND CLEOPATRA

Bonnefoy considers Desdemona's passivity, her submission to Othello, and her inability to stand up for herself as weaknesses. This is the prism through which he interprets Cleopatra's will to affirm herself as she attempts to break out of the conventional roles women are expected to play. In Bonnefoy's interpretation of *Antony and Cleopatra* the corruption of power and the aspersions cast against women are 'two sides of the same lie that paralyses life'.[66] Bonnefoy considers the insults hurled against Cleopatra's sexuality in the play to be akin to the disparagement of the dark lady of the Sonnets. Both are prejudices of societies inclined to puritanism and 'debilitated by the idolatry of material goods and power'.[67]

For Bonnefoy, Cleopatra 'existed under the burden of alienation and prejudices that have spoken in her stead, often through the very voice of a woman not yet equal to herself',[68] and when she says 'I am fire and air; my other elements | I give to baser life' (V. ii), Bonnefoy thinks that 'it is as a woman and not as queen that Cleopatra has claimed her nobility'.[69] Bonnefoy is persuaded that Cleopatra changes from a woman whose sexuality was conditioned by social patterns of female alienation to one who desires to transcend them, even if her efforts will be thwarted by social prejudices, historical events, and accidents in her romantic life. The key moment in the play, its turning point according to Bonnefoy, is the scene in which Cleopatra decides not to punish the servant who has brought the news of Antony's betrayal in his marriage to Octavian's sister. In this moment Cleopatra begins to take responsibility for her own life, and she begins to assert a different kind of nobility than the nobility of power and greed. This interpretation is more persuasive in Bonnefoy's translation than in the original. 'I myself have given myself the cause' (II. v) becomes 'c'est moi qui merite le blâme' ('I deserve the blame'). Along the same lines Bonnefoy translates 'Though it be honest, it is never good to bring bad news' as 'Il est honnête de faire part des mauvaises nouvelles' ('it is honest to deliver bad news') to suggest in his translation that she no longer holds a grudge, when in the original her annoyance at the bearer of bad news remains intact.

As Bonnefoy sees it, Cleopatra's tragedy stems from Antony's own prevarications between his love for her and his desire for worldly power, but more importantly, from her inability to convey her true self to Antony. Bonnefoy considers the scene when Cleopatra is unable to persuade Antony to remain with her a key moment in the play. The original

---

[66] Bonnefoy, *SFP*, 143.
[67] Bonnefoy, *SFP*, 147.
[68] Bonnefoy, *SFP*, 163.
[69] Bonnefoy, *SFP*, 162.

can be taken simply as an expression of her anguish that Antony will forget her: 'I am all forgotten' (I. iii), but the translation is more suggestive: 'Je me suis moi-même oubliée' ('I have forgotten myself'). It is the translation, therefore, not the original, which justifies Bonnefoy's searching explanation of the line:

> the condition of women in a man's world is such that she has been robbed even of words; language is not for her; she is forgotten in it, forgotten first of all by herself, who can speak only as people want her to speak. Her forgetting is the forgetting of her own being; she has forgotten herself in the way Antony, rejoining the world that censors her, has forgotten her. She betrays herself without wanting to, as he betrays her, giving in to his ambition.[70]

A recurrent pattern Bonnefoy identifies in the tragedies is the undermining of women by male characters who fail in their love, whether it be Romeo's failure with Juliet, Hamlet's with Ophelia, Othello's with Desdemona, or Antony's with Cleopatra. If *The Winter's Tale* consisted only of its first three Acts, it would repeat the pattern of the other plays in Leonte's humiliation of Hermione and himself through his unreasonable jealousy. But the last two Acts offer a resolution to the pattern, which Bonnefoy considers to be the highpoint of Shakespeare's oeuvre as a playwright and a poet.

36.9 *THE WINTER'S TALE*

The main theme of *The Winter's Tale*, according to Bonnefoy, is the relationship between art and nature, and more profoundly between '[art] and existence'.[71] From his perspective, the centrepiece of the play is a discussion about the beauty of flowers in which Perdita takes the side of nature, whereas Polixenes the side of gardeners who can improve the beauty of flowers through the art of grafting.

In his analysis of the discussion Bonnefoy first appears to concur with Perdita who likens human intervention in art to make-up on a woman's face, and declares that she refuses to be loved for what she appears to be as opposed to who she is: 'she feels that an art which alters nature is a snare that evil—the spirit of evil which nature is spared—makes use of and can turn to its advantage'.[72] Bonnefoy's explanation of Perdita's response is analogous to his own view, if we substitute presence for nature and poetry for art, that true poetry is able to access presence whereas bad poetry can be an obstacle to authentic experience and is susceptible to perversion. Bonnefoy makes a connection between Perdita's views, and a theme in *Lucrece*:

> in *The Rape of Lucrece* the young woman Tarquin has so cruelly abused realises to her horror that her guest has succeeded only by disguising himself with a good deal of art;

[70] Bonnefoy, *SFP*, 150.
[71] Bonnefoy, *SFP*, 38.
[72] Bonnefoy, *SFP*, 30.

which means—a painting that Lucrece tears apart with her nails is there to prove—that a work made of appearances can do more than simply deprive its audience of the truth of life; it can also simulate virtue that can lead even the most virtuous souls astray.[73]

The true problem with Leontes, according to Bonnefoy, is that he approached his relationship to Hermione like an artist prone to perversion approaches his art: 'Leontes is an artist who exemplifies the dangers of artistic creation'.[74] Bonnefoy thinks of Leontes as a poet—much like he had thought of Romeo, Hamlet, and Othello as poets—who abuses the object of his love. Hermione, therefore, is a victim of

> artistic ambition, since the artist who sees only an appearance in woman risks no longer knowing her as an authentic, living presence; at which point, either he makes an ideal image of her and, by idolizing her, stifles her needs; or turning the illusion inside out, he pours scorn on her actual ways of existing and thereby shifts onto a woman, or women in general, responsibility for the guilt he will most certainly feel at misrepresenting reality for the sake of a dream.[75]

The final recognition scene, for Bonnefoy, appears to give even more credence to Perdita's views on the superiority of nature over art since Hermione is superior to the statue she pretends to be: 'To be reunited with Leontes, Hermione has to remind him—if a reminder is needed, which it may well be—that no art can ever equal nature'.[76]

But in the end of his analysis Bonnefoy finds a way to give credence to Polixenes' point of view, to some extent, because the vindication of Perdita herself takes place in a work of art: 'Can the transcendence of nature over art be expressed only through the medium of a narrative—in other words, through art again?'[77] Bonnefoy chooses not to offer an answer to his own question, but to point out that when Shakespeare wrote *The Winter's Tale*, he must have already had in mind the critique of art as an illusion in *The Tempest*, and 'the need, at the end of the age of symbols, to think these things out anew'.[78]

Bonnefoy thinks that Prospero's pronouncement 'we are such stuff as dreams are made on' represents a view of art for which Perdita and Hermione are eloquent counterstatements:

> To say that everything is a dream, that there is nothing that is not merely an image, fleeting and insubstantial—is this to utter the truth? This pessimistic view is certainly not shared by Perdita or Hermione. We may certainly fear that this man of such ambition, so deeply troubled, may yet be incapable of the inner transformation that would open a future for him in which he would be reconciled to his finitude.[79]

[73] Bonnefoy, *SFP*, 33.
[74] Bonnefoy, *SFP*, 38.
[75] Bonnefoy, *SFP*, 39.
[76] Bonnefoy, *SFP*, 45.
[77] Bonnefoy, *SFP*, 49.
[78] Bonnefoy, *SFP*, 49.
[79] Bonnefoy, 'A Day in the Life of Prospero', *SFP*, 73.

Bonnefoy prefers Hermione's stepping down from the pedestal of art into life over what he considers to be Prospero's empty renunciation of his magic, and his success in bringing together Miranda and Ferdinand is not particularly heartening to the French poet. Unlike many readers in the English-speaking world, Bonnefoy is not enchanted by Miranda. He sees her as a woman eager to submit to social conventions and male prerogatives:

> Miranda who offered to become Ferdinand's servant if he chose not to love her, sees herself in the future, as she already does in the present, as the wife who will submit to the law, if not to the whims of her husband; as someone who will matter less to him and to others than the ambitions of the manly power he exercises in the world of other men.[80]

36.10 CONCLUSION

In a discussion of Shakespeare's achievements, Bonnefoy downplays his psychological insights, and emphasizes aspects that would apply, without much adjustment, to his own views on poetry:

> Shakespeare's greatness was his ability to perceive in each of his memorable characters their cry of separation from the human condition, and their need to repair that lost unity, that is to say to perceive the hope that endures in the *parole* above and beyond the dramas that fragment it.[81]

In his translations and explications, Bonnefoy has recreated Shakespeare as a French poet, and in so doing, he expanded the canon of his own oeuvre, while adding an important chapter in the reception of Shakespeare in the French-speaking world.

SELECT BIBLIOGRAPHY

Bonnefoy, Yves (2004) *Shakespeare and the French Poet*, John Naughton (ed.), (Chicago: University of Chicago Press).
Caws, Mary Ann (2006) 'Shakespeare, Keats, and Yeats, by Bonnefoy', in *Surprised by Translation* (Chicago: University of Chicago Press) 108–26.
Dotoli, Giovanni (2008) *Yves Bonnefoy dans la fabrique de la traduction*, (Paris: Hermann).
Edwards, Michael (2008) 'Yves Bonnefoy et les sonnets de Shakespeare', *Littérature*, 150 (2): 25–39.
Greene, Robert W. (2004) 'Presence in Delacroix and Shakespeare', *Searching for Presence. Yves Bonnefoy's Writings on Art*, (Rodopi: Amsterdam and New York) 143–54.

[80] Bonnefoy, *SFP*, 77.
[81] Bonnefoy, *L'inachevable*, 444–5.

Jackson, John E. (2004) '*Conte d'hiver* et compte de vie: Bonnefoy et Shakespeare', in Yves Bonnefoy, Jean Starobinski, John Y. Jackson, and Pascal Griener, *Goya, Baudelaire et la poésie*, (Geneva: La Dogana) 49–77.

Jasper, David (1993) »La Même Voix, Toujours »: Yves Bonnefoy and Translation, *Translating Religious Texts: Translation, Transgression and Interpretation*, David Jasper (ed.), (New York: Saint Martin's Press) 106–21.

Naughton, John (1984) *The Poetics of Yves Bonnefoy*, (Chicago: University of Chicago Press).

—— (2007) '*Readiness, Ripeness*: Hamlet, Lear. Une riche problématique *L'amitié et la réflexion*, Daniel and Stephen Romer (eds.), (Tours: Presses universitaries François-Rabelais) 77–88.

Starobinski, Jean (1985) 'Poetry Between Two Worlds', in Yves Bonnefoy, *Poems 1959–1975* (New York: Vintage Books) 179–97.

CHAPTER 37

GLOCAL SHAKESPEARE

Shakespeare's Poems in Germany

CHRISTA JANSOHN

After Bertolt Brecht, Shakespeare remains the writer whose works are performed more on German stages than those of any other dramatist; in fact, there are more performances of his plays in Germany than in England. Yet Germans not only love his plays, they also revere his poetry. In contrast to the plays, however, no translation of the Sonnets, 'A Lover's Complaint', *Venus and Adonis*, or *The Rape of Lucrece* has attained 'classical' status comparable to the Schlegel-Tieck version of the plays (1797–1833). The field of their reception has, therefore, especially since about 1900, been open to a great variety of translators, 'professionals' or amateurs, with very different biographical backgrounds and approaches. So far, more than seventy German translations of the whole sonnet sequence are extant, and more than one-hundred-and-forty enthusiasts have tried their hand at selections of individual poems. *Venus and Adonis* and *The Rape of Lucrece* have been rendered into German, chiefly during the 19th century, by more than twenty-five translators, 'A Lover's Complaint' by thirteen (only one from the 20th century, none in the present century). Out of the complete sonnet translations only twelve are by women; apart from one translation by Terese Robinson (1927), both narrative poems and 'A Lover's Complaint' were all translated by men. The majority of the German versions attempt to reproduce the verse form of the original text; only a handful are in prose or try some less restrictive metre. Some have freely translated the Sonnets to vary the order of the 1609 Quarto or offer new headings. The variations in poetic style are as striking as the degrees of faithfulness to meaning, imagery, and linguistic register. Indeed, in the course of the 20th and 21st centuries, translating the Sonnets, in particular, seems to have become almost an exercise in poetic, not to say sportive, ambition, as exemplified by a surprising number of new versions and projects, some on the printed page, some on stage or on audio CDs.

Whilst Shakespeare's Sonnets and 'A Lover's Complaint' have frequently been the subject of scholarly interest in Germany, the two narrative poems *Venus and Adonis* and *The Rape of Lucrece* have been relatively neglected in German scholarly criticism. This is all the more surprising as German interest in the two poems began earlier than interest in the Sonnets and gave rise to a remarkable number of translations, especially in the 19th century, whilst in the 20th and 21st centuries stage adaptations of *Venus and Adonis* have tended to attract more attention.

A particularly noteworthy example of an enthusiastic reception is the first German version of *Venus and Adonis* (*Venus und Adonis*) and *The Rape of Lucrece* (*Tarquin und Lukrezia*) published in 1783 by Heinrich Christoph Albrecht (1763–1800). According to Albrecht, Shakespeare's poetic works—and in this he contradicts the then prevalent opinion of several language schools—could be used for the purposes of language learning, for the learner would find in his works, specifically in the two narrative poems, 'an almost inexhaustible source of discoveries and observations on the idiosyncrasies of language, on its general capacity for expression as well as on the so varied and subtle treatment which it receives and often demands of the spirit of the English language'.[1] Albrecht's edition was bilingual, making the original available to German readers, thus encouraging and providing a direct encounter with the English language.

In his detailed introduction, Albrecht maintained that it would be possible for the 'sharp-eyed seeker' to encounter the poet William Shakespeare from a different viewpoint. For whilst, he argues, in the plays the characters 'speak and act', in the two epic poems, the poet 'narrates'. This change of viewpoint, according to Albrecht, enables the reader to broaden his knowledge of Shakespeare, but above all to become acquainted with the poet's versatility and thus to distinguish more precisely between the weaknesses and strengths of his work—at the time a frequent point of discussion.[2] For Albrecht, Shakespeare is not simply the genius of dramatic art—as for many British and German critics—but also a master of epic literature. It is this broadening of the appreciation of Shakespeare which is the particular achievement of the then twenty-year old Albrecht. At the same time, it is rather surprising that he does not mention the Sonnets at all.

In contrast to the later translation of the plays by Schlegel and Tieck, Albrecht was less concerned with the formal elements of the original than with its meaning. It is well known that Shakespeare in the 18th century was not admired for his skills as a poet. Such a view would have been inconsistent with the image of Shakespeare as an inspired natural genius who used natural, expressive language; furthermore, the verse forms of both *Venus and Adonis* and *Rape of Lucrece* were just as unfamiliar to the 18th-century German reader as blank verse. This attitude may also have played a role in Albrecht's decision to translate the poems into free verse, avoiding the original metre. Through his language, he achieves a remarkable flexibility within each line, though at the cost of an

---

[1] Heinrich Christoph Albrecht, *Versuch einer critischen englischen Sprachlehre. Vorzüglich nach dem Englischen des Dr. Lowth, Bischofs zu London* (Halle: Gebauer, 1784) 236.

[2] Albrecht (1784) iv.

exact translation of each part of the individual lines; he is, however, able to position the caesuras with greater discrimination and to emphasize particular emotional moments and thematic climaxes more effectively than in many other German versions. It is the progression of the narrative and the development of themes that dominate Albrecht's version rather than the metre.

Four years later Johann Joachim Eschenburg published a prose translation of a number of excerpts from both poems in his study *Ueber W. Shakspeare*.[3] Forty-three years later, in 1826, the second complete translation of *Venus and Adonis* was published by J. P. Sollinger, in the translation of the Viennese writer and private scholar Andreas Schumacher.[4] Schumacher's, like all the other subsequent German versions of Shakespeare's works, also included the Sonnets and the other poems, besides *Venus and Adonis* and *Rape of Lucrece*. In 1849 Ferdinand von Freiligrath (1810–1876), author of revolutionary poetry and a most gifted translator, published *Venus und Adonis* in a single volume. His main intention was to offer a high-quality translation of the poem similar to the Schlegel-Tieck translation of the plays or Gottlob Regis' translation of the Sonnets (1836). It is mainly due to Freiligrath's remarkable aesthetic power of assimilating the original for the German reader that his translation of *Venus and Adonis*, Longfellow's *Hiawatha* (1857), and Shakespeare's *Cymbeline* and *The Winter's Tale*, have all remained popular in Germany ever since. His translation of *Venus and Adonis*, in particular, was reissued in Germany (East and West) several times, sometimes with pen-and-ink sketches (for example, in 1920 by F. Heubner) in a bilingual single edition, sometimes (mostly in the former GDR) as part of a complete edition.

In the 20th century the poems became part of the canon and were no longer relegated to supplementary volumes. Friedrich Gundolf's new translation of both narrative poems came out in 1922, and Terese Robinson's versions were published in volume 10 of a revised Schlegel-Tieck edition by Levin Ludwig Schücking. The latest (unpublished) translation of *Rape of Lucrece* and *Venus and Adonis* (1939) is by the German naturalist poet Johannes Schlaf (1862–1941) better known as the co-author of *Papa Hamlet* (1889, in collaboration with Arno Holz).

37.1 *VENUS AND ADONIS* IN GERMANY

Since the second half of the 20th century scholars and translators seem to have lost interest in *Venus and Adonis*, mainly due to its gender crossing and its difficult language. At the same time, however, it has been discovered for the German stage and for opera.

---

[3] (Zürich: Orell, Füßli & Co., 1787) on *Venus and Adonis*, 527–50; on *Rape of Lucrece*, 551–71.
[4] In *William Shakspeare's Saemmtliche Dramatische Werke und Gedichte*. Vollständige Ausgabe in einem Bande. Übersetzt im Metrum des Originals von Eduard von Bauernfeld und Andreas Schumacher (Wien: Druck und Verlag von J. P. Sollinger, 1826) 103–13.

Hans Werner Henze's single-act opera *Venus and Adonis* had its premiere at the Bavarian State Opera in Munich on 11 January 1997, and a few years later in the United States (Santa Fe Opera in August 2000), Canada (2001), and in Great Britain (1997) and Tokyo (2001 in concert performance).[5] The opera, which uses both singers and dancers, was inspired by the Shakespearean poem (in Eschenburg's prose translation) and Ovid. As Allan Kozinn explains, the composer and his librettist, Hans-Ulrich Treichel, expanded the story into an operatic psychodrama with an exquisitely ornate structure. Dance, operatic vocal writing, and madrigals for a six-voice choir alternate in a series of seventeen short scenes lasting seventy minutes. The opera's structure calls to mind the masques of Purcell's time, although Mr. Henze's variegated score inhabits a different musical universe, with its dense layering, dream-like textures, and stretches of both gritty dissonance and touching lyricism.

The work is set in several worlds. One describes a mythological triangle, evoked by dancers: Mars lusts after Venus, who rejects him in favour of Adonis. Adonis is too self-absorbed and free-spirited to notice, but when, after encountering mating horses that awaken his own sexuality, he finally responds; he is killed by a wild boar.[6]

An account of *Venus and Adonis* in performance also indicates the poem's 'infinite variety' and shows the poem to be extremely stage-worthy. While British theatre still seems generally shy of staging Shakespeare's poetry, it has become quite popular in the United States and in Germany. From 1993 to the present there have been more than fifteen successful stage productions of *Venus and Adonis*. This number exceeds that of the stage productions of the Sonnets,[7] while, as far as I know, *The Rape of Lucrece* has so far been put on the German stage only once, in April 1999.[8]

The performance of Barbara Geiger, director of the Turlygood Theater Company, Berlin, was first staged in 1993 for the Berliner Globe Theater and later for the Turlygood Theater Company under the direction of Susan Graham. Barbara Geiger acted the three parts, using the original text divided into five Acts: 'The Meeting', 'The Wooing', 'The Escape', 'The Hunt', and 'The Prophesy'. There were no props, and the costume consisted merely of a plain, black, tight gym-suit with leather boots. Everything, therefore, depended on strong gesture, facial expression, and pantomimic movement. The entire performance seemed to revolve around her bright red lip-sticked mouth. This kept the spectators enthralled with its expressive changes, and was supported by the eyes which, conveying tenderness, desire, anger, resolution, and grief, added visual clarity to the poet's language. The stage was a glimmering white landscape of velvet and silk; lighting effects

---

[5] See also Christa Jansohn, 'Theatricality in *Venus and Adonis* and its Staging in Germany (1994–1998)', *Cahiers Elisabéthains. Late Medieval and Renaissance English Studies* 61 (2002): 31–41.

[6] Allan Kozinn, 'Love, Modern and Mythical', *The New York Times*, 4 August 2000.

[7] See Cordelia Borchardt, '"As an unperfect actor on the stage"? Dramatisierungen der Sonette in England und Deutschland', in *Shakespeares Sonette in europäischen Perspektiven*, Dieter Mehl and Wolfgang Weiß (eds), (Münster: LIT, 1993) 322–38.

[8] See the programme *Die Schändung der Lucretia von William Shakespeare*. Translation: Friedrich Bodenstedt. Adapted by Markus Fennert, Sylvia Kühn, Peter Pearce (premiere at the Theater am Leibnizplatz [Bremen], 14 April 1999).

FIGURE 37.1. Venus and Adonis played by Barbara Geiger, the Berliner Globe Theater, 1993.

were limited to indicating the times of the day. And when the catastrophe occurred, there was even a moment of complete darkness. After Adonis' death, the actress disappeared behind the white cloth, only to reappear again—blood-stained. These were some of the more spectacular effects. In the main, however, it was language and movement that Barbara Geiger concentrated on. Perhaps one could have wished this Venus to have been more of a woman, less boyish and athletic. Nevertheless, it was an impressively convincing stage-version of Shakespeare's poem (FIGURE 37.1).

Another remarkable example is provided by the 'Bremer Shakespeare Company'. From 1983 onwards, this enterprising venture has continually sought an innovative re-engagement with Shakespeare's text in a variety of modern translations. In September 1994, *Alles Lügen* (*All Lies*), a one-man show, was first performed by Renato Grünig in the role of Shakespeare as a scenic representation of thirty-five Sonnets, and proved a great success. It was followed by a production of *Venus and Adonis* on 9 May 1996 at the Theater am Leibnizplatz (Bremen).

For *Venus and Adonis*, three German translations from the second half of the last century, by Friedrich Bodenstedt, Felix von Mauntz, and Max Josef Wolff, were conflated and modernized, because the actor, Christian Kaiser, was unable to make up his mind which one he preferred.[9] The production, which was about one and a half hours

---

[9] See my interview with the actor: "'Geht das überhaupt?'": *Venus und Adonis* auf der Bühne. Christa Jansohn im Gespräch mit Christian Kaiser', *Anglistik. Mitteilungen des Deutschen Anglistikverbandes* 14.1. (2003) 71–6.

long, was in many ways typical of the company's own individual style, from the somewhat salesman-like programme notes introducing *Venus and Adonis* as 'a poem for lovers and those who want to become lovers', to the rather sparse set, consisting mainly of a chandelier. Metallic musical sounds in the background suggested an atmosphere of Renaissance myth. The director, Silvia Armbruster, had decided to cast one actor for all three parts, so Kaiser played the narrator, Venus, and Adonis in turn. With his face heavily painted, and wearing a decorative headband, high-heeled shoes, and long gloves, he presented a deliberately androgynous figure. His white cape, cast over a tight trouser-suit, and leaving one shoulder seductively bare, served variously as dress, cloak, veil, bed, and shroud.

Kaiser acted Venus as a grotesquely high-strung, languishing, lovesick, and madly raving Venus, indulging even in a bellydance to attract Adonis. The love-play between stallion and mare, reminiscent of an erotic flamenco, was a brilliant performance. Then Kaiser turned into an anxious, overwhelmed youth, who, in his innocent adolescence, hardly knew what was happening to him. However, there were also quieter moments where the brilliance of Shakespeare's rich imagery was fully explored. All in all, it was a production combining genuine feeling with light parody, with little of the purely gimmicky effects of some other Bremer Shakespeare Company productions.

After many years of successful performances, Christian Kaiser and Barbara Geiger decided to perform *Venus and Adonis* together. Its premiere was in February 2008 and it has been very successful on various German stages since. There were no props, apart from a chair, and the conflation of texts (spoken in English-German, occasionally German-English, with Venus, draped in paper-thin satin, wooing Adonis in the original language, while he answers in German) did not create an impression of clumsiness or awkward pedagogy. The various other parts, such as the narrator and the horses, were divided in such a way that the spectator was never left in doubt as to who was speaking at any moment. The intention behind this dual-language performance, as Barbara Geiger explains, was a 'choreographic round dance' which would convey the beauty of Shakespeare's verses to the ears and, by the translation, to the heads of the audience. The changes between original and translation were staged with genuine imagination; at one point Venus actually refused to accept the English original of Adonis cheap arguments against love (lines 769–804) and asked with terse coquetry: 'Fondling, do you really want me to translate all that???', whereupon Adonis' conclusion, 'More I could tell, but more I dare not say' (line 805) gave rise to additional laughs from the audience (FIGURE 37.2).

Another production of *Venus and Adonis* was staged in June 1997 at the Werkstatt-Café in Darmstadt to conclude the 'Theatertage' of the state theatre Darmstadt. This time, the parts of the protagonists were taken by two actors, Katharina Hofmann as Venus and Jens Ochlast as Adonis. Directed by Kirsten Uttendorf, they succeeded in relating the action to our contemporary experience and at the same time in catching the graceful spirit of Shakespeare's poetry.[10]

---

[10] Uttendorf revised and abridged Wilhelm Jordan's translation, *Shakespeare's Gedichte* (Berlin: G. Reimer, 1861). The performance was about 60-minutes long.

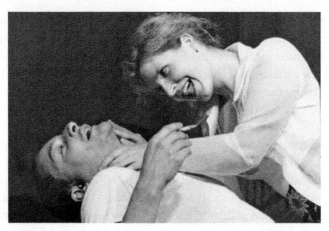

FIGURE 37.2. Venus played by Barbara Geiger and Adonis by Christian Kaiser, Pegnitz-Auen, 14 July 2008.

The performance started as a play within a play: two people were sitting in a bar, looking attractive, but rather bored. Yet they appeared to be profoundly familiar with Shakespeare's work as they began, at first simultaneously, to recite *Venus and Adonis*, stopping, however, in the midst of the first line to challenge each other to start again, saying 'You begin'—'no, you'. In this way they found themselves in the midst of a drama of seduction and resistance, between mythical past and suggested present. When, in the end, Adonis lay dead in his own blood and Venus, full of despair, resolved in the future always to add sorrow to love, the two actors suddenly broke into laughter leaving the spectators with the unanswered question whether it all was perhaps just a game.[11] In a quite different way this production also found a theatrical solution to the problem of involving an audience in the action of Shakespeare's poem, mainly by means of its language. There were brief moments of genuine seriousness, interrupted by ironic disillusioning. The actors in this production covered the full range of emotions, from tragedy to comedy, thus coming close to the poem's kaleidoscopic changes of tone and degrees of seriousness.

Besides these four productions there were other, more local readings and performances of *Venus and Adonis*. The famous German actress Jutta Lampe, for example, gave an impressive reading of the poem during the 'Shakespeare-Zyklus' organized by the Berliner Philharmonisches Orchester (30 November 1995 to 29 June 1996), and in Dresden (Theater Oben) in December 1995 and January 1996, using an abridged version of Terese Robinson's translation (1927). Lampe identified herself with the mature Venus trying to distance herself from her knowledge of the transitory nature of love.

Together with songs by Purcell an abridged version of *Venus and Adonis* was performed in the inner court of the cloister 'Unser Lieben Frauen' in Magdeburg in July

---

[11] See Nikola Herweg, 'Shakespeares Sprache eignet sich sogar für einen Flirt an der Bar', *Gießener Anzeiger*, 23 June 1998, N IIIa.

1997 and 1998. It was part of a summer theatre organized by the 'Poetenpack', which is a regional theatre company for Brandenburg and Saxony-Anhalt. The performance starts with Shakespeare meeting Count Titchfield in the garden. He is hopeful of winning him as patron, but the Countess foils his design. She confuses the young poet by continuing his lines and starting to entice him. The jealous Sir Henry Purcell makes a musical intervention and the story of *Venus und Adonis* suddenly turns into the story between the Countess of Titfield and the young poet.

Another performance of the poem took place in Freiburg in 2002. Here the director, Sybille Fabian, combined two translations (Ferdinand Freiligrath [1849] and Wilhelm Jordan [1861]) into a new dialogue about love and lust (FIGURE 37.3). The set was a radiant white box with an oversized air ventilator at the back. Venus was dressed in a dark red skirt which put one in mind of devouring fire. She kept her long-haired Adonis in this box and tried to manipulate him, sometimes even seeming to be successful – as emphasized by the music and different lighting effects. Fabian added some dream sequences where Venus and Adonis actually make love, an act interrupted in the end by the hunt. Burnt leaves falling from the sky indicated the deep loss and the tragic ending of the poem.

In view of the powerful influence in German-speaking countries of 'director's theatre', and the freedom to translate and adapt Shakespeare's text on the modern stage there, it is

FIGURE 37.3. Venus played by Nadine Geyersbach and Adonis by Alex Gamnitzer, Theater Freiburg, 20 October 2002.

perhaps not surprising that Shakespeare's poetry has been adapted to the multiplicity of modern media and that the boundaries between page and stage are getting blurred with increasing speed and thoroughness.

37.2 *THE RAPE OF LUCRECE* IN GERMANY

For the German reader of Shakespeare *The Rape of Lucrece* is a more difficult text than *Venus and Adonis* and even more so for the translator. Its first translator, Heinrich Christoph Albrecht, did not even try to reproduce the rhyme royal stanzas of the original. Rather, as in the case of *Venus and Adonis*, he used a kind of rhythmic prose in short lines which at least created the effect of a poetic diction. Albrecht showed a remarkable receptiveness to the rhetorical virtuosity and literary quality of the poem, and his comments on Shakespeare's art of characterization in *The Rape of Lucrece* deserve to be quoted at length as an early example of genuine appreciation, unique at this early stage of Shakespeare reception in Germany. Of Lucrece's first appearance in the poem, he writes:

> The poet tells the story as the progress not of a historical narrative, but of a passionate sympathy. He proceeds to the description of Lucrece; and what a demonstration of his deep-rooted art! On this portrait depends whether the story is to make a misleading or an appropriate impression on the reader's heart. Therefore, Shakespeare does not paint her beautiful form, her pleasing shape, but the charming face, the mirror of her soul. It was not his purpose to make us feel attracted by her outward, but by her inner beauty.[12]

Albrecht goes on to describe its effect on Tarquin, and his nocturnal soliloquy, the mental struggle between reason and passion, discussing with astonishing insight the dramatic potentiality of silent reflection. With keen sensibility he points out the mute 'warnings' on the rapist's way to Lucrece's bedroom: 'About the description of his terrible progress to Lucrece's room I will only remark how effectively the poet succeeds in keeping busy our attentive imagination by lending life and a sense of Tarquin's intention to inanimate or at least unthinking beings'.[13]

Albrecht's detailed analysis is important because, for the first time in German, Shakespeare's narrative poem is recognized and appreciated as a literary achievement in its own right, and it comes at a time when Goethe and many of his contemporaries were enthusiastically discussing the dramatic genius of the Bard, but apparently without any knowledge of his epic or lyrical works. Nonetheless, an anonymous review of Albrecht's translation, published in 1784, did appear to be familiar with the English original and

---

[12] Jansohn, Christa (ed.), *William Shakespeare: Venus und Adonis und Tarquin und Lukrezia in der Übersetzung von Heinrich Christoph Albrecht (1783)* (Münster: LIT, 2007) 7–8.

[13] Jansohn (2007) 7–8.

was even able to comment on variant readings between Albrecht's text and Malone's as included in the 1780 supplement to his edition.[14] The review makes the silence of Goethe and his contemporaries about this essential part of Shakespeare's oeuvre even harder to explain.

In the course of the following century a vogue for new translations of Shakespeare's poetry sprung up that included not only the Sonnets but also the narrative poems. On the whole, translators seem to have been more sensitive and enthusiastic readers than were literary critics, and no fewer than twelve translations of *The Rape of Lucrece* appeared between 1783 and 1920.

Serious literary criticism of the narrative poems in Germany began rather late. In the first fifty years of the *Shakespeare Jahrbuch*, founded in 1864 at the same time as the Deutsche Shakespeare-Gesellschaft, only one article on these poems appeared, a piece by Benno Tschischwitz (1828–90), who in 1870 had already published his translation of the complete sonnet-cycle.[15] Discussing *The Rape of Lucrece*, Tschischwitz, who was a teacher in Halle and later Professor of English in Zurich (1874–6), lays particular stress on the independence of Shakespeare's own version of the famous story as compared to earlier accounts. This, he claims, makes any further thorough source study unnecessary. Shakespeare, he argues, has practically transferred the action into the immediate present, notwithstanding that the scene is Rome. The critic's own criteria are basically moral: Tarquin is an unworthy Lord, abusing the hospitality of Collatinus, another Lord, and Lucrece feels her shame as noble women, not just Roman dames, would feel it. Tschischwitz further argues that Shakespeare in this poem makes less use of demonstrative rhetorical artifice than in *Venus and Adonis*—a reminder of Shakespeare's consummate mastery as dramatist. Like many earlier and later critics Tschischwitz finds this mastery, above all, in Tarquin's tortured reflections prior to the crime. The critic's admiration, however, leads him to emotional judgements and a genuinely high estimation of the text, rather than to strive for scholarly distance: 'Equally moving is the delicate characterization of the ruined woman hiding from every human being the shame inflicted on her; it is only to the nightingale that she offers to complain about the deep pain of her soul. The touching simplicity of the pathos of this passage makes it one of the most beautiful pearls ever created by a poet'. This kind of emphatic enthusiasm stirred by Shakespeare's poem cannot be found in any later issues of the *Shakespeare Jahrbuch* or any other German critical discussions, and only one or two of the poem's translators seem to share an equally high opinion of its literary value. Max Kahlenberg was one such

---

[14] *Allgemeine deutsche Bibliothek. 1765–90*, 59 (1784) 111–13. The reviewer finds fault with Albrecht for ignoring the critical notes and textual corrections in Malone's edition, from which he might have profited. As an example he quotes line 161, where Albrecht's source evidently read 'To sland'rous tongue and wretched hateful lays?' whereas Malone (and all later editors) read 'wretched hateful *days*' (Albrecht must have used an edition between *State* [1707] and *Evans* [1775]; see Hyder Edward Rollins (ed.), *A New Variorum Edition of Shakepeare: The Poems* (Philadelphia & London: J. B. Lippincott Company, 1938).

[15] Benno Tschischwitz, 'Ueber die Stellung der epischen Dichtungen Shakespeare's in der englischen Literatur', *Shakespeare Jahrbuch*, 8 (1873) 32–45.

fellow admirer, who in his brief preface to his 1920 translation referred to the poem as 'that apotheosis of female chastity'.[16]

Friedrich Gundolf, one of the first and most eloquent literary champions of Shakespeare in 20th-century Germany, included the two narrative poems in volume six of his much praised and influential edition of Shakespeare's complete works (1920). In his two-volume 1928 monograph, *Shakespeare. Sein Wesen und Werk*, he devotes some three pages to *The Rape of Lucrece*[17] and states that 'in *Lucrece* we find the elements of future Shakespearean tragedy make their energetic entrance for the first time, and it is not without reason that Macbeth recalls Tarquin striding towards nocturnal ravishment. He draws particular attention to the 'union of action and character' and argues that Shakespeare here abandons the 'high-Renaissance, Ariosto-like arabesque-epic inherited from Spenser' (II, 176). In the end, however, he concludes that the narrative poems do not add to our treasure of human characters and the persons depicted do not belong to Shakespeare's unforgettable figures, though these poems are invaluable as a transitional stage in Shakespeare's growth from plot-centred ('Erlebnis-art') to character-centred ('Gestaltensicht') drama (II, 179).

As for *The Rape of Lucrece*, the most comprehensive and thorough German contribution, quoted regularly even in English accounts of the story, is Hans Galinsky's dissertation of 1932, where Shakespeare's poem is described, along with Heywood's play, as an example of baroque design.[18] Galinsky observes that Lucrece's story has never before been treated at similar length and with such psychological intensity, and that Shakespeare has radically changed the proportions of the traditional plot as found in his sources by bypassing the wager at the outset and the introduction of the heroine as model of domestic virtue, not to mention the birth of Tarquin's desire before he has even set eyes on Lucrece. Galinsky was one of the earliest critics to draw attention to the subtlety of Shakespeare's characterisation and the unprecedented weight the author gives to Lucrece's complaint and agonized debate with herself and her situation.

Later German studies of the narrative poems include a substantial and valuable doctoral dissertation by Helmut Castrop,[19] and a fine article by Werner von Koppenfels, published in *Shakespeare Survey*,[20] discussing *The Rape of Lucrece* in the context of Elizabethan erotic poetry, particularly Marlowe's *Hero and Leander*. The study is also an instance of the closer ties between German and English academic Shakespeare criticism.

---

[16] *Die Schmach der Lucretia* von William Shakespeare. Deutsch von Max Kahlenberg (Berlin: Albrecht Blau, 1920).

[17] *Shakespeare. Sein Wesen und Werk* (Berlin: Georg Bondi, 1928) II, 176–9. His brilliant study *Shakespeare und der deutsche Geist* (*Shakespeare and the German Spirit*) (Berlin: Georg Bondi, 1911) 'has assumed a kind of cult status'. See Roger Paulin, *The Critical Reception of Shakespeare in Germany 1682–1914* (Hildesheim: Olms, 2003) 1.

[18] Hans Galinsky, *Der Lucretia-Stoff in der Weltliteratur* (Breslau: Priebatsch, 1932) 91–101.

[19] *Shakespeares Verserzählungen. Eine Untersuchung der Ovidischen Epik im elisabethanischen England* (Munich: PhD dissertation, 1964).

[20] 'Dis-Covering the Female Body: Erotic Exploration in Elizabethan Poetry', *Shakespeare Survey* 47 (1994): 127–37.

Another is the article by Susanne Scholz, 'Textualizing the Body Politic: National Identity and the Female Body in *The Rape of Lucrece*', evidently written in the wake of Anglo-Saxon gender criticism of the poem.[21]

37.3 THE SONNETS AND 'A LOVER'S COMPLAINT' IN GERMANY

In 1823/4 the first complete German translation of all 154 Sonnets was produced by Dorothea Tieck (1799–1841), the daughter of Ludwig Tieck. She also completed her father's translation of Shakespeare's works which he had begun together with Schlegel and Baudissin, and which since then has become something like the 'classic' translation of Shakespeare's plays. Her translation of the Sonnets, however, was buried among the papers of the Ludwig Tieck archive in Berlin and was only discovered at the beginning of the 1990s.[22] For the then twenty-four-year-old Dorothea Tieck this task constituted her first encounter with Shakespeare as a translator, dedicating herself to this work because she believed that translating was an activity for women rather than for men, since women had not been bestowed with the gift of a genuinely creative faculty. Translating for her was a real pleasure precisely because it enabled her to bury herself utterly in the creation of a great mind. A preliminary reading of her translation shows clearly the determination of this pioneering translator to stick to the poetic and rhetorical style of the original. On the whole, there are hardly any blunders of translation, although there are instances of vagueness, occasional padding, and changes to the meaning for the sake of the rhyme, as well as a number of clumsy or awkward passages. Dorothea Tieck's version was certainly not just the dutiful service of a good daughter for her busy father, who, incidentally only translated three Sonnets (1, 2, and 18), which he chose to work poetically together with other Sonnets and *Venus and Adonis* into his novella *A Poet's Life* (1825).

In spite of, or perhaps because of, the astonishing number of German sonnet translations, none of the versions has acquired the classic status that the Schlegel-Tieck translation of the plays has, even though some have established themselves more securely than others. To this group certainly belongs the Romantic version by Gottlob Regis (1836). It was most recently used for a CD recording[23] and has been reprinted many times; for example, in Leipzig in 1987. In the 'afterword' Anselm Schlösser writes: 'The translation [combines] philological fidelity to the original with a highly developed sense for the poetic potential of the German language. [...] Regis does justice to the meaning, he does not leave anything out; he neither polishes, nor does he add anything. He does not try, as

---

[21] *Shakespeare Jahrbuch*, 132 (1996) 103–13.

[22] Christa Jansohn, ed., *Shakespeares Sonette in der Übersetzung Dorothea Tiecks* (Tübingen: Francke, 1992).

[23] Bretzfeld: Noa Noa Hörbuch, 2009.

Stefan George later did, to make an overly exigent artistic virtue out of a word-for-word translation'.[24] Of the dozens of translations published in the course of the 19th century, few are of more than historical interest today.

By contrast, the celebrated 'reworking' by Stefan George (1909), a complete and surprisingly faithful, although somewhat idiosyncratic, translation of the Sonnets, was only available again for buyers in East and West Germany in the years after 1989 from the publisher Deutscher Taschenbuch Verlag in the series 'DTV Classics' as a complete bilingual edition without afterword or commentary, and at the same time from the Leipzig publishers Dietrich (with distribution also by Carl Schünemann in Bremen). Furthermore, not until 2008 was a critical edition published with extensive notes and a chapter on the genesis of the translation.[25] George's translation stands out among most of its predecessors as well as later translations on account, in particular, of its masterly rigour, a rigour that is no act of poetic self-denial, however, but an exemplary calibration of the translator's sensibility to Shakespeare's text. George, though adapting Shakespeare's rhetoric to his own very personal idiom, was admirably faithful to the rhythm and the meaning of the original: important words mostly retain their position, especially in rhymes and also at the stressed line beginnings. The sound patterns are also preserved more clearly than in other translations, for example in the opening line of Sonnet 12, in which, with the aid of the short words and the 't' alliteration, the ticking of elapsing time is expressed: 'when I do count the clock that tells the time' becomes in George's version 'Zähl ich im Glockenschlag den Schritt der Zeit' ('I count in the clock's strokes the tread of time'). The intensity of focus on linguistic detail and poetic abundance remains fluid however, even if George's use of archaisms, neologisms, and rare words often makes the reading experience difficult.

Between 1933 and 1945 we have eight complete German versions of Shakespeare's Sonnets of which those by Karl Kraus (1933), Richard Flatter (1933), Gustav Wolff (1938), Eta Harich-Schneider (1944), and Ilse Krämer (1945) were published during the Second World War, whereas three had been extant only in manuscript until their publication in 2001, when a critical bilingual edition brought together three hitherto unpublished translations from the 1930s and 1940s by the Hamburg-based grammar school teacher Sophie Zipora Heiden (1875–1945), the poet Johannes Schlaf (1862–1941), and the university lecturer and scholar in Hittite studies, Friedrich Cornelius (1893–1976).[26] Before Sophie Heiden was deported from Hamburg on 19 July 1942 to the Theresienstadt concentration camp she had sent her translation to the German Shakespeare Society in Weimar. Evidently, the typescript never reached the Society. She then sent another copy of her translation to the Folger Shakespeare Library, and two years later a slightly

[24] *William Shakespeare. Sonette. Englisch und deutsch*. Aus dem Englischen übertragen von Gottlob Regis. Nachwort von Anselm Schlösser (Leipzig: Philipp Reclam, 1987) 346–7.

[25] Ute Oelmann (ed.), *Stefan George, Shakespeare Sonnette. Vermehrt um einige Stücke aus dem Liebendem Pilgrim*, in Stefan George: Sämtliche Werke, vol. XII (Stuttgart: Klett-Cotta, 2008).

[26] Christa Jansohn (ed.), *William Shakespeare: Cupido lag im Schlummer einst. Drei neue Übersetzungen von Shakespeares Sonetten*. Englisch-deutsche Ausgabe (Tübingen: Stauffenburg, 2001).

revised typescript to the Shakespeare Memorial Library in Stratford-upon-Avon (today the Shakespeare Centre library). The director of the Folger Shakespeare Library at the time, Dr Joseph Quincy Adams, thanked her personally for sending the translation and also voiced his hope for the possibility of a later publication: 'Perhaps within a few years conditions throughout the world will be materially altered, and you can see your work in the glory of print. I sincerely hope so'. Clearly his letter was of little consequence, for the Sonnets remained unpublished and unbound in the years that followed.

The German versions from these troubled years reveal completely different approaches to the original, which is certainly a result of personal preferences and experiences as well as the translators' differing intentions and their individual skills and interest. The once celebrated harpsichordist Eta Harich-Schneider (1894–1986), for example, whose translation was produced during a six-year exile in Japan and published privately in Peking in 1944, saw a deep connection between the Sonnets and music, and she was concerned to make this link 'tangible in the translation of the Sonnets into German'.[27] This is, for example, particularly evident in Sonnet 8, where the translator places slightly too much emphasis on the musical terms. Whereas Shakespeare is attempting above all to describe a harmonious relationship ('by unions married'), the translator concentrates too much on abstract musical terminology, as a result of which the ambiguity (e.g. of 'parts') gets lost. The immediate literary context in which individual Sonnets are situated should be born in mind when we evaluate the translation. Hence, for example, Erna Grautoff's translation of several of the Sonnets in her novel *Herrscher über Traum und Leben* (Stuttgart und Berlin: Rowohlt, 1940) should be assessed differently from, for instance, Lion Feuchtwanger's use of Sonnet 66 ('Tired with all these, for restful death I cry') in his novel *Exil*. Where Grautoff used the Sonnets to refute the poet's authorship in the light of Baconian theories, the protagonist Harry Meisel in Feuchtwanger's novel accuses 'the corruption of the period with these great, desperate verses': 'Harry Meisel had taken on the bold attempt of writing a story set in the Third Reich based on every line of the sonnet, and in doing so of basing his Shakespeare poem on the events under Hitler'.[28] Accordingly, the prose version and verse translations are gruff, aggressive, and provocative in tone. In this novel, the sonnet is stylized into a political protest and also helps the protagonist to see the meaning of exile more clearly: 'Trautwein had thought he knew what exile was. That had been a mistake. Only now as he read the fictive 'sonnet' stories, did he see what it was. He understood that up until now he had only ever seen details of things as they followed each other or occurred alongside one another. Now he saw as a single whole the magnitude and abjectness of exile, its breadth, its narrowness. No description, no experience, no event is able to reveal exile, its inner truth, in its entirety: only art can do this'.[29]

This political gesture, using Sonnet 66, which saw 'art made tongue-tied by authority' (line 9), to protest against the authority of Hitler's regime, was taken up again years

---

[27] Christa Jansohn (ed.), *Eta Harich-Schneider: Die Sonette William Shakespeares und die Lyrik der 'Rekusanten': Erlebnisse und Übersetzungen einer reisenden Musikerin: 1941–1982* (Münster: LIT, 2011).

[28] Lion Feuchtwanger, *Exil*. Roman (Rudolstadt: Greifenverlag, 1939) 168–9.

[29] Feuchtwanger (1939) 170.

later, particularly in translations from the former German Democratic Republic. An interesting example is Ronald M. Schernikau's aggressive version 'Ihr kotzt mich an, ich würd jetzt gerne gehn' ('You make me puke, I feel like leaving'),[30] or most recently Rayk Wieland's parody of Sonnet 66 in his GDR novel, *Ich schlage vor, dass wir uns küssen*, where the sonnet is meticulously analysed by the Ministry for State Security. For the 'stasi' (*Staatssicherheitsdienst*, state security service) it turns out to be a most dangerous political poem. According to their report the author has 'suicidal fantasies' (lines 1 and 14); and 'art made tongued-tied by authority' is interpreted as 'Disparagement of leading authorities'.[31]

Wieland's adaptation of Sonnet 66 exemplifies one of several other original approaches to Shakespeare's poetry. For instance, German translations of Sonnets 18 and 66, including versions in various German dialects, have been gathered into a collection and there have been a few recordings and musical adaptations as well as interesting stage productions which—in contrast to the *Venus and Adonis* performances—were only put on stage for a few evenings and so far have had no influence on the reception of the Sonnets in Germany.

During the last half-century there has been an almost overwhelming outpouring of new translations of Shakespeare's sonnet-cycle, some competent and pleasing like Hanno Helbling's version of 1983, others more unconventional and provocative, and not a few have endeavoured to go with the times and appeal to present-day audiences; for example, Christa Schuenke's much-acclaimed version, or Rainer Iwersen's deliberately audacious texts for the Bremer Shakespeare Company. There is, on the one hand, Klaus Reichert's careful, although problematic, prose version, and on the other, various more or less humorous renderings in different German dialects. Daringly individual 'translations' of individual Sonnets by successful writers like Karl Bernhard or Wolf Biermann go to show that Shakespeare's poems exercise an undiminished fascination that has been part of their German reception from the beginning of the 19th century.

The first complete translation of 'A Lover's Complaint', by Johann Joachim Eschenburg, was published in his monumental work *Ueber Shakspeare* (1787). Whilst he criticizes the Sonnets' 'monotony of ideas' (Eschenburg, 574) and, to avoid tiring out both himself and his reader, only translates fifty-six (Eschenburg, 577), he provides a complete translation of 'A Lover's Complaint', which he does not, however, append directly to his sonnet translations but—clearly following Malone's edition (1790)—places it after 'The Passionate Pilgrim'. Eschenburg makes do with a few brief explanations in the footnotes, such as one annotation which informs us that he used George Steevens' edition of 1773. His remarks on the other poems suggest, however, that he also had detailed knowledge of the Malone edition, whose very positive attitude towards the poem Eschenburg also shared. He compensated for the disadvantages of a prose translation of the poems by including the original under each translated verse. This implicit appeal to the reader to

---

[30] Ronald M. Schernikau, *Legende* (Dresden: ddp goldenbogen, 1999) 532.
[31] Rayk Wieland, *Ich schlage vor, dass wir uns küssen*. Roman (Munich: Piper, 2010) 204–5.

make use of the English text clearly demonstrates Eschenburg's understanding of his own German version as a reading aid, and that it was in no way to be understood as a substitute for the original.

It was to be another fifteen years before German readers could enjoy the first metrical translation of 'A Lover's Complaint' by Karl Friedrich Ludwig Kannegießer. It was the only translation to be published in a journal (*Polychorda*, 1803), which sought to publish those foreign poems 'which have been imitated in our language and are also worthy of it' (Kannegießer, 3). It is clear that the editor valued Kannegießer's translations of twenty-six Shakespeare Sonnets, 'The Passionate Pilgrim' and 'A Lover's Complaint', all of which were published in the first year of *Polychorda* under the pseudonym 'K'. The incalculable value of this highly progressive journal for the early reception of Shakespeare in Germany becomes particularly clear when one considers the low estimation in which the poem was held for most of the following centuries.

After 1803, German translations of 'A Lover's Complaint' are sometimes included in editions of the poems. Some eleven German versions were produced during the 19th century.[32] Most later translators of the Sonnets, however, bypass the 'complaint', partly because of doubts about its authenticity and partly, it appears, because the difficulties of its language acted as a deterrent. At any rate, after a complete silence of over a century, another, and to date the last translation of 'A Lover's Complaint' (together with a new translation of the Sonnets), was produced by Günter Plessow (*b.* 1934)—again not a professional translator but an architect. He was inspired by John Kerrigan's edition and Katherine Duncan-Jones' ground-breaking work regarding this most neglected poem. In his version, published in 2003 under the title *Kritik der Liebe*[33] he tries to render the original as exactly as possible while wanting to offer a new poem to the German reader. This balance between 'faithfulness' and poetic freedom is often successfully achieved in Plessow's translation.

Let us finally return to the repeatedly asked question of why none of the translations of Shakespeare's poems has acquired the classic status which the Schlegel and Tieck translations of the plays have enjoyed for so many generations.[34] Here I can only voice a few speculations. Certainly the reason is not, for example, the inferior linguistic competence of the sonnet translators. What possibly plays a more important role, is the fact that poetic language changes more quickly and more fundamentally than dramatic language, and that it cannot be modernized as easily with a bit of retouching, as occurs continuously with the Schlegel-Tieck translation of the plays. On the contrary, at the very least one should consider the attempted sonnet translations produced during the Romantic period in the context of their time and the poetic language which characterises it. What to us sometimes seems foreign, naïve, ingenuous, or even limited, in many

---

[32] Christa Jansohn (ed.), *William Shakespeare: A Lover's Complaint. Deutsche Übersetzungen von 1787–1894. Festgabe für Dieter Mehl zum 60. Geburtstag* (Berlin: Erich Schmidt, 1993).

[33] *Kritik der Liebe* [*Criticism about Love*]. *Shakespeare's Sonnets & A Lover's Complaint*. Re-read and translated by Günter Plessow (Passau: Karl Stutz, 2003).

[34] This does not apply, or no longer, to most stage versions. In the German theatre, Shakespeare's plays are mostly presented in more or less free modern translations or adaptations.

of these texts has often nothing to do with the work of translation as such, but with the changing range of linguistic expression as a whole. The difference is that with a short poem the focus is much more on each individual word.

The question of why the Sonnets have been so often translated into German was already raised in 1871 in an anonymous article about 'Shakespeare's sonnets and German translators':

> In Germany, however, everyone who is sickly from literature and poetry throws himself into translation. There is almost no school master who does not have one translation or other in his desk at least. The longer that is spent fine-tuning it, the more pleasure he has in his idle hours when he is doing his secret reading. We indulge everyone in their pleasure but advise [...] most of these gentlemen to close their desks.[35]

The motif of the translator as one who is made 'sickly' from poetry is perhaps confirmed in a letter from Adele Schopenhauer to Annette von Droste-Hülshoff of 6 August 1838 in which she requests English sonnets: 'I need them for a friend who wants to translate in order to escape himself!' However, it seems more important to hold on to the fact that actually none of the translations produced to-date are redundant; for translation as an extreme form of poetic hermeneutics contributes to the continually renewed impact of the original, and at the same time guarantees its survival beyond the borders of national literature.

SELECT BIBLIOGRAPHY

Castrop, Helmut (1964) *Shakespeares Verserzählungen. Eine Untersuchung der ovidischen Epik im elisabethanischen England* (Munich: PhD dissertation).

Fertig, Eymar (1999) 'Nachtrag zur Bibliographie "Shakespeares Sonette in deutschen Übersetzungen 1787–1994", erweitert durch szenische und musikalische Gestaltungen. Berichtszeit: 1784–1998', *Archiv für das Studium der Neueren Sprachen und Literaturen* 236, 265–324.

Horstmann, Gesa (1995) *Shakespeares Sonette in Deutschland. Zur Geschichte der Übersetzungen zwischen dem 18. Jahrhundert und den Übertragungen von Stefan George und Karl Kraus* (Berlin: PhD dissertation), <http://deposit.ddb.de/cgi-bin/dokserv?idn=965459535>. (last accessed 1 December 2012).

Jansohn, Christa (1993) (ed.) *William Shakespeare: A Lover's Complaint. Deutsche Übersetzungen von 1787–1894. Festgabe für Dieter Mehl zum 60. Geburtstag* (Berlin: Erich Schmidt).

—— (2007) (ed.) *William Shakespeare:* Venus und Adonis *und* Tarquin und Lukrezia *in der Übersetzung von Heinrich Christoph Albrecht (1783)* (Münster: LIT).

Kahn, Ludwig W. (1935) *Shakespeares Sonette in Deutschland. Versuch einer literarischen Typologie* (Bern and Leipzig: Gotthelf).

---

[35] *Magazin für die Literatur des Auslandes*, 79–80 (1871) 520.

Leithner-Brauns, Annette (1995) 'Shakespeares Sonette in deutschen Übersetzungen 1787–1994: eine bibliographische Übersicht', *Archiv für das Studium der Neueren Sprachen und Literaturen*, 232, 285–316.

Lucas, Wilfried Irvine (1934) *Die epischen Dichtungen Shakespeares in Deutschland* (Heidelberg: J. Kruse & Söhne).

Mehl, Dieter and Wolfgang Weiß (1993) (eds.) *Shakespeares Sonette in europäischen Perspektiven.* (Münster: LIT).

Schoen-René, Otto Eugene (1941) *Shakespeare's Sonnets in Germany: 1787–1939* (Harvard, unpubl. PhD dissertation).

Volkmann, Kathrin (1996) *Shakespeares Sonette auf deutsch. Übersetzungsprozesse zwischen Philologie und dichterischer Kreativität* (Heidelberg: Universitätsdruckerei).

....

CHAPTER 38

NEGOTIATING THE UNIVERSAL

Translations of Shakespeare's Poetry In (Between) Spain and Spanish America

....

BELÉN BISTUÉ

This chapter delineates a history of Spanish translations of Shakespeare's poetry and the reflections that have accompanied them. Its guiding thread is a notion I have found repeated many times in these reflections: the idea that Shakespeare's poetry is universal and must be translated as such. In the realm of translation, this idea is more remarkable than it may seem at first, for it is precisely in the process of translating that we become most familiar with the cultural locality and linguistic particularity of a work—and with the difficulties of transposing its words to a different language, time, and place. We can argue that the translator may conceive of his task as an attempt to rescue what is universal among these particularities, so that he can carry it into a different language, yet we cannot deny that significant interpretive displacements occur in this passage anyway. In fact, I want to show that the recurrent claim that Shakespeare's poetry is universal (rather than particularly representative of early modern British literature) has less to do with the invariable shared values translators find in his writings and more with certain interpretive shifts they want to propose.

We can already find the idea that Shakespeare is a universal poet in the writings of the polemic Spanish critic and thinker Joseph Blanco White, who in the 19th century published the first known defence of the value of translating Shakespeare into Spanish. He associated the notion of universality with the idea that Shakespeare was an unbound genius, all of whose works could be detached from their historical context of composition and from the context of theatrical representation. As we will see, this strategy enabled him to discuss the translation of Shakespeare in a new aesthetic context and in a new political context as well.

Blanco White is a complex figure in Spanish letters. His migration to London in 1810, his bilingualism, his work for English patrons, his conversion to Protestantism, and, above all, his support for the autonomy of the Spanish-American colonies led influential Spanish critics and historians to exclude him—sometimes explicitly—from the official history of Spanish literature.[1] Nevertheless, his writings, in which he theorized these geographical, linguistic, and political displacements, had influence in both Spain and Spanish America, and I want to propose that his inaugural defence deserves a central place in the history of Shakespearean translations.

Later translators have continued to assert Shakespeare's universal status, relating it to different values across time: the mystical character of his love poetry, the translatable nature of the topics he chose, and the opportunities his work offers for exploring the human unconscious, to name only a few. Shakespeare's universality—in the sense that he could rework topics from many literary traditions—is even invoked as a model in the 1930s by Jorge Luis Borges when he delineates a programme for Spanish-American poets as the irreverent inheritors of the Western canon. Indeed, I want to claim that the persistent conceptualization of Shakespeare as a universal poet can also find a place in the history of Spanish and Spanish-American literatures. Above all, it can establish a productive dialogue with notions of universality developed in the search of a Spanish-American literary identity independent from the Spanish-Peninsular tradition.

Following this guiding thread, and after offering an initial survey of Spanish translations of the poems and sonnets, my chapter looks closely at the foundational defence of Blanco White. It then explores a few later instances in which Spanish and Spanish-American translators have used Shakespeare's universality as a figure of thought that helps them justify their work, ground some of their translation strategies, and propose changes in the frame of interpretation.

38.1 SPANISH TRANSLATIONS OF SHAKESPEARE'S POETRY

A comparative study of this type has become possible only recently, thanks to the publication of such works as the essay collection *Latin American Shakespeares*, edited by Bernice Kliman and Rick Santos in 2005, and the comprehensive anthology of critical reflections *Shakespeare en España: textos, 1764–1916*, compiled by Ángel Luis Pujante and Laura Campillo in 2007. Pujante also published, in 2009, an anthology of early Spanish versions of Shakespeare's Sonnets.[2] These are invaluable tools for survey and

---

[1] Marcelino Menéndez y Pelayo, founder of Spanish literary history, listed Blanco White among Spanish 'heterodox' authors, praising his translations of Shakespeare but deeming him a very 'mistaken' and 'voluble' writer. *Historia de los heterodoxos españoles* [1880–1882] (Alicante: Biblioteca Virtual Miguel de Cervantes, 2003) book 7, ch. 4.

[2] Bernice W. Kliman and Rick J. Santos (eds), *Latin American Shakespeares* (Madison: Farleigh Dickinson University Press, 2005); Ángel Luis Pujante and Laura Campillo (eds), *Shakespeare en*

analysis. What is more, they speak of a rapidly growing interest in the reception of Shakespeare in Spanish on both sides of the Atlantic.[3]

This situation, however, is the result of a relatively recent shift. For a long time, Spanish translations of Shakespeare did not receive an enthusiastic welcome. In the context of early modern rivalries between the Spanish and British empires, Shakespeare served as an emblem of English culture, and he continued to be regarded as such during European processes of national unification. Of course, the Spanish did not assign a positive value to this emblem. While for Ben Jonson Shakespeare represented Britain's happy triumph over 'all scenes of Europe', for Spanish neoclassicists, he represented the 'barbarism' of the English people. We can find an early example of this view in the bitter critique with which Leandro Fernández de Moratín accompanied his 1798 translation of *Hamlet*. Moratín was the first to render one of Shakespeare's works into Spanish directly from the English. However, espousing neoclassical ideals of unity and decorum, and following in the steps of Voltaire, he described Shakespeare's works as 'monstrous'. He even justified his translation as a means of offering Spanish readers an idea of 'Shakespeare's [lack of] poetic merit and of the English nation's [lack of] taste'. In 1881, we still find echoes of this judgement in Juan Valera's statement that, were Spain a more powerful nation than England, Shakespeare would be deemed, among other things, 'a barbaric plagiariser', while his Spanish contemporary Lope de Vega would be praised as a much more ingenious and elegant author.[4] Moving ahead in time, and in very general terms, it was not until the decline of the British Empire, on the one hand, and, on the other, of Spanish nationalist regimes (Francisco Franco's government in Spain and military dictatorships in Spanish America) that Shakespeare's works began to be perceived as less of a cultural threat.[5] In fact, as we will see, when in the early 19th century Blanco White swam against the current, attempting a defence of Shakespeare's poetry, his main strategy was to strip the English Bard's figure of national associations. His proposal to read all of Shakespeare's work as *universal poetry* generated, thus, a conceptual window for translating Shakespeare's verse.

España: textos, 1764–1916 (Granada: Universidad de Granada; Murcia: Universidad de Murcia, 2007); Ángel Luis Pujante (ed.), *Shakespeare. Sonetos escogidos. Las primeras versiones castellanas* (Molina: Nausícaä, 2009a). Although his work is centred on the dramatic works, I would also like to mention Alfredo Modenessi's 'Of Shadows and Stones: Revering and Translating "the Word" Shakespeare in Mexico', *Shakespeare Survey 54: Shakespeare and Religions*, ed. Peter Holland (Cambridge: Cambridge University Press, 2001) 152–64, and '"A Double Tongue within your Mask": Translating Shakespeare in/ to Spanish-speaking Latin America', *Shakespeare and the Language of Translation*, Ton Hoenselaars (ed.), (London: The Arden Shakespeare, 2004) 240–54.

[3] This is also visible in the context of a global interest in Shakespeare's poetry. The collection *Shakespeare's Sonnets for the First Time Globally Reprinted: A Quatercentenary Anthology* (Dozwil: Signathur, 2009), edited by Manfred Pfister and Jürgen Gutsch includes entries on translations of Shakespeare's sonnets in Argentina, Cuba, Other Latin American countries, and Spain.

[4] In Pujante and Campillo (2007) 35, 42–3, and 278–9.

[5] Pujante and Campillo see a shift in the academic perception of Shakespeare in Spain already in 1916. They note, however, that the fruits of this shift would not be seen until later. Pujante and Campillo (2007) xli–xlv.

Before we move to an analysis of Blanco White's proposal, a note of caution is warranted. As my brief overview of Shakespeare's Spanish reception suggests, the opportunities for translating Shakespeare into Spanish have not been abundant.[6] A Spanish translation of his poems did not appear until 1877 (see FIGURE 38.1). It was made by

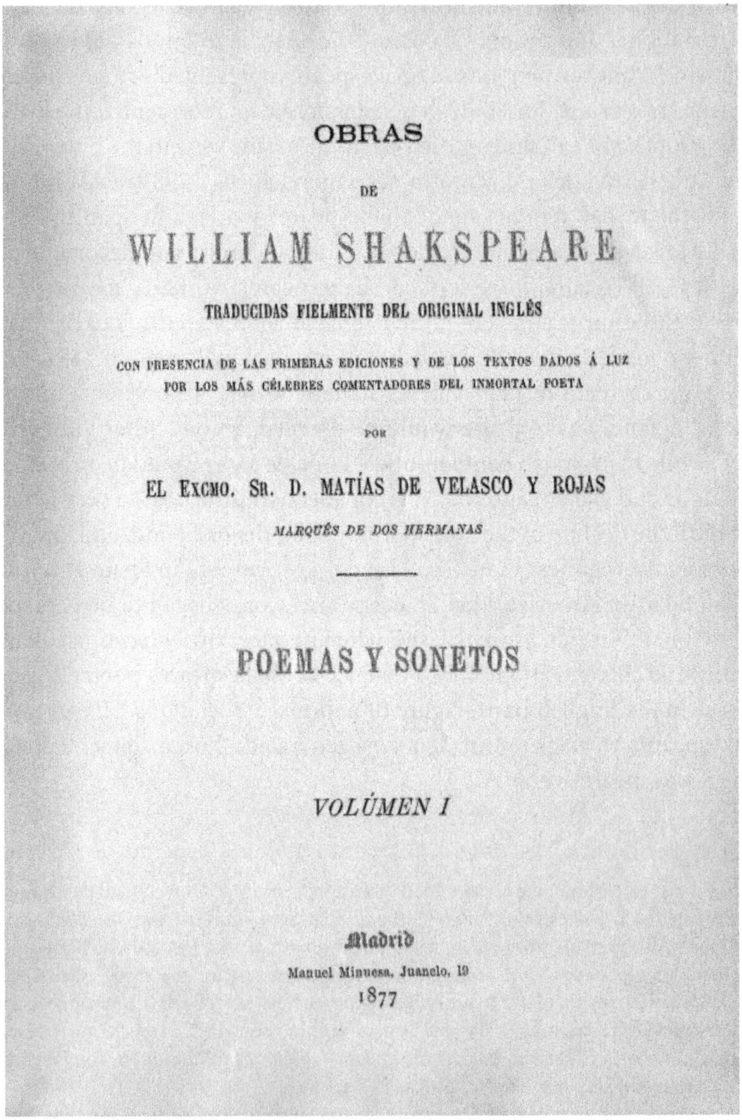

OBRAS

DE

WILLIAM SHAKSPEARE

TRADUCIDAS FIELMENTE DEL ORIGINAL INGLÉS

CON PRESENCIA DE LAS PRIMERAS EDICIONES Y DE LOS TEXTOS DADOS Á LUZ
POR LOS MÁS CÉLEBRES COMENTADORES DEL INMORTAL POETA

POR

EL EXCMO. SR. D. MATÍAS DE VELASCO Y ROJAS

MARQUÉS DE DOS HERMANAS

POEMAS Y SONETOS

VOLÚMEN I

Madrid
Manuel Minuesa, Juanelo, 19
1877

FIGURE 38.1. Title page of Matías de Velasco y Rojas' translation, 1877, courtesy of Shields Library, University of California, Davis.

---

⁶ Campillo signals the 1970s as the point when numerous Spanish versions of Shakespeare's plays begin to appear. Laura Campillo Arnaiz, 'Estudio de los elementos culturales en las obras de Shakespeare y sus traducciones al español por Macpherson, Astrana y Valverde', PhD Dissertation (Universidad de

Matías de Velasco y Rojas, lawyer and poet born in colonial Cuba. Translations of a few plays had already appeared by that time.[7] Velasco himself had published versions of *Othello* (1869) and of *The Merchant of Venice* and *Romeo and Juliet* (1872). Nevertheless, he placed the translation of the poetic works in volume 1 of his planned multi-volume translation of Shakespeare's complete works.[8] This opening volume offered prose translations of *Venus and Adonis*, *The Rape of Lucrece*, 'A Lover's Complaint', 'The Phoenix and the Turtle', and two poems from the *Passionate Pilgrim* (numbers 3 and 13 in the 1599 edition), as well as a 'Short Study' that included translations of more than thirty sonnets. Velasco produced a careful work. He valued the poems and sonnets as Shakespeare's 'first attempts', which 'announced his greatest theatre'.[9]

In spite of this promising valuation, we have to wait until the late 1920s for another translation of the poetic works comparable in scope to Velasco's work. Pujante has found versions of individual sonnets made between the late nineteenth and the early twentieth century, but these are scattered in periodicals and anthologies of English poetry in translation. Peninsular-Spanish translators who tried their hands at the sonnets include Guillermo Macpherson, Jaime Martí-Miquel, Salvador de Madariaga, Fernando Maristany, and Guillermo Belmonte Müller. And, as Pujante highlights, more versions were produced in those years by translators who, like Velasco, were of Spanish-American origin: Miguel Antonio Caro, José de Armas, Rafael Pombo, José Pablo Rivas, Carmela Eulate, Gabriel de Zéndegui, and Juan Antonio Pérez Bonalde. Pujante also notices that, compared to their Peninsular peers, Spanish-American translators showed a remarkable interest in verse translation, in maintaining the sonnet form, and in reproducing the musicality of Shakespeare's poetry.[10] Yet, it was not until 1929 that a complete Spanish translation of the sonnets and poems appeared, and this was a prose version by Peninsular scholar Luis Astrana Marín. It was the first Spanish translation not only of the complete poems but also of the complete works. It acquired and continues to hold a canonical place both in Spain and Spanish America, and it has seen sixteen editions and several reprints by Aguilar publishing house alone.

In his introduction, Astrana begins to play with the notion of Shakespeare's universality only to reassert his emblematic value as a British bard. Astrana celebrates Shakespeare as the 'greatest dramatist in the whole universe'. Yet, in a way that may have made his work agreeable to nationalistic tastes, he continues to place Shakespeare in the

Murcia, 2005) 77. We can make a similar claim for translations of the poetic works.

[7] In addition to Moratín's translation of *Hamlet* (1798), Campillo lists two translations of *Macbeth* (1838 and 1862) and translations of short passages from *Hamlet* and *Richard II* (1823), *As You Like It* (1825), *Henry IV* (1832), *Othello* (1841, 1858, and 1866), *King John* (1849), and *Macbeth* (1858). Campillo Arnaiz (2005) 36–7 and 446–8.

[8] *Poemas y sonetos*, vol. 1 of *Obras de William Shakespeare*, Matías de Velasco y Rojas (trans.), (Madrid: Manuel Minuesa, 1877). Velasco published only two more volumes of the planned *Obras*: 2 and 3, containing translations of *The Merchant of Venice* and *Romeo and Juliet* respectively. They show an earlier date of publication (1872) than vol. 1, but they were marked as the second and third volumes in the collection.

[9] Velasco y Rojas (1877) i.

[10] Pujante, 'Shakespeare's Sonnets in Spanish: Rescuing the Early Verse Translations', *1611: Revista de Historia de la traducción* 3 (2009b), <http://www.traduccionliteraria.org/1611/art/pujante.htm>.

context of Spanish-English rivalries. In the preface and in his annotations to the sonnets, he constantly establishes equivalences between Shakespeare and canonical Spanish
Golden-Age figures, such as Cervantes and Quevedo. In addition, he explains that his
translation choices reflect the norms of the most pure and elegant Castillian prose.
Regarding the poems and sonnets, Astrana did not share Velasco's opinion that they had
played a foundational role in Shakespeare's growth. In comparison to the 'universal' status of the plays, Astrana saw the poetic works as 'private and personal pieces' of 'limited
circulation'.[11] Accordingly, he relegated them to the end of the translated works.

It is not until the 1940s that we find new translations of Shakespeare's poetry. Angelina
Damians de Bulart published a version of the complete sonnet sequence in Barcelona
(1944).[12] Mariano de Vedia y Mitre published in Buenos Aires translations of *Venus and
Adonis* (1946) and of the complete sonnets (1954).[13] New characteristics in these translations are a careful attention to form and the use of verse rendering. Indeed, in 1934,
Vedia y Mitre had chosen the literary translation of Shakespeare's sonnets as the topic of
his entry speech to the Argentine Academy of Letters. After placing the love sonnets side
by side with Dante and the Greek and Roman classics, the speech engages with metrical
patterns. It emphasizes, for instance, the importance of the final couplet in Shakespeare's
sonnets, in which Vedia y Mitre sees the force of an almost autonomous distich at work,
vis-à-vis the less concentrated ending of the Italian sonnet-form.[14]

An attention to rhyme and rhythm would continue to characterize later work. Two
well-received verse translations came out in the 1960s: Manuel Mujica Lainez's forty-
nine sonnets (Buenos Aires, 1963) and José Basileo Acuña's complete sequence (Costa
Rica, 1968).[15] And in the last quarter of the 20th century, we see a substantial increase
in the number and variety of translations. We can find, at least, three translations of the
complete poetic works, twenty of the Sonnets, three of *Venus and Adonis*, two of 'The
Phoenix and the Turtle', and one of *Lucrece*, as well as three anthologies that combine different poems and sonnets, one of which includes 'poetic' passages from the plays as well.[16]
Among these translations, to cite only two representative examples, the complete poetic
works by Fátima Auad and Pablo Mañé Garzón (Barcelona, 1975) and the complete sonnets by Argentine translator Miguel Ángel Montezanti (La Plata, 1987) have seen later

[11] Vol. 1 of *Obras completas*, Luis Astrana Marín (trans.), (Madrid: Aguilar, 1981) 13 and 67. The sonnets
and poems appear at the end of vol. 2.

[12] *Sonetos*, Angelina Damians de Bulart (trans.), (Barcelona: Montaner y Simón, 1944).

[13] *Venus y Adonis*, Mariano de Vedia y Mitre (trans.), (Buenos Aires: Academia Argentina de Letras,
1946); *Los sonetos de Shakespeare*, Mariano de Vedia y Mitre (trans.), (Buenos Aires: Kraft, 1954).

[14] Mariano de Vedia y Mitre, 'Apología del traductor' [1934], *Vasos Comunicantes* 22 (2002) 82.

[15] *Cincuenta sonetos de Shakspeare*, Manuel Mujica Lainez (trans.), (Buenos Aires: Ediciones
Culturales Argentinas, 1963); *Los sonetos de Shakespeare*, José Basileo Acuña (trans.), (San José: Costa
Rica, 1968).

[16] A bibliography of all the Spanish translations of Shakespeare's poems and sonnets I have traced is
available at the website of the Centro de Literatura Comparada (CLC), at the Facultad de Filosofía y Letras
of the Universidad Nacional de Cuyo: 'Traducciones de la poesía de Shakespeare al español—Bibliografía',
<http://ffyl.uncu.edu.ar/IMG/pdf/5-5-_TRADUCCIONES_DE_LA_POESIA_DE_SHAKESPEARE_2.
pdf>.

re-editions and enjoyed a good reception among critics.[17] Other 20th-century milestones are the translations of *Romeo and Juliet* (1964), by Chilean poet and Nobel laureate Pablo Neruda, and of *King Lear* (staged in 1992; published in 2004), by Nicanor Parra, another influential Chilean poet.[18] Although these are renderings of dramatic works, they are remarkable for their translators' expressed interest in Shakespeare's poetic resources. Neruda wanted 'to preserve Shakespeare's poetic expression', and Parra saw connections between the experience of translating Shakespeare and some fundamental concepts in his own poetics. Parra is interested in the combination of prose and verse, of spoken and written grammatical features, and of different social registers he finds in Shakespeare's blank verse, as well as in the possibility of a poetic language that is accessible to a wide audience—and, therefore, open to be challenged and critiqued by it.[19]

Shakespeare's poetry continues to attract translators and editors in the 21st century. Representative of this interest is the series launched by the Colombian publishing house Norma, in which a different translator is in charge of each volume. In addition to the plays, it includes one volume dedicated to the poems ('A Lover's Complaint', *The Passionate Pilgrim*, and 'Phoenix and the Turtle'), one to *Venus and Adonis*, one to *Lucrece*, and one to the Sonnets.[20] Losada editors, in Argentina, also published a translation of the complete works that brings together the work of different translators.[21] To name only a few examples of individual projects, in Spain, poet Antonio Rivero Taravillo published translations of the complete Sonnets (2004) and the complete poetic works (2009), and in Argentina, Montezanti has recently published a new version of the Sonnets, which uses the colloquial Spanish of the Río de la Plata region (2011)—notably this last case seems to represent a departure from the main tendencies in language choice that, as we will see, have characterized the field.[22] In general, after its relatively late and slow beginnings, the translation of Shakespeare's poetic works is today an energetic field.

Interestingly, when we look at the realm of reflections on how to translate Shakespeare's poetry, we find that they precede the actual translation practice. In the context of this panoramic survey, I want to discuss these early theoretical claims, for they shed light on alternative values the figure of Shakespeare acquired in Spanish letters.

[17] *Poesía completa*, Fátima Auad and Pablo Mañé Garzón (trans.), (Barcelona: 29, 1975); *Sonetos completos*, trans. Miguel Ángel Montezanti (La Plata: Universidad Nacional, 1987).

[18] *Romeo y Julieta*, Pablo Neruda (trans.), (Buenos Aires: Losada, 1964); *Lear Rey & Mendigo*, Nicanor Parra (trans.), (Santiago, Chile: Universidad Diego Portales, 2004).

[19] Gregary J. Racz, 'Strategies of Deletion in Pablo Neruda's *Romeo y Julieta*', in Kliman and Santos (2005) 79; María de la Luz Hurtado, 'Parra traduce a Shakespeare', *Apuntes* 103 (1992), <http://www.nicanorparra.uchile.cl/estudios/shakespeare.htlm>.

[20] *Poemas*, Víctor Obiols y Olivia de Miguel Crespo (trans.), (Bogotá: Norma, 2001); *Venus y Adonis*, Jesús Munárriz (trans.), (Bogotá: Norma, 2001); *La violación de Lucrecia*, José L. Rivas (trans.), (Bogotá: Norma, 2002); *Sonetos*, William Ospina (trans.), (Bogotá: Norma, 2003).

[21] *Obras completas*, Pablo Ingberg (ed.), (Buenos Aires: Losada, 2006–2009).

[22] *Sonetos*, Antonio Rivero Taravillo (trans.), (Sevilla: Renacimiento, 2004); *Poesía completa*, Antonio Rivero Taravillo (trans.), (Córdoba, Spain: Almuzara, 2009); *Sólo vos sos vos. Los sonetos de Shakespeare en traducción rioplatense*, Miguel Ángel Montezanti (trans.), (Mar del Plata: EUDEM, 2011). Again, for an extensive list, see my bibliography, 'Traducciones de la poesía de Shakespeare al español', at the CLC website (see n. 16).

38.2 THE LYRIC UNIVERSAL: TRANSLATING SHAKESPEARE IN BETWEEN SPAIN AND SPANISH AMERICA—AND ENGLAND, AND FRANCE

In 1823, about half a century before Velasco published his inaugural translation, we find an article that highlights the need for a 'poetic translation' of Shakespeare's works. The author of the article was Joseph Blanco White, priest, journalist, political and religious thinker, literary critic, and translator. He was born in Seville, in 1775. At that time, his name was José María Blanco. His paternal grandfather, William White, had come to Spain from Ireland in the early 18th century to run a mercantile house, and, at some point, the family name was changed to 'Blanco' (Spanish for 'White'). José María had a strict Catholic formation, but, profoundly disappointed with the Church and with Spanish politics, he moved to London in 1810, he converted to Protestantism, and he changed his name to Joseph Blanco White.[23]

He kept both the Spanish and the English versions of his name side by side, and this doubling reflects an awareness of the double context in which he was writing. He became deeply interested in British literature, particularly in the new Romantic ideas, but he never lost sight of the situation in Spain. He was concerned with the relations between the Peninsula and its Spanish-American colonies, and he enthusiastically wrote in support of the colonies' autonomy from the Central Council at Seville. In fact, he published his proposal for translating Shakespeare poetically in the quarterly *Variedades, ó mensagero de Londres*, a journal he edited for the London printing house of Rudolph Ackermann but which was addressed to Spanish-American readers.

This context is important for understanding Blanco White's theoretical stance. His contact with Romanticism, for instance, gave him tools to defend Shakespeare against the attacks of French and Spanish neoclassicists. He explains that a 'poetic translation' has the benefit of conveying the general 'tone of thought' and the transcendent 'originality of Shakespeare's genius'—even when it cannot reproduce his 'particular beauties', which, for Blanco White, are inseparable from the language in which they were written.[24] But the proposal to translate Shakespeare's works as *poetry*—by which he meant lyric poetry—has other implicit benefits: it displaces the focus away from the terrain of the

---

[23] Pilar Regalado Kerson, 'José María Blanco White, intérprete de Shakespeare: pasajes traducidos y reflexiones críticas', *Actas del XII Congreso de la Asociación Internacional de Hispanistas* (University of Birmingham, 1998) vol. 4, 219–26. See also Martin Murphy's biography *Blanco White: Self-Banished Spaniard* (New Haven: Yale University Press, 1989). Blanco White's autobiographical writings are collected in Joseph Blanco White, *The Life of the Rev. Joseph Blanco White, written by himself, with portions of his correspondence*, John Hamilton (ed.), Thom (London, 1845).

[24] Joseph Blanco White, 'Shakspeare: traducción poética de algunos pasages de sus dramas', *Variedades, ó mensagero de Londres* 1.1 (1823): 74–79, in *Shakespeare en España en el marco de su recepción europea*, Universidad de Murcia, <http://www.um.es/shakespeare/traducciones/documentos/bw1.pdf>; emphasis added.

theatre and from the standards of unity and decorum that were the stronghold of neo-classicism. Indeed, he explicitly argues that Shakespeare's genius stands apart from the 'frenzies' of the theatre of his times.

In later writings, published in the Unitarian journal *The Christian Teacher*, Blanco White would continue to develop these ideas. He advises readers to approach all of Shakespeare's works as 'descriptive and lyric poetry'. He praises the abstract and universal quality of this poetry, which allows readers to detach it from particular contexts. He defines this quality in direct opposition to the constraining 'definiteness' of theatrical representations. For him, the shapes characters take in the bodies of particular actors follow the fashions of a particular time and place and destroy the 'idealities' of Shakespeare's creations. 'It is indeed in respect to the ideal of BEAUTY', he claims, 'that everyone who has studied this subject must perceive the superiority of pure poetry over dramatic representation'.[25] He even argues that, while 'Shakspere's historical dramas *seem* to have grown out without effort from the events recorded in the chronicles, ... every one of them is a fresh instance of the astonishing creative power of our bard'. In other words, 'they exhibit the powers of the poet as unlimited and universal'.[26]

Indeed, the short examples with which Blanco White had accompanied his initial proposal for poetic translation were passages from dramatic works to which he gave poetic form. The first of them is Hamlet's famous monologue in Act III, Scene i, which Blanco White calls 'Soliloquio sobre la muerte y el suicidio' [Soliloquy on Death and Suicide]. To give an idea of Blanco White's concrete translation strategies, I offer below the beginning of his version (accompanied by an instrumental English version and followed, for comparison purposes, by the same passage as it appears in Boswell's 1821 edition)[27]:

SOLILOQUIO

Sobre la muerte y el suicidio.

HAMLET.

Ser o no ser—he aqui la grande duda.
¿Qual es mas noble? ¿Presentar el pecho
De la airada fortuna a las saetas,
O tomar armas contra un mar de azares
Y acabar de una vez?—Morir—Dormirse—
Nada mas—y escapar con solo un sueño
A este dolor del alma, al choque eterno
Que es la herencia del hombre en esta vida—
Hay mas que apetecer?—Morir—Dormirse—
¡Dormir!—tal vez soñar—Aí está el daño.[28]

---

[25] 'Pictorial Shakspere. A Midsummer Night's Dream' [*The Christian Teacher* 2 (1840): 42–53], in Pujante and Campillo (2007) 454–6.

[26] Joseph Blanco White, 'The Pictorial Shakspere. Second Notice', *The Christian Teacher* 1 (1839), in Pujante and Campillo (2007) 438.

[27] Scholars have not identified the English edition Blanco White used as a source. I have chosen this edition because it is the closest one to Blanco White's translation in terms of date and punctuation.

[28] Blanco White (1823) 75.

[*SOLILOQUY*
On Death and Suicide.
HAMLET.
To be or not to be—this is the big doubt.
What is nobler? To offer the chest
(To), of mad fortune, the arrows,
Or to take arms against a sea of hazards,
And to end once and for all?—To die—To fall asleep—
Nothing more—and to escape with simply a nap
This ache of the soul, the eternal conflict
That in this life is man's inheritance—
Is there more to be wished?—To die—To fall asleep—
To sleep!—perhaps to dream—There's the damage.]

Enter HAMLET.
HAM. To be, or not to be, that is the question:—
Whether 'tis nobler in the mind, to suffer
The slings and arrows of outrageous fortune;
Or to take arms against a sea of troubles,
And, by opposing, end them?—To die,—to sleep,—
No more;—and, by a sleep, to say we end
The heart-ach, and the thousand natural shocks
That flesh is heir to,—'tis a consummation
Devoutly to be wish'd. To die;—to sleep;—
To sleep! perchance to dream;—ay, there's the rub;
..... .[29]

Using blank hendecasyllables, Blanco White offers a quite literal rendering. Of course, we can find semantic changes in his version, for instace, when he uses Spanish formulae to translate English phrases. The 'sea of troubles' becomes a Spanish 'mar de azares' [a sea of chance / sea of hazards], and he renders 'in the mind, to suffer ... slings and arrows' as 'presentar el pecho ... a las saetas' [to offer one's chest ... to the arrows]. He also places particular emphasis on the idea of suicide. He translates the English 'and by opposing end *them*' into 'y acabar de una vez' [and to end once and for all], which in Spanish can be easily read as 'to put an end to *oneself*'. Perhaps here he follows Edmond Malone, who strongly advocated this reading in his notes.[30] We can find some additions at the syntactic level, too. For instance, the hyperbaton in line 3 forces things too much even for the flexibility of Spanish syntax.[31] This might be the result of Blanco White's struggle to reflect

---

[29] *The Plays and Poems of William Shakespeare, with the Corrections and Illustrations of Various Commentators* (London: C. Baldwin, 1821) vol. 7, 321–3.

[30] Malone's notes are included in Boswell's edition. *The Plays and Poems* (1821) vol. 7, 321.

[31] A literal translation of the Spanish would read, 'To offer the chest | of mad fortune to the arrows'. The intended meaning must be 'To offer one's chest | to mad fortune's arrows', but my instrumental rendering searches to reflect the hesitation a Spanish reader might experience.

the slightly ambiguous position that 'in the mind' has in the English version (which he actually resolves with an extra question mark). Perhaps he also wants to give poetic flavour to his version by using a figure characteristic of Spanish Golden Age poetry.

In addition to these details, there are some translation choices I want to highlight because I believe they are closely related to the ideas Blanco White explored in his articles. I want to note, for example, his consistent use of punctuation to create syntactical order and pauses. This tendency is already noticeable in nineteenth-century English editions (they show many more punctuation marks than, for instance, Rowe's 1709 edition, which has only two long dashes towards the end of the cited passage and no question or exclamation marks).[32] Blanco White is careful to reproduce punctuation marks, and he goes even farther than English editors of the time. In comparison with Boswell's edition, he adds extra dashes in the first and last lines of the cited passage, a question mark in the second line, and a period in the last one. These marks can be said to limit the ambiguity and the flow of the text—a concrete strategy for fighting the variation intrinsic to dramatic representations, and thus, for detaching the text from the theatrical context. So too, Blanco White omits the stage direction for Hamlet's entrance and replaces it with a title, which helps shape the text as an autonomous poetic piece. Neither does he include Hamlet's acknowledging of Ophelia's approaching at the end of the soliloquy, even though metrically it completes the last verse of Hamlet's speech. Thus, he literally cuts the passage from its dramatic context.

What is more, at the level of semantic choices, his version also emphasizes the detachment and abstraction Blanco White finds in lyric poetry. He moves slightly away from possible concrete, bodily connotations when he renders words like 'heart-ake', 'Natural shockes', and 'flesh' as 'dolor del alma' [pain of the soul], 'choque eterno' [eternal conflict], and 'hombre' [man], respectively. Behind these translation choices and displacements lies, I believe, Blanco White's interpretation of Shakespeare's work as unbound universal poetry.

As I have mentioned, universality became a key, recurrent topic in Blanco White's later literary critique. Although the term 'universal' carries the traces of Enlightenment thought, his descriptions of the poet as a free, universal genius draw on German and British Romantic aesthetics. He mentions his familiarity with Schlegel's German version of Shakespeare and with Tieck's annotations. In addition, some of his reflections reveal a struggle to depart from neoclassic definitions while still asserting Shakespeare's universality and capacity for abstraction:

> We cannot agree with those, or rather with the form of language employed by those, who say that our poet did not paint individuals, but classes. Classes are abstractions; the living stamp of nature is found only in *individuals*. Nature spoke too clearly in Shakspere's breast that he should have attempted *generalizations*; but his individuals exhibit so abundantly the distinctive marks through which we recognize personality,

---

[32] *The Works of Mr. William Shakespear*, N. Rowe (ed.), (London, 1709) vol. 5, 2409–10.

that they might suffice to give reality to a considerable number of imperfect imitations of the original model, all of which might be taken for one class or genus.[33]

He became interested in Romantic ideas in London, where he also came in touch with British political and literary figures of the time, such as Robert Southey, Thomas Campbell, and Felicia Hemans, and where, in 1825, his sonnet on 'Night and Death' received the praise of Samuel T. Coleridge.[34]

Nevertheless, there are times when Blanco White defines abstraction and universality in different terms. This happens when he praises the 'satire' of bad poets he finds in the character of Bottom in *A Midsummer Night's Dream*. He first tells us that 'Bottom is, in his own view, a heaven-born, *universal Genius*, such as [those who] in the shape of many actors must have plagued Shakspere during the whole of his histrionic career'. Then, he gives a twist to the argument and adds that, by mocking false universal geniuses, Shakespeare is showing the truly universal value of his own poetry:

> The truth of [Shakespeare's] picture is such, that Bottom, the weaver, stands before us as *universal*, an abstract applicable to hundreds of concrete Bottoms, of all classes and professions. Whoever has made an intimate acquaintance with Bottom the Athenian, will find him repeated, though in various external disguises, at almost every social party; he will discover him under the wig of the Lawyer, and the bands of the Divine. Why not? Bottom is still ready to do every thing, to play every part, though 'his chief humour was for a tyrant.'[35]

The praise of the *universal Bottom* draws on a language very different from the one we have seen Blanco White use to define 'pure lyric poetry' and 'ideal Beauty'. His description of what we could also call the type of the *universal ass*, vis-à-vis the *universal poet*, seems to draw, instead, on Spanish Romantic *costumbrismo*. It is very much in the line of the mordant criticism of social types—actors among them—that the famous Spanish satirist Mariano José de Larra wrote in the early 1830s.[36]

If I point to Blanco White's use of different discourses, it is not to signal contradictions in his thought. My aim is to emphasize his varied efforts to define Shakespeare's poetry as *universal* and to detach it from any particular context. This definition is an important strategy in Blanco White's own historical context, where his poetics of translation

---

[33] Blanco White, 'The Pictorial Shakspere. Second Notice', in Pujante and Campillo (2007) 439.

[34] Vicente Llorens, 'Blanco White and Robert Southey: Fragments of a Correspondence', *Studies in Romanticism* 11.2 (1972): 147–52; G. Martin Murphy, 'Bacon, Philo, and Blanco White's Sonnet', *Notes and Queries* 49.4 (2002): 468.

[35] Blanco White, 'Pictorial Shakspere. A Midsummer Night' Dream', in Pujante and Campillo (2007) 463–4.

[36] In 1835 we already find a collection of Larra's articles, *Fígaro. Coleccion de artículos dramáticos, literarios, políticos y de costumbres, publicados en los años 1832, 1833 y 1834 en El Pobrecito Hablador, La Revista Española y El Observador, por D. Mariano José de Larra* (Madrid: Repullés, 1835).

intersect with aesthetic, political, and commercial values. As we have seen, the periodical in which his 1823 article appeared was part of Rudolph Ackermann's London editorial enterprise. In competition with French publishers, Ackermann dominated the
transatlantic trade of books in Spanish translation in the 1820s. His enterprise is representative of the British effort to establish cultural and commercial links with the new
Spanish-American nations in the context of a struggle with the Spanish and the French
Empires. It is telling, for instance, that, in addition to journals and books that promoted
English literature and philosophy in Spanish translation, Ackermann also printed the
bond certificates for some of the first British loans to South American governments.[37]
It is also telling that, a decade earlier, the British Foreign Office had encouraged trad-
ing firms to distribute copies, in Central and South America, of another periodical
edited by Blanco White, which was called *El Español* (1810–1814). Scholars believe that
Spanish-American presses reprinted some of its articles, and they have found echoes of
the ideas these articles promoted in some of the arguments advanced by Simón Bolivar.[38]
Many Spanish-Americans welcomed British efforts to promote free commerce—in
opposition to the closed mercantile monopoly previously established by the Spanish
Crown—and many searched to establish their cultural independence from the Spanish
Peninsula.

In this context of publication, we can better understand Blanco White's insistence on
translating Shakespeare as a universal poet. As we already saw, once he switches lenses to
consider Shakespeare's works as poetry, he can judge them beyond the frame of French
neoclassical aesthetics and dramatic units, and once he sees them as universal poetry,
he does not need to treat them as a cultural threat to Spanish literature and language. In
addition, the notion of an unbound universal poet can also be said to fit a frame of mind
in which the free circulation of commodities had become a key value. Above all, this
notion seems productive in the context of the Spanish-American search for emancipa-
tion. The access (in Spanish) to an author who was abstract and universal (but translated
from the English) offered some ground on which to begin building a cultural identity
independent from Spain's literary tradition. From his displaced position as a Spanish
exile in England, Blanco White could make this offer.

As Joselyn Almeida has claimed, Blanco White's writings give us an entry into the
transatlantic, multilingual dimension of the Romantic movement.[39] In particular, I
believe that his proposal for translating Shakespeare moves the conversation beyond an
exclusively European frame to include the emerging Spanish-American nations. In a

[37] Nanora Sweet, 'Hitherto Closed to the Spanish Enterprise: Trading and Writing the Hispanic World
circa 1815', *European Romantic Review* 8 (1997): 139–44; Eugenia Roldán Vera, *The British Book Trade and
Spanish American Independence: Education and Knowledge Transmission in Transcontinental Perspective*
(Aldershot: Ashgate, 2003) 105.

[38] D. A. Brading, *The First America: The Spanish Monarchy, Creole Patriots, and the Liberal State,
1492–1867* (Cambridge: Cambridge University Press, 1991) 545–6.

[39] Joselyn Almeida, 'Blanco White and the Making of Anglo-Hispanic Romanticism', *European
Romantic Review* 17.4 (2006): 437–9.

way, his definitions and redefinitions of Shakespeare's universality formalize the conceptual displacements he is making in the literary and political realms.

38.3 Epilogue: Irreverent Universals

The invocation of Shakespeare's universality (in the sense that he transcends his historical context and location) continued to carry a decentering force in the reflections of later translators. For instance, it sometimes worked to displace the interpretive frame away from Renaissance erotic practices. Such was the case in Matías Velasco y Rojas' 1877 translation. In his study of the Sonnets, Velasco praised those pieces in which he found no references to Shakespeare's personal amatory experiences and which spoke to him, instead, of humanity and the human soul, abstracting themselves 'from a tight historical link'. In the cases of sonnets that did speak to him of love, he read them as 'almost mystical poetry', searching for a spiritual meaning in them. He admitted that some of them spoke of a love of 'man to man', but he was quick to explain that they did so in a general and spiritual way. This, he added, was 'not similar to the base, false, and mercenary loves that during the long age of Classical Renaissance were given by protégés to their benefactors, by aspiring artists to their patrons'. More specifically, Shakespeare's love 'was not like the one distilled by the sonnets and dedications of Florio, Marlowe, and other poets of Elizabeth's time, but pure and delicate, an exquisite un-definable love'.[40]

Thus, Velasco places the Sonnets in a concrete historical context of composition, only to tell us that they do not belong there. This is a double movement, in which he advocates for a spiritual interpretation while still leaving in place the references to physical love, and even reinforcing them by the mention of Renaissance erotic practices and specific names. This strategy is not a mere rejection of an amatory relation between Shakespeare and his patron. It actually helps Velasco set a new frame of interpretation for the love sonnets: a marked contrast between bodily and spiritual love. Some of his translation choices work, indeed, to emphasize this contrast. His rendering of the opening of Sonnet 54 reads, 'Ah! ¡cuán más bella aparece la belleza cuando *lo espiritual* le presta su delicioso atractivo!' [O! how much more beautiful appears beauty when *the spiritual* lends it a delightful appeal!]. Here, Velasco has rendered the English word 'truth' ('O how much more doth beauty beauteous seem, | By that sweet ornament which *truth* doth give!') into the notion of a 'spiritual' dimension opposed to mere external beauty. The opposition between body and spirit is also emphasized in the opening lines of his version of Sonnet 146 (in the English, 'Poore soule the centre of my *sinfull earth*'), which Velasco translates as 'Pobre alma, centro de mi *barro inmundo*' [Poor soul, centre of my *filthy mud*], stressing, once more, the negative value of the body, even as he downplays the religious connotations.

---

[40] Velasco y Rojas (1877) 298–9 and 220–7.

Other instances in which translators invoke Shakespeare's universality point to displacements in the political frame of interpretation. Among them is the notion of the *adventurous universal*, developed by Spanish poet León Felipe during his exile in Mexico (1939–68) after the Spanish Civil War. Into his creative translation of *Othello*, which he entitled *Otelo, o el pañuelo encantado* [Othello, or the Enchanted Handkerchief], he incorporates the character of a jester. This character tells the audience that the 'story of the Moor' comes from an old Arabic tale, which, retold by the people (Bedouin nomads, Muslim warriors, prisoners, minstrels, Christian monks), travelled from Africa to Italy. The poet Cinthio trapped it there. Shakespeare, in turn, brought the tale to London and exhibited it at The Globe, but, after that, the story breaks free again:

> [E]l cuento es indómito, y se hace universal y
> aventurero…
> Y otro día se escapa de Inglaterra, rompe el collar
> diamantino de los versos
> con que el poeta de Stratford le sujetó gloriosa-
> mente como a un mastín, por el cuello
> y busca nuevos ritmos, otros escenarios… y otro
> acento.
> Así lo vamos a contar aquí esta noche
> en este teatro de México.[41]

> [(T)he story cannot be tamed, and it becomes *universal and
> adventurous*…
> And one day it escapes from England, it breaks the collar
> of diamond verses
> with which the Stratford poet held him glorious-
> ly as one holds a mastiff, by the neck,
> and it searches new rhythms, different stages… and another
> accent…
> This is how we are going to tell it here tonight
> in this Mexican theatre.]

This reformulation of the universal quality of Shakespeare's work is particularly insightful because it describes this quality not as something intrinsic to the work but to its translation. It is the passage from one culture to another (across places, religions, and languages) that makes the tale universal. Paradoxically—and here lies the force of this figure of thought—this *adventurous universality* is not a fixed value but the text's freedom to acquire new rhythms and accents.

León Felipe uses this freedom in the preface to his version of *Macbeth* (*Macbeth o el asesino del sueño* [Macbeth or the Murderer of Sleep]), where he tells us again that translation into new contexts lends great poets their universality. Translation lets them 'rise to the highest summits in their lands to search for other poets on the horizon.… [allowing]

---

[41] León Felipe, *Otelo; o, el pañuelo encantado* (México, 1960) 23–4; emphasis added.

the nations to find *other nations* with which to mix and lovingly cross the noble seeds of man'.[42] As Blanco White had done, he is placing his translation of Shakespeare in the context of transatlantic relationships. But he is also displacing the frame of interpretation once more: this time, it is the relations among Spain, Mexico, and *other nations* (more specifically, the International Brigades) in the aftermath of the war between Franco and the Republic. In this context, León Felipe sees translation as a force that can make Shakespeare's verse, not a free circulating value from which Spanish-Americans can build a new literary identity, but an *international* cultural space from which to oppose the Spanish *nationalism* of Franco.

These are only two examples of how the figure of a universal Shakespeare has enabled conceptual displacements. The number of translators that have invoked this figure is much larger. In yet another context, for instance, Costa Rican writer Joaquín Gutiérrez associated in the early 1980s the universal value of Shakespeare's work with a precocious capacity for exploring 'the groves of the human unconscious'.[43] Today, as the words of Argentine translator Rolando Costa Picazo attest, Shakespeare's universality can have the status of a given for the Spanish-American translator:

> Inevitably, [in our translation of Shakespeare] we started from the educated register of the Spanish we speak in Argentina, but always trying to use words whose meaning is not incomprehensible, neither for the Peninsular nor for the Spanish American register.... Shakespeare deserves a Spanish that, without being neutral is universal ...[44]

In this case, universality is associated with the potential for a Spanish-American translation to reach both a Spanish-American and a Spanish-Peninsular market. Here, the claim for a transatlantic reach has very different connotations from the ones it had for Blanco White. Yet, it is interesting to note that translations of Shakespeare continue to be placed, at least conceptually, in between Spain and Spanish America. I have but little space to enter into the dynamics of the Spanish-language publishing market. I simply want to note that, in the current situation, to reach a Spanish-Peninsular audience is a challenge for a translation published in Argentina.[45] From his position as a Spanish-American translator of Shakespeare, Costa Picazo establishes the paradoxical requirement to use a 'universal Spanish', and this paradox, I believe, is another sign of the decentering potential the figure of Shakespeare's universality continues to carry in the Spanish-American context.

---

[42] Cited and translated in Juan J. Zaro, 'Translating from Exile: León Felipe's Shakespeare *Paraphrases*', in Kliman and Santos (2005) 97; emphasis added.

[43] Joaquín Gutierrez, *Obras completas* (San José: Universidad de Costa Rica, 2002) vol. 4, 7.

[44] Rolando Costa Picazo, 'Traducir a Shakespeare', *Actas del II Simposio Nacional Ecos de la Literatura Renacentista Inglesa, 3–5 de noviembre de 2004* (Mendoza: Universidad Nacional de Cuyo, 2006) 14; translated from the Spanish.

[45] There was a marked growth of publishing houses located in such centres as Buenos Aires, Mexico, and Caracas between the 1930s and the 1960s, but these centres are today once again peripheric to Spanish-Peninsular publishing.

An exhaustive survey of uses of this conceptual figure would extend far beyond the scope of a history of Shakespearean translations into Spanish. It would need to include, for instance, Uruguayan author José Enrique Rodó's *Ariel* (1900). This is a heavily nationalistic essay in the sense that it advocates for a pan-Spanish-American *nation*, challenging what Rodó saw as 'the manifest aspiration to primacy in *universal* culture' of North American democracy. To deny such universal validity, Rodó uses the characters of *The Tempest* as timeless symbols of opposing cultural models (Ariel represents a culture that promotes spiritual development of the intellectual elite, while Caliban stands for the mediocre culture of a materialist democracy). Rodó asserts the universality of Shakespeare's characters and of the English people in general, but he denies that North America has inherited 'their ancestral poetic instinct' and their 'Germanic original traits'.[46] His symbolic-universal reading of Shakespeare's characters is remarkable, among other things, in that it fully turns around the context of interpretation. Writing from Spanish America, he uses the figure of the universal Shakespeare to create a space in between England and North America.

The proposed survey should also include such a different use of this figure as the one Jorge Luis Borges makes when he rejects literary nationalism in the early 1930s. To refute the idea that Argentine poets must write about local topics, 'instead of speaking about *the universe*', Borges cites the case of 'Shakespeare, [who] would have been surprised if somebody had tried to limit him to English topics'. Explicitly invoking the figure of the universal Shakespeare, and implicitly the practice of translation, Borges calls for South American writers to find their tradition in 'the entire Western culture', which he claims they can use 'without superstitions, with an irreverence that can have, and already has, fortunate consequences'.[47]

To conclude my chapter, I want to propose that Borges' *irreverence* establishes a productive dialogue with the definitions and redefinitions of Shakespeare's universality we have found in the realm of translation. Borges himself recognized, in a later piece, what I am arguing here: that the figure of a universal Shakespeare had become something of a theoretical tool. In the hands of critics, Shakespeare had suffered a universalizing process that Borges playfully described as 'la magnificación hasta la nada' [magnification into nothingness]. Pointing to the same literary context in which Blanco White had placed his inaugural proposal, Borges translated a passage from William Hazlitt's 1818 *Lectures on the English Poets* as a representative instance of *magnification*: 'Shakespeare se parecía a todos los hombres, salvo en lo de parecerse a todos los hombres. Íntimamente no era nada, pero era todo lo que son los demás o lo que pueden ser' [in Hazlitt's version, 'He was just like any other man, but that he was like all other men.... He was nothing in himself;

[46] José Enrique Rodó, *Ariel* [1900] (Barcelona: Linkgua, 2008) 52–61.

[47] Jorge Luis Borges, 'El escritor Argentino y la tradición', *Discusión* (1932), in *Obras Completas* (Buenos Aires: Emecé, 1974) 267–74. As Efraín Kristal has shown in *Invisible Work: Borges and Translation* (Nashville: Vanderbilt University Press, 2002), translation was central to Borges' work both as a practice and as a metaphor for the process of writing.

but he was all that others were, or that they could become'].[48] Thus, Borges redefines Shakespeare's universality as an all-encompassing multiplicity.

This sharp playful description of Shakespeare's *magnified universalization* should not leave us with the feeling that this figure is an empty rhetorical tool. In its various redeployments—the *lyric-universal*, the *mystical-universal*, the *adventurous-universal*, the *Spanish-universal*, and even Borges' earlier *irreverent-universal*—we have found traces of a recurrent specific value. The figure always carries a paradoxical force that enables conceptual displacements. This force, I believe, reflects the transatlantic and multilingual context in which Shakespeare's poetry began to be translated. The displacing value that the figure of a universal Shakespeare acquired then and continues to hold today comes from the process of translating his verse into Spanish in a context that goes beyond European relations. Thus, while the actual translation of Shakespeare's poetry into Spanish has only recently become an active field, his image as a *universal poet* already has an established place in the reflections of translators. In the history I have sketched, Shakespeare's universality emerges as a space where translators can negotiate literary and cultural relations between England, Spain, and Spanish America.

SELECT BIBLIOGRAPHY

Almeida, Joselyn (2006) 'Blanco White and the Making of Anglo-Hispanic Romanticism', *European Romantic Review* 17.4: 437–56.

Bistué, Belén (2012) 'Traducciones de la poesía de Shakespeare al español—Bibliografía', Centro de Literatura Comparada (CLC), Facultad de Filosofía y Letras, Universidad Nacional de Cuyo, <http://ffyl.uncu.edu.ar/IMG/pdf/5-5-_TRADUCCIONES_DE_LA_POESIA_DE_SHAKESPEARE_2_.pdf>.

Campillo Arnaiz, Laura (2005) 'Estudio de los elementos culturales en las obras de Shakespeare y sus traducciones al español por Macpherson, Astrana y Valverde', PhD Dissertation (Universidad de Murcia).

Kliman, Bernice W. and Santos, Rick J. (2005) (eds), *Latin American Shakespeares* (Madison: Farleigh Dickinson University Press).

Kristal, Efraín (2002) *Invisible Work: Borges and Translation* (Nashville: Vanderbilt University Press).

Murphy, Martin (1989) *Blanco White: Self-Banished Spaniard* (New Haven: Yale University Press).

Pfister, Manfred, and Gutsch, Jürgen (2009) (eds) *Shakespeare's Sonnets for the First Time Globally Reprinted: A Quatercentenary Anthology* (Dozwil: Signathur).

Pujante, Ángel-Luis and Campillo, Laura (2007) (eds), *Shakespeare en España: textos, 1764–1916* (Granada: Universidad de Granada, Murcia: Universidad de Murcia, 2007).

—— (2009a) (ed.), *Shakespeare. Sonetos escogidos. Las primeras versiones castellanas* (Molina: Nausícaä, 2009).

---

[48] Borges, 'De alguien a Nadie', *Otras Inquisiciones* (1952), in *Obras Completas*, 738; William Hazlitt, *Lectures on the English Poets* (London: Taylor and Hessey, 1818) 91.

—— (2009b)'Shakespeare's Sonnets in Spanish: Rescuing the Early Verse Translations', *1611: Revista de Historia de la traducción* 3, <http://www.traduccionliteraria.org/1611/art/pujante.htm>.

Regalado Kerson, Pilar (1998) 'José María Blanco White, intérprete de Shakespeare: pasajes traducidos y reflexiones críticas', *Actas del XII Congreso de la Asociación Internacional de Hispanistas* (University of Birmingham) vol. 4, 219–26.

Roldán Vera, Eugenia (2003) *The British Book Trade and Spanish American Independence: Education and Knowledge Transmission in Transcontinental Perspective* (Aldershot: Ashgate).

Sweet, Nanora (1997) 'Hitherto Closed to the Spanish Enterprise: Trading and Writing the Hispanic World circa 1815', *European Romantic Review* 8: 139–47.

Zaro, Juan Jesús (2007) *Shakespeare y sus traductores: análisis crítico de siete traducciones españolas de las obras de Shakespeare* (Bern: Peter Lang).

INDEX

Abbott, E. A.:
  Shakespearian Grammar, A 300, 302
Ackermann, Rudolph 696, 701
actors (performers) 21, 64, 69, 78, 81, 147,
        166, 234, 240, 247, 258–9, 264,
        267, 269, 271, 285, 288–301, 302,
        304, 307, 309–11, 316, 319–21,
        335–6, 340, 341–55, 358–9, 364,
        368, 531, 545, 575, 586, 606, 618,
        619, 632, 633, 644, 646, 659,
        674–7, 697, 700
  as metaphorical figure 384, 405, 475–8, 545,
        619, 622
  see also theatre; performances;
        individual actors
Acuña, José Basileo 694
Adams, Joseph Quincy 684
Adamson, Sylvia 81n14, 177
address, terms of 272, 363, 370, 434,
        434n16, 439, 456, 471–5, 473n10,
        481, 501, 595
Adelman, Janet 216–17, 365
Adonis 86, 113, 117
Aeschylus 578
Aesop:
  Fables 99
Africa 274–5, 643, 703
Akenside, Mark 565
Alberti, Leon Battista 490, 495
Albrecht, Heinrich Christoph 672,
        679–80
  Rape of Lucrece, The (translation) 672–3,
        679–80
  translations reviewed 679–80
  Venus and Adonis (translation)
        672–3
Alderson, Simon J, 77n
Alfar, Christina 363

allegory 121–3, 143, 231–2, 235, 237, 239, 274,
        542, 545, 547, 555–6
Alleyn, Edward 293–4
allusion 83, 122, 161, 265, 431, 567–80, 587–9,
        592, 594, 600, 605, 606, 609–10, 612,
        613, 654
  biblical 64, 83, 87, 93n52
  classical 11, 78, 83–4, 99, 102–3, 105, 106–7,
        113, 129, 408–9, 412
  to Lord's Prayer 315
  to Norse literature 83
  to Shakespeare's works 46, 567–80, 587–8,
        592, 600, 605, 606, 609–10, 612,
        613, 654
  see also citation; quotation
Almeida, Joselyn 701
Altman, Joel B. 97n4
America, United States of 633–4, 637, 640,
        641, 642, 645, 648, 674
  Americans 632, 633, 647
  literature 636
  poetry 605–13, 631–48
Americas 38, 613, 705; *see also* America,
        United States of; Spanish America
Amyot, Jacques 109
Ancaeus 88
Anderson, Christy 491, 492
Anglican church 160
Anselm of Canterbury, Saint 23
anthropology 541–2
Aphrodite 21; *see also* Venus
Aphthonius:
  Progymnasmata 102, 103, 106
Apollodorus 207
Aquinas, Saint Thomas 533
archaisms 114, 473, 509, 510, 526, 542, 683;
        see also neologisms
architecture 486–97, 500, 503

3 0 MAY 2018

Lightning Source UK Ltd.
Milton Keynes UK
UKOW05f0947040816

279945UK00004B/5/P